☆ ALMANACS OF AMERICAN LIFE ☆

CIVIL WAR AMERICA
1850 to 1875

☆ ALMANACS OF AMERICAN LIFE ☆

CIVIL WAR AMERICA 1850 to 1875

Richard F. Selcer

Richard Balkin
General Editor

Civil War America, 1850 to 1875

Facts On File, Inc.
An imprint of Infobase Publishing
132 West 31st Street
New York NY 10001

Library of Congress Cataloging-in-Publication Data
Selcer, Richard F.
Civil War America, 1850 to 1875 / Richard F. Selcer.
p.cm. — (Almanacs of American life)
Includes bibliographical references and index.
ISBN 0-8160-3867-8 (alk. paper)
1. United States—History—Civil War, 1861–1865—Miscellanea. 2. United States—History—Civil War, 1861–1865—Statistics. 3. United States—History—1849–1877—Miscellanea. 4. United States—History—1849–1877—Statistics. 5. Almanacs, American.
I. Title
E468.S45 2006
973.6—dc22 2006020068

Facts On File books are available at special discounts when purchased in bulk quantities for businesses, associations, institutions, or sales promotions. Please call our Special Sales Department in New York at (212) 967-8800 or (800) 322-8755.

You can find Facts On File on the World Wide Web at http://www.factsonfile.com

Text design by Fred Pusterla
Cover design by Cathy Rincon
Maps and graphs by Dale Williams

Printed in the United States of America

VB Hermitage 10 9 8 7 6 5 4 3 2 1

This book is printed on acid-free paper.

Note on Photos

Many of the illustrations and photographs used in this book are old, historical images. The quality of the prints is not always up to modern standards, as in some cases the originals are damaged. The content of the illustrations, however, made their inclusion important despite problems in reproduction.

Contents

List of Maps and Graphs

Acknowledgments

History books, particularly reference volumes of this sort, are not written in "splendid isolation." They are the product of a veritable army of anonymous researchers, librarians, editors, and proofreaders. The members of my writing troop on this volume must begin with a salute to "the usual suspects," who have stuck with me and provided essential support services going on four years: Lois Biege and Peggy Selcer (Nelson). They do it out of love because it sure is not for the fame or the glory.

After them, I am indebted to the historian-teacher Pete Vermilyea, who signed on at the beginning as a researcher for a pittance and then proceeded to do first-rate research for the chapters on population; popular culture; and climate, natural history, and historical geography. Also doing invaluable work as research assistants were Claude Armstrong (architecture and design; science and technology; and disasters, natural and human-made), and Dr. Jim King (Religion).

Thanks to Professor Tom Buckley of the University of Minnesota for pointing me in the right direction on the topics transportation and science and technology.

Thanks to Anne Hobart-Lang for help in selecting and assembling pictures to supplement the text. Anne gets the award for patience while I dragged this thing out far longer than anyone anticipated. Thanks also to Leslie Fields of the Gilder-Lehrman Photograph Collection at New York's Pierpont Morgan Library for similar help in locating pictures.

Thanks to Axl Grauman at the National Climactic Data Center of the U.S. Department of Commerce for invaluable help assembling weather data for the 19th century when everyone else said the kind of stuff I wanted did not exist.

Thanks to Ms. Lynn Frazier and other staff members at the Southwest Regional Library in Fort Worth for answering endless requests to do "just a quick search" for some obscure bibliographic information. All librarians should be as knowledgeable and helpful as Lynn!

Thanks to Jerry Parker of Fort Worth for crunching numbers for me to create data tables that make sense. Every historian needs a good accountant who is just a phone call away.

Thanks to Deborah Evans at the Library of Congress (LC) Photo Duplication Department, who was able to cut through procedures while correcting several mistakes in photo orders I placed with the LC—and after only a phone call or two.

Thanks to the staffs of the Mississippi, Alabama, Georgia, Arkansas, Maryland, and Tennessee Historical Societies for their kind help when I arrived on hit-and-run research trips.

Thanks to Harold Holzer at the New York Metropolitan Museum of Art, who graciously took my phone calls and patiently answered this philistine's questions about art matters.

And last, but far from least, thanks to Rick Balkin, who brought this project to me in the first place and applied the carrot and stick (liberally in both cases!) over the four years it took to get it completed. Rick went from being an editor to being a friend-mentor-adviser.

Author's Note

The quarter-century from 1850 until 1875 is dominated by the Civil War and Reconstruction, but far more occurred during those years than the two events always heard about. The era demonstrates the truth of H. G. Wells's later assessment "The most interesting history of the [entire] 19th century was the growth of the United States." In truth, the beginnings of "modern times" in the United States can be traced to developments of this time. Such familiar aspects of modern life as government bureaucracy, consumer goods, mass culture, data profiling, and professionalism all first appeared in the mid-19th century. For instance, the 1850 Census was the first to break down American religious practices by denomination, and the 1870 Census was the first to take a close look at the state of American literacy. Record keeping became a government preoccupation, prompted partly by the demands of the Civil War but already under way before. The federal government, with the states lagging only slightly behind, diligently gathered information on disease and battlefield injuries among soldiers, railroad accidents, the insane, and the illiterate. The result of all this statistics gathering was the first three-dimensional picture of the American people that far transcended the economically driven decennial census reports. The fields of medicine and weather reporting particularly benefited from the wealth of statistics being gathered.

In a parallel development, government bureaucracy multiplied enormously during these years. Two new cabinet-level departments were created by Congress, Interior (1849) and Agriculture (1862). The Patent Office was given independent status, and the Pension Office was greatly expanded to handle the flood of veterans' claims after the Civil War. The United States signed the international convention on weights and measures in 1875, and civil service reform got its start during Ulysses Grant's presidency. The nation's financial structure was also overhauled with the introduction of so-called subsidiary silver coinage into the money supply before the Civil War and the launching of the first income tax during the war.

This was a period that also saw the professionalization of American life. Physicians, engineers, and architects, among others, for the first time formed themselves into professional societies to set standards and protect their interests. Sportsmen, beginning with baseball players, divided themselves into "professional" and "amateur" ranks.

Ultimately, the Almanacs of American Life series, and *Civil War America* specifically, reflect the modern obsession of Americans with facts and figures. Spoiled by computer-based research and chronically short of time, people want their data in bite-sized bits. It would be nice if everyone could delve into the historical literature at leisure, but few have that luxury. It is the author's belief that no student of the history of 19th-century America can understand that century in all its complexities without consulting this volume. Narrative histories cannot tell the full story; nor does a concentration on the Civil War and Reconstruction to the exclusion of everything else do justice to the era. For the high school student or nonspecialist, *Civil War America* puts a wealth of facts culled from a wide range of primary and secondary sources at their fingertips. For the college student and the professional historian, this volume points the way toward deeper research with its table citations and comprehensive bibliography.

Preface

The most interesting history of the nineteenth century was the growth of the United States.

— H. G. Wells

1850 will complete the most eventful half century recorded in history. The coming year is pregnant with good for all Humanity, and so must be a happy one.

— Horace Greeley

It is ironic that the *English* historian, author, and futurist Herbert George Wells saw the United States as the most historically important of all nations in the 19th century. The eyes of the whole civilized world were focused on what was happening in the United States during those decades. But what those happenings signified was less clear to observers. In Horace Greeley's simple statement, the famed newspaper editor was wrong on two counts: Not only were the year 1851 and those following far from happy years for humanity, but the first half of the 19th century was as nothing compared to the second half in terms of grand events, tragedies, and triumphs. The half-century after 1850 was unprecedented, especially for Americans, in the rapid succession of history-making developments and in the scale and pace with which change piled on top of change. The quarter-century from 1850 to 1875 set the stage for what people now consider "modern America" on every front, which is to say society, politics, economics, religion, and technology.

There is a common misconception that "modern times" in American history began with the 20th century, or perhaps the so-called Industrial Revolution of the late 19th century, and certainly no earlier than the Civil War (1861–65). The reality is that the shadowy outlines of modern times could already be seen in the 1850s, although the idea that anything "modern" could have come out of the antebellum period seems almost ludicrous to present-day Americans. There is some justification for that way of thinking if one limits *modern* to travel via automobiles and airplanes, computer technology, total war, and global-scale economies. But if by *modern times* one means government bureaucracy, consumer goods, mass culture, data profiling, and the rise of the professions, then the foundations of the current way of life were laid down in the 1850s.

This was the time when statistics gathering became a routine activity of government and other institutions, and not just the usual vital statistics such as births, deaths, and marriages. Numerous areas of American life were quantified for the first time. Statistical profiles were compiled on the nation's religious preferences, racial makeup, inventiveness, economic output, and reading habits, to name just a few areas that attracted the attention of the bean counters. Not surprisingly, the U.S. Census Bureau took the lead in gathering these statistics. The 1850 Census was the first to break down U.S. religious practices by denomination, and the 1870 Census was the first to take a close look at the state of U.S. literacy by separating the ability to read from the ability to write, and by separating juvenile illiteracy from adult illiteracy.

With the U.S. Census Bureau leading the way, data collecting became part of the fabric of American life. In 1850 the General Land Office in its annual report included careful calculations of the land area of all the states and territories composing the national domain. This was the first time that the government had undertaken such a massive job since 1800, and in the half-century since that last measurement, the Louisiana Purchase and Mexican Cession had been added. Only in 1850 did Americans know precisely how much territory they had purchased from France and taken from Mexico. And 1854 saw the publication of the first comprehensive statistical compendium in the nation's history, the *Statistical View of the United States,* compiled by the Southern apologist J. D. B. DeBow of New Orleans.

As the era advanced, this data-gathering trend not only continued but gathered speed during the Civil War. The 1860 Census was the first officially to count the number of periodicals published in the United States (4,051 publications of all types), Uncle Sam began to collect marriage and divorce statistics in 1867, and 1874 was the first year that data on the problem of the annual Mississippi River floods were gathered.

The South was slower to jump on the bandwagon because of the Civil War and Reconstruction. During those painful years, the important work of gathering vital statistics on the population lapsed. The money and the initiative to do routine record keeping simply were not there. As a result, some important demographic trends were missed, while others could only be guessed at.

The South notwithstanding, what was being produced year by year was nothing less than a statistical profile of the American people that went far beyond the decennial work of the Census Bureau. In the new scheme of things statistics gathering became a routine activity carried out by countless private as well as public organizations. This quantification of American society produced record keeping on an unprecedented scale, whether it was counting church pews, team victories, railroad accidents, insane persons, or illiterates. Americans, it seemed, became obsessed with counting and classifying themselves. The quarter-century from 1850 to 1875 is the first era in U.S. history in which statistical record keeping becomes sophisticated enough actually to profile Americans in a variety of social, economic, political, and cultural areas.

The reasons behind all this number crunching are more difficult to gauge. Some of the motivation, such as the impetus for collecting information about economic production, undoubtedly derived from chauvinistic pride of accomplishment, allowing the nation to measure itself against European elders. The work was also driven by simple scientific curiosity as the methodology of scientists such as Louis Pasteur, Charles Darwin, and Gregor Mendel caught on among the general populace. The bureaucratic imperative also had to play a role in the heightened attention to record keeping: "Fish got to swim, birds got to fly," as the song goes, and bureaucrats have got to generate paperwork. There was also a heightened awareness in the government of its responsibility to provide for the "general welfare" of the American people. This was represented in the growing sentiment against slavery as well as in the Census Bureau's justification for counting all the newspapers and magazines published in the United States: They were seen as the "popular educators" of the day. Another motivation, however, was the post–Civil War influence of the rapidly growing insurance industry, which demanded documentation before it would pay off claims arising from accidents and natural disasters. Thus, railroad wrecks and rampaging floods, for instance, were carefully investigated and the results tabulated, although victims did not necessarily benefit. Posterity has been the greatest beneficiary, as those records that survived ultimately became the raw material for the practitioners of scientific history. As a result, the historian looking for a statistical profile of some group or activity who runs into a brick wall before about 1850—there are simply no comprehensive figures for much of American life before that date—finds that after the mid-century mark there is a relative wealth of data available for his or her purposes.

Two critical areas of American life whose modern understanding benefited greatly from all that attention to record keeping were medicine and weather reporting. The collection of medical statistics on a massive, detailed scale was a by-product of the Civil War as the Union army in particular tried to get a handle on the state of health of the hundreds of thousands of American boys who wore the blue. (Southerners were somewhat less efficient at measuring and recording medical statistics.) The result was the comprehensive and official *Medical and Surgical History of the War of the Rebellion,* published between 1870 and 1880. Its many statistical summaries, charts, tables, and color plates provide the best profile of public health in the United States in the 19th century, and of the state of the nation's medical care at that time. This priceless storehouse of information is still used by doctors and historians as a basic research tool today.

Weather observing in the United States before 1870 was the province of the army, which relied on post surgeons around the country to record observations and forward them to Washington, D.C., with their regular medical reports. With the establishment of the Weather Bureau in 1870, the era of modern weather observation began, and almost all the comprehensive weather data used in long-term analysis of weather and climate patterns date from this time. It was agents of the Weather Bureau at key locations around the country who recorded observations on a regular basis and organized those data in a useful form who are the forerunners of all scientifically trained meteorologists today. The original motivations behind creation of the bureau were to understand natural phenomena, optimize the planting and harvesting of crops by the nation's farmers, and protect lives and property from natural disasters by providing a certain measure of predictability.

All of this data profiling was welcomed by the mass of Americans in the 19th century, who saw it, not just as a way to get a handle on nature, but as necessary self-examination by the nation and as a way to distinguish themselves from their neighbors. This was more than a little ironic because today many Americans stoutly resist being pigeonholed by the Census Bureau or any other government agency, particularly on the basis of their race or religious preference, two areas that were more relevant to people of that time than were weather and public health. The government today has even been forced to respect these sentiments by cutting back on data gathering. Since 1976 Congress has barred the Census Bureau from questioning citizens about their religious affiliation.

What is important to remember is that this whole concern for data gathering and statistical profiling that is so much a part of modern society was born in the quarter-century after 1850, not just as a new area of government snooping but as a response to the needs and desires of the American people.

A parallel development in these same years is the bureaucratization of American life. It affected all areas but was most apparent in government, advancing in ways both large and small. In addition to the creation of the U.S. Weather Bureau in 1870, a variety of other government agencies were created around this time. These included two new, cabinet-level departments: the Department of the Interior (1849) and the Department of Agriculture (1862). They joined the long-standing Departments of War, State, Treasury, and Attorney-General in conducting the most important ongoing operations of the federal government. The Patent Office was given independent status in 1870, and the Pension Office underwent major expansion and reform in 1862 and again in 1873. The first small steps toward civil service reform occurred during these years, beginning in 1853, when Congress passed legislation requiring applicants for federal clerk jobs to take simple "pass examinations" to demonstrate their literacy. Seventeen years later, the first competitive *merit* examinations were administered to federal job seekers, during the much-maligned presidency of Ulysses Grant. Although these were administered on a limited basis, they set the stage for the first comprehensive civil service law, passed by Congress in 1883 (the Pendleton Act). Meanwhile, in 1875, bureaucracy was advancing on another front as the United States became a signatory to the convention that established the International Bureau of Weights and Measures. While serving beneficial purposes, all of these moves created additional layers of administration and added to the "creeping" bureaucratization of U.S. government.

The makeover of U.S. government was not confined to the executive branch. Being a congressman also began to take on more of the trappings of a "real" job. Until 1856, U.S. senators and representatives were paid a token per diem allowance only. That was officially changed to an annual salary during the Buchanan administration. Starting in 1857, congressmen drew $3,000 a year in salary, though it was still harder for a poor man to represent his constituency or his country than for a rich man.

No surer sign exists of the growth of big government than the growth of Washington, D.C., itself. The population of the nation's capital grew 75.4 percent between 1860 and 1870 (from 75,080 residents to 131,700 residents). And from 891.2 people per square mile in 1850, population density in the District soared to 2,270.7 per square mile in 1870, higher than in any place else in the United States, including New York City and Philadelphia. Without all those government office jobs, Washington, D.C., would still have been a malarial swamp on the Potomac River in those years.

While Uncle Sam's extended family was growing, he was also making his power felt in Americans' pocketbooks in unprecedented ways. First, the government entered the money printing business for the first time since the disastrous experiment with Continental notes of the Revolutionary War. During the first "four score and seven years" of the nation's history, the United States had depended on what was virtually a private banking system. The federal government left currency policy to state banks and private interests; that meant basically there was no currency policy or even a national currency worthy of the name. The initial step was taken in 1853, when the first subsidiary silver coinage was issued to serve as a practical retail currency. But it was not until 1863 that Congress legislated a full-blown revolution in the rickety American banking structure by assuming complete control of the currency, thus establishing the foundations of the modern U.S. financial system. It was another sweeping exercise of federal power unprecedented before this era.

Even more shocking was the introduction of the nation's first income tax during the Civil War. Strapped for funds to fight the war, Congress passed the tax in 1862 and proceeded to take a share of the average American's earnings for the first time in history. This prototype of the modern income tax continued even after the war, for another seven years, until it was grudgingly repealed in 1872. But the precedent that Uncle Sam could take his pound of flesh had been set.

Even American churches were swept up in the trend toward bureaucratization. Inspired by the new emphasis on scientific management and industrial efficiency all around them, spiritual leaders reexamined their traditional church practices. The primacy of the pulpit minister in church organization was felt to be antiquated, so power was shifted to boards of deacons or elders, who functioned much as corporate boards of directors do. These new church boards not only kept a tighter rein on the minister but put shepherding the flock on the same level as saving individual souls. At the same time, they also increased emphasis on hiring trained, professional clergy to run church operations. The ultimate aim of all this bureaucratization was to make the business of soul saving more efficient in the same way as industry and government were becoming more efficient at their jobs.

Amid all the changes, the big story of this era may have been the professionalization of American life. The nation's doctors, dentists, engineers, architects, and others for the first time formed themselves into professional organizations. They systematized their disciplines, started licensing procedures, and began to hold regular national conventions. They also closed ranks as exclusive fraternal associations that were not above politics or prejudice. This was particularly true in the practice of medicine, as the "regular" doctors worked hard to stamp out unconventional strains such as homeopathy and eclecticism. Other groups such as the American Institute of Architects (1857) were formed not so much to exclude certain brethren as to separate themselves from related fields and to honor their collective accomplishments.

Toward the end of this period, sports began to split into separate realms of amateur and professional players. The trend was most apparent in baseball, which formed the National Association of Base Ball Players in 1858 and then the National League in 1876. This development was soon followed by formation of the National Collegiate Athletic Association and Amateur Athletic Union.

The American scientific community was likewise caught up in the movement for a higher level of professionalization, beginning even before 1850 but accelerating greatly thereafter. Scientists and inventors aimed to separate themselves from amateur tinkerers, set their own research agenda, and conduct their investigations without moral or political restrictions. While gaining a higher measure of respect and prestige for the scientific disciplines, the professionalization movement in science also had the effect of withdrawing scientific knowledge from the public domain and making it the private preserve of the experts, the so-called men of science. Professionalization in science, as in sports, was popularly equated with superior technical knowledge and higher levels of accomplishment. It also tended to encourage snobbery and disdain for "nonprofessionals."

The ultimate effects of all this selectivity and cliquishness were to raise standards in numerous traditional occupations plus impose stringent record keeping and data gathering, another unintended boon for historians.

Professionalization was not confined to the sciences and sports, or even to government service. Even in the humanities, professionalization was the new order. The 1870s saw the establishment of the profession of dramatist in the United States. Playwrights had always practiced their art for the enjoyment of their audiences and a measure of recognition, but at least on the western side of the Atlantic had never been able to make a good living by this art. Bronson Howard and a small handful of his contemporaries changed all that, starting in the 1870s.

This era also gave birth to the modern phenomenon of mass culture, whereby millions of people are persuaded to buy alike, act alike, and in the process perhaps even think alike, as opposed to practicing regional and local patterns of living. Today many people accept this as the normal order of things, but it was not always so in the United States. As odd as it seems for an era when the principal mode of transportation was still the horse, and when wild animals and Indians could still pose a threat to a person who wandered very far beyond the narrow boundaries of "civilization," mass culture was already becoming a fact of life in the middle of the 19th century. It was manifested in new forms of mass entertainment such as the traveling circus, minstrelsy, and even professional sports. Professional sports moved the focus from participating to viewing as the level of play and commercialization took sports out of the hands of ordinary folks and delivered it to the hands of paid, full-time "players." Thus, baseball, football, horse racing, and prizefighting, to name just a few, all became big business, attracting thousands of spectators to major events and leading to the multiplication of teams, leagues, and classifications across the board.

Another form of mass culture/entertainment was popular music, which changed from being an idle pursuit for the masses to becoming, as sports became, "big business." The major change in popular music was the emergence of the commercial publishing business. The historian Daniel Kingman has called this era the "beginning of the modern age in American Popular Music" as such artists as Stephen Foster and Fannie Crosby made a very profitable living off writing songs that were sung (and played) by the masses. The songwriters, as their music did, became household names sung and played by all classes. And where there was popular affection for anything in a capitalistic democracy, there was money to be made by businesses.

Modern mass culture that first took shape during these years also included the debut of the new penny newspapers in New York City; a flood of cheap, specialized magazines that hit the market; and the beginning of the best-seller lists that helped make novels such as *Uncle Tom's Cabin* (1852) must reading for middle-class Americans. All of these phenomena cashed in on the remarkably high literacy of the American people as well as on their unquenchable curiosity about the world.

The emerging mass culture also owed a great deal to the urban explosion that occurred during this time. Fueled by immigration and natural increase, new towns sprang up all over the country while older towns were transformed into major cities. Immigrants and industrialization, trail drives and railroads were just the most visible impetus behind the waves of people who filled these towns and cities. This wave of urbanization gave rise to a distinctive urban culture that was more homogenized, more cosmopolitan, and more consumer oriented than previous generations of Americans had been. And it was a process that would only accelerate in the coming decades until it reached its full fruition with an "urban nation" in the 20th century.

At the beginning of this era the United States was already well on the road to being a consumer society by using up far more than it produced. In 1850 that meant that the country consumed $44 million more in imported goods and services than it exported. This simple statistic foreshadowed the 20th century, when the United States would be known as the most profligate consumer nation in history.

CHAPTER 1 Climate, Natural History, and Historical Geography

Americans were fortunate—or blessed—to have the most bounteous nation on Earth in terms of natural resources and salubrious climate. This fact became steadily more evident as the nation advanced westward in the 19th century. This was a rich land where starvation and pauperism were virtually unknown. Occupying roughly one-third of the North American continent by the middle of the century, the United States contained the world's largest collection of freshwater lakes, plus some of the richest soil, most extensive forests, and mightiest rivers of any region on Earth. All of this was spread out from the broad coastal tidelands of the Atlantic and Gulf coasts across the Great Plains and up to the 10,000-foot mountains of the western Cordillera range before descending again to the Pacific shores.

Climate and geography helped define the United States as much as politics, society, and economy did. In fact, the latter were in many ways dependent upon the former. Droughts and floods, growing seasons, and gold rushes contributed as much to the nation's history as did elections and industrialization.

Climate

Climate is determined by a complex combination of geographic conditions and latitude. It is weather writ large, which is to say, weather patterns considered over a long time—years, decades, even centuries. Temperature and precipitation, wind and humidity, in all their seasonal variations, characterize different geographic regions in the same way personality characterizes a person. The most visible indicator of a particular climate region is the local vegetation, whether it be swamplands, prairie grass, or giant redwoods. According to the universally used system of classification devised around 1900 by the German meteorologist Wladimir Köppen (1846–1940), the U.S. landmass has a *continental climate,* which is characteristic of the temperate regions of the globe. Such a climate is marked by sharp temperature swings, including mild to cold winters, warm to hot summers, and a broad diurnal range of temperatures. Within this broad classification U.S. climate ranges from "moist" in the eastern half of the continent to "dry" over most of the western half. The climate can only be described in the most general terms to leave room for numerous variations within any given region.

Rainfall generally declines going westward from the humid eastern zone, beginning at about 40 inches annually on the southeast side of the Appalachians, dropping to between 30 and 40 inches across most of the Central Lowland, then still further to between 10 and 30 inches annually on the plains. The intermontane basin lying between the Rockies and the Sierra Nevada receives less than four inches of precipitation annually before the pattern is thrown completely off on the upper Pacific shores.

The West Coast benefits from mild Pacific weather. As the cool moist winds from the Pacific rise over the coast ranges, they shed much precipitation so that Oregon and Washington have the heaviest rainfall of any region of the country (often as much as 70 inches annually), including Louisiana and Florida. Southern California, on the other hand, tends to have a warm, dry Mediterranean climate. As a result of these different West Coast conditions, a strong lumbering industry developed in the Pacific Northwest while farmers in California depended on irrigation or, alternatively, crops (such as grapes) that do not require much water.

Weather patterns move from west to east, so as westerly winds cross California, they dump rain or snow over the Cascade mountains and Sierra Nevada, then become warm and dry on the eastern side of both ranges, thereby helping create the forbidding deserts of Nevada and Arizona. The Great Plains likewise suffer from scant rainfall. The Central Lowland on the east and south of that broad area benefit from hot, humid air flowing off the Gulf of Mexico and as a result receive plentiful rain in the summer, which benefits cotton and sugar cultivation in particular.

Homesteaders soon learned that weather patterns over the Great Plains can swing wildly between extremes as the humid air from the south meets the colder, dry air off the Rocky Mountains. The results are seasonal thunderstorms, tornadoes, hailstorms, and blizzards that can devastate both people and crops. A broad belt running through Kansas, Oklahoma, and Missouri has been dubbed tornado alley because of the violent twisters that vacuum wide swathes through the countryside, usually in the late spring. The spring and fall seasons tend to be short, with longer winters and summers dependent at least partly on latitudinal location.

The southeast corner of the United States, wedged between the Gulf of Mexico and the Atlantic seaboard, has warm, humid conditions year-round, approaching even subtropical close to the coast. The Seminole Indians used the Florida Everglades for years as a nearly impenetrable refuge in their war against the U.S. government. The humid, subtropical climate of the Deep South did more than aid agriculture; it also encouraged the slower pace of life usually identified with that region, as well as the dreaded epidemic seasons in summer and fall that caused the ruling classes to flee north.

The Appalachians receive plenty of rainfall during the year, although their elevation and more northern latitudes preclude the semitropical conditions of the coastal regions. As a result, when the first settlers arrived, they found them covered with lush forests virtually all the way to their crests.

In the Northeast, the familiar continental climate is only slightly modified by close proximity to the Atlantic Ocean. Because the prevailing westerly winds blow offshore, the region shows relatively low winter temperatures and some very heavy snowfalls most years.

Temperatures across the United States vary seasonally, with the greatest extremes occurring on the north-central plains. The frost-free period of the year declines from south to north; Gulf Coast residents experience more than 240 days per year, whereas those living near the Canadian border experience fewer than 120 frost-free days per year. Because the climate on both oceanic coasts is generally milder than in the interior, people moving westward from the eastern settlements had to learn to adapt early on, not just their farming methods but their very lifestyle. One simple invention that caused a revolution on the Great Plains was barbed wire, which made it possible for the first time to fence in the range and put homesteaders on a par with ranchers.

The latest research by climatologists at the University of Wisconsin points toward a general warming all over North America between 1845 and 1995 (the most recent year for which data are available). Their conclusion is based, not on computer models and statistical calculations, but on direct human observation over that past 150-year period of freezing and thawing trends on lakes and other bodies of water. Regular reports made by government weather observers in major cities all over the United States from 1850 to 1870 tend to support that conclusion, too (see Chapter 10). The gradual rise in the heat quotient was most noticeable in summers, when the triple-digit highs known today were still virtually unknown, but the mean temperature during the hottest months crept steadily upward toward the 90°+ Fahrenheit values as the decades rolled by. Recognizing a trend and knowing the reasons for it are two different things, however.

TABLE 1.1 HISTORICAL MONTHLY TEMPERATURE EXTREMES, HIGHS AND LOWS, BY STATE
(temperatures in °F)

State	Year Record Keeping Began	High	Low	High	Low	High	Low	High	Low	High	Low	High	Low
		Jan.		Feb.		Mar.		Apr.		May		Jun.	
Ala.	1884	88	–27	89	–18	94	02	98	19	105	29	110	35
Ark.	1891	90	–28	95	–29	98	–14	99	12	107	24	113	35
Calif.	1897	97	–45	105	–43	105	–29	118	–30	121	–15	129	02
Conn.	1889	73	–32	77	–32	87	–24	96	–07	98	20	103	24
Del.	1895	78	–17	82	–15	91	01	99	11	100	26	104	34
Fla.	1891	92	02	94	–02	99	13	100	20	106	34	109	43
Ga.	1892	95	–17	90	–12	97	–03	99	12	108	25	110	31
Ill.	1890	78	–35	83	–32	94	–21	96	–02	107	12	108	29
Ind.	1887	80	–34	83	–35	94	–19	100	01	103	118	111	30
Iowa	1873	73	–47	82	–41	95	–35	100	–09	111	10	111	27
Kans.	1887	88	–35	92	–40	100	–25	107	–02	108	14	116	30
Ky.	1889	83	–34	86	–33	94	–14	98	12	106	20	110	29
La.	1891	92	–08	92	–16	95	10	98	24	105	30	110	41
Maine	1889	65	–48	67	–44	86	–36	94	–14	101	10	105	20
Md.	1895	83	–40	88	–29	93	–20	102	–03	102	16	105	25
Mass.	1889	72	–35	76	–31	88	–22	100	02	100	06	103	24
Mich.	1887	72	–48	70	–51	89	–45	96	–34	100	09	107	12
Minn.	1891	69	–57	73	–59	88	–49	101	–22	112	04	110	15
Miss.	1888	89	–19	91	–16	96	07	97	21	104	30	111	39
Mo.	1888	85	–36	90	–40	98	–26	100	02	110	17	112	28
Nebr.	1876	82	–45	85	–47	101	–38	106	–17	110	03	114	20
Nev.	1889	84	–50	92	–41	96	–32	106	–12	114	–07	122	12
N.H.	1889	68	–46	70	–45	87	–36	95	–17	100	–02	106	13
N.J.	1885	78	–34	80	–31	92	–15	98	03	102	18	106	29
N. Mex.	1892	89	–47	100	–50	99	–34	104	–36	110	–02	116	10
N.Y.	1890	75	–46	78	–52	91	–41	97	–24	102	10	105	21
N.C.	1887	86	–34	88	–20	100	–14	99	01	105	11	107	27
Ohio	1883	79	–37	81	–39	96	–21	97	–04	102	17	108	27
I.T.[a]	1900	92	–27	99	–27	104	–18	106	06	110	19	117	34
Ore.	1890	82	–52	89	–54	99	–30	102	–23	108	0	113	11
Pa.	1888	85	–42	83	–39	92	–31	98	–05	102	10	107	20
R.I.	1889	69	–23	72	–22	90	–10	98	01	95	25	101	30
S.C.	1887	86	–19	89	–11	99	–03	99	18	106	28	111	34
Tenn.	1883	83	–30	85	–30	94	–11	98	14	102	22	110	28
Tex.	1888	98	–22	104	–23	108	–12	113	05	116	15	119	32
Utah[b]	1891	74	–50	84	–69	89	–37	98	–19	108	0	116	10
Vt.	1889	70	–44	68	–46	84	–37	97	–13	99	05	101	19
Va.	1891	82	–30	87	–29	96	–15	100	0	105	15	107	26
W.Va.	1891	88	–36	86	–35	94	–18	101	–04	105	14	109	22
Wis.	1891	66	–54	68	–52	89	–48	99	–20	109	07	106	20

[a] I.T. = Indian Territory (Oklahoma)
[b] U.T. = Utah Territory
Source: Richard A. Wood, ed., *The Weather Almanac,* 9th ed. (Farmington, Mich.: Gale Group, 1999), 248.

It has been suggested, based on conjunction of industrial development and weather changes and what is known today about how the atmosphere works, that the documented warming trend has been one result of the intensive burning of fossil fuels that accompanied heavy industrialization from the 19th century. Historians can only note the trends.

Weather records for the third quarter of the 19th century are sparse and sketchy because they were scarcely systemized in those years. Whereas full-time weather observers were at work in Europe by the late 18th century, Americans were slow to recognize the value of such data. In 1814 the government ordered army surgeons to keep "weather diaries" in order to study the connection between weather conditions and disease, and by 1838 daily observations were being recorded at 13 army posts scattered across the country. By the 1840s, with the electric telegraph established, it became possible to gather and analyze data from many locations in a timely manner and then use it to study patterns and make forecasts. The telegraph, therefore, was as essential as the thermometer and the barometer to the scientific study of weather. Telegraph companies were charged by the U.S. government with collecting and forwarding the data on temperatures, precipitation, and other phenomena to Washington, D.C. The first national weather reports were published in the *Washington Evening Star* in 1857. The Weather Bureau was organized as part of the Army Signal Service in 1870 and before the end of the decade had established some 284 observing stations. Even with that, there were huge gaps in the national weather map until the end of the century.

The various tools for the study of climate (known as climatology) were not even widely available until the latter years of the 19th century, and all were the product of European science. The first large-scale map of precipitation was prepared in 1845, and the first maps of mean monthly temperatures three years later, both in Germany. The first modern map of global climatic zones was not devised until 1879, by Wladimir Köppen in Germany. In the United States reliable

State	Year Record Keeping Began	High	Low	High	Low	High	Low	High	Low	High	Low	High	Low
		Jul.		Aug.		Sep.		Oct.		Nov.		Dec.	
Ala.	1884	111	41	109	39	112	29	103	19	92	02	88	–10
Ark.	1891	116	40	120	38	113	28	105	12	96	0	88	–21
Calif.	1897	134	12	127	13	126	–05	117	–20	105	–28	100	–40
Conn.	1889	105	32	104	28	103	17	94	11	84	–08	75	–22
Del.	1895	110	41	107	41	102	31	97	19	88	08	76	–12
Fla.	1891	108	49	105	52	107	35	100	25	96	12	95	05
Ga.	1892	112	40	112	40	111	26	105	14	94	0	89	–09
Ill.	1890	117	35	113	31	109	14	98	01	89	–20	79	–29
Ind.	1887	116	37	111	33	108	21	100	08	91	–10	78	–30
Iowa	1873	118	35	116	20	107	10	97	–15	86	–25	74	–40
Kans.	1887	121	32	119	33	117	15	104	–03	96	–20	90	–26
Ky.	1889	114	34	113	33	110	24	98	12	93	–09	87	–24
La.	1891	111	50	114	45	110	30	103	21	95	10	90	–01
Maine	1889	105	29	104	26	100	12	92	01	78	–20	69	–42
Md.	1895	109	32	109	30	106	19	100	04	89	–16	80	–32
Mass.	1889	106	32	107	15	103	18	92	06	85	–10	74	–33
Mich.	1887	112	20	108	21	104	09	94	–03	84	–23	69	–41
Minn.	1891	114	27	110	21	111	10	95	–16	84	–45	74	–57
Miss.	1888	115	47	110	42	111	31	100	16	92	02	87	–12
Mo.	1888	118	38	116	35	110	17	110	–03	90	–13	83	–34
Nebr.	1876	118	29	117	23	113	01	104	–15	92	–32	87	–47
Nev.	1889	121	18	122	15	117	0	111	–10	98	–23	81	–45
N.H.	1889	106	25	105	20	102	13	91	–02	84	–18	70	–44
N.J.	1885	110	33	108	32	109	18	97	09	88	–07	78	–21
N.Mex.	1892	116	19	111	23	112	08	101	–15	97	–38	90	–47
N.Y.	1890	108	25	106	20	107	15	99	02	87	–24	75	–47
N.C.	1887	109	32	110	31	109	23	101	08	90	–21	86	–21
Ohio	1883	113	34	111	27	107	23	99	07	89	–17	80	–32
I.T.[a]	1900	120	41	120	38	115	25	106	09	95	–15	92	–19
Ore.	1890	119	14	119	13	111	02	104	–09	89	–32	81	–53
Pa.	1888	111	28	108	23	106	17	100	07	88	–15	82	–29
R.I.	1889	102	38	104	33	100	25	99	13	82	01	71	–17
S.C.	1887	110	45	109	45	111	28	103	16	93	–01	89	–06
Tenn.	1883	113	36	113	30	112	19	99	10	89	–08	82	–32
Tex.	1888	119	40	120	39	116	25	109	08	102	–10	98	–16
Utah[b]	1891	117	19	113	17	110	02	99	–16	86	–30	76	–49
Vt.	1889	105	24	104	24	100	15	92	–05	81	–20	72	–50
Va.	1891	110	31	108	31	108	20	101	09	91	–17	83	–27
W.Va.	1891	112	20	112	25	107	15	102	03	89	–14	84	–37
Wis.	1891	114	27	108	22	104	10	95	–07	84	–34	66	–52

weather profiles, with their highs, lows, and means, were not compiled until the 20th century, and even the most basic data, such as temperatures and precipitation levels, were not consistently gathered on the local level until the late 19th century. As a result, climate tables for the various parts of the United States covering the period from 1850 to 1875 must be extrapolated from 20th-century data. However, because long-term patterns for the 20th century show a degree of consistency, they can be projected backward into the 19th century with a fair amount of confidence in their accuracy.

Natural History

Six geographic regions can be identified in the United States, each of which helped to shape the growth of a distinctive local culture. Without the unifying political concept of "the union" these culture regions could easily have spun off into six or more separate countries, making the United States look more like the patchwork national map that is Europe than like the modern nation state it became. The six regions were (1) the narrow northeast coastal plain and northern Appalachian highlands; (2) the broad southern coastal plain between the Atlantic Ocean and the Appalachian Mountains, curving from the Chesapeake Bay all the way around the Gulf of Mexico to the Rio Grande; (3) on the western side of the Appalachians a vast central plain rising from east to west all the way to the western Cordillera range; (4) the great Cordillera, with its eastern branch (the Rockies) and western branch (Cascades on the north and Sierra Nevada on the south); (5) the great intermontane plateaus and basins lying between the two branches of the Cordillera; and (6) the narrow Pacific coastal rim.

Obviously, most states, which by definition are political units with geographic boundaries, do not fit into neat geographic categories. All of the "intermontane" states, for instance, have mountainous areas, and Pennsylvania could be two states geographically speaking, with its western, mountainous region more akin to the other Northeast states, and its eastern, rich agricultural lands closer in type to the Southeast. But these are the major categories, and by grouping the

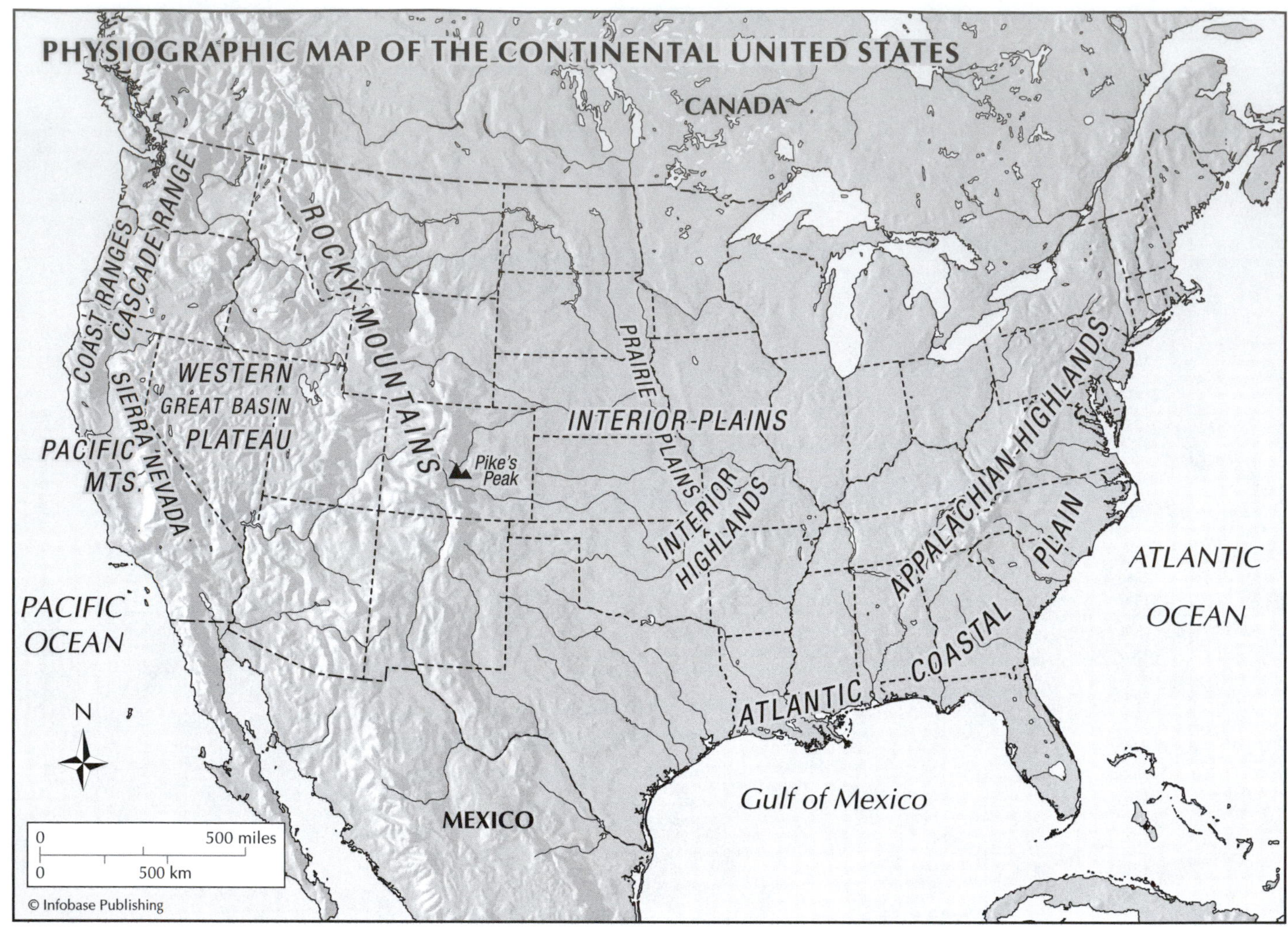

In the Great Plains and Rocky Mountains, the topography, altitudes, crops, and climate—especially the lack of rain—led to changes in a mode of settlement that had been essentially uniform from the Atlantic Coast through Kentucky, Ohio, and Missouri. The rectangular land surveys and quarter-section lots that were traditional before could not accommodate Great Plains conditions.

Source: Robert A. Divine, T. H. Breen, et al., *America Past and Present,* vol. 2, 6th ed. (New York: Longman, 2000). 490.

states by their dominant geographic and climatic features one gains a better understanding of their local cultures and economies. Although all rules have exceptions, some characteristics stand out immediately: Most states in a particular region tend to be fairly comparable in size (in square miles); the oldest states in the Northeast are, as a group, the smallest in geographic area; as the nation moved westward, the size of states tended to increase, reflecting the vast tracts of new land being acquired. There seemed to be almost a self-limiting imperative at work in each region, regardless of natural geographic boundaries, with notable exceptions such as Texas and Virginia, which were shaped as much by historic forces as by geographic considerations. Another pattern emerging from a regional grouping of states and territories is that, judging by the slow growth of their populations and their resulting slow progress toward statehood, the territories of the intermontane and mountain regions were the least hospitable areas on the continent.

The Northeast in prehistory had been shaped by glaciation, which left low highlands (mountains, ridges, and hills) carved up by numerous valleys with many lakes and rivers. North of Pennsylvania and New York, farming was poor, but vast coniferous and hardwood forests provided a strong economic foundation. Likewise, the broad continental shelf lying off the Northeast coast made fishing a lucrative activity. A hardy, highly urbanized population lived here by the mid-19th century.

The Southeast consisted of the coastal tidewater rising gradually to the Piedmont (plateau) region before abutting the southern Appalachians. The fertile plain of the tidewater was divided from the Piedmont by the fall line, where the eastward-flowing rivers drop off abruptly from the Appalachian mountain range down to the Atlantic coastal plain, and the whole region was covered with extensive deciduous forests and transected by numerous rivers that tied the interior to the coastal region both economically and politically. Just off the

TABLE 1.2 GEOGRAPHIC GROUPINGS OF STATES AND TERRITORIES BY REGION, MID-NINETEENTH CENTURY

Region	Inclusive States and Territories	Land Area
Northeast	Conn.	5,018 sq.mi.
	Del.	2,045 sq. mi.
	Maine	33,265 sq. mi.
	Mass.	8,284 sq. mi.
	N.H.	9,279 sq. mi.
	N.J.	7,787 sq. mi.
	N.Y.	49,108 sq. mi.
	Pa.	45,308 sq. mi.
	R.I.	1,212 sq. mi.
	Vt.	9,614 sq. mi.
Southeast	Fla.	58,664 sq. mi.
	Ga.	58,910 sq. mi.
	Ky.	40,410 sq. mi.
	Md.	10,460 sq. mi.
	N.C.	52,669 sq. mi.
	S.C.	31,113 sq. mi.
	Tenn.	42,144 sq. mi.
	Va.	40,767 sq. mi.
	W.Va. (after 1863)	24,232 sq. mi.
Central Lowland and Great Plains	Ala.	51,705 sq. mi.
	Ark.	53,187 sq. mi.
	Dakota Territory	147,718 sq. mi.
	Ill.	56,345 sq. mi.
	Ind.	36,185 sq. mi.
	Iowa	56,275 sq. mi.
	Kans.	82,277 sq. mi.
	La.	47,752 sq. mi.
	Mich.	58,527 sq. mi.
	Minn.	84,402 sq. mi.
	Miss.	47,689 sq. mi.
	Mo.	69,697 sq. mi.
	Neb.	77,355 sq. mi.
	Oklahoma Territory	69,956 sq. mi.
	Tex.	266,807 sq mi.
	Wis.	56,153 sq. mi.
Mountains	Colorado Territory	104,091 sq. mi.
	Idaho Territory	83,564 sq. mi.
	Montana Territory	147,046 sq. mi.
	Wyoming Territory	97,809 sq. mi.
Intermontane	Arizona Territory	114,000 sq. mi.
	Nev. (after 1864)	110,561 sq. mi.
	New Mexico Territory	121,593 sq. mi.
	Utah Territory	84,899 sq. mi.
Pacific	Calif. (after 1850)	158,706 sq. mi.
	Ore. (after 1859)	97,073 sq. mi.
	Washington Territory	68,139 sq. mi.

Source: Lands and Peoples, vol. 5, *North America* (Danbury, Conn.: Grolier, Inc., 1993), 171, 192, 208–09, 224, 236, 247, 262.

coast was a line of barrier islands and sandbars nearly a thousand miles long that had the same culture as the adjoining mainland. Large-scale agriculture and a slower, highly class-structured lifestyle characterized this region. The potent combination of soil, climate, and slave labor made this region by the mid-19th century the richest cotton producing region in the world, generating some 80 percent of the world's cotton supply. Second to cotton in importance as cash crops were sugar, tobacco, and rice, all of which benefited from the same factors that made cotton production so profitable.

This well-known portrait of the artist and naturalist John James Audubon (1785–1851), with faithful companion, is an 1861 engraving done from an 1851 painting by Alonzo Chappell. (Tennessee State Library and Archives)

Dividing this eastern region from the West early in the century was the eastern cordillera, a collection of ranges roughly grouped under the rubric Appalachians, running northeast to southwest all the way from Canada down to northern Alabama. They formed a low, almost unbroken mountain chain, heavily forested and including ranges with such charming names as Blue Ridge, Adirondacks, Alleghenies, White, Berkshire, and Green. The Blue Ridge Mountains were the most important of these, forming a steep escarpment or stair step from the Appalachians down to the tidewater. The Appalachian–Blue Ridge chain was broken by a series of valleys between the ridges, most notably the Cumberland (largest), Shenandoah, and Vermont, which developed rather insular cultures, often at odds with their closest neighbors yet still a part of their larger regions. When U.S. industrialization took off in the mid-19th century, rich veins of coal from the Appalachian mountains powered the nation's factories and drove its riverboats and trains, enriching the country as a whole while leaving the local residents themselves relatively poor.

West of the Appalachians was the vast continental basin some 1,500 miles wide at its widest point and stretching almost an equal number of miles from the Canadian border and Great Lakes on the north to the Gulf of Mexico on the south. On the eastern side was the central lowland to the north, rising to form the Kentucky-Tennessee and Ozark plateaus to the south. This fertile area rose gradually from about 2,000 feet above sea level on the east side to about 5,000 feet at the foot of the Rockies. In the middle were the Great Plains, a flat expanse of tableland covered as far as the eye could see with tall prairie grass in the north and short prairie grass in the south. It was largely treeless, with limited rainfall, and earlier in the century, incorrectly labeled "the Great American Desert." In truth, it was only semiarid, and highly suitable for cultivation by the right methods, as Americans discovered in the second half of the 19th century with the impetus of the Homestead Act (1862), which sent thousands of settlers to the plains.

In the southwest corner of the Great Plains was a desolate mesa lying south of the Canadian River (Texas) and extending westward as far as the Pecos River (New Mexico). At roughly 32,000 square miles, it was one of the largest tablelands on the continent, given the name Llano Estacado, or "Staked Plains," by the Spanish because the only landmarks for travelers crossing the region were stakes hammered into the ground by those who had passed there before. For many years it was written off by non-Indians as part of the Great American Desert and left to the Comanche and other Indians. But starting in the 1870s intrepid cattlemen saw in its vast grasslands and unfenced expanse, prime grazing range and moved onto the Staked Plains in force. In time, they would be followed by farmers, who succeeded by using dry farming techniques and tapping into the Ogalalla Aquifer.

What prevented the Great Plains from becoming a true desert were the unseen or unrecognized sources of water such as the Ogalalla Aquifer and the vast surrounding river system formed by the Mississippi, Missouri, and Ohio. The latter two drained into the Mississippi River, which was known to the American Indians long before contact with non-Indians as "the Father of Waters." (The Red River, the Tennessee, and the Cumberland were important though lesser tributaries of the Mississippi.) This 4,700-mile-long river system provided both the moisture and the transportation arteries necessary to open this region to white settlement. From Minnesota in the north to the Gulf of Mexico in the south, the Mississippi was navigable for almost 1,802 miles, but it was also subject to severe flooding in the springtime. The Mississippi's other key role in the geological scheme of things was to carry downstream the rich alluvial soil that, over eons of time, had built up the rich Mississippi delta with its familiar swamps and cotton and sugar culture. The Mississippi River was central to American life, not only geographically, but economically, politically, and culturally. Thanks to the Father of Waters and its tributaries, the upper Midwest by the 1870s was well on the way to becoming the new American "breadbasket" (i.e., producer of cereal grains), taking over the role played by Pennsylvania and New York in an earlier era.

The western Cordillera, which marked the western edge of the Great Plains, covered nearly one-third of the North American continent, an immense mountain system stretching all the way from Alaska down to South America and ranging in elevation from about 5,280 feet to above 20,000 feet. This great cordillera consists of two separate mountain systems: (1) the eastern system, towering over the Great Plains, and (2) the Cascade and Sierra Nevada ranges, paralleling the gentle curve of the Pacific coastline from north to south. The Rockies were the tallest and most forbidding mountain range on the continent, although the tallest peaks, Mount McKinley (20,320 feet) and Mount Whitney (14,494 feet) lie in the western extensions of the cordillera. The eastern range or Rockies as they are commonly known form the so-called continental divide, or watershed, causing waterways on the western side to drain into the Pacific while all those on the eastern side drain into either the Gulf of Mexico or the Atlantic Ocean.

The breathtaking beauty of the Big Horn Mountains and the Wind River was first seen by Native Americans such as these Shoshone. This scene was part of the painter Albert Bierstadt's "Rocky Mountain Landscapes" series, ca. 1859, which showed easterners the geographic wonders of the Far West. (Library of Congress)

The culture of this mountain region was mining. In fact, it is doubtful that the region would even have seen large-scale settlement if not for the discovery of rich deposits of gold, silver, and eventually other precious minerals—the bonanza era in American history. Starting with the Pike's Peak, Colorado, gold rush in 1859, this area filled up with miners, prospectors, and all the various dependents who followed the boom times—35,000 in Colorado alone by 1860. The Pike's Peak story was replayed in Nevada, Montana, Idaho, and other mountain areas. Most of the wealth that was dug out of the ground left, into the hands of businessmen and bankers on either the East or the West Coast. The Comstock Lode on the eastern slope of the Sierra Nevada produced $306 million worth of silver and gold in the 20 years after 1859. By the mid-1870s much of the gold and silver had been dug out, and copper was on the way to becoming "king" of the mining frontier. Before it was all over, the culture of mountain men and miners had entered American lore as one of the most colorful in all of U.S. history. The bonanza era also left behind an environmental disaster in the form of abandoned mines, ghost towns, and poisoned earth that would be left for people of the 20th and 21st centuries to try to clean up.

The Rockies were pierced in a few places, such as South Pass, Wyoming, and Raton Pass, Colorado, allowing travelers to get across. For most of their length, however, they were virtually impenetrable by any except the hardiest, thereby cutting off all West Coast settlements from communication, economic development, and political debate with the rest of the country. Only the discovery of gold in California in 1849 prompted those in the East to forge rail and water connections with their Pacific brethren. The several ranges of mountains that formed the Rockies were broken in places by a number of basins that early on inspired settlers from the East to brave the high crossings. The most important of these basins, the Wyoming, the Columbia, and the Great Salt Lake, provided major travel corridors as well as destinations for determined emigrants on the California, Oregon, and other historic trails.

The Great Basin—present-day Utah, Nevada, Arizona, and parts of California and New Mexico—was the most arid and inhospitable part of the United States. The area between the Sierra Nevada and the Rockies was truly a desert, formed by a 13th-century drought from which it never recovered. Different sectors were given different names as people from the East pushed into this region—Death Valley; the Mojave, Sonoran, and Chihuahuan Deserts—but all were part of the same desert. The whole area covered only about half the size of the grasslands that formed the Great Plains, but unlike the latter, it invited neither settlement nor travel across its blistering sands and alkali beds. The intermontane basin was broken by mountains, plains, and plateaus but precious few rivers, those being the Gila, Salt, and, most important, the Colorado.

The Pacific coast was more notable for its cultural isolation than for any unifying geographic characteristics. It was roughly 400 miles from the crest of the Rockies to the coast, but much of the intervening space was covered by mountains (the coast ranges) or deserts. Close to the coast, the rocky soil and lack of flatlands discouraged agriculture, while several fine, sheltered harbors encouraged the development of deep-sea fishing and oceanic trade. Great forests of pine, cedar, and fir trees also thrived in the damp climate near the coasts of Washington and Oregon, providing another economic inducement to settlers. Unfortunately, the West Coast has the distinction of being one of the most geologically active regions in the world, from active volcanoes in the north to earthquake fault lines in the south. The largest of the latter was the San Andreas Fault, which ran for 750 miles down the length of California, including the two largest cities, San Francisco and Los Angeles. Already in the mid-19th century, this break in the Earth's crust was punishing Californians who had the temerity to put down roots with occasional destructive tremors. The days when California would be one of the top agricultural states in the union were still many years ahead, awaiting major irrigation projects.

The sheer size of the continent almost guaranteed broad geographic diversity. Americans had to adapt to environmental conditions to lay possession to the vast middle of the continent between Canada and Mexico, and they did. They also exploited the diversity to build broad-based economic and political systems. Geographic size and diversity encouraged the spread of democracy, provoked frequent international clashes of interest, and posed a chronic threat to the founding fathers' grand dream of union. The railroad was more than just an improved form of transportation; it was the glue that tied the sprawling country together when so many other forces were pulling it apart.

Historical Geography

Expanding the National Domain

As Americans spread out to claim a continent, they found that roughly one-fifth of their territory was arable land, a sprawling area larger than the combined areas of France and the United Kingdom, with rangeland or pastureland making up roughly one-fourth of the total land area and forests another third. Americans considered the vast storehouse theirs by birthright and were willing to battle anyone who disagreed. The U.S.-Mexican War (1846–48) that closed out the preceding era represented just another triumph against a continental rival.

During the years 1850–75, the United States continued to expand its domain although not at the same frantic pace as in earlier decades. The only two significant additions to the national domain were the Gadsden Purchase in 1853 and the Alaska Territory in 1867. The former was a strip of barren, inhospitable land on the Rio Grande border, acquired solely as a potential southern route for the future transcontinental railroad. Alaska was the first noncontiguous territory added to the United States, setting a precedent for later politically motivated acquisitions. It was purchased from Russia for no practical purpose except to remove the last vestige of the Russian empire from the Western Hemisphere. These two new additions made the total land area of the United States some 3.5 million square miles after 1867.

Meanwhile, the population per square mile, which had been inching up for decades, took a major leap after 1850, reflecting the flood of European immigrants pouring into the country in recent years. Even with the addition of the huge Alaskan territory, population was for the first time growing at a faster rate than land area. The population would continue to grow in leaps and bounds for the rest of the century and into the next, a prospect greeted with mixed feelings. No one was yet ready to hang out a sign announcing "maximum occupancy," but the possibility had to be considered that the United States would eventually fill up its empty spaces and there would be an end to the days of free or very cheap public land for the taking. Then the country would face the same overcrowding conditions that had originally driven European colonists to its shores.

TABLE 1.3 MAJOR TERRITORIAL ADDITIONS TO THE UNITED STATES, 1850–1875

Territory	Date	Area in Square Miles	Cost
Texas Cession	1850	390,144 sq. mi.	$10,000,000
Gadsden Purchase	1853	29,640 sq. mi.	$7,200,000
Alaska Purchase	1867	586,412 sq. mi.	$10,000,000

Note: As part of the Compromise of 1850, Texas ceded its disputed western lands to the United States in return for $10 million, which was to be used in part for paying off Texas's outstanding debt to bondholders from its Republic period.
Source: U.S. Bureau of the Census, *Historical Statistics of the United States, Colonial Times to 1970,* Part 1 (Washington, D.C.: U.S. Government Printing Office, 1975), 428.

TABLE 1.4 TOTAL U.S. LAND AREA AND POPULATION DENSITY ACCORDING TO CENSUS CALCULATIONS, 1840–1880

Year[a]	Area in Square Miles[b]	Resident Population	Persons per Square Mile
1840	1,788,006	17,069,453	9.8
1850	2,992,747	23,191,876	7.9
1860	3,022,387	31,443,321	10.6
1870	3,022,387[c]	39,818,449	13.4
1880	3,022,387	50,155,783	16.9

[a] Calculated as of Jun. 1, the beginning of the government's fiscal year.
[b] There is some disparity between figures cited in different sources, including the two cited here, which is due to different ways of calculating the national domain. The figures used here are from official U.S. government calculations of 1912, "adjusted" in 1960.
[c] Excludes Alaska Purchase (1867).
Sources: U.S. Bureau of the Census, *Historical Statistics of the United States, Colonial Times to 1970,* Part 1 (Washington, D.C.: U.S. Government Printing Office, 1975), 428; Otto Johnson, ed., *1996 Information Please Almanac,* 49th ed. (Boston: Houghton Mifflin, 1996), 826.

TABLE 1.5 LAND UTILIZATION BY TYPE, 1850–1870

(land in million acres)

Year	Total Land in Farms	Cropland	Woodland	Land *Not* in Farms
1850	294	113	181	1,590
1860	407	163	244	1,496
1870	408	189	219	1,495

Source: U.S. Bureau of the Census, *Historical Statistics of the United States, Colonial Times to 1970,* Part 1 (Washington, D.C.: U.S. Government Printing Office, 1975), 433.

As the nation's population steadily increased, much of that increase occurred in the western sections of the country. As a result, the census construct known as the *center of population* (defined as the fulcrum where the country would be perfectly balanced if each resident weighed exactly the same) moved farther west and south with every census. The movement could be graphically charted on a map. In 1790 the population center was 23 miles east of Baltimore. By 1820 it was in north central Virginia and by 1850 it was in western Virginia. By the time of the 1860 and 1870 censuses, it was in southern Ohio, just above the Kentucky border. (The 2000 census found it in Phelps County, Missouri, 2.8 miles east of Edgar Springs.) These calculations serve as revealing snapshots of U.S. population growth at 10-year intervals and underscore the importance of the West in the nation's history. The demographic trend reflects long-term political and economic developments: Even at this early period the voice of the West was growing ever louder and more insistent in national affairs.

While the population marched westward, the connection of that population to the land was but slowly changing. Urbanization was a tide, not a tidal wave. The United States was still overwhelmingly an agricultural nation at this point in its history. The land devoted to farming was more than five times that devoted to commerce, shipping, and manufacturing purposes. This also meant that the population was still overwhelmingly rural.

The Frontier: A Place and a Concept

The mythical frontier, of which so much would be written later, still existed as an invisible but definite line between "civilization" and the wide, unoccupied spaces of the West (or unoccupied by non-Indians). West of that line, as Americans understood it, were free land and opportunity, but also violence and lawlessness in an area where the rule of law did not much apply. Perhaps the most distinguishing aspect of the frontier was that civilization was always catching up with it, usually sooner rather than later. In 1850 the frontier line lay to the west of the Mississippi River, with the California gold rush disrupting the earlier orderly, almost inexorable east-to-west advance of the frontier that had begun during colonial times.

Another line was recognized by Americans: the line of demarcation between "East" and "West" based on climate and geography. The Great Plains, formerly described as "the Great American Desert," was an arid, flat, inhospitable area, totally unlike anything Americans had experienced between the Atlantic coastline and the Mississippi River. The dividing line was almost arbitrarily set at the 100th meridian, roughly five miles west of Fort Dodge, Kansas, because the average rainfall beyond that longitude measured less than 20 inches per year. Homesteading and town building on the Great Plains represented a whole new phase in the settlement of the West.

Trails West

Western movement followed certain, well-defined routes, most of them beginning at jumping-off points in Missouri. St. Louis was the "Gateway City" to the West, and the Oregon Trail, Santa Fe Trail, and Butterfield Stage route all began nearby. Westward travel was hard, especially, as the saying went, on women and animals, and required weeks or even months to reach final destinations in the California goldfields or Oregon's Willamette Valley.

Emigrants were dependent on isolated trading posts en route to replenish supplies and, if necessary, seek shelter from the elements or from hostile Indians. Because trading posts were few and far between, they could charge exorbitant rates for such staples as flour, sugar, and coffee. The "consumer price index" for those staples is very sketchy because of poor record keeping at the privately owned posts. For a handful of posts it can be reconstructed from available records, and the historian John D. Unruh has done this, but even for those few posts, there are many more gaps where the information is simply not available than there are known prices. Still, even this incomplete picture is sufficient to show that emigrants were often gouged by unscrupulous post agents who possessed a monopoly on the commodities they sold as the next trading post might be 100 or more miles away.

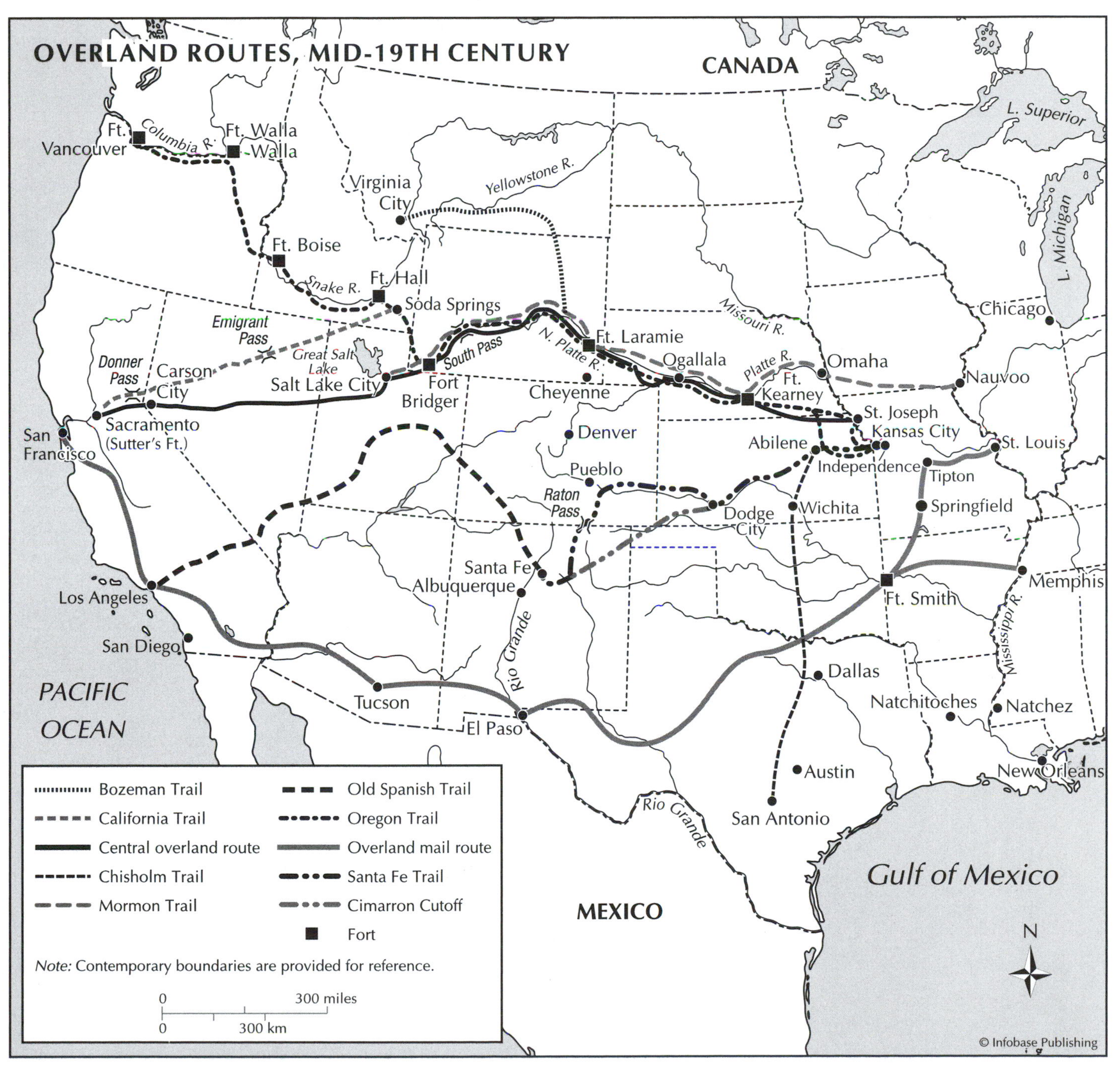

Sources: David Goldfield, Carl Abbott, et al., *The American Journey: A History of the United States.* Upper Saddle River, N.J.: Prentice Hall, 1998, 217; Stephen A. Flanders. *Atlas of American Migration,* New York: Facts On File, 1998.

TABLE 1.6 MAJOR TRAILS AND ROUTES WEST, MID- TO LATE 1800s

Trail or Route	Beginning Point	Ending Point	Length and/or Time en Route	Opened or Blazed	Traveled by	Closed	Purpose
Oregon Trail	Independence, Mo.	Astoria, Oreg.	2,000 mi. 5–6 months	1841 by John Bidwell	More than 3,000 in 1885; 4,000–5,000 in 1847	1884	Settlement cattle and sheep drives from 1870s
California Trail	Branched off the Oregon Trail at Soda Springs, Idaho	Sacramento, Calif. (Sutter's Fort)	. . .	1841 by John Bartleson and John Bidwell	Most single men: 500 in 1846	. . .	Immigration and Calif. goldfields
Bozeman Trail	Julesburg, Colo.	Virginia City, Mont.	. . .	1862–63 by John M. Bozeman	. . .	Largely abandoned, 1867–68; revived for cattle after 1877	Route to goldfields; cattle moved north from Tex. after 1877, Calif.-bound immigrants (gold)
Santa Fe Trail and Cimarron Cutoff	Franklin, Mo.; then Independence, Mo. (1830); then Westport, Mo. (now Kansas City)	Santa Fe, N.Mex.	780 mi. 2–3 months	1821 by William Becknell ("Father of the Santa Fe Trail")	Approximately 80 wagons/yr. up to 1843; 5,000 wagons/yr. by late 1860s (Conestoga wagons)	1880 (Completion of Atchison, Topeka, & Santa Fe RR)	Trade; stagecoach & mail after 1846
Overland Mail Route (Butterfield Overland Mail; Southern Overland Route)	St. Louis, Mo., and Memphis, Tenn., converge at Ft. Smith, Ark.	Los Angeles and San Francisco, Calif.	2,812 mi. 20–25 days	Sept. 15, 1858	Four-horse Concord Coaches, carrying up to nine passengers inside	Moved to central route when Civil War began	Passengers and U.S. govt. mail
Central Overland Route	St. Joseph, Mo.	Folsom, Calif.	30 days one way	1849	Stagecoach and Pony Express	1869 (after completion of first transcontinental RR)	Mail (excluding newspapers and documents)
Chisholm Trail	San Antonio, Tex.	Abilene, Kans. (later Caldwell, Kans., Ellsworth, Newton, Kans.)	1,000 mi.	1866: By Jesse Chisholm; first cattle drive 1867	1.5 million cattle by 1870	1885	Cattle drives North to railhead
Mormon Trail	Nauvoo, Ill.	Great Salt Lake Valley, Utah	1,100 mi.	1846–47 by a "Pioneer Band"	Wagons, handcarts, and on foot; some 12,000 in 1847–48; 80,000 by 1869 (estimate)	1869 (after railroad)	Route traveled by Mormons under Joseph Smith and Brigham Young, fleeing persecution
Old Spanish Trail	Santa Fe, N.M.	Los Angeles, Calif.	. . .	1829–30 by Antonio Armijo	Large pack caravans	1850s	Trade

Sources: Howard R. Lamar, ed., *The Reader's Encyclopedia of the American West* (New York: Thomas Y. Crowell, 1977); Robert M. Utley and Wilcomb E. Washburn, *The American Heritage History of the Indian Wars* (New York: Simon & Schuster in conjunction with American Heritage, 1977), passim.

Thousands of families like this pulled up roots, loaded everything they owned on a wagon, and found a wagon train headed for the West. (Arkansas History Commission)

TABLE 1.7 PRICES AT TRADING POSTS ALONG THE ROUTE FOR OVERLAND MIGRANTS GOING WEST, 1850–1860

Flour[a]				
Year	Fort Laramie, Wyo.	Ragtown, Nev.	Carson Valley, Nev.	From Ft. Hall, Idaho, to Oreg.
1850	$0.12–$0.50	$1.25–$2.50	$0.40–$2.50	. . .
1851	. . .	. . .	. . .	$0.15–$0.20
1852	$10.00–$10.50 per 100 lb.	$0.20–$0.25	$0.25–$0.40	. . .
1853	. . .	. . .	$0.50	$0.20–$0.50
1854	$10.50–$25.00 per 100 lb.	$0.40–$0.50	$0.23	. . .
1855	. . .	. . .	. . .	. . .
1856	. . .	$0.25	. . .	. . .
1857	. . .	$0.20–$0.30	. . .	. . .
1858	. . .	. . .	. . .	. . .
1859	. . .	$0.40	. . .	. . .
1860	$16.00 per 100 lb.	. . .	. . .	. . .
Sugar[a]				
Year	Fort Laramie, Wyo.	Ragtown, Nev.	Carson Valley, Nev.	From Ft. Hall, Idaho, to Oreg.
1850	$0.50–$2.00	$1.00–$2.00	$1.25–$1.50	. . .
1851	. . .	. . .	. . .	$0.37½–$0.75
1852	$0.50–$0.75	$0.50	$0.50	. . .
1853	. . .	. . .	. . .	. . .
1854	. . .	. . .	. . .	. . .
1855	. . .	. . .	. . .	. . .
1856	. . .	. . .	. . .	. . .
1857	. . .	. . .	. . .	. . .
1858	. . .	. . .	. . .	. . .
1859	. . .	$75.00 per 100 lb.	. . .	. . .
1860	$0.45	. . .	. . .	. . .

(continued)

TABLE 1.7 (continued)

Coffee[a]				
Year	Fort Laramie, Wyo.	Ragtown, Nev.	Carson Valley, Nev.	From Ft. Hall, Idaho, to Oreg.
1850	$0.50	$1.00–$1.50	$0.50–$0.75	...
1851	...	...	...	...
1852	$0.40	...	$50.00 per 100 lb.	...
1853	...	...	...	...
1854	...	...	...	...
1855	...	...	...	...
1856	...	...	...	...
1857	...	...	...	...
1858	...	...	...	...
1859	...	...	...	...
1860	...	...	...	...
Liquor[b]				
Year	Fort Laramie, Wyo.	Ragtown, Nev.	Carson Valley, Nev.	From Ft. Hall, Idaho, to Oreg.
1850	$0.75	$1.00 per drink	$2.00–$4.00	...
1851	...	...	...	...
1852	...	$1.00	...	...
1853	...	...	...	...
1854	...	...	...	...
1855	...	...	...	...
1856	...	...	...	...
1857	...	...	...	...
1858	...	...	...	...
1859	...	$1.00–$1.50	...	...
1860	$0.75	...	...	...
Bacon[a]				
Year	Fort Laramie, Wyo.	Ragtown, Nev.	Carson Valley, Nev.	From Ft. Hall, Idaho, to Oreg.
1850	$0.50	$1.00–$1.50	...	...
1851	...	...	...	...
1852	$0.15	$0.40–$0.50	$50.00 per 100 lb.	...
1853	...	...	...	...
1854	...	...	...	...
1855	...	...	...	...
1856	...	...	...	...
1857	...	...	...	...
1858	...	...	...	...
1859	...	...	...	...
1860	...	...	...	...
Beef[a]				
Year	Fort Laramie, Wyo.	Ragtown, Nev.	Carson Valley, Nev.	From Ft. Hall, Idaho, to Oreg.
1850	...	$0.25–$1.00	$0.50–$2.00	...
1851	...	...	...	...
1852	...	$0.25–$0.30	...	...
1853	...	...	...	...
1854	...	...	...	...
1855	...	...	...	...
1856	...	...	...	...
1857	...	...	...	...
1858	...	...	...	...
1859	...	...	...	...
1860	...	...	...	...

Potatoes[a]				
Year	Fort Laramie, Wyo.	Ragtown, Nev.	Carson Valley, Nev.	From Ft. Hall, Idaho, to Oreg.
1850	. . .	. . .	. . .	. . .
1851	. . .	. . .	. . .	. . .
1852	. . .	. . .	. . .	. . .
1853	. . .	. . .	. . .	. . .
1854	. . .	$0.12–$0.25	$0.10	. . .
1855	. . .	. . .	. . .	. . .
1856	. . .	. . .	. . .	. . .
1857	. . .	. . .	. . .	. . .
1858	. . .	. . .	. . .	. . .
1859	. . .	. . .	. . .	. . .
1860	. . .	. . .	. . .	. . .

Note: Ragtown, Nev., was also known as Johnson's Station. For 1853–60 these prices are for Laramie to Ragtown.
[a] Price per pound except where indicated.
[b] Price per pint except where indicated.
Source: John D. Unruh, Jr., *The Plains Across, The Overland Emigrant and the Trans-Mississippi West, 1840–60* (Urbana: University of Illinois Press, 1982), 204, 227, 234, 241.

The trails followed by wagon trains were all superseded by rail lines after 1869, when the first transcontinental railroad was completed. Both trunk and feeder lines were already multiplying across the country by the end of this period. The East had a head start and shorter distances to traverse with its railroads, but the West was already witnessing a frenzy of construction that changed basic patterns of movement and drove economic development until the end of the century and beyond. Those famous western trails were important, not just for movement of emigrants, but for trade. Before the railroad, most goods were moved by horse-drawn or ox-drawn wagons over well-known routes such as the Santa Fe Trail.

TABLE 1.8 WHAT KANSAS CITY, MISSOURI, RECEIVED FROM NEW MEXICO VIA SANTA FE TRAIL, 1858

Commodity	Amount Shipped	Value
Mexican wool	1,051,000 lb.	$167,650
Goatskins	55,000	$27,500
Dressed deerskins	60,000	$175,000
Dry hides	61,857	$170,107
Specie (gold and silver)	. . .	$1,527,789
Furs, other skins	Unknown	$50,000

Source: Kansas City *Journal of Commerce*, cited in Mike Flanagan, *The Old West, Day by Day* (New York: Facts On File, 1995), 113.

Development of the West

As Americans filled up the West, clearing the land, planting crops, and building towns, there was a subtle shift in the way they regarded the land. The conventional attitude about "the wilderness" had always been that it was a cruel enemy to be subdued; now, increasingly, it was being seen as an "American Eden," to be preserved and protected for posterity. This characterization was reflected in the national park movement that began after the Civil War.

"Opening the West," as it was picturesquely called, started with pathfinders—men such as John C. Frémont (1813–90), Jim Bridger (1804–81), and William Becknell (1788–1865). These rugged explorers—most employed by the government at one time or another; others, reclusive mountain men of the type celebrated in folklore—continued to push into the last isolated corners of the Far West, looking for mineral wealth, new routes to old places, the headwaters of mighty rivers, or more scenic wonders to report. Everybody who went west was not seeking a homestead or town site; the urge to explore and see new places still beat strongly in the American heart. Several well-known artists made names for themselves by painting the Far West for an eastern audience who never traveled west of the Adirondacks. Later, photographers aimed to provide a more realistic depiction of an area already being transformed into mythical status. As artists and photographers did, writers traveled all over the West seeking material for their stories and travelogues to sell to eager armchair adventurers back East.

Mining Bonanzas

Economics was probably the strongest draw for Americans contemplating a move to the frontier or beyond. This was the era of the greatest mining bonanzas in American history. The California gold rush (1849) and the Black Hills gold rush (1875) serve as the book ends to the period, although the first major gold rush in American history started 20 years earlier in 1829 in the Dahlonega area of north Georgia. The scenario was the same one played out later in countless strikes across the West: the rush into the area of thousands of men with dreams of instant riches, the mining claims that sprang up on every hillside and creek branch, the rumors of biscuit-sized (and larger) nuggets, the overnight appearance of complete towns, and the epidemic of lawlessness. The state set up a land lottery to auction off "gold lots" and "land lots." Through it all, a steady stream of gold was pulled out of the ground. The countless mining claims staked out by the "Twenty-niners" were so productive that the U.S. government established a branch mint in Dahlonega, Georgia, and by 1861, $6,106,569 worth of gold had been coined. When gold was discovered at Sutter's Mill near Sacramento in 1848, California became the new El Dorado (a place of fabulous wealth or opportunity derived from the country of that name believed by 16th-century explorers to exist in South America), and many of the remaining Georgia miners pulled up stakes and headed west to strike it rich in the California goldfields while Dahlonega died a slow death.

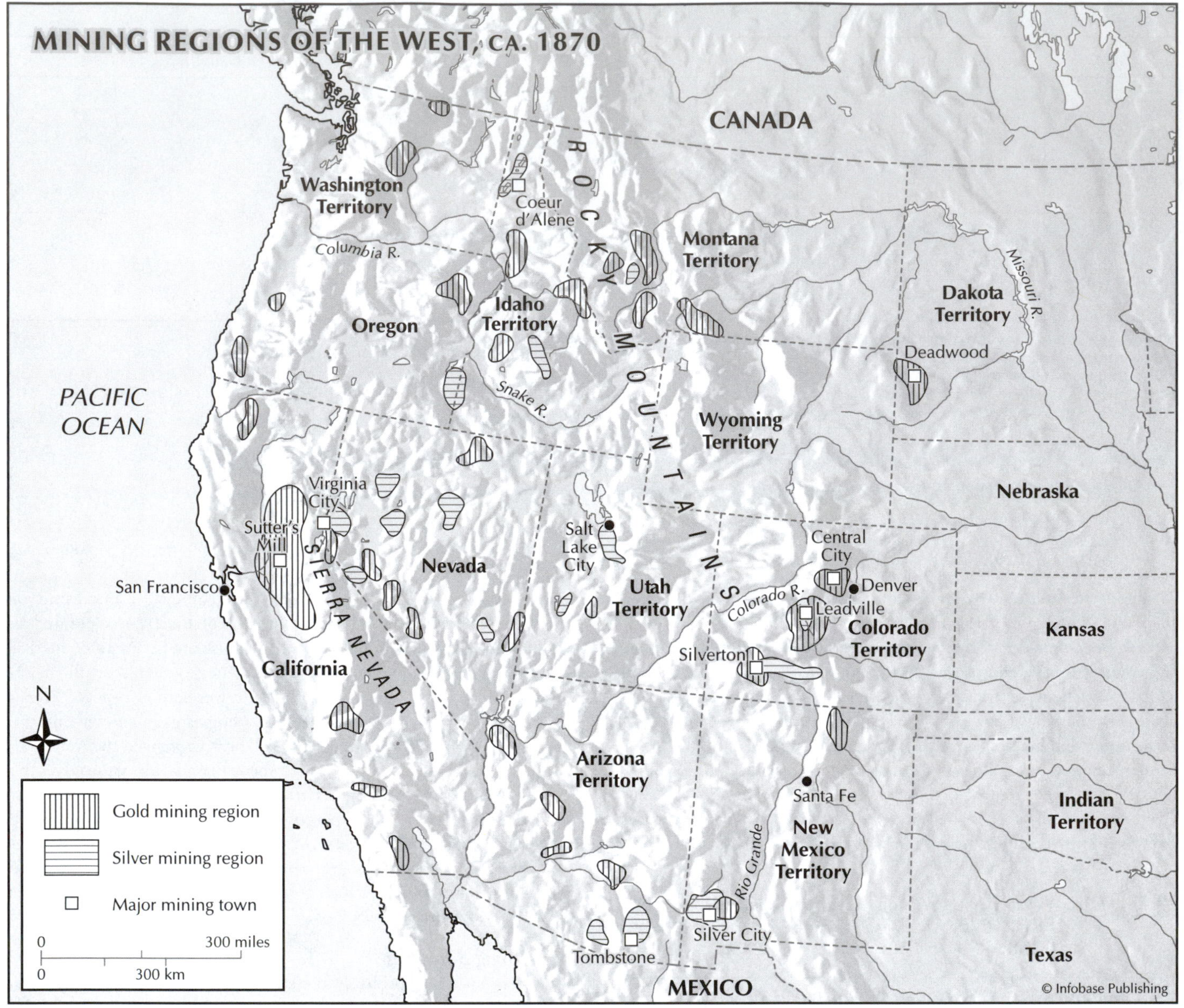

Source: Robert A. Divine et al., *America Past and Present,* vol. 2, 6th ed. (New York: Longman, 2000), 506.

After Sutter's Mill were the Pike's Peak, Comstock, and other, lesser strikes. The original strikes in each case were by independent miners who became a subculture and then a stereotype of the American West. But big companies soon moved in and took over the mining of the West, generating huge profits by turning a prospector's dream claim into a highly mechanized industry.

The 26 years between 1849 and 1875 represent the most active mining era in U.S. history. The California gold rush (1849) was followed by the Pike's Peak gold strike and the Comstock silver strike (both, 1859), and finally by the Black Hills gold rush in 1875. All these strikes produced enormous wealth and gave a healthy boost to the national economy; they also had far more negative consequences not fully appreciated until more than 100 years after most of the mines had played out. Sixty-one 19th-century mining sites have been identified in recent years as needing expensive cleanups, a process that will cost an estimated $20 billion before completed. Acid drainage, heavy-metal sediment, abandoned shafts, and piles of tailings have left permanent scars all over the West. Nobody in the mid-19th century gave much thought to this dark legacy of the great mining era as long as the mines were producing the stuff of dreams. The final bill for recklessly mining the West's vast mineral wealth was left for future generations to pay.

All that Americans took out of the ground was not gold and silver. Other minerals, less flashy, also in demand, yielded huge profits, including lead, copper, and especially iron. In the mid-19th century, most American iron was from deposits in Missouri (Pilot Knob and Iron Mountain). The opening of new iron deposits in the Mesabi Range around Lake Superior held out the promise of a practically inexhaustible supply of high-grade ore to feed burgeoning industries after the Civil War. Indeed, the mineral bonanza was an essential adjunct to American industrialization.

Fresh discoveries of gold and silver all over the West kept prospectors rushing from the site of one strike to the next, as depicted in this engraving of a miner frantically loading his horse for a quick departure from Denver, Colorado, for the Black Hills of the Dakota Territory. (Library of Congress)

Energy to Power an Economy

This was the age of wood and coal power sources. They went hand-in-glove with the development of the steam engine. Although the first oil well was brought in at Titusville, Pennsylvania, in 1859, petroleum and its by products were not used as fuel for some years. In the meantime, coal and wood drove the nation's machines. To get them, Americans cut down forests and dug in the ground with reckless abandon. Some idea of the enormous amounts of both fuel sources burned up in running the nation's growing number of steam engines can be gleaned from the amount of each required to power steamboats on the western rivers. To keep the vessels running, it was necessary to have enormous stacks of wood and piles of coal always on hand at the landings where they made regular stops. Such "fuel dumps" were unsightly, created fire hazards, and provided breeding grounds for rats.

TABLE 1.9 FUEL CONSUMPTION OF SOME TYPICAL STEAMBOATS ON WESTERN RIVERS, CA. 1870s
(per trip)

Boat	Route	Bushels of Coal per Trip	Cords of Wood per Trip	Pounds of Coal/Wood (Equivalent) Burned per Hour
Clipper No. 2	Pittsburgh–Cincinnati	3,200	None	2,545
Brilliant	Pittsburgh–Cincinnati	4,000	50	3,892
Keystone State	Pittsburgh–Cincinnati	3,000	72	3,409
Buckeye State	Pittsburgh–Cincinnati	4,000	50	4,281
Messenger No. 2	Pittsburgh–Cincinnati	3,000	60	3,032
Cincinnati	Pittsburgh–Cincinnati	3,000	20	Unknown
Hibernia No. 2	Pittsburgh–Cincinnati	2,500	80	2,989
Bostona	Louisville–New Orleans	None	660	3,125

Note: For conversion purposes, it is helpful to know that one ton of coal was reckoned approximately equal to two cords of wood.
Source: Louis C. Hunter, *Steamboats on the Western Rivers* (New York: Octagon Books, 1969), 650–51.

The Cattle-Driving Era

The exploitation of nature took an entirely different form on the Great Plains in these same years—the range cattle industry. Beef on the hoof and cattle drives to market were nothing new to Americans, but after the Civil War the combination of herds of wild longhorns in south Texas; vast open grasslands; and an insatiable market for beef back East created a booming industry. The combination also produced enormous environmental and social consequences. Beef became a staple of Americans' diet, longhorns displaced buffalo, railroads pushed westward to establish railhead destinations for cattle drives, and fencing parceled off the wide open spaces of the Great Plains into private fiefdoms. Beginning with the first long drive in 1866, cattle trails added a new type of migratory route to the familiar mix. From 1866 to 1885 they were the most widespread and important means of transportation for the range cattle industry. They tended to follow old Indian or pioneer trails across public land, where there was plenty of water and grass free for the taking. The five principal cattle trails during the heyday of the range cattle era all originated in south Texas before wending their way northward to either grazing ranges on the northern plains or railheads in the Midwest: the Shawnee Trail, the Chisholm Trail, the Eastern Trail, the Western Trail, and the Goodnight-Loving Trail.

The exact numbers of cattle that were moved up these trails could never be accurately calculated, but according to the best estimates, some 35,000 cattle were driven north the first big year (1867); that number grew to 600,000 in the peak year of 1871 and declined until it reached 250,000 in 1881, the last major year of the long drives before the railroads took over most of the business of moving cattle.

Long before then, cattle drives had changed the face of the West far beyond the trails, huge ranches, and ever-advancing railheads. They put Kansas on the map and created a whole new urban culture quickly dubbed cowtowns. Among the major cowtowns were Fort Worth, Texas, and Abilene and Dodge City, Kansas. Cattlemen became the first land barons in the West. They were able to thrive as long as there was free grass, plenty of water, and open country to drive their herds through on the way to market. The importance of the cattle industry also explains the surge of several cities, including Chicago and Kansas City, which became important for their stockyards and slaughterhouses, which transformed beef on the hoof to beef on the table.

Together, cattle and mining filled up many of the empty spaces of the West and solidified Americans' claim to a continent. Later, the historian Frederick Jackson Turner in his "frontier thesis" enshrined them as defining two stages in the long, evolutionary development of the American West.

Abilene, Kansas, was nothing but a dot on the Great Plains when the first cattle drives began to travel there in 1867. Four years later it was a wild and woolly cowtown and railhead. In this engraving from *Frank Leslie's Illustrated Newspaper*, ca. 1871, Texas longhorns are being loaded onto cars of the Kansas Pacific Railroad via a "cattle-shoot." (Library of Congress)

TABLE 1.10 PRINCIPAL WESTERN CATTLE TRAILS NORTH FROM TEXAS, 1840–1880s

Trail	Alternate Name or Branch(es)	Developed by or Named for	Starting Point	Ending Point(s)	Length	Rail Connection[a]	Active Years
Shawnee	Sedalia and Baxter Springs	Unknown	Brownsville, Tex.	Kansas City, Mo. Sedalia, Mo.	800 mi.	Atchison, Topeka & Santa Fe at Kansas City; Missouri-Kansas & Texas at Sedalia	1840s–Civil War
Chisholm	Chisholm Trail Cutoff, or Cox Trail	Cherokee trader Jesse Chisholm and Joseph McCoy	Brownsville, Tex. (San Antonio, Tex.)	Abilene, Kans. (Dodge City, Caldwell, Wichita, Newton, Ellsworth, Kans.)	600 mi.	Kansas-Pacific at Abilene; Atchison, Topeka & Santa Fe at Newton and Dodge City	1867–78
Eastern	Merged with Chisholm and Shawnee Trails above Sabine R.; split with Shawnee near Red R.; roughly paralleled Chisholm to Abilene	Unknown	King Ranch and Laureles Ranch (Austin, Waco, Fort Worth)	Abilene, Kans.	600 mi.	Kansas-Pacific	1867–70s
Western	Jones and Plummer, or Texas	Lucien Maxwell	San Antonio, Tex. (Bandera, Tex.)	Ogallala, Nebr., via Dodge City, Kans.	900 mi.	Atchison, Topeka & Santa Fe at Dodge City	1872–86
Goodnight-Loving	Goodnight or Dodge Trail	Cattlemen Charles Goodnight and Oliver Loving	Just west of Fort Worth, Tex.	Cheyenne, Wyo.	700 mi.	Kansas-Pacific at Denver; Atchison, Topeka & Santa Fe at Pueblo, Colo.	1866–85

Note: Cattle trails were not interstate highways that always went from point A to point B over the same road every time. They shifted to find grass and water, were known by different names to different people, and had no precise starting points. Where more than one point of origin or termination is recognized, alternate points appear in parentheses.
[a] The Missouri, Kansas & Texas Railroad is generally known as "the KATY."
Sources: Harry Sinclair Drago, *Great American Cattle Trails* (New York: Dodd, Mead & Company, 1965), passim; Howard R. Lamar, ed., *The Reader's Encyclopedia of the American West* (New York: Thomas Y. Crowell, 1977), passim.

Land Policy and the National Domain

For many Americans, their first encounter with the federal government occurred when they tried to lay claim to a piece of the public domain. The government controlled millions of acres of western territory through the ancient principle of eminent domain. Unofficial—and often official—policy was to transfer as much of that bounty as possible, as quickly as possible, to private hands. The challenge was to ensure as fair and equitable a transfer as possible, and this is where problems often arose. The major problem was that many settlers moved out west before government surveyors did, and they squatted on the land claiming it as their own by right of getting there first. The government recognized their rights with the Pre-Emotion Act of 1841 but thereafter tried to increase organization and control of the distribution of western lands with legislation such as the Homestead Act of 1862, the Morrill Act of 1862, and the Timber Culture Act of 1873. Under these and other official acts, parcels of land were liberally allotted to states, industries, local communities, and individuals to encourage such worthy objectives as economic development, education, and national security. Federal land policy as it evolved proved to be quite generous, even to a fault, favoring speculators rather than homesteaders thanks to initially pricing the acreage too high, setting no limits on the amount one might purchase, and not enforcing provisions about improving the land. The Homestead Act (1862) is often seen as the ultimate government response to calls by ordinary citizens for free land and the crowning glory of a beneficent national land policy. In truth, however, much of the best land in the West had already been given away to states and railroads. In terms of sheer acreage, however, the amount of land transferred to various public and private entities over the years is staggering. Under the Homestead Act alone, 48,000,000 acres was transferred to private individuals by 1890. The Morrill Act made available to the states 30,000 acres for each representative they had in Congress, and eventually every state claimed its share. And the Timber Culture Act disposed of another 10,000,000 acres, most of it under fraudulent claims, before its repeal in 1891. The Desert Land Act of 1877 and the Timber and Stone Act of 1878, which fall outside the scope of this volume, also transferred millions of acres of public domain to private hands. For the years 1850–75 alone, some 139,000,000 acres of land was either given away or sold at cut-rate prices under a prevailing philosophy that the best use of the public domain was to put it into private hands. The largest single packages were railroad grants (beginning with the Illinois Central in 1850) created to encourage more construction, an exercise in free enterprise backed by government subsidy that paid huge dividends in the long run.

The Environmental Cost of Conquering a Continent

The conquest and settlement of a continent could be thrilling, even heroic; it could also be hard on the native flora and fauna. The American cornucopia produced an unforeseen consequence: wastefulness and destructiveness on a grand scale. The white man was most to blame for this. Conservation and ecological stewardship were practically unknown to the American people historically and had few advocates in the rush to settle a continent. They saw the land as something to be possessed and exploited to the maximum, not nurtured and conserved for future generations. In fact, conservation stood in the way of the cherished ideal of self-advancement. This bounteous land was the rock on which the great U.S. commonwealth was built.

TABLE 1.11 DISPOSAL OF U.S. PUBLIC LANDS FOR SELECTED YEARS, 1850–1875

Year	Transferred to States (acres)	Land Sales and Grants to Citizens (acres)	Number of Homesteads under 1862 Law	Land Transferred under Homestead Law (acres)
1850	55,401,000	. . .	. . .	. . .
1853	5,587,000	. . .	. . .	. . .
1855	46,000	. . .	. . .	. . .
1857	2,974,000	. . .	. . .	. . .
1859	3,498,000	. . .	. . .	. . .
1861	3,052,000	. . .	. . .	. . .
1862	9,420,000	. . .	. . .	. . .
1863	. . .	. . .	8,223	. . .
1864	4,955,000	. . .	9,405	. . .
1865	. . .	. . .	8,924	. . .
1866	226,000	. . .	15,355	. . .
1867	4,000	. . .	16,957	. . .
1868	. . .	. . .	23,746	355,000
1869	. . .	6,678,000	25,628	504,000
1870	. . .	6,663,000	33,972	520,000
1871	. . .	7,119,000	39,768	629,000
1872	. . .	7,248,000	38,742	707,000
1873	. . .	6,386,000	31,561	1,225,000
1874	. . .	4,784,000	29,126	1,586,000
1875	3,842,000	3,792,000	20,668	2,069,000

Source: Historical Statistics of the United States: Colonial Times to 1970, Part 1, (Washington, D.C.: U.S. Government Printing Office), 430.

TABLE 1.12 DISPOSING OF THE PUBLIC DOMAIN: FEDERAL GOVERNMENT LAND GRANTS AND ALLOTMENTS, NINETEENTH CENTURY

Policy or Legislation	Date	Amount	Recipient(s)	Purpose
Implementing treaties of annexation and cession with foreign governments	19th century	35 million acres	Individual land grant holders	To resolve all title claims from predecessor governments
Railroad land grants	1850–71	181 million acres[a]	Railroad companies	To encourage construction and development in the West
Homestead Act	1862	80 million acres	Private individuals	To encourage settlement on the Great Plains
Land Grant Act (Morrill Act)[b]	1862	11 million acres[c]	The states	To sell off in order to fund agricultural colleges and universities
Dawes Severalty Act	1887	75 million acres	Individual Indians and later whites	To break up the Indian reservations and tribal structure
Various other grants	19th century	129 million acres[c]	The states	To sell off in order to fund general education and other public institutions

[a] Some sources say 174 million acres.
[b] A second Morrill Act was passed in 1890 providing cash allotments for "land-grant" colleges.
[c] Some sources use 72 million acres for total grants to states for all educational purposes and other public institutions, instead of splitting off the Morrill and other acreage from the total.
Source: David Goldfield et al., *The American Journey: A History of the United States* (Upper Saddle River, N.J.: Prentice-Hall, 1998), 394; Howard R. Lamar, *The Reader's Encyclopedia of the American West* (New York: Thomas Y. Crowell, 1977), passim.

TABLE 1.13 PUBLIC LAND GRANTS BY UNITED STATES TO AID IN CONSTRUCTION OF RAILROADS, WAGON ROADS, AND CANALS, 1851–1871

Year	Total Grants	Purpose			
		Railroads	Wagon Roads	Canals	River Improvements
1851	3,752	3,752	0	0	0
1852	1,773	1,773	0	0	0
1853	3,379	2,629	0	750	0
1854	. . .	. . .	. . .	. . .	. . .
1855	. . .	. . .	. . .	. . .	. . .
1856	14,085	14,085	0	0	0
1857	6,689	6,689	0	0	0
1858	. . .	. . .	. . .	. . .	. . .
1859	. . .	. . .	. . .	. . .	. . .
1860	. . .	. . .	. . .	. . .	. . .
1861	. . .	. . .	. . .	. . .	. . .
1862	. . .	. . .	. . .	. . .	. . .
1863	31,401	30,877	524	0	0
1864	2,349	2,349	0	0	0
1865	42,794	41,452	941	401	0
1866	200	0	0	200	0
1867	25,173	23,535	1,538	100	0
1868	. . .	. . .	. . .	. . .	. . .
1869	105	0	105	0	0
1870	129	129	0	0	0
1871	3,253	3,253	0	0	0

Source: U.S. Bureau of the Census, *Historical Statistics of the United States, Colonial Times to 1970,* Part 1 (Washington, D.C.: U.S. Government Printing Office, 1975), 430.

Most 19th-century Americans would have agreed with the historian Frederick Jackson Turner, who wrote in 1920, "Free land in the West promoted a uniquely egalitarian society in the United States, and migration to the frontier provided a safety valve for urban discontent and preserved the peace of American politics." The downside to this rosy picture was the sheet wastefulness of westward expansion, expressed by one old homesteader to his young protégé this way: "Why, son, by the time I was yore age I'd wore out three farms." Only late in the game did Americans wake up to the fact that the bounty was not limitless and that resources heedlessly squandered were lost forever.

The desirability of *managing* the environment, as opposed to *subduing* it, led to the beginnings of a small but vocal conservation movement. The few advocates actively preaching conservation found themselves lonely voices in the wilderness, the object of scorn and sometimes worse. Ulysses Grant's secretary of the interior, the liberal Jacob D. Cox, former governor of Ohio, began in 1870 urging the prudent, even restrained, use of the nation's natural resources. For his efforts he found himself forced out of office by a Congress in thrall to developers, mining companies, and railroads.

One victim of civilization in the 19th-century was the buffalo, or American bison. The destruction of the vast buffalo herds that once roamed the Great Plains was motivated by the misguided war against the Plains Indians, plus the valuable profits to be made from selling buffalo parts on the open market. When Europeans arrived on the continent, the buffalo, or American bison, ranged from the Rocky Mountains to the Atlantic coast and from southern Canada to northern Mexico. In 1853, according to some authorities, the bison population still numbered between 60 and 70 million animals. Most authorities place their estimates at a more conservative 15 to 20 million. Either way, the slaughter is truly mind-boggling. In the next 40 years the once-vast herds were reduced, through deliberate extermination, to less than 1,000 known animals. This was the result of human greed, uncontrolled exploitation, and the U.S. government's strategy of defeating the Plains Indians by eliminating the source of their sustenance.

Nobody kept careful count of the slaughter; however, some numbers are known. An 1869 report noted that in a good year, about 250,000 hides were shipped to the New York market alone. Railroad shipments between 1872 and 1874 totaled 1,378,359 hides. When commercial exploitation and sport hunting of the buffalo peaked in 1872, some 2,000 hunters were working in western Kansas alone, bringing down about 15 bison per hunter per day. This added up to some 30,000 animals killed daily, not for meat, but for the hides, horns, and tongues (considered a delicacy), and this was just in Kansas. Similar scenarios were being played out in Texas,

TABLE 1.14 A HISTORY OF SLAUGHTER: DECIMATION OF THE AMERICAN BISON, NINETEENTH CENTURY

Year	Estimated Number of Animals
1800	40,000,000
1850	20,000,000
1865	15,000,000
1875	1,000,000
1880	395,000
1885	20,000
1895	Fewer than 1,000

Source: Arlene Hirschfelder and Martha Kreipe de Montaño, *The Native American Almanac* (New York: Macmillan USA, 1993), 18.

Colorado, Indian Territory, and the Dakotas. When the herds in one area were decimated, after about four years of aggressive hunting, the hunters moved on to another area and the process resumed. They took what they wanted from the still-warm carcass and left the rest to rot in the sun. Adding to the tragedy, the hunts were not controlled or managed; the slaughter was indiscriminate, with each hunter or hunting party taking as many animals as they could shoot. Farmers followed the hunters and gathered the sun-bleached bones to sell for fertilizer.

The mass slaughter was virtually over by 1883, not because buffalo killing had gone out of style, but because the vast herds that had been the objects of the slaughter were gone. No one could believe at first that an entire native species had been practically wiped out in less than a generation, particularly the Plains Indians, who depended on the buffalo for food. But the evidence was inescapable. Except for a few isolated animals in Yellowstone National Park, the Texas Panhandle, and Canada, there were no more American bison. It was an ecological disaster.

Only a thoughtful few recognized what was being done to the environment. One of those was George Perkins Marsh, a diplomat, historian, philologist, and scientist, who wrote what is widely regarded as the most influential American geographical work of the 19th century. *Man and Nature* (1864) examined the consequences of people's heedless destruction of nature. Later Marsh republished it as *The Earth as Modified by Human Action,* and it helped launch the conservation movement in both the United States and Europe.

In the rush to subsidize railroad construction and mining and generally to encourage economic development, the government seldom gave much thought to stewardship of the nation's land and resources. Congress was, as a rule, much more interested in development than in conservation in these years, in giving land away rather than in setting it aside. Under the Swamplands Act of 1850, swampy or flood-prone lands deemed unfit for cultivation were given to the states where they were located as an inducement for draining them. This act applied only to states that entered the union before 1860, however. One misguided attempt at ecological management was the Timber Culture Act of 1873, which supplemented the 1862 Homestead Act by promising an additional 160 acres of land to settlers for every 40 acres (later reduced to 10 acres) of trees they planted on the Great Plains and maintained for 10 years. Well intentioned to be sure, the Timber Culture Act in the end made snapping up huge chunks of land practically free even easier for speculators and had no visible effect on alleviating the dry conditions of the Great Plains. (It would be repealed in 1891.)

Congress took the first hesitant steps toward preserving some of the unspoiled natural wilderness for future generations in 1864, when it granted the Yosemite Valley and nearby Mariposa Grove of magnificent redwoods to the state of California as a public park. It would

This engraving by W. Measom, from a sketch by Ernest Griset, shows the slaughter of the buffalo on the Kansas Pacific Railroad. One of the unforeseen consequences of pushing the railroad across the Great Plains was the opportunity to shoot at the mighty creatures from the safety of the train. Thousands were killed in this way and left lying on the plains for the buzzards. (Library of Congress)

remain the state's jewel until 1890, when it was incorporated into the nascent national park system. The idea that Congress should take the responsibility for preserving the nation's natural wonders had developed only slowly. The first real measure of what could be considered a federal conservation policy by modern sensibilities was the creation of Yellowstone National Park in 1872. Congress passed the legislation setting aside 2,221,773 acres from the public domain as a "pleasuring-ground" for the American people, protected for all time from commercial exploitation. The establishment of the Yellowstone preserve set the precedent for all subsequent national parks and made such set-asides national policy. Other nations would model their own national park systems on the U.S. example.

It is doubtful that Yellowstone would ever have been set aside in its pristine state if not for the efforts of the Hayden expedition in 1871–72. Ferdinand Vendeveer Hayden led this first scientific (as opposed to hunting and trapping) party into the region; when the party returned, it publicized Yellowstone's natural beauties, thanks largely to the work of the pioneer photographer William H. Jackson and the artist Thomas Moran, both of whom were members of the expedition. The self-styled naturalist John Muir was one of the first explorers of the Yosemite Valley. In 1871 he invited the philosopher Ralph Waldo Emerson "to join me," as he put it, "in a month's work-shop with Nature in the high temples of the great Sierra Crown. No temple made with hands can compare with Yosemite. Every rock in its walls seems to glow with life." Emerson accepted the invitation and was impressed enough to write in his journal, "This valley is the only place that comes up to the brag about it, and exceeds it."

Hayden and Muir were members of a remarkable fraternity of people who fanned out across the West in these years seeking to unlock the secrets of America's vast natural storehouse. They created a new calling in American life, that of naturalist—one who studies nature in all its forms, a broader calling than the profession of botanist or geologist. Perhaps the most famous member of that fraternity in America was John Jacob Audubon (1785–1851). Interested in ornithology and art, he combined them in his career, becoming the acknowledged expert on birds and mammals of North America. Unfortunately he died just as this period was beginning, but he left a legacy that others carried on.

Explorers and Pathfinders

There were other explorers at work during these years who did not call themselves naturalists, but who nonetheless advanced the cause of knowledge in numerous fields. The middle decades of the 19th century represent the tail end of the last great age of discovery, which began with the expedition of Meriwether Lewis and William Clark in 1804–06. From 1851 to 1875 U.S. explorers headed for distant unknown corners of the continent to explore and survey the trackless wilderness. The military took an active interest in the exploration of the West because of its concern for national defense. The Corps of Topographical Engineers (created in 1831) was the section of the War Department charged specifically with surveying routes for roads, canals, and railroads; supervising harbor and river improvements; conducting western explorations and carrying out various boundary and coastal surveys; and constructing wagon roads in the trans-Mississippi West. They split their time between civil and military projects, and they were the principal arm of the federal government responsible for internal improvements. The Department of the Interior (created in 1848) was also active in exploring and mapping terra incognita, specifically in the collection of geological and geographical data for government use. Smaller contributions were made by the scientific community in the form of the Academy of Natural Sciences of Philadelphia, the Boston Society of Natural History, and particularly the Smithsonian Institution.

Survey teams funded by the federal government and organized by the War Department led the way in the aftermath of the U.S.-Mexican War (1846–48). One of the first areas to be explored was the Great Salt Lake basin. Mormons had already settled there in 1847, and the next year the territory of Utah was officially acquired from Mexico as part of the Treaty of Guadalupe-Hidalgo. In 1849 Captain Howard Stansbury of the Topographical Engineers was ordered to make a survey of the area, from the location where the Weber River entered the lake from the east. His guide was the famed mountain man Jim Bridger, and his assistant was John Williams Gunnison, who subsequently led one of the Pacific Railroad surveys. Stansbury carried out his mission without arousing the hostility of the resident Mormons, and an account of his work was published in the *Congressional Record* in 1853. *Exploration and Survey of the Valley of the Great Salt Lake of Utah* contained excellent geographical and environmental data and, according to the *Congressional Record,* "a matchless picture of the Mormon community."

While Captain Stansbury was roaming through Utah, another group of army officers constituting the Southwestern Boundary Survey were ordered into the Southwest to determine the international boundary between Mexico and the United States after the transfer of the Mexican Cession provided for in the Treaty of Guadalupe-Hidalgo. They spent three years (1850–53) at their task, in the course of which they also gathered a wealth of scientific, ethnological, and historical information that was published by Congress in 1854.

The next major assignment for the topographical engineers likewise was from Congress: to fan out across the Far West from 1853 and "ascertain the most practicable and economical route for a railroad from the Mississippi River to the Pacific Ocean." An amendment to the annual Army Appropriation Bill appropriated $150,000 for the purpose, eventually increased to $340,000. Jefferson Davis, the secretary of war, took a special interest in this project, recognizing the great economic benefits that would accrue to whichever section of the country the proposed transcontinental railroad traversed. Five survey teams were dispatched to explore the same number of possible routes: (1) between the 47th and 49th parallels, (2) between 41st and 42nd parallels, (3) between the 38th and 39th parallels, (4) along the 35th parallel, and (5) along the 32nd parallel.

Each route had its supporters, for political as much as geographic reasons. All the survey parties included, in addition to the requisite number of military officers and engineers, cartographers, geologists, naturalists, botanists, artists, and photographers. In truth, they represented as remarkable an assemblage of talent and brains as was gathered anywhere in the United States in the 19th century.

The northern survey, which stuck close to the 47th parallel, was led by Washington Territory's governor, Isaac Ingalls Stevens, and included Captain George B. McClellan of future Civil War fame and the artist John Mix Stanley. Although the northern route lost out in the sweepstakes to become the site of the first transcontinental railroad, the Stevens group did produce such a valuable report it was subsequently reprinted by a commercial publisher as *The Natural History of Washington Territory* (1859).

A second party, led by Captain John W. Gunnison, followed the 38th and 39th parallels starting from Fort Leavenworth, Kansas Territory, then down the Santa Fe Trail before veering north to cross the continental divide. Reaching central Utah in October 1853, after crossing the Wasatch Mountains, they were attacked near Sevier Lake by Paiute Indians. Gunnison and seven members of his party, including the artist Richard H. Kern, were killed, thus ending their expedition prematurely.

In spring 1854 a third survey party set out to follow a central route between the 41st and 42nd parallels. Led by Lieutenant E. G. Beckwith, it followed a middling route across the waist of the continent (the 41st–42nd parallels), using Council Bluffs, Nebraska, as a jumping off point. They had a relatively easy time of it because they used the same routes (trails) favored for years by immigrants migrating to California and Oregon. They identified two passes over the Sierra Nevada that looked promising before they reached California in early 1855. This party was notable both because it mapped the central route eventually selected for the first transcontinental railroad and because it included among its military escort the future head of the National Museum of Hungary, doing work as a field naturalist. Lieutenant Gouverneur K. Warren, also a member of this party, contributed a number of excellent maps, including the first general map of the entire Trans-Mississippi West, to the final report.

Lieutenant Amiel Weeks Whipple led the Thirty-fifth Parallel Survey from Fort Smith, Arkansas, to Los Angeles, California (then known as San Pedro). They roughly followed a route blazed earlier by Josiah Gregg (1839) and Captain Randolph B. Marcy, passing by the Zuni Pueblo. The artist of record on the expedition was H. B. Möllhausen. As would be the case with Thomas Charlton Henry's route, Whipple's appeared to be too difficult and, therefore, expensive to be selected, though later it was used by the Santa Fe Railroad.

The party that received the least public recognition was led by T. C. Henry through the southwest desert along the 32nd parallel. They were hardly trailblazers opening new territory. The trail had already been pioneered by Brigadier General Stephen W. Kearny leading the Army of the West to California in 1846. Nor did their assigned route hold much promise to win the transcontinental railroad sweepstakes: The mountains and desert were too daunting. But the 32nd survey party was not without its accomplishments. Henry's correspondence and final report, especially on the subject of ornithology, subsequently proved a gold mine to scientists and government officials alike. And his survey work also did not go for naught; it became the route of the Overland Mail.

The final reports of the five teams who completed their missions were not completed and turned in until 1856, two years after the original target date given by Congress. Altogether, it had taken nearly three years from inception to complete the job. The full account was first presented by Secretary Davis in his annual War Department report to Congress in December of that year. In 1857 the compiled reports were published by order of Congress in 13 volumes as *Reports of Explorations and Surveys . . . for a Railroad from the Mississippi River to the Pacific Ocean* (usually referred to as The Pacific Railroad Survey Reports).

Less famous than Lewis and Clark's Corps of Discovery, the railroad survey expeditions did far more than simply look for likely routes for the railroad; they also acquired a wealth of geological, zoological, and botanical information. And their reports proved so valuable that they were recorded not only in stuffy government volumes but as newspaper articles, scientific studies, and commercial publications. They produced a remarkable scientific record that would serve the government and scholars for generations.

Other army officers posted at western forts also routinely gathered information on their surroundings, such as Doctors Edward Perry Vollum at Fort Belknap, Texas; John Frazier at Fort Ripley, Minnesota; and Wylie Crawford at Fort McKavett, Texas. Colonel George Armstrong Custer was an amateur paleontologist and zoologist who shipped some of the native fauna of the Great Plains back to the Central Park Zoo in New York. Other army officers who had far less press than Custer contributed substantially to the store of scientific knowledge of the fauna and flora of the Far West. They were in a much better position to observe and collect information than the occasional academician from some eastern institution traveling West on sabbatical.

Between 1869 and 1879 four government survey teams expanded the knowledge of the West exponentially. Two were sponsored by the Interior Department, namely, the U.S. Geological and Geographical Survey and the U.S. Geographical Survey of the Rocky Mountain Region. The former was led by Dr. Hayden and the latter by Major John Wesley Powell. Hayden spent two seasons in the Yellowstone region, then in 1873 led a surveying party into the Colorado mountains. His photographer on that expedition, W. H. Jackson, the following year led another expedition into southwestern Colorado, where they became the first who officially observed and reported on prehistoric cliff dwellings. In 1875 Jackson returned to study the hundreds of cliff dwelling ruins in the canyons of southwestern Colorado.

In 1869, Major Powell led the first party of non-Indians in exploring the Grand Canyon, at the time one of the nation's last geographical mysteries. The one-armed major and nine companions navigated the tricky rapids of the Colorado River in four supposedly unsinkable boats, passing through the towering walls of the Grand Canyon and traveling more than 1,000 miles between May 24 and August 30 and emerging at the mouth of the Virgin River. He made a second trip through the canyon in 1871. A serialized account of his epic journeys appeared in *Scribner's Monthly Magazine* between January and March 1875, cementing his place in American history as an explorer, surveyor, geologist, and anthropologist (of Native American life) par excellence. His ideas on protecting the environment were far ahead of his time, and his latest biographer Donald Worster even calls him "an American renaissance man."

The two other U.S. government survey teams that rewrote the book between 1867 and 1879 were sponsored by the War Department—the U.S. Geological Exploration of the Fortieth Parallel under Clarence King and the U.S. Geographical Surveys West of the One Hundredth Meridian (also known as the One Hundredth Meridian Survey) under Lieutenant George M. Wheeler. The Wheeler expedition turned in 164 detailed maps and 41 reports describing 219 mining districts, 143 mountain ranges, 202 mountain passes, 90 streams, 25 lakes, and 395 peaks. They also gathered 61,659 specimens, which ended up ultimately in the Smithsonian. The four surveys were consolidated into the monumental U.S. Geological Survey of 1879, which unified government policy and administration into a single agency.

These were just the high-profile expeditions. There were others during this period that also did much to help expand geographical knowledge and open up the West to settlement. The upper Colorado River was practically unknown to non-Indians until Captain Lorenzo Sitgreaves visited it in 1851. Then in 1857 Lieutenant Joseph C. Ives was placed in charge of an expedition to explore the river thoroughly. He carried a disassembled shallow-draft steamboat overland, assembled it on the bank of the river, and headed upstream four days before Christmas 1857. He gained valuable knowledge of both the river's geography, including the Grand Canyon, and the local Indians, which was published as *Report upon the Colorado River of the West* in 1861.

Some U.S. military officers carved out remarkable careers as explorers and surveyors, which were largely overshadowed by the combat records of brother officers in the U.S.-Mexican and Civil Wars. Captain Sitgreaves, in addition to visiting the upper Colorado River, surveyed Sault Sainte Marie, served on the Texas boundary survey after the U.S.-Mexican War, and helped survey the Florida reefs. Captain Randolph B. Marcy led his first expedition through the Far West in 1849 when he guided an immigrant train to the California gold fields. He followed that up with four more. On his 1852 expedition he traced the course of the Red River to its source, the first non-Indian to do so. He also drafted what experts consider "the first reasonably accurate" maps of the Southwest and was instrumental in establishing a chain of forts across the Indian Territory and west Texas. He kept careful journals of his travels, which were later published.

All the information-gathering expeditions of the period were not devoted to opening up virgin wilderness. Some had more modest goals, such as gathering ornithological material on the Platte River, exploring the Agate Fossil Beds in northwestern Nebraska, and conducting other purely scientific research, sometimes at great physical peril. The scientific explorations of this period climaxed

This photo by William H. Jackson, photographer of several government expeditions into the West in the 1870s, shows the U.S. Geological Survey of the Territories, ca. 1879. (Tennessee State Library and Archives)

with Colonel Richard Dodge's expedition into the Black Hills of the Dakotas in summer 1875, escorting a party of geologists and mining experts. Their labors confirmed the presence of gold in the region, thereby prompting the last great gold rush in the continental United States and in turn provoking the last great Indian war in American history.

In addition to the scientists and military officers, almost all of these various expeditions included respected artists or photographers to furnish a visual record of what they saw. That visual record often proved to be a godsend when it came time to ask Congress for appropriations or to enlist public support in the cause of creating the first national park. William H. Jackson's photo spread of the Yellowstone during his 1871 trip was instrumental in gaining national park status for that area. Besides the artists and photographers, Captain Seth Eastman accompanied the Southwestern Boundary Survey of 1850–53 as official painter, and Carleton Watkins, one of the greatest of 19th-century American photographers, accompanied an expedition to the Yosemite Valley. Some of the most stunning views ever produced of the unspoiled West were the work of these brush and camera artists. When they were published, the Pacific Railroad Surveys included 147 lithographs, contributed by 11 civilian and military artists.

Americans' thirst for knowledge and adventure did not stop at the country's borders. U.S. citizens were active in exploring exotic climes from the Amazon River basin to the Arctic. One expedition under the American flag, led by William L. Herndon, explored the Amazon River in 1851–52, thanks largely to the support of the famed oceanographer Matthew F. Maury. And Americans were at the forefront of national efforts to reach the North Pole, for both chauvinistic and scientific reasons. Captain Charles Francis Hall died under mysterious circumstances in 1872 trying to accomplish the feat. Emil Bessels led another star-spangled expedition, likewise unsuccessful and equally controversial, in 1875, with the North Pole as its goal. As the expeditions to the Far West were, these were jointly sponsored by the U.S. military (the navy in the case of Arctic expeditions), the Smithsonian Institution, and private individuals willing to put their money and their lives on the line.

By 1875 the areas on the map of the United States not filled in had dwindled to insignificance. Although a frontier line still divided "East" from "West," the days when the West was a vast empty space or a cipher waiting to be opened were over.

CHAPTER 2 Disasters, Natural and Human-Made

Disasters are a part of life, but they become historical events only when they kill large numbers of people and/or cause major property damage. The mid-19th century saw the usual assortment of tornadoes, fires, locust infestations, and earthquakes. About the only one of the original biblical plagues the United States never suffered from was widespread famine, thanks to the bountiful land and the scattered, mobile population, which was constantly moving on to more fertile areas. But in the 19th-century, humans invented new forms of catastrophe and the old, familiar forms became much worse. The growing density of urban populations and the impact of modern technology proved to be a recipe for disasters as well as for progress. Railroads and steam power were technological wonders, but they also produced train wrecks and boiler explosions aboard the new steamships. Old categories of disaster such as shipwreck and urban fires became much more lethal because of the large numbers of people crammed onto the new ships and living in the booming urban centers. When disaster struck those large ships and grand cities, the result was longer casualty lists, running into the hundreds or even thousands.

No government agency in these years was charged with gathering statistics on disasters, and the insurance business was still in its infancy in terms of record keeping, so the historical record of casualties and property damage is incomplete. Mostly what has come down to researchers today are contemporary newspaper reports, which are anecdotal and often more sensationalist than helpful. But they paint a picture of a time when natural and human-made disasters struck with frightening regularity.

Dealing with Disasters in the 19th Century

One important difference from today was that even great disasters often remained local affairs, not widely known until weeks after the event. This was not the result of callousness or a conspiracy of silence but simply of slow communications. News had to travel by word of mouth or by telegraph, so *national disaster* was understood in a limited context of war or invasion, not flood or earthquake. *Frank Leslie's Illustrated Newspaper* was normally the first to get the news out nationally, but that still meant days or even weeks after the event before the country at large could read about it. The magazine discovered one of the verities of mass publishing: the instant appeal of human tragedy, especially when coupled with powerful visuals. Every *Frank Leslie's* disaster story included graphic woodcuts accompanied by lurid descriptions of crushed bodies and broken lives. In fact, *Leslie's* made a name for itself with such sensational stories. Other newspapers and magazines were quick to jump on the bandwagon to feed the public's insatiable appetite for gory disaster news.

Another difference between then and now lay in the immediate follow-up to the disaster. At that time emergency response measures were primitive or nonexistent, and troubling questions of legal liability did not get much attention in the judicial system. Neither tort law nor criminal law was as highly developed as today in identifying the guilty party or parties and suing them. Most people of the time, and the legal system as well, tended to ascribe disasters to either the will of God or plain bad luck. There was widespread belief that nature in its mystery and awesomeness, whether in the form of Indians, wild animals, weather, or other natural phenomena, was almost wilfully perverse, an entity that people had to battle constantly. In the thinking of the time, nature was human beings' enemy; it was that simple. This sort of thinking produced an almost fatalistic attitude in the public mind that made judges and juries less than sympathetic to victims' claims after fires, floods, and explosions.

Nor was disaster relief regarded as the proper business of legislatures. Only once before had Congress stepped in to help disaster victims. That was after the unprecedented destruction of the New Madrid earthquakes of December 1811–February 1812, when Congress had passed the first national disaster relief act, providing landowners of ruined property with equal amounts of land elsewhere in the territory of Missouri. On every other occasion in the 19th century, disaster relief was left to the private sector.

Even on the local level the combination of shortsightedness and penuriousness kept organized disaster prevention and response in the primitive stages even when better ways of doing things were available. For instance, only a handful of cities before 1875 had professional fire or police departments to take over after a disaster. There were no emergency evacuation plans, emergency medical personnel, first aid, search and rescue procedures, or public relief agencies until 1881, when Clara Barton founded the American Association of the Red Cross. Boston in 1852 became the first city to have fireboxes, based on telegraphic communications, but they were kept locked to prevent pranksters from sending in false alarms, and only policemen had keys. Boston also had one of the nation's first professional fire departments, with the latest equipment and 475 trained men on call, but in 1872 when the city's worst fire hit, the department had no horses to pull the fire engines because their stables had recently been hit by a distemper epidemic.

Likewise, when it came to natural disasters, the concept of emergency planning was virtually unknown in an age when weather forecasting meant the *Farmer's Almanac* and *early warning* still meant Paul Revere–type rides.

Urban Fires

Fire was an ever-present danger in the largely wood-built American cities of the 19th century. In fact, it was often said to be the urban dweller's worst nightmare. Of course, at other times, cholera was given top billing; the lesson here is that whatever type of disaster was most recent was considered the worst. Still, the potential for fires to get out of control quickly was greatly increased by two other factors: (1) the prevailing use of gas lighting, not only on the main streets but also for interior illumination at night, and (2) the almost complete lack of municipal fire codes in any U.S. city.

The danger was highest in large public buildings such as theaters and hotels. Because most of those did not keep fire hoses or filled water buckets on hand, in the beginning stages of a fire witnesses had only their coats and bare hands to try to extinguish it. When those inevitably failed, panic usually followed as people stampeded for the nearest exit. People were as likely to be trampled to death as burned to death.

This period saw three great urban fires in the United States—in San Francisco, Chicago, and Boston—although as a myth-spawning and history-making event Chicago's fire easily overshadows the other two.

San Francisco

San Francisco's occurred on May 3, 1851, and there were plenty of advance warning signs in the form of previous blazes that had been barely contained. This fire was far worse, destroying more than half the city and killing 30 people. San Franciscans showed even at this early date a tenacity and survivor's mentality that led them to start rebuilding immediately. That sort of persevering spirit would stand them in good stead in the decades to come.

The Chicago fire caused chaos, shown here at the Randolph Street bridge on the night of October 8, 1871, as the city's residents flee the inferno. Before it was over, some 250 were killed and 95,000 left homeless. (Library of Congress)

Chicago

The Chicago conflagration has been given the title "the Great Chicago Fire," just as San Francisco's 1906 earthquake has been labeled "the Great San Francisco Earthquake," thus putting all others on a lower plane. The 1871 fire struck what one post-fire newspaper report called "the city of everlasting pine, shingles, shams, veneers, stucco and putty" on October 8, a Sunday night, as number 31 in series of fire alarms starting the previous week that had called out the exhausted and understaffed fire department. It was actually the second major blaze in two days. The blaze quickly grew out of control, leaped the Chicago River, and was still going strong on Monday morning, October 9. People were driven into the streets, where they joined existing mobs either seeking safety or looting whatever they could carry off. The fire finally burned itself out Monday night, leaving a three-and-a-half-square-mile section of the business district a smoking ruin. In addition to the known dead, there were 98,500 left homeless and 17,450 buildings wiped out of existence. With property damage soaring above $200 million, it was by far the costliest fire of the 19th century.

Ten days later the citizens had rolled up their sleeves and gotten busy rebuilding, bigger and better than ever, while the city's business life resumed in temporary structures. The disaster caused the city to invest in better fire protection, but it also drew the doomsayers out of the woodwork, as often happens after such events. Preachers and self-proclaimed prophets such as the Reverend Granville Moody of Cincinnati pronounced it the wrath of God visited upon Sodom on the shores (of Lake Michigan). If so, God's wrath quickly cooled because the city was soon back in business and rising phoenixlike from the ashes.

A different type of mythology that grew up about the Great Fire wove together fact and fancy about the single most famous urban disaster of the 19th century. Where the historic record was silent or incomplete, the public's imagination took over, creating two enduring legends: one, that the fire was started when Mrs. O'Leary's cow kicked over a lantern; two, that at the height of the blaze the mayor ordered the city's jails thrown open to allow the prisoners to flee for safety. Neither story has borne up to the harsh scrutiny of historians, but they illustrate one of the characteristics of great disasters: that people create stories of heroism and fantastic occurrences.

Peshtigo

The most fantastic aspect of the Great Chicago Fire is that it was not the worst fire of the era, nor even the worst fire on that particular date. While much of Chicago's central business district was burning, a much larger, more destructive fire was raging at the same hour at Peshtigo, Wisconsin, 250 miles north of Chicago. It devastated 400 square miles and caused more than four times as much human misery as the Chicago fire (2,682 dead versus 250 dead). The Peshtigo fire was the worst fire in U.S. history. It is sometimes called a "forest fire" because the forest is where it started, but its ultimate impact was that it was an urban fire that wiped out not just Peshtigo but 23 other towns as well.

The locus of the tragedy was Peshtigo. Before its immolation Peshtigo was a woodworking town of 2,000 dependent on the bounty of the nearby forests. On the night of October 8, a forest fire propelled by high winds swept through the town, turning it in a matter of minutes into a raging inferno. Brick buildings exploded, people's clothing burst into flames, and trees were consumed down to their roots. Even the river running through the center of town offered no refuge as the heat was so intense it sucked the oxygen out of the air and cooked anything above water. Those citizens who lived to see the dawn on October 9 forever remembered their ordeal as a "night of hell." As for Peshtigo, it had been wiped off the map. Yet the nation's attention and sympathy focused on Chicago, so much so that the governor of Wisconsin had to beg for medical and other forms of aid for the Peshtigo survivors. It was not until weeks later that the full story of the night Peshtigo died was relayed across the country, and by then it was old news.

Boston

Just 13 months later, almost to the day, another great American city was engulfed in flames. On November 9, 1872, fire broke out in the business district of Boston. In no time at all it was raging out of control because, as in the case of San Francisco and Chicago, carelessness and negligence were rampant among city officials. The fire gathered force that night and continued into the next day, eventually burning 60 acres of central Boston to the ground. But the disaster was less costly in terms of both property destruction and human life than the Chicago fire.

Other Fires

In the second rank of urban disasters were the fires that struck Washington, D.C., and Portland, Maine, in 1851 and 1866, respectively. Both caused considerable damage but no loss of life. The Washington, D.C., fire occurred on Christmas Eve in the Capitol wing that housed the Library of Congress. It was the third major fire since the library had been established in 1800. This one destroyed some 35,000 volumes, including two-thirds of the Jefferson collection, donated by the third president. The Portland, Maine, fire occurred on July 4 during the city's celebration of Independence Day. A young boy threw a firecracker into a pile of wood shavings in the docks area, causing a blaze that destroyed 1,500 buildings (half the city) with an estimated property loss of some $10 million.

Making even relatively minor fires catastrophic was the fact that property insurance was still in its infancy in the United States. Few owners bothered to insure their buildings, and when they did, it was

Fire was perhaps the greatest fear of urban dwellers in the 19th century and for good reason. Chicago's was only the most famous of the great city fires of the century. A year after Chicago, Boston suffered a devastating conflagration on November 9–10, 1872, which destroyed 60 acres of the downtown district and did about $150 million damage. (Library of Congress, Prints and Photographs Division [LC USZ62 - 124128])

The "Great Fire" at Savannah, Georgia, January 27, 1865. Soldiers of the Union army's XIX Corps put out a blaze while removing ammunition stores to safety. Urban fire was an ever-present 19th-century danger at a time of wooden buildings, volunteer fire departments, and primitive fire-fighting equipment. (Courtesy of the Georgia Historical Society)

far less than the value of the structure and its contents. For their part, states did not require property insurance or attempt to oversee the business until New Hampshire enacted the first regulatory legislation in 1851, and even then other states were slow to follow. Not until 1873 and the Massachusetts Standard Policy law was there any attempt to standardize policies. In the meantime, the prevailing principle in the insurance business was caveat emptor (let the buyer beware). P. T. Barnum suffered three disastrous fires at his show places in New York City in seven years yet never learned his lesson. When the third of those fires burned down his "Hippotheatron" on Christmas Eve 1872, with the total loss of the building and its contents valued at above $300,000, he was carrying only $90,000 in insurance coverage. He was forced to scour two continents and spend half a million dollars to replace the exhibits and never fully recovered. Casualty and property insurance for other disasters was similarly slow to catch on. Insurance was costly and smacked of pessimism, policies were often unreliable, and the whole idea seemed to challenge God's will for people. As a result, only after a long, catastrophic string of disasters were skeptics eventually convinced of the universal need for insurance.

Chicago and San Francisco were classic examples of the dangers of unregulated urban growth. The latter, which virtually sprang into existence overnight between 1849 and 1850, suffered five major fires in less than two years, and Chicago's record was more than 100 times worse. It had suffered a major blaze in 1857 that killed 20 people and more than 600 fires in 1870. One day before the Great Chicago Fire (October 7, 1871), the worst blaze in the city's history up to that time struck the Western District, causing more than half a million dollars in property damage although no fatalities. Almost every U.S. city of the 19th century had a similar tale to tell of repeated urban conflagrations. The fires were seldom small affairs because fire fighting was given a low priority by most municipal governments. Whenever a blaze broke out, typically there were an inadequate water supply and precious little equipment. The first line of defense was usually volunteer companies armed with shovels, buckets, and dampened gunny sacks.

Besides the loss of human life and livestock and property damage, irreplaceable historic records, including property deeds and titles, were lost. Today the vital records of many cities in the United States are incomplete for the 19th century as a result of disastrous courthouse fires. The burning up of a large portion of Jefferson's personal library in the Library of Congress fire in 1851 was not the only major loss of historic works during this time. The Great Chicago Fire destroyed the newly built Chicago Historical Society and all its holdings, including the original draft of Lincoln's Emancipation Proclamation. The wonder is that such frequent and severe fires did not inspire any of these cities to invest in the latest fire-fighting equipment and professional fire departments after the news of just one big blaze got around.

TABLE 2.1 WORST URBAN FIRES OF THE MID-NINETEENTH CENTURY, 1850–1872

Site	Date	Loss of Life	Property Damage
San Francisco, Calif.	Sep. 17, 1850	Unknown	130 buildings destroyed, estimated value $300,000
Insane hospital in Augusta, Maine	Dec. 4, 1850	Unknown	Unknown
Michigan railroad depot, Detroit, Mich.	Nov. 18, 1850	None	Unknown
Nevada City, Calif.	Mar. 12, 1851	Unknown	More than 200 houses, estimated worth $1,300,000
San Francisco, Calif., business district	May 3–5, 1851	"Many persons burned to death"	Nearly 2,500 buildings destroyed, estimated value $1–$5 million
San Francisco, Calif.	Jun. 22, 1851	Unknown	500 Houses destroyed, estimated worth $3 million
Concord, N.H.	Aug. 24, 1851	Unknown	Most of business district destroyed
Marysville, Calif.	Aug. 30, 1851	Unknown	Unknown
Washington, D.C. (Library of Congress)	Dec. 24, 1851	None	Some 35,000 priceless volumes, including 60% of Jefferson collection
San Francisco, Calif.	May 31, 1851	30 dead; unknown numbers of injured	70% of city destroyed
Syracuse, N.Y.	Nov. 8, 1856	Unknown	More than 12 acres of city destroyed, including 100 buildings
Montpelier, Vt.	Jan. 6, 1857	Unknown	Vermont State Capitol destroyed, estimated value $132,007
Toledo, Ohio	Feb. 13, 1857	Unknown	Consumed five hotels plus other buildings
Baltimore, Md.	Apr. 14, 1857	At least 15 killed	Property on Charles and Lombard Streets, estimated worth $400,000
New York City, N.Y.	Oct. 5, 1858	None	Crystal Palace Exhibition Building and all exhibits destroyed
Memphis, Tenn.	Mar. 1, 1859	Unknown	One of the principal squares on Main St. destroyed, including several newspaper offices, estimated worth $150,000
Dubuque, Iowa	May 26, 1859	Unknown	Post office, land office, and other buildings destroyed
Salem, Mass.	Jun. 8, 1859	Unknown	"Large amount of property," estimated value $100,000
Salisbury, Md.	Aug. 2, 1860	Unknown	60 houses consumed; estimated value $200,000
New York City, N.Y. (Broadway and Ann Streets)	Jun. 13, 1865	None reported	P.T. Barnum's American Museum completely destroyed [a]
Portland, Maine	Jul. 4, 1866	None; unknown numbers injured	Estimated $10 million in property damage
New York City, N.Y. (Broadway, between Spring and Prince Streets)	Mar. 3, 1868	None reported	Barnum's New American Museum completely destroyed
Chicago, Ill.	Oct. 7, 1871	None; 30 firemen injured	$700,000 in property damage to city's West Division
Chicago, Ill.	Oct. 8–10, 1871	250–300 known dead; another 200 injured	3½ sq. mi. burned, more than 17,000 buildings destroyed; total losses estimated at more than $200 million, bankrupting 60 insurance companies
Peshtigo, Wis.[b]	Oct. 8–9, 1871	1,182 dead; hundreds more injured	Entire town destroyed
San Diego, Calif.	Apr. 10, 1872	None; injuries unknown	Destroyed most of the city's "Old Town" district
Boston, Mass.	Nov. 9–10, 1872	14 dead, including 9 firemen; unknown numbers of injured	Estimated $75 million in property damage
New York City, N.Y. (14th Street and Broadway)	Dec. 24, 1872	None reported	Barnum's third showplace, the Hippotheatron, recently remodeled, destroyed with all its facilities and equipment and most of its performing animals, for a loss of $300,000

[a] Barnum's museum had already been heavily damaged in November 1864, when Confederate agents attempted to burn New York City. This time the fire was an accident, but the museum was still a complete loss.

[b] At the same time the fire that destroyed Peshtigo also hit 23 other Wisconsin towns, of which the worst hit were Casco, DePere, Shite Rock, Ahnepee, Elm Creek, Forestville, Little Sturgeon Bay, Lincoln, Brussels, and Rosiere. The total of deaths recorded at those other sites adds another 1,500 to the list of victims at Peshtigo. Coupled with the sheer scale of destruction, that makes this the worst fire in U.S. history.

Sources: James Cornell, *The Great International Disaster Book,* 3d ed. (New York: Charles Scribner's Sons, 1982); Mike Flanagan, *The Old West: Day by Day* (New York: Facts On File, 1995); Lee Davis, *Man-Made Catastrophes* (New York: Facts On File, 2002); Ben Kartman and Leonard Brown, eds., *Disaster!* (New York: Berkley, 1960), 18–28; *The American Almanac and Repository of Useful Knowledge for the Years 1850–1861* (Boston: Chas. C. Little & James Brown, 1849–51, Crosby, Nichols, Lee & Co., 1860–75), *passim;* John Culhane, *The American Circus* (New York: Henry Holt, 1990), 398.

Industrial Accidents

A new category of horrific disaster began making news with shocking regularity in these years—industrial accidents, specifically those that struck America's mines and factories. Both types were a product of the new industrial age, which upped the ante in workplace accidents to shocking levels. The factory system put heavy machinery, combustible material, and large numbers of workers all together in one place—a surefire recipe for disaster. Even when industrial accidents did not kill, they usually left the victim disabled for life. High-speed power equipment was unforgiving when fingers and limbs got in the way of its operation. And as machinery grew more complex, the risk of death or injury rose accordingly. Callous attitudes in management did not improve a bad situation. Employers considered safety precautions an unnecessary expense and, when accidents inevitably occurred, blamed workers for "imprudence" or general carelessness. It is safe to say that industrialization caused the rate of death on the job to rise dramatically in the 19th century.

Mining has always been a dangerous occupation, but in the 19th century it was even more so. New technology such as pneumatic drills and dynamite increased both the intensity and the inherent risks of mining. Mines became deeper and more extensive, employing more workers, and the pace of work sped up to meet the demands of industrialism for the Earth's riches.

Fires, underground explosions and cave-ins were facts of life for men who worked in the bowels of the Earth, whether digging coal in Pennsylvania, gold in Colorado, or silver in Nevada. Veteran miners figured a man's probability of becoming a victim in a mine accident was one in eight if he spent 10 years in the mines. Only logging was as dangerous, and it did not have the record for mass deaths of the mining industry. In 1869, at the 700- to 1,000-foot level of the Comstock mine in Nevada, a flash fire claimed the lives of 45 men. Mining communities traditionally buried their dead and went back to work the next day. During Comstock's boom years of the 1870s, some 300 of an estimated 10,000 men employed died below ground, and another 600 were maimed or disabled. During some periods, the rate of death reached one man per week.

Comstock was hardly unique. The mine town names—Goldfield, Leadville, Cripple Creek, Virginia City, Scofield—were also a roll call of accidents over the years. Mining accidents were so frequent they rarely made the news outside the small community that was personally affected. Only the occasional great disaster made headlines. The new technology that made mining more efficient proved to be a mixed blessing for the miner. For instance, in the 1870s dynamite replaced black powder as the explosive of choice in mining because it was four times more powerful. But it also happened to be so hypersensitive and unstable that it would explode if even jostled too vigorously. The price of carelessness suddenly accelerated. From the coal fields of western Pennsylvania to the gold mines of the Sierra Nevada, death was the miner's constant companion. Disasters punctuated the steady litany of deaths in the mines. Today history remembers even relatively minor skirmishes of the Civil War that produced 100 casualties but not the coal mine disaster at Avondale, Pennsylvania, on September 6, 1869, that left as many as 179 miners dead after they were trapped by a fire. One was a glorious clash of arms, the other, a bad day at work.

Mine disasters were always a danger. A group of miners volunteers to go back down into the mine to search for missing comrades in this engraving from *Frank Leslie's Illustrated Newspaper,* September 25, 1869. (Library of Congress, Prints and Photographs Division [LC-USZ62-18148])

Natural Disasters

Even without human help, nature could wreak devastation. In one form or another, the Four Horsemen of legend rode across America in these years: Droughts, floods, storms, blizzards, and even the occasional earthquake all devastated unwary communities with frightening regularity. The first natural disaster in the United States to capture national attention was an avalanche in the White Mountains of New Hampshire in 1826 that wiped out a family of seven and their two hired men. The "Willey Tragedy," as it was called, was widely reported in the newspapers, literature, travel writing, and scientific journals of the day, although it pales when compared to the body counts of the Civil War and later disasters.

Drought, Rain, and Snow

Drought was almost common on the Great Plains, where less than 20 inches of rain fell in *good* years. Nevertheless, eager homesteaders disregarded the climatic warning signs as they swarmed over the region after the Civil War. The conventional wisdom, disingenuously encouraged by railroads with land to sell, was "Rain follows the plow": Turning the soil, planting trees, and other agricultural activities retarded evaporation and thereby shortened the rain cycle. It was all pseudoscience, of course, but it was accepted as gospel by thousands of homesteaders. Drought's effects did not stop with parching the land and withering the crops; as one Kansas editor wrote, "A drought nourishes chinch bugs, sun-strokes, grasshoppers and profanity."

Nature initially lulled residents of the Great Plains into a sense of security with a prolonged period of abundant rainfall, from the mid-1860s until 1870. Then two short spells of drought struck in the next three years. The rains returned in 1875, and nature was on its best behavior for another six years, until the early 1880s produced a brutal combination of summer droughts and winter blizzards that ultimately drove fully half the settlers in Kansas and Nebraska off the land.

The same weather patterns that produced no rainfall for a year or more might also produce an overabundance of rain ("gully washers") and snowfall in other years. Raging snowstorms might arrive without warning, then last for either a few hours or several days. The snow falls were such a dramatic weather phenomenon that they caused settlers to grope for the right descriptive words, inspiring the editor of Estherville, Iowa's *Northern Vindicator,* O. C. Bates, in April 1870 to create the word *blizzard* to describe a particularly nasty snowstorm with gale-force winds and low temperatures. The lexicographer Stuart Flexner has suggested that European colonists were so struck by the severity of the New World's weather that they immediately began coining a plethora of new words to describe it, a tendency continued by Americans after independence; this period generated such terms as, *snowed in* (1859), *snow fence* (1872), and *sugar snow* (1861). *Blizzard* did not enter common usage until after 1875, but the relevant conditions were already well known. These storms could kill any human caught out in them and destroy livestock on the open range. There are no statistics on the numbers of people killed by blizzards or by the sudden arctic blasts known as blue northers, which could sweep down off the high plains, dropping temperatures as much as 25 degrees in an hour.

TABLE 2.2 HISTORICAL DROUGHTS IN THE CONTINENTAL UNITED STATES, 1850–1880s

Year(s)	Area Affected	Consequences or Effects
1850–51	Calif.	Rainfall one-third the normal rate
1854	N.Y. to Mo.	Widespread crop failures
1860	Kans., Mo., Iowa, Minn., Wis., and Ill.	Burned crops, dry streams, low lakes and ponds
1862–64	Calif.	Put an end to extensive cattle industry
1870–71	Midwest, particularly Wis. and Ill.	Devastating fires in Chicago, Ill., and Peshtigo, Wis., in October
1873	Great Plains	Described as a record setter at the time; followed by infestations of grasshoppers
1881–87	Great Plains	Coupled with unusually hard winters; burned out crops and killed off cattle herds

Source: Norman J. Rosenberg, ed., *North American Droughts* (Boulder, Colo.: Westview Press, 1978), 19.

Fire

Fire on the plains could be as fearsome as in any big city, taking the form of prairie fires that raced over the ground so fast and covered such a wide front that there was no escape. Worse, these conflagrations were just as likely to be started by lightning as by human carelessness. Whatever the origins, the results could be deadly for people and livestock. The only protection besides running away was preparing fire breaks around a home ahead of time, but that required a far-sighted and energetic person to do so when there was no danger in sight. Two of the worst prairie fires occurred in Nebraska in 1860 and 1872, scorching dozens of square miles of land. Kansans were no strangers to prairie fires. In 1867 the Ottawa *Western Home Journal* reported, "The fires this fall have been unusually terrific and destructive," and attributed the situation to a long dry spell and high winds.

Flood

Residents of the high plains did not have to worry about flooding, but those in the river valleys of the Mississippi, the Missouri, and other major streams did. The 1855 edition of Noah Webster's *American Dictionary of the English Language* noted that "there is an annual flood in the Nile and the Mississippi." Thousands of years of such flooding had produced the great alluvial tideland that New Orleans was built on, but it also gave rise to the writer Mark Twain's characterization of the mighty Mississippi as "this lawless stream."

Flooding often seemed to wreak the worst havoc on small western communities that sprang up along creeks and then grew helter-skelter without a thought for preventive measures such as constructing levees and runoff channels. On May 19, 1864, Cherry Creek, running through the heart of Denver, overspilled its banks after heavy rains and sent a wall of water sweeping through the town. The result was a "night of terror" that left at least 15 dead and property damage estimated at $250,000 to $1 million. On June 7, 1867, torrential rains at Fort Hays, Kansas, caused Big Creek to overflow its banks, and only the foresight of Lieutenant Colonel George Custer, post commander, prevented more than the seven deaths that occurred among 7th Cavalry soldiers and their families. Then on July 24, 1874, another flash flood killed 30 residents of Eureka, Nevada, another mining boom town that had developed without any town planning whatsoever. The concept of a flood plain did not even enter the public consciousness until about 1873.

The worst inundation of this era was the Mississippi River flood of April 1874, which also has the distinction of being the first to be extensively reported and systematically documented. Its occurrence in April should have been no surprise. As the historian Lee Davis has pointed out, "April has always been the cruelest month for those who live along the banks of the Mississippi."

This lithograph from *Harper's Weekly,* May 14, 1859, shows a Mississippi River flood sweeping everything before it. (Courtesy of Mississippi Department of Archives and History)

The Great Flood of '74 began with melting snow far upriver and unusually heavy spring rains. Before the waters subsided, 200 to 300 persons were dead along with more than 1,000 head of livestock. A dozen or more river towns in Mississippi and Louisiana were heavily damaged, and tens of thousands of acres left covered in mud and debris. The river valley's residents would not experience another flood of this magnitude for another 16 years.

Insects

One natural disaster that singled out the unfortunate residents of the Great Plains was grasshopper infestations. Biblical plagues of locusts were well known to Americans, but until settlers arrived on the Great Plains, most had no personal experience of them. In 1848 the Mormons at Salt Lake City had experienced a grasshopper invasion, which was defeated by the timely arrival of a flock of seagulls. In 1866 the citizens of northern Kansas experienced their own grasshopper plague, but that was nothing compared to the history-making infestation of 1874, known as "the Year of the Grasshopper." The culprit then, as in 1848, was the Rocky Mountain locust, also known as the American grasshopper, which is about two inches long and has a reddish-colored body. The pesky creatures were harmless singly or even by the dozens, but when numbers reached the millions, enough to blot out the Sun over an area of 2,000 square miles, they posed a danger to living animals and property alike. They devoured everything in their path, stripping clothes off the body and making it impossible to breathe when they descended out of the sky to feed. As with most other disasters of the 19th century, no statistics are known on fatalities directly attributable to them or even property damage from the 1874 infestation, just horror stories of how they swarmed over the West from Oregon to Minnesota and as far south as Texas, wiping out crops in the fields, eating leather harnesses and even soft wood, and stopping train travel because locomotives could not gain traction on tracks covered with goo from their smashed bodies. In some places in Kansas dead grasshoppers covered acres of ground two inches deep. The state of Minnesota offered a bounty of 50 cents a bushel for dead grasshoppers, and farmers with nothing else to do took in so many bags they bankrupted the state treasury. As suddenly as they had arrived, the horde of six-legged invaders disappeared, leaving behind incalculable economic devastation. The swarms were back in 1875 and 1876 but, except in Minnesota, were milder than in 1874. After summer 1876, nature seemed to take pity on the Midwest and the grasshoppers stayed away.

Hordes of grasshoppers, resembling the biblical plague of locusts, were a terrifying and inevitable occurrence on the Great Plains. The only way to fight them was to sweep them into piles and burn them, but even that was usually too little and too late to save the crops. This engraving is from a sketch by Mrs. Clara Knapp in *Harper's Weekly,* July 3, 1875. (Library of Congress)

Wind

Farmers prayed for winds to blow the grasshoppers away, but those same winds could also turn deadly when they became tornadoes or hurricanes. Americans in the 19th century were quite familiar with killer hurricanes and killer tornadoes. The popular understanding of a hurricane is a storm that arises over water and a tornado is one that originates over land. Meteorological science defines a hurricane as a type of tropical cyclone, which produces violent winds and rain. The pattern for hurricanes in U.S. history has always been that the worst ones hit between the beginning of August and the end of October, and their life span is measured in days as they slowly build up gale-force winds. Much smaller than hurricanes, tornadoes, often resulting from storm clouds contained within a tropical cyclone, have always been distinguished by the giant, funnel-shaped whirlwind form they take. The midwestern prairie states have always seemed to be particularly vulnerable to such storms. All the prairie states, including Wisconsin, Illinois, and Indiana, were victimized at one time or another, but Kansas was hit more often than any other in the 19th century. It made sense for L. Frank Baum later to set the beginning and end of his fable *The Wonderful Wizard of Oz* in Kansas. The life of a tornado could be measured in terms of minutes or sometimes hours. They were usually named for the town where they caused the worst damage.

Americans were first introduced to killer hurricanes, or tropical cyclones, in July 1819, when one hit Mobile, Alabama, killing more than 200 people. People living along the Gulf Coast then used the term *hurricane,* from the Spanish word meaning "big wind," as it had been a part of the English lexicon since at least 1589. *Cyclone* as a meteorological term was first used in England in 1856 and arrived in America soon thereafter.

Another massive hurricane hit Saint Jo, Florida, in September 1841, destroying the town and taking nearly 4,000 lives. Then in October that same year, one attacked Cape Cod, wiping out the fishing fleet and killing hundreds of fishermen. Between 1850 and 1870, no fewer than 35 hurricanes struck land on the south Atlantic and Gulf coasts. Alabama and Louisiana were the most frequent targets. No major storms struck the New England coast during these years. As luck would have it, the 18th and early 19th centuries were much worse for hurricanes in the United States than the mid- to late 19th century. The worst of this era was the "colossal hurricane" that struck the Isles Dernieres of Louisiana, in 1856, completely inundating the barrier islands and killing hundreds of people, the largest single group

TABLE 2.3 HURRICANES HITTING THE GULF COAST, 1852–1877

Year	Date	Area Hit	Intensity[a]	Miscellaneous Notes
1852	Aug. 23–25	Mobile, Ala.	Minimal	Tides 8.8 feet above normal
1856	Aug. 10–11	Isles Dernieres, La.	Major	400 Killed
1856	Aug. 30	Mobile, Ala.	Minimal	. . .
1860	Aug. 11	Mobile, Ala.	Minor	Tides just 18 inches lower than in 1852
1860	Sep. 15	Mobile, Ala.	Minimal	High tides
1865	Sep.	La. coast	Minimal	. . .
1870	Jul. 3 or 30	Mobile, Ala.	Minor	. . .
1877	Sep. 19–20	Entire Gulf Coast from La. to Ala.	Minor	Storm center remained off coast

[a] The standard meteorological classification for hurricane winds is as follows: Minor, less than 74 miles per hour (mph); minimal, 74–100 mph; major, 101–135 mph; extreme, 136 mph and above.
Source: Gordon E. Dunn and Banner I. Miller, *Atlantic Hurricanes* (Baton Rouge: Louisiana State University Press, 1960), 302.

of whom were a party of revelers at a resort hotel. But for sheer frequency, Mobile, Alabama, was the hurricane capital of the United States during these years.

Tornadoes, probably from the Spanish for "thunderstorm," were nothing new to residents of the Great Plains in the mid-19th century; the word had been part of the English lexicon since at least 1804. But the danger posed by tornadoes grew enormously after homesteaders began to rush onto the Great Plains after the Civil War. Lethal "twisters" were also known before the Civil War. One of the most severe tornadoes on record up to this time hit Natchez, Mississippi, in May 1840, killing 317 and injuring another 109 while causing $1.26 million in property damage. In May 1859, another monster tornado tore through Iowa farm country, causing widespread ruin although minimal loss of life. The only factor that prevented larger numbers of casualties was that it was farm country with relatively low population.

Although mainly identified with the Midwest, tornadoes were not unknown to New Englanders. One touched down between Cambridge and Medford, Massachusetts, on August 23, 1851, causing an unknown number of casualties and considerable property damage. The next major New England tornado occurred on August 9, 1878, hitting Wallingford, Connecticut, and causing 34 deaths and some $200,000 in property damage.

Judging by the historical records, tornadoes were by far the most common destructive weather phenomenon in the 19th century, just as they are today, when roughly 1,000 a year are sighted. According to the U.S. Weather Service, the death rate from tornadoes in that era was roughly 1.1 fatalities per million people in the U.S. population, a figure derived from combing the contemporary accounts. No exact figures are available for the years 1850–75, but by comparison, the Weather Service calculates that 18,000 Americans have been killed by tornadoes since 1880.

Weather Prediction

What is clear is that Americans were hit by a variety of severe storms in the mid-19th century, usually without warning and with little assistance afterward in cleaning up the damage. These events were regarded as acts of God, a fatalistic view that did little to alleviate suffering afterward and preempted serious efforts at advance planning.

Scientific weather observation and record keeping were new practices that appeared in the United States at this time. The first regular observations originated from a network of 600 telegraph stations under the aegis of the Smithsonian Institution from 1849. These were augmented the following year when the U.S. Army Signal Corps began gathering data from its various posts around the country. (It was the post surgeon's job to make the daily readings.) New Yorker Ebenezer Merrian used the Smithsonian's data to begin publishing weather forecasts in the New York City newspapers in 1853; six years later the term *weatherman* entered the language. In the meantime, in 1857 U.S. government officials began discussing the need for a national weather bureau, which was established by act of Congress in 1870. The first weather maps were produced for the War Department in 1871. For the first time, Americans were doing more than just talking about the weather.

Riverboat Disasters

One of the paradoxes of progress was that the same technology that was such a boon to transportation could be a deadly killer—the steam engine. Whether powering a riverboat or a train, steam engines were dangerous and fickle. Their boilers were often ticking time bombs. They could blow without warning and all too frequently did. The combination of barely contained fire, high-pressure steam, and primitive metallurgy was a lethal one even without the human element. And when accidents happened, the reasons most often offered were not defective manufacturing, poor maintenance, or improper operation but "unpreventable causes," a catch-all excuse that provided legal cover for owners and operators. Sinkings caused by storm, collision, or snagging were also familiar disasters on water; however, the most dreaded and dramatic sinkings were the result of boiler explosions. Passengers and crew were immediately exposed to fire and scalding steam, and if they escaped both of those, they risked drowning when they jumped into the water.

The first major steamboat disaster in U.S. history occurred in 1816, when a packet boat on the Ohio River blew up with great loss of life. This was only nine years after Robert Fulton had first demonstrated the new technology. No records were kept of the casualties or the damage from that first disaster; in the next 30 years there were another 230 steamboat explosions, costing thousands of lives and millions of dollars of damage. Still no comprehensive records were kept by either the industry or the government.

In 1856 the St. Louis *Democrat* finally assembled a list of all steamboat disasters on the western rivers during the first six months of the year (ending June 30). Their listing showed an average loss of eight boats per month, which was as clear an indication as needed that steamboat technology was still in its infancy and remained a highly risky venture for anyone stepping foot on a riverboat.

When steamboat disasters occurred, the crew and wealthy cabin passengers routinely fared better than the poor deck passengers. The crew were usually the first to be aware of a catastrophe and knew how to save themselves; the cabin passengers enjoyed more protection

Steamboats with their fragile high-pressure boilers were ticking time bombs. They had a nasty habit of exploding, as this one has, usually with great loss of life. This illustration is from *Harper's Weekly,* September 16, 1871. (Courtesy of Mississippi Department of Archives and History)

TABLE 2.4 STEAMBOATS IN THE WESTERN TRADE LOST TO VARIOUS CAUSES, JANUARY–JUNE 1856

Cause of Accident	Number of Boats Lost	Lives Lost	Value of Property Lost
Fire	10	. . .	. . .
Explosion	2	. . .	. . .
Other (collision, ice, snags, etc.)	36	. . .	. . .
TOTALS	48	43	$1,200,000

Source: Reprinted in *Frank Leslie's Illustrated Newspaper,* 26 July 1856, 130.

from fire and explosion than did people on an open deck. The result was a clear class division in relative numbers of victims whenever a steamboat disaster occurred. Typical of such disasters was the casualty list of the Mississippi riverboat *John Adams,* which struck a snag and sank within minutes in 1851.

Steamboat accidents, frequent and deadly, were a fact of life on the river. The high-pressure boilers, roaring furnaces, and flimsy construction that characterized the vessels seemed designed to produce disasters. Some boats carried as many as seven boilers, and the pressures to turn a profit made most owners run their boats at night, even when the only illumination was provided by torches or oil lamps. The odds of an engine malfunction's turning into a fiery inferno were increased by the practice of cramming highly flammable cotton bales

TABLE 2.5 CASUALTIES AMONG PASSENGERS AND CREW IN THE SINKING OF THE STEAMBOAT *JOHN ADAMS*, FEBRUARY 4, 1851

Category	On Board	Saved
Cabin passengers	100	84
Deck passengers	87	5
Ordinary crewmen	32	7
Officers	11	11

Source: Louis C. Hunter, *Steamboats on the Western Rivers* (New York: Octagon Books, 1969), 436.

TABLE 2.6 STEAMBOAT ACCIDENTS AND FATALITIES IN THE UNITED STATES, 1860–1879

	Mississippi and Ohio River Systems		United States Total	
Period[a]	Number of Accidents	Lives Lost	Number of Accidents	Lives Lost
1860–64	188	101	341	821
1865–69	196	2,883	385	4,416
1870–74	403	381	775	1,274
1875–79	332	236	954	1,044

[a] Data on accidents and fatalities are not available for 1863 and 1870; therefore, averages for the remaining years in these periods have been interpolated from the existing data.
Source: Louis C. Hunter, *Steamboats on the Western Rivers* (New York: Octagon Books, 1969), 656–57.

TABLE 2.7 STEAMBOAT ACCIDENTS AND FATALITIES IN THE UNITED STATES BY TYPE, 1860–1879

	Mississippi River System		Ohio River System		United States Total	
Kind of Accident	Number of Accidents	Lives Lost	Number of Accidents	Lives Lost	Number of Accidents	Lives Lost
Explosions	. . .	. . .	. . .	. . .	. . .	. . .
1860–69	28	1,983	19	283	93	2,503
1870–79	38	175	18	72	116	562
Fire	. . .	. . .	. . .	. . .	. . .	. . .
1860–69	75	351	24	26	172	705
1870–79	79	105	28	51	334	563

Note: Before 1868 the Board of Supervising Inspectors for Steamboats calculated the "accident year" as Oct. 1–Sep. 30; starting in 1868 the accident year was calculated as Jan. 1–Dec. 31. The figures here for 1868 cover the period from Oct. 1, 1867, to Dec. 31, 1868.
[a] Because the necessary data for 1863 and 1870 are lacking, no attempt has been made to interpolate figures for those two years in the table.
Source: Louis C. Hunter, *Steamboats on the Western Rivers* (New York: Octagon Books, 1969), 656–57.

into every available space on board. Finally, the fact that most Americans in the 19th century could not swim increased the potential for human tragedy any time an accident occurred on the river.

Many captains also liked to race their boat whenever they encountered each other traveling the same direction. The contests, which could continue for hours, relieved the tedium of long journeys, won bragging rights for owners, and were cheered on by passengers. After 1870, the *Robert E. Lee* held the record as the fastest boat on the Mississippi.

There are only the sketchiest of statistics for the total number of accidents and fatalities in the riverboat trade over the years. The wonder is, with an estimated 3 million people annually traveling the western rivers via steamboat, that more deadly accidents did not occur.

Maritime Disasters

Traveling the western rivers had its special dangers in the form of snags, tricky currents, and continuously shifting channels; however, boat travel on the Great Lakes and the oceans was also not risk-free. The larger the body of water, the bigger and more violent the storms were, and the farther from land in the event of an accident. This era did not have wireless communications, so a captain had no way of signaling his vessel was in distress and calling for help except to send up flares. And as the age of steam dominated shipping, people discovered that as is every other form of new technology, it was a mixed blessing. On the one hand, it gave captains more control over their vessels than when they were dependent on sail and wind power. But it also entailed all the dangers of steam power, made worse because most veteran sea captains had little or no experience with steam engines—how they operated or how to care for them. The master of the ship was therefore totally dependent on his engineers to keep him afloat. And those engineers as a rule had received no formal training in their craft, being self-taught men. Temperamental technology, untrained operators, and primitive communications made for an adventure every time someone set foot on a boat or ship. For all these reasons, most shipwrecks at sea entailed the loss of all persons on board.

As travel via water increased, and as vessels grew larger and therefore able to carry more passengers, the potential for maritime disasters increased. Two of the worst of all time occurred during these years, the sinking of the ocean steamer SS *Central America* in 1857 and of the Mississippi river steamer SS *Sultana* in 1865. The sidewheeler *Central America* was steaming up the eastern seaboard en route from California carrying 600 passengers and 21 tons of gold bars and coins when caught in a hurricane. It sank on September 12 after a hopeless three-day battle to stay afloat, taking down 450 victims and all its cargo. To his credit Captain William Lewis Herndon saw to it that every woman and child on board was saved before he went down with his ship. The

TABLE 2.8 MAJOR MARITIME DISASTERS AT SEA AND ON THE GREAT LAKES, 1850–1875

Name of Vessel(s)	Type of Vessel(s)	Date	Location	Details	Loss of Life
SS *G.P. Griffith*	Paddle-wheel steamer	Jun. 17, 1850	Lake Erie, off Mentor, Ohio	Caught fire and burned	286 dead
1) SS *Atlantic* 2) Smaller sailboat	1) Paddle-wheel steamer 2) Fishing boat	Aug. 20, 1852	Offshore	Collision	250 dead
SS *Powhatan*	Paddle-wheel steamer	Apr. 16, 1854	Off Long Beach, N.Y.	Ran aground and sank	311 dead
SS *New Era*	Paddle-wheel steamer	Nov. 13, 1854	Off N.J. shore, 15 mi. below Sandy Hook	Immigrant ship en route from Bremen, Germany, to New York City	More than 300 dead (mostly immigrants)
SS *Guiding Star*	Paddle-wheel steamer	Jan. 9, 1855	Mid-Atlantic	. . .	Unknown
SS *Niagara*	Paddle-wheel steamer	Sep. 24, 1856	Lake Michigan near Ft. Washington	Burned	60–70 passengers
SS *Monarch of the Sea*	Paddle-wheel steamer	Apr. 3, 1866	Mid-Atlantic	. . .	Unknown
SS *Metropolis* and SS *J. N. Harris*	Paddle-wheel steamer and propeller-driven steamer	Aug. 15, 1857	Long Island Sound, N.Y.	Collision that caused the *J. N. Harris* to sink in matter of minutes	15 dead
SS *Central America*	Paddle-wheel steamer	Sep. 12, 1857	North–south shipping lanes, about 100 mi. east of Cape Romain, S.C.	Sailing from Havana, Cuba, to New York carrying 576 crew and passengers; battered for 2 days by a hurricane, capsized, and sank	423 passengers and crew dead
SS *Pomona*	Paddle-wheel steamer	Apr. 27, 1859	Mid-Atlantic	En route from New York City to Liverpool, England; sank after causes unknown	All 400 people aboard lost at sea
1) SS *Lady Elgin* 2) SS *Augusta*	1) Paddle-wheel steamer 2) Paddle-wheel cargo schooner	Sep. 7–8, 1860 (night of)	Lake Michigan, about 30 mi. north of Chicago	Excursion boat with 421 passengers returning home to Milwaukee from Chicago; collided with cargo vessel *Augusta* carrying lumber to Chicago; *Lady Elgin* broke up and sank	339 on passenger list dead
SS *Golden Gate*	Paddle-wheel steamer	Jul. 27, 1862	Off west coast of Mexico, near Manzanillo	Sailing for East Coast out of San Francisco with gold shipment; burned and sank	175 lost at sea
1) USS *Miantonomoh* 2) SS *Sarah*	1) Ironclad monitor 2) Sailing schooner	Dec. 4, 1869	New York harbor	Collision; sank the *Sarah*	Unknown
1) USS *Miantonomoh* 2) SS *Maria*	1) Ironclad monitor 2) Steam-powered tugboat	Jan. 4, 1870	Off Martha's Vineyard, Mass.	Collision; sank the *Maria*	Unknown
SS *City of Boston*	Paddle-wheel steamer	Jan. 20, 1870	Mid-Atlantic	En route from New York to Liverpool, England	All 177 passengers and crew lost at sea
Westfield	Staten Island ferryboat, steam-powered	Jul. 30, 1870	New York harbor	Boiler explosion that caused onboard fire	100 dead
SS *Mary Celeste*	Brigantine-rigged sailing ship	Nov.–Dec. 1872[a]	Eastern Atlantic between Azores and Portugal	Discovered drifting at sea with no one aboard and scant damage	Captain, wife, and child and eight crewmen missing; never found
SS *Atlantic*	Steam-powered ocean liner	Apr. 1, 1873	Off Halifax, Nova Scotia, near Piggy's Point	En route from Liverpool to New York, with 975 passengers and crew; ran aground during heavy rainstorm because of captain's navigational error	560 total dead; 481 passengers, including all but one of 295 women and children
1) SS *Pacific* 2) SS *Orpheus*	1) Stern-wheel steamer 2) Paddle-wheel steamer	Nov. 1875	Off Cape Flattery, Washington Territory	Collision at sea	236 dead

Note: The *SS* before a vessel's name identifies it as a privately owned steamship; *USS* identifies it as a United States Navy warship.
[a] The *Mary Celeste* left New York harbor on Nov. 7 en route to Genoa, Italy, and was found drifting at sea and abandoned on Dec. 4.
Sources: James Cornell, *The Great International Disaster Book,* 3d ed. (New York: Charles Scribner's Sons, 1982), 396–400; Lee Davis, *Man-Made Catastrophes* (New York: Facts On File, 1993), 206–25.

gold and the ship rested on the bottom under 8,000 feet of water until finally salvaged by a privately financed expedition in 1989.

The *Sultana* was an overloaded river steamer carrying home 2,134 Union prisoners of war after the Civil War among its 2,300 passengers and crew *and* 160 head of livestock. On April 27, 1865, when it was just eight miles north of Memphis and beating its way upriver toward Cairo, Illinois, one of its boilers exploded. The explosion ripped the guts out of the boat and left the hulk burning as it drifted down-river powerless and sinking. The *Sultana* was in midstream when the disaster occurred; most of the passengers were in weakened condition from their time in captivity and unable to swim anyway, and the night was unseasonably cool. While most of the crew saved themselves, some 1,700 of their charges died of drowning or scalding. It was the greatest maritime disaster in U.S. history, taking 200 more lives than the *Titanic* did in 1912 and almost 700 more than died on the *General Slocum* in 1904. In a five-month trial that followed, the cause of the human disaster was fixed not on the boiler but on overloading of the ship, the responsibility of Captain Frederic Speed of the U.S. Army, who had directed their boarding at Vicksburg, Mississippi. Speed was cashiered from the service, but the lingering suspicion remained that he was the scapegoat for major problems with the vessel's design and power plant.

The Mississippi riverboat *Sultana* stops over at Helena, Arkansas, on its last ill-fated voyage upriver. It is heavily overloaded with some 2,000 recently released Union prisoners of war, plus 200 other crew and passengers. Just above Memphis, Tennessee, on April 27, 1865, one of its boilers explodes, and it burns up in 20 minutes, causing the death of 1,500 people, the worst maritime disaster in U.S. history. (Arkansas History Commission)

Railroad Deaths

The first fatal railroad accident on record in the United States occurred in 1833. By the mid-century mark, train wrecks had become a surprisingly frequent form of disaster, caused by poor equipment, lack of standardization, unregulated operations, and often shocking carelessness of the operators. Vague and conflicting timetables were one major problem because trains traveled on "local time," and until telegraphy was widely adopted in the 1850s, communication between distant stations on the line was impossible. The result was more than a few head-on collisions when glitches in scheduling put trains on the same track heading in opposite directions. Scheduling traffic by printed timetables rather than telegraph communication remained the norm until 1855. Unfortunately railroad owners were slow to embrace telegraphy because of conservatism and the expense of making the change. As late as 1875 the *Railroad Gazette,* a trade publication, reported 104 head-on collisions on U.S. lines.

The single worst type of railroad accident after 1870, not to say the most frequent, was the rear-end collision. Caused by inability to stay on schedule or by breakdowns in equipment, they were not a problem in the early years because most trains never exceeded 15 miles per hour. But when speeds increased to 40 and 45 miles an hour after the Civil War, when trains were still using the same primitive hand-braking and flagman-signaling systems, both the numbers and severity of accidents increased. What caused such horrific casualties was that the trains collided with such force that the flimsy passenger cars "telescoped" through each other. This tendency was finally alleviated after Ezra Miller patented an effective trussed platform and compression buffer system in 1869. Thereafter, telescoping became less of a nightmare although the potential could never be completely eliminated as long as trains traveled at ever-increasing speeds on the same line.

Numerous other factors contributed to the inherent dangers of rail travel. Passenger cars were framed and paneled with wood, heated by coal stoves, and illuminated by oil or kerosene lamps. During violent accidents, they could turn into human-crushing machines or fiery infernos. Beginning about 1850, most railroad companies began nighttime operations, creating two potential hazards: Visibility on the lines was dramatically reduced, even with headlamps installed on the engines, and those headlamps burned kerosene, which created an additional source of fire in the event of an accident.

Even under the best of conditions in the daytime, tracks were dangerous. Near cities, where major lines often joined, companies refused to invest in either crossing guards or warning signals to mark the sites, though the money invested in prevention had to be far less than the cost in equipment and lives when serious accidents occurred. In 1867, the commissioner of Ohio Railroads publicly warned that accidents at railroad crossings would continue until the companies installed the necessary safety devices. The most curious aspect of the warning is that he obviously considered it the business of the companies and not the state of Ohio to see that such devices were installed.

Until about 1850, trains traveled on strap rails, which were formed of wood with strips of iron laid across the top or track portion. Heavy use caused such rails to warp and break apart, producing countless derailing between the 1830s and 1850s. Only as U.S. mills

Train wrecks were almost as common in the 19th century as automobile wrecks are today, but they were far more costly in human lives and property damage. An 1855 accident on the Camden & Amboy line near Burlington, New Jersey, left cars crushed and bodies of passengers and livestock scattered about the site. This lithograph was done from a drawing made immediately after the accident. (Library of Congress, Prints and Photographs Division [LC-USZ62-1383])

gained the capability of rolling the all-iron T rails and those were installed on a leisurely maintenance schedule did the situation improve by the 1850s. In the meantime, wrecks caused by the old-fashioned rails were called snakehead accidents in the industry. Starting in 1863 on the Pennsylvania Railroad line, steel rails replaced the iron variety, improving safety and weight-carrying capacity at the same time. Another design failing that did not cause accidents but made them much worse when they occurred was the conventional link-and-pin coupling between cars, which allowed the cars to telescope in the event of a head-on or rear-end collision.

Train accidents were not just a problem for long-distance service; they were also occurring regularly on local commuter lines by the 1870s. New York City's elevated trains were plagued by misplaced switches, flawed timetables, and incompetent conductors. And accidents on urban commuter lines had the potential for even greater casualties because of the surroundings and the typically high passenger occupancy rates.

No comprehensive figures are available on 19th-century railroad accidents because the companies were not even required to report all collisions and derailments until 1901, when the Interstate Commerce Commission assumed control over railroad safety standards. Anecdotal evidence for this period drawn from newspaper accounts suggests that the numbers of accidents and victims of train wrecks exceeded even those of steamboat accidents. Adding to the scope of the tragedy, human error was involved in almost every reported train wreck of the time.

The year 1853 is considered to be the worst for 19th-century railroad accidents for several reasons: First is the sheer number of accidents that occurred that year; no fewer than eight major accidents were recorded in addition to innumerable "minor" accidents—a very relative term. Second, the worst accident in U.S. railroad history up to that date occurred near South Norwalk, Connecticut, when the year was only five months old. The rest of that terrible year continued in the same vein.

TABLE 2.9 NOTABLE WRECKS, ACCIDENTS, AND COLLISIONS ON U.S. RAIL LINES, 1850–1875

(1853 saw many train accidents; for more, see table 2.10)

Date	Location	Equipment and/or Companies Involved[a]	Cause(s)	Casualties
Sep. 9, 1850	"Near the Washington Summit"	Albany to Springfield passenger train	Unknown	Three killed, "several others" seriously injured
Jan. 6, 1853	One mile outside Boston, Mass.	Boston-to-Concord (N.H.) RR	Derailing	Bennie, 11-year-old son of Jane Pierce and President-elect Franklin Pierce, killed and two others injured
Jul. 4, 1854	Riverwood, Md.	Unknown	Conductor disobeying of orders	34 dead
Aug. 29, 1855	Near Burlington, N.J.	Camden and Amboy train	Collision with a surrey at a RR crossing because surrey driver unable to hear train whistle	Surrey's driver and 20 passengers dead; 75 injured
Nov. 1, 1855	Gasconade River, Mo. ("the Gasconade Bridge Disaster")	Pacific Railroad	New bridge trestle that collapsed during testing by loaded train on inaugural run	22 dead (most V.I.P.s); many injured
Jul. 17, 1856	Camp Hill, Pa.	Northern Pennsylvania RR local and excursion trains	Head-on collision due to missed schedules, inadequate signals, and human error	66 dead (all children); 60 injured
May 11, 1858	Near Utica, N.Y.	Two New York Central trains: passenger train and freight train	Attempt by two trains to pass on same, overloaded bridge, causing its collapse	Nine dead; 55 seriously injured including man whose throat was cut and woman who was scalped
Jun. 27, 1859	Near South Bend, Ind.	Michigan Southern RR passenger train	Culvert was washed away and cars thrown into the chasm	38 dead; more than 50 injured
Aug. 25, 1861	Huron, Ind.	Unknown	Bridge collapse	23 dead
Jul. 15, 1864[b]	Near Shohola, Pa.	Union army troop train (carrying POWs) and Erie RR coal train	Long delay that disrupted regular schedule and resulted in head-on collision	74 dead; no record of number injured
Sep. 1, 1864	Barnesville, Ga.	Unknown	Head-on collision	30 dead
Aug. 25, 1865	Reynolds, Tenn.	Unknown	Trestle collapse	35 dead
Aug. 28, 1865	Jamaica, N.Y.	Long Island RR (the *General Grant* and the *General Sherman*)	Head-on collision after conductor failed to follow prescribed timetable	5 dead; number of injured unknown
Nov. 21, 1867	Lockland, just north of Cincinnati, Ohio	Two Cincinnati, Hartford and Dayton (C.H. & D.) trains; the *Franklin* and the *Lightning Express*	*Franklin* rear-ending of *Express*, igniting fire among *Express's*, passenger cars	Numbers of dead and injured unknown
Dec. 18, 1867	Angola, N.Y. ("the Angola Horror")	The Lakeshore and Michigan Southern's New York express	Derailing caused by defective axle on speeding train; followed by fire in passenger cars	43 burned to death; hundreds injured
Apr. 15, 1868	Carr's Point, N.Y. (Carr's Rock)	Erie RR Express	Defective iron rail that caused train to run off track, plunge down 100 feet into gorge, and catch fire	26 dead; 63 severely injured

(continued)

TABLE 2.9 (continued)

Date	Location	Equipment and/or Companies Involved[a]	Cause(s)	Casualties
Feb. 26, 1870	Oxford, Mich.	Unknown	Trestle collapse	19 dead
May 12, 1870	Eureka, Mo.	Unknown	Switchman disobeying of procedure	19 dead
Feb. 6, 1871	Wappingers Creek, N.Y.	Unknown	Derailing	21 dead
Aug. 26, 1871[c]	Revere, Mass.	Two Eastern RR excursion trains: an express and a local	Express rear-ending of local, unable to stop with outdated hand brakes; resulting fire and boiler explosion	32 dead; more than 100 injured
Dec. 24, 1872	Prospect Station, Pa.	Unknown	Broken wheel that caused train to derail and fall into a creek bed, where passenger cars caught fire	25 passengers dead of fire and crushing
1873	Wood River Junction, R.I.	Stonington and Providence express	Washout that carried the Wood River bridge away and train plunge into chasm; followed by fire	Nine passengers dead
Apr. 29, 1874	Near Franklin Grove, Ill.	Two Chicago and Northwestern Railway trains (the *Lyons* and the *Lucifer*)	Head-on collision caused by signal error	Unknown

Note: Figures vary in different sources. Those cited here are the most credible.
[a] Most companies identified their trains by either the regular route they ran (i.e., the Boston to Concord express) or the name assigned to the engine (i.e., the *General Sherman*).
[b] The worst head-on collision in U.S. railroading history.
[c] One of the most infamous disasters in U.S. railroad history, and the worst rear-end collision on record before 1880.
Sources: Lee Davis, *Man-Made Catastrophes* (New York: Facts On File, 1993), 298–309; Oliver Jensen, *The American Heritage History of Railroads in America* (New York: American Heritage, 1981) 178–83; Robert C. Reed, *Train Wrecks* (reprint, New York: Bonanza Books, 1968), 17–31, 55, 71–74, 85–86, 119–20.; *The American Almanac and Repository of Useful Knowledge for the Years 1850–1861* (Boston: Chas. C. Little & James Brown, Crosby, Nichols, Lee & Co., 1860–75), 344–52, 353–55, 365–67, 368–75, 383–91, 406–13.

TABLE 2.10 RAILROAD ACCIDENTS, 1853

(The year 1853 was an especially bad one in terms of number of train accidents.)

Month	Train(s) involved	Location	Casualties	Cause/Details
Jan.	Boston and Maine Express derailment	Andover, Mass.	One killed; two injured	Broken axle
Mar.	Pennsylvania RR	Mount Union, Pa.	Seven dead; several injured	Mail train ramming of another train halted on tracks ("human error")
Apr. 23	Camden and Amboy express	Rancocas Creek, near Philadelphia, Pa.	No one killed; injuries unknown	Engineer inability to see signals and driving of train off open drawbridge and into creek
Apr. 25	Michigan Central express and Michigan Southern emigrant train	Grand Crossing (near Chicago, Ill.)	21 dead	Michigan Central hit broadside by Michigan Southern at RR crossing when trains off schedule (investigation ruling of "human error")[a]
May 6	New York and New Haven RR, Boston Express	Norwalk River Bridge, near South Norwalk, Conn.	46 dead; 25 injured	Careless train engineer who disregarded signal and speed limit and failed to see raised drawbridge
May 8	Two trains, unknown ownership	Secaucus, N.J.	Several	Head-on collision caused by failure to follow timetable
Aug.	Excursion train and regular train	Valley Falls Station, R.I.	13 dead	Head-on collision caused by failure to follow timetable
Aug. 2	Unknown	Bulls Island, N.J.	11 dead	Hitting of cow on tracks

[a] The deadliest rail accident in U.S. history up to this time, and the worst crossing accident in the United States in the 19th century.
Sources: Lee Davis, *Man-Made Catastrophes* (New York: Facts On File, 1993), 298–99; Oliver Jensen, *The American Heritage History of Railroads in America* (New York: American Heritage, 1981), 178–83; Robert C. Reed, *Train Wrecks* (reprint, New York: Bonanza Books, 1968), 17–24.

Learning from Mistakes

Although all disasters were tragedies and many were preventable, at least good resulted from some of them in the form of improved safety measures. After the sinking of the luxurious wooden-hulled paddle steamer *Arctic* in 1854, new shipping regulations that required watertight bulkheads, better provisioned lifeboats, steam whistles, and separate east-west shipping lanes for the North Atlantic trade were introduced. Then, after a series of shipping disasters in the 1850s and 1860s, the U.S. Life-Saving Service was founded in 1870 "to aid mariners in distress along the American shores." In the years following, the American Red Cross, as it would become, was a welcome presence at countless maritime disasters in U.S. waters, never failing to respond promptly and courageously in an emergency. The service adopted the fatalistic motto "You have to go out—you don't have to come back." (In 1915 the Life-Saving Service merged with the Revenue Cutter Service to form the U.S. Coast Guard.)

The riverboat industry also learned some hard lessons from its mistakes. After the *Sultana* sank, a different type of boiler was mandated for boats on the Upper Mississippi River. The *Sultana* had been built with the old-fashioned tubular boilers used in boats in the upper river trade. Boats in the lower river trade used flue-type boilers, which were better suited to the muddy waters closer to the mouth of the river. On its last run the *Sultana* had started in New Orleans and worked its way upriver to its date with disaster. A similar though less lethal boiler explosion on the *Sultana*'s sister boat *Missouri* not long afterward seemed to confirm the hunch that tubular boilers were the problem, and led to the boiler ruling.

And in the mining industry the Avondale coal mine disaster of 1869 spurred shocked politicians in Scranton to enact legislation that required all the state's mines to have at least two exits and prohibited the building of enclosed structures directly over shaft entrances that might block quick escape in the event of an emergency. These measures, meager and long-overdue as they were, did not prevent future accidents, but at least they helped reduce the catastrophic nature of such accidents.

CHAPTER 3 Native American Life

Native Americans were neither bloodthirsty savages nor the noble red men of popular imagination, but whites tended to see them in terms of those stereotypes. Seemingly there was not room on the continent for both races to live freely. Of the estimated 360,000 American Indians who were still alive at mid-century (down from pre-Columbian times), some 200,000 lived on lands newly acquired in the 1840s by war, treaty, or annexation. The most unbowed were the 75,000 Plains Indians. They had battled the Spanish and the Mexicans before the Europeans arrived and were unlikely to back down to the latest interlopers. Another 84,000 Indians living on the Plains represented tribes uprooted from their eastern lands and transplanted west of the 95th meridian. The Mexican Cession held another 150,000, and Oregon Country could claim 25,000. By comparison, the United States at the mid-century mark had a population of 20 million and counting. In the next decades the Native American population would continue to drop precipitously, victimized by war, disease, and what might be called "rootlessness."

U.S. Government Policy

During the course of the century to 1850, government policy from Washington had undergone a profound change in relations with

TABLE 3.1 NATIVE AMERICAN POPULATION IN THE UNITED STATES, ESTIMATED FOR SELECT YEARS, BASED ON BEST AVAILABLE EVIDENCE, 1850–1875

Year	Estimated Number of Indians	Source or Authority
1850	388,229	Report of H. R. Schoolcraft[a]
1853	400,764	Report of U.S. Census Office (from 1850 count, delayed)
1855	314,622	Report of Bureau of Indian Affairs
1857	379,264	Report of H. R. Schoolcraft
1860	254,300	Report of Bureau of Indian Affairs
1865	294,574	Report of Bureau of Indian Affairs
1870	313,712[b]	Report of U.S. Census Office (1870)
1875	305,068	Report of U.S. Census Office

Note: In general a new census was taken whenever a new commissioner of Indian Affairs or a new administration took office. The official U.S. Census every 10 years provided another occasion to conduct a count. Because some Indians were nomadic and many tried to live as far away from white settlement as possible, no census count of their numbers can be considered anything but a rough estimate.

[a] See Schoolcraft, *Historical and Statistical Information* (1851–57).

[b] An alternate figure of 278,000 is cited in U.S. Bureau of the Census, *Indian Population in the United States and Alaska, 1910* (Washington, D.C., 1915), 10.

Source: Warren K. Moorehead, *The American Indian in the United States . . . 1850–1914* (Andover, Mass.: The Andover Press, 1914), 22.

Bloody Indian raids were a fact of life on the frontier. Here a fanciful engraving that appeared in George Custer's *My Life on the Plains* (1874) shows Indians who, the author claims, were under government protection while committing outrages on settlers. (Library of Congress)

the remaining American Indian population: from treating them as "domestic independent nations" sharing the national domain with the United States to treating them generally as wards of a beneficent government. However, official policy and popular attitudes were at great variance. During the same period, white attitudes toward Indians had also changed, from seeing them as a minor irritant to be shunted aside, to seeing them as a serious threat and impediment to "manifest destiny" (i.e., westward progress). The principal reason for this change was the fierce resistance of the Plains Indians. Matters came to a head after the U.S.-Mexican War (1846–48), which gave the United States sovereignty over a vast new area of the West, thus opening the door for a fight to the death between whites and the Plains Indians. A new phase of the Indian Wars was about to begin.

In 1849, the Bureau of Indian Affairs (BIA), which had the official responsibility for "all matters arising out of Indian relations," was moved from the War Department, in which it had resided since its beginnings in 1824, to the newly created Department of the Interior. The move set up a turf battle between the two cabinet departments because the U.S. Army continued to be the primary agent in dealing with the Indians so long as they remained defiant and engaged in armed resistance. The commissioner of Indian Affairs, an office created by Congress in 1832, was responsible only to the secretary of the interior, the president, and the Senate (who had to confirm his appointment). He commanded a small army of field agents and superintendents but was still forced to rely on the army to back up his authority in any confrontation with the Indians. The real strength of the BIA lay in Washington, D.C., where a byzantine bureaucracy provided fertile soil for political patronage but little training in understanding Native American culture.

As a generality, it is fair to say that the BIA took a humanitarian approach to the Indians while the army continued to favor the traditional forceful approach. Westerners tended to side with the army. The bureau viewed their charges through the lens of the bureaucracy, pigeonholing them in neat categories according to their perceived friendliness, "teachability," and level of "civilization." This approach made for painfully simplistic, even bigoted appraisals by field agents and superintendents, but it was on these reports that policy, such as it was, had to be based.

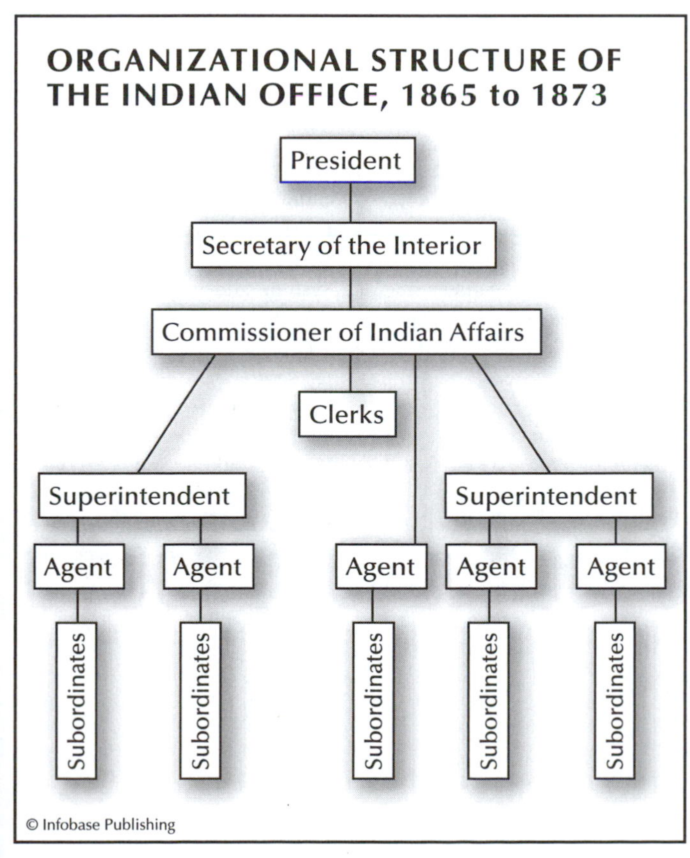

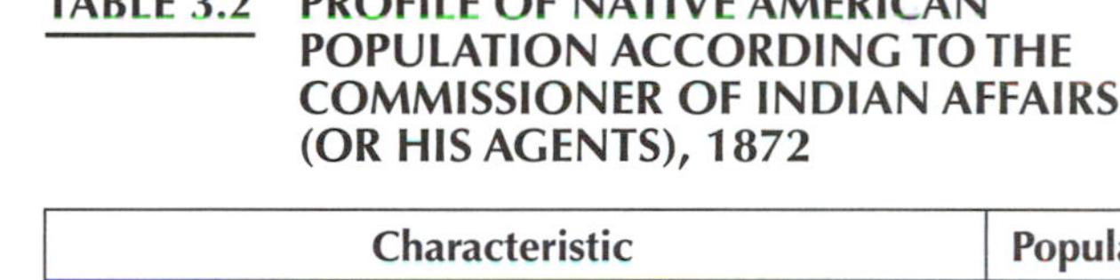

TABLE 3.2 PROFILE OF NATIVE AMERICAN POPULATION ACCORDING TO THE COMMISSIONER OF INDIAN AFFAIRS (OR HIS AGENTS), 1872

Characteristic	Population
Means of support	
"Supporting themselves on reservations, receiving nothing from government except interest on their own funds or annuities pursuant to treaties"	130,000
"Entirely subsisted by the government"	31,000
"In part subsisted by the government"	84,000
"Subsisting by hunting, fishing, roots, berries; begging or stealing"	55,000
Connection with the government	
"On reservations under complete control of agents"	150,000
"Visited agency at times for food or gossip, but generally roaming on or off their reservations, engaged in hunting or fishing"	95,000
"Never visited agency, and over whom government exercised practically no control, but most of whom were inoffensive"	55,000
Treaties and reservations	
"Had treaties with the government, 92 reservations"	180,000
"No treaties, but 15 reservations with agents in charge"	40,000
"No treaties, no reservations, but were more or less under the control of agents appointed for them and received more or less subsistence"	25,000
"No treaties, no reservations, practically no government control"	55,000
Degree of "civilization" (with no degree of assurance)	
"Civilized"	97,000
"Semi-Civilized"	125,000
"Wholly barbarous"	78,000

Source: Marlita A. Reddy, ed., *Statistical Record of Native North Americans* (Detroit: Gale Research, 1993), 9.

According to this *Harper's Weekly* cover, the "New Indian War" was between the Interior Department and the War Department over Indian policy (General William T. Sherman looks on from the background). Meanwhile, the poor Indian is caught in the middle. The caption reads, "The New Indian War. Now, no Sarcastic innuendoes, but let us have a square fight." (Library of Congress)

The bureau did not actually make official policy—that right was reserved to Congress and sometimes the army—and the post of commissioner was purely a political appointment, where loyalties were more important than any expertise or experience in dealing with Native Americans. In the heyday of the spoils system, this meant that the BIA soon established a reputation as one of the most corrupt and mismanaged government departments of all time, and this on top of its generally poor relations with the War Department. The constant cry in Congress was to "clean up the Indian mess" that was the bureau's job. The commissioners were judged on the basis of the number of treaties they successfully negotiated and the satisfaction of the majority party in Congress. It is indicative of the general attitude toward the bureau that to that date only one Native American (Ely Parker) was ever appointed commissioner, and the records do not indicate that any was appointed either to clerk positions in Washington, D.C., or to high-level field positions. The bureau's mission was to "pacify" and manage the Indians, not act as their advocate.

The principal policies of the U.S. government were extinguishing Indian land claims and concentrating the tribes on distant reservations, by force if necessary. These policies produced a system of forced treaties and annuity payments that pleased no one. The army enforced government policy and protected the ever-increasing numbers of non-Indian settlers moving west. The protection policy also led to the establishment of army forts all across the West, which in turn served as magnets for further settlement.

The New "Peace Policy" of 1867

A radical new policy toward the Indians was launched after the Civil War by a Congress tired of hearing of massacres and of footing the bill for forts and garrisons all over the West. The new "peace policy" began with the creation of a "peace commission" in July 1867 to hammer out equitable treaties and move the Indians onto reservations through persuasion rather than coercion. One commission policy ended the practice of negotiating formal treaties with the tribes after 1871; treaties were replaced by more flexible "agreements" that had to be approved by both houses of Congress. Another change that resulted from the new policy was initiated by the Grant administration: Responsibility for running the Indian agencies was turned over to the Society of Friends (the Quakers) and other churches. The thinking behind this was that they might accomplish with love what the government had not been able to accomplish with naked force over the years.

The immediate inspiration for the change arose in July 1870, when Congress made it illegal for military officers to hold high civil office (e.g., Indian agents for the BIA). In response, Grant, on the advice of religious friends, decided to appoint church leaders to the open positions at the Indian agencies. All the major Christian denominations, except the Mormons, received appointments on the basis of the group's willingness to participate and their record of mission work with a particular tribe.

With Quakers supervising the system, different denominations were allowed to run the agencies virtually as church missions. This experiment in Indian–white *and* church–state relations failed, partly because hard-liners and professional soldiers bitterly opposed it, partly because good intentions do not compensate for poor management skills and organization, and partly because some Indian groups resented having the beliefs and customs of another religion forced on them. Twenty years after it was inaugurated with great fanfare, the "Quaker Plan" ended and the politicians reclaimed supervision of Indian affairs. It had been another one of those "noble experiments" for which Americans are famous.

Fort Smith, Arkansas, was part of Indian Territory when a great Indian council was held on this spot and a treaty of peace was signed September 14, 1865. (Arkansas History Commission)

The Indian Wars Resume

In the meantime, peace policies not withstanding, most relations between whites and Indians occurred at the point of a gun or lance. Unfinished business from the previous era was the Third Seminole War (1855–58), which aimed to remove the last members of that tribe from the Florida Everglades. The final phase of the Seminole Wars ended not on the battlefield but in the peace circle with the United States negotiating a cash settlement with Chief Billy Bowlegs in return for moving most of his people to the Indian Territory. A handful remained behind, still defiant in their swampy redoubt, but their days as a military threat were ended at a final cost to the government of $30 million and some 3,000 military casualties.

During the 1850s the arena of Indian-white warfare shifted to the trans-Mississippi West. The Yakama (Yakima) of Washington Territory were defeated in the Puget Sound War of October 1855 to March 1856. The war was part of an uprising by Yakama after one of their leaders was ordered arrested by Governor Isaac Stevens. The Indians resented a series of one-sided peace treaties forced on them by the governor and his representatives. At the signing of one of those treaties, Chief Seattle commented glumly, "It matters little where we pass the remnant of our days. They will not be many."

But it was perhaps the California Indians who suffered most of any group of Native Americans at the hands of non-Indians. Although genocide was never official government policy at any time in U.S. history, this was the de facto approach, as "Indian hunts" were regularly organized against the Hoopa, Shasta, Yana, Yurok, Wiyot, and other California tribes. From a high of more than 100,000 in 1850, the number of California Indians dropped to only 35,000 in the next 10 years and eventually to fewer than 20,000 by the end of the century. Those who were still alive after 1860 were starving refugees hiding out in the mountains.

Much less powerless in the face of open white aggression were the tribes of the Great Plains, who defended their lands and way of life for some four decades against white encroachment. Open warfare with the Plains Indians first flared in the 1850s, but the worst was yet to come. The U.S. Army took a tough stance against the Sioux (Dakota, Lakota, Nakota), Cheyenne, and Comanche in particular, winning several unequal campaigns, but never completely cowing the foe.

Although the Civil War was not an Indian war, it severely strained relations between whites and Indians. Partisans on both sides believed the Indians could be used against the other side. A slight variation on that idea was proposed by the novelist William Gillmore Simms, who advised the Confederate general P. G. T. Beauregard in 1861 to raise a guerrilla band dressed and painted to resemble Indians, then turn them loose behind Northern lines. Everybody, he continued blithely, "is familiar with the Indian mode of warfare . . . and if there be anything which will inspire terror in the souls of the citizen soldiery of the North, it will be the idea that scalps are to be taken." Just the suggestion of "Indian warfare," especially in the West, stirred great fear.

There is no record that Beauregard took Simms's advice, but some Native Americans chose sides for different reasons, including the Cherokee of Oklahoma, who were drawn into the fighting. More important, the war stripped the frontier regions of regular army protection, leaving the job to local militia or to no one at all. In either case, Indians seized the opportunity to reassert themselves and to roll back the frontier.

Two wartime incidents sparked the latest round of bloody conflict between whites and Indians: the Dakota Uprising in Minnesota in 1862 and the Sand Creek massacre in Colorado in 1864. Together they provoked the final round of a war that many believed the Indians were destined to lose from the start. The inability to settle the "Indian problem" peaceably frustrated Abraham Lincoln even in the midst of the great sectional conflict. In 1864 he remarked to a friend, "If we get through this war, and I live, this Indian system shall be reformed."

With a few minor exceptions during this period the military solution was preferred to negotiation for settling differences. The only significant departure occurred in 1867, when a scathing Senate report on government policy led to formation of a peace commission, which

After the Dakota Sioux Uprising of August to September, 1862, 392 Santee Dakota were found guilty of "extreme barbarity," and 307 sentenced to hang. Ultimately only 38 are actually hanged, on December 26 from a large gallows built for the occasion at Mankato, Minnesota. Here a crowd looks on approvingly after the deed is done. (Library of Congress, Prints and Photographs Division [LC-USZ62-37940])

was dispatched by Washington to negotiate the sweeping Medicine Lodge Treaty.

As the U.S. population grew rapidly and settlers pushed the boundaries ever westward, the basis of relations between Indians and non-Indians had to change to reflect the new arrangements. Treaty negotiations had a long history of relations between non-Indians, represented by the federal government, and Indians, represented by their tribal leaders (at least in the eyes of the non-Indians, who often did not understand the direct democracy of many tribes). In 1856, George W. Manypenny, commissioner of Indian Affairs, identified three different kinds of treaties: (1) "treaties of peace and friendship"; (2) "treaties of acquisition with a view of colonizing the Indians on reservations"; and (3) "treaties of acquisition . . . providing for the permanent settlement of the individuals of the tribes, at once or in the future, on separate tracts of lands or homesteads, and for the gradual abolition of the tribal character." Most of the treaties, regardless of category, were named for the place (often a fort) where they were negotiated and, flowery language and promise of annuities aside, were aimed at coaxing the Indians onto reservations so that their traditional lands might be taken over for settlement. On the U.S. side treaty negotiations were usually conducted by specially appointed civilian peace commissioners rather than army officers. Between 1778 and 1871, the U.S. government concluded more than 370 treaties with various tribes; 245 of those were signed before 1850. Those 245 treaties appropriated more than 450 million acres of tribal lands at an estimated cost of $90 million in public funds. In return the Indian signatories were moved onto designated reservations and promised annual payments in the form of food and trade goods. Most of those treaties also contained wording to the effect that the new reservations would be guaranteed so long as grass shall grow and waters run. The last major treaties under the old policy were negotiated with the Plains Indians in 1868. Three years later a policy that had stood since 1795 changed dramatically when Congress passed the 1871 Indian Appropriation Act to fund the operations of the Bureau of Indian Affairs plus the various annuities promised to the Indians for another year. One provision of the act also decreed that the tribes would no longer be treated as sovereign nations with treaty-making powers. Henceforward, they would be treated as wards of the government, dictated to rather than negotiated with as before. It was the beginning of a new era.

Most Indian treaties were ad hoc arrangements, negotiated by local commanders, territorial governors, or Indian agents. They lasted only as long as the whites could force the Indians to live up to them and as long as it suited the interests of the whites to honor their end of the bargain. Very few were ever submitted to the U.S. Senate for formal ratification, which would make them no more or any less binding on either side. So, while hundreds of treaties were negotiated over the years, few were ever seen by Congress, fewer still were actually funded by the chronically cash-strapped federal government, and only a handful actually changed anything.

The executive and judicial branches quickly fell in step with the new Peace Policy. The Supreme Court helped define and harmonize the new with the old by ruling that new legislation by Congress superseded all the old treaties, even those guaranteeing arrangements in perpetuity. Executive orders replaced treaties and legislation as the supposedly new, improved way of making Indian policy because they did not involve the grueling process of negotiating treaties. In 1874, the Indian commissioner recommended a new, determined push to "civilize" Indians by granting citizenship, placing all under U.S. law, and breaking up reservations into individual plots of land. This policy was known as Allotment. It is fair to say that U.S. government policy during this time was confused and inconsistent in the extreme.

The Civil War had barely ended when a new round of violent uprisings scorched the West, sparked by a combination of causes, especially white encroachment and smoldering Indian resentment of being confined to reservations. What made the conflict different after 1865 was the large number of veteran soldiers fresh from Civil War battlefields who were dispatched to the Plains to subdue the tribes. For years, one of the major problems in maintaining peaceful relations with the Indians had been the disgraceful, brutal behavior of undisciplined militia troops (many of them volunteers), who got the job when the regulars went off to the Civil War. Repeatedly, the volunteers violated flags of truce, made war on women and children and peaceful Indians, and disregarded treaty provisions by trespassing on Indian lands without permission. When the regulars returned, at least the war was fought with a higher degree of professionalism as well as efficiency. By applying the tactics learned in the Civil War, wide-ranging, well-coordinated military campaigns were launched for the first time against the Plains Indians, and the results were impressive. The southern Plains Indians were already on the defensive even before the regulars took over the fighting. By 1863–64, the majority of the Apache and Navajo (Dineh) had been rounded up and dispatched to reservations. Only the Comanche and Kiowa remained active in Texas and New Mexico in 1865, and in short order the tribes of the Indian Territory (later Oklahoma) were subjugated. The first half of the 1870s saw the last gasp of the wars on the southern plains, beginning with the Kiowa in Texas and ending in the Red River War versus the Comanche, Cheyenne, and Kiowa, in which George Armstrong Custer won his Indian-fighting spurs. Already, by March 1872, the government could report that the Indians of Kansas "are absolutely destitute . . . living on a little corn and dead animals they can find lying around." It was a pitiful state for a once-great people. The northern Plains Indians, however, would prove tougher to whip than their southern cousins.

A sideshow to the main war against the Plains Indians was fought in northern California, 1872–73, against the Modoc, who were refusing to be resettled on a reservation. The Modoc War produced the highest-ranking casualty on the non-Indian side: Brigadier General Edward R. S. Canby, ambushed during peace talks with tribal representatives on April 11, 1873. The swift and merciless response of the army crushed the Modoc, who were shipped off to a reservation in Oklahoma (Indian Territory). The human and monetary cost ($300,000) of the Modoc War doomed Grant's Peace Policy.

Meanwhile, the Apache of the Southwest waged low-level but almost continuous war against settlers on both sides of the Mexican border—mostly in the form of raids by small bands hiding out in the mountains. The majority of the Apache were confined to the miserable San Carlos Reservation in Arizona while a handful defied government authority and terrorized isolated settlers.

The U.S. Army during all these campaigns perceived its mission in clear terms: to establish the Indians on reservations—peacefully or otherwise—and then to keep them there. Ironically the Great Plains had once been promised to the tribes as their permanent homeland. But that was back when conventional wisdom still regarded the Plains as the Great American Desert, unfit for non-Indian settlement. Now as settlers and immigrants poured onto the Plains, those promises proved impossible to keep.

Altogether, hundreds of battles, raids, campaigns, skirmishes, ambushes, and sieges were fought between Native Americans and non-Indians during these years. Most were of minor significance except to those who fought in them and have been largely forgotten in the passage of time. Only a relative handful stand out as major engagements, because of the numbers involved or the stakes at issue. Only the worst in terms of savagery or annihilation were labeled *massacres,* thereby guaranteeing that they would become history. More often than not, neither side gave any quarter once the bullets and arrows started flying.

And the Indians did not have a monopoly on massacring their enemies. Whites could be equally merciless, and not just at Sand Creek. On

TABLE 3.3 KEY TREATIES AND AGREEMENTS BETWEEN THE U.S. GOVERNMENT AND INDIAN TRIBES, 1851–1875

Name/Site of Treaty	Date Signed	Participating Tribe(s)	Indian Representative(s)	U.S. Government Representatives[a]	Ratified by U.S. Senate	Key Provision(s)	Duration
Canyon de Chelly (Arizona Territory) Treaty	1849	Navajo	Zarcillos Largos (i.e., Long Earrings)	Lieutenant Colonel John Washington	Yes[b]	Navajo agreed to stop raids and settle down peaceably	Until 1863, when fighting resumed
(First) Fort Laramie (Wyo.) Treaty (Treaty of Horse Creek)	Sep. 17, 1851[c]	Sioux (Dakota, Lakota, Nakota), Cheyenne, Arapaho, Crow, Arikara, Gros Ventre (Atsina), Mandan, Assiniboine	Various chiefs and "headmen"	Superintendent David Dawson Mitchell and Indian agent Thomas "Broken Hand" Fitzpatrick	Yes (with revisions)	Tribes agreed to end all hostilities, surrender traditional lands, and move to new lands; allow roads through new lands. Government was to pay $50,000 annual annuity for 50 yr. (later reduced to 10 yr.); established tribal boundaries for first time, e.g., Northern and Southern Cheyenne	Until 1865
Second Table Rock (Oreg.) Treaty (cf. 1851)	1853	Yakima, Klickitat, Molala, others	Various chiefs and "headmen"	Oregon Territory governor John P. Gaines	No	Prototype for subsequent Indian cession treaties in Pacific Northwest	
Fort Atkinson (Kans.) Treaty	1853	Kiowa, Comanche, Plains Apache	Various chiefs and "headmen"	Thomas Fitzpatrick	Yes	Indians promised not to raid across border into Mexico and to allow road and fort construction on their lands	Unspecified
Missouri Treaty	Mar. 16, 1854	Otoe, Missouria, Delaware (Lenni Lenape), Peoria, Shawnee, Omaha, Piankashawa, Wea, Miami	Various chiefs and "headmen"	Indian agent James M. Gatewood	Yes	Tribes ceded 43 million acres in Kans. and Nebr. territories, and retained 300,000 acres, received annuities and "necessary services"; recognized president as chief agent of U.S. government in all dealings with Indians	Unspecified
Oregon Country Treaty	Dec. 26, 1854	Nisqualli	Various chiefs and "headmen"	Washington Territory governor Isaac Stevens[d]	Yes	Government guaranteed historic fishing rights	Unspecified
Oregon Country Treaty	Jan. 26, 1855	Dwamish, Suquamish, S'Kallam, others	Various chiefs and "headmen"	Washington Territory governor Isaac Stevens	Yes	Extinguished all Indian claims in western Washington Territory	Unspecified
Treaty of Hell Gate (Washington Territory) (Walla Walla Valley Treaty Council)	Jul. 16, 1855	Columbia Basin tribes (included Nez Perce, Flathead, Kootenay, Akima)	Yakima chief Kamiakin	Washington Territory governor Isaac Stevens	Yes	Established Nez Perce Reservation in east Idaho and extinguished all other Indian claims in eastern Washington Territory	Unspecified
Unnamed	Jul. 31, 1855	Ottawa, Chippewa	Various chiefs and "headmen"	Indian Affairs commissioner George W. Manypenny and Agent Henry Gilbert	Yes	Government granted permanent residence to these tribes in upper Mich., lifting threat of removal across Mississippi River	Unspecified
Laguna Negra Treaty	Jul. 18, 1855	Navajo and other N. Mex. tribes	Manuelito, Zarcillos Largos, others	N. Mex. territorial governor David Meriwether	No	Created "dividing line" between Indian lands and whites' lands; Indians ceded lands in return for cash annuities; honored by neither side	Superseded in 1868 by new treaty
Latah Creek Treaty	Sep. 23, 1858	Spokane, Coeur d'Alene, Palouse	Chief Garry	Colonel George Wright	No	Indians agreed to cede lands and keep the peace	Unspecified
Fort Wise Treaty (Colorado Territory)	1861	Southern Cheyenne and Arapaho	Black Kettle	Colo. territorial governor John Evans	Yes	Extinguished Indian claims to east Colo. in return for reservation south of Arkansas River	Unspecified
Unnamed	1861	Cherokee, Creek, Choctaw, Chickasaw, Seminole ("Five Civilized Tribes")[e]		Albert Pike, representing Confederate States	Yes (Confederate States Senate)	Granted fee-simple ownership of lands in Indian Territory to tribes in perpetuity in return for Indian allegiance to Confederate States of America	Unspecified
Fort Sully Treaty (Dakota Territory)	Oct. 1865	Teton and Yankton Sioux	Various chiefs	Generals Samuel Curtis and Henry H. Sibley; Governor Newton Edmunds of Dakota Territory	Yes	Whites to abandon the emigrant routes through Northern Sioux territory; U.S. government to make regular annuity payments to Indians	Unspecified

Name/Site of Treaty	Date Signed	Participating Tribe(s)	Indian Representative(s)	U.S. Government Representatives[a]	Ratified by U.S. Senate	Key Provision(s)	Duration
Little Arkansas River Treaty (Indian Territory)	Oct. 1865	Cheyenne, Arapaho, Comanche, Kiowa, Kiowa Apache	Satanta, Lone Wolf, Kicking Bird, Dohäsan		Yes by U.S. Senate but not by states of Tex. and Kans.	Tribes sign away lands in return for reservations in Kans., Tex., and Indian Territory	Unspecified
Medicine Lodge Creek Treaty (Kans.)	Oct. 21 and Oct. 28, 1867	Kiowa, Apache, Comanche, Arapaho	Satanta, Black Kettle, Stumblng Bear, Little Raven, Quanah Parker	Nathaniel G. Taylor, William S. Harney, C. C. Auger, Alfred H. Terry, John B. Sanborn, Samuel F. Tappan, John B. Henderson	No	Tribes to move to reservations in Indian Territory and receive $25,000 annuity in return for keeping the peace and allowing RRs to cross lands	Unspecified
(Second) Fort Laramie Treaty	May 1868	Hunkpapa Sioux	Sitting Bull, Gall		No	Set aside Great Sioux Reserve for Hunkpapa	Unspecified
Peace Commission Treaties	Various, spring 1868	Brulé Sioux (Apr. 29), Crow (May 7), Northern Cheyenne, Northern Arapaho (May 10)	Various chiefs and "headmen"	General William T. Sherman and six other commissioners	Yes	Tribes agreed to move onto reservations; usual cash annuities replaced by payment in goods plus promise of cash bonuses to encourage agriculture	30 years
Treaty of Bosque Redondo	Jun. 1, 1868	Navajo	Various chiefs and "headmen"	Peace commissioners William T. Sherman and Samuel F. Tappan	Yes	Terminated hostilities and established permanent boundaries of Navajo reservation	Unspecified
Fort Bridger Treaty	Jul. 3, 1868	Shoshone, Bannock	Chief Washakie (of Eastern Shoshone)	Various peace commissioners	Yes	Tribes to move to 3 million–acre reservation in Wyo. and Idaho	Unspecified
Unnamed	Aug. 3, 1868	Nez Perce	Looking Glass, White Bird, Toohoolhoolzate, Chief Joseph	Representatives of Indian Peace Commission	Yes	Tribe to move to new reservation	Unspecified
(Third) Fort Laramie Treaty	Nov. 6, 1868	Sioux	Red Cloud	General William T. Sherman	Yes	Ended Red Cloud's War, closed Bozeman Trail, guaranteed annuities to Indians	Unspecified

[a] Except the 1861 treaty negotiated with the "Five Civilized Tribes" by the Confederate States government.
[b] This is the first Indian treaty formally ratified by the U.S. Senate, setting a precedent and provoking jealousy of the U.S. House of Representatives.
[c] Never ratified by U.S. Senate but followed nonetheless.
[d] Stevens negotiated more Indian treaties than any other government official during these years.
[e] So designated in a compact signed among themselves in 1843 to make common cause against the "wild tribes" of the Plains.
Source: Candy Moulton, *The Writer's Guide to Everyday Life in the Wild West* (Cincinnati: Writer's Digest Books, 1999), 36–40.

In an unintended caricature of Indian-white relations, a well-armed Indian has hurled his lance into the ground to warn away a grizzled scout leading a wagon train across the Great Plains. Such dramatic confrontations made good copy for eastern readers of *Harper's Weekly Magazine,* which ran this engraving September 19, 1874. (Library of Congress)

January 23, 1870, 173 Piegan (a subtribe of the Blackfeet)—men, women, and children—were massacred in their undefended camp on the Marias River in Montana by U.S. Cavalry troops, and on April 30, 1871, more than 100 Apache under federal military protection at Camp Grant, Arizona, were massacred by a civilian mob. The Indians had plenty of cause to hate and distrust whites aside from broken treaties.

The 28-year war against the Plains Indians that began with the Minnesota Uprising (Dakota Uprising) in 1862 did not confer much glory on the army. Yet it was desirable to recognize soldiers who performed heroically even in an ugly war. The only medal available to U.S. soldiers at the time was the (congressional) Medal of Honor, awarded generously during the Civil War, but much more stingily in the Indian Wars. As a result, the army created its own form of recognition, the "campaign badge." Unfortunately, it has been largely overshadowed in history by the medals and ribbons awarded for service in foreign wars during the years that followed.

By 1875 the Indian Wars, the longest-running military conflict in U.S. history, were by all appearances in the final stages. From 1862 until 1890 the fighting would be practically continuous, albeit low-level and uncoordinated. Yet ultimate victory was within sight in 1875 for the U.S. troops, who were better organized, more numerous, and had technologically superior arms. The decimation of the buffalo herds merely hastened the end. However, the bloodletting was not over yet. At the end of this period, non-Indian prospectors, pushing into the Black Hills of the Dakotas, were on the verge of provoking the last great clash with the Plains Indians.

TABLE 3.4 MAJOR ENGAGEMENTS IN THE PLAINS INDIAN WARS, 1850–1875

Name/Site of Battle	Date	State/Territory	Combatants	Outcome
Fort Pueblo Massacre	Dec. 24, 1854	Colorado Territory	Party of Moache Ute versus civilian inhabitants of trading post (fort)	At least a dozen whites killed, woman and two children carried off; only about six Indians killed
Blue Water Creek	Sep. 3, 1855	Nebraska Territory	Colonel William S. Harney and 600 troops versus Sioux village	150 Indians killed versus four dead and seven wounded soldiers
Solomon Fork	Jul. 29, 1857	Kansas Territory	Colonel Edwin V. Sumner and 300 troops versus equal number of Cheyenne	Nine Cheyenne killed; tribe remained passive until 1863
"Steptoe's Last Stand"	May 18, 1858	Washington Territory (near Rosalia)	Lieutenant Colonel Edward Steptoe and 158 troops versus 800–1,200 Palouse, Spokane, Coeur d'Alene, Yakima under Kamiakin	Five soldiers killed, 15 wounded, the rest driven away; nine Indians killed, 40–50 wounded; "disastrous affair" for army (Winfield Scott)
Battle of Four Lakes	Sep. 15, 1858	Washington Territory (near Spokane)	Colonel George Wright and 600 troops versus Spokane, Coeur d'Alene, and Palouse war party	18–20 Indians killed, numerous wounded, one chief taken hostage; complete Indian defeat
Poncha Pass	Apr. 28, 1855	Colo.	Colonel Thomas T. Fauntleroy and 500 troops versus 150 Ute	40 Indians killed, the rest dispersed; ended Ute power in eastern Colo.
Canadian River	May 11, 1858	Indian Territory (Okla.)	John S. "Rip" Ford and 200 Texas Rangers and allied Indians versus Cheyenne village	76 Cheyenne warriors killed, 300 routed
Rush Springs	Oct. 1, 1858	Indian Territory (Okla.)	Captain Earl Van Dorn and four companies of 2nd Cavalry and "Texas tribal auxiliaries" versus Comanche encampment under Buffalo Hump	83 Comanche killed or wounded, 120 lodges destroyed; five U.S. fatalities (included Van Dorn, wounded)
Crooked Creek	May 13, 1859	Kans.	Brevet Major Van Dorn and troop of U.S. dragoons versus 90–100 Cheyenne	49 Indians killed, five wounded, 37 captured; two soldiers wounded
Apache Pass	Jul. 15–16, 1862	Arizona Territory	James Carleton and 1,800 men of "California Column" versus Apache war party under Mangas Coloradas and Cochise	Indians driven off and Mangas Coloradas wounded
Fort Ridgley[a]	Aug. 21–22, 1862	Minn.	400 Sioux under Little Crow in attack on 180-man garrison; 800 Sioux in another attack the next day	More than 100 Sioux killed and wounded; the rest driven off
Wood Lake[a]	Sep. 23, 1862	Minn.	Colonel Henry H. Sibley and 1,500 state militia versus 700 Sioux under Little Crow	Seven soldiers killed and 30 wounded; 30 Indians killed and 30 wounded; Indians routed, ending Sioux War
Birch Coulee[a]	Sep. 2–3, 1862	Minn. (near Fort Snelling)	Captain John L. Marsh and 135 soldiers versus Sioux war party under Little Crow	23 soldiers killed or wounded before Indians driven off by relief force from Fort Snelling
Sacred Heart Creek[a]	Aug. 18, 1862	Minnesota	Dakota Sioux war party ambush of 28 farmers	27 whites killed
Bear River	Jan. 1863	Utah	Patrick E. Connor and Calif. militia versus Shoshone village under Bear Hunter	Village destroyed; Bear Hunter and 200 followers killed
Canyon de Chelly	Jan. 1864	Arizona Territory	Colonel Kit Carson and 1st N. Mex. Volunteer Cavalry versus 60 Navajo in their redoubt	Navajo home base destroyed and inhabitants surrendered
Sand Creek Massacre[b]	Nov. 29, 1864	Colorado Territory	Colonel John Chivington and 3rd Colo. Volunteers versus peaceful Cheyenne encampment	200^{+} Indians killed (most women and children); military and congressional investigations
Adobe Walls	Nov. 26, 1864	Tex. Panhandle	Colonel Kit Carson and 321 soldiers and 75 Indian auxiliaries versus Kiowa Apache village of 3,000–7,000	Three soldiers killed, 25 wounded; 100–150 Indians killed, 176 lodges destroyed
Killdeer Mountain	Jul. 28, 1864	Dakota Territory (North)	General Alfred Sully and 3,000 troops in attack on camp of 1,600 (?) Sioux	Five soldiers killed, 10 wounded; 31 (?) Indians killed; Sioux forced to flee, leaving all stores behind
Dove Creek	Jan. 8, 1865	Southwest Tex. frontier (near Concho River)	325 Tex. militia and Confederate Regulars under Captain S. S. Totton versus 700 Kickapoo under Chiefs Papequah, Pecan, and Nokowhat	22 whites killed and 24 wounded; 11 Indians killed and seven wounded; soldiers' unwarranted attack caused decade of warfare between Kickapoo and Texans
Fetterman Fight	Dec. 21, 1866	Wyo. (near Fort Phil Kearny)	Lieutenant Colonel William J. Fetterman and 80 soldiers ambushed by band of Sioux, Cheyenne, Arapaho	Soldiers all killed; official army investigation relieved fort commander
Fort Phil Kearny	Aug. 1867	Wyo.	Captain James W. Powell and 32-man garrison versus 3,000 attacking Sioux, Cheyenne, and Arapaho	Three Indian attacks beaten off and 1,137 Indians killed
Hayfield Fight	Aug. 1867	Mont. (near Fort C. F. Smith)	Party of civilian hay cutters versus Sioux, Cheyenne, and Arapaho war party	Indians driven off but Bozeman Trail virtually closed to regular traffic

(continued)

TABLE 3.4 (continued)

Name/Site of Battle	Date	State/Territory	Combatants	Outcome
Wagon-Box Fight	Aug. 2, 1867	Wyo. (near Fort Phil Kearny)	Party of civilian wood cutters versus Sioux, Cheyenne, and Arapaho war party under Red Cloud	See Hayfield Fight
Battle of the Washita	Nov. 27, 1868	Indian Territory (Okla.)	Lieutenant Colonel George Custer and 7th Cavalry Regiment versus peaceful village of Cheyenne and Arapaho under Black Kettle	19 soldiers killed; village destroyed, Indians scattered, Black Kettle killed
Beecher's Island	Sep. 17–25, 1868	Colo. (Republican River)	Major George A. Forsyth and 50 militia troops versus 600 Sioux and Cheyenne warriors	22 soldiers killed or wounded; many Indians killed, included Chief Roman Nose, before relief force arrived
Soldier Spring	Dec. 25, 1868	Indian Territory (Okla.)	Major Andrew Evans and 300 soldiers of 3rd U.S. Cavalry in attack on Comanche and Kiowa village of 200^{+} warriors	60 lodges destroyed and Indians driven off without provisions
Summit Springs	Jul. 11, 1869	Colorado Territory (near Republican River)	General Eugene A. Carr and troop of U.S. Cavalry versus Cheyenne "Dog Soldiers" under Tall Bull	Forced Southern Cheyenne onto reservation
Camp Grant (Reservation) Massacre	Apr. 30, 1871	Arizona Territory	Band of Tucson citizen militia in attack on peaceful camp of Pinal and Aravaipa Apache	83 Indians killed, most women and children; 29 children seized and held in bondage
Warren Wagon Train Massacre	May 18, 1871	Salt Creek, Tex.	War party of 150 Kiowa and Comanche led by Satanta and others in attack on wagons hauling grain from Weatherford to Fort Griffin	Wagon master Nathan Long and six other whites killed vs. unknown number of Indians
Skull Cave	Dec. 28, 1872	Arizona Territory (Salt River Canyon)	General George Crook and elements of 5th U.S. Cavalry versus 100 Yavapai Apache	76 Indians killed; no soldier casualties
Turret Park	Mar. 27, 1873	Arizona Territory	Captain George M. Randall and 23rd U.S. Infantry in attack on Apache encampment	23 Indians killed; no soldier casualties; forced Apache back to reservation for next four years
Lost River	Nov. 29, 1872	Calif.	Captain David Jackson and 38 soldiers versus 160 Modoc under Captain Jack	Soldiers prevented from arresting Captain Jack; several soldiers killed; start of Modoc War (1872–73)
Lava Beds	Apr. 11, 1873	Calif.	Peace commissioners versus Modoc	Two commissioners killed, including General E. R. S. Canby, one badly wounded, one escaped; four Modoc hanged, tribe scattered
Adobe Walls (Second Battle of)	Jun. 27–29, 1874	Tex. Panhandle	28 Buffalo hunters versus 700 Southern Cheyenne, Arapaho, Comanche, and Kiowa warriors under Quanah Parker and Isa-Tai	Three hunters killed; 13 Indians killed; dozens wounded; the rest driven off; led to Red River War of 1874–75
Palo Duro Canyon	Sep. 28, 1874	Tex. Panhandle	Colonel Ranald Mackenzie and 4th U.S. Cavalry versus Cheyenne, Kiowa, and Comanche war party under Iron Shirt, Poor Buffalo, and Lone Wolf	One soldier killed; three Indians killed; 1,400 Indian horses captured, most destroyed; last stand-up fight by Southern Plains Indians

[a] Part of the larger action known as the Sioux Uprising or Minnesota Massacre in the summer and fall of 1862. During the course of four weeks, 357 settlers, 90 soldiers, and about 30 Indians had been killed. After peace was restored, 392 Indians were taken into custody for various crimes and tried before a military tribunal.
[b] Known locally as Big Sandy Creek, it has been recorded in history as "Sand Creek," and therefore the event is popularly if inaccurately referred to as the "Sand Creek Massacre."
Sources: Harvey Markowitz, ed., *Ready Reference: American Indians,* vol. 1 (Englewood Cliffs, N.J.: Salem Press, 1995); Charles R. Shrader, ed., *Reference Guide to United States Military History, 1815–1865* (New York: Facts On File, 1993); Alan Axelrod, *Chronicle of the Indian Wars* (New York: Prentice-Hall, 1993); Frederick J. Dockstader, *Great North American Indians* (New York: Van Nostrand Reinhold, 1977), passim.

A New Field of Study

At the same time popular sentiment favored exterminating or relocating all the Indians, there were insistent voices calling out to preserve and protect Native American culture. It was during these years that some of the earliest ethnographic studies were done. Almost to a person, the ethnologists who studied and wrote about the Indians were amateurs, and ethnographic studies were a side line to their regular jobs: soldiering, exploring, administering Indian policy, doing mission work, or making surveys. Their work was underwritten by scientific groups such as the Smithsonian Institution, the American Philosophical Society, and the Anthropological Institute of New York. At a time when Indian culture was being ground down and Indian population decimated, ethnologists felt an urgency to work fast before the subjects of their works were no more. Much of what is known today about 19th-century Native American life was collected by those self-taught ethnologists.

Native Americans of the 19th century are thought of today by most people as either obstacles in the way of westward progress or victims of non-Indians. Truth be told, they were never simply one or the other. At the beginning of this era they were still formidable enemies of settlers and the government, in retreat but managing to hold their own in some remote corners of the United States. They were numerous and dangerous enough to be major objects of U.S. policy makers in Washington. At one time or another, Congress, the president, the army, and the bureaucracy all devoted enormous amounts of time and energy, not to mention money, to the problem of what to do with the Native Americans. By the end of this era they had been reduced to such a state of feebleness that Custer's defeat by Teton Lakota and Cheyenne at the Little Bighorn in 1876 was almost beyond the comprehension of most Americans. And Custer's Last Stand was an aberration. Already by 1875 most Indians were on the way to becoming wards of the state or Wild West Show characters. They were on the losing end of a historic clash of cultures.

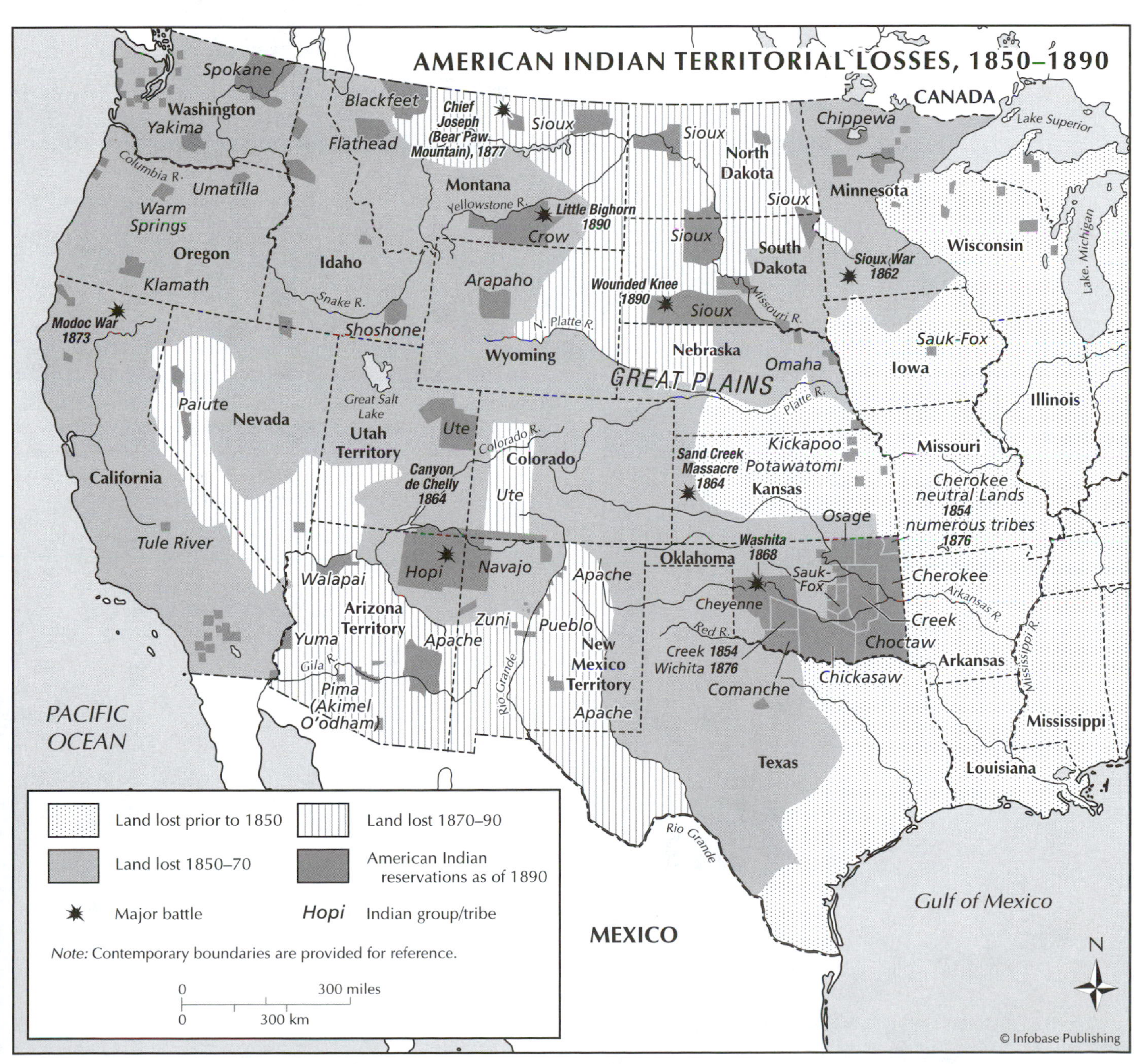

These Mojave were drawn by an official artist on the U.S. Pacific Railroad survey of the 35th parallel in 1853–54. At this time, the Mojave were a small tribe, living along the Colorado River astraddle one of the major immigrant trails to Georgia. This lithograph appeared in the Pacific Railroad Survey Reports (1856). (Tennessee State Library and Archives)

A Choctaw Indian wears a traditional sash over "a ball player's costume," ca. 1870. (Courtesy of Mississippi Department of Archives and History)

CHAPTER 4 Chronology, 1850 to 1875

January 1, 1850 The D'Avignon Press publishes the first edition of Mathew Brady's *The Gallery of Illustrious Americans,* a lifetime project "containing portraits of twelve of the most eminent citizens of the American Republic since the days of Washington." It weighs five pounds, sells for $30, and proves to be a financial failure though a landmark in the history of photography.

January 20, 1850 The opening salvo in the Compromise of 1850 is fired when Henry Clay of Kentucky introduces a complex omnibus bill in the Senate to deal with what he calls the nation's "5 Bleeding Wounds" (i.e., sectional issues).

March 4, 1850 Senator John C. Calhoun of South Carolina predicts the nation is headed for disunion in his last speech to Congress. (Because Calhoun is too sick to deliver it himself, it is read by Senator James Mason of Virginia.)

March 7, 1850 Daniel Webster delivers what many consider one of the greatest orations ever presented on the floor of the U.S. Senate in defense of the Compromise of 1850 and of the Union itself, pleading for compromise, "not as a Massachusetts man, not as a Northern man, but as an American."

March 30, 1850 The Webster-Parkman murder case closes in Boston with a jury conviction of Professor John W. Webster, becoming an instant classic of American jurisprudence.

March 31, 1850 Senator John C. Calhoun, one of the famed triumvirate of giants who dominated Congress and shaped national policy for half a century, dies.

March 1850 The Massachusetts Supreme Court rejects racial integration of public schools, using the "separate but equal" doctrine for the first time in U.S. judicial history.

April 8, 1850 The U.S. Supreme Court hands down its decision in the first school desegregation case: *Sarah C. Roberts v. the City of Boston.* The Court finds against the five-year-old African-American plaintiff in a unanimous decision written by Justice Lemuel Shaw; five years later the state legislature bans segregation of public schools in Massachusetts.

April 19, 1850 The Clayton-Bulwer Treaty is signed by the United States and Great Britain pledging the two nations to cooperate in the construction, operation, and defense of any canal built across the isthmus of Central America.

May 6, 1850 The Bloody Island Massacre (sometimes called the Clear Lake Massacre) occurs in California, when about 60 Pomo Indians are killed by army troops and civilian volunteers in retaliation for the murders of Charles Stone and Andrew Kelsey (who had been abusing the Pomo) in December 1849.

July 1, 1850 The first regular overland mail service to the West is launched, connecting Kansas City, Missouri, and Salt Lake City, Utah; it is a monthly service. On the same date, mail service from Independence, Missouri, to Santa Fe, New Mexico, begins.

July 9, 1850 President Zachary Taylor, U.S.-Mexican War hero, dies in office after delivering a July 4 speech in the broiling sun and then having cold refreshments, leading to the stubborn myth that he died of eating cherries and milk. The truth is that he died of either acute gastroenteritis or cholera morbus.

July 10, 1850 Zachary Taylor's cabinet resigns en masse rather than support the "accidental president" Millard Fillmore, causing a small-scale political crisis in the federal government.

July 15, 1850 The first recorded casualty in the 19th-century U.S. labor wars: A worker is killed in a clash between striking New York City tailors and management.

July 31, 1850 The U.S. Senate passes a bill creating the Territory of Utah, incorporating the former Mormon state of Deseret and appointing Brigham Young the first governor.

August–September 1850 Congress passes the five bills that together compose the Compromise of 1850, providing something for both sides in the growing sectional controversy.

September 9, 1850 California is admitted to the Union as a free state under the provisions of the Compromise of 1850. It is the 31st state.

September 18, 1850 President Millard Fillmore signs into law the Second Fugitive Slave Act, making the pursuit and return of runaway slaves a federal matter, with penalties for those who break the law or help others break the law. The new law is part of the Compromise of 1850.

September 20, 1850 The first federal land grant for railroad construction is awarded by Congress to build a line between Chicago, Illinois, and Mobile, Alabama, beginning a practice that will see millions of acres handed out to railroad companies in the years that follow.

September 28, 1850 By act of Congress (part of the Naval Appropriations Bill), flogging is abolished in the U.S. Navy and merchant marine.

October 1850 The first national woman's rights convention meets in Worcester, Massachusetts, the result of a call issued by Elizabeth Cady Stanton and Lucretia Mott. It is presided over by Paulina Wright Davis. Although this is the first truly national convention of women, it has been overshadowed in history by the more locally oriented Seneca Falls, New York, convention two years earlier.

October 1850 The first medical school for women in the world, the Female Medical College of Pennsylvania, admits its inaugural class. Located in Philadelphia and opened with the help of sympathetic Quakers, the college is originally allied with the eclectic philosophy of medicine. Later the name is changed to the Woman's Medical College of Pennsylvania.

January 1, 1851 The slave trade in the District of Columbia is ended by the terms of the Compromise of 1850.

May 15, 1851 The first rail connection between New York City and the Great Lakes is inaugurated when a train carrying President Millard Fillmore and Secretary of State Daniel Webster arrives at Dunkirk, New York, on Lake Erie.

May 1851 A group of 1,700 Sac and Fox Indians are vaccinated for smallpox, becoming the first non-whites to be inoculated en masse.

June 2, 1851 The governor of Maine signs the first statewide prohibition legislation into law. This so-called Maine Law provides the model used by 13 other states in the next decade to pass legislation aimed at the trade in "intoxicating liquors."

June 3, 1851 The New York Knickerbockers play a baseball game with every player outfitted in identical straw hats and baggy blue pants, becoming the first professional baseball team to wear uniforms.

June 5, 1851 The first installment of *Uncle Tom's Cabin* by Harriet Beecher Stowe appears in serialization form in the antislavery newspaper *National Era.*

June 1851 Isaac Merrit Singer and Edward Clark form a partnership to begin mass production of Singer's invention, the sewing machine. By 1860 their company is the largest producer of such machines in the world, allowing the inventor to retire in comfort in 1863.

August 16, 1851 Fifty American "volunteers" (filibusterers) are executed by authorities in Cuba after a failed attempt to overthrow the Spanish colonial government there.

August 22, 1851 The U.S.-built yacht *America* beats the British-built *Aurora* in the first of the annual challenge races for the "cup of all nations" offered by the Royal Yacht Society of England; the prize is renamed the America's Cup in later years.

Isaac Singer may have made his name synonymous with sewing machines, but numerous other companies sprang up in the years following to cash in on the popularity of the new technology. The United States Sewing Machine Co. produced this "family" model, priced at only $12, beginning in 1869. Sewing machine makers were also pioneers in consumer advertising. (Library of Congress, Prints and Photographs Division [LC-US262-40750]).

September 11, 1851 The so-called Christiana Riot occurs at this small community near Philadelphia when a band of slave hunters try to seize four runaways from their local protectors. In the resulting gun battle the head of the slave hunters is killed and four of his colleagues are wounded. President Millard Fillmore orders U.S. Marines to the scene, where they arrest 36 African Americans and two whites. The incident hardens feelings on both sides about the new Fugitive Slave Law.

September 14, 1851 The noted author James Fenimore Cooper dies at his home in Cooperstown, New York.

September 18, 1851 The *New York Times* begins publishing with issue no. 1 and has been publishing continuously ever since. The paper costs one cent on the street.

December 24, 1851 A disastrous fire in the Library of Congress destroys some 35,000 volumes, including two-thirds of the works donated by Thomas Jefferson from his personal collection to begin the library.

December 29, 1851 The first U.S. branch of the Young Men's Christian Association (YMCA) opens in Boston, based on the founding British model (1844). The first Young Women's Christian Association (YWCA), in New York City, does not open until 1858.

February 16, 1852 The Studebaker brothers, Henry and Clement, open a blacksmith and wagon business in South Bend, Indiana, that in a few years will supply farm wagons, carriages, and prairie schooners throughout the West. (Eventually they will shift to manufacturing automobiles.)

February 20, 1852 The first rail connection between Chicago, Illinois, and the East Coast is established when a train owned by the Michigan Southern Railway arrives in the "Windy City."

March 20, 1852 *Uncle Tom's Cabin* by Harriet Beecher Stowe is available in book form for the first time in Boston, Massachusetts.

March 1852 The freighting and banking firm of Wells Fargo & Company is founded as a joint stock association in New York by Henry Wells, William G. Fargo, and others. It begins business in California four months later.

Summer 1852 The first trainload of cattle in U.S. history is sent to market via rail, at least in part. They are first driven on the hoof from Lexington, Kentucky, to Cincinnati, Ohio; then entrained to Cleveland on Lake Erie; then by boat to Buffalo, New York; by rail again to Albany; and finally the final leg by boat once again, down the Hudson River to New York City.

June 29, 1852 The longtime statesman and Whig leader Henry Clay dies in the city where he spent most of his career, Washington, D.C. He will be remembered as "the Great Compromiser."

August 24, 1852 The first dramatization of *Uncle Tom's Cabin* is staged in New York City.

August 29, 1852 Brigham Young announces his revelation on "celestial marriage," thus sanctioning the Mormon practice of polygamy.

October 24, 1852 Daniel Webster dies at home in Marshfield, Massachusetts, after a 42-year career in national government; he is considered by many to be America's greatest statesman of any era.

November 2, 1852 The Democrat Franklin Pierce defeats two other candidates for the presidency, becoming the 14th president of the United States.

November 24, 1852 Commodore Matthew C. Perry leaves the United States with four ships on a mission to establish diplomatic and trade relations with the closed kingdom of Japan.

February 21, 1853 The Coinage Act of 1853 reduces the amount of silver in most U.S. coins and launches the three-dollar gold piece.

March 2, 1853 Congress creates the Territory of Washington by dividing the old Oregon Territory.

March 4, 1853 Congress appropriates $150,000 to survey potential western routes for the country's first transcontinental railroad, a dream since the early 1840s.

March 5, 1853 After anglicizing his name to Henry Steinway, the German immigrant Heinrich Steinweg and his five sons open a factory at 85 Varick Street in Manhattan, where they make and sell pianos, the beginning of the world-famous Steinway Piano Company.

July 6, 1853 The National Council of Colored People is founded in Rochester, New York, after a three-day convention organized by Frederick Douglass and attended by more than 100 delegates from around the United States. They call for repeal of the Fugitive Slave Law plus civil and political rights for blacks.

July 8, 1853 An armed squadron of the U.S. Navy under Commodore Matthew Perry anchors in Tokyo harbor in Japan, making the United States the first Western nation to "open the door" to trade with the intensely insular country.

July 14, 1853 The nation's first world-class fair opens in New York City.

July 18, 1853 The first international train service in the Western Hemisphere begins service between Portland, Maine, and Montreal, Canada; the 292-mile trip takes about 12 hours.

August 1853 The worst yellow fever outbreak in U.S. history, raging in New Orleans, peaks with nearly 5,000 deaths in this month alone, producing a public health crisis in the South's largest and most important city.

December 30, 1853 The Gadsden Treaty (named for the railroad magnate James Gadsden) is signed between the United States and Mexico, transferring some 45,535 square miles of territory on the Gila River border to the United States in return for $15 million in cash. Both the purchase price and the area are reduced by the U.S. Senate before the final treaty is ratified.

March 31, 1854 The Treaty of Kanagawa allows the United States to establish a consulate in Japan, assures good treatment of castaways, and permits U.S. vessels to visit certain Japanese ports for supplies and repairs.

April 3, 1854 By act of Congress, private coinage of gold is no longer legal now that a branch mint has been established for that purpose in San Francisco, California.

May 9, 1854 A group of 30 congressmen meeting at Ripon, Wisconsin, open discussions on forming a new party to challenge the Democrats and rapidly dying Whigs.

May 30, 1854 The Kansas-Nebraska Act, signed into law by President Franklin Pierce, creates two separate territories of Kansas and Nebraska with the question of slavery in each to be decided by the residents themselves (popular sovereignty), thus in effect repealing a key portion of the Missouri Compromise of 1820. The slave debate is reopened with a vengeance.

May 1854 President Pierce vetoes a bill that would grant 10 million acres of public land to the states to be used exclusively "for the relief and support of the indigent insane in the United States." The bill, a longtime goal of Dorothea Dix, enjoys bipartisan support in both houses of Congress.

July 3, 1854 The first herd of Texas longhorns reaches New York City in an unsatisfactory experiment to transport beef on the hoof from the western plains to eastern markets. Successful cattle drives up to Kansas railheads start after the Civil War.

July 6, 1854 The Republican Party is formally organized at Jackson, Missouri, to oppose the extension of slavery into the territories. (A legend grows up that the first organizational meeting was at Ripon, Wisconsin; however, that is not true.)

July 31, 1854 Sam Wilson of Troy, New York, dies at the age of 88. He is the inspiration for the famous "Uncle Sam" figure representing the United States in countless political cartoons, a fact officially recognized by the 87th Congress in 1961.

August 19, 1854 The first clash between the Brulé Lakota Sioux (under Conquering Bear) and the U.S. Army (under Lieutenant John Grattan) occurs near Fort Laramie, Wyoming, over a cow. The soldiers are wiped out and what becomes known as the Grattan Massacre is the opening round in 36 years of warfare between the Lakota and U.S. government.

October 16, 1854 A young, relatively unknown Abraham Lincoln gives a speech in Peoria, Illinois, taking a new, antislavery stand for the first time, although couched in sympathetic terms calculated not to offend slave-owners unduly.

February 1, 1855 Six midwestern railroads hire the self-described detective Allan Pinkerton to provide security for their property, giving birth to the North West Police Agency—soon to become world renowned as the Pinkerton Detective Agency.

March 3, 1855 Congress appropriates $30,000 at the urging of Secretary of War Jefferson Davis to launch an experimental program that will import Egyptian camels into the Southwest for army transport purposes. The idea ultimately dies for lack of interest.

March 30, 1855 Elections in Kansas to select the first territorial legislation produce bloody conflict between pro- and antislavery factions and ultimately, two rival governments in the state.

April 11, 1855 The Delafield Commission (Majors Richard Delafield, Alfred Mordecai, and George B. McClellan) depart for Europe to observe the Crimean War in order to report on the state of military art in Europe. This is the first U.S. military observation of a foreign war in progress, and their reports are subsequently published in the *Congressional Record.*

April 28, 1855 The Massachusetts legislature prohibits segregation in the state's schools.

May 4, 1855 New York Women's Hospital opens as the world's first institution devoted solely to "the treatment of diseases peculiar to women," with a 40-bed capacity.

September 2, 1855 In retaliation for the so-called Grattan Massacre (1854), U.S. troops under Brigade General William S. Harney attack a band of Brulé Lakota Sioux at Blue Water Creek, Nebraska, wiping out between 85 and 135 men, women, and children.

October 16–19, 1855 The National Black Convention, devoted to the cause of abolition, meets in Philadelphia with more than 100 delegates from six states in attendance.

November 3, 1855 An anti-Chinese mob in Tacoma, Washington Territory, drives all the Chinese out of the town.

December 15, 1855 *Frank Leslie's Illustrated Newspaper,* soon to be the leading periodical of its day, begins publication in New York City.

December 1855 The third and final Seminole War begins in Florida when the U.S. Army resumes its campaign to resettle the tribe's holdouts in the Indian Territory (Oklahoma).

April 18, 1856 Congress enacts the first U.S. copyright law, giving authors of original works exclusive rights to print, publish, act, perform, or otherwise present their works.

April 21, 1856 The first railroad bridge spanning the Mississippi River, connecting Rock Island, Illinois, with Davenport, Iowa, is completed.

May 21, 1856 The "free-soil" community of Lawrence, Kansas, is destroyed in a bloodless raid of 800 proslavers led by Sheriff S. J. Jones. This "Sack of Lawrence" launches the ordeal of "Bleeding Kansas" in the run-up to the Civil War.

May 22, 1856 The South Carolina congressman Preston Brooks canes the Massachusetts senator Charles Sumner into insensibility in the Senate chamber of the U.S. Capitol, launching a frightening new phase in the growing sectional crisis.

May 24–25, 1856 The abolitionist John Brown and seven followers butcher five proslavery settlers along Pottawatomie Creek, Kansas, in retaliation for the murders of several abolitionists and the "Sack of Lawrence" three days earlier.

August 18, 1856 Congress passes the Guano Island Act allowing U.S. citizens to claim uninhabited atolls with the fertilizer deposits; over the next 30 years the U.S. flag is planted on some 70 islands in the Pacific and Caribbean using this law as justification.

November 4, 1856 The Democrat James Buchanan of Pennsylvania is elected 15th president of the United States.

November 16, 1856 Laura Keene, a noted British actress, opens her own theater in New York City, breaking new ground for women in the U.S. theater: She is the first woman to manage a large metropolitan venue.

January 1, 1857 The Ashmun Institute in Ohio begins classes (with just one professor and two students) as the first U.S. institution of higher learning exclusively for African Americans.

March 6, 1857 The *Dred Scott* decision is handed down by the Supreme Court. There are nine separate opinions given by the justices. It declares the Missouri Compromise of 1820 unconstitutional because "slavery follows the flag," and "Negroes are so inferior that they [have] no rights which a white man [is] bound to respect." This is only the second time the Supreme Court has declared an act of Congress unconstitutional; it is the second part of the decision that drives a fatal wedge between the North and South.

March 1857 Congressional action creates the first overland mail service to the Far West with delivery on a semiweekly schedule, to be subsidized at $600,000 a year and with oversight by the postmaster general.

April 21, 1857 The Genesee suspension bridge, completed just the year before, collapses from the heavy weight of accumulated snow on it, the result of New York's worst winter in living memory. No lives are lost.

May 10, 1857 A mass breakout by about 60 prisoners at New York's Sing Sing Prison is narrowly prevented after guards are overpowered; the escape is averted only after reinforcements arrive.

May 12, 1857 The New York Infirmary for Indigent Women and Children opens on Bleeker Street in New York City to address the specific needs of women and children; it includes the first nursing school in the United States.

May 20, 1857 President Buchanan declares Utah to be in open rebellion because the Mormons are harassing migrant wagon trains on the way to California.

August 4, 1857 The first national convention of the American Association for the Advancement of Education is held in Albany, New York, signaling a new concern for the state of the nation's schools; it becomes an annual event.

August 24, 1857 A major financial panic is sparked by the failure of the Ohio Life Insurance and Trust Company, causing a two-year depression and inspiring the so-called Businessmen's Revival to begin at the North Dutch Church on Fulton Street in New York City.

August 26, 1857 The National Teachers Association is organized in Philadelphia; it becomes the present-day National Education Association in 1870.

August–December 1857 The so-called Cart War in Texas occurs when a series of armed raids against Tejano cartmen by their Anglo neighbors ends a profitable ethnic business enterprise and guarantees Anglo economic ascendancy in the state.

September 16, 1857 The Butterfield Overland Mail Company receives a government contract to provide regular service from St. Louis and Memphis to Los Angeles and San Francisco for an annual subsidy of $600,000.

October 3, 1857 The first mention of the "Molly Maguires," a secret Irish society in the coalfields of Pennsylvania, appears in *Miners' Journal*.

November 7, 1857 The proslavery Lecompton Constitution is adopted by delegates to a constitutional convention in Kansas Territory, stirring up a storm of controversy.

February 6, 1858 A full-scale brawl breaks out on the floor of the U.S. House of Representatives after the Democrat Lawrence Keitt insults the Republican Galusha Grow. The personal confrontation quickly explodes into a proslavery versus antislavery free-for-all that only ends when the participants are too tired to continue.

March 4, 1858 Senator James Hammond of South Carolina gives his "King Cotton" speech, bragging, "No power on earth dares to make war on cotton. Cotton is king!"

May 11, 1858 Minnesota enters the Union as the 32nd state, and as a free state in the slave versus free state controversy.

June 17, 1858 Abraham Lincoln delivers his "House Divided" speech to a state Republican convention in Springfield, Illinois, leading them to make him the party's candidate in the U.S. Senate race against Stephen Douglas later that year. He did not invent the phrase, but he made it immortal.

August 16, 1858 Queen Victoria of England sends the first transatlantic telegraph message via the new transatlantic cable (completed August 4) to President James Buchanan.

August 21, 1858 The first of seven Lincoln–Douglas debates on slavery and other issues takes place in Ottawa, Illinois, part of their campaign for one of the state's U.S. Senate seats. The debates are attended by thousands and catapult Abraham Lincoln to national prominence, though they have little impact on who is appointed to fill the Senate seat by the Illinois legislature.

August 23, 1858 William W. Pratt's stage adaptation of the famous temperance novel *Ten Nights in a Bar-Room* opens at New York City's National Theater. It is an immediate sensation and a huge hit.

August 27, 1858 The first news dispatch via international telegraph is received from England and subsequently published in the *New York Sun*. It concerns a peace agreement signed by China, England, and France.

September 1, 1858 The transatlantic telegraph cable between the United States and Great Britain breaks down after a mere two weeks of operation; it will not be restored until after the Civil War.

September 15, 1858 Semiweekly passenger and mail service begins between Tipton, Missouri, and San Francisco, California, via stagecoach, operated by the Butterfield Overland Mail. The one-way trip takes 25 days and costs $200.

September 15, 1858 The American Express Company, owned by John Butterfield, begins delivery of mail to the West under a U.S. government contract. Butterfield's stages will carry more mail than those of any other private firm contracted by government during this era.

October 5, 1858 New York City's magnificent Crystal Palace, modeled on the popular London exhibition hall, is torched by an unknown arsonist, destroying the building and $2 million worth of art inside.

October 25, 1858 U.S. senator William H. Seward first uses the expression "irrepressible conflict," describing the slavery issue, in a political speech at Rochester, New York; the expression subsequently becomes one explanation for the Civil War.

October 1858 R. H. Macy Company opens its first department store in New York City.

January 4, 1859 The U.S. Senate formally abandons its old chamber in the Capitol building, moving into a new hall in the same building.

February 14, 1859 Oregon enters the Union as the 33rd state, on the free-state side of sectional debate.

February 23–24, 1859 The first national convention of Sunday school teachers is held in Philadelphia.

February 27, 1859 On a Washington, D.C., street, U.S. congressman Dan Sickles shoots U.S. attorney Philip Barton Key, who is having an affair with Sickles's wife. The code of the day portrays Sickles as the "victim," and he receives the support of even the president of the United States. The resulting "trial of the century" breaks new legal ground by introducing the "temporary insanity" defense.

April 4, 1859 Dan Emmett's "Dixie" is first performed publicly by Bryant's Minstrels in Mechanic's Hall, New York City. The composer's name is not attached to the song at this time because he does not consider it "serious" music, but by the time of the Civil War it will be the South's unofficial anthem, as well as Abraham Lincoln's favorite song.

June 10, 1859 What will soon be known as the Comstock Lode (from "mother lode") is discovered in Six Mile Canyon in Nevada's Washoe Mountains by Patrick McLaughlin and Peter O'Riley. Henry Comstock, another partner, realizes little from the fabulous silver and gold bonanza except having his name associated with it.

June 1859 Gold is discovered at Plymouth, Vermont, and before the end of the month, 300 miners have rushed into the area, but the strike is completely overshadowed by the much bigger strike in Nevada.

July 9, 1859 U.S. troops are ordered onto San Juan Island, off the coast of Washington Territory, by General William S. Harney, in open defiance of the British government, who also claim the island. Open conflict threatens.

July 1859 The last slave ship in the outlawed slave trade docks at Mobile Bay, Alabama; the subsequent arrest and prosecution of the crew of the *Clothilde* finally end the illegal commerce in human beings in the United States.

August 1, 1859 An announcement in the newspapers proclaims the opening of the nation's first "Rogue's Gallery" of wanted criminals in the New York City Police headquarters building, displaying 450 daguerreotypes of various felons.

August 27, 1859 The world's first commercial oil well is brought in by Edward L. Drake in Titusville, Pennsylvania, and begins producing 25 barrels a day.

September 17, 1859 Henry McCarty is born in New York City and grows up anonymously until launching his murderous career in the New Mexico Territory as Billy the Kid. After his death at age 22, later, he becomes the most celebrated of all 19th-century outlaws, reputed to have killed 21 men (but more likely nine or fewer).

October 16–17, 1859 John Brown leads a force of 13 whites (including his three sons) and five blacks in a raid on Harper's Ferry, Virginia, killing the town's mayor and taking leading townspeople hostage. The next day Colonel Robert E. Lee arrives at the head of a company of U.S. Marines and captures Brown. He is tried for treason and hanged 40 days later. The "raid" electrifies the nation.

December 2, 1859 John Brown is executed by hanging at Charlestown, Virginia, creating an instant martyr for the abolitionist cause. Ralph Waldo Emerson declares him a new saint, who will "make the gallows glorious like the cross."

March 6, 1860 The revolutionary seven-shot, lever-action Spencer rifle is patented by Christopher M. Spencer of Boston, Massachusetts. It helps rewrite the infantry tactics manual after being adopted by some Union troops during the Civil War.

March 29, 1860 The Japanese Grand Embassy arrives in San Francisco, California, aboard the USS *Powhatan,* marking the beginning of diplomatic exchanges by the two nations.

April 3, 1860 The first Pony Express rider departs Saint Joseph, Missouri, for Sacramento, California, at 7:15 P.M., carrying 49 pieces of mail, including newspapers, telegrams, and special dispatches for West Coast residents. (The Pony Express halts operations in mid-October 1861.)

April 23, 1860 The Democratic National Convention assembles in Charleston, South Carolina, but adjourns nine days later, unable to settle on a candidate for the upcoming presidential race.

April 30, 1860 Delegations from Alabama, Georgia, Florida, Louisiana, and Arkansas withdraw from the Democratic convention.

May 1860 The Republican National Convention assembles in Chicago in the specially constructed "Wigwam," where they select Abraham Lincoln as their candidate and adopt "Dixie's Land" as the party's campaign song.

May 1860 The first U.S. edition of Charles Darwin's *On the Origin of Species* appears, a year after the English edition. It causes a sensation as the author's theories on natural selection are accused of trying to "dethrone God."

June 9, 1860 The first "dime novel," *Malaeska: The Indian Wife of the White Hunter* by Ann Sophia Stevens, goes on sale in New York City.

June 23, 1860 The U.S. Government Printing Office is established by act of Congress; henceforward, it will be the official printer of record for all government documents and publications.

June 26, 1860 Democratic "seceders," representing the Deep South, nominate John C. Breckenridge of Kentucky for president.

September 12, 1860 William Walker, the self-styled "freedom fighter" and "voice of Manifest Destiny," is executed by a Honduran firing squad, thus effectively ending the era of the American filibuster.

Thomas Hovenden's *The Last Moments of John Brown* (1885), an etching based on the artist's popular 1884 painting. This completely apocryphal incident starts the fanatical abolitionist and convicted traitor on his long walk from the Charles Town, Virginia, jailhouse to the gallows, where he will be hanged for his murderous raid on Harper's Ferry, Virgina. The painting/etching reinforces the sympathetic Northern view of Brown as a martyr to the cause of abolition. (The Gilder Lehrman Collection at the Pierpont Morgan Library, New York. GLC 737)

October 24, 1860 The first transcontinental telegraph line begins operation, marking the end of the Pony Express as a viable form of communication.

November 6, 1860 Lincoln wins the presidential campaign of 1860 to become the 16th president of the United States, making him the first modern Republican president and provoking the secession of Southern states from the Union.

December 18, 1860 The Crittenden Compromise is proposed by Senator John J. Crittenden of Kentucky in a last-ditch attempt to save the Union; it is discussed for the next two months before being rejected as too little, too late.

December 20, 1860 The South Carolina legislature meets at Charleston and unanimously declares that "the Union now subsisting between South Carolina and the other states under the name of 'the United States of America' is hereby dissolved." The stampede to secession is on, and civil war follows in four months.

January 29, 1861 Kansas enters the Union as the 34th state, after six years of sectional conflict as "Bleeding Kansas."

February 4–8, 1861 Delegates from seven seceded states meet in Montgomery, Alabama; at the end of the meeting they proclaim the Confederate States of America.

February 6, 1861 The first clashes between white settlers and Apache mark the beginning of the Apache Wars in the Southwest.

In 1860 Chicago, Illinois, was poised to become a great metropolis, so it seemed fitting to hold the Republican national nominating convention there that year. A vast meeting hall able to hold up to 15,000 people was constructed for the occasion at the corner of Lake and South Water Streets, almost on Lake Michigan. Promptly dubbed "The Wigwam" by local citizens, it was the site of Abraham Lincoln's nomination for president on the third ballot on May 18. (Library of Congress, Prints and Photographs Division [LC-US262-30971])

February 9, 1861 At a meeting in Montgomery, Alabama, the Congress of the newly formed Confederate States of America elects Jefferson Davis of Mississippi as provisional president, and Alexander H. Stephens as vice president.

February 11, 1861 Lincoln departs from Illinois for Washington, D.C., to assume the presidency.

February 18, 1861 Jefferson Davis is inaugurated as the first (and last) president of the Confederate States of America in Montgomery, Alabama.

February 20, 1861 The Morrill Tariff is passed by the U.S. Congress sans Southern states; it is the most aggressive protective tariff since 1832.

February 28, 1861 Congress creates Colorado Territory, formerly part of Kansas Territory.

March 2, 1861 Congress creates Dakota Territory, formerly part of Nebraska Territory.

March 4, 1861 Abraham Lincoln is inaugurated as 16th president of the United States; he refers in his inaugural address to "the momentous question of civil war" facing the country.

March 11, 1861 The new constitution of the Confederate States of America is signed by delegates at the Montgomery, Alabama, convention, creating a political structure for the 11 secessionist states; it is modeled on the U.S. Constitution but includes more safeguards against centralized power.

April 12, 1861 At 4:30 A.M. Confederate batteries around Charleston harbor, South Carolina, open fire on Fort Sumter, occupied by federal soldiers. Four thousand shells are fired into the fort during the next two days, forcing it to surrender on April 14. The Civil War is begun.

April 15, 1861 President Lincoln issues a "call to arms" for 75,000 volunteers to put down the "rebellion" in the Southern states.

April 17, 1861 President Davis invites applications from Southern shipowners for letters of marque, authorizing them to attack U.S. shipping on the high seas without being branded pirates.

April 19, 1861 President Lincoln proclaims a naval blockade of all Southern parts, rather than declaring them closed, and the resulting "paper blockade" proves to be a diplomatic misstep.

May 6, 1861 President Jefferson Davis responds to Lincoln's call to arms by issuing his own call for 100,000 (Southern) volunteers to aid in resisting Northern aggression.

May 13, 1861 The British government announces a policy of formal neutrality in the U.S. Civil War, thus stealing a page from U.S. foreign policy dating back to President George Washington. The British pronouncement forbids British subjects to fight for either side and prohibits the sale of war matériel to either "belligerent."

May 24, 1861 The Union general Benjamin F. Butler, commander at Fortress Monroe, Virginia, issues orders declaring all runaway slaves reaching his lines to be "contraband of war" and therefore subject to being "confiscated" and put to work as "free blacks." This novel interpretation of an ancient wartime principle covering enemy property appeals to escaping slaves and Northern abolitionists but presents a thorny problem for the Lincoln administration.

May 1861 Yale University graduate school grants the first Ph.D.s in the nation's history to three students.

June 1, 1861 Robert E. Lee takes command of Confederate forces in northern Virginia after General Joseph Johnston is wounded. General Lee will command the Army of Northern Virginia for the next four years, putting his personal stamp on one of the finest armies in U.S. history.

June 8, 1861 Tennessee becomes the last Southern state to secede from the Union after a bitter partisan political fight, making it 11th of the Confederate States of America.

June 9, 1861 The U.S. Sanitary Commission is officially launched with the approval of President Lincoln and Secretary of War Simon Cameron to put civilians to work providing for the comfort and health of U.S. volunteer forces. The service changes the way medicine is practiced in the United States and becomes the forerunner of the American Red Cross.

June 13, 1861 President Lincoln signs the instrument creating the quasi-official U.S. Sanitary Commission as a volunteer organization to provide health care and other humanitarian services to Union soldiers in the Civil War.

June 30, 1861 The last legal U.S. mail delivery in any Southern state is made without incident in South Carolina.

July 2, 1861 President Lincoln suspends the writ of habeas corpus indefinitely, making the preservation of the Union a higher ideal than constitutional guarantees of individual rights.

July 4, 1861 President Lincoln calls for 400,000 three-year volunteers to suppress the expanding "rebellion" in the South.

August 5, 1861 President Lincoln signs the Legal Tender Act to help finance the Civil War. Included in its provisions are the nation's first income tax (3 percent on annual income above $800, 5 percent on income above $10,000), as well as new levies on tobacco, liquor, and distilled spirits.

August 6, 1861 Congress passes the first Confiscation Act of the Civil War, authorizing Union forces to seize rebel property, including slaves, as "contraband." President Lincoln opposes it as likely to push border states into the arms of the Confederates.

October 24, 1861 The first transcontinental telegraph is completed when lines from the East and the West are connected at Salt Lake City, Utah. The first message is sent to President Lincoln from Sacramento, California.

November 1, 1861 The 75-year-old Winfield Scott resigns from the U.S. Army after a 53-year military career, the last 20 as general-in-chief, a post created especially for him. He is replaced by 34-year-old George B. McClellan, who is fired in less than a year.

November 8, 1861 The USS *San Jacinto,* Captain Charles Wilkes commanding, stops the British mail steamer *Trent* on the high seas and removes the Confederate envoys James Mason and John Slidell, in flagrant violation of international law, thus provoking an international incident between the United States and Great Britain that nearly leads to war.

December 30, 1861 The U.S. Treasury and all national banks suspend specie payments (i.e., payments of gold or silver) for the duration of the Civil War.

January 27, 1862 President Lincoln issues General War Order No. 1 in his capacity as commander in chief of the United States, ordering all Union forces to launch a unified assault on the Confederacy to end the rebellion. Nothing happens immediately.

January 30, 1862 The world's first ironclad warship built entirely without rigging or sails is launched: The turreted USS *Monitor* will spark a naval revolution.

February 20, 1862 Abraham and Mary Todd Lincoln's son, Willie, dies at age 12 of typhoid fever.

February 21, 1862 The captured slave trader Nathaniel Gordon of Portland, Maine, is hanged at New York City's Tombs Prison for violating the 1808 federal law against slave trading, the only person in U.S. history executed under that law.

February 25 and 26, 1862 Alarmed by lack of funds to prosecute the Civil War, Congress passes and the next day Lincoln signs the (first) Legal Tender Act, creating the country's first national currency, $150 million in Treasury notes (i.e., "greenbacks") to be issued as soon as they can be printed.

March 9, 1862 The duel between USS *Monitor* and CSS *Virginia* (formerly the *Merrimack*) at Hampton Roads, Virginia, is the first clash in history between ironclad warships. The battle, a draw, nevertheless "revolutionizes the navies of the world."

April 7, 1862 The Battle of Shiloh (Tennessee) ends, shocking the nation with its 24,000 casualties on the two sides, more than the United States has lost in any conflict up to this date.

April 16, 1862 President Lincoln orders the emancipation of the slaves in the District of Columbia.

May 20, 1862 Lincoln signs the Homestead Act into law; it is the government's response to popular demand for land in the West and stimulates settlement of vast territories after the Civil War.

July 1, 1862 Lincoln signs the Pacific Railroad Act, authorizing the Union Pacific to build westward from Omaha, Nebraska, and the Central Pacific eastward from Sacramento, California. They will join somewhere in between.

July 2, 1862 The Morrill Land Grant Act is passed by Congress, putting the federal government in the education business on a large scale by using public lands (some 17 million acres) to endow land-grant colleges in numerous states.

July 12, 1862 By resolution of Congress the president is authorized to issue "medals of honor" to deserving enlisted men and noncommissioned officers who have distinguished themselves by their gallantry in action; this is the origin of the modern U.S. Medal of Honor, the nation's highest military medal.

July 17, 1862 Congress passes the Second Confiscation Act, declaring slaves of Confederate civilian or military officials "forever free."

August 18, 1862 War erupts in southern Minnesota after Dakota Indians, starving because they have not received promised government rations, attack white settlements, ultimately leading to the death of some 400 whites before the war ends.

September 1, 1862 The long-standing practice of issuing a daily grog ration to sailors officially ceases in the U.S. Navy by act of Congress, acceding to a request by Assistant Secretary of the Navy Gustavus Fox.

September 13, 1862 The *Southern Illustrated News* begins publication in Richmond, Virginia, aiming to give Southern readers the same timely news and arts coverage, with pictures, that Northern readers get from the New York–based *Harper's Weekly Magazine* and *Frank Leslie's Illustrated Newspaper.*

September 15, 1862 The Union garrison at Harper's Ferry, Virginia, surrenders to Confederates under Stonewall Jackson, constituting the largest capitulation of U.S. forces in American history until the fall of Bataan and Corregidor to the Japanese in 1942: 12,500 prisoners with all their muskets, cannons, and supplies.

September 17, 1862 The Battle of Antietam (Sharpsburg), Maryland, rages all day as General George McClellan's Army of the Potomac tries to destroy Robert E. Lee's Army of Northern Virginia. Lee survives to fight another day, but his first invasion of Northern soil is turned back, and it is the bloodiest single day in U.S. history.

September 22, 1862 Lincoln issues the Preliminary Emancipation Proclamation declaring all slaves in the Confederacy to be free persons after January 1, 1863. The Proclamation does not cover slaves in neutral or Union states.

November 1862 The former president James Buchanan completes the manuscript for his memoirs, *Mr. Buchanan's Administration on the Eve of the Rebellion;* published in 1866, it becomes the first presidential memoir in U.S. history.

December 17, 1862 Major General Ulysses S. Grant issues General Order No. 11 expelling all Jews from the Department of the Tennessee [River], giving them 24 hours to be gone. It is an embarrassment to Grant and to the Lincoln administration that is soon revoked by order of the president.

December 26, 1862 Thirty-eight Dakota Sioux are hanged in Mankato, Minnesota, from a single scaffold as a punishment for the Minnesota Uprising, which killed more than 400 whites. Subsequently, Congress confiscated the Dakota reservation in Minnesota without providing hunting grounds elsewhere in the national domain. Originally more than 300 were sentenced to death, but Lincoln commuted the sentences of all but 38.

December 31, 1862 The USS *Monitor* founders in heavy seas off the North Carolina coast, marking the end of the first U.S. ironclad, but not of its type, which dominates naval operations for the rest of the war.

January 1, 1863 Lincoln's Emancipation Proclamation officially takes effect, declaring all slaves in any state under rebellion to be free, but without defining their new legal status. The Civil War is thus transformed into a war to end slavery as well as to preserve the Union.

January 1, 1863 The Homestead Act takes effect.

February 10, 1863 The first great celebrity wedding in American history, staged by P. T. Barnum, sees the famous little people "General Tom Thumb" and Lavinia Warren married in New York City.

February 24, 1863 Congress creates Arizona Territory, formerly part of New Mexico Territory.

February 25, 1863 The National Bank Acts are passed by Congress to help finance the Civil War. They effectively give complete control over the nation's banking and monetary system to the federal government for the first time.

March 3, 1863 Congress passes the first U.S. Conscription Act, "a most imperfect law" that adds fewer than 170,000 men to the army. A total of four draft calls are conducted under this law.

March 3, 1863 The National Academy of Sciences is established by act of Congress to serve as official adviser to the government in all matters scientific and technological.

March 3, 1863 Congress increases the number of Supreme Court justices from nine to 10 in order to win leverage in the battle shaping up over Reconstruction.

March 3, 1863 Congress creates Idaho Territory, formerly part of Washington Territory.

April 24, 1863 The U.S. War Department, through General Order No. 100, *Instructions for the Government of Armies of the United States in the Field by Order of the Secretary of War,* puts the United States at the forefront of the world's nations in creating the first comprehensive rules of war for international conflict.

June 17, 1863 The nation's first accident insurance company (Travelers) is chartered in Hartford, Connecticut.

June 20, 1863 West Virginia, after "seceding" from Virginia at the beginning of the war, enters the Union as the 35th state, driven by wartime politics despite questionable constitutional legality.

July 1–3, 1863 The three-day Battle of Gettysburg (Pennsylvania) ends Robert E. Lee's second invasion of the North, marking the high point of Confederate hopes and the bloodiest single battle in American history.

July 13–16, 1863 New York City draft riots rage for four days; at least 1,000 are dead and wounded (mostly blacks), 100 buildings are torched, and property damage exceeds $1.5 million. Rioting is finally quelled by federal troops rushed up from Gettysburg.

August 1863 The Long Walk of the Navajo (Dineh): Forced to walk from their ancestral lands to an arid reservation 300 miles away, the Navajo lose their home and many of their people.

September 15, 1863 Without even seeking authorization from Congress, President Lincoln suspends the right of habeas corpus for citizens in cases in which officers hold them for offenses against the military or naval service.

September 1863 The Denver mint goes into operation as the third U.S. mint after Philadelphia and San Francisco, reflecting the productivity of recent western gold strikes and the growing importance of the West in general.

September 1863 Six imperial Russian warships under Rear Admiral Lisovskii arrive in New York harbor, the first elements of the czar's navy to pay a formal visit to the United States up to this date. They receive a royal welcome from the Lincoln administration and stay until April 1864.

October 21, 1863 William "Bloody Bill" Anderson and William Clarke Quantrill, Confederate guerrilla captains, lead 450 men in a raid on Unionist Lawrence, Kansas, killing at least 150 unarmed men and boys. This is the most famous guerrilla raid of the Civil War.

November 19, 1863 Lincoln delivers his Gettysburg Address to a modest-sized, shivering crowd at Gettysburg, Pennsylvania, on the occasion of dedicating a new national cemetery there.

December 8, 1863 President Lincoln issues his Proclamation of Amnesty and Reconstruction, which includes the generous "10% Plan" for Confederate states to be readmitted to the Union. This is the first significant step toward Reconstruction.

January 13, 1864 The composer Stephen Foster dies virtually penniless at the age of 37, a patient in New York City's Bellevue Hospital. During his short career he composed "The Old Folks at Home," "Camptown Races," "Beautiful Dreamer," "Oh, Susannah!" and dozens of other song.

February 17, 1864 The Confederate warship *H. L. Hunley* makes naval history as the first submarine to sink an enemy vessel, when it attacks the USS *Housatonic* in Charleston Harbor.

March 9, 1864 President Lincoln names General U. S. Grant commander of all federal forces, an organizational move that marks a new phase in the war and in Grant's meteoric career.

April 10, 1864 Senator Charles Sumner introduces the first civil service bill in Congress, aiming to replace the corrupt patronage system in federal politics with a merit system. This first effort and subsequent reform efforts until 1883 are fruitless.

May 5–6, 1864 The Battle of the Wilderness in northern Virginia marks the first meeting between Robert E. Lee and Ulysses Grant on the field of battle. Two days of fighting leave nearly 30,000 dead on both sides and lead Grant to observe, "More desperate fighting had not been witnessed on this continent."

May 26, 1864 Congress creates Montana Territory, formerly part of Dakota Territory.

June 19, 1864 The USS *Kearsarge* meets the CSS *Alabama* off the coast of Cherbourg, France, in the second-most famous naval engagement of the Civil War (after that of the *Monitor* versus the *Virginia*). The *Alabama* is sunk, but its captain, Raphael Semmes, escapes.

June 30, 1864 Congress turns over the Yosemite Valley and the nearby Mariposa Grove of redwoods to the state of California as a public park.

July 4, 1864 Congresses passes an immigration bill allowing companies to import Chinese laborers. The act is aimed at helping western railroads such as the Central Pacific secure sufficient cheap labor to lay their tracks.

August 5, 1864 The U.S. Navy admiral Davie Farragut, trying to force an entrance into Mobile Bay, Alabama, reportedly declares, "Damn the torpedoes, full steam ahead!" creating a historic moment in U.S. naval history.

September 2, 1864 General Sherman's army captures Atlanta, Georgia, after a short siege, opening the door to the Confederate heartland and practically guaranteeing Lincoln's reelection in November.

September 15–16, 1864 The Confederate general Wade Hampton's famous "Beefsteak Raid" on a federal supply depot in Virginia delivers more than 2 million pounds of meat on the hoof to Lee's starving army at Petersburg, "as brilliant an operation as any completed during the war," say historians.

October 4, 1864 The nation's first African-American daily newspaper, the *New Orleans Tribune,* begins publication, under the editorship of Louis C. Roudanez.

October 19, 1864 Confederate raiders, striking from Canada, hit Saint Albans, Vermont, kill one citizen and take $208,000 before escaping back across the border. It is the northernmost action of the war, but whether it is a bold military operation or a simple bank robbery is open to question.

October 20, 1864 President Lincoln proclaims the last Thursday in November as (national) Thanksgiving Day, beginning an American tradition. Already, 30 of the states celebrate it on the same date yearly. The presidential proclamation culminates a seven-year campaign by Sara Josepha Hale.

October 31, 1864 Nevada enters the Union as the 36th state, its admission rushed through Congress to secure more votes for passage of the Thirteenth Amendment.

October 1864 Sojourner Truth becomes the second black person formally received by a president of the United States when she meets Abraham Lincoln in the White House.

November 8, 1864 Abraham Lincoln is elected to a second term in office, defeating the Democrat former general George B. McClellan. The way is open for Lincoln to finish the job of preserving the Union begun three years earlier.

November 29, 1864 At Sand Creek, Colorado, Colonel John M. Chivington leads a group of territorial militia who massacre more than 500 Arapaho and Cheyenne, mostly women and children, who thought they were under government protection at the time. This outrage opens the last phase in the war to subjugate the Plains Indians.

December 22, 1864 General William T. Sherman completes his historic "March to the Sea" by capturing Savannah, Georgia, and sends a telegram to President Lincoln, saying, "I beg to present you as a Christmas gift the city of Savannah." Southerners will never forgive Sherman for the devastation he causes.

January 31, 1865 The Thirteenth Amendment to the Constitution (abolishing slavery) is ratified by the necessary two-thirds majority of states to become the law of the land.

February 1, 1865 The U.S. Supreme Court for the first time admits a black man, John Rock of Massachusetts, to practice law before the nation's highest court, an ironic reversal from the Court's stand eight years earlier in the *Dred Scott v. Sanford* decision.

February 4, 1865 Jefferson Davis names Robert E. Lee general-in-chief of all Confederate armies, although the action is too little, too late, to have any effect on the outcome of the war.

February 18, 1865 Charleston, South Carolina, the "cradle of rebellion," falls to Union forces, thus bringing the war full circle to where it began in 1861.

February 1865 Martin R. Delany, surgeon for the black 54th Regiment of Massachusetts Volunteers, is commissioned a major in the Regular Army, the first African American to receive an officer's commission.

March 3, 1865 Congress creates the Bureau for the Relief of Refugees, Freedmen, and Abandoned Lands (Freedmen's Bureau) to assist newly freed African Americans in making the transition from slavery to freedom by providing them with food, fuel, clothing, and land. The historian W. E. B. Du Bois, writing in 1935, calls it "the most extraordinary and far-reaching institution of social uplift that America has ever attempted."

March 3, 1865 Congress passes an act requiring that a copy of all books "and other materials" holding a U.S. copyright be deposited in the Library of Congress. Failure to do so will result in loss of copyright.

March 4, 1865 In Washington, D.C., Lincoln delivers his second Inaugural Address, classic oration couched in conciliatory terms and containing the immortal words "with malice toward none; with charity for all; with firmness in the right, as God gives us to see the right, let us strive on to finish the work we are in."

April 3, 1865 After four years of fighting, Richmond, Virginia, the Confederacy's capital city, falls to Union forces, although there is nothing left to occupy but a smoldering ruin left behind by its retreating defenders.

April 9, 1865 General Robert E. Lee meets with General Ulysses. S. Grant at the McLean house in Appomattox Court House, Virginia, to surrender his Confederate army. The Confederacy is, for all practical purposes, dead.

April 14, 1865 Lincoln is assassinated at Ford's Theatre in Washington, D.C., by the actor John Wilkes Booth, a Southern sympathizer. The president dies the next day.

April 15, 1865 Andrew Johnson, Lincoln's vice president, is inaugurated as president shortly after Lincoln is pronounced dead.

April 26, 1865 The last Confederate army still in the field, led by Joe Johnston, surrenders to William T. Sherman at Durham, North Carolina, virtually ending organized resistance to federal authority in the Civil War.

April 26, 1865 The presidential assassin, John Wilkes Booth, is trapped in a barn near Bowling Green, Virginia, and shot to death, eliminating the possibility of a trial or an explanation for his deed.

May 2, 1865 The country's first professional fire department (i.e. full-time, paid firemen) is established in New York City by act of the state legislature.

May 5, 1865 Thieves commit the first U.S. train robbery by derailing an Ohio & Mississippi Railroad train at North Bend, Ohio, then holding up male passengers and looting the express car. Over the next few decades, the methods are considerably refined (on July 21, 1872, the James gang robs its first train after perfecting their technique for six years with banks and stagecoaches).

May 10, 1865 The Confederate president, Jefferson Davis, is captured in flight on the way through Georgia, more than a month after Richmond was evacuated and Lee surrendered. Rumors will circulate that he was wearing his wife's clothes.

May 19, 1865 President Andrew Johnson officially declares the "armed insurrection" against the lawful U.S. government to be at an end, concluding the Civil War.

May 29, 1865 President Andrew Johnson issues his own Amnesty Proclamation, covering a limited number of Southerners recently engaged in rebellion; it specifically excludes former Confederate civil officials, military officers, and wealthy landowners.

May 1865 In the Capitol's Hall of Representatives, President Lincoln's assassinated body lies in an open casket while approximately 75,000 mourners file past to pay their final respects.

June 19, 1865 The Union general Gordon Granger lands at Galveston, Texas, and promptly issues General Order No. 3, proclaiming emancipation of all slaves in the former Confederate state. This is the first the state's black population have heard of Lincoln's Emancipation Proclamation. The joyous event is subsequently celebrated as "Juneteenth" every year by African Americans in Texas.

June 23, 1865 The last vestige of organized Confederate forces, a group of Cherokee Indians under General Stand Watie, formally surrender.

July 1, 1865 The four-year blockade of Southern ports proclaimed by President Lincoln at the start of the Civil War is terminated by President Andrew Johnson; all U.S. ports are now open to commerce.

July 7, 1865 After a speedy, even hasty trial, four of the convicted Lincoln assassination conspirators are hanged at the Old Penitentiary Building in Washington, D.C.

July 13, 1865 Phineas T. Barnum's American Museum in New York City, the nation's first public museum and most popular performing venue, is completely gutted by fire. Four months later, the irrepressible showman will reopen, calling it the New American Museum.

July 21, 1865 The first genuine Western "showdown on Main Street" occurs in Springfield, Missouri, albeit not at "high noon," when James Butler "Wild Bill" Hickock squares off against Dave Tutt to settle a feud involving a woman and a card game. Standing 75 yards apart while a large crowd looks on, Tutt fires first, but Hickock fires straighter, leaving Tutt dead in the street and further aggrandizing Hickock's reputation. The situation becomes a staple of dime novels and Hollywood movies.

September 26, 1865 After a false start in 1861, Vassar College in Poughkeepsie, New York, begins its inaugural school year as the first liberal arts college exclusively for women.

November 6, 1865 Captain Henri Wirz is found guilty by a specially assembled military commission of committing murder and otherwise inflicting "wanton cruelty" on Union prisoners of war in his care at Andersonville prison camp in Georgia during the last 12 months of the war.

November 7, 1865 The Confederate cruiser CSS *Shenandoah* arrives in Liverpool, England, and surrenders to British authorities, lowering the last Confederate flag still defying U.S. authority—more than six months after the Confederacy has surrendered.

November 10, 1865 Captain Henri Wirz is hanged at Washington, D.C.'s Capitol Prison, the only Confederate executed for war crimes after the Civil War.

November 13, 1865 P. T. Barnum's new American Museum opens for business on the west side of Broadway, between Spring and Prince Streets, in New York City.

November 18, 1865 Samuel Langhorne Clemens (Mark Twain) publishes his first story, "The Celebrated Jumping Frog of Calaveras County," in the New York *Saturday Press.*

November 25, 1865 Mississippi becomes the first of the former Confederate states to introduce black codes when the legislature enacts laws aimed at preserving the form if not the substance of slavery; other Southern states quickly follow.

November 29, 1865 Horace Greeley dies at the age of 61 in Pleasantville, New York, just 24 days after losing a race for president. He will be best remembered for his radical stands on the issues of slavery, women's rights, and Reconstruction.

December 1, 1865 President Andrew Johnson restores the writ of habeas corpus, which Lincoln suspended four years previously in the early days of the Civil War.

December 18, 1865 The Thirteenth Amendment to the Constitution is formally ratified by the necessary three-fourths of the state legislatures, just 11 months after Congress submitted it to the states; thus ends the institution of slavery in the United States.

December 24, 1865 The Ku Klux Klan is organized in Pulaski, Tennessee, by six Southern veterans as a social club for former Confederate soldiers; it quickly becomes a terrorist organization.

December 25, 1865 On a 325-acre tract where nine railroads converge the Chicago Union Stock Yards slaughterhouse opens for business after incorporation by the Illinois legislature; it will soon be the biggest stockyard in the world.

February 13, 1866 The James brothers outlaw gang is born when they rob their first bank: Ten men led by Jesse and Frank James hit the Clay County Savings and Loan in Liberty, Missouri, escaping with $60,000 in gold and securities and launching a 10-year crime spree.

March 1866 Horatio Alger is removed from his pulpit at the First Unitarian Church of Brewster, Massachusetts, after being accused of "the abominable and revolting crime of unnatural familiarity with boys." It is the end of his ministerial career but the beginning of a new career as an author of juvenile fiction.

April 9, 1866 Congress passes the Civil Rights Act of 1866 over President Johnson's veto, marking the first time that legislation is passed over an executive veto. It is the first piece of legislation after ratification of the Thirteenth Amendment to protect the rights of newly freed African Americans.

April 10, 1866 The American Society for the Prevention of Cruelty to Animals, patterned after the similar Royal Society in England, is chartered in New York City by Henry Bergh.

July 2, 1866 Representative Nathaniel P. Banks of Massachusetts proposes a bill in the House to admit Canada into the Union as a state; it is quickly voted down.

August 20, 1866 An estimated 64 delegates, representing 60,000 workingmen and 52 unions, meet in Baltimore to form the National Labor Union, the first "permanent" national labor organization in the history of U.S. labor movement.

August 28, 1866 President Johnson launches his great speaking tour by train out West to Chicago and other points, trying to whip up public support for his Reconstruction policies heading into the off-year elections in November. His journey is dubbed the "swing around the circle" and becomes a standard part of political campaigning.

September 12, 1866 The first burlesque show staged in the United States, a European import called "The Black Crook," opens at Niblo's Garden in New York City. It produces a mixed reaction of outrage and titillation.

November 1, 1866 In a deal known as "the Great Consolidation," Wells, Fargo takes over Ben Holladay's Overland Mail and Express Company, creating the firm of Wells, Fargo & Company, which now has a virtual monopoly on mail and express business in the West.

January 31, 1867 Congress grants suffrage to all males older than 21 years of age in all U.S. territories.

January 1867 Horatio Alger publishes the first installment of "Ragged Dick" in *Student Schoolmate* magazine. This serialized novel launches a new genre of rags-to-riches stories.

February 1867 The "nonfiction" story "Wild Bill" by George Ward Nichols is published in *Harper's New Monthly Magazine,* launching the legend of James Butler "Wild Bill" Hickock, gunfighter.

February 1867 Napoléon III withdraws the last French troops from Mexico, where they had been propping up the puppet Maximilian in open defiance of U.S. wishes, thus ending the last armed threat to U.S. hegemony in the Western Hemisphere.

March 1, 1867 Nebraska enters the union as the 37th state.

March 2, 1867 Congress passes three partisan pieces of legislation—the Tenure of Office Act, the Army Act, and the first Reconstruction Act—severely limiting presidential powers as a slap at the unpopular Andrew Johnson, thereby provoking a fight that will culminate in Johnson's impeachment.

March 2, 1867 Congress creates the Department of Education, headed by a commissioner, in a major commitment to public education; it becomes part of the Department of the Interior in 1889.

March 30, 1867 The Russian–American Treaty transferring Alaska to the United States is signed at 4:00 A.M. in Washington, D.C., by Secretary of State William Seward and the Russian minister, Edouard de Stoeckl.

July 20, 1867 Congress creates a Peace Commission to seek to negotiate an end to the bloody and long-running wars against the Plains Indians.

August 1867 The first Texas cattle herds begin arriving at the railhead in Abilene, Kansas, having followed a vaguely marked trail up from San Antonio, Texas. That trail will eventually be known as the Chisholm Trail after the Indian trader Jesse Chisholm, although the entrepreneur Joseph McCoy played the key role in making it a cattle route. This first herd is shipped out on the Kansas-Pacific Railroad to Chicago the following month.

October 21, 1867 Some 7,000 Plains Indians and representatives of the U.S. government gather at Medicine Lodge Creek, Kansas, to negotiate an end to their long-running war. The resulting treaty requires the Indians to give up their free-roaming practices and move onto reservation lands.

November 25, 1867 In a vote along party lines, the Senate Judiciary Committee votes to impeach President Andrew Johnson for "high crimes and misdemeanors."

November 25, 1867 In one of the most famous court-martial trials in U.S. history, Lieutenant Colonel George A. Custer is court-martialed for ordering deserters to be shot and for being absent from his command in the field. For his crimes he is suspended from rank and pay for one year.

December 4, 1867 The Patrons of Husbandry (the Grangers) organization is founded in Washington, D.C., by Oliver H. Kelley to work for fairer railroad rates and to draw together isolated farmers for educational and social functions: Within 10 years 20,000 local chapters with some 800,000 members are established.

December 7, 1867 The House of Representatives by a vote of 108 to 57 rejects the recommendation of its own Judiciary Committee to impeach President Andrew Johnson, but this is just the second round in the bitter affair.

February 16, 1868 The Benevolent and Protective Order of Elks is launched in New York City as a fraternal organization with charitable purposes for people connected with the theater. (This original theater connection is lost by the end of the century.)

February 24, 1868 President Andrew Johnson is formally impeached by a vote of 126 to 47 in the U.S. House of Representatives. An ad hoc committee of two Republicans is appointed to head the proceedings, which will soon lead to the first impeachment trial in American history.

March 2, 1868 P. T. Barnum's New American Museum burns to the ground, taking with it all of his exotic exhibits and most of his animals and leading the legendary owner to retire from show business for the next three years.

March 21, 1868 The first women's professional club, Sorosis, is founded in New York City by Jane Cunningham Croly and Ellen Curtis Demorest; it is modeled on the Elks, the Masons, and other male fraternal organizations.

April 1868 The Fort Laramie (Wyoming) Treaty of 1868 ends the First Sioux War, marking a significant defeat for the U.S. Army in its war against the Plains Indians.

May 30, 1868 Decoration Day (the predecessor of Memorial Day) is celebrated for the first time as a national holiday, thanks to the combined efforts of the former Union general John A. Logan and the veterans of the Grand Army of the Republic. It is a day "for the purpose of strewing with flowers or otherwise decorating the graves of comrades who die in defense of their country during the late rebellion" (i.e., Union soldiers killed in the Civil War). It is recognized first as a legal holiday by the state of New York (1873) then by Rhode Island (1874) and ultimately the whole nation.

June 23, 1868 Christopher L. Sholes receives a patent for inventing the first practical typewriter.

June 24, 1868 Congress passes the first eight-hour-day work law, introduced by Nathaniel P. Banks of Massachusetts, applied only to mechanics and laborers employed by the federal government. President Andrew Johnson signs it a few days later, but the law's good intentions are immediately frustrated when wages are cut 20 percent.

July 25, 1868 Congress creates Wyoming Territory out of parts of western Dakota, eastern Idaho, and northern Utah Territories, with its capital at Cheyenne.

July 28, 1868 The Burlingame Treaty is signed by Secretary of State William Seward for the United States and representatives of China, becoming the first formal agreement between the two nations. It establishes reciprocal rights, mutual respect for territorial sovereignty, and unrestricted bilateral immigration, the latter mainly important for Chinese who wish to enter the United States. However, it does not grant the right of naturalization to Chinese residents in the United States.

July 28, 1868 The Fourteenth Amendment is ratified by the necessary three-fourths of the states, thereby becoming part of the U.S. Constitution; it provides a new definition of citizenship that includes former slaves and enshrines the concept of due process in U.S. jurisprudence.

November 3, 1868 Republican Ulysses S. Grant of Ohio is elected the 18th president of the United States.

November 6, 1868 The Sioux chief Red Cloud signs a peace treaty with General William T. Sherman at Fort Laramie, Wyoming, ending Red Cloud's War and establishing the Great Sioux Reservation. The army agrees to abandon posts in order to end Indian raids.

November 27, 1868 Colonel George A. Custer and the 7th U.S. Cavalry attack and wipe out an entire Cheyenne village on the Washita River in the Indian Territory (present-day Oklahoma).

December 1, 1868 A group of New York and Philadelphia photographers meeting in Philadelphia form the National Photographic Association, the first professional association of photographers in the United States. The organization changes its name in 1880 and, as the Photographic Association of America, still exists today.

December 3, 1868 The treason trial of the former Confederate president, Jefferson Davis, begins in Richmond, Virginia.

December 25, 1868 President Andrew Johnson issues a proclamation of "unconditional pardon and amnesty" to all involved in the recent "insurrection" (the Civil War), including Jefferson Davis.

January 12, 1869 The National Convention of Negroes meets in Washington, D.C., in the first postslavery effort to organize a national movement to protect their rights and fight for justice.

January 19, 1869 The American Equal Rights Association is formed in Washington, D.C., with Susan B. Anthony as its first president. This is the beginning of an organized national women's movement in the United States.

March 4, 1869 Ulysses S. Grant is sworn in as 18th president of the United States and delivers his inaugural address on the east portico of the Capitol building. His simple message to the people of the United States: "Let us have peace."

April 10, 1869 Congress passes legislation creating the Board of Indian Commissioners to oversee U.S. government relations with Native Americans and prod the U.S. Army to secure permanent peace.

May 10, 1869 The first transcontinental railroad is completed with the driving of the golden spike at Promontory Point, near Ogden, Utah; this historic moment opens a new phase in the settlement of the West, which will eventually lead to the end of the frontier.

May 15, 1869 The National Woman Suffrage Association is formed with Elizabeth Cady Stanton as its first president to promote voting rights for women in national elections.

May 27, 1869 The first group of Japanese immigrants arrive in the United States and settle in Gold Hill, California.

July 22, 1869 Washington Roebling, designer of the Brooklyn Bridge, dies of complications of an accident suffered while work-

The impeachment trial of President Andrew Johnson in the U.S. Senate, 1868, breaking new ground in American politics. Johnson was acquitted by a single vote. (Tennessee State Library and Archives)

ing on his bridge-building project; he is the first of 20 men who will die on the 14-year construction job.

September 1, 1869 Cleveland Abbe, director of the Cincinnati Observatory, begins issuing regular weather reports, anticipating the creation of the U.S. Weather Bureau two years later.

September 1, 1869 The Prohibition Party is launched in Chicago at a national convention of 500 delegates from 19 states. Women delegates participate as equals with men for the first time in any political party's history.

September 24, 1869 This is the first "Black Friday" in the history of Wall Street: the day that President Grant belatedly orders the release of federal gold reserves to prevent Jim Fisk and Jay Gould from cornering the gold market. The result is a national financial crisis.

October 15, 1869 A 10-foot object, which appears to be the petrified remains of an ancient man, is unearthed by laborers digging a well on the farm of "Stub" Newell near the town of Cardiff in upstate New York. Declared genuine by experts, it is later proved to be a fake perpetrated by Newell's cousin, George Hull, but it enters history as the "Cardiff Giant."

December 10, 1869 The Wyoming territorial legislature passes the Democrat William H. Bright's women's suffrage bill, which is signed by Governor John Campbell, making Wyoming the first state or territory to grant women the right to vote, hold office, and serve on juries.

January 10, 1870 Forty-one-year-old John D. Rockefeller and associates organize Standard Oil Company of Ohio, capitalized at $1 million.

February 9, 1870 The National Weather Service (forerunner of the U.S. Weather Bureau) is established as an independent agency by act of Congress. It will later become part of the Department of Agriculture (1891), before ultimately finding a home in the Department of Commerce (1940).

February 25, 1870 The Republican Hiram R. Revels of Mississippi takes his seat as the first African-American member of the U.S. Senate.

February 26, 1870 The first subway in the Western Hemisphere, based on experimental pneumatic technology, begins service in New York City on a stretch of Broadway Street; the pneumatic version never advances beyond the prototype stage.

March 30, 1870 The Fifteenth Amendment to the Constitution is ratified after being approved by the necessary 29 states (three-fourths). It guarantees all male citizens the right to vote regardless of "race, color, or previous condition of servitude."

June 1870 The U.S. Senate handily votes down a treaty to annex the Caribbean republic of Santo Domingo (the Dominican Republic), a measure that has been enthusiastically supported by President Grant and U.S. expansionists.

July 8, 1870 By act of Congress, the U.S. government begins officially registering trademarks with the U.S. Patent Office, which already possessed responsibility for patents and copyrights.

July 14, 1870 Congress passes the Naturalization Act (c. 254, 16 Statutes at Large 254), limiting U.S. citizenship to "white persons and persons of African descent," thereby excluding all Asians and Native Americans.

July 15, 1870 Georgia officially rejoins the Union, becoming the last former Confederate state to be readmitted. The delay has been caused by Georgia's reluctance to ratify the Fifteenth Amendment and seat African Americans in its legislature.

July 16, 1870 Chief Red Cloud of the Oglala Lakota Sioux speaks to a large respectful audience at the Cooper Union lyceum in New York City, allowing many non-Indians for the first time to see a kinder, gentler side of Native Americans. His eloquent review of Indian-white relations and plea for understanding are recorded verbatim by reporters, and he receives a standing ovation when he finishes.

July 24, 1870 The first through train from the nation's Pacific shores reaches the Atlantic coast, arriving at New York City on this date and thereby fulfilling for the first time the promise of the transcontinental railroad.

August 1, 1870 The first women to exercise the franchise in the United States vote in Utah Territory elections, but the action is overshadowed by events in Wyoming the following month.

September 6, 1870 Louisa Swain casts the first woman's vote in Wyoming Territory, and Wyoming, according to lore, gets the credit for being the most progressive state or territory on this issue in U.S. history.

October 12, 1870 The former Confederate general Robert E. Lee dies peacefully at the age of 63 at his home in Lexington, Virginia.

October 25, 1870 Baltimore's Pimlico Race Track holds its first horse race—won by a bay colt named Preakness. The horse enjoys a fine career, and a few years later an entire race, a premier event of the racing season, is named for that bay.

November 1870 The Wild West's first train robbery is carried out on the Central Pacific line near Verdi, Nevada, by A. J. "Big Jack" Davis and gang.

December 5, 1870 For the first time since December 1860, representatives of every state in the Union are gathered in the Capitol for a session of Congress. The occasion is the opening of the 41st Congress.

December 12, 1870 Joseph H. Rainey of South Carolina is sworn in as the first black member of the U.S. House of Representatives.

January 1871 The National Suffrage Convention demanding the right to vote for women meets in Washington, D.C., where they can appeal directly to Congress for their cause.

February 24, 1871 With the seating of the senators from Georgia, the South for the first time in more than a decade is fully represented in Congress.

March 3, 1871 President Grant signs the Indian Appropriation Act, ending the long-standing treaty system that has governed relations between whites and Native Americans. The government is barred henceforward from ever again negotiating with the Indians on sovereign terms. Henceforward, Native Americans will be treated as "wards of the state."

March 4, 1871 The first professional baseball league, the National Association of Professional Base-Ball Players, is formed in New York.

April 30, 1871 More than 100 Apache supposedly under federal protection are massacred by a mob at Camp Grant, Arizona. This is the second time this has happened in seven years (the first was Sand Creek in 1864).

May 8, 1871 The United States and Great Britain sign the Treaty of Washington to settle all outstanding issues between the two nations, especially the destruction wrought by the *Alabama* and other Confederate commerce raiders built or bought in Britain during the Civil War. Under terms of the treaty, Britain agrees to pay $15 million for depredations against U.S. shipping by CSS *Alabama,* CSS *Florida,* and CSS *Shenandoah.*

July 1871 Anthony J. Drexel merges his investment firm with J. P. Morgan's to establish the firm of Drexel, Morgan, and Company and quickly assume a leading role in U.S. finance.

September 17, 1871 Twenty-two convicts escape from the Nevada State Penitentiary in Carson City in one of the largest breakouts in U.S. history. Six are recaptured after a long pursuit and gun battle, but most are never caught.

October 8–10, 1871 The disastrous Chicago fire kills more than 300, destroys 17,450 buildings, and causes $196 million in damage.

October 23–24, 1871 The first anti-Chinese riot in U.S. history occurs in Los Angeles, California. Fifteen Chinese are lynched and another six are shot before it ends.

October 1871 Montgomery Ward, the first mail-order company, begins operation in Chicago, but after the Great Chicago Fire destroys their entire inventory, they are forced to begin again the next spring.

November 10, 1871 The *New York Herald*'s ace reporter Henry Stanley, on assignment for his publisher, finds the "lost" Scottish missionary David Livingstone at Ujiji, central Africa, and utters the historic greeting, "Dr. Livingstone, I presume?"

November 24, 1871 The National Rifle Association is founded in New York City as a sporting club. It will eventually evolve into a political lobby. Its first president is the former Union general Ambrose Burnside.

January 7, 1872 Death strikes the nouveau riche as "Jubilee Jim" Fisk, tycoon and bon vivant, dies in a hail of bullets in New York City's swank Broadway Central Hotel, shot down by a jealous rival for the affections of his showgirl mistress, Helen Josephine Mansfield.

January 1872 An informal discussion group of Harvard intellectuals calling itself "the Metaphysical Club," which includes Oliver Wendell Holmes, Jr., William James, Charles Sanders Pierce, and John Dewey, begins meeting in Cambridge, Massachusetts. Although the group is short-lived (nine months), its members have a major influence on each other and on U.S. intellectual history.

February 1872 Thomas Adams secures a patent for his process of producing chewing gum from chicle.

February 1872 William F. "Buffalo Bill" Cody on a visit to New York City sees a performance of the stage version of his life (written by Edward Z. C. Judson). He returns to the West and begins living the legend.

March 1, 1872 President Ulysses Grant signs the Yellowstone National Park bill into law, creating the nation's first national park out of 2,221,773 acres straddling Wyoming, Montana, and Idaho.

May 1–3, 1872 The breakaway Liberal Republican Party meets in Cincinnati, Ohio; chooses the eccentric newspaperman Horace Greeley as its presidential candidate; and announces its platform for the upcoming election. Nine weeks later the Democratic Party at their national convention in Baltimore also nominates Greeley.

May 22, 1872 Congress passes the Amnesty Act, restoring civil rights to all former Confederates with the exception of approximately 600 important leaders.

June 30, 1872 After five years the Freedmen's Bureau is shut down by Congress.

June 1872 Congress repeals the wartime-related income tax but maintains taxes on distilled spirits, liquor, and tobacco.

August 19, 1872 One of the greatest scams of all time is launched after Philip Arnold and John Slack of Kentucky "salt" a piece of land in Colorado with uncut diamonds. It sets off a rush to "the Great Diamond Fields of America" by eager prospectors from two continents before it is exposed by the geologist Clarence King as a fraud.

September 4, 1872 The *New York Sun* breaks the story of the Crédit Mobilier, a swindle by officers of the Union Pacific Railroad in cahoots with members of Congress and the Grant administration.

The resulting investigation becomes the major political scandal in U.S. history until the Teapot Dome and Watergate events of the 20th century.

November 5, 1872 The Republican Ulysses Grant is elected to a second term as president of the United States.

November 5, 1872 On national election day, the suffragist Susan B. Anthony goes to the polls and casts a vote illegally in the presidential election, hoping to draw attention to her cause. She is subsequently arrested and convicted of breaking the law, although her case does not reach the Supreme Court as she had hoped.

November 9–10, 1872 A massive fire sweeps through Boston, killing 13 people and destroying 60 acres of the downtown district.

November 15, 1872 A ceremony is held in San Francisco celebrating completion of the first transcontinental telegraph link between the United States and Australia (via Europe).

December 11, 1872 Pinckney Benton Stewart Pinchback, a Union army veteran, becomes acting governor of Louisiana, the first African American to occupy that office in any state of the Union.

February 12, 1873 Congress passes the Coinage Act of 1873, discontinuing the coinage of silver dollars and setting the stage for the demonetization of silver the following year. The reaction provoked by this legislation leads it to be labeled the "Crime of '73" by outraged silver interests.

March 3, 1873 The lame-duck 42nd Congress passes and President Grant signs into law "An Act for the Suppression of Trade in and Circulation of Obscene Literature and Articles of Immoral Use," soon to be known as the Comstock Act after the man who was instrumental in getting it enacted. The law makes it a crime to send any material broadly deemed "obscene" through the mails.

The upper falls of the Yellowstone River as photographed by William H. Jackson, official photographer of the Hayden Survey in 1871. Jackson is the first person to photograph the Yellowstone region, and his pictures are instrumental in inducing Congress to pass the 1872 legislation that creates Yellowstone National Park. (Tennessee State Library and Archives)

March 3, 1873 The 42nd Congress passes the notorious "Salary Grab" Act giving raises beginning at 50 percent to all federal officials from the president down, then adds insult to injury by making the raises retroactive. The act was repealed by the next Congress.

March 3, 1873 The 42nd Congress passes the Timber Culture Act, expanding the original (1862) homestead legislation by making it possible to stake a claim on the Great Plains by planting trees on the homestead.

May 1, 1873 The U.S. Post Office issues the first penny postcards, a revolution in mail service that allows people to send a brief message anywhere in the United States for one cent.

May 20, 1873 The Bavarian immigrant Levi Strauss and partners secure a patent for a new type of rugged work pants with copper rivets at stress points, which they call 501 Double X overalls. This uniquely American form of clothing, eventually known as "blue jeans," is favored by gold miners and lumberjacks.

July 1, 1873 The African American Henry O. Flipper enters West Point, the first member of his race to graduate from the academy. Four years later he graduates 50th of 76 in his class. Later accused of embezzlement and lying, he is dismissed from the U.S. Army, an action that is reversed by a review board in 1976 and confirmed by a full pardon granted by President William Clinton in February 1999.

July 8–10, 1873 The first national organization of Jewish congregations in the United States is formed, the Union of American Hebrew Congregations.

July 1873 Dr. Silas Weir Mitchell publishes a paper in the *American Journal of Medical Science* that first describes his revolutionary "rest cure" for the treatment of nervous exhaustion (neurasthenia). It remains a popular treatment among the well-to-do for the rest of the 19th century.

September 1, 1873 The world's first cable-car system, invented by Andrew Smith Hallidie, begins operation on Clay Street in San Francisco, covering six-tenths of a mile. Eventually 28 other U.S. cities build the same sort of transit system.

September 18, 1873 The great brokerage house of Jay Cooke & Company fails, causing all trading to shut down on Wall Street two days later and sparking the worst financial crash in U.S. history to that date.

October 27, 1873 Joseph Glidden of De Kalb, Illinois, applies to the U.S. Patent Office for a patent for his improved form of barbed wire.

October 31, 1873 Another Cuba-related crisis with Spain erupts when the U.S.-flagged gun-running ship *Virginius* is captured by Spanish authorities and 53 crew members and passengers are executed as pirates. War is narrowly avoided when the Spanish government apologizes and pays an indemnity.

November 19, 1873 William Marcy "Boss" Tweed, ringleader of the most notorious political machine in U.S. history, is convicted in a New York City court on 204 misdemeanor counts of criminal activity, a small fraction of the activities that may have netted him and his cronies as much as $200 million in graft between 1865 and 1871. (He is in and out of jail for the next eight years until he dies in debtor's prison in 1878.)

January 24, 1874 The world's original "Siamese twins," Chang and Eng of Siam, die at their home in Trap Hill, North Carolina, at the age of 63. Joined at the chest by a narrow band of ligament, they have managed to marry different women and father 21 children while living reasonably normal lives. They were forced to earn their living, however, touring the world as "sideshow freaks." The state of medical knowledge was not yet capable of safely separating them.

April 6, 1874 Alfred E. Packer, a 42-year-old epileptic mountain guide, emerges from the Rocky Mountains near Lake City, Colorado, to admit that he had eaten five fellow gold prospectors while they were stranded in the mountains for the winter. Convicted on five counts of manslaughter in 1886, he is sentenced to 40 years in prison but serves only 14 before being paroled.

April 1874 Adolph Herman Joseph Coors begins brewing beer in Golden, Colorado, initially in partnership with Jacob Schueler.

April 1874 P. T. Barnum's Great Roman Hippodrome opens on Madison Square in New York City as the first permanent home of his traveling circus. Barnum will sell the building this same year, and in 1879 it will become the first Madison Square Garden.

May 14, 1874 The first intercollegiate football game is played between Harvard University and McGill University of Montreal, using U.S. rules. Harvard wins, 3-0. It also begins the tradition of the home-and-away series as Harvard has already agreed to go to Montreal in October for a rematch with Canadian rules.

May 1874 The African American Edward Alexander Bouchet graduates from the Yale University undergraduate program and immediately enters the doctoral program, becoming two years later the first of his race to earn a Ph.D. in the United States and only the sixth person of any race or nationality to receive a doctorate in the field of physics.

June 1874 The Red River War begins against the Cheyenne, Kiowa, and Comanche, as the U.S. Army attempts to open new areas of the Southwest to non-Indian settlement.

July 4, 1874 The revolutionary Eads Bridge (named for James B. Eads) spanning the Mississippi River at Saint Louis, Missouri (Missouri to Illinois), is formally opened to great fanfare, reflecting its status as "an engineering miracle": the first bridge to span the mighty Mississippi and the largest bridge in the world at the time.

August 4, 1874 A group of 142 Methodist Sunday school teachers conclude a two-week instructional camp at Lake Chautauqua in western New York, led by John H. Vincent and Lewis Miller. The unqualified success of their "teacher training institute" persuades them to make it an annual event with a changing program, known as the Chautauqua Institution.

October 1874 In *Minor v. Happersett,* the U.S. Supreme Court holds that a state can constitutionally forbid a woman to vote, despite her U.S. citizenship.

November 18–20, 1874 The Woman's Christian Temperance Union is founded at a Cleveland, Ohio, temperance convention by 135 "concerned women" to provide political clout for the unenfranchised women in their fight against the drinking of alcohol.

November 24, 1874 Joseph F. Glidden of DeKalb, Illinois, receives U.S. patent no. 157,124 for his barbed wire, an invention that ranks alongside the railroad and Colt .45 revolver as technology that opened the West.

January 11–July 2, 1875 The Beecher-Tilton trial becomes the latest in a long list of "Trials of the Century." Theodore Tilton sues Henry Ward Beecher for $100,000 for alienating him from his wife's (Libby Tilton) affections. The result, a hung jury after 52 ballots, is interpreted by Beecher's congregation as a victory.

January 14, 1875 Congress passes an act for the Resumption of Specie Payments, which authorizes the Treasury to buy back Civil War greenbacks in circulation for gold or silver until the amount of greenbacks in circulation is reduced to $300 million.

February 9, 1875 The Hoosac Railway Tunnel in western Massachusetts is officially opened for traffic after 24 years of delays, setbacks, and problems in construction. At 4.7 miles, it is the longest tunnel built in North America in the 19th century.

February 10, 1875 The California congressman Horace F. Page introduces federal legislation designed to prohibit the immigration of Asian female prostitutes into the United States. Eventually it restricts the immigration of Chinese contract workers and Asian women in general.

February 1875 A lame duck Congress passes the Civil Rights Act of 1875, marking the last race-related civil rights legislation passed in the 19th century.

March 1, 1875 The latest in a series of Reconstruction-era Civil Rights Acts is signed into law by President Ulysses Grant, guaranteeing "full and equal enjoyment" of all public facilities to every citizen, regardless of "race, color, or previous condition of servitude." It is the last such legislation of its kind for the next 90 years.

April 6, 1875 Alexander Graham Bell is granted a patent for the multiple telegraph, which allows two signals to be sent at the same time over the same line.

May 1, 1875 The first Kentucky Derby is run in Louisville, Kentucky, and the tradition that it is always run on the first Saturday in May is started.

May 2, 1875 Isaac Parker arrives in Fort Smith, Arkansas, to begin his tenure as the first federal judge of the Indian Territory. In time he will win a reputation among lawbreakers as "the Hanging Judge."

May 13, 1875 The murder of a cattleman, Timothy P. Williamson, near Willow Creek, Texas, sparks the bloody Mason County War, destined to be known as the most bitter and vicious feud Texas ever experienced.

May 20, 1875 The United States joins 16 other nations in signing a convention for the establishment and maintenance of a permanent International Bureau of Weights and Measures, to set worldwide standards. This is more than 50 years after such an organization was recommended by John Quincy Adams.

May 31, 1875 A reciprocity treaty between the United States and the Kingdom of Hawaii is signed into law by President U.S. Grant. It mainly affects sugar imports from the islands.

May 1875 The U.S. government offers the northern Sioux $6 million for their tribal lands in the Black Hills of the Dakotas, where, not coincidentally, gold has just been discovered. The Sioux reject the offer.

June 2, 1875 James Augustine Healy becomes the first African American elevated to bishop in the American Catholic Church when he is consecrated to the See of Portland, Maine. He presides for the next 25 years over a diocese that includes Maine and Rhode Island. (Six African Americans lead Roman Catholic dioceses in the United States 125 years later.)

June 1875 The first intercollegiate football game between two U.S. teams is played between Harvard University and Tufts University; Tufts wins. A uniform code of rules is not established until the following year.

October 1875 The special Pinkerton agent James McParland, after working undercover in the Pennsylvania coalfields for more than two years, turns in the names of 374 members of the radical Irish society the Molly Maguires, who had committed violent crimes, opening the way for the first prosecutions of the group.

CHAPTER 5 The Economy

A Booming Economy

The 25 years 1850 to 1875 saw the United States in the midst of a profound transformation from an agrarian economy into one of the world's top industrial powers. The change was more evolutionary than revolutionary because, at least in the beginning, most native industries were adjuncts of agriculture—textiles, lumber, flour, clothing, distilling—with iron production and machinery making being the only significant exceptions.

By any measure, the U.S. economy grew at a phenomenal rate. This was true across the board, whether in agriculture or industry, exports or imports, mining or banking. And while per capita productivity was rising, so was the income of U.S. workers. Between 1846 and 1856 the average rate of growth in almost every sector of the economy was somewhere above 100 percent, with even the most slowly growing segment increasing a healthy 70 percent. The 1850s has rightly been called a "prosperity decade" despite the setback of a major business panic in 1857.

TABLE 5.1 LEADING STATISTICAL INDICATORS OF ECONOMIC GROWTH, 1844–1856

Indicator	Percentage Growth in 10 Years
Population	0.44%
Value of exports	200%
Value of imports	200%
Tonnage of coal mined	270%
Amount of banking capital	100%
Amount of industrial capital	100%
Industrial output	100%
Value of farmland	100%
Amount of cotton, wheat, and corn harvested	70%

Source: John M. Murrin et al. *Liberty, Equality, Power: A History of the American People* (Fort Worth, Tex.: Harcourt Brace, 1996), 465.

General view of the Savannah, Georgia, city market before the Civil War, when life was good (if one's business was in cotton) and the local economy was booming. Southern ports were the busiest and most prosperous in the United States. The Civil War would change all that. (Courtesy of the Georgia Historical Society)

Agriculture

While industrialization got all the press, agriculture was still the engine that drove the economy, as farming was both a way of life and a commercial enterprise for most Americans. In 1860, 84 percent of the South's workforce was engaged in agriculture; in the more heavily industrialized North the proportion was 40 percent. U.S. farmers were known as the most efficient and productive in the world. They were quick to adopt the latest technology, and the U.S. government was supportive with laws such as the Homestead Act (1862) and the Morrill Land Grant Act (1862).

In the decade before the Civil War, thousands of pioneers settled on the rich lands of the Ohio and Mississippi River valleys, raising bumper crops of cotton, corn, and wheat. The nation's booming population produced an ever-growing home market, and an expanding transportation network provided the means to move crops to market. Productivity was high and production costs low thanks to long growing seasons and new technology.

The commercialization of agriculture made certain crops—cotton, tobacco, sugar, wheat—more important than the rest and favored certain regions—the South and the upper Midwest—over others. In the decade before 1855, the market price of cotton, tobacco, and sugar, the South's principal cash crops, doubled. Southern agriculture produced 60 percent of all U.S. exports with cotton alone amounting to more than 50 percent of the total. Development of upland cotton strains had made Southern cotton the most desired in the world. But the downside of those figures was that the economics of Southern cotton made the slave system inviolable and economic diversity almost impossible. In 1860, 80 percent of the South's labor force was committed to agriculture, while its share of the nation's manufacturing capacity was only 16 percent. Industrialization was passing the South by.

As cotton was "king" south of the Mason-Dixon line, wheat was "queen" in the upper Midwest. By the time of the Civil War it was challenging cotton as the nation's principal export crop, and it surpassed it during the war while Southern cotton sat on the docks in Confederate ports. Wheat prices reached a high of four dollars per bushel in 1864, and although that price dropped precipitously in the postwar economic contraction, wheat had permanently replaced cotton as the number one export crop. An important consideration was that wheat production was not based on slave labor, making it not only profitable but politically correct for its day.

The sheer number of farms grew enormously between 1850 and 1875. Western expansion was opening up new areas to agriculture, and it seemed every day sent new boatloads of immigrants into the nation's ports. Most of those immigrants were people of the land, not city dwellers. And after the Civil War, large numbers of African Americans, former slaves, joined the farm population, each eager to acquire

Even after the Civil War led to the abolition of slavery, Southern cotton continued to be picked and pressed into bales by the same system used in the first half of the century. All the work of ginning and baling was done on the plantation. Horses hitched to long sweeps turned the great screw that compressed the fiber into bales. This engraving is from *Frank Leslie's Illustrated Newspaper,* October 7, 1871. (Library of Congress)

TABLE 5.2 A NATION OF FARMERS

Region	1850			1860			1870		
	Number of Farms	Millions of Acres	Average Acreage per Farm	Number of Farms	Millions of Acres	Average Acreage per Farm	Number of Farms	Millions of Acres	Average Acreage per Farm
New England	167,000	18	N/A	185,000	20	N/A	182,000	21	N/A
Middle States	351,000	43	N/A	413,000	47	N/A	456,000	49	N/A
Southern States	488,000	165	N/A	640,000	220	N/A	849,000	185	N/A
Western States	444,000	67	N/A	716,000	120	N/A	1,167,000	155	N/A
TOTAL	1,450,000	293	202	1,954,000	407	200	2,654,000	410	154

Source: Michael G. Mulhall, *The Dictionary of Statistics*, 4th ed. rev. (London: George Routledge and Sons, Ltd., 1899), 348.

TABLE 5.3 U.S. FARMS AND THEIR DOLLAR VALUE BY STATES, TERRITORIES, AND REGIONS, 1850, 1860, 1870

State, Territory, or Region	Number of Farms			Value of Farmland		
	1850	1860	1870	1850	1860	1870
North	928,000	1,337,000	1,727,000	$2,207	$4,252	$5,979
Maine	47,000	56,000	60,000	$55	$79	$82
N.H.	29,000	31,000	30,000	$55	$70	$64
Vt.	30,000	32,000	34,000	$63	$94	$111
Mass.	34,000	36,000	27,000	$109	$123	$93
R.I.	5,000	5,000	5,000	$17	$20	$17
Conn.	22,000	25,000	26,000	$73	$91	$99
N.Y.	171,000	197,000	216,000	$555	$803	$1,018
N.J.	24,000	28,000	31,000	$120	$180	$206
Pa.	128,000	156,000	174,00	$408	$662	$835
Ohio	144,000	180,000	196,000	$359	$678	$844
Ind.	94,000	132,000	161,000	$136	$357	$508
Ill.	76,000	143,000	203,000	$96	$409	$736
Mich.	34,000	62,000	99,000	$52	$161	$319
Wis.	20,000	69,000	103,000	$29	$131	$240
Minn.	N/A	18,000	47,000	N/A	$28	$78
Iowa	15,000	61,000	116,000	$17	$120	$314
Mo.	54,000	93,000	148,000	$63	$231	$314
Nebr.	N/A	3,000	12,000	N/A	$4	$24
Kans.	N/A	10,000	38,000	N/A	$12	$72
South	515,000	672,000	885,000	$1,056	$2,323	$1,289
Del.	6,000	7,000	8,000	$19	$31	$37
Md.	22,000	25,000	27,000	$87	$146	$136
Va.	77,000	93,000	74,000	$216	$372	$170
W.Va.	N/A	N/A	40,000	N/A	N/A	$81
N.C.	57,000	75,000	94,000	$68	$143	$63
S.C.	30,000	33,000	52,000	$82	$140	$36
Ga.	52,000	62,000	70,000	$96	$157	$76
Fla.	4,000	7,000	10,000	$6	$16	$8
Ky.	75,000	91,000	118,000	$155	$291	$249
Tenn.	73,000	82,000	118,000	$98	$271	$175
Ala.	42,000	55,000	67,000	$64	$176	$54
Miss.	34,000	43,000	68,000	$55	$191	$65
Ark.	18,000	39,000	49,000	$15	$92	$32
La.	13,000	17,000	28,000	$76	$205	$55
Tex.	12,000	43,000	61,000	$17	$88	$48
West	7,000	35,000	48,000	$9	$70	$177
Colo. (Territory)	N/A	N/A	2,000	N/A	N/A	$3
N.Mex. Territory	4,000	5,000	4,000	$2	$3	$2
Utah (Territory)	1,000	4,000	5,000	N/A	$1	$2
Nev.	N/A	N/A	1,000	N/A	N/A	$1
Wash. Territory	N/A	1,000	3,000	N/A	$2	$4
Oreg.	1,000	6,000	8,000	$3	$15	$22
Calif.	1,000	19,000	24,000	$4	$49	$141
United States (Total)	1,449	2,044	2,660	$3,272	$6,645	$7,444

Note: Multiply each dollar value by 1,000,000.

Source: U.S. Bureau of the Census, *Historical Statistics of the United States, Colonial Times to 1970,* Part I (Washington, D.C.: Government Printing Office, 1975), 459, 462.

his or her own piece of land. As a result of all these factors, the number of farms grew by almost a half-million between 1850 and 1860, and by another 700,000 between 1860 and 1870. Before 1865, U.S. farmers put some 407 million acres under the plow; that number more than doubled to 841 million acres by the end of the century. The major gains occurred on the northern plains (Kansas, Nebraska, and the Dakotas), an area once known as "the Great American Desert" but soon to be dubbed the nation's "breadbasket."

Yet while the agricultural sector was expanding, the nature of farming itself was changing. From 1850 to 1870, as the number of farms and the total acreage under cultivation increased every reporting period, the size of the average farm was shrinking, a result of the breakup of the South's plantation system. The trend would reverse itself before the end of the century as large-scale commercial agriculture took over, but this was still the era of the family-owned farm.

TABLE 5.4 COMPARATIVE SIZE OF AMERICAN FARMS, 1860 AND 1870

Acreage	1860		1870	
	Number of Farms	As a Percentage of the Total Number of Farms	Number of Farms	As a Percentage of the Total Number of Farms
Less than 20 acres	306,000	15.0%	467,000	17.6%
20–50 acres	617,000	30.1%	848,000	32.0%
50–100 acres	609,000	29.8%	754,000	28.4%
100–500 acres	487,000	23.9%	565,000	21.3%
More than 500 acres	25,000	1.2%	20,000	0.7%
Totals	2,844,000	100.0%	2,654,000	100.0%

Source: Michael G. Mulhall, *Dictionary of Statistics*, 4th ed. rev. (London: George Routledge and Sons, Ltd., 1899), 348.

The Revolution Down on the Farm

U.S. farmers produced a stunning abundance from the soil. In the single year of 1860, they grew 838 million bushels of corn, 172 bushels of wheat, 5.4 million bales of cotton, plus uncounted millions of pounds of tobacco, fruits, vegetables, and other crops for market. Much of that cornucopia was sold abroad, as 82 percent of the country's exports in 1860 were from its farms.

The remarkable productivity of U.S. farms depended as much on new technology as on the ability of the farmer and the fertility of the soil. Beginning with John Deere's famous "singing plow" in 1837, a succession of mechanical marvels went on the market in the next 40 years: reapers, threshing machines, grain drills, iron harrows, cultivators, and binders. Even better, they were priced so that most U.S. farmers could afford them, albeit often through generous financing arrangements or cooperative associations with their neighbors. On the Great Plains, a farmer in 1875 might have $700 tied up in equipment, above the expense of the land, hired help, and transportation costs. That was a substantial investment, but market-minded farmers looked on such machines not as luxuries but as necessities.

And there was no arguing with the results: Technology paid for itself in a fatter bottom line. Simple calculations showed an immediate surge in productivity and efficiency after every new generation of farm machinery was introduced. In 1800, 56 man-hours were required to raise and harvest an acre of wheat; by 1850 that number was below 35 man-hours, and it continued to drop. The initial payoff of mechanization occurred when a new machine was introduced, but it did not stop then. Redesigns and improvements were constantly added to the existing technology so that the efficiency curve continued to rise; for instance, steam power was added to reapers and threshers. Bringing in a harvest of wheat or corn or oats in 1880 took a fraction of the time and money that it had before the Industrial Revolution. The long-term results were the transformation of the United States into the "breadbasket of the world" and of the U.S. farmer into the most mechanized and productive of any in the world. Before the end of the century, the average farmer could, with the help of machines, produce up to 10 times more than was possible in the old days when humans and animals did all the work. The increased efficiency was most apparent in the production of wheat but was nearly as impressive with other crops. Only cotton and tobacco, among major crops, stubbornly resisted the benefits of technology to produce quantum gains in productivity.

TABLE 5.5 TOTAL HORSEPOWER OF ALL PRIME MOVERS (ANIMAL AND MECHANICAL), 1850–1880

Year	Total Horsepower (hp)
1850	8,494,000 hp
1860	13,763,000 hp
1870	16,931,000 hp
1880	26,314,000 hp

Source: Charles Van Doren and Robert McHenry, eds., *Webster's Guide to American History* (Springfield, Mass.: G.&C. Merriam, 1971), 739.

TABLE 5.6 HAND VERSUS MACHINE LABOR ON THE FARM, CA. 1880

Crop	Time Worked		Labor Cost	
	By Hand	By Machine	By Hand	By Machine
Wheat	61 hours	3 hours	$3.55	$0.66
Corn	39 hours	15 hours	3.62	1.51
Oats	66 hours	7 hours	3.73	1.07
Loose hay	21 hours	4 hours	1.75	0.42
Baled hay	35 hours	12 hours	3.06	1.29

Source: John Mack Faragher et al., *Out of Many: A History of the American People*, 2d ed. (Upper Saddle River, N.J.: Prentice Hall, 1997), 566.

Output from the nation's farms increased at more than double the rate of population growth in the late 1800s. U.S. farmers were able to feed themselves and the nation's growing industrial workforce with an ease that astounded Europeans but seemed perfectly normal to Americans. Agricultural exports also fed the world and earned valuable foreign exchange to be used in developing U.S. industries and infrastructure.

Industry

The major economic story of the 19th century was the building of a modern industrialized state, for it was there that Americans truly made their mark on history, not in a single year or even a single decade but over the second half of the century. It was a time when the expression *Yankee ingenuity* became synonymous all over the world with creativity and efficiency. Although while the Industrial Revolution; had begun on the western side of the Atlantic at the end of the 18th century with the invention of the cotton gin and the creation of a U.S. textile industry, by the 1850s U.S. manufacturers were turning out a profusion of firearms, sewing machines, and farm implements through the fabrication and assembly of standardized parts.

The United States so dominated the new manufacturing methods that those methods were dubbed "the American system" by British rivals after they observed them in action at the Crystal Palace Exhibition in 1851. The American system was several steps ahead of the European: to cite three examples, Americans pioneered the manufacture of interchangeable parts, which allowed quick replacements for broken or worn-out machinery; pioneered high-quality machine tools capable of turning out closely calibrated parts; and significantly shortened the lead time from invention to mass production. Not part of the American system but equally important, Americans also invented new ways of raising the enormous amounts of capital necessary to fund the research and development side of new technology. Thanks to all of these characteristics, before the end of the 1850s the United States had replaced France as the second leading industrial producer in the world, behind only Great Britain.

Few Americans at mid-century understood the transformation that was going on. Most still viewed the country in Jeffersonian terms, that is, as a nation of farmers and small producers, whereas in reality the nation was well on the way to being an urban, industrial society. By 1850, 20 percent of the labor force was engaged in manufacturing, producing about 30 percent of the national output. Those numbers would only grow in the next years. One national character trait that aided and abetted the transformation was that Americans proved particularly open to new technology, willing both to invest in it and to use it. The nation's inventors became partners with its industrialists and financiers in propelling the economy forward.

The industrial sector included a wide range of products, underscoring the diversity of the people themselves. The leading products were tied to the output of the land: flour, cotton, lumber. But the presence of machinery and distilled spirits among the top 10 manufactured products indicates a healthy, balanced economy.

TABLE 5.7 THE 10 LEADING U.S. INDUSTRIES LISTED IN THE CENSUS OF MANUFACTURES, 1860

Industry	Approximate Value of Product
Flour	$249,000,000
Cotton goods	$110,000,000
Lumber	$105,000,000
Boots and shoes	$88,000,000
Men's clothing	$80,000,000
Iron	$73,000,000
Leather	$65,000,000
Woolen goods	$62,000,000
Liquor	$60,000,000
Machinery	$52,000,000

Source: Winthrop D. Jordan et al., *The United States,* combined ed., 5th ed. (Englewood Cliffs, N.J.: Prentice-Hall, 1982), 317.

The demands of a wartime economy between 1861 and 1865 gave a tremendous boost to industrialization. In 1860 the nation possessed some 128,300 industrial establishments, 86 percent of them in the North. By 1865 the North alone was producing 29 percent more than the entire country had produced in the busiest antebellum year on record, 1856. But it was still a limited economy built on a handful of

W. S. & C. H. Thomson's Skirt Manufactory was typical of the booming American garment industry centered in the Northeast. In this engraving from *Harper's Weekly Magazine,* February 19, 1859, women are making hoop skirts, encouraged by their employer's sign on the wall, "Strive to Excel." In little more than two years, many of these same workers will be busy producing uniforms for Civil War armies. (Library of Congress)

industries, specifically firearms, gunpowder, wagons, shoemaking, and leather tanning. The Civil War, far from being the mother of U.S. industry, actually gave birth to no important new industries and even retarded the growth of some, such as railroads and coal mining.

By 1865, however, the country was primed for a takeoff that would leave all previous industrial booms in the dust. Everything was in place: an abundance of national resources, especially coal and iron; a skilled labor force willing to work cheaply; an agricultural base capable of producing enough food for a large urban population; access to investment capital through banks, stock exchanges, and wealthy financiers; and, not least, a capitalismt-friendly government. Combine these elements with a remarkable pool of entrepreneurial talent to organize it all, and it is no wonder the United States was the industrial colossus of the Western world by the end of the 19th century. The North had won the Civil War on the battlefields and in the factories. Now it was ready to lead the nation into the modern age.

The Maritime Economy

The U.S. maritime economy in the mid-19th century focused on the nation's coastal and inland waters, which composed such an extensive and profitable market that there was little need to look abroad. From the Chesapeake to the Rio Grande there was more than 3,500 miles of coastline, including 189 navigable harbors, inlets, bays, and river mouths. The network of inland waterways in the eastern half of the country exceeded 8,000 miles, not counting canals and the Great Lakes. This network was often referred to picturesquely as "the Inland Sea." It was the private preserve of U.S. commercial interests, and they set the tone of the government's maritime policies, which were resolutely laissez faire and inward-looking. U.S. investors, inventors, and shipbuilders found it more profitable to put their efforts into coastal and river shipping than transoceanic shipping. As a result the tonnage of domestic waterborne commerce increased some 200 percent from 1860 to the end of the century. Coastal trade even grew in three of the four Civil War years. Meanwhile, the gross tonnage of U.S. vessels involved in foreign trade fell by nearly half in the same 40-year period.

The two most profitable sectors of the U.S. maritime industry were the clipper-ship trade and whaling. Both belonged to the age of sail and enjoyed their peak years just before the Civil War. Clipper ships are discussed at greater length in chapter 6; analysis of their contribution to the nation's seaborne trade belongs here. The slim, rakish ships were, as a class, short on cargo-carrying capacity but long on speed. For commodities that had a high profits-to-weight ratio, such as tea, opium, wool, and fresh fruits, clipper ships were the perfect carrier.

TABLE 5.8 U.S. COASTAL TRADE, TONNAGE, 1850–1875

Year	Tonnage	Year	Tonnage
1850	1,755,797	1863	2,918,614
1851	1,854,318	1864	3,204,227
1852	2,008,022	1865	3,353,657
1853	2,082,782	1866	2,689,152
1854	2,273,900	1867	2,627,151
1855	2,491,108	1868	2,658,404
1856	2,211,935	1869	2,470,928
1857	2,300,399	1870	2,595,328
1858	2,361,596	1871	2,722,372
1859	2,439,320	1872	2,883,906
1860	2,599,319	1873	3,116,373
1861	2,657,293	1874	3,243,656
1862	2,578,546	1875	3,169,687

Source: Winthrop Marvin, *The American Merchant Marine—Its History and Romance from 1620–1902* (New York: Charles Scribner's Sons, 1902), 380.

Most U.S. clippers ran between Britain and the Far East because profits were greater than between U.S. ports and the Far East. They could make the long runs between London and Australian or Chinese ports of call in fewer than 60 and 90 days, respectively. Between 1850 and 1855 U.S.-built clippers held a virtual monopoly in the China-to-England tea trade. They were also the preferred carriers for passengers and mail from the East Coast around Cape Horn to San Francisco during the California gold rush. The Civil War, more than the introduction of steam power, ultimately destroyed the U.S. clipper ship trade.

Although Americans were important players in the international carrying trade before the Civil War, U.S.-flagged vessels were far from the preferred carriers even for their own producers. In the largest U.S. ports on any given day, foreign flags probably outnumbered Old Glory along the wharves and loading docks. In 1860 about 66 percent of the total ocean-borne commerce of the nation was handled by U.S. ships, a share that declined steadily from that point to the end of the century. Ironically, the U.S. government, while willing to protect zealously the nation's struggling manufacturers with protective tariffs, did almost nothing to help U.S. shippers. For a time before the Civil War, Congress subsidized the Collins line, but even that support ended in the late 1850s. Most of the government's attention was focused on the domestic market, which was constantly expanding thanks to immigration and westward expansion, but still only a small share of the world market. In international commerce, the United States was hardly more than a niche player, carrying tea, specie, small items, and travelers to and from the West Coast. The major U.S. exports, cotton and grain, were more often than not transported under the Union Jack or other European flags. Even U.S.-flagged vessels profited more from serving the international carrying trade than from working for U.S. business interests, for example, carrying tea between the China and Britain.

TABLE 5.9 U.S. SHIPPING TONNAGE AND FOREIGN TRADE, 1850–1875

Year	Shipping Tonnage	Total Value, Foreign Trade	Proportion Carried in U.S. Ships		
			Imports	Exports	Combined
1850	1,439,694	$317,885,252	77.8%	65.5%	72.0%
1851	1,544,663	$399,686,688	75.6%	69.8%	72.7%
1852	1,705,650	$374,424,629	74.5%	66.5%	70.5%
1853	1,910,471	$467,266,547	71.5%	67.1%	69.5%
1854	2,151,918	$534,847,588	71.4%	69.3%	70.5%
1855	2,348,358	$476,718,211	77.3%	73.8%	75.6%
1856	2,302,190	$591,651,733	78.1%	70.9%	75.2%
1857	2,268,196	$642,252,102	71.8%	60.2%	70.5%
1858	2,301,148	$535,349,928	72.0%	75.0%	73.7%
1859	2,321,674	$624,235,392	63.7%	69.9%	66.9%
1860	2,379,396	$687,192,176	63.0%	69.7%	66.5%
1861	2,496,894	$508,864,375	60.0%	72.1%	65.2%
1862	2,173,537	$380,027,178	44.8%	54.5%	50.0%
1863	1,926,886	$447,300,262	43.3%	40.0%	41.4%
1864	1,486,749	$475,285,271	24.6%	30.0%	27.5%
1865	1,518,350	$404,774,883	29.9%	26.1%	27.7%
1866	1,387,756	$783,671,588	25.1%	37.7%	32.2%
1867	1,515,648	$690,267,237	28.0%	39.1%	33.9%
1868	1,494,389	$639,389,339	33.0%	36.6%	35.1%
1869	1,496,220	$703,624,076	31.3%	34.9%	33.1%
1870	1,448,846	$828,730,176	33.1%	37.7%	35.6%
1871	1,363,652	$963,043,862	31.0%	32.6%	31.8%
1872	1,359,040	$1,070,772,663	26.8%	29.8%	29.1%
1873	1,378,533	$1,164,616,132	27.0%	25.7%	26.4%
1874	1,389,815	$1,153,689,382	30.2%	24.6%	27.2%
1875	1,515,598	$1,046,448,147	29.2%	23.7%	26.2%

Source: Winthrop Marvin, *The American Merchant Marine—Its History and Romance from 1620–1902* (New York: Charles Scribner's Sons, 1902), 284, 353.

The whaling business was one area in which Americans were able not just to compete with but surpass longtime European maritime nations. Whaling had been a New England specialty since colonial days, prospering because whale oil was the principal source of lighting and lubrication until the introduction of petroleum products, and because whalebone was a prime material for corsets and gewgaws. Nantucket, Rhode Island; New Bedford, Massachusetts; and New London, Connecticut, were the main home ports for the U.S. whaling industry before the Civil War. Tough New England whalers ranged over the world's oceans seeking out the great sperm and baleen whales and outdoing the fleets of all other nations between 1820 and 1859. The average annual U.S. production of whale products before the Civil War was 118,000 barrels of sperm oil, 216,000 barrels of whale oil, and 2,324,000 pounds of whalebone. Most of this production was used domestically, but a portion was exported to the West Indies, South America, and Europe. Confederate commerce raiders virtually swept U.S. whalers from the seas during the Civil War, and the industry never recovered.

The U.S. fishing industry mainly served the domestic market. The most popular commercial fish were cod, mackerel, herring, and halibut. Cod fishing was easily the major moneymaker with revenues of approximately $3 million annually. Tonnage in cod fishing peaked at 136,700 in 1860. The mackerel catch ranked second in both value and tonnage. Maine and Massachusetts were the centers of the nation's fishing industry.

TABLE 5.10 U.S. DEEP-SEA FISHING AND WHALING TONNAGE, 1850–1875

Year	Fishing Tonnage	Whaling Tonnage	Year	Fishing Tonnage	Whaling Tonnage
1850	143,758	146,017	1863	157,579	99,228
1851	138,015	181,644	1864	148,244	95,145
1852	175,205	193,798	1865	100,436	84,233
1853	159,840	193,203	1866	89,386	105,170
1854	137,235	181,901	1867	68,207	52,384
1855	124,553	186,848	1868	74,763	78,486
1856	125,703	189,461	1869	55,165	70,202
1857	132,901	195,842	1870	82,612	67,954
1858	140,490	198,594	1871	82,902	61,490
1859	147,647	185,728	1872	87,403	51,608
1860	153,619	166,841	1873	99,532	44,755
1861	182,106	145,734	1874	68,490	39,108
1862	193,459	117,714	1875	68,703	38,229

Source: Winthrop Marvin, *The American Merchant Marine—Its History and Romance from 1620–1902* (New York: Charles Scribner's Sons, 1902), 172, 317–18.

In the antebellum period American whalers out of New England spread all over the globe seeking the great whales for their oil. Whaling was hard and dangerous work, as Herman Melville described in *Moby Dick* (1851). (Library of Congress, Prints and Photographs Division [LC-USZ62-065469])

While fishing held steady as a share of the U.S. economy, the shipbuilding industry and carrying trade suffered from the twin blows of the Civil War and betting on the wrong horse. The Civil War put half the U.S. merchant fleet on the bottom of the sea and drove the rest into hiding, and the shipbuilding industry made the fatal mistake in the antebellum period of putting their money on clipper ships while the British and other maritime powers made the conversion to steam power. In 1870 steamships accounted for just 16 percent of worldwide shipping, but that percentage grew rapidly thereafter while the percentage of the world's trade carried in sailing ships steadily declined.

Other Major Industries

Cattle

Two of the most important industries of this era were mining and cattle, both dependent more on luck and the bounty of nature than on the efficiency of the nation's factories. The cattle industry was a legacy of Spanish colonialism, taken over and Americanized by cattle barons and the cowboys. By 1865 there was an estimated glut of some 4 million longhorn cattle roaming south Texas. The process of rounding up those animals, driving them to market in Kansas, and shipping them to eastern markets constituted the most uniquely American industry in history. The "beef bonanza," which arrived in the 1870s, made enormous fortunes for bankers, ranchers, railroaders, and meatpackers, but not cowboys, the working stiffs of the industry. In 1875, the cattle industry entered a new phase when U.S. beef became a prime export commodity to Europe. Although the industry involved relatively few workers or entrepreneurs, it had an enormous impact on both national culture and the economy.

Mining

The simple term *mining* covered a remarkably diverse industry that included everything dug out of the ground from coal to gold, silver, and copper, although most of the attention has focused on precious metals. It included both surface and underground mining, "jack-ass miners" and large corporations, panning and hydraulic mining. The years 1848–59 constitute the first mining era, when attention focused on the California goldfields. Before the decade was out, wealthy corporations had squeezed out the independent and underfunded prospectors. California became the training ground for all subsequent mining enterprises. With new gold and silver strikes making headlines, attention shifted to Colorado, Nevada, and finally the Dakotas. While a certain romantic mythology grew up around the gold and silver bonanzas, equally important to the economy were the coal mines of Pennsylvania, the iron mines of Minnesota, and the lead mines of Illinois. Along the way the industry made great advances in engineering, metallurgy, and chemistry in ever more sophisticated efforts to wring more profits out of the Earth. The mines of California and Nevada also played a major role in financing the Union effort in the Civil War, holding down both inflation and the need for borrowing. The late 1860s and early 1870s became a transition era as sophisticated, heavily capitalized companies took over operations, driving individuals and marginal mines out of business. While the mining industry underwrote U.S. economic expansion during the rest of the 19th century, it also exacted a terrible cost in terms of environmental damage and labor strife.

The Economy and Federal Spending

In the 19th century, the federal government was nothing like the major player in the national economy that it is today. The first year it is possible to calculate statistically the gross national product (GNP: the sum of all goods and services produced by the nation) is 1870, when it was $7.4 billion. But the wealth of anecdotal evidence coupled with the limited statistical evidence point to the same inescapable fact, that the federal budget was only an insignificant fraction of GNP, even during the profligate Civil War years. Between 1850 and 1875, the budget was less than $500 million annually.

TABLE 5.11 FEDERAL SPENDING AS A PROPORTION OF THE NATIONAL ECONOMY WITH SURPLUS, DEFICIT, AND DEBT FOR DECENNIAL YEARS, 1850–1875

Fiscal Year[a]	Federal Expenditures	Surplus (+) or Deficit (–)	Total Federal Debt
1850	$40 million	(+) $4 million	$64 million
1851	$48 million		
1852	$44 million		
1853	$48 million		
1854	$58 million		
1855	$60 million		
1856	$70 million		
1857	$68 million		
1858	$74 million		
1859	$69 million		
1860	$63 million	(–) $1 million	$65 million
1861	$67 million		
1862	$475 million		
1863	$715 million		
1864	$865 million		
1865	$1.298 billion		
1866	$521 million		
1867	$358 million		
1868	$377 million		
1869	$323 million		
1870	$310 million	(+) $10 million	$2.4 billion
1871	$292 million		
1872	$278 million		
1873	$290 million		
1874	$303 million		
1875	$275 million		

[a] The fiscal year for the federal government was Jul. 1–Jun. 30, not the conventional Jan.–Dec. calendar year.

Sources: U.S. Office of Management and Budget, annual budget reports, cited in John Mack Faragher et al., *Out of Many,* 2d ed. (Upper Saddle River, N.J.: Prentice, Hall, 1997), A-18 (appendix); B. R. Mitchell, *International Historical Statistics: The Americas and Australasia* (Detroit: Gale Research, 1983), 790–91.

Government expenditures were small at least partly because government revenues were small during these years. This was before the income tax became a fact of American life, so most of the federal revenue was derived from customs duties on imports plus various sources of "internal revenue." The latter consisted mostly of excise taxes on such items as liquor, state bank notes, and a handful of other lucrative commodities, plus sales of public lands to homesteaders and developers. Noncustoms income (or internal revenue) amounted to less than 10 percent of total revenues before the Civil War, but it became the principal source of federal monies for a few years in the late 1860s. The turnabout was largely the result of the income tax imposed by Congress on personal income during the war years, which put $2 million in the treasury in 1863 and 10 times that amount the next year. Revenues from it peaked in 1866, then declined until it was repealed in 1872.

TABLE 5.12 FEDERAL GOVERNMENT REVENUES, 1850–1875

Fiscal Year[a]	Customs Revenue	Internal Revenue[b]	Total Federal Revenues
1850	$40 million	N/A	$44 million
1851	$49 million	N/A	$53 million
1852	$47 million	N/A	$50 million
1853	$59 million	N/A	$62 million
1854	$64 million	N/A	$74 million
1855	$53 million	N/A	$65 million
1856	$64 million	N/A	$74 million
1857	$64 million	N/A	$69 million
1858	$42 million	N/A	$47 million
1859	$50 million	N/A	$53 million
1860	$53 million	N/A	$56 million
1861	$40 million	N/A	$42 million
1862	$49 million	N/A	$52 million
1863	$69 million	$38 million	$113 million
1864	$102 million	$110 million	$265 million
1865	$85 million	$209 million	$334 million
1866	$179 million	$309 million	$558 million
1867	$216 million	$266 million	$491 million
1868	$164 million	$191 million	$406 million
1869	$180 million	$158 million	$371 million
1870	$195 million	$185 million	$411 million
1871	$206 million	$143 million	$383 million
1872	$216 million	$131 million	$374 million
1873	$188 million	$114 million	$334 million
1874	$163 million	$102 million	$305 million
1875	$157 million	$110 million	$288 million

[a] The fiscal year for the federal government was Jul. 1–Jun. 30, not the conventional Jan.–Dec. calendar year.
[b] *N/A* (not available) indicates that comprehensive figures do not exist for internal revenues, specifically, the years prior to 1863.
Source: B. R. Mitchell, *International Historical Statistics: The Americas and Australasia* (Detroit: Gale Research, 1983), 809–11.

TABLE 5.13 THE FIRST FEDERAL INCOME TAX, 1862–1872

Fiscal Year[a]	Income Tax Collections
1863	$2.7 million
1864	$20 million
1865	$61 million
1866	$73 million
1867	$66 million
1868	$41 million
1869	$35 million
1870	$38 million
1871	$19 million
1872	$14 million
1873	$5.1 million

Note: This was actually the second income tax measure enacted by Congress; the first, in Aug. 1861, was never implemented. The second law was passed by Congress in Jul. 1862, but the first collections not until 1863; it was repealed in 1872, but the last collections extended into 1873.
[a] The fiscal year for the federal government was Jul. 1–Jun. 30, not the conventional Jan.–Dec. calendar year.
Source: B. R. Mitchell, *International Historical Statistics: The Americas and Australasia* (Detroit: Gale Research, 1983), 832.

Finance and Banking

During most of the 19th century, the United States barely qualified as a money economy. On the local level, most business was still conducted by the ancient system of barter and exchange—goods for goods, goods for services, services for goods. This was particularly true in rural areas, where wealth was measured in terms of land and servants/slaves, not bank balances. Cash transactions were rare as much because of an inadequate money supply as of simple poverty. Gold and silver coins had both been legal tender since 1792 (bimetallism), but a shortage of specie and the inconvenience of coinage in general prevented them from greasing the wheels of commerce. Gold and silver circulated freely but in an uneasy balancing act between their mint value and their market value, that is, the face value of the coin versus the value of the metal it contained. When the value of the gold or silver in either type of coin rose higher than the monetary value of the coin itself, people simply melted their down coins, thereby effectively driving that form of coinage out of circulation.

This was a particular problem with so-called fractional or subsidiary coins, for example, 10-cent, 25-cent, and half-dollar pieces. Congress created the problem by setting the percentage of gold or silver in each coin. When the price of gold soared in the 1830s, gold coins virtually disappeared from circulation because they were undervalued. Much of the nation's coinage in the years that followed flowed out of the country almost as soon as it was minted, leaving frustrated Americans with a nondescript assortment of wildcat bank notes and underweight foreign coins for conducting business. Major strikes out West after 1848 (e.g., at Sutter's Mill, California; Pike's Peak, Colorado; and Comstock, Nevada) alleviated the shortages of both gold and silver, but without solving the problem. The Subsidiary Coinage Act of 1853 reduced the weight of precious metal in fractional coins to ensure that their market value remained below mint value. The first "modern" U.S. fractional coin to achieve wide circulation was the three-cent piece, an odd duck that was later widely ridiculed.

In 1873 Congress attempted to legislate confidence in the money supply by "demonetizing" silver, that is, making gold the sole U.S. monetary standard, but the problem would not go away by government fiat.

Making change was always a problem in commercial transactions because of the chronic shortage of small coinage in circulation, and that was purely due to government short sightedness. Congress tried to alleviate the problem by authorizing smaller denominations, including one-, two-, and three-cent coins, but with mixed success. Merchants and government agencies alike continued to accept foreign coins as legal tender until 1857, when Congress passed a law removing them all from circulation and prohibiting their further official use. But the use of foreign coins, especially British shillings and Spanish reales, was a hard habit to break. Even after 1857, merchandise in major port cities was as likely to be marked in shillings as in cents. The most popular U.S. coins at mid-century were the silver half-dollar and the gold dollar; the least popular were the three-dollar gold piece and the 20-cent piece.

This was a transition era between large-denomination coinage and bills. A man carrying around a substantial amount of money was said to have a "pocketful of rocks" because of the sheer weight of gold and silver dollar pieces. Because generally speaking coins were worth more than bills, a wallet full of money would probably have less buying power than a pocketful of money. Most of the coinage was stamped with some version of Lady Liberty and/or an eagle, a practice reflected in their popular nicknames.

TABLE 5.14 THE MOST POPULAR U.S. NOTES AND COINS IN CIRCULATION, 1850–1875

Coin or Bill	Nickname or Distinguishing Feature	Composition	In Circulation[a]
$50 gold piece	"Quintuple eagle," five-eagle piece, or "slug"	100% gold	1851–Civil War (mostly in Calif.)
$20 gold piece	"Double eagle"	100% gold	1849–1907
$10 gold piece	"Eagle"	100% gold	1838–1907
$5 gold piece	"Half-eagle" (Liberty head)	100% gold	1839–1908
$3 gold piece	Indian princess head	100% gold	1854–89
$2.50 gold piece	"Quarter-eagle" (Liberty head)	100% gold	1840–97
$1 gold piece	Liberty/Indian head	100% gold	1849–89
Silver dollar	Liberty head and flying eagle	100% silver	1836–1921
Silver half-dollar	Liberty head	100% silver	1838–91
25¢ piece	Quarter, "two bits"; Liberty head	Silver mixture	1838–91
20¢ piece	Liberty head	Mixture	1875–78
12½¢ piece	Shilling, York shilling, a "bit," a levy, ninepence, or real	Mixture	19th century–Civil War
10¢ piece	Liberty dime	Silver mixture	1837–91
Half-dime piece	Liberty head	Silver mixture	1837–73
5¢ piece	Shield and stars (until 1883)	Nickel	1866–83
3¢ piece	Star head (six-pointed)[b]	Silver mixture initially; later made out of nickel	1851–73
2¢ piece	Shield and wreath[c]	Bronze	1864–73
1¢ piece	"Large cent" (until 1857); "small cent" (1857–1859); "Indian head penny" (1859–1909)	Copper (large cent) nickel (small cent) copper amalgam (Indian head penny)	1793–present (all 1-cent pieces) 1859–1909 (Indian head penny)
Half-cent piece	Liberty and wreath	Copper	1793–1857
3¢, 5¢, 10¢, 25¢, and 50¢ U.S. Treasury notes	Fractional currency or "shinplasters"	Paper	1860s (during Civil War)
$1 and $2 U.S. Treasury notes	"Greenbacks"	Paper, engraved with green ink.	1862–present
12½¢ coins	(Spanish) real, ninepence, elevenpence, "one bit"	Mixture	Until 1857
6¼¢ coins	(Spanish) half-real, "*medio,*" sixpence, picayune	Mixture	Until 1857

[a] The first date is the date of issuance for this particular design. The U.S. Mint issues new designs of popular coins periodically, and for a certain number of years thereafter. They continue in circulation even after no more new ones are issued. Meanwhile, old versions of the same coin also continue to circulate.
[b] The silver three-cent piece has been called "the most useless American coin ever [produced]," although it exactly paid for the cost of sending a letter in the United States after the postage rate was set at that in 1851.
[c] The first U.S. coin to bear the motto "In God We Trust."
Source: Marc McCutcheon, *The Writer's Guide to Everyday Life in the 1800s* (Cincinnati: Writer's Digest Books, 1993), 142–54.

Paper money was another problem altogether, first because it was mistrusted by the mass of Americans on general principles: It was not easily convertible in a pinch, and it tended to depreciate swiftly even in the best of times. Nonetheless, paper money did circulate in the form of interest-bearing Treasury notes and state bank issues backed only by the promise of the banks to redeem them on demand. From 1820 to 1860 the number of notes issued by state-chartered banks soared from 16.6 million to 207 million. This was a sign of a flourishing economy but also of an unregulated and inadequate money supply.

An adequate money supply was more than a matter of simple consumer inconvenience or even the occasional bank crash; it was necessary to fund the expansion of the national economy. In the early 19th century, the major projects to be financed were wars, not industrial plants or public works programs. The federal government issued millions of dollars worth of short-term, interest-bearing notes to pay for the three major wars of the 19th century through 1875, but even that proved inadequate by the time of the Civil War, so beginning in 1862, the Treasury issued non-interest-bearing notes to augment the dwindling supply of specie (gold and silver) in circulation. This was genuine paper money, quickly dubbed greenbacks because they were printed in green ink. In all, $450 million worth of greenbacks was issued in the next three years. Reluctantly accepted by Americans, they depreciated to 35 cents on the dollar in 1864 before rising back up to 75 cents on the dollar by the end of the war. Both government and the public had mixed feelings about greenbacks. Congress tried to retire them all in the 1870s and return the nation to a "hard currency." That move failed, and some $348 million worth of paper money was in circulation by 1878. Greenbacks finally recovered their full face value in 1879, an indication that they had at last earned the public's trust.

TABLE 5.15 AMOUNT OF U.S. MONEY IN CIRCULATION, 1850–1875

Year	Currency	Notes
1850	$279,000,000	$131,000,000
1851	$330,000,000	$155,000,000
1852	$361,000,000	$172,000,000
1853	$402,000,000	$188,000,000
1854	$426,000,000	$205,000,000
1855	$418,000,000	$187,000,000
1856	$426,000,000	$196,000,000
1857	$457,000,000	$215,000,000
1858	$409,000,000	$155,000,000
1859	$439,000,000[a]	$193,000,000
1860	$435,000,000[a]	$207,000,000
1861	$484,000,000[a b]	$202,000,000
1862	$606,000,000[a b]	$$257,000,000
1863	$931,000,000[a b]	$551,000,000
1864	$1,008,000,000	$626,000,000
1865	$1,084,000,000	$668,000,000
1866	$940,000,000	$634,000,000
1867	$859,000,000	$629,000,000
1868	$772,000,000	$644,000,000
1869	$741,000,000	$639,000,000
1870	$775,000,000	$658,000,000
1871	$794,000,000	$674,000,000
1872	$829,000,000	$703,000,000
1873	$838,000,000	$723,000,000
1874	$864,000,000	$731,000,000
1875	$834,000,000	$709,000,000

Note: Includes all specie *and* paper money in general circulation outside the Treasury (including banknotes and Treasury notes) at the end of the fiscal year (Jun. 30).
[a] Includes total stock of silver coins in circulation, 1860–63.
[b] Includes total stock of gold coin and bullion in circulation, 1862–63.
Source: B. R. Mitchell, *International Historical Statistics: The Americas and Australasia* (Detroit: Gale Research, 1983), 763.

TABLE 5.16 SUMMARY OF STATE BANKING OPERATIONS FOR VARIOUS YEARS, 1840–1860

Year	Number of Banks	Capital	Value of Notes in Circulation
1840	901	$358,400,000	$107,000,000
1842	692	$260,200,000	$83,700,000
1845	707	$206,000,000	$89,600,000
1848	751	$204,800,000	$128,500,000
1850	824	$217,300,000	$131,400,000
1853	750	$207,900,000	$146,100,000
1854	1,208	$301,400,000	$204,700,000
1857	1,416	$370,800,000	$214,800,000
1860	1,562	$421,900,000	$207,100,000

Note: State banking shrank greatly after 1860 as the federal government centralized control and squeezed the profitability of their operations.
Source: Francis G. Walett, *Economic History of the United States,* 2d ed. (New York: Barnes & Noble, 1963), 105.

TABLE 5.17 U.S. SAVINGS BANK DEPOSITS, 1850–1875

Year	Savings	Year	Savings
1850	$43,000,000	1863	$206,000,000
1851	$51,000,000	1864	$236,000,000
1852	$60,000,000	1865	$243,000,000
1853	$72,000,000	1866	$283,000,000
1854	$78,000,000	1867	$337,000,000
1855	$84,000,000	1868	$393,000,000
1856	$96,000,000	1869	$458,000,000
1857	$99,000,000	1870	$550,000,000
1858	$108,000,000	1871	$651,000,000
1859	$129,000,000	1872	$735,000,000
1860	$149,000,000	1873	$802,000,000
1861	$147,000,000	1874	$865,000,000
1862	$169,000,000	1875	$924,000,000

Source: B. R. Mitchell, *International Historical Statistics: The Americas and Australasia* (Detroit: Gale Research, 1983), 783.

While the banks were spectators of most of the currency debate, they were not inconsequential. Banking in the first half of the 19th century was local, small-scale, and unregulated. The enormous fight over whether or not to have a national bank (the First and Second Banks of the United States) reflected the widespread fear of a centralized banking system. Banking was generally considered a state prerogative and was jealously guarded by state legislatures. It was a system that encouraged easy credit policies and loose operations whereby banks engaged in speculation and made unwise loans. The results were frequent bank failures and even occasional panics (the 19th-century name for financial crises).

Americans had little faith in banks, but they did have enormous faith in the old-fashioned Puritan value of saving. That plus the relative lack of consumer goods made them a remarkably thrifty people in the 19th century. Private savings climbed spectacularly even after adjustment to account for the booming population growth. In the 25 years between 1850 and 1875, personal savings grew by more than 2000 percent while population grew by little more than 100 percent. Even the Civil War with its inflated prices and wartime scarcities hardly dampened the thrifty ways of Americans, and after 1865 the pace of savings actually picked up during the dark days of Reconstruction. Although much of this massive savings was the work of nouveau riche tycoons, it was nonetheless an impressive accomplishment that helped fuel the dramatic economic expansion in these same years.

U.S. economic expansion was so great it even overwhelmed the domestic money market. The United States was forced to look to Europe for investment capital starting in the 1850s, and some $190 million poured into the country from European sources during the decade. A high rate of return, a bright economic future, and a stable political system all had investors across the Atlantic eager to underwrite everything from cattle ranches to railroad projects. But the major recipients of European largesse were federal, state, and municipal governments, who found eager buyers for their bonds on the eastern side of the Atlantic—at least until the financial panic of 1873.

Financial panics were an intrinsic part of the hurly-burly U.S. economy. Two major depressions hit the nation during these 25 years, each preceded by a financial crisis recorded in history as "Black Friday." The first depression lasted from 1857 to 1858 and the second from 1873 to 1878. The 1857 Panic began when a branch of the Ohio Life Insurance and Trust Company failed as a result of questionable investments, sparking a wave of panic selling in the stock market, which rippled through the nation. It coincided with an agricultural recession and a speculative "bust" in railroads and real estate. In the next 18 months, some 7,200 business houses failed with total losses estimated at $111 million. It was the worst financial loss suffered by any Western nation in history up to this time.

The Panic of 1873 was sparked by the failure of Jay Cooke and Company, who had invested heavily in the nation's railroads. Their

During the Panic of 1857, many banks went under while others temporarily suspended specie payments. This suspension caused runs on the banks in many major cities, such as New York, shown here. A group of angry depositors mill around outside the Seaman's Savings Bank, waiting to withdraw their money, 1857. (Library of Congress, Prints and Photographs Division [LC- US262-5358])

collapse dragged down some 5,000 other business firms with them before the end of the year. By the time the depression had run its course, some 100 banks and 18,000 businesses had gone under.

Civil War Finances

Despite their common financial background, North and South paid for the Civil War quite differently. Both sides had to be quite creative in financing the most expensive conflict in history to that date, but they followed different paths out of necessity. The difference was credit; the government in Washington, D.C., had it in abundance, whereas the government in Richmond never had it and made matters worse through a series of bad decisions. The North was able to finance the war through a judicious assortment of measures, including borrowing, taxation, and printing of money. The South, on the other hand, was forced to begin to print money early in the war and continued that suicidal practice until Southerners were buried under piles of useless Confederate currency.

TABLE 5.18 DIFFERENT SOURCES OF INCOME AS A PERCENTAGE OF NORTHERN AND SOUTHERN FINANCING DURING THE CIVIL WAR

Income Source	South	North
Fees and revenues[a]	5%	4%
Foreign loans[b]	30%	62%
Paper (money)[c]	60%	13%
Taxes[d]	5%	21%
TOTAL	100%	100%

Note: These calculations refer strictly to the central governments (Richmond and Washington, D.C.), not to the financial arrangements of the several states. All percentages are rough approximations because no exact figures are available for either side.

[a] Includes import duties, port fees, licenses, and the like.

[b] Includes only loans from the British and French.

[c] Includes only issues by the two central governments, not the states or private banks.

[d] Includes excise taxes and the federal-government-imposed income tax on net income in excess of $600 a year after 1862.

Source: Albert A. Nofi, "Profile: [Civil War] Money and Inflation," *North & South Magazine* 3, no. 2 (January 2000): 15.

TABLE 5.19 THE VALUE OF THE U.S. DOLLAR, 1860–1875

Year	Value	Year	Value
1860	$100	1868	$156
1861	$100	1869	$148
1862	$100	1870	$148
1863	$111	1871	$141
1864	$137	1872	$133
1865	$174	1873	$133
1866	$170	1874	$133
1867	$163	1875	$126

Note: 1860 is used as the baseline.
Source: Scott Derks, ed., *The Value of a Dollar, Prices and Incomes in the United States, 1860–1999,* 2d ed. (Lakeville, Conn.: Grey House, 1999), 2.

TABLE 5.20 APPROXIMATE VALUE OF CONFEDERATE CURRENCY COMPARED TO $100 IN GOLD, 1862–1865

Date	Confederate Currency Equivalent to $100 in Gold
Jan. 1, 1862	$120
Dec. 20, 1862	$300
Dec. 20, 1863	$1,700
Jan. 1, 1864	$1,800
Dec. 20, 1864	$2,800
Jan. 1, 1865	$3,400
Feb. 1, 1865	$5,000
Mar. 1, 1865	$4,700
Apr. 10,1865	$5,500

Source: Philip Katcher, *The American Civil War Source Book* (London: Arms and Armour, 1992), 303.

Inflation

Inflation was not a problem before the Civil War. In fact, the depression caused by the Panic of 1857 was still lingering as the new decade opened. But unlike the dramatic events of a panic, inflation is a silent thief that steals the value of the dollar little by little, year by year, only occasionally taking a large bite out of the pocketbook. Inflation is measured by the consumer price index, a theoretical construct used by economists to calculate the value of the dollar at different times in history. It is a relative measurement that is derived by establishing a base year (100) for a standard basket of goods, then following the rise and fall of that basket's value over several years. Using 1860 as the base year, a basket of goods that cost $100 in 1860 cost only $92 in 1851, $105 in 1857 thanks to inflation, then back down to $100 in 1859.

Americans experienced runaway inflation for the first time during the Civil War. The wartime shortages of even the most mundane commodities coupled with the breakdown of the normal market mechanisms resulted in shortages and higher prices. Between 1861 and 1865 inflation affected both sides but the South much more severely because they financed approximately 60 percent of wartime expenditures by the simple expedient of printing money. By the end of the war, it has been estimated, $1 billion in paper money was in circulation in the South. That included 582 different types of notes issued by the Confederate government, state governments, and various banks. After two years of war, $100 in Confederate currency had lost $95.40 of its value, and conditions worsened thereafter. Before the end of the war, inflation reduced the value of 100 Confederate dollars to $1.76, an inflation rate greater than 9,000 percent. The Confederate first lady, Varina Howell Davis, kept a record of the depreciation of Southern currency, which parallels the decline and fall of the Confederacy.

A weekly grocery list for a typical middle-class family living in the Confederate capital was published in the *Richmond Dispatch* on January 29, 1863, showing the effect of inflation after two years of war. The newspaper compared the prices for a group of standard items in 1860 with the prices for those same items in 1863. Not included in the equation was the fact that some of these items were rarely available by 1863 except on the black market or at such an exorbitant cost that they were almost unaffordable.

Meanwhile, in the North the strength of the economy protected the U.S. dollar against the most severe inflation. Not only was inflation kept well below 100 percent, but the dollar *increased* slightly in value between 1860 and 1865. After the war ended, postwar demobilization naturally took its toll, and reunification of the thriving Northern economy with the crippled Southern economy also dragged down the dollar. Prices rose rapidly after 1865, and the value of the dollar went into a long-term decline that did not reverse itself until the 20th century.

TABLE 5.21 THE WEEKLY GROCERY BILL FOR A RICHMOND FAMILY, 1860 VERSUS 1863

Item	Amount Per Week	Unit Cost 1860	Unit Cost 1863	Total Cost 1860	Total Cost 1863
Bacon	10lbs.	12½¢/lb.	$1.00/lb.	$1.25	$10.00
Flour	30 lbs.	5¢/lb.	12½¢/lb.	$1.50	$3.75
Sugar	5 lbs.	8¢/lb.	$1.15/lb.	$0.40	$5.75
Coffee	4 lbs.	12½¢/lb.	$5.00/lb.	$0.50	$20.00
Tea (green)	½ lbs.	$1.00/lb.	$16.00/lb.	$0.50	$8.00
Lard	4 lbs.	12½¢/lb.	$1.00/lb.	$0.50	$4.00
Butter	3 lbs.	25¢/lb.	$1.75/lb.	$0.75	$5.25
Meal	1 peck	25¢/lb.	$1.00/lb.	$0.25	$1.00
Candles	2 lbs.	15¢/lb.	$1.25/lb.	$0.30	$2.50
Soap	5 lbs.	10¢/lb.	$1.10/lb.	$0.50	$5.50
Pepper and salt	Unknown	Unknown	Unknown	$0.10 (approximate)	$2.50 (approximate)

Sources: John B. Jones, *A Rebel War Clerk's Diary at the Confederate States Capital* (Philadelphia: J. B. Lippincott, 1866), vols. 1 and 2, passim, summarized in Henry Steele Commager, ed., *The Civil War Archive: The History of the Civil War in Documents,* rev. ed. by Erik Bruun (New York: Black Dog & Leventhal, 2000), 501.

Workers and Jobs

Jobs and employment statistics are difficult to calculate for the 19th century because many jobs were undefined and statistical gathering was still a very inexact science. Once every decade the U.S. government gathered statistics as part of the census, but the breakdown of occupations was rudimentary, and the job categories were determined by untrained census takers. The best figures for the era are collected from enlistment records for Union and Confederate soldiers during the Civil War. The value of those figures derives from the sheer numbers of men (no women) sampled in the records. There are also some controls present because the statistics gathering was done by the U.S. War Department, the U.S. Census Bureau, and the U.S. Sanitary Commission. The resulting figures can also be tallied against numbers assembled by the pre-eminent historian of the common soldier, Bell A. Wiley, from a lifetime of researching soldiers' accounts, published as *The Life of Johnny Reb* (1943) and *The Life of Billy Yank* (1952). The figures show a remarkable consistency across the board. Unfortunately, they are not equally useful for Northern and Southern men because the Confederate government and its various constituent bureaucracies were much less conscientious about statistics gathering than their opposite numbers.

That said, however, several points are apparent: The Southern workforce had far more agricultural workers than the Northern, fewer skilled and unskilled workers, but comparable numbers of white-collar and professional workers. The statistics also show that the total number of workers in the South, both men and women, increased steadily throughout the century while the percentage of workers engaged in agriculture declined steadily.

The forgotten member of the U.S. workforce was not the factory worker or even the black slave but the woman. The historian Jane Pitt speaks of "gender invisibility" in describing the way women's significant achievements in business and the professions have traditionally been treated. In 1850 women made up an insignificant proportion of the nation's paid labor force, most of them employed in agriculture or as domestic servants. (No statistics are available on "the world's oldest profession," prostitution.) Working women were shunned by their upper-class sisters as less than ladies, and by men as threatening the sanctity of the "two spheres."

Black laborers on a Mississippi steamboat are shown in this lithograph from *Harper's Weekly,* September 2, 1871. (Courtesy of Mississippi Department of Archives and History)

TABLE 5.22 PREVIOUS OCCUPATIONS OF UNION AND CONFEDERATE SOLDIERS DERIVED FROM U.S. CENSUS RECORDS AND OTHER SOURCES

Occupational Categories	From U.S. Sanitary Commission Sample	From Bell Wiley Sample[a]	From 1860 Census Records
Farmers and farm laborers	47.5%	47.8%	42.9%
Skilled laborers	25.1%	25.2%	24.9%
Unskilled laborers	15.9%	15.1%	16.7%
White-collar and commercial laborers	5.1%	7.8%	10.0%
Professional	3.2%	2.9%	3.5%
Miscellaneous and unknown	3.2%	1.2%	2.0%

[a] The respected Civil War historian Bell A. Wiley, author of *The Life of Johnny Reb: The Common Soldier of the Confederacy* (1943) and *The Life of Billy Yank: The Common Soldier of the Union* (1952), definitive studies of the common soldier during the Civil War based on a wealth of primary sources.
Source: James M. McPherson, *Ordeal by Fire: The Civil War and Reconstruction* (New York: Alfred A. Knopf, 1982), 359.

TABLE 5.23 PREVIOUS OCCUPATIONS OF CONFEDERATE SOLDIERS DERIVED FROM SELECTED STATE RECORDS AND THE U.S. CENSUS

Occupational Categories	From State Records	From 1860 Census Records
Planters, farmers, and farm laborers	61.5%	57.5%
Skilled laborers	14.1%	15.7%
Unskilled laborers	8.5%	12.7%
White-collar and commercial laborers	7.0%	8.3%
Professional	5.2%	5.0%
Miscellaneous and unknown	3.7%	0.8%

Note: State records utilized include those of Ala., Ark., Ga., La., Miss., N.C., and Va.
Source: James M. McPherson, *Ordeal by Fire: The Civil War and Reconstruction* (New York: Alfred A. Knopf, 1982), 359.

The rise of manufacturing opened more jobs to women, but this concession to equal opportunity was a mixed blessing at best as many were now forced to go out of the home to work to help support the family. And only the lowest-paying and most exploitive jobs were open to them. Young girls were favored over mature women for such jobs as mill workers in New England factory towns or seamstresses doing piecework out of their home in New York City. In 1860 there were 25,000 girls and women employed in manufacturing in New York City, two-thirds of them in the clothing trades. The job situation changed, not to say improved, in the 1870s, when teaching and office work began to be regarded as suitable employment for "nice girls."

The workday at a typical New England factory in 1868 began when a bell sounded. Then workers of both sexes and all ages filed in carrying their lunch pails. (Library of Congress, Prints and Photograph Division [LC- USZ62- 5292])

The first time women were counted as a separate group in the workforce by the Census Bureau was 1850. Up until then their work was not considered "gainful employment." The new technology introduced after mid-century in the form of sewing machines, typewriters, and telephones opened up new job opportunities but also helped hasten the end to the "age of innocence."

A survey of the U.S. workforce in these years shows an overwhelming preponderance of men, the contribution of slaves before 1865, and the shrinking agricultural sector. One more characteristic of the U.S. workforce is clear: its work ethic. The dominant attitude among free labor regardless of race was "Work hard or go under!" This was the popular expression of the classic Protestant work ethic, or "go-getter spirit" as contemporaries called it, that was a wonder to the rest of the world. This attitude was common among wage earners, middle-class professionals, and tycoons alike; among immigrants and native-born; and among whites and blacks. Americans noticed it, and so did foreign visitors to the shores. In 1869, Wendell Phillips described U.S. industrial workers in terms that applied equally to the rest of the nation's workforce as a class "that only rises to toil and lies down to rest." The only significant group among whom this attitude was missing were slaves, for reasons that are obvious.

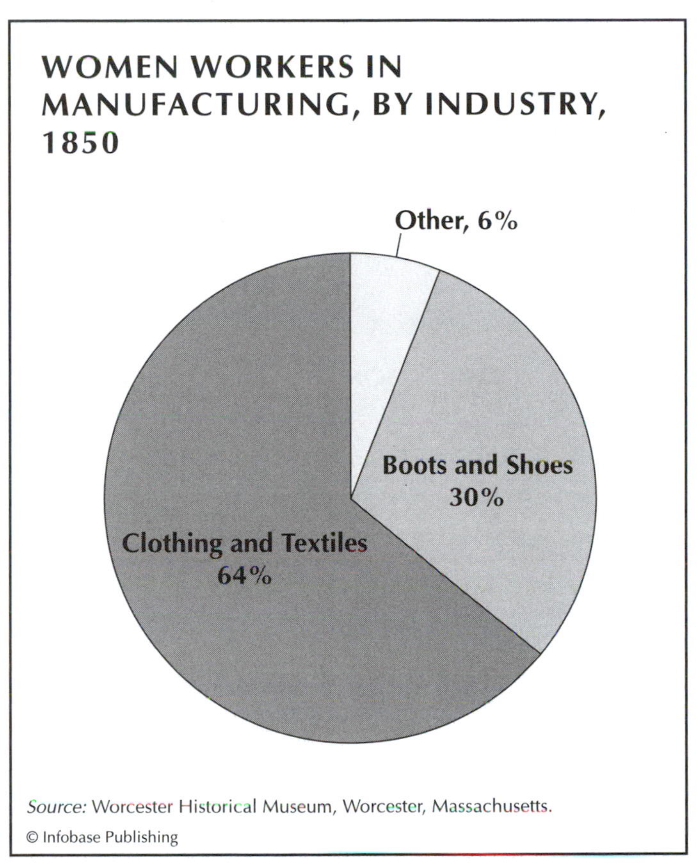

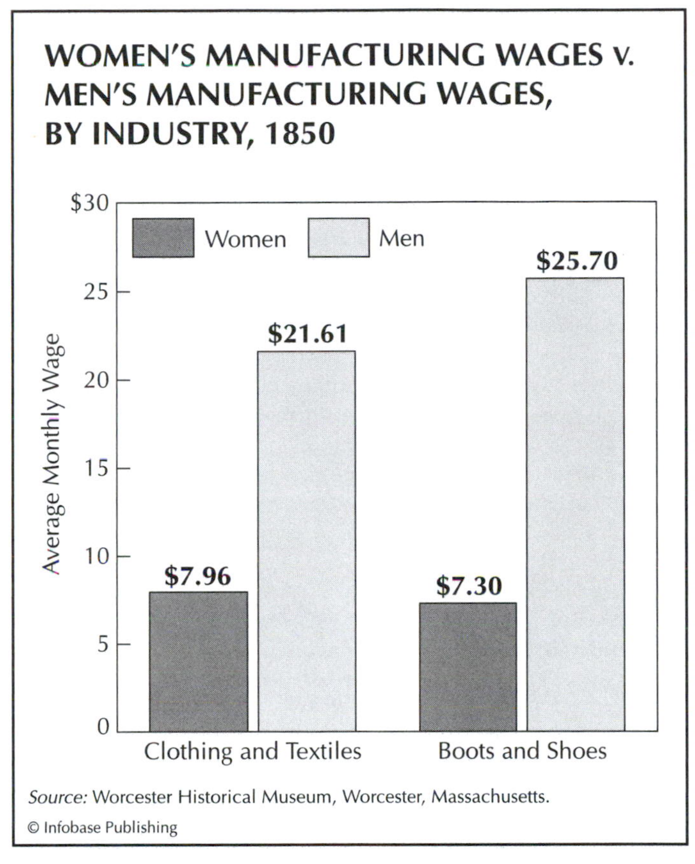

TABLE 5.24 THE AMERICAN WORKFORCE, 1840–1880

Year	Total Number of Workers	Farmers as Percentage of Total	Women as Percentage of Total
1840	5,660,000	75%	N/A
1850	N/A	N/A	13%
1860	11,110,000	53%	13+%
1870	12,506,000	53%	15%
1880	17,392,000	52%	15%

Note: N/A, information not available.
Source: John Mack Faragher et al., *Out of Many: A History of the American People,* 2d ed. (Upper Saddle River, N.J.: Prentice-Hall, 1997), A-17.

TABLE 5.25 AMERICAN MALE WORKERS, THEIR NUMBERS AND OCCUPATIONS, 1850–1875

Year	Agriculture		Manufacturing		Commerce[a]		Total		Persons of Working Age	Ratio of Workers to Total Adult Male Population
	Free Adult Males	All Adult Males	Free Adult Males	All Adult Males	Free Adult Males	All Adult Males	Free Adult Males	All Adult Males		
1850	2,401,000	3,329,000	958,000	958,000	2,013,000	2,950,000	5,372,000	7,237,000	12,596,000	57.4%
1860	3,220,000	4,342,000	1,311,000	1,311,000	3,756,000	4,878,000	8,287,000	10,531,000	17,301,000	60.7%
1870	5,923,000	5,923,000	2,054,000	2,054,000	3,756,000	4,529,000	12,506,000	12,506,000	21,561,000	58.2%

Note: Actual census figures show only free adult males. Demographic analysis that assumes 50 percent of the adult male *black* population were in the workforce provides the second column.
[a] Commerce category cover all things not included in Agriculture and Manufacturing.
Source: Michael G. Mulhall, *The Dictionary of Statistics,* 4th ed. rev. (London: George Routledge and Sons, Ltd., 1899), 432.

In 1855 some 77 percent of the working population still earned their living from the land: farming, ranching, or herding. (Separating ranching and herding from farming produces a much lower percentage.) Life for most people continued to be rural and agrarian, as it had been for their parents and grandparents. A statistical breakdown of occupations from the 1850 census shows agriculture (farming) as by far the leading occupation.

African Americans, as a class of workers, were confined to agricultural work or menial service jobs. This was true of both slaves and free blacks. The numbers of black educators, professionals, and entrepreneurs was too small to count. The situation was somewhat better in the North than in the South, in urban areas than in rural areas. A small number of slaves in the antebellum period were permitted by their master to find their own work in cities and towns (e.g., Richmond, and Baltimore). Such slaves generally remitted two-thirds to three-quarters of their wages to the master and paid their own living expenses. This practice, known as hiring their own time, allowed some slaves to save enough to purchase freedom for themselves and even their family after long years of indentured toil. In South Carolina, a slave allowed to contract his labor independently could over several years earn enough to purchase his wife and child for $700 to $800. Illustrative of blacks' place in the workforce are lists of racially approved jobs on a Southern plantation and in New York City from the mid-1850s compiled from the New York State Census of 1855.

TABLE 5.26 OCCUPATIONAL DISTRIBUTION OF WORKERS AS A PERCENTAGE OF FREE MALE POPULATION, 1850

Occupation[a]	Number of Workers as a Percentage of Total
Agriculture	45.2%
Commerce/banking	5.9%
Professional	2.5%
Manufacturer/artisan	22.1%
Mariner/fisherman	2.2%
Servant/semiskilled worker	3.7%
Laborer (nonagricultural)	16.9%
Government service	0.5%
Miscellaneous	0.9%
TOTAL	**99.9%**

[a] The categories here, as derived from Census data, are very imprecise, making it difficult to distinguish between, for instance, industrial workers and artisans, skilled and semiskilled workers, and men employed in more than one occupation. Therefore the data are best used as a general guide to the *distribution* of occupations, not to the absolute numbers in each.
Source: Compiled from U.S. Census reports (1850) by William B. Skelton, *An American Profession of Arms* (Lawrence: University Press of Kansas, 1992), 160.

TABLE 5.27 COMPARISON OF WORK PERFORMED BY FREE BLACKS IN THE NORTH (NEW YORK CITY) VERSUS SLAVES ON A LARGE SOUTHERN PLANTATION, 1854–1855

New York State, 1855[a]	Large Southern Plantation, 1854[b]
1,025 domestic servants	22 hoe hands (field workers)
536 laborers	5 masons (brick and stone masons)
499 waiters	5 spinning girls
366 laundresses	4 housemaids (cleaning girls)
176 porters	4 plowmen
151 cooks	4 drovers
129 whitewashes	2 parlor maids (serving girls)
111 dressmakers or seamstresses	2 wagon drivers
102 drivers, coachmen, or hackmen	2 stable hands
78 barbers	2 carpenters
56 stewards	2 smiths (blacksmiths)
55 cartmen, draymen, or teamsters	2 shoemakers
19 butchers	1 butler
19 tailors	1 cook
18 clerks	1 nursemaid
17 boatmen	1 washerwoman
16 longshoremen	1 seamstress
15 chimney sweeps	1 gardener
15 musicians	1 coachman
14 hotel keepers or boardinghouse keepers	1 cowman
13 boot makers or shoemakers	1 pigman
13 nurses	1 miller
13 teachers	1 weaving girl
12 clergymen	. . .
12 carpenters	. . .
11 peddlers or traders	. . .
10 sawyers	. . .

[a] Occupations of 3,501 free blacks.
[b] Job description of 67 slaves. Normally, when slaves finished their regular tasks, they helped with others; for instance, the parlor maids and housemaids might help in the kitchen or the laundry. However, indoor and outdoor servants rarely mixed together or did each other's work.
Sources: Compiled from the New York State Census of 1855 by Marc McCutcheon, *The Writer's Guide to Everyday Life in the 1800s* (Cincinnati: Writer's Digest Books, 1993), 217–18.

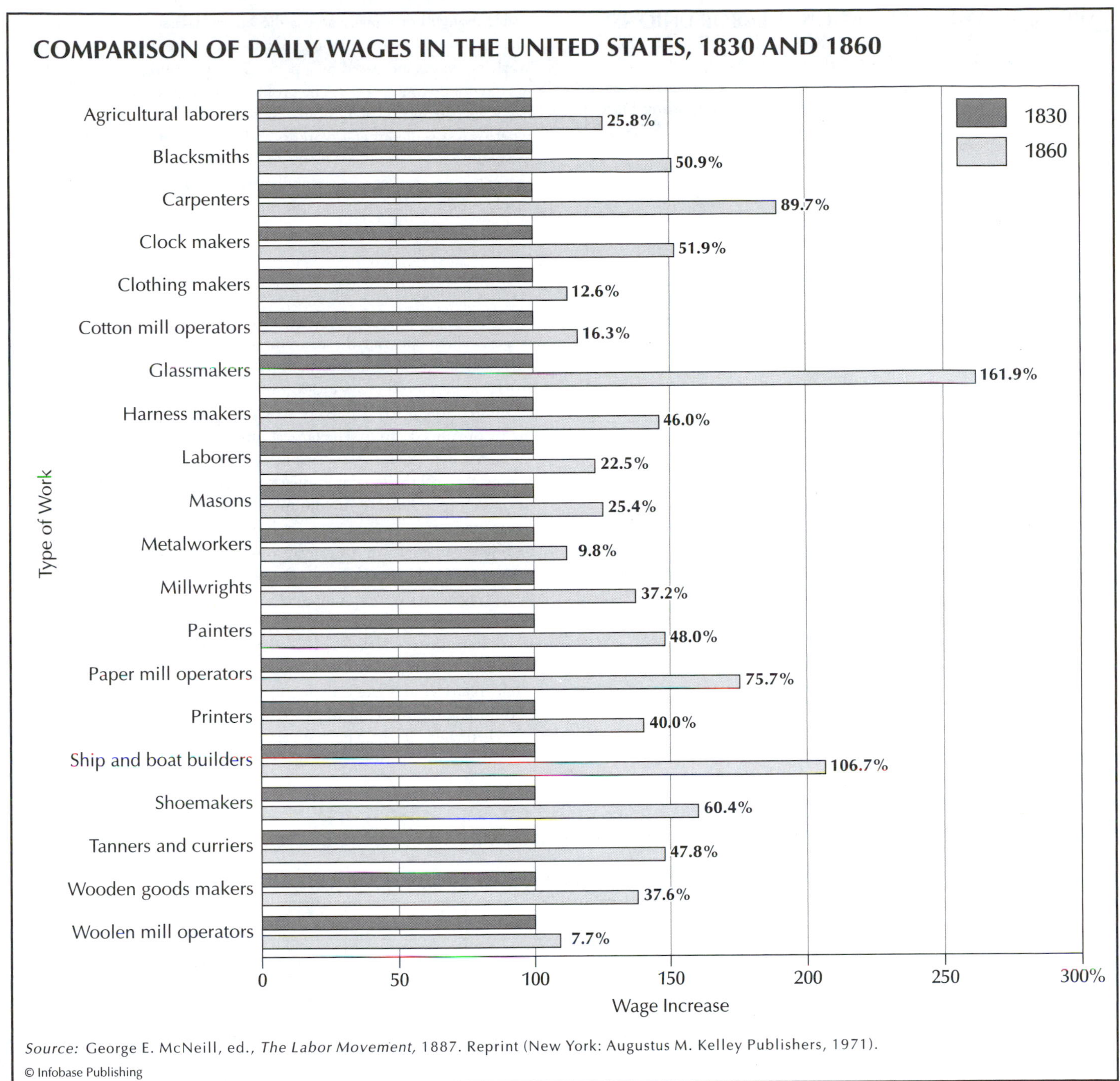

Source: George E. McNeill, ed., *The Labor Movement,* 1887. Reprint (New York: Augustus M. Kelley Publishers, 1971).

Organized Labor

Industrialization introduced a new culture of labor, which depersonalized the relationship between employer and employees and ultimately made daily wages the principal livelihood of a majority of the U.S. workforce. The introduction of the factory system started in the early 1800s and accelerated rapidly after mid-century. The cooperative environment of the small workshop or family-run business of former days was replaced by the impersonal wage system with emphasis on the bottom line. The worker's growing sense of isolation from the employer and the antagonistic work environment produced a nascent union movement during this era.

The earliest unions were local, covering only workers in a single trade (e.g., shoemaking) and a single community, and they usually adopted the fraternal forms of the Masonic order, which was a successful organization with which most men were already familiar. These early associations were craft unions, composed exclusively of skilled workers who enjoyed some bargaining leverage. Skilled workers maintained a stranglehold on the movement until well into the 20th century. As unionization spread, city federations were the next logical step in the organization process. The first *permanent,* nationwide association of workers was the National Typographical Union, established in 1852. And when the typographers organized in Canada that same year, the labor movement entered a new, international phase. By the 1870s the most thoroughly unionized industry in the United States was the railroad industry.

Although no more than 1 percent of all U.S. workers were unionized around this time, wages for all workers climbed between 1830 and

TABLE 5.28 THE FIRST NATIONAL LABOR UNIONS OF SKILLED WORKERS IN THE UNITED STATES, 1852–1873

Workers' Group	Founding Date
National Typographical Union[a]	1852
Hat Finishers	1854
Journeyman Stone Cutters Association	1855
United Cigarmakers[b]	1856
United Hatters	1856
Iron Moulders Union of North America[c]	1859
Machinists and Blacksmiths[d]	1863
Locomotive Engineers	1863
National Labor Union[e]	1866
Order of the Knights of Saint Crispin (shoemakers)[f]	1867
Railway Conductors	1868
Workingmen's Benevolent Association (of anthracite coal miners)	1868
Railway Firemen	1873

[a] Still in existence today.
[b] The union in which Samuel Gompers, father of the American Federation of Labor (AFL), got his start.
[c] The union had 300,000 international members by the late 1860s.
[d] Historically a blacksmith was not the same as a farrier; the latter made a living shoeing horses, the former was anyone who worked iron using anvil, hammer, and forge.
[e] An "umbrella organization" of several independent unions started by William H. Sylvus of Pennsylvania. It was committed more to humanitarian reforms than to simple "bread-and-butter" issues. The National Labor Union (NLU) grew to some 640,000 members by 1868 before the death of Sylvanus and its subsequent rapid decline.
[f] The union had 50,000 nationally by 1870.
Source: Thomas C. Cochran and Wayne Andrews, eds., *Concise Dictionary of American History* (New York: Charles Scribner's Sons, 1962), 524.

1860, though not equally across the board. Glassmakers, for instance, saw their wages increase by more than 150 percent, while woolen mill workers' wages increased by a paltry 7.70 percent. Agricultural laborers did not do much better. The problem, then as always, was that workers who had the most desirable skills received the largest increases, whereas less skilled metal workers and mill operators saw much less of the bounty being produced by the U.S. economy. A related problem was that the labor market was generally "soft" during the antebellum years, thanks to the influx of European immigrants who had industrial skills and were willing to work for minimal wages. In 1860, most skilled laborers worked 60 hours or more per week for less than $2 per day. In the next 15 years, the wage rate rose appreciably for all but farm laborers, but the hours per week remained the same.

The Civil War created labor shortages and pressures for higher wages, which spurred the movement toward unionization. By 1865 there were 1,500 local and national unions, and by 1870 unionized workers numbered at least 300,000, more than ever before. Miners accounted for nearly a third of that total; shoemakers were the most highly organized group. The largest union of the period was the Workingmen's Benevolent Association, organized in 1868 by John Siney among the anthracite coal miners of eastern Pennsylvania. In the face of open "union busting" by the mine owners, it did not last long. Sad to say, the mine owners were only reflecting the prevailing attitude among the majority of Americans toward labor organization.

In these early years the union movement displayed a strong idealist bent. Organizers were not interested only in improving working conditions: They wanted to reform the entire labor system and even the political system that underlay it. This very idealism sometimes made them unwilling to compromise and prone to revolutionary rhetoric. Meanwhile, management was claiming that they were protecting not just the bottom line but the U.S. way of life. Confrontation was inevitable and quickly turned violent. The first recorded strike fatalities in U.S. history were the deaths of two New York City tailors killed in 1850 by police

TABLE 5.29 WORKING PEOPLE'S WAGES AND HOURS FOR SOME COMMON JOBS, 1860–1874

Job Type	Wages per Day (average hours per week)							
	1860	1862	1864	1866	1868	1870	1872	1874
Bricklayer[a]	$1.53 (60)	$1.79 (60)	$2.31 (60)	$2.95 (60)	$3.76 (60)	$3.97 (60)	$3.86 (60)	$3.50 (60)
Carpenters and joiners,[b]	$1.65 (61)	$1.48 (60)	$2.05 (60)	$2.63 (61)	$3.05 (60)	$2.77 (60)	$2.73 (60)	$2.89 (60)
Engineers (stationary)[c]	$1.63 (68)	$1.77 (70)	$2.04 (73)	$2.43 (70)	$2.66 (70)	$2.97 (66)	$2.62 (65)	$2.94 (67)
Farm laborers (hired)[d]	$0.88 (66)	$1.00 (66)	$ 1.50 (66)	$1.50 (66)	$1.50 (66)	$1.50 (66)	$1.50 (66)	$1.25 (66)
Firemen[e]	$1.33 (70)	$1.41 (66)	$1.25 (72)	$1.58 (66)	$1.64 (66)	$1.73 (66)	$1.61 (66)	$1.72 (66)
Glassblowers (bottles)[f]	$2.59 (N/A)[g]	$2.95 (N/A)	$2.95 (N/A)	$3.95 (N/A)	$5.19 (N/A)	$5.19 (N/A)	$5.19 (N/A)	$4.96 (N/A)
Hod carriers[h]	$1.00 (56)	$1.18 (63)	$1.43 (63)	$1.74 (60)	$2.00 (60)	$2.12 (60)	$1.98 (60)	$1.95 (60)
Marble cutters[i]	$2.04 (60)	$1.58 (60)	$2.52 (60)	$2.94 (60)	$3.46 (60)	$3.19 (60)	$3.27 (60)	$3.19 (60)
Painters[j]	$1.97 (60)	$1.98 (60)	$2.93 (60)	$3.35 (60)	$3.43 (60)	$3.15 (60)	$3.12 (60)	$3.02 (60)
Plasterers[k]	$1.69 (60)	$1.67 (60)	$1.93 (60)	$2.60 (60)	$3.67 (60)	$2.86 (60)	$2.86 (60)	$2.86 (60)
Plumbers[l]	$1.88 (60)	$1.93 (60)	$3.50 (60)	$3.50 (60)	$3.85 (60)	$3.37 (57)	$3.22 (57)	$3.11 (57)
Stonemasons[m]	$2.50 (60)	$2.05 (60)	$2.35 (60)	$2.73 (60)	$2.72 (60)	$3.41 (60)	$3.38 (60)	$2.95 (60)

Note: Using the base line of 1860 for the dollar's value in these years. Unfortunately, the data are limited because only a handful of states, all of them in the Northeast, kept the records that allow modern economists to calculate contemporary incomes. The source of the data for each job type is indicated in notes [a] through [m].
[a] Mass.
[b] Conn.
[c] N.Y.
[d] N.Y.
[e] Mass.
[f] N.J.
[g] N/A: figures are not available.
[h] Mass.
[i] N.Y.
[j] N.Y.
[k] Pa.
[l] N.Y.
[m] N.Y.
Source: Scott Derks, ed., *The Value of a Dollar: Prices and Incomes in the United States 1860–1999*, 2d ed. (Lakeville, Conn.: Grey House, 1999), 11–13.

dispersing a street demonstration. The first mass strike occurred in February and March 1860 when 20,000 workers in the Massachusetts shoe industry stopped working to protest the introduction of labor-saving machinery. The strike was broken after six weeks.

The most important issue after the Civil War was the eight-hour workday at a time when most worker were laboring 10- or even 12-hour days. Progress occurred in increments. In 1868 Congress enacted an eight-hour day for laborers and mechanics on federal projects. This was followed by unsuccessful strikes for the eight-hour day among Pennsylvania coal miners in 1870. New York construction workers organized a huge, peaceful parade through Manhattan on June 10, 1872, that drew attention but no reduction in the workday. The best estimate is that no more than 100,000 workers had the eight-hour day by 1872. For the rest, the battle went on.

When this period ended, the union movement in the United States was in full retreat in every industry. Ownership was adamantly hostile to labor organization of any kind, and the country was on the threshold of the bloodiest era in labor history of any industrialized nation.

Big Business

The years 1850–75 represented the dawn of big business in the United States. Large-scale business was not new, but the rapid consolidation and combination of American business, the staggering accumulation of wealth, and the unbridled exercise of political clout on all levels of government were. This era witnessed the growth of trusts and other forms of monopoly that ultimately reshaped Western civilization. Some industries were more susceptible to the process of combination and consolidation than others. The transformation of business into big business began in the railroad and communication industries even before the Civil War. In 1851, Western Union Company was formed out of several small telegraph firms, and in 1853, the New York Central Railroad was created out of 10 smaller lines. The pace picked up after the Civil War. In 1869 John D. Rockefeller gobbled up several smaller oil companies to create Standard Oil of Ohio, thereby inaugurating the age of trusts. Alone among Western nations, the United States saw the rise of big business before the rise of big government.

At the forefront of the age of trusts were a group of men who have been variously described by historians as either captains of industry (by admirers) or robber barons (by critics). Early members of this fabled group were John D. Rockefeller and Jay Cooke. They represented a new breed in the United States: the tycoons of finance and industry who transformed the national economy with their ruthless methods, at the same time accumulating immense personal fortunes. They formed an exclusive fraternity of multimillionaires whose membership grew along with the class of nouveau riche as the years passed.

On a list of the 50 richest tycoons in U.S. history, more men got their start during the 25 years than in any other similar period. The ranks of U.S. millionaires already stood at 40 in 1840, and it reached 100 in the next 40 years. These men lived a life of conspicuous consumption and exercised inordinate influence over the political system, whether trying to corner the gold market or build the first transcontinental railroad.

TABLE 5.30 LEADING TYCOONS OF THE MID-19TH CENTURY, HOW THEY MADE THEIR MARK, AND HOW MUCH THEY WERE ULTIMATELY WORTH

Name	Life Dates	Industry or Business	First Went into Business for Himself	Net Worth at Time of Death[a]
John D. Rockefeller	1839–1937	Oil	1858	$1.4 billion
Andrew Carnegie	1835–1919	Steel	1865	$475 million
Cornelius Vanderbilt	1794–1877	Shipping, railroads	1829	$105 million
A. T. Stewart	1803–76	Retail, wholesale, and real estate	1823	$50 million
Frederick Weyerhaeuser	1834–1914	Lumber	Panic of 1857	$200 million
Jay Gould	1836–92	Investments, railroads	1857	$77 million
Marshall Field	1834–1906	Department stores	1881	$140 million
Andrew W. Mellon	1855–1937	Banking	1874[b]	$350 million
and Richard B. Mellon	1858–1933	Banking		$350 million
James G. Fair	1831–94	Mining	1865	$45 million
William Weightman	1813–1904	Chemicals	1836	$80 million
Moses Taylor	1806–82	Banking	1832	$40 million
Russell Sage	1816–1906	Finance	N/A	$100 million
John I. Blair	1802–99	Railroads	1820	$60 million
John Pierpont Morgan	1837–1913	Finance	1861	$119 million
Edward Henry Harriman	1848–1909	Railroads	1869	$100 million
Henry Huddleston Rogers	1840–1909	Oil	ca. 1860	$100 million
Oliver Hazard Payne	1839–1917	Oil	ca. 1865	$178 million
Henry Clay Frick	1849–1919	Steel	1870	$225 million
Collis Potter Huntington	1821–1900	Railroads	California gold rush	$50 million
Peter A. Widener	1834–1915	Streetcars	1875	$100 million
Nicholas Longworth	1782–1863	Real estate	ca. 1819	$15 million
Philip Danforth Armour	1832–1901	Meatpacking	Gold rush 1849	$50 million
James C. Flood	1826–88	Mining	Gold rush 1849	$30 million
Mark Hopkins	1813–78	Railroads	ca. 1849	$20 million
Edward Clark	1811–82	Sewing machines	1851	$25 million
Leland Stanford	1824–93	Railroads	1852	$30 million
Hetty Green	1834–1916	Investments	1865[c]	$100 million
William Rockefeller	1841–1922	Oil	ca. 1861	$150 million
Claus Spreckels	1828–1908	Sugar	ca. early 1850s	$50 million

Note: N/A indicates that the information is not available.
[a] In "real dollars," i.e., not adjusted for inflation.
[b] Andrew W. Mellon was the first brother to enter the banking business.
[c] At age 31 Hetty Green inherited $6 million from her father, launching her on her career as the first woman tycoon.
Source: Michael Klepper and Robert Gunther, *The Wealthy 100* (Secaucus, N.J.: Carol Publishing Group, Citadel Press, 1996), vii–xiii

The Export-Import Trade

Neither cyclical panics nor civil war could put a permanent dent in U.S. foreign trade. When this period opened, foreign trade was on an impressive 30-year growth curve; that statistic, however, is misleading. In 1850 the nation was still a net importer, meaning Americans bought more from their trading partners than they sold to them. The principal imports were British-made textiles and foodstuffs. In 22 of the next 25 years the nation ran an annual trade deficit. That little bookkeeping problem, however, did not prevent international trade from constituting a significant part of the U.S. economy.

In the export mix, U.S. agricultural products were far more valuable than U.S. manufactured goods. In 1850, manufactured goods accounted for only one-eighth of the nation's exports; agriculture provided the other seven-eighths. The rivalry took on political overtones because the economic well-being of the South depended on its cash crops, whereas that of the North depended on its nascent industrial system. North and South were more competitors than allies in international trade.

Some of the most important manufactured items seem very strange today. Barrels, for instance, were essential for shipping and storing virtually everything, and high-quality U.S. barrel staves from the Great Lakes region were a valuable export commodity to the European market. When a shortage of experienced coopers during the Civil War slowed production, a worldwide barrel shortage followed.

With attention focused on the rivalry between Northeastern manufacturing and Southern cotton production, scarcely anybody noticed the growing share of U.S. exports represented by midwestern farmers. By 1860 the production of grains, flour, and livestock had risen to 20 percent of total national exports—and those commodities would soon surpass cotton in value on the world market. As U.S. grain battled U.S. cotton on the international market for primacy, U.S. manufactures ranked no better than fourth or fifth in the nation's export mix.

Most U.S. overseas trade was with European countries or their colonial possessions (e.g., Canada and Cuba) because the countries had traditional ties and because they were the most active in international trade. Latin America and China were far less valuable as trading partners but still an important part of the equation. Beginning in the late 1840s the trans-Pacific trade picked up, starting with China after a treaty was signed in 1844, then Japan after 1854, and Korea after 1878. In 1854 one West Coast newspaper boasted, "We shall have the boundless Pacific for a market in manifest destiny. We were born to command it." Americans saw the new Asian markets as a way to reverse the long-standing trade imbalance with Europe. The United States could be the provider of processed goods for Asia as Europe was for America. Regardless of the area, U.S. overseas trade grew by leaps and bounds in every decade, in some cases doubling, during the antebellum period.

The importance of international commerce to the U.S. economy could not be simply measured by the balance of trade. The nation consistently ran a negative balance because even at that point it was a consumer society. The true value was reflected in the economic activity generated within the nation by international trade and the strong trading ties forged with several foreign countries.

TABLE 5.31 MOST IMPORTANT FOREIGN TRADE COMMODITIES, EXPORTED AND IMPORTED, 1840–1860

Exports			
Commodity	**Value in 1840**	**Value in 1850**	**Value in 1860**
Cotton	$63,800,000	$71,900,000	$191,800,000
Wheat and flour	$11,700,000	$7,700,000	$19,500,000
Tobacco	$9,800,000	$9,900,000	$15,900,000
Lumber and wood manufactures	$2,900,000	$4,800,000	$14,600,000
Cotton manufactures	$3,500,000	$4,700,000	$10,900,000
Imports			
Commodity	**Value in 1840**	**Value in 1850**	**Value in 1860**
Woolens	$10,800,000	$19,600,000	$43,100,000
Cotton manufactures	$6,500,000	$20,700,000	$33,200,000
Coffee	$8,500,000	$11,200,000	$21,800,000
Sugar	$5,500,000	$7,500,000	$31,000,000
Hides, skins, and furs	$3,100,000	$5,800,000	$12,300,000

Source: Francis G. Walett, *Economic History of the United States,* 2d ed. (New York: Barnes & Noble, 1963), 96.

TABLE 5.32 PATTERNS OF U.S. TRADE BEFORE THE CIVIL WAR

Nation or Region	1841	1851	1860[a]
United Kingdom[b]	$96,000,000	$211,000,000	$340,000,000
France	$41,000,000	$55,000,000	$105,000,000
Cuba	$17,000,000	$23,000,000	$46,000,000
British North America[c]	$8,000,000	$18,000,000	$46,000,000
Germany (the Hanse)[d]	$6,000,000	$16,000,000	$36,000,000
Brazil	$9,000,000	$18,000,000	$27,000,000
China	$4,000,000	$9,000,000	$22,000,000

Note: The figures for each area represent the value of exports and imports combined.

[a] A census year *and* the last year of normal trading relations before the Civil War disrupted commerce.

[b] England, Ireland, and Scotland.

[c] Canada and the islands of the Caribbean (Jamaica, Bermuda, and others).

[d] Germany was not a unified nation-state at this time. The Hanse was a commercial league of north German cities dating back to the 14th century that had worldwide trade connections.

Source: Francis G. Walett, *Economic History of the United States,* 2d ed. (New York: Barnes & Noble, 1963), 95.

The American Consumer

Until the second half of the 19th century, U.S. manufacturing was concentrated in the heavy industry sector, producing farm machinery, engines, and the like. Only slowly did U.S. industry discover the consumer market. The first two nationally known brand names of consumer products were Smith Brothers cough drops and Arm & Hammer baking soda, introduced in 1866 and 1867, respectively. Such items as meat biscuits and bath soap had not even been patented yet when they first began to be mass-marketed; neither inventors nor manufacturers recognized their profit-making potential early on.

A number of consumer milestones occurred during these years. In 1860 New York's Tiffany & Co. jewelers rang up the first million-dollar sale, a pearl necklace sold to one of the new tycoons. Congress passed the first consumer protection law in 1872, making it illegal to use the mails to defraud citizens. Similar laws did not follow for many years.

Even at this early date, the American standard of living was the wonder of the world. Between 1759 and 1859 the per capita real income of the nation rose gradually from about $211 to $300, most of that the result of increasing production rather than improvements in living conditions. But the rising tide of the U.S. economy raised many boats. The standard of living then can best be gauged by looking at the cost of certain activities and products. Items such as shoes, concert tickets, and books were as common to people of the mid-19th century as they are to American today, and the newspapers and magazines of that day, with their consumer-oriented advertisements, are a rich source of information on such prices.

TABLE 5.33 INTRODUCTION OF CONSUMER PRODUCTS BY AMERICAN INDUSTRY, 1850–1875

Product	Manufacturer/ Seller	Date Introduced
Meat biscuit [a]	Mr. Gail Borden	1851
Bath soap	Palmolive	1860
Board games	Milton Bradley [b]	1860
Cylinder lock	Linus Yale, Jr.	1865
Ice cream [c]	Breyer's	1866
Tabasco sauce	Edmund McIlhenny	1868
Mass-produced toys	F.A.O. Schwartz (of New York)	1870
Cough drops	Smith Brothers (Andrew and Mark)	1870
"Infant Milk Food"	Henri Nestlé (Swiss)	1873
Typewriter	F. Remington & Sons Fire Arms Co.	1874
Improved blue jeans with rivets [d]	Levi Strauss	1874
Margarine (oleomargarine)[e]	Unknown	1874
Vaseline petroleum jelly	Cheesebrough Manufacturing Co.	1875
Canned milk	New York Condensed Milk Co.	1875

[a] A hit with exhibition judges, who awarded it gold medals, Borden's portable meat-and-flour loaf proved a decided flop with consumers.
[b] A Springfield, Mass., lithographer. The game was named the Checkered Game of Life.
[c] Philadelphia was the ice cream capital of the United States; it was there the ice cream soda, among other concoctions, was invented.
[d] Selling for $13.50 per dozen.
[e] Consumers were simply calling it "oleo" by 1884.
Sources: Scott Derks, ed., *The Value of a Dollar: Prices and Incomes in the United States, 1860–1999,* 2d ed. (Lakeville, Conn., Grey House, 1999), 5–7; Charles Panati, *Extraordinary Origins of Everyday Things* (New York: Harper & Row, 1987), 247–48, 258–60, 302–03, 368–87, 404–05, 418–21; Reader's Digest, *Stories behind Everyday Things* (Pleasantville, N.Y.: Reader's Digest, 1980), 53, 188, 210–11, 218–20, 195–96, 340, 380–81.

The former president of the Confederacy Jefferson Davis is reduced to shilling for beauty lotions in his later years. This broadside is an example of early-day advertising. Dr. Harter's Medicine Co. of Saint Louis (established 1855) proclaims its tonic "the first of its kind on the market . . . registered with the U.S. Patent Office." (Courtesy of the Georgia Historical Society.)

TABLE 5.34 COST OF SOME POPULAR CONSUMER ITEMS, CA. MID-19TH CENTURY

Item	Year(s)	Location Offered	Description	Price[a]
Stereoscopic photographs	1863	New York City	"Magnificent colored pictures"	$1.50/doz.
Concert ticket	1875	San Francisco	Opera music with performance by Madame Z. of Paris	$1.00
Museum ticket	1863	New York City	General admission, Barnum's American Museum	15¢ (younger than 10 yr); 25¢ (adults)
Men's and women's shoes	1875	Unspecified	"Button boats"	60¢
Man's shirt collar	1865	Unspecified	"Snow-white, linen-finished, illusion-stitched	$1.25
Man's necktie	1873	Unspecified	Bow tie, with fastener for turn-down collar	10¢
Man's suite	1875	Unspecified	Imported from Scotland	$10.00
Woman's cape	1875	Unspecified	"Storm garment: gossamer and waterproof"; 56 in. long	$8.25
Currier & Ives prints	1877	Unspecified	"Pictures of the great trotters"; 13½ by 17¾ in.	20¢ each
Piano lessons	1863	New York City	24 private lessons at pupil's home	$8.00
Tuition at a private school	1868	New York State	Rockland Female Institute ("for board and English tuition")	$360 per year
Books	1865	Unspecified	1) *Portrait Gallery of the War* by Frank Moore; "full gilt" binding	1) $7.50
	1875		2) *The Ugly Girl Papers; Or, Hints for the Toilet*	2) $1.00
Magazine subscription	1865	Unspecified	1) *Demarest's Monthly Magazine,* "the model parlor magazine of America"	1) $3.00/yr
			2) *Harper's Weekly*	2) 10¢/wk
Steamship ticket	1863	Unspecified	1) New York to Nassau	1) $45
	1868		2) New York to Liverpool, one-way	2) $80 (first class), $30 (steerage)

[a] All prices are from major newspapers and magazines of the day, e.g., the *New York Times* and *Harper's Weekly.*
Source: Scott Derks, ed., *The Value of a Dollar: Prices and Incomes in the United States 1860–1999,* 2d ed. (Lakeville, Conn.: Grey House, 1999), 17–44.

A National Economy

At the beginning of the 19th century, the United States was hardly more than a frontier of Europe, absorbing the Old World's excess population and furnishing raw materials for its industries. By 1860 America had a national economy that, although still dependent on the outside world in ways large and small, had nonetheless managed to achieve self-sufficiency in food, a solid industrial foundation, and a healthy export trade. The Civil War hastened the shift from an agrarian to an industrial economy, put a premium on technology, and made the corporate form of business organization dominant.

Several developments marked that quiet revolution. Before 1870 there was no such entity as gross national product (GNP), or at least it was impossible to calculate the total of all goods and services produced by the nation. A very sophisticated calculation, GNP is derived by adding up personal consumption expenditures, gross private domestic investments, net foreign investments, and government purchases of goods and services (as opposed to interest payments and subsidies). In modern times, GNP has been figured by the Department of Commerce; in these years the Department of Commerce did not even exist. Furthermore, trying to calculate precisely 19th century GNP is virtually impossible because the necessary raw data simply do not exist. Exports and imports and balance of trade were all measured by the government, GNP was not. Therefore, it is necessary to extrapolate from the available figures and make educated guesses. What the numbers do show for the three census periods surveyed is that the U.S. economy grew at nearly twice the rate of the population from 1870 to 1880 (roughly 26 percent versus 50 percent), and even after 1880, it grew at a healthy 17 percent in the next decade versus roughly 25 percent for population).

TABLE 5.35 CALCULATING THE U.S. NATIONAL ECONOMY, 1850–1890

Year	Population	Gross National Product[a]
1850	23,191,876	N/A
1860	31,443,321	N/A
1870	39,818,449	$7.4 billion
1880	50,155,783	$11.2 billion
1890	62,947,714	$13.1 billion

Note: The figures given are in current dollars (i.e., dollars measured at what they can currently purchase) as opposed to constant dollars (i.e., dollars adjusted for inflation).

[a] There are not even enough rudimentary data from the years 1850 and 1860 to allow an educated guess about the GNP. Therefore, GNP for those years is "not accessible."

Sources: U.S. Office of Management and Budget, (Annual) Budget of the United States Government, cited in John Mack Faragher et al., *Out of Many,* 2d ed. (Upper Saddle River, N.J.: Prentice-Hall, 1997), A-17, A-18.

Writing later, Congressman William Kelly of Pennsylvania would call this the period when "the American people woke each morning to feel that there were great duties before them . . . mines to be opened, forges and furnaces to erect, new houses to be built: our wealth grew as it had never grown [before]." The U.S. economy was on its way to becoming the world leader.

CHAPTER 6 Transportation

The 19th century witnessed a transportation revolution that was just gathering steam at the mid-century mark. That it occurred at this time and in this place was not coincidental. The vast empty spaces, extensive inland waterways, and restless population of the United States made such a revolution almost inevitable given the expansionist imperative of Manifest Destiny. At the beginning of the 1800s people traveled over long distances just as they had for centuries, via horse, wagon, and sailing vessel. Before this era was out, Americans had progressed to railroads and steamships, and canals and clipper ships were also contributing to the transportation revolution.

Mass transportation helped define the United States as a nation knit together not by blood or a common culture but by rivers, roads, and rails. The free movement of people between different geographic sections (i.e., the South, the North, and the West) broke down provincial barriers and encouraged the development of a national identity transcending various regional identities.

The mid-19th century experienced an urgency to develop new forms of transportation resulting from several factors. The needs of internal trade and military defense, especially after the war with Mexico and the discovery of gold in California in 1848, played a part. Ties of trade and kinship to Europe likewise inspired the search for ways to shorten the transatlantic crossing. Immigrants, both native-born and European, were filling the distant corners of the country and demanding good connections to older population centers. Finally, joining resources with markets required efficient transportation. And neither empty spaces, hostile Indians, nor difficult terrain would be allowed to halt development.

Canals

Canals were principally important not as people movers but as a means of shipping bulk goods. The concept of a canal transportation system dated to pre-Revolutionary days when it enjoyed the support of such important leaders as George Washington. But it took the completion of the profitable Erie Canal (1825) to usher in the canal-building age, which continued for the next three decades. The enlarged Erie Canal, at 70 feet wide and seven feet deep, began operations in 1862 and was typical of these human-made waterways. Linking key points on lakes and rivers in the eastern half of the country, they created a vast network of inland waterways that provided a cheap if not fast form of transportation. The motto of the canal-boat man was "A cent and a half a mile, a mile and a half an hour." They were most efficient at moving bulk cargoes such as meat, grain, and iron ore because they could charge as little as $12 a ton versus $100 a ton to move the same load by wagon. One of the last canals built during the golden age of canal building was the Chesapeake & Ohio, which opened in 1850, linking Washington, D.C., to Cumberland, Maryland. The Chesapeake & Ohio enjoyed its finest hour during the Civil War, when towboat traffic on it peaked. In 1855 the Sault Sainte Marie Canal opened, destined to become the world's busiest and marking the apogee of the U.S. canal-building age.

Unfortunately for their backers, even at the low prices the towboat operators charged, and with customers lined up on the wharves waiting to ship goods, canals still could not consistently make money, particularly after railroads offered competition. Until

The Erie Canal was an engineering and commercial marvel that launched the canal era in U.S. history. It was 363 miles long (connecting Buffalo, New York, with Albany, New York) and only four feet deep. In this engraving from *Frank Leslie's Illustrated Newspaper,* November 22, 1856, the first of 83 locks can be seen at the Albany end of the canal, with the Hudson River in the foreground. (Library of Congress)

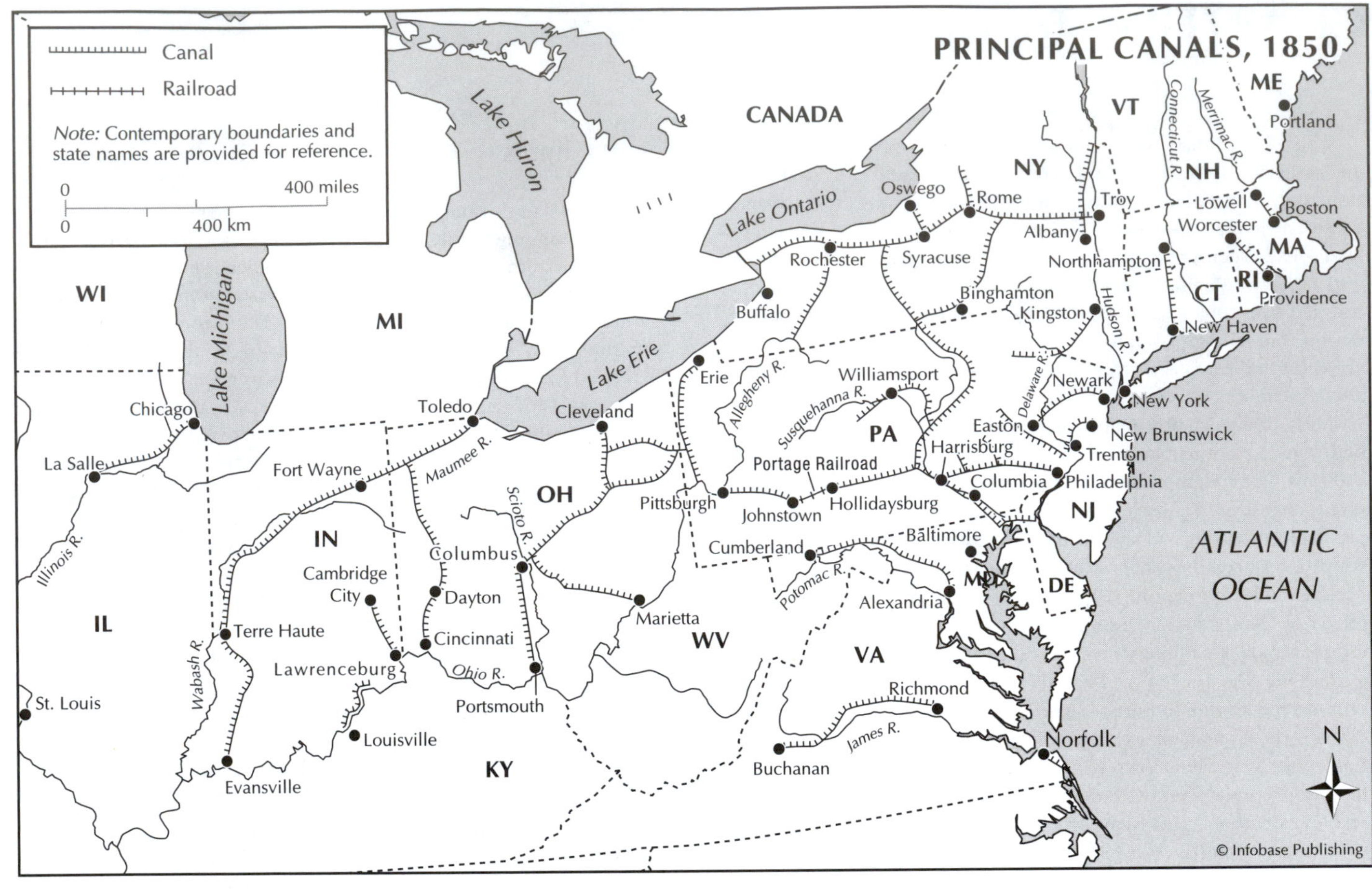

Source: John M. Murrin, Paul E. Johnson, et al. *Liberty, Equality, Power: A History of the American People,* 2d ed. Forth Worth, Tex.: Harcourt Brace, 1999, 482.

1840, canals still carried a larger volume of goods than railroads, but from that time onward, the balance shifted inexorably in favor of the railroads. By 1850 there were more than three times as many miles of track as of canals. Only habit and political considerations slowed the changeover from canal boats to freight trains. Some states such as Pennsylvania and New York had invested so heavily in canal construction that their legislatures resisted chartering railroads even when railroads offered more routes and comparable unit shipping costs. Most canals, built by state funds and public bond drives, never got out of debt because their golden age was not long enough to earn back their initial investment. Many only survived through continuing state subsidies. In the end, loaded down with debt and high maintenance costs, most were bankrupt before mid-century. Only one totally new canal was started after 1850, the Saint Mary's Falls Ship Canal between Lakes Superior and Huron, which opened in late 1855.

TABLE 6.1 MILES OF CANALS IN THE UNITED STATES AND PERCENTAGE INCREASE PER DECADE, 1830–1850

State and Region	Miles of Canals			Miles Added		Percentage Increase	
	1830	1840	1850	1830–40	1840–50	1830–40	1840–50
North (Total)	1,041	2,630	3,005	1,589	375	153	14.3
N.Y.	546	640	803	94	163	17.2	25.45
N.J.	20	142	142	122	0	625	N/A
Pa.	230	954	954	724	0	312	N/A
Ohio	245	744	792	499	48	204	6.5
Ind.	0	150	214	150	64	N/A	42.7
Ill.	0	0	100	0	100	N/A	N/A
South (Total)	68	361	361	293	0	435	N/A
Va.	0	216	216	216	0	N/A	N/A
N.C.	0	13	13	13	0	N/A	N/A
Ga.	16	28	28	12	0	75.2	N/A
S.C.	52	52	52	0	0	N/A	N/A
Ala.	0	52	52	52	0	N/A	N/A
Miss.	0	0	0	0	0	N/A	N/A

Sources: Eugene Alvarez, *Travel on Southern Antebellum Railroads, 1828–1860* (University: University of Alabama Press, 1974), 171; Gavin Wright, *Old South, New South* (New York: Basic Books, 1986), 21.

Clipper Ships

Clipper ships were another form of 19th-century transportation that had a short but glorious golden age. As canals were, they were built to move goods, not people, and as canals were, they were an interim solution to a long-term problem, that is, moving bulk cargo cheaply and swiftly across the great distances. But clipper ships crossed the world's oceans. For their brief reign as the "queens of the sea," U.S.-made clipper ships set the benchmark for sailing vessels in terms of beauty, speed, and craftsmanship.

They represented an evolution, not a revolution in ship design, being based on the familiar schooner form pioneered by U.S. smugglers during colonial times and perfected thereafter. They were cut low to the water and rigged fore and aft to carry a cloud of jibs, with slim lines starting at the graceful concave bow and flowing back to a rounded, overhanging stern—all of which made them instantly recognizable. They were not especially large ships in the beginning. Most displaced less than a thousand tons, making them about the same size as the riverboats that plied the Mississippi. Pride and the profits to be made from the California run led to a dramatic increase in size after 1850, up to 1,500 then 2,000 tons, until the giantess *Great Republic* at 4,000 tons made its debut in 1853. The largest thing about them was the expanse of sail high overhead that gave them their amazing speed but also made them top-heavy, requiring a deep draft to prevent keeling over in a strong wind. Thus, despite tonnage, comparable clipper ships drew two or more times the depth of water required by the plodding, flat-bottomed riverboats or even the deeper-draft, seagoing brigs. The thousands of yards of canvas they typically carried also required extra large and highly trained crews to keep the sails trimmed properly while they were under way.

The clipper design reached its classic form with the 750-ton *Rainbow,* launched in January 1845. The timing was fortuitous because the California gold rush that followed just four years later made swift passage to the West Coast suddenly very popular. Clipper ships out of New York, Boston, or Baltimore made regular runs around Cape Horn to San Francisco, carrying passengers and manufactured goods on the outward voyage, and tea, spices, or even gold dust on the return voyage. Others traveled to Asia and carried back cargoes of tea and spices directly to the East Coast or even on to England, where they could get top dollar for John Bull's national drink. And with the discovery of a huge gold strike in Australia in 1851 that destination was also added to the globe-girdling itinerary.

Every time a clipper ship left port the captain had reasonable expectations of breaking the old speed record to his destination, and during these years new records were made and broken almost routinely. Racing in front of a good wind, a clipper could reach and maintain speeds of 18 to 20 miles per hour, riding on top of the water instead of through it. The *Sovereign of the Seas* once covered an amazing 378 miles a day for four straight days. The *Oriental* made the passage from New York to Hong Kong in a record-shattering 81 days. In 1854 the *Flying Cloud* set a new mark for the voyage between Sandy Hook, New Jersey, and San Francisco's Golden Gate of 89 days, eight hours. They were faster than the steamships of their day and remained so for another quarter-century. They also established speed records for sailing vessels that have still not been broken to this day.

Clipper ships like the one pictured here were the pride of both the U.S. merchant fleet and American shipbuilding before the Civil War. The *Three Brothers* was not only fast but also the largest sailing ship in the world in its day. (Library of Congress, Prints and Photographs Division [LC-USZ62-690])

The *Flying Cloud* was merely the most famous of a family of clipper ships built by the brilliant Donald McKay in his Boston shipyard. McKay's skills as a shipbuilder were only exceeded by his chutzpah. He was the Stradivarius of clipper ships. McKay started the race to build ever-bigger clippers and gave his ships such chauvinistic names as *Sovereign of the Seas* and *Great Republic*. In the first four years of the California gold rush, McKay's yards turned out 160 examples of what became known as "extreme clippers." His ships quickly dominated the trade to Hawaii, China, Australia, and the East Indies. When the Panic of 1857 swamped his business, he went to England and later returned home an advocate of the new steam-and-screw-powered iron vessels being pioneered in British shipyards. McKay and a few other builders on the East Coast made U.S. shipyards the envy and the standard of the world for a few short years.

Even while U.S.-built clipper ships were setting speed records all over the world, they were already outdated. Their twin blessings of speed and beauty were also their curse, for their cargo capacity was extremely limited and they were always dependent on favorable wind conditions to justify the meager cargoes they delivered. On trade routes in which volume and quantity counted more than speed, they were hopelessly uncompetitive. The pride they took in shattering speed records could not make up for the loss of profits when the cargo was unloaded at the destination. And even their speed was nullified if there was not a brisk wind behind them. The development of more reliable and faster steamers steadily eroded their share of international trade. Clipper ships were most efficient over vast oceanic distances; for shorter voyages, especially intercoastal trade, they were beautiful but useless. After the Suez Canal opened in 1869, significantly cutting the distance from Europe and the East Coast to Asia, clipper ships suffered a rapid decline. Orders dried up and those in service were allowed to deteriorate because keeping up their sleek wooden hulls required more expense than it was worth. Most sadly of all perhaps, what should have been their most profitable years, the 1860s, were taken away by the Civil War, which swept U.S. shipping from the high seas. By the time peace and prosperity returned, they had been overtaken by newer technology and shifting trading patterns. They continued for many years to ply the seas mainly as museum pieces and classic collectibles, but not as front-line commercial vessels. After a brief reign as "queens of the sea," clipper ships were replaced by products of the new industrial age—slower, more seaworthy steamships with larger carrying capacity.

Ironically, the clipper ships' nearest relative as a representative of the U.S. shipbuilding arts was the relatively ugly, plodding river steamer, which Americans perfected during these same years as the answer to the need for efficient vessels in the inland waterways trade. Both met a need and were built for the conditions of a specific water environment, and both got the job done.

TABLE 6.2 COMPARISON OF THE SIZE AND DRAFTS OF SOME TYPICAL CARGO-CARRYING CLIPPER SHIPS AND RIVER STEAMBOATS, CA. 1850

Vessel	Type	Year Built	Tonnage	Draft When Loaded (in feet)
Aramingo	Clipper ship	1851	716	18
Argonaut	Clipper ship	1849	575	17
Antelope	Clipper ship	1851	587	17
Uncle Sam	Steamboat	1848	741	9
L. M. Kennett	Steamboat	1852	597	7
Daniel G. Taylor	Steamboat	1855	543	6

Source: Louis C. Hunter, *Steamboats on the Western Rivers* (New York: Octagon Books, 1969), 653.

Steamboats

It was the advent of steam power in the early part of the 19th century that truly revolutionized mass transportation on both land and water. In the United States its first application was riverboats; railways would follow by a couple of decades. This was the result of a curious twist of fate. Early in the game the road forked and U.S. engineers committed themselves to developing paddle-wheel steamers, a form of technology best suited for river navigation, while their European counterparts invested in screw propellers and oceangoing vessels. As in later technological battles between short-wave versus long-wave radar, or supersonic versus subsonic airliners, it proved fateful. U.S. marine engineers were seemingly so mesmerized by the nation's vast network of inland waterways, by the limitations of their home-grown industrial base, and by the myth of British superiority that they did not recognize until too late that they were conceding the ocean trade to Great Britain without a fight. Instead, Americans made a decision to place their bets on paddle wheel riverboats and sail-powered clipper ships, which proved to be the wrong horses in the race to dominate waterborne transportation.

The first practical steam engine was developed by the American Robert Fulton in the early part of the century to power waterborne vessels. The steam engine did not take long to revolutionize not only transportation but also, indirectly, U. S. constitutional law in the area of interstate commerce: In a landmark case (*Gibbons v. Ogden*, 1824) the Supreme Court ruled that the state of New York could not grant a monopoly to a steamboat company engaged in interstate trade, reserving the power to "regulate" interstate commerce to Congress. The first steamboats traveled the Hudson River, but beginning with the appropriately named *New Orleans* in 1811, they took the western rivers by storm, steaming up and down the Ohio, Mississippi, Missouri, and all their tributaries. Form followed function in their development. Steam propulsion led to a revolution in boat design: long, flat-bottomed, shallow hulls; paddle wheels; high-pressure engines; and towering smokestacks to take away the dangerous sparks. Paddle wheels might be either side-wheelers or stern-wheelers, both of which were suited to shallow streams and narrow channels. Stern-wheelers could generate more power on the straightaway, but side-wheelers were more maneuverable and easier to load and unload at undeveloped landings. Both were built in large numbers.

Steam power conquered the lower Mississippi and its tributaries first, then moved upriver to one town or landing after another. There was regular service between New Orleans and Louisville, Kentucky, after 1815, and daily departures for the Upper Mississippi starting in 1823. Having reached the upper Mississippi, steamboats next pushed up the Missouri River, reaching Fort Benton, Montana, in 1850. The first boat built specifically for the Missouri River trade was a stern-wheeler capable of carrying 350 tons, which went into service in 1859. Regular service was inaugurated on the upper Missouri the following year. Steamboats also saw limited use on the Sacramento River (California) and Columbia River (Washington Territory). On most of these routes, the journey was hard, facilities primitive, and local accommodations limited even at the regular ports of call, but such considerations hardly slowed the march of progress. The 1,350-mile journey between New Orleans and Louisville, which could take months of grueling overland travel before, now took 25 days by boat going upriver under favorable conditions, half as long returning pushed by the current. Bigger, better boats were soon whittling away at even those remarkable times.

Slowly steamboats took the carrying trade away from old-fashioned flatboats and keelboats, lowering shipping rates over the next 40 years from about five dollars per 100 pounds to as little as 25 cents per 100 pounds. Their major advantages, besides speed, were less

Small river towns such as Jefferson City, Missouri, lived and died by the steamboat traffic on the river. Jefferson City derived more value from its position as a port on the Missouri River than as the state capital. The capitol building is on the hill above the river. (author's collection, 1852 woodcut engraving by Hermann J. Meyer of New York City)

work for the crew and regularity of service. Although keelboats could be poled either upstream or downstream, or, alternatively, dragged with ropes stretching to the bank, either form of motive power required a sizable crew of burly men. Flatboats (also known as mackinaws) could drift with the current or be propelled with oars or a small sail, but they still made only down-river journeys. Once they reached their final destination they could only be sold and broken up for scrap lumber. Steamboats could travel upriver as well as downriver, carrying cargo both ways, and with minimal demands on the crew. Furthermore, the trip was measured in terms of hours, not days. A good steamboat could maintain a speed of approximately 10 miles per hour against a steady Mississippi current hour after hour.

Steamboats also had a much greater carrying capacity than either keelboats or flatboats, which had reached the natural limits of their technological development centuries earlier. Steamboats had no such built-in limitations. By 1850 the typical paddle wheeler could carry more than 300 tons of freight plus 100 or more passengers and still draw as little as six or seven feet of water fully loaded. The largest, such as the *Sultana,* could carry 1,700 or more tons. Even at that size, their light draft enabled them to reach remote river landings on shallow waterways such as the Yazoo and Red Rivers.

A certain glamorous image grew up around steamboats in the passenger trade that led some of them to be described as "floating palaces." Boat owners competed for passengers at least as fiercely as they did for cargo, and passenger lists included more than travelers trying to get from point A to point B. There was a whole subculture of

TABLE 6.3 AVERAGE TRAVEL TIMES AND SPEEDS BY SELECTED PACKET BOATS ON THE MISSISSIPPI, 1846–1850

Boat Name	Entered Service	Average Freight Trip in Hours Between New Orleans and Memphis: Going Downriver	Going Upriver	Average Speed against a 4-mph Current
Clipper No. 2	1848	36 hours	52 hours	10 mph
Brilliant	1846	36 hours	52 hours	10 mph
Keystone State	1850	36 hours	52 hours	10 mph
Buckeye State	1850	30 hours	50 hours	12 mph
Messenger No. 2	1848	42 hours	52 hours	9 mph
Cincinnati	1850	38 hours	52 hours	10 mph
Hibernia No. 2	1847	40 hours	52 hours	10 mph
Ben Franklin	1848	9 hours	15 hours	10 mph
Telegraph No. 2	Unknown	10 hours	15 hours	12 mph
Bostona	1848	132 hours	132 hours	12 mph
Alexander Scott	Unknown	144 hours	144 hours	11 mph
Cabinet	Unknown	3 hours	3 hours	7 mph

Note: Packet boats traveled a particular route at scheduled times. In the case of the boats listed here their specific routes are not identified, but the number of hours indicates the distance upriver they had to travel from New Orleans; for example, boats taking 11 or 12 days (132 hours or 144 hours) were headed for destinations on the upper Mississippi, such as Cairo, Ill., or Louisville, Ky.
Source: Louis C. Hunter, *Steamboats on the Western Rivers* (New York: Octagon Books, 1969), 651.

TABLE 6.4 TONNAGE AND CARGO CAPACITY OF TYPICAL WESTERN STEAMBOATS, 1826–1848

Steamboat	Year Built	Measured Tonnage of Boat	Cargo Capacity (in tons)
Philadelphia	1826	325	350
Factor	1838	173	250
Diamond	1842	308	450
Harry of the West	1843	490	750
Martha Washington	1847	299	600
United States	1847	332	650
Sultana	1848	924	1700
Uncle Sam	1848	741	1300

Source: Louis C. Hunter, *Steamboats on the Western Rivers* (New York: Octagon Books, 1969), 652.

regular riverboat riders, who included performers, gamblers, and sightseers. Many of these would settle for nothing less than first-class accommodations. On the most popular runs ornate decorations and luxurious accommodations became standard, although hauling cargo was still the major revenue producer of the business.

Some boat owners catered to passengers more than others. This was especially true of those running boats between the major river towns such as New Orleans, St. Louis, and Louisville. They provided separate gangplanks for passengers and for cargo being taken aboard and assigned crew members to look after first-class passengers' needs. For the upper classes, there were private cabins and "saloons" (i.e., lounges); for the rest, there was space on the deck, which meant even under the best of circumstances providing one's own food, sleeping on cotton bales, and dealing with the ever-present cinders. But deck passengers also paid a fraction of what cabin passengers paid.

Steamboats service, as would coming of the railroad a few years later, had the power to create new towns or turn older communities into boom towns. New towns included Cairo, Illinois; Hannibal, Missouri; and Natchez and Port Hudson, Mississippi, all of which grew up around river landings. Already established towns that steamboat service put on the map included Cincinnati, Ohio; Louisville, Kentucky; and St. Louis, Missouri. In a category all by itself was New Orleans, which was transformed into a major international commercial port and transshipment point for the import-export trade. Saint Louis and Cincinnati became famous not only as shipping centers but for boatyard facilities that built most of the boats on the rivers. Louisville on the Ohio River became the most important port in the upper Midwest and developed a very profitable trade with New Orleans and other cities in the lower Mississippi Valley. The major inland ports rivaled their older Atlantic cousins as "shipbuilding" centers, although technically ships were oceangoing vessels and boats plied inland waterways. Without a seafaring tradition to draw from, the boat-building industry nurtured its own highly skilled workforce of shipwrights, carpenters, ironworkers, and mechanics who could turn out as many as four complete boats a year at a single yard. In the last peacetime year before the Civil War, boatyards in the upper Midwest put more than 52 new vessels into service.

TABLE 6.5 COMPARISON OF FREIGHT REVENUES VERSUS PASSENGER REVENUES FOR A TYPICAL GROUP OF WESTERN STEAMBOATS, 1862–1869

Steamboat	Trade Route	For the Year(s)	Freight Revenue (in dollars)	Passenger Revenue (in dollars)	Total Revenue (in dollars)	Percentage of Total from Passengers
Volunteer	Upper Ohio River	1862	4,375	605	4,980	12
Ida Rees	Allegheny River	1864–65	13,079	2,523	15,602	16
Lorena	Pittsburgh to St. Louis	1865–66	120,530	22,527	143,057	16
Silver Lake	Pittsburgh to St. Louis	1867–69	52,985	11,291	64,276	18

Source: Louis C. Hunter, *Steamboats on the Western Rivers* (New York: Octagon Books, 1969), 663.

TABLE 6.6 FARE SCHEDULE FOR REGULAR BOATS BETWEEN NEW ORLEANS, LOUISIANA, AND LOUISVILLE, KENTUCKY, 1850–1860

Accommodations (or Passenger Class)	Fares (in dollars)		Typical Passenger Load	
	Upstream	Downstream	Upstream	Downstream
Cabin	15	15	58	43
Deck	3	3	86	65

Source: Erik F. Haites, James Mak, and Gary M. Walton, *Western River Transporation* (Baltimore: Johns Hopkins University Press, 1975), 162.

TABLE 6.7 STEAMBOAT-BUILDING INDUSTRY ON WESTERN RIVERS, 1860

Industry Aspect	Pittsburgh, Pa.	Cincinnati, Ohio	Louisville, Ky.[a]	Saint Louis, Mo.[b]
Existing steamboats	91	Unknown	33	168
New steamboats built	Unknown	24	22	6
Steamboats repaired	53	81	50	30
Boatyards	11	6	14	2
Number of workers in boatyards	450–500	500	355	200–300
Machine shops doing steamboat work	24	6	8	30
Number of workers in machine shops	1,800	700–800	800	1,500
Foundries doing steamboat work	46	12	13	28
Number of workers in foundries	2,494	1,200–1,400	533	1,500–1,800

Note: Because of incomplete data, the picture given here of the steamboat building industry is not comprehensive. For instance, only certain cities kept such statistics, and even then the numbers simply do not exist for some categories.
[a] Statistics for Louisville include facilities at New Albany.
[b] Statistics for St. Louis include facilities at Carondelet, Ill. (across the river).
Source: Louis C. Hunter, *Steamboats on the Western Rivers* (New York: Octagon Books, 1969), 654.

In the years from 1811 to 1880, thousands of boats were built at Pittsburgh, Cincinnati, and Louisville. The best years were those between 1841 and 1880 when huge floating palaces weighing 212 tons or more were launched. Facilities at these three places turned out 81 percent of all steamboats built on western rivers, in addition to doing repair work and filling steady orders for the old-fashioned flatboats, keelboats, and barges.

Steamboats were commonly designated by the trade or route that they served, for instance, the "Louisville–to–New Orleans" boat. Vessels making regularly scheduled runs were called packet boats, and many of them made the same run year after year, either going directly from point A to point B (trunk routes) or making "whistle stops" at numerous little landings up this branch stream or that one to pick up and unload cargo and passengers (tributary routes). It was in the latter service that paddle-wheel technology really proved its worth by allowing vessels to back in and out of narrow places. The leading ports kept extensive records that showed how their trade increased (or decreased) over the years. But even the busiest showed a steady decline in traffic after 1860, the result of war and changing trade patterns.

TABLE 6.8 STEAMBOAT CONSTRUCTION ON THE WESTERN RIVERS, 1841–1880

	Pittsburgh, Pa.		Cincinnati, Ohio		Louisville, Ky.		Total in West	
Years	Number of Boats Built	Tonnage of Boats Built	Number of Boats Built	Tonnage of Boats Built	Number of Boats Built	Tonnage of Boats Built	Number of Boats Built	Tonnage of Boats Built
1841–50	423	65,291	295	61,566	296	62,694	1,133	212,085
1851–60	533	98,234	288	76,157	266	75,133	1,346	307,618
1861–70	435	84,594	263	55,550	203	52,717	1,210	236,422
1871–80	159	36,002	195	43,266	201	42,425	1,184	174,099

Source: Louis C. Hunter, *Steamboats on the Western Rivers* (New York: Octagon Books, 1979), 106.

TABLE 6.9 PACKET BOAT TRADE OUT OF LOUISVILLE, KENTUCKY, 1850

Route[a]	Number of Boats in the Trade	Type of Trade
Louisville to New Orleans	22	Trunk
Louisville to St. Louis	4	Trunk (including three regularly scheduled packets)
Louisville up the Tennessee River	5	Tributary
Louisville to Henderson	2	Trunk
Louisville to Frankfort	2	Tributary
Louisville to Cincinnati	2	Trunk (including 2 regularly scheduled packets)
Louisville up the Green River	3	Tributary
Louisville up the Wabash River	3	Tributary
Louisville up the Kninhaus River	1	Tributary
Louisville to Madison	1	Trunk

[a] The Louisville–St. Louis and Louisville-Cincinnati routes were considered high-volume, prestige routes for passenger service, thus the number of packets (regularly scheduled boats) on these routes.
Source: Erik F. Haites, James Mak, and Gary M. Walton *Western River Transportation* (Baltimore, Md.: Johns Hopkins University Press, 1975), 171.

TABLE 6.10 ANNUAL STEAMBOAT ARRIVALS AT FIVE LEADING RIVER PORTS, 1850–1860

Year	Pittsburgh, Pa.	Cincinnati, Ohio	Louisville, Ky.	St. Louis, Mo.	New Orleans, La.
1850	N/A	3,653	N/A	2,897	2,784
1851	N/A	3,698	N/A	2,628	2,918
1852	N/A	3,675	N/A	3,184	2,778
1853	N/A	4,058	N/A	3,307	3,252
1854	N/A	3,887	N/A	N/A	3,076
1855	1,987	2,845	2,427	3,449	2,763
1856	N/A	2,796	N/A	3,065	2,956
1857	N/A	2,703	N/A	3,443	2,745
1858	587[a]	3,168	N/A	3,160	3,264
1859	N/A	3,106	N/A	3,149	3,259
1860	N/A	2,985	2,048	N/A	3,566

Note: In some cases statistics are not available (N/A) for particular cities for particular years.
[a] Does not include towboats and boats carrying pig iron exclusively.
Source: Louis C. Hunter, *Steamboats on the Western Rivers* (New York: Octagon Books, 1969), 644–45.

Steam technology had profound economic and social consequences, far beyond the mere movement of people and goods. It was the steamboat that transformed traditional farming in the West from subsistence into commercial agriculture, connecting western farmers with markets outside their region. In the 30 years after 1810 tonnage shipped grew an amazing 1,000 percent. The West was no longer just the frontier but a busy commercial region, producing and shipping crops for a worldwide market. The steamboat not only made western farmers major exporters; it also made them consumers of eastern and even foreign goods heretofore unavailable or too expensive to be appealing. For the next 50 or 60 years, steamboats also reoriented internal trade from its traditional east-west axis to a north–south axis by tying the upper Mississippi basin to New Orleans via the water connections rather than with eastern cities via primitive rail or road connections. Already by the mid-1850s, the tonnage of freight carried on east-west rail and water routes was more than double the north-south tonnage transported on rivers alone. And these economic ties helped determine political developments during the antebellum period.

Riverboats also changed traditional entertainment patterns. They brought fresh entertainment to culture-starved river towns that might not otherwise have seen the touring minstrel shows, Shakespeare performers, and opera companies. The legendary showboats became as eagerly anticipated as the regular passenger and cargo boats.

In 1850 there were 740 steamboats operating on western rivers by one reliable estimate (authorities are not unanimous). Three million passengers annually were using this form of transportation to get about the region before the end of the decade. Some boats became like old friends to regular passengers. The average boat stayed in service for many years because regular safety inspections and forced retirement of older vessels were not mandated. Rust buckets continued to beat their way up and down the river until they literally fell apart or suffered some catastrophic accident. Some of the boats in the trade by the 1850s were 25 or more years old, their machinery and superstructures barely holding together. In fact, the main retirement plan seemed to be boiler explosions, which happened with alarming frequency.

But it was not primarily boiler explosions or decrepit equipment that caused steamboat commerce to decline after 1850; it was a complex combination of political, social, and economic factors. Five years after the peak year of 1850, when there were 740 boats in the trade, the number was down to 727. By 1870 the total number of boats on western rivers was down to 435. In some cases age had finally caught up with vessels that had been in service for many years, and after they were retired they were not replaced. Between 1840 and 1849, 166 boats in the western trade had to be destroyed, not all of them with replacements waiting to take over. But the biggest hits on the business were yet to come. In the next decade the Civil War would disrupt travel on the rivers; trade patterns would change once again as the railroads pushed westward, renewing old east-west links; and there would be an economic downturn in the South after the Civil War. For decades the cotton trade and its related activities had kept the river trade alive, but that trade never recovered from the war. The railroad industry also had greater political clout than did the steamboat industry in both Washington, D.C., and state legislatures, and railroad transportation was not limited by geography as was river transportation. As late as 1850, on competitive routes, river transportation still easily beat rail in cost efficiency for heavy shipping. For instance, shipping 2,000 pounds (one ton) from St. Louis, Missouri, to St. Joseph, Missouri, a distance of more than 300 miles as the crow flies, cost $1,498.91 by rail but only $15 by steamboat! Similarly, St. Louis to Council Bluffs, Iowa, cost $2,000.28 by rail but only $20 by boat. Conditions were the same for all cities served by both rail and river transportation.

TABLE 6.11 COMPARATIVE FREIGHT RATES FOR SELECTED STEAMBOAT/RAILROAD ROUTES, 1850

	Distance (in miles)		Rates (in dollars and cents)	
Route	By Rail	By River	Per 100 Pounds	Per Ton-mile (railroad routes)
Pittsburgh-Brownsville	55	55	0.10	3.63
Pittsburgh-Franklin	122	127	0.30	4.91
Pittsburgh-Zanesville	152	248	0.25	3.29
Louisville–Bowling Green	113	360	0.35	6.19
Louisville–Terre Haute	283	479	0.325	2.29
Louisville–Florence	266	577	0.50	3.76
Louisville–Nashville	186	506	0.38	3.76
St. Louis–Peoria	162	205	0.18	2.22
St. Louis–St. Joseph	343	498	0.75	4.37
St. Louis–Council Bluffs	474	678	1.00	4.22

Source: Louis C. Hunter, *Steamboats on the Western Rivers* (New York: Octagon Books, 1969), 659.

The problem was that navigable rivers only reached certain points whereas rail service could be extended to any point on the map, as the completion of the first transcontinental railroad proved in 1869. In the years after the Civil War, the combination of a powerful lobby, aggressive construction, and improving technology won practically all of the all-important freight trade for the railroads.

Meanwhile steamboats were left mostly to fill the entertainment and passenger niches, and mostly the former, as celebrated in Edna Ferber's famous novel *Showboat* and the musical made from it. Their days as the "queens of commerce" were over. As Mark Twain noted in *Life on the Mississippi,* in the span of roughly 60 years after 1812, "Mississippi steamboating" was born, grew to "mighty proportions," and died.

While they dominated river commerce, steamboats also provided another link in the western transportation network. Many river ports were also terminals for stagecoach service to outlying regions. Passengers disembarking from steamboats could make connections to continue their journey westward. A major link in that network took emigrants via steamboat from Saint Louis to gateway towns of Independence and Saint Joseph, Missouri, and Council Bluffs, Iowa.

The Shipping and Passenger Trades

As U.S. commercial interests expanded, new patterns in waterborne trade followed. The clipper ships opened up Asia the Far East to U.S. shipping. Completion of the Erie Canal In 1825 connected the Great Lakes to the transatlantic trade via New York City, and with expanded Great Lakes shipbuilding facilities, vessels capable of making that transatlantic voyage were soon being built on the lakes. All of the early oceangoing vessels were built on the Canadian side until the U.S.-built *Dean of Richmond* entered service in 1856.

In the 1850s, paddle-wheel steamers such as the *Mississippi,* built in 1853 for the Michigan Southern Railroad, enjoyed a virtual monopoly of the trade around the Great Lakes. But the very fact that it was owned by a railroad company signaled the changing times. The *Mississippi* was laid up as a money-saving measure during the financial panic of 1857, and by the time the panic ended and the Civil War was resolved, it was no longer needed; the major Great Lakes ports were being linked by rails, which could move heavy cargo more cheaply and safely than steamboats. The Michigan Southern also ran a fleet of six to eight luxury boats serving Buffalo, Toledo, Detroit, Sandusky, and other lake ports starting in the mid-1850s. But as it did their cargo-carrying cousins, the railroad eventually made them obsolete. Only in cross–Great Lakes trade did steamboats continue to play a major role for many years because rail connections could not easily replace the direct water routes between Canadian and U.S. ports.

The one significant area of mass transportation unconquered by the United States in these years was transatlantic passenger service. The British Cunard Line dominated the business in 1850 when the newly founded American Collins Line challenged it. Starting with the SS *Atlantic* on April 27, the first of four fast steamers designed for Collins by the naval architect John Wills Griffiths, regular U.S. service to Europe was inaugurated. But without the kind of government support given to the railroads, and without the name or experience that Cunard had, U.S. competition on the transatlantic routes could not overcome the British monopoly. Americans preferred to place their money on the iron horse.

Whether on inland waters or over the seven seas, however, the U.S. shipping trade remained an important element of the antebellum economy. The nation still possessed fine shipbuilding and docking facilities from the Great Lakes to the Gulf of Mexico, a world-class merchant marine, and a global network of commercial treaties. The overwhelming majority of that international trade was with Western Europe, as it had always been, but around mid-century the United States opened regular trade with the Far East and with Australia. The passenger business never represented more than a very small percentage of the carrying trade, limited almost entirely to Europe and the West Indies. Except for commercial gain, most Americans had no desire to see the world. More than 90 percent of U.S. carrying trade in terms of dollar value was cargo, and most of that cargo was U.S.-made or U.S.-grown.

The U.S. merchant marine was almost wiped out by the Civil War; what was not destroyed was driven from the seas, and it never achieved its prewar levels after 1865. Slowly the merchant marine was rebuilt to respectable levels. Still, by 1875, the United States lagged behind Europe in the conversion from sail to steam power with less than half as many steamships as sailing ships in service.

TABLE 6.12 CARGO VESSELS BUILT ON THE GREAT LAKES FOR TRANSATLANTIC TRADE, 1844–1858

Vessel	Type (rigging)	Entered Service	Nationality	Route	Cargo[a]
Pacific	Brigantine	1844	Canadian[b]	Toronto to Liverpool	Flour and wheat
Lillie	Schooner	1848	Canadian	Kingston to Liverpool	Flour
Sophia	Schooner	1850	Canadian	Kingston to Liverpool	Flour
Cherokee	Schooner	1853	Canadian	Toronto to Liverpool	Lumber
Arabia	Barquentine	1854	Canadian	Kingston to Liverpool	General cargo
Cataraqui	Barque	1854	Canadian	Kingston to Liverpool	General cargo
Eliza Mary	Barque	1854	Canadian	Kingston to Liverpool	Lumber
Reindeer	Barque	1854	Canadian	Toronto to Liverpool	Lumber
City of Toronto	Ship	1855	Canadian	Toronto to Liverpool	Lumber
Dean Richmond	Schooner	1856	United States	Milwaukee to Liverpool	Wheat
C. J. Kershaw	Barquentine	1857	United States	Detroit to Liverpool	Staves and lumber
Parmelia J. Flood	Barquentine	1858	United States	Detroit to West Indies	Lumber; sugar and molasses on return[c]

[a] All vessels listed here begin their voyages at Great Lakes ports en route to foreign destinations. Kingston is Kingston, Canada, on the "upper" Saint Lawrence River, where it enters Lake Ontario, not Kingston, Jamaica.
[b] Strictly speaking, all Canadian-registered vessels were actually British because Canada at this time was part of the British Empire.
[c] First recorded direct cargo loading from a Great Lakes port to the West Indies.
Source: George A. Cuthbertson, *Freshwater: A History and a Narrative of the Great Lakes* (New York: Macmillan, 1931), 284–85.

The legendary *Robert E. Lee* gets under way with a crowd at the wharf to see it off. This lithograph is from *Harper's Weekly,* September 2, 1871. (Courtesy of Mississippi Department of Archives and History)

TABLE 6.13 U.S. MERCHANT MARINE, 1865–1875

Year	Total Numbers of Ships Registered[a]	Tonnage Transported by Sail Power[a,b]	Tonnage Transported by Steam Power[b]
1865	N/A	4,030	1,067
1866	N/A	3,227	1,084
1867	N/A	3,113	1,192
1868	28,167	3,153 (including canal and barge tonnage)	1,199
		2,509 (sailing tonnage only)	
1869	27,487	2,400	1,104
1870	28,998	2,363	1,075
1871	29,651	2,286	1,088
1872	31,114	2,325	1,112
1873	32,672	2,383	1,156
1874	32,486	2,474	1,186
1875	32,285	2,585	1,169

Note: Includes all vessels registered with the U.S. government, both inland and oceangoing. *N/A* (not available) indicates that the number of U.S.-registered vessels is not known. Changes were made in the official method of calculating tonnage between 1865 and 1868; one change is explained in [b], but the full scope of the changes is not clarified in the relevant government records, so the figures for those years represent "mixed tonnage."

[a] These numbers combine canal boat and barge tonnage with sailing tonnage until 1868, at which time separate figures are given for sailing tonnage versus canal and barge tonnage.

[b] Gross tonnage = total of vessel + cargo; net tonnage = weight of cargo alone.

Source: B. R. Mitchell, *International Historical Statistics: The Americas and Australasia* (Detroit: Gale Research, 1983), 694.

Wagons and Stagecoaches

Moving people overland in large numbers before the advent of the railroads required either wagons or stagecoaches, the former mostly for immigration purposes and the latter for commercial transportation. The wagon of choice for many immigrants and for most heavy-duty freight hauling was the Conestoga wagon, named for the valley in Pennsylvania where it had been produced by German craftsmen since the early 18th century and still going strong in the mid-19th century. Sturdy, practical, and well crafted, Conestoga wagons hauled cargo and pioneering families across the trackless wilds of the continent, becoming homes on wheels for weeks or even months, converting into "forts" during Indian attacks and even into boats at deep river crossings.

Conestogas, also known as prairie schooners, were instantly recognizable for the distinctive bowed construction of the wagon box and the high canvas cover (known as an osnaburg cover), giving them a sweeping nautical look, which was reinforced by the rocking motion when they moved. The typical prairie schooner could carry as much as three to four tons of cargo, pulled by up to six oxen yoked in pairs, or a like number of mules harnessed in pairs. Oxen were slower but more durable. A fully loaded freight wagon pulled by a team of oxen could travel about two miles per hour; that same wagon pulled by mules could travel about three miles per hour.

After Conestogas became the wagon of choice for pioneers, their manufacture was largely taken over by the Studebaker Brothers Manufacturing Company of South Bend, Indiana, which also had plants in Missouri, Iowa, and Ohio. A genuine Conestoga cost about $1,500 brand-new, making it prohibitive in both size and cost for the average freight hauler.

Other prominent wagon manufacturers, such as the J. Murphy Company of Saint Louis and Peter Schuttler of Chicago, mainly turned out generic freight wagons. These less distinctive-looking vehicles were 16 to 18 feet long and four and a half feet wide and had a carrying capacity of one to 10 tons. Lacking the Conestoga designation, these simple wagons cost less than $200 and were more than adequate for most jobs.

Despite the greater attention given to railroads, in these years many more Americans traveled on wagon wheels, especially in the West, where availability of alternative forms of transportation such as the railroad and steamboat was still limited. In 1858 the shipping firm of Russell, Majors & Waddell employed 3,500 wagons to haul some 25 million pounds of freight, and they were just one of many express companies hauling U.S. goods overland. At Atchison, Kansas, a major shipping center by 1860, no fewer than 1,338 wagon teams were available for hire, and those wagons transported nearly 7 million pounds of merchandise across the western plains annually.

The heyday of the Conestoga wagon and its imitators was between 1820 and 1850 when they were familiar sights on western trails to California and Oregon country. Never comfortable or fast, they were nonetheless ideally suited to a restless nation with few roads and vast distances.

The revolution in transportation wrought by the railroad can be seen in the time overland emigrants traveling by foot and wagon (oxen- or mule-drawn) took to go from jumping-off points in Missouri to either California or Oregon country. The journey was measured in grim, wearying months that destroyed both humans and animals before the destination was reached. Even after a routine was established and the route well mapped, veteran trail guides would only estimate the journey in terms of weeks, and even then they made no promises. After 1869, the journey from Missouri to the West Coast became a matter of days, riding in the relative comfort and safety of a railroad car. Before that, it was typically a trip through hell "with the fires banked," as one survivor described it.

TABLE 6.14 AVERAGE TRAVEL TIMES FOR THE OVERLAND JOURNEY FROM MISSOURI TO CALIFORNIA AND OREGON BY FOOT AND MULE-DRAWN OR OXEN-DRAWN WAGON, 1841–1860

Years	Days to California	Days to Oregon	Days to West Coast
1841–48	157.7	169.1	164.5
1849	131.6	129.0	131.6
1841–49	134.6	166.2	139.5
1850	107.9	125.0	108.6
1850–60	112.7	128.5	116.3
1841–60	121.0	138.6	124.6

Note: As travelers learned the routine and the optimal routes were discovered, the time on the trail dropped. The earliest travelers had the hardest go of it and took the longest time to reach their destination. Seasonal weather conditions such as early snows or heavy rains could also cause delays, as could hostile Indians or sickness.

Source: John D. Unruh, Jr., *The Plains Across* (Urbana: University of Illinois Press, 1979), 341.

As public transportation the stagecoach was the bus, train, and airline of its day all rolled into one. Still, people did not lightly embark on a long overland journey by stage. The trip was guaranteed to be cramped, jolting, dust-eating, and stomach-churning. The classic stagecoach was primarily identified with the West, but it had traversed the nation's roads since colonial times and had a long history in Europe before that. They were the nation's principal carriers of both passengers and mail.

To suit primitive American road conditions U.S. coach makers advanced the technology considerably, improving on the inherited European designs in suspension, running gear, and superstructure. The acme of U.S. craftsmanship was the Concord coach, manufactured in New Hampshire from 1826 and exported all over the world. It stood eight and a half feet tall, weighed about 2,500 pounds empty, and retailed at $1,050 new. It could carry a standard load of nine to 12 passengers plus the driver. Each was a masterpiece of sturdy construction and beautiful hand-finishing. Good drivers who could handle a team of horses six-in-hand and maneuver more than three tons of loaded coach were as highly valued and skilled at their profession as airline pilots are today. Although mules were also used successfully with stagecoaches, it was the horse-drawn coaches that created the glamorous image of "overland coaching." In 1868 Wells, Fargo & Co. contracted with the industry-leading firm of Abbott and Downing for 30 Concord coaches, the largest order ever placed by a single company.

A Concord coach behind a six-horse team could make about four and a half miles per hour over level ground. On long-distance routes, such as the Overland Trail between St. Louis, Missouri, and the West Coast, relay stations were spaced every 10 to 15 miles over the 2,800-mile route, with U.S. Army posts at more widely separated intervals providing some protection from Indians. A one-way ticket to California that could be purchased in St. Louis or Memphis (the other end point) for $200 included a 40-pound luggage allowance. The trip required 24 days of round-the-clock travel.

The California gold rush was the driving force behind the development of efficient long-distance coach service, and after 1850 the "Bear flag" state became the most important market for both intrastate and interstate lines. The first of many Concord coaches arrived in California in 1850 after making the trip around the Horn lashed aboard a sailing ship. In 1858 John G. Butterfield and William G. Fargo launched the nation's first long-distance service linking East and West, from Tipton, Missouri, to San Francisco, California. Two of the large, heavy-duty coaches made the trip in each direction every week. Later the routes were expanded and the frequency of service increased. Another stagecoach left St. Louis, Missouri, for Los Angeles, California, every 24½ hours loaded down with mail and eager "argonauts", hoping to get rich quick. Throughout the 1850s and 1860s stage lines crisscrossed the West, tying distant communities together. After 1869 the railroad rang the death knell for long-distance coaches on the longest routes and between principal cities, but they continued service past the end of the century as feeder lines. For a time the Concord name was to overland transportation what Singer was to sewing machines or Baltimore was to clipper ships: the benchmark of the industry worldwide and a proud symbol of U.S. technological superiority.

Stagecoach travel had peaked by 1870, and a steady decline followed, hitting the long-distance east-west routes hardest because the railroads were not only faster but safer and more reliable. But as late as 1874, *Harper's Weekly* could still call the rugged stagecoaches "the advance guard of civilization in the far West" Along the way, several companies carved out a place in transportation history as major carriers of goods and people across the width and breadth of the country, operating both stagecoaches and freight wagons and in some cases even pony express. Just as the airlines and railroads that succeeded them, they had to carry both passengers and "express" to make a go of it. *Express* in the vernacular of the day meant small packages, newspa-

The Butterfield Overland Mail stagecoach began its inaugural journey eastward from San Francisco in September 1858. The six-horse coach is loaded to the gunwales with passengers, mail, and baggage. It will be at least 24 days before it reaches its final destination in Tipton, Missouri, 2,600 miles away. (Library of Congress)

pers, and mail. Some firms also transported heavier freight, such as machinery, bullion, and bulk foodstuffs, but their bread and butter was express service. Four great names dominated the express business: Adams, American, National, and Wells Fargo.

The real moneymaker on long-distance routes was neither passengers nor goods, but mail. So important was mail service that the U.S. government was willing to pay premium prices to anyone willing to take on the job. Congress authorized subsidies from 1857, and contracts were signed that same year paying John Butterfield's Overland Mail Company $290,000 a year to transport the mail to the West Coast. By 1860 Butterfield's subsidy had risen to $600,000 annually, and in 1868 when Wells, Fargo & Company took over the job, their first contract was for $1.75 million per year. After 1869, however, the major contracts went to the railroads, not the stagecoach companies.

For some 20 years stagecoaches monopolized mass transportation in the West. A handful of giants built the coaching industry, starting with Ben Holladay (the "Stagecoach King") and including John Butterfield, Alvin Adams, Henry Wells, and William G. Fargo. Several big operators got their start in California during the gold rush, but the two largest, Adams & Company and Wells, Fargo & Company, began by paying others to carry their express. They were not in the coach or horse business. That changed soon enough, however, as they began to buy their own equipment to operate on their own lines. Between 1858 and 1866, John Butterfield's Overland Mail Company operated the "longest stage run in the world"—2,600 miles from Tipton, Missouri, to San Francisco, California, a 24-day trip one way. Just as the railroads did, the stagecoach business went through a consolidation period as rivals first fought over the most choice routes, then bought out each other. In this way, Ben Holladay took over Butterfield; then Wells, Fargo bought out Holladay. Eventually Wells, Fargo & Company stood alone as the king of the mountain. But in the mid-century years they were still fierce competitors aiming to extend their reach into new corners of the West. In 1856, the California Stage Company, which operated only in California and Nevada, was the largest stagecoach firm in the United States, but it proved unable to compete with the likes of Wells, Fargo and Butterfield. The contribution of the stagecoach kings to national growth has largely been overshadowed by the larger-than-life image of the railroad tycoons who built on what the stagecoach kings started.

TABLE 6.15 THE STAGECOACH LINES AND EXPRESS COMPANIES THAT BUILT THE WEST, 1840 AND LATER

Name of Company	Founder(s) or Owner(s)	Type of Service	Headquarters	Principal Route(s)	Years of Operation	Fate
Adams & Company[a]	Alvin Adams	Freight and express	New York City; San Francisco after 1849	Calif. intrastate	1840–55	Bankrupted by business panic during mid-1850s
Adams Express Company[b]	Alvin Adams and William Dinsmore	Passengers, express, and mail	New York City	East of the Mississippi Route, particularly North–South trade during Civil War	1854–1918	Merged with three other companies to form American Railway Express Company
California Stage Company	James Birch[c]	Express and passengers	Sacramento, Calif.	Calif. intrastate and between Calif. and Nev.	Jan. 1, 1854–post–Civil War	Absorbed by Wells, Fargo & Company
American Express Company	Henry Wells, William G. Fargo, John Butterfield, and James D. Wasson	Express and passengers	New York City	National	1850–present	Evolved into banking and travel business
Wells, Fargo & Company	Henry Wells, William G. Fargo	Mail, passengers, express, luxury items for wealthy customers, banking	New York City and San Francisco	National, with monopoly of mail and passenger service west of Mississippi by 1868	Jul. 1852–present	Evolved into financial and private security business
Pioneer Stage Company	Louis McLane	Express mail and passengers	Sacramento, Calif.	Calif. to Virginia City and Carson City, Nev.	1855–64	Purchased by Wells, Fargo & Company
Holladay Overland Mail & Express Company (Holladay Overland Stage Line)	Ben Holladay[d]	Express, mail, passengers	Atchison, Kans.	Kans. and Nebr. west through Colo. as far as Salt Lake City, Utah	1862–Nov. 1866	Sold out to Wells, Fargo & Company Nov. 1, 1866, for $1.5 million cash + $3 million stock
Overland Mail Company[e]	John Butterfield, William G. Fargo, John Dinsmore (directors)	Mail and passengers	New York City	Tipton, Mo., to San Francisco, Calif.	Sep. 15, 1858–Feb. 1866[f]	Taken over by Ben Holladay; ultimately put out of business by transcontinental Railroad Routes
Russell, Majors and Waddell	William Russell, James Waddell, Alexander Majors	Freight and U.S. govt. stores, especially under army contract	Leavenworth, Kans.; later Nebraska City, Nebr.	U.S. forts and depots in Kans., N. Mex., and Utah	Dec. 1854–62	Failed because of bankruptcy and charges of corruption
Butterfield Overland Despatch Company	David Butterfield[g]	"Fast freight," express, and passengers	Atchison, Kans., and New York City (after 1865)	Atchison, Kans., westward through intermountain region but not Calif.	Dec. 1864–Mar. 1866	Sold out to Ben Holladay

[a] Reorganized briefly in 1850s as the Pacific Express Company.
[b] Originally known as the New York & Boston Express Company.
[c] Starting in 1849 on his own, Birch was the first commercial stagecoach operator in California.
[d] Holladay purchased the nearly bankrupt Central Overland and California and Pikes Peak Express Company in 1859 and expanded into mail and passenger service by 1862.
[e] Also known as the Butterfied Overland Mail Company because John Butterfield was the high-profile president of the company.
[f] The company was organized in 1857, but the first stagecoaches departed from opposite ends of the line (St. Louis, Mo., and San Francisco, Calif.) on Sep. 15, 1858.
[g] David Butterfield of Denver, Colo., was no relation to John Butterfield of the Overland Mail and American Express companies.

Sources: Ralph Moody, *Stagecoach West* (New York: Thomas Y. Crowell, Promontory Press, 1967); Howard R. Lamar, ed., *The Reader's Encyclopedia of the American West* (New York: Thomas Y. Crowell, 1977), passim; Denis McLoughlin, *Wild and Woolly: An Encyclopedia of the Old West* (New York: Barnes & Noble Books, 1975), passim; Candy Moulton, *The Writer's Guide to Everyday Life in the Wild West* (Cincinnati: Writer's Digest Books, 1999), 242–51.

Railroads

Throughout the 19th century, the railroad was the embodiment of mechanical progress and the icon of modern travel. Americans had a long love affair with the iron horse. Industrial growth in the 19th century was led by the railroads, which became the first big business and even enjoyed firm support among the majority of congressmen, who were seldom so farsighted in spending public monies. Some of the most powerful senators and representatives, including Stephen A. Douglas and Thomas Hart Benton, became spokesmen for the railroads. Most congressional aid to railroads was in the form of land grants, which the government had more of than money to hand out. Congress made the first federal land grant to promote railroad development in 1850, and the decade that followed was the most beneficial to the booming industry to date. Between 1850 and 1871, some 80 companies received more than 170 million acres of public land (mostly west of the Mississippi). The value of those lands was estimated by the Interior Department in November 1880 at $391,804,610. On top of that, Congress passed out $64,623,512 in generous 30-year loans to the same companies. Taken altogether, it was the biggest incentive program in national history to that date, but it was hardly the give away its critics have charged. When the government settled up with the railroads in 1898–99, the U.S. government received back $167,746,490 in, principal and interest on its initial $64 million corporate loan. More important, the country achieved the desired objective of inducing private enterprise to take on the enormous task of constructing a continental-sized rail network that became the envy of the world.

Source: Magellan Geographic U.S. History Atlas, supplement. New York: Harcourt College Publications, 2000, 23.

By the usual terms of the land-grant system, a belt of land from two to 10 miles wide along either side of the tracks was set aside right of way; then alternating sections were awarded to the builder of the line. These grants were a major factor in attracting the enormous capital investment necessary to build the roads. The railroads could earn back their investment by selling off their right of way to settlers or speculators at top dollar. Land-grant railroads thus became the standard arrangement in construction of the nation's rail network in the decades that followed. By the 1870s railroad companies were the largest private land landholders in the United States, and the U.S. Congress was the principal partner for the nation's railroads.

States competed just as local communities did to attract the railroads. State legislatures granted charters to build them, subsidized construction with cash and land grants, and as a result often wound up in the pockets of the railroad tycoons. But all the wheeling and dealing had the desired effect: Railroad mileage increased dramatically in every state and territory between 1850 and 1875. At the beginning of the period, northeastern states led in the laying of new track, but by the end of the period 25 years later, the midwestern agricultural states were threatening to overtake them. Even the most remote territories counted their increase in hundreds of miles of new track crossing mountains, prairies, and swamps with equal vigor.

From 1830 on, railroads were the most quantified sector of the U.S. economy or society, and second only to the statistics gathered about the electorate. Figures were kept for railroad mileage, new construction, rolling stock, amount of freight and passengers carried, and so forth; if it could be measured, the U.S. government kept track of it. The reasons for such meticulous record keeping are not hard to understand. The railroad was widely recognized as the engine driving the U.S. economy. To paraphrase a later quotation, as the railroads went, so went the nation. States and territories competed fiercely to attract railroads, and the carrying trade was a major measure of economic prosperity. The number of miles added to the national total every year was an almost magical economic indicator, just as automobile production or housing starts were in the next century. Therefore, as figures on imports and exports were important to economists and government bureaucrats, the expansion of the nation's railroad network was a measurement that ordinary citizens could easily understand.

There was money to be made in railroading, vast amounts of money, but from moving goods, not people. Freight hauling was the name of the business, and companies conducted bitter "rate wars" to win and keep the business of the big shippers. For most railroads, passenger service was almost an afterthought, as demonstrated by the production of railroad equipment. Of the thousands of cars turned out by the major producers every year, the overwhelming majority were freight cars, not passenger cars. It was this lack of interest in passengers that opened the door for George Pullman and his Pullman Palace Car Company to fill a virtual void in the industry by producing truly comfortable, well-appointed passenger cars, in the process establishing a near monopoly of that type of rolling stock.

Not for nothing were the nation's railroads described as "arteries" of commerce, for farmers and manufacturers alike depended on them for their economic livelihood, even their survival. And no one was more dependent than the homesteader. In the farm belt, there was a direct connection between the railroad and the expansion of farmland. Not only did the railroads sell off their right-of-way to local farmers at cut-rate prices, but the very presence of the railroad tended to cause a land rush of new homesteaders foreseeing a bright economic future for the region. In the 11 leading agricultural states between 1871 and 1880, the expansion of the rail network by 88 percent led to a concomitant 60 percent expansion of land under cultivation. That represented a net gain of $520 million in agricultural value in those states, or 39 percent of the cost of constructing the new rail lines ($1.35 billion).

TABLE 6.16 GROWTH OF RAILROAD MILEAGE IN THE UNITED STATES, 1850–1875

Year	Miles Already in Service	New Mileage Added	Percentage Increase
1850	9,021	1,656	18.3
1851	10,982	1,961	17.9
1852	12,908	1,926	14.9
1853	15,360	2,452	15.9
1854	16,720	1,360	8.1
1855	18,374	1,654	9.0
1856	22,016	3,642	16.6
1857	24,503	2,487	10.1
1858	26,963	2,465	9.2
1859	28,789	1,821	6.3
1860	30,635	1,846	6.0
1861	31,286	651	2.1
1862	32,120	834	2.6
1863	33,170	1,050	3.2
1864	33,908	738	2.2
1865	35,085	1,177	3.4
1866	36,801	1,716	4.7
1867	39,250	2,249	5.7
1868	42,229	2,979	7.0
1869	46,844	4,615	9.9
1870	52,914	6,070	11.5
1871	60,293	7,379	12.2
1872	66,171	5,878	8.9
1873	70,268	4,097	5.8
1874	72,385	2,117	2.9
1875	74,096	1,711	2.3

Note: Different authorities use different methods and different primary sources for their calculations. Statistical discrepancies between 19th-century "modern" figures are almost guaranteed. Thus, the numbers in this table vary in some cases from those given in Table 6.17, e.g., total railroad mileage in 1871.
Source: Alfred D. Chandler, Jr., ed., *The Railroads: The Nation's First Big Business,* The Forces in American Economic Growth series (New York: Harcourt Brace, & World, 1965), 429.

TABLE 6.17 RAILROAD MILEAGE IN THE UNITED STATES BY REGION AND YEAR, 1850–1871

Year	New England	Middle States	South	West	Total
1850	2,510	3,200	1,280	2,030	9,020
1860	3,660	6,350	8,540	12,080	30,630
1871	4,490	10,580	12,560	25,290	52,920

Note: Different authorities use different methods and different primary sources for their calculations. Statistical discrepancies between 19th-century and "modern" figures are almost guaranteed. Thus the numbers in this table vary in some cases from those given in Table 6.16 e.g., total railroad mileage in 1871. All mileage was owned by private companies, not the government.
Source: Michael G. Mulhall. *The Dictionary of Statistics,* 4th ed. (London: George Routledge & Sons, 1899), 507.

TABLE 6.18 NUMBERS OF RAILROAD CARS PRODUCED BY U.S. COMPANIES, 1871–1875

Year	Freight Cars	Passenger Cars
1871	185,000	9,000
1872	256,000	5,000
1873	280,000	6,000
1874	387,000	9,000
1875	185,000	2,000

Source: U.S. Bureau of the Census, *Historical Statistics of the United States,* vol. 2 (Washington, D.C.: U.S. Government Printing Office, 1960), 697.

TABLE 6.19 THE ECONOMIC IMPACT OF RAILROADS: THE STATES WITH THE GREATEST INCREASE IN MILEAGE AND THE GREATEST EXPANSION OF FARMLAND, 1871–1880

State	Railroad Mileage			Farm Acreage		
	1871	1880	Percentage Increase 1871–80	1871	1880	Percentage Increase 1871–80
Ill.	5,904	8,326	41	25,883,000	31,674,000	21
Ohio	3,740	6,664	78	21,713,000	24,529,000	13
Iowa	3,160	6,113	93	15,542,000	24,753,000	61
Tex.	865	5,344	520	18,397,000	36,292,000	98
Ind.	3,529	4,765	36	18,120,000	31,674,000	74
Mich.	2,116	4,284	102	10,019,000	13,807,000	38
Mo.	2,580	4,211	62	21,707,000	27,879,000	27
Kans.	1,760	3,718	111	5,657,000	21,417,000	282
Wis.	1,725	3,442	99	11,715,000	15,353,000	31
Minn.	1,612	3,391	110	6,484,000	13,403,000	106
Nebr.	943	2,310	146	2,074,000	9,945,000	380
11-State Total	27,934	52,568	88	157,311,000	250,726,000	60

Source: Michael G. Mulhall, ed., *The Dictionary of Statistics,* 4th ed. (London: George Routledge and Sons, 1899; republished by Gale Research, 1969), 508.

Railroads were vital to economic prosperity, but more than that, they were the vehicle of western expansion, tying East and West into a single commonwealth. Most pioneers may have first traveled west by wagon or on foot, but they depended on the railroad to maintain their ties with the rest of the country. Frontier communities began to clamor for a railroad almost as soon as they began to clamor for organized government. Spurred by popular demand, the nation's rail network grew in the form of trunk lines and feeder lines. The trunk lines tied together major points on the map and were guaranteed heavy usage. Feeder lines connecting smaller communities to the nearest major line were then added. The most powerful regional carriers tried to control both the region's trunk line and the various lesser lines feeding into it. Where there was more than one major carrier in a region, the resulting competition could be ruthless, reflecting the high stakes involved for winners and losers.

By 1874 the age of railroads was in full swing, as this scene at some unnamed junction depicts, with at least five lines converging at the station. Two "lightning express trains" have their steam up and are ready to depart. (Library of Congress, Prints and Photographs Division [LC - USZ62-635])

TABLE 6.20 ANNUAL CONSTRUCTION OF NEW RAILROADS, AVERAGED BY YEAR FOR EACH REGION OF THE UNITED STATES, 1851–1880

(in miles)

Decade	New England	Middle States	South	West	Total
1851–60	115	315	726	1,005	2,161
1861–70	83	423	402	1,321	2,229
1871–80	149	460	701	2,728	4,038

Note: Figures show the average new mileage constructed yearly in each region.
Source: Michael G. Mulhall, ed., *The Dictionary of Statistics,* 4th ed. (London: George Routledge and Sons, 1899; republished by Gale Research, 1969), 507–08.

For much of the 19th-century, U.S. railroad companies could not lay track fast enough to satisfy the demand for new lines. New construction was always greatest in the West, least in New England, reflecting the growth patterns of the country. Construction slowed everywhere during the decade of the Civil War, as more railroads were destroyed than built during the years 1861–65.

Meanwhile, the business side operated almost as a separate entity from the construction side of the industry. After a period of rapid growth, the railroad business (as opposed to construction of new track) underwent a period of consolidation, beginning in 1853, when Erastus Corning founded the first large unified system by combining 10 small local companies into the New York Central, linking New York City to Buffalo, New York. Further consolidation followed with the adoption of a standard track gauge for the nation, which allowed rolling stock of different companies all to use the same tracks all over the country.

The vital issue of track gauge was a drag on the growth of the railroad industry for too many years. *Gauge* is the width between the rails, and in the days of rampant free enterprise every line was free to set its own standard. A few reached "gentlemen's agreements" with their competitors, but there was little business incentive to establish a single standard so long as short haulers and regional lines focused on local markets. By 1872, with more than 66,000 miles of railway crisscrossing the country, there were still 23 different track gauges, varying from three to six feet. In the Northeast, a consortium of lines had settled on a four-inch to three-and-a-half-inch gauge, while in the Deep South, a five-inch gauge was in general use. It would take years to get a uniform standard adopted all over the country, with most of the push for standardization from an odd alliance of long-haul shippers and touring circus companies who traveled by their own railroad cars.

Nineteenth-century railroads filled two vital roles for the nation, hauling both passengers and goods across country. Beyond the reach of the great eastern rivers (Ohio, Missouri, Mississippi), railroads provided the only option for reasonably quick and efficient mass transportation. It would not be until well into the 20th century that alternate forms of transportation for both passengers and bulk goods would become available. Focusing on two years alone, 1872 and 1875, the balance between passengers and goods carried by the nation's railroads is apparent. In the years that followed, freight hauling would steadily gain in importance over passenger service as the bread and butter of the railroads.

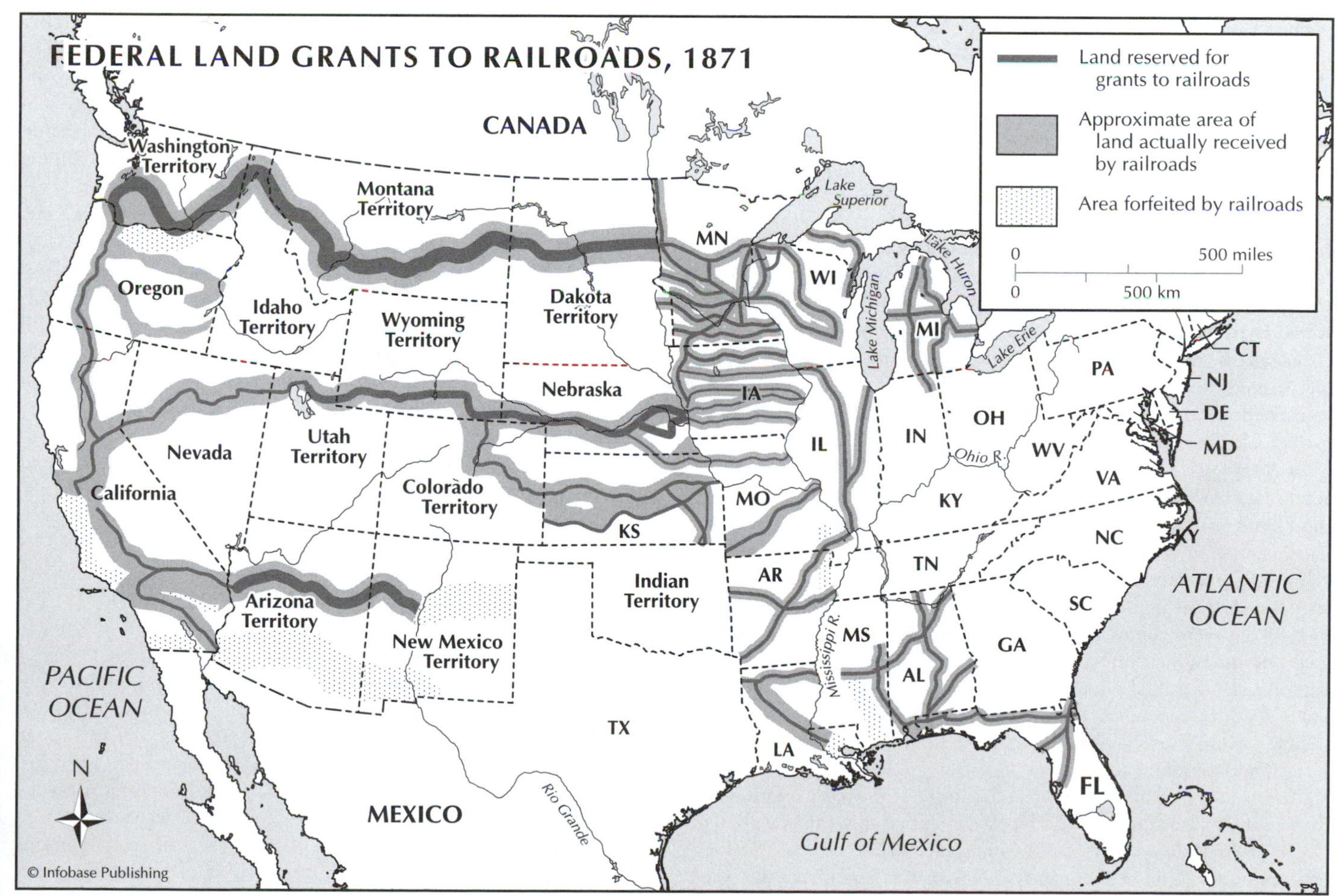

Source: Robert A. Divine, T. H. Breen, et al. *America Past and Present,* 6th ed. New York: Longman, 2000, 522.

TABLE 6.21 PASSENGERS AND GOODS CARRIED BY U.S. RAILROADS, 1872 AND 1875

Year	Number of Passengers	Passenger Miles	Average Passengers per Mile	Goods Carried (tonnage)	Average Tonnage per Mile	Total Receipts of All Railroads (in dollars)
1872	150,000,000	66,200	2,300	170,000,000	2,500	405,407,000
1875	191,000,000	74,370	2,600	202,000,000	2,700	504,593,000

Source: Michael G. Mulhall, ed., *The Dictionary of Statistics,* 4th ed. (1899; reprint, Farmington Hills, Mich.: Gale Research, 1969), 508.

One of the major services provided by railroads was mail delivery. By 1859, trains delivered mail in bulk across the eastern half of the country and as far west as Missouri, where wagon trains and stagecoaches took over.

The railroad as a historical entity was more than a form of transportation or even an economic juggernaut; it was also a profound sociological force. The railroads had the power to make and break cities according to where they laid their tracks. Fort Worth, Texas, and Ellsworth, Kansas, for instance, owed their very survival to the coming of the railroad in the 1870s. By the same token, the great hub cities of Chicago, Illinois; Atlanta, Georgia; and Chattanooga, Tennessee, would have remained small towns if not for the iron horse.

Geographic barriers could not stop the inexorable advance of the railroads, only slow it. By the 1850s, the railroads had reached the Midwest and leaped the Mississippi River (1854). In 1866 the Ohio River was spanned with rails. Railroads were the stuff transcontinental dreams were made of; only the route remained to be determined. The major obstacle to transcontinental rail service was the forbidding altitudes of the Rocky Mountains, which were broken by only a limited number of passes. To connect California to the rest of the country, one of these passes would have to be used, but which one involved politics as much as geography because the chosen route would connect the West Coast directly to either the North or the South with all the economic advantages that entailed. Southern political leaders lobbied for a Southern route and Northern leaders for a Northern route. One proposal from Secretary of War Jefferson Davis of Mississippi was to have the main rail line run along the 32d parallel, thereby bisecting Mississippi, Louisiana, and Texas with its western terminus near San Diego. As Davis explained, with more than a hint of what one historian calls "overweening sectional bias," this route was "not only the shortest and cheapest [by a third] but could be completed much more quickly and would enjoy much less interruption of service once built."

Congress got in on the debate in 1853 when it authorized the War Department to survey four possible transcontinental routes for future construction. Years of negotiation and surveying followed, and Congress took the next step when it purchased the Gadsden Territory from Mexico in 1853 with a Southern route in mind. The people's representatives finally kick-started construction with the passage of the Pacific Railroad Act in 1862, granting right-of-way to the Union Pacific and Central Pacific companies to lay track between Omaha, Nebraska, and Sacramento, California. The Civil War slowed construction, but the first transcontinental railroad was finally completed in 1869, an event commemorated by the "driving of the golden spike" at Promontory Summit, Utah. (This historic event has often been erroneously identified with Promontory Point, a site that is some 30 miles south of the actual site where the two lines were joined.) It required more than six years to complete this final 1,775-mile gap in service between the East and West Coasts.

The paradox of the Civil War is that while it slowed expansion of the national railroad network, it focused attention more than anything else ever could have on the vital importance of the railroads to the nation's future. One of the principal reasons the North won the war was that its extensive rail network allowed it to move soldiers from theater to theater to meet developing threats, to outflank the Confederates, and to supply armies in the field with everything they could possibly need rather than periodically needing to pull them back to supply bases. In all these respects the Northern railroads far outperformed their Southern counterparts. The optimum in effective railroad use for both sides occurred in the late summer of 1863. The Confederates managed by heroic effort to shift 12,000 troops of General Longstreet's corps from Virginia to north Georgia, a distance of some 840 miles, between September 8 and 25, in time to win a major victory at Chickamauga. As impressive as that accomplishment was, it could not compare to what the U.S. Military Railroad Service under Daniel C. McCollum accomplished around the same time. In eight days at the end of September, the North moved 20,000 members of the XI and XII Corps some 1,200 miles from Virginia through northern territory to Chattanooga, Tennessee, to lift a Confederate siege of the city. These two events represented the largest mass transfer of troops by rail during the Civil War, and more than that, the largest ever attempted by any government in history up to that point. The fact that the North was able to move more troops farther scarcely diminishes the accomplishment of the South, which had a far more rickety system.

The Civil War was a tremendous setback to railroad growth in the South, which started the 1860s already behind with only 10,000 miles of track to the North's 20,000 miles. Before the war, railroad construction had forged both economic and political ties between the Northeast and the Midwest, which left the Deep South isolated and pushed it toward secession in 1861. Four years of war and destruction did not help, and even after 1865 the South never caught up with the North's track mileage. But the South was part of the national rail network that helped reunite the nation and wipe out traditional sectional differences in the late 19th century.

After the Civil War the "age of empire building" in U.S. railroad history began as a group of tycoons such as Jay Gould, Cornelius Vanderbilt, Collis P. Huntington, Edward H. Harriman, and James J. Hill accumulated railroad companies and multimillion-dollar fortunes with equal felicity. The railroads took the leading role in bringing in foreign immigrants, deciding where towns should be planted, politicizing U.S. farmers, and setting the economic agenda of the nation. The year 1873 marked the beginning of a 25-year period of rapid expansion of track mileage and declining shipping costs that made the U.S. rail network the admiration of the world.

Comparing Modes of Transportation

Comparisons are difficult to make among the various forms of mass transportation in place in the mid-19th century. Options were not often available to the average traveler, but where they were available, there were trade-offs. For passengers travel by rail was faster and more comfortable than by horse-drawn coach, but also more dangerous because of poor safety standards and mechanical breakdowns. For shippers there was no real alternative where rail transportation was available, and the larger the cargo, the more cost-efficient it was. Even in their first decade of operation, trains were seven to 12 times faster than wagon transport. The only real considerations were the expense and availability of rail transport, and

TABLE 6.22 COMPARATIVE SPEED AND RATES OF DIFFERENT MODES OF TRANSPORTATION, CA. 1850

Speed and Rates	Horse-Drawn Wagon	Stagecoach	Canal	Steamboat	Railroad[a]		
					1830s	1840s	1850s
Estimated Speed (in miles per hour)[b]	2	6–8	15–20	10–15	15–25	10–14 (24)[c]	26
Freight Rates (in cents per ton-mile)	10–15	N/A	1.5	0.5–1.5	N/A	N/A	2.5

[a] Based on data from operation of trains on New York lines.
[b] Under normal operating conditions, i.e., in good weather and over flat terrain. As a rule, roads were unpaved except in a few large eastern cities.
[c] Higher speed (X) is for passenger trains only.
Source: Glenn Porter, ed., *Encyclopedia of American Economic History,* vol. 1 (New York: Charles Scribner's Sons, 1980), 325.

both of those improved steadily over the years. All else being equal, for bulk transport, canals provided the best value for the shipper's dollar, but their availability was limited to a handful of routes in the East and upper Midwest. Beyond the Mississippi, there were no canals. It is safe to say that competition among various forms of transportation was more apparent than real.

Almost regardless of the form of transportation chosen, shipping rates were dropping at mid-century. This delightful development occurred because of the growing competition for shipping business and because, with the exception of the two panics in the mid-1850s and mid-1870s, the U.S. economy was booming. Naturally the Civil War threw all calculations out of kilter, but afterward the economic boom picked up almost where it had left off, at least in the North and the West. Available options varied from region to region; where a shipper could choose among railroad, canal, and graded road (turnpike), he or she could save even more by negotiating the best price. Although comparable figures are sketchy, they reveal a pattern, showing waterborne transportation to be generally cheaper than rail, and 1860 prices to be slightly lower than 1853 prices over the same route, the only exception being turnpikes.

TABLE 6.23 AVERAGE SHIPPING RATES IN DOLLARS AND CENTS PER TON-MILE, 1853 AND 1860

Means of Transportation	1853	1860
Turnpikes	15.00	15.00
River Transportation		
Mississippi and Ohio Rivers (downstream)	N/A	0.37
Mississippi and Ohio Rivers	N/A	0.37
Ohio River	0.80	N/A
Hudson River	0.70	N/A
Illinois River	1.20	N/A
Canals		
Erie Canal	1.10	0.99
Ohio Canal	1.00	N/A
Wabash-Erie Canal	1.90	N/A
Illinois Canal	1.40	N/A
Pennsylvania Main Line Canal	2.40	N/A
Chesapeake & Ohio Canal[a]	0.25	0.25
Railroads		
New York Central Railroad	3.40	2.06
Erie Railroad	2.40	1.84
Western Railroad (Buffalo, N.Y., to Chicago, Ill.)	2.50	N/A
Western Railroad (Boston, Mass., to Albany, N.Y.)	2.30	N/A
Pennsylvania Railroad	3.50	1.96
Great Lakes		
Western lakes (short voyage)	0.10	N/A
Western lakes (long voyage)	0.05	N/A

[a] Rates available for coal shipments only.
Source: George Rogers Taylor, *The Transportation Revolution, 1815–1860* (New York: Rinehart, 1957), 442.

Local Transportation

Railroads tied U.S. cities into a vast network of urban communities that fostered trade and communication. Unfortunately, they also had a nasty habit of laying their tracks right through the middle of small towns and great cities alike without the slightest regard for safety or aesthetics. The railroad companies carved up urban communities so routinely that it became a cliché to speak of somebody's living on the "right" versus the "wrong side of the tracks." Trains barreled through the heart of towns such as Altoona, Pennsylvania, at all hours with impunity because they had the city fathers under their thumb and the city's economy in their pocket.

But there was a positive side of the impact of mass transportation on U.S. cities, and that was the development of new and more efficient means of moving large numbers of people. As the long-distance variety did, local mass transportation made a great leap forward in the mid-19th century, though it also had several painful tumbles. The changes were driven by social factors (urbanization) as much as by technological advances. New modes of local transportation that first made their appearance during these years include trolleys, cable cars, even subways, and elevated trains. They were all designed to meet the needs of the growing crush of people trying to travel around in the nation's cities. With no existing mass transportation beyond the horse-drawn wagon or carriage, the way was open for any successful, cost-efficient system to set the standard.

Eliminating the horse from the equation was the first challenge. One of the chief problems of urban transportation was reliance on horses, which were high-maintenance and left excrement on the streets. What was needed was an effective, urban-friendly "streetcar" that was not literally horse-powered. In 1872 George Brayton patented a natural-gas-powered streetcar, which he demonstrated in Providence, Rhode Island, the following year, but a power source that worked for street lamps did not work for streetcars. Then in 1874 Charles Dudley Field successfully tested an electric street car that operated from a central electrical dynamo. The idea caught on first in New York City, but not immediately. Field patented his idea four years later, but the first electric streetcar (trolley) system would not debut in New York City until 1887, introducing a forest of overhead wires and endless confrontations with horse-drawn vehicles for right-of-way. But as the first form of urban mass transportation specifically created for the industrial city, electric trolleys eventually became the norm.

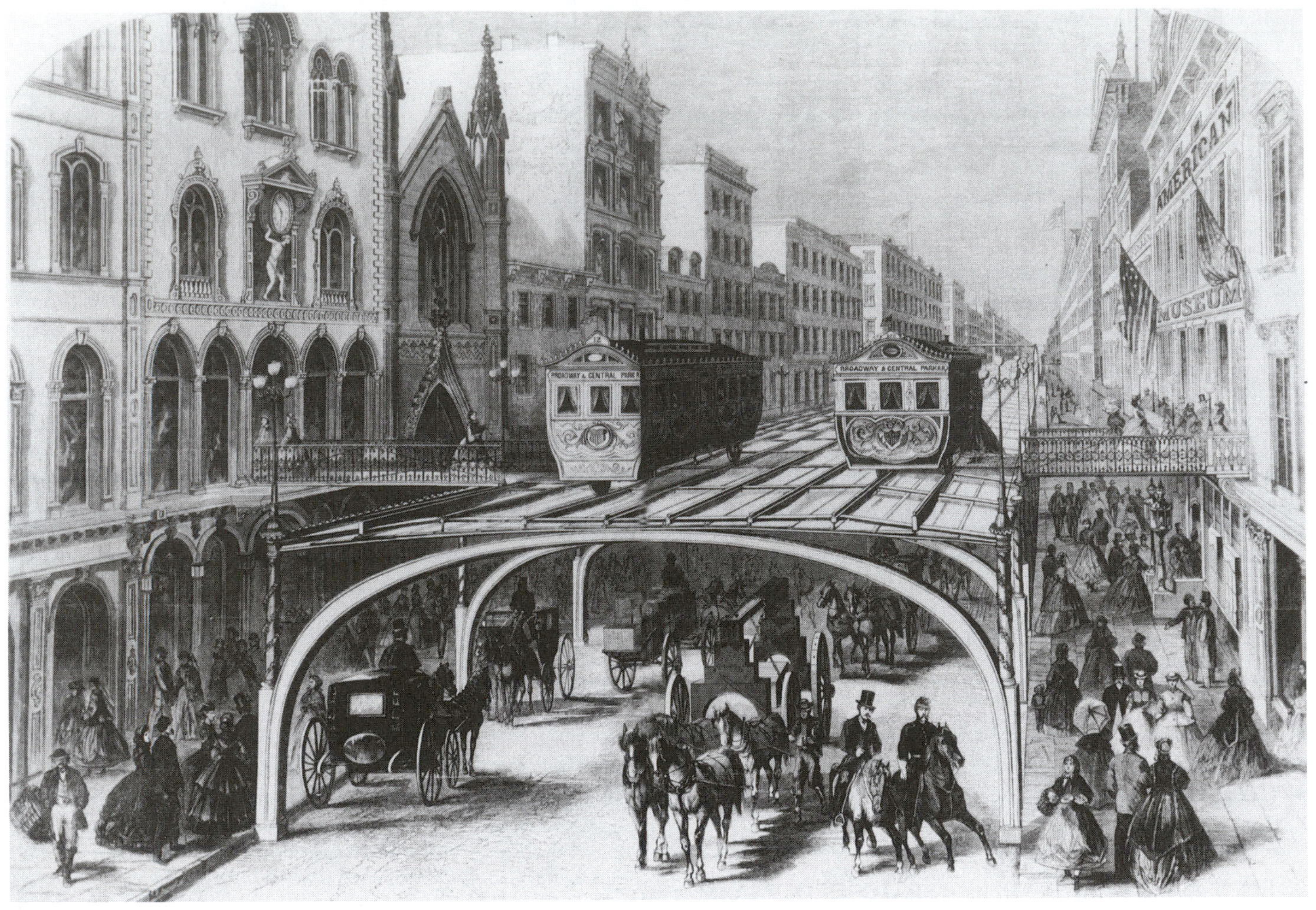

The U.S. nation's first elevated railway was in New York City, going from Battery Place to 30th Street via Greenwich Street and Ninth Avenue. This engraving by William Hemstreet in *Frank Leslie's Illustrated Newspaper,* March 3, 1866, drawn a year before the railway opened, shows a multitrack line traversing Broadway, with elegant cars. (Library of Congress)

The second problem for any urban public transportation system to overcome after motive power was space limitations. Already in 1872 New York City was experiencing modern traffic jams, described by one contemporary as "stages, carriages, cart-men, express-men, pedestrians all melted together in one agglomerate mess!" Inventive minds were already working on the problem. If street level was already what the newspapers called "a serried mass of seething humanity," the place to look was either above ground or underground. In 1867 Alfred Beach invented a pneumatic passenger subway system, which proved technologically and economically feasible but lost the public relations war. That same year, the first elevated railroad was completed in New York City by the West Side Elevated Railroad Company, a single track running from Battery Place (downtown Manhattan) up Ninth Avenue to 30th Street. It got off to a rough start. The first trains operated on a continuous chain or cable, but that was soon replaced by small steam locomotives pulling three to six cars each. The company rushed it into service, but it failed financially within three years. A new company took over the line and in the face of growing public resistance expanded service up Sixth and Third Avenues. The city franchised private companies to operate various parts of a growing system that New Yorkers were soon calling "the El." These included the Gilbert Elevated Railway, which ran along Greenwich Street, and the Third Avenue Railroad, running between City Hall Park and 42nd Street. Manhattan's system was extended into the Bronx, and Brooklyn built its own "El" line.

It was the beginning of a love-hate relationship that would endure well into the 20th century as the tracks blocked out the sky, and the trains rained ashes and cinders on pedestrians below while their rumbling made nearby buildings shake every time they passed. The concept was always more beloved by city officials and private enterprise that stood to profit by operating it than by urban dwellers forced to live in its shadow. When this era ended in 1875, Boston officials were discussing plans to build an elevated railway in their city.

Most cities, without New York City's traffic problems yet, preferred street-level, horse-drawn streetcars, which were easy to set up and operate even for small towns and required no great investment in new technology. But it was still the big cities that drove developments, and within 20 years electric streetcars were a common sight on Main Street, U.S.A.

Despite the occasional setback, the steam-powered railroad industry was one of the most vital parts of the U.S. economy. It represented more than one-third of the total dollar value of U.S. industry by 1870, and its political clout was commensurate with its economic power. By contrast, in the entire transportation industry, street and electric railways represented only a fraction of a percentage of the total dollar value. Clearly in U.S. cities, horse-drawn transportation was still the order of the day at the end of this period.

Between the needs of short-haul local transportation and long-distance needs there was a third area that demanded attention: interurban transportation. With the improving speed and comfort of modern trans-

TABLE 6.24 COMPARATIVE VALUE OF STEAM, STREET, AND ELECTRIC RAILWAYS WITH ALL U.S. INDUSTRIES, 1870–1875

(in millions of dollars)

Year	Value of All U.S. Industries	Value of Steam Railroads	Value of Street and Electric Railways
1870	4,437	3,787	65
1871	4,484	3,829	61
1872	4,899	4,172	68
1873	5,656	4,799	81
1874	5,993	5,076	90
1875	5,729	4,844	91

Note: Value includes industrial plants and equipment.
Source: U.S. Bureau of the Census, *Historical Statistics of the United States,* vol. 2 (Washington, D.C.: U.S. Government Printing Office, 1960), 940.

portation, trips to nearby cities no more than a few hours away became increasingly attractive. Charles Grafton Page invented an electric locomotive powered by galvanic storage batteries and successfully demonstrated it in a trial run from Washington, D.C., to Blandensburg, Maryland, in April 1851. But the technology of storing an electrical charge was still too primitive to be practical. The benefits of steam-powered locomotion were obvious, even if it was unwieldy and dangerous in an urban setting. In 1856 the first interurban "steam trains" were put in service in Massachusetts over a route from Boston to Cambridge, but the venture failed for technological as well as financial reasons.

Special conditions required creative solutions. Thus, in 1873, an Englishman, Andrew Hallidie, patented a successful cable car system for overcoming the hills of San Francisco, California, and other vertically challenged cities. He was the first to sell an entire system to a city, but he was not the first to have the idea. In 1858 Elaezer A. Gardener of Philadelphia received a patent for a cable car that operated on pulleys and cables, but his hometown—unlike San Francisco—had no particular need for it. In mountainous regions, cogwheel railways offered another solution to the problem of moving people up and down from point A to point B in a timely and efficient manner. The world's first cog railroad was the Mount Washington Cog Railway, invented by Sylvester Marsh and in operation after August 1866.

By the end of this period, a variety of creative solutions were moving Americans around cities and between cities. The constant demand for faster, cheaper transportation and the lure of enormous profit were all that was needed to motivate U.S. inventors to produce a better set of wheels. The results ranged from the exotic and totally impractical, such as the horse-powered ferries (horseboats) that operated on the same principle as a treadmill, to ideas just a little ahead of their time, such as Charles Grafton Page's electric-powered locomotive. A few mass transportation proposals represented nothing more than faulty thinking or the misapplication of existing technology, for instance, Alfred Beach's pneumatic subway and Henry Alonzo and James A. House's 1866 steam-powered "automobile." All forms of mass urban transportation, however, had one feature in common: They were an attempt to answer the age-old urban problem of how to move large numbers of people swiftly and efficiently about the city. As cities grew larger in the 19th century, so did the problem. New technology could alleviate the problem; it could never solve it.

TABLE 6.25 ADVANCES IN LOCAL TRANSPORTATION IN U.S. CITIES, 1850–1875

Mode of Transportation	Inventor or Operator	Locale or Area Served	Built or Introduced
Steam-powered street trains ("interurbans")	Unknown	Boston to Cambridge, Mass.	Mar. 1856
Horse-drawn trolley	Unknown	Boston Philadelphia Chicago	1852 1858 1859
Elevated railway	West Side Elevated Railroad Company	New York City	1867–69
Cable car	Andrew Smith Hallidie[a]	San Francisco	1871–73
The "third rail" for electric railways	Stephen Field	New York City	1874–87

[a] Hallidie invented the technology that made the cable car possible: an underground continuous moving cable and a mechanical grip for the underside of the cars.
Source: Gorton Carruth, *The Encyclopedia of American Facts and Dates,* 8th ed. (New York: Harper & Row, 1987), passim.

With new and unregulated technology, it was only natural that a rash of accidents follow, and with tragic consequences. The use of contained combustion for locomotion, the high speeds attainable through powerful steam engines, the flimsy construction of trains and boats alike, and finally the large numbers of passengers crammed together all contributed to the appalling mortality rate associated with early steam travel. The manufacturers were learning as they went, and safety was low on the list of concerns. Besides, the United States was a nation built on free choice; no one was forced to ride on trains or riverboats. Travelers of necessity adopted an attitude of fatalism when embarking on any trip. Reports of crashes and derailings, of sinkings and boiler explosions, became almost routine fare in the newspapers of the day, accompanied by shocking casualty figures unmatched heretofore in peacetime. The story of those accidents, along with other disasters, is the subject of another chapter, however (chapter 2).

The rise of any new form of transportation is always accompanied by the decline of some older form. The mid-19th century was no exception as wagons and stage coaches began to play an ever-diminishing role in the nation's transportation mix. This was not necessarily evident in 1850, when emigrant wagon trains were still the principal way settlers moved west and stage coaches still carried most mail and passenger traffic. The opening of regular coach service between Missouri and California in 1858 was actually more of a last hurrah than an affirmation of strength. The Butterfield stagecoach company and its successors on the Overland route were never wildly profitable nor even particularly popular among either passengers or investors. As a rule, traveling in the 19th century was still a necessity rather than a pleasure. Seventeen years later, at the end of this era, it was apparent that the future of mass transportation lay in mechanical, steam-powered modes.

CHAPTER 7 Population

Demographic Trends

These were years of rapid population growth in the United States, which was attributable mostly to the vast tide of arriving immigrants. The number of Americans increased more than 500 percent between 1800 and 1850 and averaged nearly a one-third increase every decade between 1840 and 1880. The four years of Civil War in the 1860s exerted a powerful downward pull, both by killing off a generation of men and by discouraging immigration while the conflict raged. During that decade the rate of population growth declined 10 percent. Still, most of the demographic loss attributable to the conflict was replaced in the years that followed by successive waves of immigrants. The same scale of deaths in European countries from two great 20th-century wars produced permanent declines in national populations. By comparison, the U.S. population absorbed the deaths of 1861–65 and kept right on expanding without missing a beat, truly an amazing accomplishment.

TABLE 7.1 POPULATION GROWTH OF THE UNITED STATES, 1850–1875, 1880

Year[a]	Population	Increase over Previous Census	Percentage Increase
1850	**23,261,000**	**6,122,000**	**35.9**
1851	24,086,000	. . .	. . .
1852	24,911,000	. . .	. . .
1853	25,736,000	. . .	. . .
1854	26,561,000	. . .	. . .
1855	27,386,000	. . .	. . .
1856	28,212,000	. . .	. . .
1857	29,037,000	. . .	. . .
1858	29,862,000	. . .	. . .
1859	30,687,000	. . .	. . .
1860	**31,513,000**	**8,251,000**	**35.6**
1861	32,351,000	. . .	. . .
1862	33,188,000	. . .	. . .
1863	34,026,000	. . .	. . .
1864	34,863,000	. . .	. . .
1865	35,701,000	. . .	. . .
1866	36,538,000	. . .	. . .
1867	37,376,000	. . .	. . .
1868	38,213.000	. . .	. . .
1869	39,051,000	. . .	. . .
1870	**39,905,000**	**8,375,000**	**26.6**
1871	40,938,000	. . .	. . .
1872	41,972,000	. . .	. . .
1873	43,006,000	. . .	. . .
1874	44,040,000	. . .	. . .
1875	45,073,000	. . .	. . .
1880	**50,155,783**	**10,337,000**	**26.0**

Note: The census numbers for the 19th century, depending on the source consulted, can vary by as much as 60,000 to 70,000 people for a particular decennial year. The original numbers have been recalculated in modern times using more sophisticated statistical models and, wherever possible, rechecking historical sources. The numbers here are rounded off to the nearest thousand, reflecting the corrections of the U.S. Census Bureau, ca. 1875.

[a] Census years in boldface type.

Sources: U.S. Bureau of the Census, *Historical Statistics of the United States, Colonial Times to 1970,* series A (Washington, D.C.: Government Printing Office, 1975), 8; Chris Cook and David Waller, *The Longman Handbook of Modern American History, 1763–1996* (New York: Addison Wesley Longman, 1998), 177; Thomas C. Cochran and Wayne Andrews, eds. *Concise Dictionary of American History* (New York: Charles Scribner's Sons, 1962), 747.

Immigration was the great multiplier of U.S. population growth. If demographics is destiny, the nation was indeed fortunate that it did not have to depend on natural increase to grow during these years. Among the native white population, fertility dropped steadily during the 19th century. The typical white woman bore seven or eight children in 1800; by 1860 that number had dropped to five or six. Over the course of the century, the decline amounted to a 50 percent drop, falling fastest after about 1830. Shifting family values and declining economic necessity for large families are usually cited as the reasons for this phenomenon. Early in the century, natural increase contributed more than 95 percent of the population growth; by 1880 that percentage was down to 71.5 percent, meaning that immigration accounted for the remaining 28.5 percent. These statistics help explain why as the century advanced, old-stock Americans grew increasingly alarmed about the social, political, and economic impact of all those new immigrants.

Not only were white women having significantly fewer children every decade, but so were black women, at least up to 1870. Black women were in a different situation than their white counterparts because under slavery stable family life was an impossibility and even the institution of marriage was denied them. Instead, they were practically bred as livestock to keep the system going, and that system discouraged bringing children into the world. The maternal image of the slave "mammy" was as a nursemaid or surrogate mother for her master's children, not her own. It took emancipation in 1865 to reverse the decline in African-American birth rate by opening the door to marriage and stable family life, thus the higher birth rate revealed in the 1870 census figures: Free women were more likely to embrace motherhood than enslaved women.

The standard demographic model calculates birth rates by using a complicated formula that counts the number of children ages zero to four years of 1,000 women, ages 15 to 44. Dividing the number of births by the census population for the decennial then yields an estimated birth rate. The estimated white birth rate has been calculated by the demographers Warren S. Thompson and P. K. Whelpton, along with the ratio of natural increase to immigration as sources of U.S. population growth. Information from that time is incomplete for black women, and Hispanics were lumped together with whites.

TABLE 7.2 BIRTH RATES IN U.S. POPULATION BY RACE, 1850–1880

Decennial Year	Children per 1,000 Women[a]		White Birth Rate per 1,000 Population	White Birth Rate per 1,000 Women[b]
	White	Black		
1850	659	741[c]	43.3	194
1860	675	724	41.4	184
1870	610	692	38.3	167
1880	586	750[c]	35.2	155

[a] Counting only those children zero to four years of age, and those women 15 to 44 years of age.

[b] Counting only those women 15 to 44 years of age.

[c] This category would have included both blacks and mulattos (mixed race), all of them lumped together in the vernacular of the day as "negroes" or "coloreds."

Source: Thomas C. Cochran and Wayne Andrews, eds. *Concise Dictionary of American History* (New York: Charles Scribner's Sons, 1962), 748.

TABLE 7.3 WHITE POPULATION GROWTH FROM NATURAL INCREASE VERSUS IMMIGRATION, 1840–1880

Decade	White Population Growth	Population Growth by Natural Increase	As Percentage of Population Growth	Population Growth by Immigration	As Percentage of Population Growth
1841–50	5,357,000	3,937,000	73.5	1,420,000	26.5
1851–60	7,369,000	4,811,000	65.3	2,558,000	34.7
1861–70	7,415,000	5,341,000	72.0	2,074,000	28.0
1871–80	9,066,000	6,486,000	71.5	2,580,000	28.5

Source: Thomas C. Cochran and Wayne Andrews, eds. *Concise Dictionary of American History* (New York: Charles Scribner's Sons, 1962), 748.

TABLE 7.4 GROWTH IN POPULATION PER SQUARE MILE BY STATE AND REGION, 1850–1870

Region and State[a]	1850	1860	Percentage Increase over 1850	1870	Percentage Increase over 1860[b]
North					
Mass.	123.7	153.1	24	181.3	18
Conn.	76.9	95.5	24	111.5	17
Del.	46.6	57.1	22	63.6	11
N.H.	35.2	36.1	03	35.2	(–) 02
N.Y.	65.0	81.4	25	92.0	13
Pa.	51.6	64.8	26	78.6	21
Ohio	48.6	57.4	18	65.4	14
Ind.	27.5	37.6	37	46.8	24
Ill.	15.2	30.6	101	45.4	48
Iowa	3.5	12.1	256	21.5	78
Ky.	24.4	28.8	18	32.9	14
Maine	19.5	21.0	08	21.0	0
Mich.	6.9	13.0	88	20.6	58
N.J.	65.2	89.4	37	128.6	44
R.I.	138.3	163.7	18	203.7	24
Vt.	34.4	34.5	0.3	36.2	05
Wis.	5.5	14.0	61	19.1	36
South					
Washington, D.C.	891.2	1294.5	45	2270.7	75
Ala.	15.0	18.8	25	19.4	03
Ark.	4.0	8.3	110	9.2	11
Fla.	1.6	2.6	62	3.4	31
Ga.	15.4	18.0	17	20.2	12
La.	11.4	15.6	37	16.0	03
Md.	58.6	69.1	18	78.6	14
Miss.	13.1	17.1	31	17.9	05
Mo.	9.9	17.2	74	25.0	45
N.C.	17.8	20.4	15	22.0	08
S.C.	21.9	23.1	05	23.1	0
Tenn.	24.1	26.6	10	30.2	14
Va.	27.8	30.3	09	30.4	0.3
W.Va.	N/A	N/A	N/A	18.4	N/A
West					
Calif.	0.6	2.4	300	3.6	50
Kans.	N/A	1.3	N/A	4.5	246
Minn.	N/A	2.1	N/A	5.4	157
Nebr.	N/A	0.2	N/A	1.6	700
Nev.	N/A	0.1	N/A	0.4	300
Oreg.	N/A	0.5	N/A	1.0	100
Tex.	0.8	2.3	187	3.1	35
Utah	N/A	0.3	N/A	1.1	267

[a] Regional groupings are based on cultural and geographical identity, not political alignment during the Civil War. In some cases, e.g., Ky. and Mo., the designation is more subjective. The "West" includes any state with a defined frontier area plus a population density of less than one person per square mile in 1850.
[b] Only one state in the Union, N.H., had negative (–) population growth during these years.
Sources: Donald B. Dodd, compiler, *Historical Statistics of the States of the United States: Two Centuries of the Census, 1790–1990* (Westport, Conn.: Greenwood Press, 1993), 2–99; Gavin Wright, *Old South, New South* (New York: Basic Books, 1986), 25.

The spectacular population growth of these years was not uniformly distributed across all regions: The West grew fastest, averaging 232 percent growth across the board between 1860 and 1870, but the most significant difference was between the states collectively known as the North versus those collectively known as the South. The rate of growth in the North was consistently higher than in the South, with profound political and economic consequences. Even Virginia, the exemplar of Southern pride and progress, did not experience any statistically meaningful growth in the 1860s. What growth the South did enjoy during the years 1850–70 was more apparent than real. Most of it occurred in the region's westernmost states as the result of internal migration from the Old South, not of immigration from abroad. Meanwhile the North was snaring the lion's share of foreign immigrants, and it was those same immigrants who had the highest birth rate of any segment of the population.

The diverging demographics can be seen in the relative population densities of the two sections in the three census counts between 1850 and 1870. If one disregards the top and bottom states, the Northern states on average increased their population per square mile by more than 38 percent during the 1850s, while the Southern states on average increased only about 22 percent. The same imbalance can be seen in the following decade, only made worse by civil war. In general, birth rates and immigration both greatly favored the North during these years.

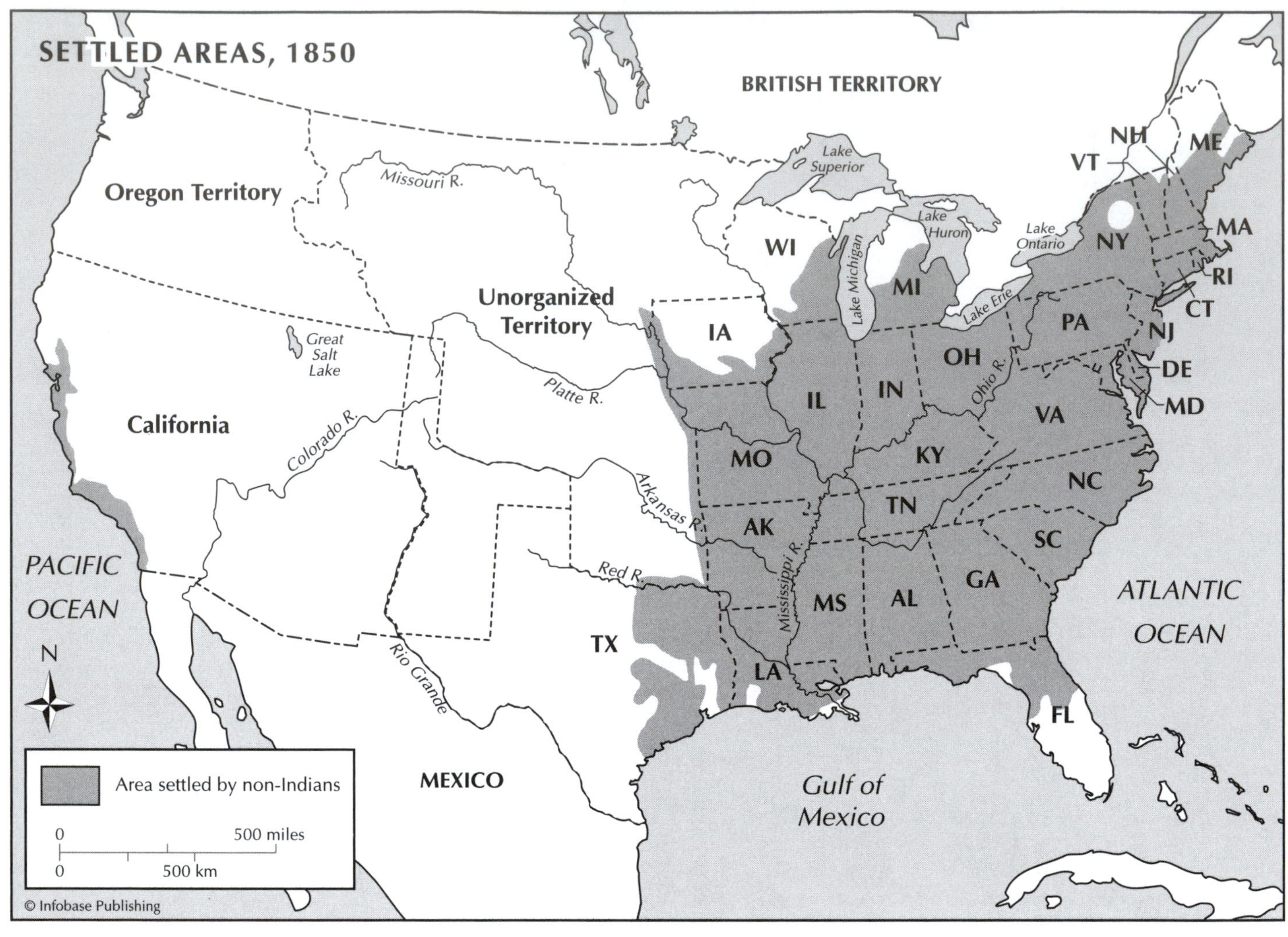

Source: Sandra Opdycke. *The Routledge Historical Atlas of Women in America.* New York: Routledge, 2000, 35

Age and Mortality Statistics

The median age of the U.S. population around mid-century was remarkably young. In 1850, it was slightly less than 19 years for both whites and blacks, with whites slightly older and blacks almost two full years younger than the median. In 1860, the black median age had declined while the white was approaching 20 years. After another 10 years the median age for both races was still younger than age 21, but whites were only slightly younger while blacks still hovered below 19 years old. Thus, it is apparent that while the life span for whites was rising steadily year after year, for blacks it was lagging chronically behind, in fact barely improving over two decades. Longevity for African Americans did rise significantly between 1860 and 1870, likely reflecting the end of slavery and the brutal conditions associated with it.

For women as a whole, the median age was lower than for men. Although solid statistical proof is lacking, it is nonetheless fair to say that more women died as a result of childbirth and overwork than men died as a result of war and violence, even during the decade of the Civil War. As a result of poor hygiene, poor eating habits, lack of effective medicines, and other factors, the average U.S. child in 1850 or 1860 was unlikely to even survive the teenage years. This is not to say that people suddenly dropped dead at age 19. What skewered the numbers were infant mortality and childhood diseases. If a child survived infancy, his or her chance of living to a "ripe old age" improved dramatically.

The United States was fortunate to have a population in its most productive and healthy years: 15 to 64 years old. But even among the "elderly" (those 65 years and older), a remarkable number were able to live independently in their advanced years, suggesting that anyone who survived to age 64 had already proved to be hardy, not susceptible to diseases or physical breakdown.

TABLE 7.5 MEDIAN AGE OF THE U.S. POPULATION, 1850–1870

Demographic Category	1850	1860	1870
Total Population	18.9	19.4	20.2
Male	19.2	19.8	20.2
Female	18.6	19.1	20.1
All whites	19.2	19.7	20.4
White males	19.5	20.1	20.6
White females	18.8	19.3	20.3
All blacks	17.4	17.5	18.3
Black males	17.3	17.5	17.8
Black females	17.4	17.5	18.8
All others[a]	N/A	26.1	28.1
Other males	N/A	27.5	29.1
Other females	N/A	20.5	23.0

[a] Includes Asians and Native Americans, for whom statistics are "not available" from 1850, and not entirely reliable on the next two census counts.
Source: U.S. Bureau of the Census, *Historical Statistics of the United States, Colonial Times to 1970,* series A (Washington, D.C.: Government Printing Office, 1975), 8.

TABLE 7.6 PERCENTAGE OF ELDERLY AND CHILDREN IN THE GENERAL POPULATION OF THE UNITED STATES AND RATIO OF DEPENDENCY FOR THE SAME GROUPS ON THE GENERAL POPULATION, 1850–1870

	1850			1860			1870		
Categories	Male	Female	Both Sexes	Male	Female	Both Sexes	Male	Female	Both Sexes
Less than 15 years of age as percentage of general population	41.2	41.8	41.5	40.2	40.9	40.6	39.3	39.1	39.2
Older than 64 years of age as percentage of general population	4.1	4.2	4.1	4.2	4.4	4.3	3.0	3.0	3.0
Dependency ratio for combined under 15 and over 64[a]	42.6	41.5	84.1	41.1	40.0	81.4	37.0	36.0	73.0

Note: Children by the applicable census reports are defined as persons less than 15 years of age; the *elderly* are defined as persons 65 years and older.
[a] This includes those on the upper and lower ends of the population, agewise, between the ages of 15 and 64, who were supported by others, probably family members.
Source: Douglas L. Anderton et al., *The Population of the United States,* 3d ed. (New York: The Free Press, 1997), 428.

TABLE 7.7 COMPARATIVE MORTALITY AMONG SELECTED STATE POPULATIONS AS A PERCENTAGE OF THE TOTAL STATE POPULATION, 1850

	Mortality Rate				
Condition/Category	La.	Ark.	Miss.	Tex.	Md.
Zymotic[a]	10.17	6.01	6.04	6.28	5.65
Sporadic	6.45	5.29	5.25	4.18	6.47
External	1.68	0.78	1.34	1.27	0.74
Epidemic/endemic	7.33	4.96	4.80	5.96	4.19
Monoxysragl[b]	0.42	0.85	0.89	0.43	1.40
Variable	0.92	0.69	1.01	0.76	9.53
Nervous disorder	1.60	0.80	0.98	0.95	1.55
Respiratory	1.31	1.88	1.63	1.83	2.29
Circulatory	0.08	0.02	0.06	0.05	0.22
Digestive	0.60	1.90	1.02	0.75	0.58
Urinary	0.01	0.03	0.02	0.03	0.04
Locomotive	0.06	0.08	0.07	0.08	0.12
Integumentary[c]	0.01	N/A	0.03	0.02	0.01
Old age	0.17	0.17	0.23	0.17	0.43
Stillborn	0.06	0.10	0.05	0.04	0.04
Casualties	0.57	0.53	0.93	0.94	0.58
Exopathic[d]	0.05	0.18	0.31	0.28	0.05
Esopathic[e]	0.14	0.08	0.08	0.03	0.09
Medical treatment	N/A	N/A	0.01	N/A	N/A
Female	0.16	0.32	0.20	0.44	0.18
Total mortality as a percentage of population	21.49	14.34	14.62	15.72	16.85

Note: N/A, not available.
[a] An infectious or contagious disease, especially one caused by a fungus.
[b] Caused by a parasite.
[c] Pertaining to the skin or epidermis.
[d] Any disease due to external causes.
[e] Any disease due to internal causes.
Source: U.S. Department of Commerce and Labor, *A Century of Population Growth* (Washington, D.C.: Government Printing Office, 1909), 106.

Americans were constantly reminded of their own mortality because death was all around them. The ill and dying were not whisked away to hospitals and hospices to die out of sight but died at home surrounded by friends and family. Families were routinely hit by the deaths of loved ones. A woman might give birth to eight children, only to bury six of them before they reached maturity. A husband might lose his wife as a result of repeated pregnancies, and many of those pregnancies terminated in miscarriage. Surviving childbirth merely meant a life of disease and accident, and medical knowledge of the day was able to save precious few even when doctors and hospitals were available, and in many isolated areas they were not. Lack of medical care was a mixed blessing because without effective treatment, the mortally ill did not suffer long. As a result of all these factors, average life expectancy in the 1850s was about age 40, and while comprehensive statistics are not available for every state, the figures that exist show a mortality rate of between 14 percent and 21 percent among whites at the beginning of this period. (Almost all the contemporary statistics are for whites only.) As a general rule, the mortality rate due to sickness and disease tended to be higher in the West than in the South, and higher in the South than in the North. The differences are explained by climate, lifestyle, and the availability of medical care. Urban life in one of the major cities was a trade-off: Good medical care was more often available, but crowded living conditions made some diseases more dangerous.

It is virtually impossible to calculate comprehensive mortality figures for either the black or the Native American population because of lack of statistical data. In general, most authorities thought of slaves (the overwhelming majority of blacks) as property, not as actuarial subjects or even as members of the "regular population." A similar bias applied to the American Indian population, who, instead of being regarded as property, were regarded as savages, not "Americans," and therefore excluded from demographic calculations.

TABLE 7.8 DEATHS PER 100,000 POPULATION IN NEW YORK CITY, PHILADELPHIA, AND NEW ORLEANS, 1864–1888

Cause of Death	Average Annual Death Rate per 100,000 Population
Tuberculosis	365
Stomach and intestinal disorders	299
Diphtheria	123
Typhoid	66
Smallpox	53

Source: Stephan Thernstrom, *A History of the American People* (San Diego: Harcourt Brace Jovanovich, 1989), 467.

Defining U.S. Society

The United States was home to four distinct racial-ethnic groups: native-born whites, European immigrants, African Americans, and Native Americans. Native Americans are discussed in chapter 3; the others groups lived in uneasy peace within the boundaries of the United States. Race and ethnicity were also tied to economic status and lifestyle.

After race, probably no characteristic defined Americans more than whether they were rural or urban dwellers. In mid-19th century, the U.S. population was still overwhelmingly rural, not so much by choice as by necessity. It was still a country of vast, empty spaces and relatively few cities, and most people were still tied to the land because that was the only way of life they had ever known. Many had immigrated to the United States looking for a piece of land to call their own, and nearing the end of the nation's first century, many Americans still drew both their livelihood and their identity from the land. Rural folks tended to be conservative, independent, and hard-working. Concepts of leisure and play and the luxuries of "high culture" were practically unknown to them.

The New York Colonization Society was one of several U.S. groups that thought the solution to the "slave question" was to repatriate all American blacks back to Africa. In this depiction, a thankful naked black man gratefully shakes hands with his white benefactor while his transportation "home" awaits in the background. This certificate of lifetime membership in the society honors Alexander Fraser and is signed by the society president, Anson Philps. (The Gilder Lehrman Collection on deposit at the Pierpont Morgan Library, New York. GLC 5781)

In an agrarian society, there are basically two classes: the propertied class (landowners) and the landless working class. This general rule did not apply in 19th-century America however, for two reasons: (1) Land was so plentiful that even many of the poor could acquire a little piece of their own, and (2) urbanization and a booming economy were creating a middle class with significant clout in national life. As a result, Americans did not have to settle for a class system virtually frozen in place such as they had left behind in the Old World.

Regional Character

The South

The three major regions of the country—South, Northeast, and West—each had its own distinctive social structure. The Civil War would blur these distinctions into North versus South, but in the antebellum period there were still three distinct sections competing for influence and recognition. The South's social structure included a white slave-owning aristocracy, a yeoman class of small nonslaveholding farmers, a lower class of poor or "backwoods" whites, and black slaves. All four groups depended on agriculture for their livelihood. There was also a small professional class of lawyers, merchants, artisans, and physicians who were scarcely represented in the region's demographics. In every Southern state nonslaveholding farmers composed the majority of the white population before the Civil War, but their political and economic influence was disproportionately small compared to their numbers. In 1860 only one-fourth of all white families owned slaves, and of those, about half owned five or fewer. The large slave owners were a minority even in their own region, and a declining minority at that. The slaveholding class represented 31 percent of the South in 1850 but had shrunk to 25 percent by 1860, because many had been ruined by the high cost of owning slaves, and there were growing numbers of Southerners occupying the bottom rungs of society. Despite the inequities of the slave system for whites and blacks alike, slavery was the strongest bond uniting white Southerners; its preservation and defense extended across all class and state lines. Slaveholders and nonslaveholders alike generally agreed on the necessity and benefits of slavery to their society as a whole.

In the last census count before the Civil War, there were 3,957,700 slaves in the Southern states. They represented a permanent black underclass, locked into a caste system almost as rigid as India's. It was not a benevolent, paternalistic system, as its defenders asserted, nor a hopelessly cruel and brutal system, as its critics charged. It was a system ingrained in Southern society, questioned by few, vigorously defended by many, and in many ways it worked. It was much more complex than the simplistic image of field hands and house slaves would suggest. There were rural and urban bondsmen, agricultural and industrial, faithful and rebellious individuals in the system. But the majority were employed in producing cash crops for sale to distant markets. In 1850 the typical slave worked on a large farm or plantation with no more than nine fellow bondsmen and bondswomen. Men and women worked side by side under the watchful eye of an overseer subclass, totally dependent on the whims of their master.

Life as a slave on the plantation was defined by the "quarters," the Southern version of the urban ghetto. Only in recent years has scholarship focused on the slave quarters as the center of slave life, and in so doing moved beyond the stereotypes of the "happy" slave or the submissive Uncle Tom. There existed in the quarters a unique exile community built on extended kinship, folk tales and African lore, spirituals, and an Afro-Christianity that flourished either behind the master's back or with his tacit approval. It was in the slave quarters that a distinct African-American culture was born, neither fully American nor fully African, with its own pidgin language, music, oral history, and religious practices capable of sustaining a people in bondage.

The great unmentionable in race relations was miscegenation, or the mixture of the races through sexual relations. Even so-called liberals considered this a crime against "nature's law," and most states legislated against it, although it was a fact of life wherever whites and blacks lived in close proximity. In point of fact, it was the dirty little secret of the plantation South that might be winked at in polite society but was acknowledged in census tallies. Mulattoes made up 11.2 percent of the total black population in 1850 (159,000 of them "free"), 13.2 percent in 1860, and 12.0 percent in 1870. Ironically the number of mulattoes counted in the former slave states was less than half the number counted in the North and less than one-fourth in western states and territories, suggesting that there were other factors at work in the numbers being reported than simple demographic characteristics.

For all its built-in safeguards and solid institutional basis, slavery was a very fragile system, built on fear, intimidation, and rigid traditions. The South, as Jefferson had once observed, had a "wolf by the ears" in slavery and could not let go. Its economy, its class system, and its political power were inseparably tied to the abhorrent system of human bondage. What had once been a geographic location ("the South") by the 1850s had become a regional identity ("the Old South"), celebrated in such books as *Sociology for the South* and *Social Relations in Our Southern States,* written by Southern authors not surprisingly. And slavery to Southerners was "our peculiar institution."

The institution of slavery, implicitly protected in the Constitution, affected the whole nation, not just the South. Although most Northerners frowned on slavery and considered it a Southern problem, only three states in the Union had taken the step of abolishing it by law before the Civil War: Pennsylvania and California (both in 1850) and Minnesota (1858). Every other state in the Union accepted the *legal* existence of slavery, and this despite the fact that both the northern and western sections of the country had their own resident black populations, although in both cases composed overwhelmingly of free blacks, not slaves. The black populations in those two regions ranged from a high of 3.8 percent of the total population in New Jersey to a low of 0.1 percent in the western territories of Montana, Colorado, and New Mexico. By contrast, in the Old South, black populations ranged upward to a high of more than 50 percent of the total population; in South Carolina, nearly 98 percent of those were slaves.

Free blacks were in the most awkward position; neither being full members of society nor possessing the dubious security of slaves, they existed in a twilight zone of prejudice, mistrust, and limited opportunity. By 1860 there were nearly a half-million free blacks in the United States, constituting about 11 percent of the total black population. More than half lived in the North, mostly in cities, where they enjoyed more protection from the law, but where they also had to compete with immigrants and the poorest members of society for the most menial jobs.

Segregation in public transportation was practiced as early as 1838, even in Massachusetts. This picture from the *Illustrated London News* of September 27, 1856, shows the conductor expelling a well-dressed black man from a railroad car in the "City of Brotherly Love," apparently so that a white woman and child can sit down. (Photographs and Prints Division, Schomburg Center for Research in Black Culture, The New York Public Library, Astor, Lenox, and Tilden Foundations)

At mid-century, blacks were by far the largest racial minority in the United States. Natural increase and years of importation (legal until 1808) produced numbers that were probably four times greater than that of the dwindling Native American population, while the Asian population was barely a line on the demographic chart. The relative proportions of the three races did not change much after 1850.

One should note that slavery only appears to be declining in the U.S. population during the last two decades before the Civil War: In absolute terms, the number of slaves was actually growing. The numbers were decreasing as a percentage of the general population only because of the enormous flood of European immigrants during those same years. The inference to be drawn from these figures is that the numbers of white Americans were increasing at a faster *rate* than the numbers of African Americans. Yet the statistics have allowed Southern apologists to argue that slavery was gradually declining as a demographic factor in the nation and therefore would have ultimately died a natural death, that is, without forceful intervention.

Obviously most African Americans were to be found in the South, and the states of the "Old South," because of their plantation-based economies had the greatest numbers. Slavery was also carried into the "South West" (written as two words before 1853) as slave-based agriculture aggressively expanded into Mississippi, Louisiana, and Texas. In the West as a whole, however, the black population was almost negligible until after the Civil War, when emancipation allowed blacks the freedom to choose where they wanted to live. The same characteristics that drew white settlers to the West also attracted blacks, although the great migration of blacks known as the Exodusters did not occur until after this period.

TABLE 7.9 RACIAL COMPOSITION OF THE U.S. POPULATION BY MAJOR GROUPS, 1850–1870

	Numbers				Percentage Distribution			Percentage Change Since Previous Decade		
Year	Whites	Blacks	American Indians	Chinese	White	Black	Other	White	Black	Other
1850	19,553,000	3,639,000	N/A	N/A	84.3	15.7	N/A	+37.7	+26.6	N/A
1860	26,923,000	4,442,000	44,000	35,000	85.6	14.1	0.3	+37.7	+22.1	N/A
1870	33,589,000	4,880,000	26,000	64,000	87.1	12.7	0.2	+24.8	+9.9	+13.9

Source: U.S. Bureau of the Census, *Historical Statistics of the United States, Colonial Times to 1970,* Series A (Washington, D.C.: U.S. Government Printing Office, 1975), 91–104.

TABLE 7.10 WHITE AND BLACK POPULATION OF THE UNITED STATES BY CENSUS COUNT, 1850–1880

			Black Population				
Census Year	Total Population	White Population	Total	Slave	Free	As Percentage of Total Population	Percentage Increase or Decrease over Previous Decade
1850	23,191,876	19,553,068	3,638,803	3,204,313	434,490	15.7	–1.1
1860	31,443,321	26,922,537	4,441,830	3,953,760	488,070	14.1	–1.6
1870	38,558,371	33,589,377	4,880,009	N/A	4,880,009	12.7	–1.4
1880	50,155,783	45,275,783	6,581,000	N/A	6,581,000	13.1	+0.4

Note: Not applicable for 1870 or 1880 because slavery was abolished by the Thirteenth Amendment to the Constitution in 1865.
Sources: U.S. Census Office, *A Compendium of the 9th Census, June 1, 1870,* compiled by Frances Amasa Walker (Washington, D.C.: U.S. Government Printing Office, 1872) passim; Chris Cook and David Waller, *The Longman Handbook of Modern American History, 1763–1996* (New York: Addison Wesley Longman, 1998), 147.

TABLE 7.11 U.S. BLACK POPULATION BY STATE AND REGION ON THE EVE OF THE CIVIL WAR, 1860

State and Region	Black Population in 1860	Percentage of Black Population in State/Region in 1860
North	340,240	1.7
New England	24,711	0.8
Maine	1,327	0.2
N.H.	494	0.2
Vt.	709	0.2
Mass.	9,602	0.8
R.I.	3,952	2.3
Conn.	8,627	1.9
Middle Atlantic	131,290	1.8
N.Y.	49,005	1.3
N.J.	25,336	3.8
Pa.	56,949	2.0
East North-Central	63,699	0.9
Ohio	36,673	1.6
Ind.	11,428	0.9
Ill.	7,628	0.5
Mich.	6,799	0.9
Wis.	1,171	0.2
West North-Central	120,540	5.6
Minn.	259	0.2
Iowa	1,069	0.2
Mo.	118,503	10.0
Nebr.	82	0.3
Kans.	627	0.6
South	4,097,111	36.8
South Atlantic	2,058,198	38.4
Del.	21,627	19.3
Md.	171,131	24.9
District of Columbia	14,316	19.1
Va.	548,907	34.4
N.C.	361,522	36.4
S.C.	412,320	58.6
Ga.	465,698	44.1
Fla.	62,677	44.6
East South-Central	1,394,360	34.7
Ky.	236,167	20.4
Tenn.	283,019	25.5
Ala.	437,770	45.4
Miss.	437,404	55.3
West South-Central	644,553	36.9
Ark.	111,259	25.6
La.	350,373	49.5
Tex.	182,921	30.3
West	4,479	0.7
Mountain	235	0.1
Colo.	46	0.1
N.Mex.	85	0.1
Utah	59	0.2
Nev.	45	0.7
Pacific	4,244	1.0
Wash.	30	0.3
Oreg.	128	0.2
Calif.	4,086	1.1
U.S. Total	**4,441,830**	**14.1**

Source: Mabel M. Smythe, ed., *The Black American Reference Book* (Englewood Cliffs, N.J.: Prentice-Hall, 1976), 168–69.

Slavery was not a monolithic institution even in the South. There were significant differences between what was known as the Upper South and the Lower South, and lesser differences between the Old South and the Southwest, apart from simple geographical variations. ("Deep South" is a 20th-century designation.) The more northerly subregion also differed from the area farther south in terms of economy, living conditions, and commitment to slavery. The Upper South was characterized by milder climate; more land area devoted to tobacco, hemp, wheat, and vegetables and less to cash crops such as sugar and cotton; and generally less stridency on the twin issues of slavery and secession. The more tolerant racial attitudes in such states as Virginia, Tennessee, and Kentucky explain the enormous difference (more than five to one) in the numbers of free blacks living in each subregion. Free blacks found more opportunities and more acceptance in the Upper South. As a percentage of total population, the Lower South also had a far larger proportion of blacks, most notably in South Carolina, a fact that encouraged more repression by a fearful white population. There was also an important internal slave trade between the two subregions, with masters in the Upper South finding it very profitable to sell their surplus slaves to planters in the Lower South. As early as 1832, Virginia was being described as "a *negro*-raising State capable of furnishing as many as 6,000 slaves per year to buyers farther south." Slave-trading "hubs" in this internal trade included Richmond, Charleston, Savannah, Montgomery, Mobile, New Orleans, and Memphis.

The whole system of slavery, far from being on a long, slow decline as many apologists have stated, was actually becoming more entrenched in the South as the years went by. This is apparent from the statistics on slaveholdings gathered by the last two censuses before the Civil War. Although a great many Southerners were not slave owners, those who had slaves were heavily invested in the system, owning more than 32 slaves each in the Lower South in 1860 and more than 15 each in the Upper South. The average number of slaves per master rose in every Southern state save three (Florida, Tennessee, and Missouri) between 1850 and 1860. And because the African slave trade had been outlawed since 1808, this meant either that slaves were being smuggled in illegally or that they were being bred and sold as cattle are to supply the voracious demand. There was a need for a continuous, fresh supply of slaves because new lands were being opened to cultivation in the western territories, and the labor-intensive system "used up" slaves at a high rate. Clearly, slavery was not an archaic and deplorable by-product of plantation-style agriculture but a matter of big business for the South.

TABLE 7.12 FREE AND SLAVE POPULATIONS IN THE UPPER VERSUS LOWER SOUTH, 1860

State or Region	Number of Slaves	As Percentage of Total (Regional) Population	Number of Free Blacks[a]	As Percentage of Total (Regional) Black Population
United States (total)	3,953,760	12.6	488,070	11.0
Upper South	1,530,229	22.1	224,963	12.8
Del.	1,798	1.6	19,829	91.7
Md.	87,189	12.7	83,942	49.1
District of Columbia	3,185	4.2	11,131	77.8
Va.	490,865	30.7	58,042	10.6
N.C.	331,059	33.4	30,463	8.4
Ky.	225,483	19.5	10,684	4.5
Mo.	114,931	9.7	3,572	3.0
Tenn.	275,719	24.8	7,300	2.6
Deep South	2,423,467	44.8	36,955	1.5
S.C.	402,406	57.2	9,914	2.4
Ga.	462,198	43.7	3,500	0.8
Fla.	61,745	44.0	932	1.5
Ark.	111,115	25.5	144	0.1
Ala.	435,080	45.1	2,690	0.6
La.	331,726	46.9	18,647	5.3
Miss.	436,631	55.2	773	0.2
Tex.	182,566	30.2	355	0.2

[a] Calculated by subtracting the number of slaves in census counts from the total "Negro population" of each state.
Sources: Peter Kolchin, *American Slavery, 1619–1877* (New York: Hill & Wang, 1993), 241; John P. Davis, ed., *The American Negro Reference Book* (Englewood Cliffs, N.J.: Prentice-Hall, 1966); Ira Berlin, *Slaves without Masters* (New York: Pantheon Books, 1974), 396–99 (Appendix 1).

TABLE 7.13 AVERAGE NUMBER OF SLAVES PER HOLDING IN SOUTHERN STATES, 1850 AND 1860

State or Region	1850	1860
Total South	**20.6**	**23.0**
Total Upper South	**15.3**	**15.6**
Tenn.	15.2	15.1
Md.	12.2	14.0
Ky.	10.3	10.4
Mo.	8.6	8.3
Del.	5.7	6.3
N.C.	18.6	19.3
Va.	18.1	18.8
Total Deep South	**30.9**	**32.5**
La.	38.9	49.3
S.C.	38.2	38.9
Miss.	33.0	35.0
Ala.	29.9	33.4
Fla.	28.5	28.4
Ga.	26.0	26.4
Ark.	18.4	23.4
Tex.	14.9	17.6

Note: Holding can refer to a business firm (e.g., plantation) or an individual's personal property.
Source: Peter Kolchin, *American Slavery, 1619–1877* (New York: Hill & Wang, 1993), 244.

The North

In Northern society the most obvious characteristics were industrialization and city life. Unlike in the South, where the rhythms and patterns of life did not change all that much during the first half of the century, in the North, society was changing greatly in the nature of work, life, and social relationships. The North had built a social system based on Protestant, middle-class morality and obsessive industriousness. These ideals failed to truly connect with the tide of foreign immigrants on the one hand or with old-fashioned rural inhabitants on the other. One unexpected outcome of industrialization was that Northern society began to pull apart at the seams, dividing into three distinct socioeconomic classes, each with its own culture and values: a "genteel" class, a middle class, and a working class. The *Philadelphia Ledger* observed sadly in 1849, "There is now in our country . . . a high class and a low class . . . as divided as the white and red roses of York and Lancaster."

The largest class was the industrial working class. With the rise of industrialization, the labor of many citizens no longer centered on the field, the home, or the nearby shop, but on the factory. Owners and employees no longer worked side by side or lived in close proximity, and cities were no longer close-knit communities. Instead, workers became estranged from bosses, neighbors from neighbors, and city life from country life. The rise of the factory system necessitated new labor arrangements. Some employers aggressively recruited workers from among farm and immigrant populations. The increasing sophistication of machinery allowed the hiring of more unskilled and inexperienced workers than before. The new industrial working class lived in slums, had no job security, and labored for the lowest wages the market would bear.

As factories grew more complex and employed greater numbers of workers, a new class of managers and clerks arose to run operations for absentee owners. They swelled the ranks of the existing middle class of professionals and artisans, and they acted as a buffer between the working poor and the wealthy "genteel" class. The new middle class lived in nice city houses, ate better and dressed better, and had running water and an indoor toilet. Hygiene lagged behind as bathing, deodorant, and toothbrushing were not yet part of daily life.

Members of the genteel class were able to remove themselves from the workaday world, pursue leisure and cultural interests, and isolate themselves from those below them. Women of this class were able to reduce their traditional work burden and focus instead on running a household ("the cult of domesticity"). They turned their backs on the workforce, retreating to the home, where creative idleness became the hallmark of the genteel-class woman.

The upper class saw its wealth multiply rapidly, thanks to all the get-rich-quick possibilities created by industrialization; their wealth was in the form of liquid assets rather than land and slaves as that of their Southern counterparts was. Because wealth and breeding tended to set them apart anyway, they withdrew into social enclaves to live with their own, "far from the madding crowd."

In the mid-19th century the middle class was often referred to as "the middling sort," the *-ing* form of the modifier suggesting their transitory state. They were considered to be either on their way up or on their way down; they were not seen as a permanent, well-defined class of citizens. Reflecting their uncertain social status, the middle class strove to separate themselves from the working class, and to emulate their betters, but they had only indifferent success in the latter. What distinguished the middle from the upper class, apart from the smaller size of their bank accounts, was the high level of their commitment to moral reform, especially as it concerned alcoholism and slavery. City life defined and nurtured the middle class, so as U.S. cities grew, so did the middle class.

Meanwhile, for African Americans, the industrialized North was hardly a utopia despite the inspiring success stories of people like Frederick Douglass and Harriet Tubman. Outside a few pockets of abolitionist aid and comfort for runaway slaves, the white majority was hardly more hospitable to blacks than the plantation South. New York City, for instance, was not a markedly more enlightened city than Richmond or Baltimore. Free blacks there were limited in where they could live and what occupations they could enter, plus they had to compete with recently arrived immigrants for the lowest jobs.

TABLE 7.14 NUMBERS AND OCCUPATION OF "FREE BLACKS" IN NEW YORK STATE, 1855

Occupation	Number
Domestic servants	1,025
Laborers	536
Waiters	499
Laundresses	366
Clerks	18
Boatmen	17
Longshoremen	16
Chimney sweeps	15
Porters	176
Cooks	151
Whitewashers	129
Dressmakers, seamstresses	111
Drivers, coachmen, and hackmen	102
Barbers	78
Stewards	56
Cartmen, draymen, and teamsters	55
Butchers	19
Tailors	19
Musicians	15
Hotel and boardinghouse keepers	14
Boot makers and shoemakers	13
Nurses	13
Teachers	13
Clergymen	12
Carpenters	12
Peddlers and traders	11
Sawyers	10
Total	**3,501**

Source: New York State Census of 1855, cited in Marc McCutcheon, *The Writer's Guide to Everyday Life in the 1800s* (Cincinnati: Writer's Digest Books, 1993), 217.

The West

In addition to the familiar differences between North and South and between urban and rural, there was a significant division in the U.S. population between East and West. Part of it was cultural. Westerners were long considered backwoods bumpkins, and before the term *frontier* came into vogue, their region was commonly described, with considerable condescension, as the "back country." But there was a demographic dividing line between East and West even stronger than the ephemeral Mason-Dixon Line that was supposed to divide North from South, and that was the frontier. The U.S. government recognized an invisible line that separated the "settled" from the "unsettled" sections of the country. This "frontier" region, by Census Bureau calculations, was characterized by fewer than six persons per square mile, a number arrived at by dividing the square miles by the resident population. The resulting number distinguished territorial status from statehood, and therefore had enormous political impact. Socially the frontier was important because settling and developing those lands were widely seen as the unfinished business of the country. And the people who populated that region were seen as the best examples of "the American race."

Westerners had come into their own with the age of Jackson (1820s–40s), priding themselves on their rough ways, self-reliance, and lack of refinement. By contrast, easterners took more pride in their level of education, culture, and sophistication. In time western values were cherished above all others and to be seen as peculiarly American. Just exactly who was a "westerner" and when could one legitimately claim to be a "westerner" are sociological conundrums with no easy answers. The West was a state of mind as much as a geographic region, and, as generations of historians raised on Frederick Jackson Turner have pointed out, the frontier line dividing East from West was constantly moving, turning westerners into easterners while marking the march of civilization across the continent. What is clear is that tens of thousands of old-stock Americans and recently arrived immigrants formed a continuous stream of argonauts heading into the setting Sun to make a new life for themselves. Between 1840 and 1870, more than 350,000 people traveled by covered wagon over various trails to Oregon and California. Others made the trip by clipper ship around the tip of South America. And these were just the tail end of a mass westward migration that had already reached the Great Plains and the Rockies. Americans living in the mid-19th century had never known a time when there was not the "Promised Land" of the West.

On the frontier women were every bit as adept as the menfolk at lighting up a corncob pipe or dipping snuff. In this lithograph based on a "drawing by a German officer in the Rebel Army" during the Civil War, a relaxing threesome sit around the fire enjoying a little tobacco. (Arkansas History Commission)

What attracted both Americans and foreign-born immigrants to the West was a broad range of factors, termed by the historian Walter Nugent "universal impulses." These included (1) free land; (2) quick wealth; (3) quality of life issues, such as freedom, unspoiled nature, and healthful climate; (4) spiritual fulfillment; and (5) the search for a mythic Eden, where such ideals as heroic purpose, rugged individualism, and self-realization existed. It is doubtful that most westward migrants could articulate these motives, and a combination of two or more were probably at work in any given case. Regardless of what drove them, an estimated 300,000 or more made their way west in the 20-year span between 1840 and 1860. Of that number the overwhelming majority settled in one of three areas: Oregon, California, or Utah. The movement accelerated greatly after 1849 as a result of the California gold rush and the "Macedonian Call" of the Mormon Church in Utah.

Westward migration slowed greatly as a result of the Civil War but resumed after 1865, encouraged by the 1862 Homestead Act, which promised a 160-acre spread to any citizen (or intended citizen) who would settle on it and work it for five years. At the end of that period the settler would receive free and clear title to the land. And the Homestead Act was just one of several ways of claiming public lands available to speculators and settlers alike. All of the various land giveaways yielded a rush of farmers to the West to join the host of miners, cattlemen, fur trappers, and pioneers who were already there. Between 1862 and 1890 (when the frontier was officially declared "closed" by the Census Bureau), approximately 2 million people settled on 377,659 farms claimed under the provisions of the Homestead Act. In the act's first eight years alone, nearly 14 million acres carved out of the public domain were distributed to eager claimants.

The popular image of the homesteader is of a young white male, perhaps with a family, moving west with all the family possessions in a wagon, re-creating the farm life back East. There is a great deal of truth to this image, but it is not the complete story. The Homestead Act was open to women as well as men. After the Civil War the West was also home to a resident black population that grew slowly but steadily. Generally, African Americans found the principles of freedom and equality more respected in the West than back East. More than 5,000 black cowboys, it has been estimated, participated in the cattle-drive era. Thousands more became homesteaders on the Great Plains. More than a few tried their luck in the gold fields of the Rocky Mountain region, either staking claims or opening businesses to serve the miners. The remarkable tolerance they experienced is represented by the story of "Aunt Clara" Brown, a former slave who was certified in 1881 as a full-fledged member of the Society of Colorado Pioneers because she had arrived with many white pioneers in 1859 and stayed to become a leading citizen of Central City and Denver until her death in 1885.

Farther west other black communities put down roots in California, Oregon, and Washington. In 1870 San Francisco had more than 1,000 black citizens, while Los Angeles county that same year counted more than 100. The black population in the entire state of Oregon that same census year was 300, and in Washington Territory, 200.

To their detriment, African Americans, Asians, and Native Americans in the West never made common cause, which was probably impossible because of their different cultures, scattered presence, and differing agendas. On the contrary, African Americans were employed against the Plains Indians in the form of the "buffalo soldiers," members of the black 9th and 10th U.S. Cavalry Regiments.

TABLE 7.15 NUMBERS OF NEW IMMIGRANTS IN THE FAR WEST, 1840–1860

Year	Oreg.	Calif.	Utah	Cumulative Grand Total for All Three Areas to Date
1840–48	11,512	2,735	4,600	18,847
1849	450	25,000	1,500	45,797
1850	6,000	44,000	2,500	98,297
1851	3,600	1,100	1,500	104,497
1852	10,000	50,000	10,000	174,497
1853	7,500	20,000	8,000	209,997
1854	6,000	12,000	3,167	231,164
1855	500	1,500	4,684	237,848
1856	1,000	8,000	2,400	249,248
1857	1,500	4,000	1,300	256,048
1858	1,500	6,000	150	263,698
1859	2,000	17,000	1,431	284,129
1860	1,500	9,000	1,630	296,259
Grand Totals[a]	53,062	200,335	42,862	296,259

[a] Grand totals cover the years 1840–60.
Source: John D. Unruh, Jr., *The Plains Across* (Urbana: University of Illinois Press, 1979), 84–85.

TABLE 7.16 REGIONAL BLACK POPULATION IN THE NORTHEAST AND THE WEST, 1860

Region or State	Black Population in 1860	Blacks as a Percentage of Population
North (total)	340,240	1.7
New England	24,711	0.8
Maine	1,327	0.2
N.H.	494	0.2
Vt.	709	0.2
Mass.	9,602	0.8
R.I.	3,952	2.3
Conn.	8,627	1.9
Middle Atlantic	131,290	1.8
N.Y.	49,005	1.3
N.J.	25,336	3.8
Pa.	56,949	2.0
East North-Central	63,699	0.9
Ohio	36,673	1.6
Ind.	11,428	0.9
Ill.	7,628	0.5
Mich.	6,799	0.9
Wis.	1,171	0.2
West North-Central	120,540	5.6
Minn.	259	0.2
Iowa	1,069	0.2
Mo.	118,503	10.0
Nebr.	82	0.3
Kans.	627	0.6
West (total)	4,479	0.7
Mountain	235	0.1
Colorado Territory	46	0.1
New Mexico Territory	85	0.1
Utah Territory	59	0.2
Nevada Territory	45	0.7
Pacific	4,244	1.0
Washington Territory	30	0.3
Oregon Territory	128	0.2
California	4,086	1.1

Note: Figures almost exclusively represent free blacks, except in the "border" states Mo. and Kans.
Source: Mable M. Smythe, ed., *The Black American Reference Book* (Englewood Cliffs, N.J.: Prentice-Hall, 1976), 168–69.

Urbanization

As the century progressed, cities played an ever-increasing role in U.S. society. The lure of the city even began to supplant the traditional lure of the West, particularly among young men of spirit and ambition. In the North, urban areas were the center of life as city dwellers put more and more distance between themselves and their country cousins. The first generation of U.S. cities had been political capitals and trading centers. This second generation were industrial powerhouses, population centers, and cultural oases. Beginning in this era, a third generation sprang up in the Far West, on the Great Plains, in the Rockies, and on the Pacific coast. They began life as territorial capitals, cow towns, army posts, and mining centers, especially as railroad junctions.

The main impetus behind many new towns across the West were the railroad companies, which could only make money when people used their trains for riding or shipping. They had to attract settlers to pay the massive costs of construction and maintenance on their lines. By the same token, frontier communities had to lure the railroad to town if they were to survive and prosper. Fort Worth, Texas, and Abilene, Kansas, succeeded becasue they got their rail connections; Tascosa, in the panhandle of Texas, turned into a ghost town after the railroad passed it by.

Town boosters proclaimed the access to the railroad and industry in promoting their communities to potential settlers. Sometimes it was true; sometimes it was wishful thinking or mere hype. One wag described the rosy prospects of his frontier town by saying it had a population of 150,000, "only they are not all here yet."

Census numbers bore witness to the apparently irresistible spread of urbanization all across the country. For census purposes, the U.S. government included in the urban population any town having more than 800 people. From 1840 to 1850, the population of urban areas (i.e., cities) increased 90 percent while the population of the nation as a whole increased only 36 precent. The onrush of urbanization meant that by 1860 the total capital investment in industry, railroads, commerce, and urban property was greater than the combined value of all the farms from the Atlantic to the Pacific.

TABLE 7.17 THIRD GENERATION OF U.S. CITIES: TAKING URBANIZATION TO THE FAR WEST, 1850–1873

City	State or Territory	Date Founded	Origins of Name	Raison d'Être	Platted or Incorporated
Fort Worth	Tex.	ca.1850	Major William Jenkins Worth was a Mexican War hero	Proximity to U.S. Army post	Chartered by state legislature 1873
Seattle	Wash.	Nov. 1852	Seathl was a local Indian headman who owned the site	Vast nearby forests suitable for logging	Unknown
Omaha	Nebr.	1854	From the Maha or Omaha Indian tribe	Territorial capital, river port, and trail town	320-block townsite platted (May 1854)
Denver City	Colo.	1858	Territorial governor of Kansas James W. Denver, a supporter of the community	Close to the goldfields	Incorporated 1861
Virginia City	Nev.	Sep. 1859	Legend of "Old Virginny" (James Finney or Fennimore)	Nearness to Comstock silver strike	Never; virtual ghost town after 1878
Helena	Mont.	Oct. 30, 1864	Named for Helena, Minn.	Gold discovery at Last Chance Gulch	Third capital of territory in 1875
Prescott	Ariz.	1864	In honor of the famed western historian William H. Prescott	Territorial capital	Never; Prescott seat of government lost to Tuscon in 1867
Phoenix	Ariz.	1865	Named for the mythical bird	Ranching and farming in Salt River Valley	Incorporated, 1881; seat of government from 1889
Lincoln	Nebr.	1867	Named after martyred president	State capital and cultural center	Unknown
Cheyenne	Wyo.	July 1867	Named for Plains Indian tribe	Union Pacific Railroad Routes town and territorial capital	Unknown
Reno	Nev.	May 9, 1868	Named in honor of Union general Jesse Reno, killed in Civil War	Central Pacific Railroad Routes town	Unknown
Bismarck	Dakota	1873	Named by Northern Pacific officials after Germany chancellor Otto von Bismarck as thanks to German investors	Northern Pacific Railroad Routes town and gateway to Black Hills gold country	Officially registered as Bismarck with U.S. Post Office Dept. in 1873

Source: John W. Reps, *Bird's Eye Views* (New York: Princeton Architectural Press, 1998), passim.

TABLE 7.18 PERCENTAGE OF U.S. POPULATION CLASSIFIED AS URBAN BY REGION, STATE, AND (ORGANIZED) TERRITORY, 1850–1870

Region or State	Percentage in 1850	Percentage in 1860	Percentage in 1870
Northeast	26.5	35.7	44.3
Maine	13.5	16.6	21.0
N.H.	17.1	22.1	26.2
Vt.	1.9	2.0	6.9
Mass.	50.7	59.6	66.7
R.I.	55.6	63.3	74.6
Conn.	16.0	26.5	33.0
N.Y.	28.2	39.3	50.0
N.J.	17.6	32.7	43.7
Pa.	23.6	30.8	37.3
Midwest	**9.2**	**13.9**	**20.8**
Ohio	12.2	17.1	25.6
Ind.	4.5	8.6	14.7
Ill.	7.6	14.3	23.5
Mich.	7.3	13.3	20.1
Wis.	9.4	14.4	19.6
Minn.	N/A	9.4	16.1
Iowa	5.1	8.9	13.1
Mo.	11.8	17.2	25.0
Dakota	N/A	N/A	18.0
Nebr.	N/A	N/A	18.0
Kans.	N/A	9.4	14.2
South	**8.3**	**9.6**	**12.2**
Del.	15.3	18.9	24.7
Md.	32.3	34.0	37.8
District of Columbia	93.6	93.0	91.6
Va.	8.0	9.5	11.9
W.Va.	3.8	5.3	8.1
N.C.	2.4	2.5	3.4
S.C.	7.3	6.9	8.6
Ga.	4.3	7.1	8.4
Fla.	N/A	4.1	8.1
Ky.	7.5	10.4	14.8
Tenn.	2.2	4.2	7.5
Ala.	4.6	5.1	6.3
Miss.	1.8	2.6	4.0
Ark.	N/A	0.9	2.6
La.	26.0	26.1	27.9
Tex.	3.6	4.4	6.7
Far West	**6.4**	**16.0**	**25.8**
Mont.	N/A	N/A	15.1
Colo.	N/A	13.9	11.9
N.Mex.	7.4	5.0	5.2
Ariz.	N/A	N/A	33.4
Utah	N/A	20.5	18.4
Nev.	N/A	N/A	16.6
Oreg.	N/A	5.5	9.1
Calif.	7.4	20.7	37.2
United States (total)	**15.3**	**19.8**	**25.7**

Note: For some territories the statistics are not available (N/A) because the number of urban dwellers was too insignificant to count.
Source: Douglas L. Anderton, Richard E. Barrett, and Donald J. Bogue, *The Population of the United States,* 3d ed. (New York: The Free Press, 1997), 40–41.

TABLE 7.19 THE SPREAD OF URBANIZATION IN THE UNITED STATES, 1860–1880

Year	Total U.S. Population	Urban Population	Rural Population	Percentage of Population Considered Urban
1860	31,440,000	5,070,000	26,370,000	16.1
1870	38,560,000	8,070,000	30,490,000	20.9
1880	50,155,000	11,320,000	38,835,000	22.6

Source: Michael G. Mulhall, ed., *The Dictionary of Statistics,* 4th ed. (London: George Routledge & Sons, 1899), 789.

The Poor

In the "land of opportunity," pauperism, as opposed to poverty, was considered a character failure if not an outright sin in the 19th century. The latter class of citizens were simply poor in the things of the world; the former were freeloaders living off charity. Pauperism was commonly linked with both criminality and imbecility as chronic conditions among those on the lower end of the social scale. Government officials kept careful records of persons living on the public dole and debated their moral responsibility to provide for the poorest members of society.

TABLE 7.20 PAUPER POPULATION OF THE UNITED STATES BY NATIONAL ORIGIN, FOR ALL STATES AND ORGANIZED TERRITORIES REPORTING, 1850

State or Territory	Total Population	Native-Born Population[a]	Foreign-Born Population[a]	Total Pauper Population	Native-Born Paupers[a]	Foreign-Born Paupers[b]
Ala.	771,623	763,089	7,509	363	306	9
Ark.	209,897	207,636	1,471	105	67	N/A
Conn.	370,792	331,560	38,518	2,337	1,463	281
Del.	91,532	86,268	5,243	697	240	33
Fla.	87,445	84,665	2,769	76	58	4
Ga.	906,185	899,132	6,488	1,036	825	29
Ill.	851,470	736,149	111,892	797	279	155
Ind.	988,416	930,458	55,572	1,182	446	137
Iowa	192,214	170,931	20,969	135	27	17
Ky.	982,405	949,652	31,420	1,126	690	87
La.	547,762	448,848	68,233	423	76	30
Maine	583,169	550,878	31,825	5,503	3,209	326
Md.	583,034	531,476	51,209	4,494	1,681	320
Mass.	994,514	827,430	164,024	15,777	4,059	1,490
Mich.	397,654	341,656	54,703	1,190	248	181
Miss.	606,526	601,230	4,788	260	245	12
Mo.	682,044	604,522	76,592	2,977	251	254
N.H.	317,976	303,563	14,265	3,600	1,998	186
N.J.	489,555	429,176	59,948	2,392	1,339	239
N.Y.	3,097,394	2,436,771	655,929	59,855	5,755	7,078
N.C.	869,039	866,241	2,581	1,931	1,567	13
Ohio	1,980,329	1,757,746	218,193	2,513	1,254	419
Pa.	2,311,786	2,006,207	303,417	11,551	2,654	1,157
R.I.	147,545	123,564	23,902	2,560	492	204
S.C.	668,507	659,743	8,707	1,642	1,113	180
Tenn.	1,002,717	995,478	5,653	1,005	577	14
Tex.	212,592	194,433	17,681	7	4	N/A
Vt.	314,120	280,055	33,715	3,654	1,565	314
Va.	1,421,661	1,398,205	22,985	5,118	4,356	102
Wis.	305,391	194,099	110,477	666	72	166
United States (total)	23,191,876	20,912,612	2,244,602	134,972	36,916	13,437

Note: All dates are for the fiscal year (ending Jun. 1), not the calendar year. *Pauperism* in the 19th century was defined as being supported at the public expense, as distinguished from mere poverty, which did not have the same social stigma. Figures are taken from U.S. Census reports, based on returns from asylums, county poorhouses, city workhouses, and city almshouses.

[a] Figures cover only those persons receiving public support on Jun. 1, 1850.

Source: U.S. Census Office, *A Compendium of the 9th Census, June 1, 1870,* compiled by Frances Amasa Walker (Washington, D.C.: U.S. Government Printing Office, 1872), 535.

TABLE 7.21 PAUPER POPULATION OF THE UNITED STATES BY NATIONAL ORIGIN, FOR ALL STATES AND ORGANIZED TERRITORIES REPORTING, 1860

State or Territory	Total Population	Native-Born Population	Foreign-Born Population[a]	Total Pauper Population	Native-Born Paupers[a]	Foreign-Born Paupers[a]
Ala.	964,201	951,849	12,352	582	431	18
Ark.	435,450	431,850	3,600	289	175	3
Calif.	379,994	233,466	146,528	2,183	105	188
Conn.	460,147	379,451	80,696	4,044	1,548	690
Del.	112,216	103,051	9,165	742	331	116
District of Columbia	75,080	62,596	12,484	2,081	95	47
Fla.	140,424	137,115	3,309	168	105	2
Go.	1,057,286	1,045,615	11,671	1,451	1,106	90
Ill.	1,711,951	1,387,308	324,643	4,628	707	1,149
Ind.	1,350,428	1,232,144	118,284	3,565	1,120	469
Iowa	674,913	568,836	106,077	2,165	322	361
Kans.	107,206	94,515	12,691	21	7	14
Ky.	1,155,684	1,095,885	59,799	1,265	749	150
La.	708,002	627,027	80,975	194	146	16
Maine	628,279	590,826	37,453	8,946	4,147	471
Md.	687,049	609,520	77,529	4,275	621	99
Mass.	1,231,066	970,960	260,106	51,880	5,206	1,297
Mich.	749,113	600,020	149,093	9,104	679	744
Minn.	172,023	113,295	58,728	350	39	117
Miss.	791,305	782,747	8,558	374	270	31
Mo.	1,182,012	1,021,471	160,541	958	513	271
Nebr.	28,841	22,490	6,351	30	3	3
N.H.	326,073	305,135	20,938	4,394	2,072	239
N.J.	672,035	549,245	122,790	8,200	1,308	553
N.Y.	3,880,735	2,879,455	1,001,280	164,782	7,666	11,549
N.C.	992,622	989,324	3,298	1,922	1,422	9
Ohio	2,339,511	2,011,262	328,249	5,953	5,700	8,392
Oreg.	52,465	47,342	5,123	50	15	10
Pa.	2,906,215	2,475,710	430,505	16,463	4,495	3,281
R.I.	174,620	137,226	37,394	1,108	445	168
S.C.	703,708	693,722	9,986	1,640	1,404	35
Tenn.	1,109,801	1,088,575	21,226	3,038	776	159
Tex.	604,215	560,793	43,422	139	108	14
Utah	40,273	27,519	12,754	4	1	N/A
Vt.	315,098	282,355	32,743	3,387	1,510	340
Va.	1,596,318	1,561,260	35,058	6,027	4,320	214
Wash.	11,594	8,450	3,144	7	1	1
Wis.	775,881	498,954	276,927	5,256	815	1,149
United States (total)	31,413,321	27,304,624	4,138,697	321,665	50,483	32,459

Note: All dates are for the fiscal year (ending Jun. 1), not the calendar year. *Pauperism* in the 19th century was defined as being supported at the public expense, as distinguished from mere poverty, which did not have the same social stigma. Figures are taken from U.S. Census reports, based on returns from asylums, county poorhouses, city workhouses, and city almshouses.

[a] Figures cover only those persons receiving public support on Jun. 1, 1860.

Source: U.S. Census Office, *A Compendium of the 9th Census, June 1, 1870,* compiled by Frances Amasa Walker (Washington, D.C.: U.S. Government Printing Office, 1872), 532–33.

TABLE 7.22 PAUPER POPULATION OF THE UNITED STATES BY NATIONAL ORIGIN, FOR ALL STATES AND ORGANIZED TERRITORIES REPORTING, 1870

State or Territory	Total Population	Native-Born Population	Foreign-Born Population	Total Pauper Population[a]	Native-Born Paupers[a]	Foreign-Born Paupers[a]
Ala.	996,992	987,030	9,962	890	681	6
Ark.	484,471	479,445	5,026	626	490	48
Calif.	560,247	350,416	209,831	2,317	354	637
Colo.	398,647	33,265	6,599	73	8	11
Conn.	537,454	423,815	113,639	1,728	1,237	468
Del.	125,015	115,879	9,136	556	403	50
District of Columbia	131,700	115,446	16,254	303	234	45
Fla.	187,748	182,781	4,967	147	142	5
Ga.	1,184,109	1,172,982	11,127	2,181	1,777	39
Idaho	14,999	7,114	7,885	41	3	1
Ill.	2,539,891	2,024,693	515,198	6,054	1,254	1,109
Ind.	1,680,637	1,539,163	141,474	4,657	2,790	862
Iowa	1,194,020	989,328	204,692	1,543	542	311
Kans.	364,399	316,007	48,392	361	190	146
Ky.	1,321,011	1,257,613	63,398	2,059	1,667	117
La.	726,915	665,088	61,827	590	409	98
Maine	626,915	578,034	48,881	4,619	3,188	443
Md.	780,894	697,482	83,412	1,857	1,347	265
Mass.	1,457,351	1,104,032	353,319	8,036	5,396	381
Mich.	1,184,059	916,049	268,010	3,151	853	1,189
Minn.	439,706	279,009	160,697	684	126	266
Miss.	827,922	816,731	11,191	921	793	16
Mo.	1,721,295	1,499,028	222,267	2,424	1,415	439
Mont.	20,595	12,616	7,979	104	8	15
Neb.	122,993	92,245	30,748	93	54	38
Nev.	42,491	23,690	18,801	196	29	25
N.H.	318,300	288,689	29,611	2,636	1,754	375
N.J.	906,096	717,153	188,943	3,356	1,669	721
N.Y.	4,382,759	3,244,406	1,138,353	26,152	5,953	8,147
N.C.	1,071,361	1,068,332	3,029	1,706	1,647	5
Ohio	2,665,260	2,292,767	372,493	6,383	2,860	814
Oreg.	90,923	79,323	11,600	133	62	19
Pa.	3,521,951	2,976,642	545,309	15,872	4,822	3,974
R.I.	217,353	161,957	55,396	1,046	442	192
S.C.	705,606	697,532	8,074	2,343	1,904	77
Tenn.	1,258,520	1,239,204	19,316	1,349	1,280	52
Tex.	818,579	756,168	62,411	204	177	25
Utah	86,786	56,084	30,702	56	20	31
Vt.	330,551	283,396	47,155	2,008	1,262	523
Va.	1,225,163	1,211,409	13,754	3,890	3,254	26
Wash.	23,955	18,931	5,024	34	15	5
W.V.	442,014	424,923	17,091	1,102	948	46
Wis.	1,054,670	690,171	364,449	1,553	390	736
United States (total)	38,558,371	32,991,142	5,567,229	116,102	53,939	22,798

Note: All dates are for the fiscal year (ending Jun. 1), not the calendar year. *Pauperism* in the 19th century was defined as anyone supported at the public expense, as distinguished from mere poverty which did not have the same social stigma. Figures are taken from U.S. Census reports, based on returns from asylums, county poorhouses, city workhouses and city almshouses.

[a] Figures cover only those persons receiving public support on Jun. 1,1870.

Source: U.S. Census Office, *A Compendium of the 9th Census, June 1, 1870,* compiled by Frances Amasa Walker (Washington, D.C.: U.S. Government Printing Office, 1872), 530–31.

TABLE 7.23 PAUPER POPULATION OF THE UNITED STATES BY RACE FOR ALL STATES AND ORGANIZED TERRITORIES, 1870

State or Territory	Population			Pauper Population[a]		
	Total	White	Black	Total	White	Black
Ala.	996,992	521,384	475,510	890	354	327
Ark.	484,471	362,115	122,169	626	288	292
Calif.	560,247	499,424	4,272	2,317	351	3
Colo.	39,864	39,221	456	73	8	0
Conn.	537,454	527,549	9,668	1.728	1,123	114
Del.	125,015	102,221	22,794	556	223	180
District of Columbia	131,700	88,278	43,404	303	135	99
Fla.	187,748	96,057	91,689	147	80	62
Ga.	1,184,109	638,926	545,142	2,181	270	507
Idaho	14,999	10,618	60	41	3	0
Ill.	2,539,891	2,511,096	28,762	6,054	1,213	41
Ind.	1,680,637	1,655,837	24,560	4,657	2,583	207
Iowa	1,194,020	1,188,207	5,762	1,543	486	56
Kans.	364,399	346,377	17,108	361	105	85
Ky.	1,321,011	1,098,692	222,210	2,059	963	704
La.	726,915	362,065	364,210	590	279	130
Maine	626,915	624,809	1,606	4,619	3,149	39
Md.	780,894	605,497	175,391	1,857	781	566
Mass.	1,457,351	1,443,156	13,947	8,036	5,323	73
Mich.	1,184,059	1,167,282	11,849	3,151	768	85[b]
Minn.	439,706	438,257	759	684	120	6
Miss.	827,922	382,896	444,201	921	413	380
Mo.	1,721,295	1,603,146	118,071	2,424	1,090	325
Mont.	20,595	18,306	183	104	8	0
Nebr.	122,993	122,117	789	93	54	0
Nev.	42,491	38,959	357	196	27	2
N.H.	318,300	317,697	580	2,636	1,739	15
N.J.	906,096	875,407	30,658	3,356	1,368	301
N.Y.	4,382,759	4,330,210	52,081	26,152	5,289	664
N.C.	1,071,361	678,470	391,650	1,706	1,119	528
Ohio	2,665,260	2,601,946	63,213	6,383	2,659	201
Oreg.	90,923	86,929	346	133	62	0
Pa.	3,521,951	3,456,609	65,294	15,872	4,354	468
R.I.	217,353	212,219	4,980	1,046	497	35
S.C.	705,606	289,667	415,814	2,343	888	1,106
Tenn.	1,258,520	936,119	322,331	1,349	966	314
Tex.	818,579	564,700	253,475	204	73	104
Utah	86,786	86,044	118	56	19	1
Vt.	330,551	329,613	924	2,008	1,231	31
Va.	1,225,163	712,089	512,841	3,890	1,942	1,312
Wash.	23,955	22,195	207	34	13	2
W.V.	442,014	424,033	17,980	1,102	839	109
Wis.	1,054,670	1,051,351	2,113	1,553	374	16
United States (total)	38,558,371	33,589,377	4,880,009	116,102	44,539	9,400[a]

Note: All dates are for the fiscal year (ending Jun. 1), not the calendar year. *Pauperism* in the 19th century was defined as being supported at the public expense, as distinguished from mere poverty, which did not have the same social stigma. Figures are taken from U.S. Census reports, based on returns from asylums, county poorhouses, city workhouses, and city almshouses. The figures cover only those receiving support as of Jun. 1, 1870.

[a] The 1870 census is the first to break down the pauper population by race, because slaves constituted more than 90 percent of the black population in previous censuses. Figures cover only those persons receiving public support on Jun. 1, 1870.

[b] This number includes 33 Indians identified as paupers in Michigan and therefore likewise included in the total pauper population of the United States.

Source: U.S. Census Office, *A Compendium of the 9th Census, June 1, 1870,* compiled by Frances Amasa Walker (Washington, D.C.: U.S. Government Printing Office, 1872), 530–31.

In both social and financial calculations, Americans made a careful distinction between poverty and pauperism, and a further distinction should be made between *poverty* as understood in the 19th century and the current official definition. Today *poverty* describes the living conditions of that proportion of the U.S. population whose income falls below an arbitrary standard established by the federal government (adjusted annually for inflation). Most people in the 19th-century United States did not see poverty as a problem with a government solution. And although many Americans then would admit to being poor, they were not judged to be the same as those dependent on public assistance for survival, at least in part because the frontier was still viewed as a "fresh start," where anyone could succeed with a little exertion.

During Reconstruction four children of a tenant farm family pose for a photographer on a cotton farm between Ackerman and Louisville, Mississippi. (Courtesy of the Mississippi Department of Archives and History)

Immigration

Immigration has been a part of U.S. life right from the beginning, but it has always produced mixed feelings, too, and that ambivalence to a head in the mid-19th century. A new wave of immigrants at that time changed the national demographic and alarmed older-stock Americans by their "exotic" cultures and sheer numbers. After 1840 a sharply increasing percentage of the population was of foreign birth. The 1850s witnessed the largest influx of immigrants in proportion to the population of any decade in U.S. history; in the single year 1854, almost a half-million entered, a ratio of about 20 foreign arrivals for every 1,000 U.S. residents. In other words, almost 2 percent of the nation's population were new immigrants. From 1850 to 1860 the number of foreign-born increased 84.4 percent. There were 4.1 million immigrants in a total U.S. population of 31.4 million in 1860. The Civil War caused a temporary lull in the immigrant flood as the land of opportunity became a war zone for four years, but even with that disruption the numbers did not significantly decrease during the decade. The same year that the war ended (1865), 248,120 immigrants arrived. Altogether from 1860 to 1870 the number of foreign-born in the population increased another 34.5 percent.

The newcomers were overwhelmingly from western Europe, heavily weighted toward two countries, Germany and Ireland. They immigrated for a variety of reasons: religious freedom, economic opportunity, utopian dreams of improving their station in life. Unlike earlier generations, who were fairly well equipped for their new life, many of these arrivals had nothing but the clothes on their back and a desperate desire to succeed. They found not a land of opportunity but a harsh and merciless country where they were regarded with fear and suspicion. Antiforeign and anti-Catholic sentiment was flogged by the New York–based Protestant Association and the Protestant Reformation Society, forerunners of the Ku Klux Klan as self-styled defenders of U.S. ethnic and religious "purity." Even the staid Boston Public Library barred Irish from using its facilities because, as the directors told the city council in 1852, "They [the Irish] think little of moral and intellectual culture."

Despite this sort of bigotry in their new country, Germans and Irish crowded into Northern cities or headed for the Midwest to stake out farms. Some states by chance or design became home to large concentrations of one or another nationality: Germans in Texas, Wisconsin, and Missouri; Scandinavians in Minnesota and the Dakota Territory.

Before there was Ellis Island as an entry port for European immigrants, there was Castle Garden, a former theater in Manhattan's Battery Park, that was turned into an immigrant receiving station in 1855. There newcomers could change money, buy railroad tickets, and find a place to stay. It was owned and operated by the state of New York. This image shows it in its theater days in 1852. (Library of Congress, Prints and Photographs Division [LC-US262-092275])

TABLE 7.24 FOREIGN-BORN POPULATION OF THE UNITED STATES BY NUMERICAL COUNT AND AS A PERCENTAGE OF THE TOTAL POPULATION, 1850, 1860, AND 1870

Race	1850		1860		1870	
	Foreign-born[c]	Percentage of Foreign-born among Resident Ethnic Group	Foreign-Born	Percentage of Foreign-born among Resident Ethnic Group	Foreign-Born	Percentage of Foreign-born among Resident Ethnic Group
White	2,240,000	11.5	4,096,000	15.2	5,494,000[d]	16.4
Black[a]	4,000	N/A	7,000	N/A	10,000	0.2
American Indian[b]	N/A	N/A	44,000	N/A	1,000	3.8
Chinese	N/A	N/A	N/A	N/A	63,000	98.4

[a] For free blacks only; relevant data for slaves were not collected.
[b] Born in Mexico or Canada.
[c] As a percentage of total United States population: 9.7% in 1850; 13.2% in 1860; and 14.0% in 1870.
[d] *Cf.* Roger Daniels's figure: 5,567,000.
Sources: Douglas L. Anderton et al., eds., *The Population of the United States,* 3d ed. (New York: The Free Press, 1997), 387; Roger Daniels, *Coming to America: A History of Immigration and Ethnicity in American Life* (New York: Harper Collins, 1990), 125.

TABLE 7.25 IMMIGRATION TO THE UNITED STATES, 1851–1880

Decade	Number of Immigrants Arriving	Rate of Immigration per Thousand Population[a]
1851–60[b]	2,598,214	9.3
1861–70	2,314,824	6.4
1871–80	2,812,191	6.2

[a] This number is a decennial average of the annual figures for the 10-year period.
[b] Includes the largest single immigration year in this period, 1854, when almost 1 million immigrants entered the United States, constituting a rate of about 20 per 1,000.
Source: Roger Daniels, *Coming to America: A History of Immigration and Ethnicity in American Life* (New York: Harper Collins, 1990), 124–25.

TABLE 7.26 CONTRIBUTION OF MAJOR NATIONAL GROUPS TO U.S. IMMIGRATION, 1851–1880

Decade	Germans		Irish		Swedes	
	Number of Immigrants	As a Percentage of Total Immigrants	Number of Immigrants	As a Percentage of Total Immigrants	Number of Immigrants	As a Percentage of Total Immigrants
1851–60	951,667	36.6	914,119	35.2	N/A[a]	N/A[a]
1861–70	787,468	34.0	435,778	18.8	37,667	1.63
1871–80	718,182	25.5	436,871	15.5	115,922	4.12

Decade	Norwegians		Danes		Italians	
	Number of Immigrants	As a Percentage of Total Immigrants	Number of Immigrants	As a Percentage of Total Immigrants	Number of Immigrants	As a Percentage of Total Immigrants
1851–60	N/A[a]	N/A[a]	3,749	0.01	9,231	0.36
1861–70	71,631	3.09	17,094	0.74	11,725	0.51
1871–80	95,323	3.39	31,771	1.13	55,759	1.98

[a] It is impossible to calculate Swedish and Norwegian immigrants separately in this period because until 1861 Norwegian immigrants were counted as part of Sweden's population. Between 1851 and 1860, there were 20,931 immigrants of Swedish/Norwegian stock, who constituted 0.81 percent of the total immigrant population.
Sources: Roger Daniels, *Coming to America: A History of Immigration and Ethnicity in American Life* (New York: Harper Collins, 1990), 124, 129, 146, 165; Stephan Thernstrom et al., eds., *Harvard Encyclopedia of American Ethnic Groups* (Cambridge, Mass.: Harvard University Press, 1980), 547.

TABLE 7.27 RESIDENT FOREIGN-BORN POPULATION OF THE UNITED STATES, DISTRIBUTED ACCORDING TO PRINCIPAL COUNTRIES OF BIRTH, 1850, 1860, AND 1870

Country of Birth	1850		1860		1870	
	Number	As a Percentage of Total Foreign-Born Population	Number	As a Percentage of Total Foreign-Born Population	Number	As a Percentage of Total Foreign-Born Population
Canada and Newfoundland	147,711	6.58	249,970	6.04	493,464	8.86
Mexico	13,317	0.59	27,466	0.66	42,435	0.76
England	278,675	12.42	433,494	10.47	555,046	9.97
Scotland	70,550	3.14	108,518	2.62	140,835	2.53
Wales	29,868	1.33	45,763	1.11	74,533	1.34
Ireland	961,719	42.85	1,611,304	38.93	1,855,827	33.34
Germany	583,774	26.01	1,276,075	30.83	1,690,533	30.37
Austria	946	0.04	25,061	0.61	30,508	0.55
Holland	9,848	0.44	28,281	0.68	46,802	0.84
Switzerland	13,358	0.60	53,327	1.29	75,153	1.35
Norway	12,678	0.57	43,995	1.06	114,246	2.05
Sweden	3,559	0.16	18,625	0.45	97,332	1.75
Denmark	1,838	0.08	9,962	0.24	30,107	0.54
Russia	1,414	0.06	3,160	0.08	4,644	0.08
Hungary[a]	N/A	N/A	N/A	N/A	3,737	0.07
Bohemia[a]	N/A	N/A	N/A	N/A	40,289	0.72
Poland[a]	N/A	N/A	7,298	0.18	14,436	0.26
France	54,069	2.41	109,870	2.66	116,402	2.09
Italy	3,645	0.16	10,518	0.25	17,157	0.31
China	758	0.03	35,565	0.86	63,042	1.13
Others	56,875	2.53	40,445	0.98	60,701	1.09
Total	2,244,602	100.00	4,138,697	100.00	5,567,226	100.00

[a] *N/A*, not available, indicates population too insignificant to count.
Source: Stephan Thernstrom et al., eds., *Harvard Encyclopedia of American Ethnic Groups* (Cambridge, Mass.: Harvard University Press, 1980), 1052.

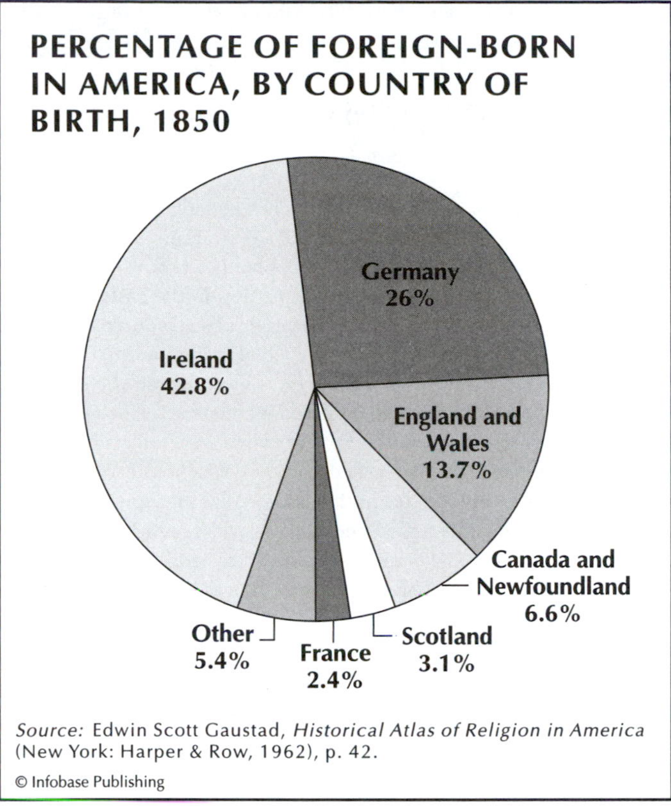

PERCENTAGE OF FOREIGN-BORN IN AMERICA, BY COUNTRY OF BIRTH, 1850

Source: Edwin Scott Gaustad, *Historical Atlas of Religion in America* (New York: Harper & Row, 1962), p. 42.

Hispanics and Asians

Practically lost among the other, more numerous and more visible ethnic and racial groups were the Hispanics and Asians. The Hispanics (a name assigned by the U.S. Census Bureau in the 20th century) became a significant segment of U.S. society only after 1848, when the Mexican Cession introduced tens of thousands into the national mix. But because they were at this time still distant from the main population centers, they did not attract much attention until Anglos began to crowd into the Southwest and California. Generally Hispanics shared the fate of Native Americans at the hands of the Anglo-Saxon majority: dispossessed of their land, denied political power, their culture suppressed. In 1850 Mexican-American miners were forced out of the California goldfields by a pair of bigoted laws of questionable legality, the Greaser Act (its official name) and the Foreign Miners Tax. Anglo squatters settled on historically Mexican-American lands and were supported by the courts. As a result, most Mexican-American landowners in the Southwest were forced to sell out or face ruin. Where they shared urban areas (e.g., San Antonio, Texas; Santa Fe, New Mexico; San Diego, California), they were forced into segregated barrios. Ironically while they were losing in the courts and legislatures, Mexican Americans passed on important elements of their culture in the form of cattle herding, mining techniques, and water management law.

In the mid-19th century, Asians in the United States were either Chinese or Japanese, primarily the former and mostly in California. The term *Asian American* did not have any meaning then because Asians were barred by law from becoming naturalized citizens of the United States, and, besides, there were too few to form a distinct community within the national population.

The Chinese immigrated to the United States at this time primarily because of the California gold rush and the transcontinental railroad. In 1850 there were 4,000 Chinese enumerated in the census, all of them living in California. They represented the first surge. Ten years later there were 34,933 Chinese enumerated for the entire United States, and from that time forward the numbers increased dramatically, although it was a very skewed demographic. At least 95 percent of the Chinese who immigrated to the United States in the mid-1800s were men. In the single year of 1867, some 50,000 arrived, mostly laborers (called coolies) hired to work on the railroads or in the gold mines for wages of 60 to 75 cents a day. Between 1864 and 1869 more than 10,000 Chinese were brought in by the Central Pacific alone to fill out construction crews building the transcontinental railroad. This second surge is usually "credited" to the railroad tycoon Charles Crocker, a member of the so-called Big Four who introduced railroads and "civilization" to California. Actually the idea of importing an army of 10,000 Chinese laborers to build the Union Pacific half of the transcontinental railroad arose from an idea of Crocker's Chinese servant Ah Ling. The chief appeal of an Asian workforce was their willingness to work under slavelike conditions for a dollar a day.

Numerous other Chinese entered the country around this same time to work in other labor-intensive, low-wage industries and as domestic help, mostly in the West. Chinese young women were imported in shockingly large numbers after 1850 to work as prostitutes in the ports and mining camps. By the 1870s, there were an estimated 1,500 to 2,000 in San Francisco alone, and another stereotype was added to the Chinese laundryman and coolie laborer. Inevitably there was a white backlash against these foreign people who uncomplainingly built the railroads and provided comfort to lonely men. After the transcontinental railroad was completed in 1869, some 15,000 Chinese workers were pressured into leaving the country, although others were arriving almost daily in search of the elusive American Dream. In the 1880s Congress would pass exclusionary laws specifically aimed at barring Chinese entry into the United States for any reason.

Far less visible to the public eye than the Chinese laborers were the Chinese who entered as students, beginning with an initial 30 (ages 10 to 15) in January 1872. The student program was organized by the Chinese Educational Mission but disbanded under pressure after only three years.

As their numbers increased, so did the hostility toward Chinese by Anglo-Americans. It was the same old problem: Their culture was seen as strange and they were seen as a threat to U.S. Workers. Outside the Far West, the Chinese were practically mythical creatures in the consciousness of most Americans. They were singled out for the sound of their language, their clothing, and their taste for opium and "strange" foods. But to people in the East who had never encountered an Asian, these were harmless eccentricities. The public reaction on the West Coast was considerably more hostile than curious. In California nonwhites were not allowed to testify in court against whites until 1862, and even after that they could not get a fair hearing in the judicial system. In 1871 the first anti-Chinese riot occurred, in Los Angeles, punctuated by the lynching of several men for no other reason than that they were Chinese. Nativist sentiment continued to grow through the 1870s. In 1874 a "Buy American" movement sprang up in San Francisco against Chinese-made cigars, organized by white-dominated unions. Westerners took their anti-Chinese prejudices with them when they went East. In 1877 Mark Twain and Bret Harte joined forces to write a stage play about the "heathen chinee," which debuted on the New York stage. On opening night Twain informed the boisterous audience, "The Chinaman is getting to be a pretty frequent figure in the United States, and is going to be a great political problem and we thought it well for you to see him on the stage before you had to deal with that problem." The Chinese continued to suffer because of their "differentness" and their generally unconfrontational behavior for the rest of the century. In response to the violence and prejudice, they formed their own culture within a culture of business and fraternal organizations, self-defense groups, and even criminal gangs (tongs).

The Japanese followed a different script. Anglo Americans first became aware of them after Commodore Perry opened up Japan to the West in 1854 and then six years later when the first personnel arrived to staff a Japanese embassy in Washington, D.C. Thereafter Japanese immigration was far less extensive than Chinese, and therefore the Japanese remained less visible than the Chinese, and as a result life was easier for them. In 1869, the same year the transcontinental railroad was completed and deportation sentiment began to run high against the Chinese, the first group of Japanese immigrants arrived in the United States and settled in Gold Hills, California, where they started the Wakamatsu Tea & Silk Farm Colony. In the years that followed the Japanese government allowed only select, highly sophisticated persons to emigrate. Those included, in 1870, a group of 12 Japanese students who were admitted as cadets at the U.S. Naval Academy. Two years later 53 more students entered the United States to study. A small community of Japanese on the East Coast grew out of the Washington, D.C.–Annapolis groups, but they were spared the humiliations and hostility experienced by Asians in the Far West. Mostly they were objects of caricature, as in the fad for kabuki performances on stage between 1865 and 1867. The *New York Clipper* dismissed all Japanese as "outside barbarians" in June 1860. (After 1885, there was Japanese immigration to Hawaii but that was not yet part of the United States.) By a combination of circumstance and planning, the Japanese would maintain a very low profile in the United States until the 20th century.

American National Traits

Unlike the United States today, 19th-century America was overwhelmingly white and western European, and the concept of a multicultural society was incomprehensible. Regardless of their particular heritage or European country of origin, most white Americans shared certain traits: They were restless, acquisitive, eager to make money, democratically minded, and fiercely independent. The United States was a highly mobile, individualistic society, also a violent one, but its people had an abiding faith in egalitarian principles—the vague, abstract belief in some sort of generic equality. It was a highly limited belief because the democratic promise extended only to white males at this time, but it was open to negotiation. In practice it meant that anyone could grasp the basics of law, government, medicine, and art; that taste was a matter of opinion; that native intelligence was as good as book learning; and that self-improvement was everybody's right. It was what Ralph Waldo Emerson called "the democratizing spirit of the age." Most Americans worked hard to break down traditional class barriers by "popularizing" everything, including art and schooling. In the process, mediocrity became a badge of pride, not shame. It meant the great American middle class in the public mind.

Equality, even as a vague principle, required raising up the lowest classes to a higher level, and that required broad reforms of the worst inequalities of the system. There was a reformist spirit abroad in the land at mid-century, the last gasp of a movement launched by Jacksonian Democrats a generation before with such high hopes. It was directed against drunkenness, slavery, mental illness, popery, illiteracy, pauperism, and other "evils" of American society. Naturally agreement was not universal on how far reformers should be allowed to change traditional ways or even on whether there was a need for reform in so many areas. The reform spirit was strongest in New England, the cradle of the Puritan zeal that drove many reformers. The U.S. branch of the British-originated Young Men's Christian Association (YMCA) opened in Boston in 1851 thanks to the efforts of a retired sea captain and Baptist lay missionary, Thomas Valentine Sullivan. As an alternative gathering place to brothels and taverns for young men living in the city, it was equal parts theology and character building, and its being a British import did not seem to harm its popularity any.

Impact of the Civil War on American Society

The Civil War mainly accelerated trends already under way, especially the gradual transformation from an agrarian to an industrial society. Although more than half the population still worked on the land in 1870, the future belonged to the cities. In the East, farms and small towns lost population steadily to larger urban industrial centers. In the South, the transformation was sped along by the fact that one-fourth of Southern white farmers were killed during the war. The large numbers of unproductive or abandoned farms opened opportunities for the "freedmen," as the former slaves were officially known, but they found that prejudice and a rickety economic system prevented most of them from becoming independent landowners.

The freedmen represented the biggest consequence of the Civil War for U.S. society as 4.1 million slaves were suddenly transformed into free citizens by the Thirteenth Amendment. What the freedmen wanted was not just freedom from enslavement, but, in the words of the historian Eric Foner, "freedom from white control . . . and autonomy both for themselves as individuals and for their community." With emancipation, African Americans had gained their freedom, but few had the means to start a new life, and with the social order stacked against them, they quickly slipped into dependency as tenant farmers and sharecroppers. New social barriers in the form of "Black Codes" were thrown up. These required freedmen to have employment contracts and passes to travel but denied them such basic rights as owning weapons and changing jobs. The codes were so outrageous that Congress finally declared them unlawful in 1867 after looking the other way for almost two years.

In the end the South underwent a true social revolution such as no other section of the nation has ever experienced in U.S. history. For the duration of Reconstruction, the former Confederacy became a "social laboratory" for implementation of racial equality under federal oversight. This was going on while bigotry and racism were being widely ignored in Northern communities. By 1875, however, the experiment had been called off and its enforcers had gone home. Southern society was left even more polarized along racial lines than it was before the war because the security of the slave system that had allowed blacks to live and work alongside whites without arousing whites' fears of racial mixing had disappeared. Instead of the old slave system second-class citizenship was the status of blacks by both law and custom. To keep the social structure as close to the antebellum model as possible, terror tactics that included "night riding" and even lynching were employed. These methods were successful in freezing Southern society in what amounted to an antebellum time warp scarcely affected by 12 years of Reconstruction.

Yet Reconstruction was not a total loss for African Americans. During the time that they enjoyed federal protection, they managed to establish a beachhead in Southern society ("Black Reconstruction"), which they slowly built on in the generations that followed: Black business districts (e.g., Richmond), a black professional class, black fraternal organizations, and black colleges (e.g., Howard University) all helped African Americans claim their rightful place in the nation, although not for many more decades.

White Southern society had to deal with more than one kind of painful social change. Class and regional solidarity were challenged by two new types: Northern "carpetbaggers" who descended on the postwar South and Southern "scalawags" who cooperated with the carpetbag regimes. Thousands of Southern whites pulled up stakes and joined the exodus to the West, providing a new generation of cattle ranchers, entrepreneurs, and outlaws. Most white Southerners, former slaveholders and nonslaveholders alike, closed ranks against

This lithograph from *Harper's Weekly,* June 30, 1866, shows a member of the U.S. Colored Troops being married at Vicksburg, Mississippi, by Chaplain Warren of the Freedmen's Bureau: a great improvement over the old days, when slaves only had to jump over a broomstick to be considered "married." (Courtesy of Mississippi Department of Archives and History)

Republican rule and black equality. The strongest sentiments they shared were hatred of Yankees and love for the "Lost Cause" of Confederate independence, which found expression in the creation of the Ku Klux Klan and white supremacist philosophy. They hoped to recreate antebellum society in every facet except slavery, and they were willing to use violence to do it.

The popular reaction of the white South to defeat seemed to follow one of two lines of thinking—either nostalgia for the Lost Cause or commitment to economic makeover in the image of the North. Most Southerners seemed to retreat into a mythology that explained away defeat and elevated the nobility of the Confederacy's fight to heroic proportions. The newspaperman Edward A. Pollard first popularized the term *Lost Cause* as the title of a history of the war he published in 1867. The other reaction, favored by thoughtful Southerners, was to embrace the more progressive values and economic principles of the North, thereby beating the Northerners at their own game. The "New South" would be a South built on freedom, union, and industrialization. The term was popularized from the 1870s by Southern journalists such as J. D. B. DeBow *(DeBow's Review),* Edwin DeLeon *(Putnam's Magazine),* and especially Henry W. Grady *(Atlanta Constitution).* Unfortu-

Henry W. Grady (1850–89), a symbol of the "New South" that began to emerge from the ruins of Civil War and Reconstruction, became editor of the *Atlanta Constitution,* a position he used to decry "Lost Cause" mythology and champion Union, freedom, and economic development. (Courtesy of the Georgia Historical Society)

This view of the "business house," or general merchandise store, of Thomas W. Anderson & Co. in Cambridge, Maryland, as it appeared in the mid-1870s, shows that such shopping was still an activity limited to the upper classes. (The Maryland Historical Society, Baltimore, Maryland)

nately the New South never became much more than a concept used by boosters and apologists, while the Lost Cause became practically a secular religion among unreconstructed Confederates. The reality of the so-called New South, which emerged at the end of this period, was that it was as provincial as the antebellum South, but now it was built on the ideas of material progress, segregation, and home rule.

The Rise of an Industrial Working Class

Industrialization, urbanization, and immigration were a three-headed monster that threatened to overwhelm the nation after the Civil War. The industrial working class that had been steadily growing since the antebellum period continued to increase in both absolute and relative numbers if not in political power. A great proportion of that growth resulted from the influx of women, children, and new immigrants into the ranks of labor. Traditionally men had been the breadwinners, and now women and children were also taking home a paycheck. And the new immigrants introduced new ideas about labor relations and class conflict.

Workers flocked to the new industrial centers from rural areas and foreign countries, creating urban metropolises and a social transformation. In some cases the factory became the new center of communal life because the larger corporations built "company towns" that extended their control over every aspect of the workers' lives both on the job and off. The urban working class was completely dependent on others to provide the raw materials that kept the factories open and the food and shelter that kept them alive. Unlike in agrarian society, there was no "safety net" of homestead and vegetable garden to sustain them in tough times. They were vulnerable to every economic and social shift. As workers lost control over their own lives, they drew together with an increased sense of class consciousness heretofore unknown in the United States.

Not only did the tasks change (from farming to factory work), but the very nature of work itself changed. The emphasis now was on efficiency and high productivity, so the worker became a disposable commodity, his/her work repetitious and dehumanizing and subject to cycles of employment and unemployment. The system was often compared, unfavorably, with slavery because at least slavery had a paternal side. Open class warfare did not occur because Americans both high-born and low- still shared an abiding faith that anyone who worked hard and saved frugally could eventually be a success regardless of his/her circumstances. The built-in inequities of the capitalist system were justified not just by the bottom line on the business ledger but by such intellectual rationalizations as Social Darwinism ("survival of the fittest"), rags-to-riches fables, and McGuffey's school readers. The traditional U.S. belief in individualism over collectivism was also co-opted because such ideas as every man his own master, self-reliance, and personal responsibility were all readily adaptable to the new order. By contrast anything that smacked of collectivism, such as Marxist philosophy, was anathema.

The Wealthy Class

Historically wealth had been based on land. But with industrialization a new wealthy class, the nouveau riche, based their wealth on financial holdings, not acreage. They first became a powerful segment of society in the urban North, where they controlled the new industries. Slavery and the plantation economy in the South retarded development of a nouveau riche class there but could not keep it at bay forever. Meanwhile in the North the rich were acquiring financial wealth beyond the wildest dreams of anyone before them who was not a member of a royal family, In fact, this was a new, peculiarly American, kind of "royalty."

Their "conspicuous" lifestyle as much as their wealth defined them. Their food, the size of their homes, luxurious travel accommodations, all these and more, set them apart from the mass of Americans. The masses regarded the superwealthy with mixed feelings of envy and admiration. On the one hand, they were seen as the recipients of God's blessings and even the benefactors of society ("captains of industry"); on the other hand, they were denounced as parasites and greedy, rapacious "robber barons."

The very rich added a fifth season to the traditional four of nature—the "social season," when parties were given, the ranks were opened to newcomers who met their high standards, and everyone tried to top everyone else in showing off wealth. One of the premier events of the social season in the Northeast was the Grand Showman's Ball, held every February at the Elephant Hotel in Westchester County, New York, from 1847. Described as a "brilliant fete," it continued to be held annually for many years thereafter. Its organizers and leading lights were all men in show business who styled themselves "the Syndicate." For the 1849 affair, 300 couples were in attendance, a 12-hour banquet was served, the dancing stretched on into a second day, and the aggregate wealth of the family fortunes present was estimated at $5 million by one newspaper reporter—a fabulous sum for that day. A major focus of the new penny press that arose in the 1850s was chronicling the affairs of the superrich, who held such fascination for the masses of Americans barely scraping by.

Women

Women were of course not a single demographic group. Rather, representative types ranged from the plantation mistress of the South to the New England factory girl. What was consistent was that their legal and civil rights were severely restricted and firmly in the hands of a male relative or a spouse. That United States was still very much a patriarchal society is neither outrageous nor shocking in the context of the times. At least there was enough tolerance among the ruling male establishment to allow the formation of an active women's movement. The 19th-century women's rights crusade, still in its infancy, was, however, a middle-class phenomenon that scarcely affected the overwhelming number of U.S. women.

The fact is that although women were largely excluded from civic life—meaning voting, serving on juries, and holding elective office—they were far from being an oppressed class in the usual sense of that term. They had several important roles in the society outside of the home. Education (including in universities), business, and the professions (i.e., law and medicine) were open to women, albeit on a limited basis. The literary societies and self-help and charitable groups that were founded by women in the 19th century are only part of the story. Women were also prominent in American literature (see chapter 15), church work (see chapter 8), and major reform movements (e.g., temperance and abolition). A portrayal of them as powerless

A pair of Southern ladies pass along the sidewalk in Vicksburg, Mississippi, while a group of gents look on. (Courtesy of Mississippi Department of Archives and History)

and virtually banished from national life is not supported by the historical evidence.

Before the Civil War the women's movement achieved some modest gains:

1. Most states enacted laws allowing women to own property independently of their husband.
2. Academies for secondary education were established and the first coed institution (Oberlin College) opened its doors.
3. A handful of women were admitted into the professional ranks (i.e., as physicians, members of the clergy, et al).
4. In 1860 for the first time in U.S. history, as many girls as boys attended elementary schools and as many women as men could read and write.
5. They were a powerful, even disproportionate, voice in national literature as the authors of so-called sentimental novels.

During the Civil War Northern and Southern (white) women reacted very differently to wartime demands. Southern women mostly tended the home fires and prayed that the slaves would remain docile while the menfolk were away. Some also expanded on the traditional women's roles of sewing and cooking for and nursing the soldiers. In the North female leaders put aside their own interests to work for the twin causes of preserving the Union and ending black slavery. They helped found the U.S. Sanitary Commission, organized the Loyal National League to crusade for emancipation, and served as nurses in hospitals. But North or South, they had little to show for the cause of equality when the war ended.

After the Civil War the immediate problem for many women was a shortage of men. Between battlefield casualties and disease, the war had taken away nearly 134,000 men from the South, and at least another 310,000 from the North. Those men left behind them widows and sweethearts who faced the prospect of finding a mate in a severely reduced pool of eligible men. That was a need that could not be as easily satisfied from the ranks of incoming immigrants as the labor market could. In Massachusetts immediately after the war it was reported there were 50,000 "extra" women with no mate and little prospects of finding one. Some women who had lost their husband in the war simply removed themselves from the competition. The sight of women in widow's black was common during the rest of the century. Mail-ordering brides became an acceptable method of getting a wife in many parts of the country, and "old maid" jokes became a staple of American humor. In New Haven, Connecticut, the story was told that a student threw a stone at a dog and missed the pooch but hit seven old maids! The widows and single women were the forgotten victims of the Civil War.

Perhaps for some of the same reasons a significant number of women chose to forgo marriage and instead devote their life to a writing career or even the noble cause of women's rights. The slow progress toward female equality that had begun in the antebellum period continued after the Civil War. In 1865 the first all-women's college, Vassar College, opened its doors, and in the years that followed women also began to be admitted to such major universities as Cornell, Michigan, Pennsylvania, and California. The golden age of the movement was still ahead; it would have to wait until the first generation of trained, educated feminine leadership could make its mark on society. The first women's rights convention since 1848 met in May 1866, and those who attended founded the American Equal Rights Association with the intention of tying their cause to the freedmen's—on the basis of the arguments of "common humanity" and "equal natural rights." But black civil rights leaders quickly distanced themselves from the women's movement, preferring to focus on racial over gender issues. The resulting bitter split between the two groups in 1869 ended a historic alliance and set the cause of gender equality back at least a generation.

TABLE 7.28 MALE-TO-FEMALE RATIO OF U.S. POPULATION BY RACE AND ETHNIC GROUP, 1850–1870

Year	Total (men: women)	White (men: women)	Black (men: women)	American Indian (men: women)	Japanese (men: women)	Chinese (men: women)
1850	1.04:1	1.05:1	0.99:1	N/A	N/A	N/A
1860	1.05:1	1.05:1	1.00:1	1.19:1	N/A	18.58:1
1870	1.02:1	1.03:1	0.96:1	0.95:1	5.88:1	12.84:1

Note: For some groups statistics are not available (N/A) either because the total numbers were so insignificant that the government did not do the counting or because the statistical methodology excluded the group.
Source: U.S. Bureau of the Census, *Historical Statistics of the United States, Colonial Times to 1970,* series A (Washington, D.C.: Government Printing Office, 1975), 91–104.

The baby-step advances made by the women's rights movement in these years did little to change the major obstacles to victory: (1) Women still could not vote on either the state, the local, or the national level; and (2) the ingrained belief was that women were not just different biologically but weaker and more easily led than men. For reformers the principal goal of the movement in the years ahead was to secure the right to vote. That defined the debate and outweighed all other issues.

Children

The forgotten demographic of society were the children, who were either exploited as cheap labor or doted on by middle-class Victorian parents. The problem of a high infant mortality rate was a constant factor, but family size among whites also declined steadily during the century as a factor of the falling birth rate. This not only meant fewer children in the general population but made those who survived even more precious to their parents.

Childhood followed two divergent paths: the sheltered, privileged existence of middle-class children versus growing up quickly in the harsh world of the working classes. There were no child protection laws yet, so children formed their own subculture of the labor force. They enlisted as soldiers in Civil War armies, worked in mines, and drove cattle up the western trails. Some menial jobs were virtually reserved for children: selling newspapers, running errands, shining shoes, and cleaning chimneys, for instance. In 1870 child workers in factories, mills, and mines numbered about 700,000, earning an average of $2.50 per week. Few children spent much time in school, and this was particularly true of blacks, immigrants, farm children, and the working classes in general.

Children in poor families were forced to survive by their own wits, especially in big cities, where many lived on the streets by peddling, scavenging, and thieving. In the 1850s reformers introduced the idea of foster care for street urchins in several eastern cities, and in 1874 child advocacy became a reality thanks to New York City's Society for the Prevention of Cruelty to Children.

A revolutionary solution to the problem of a juvenile underclass in New York City was offered by Charles Loring Brace, founder of the Children's Aid Society, in 1853. Reflecting the conventional wisdom that children grow up better in the country than in the city, the society's mission was to round up thousands of poor waifs from the streets and tenements of New York and ship them west by rail to new foster homes in rural America. The New York Foundling Hospital participated in the program for 50 years, starting in 1870. Society members such as the Reverend E. P. Smith roamed the slums of New York gathering homeless and unwanted children. Meanwhile prospective parents on the other end of the pipeline answered ads in local newspapers and signed up in advance for their orphans or sometimes just met the train and selected on the spot from among unclaimed kids. The first "Orphan's Train," as they were eventually dubbed, left New York City for Dowagiac, Michigan, in 1854 carrying 46 boys, seven to 15 years old. In the next 20 years some 25,000 boys and girls were placed in "country homes." By August 1873 nearly 3,000 a year were being sent off, and by 1875 that number had reached 4,000 a year. They usually made the journey in groups of 20 to 40 with members of the society as chaperones, and some groups were as large as 100. The program continued until 1929 when reform legislation finally ended all such "placing out" programs. It was the nation's first organized foster care program, and one of the most important social experiments in U.S. history.

All the children were not orphans; some were members of large, poor families living in the slums of New York, Philadelphia, and other eastern cities whose parents could not afford them. They became de facto orphans transported with the rest. This transportation system, for that is what it was, bore an uncomfortable resemblance to the English 17th-century practice of transporting convicts and paupers to the colonies. Brace's orphan placement program rid the cities of a social problem and met a need in western rural communities succinctly expressed in the society's literature: "A child's labor is needed for a thousand things on a Western farm." Eventually more than 150,000 children were relocated to rural communities all over the West, and some 7,000 of those were from the New York Foundling Hospital. The society's official line used to justify trafficking in children was that "they share fully in the active and inspiring Western life. They are moulded by the social tone around them, and they grow up under the very best circumstances which can surround a poor boy or girl." The record of the orphan trains was mixed. No doubt many did benefit by the change of scenery, but many others were shamefully exploited as cheap labor by their foster parents, who ignored whatever legal rights they had. Life for most children in the 19th century was more Oliver Twist than Little Lord Fauntleroy, though there is accuracy in both literary images.

American society experienced profound and painful changes during these years as a result of immigration, war, and westward expansion. Immigrants formed a higher percentage of the total population than at any other time in the nation's history. Consequently the old Anglo-Saxon type, English values and culture, and the Protestant religion no longer defined the nation. And with national emancipation in 1865, a whole race of people, nearly 4 million strong, was suddenly transformed from chattel into citizens. Freedom did not mean equality, but it did place new stresses on the social fabric of the nation. And the West was producing a new type of American, more rude, more rugged, and more independent than ever before. It also encouraged traits that were already present, such as violence and egalitarianism. The western experience was so crucial in shaping national character that near the end of the 19th century the historian Frederick Jackson Turner would call it the primary influence in the nation's history.

This was a transitional period in other ways. One can see the steady transformation from an agrarian society into an urbanized and industrialized one. The heartbeat of America increasingly was to be found in the city and the factory, not the farm and the small town. This change produced great differences in wealth, power, and living conditions from top to bottom. The gulfs among the working class, middle class, and upper class grew with each passing year. Each class developed its own distinctive cultures of work and play, which were reflected in value systems, too. For the very rich there was a sense of entitlement justified by the philosophy of Social Darwinism. For the working class there was a growing sense of alienation and resentment that fueled, among other things, a smoldering labor movement. The middle class, many of whom had not long before been members of the working class, cherished the certainty of Victorian morality, which emphasized appearances, family values, and the "gospel of success." What held the classes together and made U.S. society work was a degree of social mobility unknown in the rest of the world. In a single lifetime that poor working-class "schlub" could rise through the middle class and become one of the "swells" at the top, precisely as Andrew Carnegie and countless others did. So numerous were they in fact that they constituted a new class, the nouveau riche (new rich). Hope sprang eternal in the American breast regardless of color or gender. The rags-to-riches story became an integral part of American mythology. The two groups who found the path to the top strewn with the most obstacles were women and Native Americans, because the traditional power structure accepted the conventional wisdom that women were by nature inferior to men, while Indians lacked even the meager advantages of the freedman in U.S. society. But even for these two groups the situation was not hopeless, as the cases of Clara Barton, founder of the Red Cross, and Ely Parker, first commissioner of Indian Affairs, proved.

Freedom in U.S. society meant that a bobbin boy could become a captain of industry, but it also meant that the white male majority was "free" to subjugate, oppress, and disenfranchise the various minorities with impunity. But the strong social conscience of the American people and the universal faith in the rule of law meant that conditions could improve and that, to use the words of the jubilant freedmen, the "bottom rail could become the top."

TABLE 7.29 STATES AND TERRITORIES THAT RECEIVED "ORPHANS" UNDER THE CHILDREN'S AID SOCIETY PROGRAM, 1854–1929

State or Territory	Approximate Number of Children Received
Ohio	7,000
Ind.	4,000
Ill.	9,000+
Iowa	6,000+
Mo.	6,000+
Minn.	4,000
Nebr.	4,000
Kans.	4,000
Tex.	4,000
Colo.	1,500
Indian Territory (Okla.)	59

Note: All the numbers are approximate because both the society's and the Foundling Hospital's records are sealed for reasons of client confidentiality. Barring some future legislative action, they can only be opened by court order.
Source: Marilyn Holt, *Orphan Trains* (Lincoln: University of Nebraska Press, 1992), passim.

CHAPTER 8 Religion

The United States has been described as "a nation with the soul of a church," meaning that from the beginning it has had a very devout people whose strong faith has shaped their morality, their public policy, and their view of the world. The number of "churched" Americans climbed steadily during the 19th century, although a significant decline occurred during the Civil War years. (The dip during those years was the normal result of the dislocations and disillusionment caused by war.) By one estimation the percentage of U.S. church members in 1800 was no more than 10 percent, climbing to 35 percent by 1870, so that a little more than one-third of Americans in 1870 could be considered religious by conventional standards.

TABLE 8.1 CHURCH MEMBERSHIP IN THE UNITED STATES AS A PERCENTAGE OF TOTAL POPULATION AT MID-CENTURY, 1850–1870

Year	Total U.S. Population	Percentage of Adherents among General Population
1850	23,191,876	34
1860	31,443,321	37
1870	39,818,449	35

Note: Based on the Fiske-Stark statistical model, whereby the number of "adherents" (*cf.*, "members") is calculated by adding in members' children and other historical factors not calculated in regular church records. Adherents are those who profess a particular faith as opposed to those who hold membership on a church roll.
Source: Roger Finke and Rodney Stark, "Turning Pews into People: Estimating 19th Century Church Membership," *Journal for the Scientific Study of Religion* 25, no. 2 (1986): 180–92.

Church Membership

There are problems trying to calculate church membership at this late date because of incomplete records, primitive statistical methodology, and the fact that the U.S. Census Bureau counted *the number of seats in each church building,* not the actual number of members, in their decennial counts. The available raw data from census enumerations and church records are still sufficient to show that, contrary to popular belief, church membership in the 19th century was much lower than at any time during the 20th century. Modern scholars have used sophisticated statistical methods to reconstruct the numbers of churches and members in the 19th century, providing a good profile of American religious practices.

By 1850 there was one church for every 609 inhabitants, down from earlier in the century, but a higher ratio than it would ever be again according to *The Historical Atlas of Religion in America.* Ten years later, despite a massive surge in population that resulted from immigration, the number was down only slightly, with one church for every 608 Americans, served by 36,000 full-time or part-time clergy. In general, it can be said that easterners were more religious than westerners, rural folk more religious than city dwellers. In 1870, 35 percent to 40 percent of the population of the eastern seaboard states were regular churchgoers. Farther west the rate dropped to about 25 percent on the Great Plains, then rose again slightly in the Rocky Mountain and Pacific Coast regions. Why some regions were "more religious" than others is impossible to say, but it was probably a combination of several factors, including the nearness of a place of worship, the numbers of women and family men in the local population, and the historic presence of a particular church, for example, the Catholic Church in the Southwest.

TABLE 8.3 CHURCH MEMBERSHIP BY REGION, AS A PERCENTAGE OF TOTAL REGIONAL POPULATION, 1850–1870

Region	1850	1860	1870
New England[a]	32	36	36
Middle Atlantic[b]	35	39	37
East North Central[c]	37	39	36
West North Central[d]	22	26	26
South Atlantic[e]	36	39	35
East South Central[f]	34	35	36
West South Central[g]	20	32	23
Mountain[h]	53	69	56
Pacific[i]	19	26	37

Note: Based on the Fiske-Stark statistical model, which calculates "adherents" rather than recorded members.
[a] Conn., Maine, Mass. N.H., R.I., Vt.
[b] N.Y., N.J., Pa.
[c] Ill., Ind., Ohio, Wis., Mich.
[d] Iowa, Kans. (1861), Minn. (1858), Mo., Nebr. (1867), Dakota Territory.
[e] Del., Md., District of Columbia, Va., W.Va. (1863), Fla., Ga. N.C., S.C.
[f] Ala. Ky., Miss. Tenn.
[g] Indian Territory, La., Ark., Tex.
[h] Arizona Territory, Colorado Territory, Idaho Territory, Montana Territory, New Mexico Territory, Nev. (1864), Utah Territory, Wyoming Territory.
[i] Calif., Washington Territory, Oreg. (1859).
Source: Roger Finke and Rodney Stark, "Turning Pews into People: Estimating 19th Century Church Membership," *Journal for the Scientific Study of Religion* 25, no. 2 (1986): 180–92.

TABLE 8.2 MEMBERSHIP OF MAJOR DENOMINATIONS BASED ON AVAILABLE CHURCH RECORDS AND ON STATISTICAL MODEL, 1850–1870

Denomination	1850		1860		1870	
	Church Records	Statistical Model	Church Records	Statistical Model	Church Records	Statistical Model
Methodist	1,247,000	1,615,000	1,803,000	2,306,000	2,012,000	2,330,000
Presbyterian	347,000	548,000	428,000	697,000	447,000	763,000
Episcopal	89,000	172,000	146,000	243,000	218,000	289,000
Roman Catholic	1,606,000	1,088,000	3,103,000	2,439,000	4,504,000	3,555,000
Baptist	N/A	1,566,000	N/A	1,955,000	N/A	2,031,000
Congregational	N/A	345,000	N/A	427,000	N/A	482,000
Lutheran	N/A	200,000	N/A	308,000	N/A	441,000

Note: Based on the Fiske-Stark statistical model.
Source: Roger Finke and Rodney Stark, "Turning Pews into People: Estimating 19th Century Church Membership," *Journal for the Scientific Study of Religion* 25, no. 2 (1986): 180–92.

Certain denominations also tended to be more heavily represented in certain states and territories than in others. For example, the Lutheran Church was strong in Pennsylvania but virtually nonexistent in Florida; the Baptists were strong in every Southern state, much weaker in New England. The explanation for this is easier to deduce: It had to be related to the socioreligious background of the people who settled the state. For instance, the large number of Germans Protestants who settled in Pennsylvania during colonial times explains the strong Lutheran presence in that state.

Separation of church and state, embedded in the Constitution in the form of the establishment clause, was unquestioned, yet a shared Protestant faith was one of the bonds that held Americans together. The United States was the first Western nation founded by Protestants after the Protestant Reformation of the 16th century, and Americans never stopped believing that they should be "a shining example to the world," as the Puritan John Winthrop had expressed it. At mid-century, Protestants outnumbered Roman Catholics (the second largest group) by more than three to one.

Although the unbending Puritanism of Cotton Mather was dead, Americans of the mid-19th century still believed they were on a divine mission from God. Americans saw God's hand in everything, from the relentless settlement of the West to the tragedy of the Civil War. What had changed since Cotton Mather's day was that American Protestantism had shifted its focus from the old-fashioned Puritan obsession with an angry, awesome God to a faith based on the gentle, loving Jesus. This was best exemplified by the popular hymns of the day: "Jesus Loves Me" (Anna B. Warner, 1860), "Jesus, Meek and Gentle" (George R. Prynne, 1856), and "Jesus, Keep Me near the Cross" (Fanny J. Crosby, 1869).

Religion in America was marked by pluralism, optimism, and conservatism. There were 14 major denominations and numerous small sects practicing their particular faiths and exhibiting an amazing level of toleration among themselves. Unlike rival faiths and sects in the Old World, American denominations did not make war on each other; nor did American believers, as a rule, try to exterminate each other. The glaring exceptions to this rule were the widespread hostility to and suspicion of Catholics and Mormons, which occasionally broke out into violence as it did in the Philadelphia Bible Riots of Catholics and Protestants in 1844. Persecution drove the Mormons completely out of the United States and to the Great Salt Lake Valley (now Utah, then still part of Mexico), where they established a safe homeland.

Persecution of Mormons was spontaneous and unorganized, that of Catholics was both organized and formal. In fact, it is fair to say that during this era in the United States the Roman Catholic Church was under siege from all sides by those who believed that Catholicism and the American way of life were fundamentally incompatible. The movement was closely tied to nativist (i.e., antiforeign) fears that a

TABLE 8.4 NUMBER OF CHURCHES, BY DENOMINATION, IN EACH STATE AND (ORGANIZED) TERRITORY OF THE UNITED STATES, 1850

State or Territory	Baptist	Congregational	Episcopal	Lutheran	Methodist	Presbyterian	Quaker	Dutch Reformed	German Reformed	Roman Catholic
Maine	326	180	9	0	199	7	26	0	0	12
N.H.	193	176	11	0	103	13	15	0	0	2
Vt.	102	175	26	0	140	11	7	0	0	8
Mass.	266	448	54	1	262	15	39	0	0	41
R.I.	106	21	26	0	23	0	18	0	0	7
Conn.	114	252	101	0	185	17	5	0	0	12
N.Y.	781	215	279	81	1,231	671	133	233	1	176
N.J.	108	8	52	7	312	149	52	66	0	22
Pa.	320	0	136	498	889	775	149	7	209	139
Del.	12	0	21	0	106	26	9	0	0	3
Md.	45	0	133	40	497	56	26	0	22	65
District of Columbia	6	0	8	2	16	6	1	0	0	6
Va.	649	0	173	50	1,025	240	14	0	9	17
N.C.	615	0	50	49	784	151	31	0	16	4
S.C.	413	1	72	41	484	136	1	0	0	14
Ga.	879	1	20	8	795	97	2	0	0	8
Fla.	56	0	10	0	87	16	0	0	0	5
Ala.	579	0	17	1	577	162	0	0	0	5
Miss.	385	0	13	0	454	143	0	0	0	9
La.	77	0	14	0	125	18	0	0	1	55
Tex.	82	0	5	0	176	45	0	0	0	13
Ark.	114	0	2	0	168	52	0	0	0	7
Tenn.	646	0	17	12	861	363	4	0	0	3
Ky.	803	0	19	5	530	224	0	0	0	48
Mo.	300	0	11	21	250	125	0	0	0	65
Ill.	282	46	27	42	405	206	6	2	3	59
Ind.	428	2	24	63	778	282	89	5	5	63
Ohio.	551	100	79	260	1,529	663	94	5	71	130
Mich.	66	29	25	12	119	72	7	10	0	44
Wis.	49	37	19	20	110	40	0	2	0	64
Iowa	20	14	5	4	71	38	5	0	1	18
Calif.	1	0	1	0	5	3	0	0	0	18
Minn.[a]	0	0	0	0	1	1	0	0	0	1
N.Mex.[a]	0	0	0	0	0	0	0	0	0	73
Oreg.[a]	1	1	0	0	1	1	0	0	0	5
Utah[b]										

[a] Organized territory in 1850.
[b] Nine churches unclassified but probably Mormon.
Source: Edwin Scott Gaustad, *Historical Atlas of Religion in America* (New York: Harper & Row, Publishers, 1962), 168 (from information contained in *The Seventh Census of the United States, 1850*).

flood of predominantly Catholic Irish and Germans were overrunning the country. It included in its ranks such notables as the minister Lyman Beecher and the artist-inventor Samuel F. B. Morse. Three bitterly anti-Catholic groups operated in the United States: the American Protestant Association (organized, 1842), the Know-Nothing Party (organized, 1854), and the Ku Klux Klan (organized, 1865).

TABLE 8.5 MAJOR DENOMINATIONS AND STATES WHERE THEY REPRESENTED THE MAJORITY BY NUMBERS OF CONGREGATION, 1850

Denomination	Number of States/Territories Where They Were in the Majority
Methodists	20 (N.Y., N.J., Pa., Del., Md., Va., N.C., S.C., Fla., Miss., La., Tex., Ark., Tenn., Ill., Ind., Ohio, Mich., Wis., Iowa)
Baptists	7 (Maine, N.H., R.I., Ga., Ala., Ky., Mo.)
Congregationalists	3 (Mass., Conn., Vt.)
Roman Catholics	3 (Calif., Oreg., N.Mex.)[a]

[a] Oreg. and N.Mex. were territories in 1850.
Source: Edwin Scott Gaustad, *Historical Atlas of Religion in America* (New York: Harper & Row, 1962), 64.

TABLE 8.6 PROPORTION OF CHURCH ADHERENTS FOR SELECTED MAJOR GROUPS IN THE GENERAL POPULATION OF 31,500,000, 1860

Church-Ethnic Group	Percentage of Adherents in Total Population
White Protestants of Anglo-Saxon background	69.4
Roman Catholics	21.4
Black Methodists and Baptists	1.7
Lutherans	2.6
Jews	1.3
Eastern Orthodox	1.3

Source: Mark A. Noll, *A History of Christianity in the United States and Canada* (Grand Rapids, Mich.: William B. Eerdmans, 1992), 361.

The virulent bigotry against Roman Catholics produced riots and assassinations as well as a flood of anti-Catholic propaganda in the form of sermons, broadsides, editorials, and even a literary genre known as convent exposés. These were tell-alls supposedly written by former nuns revealing the debauchery that occurred behind the convent walls. Some U.S. leaders attempted to draw a line between ordinary Catholic believers and the church itself by calling their movement antipopery, but the distinction was lost on the majority of Americans.

In terms of the number of new congregations planted, all of the major denominations except Quakers increased their membership during this 25-year period.

By contrast, the number of Quaker congregations actually declined from 726 in 1850 to 692 20 years later. The overwhelming majority of Americans counted themselves Protestants, and they clearly had denominational preferences. Up to around 1850, more Americans identified themselves as Methodists than as members of any other church—about 1.25 million. They had more congregations in more states than any other denomination. Their historic "March to the Pacific," beginning in Natchez, Mississippi, in 1805, swept across the country almost inexorably, reaching Oregon in 1834 and California the same year as the "forty-niners." Their numbers dropped after 1860, but so did those of all denominations except one, the result of dislocations and cynicism caused by the Civil War.

The one group that continued to increase its numbers right through the Civil War was the Catholic Church, continuing a trend that had started before the war. When the Great Sectional Conflict occurred the Catholic Church proved to be "war-proof." It benefited from a demographic shift that first became apparent when the 1850 Census was calculated. Thanks to a flood of some 2.5 million European immigrants who poured into the country in the 10 years after that, the nation's religious makeup changed dramatically. Roman Catholics became the single largest religious body in the United States. This was ironic considering America's Calvinist religious roots and the popular suspicion of anyone who venerated the pope in Rome. But it was more the acceleration of a trend than a radical departure. Catholics had been increasing their numbers quietly for two decades. Between 1830 and 1860, the Catholic population of the United States increased 10-fold—from 300,000 to 3 million, a proportional increase from 3 percent to 13 percent of the religious population. And there was more to the story than sheer numbers. The labors of the U.S. priesthood were remarkable enough to merit official recognition by the Holy See in later years.

TABLE 8.7 NUMBER OF CONGREGATIONS, IN THE UNITED STATES AS REPRESENTED BY MAJOR DENOMINATIONS, 1850 AND 1860

Denomination	Number of Congregations in 1850	As a Percentage of Total Congregations	Number of Congregations in 1860	Percentage Increase, 1850–60
Baptist	9,375	25.2	12,150	29.6
Congregational	1,706	4.6	2,234	32.0
Episcopalian	1,459	3.9	2,145	46.9
Lutheran	1,217	3.3	2,128	74.6
Methodist	13,280	35.7	19,883	49.7
Presbyterian	4,824	13.0	6,406	32.8
Quaker	726	2.0	726	0.0
Dutch Reformed	330	1.8	440	33.3
German Reformed	338	c	676	100.0
Roman Catholic	1,221	3.3	2,550	108.8
Disciples of Christ	1,898	5.1	2,100	10.6
Unitarian[a]	246	2.1	264	N/A
Universalist[b]	285	c	664	N/A
Jewish	30[d]	0.1	N/A	N/A

[a] A Protestant group dating from the 16th century that denied the doctrine of the Trinity and rejected the belief in Jesus as the Christ.
[b] A Protestant group that believed that salvation was not for a chosen few (the "elect") but a gift of God available to all.
[c] All "Reformed" churches are counted together here, as are the Unitarian and Universalist Churches.
[d] Cf. Table 8.10, in which the U.S. Census cites a different number (29) than Gaustad, the reference used here.
Source: From Seventh census of the United States, 1850, and Eighth census of the United States, 1860, social statistical schedules, cited in Edwin S. Gaustad, *Historical Atlas of Religion in America* (New York: Harper and Row, 1962), 43, 160–61.

Three members of the U.S. clergy who were active during this period have been raised to sainthood by the Catholic Church, and another three beatified, a lengthy and complicated process under canon law.

TABLE 8.8 MAJOR DENOMINATIONS IN THE UNITED STATES AS A PERCENTAGE OF TOTAL U.S. POPULATION AT MID-CENTURY, 1850–1870

Denomination	1850	1860	1870
Baptist	6.8	6.2	5.3
Congregational	1.5	1.4	1.2
Episcopal	1.2	1.3	1.1
Lutheran	0.9	1.0	1.1
Methodist	11.3	12.0	9.2
Presbyterian	3.9	3.6	3.0
Roman Catholic	4.6	7.8	9.2

Note: Based on the Fiske-Stark statistical model.
Source: Roger Finke and Rodney Stark, "Turning Pews into People: Estimating 19th Century Church Membership," *Journal for the Scientific Study of Religion* 25, no. 2 (1986): 190.

Denominational Numbers

Among mainline denominations the Catholics and Methodists were clearly dominant. No other churches even approached these two in sheer numbers of adherents or congregations during these years. The Methodists, for instance, had more congregations in the state of New York than any other church had in the entire country. At the other end of the spectrum were the small denominations who barely registered on the census rolls. For instance, the United States counted very few Jews at mid-century. In fact, there were more Methodist congregations in the frontier region of Iowa alone than there were Jewish synagogues in the entire country. And the Disciples of Christ were still a break-away denomination struggling to establish an identity independent of the Presbyterians. The bean counters in the Census Bureau considered the Disciples to be a sect of the Presbyterians, so the only figures available on them from this period are those of their founder, Alexander Campbell. Because no one knows how he gathered his data and because he had good reason to inflate the numbers, care must be taken in using his figures. Unfortunately for comparison purposes Campbell did not attempt to calculate the number of congregations in his flock.

Chicago's Church of the Holy Family (run by the Jesuit order) attracted a sizable crowd to worship services from the city's large Catholic population in 1866. (Library of Congress, Prints and Photographs Division [LC-USZ62-11557])

TABLE 8.9 NUMBERS AND DISTRIBUTION OF METHODIST CHURCHES IN THE UNITED STATES, 1850

State	Number of Congregations
N.Y.	1,231
N.J.	312
Pa.	889
Del.	106
Md.	479
Va.	1,025
N.C.	784
S.C.	484
Fla.	87
Miss.	454
La.	125
Tex.	176
Ark.	168
Tenn.	861
Ill.	405
Ind.	778
Ohio	1,529
Minn.	119
Wis.	110
Iowa.	71

Source: Edwin Scott Gaustad, *Historical Atlas of Religion in America* (New York: Harper & Row, 1962) 78.

TABLE 8.10 MEMBERSHIP OF THE DISCIPLES OF CHRIST (DENOMINATION) AS ESTIMATED BY ALEXANDER CAMPBELL (FOUNDER), 1852

State/Region	Numbers of Members
N.Y., Pa., Va., Md.	25,000
Ohio, Ky., Tenn., Mo.	110,000
Ind., Ill.	60,000
Iowa, Wis., Mich.	15,000
Ga., Ala., N.C., S.C.	5,000
Tex.	5,000
All other states	5,000
Total	225,000

Source: Edwin Scott Gaustad, *Historical Atlas of Religion in America* (New York: Harper & Row, 1962), 64.

African-American Christianity

In American religious life before the Civil War there was a deep racial divide separating white believers from black believers. Mainstream Christian churches made a regrettable accommodation with slavery, decrying its baneful effects in general terms but not actively opposing its actual practice where it existed. In both the North and the South, they virtually abandoned blacks to their fate, with only individual voices crying out for abolition. Instead of fighting slavery root and branch, the various denominations were content to launch missions among slave communities, focusing on the Bible's message of submissiveness rather than freedom. The black church was always firmly under the thumb of white authorities. Thus it functioned as both a comfort to its membership and a method of racial control for the white ruling class.

Neither the Muslim nor the Jewish faith was represented in African-American religious practices at this early date in U.S. history. Catholicism likewise had little influence on 19th-century African Americans. Blacks encountered Christianity only in its Protestant form when they reached American shores.

The Baptists and Methodists were the most active denominations in evangelizing Southern blacks. By contrast, some other denominations, such as the Lutherans and Episcopalians, continued to operate as they had for centuries, firmly rooted in European traditions. As a result of the accommodation of institutional Christianity with the slave system, parallel church structures grew up, one black and the other white. Even with good intentions, the organization of black churches in the South was greatly hindered by almost universal illiteracy among the slave population and legal prohibitions against public assembly of blacks for any reason. By the time of the Civil War the best estimate is that between one-eighth and one-sixth of the South's slave population of roughly 4 million were affiliated with one denomination or another, led by some 225,000 Methodists and 175,000 Baptists. Some historians, citing oral history traditions and anecdotal evidence, believe that acceptance of Christianity among blacks during the years of slavery was far higher than church records suggest. Numbers aside, the slave question eventually split the three largest Protestant denominations—Methodist, Presbyterian, and Baptist—producing what is known as the Great Schism in U.S. church history, which still reverberates today. Ministers chose sides along with their congregations, and many even laid their vestments aside in 1861 to join the army.

Black Christianity in the South operated in a shadow world between paternalistic toleration and furtive practice. And as it evolved in the slave quarters, the African-American church was a mixture of regular Christian worship forms and traditional (i.e., pre-Christian) African religious practices. In many ways, it was more emotional and more personal than white worship, with strong elements of sadness and longing. In some areas slaves were allowed to have their own churches and even their own places of worship. They held their services quietly, out of sight of white authorities. In most locales, however, they attended white churches, sitting in segregated sections of the sanctuary. Ironically, while slavery was denounced from the pulpit in some white Northern churches, Southern churches were the most interracial institutions in the Old South. Whites and blacks had the same denominational affiliation, read the same Bible, sang the same hymns, and listened to the same sermons. This apparent unity of spirit was only superficial, however.

The Civil War destroyed the well-established segregated, paternalistic system of worship in the South. As Union armies pushed deeper into the Confederacy, mainline churches expanded their mission work among the new freedmen who came to them. After 1865 those missions served as beachheads in the aggressive organization of separate black churches across the South, such as the African Methodist Episcopal Church. These remained loosely affiliated with their parent denominations but operated semi-independently. After the war the Presbyterians and Methodists led the way in establishing both seminaries (to train clergy) and new congregations across the South. Evangelizing was hurt by the intrusion of political issues. During Reconstruction black churches expanded their efforts beyond soul saving to become centers not just of religious activities, but also of political activism. Many worked with the Freedmen's Bureau and openly supported carpetbag regimes. This political activism would haunt them after Reconstruction ended and white "Redeemers" took over.

In the face of segregation and prejudice, black churches composed the most important social unit among the newly freed, furnishing leadership, organizing relief, serving as a bridge between blacks and whites, and providing convenient forums for the discussion of issues and problems. One scholar has called those postwar churches America's "first social institutions fully controlled by black men."

The organization of separate black churches in the middle years of the 19th century expanded the church rolls of the traditional mainline denominations, while also producing some new denominations. While Methodists, Baptists, and Presbyterians split or formed separate African-American branches, other mainline denominations either kept their racial differences in-house or else dodged the issue altogether.

TABLE 8.11 INSTITUTIONALIZATION OF THE AFRICAN-AMERICAN (CHRISTIAN) CHURCH, 19TH CENTURY

Denomination/Name of Group	Date of Organization
Providence Baptist Association[a]	1834
American Baptist Missionary Convention	1840
Colored Primitive Baptists	1866
(Colored) Cumberland Presbyterian Church	1869
Colored Presbyterian Church	1874
Colored Methodist Episcopal Church	1870[b]
Northern Methodist Church (Negro Conference)	1866
African Methodist Episcopal Church	1816
African Methodist Church Zion	1821
American Missionary Association (AMA) (Congregational Church)[c]	1846

[a] Of Providence, R.I., the first association of black Baptist churches in U.S. history. Others followed, climaxing in the National Baptist Convention in 1895, still the largest single African-American denominational group today.
[b] In 1956, the Colored Methodist Episcopal Church changed its name to the Christian Methodist Episcopal Church.
[c] The AMA was founded in Albany, N.Y., as an umbrella organization for several antislavery Congregational churches. By 1865 it had 528 missionaries and teachers working in the South.
Sources: Sydney E. Ahlstrom, *A Religious History of the American People* (New Haven, Conn: Yale University Press, 1972), 694, 707–09; "Bound for Canaan," special edition of *Christian History Magazine* 62, 18, no. 2: 37.

TABLE 8.12 SNAPSHOTS OF THE AMERICAN JEWISH POPULATION AT VARIOUS TIMES, 19TH CENTURY

Year	(Estimated) Numbers
1826	ca. 5,000–6,000[a]
1840	15,000
1850	ca. 50,0000[b]
1855	100,000
1860	150,000
1871	250,000
1880	ca. 230,000–280,000[c]
1888	400,000

Note: The scholarship is far from agreement on this subject. Different experts cite figures that vary up to 20 percent, which amount to tens of thousands of people. The conflicting numbers are noted without any attempt to judge their relative merits. What they provide is a *reasonable* range of numbers.
[a] Cf. Wigoder says "about 6,000" in 1825; Shamir and Shavit say 5,000 in 1826; Bar-Lev and Sakkal say 6,000 in 1826.
[b] Cf. Bar-Lev and Sakkal say 50,000 already in 1848.
[c] Cf. Bar-Lev and Sakkal say 230,000 in 1880; Shamir and Shavit calculate 230,200 in 1878 (see Table 8.13); Shamir and Shavit agree with Auerbach in citing "about [or "approximately"] 280,000" in 1880.
Sources: Geoffrey Bar-Lev and Joyce Sakkal, *Jewish Americans Struggle for Equality* (Vero Beach, Fla.: Rourke, 1992), 51; Susan Auerbach, ed., *Encyclopedia of Multiculturalism,* vol. 4 (New York: Marshall Cavendish, 1994): 968–69; Ilana Shamir and Shlomo Shavit, eds., *Encyclopedia of Jewish History* (New York: Facts On File, 1986), 128–29; Martin Gilbert, ed., *The Illustrated Atlas of Jewish Civilization* (New York: Macmillan, 1990), 99; Geoffrey Wigoder, ed., *The New Standard Jewish Encyclopedia* (New York: Facts On File, 1992), 941–42.

American Jews

Jewish Americans represent both an ethnic group and a religion in U.S. history, so that pigeonholing them in a reference work such as this is awkward. Not only is the general public unclear about making a distinction, but scholars are as well. Respected historians such as Susan Auerbach treat Jews as more a distinctive ethnic minority than a religious group, noting that they have never represented "more than 2 to 3 percent of the country's total population." Yet representatives of other faiths have always regarded Judaism as a rival religious group. In this volume, they are discussed as a religion because Jewish Americans' ethnic and national backgrounds have always been diverse and because U.S. Jews today consider themselves to be a religious body, not an ethnic minority.

The U.S. Jewish population leaped during the 1840s and 1850s as a result of heavy immigration from the German states of Bavaria and Prussia and from Central Europe. An earlier wave of European Jews (the Sephardic period) had immigrated from Spain and Portugal. In the decade after 1850 the rapid growth of numbers of German Jews overwhelmed the Sephardic community and contributed to a total Jewish population on the eve of the Civil War numbering some 150,000 believers. About half of this second wave were from the southern German region of Bavaria; most of the remainder were from the non-German lands of Bohemia, Moravia, and Poland. They all sought political freedom and economic opportunity, and most were already well educated by contemporary standards, a characteristic that eased their assimilation into the upper levels of U.S. society. In 1871 German Jewry was "emancipated" from religious persecution, and thereafter the flow across the Atlantic dwindled to a trickle for a time. A third wave of European Jews, however, began to arrive in about 1881 from the Slavic lands of Eastern Europe, particularly Russia. As the first wave were, they were fleeing persecution. By the end of the 1870s the best estimates are that between 230,000 and 250,000 Jews lived in the United States. The number is difficult to determine because all Jews were not willing to proclaim their faith publicly because of their experiences in the old country. And because they had different cultural backgrounds and spoke different languages, they were often identified as, for instance, Germans or Poles rather than as Jews. Most quickly settled into familiar occupations they had known in the old country, becoming clerks, peddlers, artisans, tailors, shopkeepers, and petty merchants. Bigoted gentile Americans tended to regard them all as "Wandering Jews," that is, citizens of no country, who were cowardly, dishonest, and untrustworthy. This sort of mindless prejudice, however, did not prevent U.S. Jews from joining in to help build their new country, nor from fighting to defend it whenever the need arose.

The geographic distribution of the U.S. Jewish population is almost impossible to gauge for most of the 19th century. Some cities are known to have had significant Jewish populations before the Civil War. These include New York City, Boston, Cleveland, Cincinnati, Detroit, Chicago, St. Louis, Portland (Oreg.), and San Francisco. At opposite ends of the spectrum and of the country were San Francisco and New York City. Most of San Francisco's Jewish population arrived with the gold rush and departed after it played out, while New York's grew steadily, reaching 73,000 by 1880. At the time of the Civil War, Louisiana—especially New Orleans—was home to approximately one-third of all Jews living in the South. The first year for which there is a reliable regional breakdown of the nation's Jewish population is 1878. Thereafter, regional profiles were compiled at regular intervals by the Jewish community itself.

After settling in their new land, most of the German Jews of the second wave made their contribution in the fields of culture (e.g., music) or business (e.g., merchants, peddlers, wholesalers). The dominant sectarian practice among members of this wave was Reform Judaism, and its leaders were Rabbis Isaac Mayer Wise (1819–1900) of Cincinnati and Isaac Leeser (1806–68) of Philadelphia. They accepted the U.S. constitutional principle of separation of church and state, and they established a new tradition of moderately liberal theology, which they institutionalized by establishing the first rabbinical seminary in the United States, Hebrew Union College in Cincinnati (1875). The third wave of Jewish immigration would be dominated by Yiddish culture and Orthodox or Conservative beliefs and, unlike the individuals of the second wave, immigrants less eager to integrate themselves into the mainstream of American society. Still all of the new immigrants followed a familiar pattern of becoming more secularized as they settled into their new country. Fraternal lodges and social clubs arose to

TABLE 8.13 REGIONAL PROFILE OF U.S. JEWISH POPULATION, 1878

Region	Number
New England	11,800
Central Atlantic Coast	104,300
Southern Atlantic Coast	21,900
North Central East	36,400
North Central West	10,100
South Central East	11,700
South Central West	12,300
Mountain Region	2,000
Pacific Coast	19,700
Total	230,200

Source: Ilana Shamir and Shlomo Shavit, eds., *Encyclopedia of Jewish History* (New York: Facts On File, 1986), 129.

TABLE 8.14 NUMBERS AND DISTRIBUTION OF JEWISH SYNAGOGUES IN THE UNITED STATES, 1850

State	Number of Synagogues
N.Y.	9
Pa.	7
S.C.	3
Ohio	2
Conn.	2
Mass.	1
R.I.	1
Va.	1
Ky.	1
Mo.	1
La.	1
Total	29[a]

[a] The number here is disputed by some scholars, who claim there were "closer to 50" synagogues in the United States in 1850. These are the synagogues documented in the Census of 1850.
Source: Edwin Scott Gaustad, *Historical Atlas of Religion in America* (New York: Harper & Row, 1962), 145.

TABLE 8.15 RELIGIOUS AFFILIATIONS OF U.S. PRESIDENTS FROM GEORGE WASHINGTON TO ULYSSES S. GRANT

President	Religious Affiliation
George Washington	Episcopalian
John Adams	Unitarian
Thomas Jefferson	Deist
James Madison	Episcopalian[a]
James Monroe	Episcopalian
John Quincy Adams	Unitarian
Andrew Jackson	Presbyterian
Martin Van Buren	Dutch Reformed
William Henry Harrison	Episcopalian
John Tyler	Episcopalian
James K. Polk	Methodist
Zachary Taylor	Episcopalian
Millard Fillmore	Unitarian
Franklin Pierce	Episcopalian
James Buchanan	Presbyterian
Abraham Lincoln	"Liberal"[b]
Andrew Johnson	No specific denomination[c]
Ulysses S. Grant	Methodist

[a] James Madison attended the services of the Episcopal Church, although he never became a member.
[b] Lincoln never identified himself with any particular denomination, although while president he attended Presbyterian services in Washington, D.C.
[c] Sources disagree on Andrew Johnson. Some say he was not a member of any particular church, although he "admired the Baptist Principles of Church Government." Some other sources list him as a Methodist.
Source: Leo Rosten, ed., *Religions of America: A New Guide and Almanac* (New York: Simon & Schuster, 1975), 620.

challenge the synagogue as the central institution of the community. The first Jewish hospitals were established in the 1850s. In 1859 the Board of Delegates of American Israelites was formed, putting Jews at the forefront of the fight to separate church and state in the United States and oppose persecution of Jews in other countries.

Jews fought on both sides during the Civil War: between 6,000 and 7,000 represented in Union ranks and about 1,000 to 1,200 in Confederate ranks. They liked to call themselves "Israelite soldiers," a practice that only emphasized their differentness from their comrades in arms. It is perhaps ironic that the South seemed to be less prejudiced than the North. Judah P. Benjamin, a Jew, was a valued member of the Confederate president Jefferson Davis's cabinet, by contrast, the Union hero Ulysses Grant while commanding the Department of Tennessee in 1862 issued General Order No. 11 expelling all Jews "as a class" from his jurisdiction. Abraham Lincoln rescinded the order, but it remained forever a black mark on General Grant's otherwise admirable wartime record. That same year Congress passed a law authorizing the U.S. Army to employ rabbis as military chaplains.

Jewish worship during this period was overwhelmingly aligned in the Reform tradition, which adopted the organizational form of a national "congregational union" in 1873 through the efforts of Rabbi Wise. Reform Judaism had its roots in the German immigrant community; the earlier Sephardic Jews did not practice this form of worship. There were nine organized Jewish synagogues in 1825, not identified with any particular sect. That number increased to 18 by 1840, then quadrupled in the next decade. By 1877 there were 278 Jewish congregations in the United States, serving an estimated population of 230,000 practicing Jews. The majority of those synagogues, more than 200, were Reformist, while the remainder followed the Orthodox tradition.

If in a democracy majority rules, then Catholics and Methodists should have occupied most of the top positions of U.S. leadership. But U.S. Christians were a notoriously fractious group and were generally adept at separating their political beliefs from their religious convictions, at least until the Civil War.

Certain denominations were, however, disproportionately represented in the higher reaches of U.S. leadership. The Episcopalian Church could claim more U.S. presidents and members of the military officers corps than any other denomination, at least in part because of its stately liturgy and historic identification with the upper classes of society. Jews, Mormons, and Quakers, on the other hand, had thousands of practicing members but were virtually unrepresented at the highest levels of political and military leadership. At a time when Americans still identified themselves at least in part by church affiliation, piety and depth of beliefs were less important than membership in a church.

Americans' spiritual beliefs reflected U.S. culture in general. The optimism of the American dream and the land of opportunity pervaded religion as it did all of society. And religion was generally a conservative force in national affairs. It girded the capitalist system, preached obedience to law and respect for individuals and their property, and acceptance of the social order, and championed old-fashioned

TABLE 8.16 RELIGIOUS PREFERENCES OF SENIOR U.S. MILITARY OFFICERS AS REPORTED IN ARMY REGISTERS, 1860

Denomination	Number of Practicing Officers	As a Percentage of Officer Corps
Episcopalian	32	41.0
Presbyterian	13	16.7
Congregational	6	7.7
Methodist	5	6.4
Baptist	8	10.3
Lutheran	1	1.3
Unitarian/Universalist	3	3.8
Catholic	8	10.3
Jewish	2	2.6
Total	78	

Source: William B. Skelton, *An American Profession of Arms* (Lawrence: University of Kansas Press, 1992), 162.

values (for instance, "blue laws," which prohibited doing most business on Sundays.)

Other characteristics of U.S. religious practices were eclecticism, a lack of orthodoxy, an assertive social conscience, strong charitable impulses, and a passion for novelty. The passion to join in with "the next big thing" made the United States fertile soil for new faiths or old faiths recast in new form. Nearly a score of new cults or denominations sprang up over 25 years, following one of two paths: They either split off from an old group (the Presbyterian Church) or rallied around a charismatic leader (the Latter-Day Saints and Jehovah's Witnesses).

The freedom of thought and action generally accorded such upstart groups was a reaffirmation of basic American principles, but all was not sweetness and light. On the negative side, U.S. Protestantism during these years also became strongly identified with nationalism and xenophobia in U.S. relations with other countries and in the popular attitude toward immigrants.

Evangelicalism

The strongest forces at work in U.S. religion at mid-century were reformism and evangelicalism. The drive to uplift American society was particularly strong among Protestants. Public-spirited believers were convinced the key to creating a moral, humane nation was to convert to the faith individuals who would ultimately form the sort of high-minded, devout society spoken of in the Scriptures. Reformers took aim at drinking, slavery, prisons, the mentally deficient, and numerous other evils in American society, but the reformist spirit burned hottest in the commitment to abolishing slavery, prohibiting use of alcohol, and securing women's rights. All three causes attracted thousands of adherents in the antebellum period and eventually succeeded in winning constitutional endorsement with the abolition of slavery (Thirteenth Amendment), national prohibition (Eighteenth Amendment), and women's suffrage (Nineteenth Amendment).

Evangelicalism, almost indistinguishable from classic revivalism, dominated U.S. Protestantism in this era, replacing the old-fashioned Calvinism of the colonial and early national periods with Arminianism. The former emphasized the helplessness of an individual to affect his/her own destiny; the latter believed in the individual's ability to play a role in his/her own salvation: That is, humans could choose to be saved. This "new" thinking fit in well with other powerful beliefs about an expanding and progressive nation. According to this view, Americans could annex new lands and save souls all at the same time, pleasing God in the process! It was a very convenient ideology summed up in the idea of "manifest destiny."

Evangelicalism encompassed both aggressive proselytizing and the moral reform of society. It began with a personal relationship to God and grew from there to advocate emotional displays of faith and living a "holy life." It has been called "America's public theology." The roots of the movement can be found in the two outbursts of revivalist fervor (Great Awakenings) that swept the country in the 18th and early 19th centuries, injecting new life into U.S. churches and filling believers with righteous zeal. What began with the Union Prayer Meeting Revival in 1857 is sometimes called the Third Great Awakening in U.S. history. It mixed the new doctrines of "holiness" and "usefulness" with a commitment to social reform and focused on the cities rather than rural areas. This third and final Great Awakening lasted until about 1870, by which time the initial fever had faded and the concerns of the movement had been institutionalized within the existing church structure.

Evangelicalism held sway across the entire spectrum of mainstream U.S. religion in these middle years, but it was strongest among the Protestants. It inspired missions to American Indians, to unchurched frontier communities, even abroad to China and the Pacific Islands. No group was more aggressively evangelical overseas than the Mormons. Beginning in the late 1840s and continuing through the 1850s, Mormon missionaries carried this peculiarly American brand of Christianity back to the Old World. They proselytized tirelessly across Scandinavia and the British Isles, ultimately enrolling and sending to the United States some 85,000 Mormon converts. Most settled in Utah.

But for all of its good intentions, evangelicalism could not solve or even reach an agreement to disagree on the thorny issue of slavery. This issue would rip apart U.S. denominations before the Civil War, leaving rifts that would not be healed for decades.

Because of the great diversity of U.S. religion and the constitutional protections guaranteed all beliefs, it is no surprise that fringe cults and sects thrived on American soil. Some freethinkers saw America as "the land of Utopia" incarnate, and they used their personal charisma and wealth to set up spiritual communities in isolated locales. Their idealistic and often eccentric beliefs attracted some Americans and frightened others. Among the utopian groups that flourished during this time were the Shakers, Oneida (New York) Community, and Amana Society (Iowa). A few other groups, most notably the Mormons, began as cults or sects before growing into mainstream churches.

In the antebellum period Protestant evangelicalism and suspicions of any creed deemed "undemocratic" could make life hard not just for Roman Catholics and Mormons but for Jews as well. By 1850 there were more than 50,000 Jews in the United States, a relatively small number but highly visible in their "differentness." As other persecuted groups have historically, they tended to congregate in certain tolerant communities, most in the East and in larger cities. Jews, Roman Catholics, and Mormons suffered from periodic violence, not just because they were perceived as un-American, but because they were identified in the public mind with great "evils": the Inquisition and popery for Catholics, the Crucifixion of Christ for Jews, and polygamy for Mormons. Despite haphazard and relatively mild persecution, all three groups were grudgingly accepted by the majority of Protestants.

The Civil War's Impact on U.S. Churches

The Civil War interrupted deep-rooted U.S. religious traditions, in particular evangelicalism and denominational unity. Many contemporary observers believed that the final break between North and South began with the split within the churches. Henry Clay on the eve of his death in 1852 warned, "I tell you, this sundering of the religious ties which have bound our people together I consider the greatest source of danger to our country." When the war began, a majority of white Southerners accepted it as gospel that their society, slavery and all, was pleasing to God, and if they kept the faith, they would triumph. Of course, Northerners had the same belief. In defeat, Southerners faced not just national humiliation, but a crisis of faith.

The post–Civil War years saw a determined effort to restore the religious cords that had formerly bound the nation together. This began by trying to reunite the denominations sundered by issues of slavery and sectionalism. The healers' efforts achieved mixed results at best, and some of the splits were not overcome for decades. In the meantime most churches launched vigorous new campaigns to save "the lost." And there were many lost souls to be saved in the years immediately after the Civil War, beginning on the Western frontier, where, it was said, "there was no law west of the Pecos [River], and no God west of the Rio Grande." Methodists, who had always been the most fractious of denominations, managed to ignore their differences long enough to lead "the westward march of churches," followed closely by the Presbyterians, Congregationalists, and Baptists. The Baptists combined modern technology (the railroad) with evangelical Christianity by attaching "chapel cars" to western trains. But the greatest growth among postwar churches occurred among the Roman Catholics, whose immigration-fueled numbers surpassed those of the Methodist Church as the nation's largest denomination.

New Directions

The most notable developments in mainstream religion in the United States after 1865 were the urban revival and Sunday school movements. The former actually began in late 1857 as the so-called Businessman's Revival, sparked by the financial panic that year, and picked up speed after the war. In the beginning it took the form of prayer meetings among the new urban business class and represented a departure from the typical revival meetings of former times by being both city-centered and lay-led. As it grew, the movement was "shaped and systematized" by Dwight L. Moody (1837–99), who introduced old-fashioned gospel teaching to the new booming metropolises of New York, Philadelphia, Boston, and Chicago. The movement produced at least 100,000 public conversions in the four months after it began in New York City, and perhaps as many as 1 million before it ran its course. Urban revivalism received additional impetus from the work of the Young Men's Christian Association (YMCA), which arrived from Britain in 1851 and aimed at the same audience.

The Sunday school movement was one of the biggest evangelistic enterprise among Protestant churches after the Civil War. The agency for its spread was the lay-led International Sunday School Association, which aimed to provide basic scriptural instruction for both children and adults. It was a response to the spread of Roman Catholicism with its powerful training in the catechism. The Sunday school movement became the primary recruiting device of the [Protestant] churches, replacing old-style revivals and adding the modern flourish of public relations slogans, such as "Each one win one."

Religious Education

American churches have always been strong supporters of religious education, going all the way back to the Puritans in colonial times. In the 19th century it was no different. Mainstream denominations competed to establish seminaries and colleges all over the United States, loosely linked to parent churches through finances and doctrine. Most foundered after a short time, but some survived into the 20th century, notably Wilberforce University (founded by Methodists, 1856), Brigham Young University (by Mormons, 1875), and Hebrew Union College (by Jews, 1875). Their institutional role was less related to academic education than to protection of orthodoxy, training of clergy, and recruitment of new members. The respective numbers of these denominational colleges do *not* reflect the relative popularity of their parent churches, just their devotion to religious training.

TABLE 8.17 DENOMINATIONAL COLLEGES IN 1850 THAT SURVIVED TO THE END OF THE CENTURY

Denomination	Number of Colleges/ Seminaries in 1850
Presbyterian	29
Methodist	25
Baptist	24
Roman Catholic	18
Congregational	11
Congregational and Presbyterian (jointly)	9
Lutheran	7
Reformed	5
Episcopal	4
Disciples of Christ	3
Quaker	3

Source: Edwin Scott Gaustad, *Historical Atlas of Religion in America* (New York: Harper & Row, 1962), 40.

Byways in American Religion

As did American medicine and politics, American religion went down some strange paths during these years. The same powerful forces of populism and pluralism were at work in all three fields. The United States had always been fertile soil for new ideas, and popular theology was not immune to unorthodox thinking. Institutionalism, tradition, and dogma were weaker than in the Old World. Instead, Americans tended to place their faith in individualism and liberty of conscience. This sort of thinking produced a number of splinter groups that might be called cults today but were all part of the religious mix in the mid-19th century.

Some of the more notable "isms" in American religion during these years were the "Gospel of Health," preaching the spiritual benefits of fresh air, sunshine, and proper diet; spiritualism, which believed it possible to communicate with the spirit world; communitarian societies such as the Shakers; transcendentalism, with its emphasis on intuition and the "inner experience"; millennialism, which looked forward to the second coming of Christ and his thousand-year reign, which would follow; occultism, represented by the New York Theosophical Society; the Free Love disciples of John Humphrey Noyes; and the "Awakeners," who believed in the possibility of attaining perfection on Earth. These and similar groups comprised only a small percentage of U.S. believers, but they had high visibility and were a source of great alarm among mainstream churches. They tended to be anti-establishment, experimental, and iconoclastic to a degree that tested even the broad toleration of Americans. Some were also reformist and deeply pious. Taken together, they were another manifestation of American democracy, because a person who did not agree with the mainline churches was free to start his or her own church. Only a few achieved anything like the long-term success of the Mormons or Christian Scientists. The rest tended to come and go rather quickly, brought down by the death of their founder, internal bickering, or simple lack of broad popular appeal.

At the end of this period the nation's religious life was still overwhelmingly Protestant and organized into white denominations of English origin, just as at the beginning. What was different was that traditional U.S. faith was being strongly challenged by the new intellectual climate (influenced by the work of individuals such as Charles Darwin and Herbert Spencer) and the new immigrant-filled urban society (represented by such cities as New York and Chicago). In many respects traditional beliefs would have to fight a losing rear-guard action from this time on.

CHAPTER 9 Government and Politics

The third quarter of the 19th century was a period of great political ferment: secession and civil war, the rise and fall of political parties, and three new amendments to the Constitution. The 1850s stands out as a decade that began in compromise and ended in conflict, while the end of this quarter-century saw the curtain ring down on Reconstruction, remembered as one of the most painful times in the nation's history. The political system survived war and reconstruction but was sorely tried and forever changed by the ordeal.

At the beginning of the era traditional political issues such as the tariff, internal improvements, and control of the national currency were still important, but the hot-button issue was the expansion of slavery into the western territories. As did every other issue at this time, it divided along sectional lines between the North and the South. Southern leaders spoke of defending their constitutional rights, while Northerners spoke in generic terms of freedom and liberty, but slavery was the specter behind every debate. In June 1850 a convention of Southern slaveholders met in Nashville to discuss withdrawing from the Union. This was hardly the first time such talk had occurred, but it showed that the secession sentiment was becoming stronger.

What Southerners and Northerners were fighting over was not just slavery, or even tariff and land policies. Rather, it was competing visions for the future of America, and opposing opinions on just what constituted the nation's destiny divided political parties as much as it divided private citizens. While many Southerners stubbornly defended what they liked to call their "peculiar institution," Northerners spoke of "Free Soil, Free Labor, and Free Men." Those who tried to finesse the issue, such as Stephen Douglas of Illinois with his talk of "popular sovereignty" in the territories, ultimately pleased neither side. Almost all the party activity between 1850 and 1865 tended to align along sectional lines, demonstrating that for all its partisan rhetoric, the Civil War would not be a conflict of Democrats versus Republicans or state versus state, but of Northern interests versus Southern interests.

Slavery as an Institution

The debate over slavery colored every issue in these years. It was a moral and an economic question, as well as a political and constitutional question that no party or candidate for elected office could ignore. Whatever the rights and wrongs of slavery, it had always been protected by the Constitution in several ways:

1. Slavery was implicitly recognized as a legal institution, and therefore slave owners were entitled to protection of their "property."
2. Slaves counted as three-fifths of a free citizen for purposes of taxation and representation.
3. The African slave trade had been protected until 1808.
4. The federal government was obligated to help return fugitive slaves to their owners.
5. The militia could be called out to suppress any insurrection, including slave insurrections.
6. States were guaranteed national support against domestic violence.

For these reasons, slavery could never be rooted out in the Deep South where it already existed.

The thornier question concerned the introduction of slavery into territories where it did not already exist, and with rapid westward expansion during this era (driven by Manifest Destiny), that question could not be dodged. Slavery affected every aspect of national life, from the building of a transcontinental railroad (northern versus southern routes) to the literature Americans were reading (e.g., *Uncle Tom's Cabin*).

The Union was divided into those states where slavery was tolerated and even protected versus those states where it was barred as an institution. (A separate issue was the status of slaves taken by their owners into "free" states as legal property.) Four new states were added to the Union in the decade before 1850; Florida and Texas as

TABLE 9.1 THE BALANCE BETWEEN SLAVE AND FREE STATES, 1850 AND 1861

State or Territory[a]	Status at the Beginning of 1850	Status in the Civil War[b]
Conn.	Free	Union
Ill.	Free	Union
Ind.	Free	Union
Iowa	Free	Union
Maine	Free	Union
Mass.	Free	Union
Mich.	Free	Union
N.H.	Free	Union
N.J.	Free	Union
N.Y.	Free	Union
Ohio	Free	Union
Pa.	Free	Union
R.I.	Free	Union
Vt.	Free	Union
Wis.	Free	Union
Minnesota	Territory	Union (as a state)
Oregon	Territory	Union (as a state)
Ala.	Slave	Confederate
Ark.	Slave	Confederate
Del.	Slave	Union
Fla.	Slave	Confederate
Ga.	Slave	Confederate
Ky.	Slave	Officially neutral
La.	Slave	Confederate
Md.	Slave	Union
Miss.	Slave	Confederate
Mo.	Slave	Confederate
N.C.	Slave	Confederate
S.C.	Slave	Confederate
Tenn.	Slave	Confederate
Tex.	Slave	Confederate
Va.	Slave	Confederate
Indian Territory (later Okla.)	Open to slavery	Confederate
New Mexico	Territory	Union (as territory)
Utah	Territory	Union (as territory)
Calif.	Free[c]	Union
Kansas	Territory	Union[d]
Nebraska	Territory	Union (as territory)

[a] Includes all states and organized territories as of Jan. 1, 1850.
[b] In 1861 Del. and Md. had significant slave-owning populations but remained in the Union in the secession crisis through a combination of heroic individual efforts and the abiding loyalty of their citizens.
[c] By terms of the Compromise of 1850, California entered the Union as a Free State.
[d] Kansas becomes a Free State in 1861, after the war begins.
Source: Samuel Eliot Morison, Henry Steele Commager, Wm. E. Leuchtenburg, *The Growth of the American Republic,* 6th ed. (New York: Oxford University Press, 1969), vol. I, 608, 859.

A slave auction is held on Courthouse Square, in Montgomery, Alabama. The well-dressed black men on display are most likely house slaves who will fetch less on the block than good field hands would. (Alabama Department of Archives and History, Montgomery, Alabama)

slave states, Iowa and Wisconsin as free states. As had the animals entering Noah's ark, new states for years had come in two by two, slave and free. But 1850 was the last time that slave and free states would exist in the sort of delicate equilibrium envisioned by the men who had crafted the 1820 Missouri Compromise. California's admission threatened to change all that. Southerners had watched their influence in national politics—and therefore their ability to protect slavery—wane over the years. In the House their numbers were down to 90 slave-state representatives versus 144 men from free-soil states. The Senate balance had been an effective line of defense for 30 years, but with California knocking on the door and other western territories lining up behind, that balance would soon end. At the beginning of 1850 there were 15 "free" states plus two organized territories that were virtually guaranteed to join the "free" column some day. There were contemporaneously 15 states where slavery was entrenched, plus three organized territories where slavery was not barred by law but also not likely to take root. Then there was California. It was the chief battleground because its strategic location, mineral wealth, and booming population after 1848 all combined to make its admission to the Union a vital issue for both sides.

If California went into the free state column, followed by other like-minded territories, then the South would become a permanent minority section and die-hard slave owners would face the alarming prospect of a future when they could not kill or sidetrack abolitionist legislation as in former decades. To protect their interests, short of secession, they set their sights on capturing control of the White House (still called the Executive Mansion) and/or the Supreme Court, setting the stage for a series of political donnybrooks in the late 1850s. In the meantime a survey of slave states versus free states at the beginning of this period shows that the slave states were not a monolithic bloc; being a slave state did not dictate membership in the Confederacy when the Civil War began.

As the political situation heated up, there was a passing of the torch in the nation's political leadership. The legislative giants who had held the sections together for 40 years, in particular Henry Clay of Kentucky, Daniel Webster of Massachusetts, John C. Calhoun of South Carolina, and Martin Van Buren of New York, were tired old men. The end of their reign in the Senate was in sight. Calhoun died in March 1850; Clay and Webster were gone before the end of 1852; Van Buren drifted in political limbo between parties. Taking their places were unbending sectional partisans such as New York's William H. Seward, Ohio's Salmon P. Chase, Mississippi's Jefferson Davis, and Georgia's Alexander Stephens. Some other natural leaders in Congress were opportunists, such as Stephen A. Douglas of Illinois. These men held the future of the nation in their hands in the 1850s, and their decisions would ultimately determine whether compromise or war would follow.

The latest chapter in the great slave debate opened with the Treaty of Guadalupe-Hidalgo (1848), which gave the United States title to an enormous western territory (north of Texas and west of the old Louisiana Purchase). Frederick Douglass described the area acquired from Mexico as a "vast wilderness 1500 miles in breadth," but it was actually far more than just an empty space on the map waiting to be filled. When the Mexican Cession threw open the Far West to American settlement, it also threw it open to sectional politics. The discovery of gold in California (1848) only exacerbated the tension between the two hostile sections, North and South. To deal with a variety of related issues, Henry Clay on January 29, 1850, introduced an omnibus bill in the U.S. Senate. Debate dragged on for nine months before Congress finally passed not one but five separate measures to deal with the five "Bleeding Wounds of the Republic." The so-called Compromise of 1850 contained these key provisions:

1. Immediate admission of California into the Union as a free state
2. The formal organization of New Mexico and Utah into territories with the residents of each deciding later on the status of slavery within their borders (the "popular sovereignty" principle)
3. Adjustment of the Texas–New Mexico boundary in favor of New Mexico in return for the federal government's assuming a large part of Texas's public debt (left over from its days as a republic)
4. Abolition of the slave trade (but not slavery itself) in the District of Columbia
5. Passage of a new, more stringent Fugitive Slave Law that would place the full power of the federal government behind the apprehension and return of runaway slaves

During the heated debates a president (Zachary Taylor) died in office, to be succeeded, for only the second time in U.S. history, by the vice president, Millard Fillmore, a man of fine presidential appearance, but without presidential-caliber intellect or backbone. Fillmore quickly signed the compromise of 1850 before fading forever into the background of U.S. history. Critics of the compromise, which included virtually everybody, split right down sectional lines arguing over what they hated most about it. The compromise directly—and slavery indirectly—destroyed two parties (the Whigs and the Know-Nothings), split another (the Democrats), and caused the rise of two new parties (the Free-Soilers and the Republicans). It also set the political agenda for the rest of the decade.

Congress

The debate over the Compromise of 1850 put Congress at center stage in national politics. Although that body represented all Americans, its workings were still a mystery to most citizens and significantly different from those of today's House and Senate. To begin with, senators were still appointed by state legislatures and therefore easily controlled by special interests such as the "slaveocracy" in the South. In 1850 the membership of the House of Representatives stood at 232, but that number was increased after every census until 1929, when it was permanently set at 435. Congress routinely convened on March 4 to begin its deliberations, a practice that left the president in virtual control of the government for the first three months of every year.

There were 14 congressional terms between 1850 and 1875, beginning with the 31st (1849–50) and ending with the 44th (1875–77). Each two-year term was divided into two sessions. Both houses had long been accustomed to operating with two parties, positioned by tradition on opposite sides of the aisle. With stable membership and well-oiled party organization, the business of government was conducted relatively smoothly. In 1850 the two major parties were the Democrats and Whigs, who had shared power more or less peacefully since the early 1830s. That would all change in the 1850s as both the organization and the workings of Congress entered a period of upheaval that lasted through the 1860s. With the return of peace after the Civil War, the traditional two-party system was restored and business returned to normal.

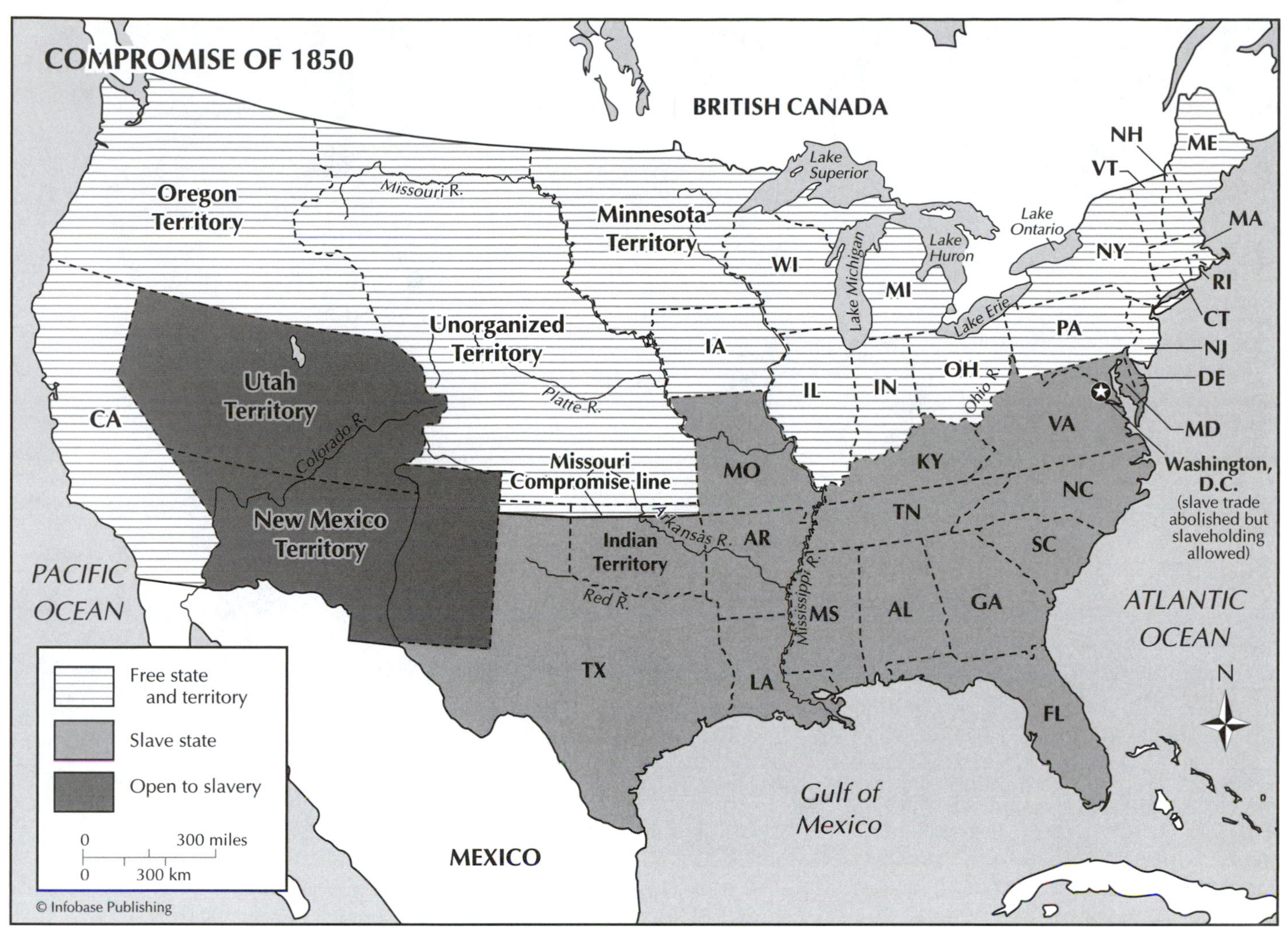

Source: David Goldfield, Carl Abbott, et al. *The American Journey: A History of the United States.* Upper Saddle River, N. J.: Prentice Hall, 1998, 268; Facts On File. *Historical Maps On File,* New York, Facts On File, 2001.

Seldom have the members of Congress been called upon to decide on the impeachment of a president, in fact, only three times in all of U.S. history. The first was the impeachment of Andrew Johnson in 1868. The managers of the impeachment proceedings in the House of Representatives pose at Mathew Brady's Washington, D.C., studio for posterity. *Left to right, standing:* James F. Wilson (Iowa), George S. Boutwell (Massachusetts), John A. Logan (Illinois). *Left to right, sitting:* Benjamin F. Butler (Massachusetts), Thaddeus Stevens (Pennsylvania), Thomas Williams (Pennsylvania), and John A. Bingham (Ohio). (National Archives)

TABLE 9.2 THIRTY-FIRST CONGRESS, MARCH 4, 1949, TO MARCH 3, 1851

President of the Senate	Presidents Pro Tempore of the Senate	Speaker of the House of Representatives
Millard Fillmore	David R. Atchison William R. King	Howell Cobb

Alabama	
Senators	Representatives
William R. King (D) Benjamin Fitzpatrick (SRD) r. Dec. 1849 Jeremiah Clemens (D)	William J. Alston (W) Franklin W. Bowdon (D) Williamson R. W. Cobb (D) Sampson W. Harris (D) Henry W. Hilliard (W) David Hubbard (SRD) Samuel W. Inge (D)
Arkansas	
Senators	Representative
Solon Borland (D) William K. Sebastian (D)	Robert W. Johnson (D)
California	
Senators	Representatives
William M. Gwin (D) s. 1850 John C. Fremont (D) s. 1850	Edward Gilbert (D) s. 1850 George W. Wright s. 1850
Connecticut	
Senators	Representatives
Roger S. Baldwin (W) Truman Smith (W)	Walter Booth (Free-Soiler) Thomas B. Butler (W) Chauncey F. Cleveland (D) Loren P. Waldo (D)
Delaware	
Senators	Representative
Presley Spruance (W) John Wales	John W. Houston (W)
Florida	
Senators	Representative
David Levy Yulee (W) Jackson Morton (W)	Edward C. Cabell (W)

Georgia

Senators	Representatives
John M. Berrien (W) William C. Dawson (SRW)	Howell Cobb (D) Thomas C. Hackett (D) Hugh A. Haralson (D) Joseph W. Jackson (D) s. 1850 Thomas B. King (W) r. 1850 Allen F. Owen (W) Alexander H. Stephens (D) Robert Toombs (SRD) Marshall J. Wellborn (D)

Illinois

Senators	Representatives
Stephen A. Douglas (D) James Shields (D)	Edward D. Baker William H. Bissell (D) Thomas L. Harris (D) John A. McClernand (D) William A. Richardson (D) John Wentworth (D) Timothy R. Young (D)

Indiana

Senators	Representatives
Jesse D. Bright (D) James Whitcomb (D)	Nathaniel Albertson (D) William J. Brown (D) Cyrus L. Dunham (D) Graham N. Fitch (D) Willis A. Gorman (D) Andrew J. Harlan (D) George W. Julian (Free-Soiler) Joseph E. McDonald (D) Edward W. McGaughey (W) John L. Robinson (D)

Iowa

Senators	Representatives
Augustus C. Dodge (D) George W. Jones (D)	Shepherd Leffler (D) Daniel F. Miller (W) s. 1850 William Thompson (D) r. June 1850

Kentucky

Senators	Representatives
Joseph R. Underwood (W) Henry Clay (W)	Daniel Breck (W) Linn Boyd (D) George A. Caldwell (D) James L. Johnson (W) Finis E. McLean (W) Humphrey Marshall (W) John C. Mason (D) Charles S. Morehead (W) Richard H. Stanton (D) John B. Thompson (W)

Louisiana

Senators	Representatives
Solomon W. Downs (D) Pierre Soule (SRD)	Henry A. Bullard (W) s. 1850 Charles M. Conrad (W) r. Aug. 1850 John H. Harmanson (D) d. Oct. 1850 Emile LaSere (D) Isaac E. Morse (D) Alexander G. Penn (D) s. 1850

Maine

Senators	Representatives
James W. Bradbury (D) Hannibal Hamlin (D)	Thomas J. D. Fuller (D) Elbridge Gerry (D) Rufus K. Goodenow (W) Nathaniel S. Littlefield (D) John Otis (W) Cullen Sawtelle (D) Charles Stetson (D)

Maryland

Senators	Representatives
James A. Pearce (W) Reverdy Johnson (W) r. Mar. 1849 David Stewart (W) ta. 1849 Thomas G. Pratt (W) s. 1850	Richard J. Bowie (W) Alexander Evans (W) William T. Hamilton (D) Edward Hammond (D) John B. Kerr (W) Robert M. McLane (D)

Massachusetts

Senators	Representatives
Daniel Webster (W) r. July 1850 Robert C. Winthrop (W) ta. 1850 Robert Rantoul, Jr. (D) s. 1851 John Davis (W)	Charles Allen (Free-Soiler) George Ashmun (W) James H. Duncan (W) Samuel A. Eliot (W) s. 1850 Orin Fowler (W) Joseph Grinnell (W) Daniel P. King (W) d. July 1850 Horace Mann (W) Julius Rockwell (W) Robert C. Winthrop (W) r. July 1850

Michigan

Senators	Representatives
Lewis Cass (D) Alpheus Felch (D)	Kinsley S. Bingham (D) Alexander W. Buel (D) William Sprague (W)

Mississippi

Senators	Representatives
Henry S. Foote (Un) Jefferson Davis (D)	Albert G. Brown (D) Winfield S. Featherston (D) William McWillie (D) Jacob Thompson (D)

Missouri

Senators	Representatives
Thomas H. Benton (D) David R. Atchison (W)	William V. Bay (D) James B. Bowlin (D) James S. Green (D) Willard P. Hall (D) John S. Phelps (D)

New Hampshire

Senators	Representatives
John P. Hale (Anti-Slavery) Moses Norris, Jr. (D)	Harry Hibbard (D) George W. Morrison (D) s. 1850 Charles H. Peaslee (D) Amos Tuck James Wilson (W) r. Sept. 1850

New Jersey

Senators	Representatives
Jacob W. Miller (W) William L. Dayton (W)	Andrew K. Hay (W) James G. King (W) William A. Newell (W) John Van Dyke (W) Isaac Wildrick (D)

(continued)

TABLE 9.2 (continued)

New York	
Senators	**Representatives**
Daniel S. Dickinson (D)	Henry P. Alexander (W))
William H. Seward (W)	George R. Andrews (W)
	Henry Bennett
	David A. Bokee (W)
	George Briggs (W)
	James Brooks (W)
	Lorenzo Burrows (W)
	Charles E. Clarke (W)
	Harmon S. Conger (W)
	William Duer (W)
	Daniel Gott (W)
	Herman D. Gould (W)
	Ransom Halloway (W)
	William T. Jackson (W)
	John A. King (W)
	Preston King (D)
	Thomas McKissock (W)
	Orsamus B. Matteson (W)
	William Nelson (W)
	J. Phillips Phoenix (W)
	Harvey Putnam (W)
	Gideon Reynolds (W)
	Elijah Risley (W)
	Robert L. Rose (W)
	David Rumsey, Jr. (W)
	William A. Sackett (W)
	Abraham M. Schermerhorn (W)
	John L. Schoolcraft (W)
	Peter H. Silvester (W)
	Elbridge G. Spaulding (W)
	John R. Thurman (W)
	Walter Underhill (W)
	Hiram Walden (D)
	Hugh White

North Carolina	
Senators	**Representatives**
Willie P. Mangum (W)	William S. Ashe (D)
George E. Badger (W)	Joseph P. Caldwell (W)
	Thomas L. Clingman (W)
	John R. J. Daniel (D)
	Edmund Deberry (W)
	David Outlaw (W)
	Augustine H. Shepperd (W)
	Edward Stanly (W)
	Abraham W. Venable (D)

Ohio	
Senators	**Representatives**
Thomas Corwin (W) r. July 1850	John Bell (W) s. 1851
Thomas Ewing (W) s. 1850	Joseph Cable (D)
Salmon P. Chase (D)	Lewis D. Campbell (W)
	David K. Cartter (D)
	Moses B. Corwin (W)
	John Crowell (W)
	Rodolphus Dickinson d. Mar. 1849
	David T. Disney (D)
	Nathan Evans (W)
	Joshua R. Giddings (W)
	Moses Hoagland (D)
	William F. Hunter (W)
	John K. Miller (D)
	Jonathan D. Morris (D)
	Edson B. Olds (D)
	Emery D. Potter (D)
	Joseph M. Root (W)
	Robert C. Schenck (W)
	Charles Sweetser (D)
	John L. Taylor (W)
	Samuel F. Vinton (W)
	William A. Whittlesey (D)
	Amos E. Wood (D) d. Nov. 1850

Pennsylvania	
Senators	**Representatives**
Daniel Sturgeon (D)	John Brisbin (W) s. 1851
James Cooper (W)	Chester P. Butler (W) d. Oct. 1850
	Samuel Calvin (W)
	Joseph Casey (W)
	Joseph R. Chandler (W)
	Joel B. Danner (D) s. 1850
	Jesse C. Dickey (W)
	Milo M. Dimmick (D)
	John Freedley (W)
	Alfred Gilmore (D)
	Moses Hampton (W)
	John W. Howe (W)
	Lewis C. Levin (Amer)
	James X. McLanahan (D)
	Job Mann (D)
	Henry D. Moore (W)
	Henry Nes d. Sept. 1850
	Andrew J. Ogle (W)
	Charles W. Pitman (W)
	Robert R. Reed (W)
	John Robbins, Jr. (D)
	Thomas Ross (D)
	Thaddeus Stevens (W)
	William Strong (D)
	James Thompson (W)
	David Wilmot (D)

Rhode Island	
Senators	**Representatives**
Albert C. Greene (W)	Nathan F. Dixon (W)
John H. Clarke (W)	George G. King (W)

South Carolina	
Senators	**Representatives**
John C. Calhoun (D) d. Mar. 1850	Armistead Burt (D)
Franklin H. Elmore (D) s. d. 1850	William F. Colcock (D)
Robert W. Barnwell (D) ta. 1850	Isaac E. Holmes (D)
R. Barnwell Rhett (D) s. 1851	John McQueen (D)
Andrew P. Butler (SRD)	James L. Orr (D)
	Daniel Wallace (W)
	Joseph A. Woodward (D)

Tennessee	
Senators	**Representatives**
Hopkins L. Turney (D)	Josiah M. Anderson (W)
John Bell (W)	Andrew Ewing (D)
	Meredith P. Gentry (W)
	Isham G. Harris (W)
	Andrew Johnson (D)
	George W. Jones (D)
	John H. Savage (D)
	Frederick P. Stanton (D)
	James H. Thomas (D)
	Albert G. Watkins (W)
	Christopher H. Williams (W)

Texas	
Senators	**Representatives**
Sam Houston (D)	Volney E. Howard (D)
Thomas J. Rusk (D)	David S. Kaufman (D) d. Jan. 1851

Vermont	
Senators	Representatives
Samuel S. Phelps (W) William Upham (W)	William Hebard (W) William Henry (W) George P. Marsh (W) r. 1849 James Meacham (W) Lucius B. Peck (D)

Virginia	
Senators	Representatives
James M. Mason (D) Robert M. T. Hunter (D)	Thomas H. Averett (D) Thomas H. Bayly (SRD) James M. H. Beale (D) Thomas S. Bocock (D) Henry A. Edmundson (D) Thomas S. Haymond (W) Alexander R. Holladay (D) James McDowell (D) Fayette McMullen (D) Richard K. Meade (D) John S. Millson (D) Jeremiah Morton (W) Alexander Newman (D) d. Sept. 1849 Richard Parker (D) Paulus Powell (D) James A. Seddon (D)

Wisconsin	
Senators	Representatives
Henry Dodge (D) Isaac P. Walker (D)	Orsamus Cole (W) James D. Doty (Free-Soiler) Charles Durkee (Free-Soiler)

Note: * D, Democrat; W, Whig; SRD, States Right Democrat; SRW, States Right Whig; R, Republican (after 1856); Un, Union Party (Civil War only); Amer, American or "Know-Nothing" Party. Some members did not serve a full term, usually because somebody died in office or resigned. Where that occurred: r, resigned; d, died in office; s, started.
Source: Notable Names in American History: A Tabular Register, 3d ed. (Clifton, N.J.: James T. White, 1973), 92–120.

TABLE 9.3 THIRTY-SECOND CONGRESS, MARCH 4, 1851, TO MARCH 3, 1853

President of the Senate	Presidents Pro Tempore of the Senate	Speaker of the House of Representatives
Millard Fillmore	William R. King David R. Atchison	Linn Boyd

Alabama	
Senators	Representatives
William R. King (D) r. Dec. 1852 Benjamin Fitzpatrick (SRD) s. 1853 Jeremiah Clemens (D)	James Abercrombie (W) John Bragg (SRD) Williamson R. W. Cobb (D) Sampson W. Harris (D) George W. Houston (D) William R. Smith (W) Alexander White (W)

Arkansas	
Senators	Representative
William K. Sebastian (D) Solon Borland (D)	Robert W. Johnson (D)

California	
Senators	Representatives
William M. Gwin (D) John B. Weller (D) s. 1852	Joseph W. McCorkle (D) Edward C. Marshall (D)

Connecticut	
Senators	Representatives
Truman Smith (W) Isaac Toucey (D) s. 1852	Charles Chapman (W) Chauncey F. Cleveland (D) Colin M. Ingersoll (D) Origen S. Seymour (D)

Delaware	
Senators	Representative
Presley Spruance (W) James A. Bayard (D)	George R. Riddle (D)

Florida	
Senators	Representative
Jackson Morton (W) Stephen R. Mallory (D)	Edward C. Cabell (W)

Georgia	
Senators	Representatives
John M. Berrien (W) r. May 1852 Robert M. Charlton s. 1852 William C. Dawson (SRW)	David J. Bailey (SRD) Elijah W. Chastain (D) Junius Hillyer (D) Joseph W. Jackson (D) James Johnson (D) Charles Murphey (D) Alexander H. Stephens (D) Robert Toombs (SRD)

Illinois	
Senators	Representatives
Stephen A. Douglas (D) James Shields (D)	Willis Allen (D) William H. Bissell (D) Thompson Campbell (D) Orlando B. Ficklin (D) Richard S. Molony (D) William A. Richardson (D) Richard Yates (W)

Indiana	
Senators	Representatives
Jesse D. Bright (D) James Whitcomb (D) d. Oct. 1852 Charles W. Cathcart (D) ta. 1852 John Pettit (D) s. 1853	Samuel Brenton (W) John G. Davis (D) Cyrus L. Dunham (D) Graham N. Fitch (D) Willis A. Gorman (D) Thomas A. Hendricks (D) James Lockhart (D) Daniel Mace (D) Samuel W. Parker (W) John L. Robinson (D)

Iowa	
Senators	Representatives
Augustus C. Dodge (D) George W. Jones (D)	Lincoln Clark (D) Bernhart Henn (D)

Kentucky	
Senators	Representatives
Joseph R. Underwood (W) Henry Clay (W) d. June 1852 David Meriwether (D) ta. 1852 Archibald Dixon (W) s. 1852	John C. Breckinridge (D) Linn Boyd (D) Presley U. Ewing (W) Benjamin E. Grey (W) Humphrey Marshall (W) r. Aug. 1852 John C. Mason (D)

(continued)

TABLE 9.3 (continued)

	William Preston (W) s. 1852 Richard H. Stanton (D) James W. Stone (D) William T. Ward (W) Addison White (W)
Louisiana	
Senators	Representatives
Solomon W. Downs (D) Pierre Soule (SRD)	J. Aristide Landry (D) John Moore (W) Alexander G. Penn (D) Louis St. Martin (D)
Maine	
Senators	Representatives
James W. Bradbury (D) Hannibal Hamlin (D)	Charles Andrews (D) d. Apr. 1852 John Appleton (D) Thomas J. D. Fuller (D) Robert Goodenow (W) Moses Macdonald (D) Isaac Reed (W) s. 1852 Ephraim K. Smart (D) Israel Washburn, Jr. (W)
Maryland	
Senators	Representatives
James A. Pearce (W) Thomas G. Pratt (W)	Richard J. Bowie (W) Joseph S. Cottman (W) Alexander Evans (W) William T. Hamilton (D) Edward Hammond (D) Thomas Yates Walsh (W)
Massachusetts	
Senators	Representatives
John Davis (W) Charles Sumner (D)	Charles Allen (Free-Soiler) William Appleton (W) George T. Davis (W) James H. Duncan (W) Francis B. Fay (W) s. 1852 Orin Fowler (W) d. Dec. 1852 John Z. Goodrich (W) Edward P. Little (D) s. 1852 Horace Mann (W) Robert Rantoul, Jr. (D) d. Aug. 1852 Lorenzo Sabine (W) s. 1852 Zeno Scudder (W) Benjamin Thompson (W) d. Sept. 1852
Michigan	
Senators	Representatives
Lewis Cass (D) Alpheus Felch (D)	James L. Conger (W) Ebenezer J. Penniman (W) Charles E. Stuart (D)
Mississippi	
Senators	Representatives
Henry S. Foote (Un) r. Jan. 1852 Walker Brooke (W) s. 1852 Jefferson Davis (D) r. Sept. 1851 John J. McRae (D) ta. 1852 Stephen Adams (D) s. 1852	Albert G. Brown (D) John D. Freeman (Un) Benjamin D. Nabers (Un) John A. Wilcox (W)
Missouri	
Senators	Representatives
David R. Atchison (W) Henry S. Geyer (D)	John F. Darby (W) Willard P. Hall (D) John G. Miller (W) John S. Phelps (D) Gilchrist Porter (W)
New Hampshire	
Senators	Representatives
John P. Hale (Anti-Slavery) Moses Norris, Jr. (D)	Harry Hibbard (D) Charles H. Peaslee (D) Jared Perkins (W) Amos Tuck
New Jersey	
Senators	Representatives
Jacob W. Miller (W) Robert F. Stockton (D)	George H. Brown (W) Rodman M. Price (D) Charles Skelton (D) Nathan T. Stratton (D) Isaac Wildrick (D)
New York	
Senators	Representatives
William H. Seward (W) Hamilton Fish (W)	Leander Babcock (D) Henry Bennett (W) Obadiah Bowne (W) John H. Boyd (W) George Briggs (W) James Brooks (W) Alexander H. Buell (D) d. Jan. 1853 Lorenzo Burrows (W) Gilbert Dean (D) John G. Floyd (D) Emanuel B. Hart (D) Augustus P. Hascall (W) Solomon G. Haven (W) J. H. Hobart Haws (W) Jerediah Horsford (W) Thomas Y. Howe, Jr. (D) Willard Ives (D) Timothy Jenkins (D) Daniel T. Jones (D) Preston King (D) Frederick S. Martin (W) William Murray (D) Reuben Robie (D) Joseph Russell (D) William A. Sackett (W) Abraham M. Schermerhorn (W) John L. Schoolcraft (W) Marius Schoonmaker (W) David L. Seymour (D) William W. Snow (D) Abraham P. Stephens Josiah Sutherland (D) Henry S. Walbridge (W) John Wells (W)

North Carolina	
Senators	Representatives
Willie P. Mangum (W) George E. Badger (W)	William S. Ashe (D) Joseph P. Caldwell (W) Thomas L. Clingman (W) John R. J. Daniel (D) Alfred Dockery (W) James T. Morehead (W) David Outlaw (W) Edward Stanly (W) Abraham W. Venable (D)

Ohio	
Senators	Representatives
Salmon P. Chase (D) Benjamin F. Wade (W)	Nelson Barrere (W) Hiram Bell (W) George H. Busby (D) Joseph Cable (D) Lewis D. Campbell (W) David K. Cartter (D) David T. Disney (D) Alfred P. Edgerton (D) James M. Gaylord Joshua R. Giddings (W) Frederick W. Green (D) Alexander Harper (W) William F. Hunter (W) John Johnson Eben Newton (W) Edson B. Olds (D) Benjamin Stanton (W) Charles Sweetser (D) John L. Taylor (W) Norton S. Townshend (D) John Welch (W)

Pennsylvania	
Senators	Representatives
James Cooper (W) Richard Brodhead (D)	John Allison (W) Thomas M. Bibighaus (W) Joseph R. Chandler (W) Carlton B. Curtis (D) John L. Dawson (D) Milo M. Dimmick (D) Thomas B. Florence (D) Henry M. Fuller (W) James Gamble (D) Alfred Gilmore (D) Galusha A. Grow (D) John W. Howe (W) Thomas M. Howe (W) J. Glancy Jones (D) Joseph H. Kuhns (W) William H. Kurtz (D) James X. McLanahan (D) John McNair (D) Henry D. Moore (W) John A. Morrison (D) Andrew Parker (D) John Robbins, Jr. (D) Thomas Ross (D) Thaddeus Stevens (W)

Rhode Island	
Senators	Representatives
John H. Clarke (W) Charles T. James (D)	George G. King (W) Benjamin B. Thurston (D)

South Carolina	
Senators	Representatives
Andrew P. Butler (SRD) R. Barnwell Rhett (D) r. May 1852 William F. DeSaussure (D) s. 1852	William Aiken (D) Armistead Burt (D) William F. Colcock (D) John McQueen (D) James L. Orr (D) Daniel Wallace (W) Joseph A. Woodward (D)

Tennessee	
Senators	Representatives
John Bell (W) James C. Jones (W)	William M. Churchwell (D) William Cullom (W) Meredith P. Gentry (W) Isham G. Harris (D) Andrew Johnson (D) George W. Jones (D) William H. Polk (D) John H. Savage (D) Frederick P. Stanton (D) Albert G. Watkins (W) Christopher H. Williams (W)

Texas	
Senators	Representatives
Sam Houston (D) Thomas J. Rusk (D)	Volney E. Howard (D) Richardson Scurry (D)

Vermont	
Senators	Representatives
William Upham (W) d. Jan. 1853 Samuel S. Phelps (W) s. 1853 Solomon Foot	Thomas Bartlett, Jr. (D) William Hebard (W) James Meacham (W) Ahiman L. Miner (W)

Virginia	
Senators	Representatives
James M. Mason (D) Robert M. T. Hunter (D)	Thomas H. Averett (D) Thomas H. Bayly (SRD) James M. H. Beale (D) Thomas S. Bocock (D) John S. Caskie (D) Sherrard Clemens (D) s. 1852 Henry A. Edmundson (D) Charles J. Faulkner Alexander R. Holladay (D) John Letcher (D) Fayette McMullen (D) Richard K. Meade (D) John S. Millson (D) Paulus Powell (D) James F. Strother (W) George W. Thompson (D) r. July 1852

Wisconsin	
Senators	Representatives
Henry Dodge (D) Isaac P. Walker (D)	James D. Doty (Free-Soiler) Charles Durkee (Free-Soiler) Ben C. Eastman (D)

Note: * D, Democrat; W, Whig; SRD, States Right Democrat; SRW, States Right Whig; R, Republican (after 1856); Un, Union Party (Civil War only); Amer, American or "Know-Nothing" Party. Some members did not serve a full term, usually because somebody died in office or resigned. Where that occurred: r, resigned; d, died in office.; s, started.

Source: Notable Names in American History: A Tabular Register, 3d ed. (Clifton, N.J.: James T. White, 1973), 92–120.

TABLE 9.4 THIRTY-THIRD CONGRESS, MARCH 4, 1853, TO MARCH 3, 1855

President of the Senate	Presidents Pro Tempore of the Senate	Speaker of the House of Representatives
William R. King	David R. Atchison Lewis Cass Jesse D. Bright	Linn Boyd

Alabama

Senators	Representatives
Benjamin Fitzpatrick (SRD) Clement Claiborne Clay (D)	James Abercrombie (W) Willamson R. W. Cobb (D) James F. Dowdell (SRD) Sampson W. Harris (D) George S. Houston (D) Philip Phillips (D) William R. Smith (W)

Arkansas

Senators	Representatives
William K. Sebastian (D) Solon Borland (D) r. Apr. 1853 Robert W. Johnson (D) s. 1853	Alfred B. Greenwood (D) Edward A. Warren (D)

California

Senators	Representatives
William M. Gwin (D) John B. Weller (D)	Milton S. Latham (D) James A. McDougall (D)

Connecticut

Senators	Representatives
Truman Smith (W) r. May 1854 Francis Gillette (W) s. 1854 Isaac Toucey (D)	Nathan Belcher (D) Colin M. Ingeroll (D) James T. Pratt (D) Origen S. Seymour (D)

Delaware

Senators	Representative
James A. Bayard (D) John M. Clayton (W))	George R. Riddle (D)

Florida

Senators	Representative
Jackson Morton (W) Stephen R. Mallory (D)	Augustus E. Maxwell (D)

Georgia

Senators	Representatives
William C. Dawson (SRW) Robert Toombs (SRD)	David J. Bailey (SRD) Elijah W. Chastain (D) Alfred H. Colquitt (D) William B. W. Dent (D) Junius Hillyer (D) David A. Reese (W) James L. Seward (D) Alexander H. Stephens (D)

Illinois

Senators	Representatives
Stephen A. Douglas (D) James Shields (D)	James C. Allen (D) Willis Allen (D) William H. Bissell (D) James Knox (W) Jesse O. Norton William A. Richardson (D) Elihu B. Washburne (W) John Wentworth (D) Richard Yates (W)

Indiana

Senators	Representatives
Jesse D. Bright (D) John Pettit (D)	Ebenezer M. Chamberlain (D) John G. Davis (D) Cyrus L. Dunham (D) Norman Eddy (D) William H. English (D) Andrew J. Harlan (D) Thomas A. Hendricks (D) James H. Lane (D) Daniel Mace (D) Smith Miller (D) Samuel W. Parker (W)

Iowa

Senators	Representatives
Augustus C. Dodge (D) George W. Jones (D)	John P. Cook (W) Bernhart Henn (D)

Kentucky

Senators	Representatives
Archibald Dixon (W) John B. Thompson (W)	Linn Boyd (D) John C. Breckinridge (D) Francis M. Bristow (W) s. 1854 James S. Chrisman (D) Leander M. Cox (W) John M. Elliott (D) Presley U. Ewing (W) d. Sept. 1854 Benjamin E. Grey (W) Clement S. Hill (D) William Preston (W) Richard H. Stanton (D)

Louisiana

Senators	Representatives
Pierre Soule (SRD) r 1853 John Slidell (SRD) s. 1853 Judah P. Benjamin (W)	William Dunbar (D) Theodore G. Hunt (W) Roland Jones (D) John Perkins, Jr. (D)

Maine

Senators	Representatives
Hannibal Hamlin (D) William P. Fessenden (W) s. 1854	Samuel P. Benson (W) E. Wilder Farley (W) Thomas J. D. Fuller (D) Moses Macdonald (D) Samuel Mayall (D) Israel Wash burn, Jr. (W)

Maryland

Senators	Representatives
James A. Pearce (W) Thomas G. Pratt (W)	John R. Franklin (W) William T. Hamilton (D) Henry May (D) Jacob Shower Augustus R. Sollers (W) Joshua Van Sant (D)

Massachusetts

Senators	Representatives
Charles Sumner (D) Edward Everett (R) r. June 1854	William Appleton (W) Nathaniel P. Banks (D)

Julius Rockwell (R) ta. 1854 Henry Wilson (Free-Soiler) s. 1855	Samuel L. Crocker (W) Alexander De Witt (Amer) Edward Dickinson (W) J. Wiley Edmands (W) Thomas D. Eliot s. 1854 John Z. Goodrich (W) Zeno Scudder (W) r. Mar. 1854 Charles W. Upham (W) Samuel H. Walley (W) Tappan Wentworth (W)

Michigan

Senators	Representatives
Lewis Cass (D) Charles E. Stuart (D)	Samuel Clark (D) David A. Noble (D) Hestor L. Stevens (D) David Stuart (D)

Mississippi

Senators	Representatives
Stephen Adams (D) Albert G. Brown (D) s. 1854	William Barksdale (SRD) William T. S. Barry (D) Wiley P. Harris (D) Otho R. Singleton (D) Daniel B. Wright (D)

Missouri

Senators	Representatives
David R. Atchison (W) Henry S. Geyer (D)	Thomas H. Benton (D) Samuel Caruthers (W) Alfred W. Lamb (D) James J. Lindley (W) John G. Miller (W) Mordecai Oliver (W) John S. Phelps (D)

New Hampshire

Senators	Representatives
Moses Norris, Jr. (D) d. Jan. 1855 John S. Wells (D) s. 1855 Charles G. Atherton (D) d. Nov. 1853 Jared W. Williams (D) s. 1853	Harry Hibbard (D) George W. Kittredge (D) George W. Morrison (D)

New Jersey

Senators	Representatives
John R. Thomson (D) William Wright (D)	Samuel Lilly (D) Alexander C. M. Pennington (W) Charles Skelton (D) Nathan T. Stratton (D) George Vail (D)

New York

Senators	Representatives
William H. Seward (W) Hamilton Fish (W)	Henry Bennet (W) Davis Carpenter (W) George W. Chase (W) Thomas W. Cumming (D) Francis B. Cutting (D) Gilbert Dean (D) r. July 1854 Reuben E. Fenton Thomas T. Flagler (W) Henry C. Goodwin s. 1854 George Hastings (D) Solomon G. Haven (W) Charles Hughes (D) Daniel T. Jones (D) Caleb Lyon (D) Orsamus B. Matteson (W) James Maurice (D) Edwin B. Morgan (D)
	William Murray (D) Andrew Oliver (D) Jared V. Peck (D) Rufus W. Peckham (D) Bishop Perkins (D) Benjamin Pringle (W) Peter Rowe (D) Russell Sage (W) George A. Simmons (W) Gerrit Smith (Abolitionist) r. Aug. 1854 John J. Taylor (D) Isaac Teller (D) s. 1854 William M. Tweed (D) Hiram Walbridge (D) William A. Walker (D) Mike Walsh (D) Theodore R. Westbrook (D) John Wheeler (D)

North Carolina

Senators	Representatives
George E. Badger (W) David S. Reid (d) s. 1854	William S. Ashe (D) Thomas L. Clingman (W) F. Burton Craige (D) John Kerr. Jr. (W) Richard C. Puryear (W) Sion H. Rogers (W) Thomas Ruffin (D) Henry M. Shaw (D)

Ohio

Senators	Representatives
Salmon P. Chase (D) Benjamin F. Wade (W)	Edward Ball (W) George Bliss (D) Lewis D. Campbell (W) Moses B. Corwin (W) David T. Disney (D) Alfred P. Edgerton (D) Andrew Ellison (D) Joshua R. Giddings (W) Frederick W. Green (D) Aaron Harlan (W) John Scott Harrison (W) Harvey H. Johnson (D) William D. Lindsley (D) Matthias H. Nichols (W) Edson B. Olds (D) Thomas Ritchey (D) William R. Sapp (W) Wilson Shannon (D) Andrew Stuart (D) John L. Taylor (W) Edward Wade (W)

Pennsylvania

Senators	Representatives
James Cooper (W) Richard Brodhead (D)	Samuel A. Bridges (D) Joseph R. Chandler (W) Carlton B. Curtis (D) John L. Dawson (D) John Dick (W) Augustus Drum (D) William Everhart (W) Thomas B. Florence (D) James Gamble (D) Galusha A. Grow (D) Isaac E. Hiester (W) Thomas M. Howe (W) J. Glancy Jones (D) s. 1854 William H. Kurtz (D) John McCulloch (W) John McNair (D)

(continued)

TABLE 9.4 (continued)

Senators	Representatives
	Ner Middleswarth (W) Henry A. Muhlenberg (D) d. Jan. 1854 Asa Packer (D) David Ritchie John Robbins, Jr. (D) Samuel L. Russell (W) Christian M. Straub (D) Michael C. Trout (D) William H. Witte (D) Hendrick B. Wright (D)
Rhode Island	
Senators	Representatives
Charles T. James (D) Philip Allen (D)	Thomas Davis (D) Benjamin B. Thurston (D)
South Carolina	
Senators	Representatives
Andrew P. Butler (SRD) Josiah J. Evans (SRD)	William Aiken (D) William W. Boyce (SRD) Preston S. Brooks (SRD) Laurence M. Keitt (D) John McQueen James L. Orr (D)
Tennessee	
Senators	Representatives
John Bell (W) James C. Jones (W)	Robert M. Bugg (W) William M. Churchwell (D) William Cullom (W) Emerson Etheridge (W) George W. Jones (D) Charles Ready (W) Samuel A. Smith (D) Frederick P. Stanton (D) Nathaniel G. Taylor (W) s. 1854 Felix K. Zollicoffer (SRW)
Texas	
Senators	Representatives
Sam Houston (D) Thomas J. Rusk (D)	Peter H. Bell (D) George W. Smyth
Vermont	
Senators	Representatives
Solomon Foot Samuel S. Phelps (W) r. Mar. 1854 Lawrence Brainerd (W) s. 1854	James Meacham (W) Alvah Sabin (W) Andrew Tracy (W)
Virginia	
Senators	Representatives
James M. Mason (D) Robert M. T. Hunter (D)	Thomas H. Bayly (SRD) Thomas S. Bocock (D) John S. Caskie (D) Henry A. Edmundson (D) Charles J. Faulkner William O. Goode (D) Zedekiah Kidwell (D) John Letcher (D) Charles S. Lewis (D) s. 1854 Fayette McMullen (D) John S. Millson (D) Paulus Powell (D) William Smith (D) John F. Snodgrass d. June 1854
Wisconsin	
Senators	Representatives
Henry Dodge (D) Isaac P. Walker (D)	Ben C. Eastman (D) John B. Macy (D) Daniel Wells, Jr. (D)

Note: * D, Democrat; W, Whig; SRD, States Right Democrat; SRW, States Right Whig; R, Republican (after 1856); Un, Union Party (Civil War only); Amer, American or "Know-Nothing" Party. Some members did not serve a full term, usually because somebody died in office or resigned. Where that occurred: r, resigned; d, died in office.; s, started.
Source: Notable Names in American History: A Tabular Register, 3d ed. (Clifton, N.J.: James T. White, 1973), 92–120.

TABLE 9.5 THIRTY-FOURTH CONGRESS, MARCH 4, 1855, TO MARCH 3, 1857

President of the Senate	Presidents Pro Tempore of the Senate	Speaker of the House of Representatives
Vacant	Jesse D. Bright Charles E. Stuart James M. Mason	Nathaniel P. Banks

Senators	Representatives
Alabama	
Senators	Representatives
Clement Claiborne Clay (D) Benjamin Fitzpatrick (SRD)	Williamson R. W. Cobb (D) James F. Dowdell (SRD) Sampson W. Harris (D) George S. Houston (D) Eli S. Shorter (D) William R. Smith (Amer) Percy Walker (Amer)
Arkansas	
Senators	Representatives
William K. Sebastian (D) Robert W. Johnson (D)	Alfred B. Greenwood (SRD) Albert Rust (D)
California	
Senators	Representatives
John B. Weller (D) William M. Gwin (D) s. 1857	James W. Denver (D) Philemon T. Herbert (D)
Connecticut	
Senators	Representatives
Isaac Toucey (D) Lafayette S. Foster (R)	Ezra Clark, Jr. (Amer) Sidney Dean (Amer) William W. Welch (Amer) John Woodruff (Amer)
Delaware	
Senators	Representative
James A. Bayard (D) John M. Clayton (W) d. Nov. 1856 Joseph P. Comegys (W) s. 1856 Martin W. Bates (D) s. 1857	Elisha D. Cullen (Amer)
Florida	
Senators	Representative
Stephen R. Mallory (D) David Levy Yulee (D)	Augustus E. Maxwell (D)

Georgia	
Senators	Representatives
Robert Toombs (SRD) Alfred Iverson (D)	Martin J. Crawford (D) Howell Cobb (D) Nathaniel G. Foster (Amer) John H. Lumpkin (D) James L. Seward (D) Alexander H. Stephens (D) Robert P. Trippe (W) Hiram Warner (D)

Illinois	
Senators	Representatives
Stephen A. Douglas (D) Lyman Trumbull (R)	James C. Allen (D) s. 1856 Jacob C. Davis (D) s. 1856 Thomas L. Harris (D) James Knox (W) Samuel S. Marshall (D) James L. D. Morrison (D) s. 1856 Jesse O. Norton William A. Richardson (D) r. Aug. 1856 Elihu B. Washburne (W) James H. Woodworth

Indiana	
Senators	Representatives
Jesse D. Bright (D) Graham N. Fitch (D) s. 1857	Lucien Barbour (Free-Soiler) Samuel Brenton (W) Schuyler Colfax (R) William Cumback George G. Dunn William H. English (D) David P. Holloway (People's Party) Daniel Mace (D) Smith Miller (D) John U. Pettit (R) Harvey D. Scott

Iowa	
Senators	Representatives
George W. Jones (D) James Harlan (W) s. 1857	Augustus Hall (D) James Thorington (W)

Kentucky	
Senators	Representatives
John B. Thompson (W) John J. Crittenden (Un)	Henry C. Burnett (D) John P. Campbell, Jr. (Amer) Leander M. Cox (Amer) John M. Elliott (D) Joshua H. Jewett (D) Alexander K. Marshall (Amer) Humphrey Marshall (Amer) Samuel F. Swope (Amer) Albert G. Talbott (D) Warner L. Underwood (Amer)

Louisiana	
Senators	Representatives
Judah P. Benjamin (W) John Slidell (SRD)	Thomas G. Davidson (D) George Eustis, Jr. (Amer) John M. Sandidge (D) Miles Taylor (D)

Maine	
Senators	Representatives
Hannibal Hamlin (D) r. Jan. 1857 Amos Nourse s. 1857 William P. Fessenden (W)	Samuel P. Benson Thomas J. D. Fuller (D) Ebenezer Knowlton John J. Perry Israel Washburn, Jr. John M. Wood

Maryland	
Senators	Representatives
James A. Pearce (W) Thomas G. Pratt (W)	Thomas F. Bowie (D) H. Winter Davis (Amer) J. Morrison Harris (Amer) Henry W. Hoffman (Amer) James B. Ricaud (Amer) James A. Stewart (D)

Massachusetts	
Senators	Representatives
Charles Sumner Henry Wilson (Free-Soiler)	Nathaniel P. Banks (Amer) James Buffinton (Amer) Anson Burlingame (Amer) Calvin C. Chaffee (Amer) Linus B. Comins (Amer) Timothy Davis (Amer) William S. Damrell (Amer) Alexander De Witt (Amer) Robert B. Hall (Amer) Chauncey L. Knapp (Amer) Mark Trafton (Amer)

Michigan	
Senators	Representatives
Lewis Cass (D) Charles E. Stuart (D)	William A. Howard George W. Peck (D) David S. Walbridge Henry Waldron

Mississippi	
Senators	Representatives
Stephen Adams (D) Albert G. Brown (D)	William Barksdale (SRD) Hendley S. Bennett (D) William A. Lake (W) John A. Quitman (D) Daniel B. Wright (D)

Missouri	
Senators	Representatives
Henry S. Geyer (D) James S. Green (D) s. 1857	Thomas P. Akers (Amer) s. 1856 Samuel Caruthers (W) Luther M. Kennett (Amer) James J. Lindley (W) Mordecai Oliver (W) John S. Phelps (D) Gilchrist Porter (W)

(continued)

TABLE 9.5 (continued)

New Hampshire	
Senators	**Representatives**
John P. Hale James Bell (W)	Aaron H. Cragin (Amer) James Pike (Amer) Mason W. Tappan (R)
New Jersey	
Senators	**Representatives**
John R. Thompson (D) William Wright (D)	James Bishop (W) Isaiah D. Clawson (W) Alexander C. M. Pennington (W) George R. Robbins (W) George Vail (D)
New York	
Senators	**Representatives**
William H. Seward (R) Hamilton Fish (W)	Henry Bennett (W) Bayard Clarke (Amer) Samuel Dickson (W) Edward Dodd (W) Francis S. Edwards (Amer) r. Feb. 1857 Thomas T. Flagler (W) William A. Gilbert (W) r. Feb. 1857 Amos P. Granger (W) Solomon G. Haven (W) Thomas R. Horton Jonas A. Hughston (W) John Kelly (D) William H. Kelsey (W) Rufus H. King (W) Andrew Z. McCarty (W) Orsamus B. Matteson (W) r. Feb. 1857 Killian Miller (W) Edwin B. Morgan (D) Ambrose S. Murray Andrew Oliver (D) John M. Parker (W) Guy R. Pelton (W) Benjamin Pringle (W) Russell Sage (W) George A. Simmons (W) Francis E. Spinner (D) James S. T. Stranahan (W) William W. Valk (Amer.) Abram Wakeman (W) John Wheeler (D) Thomas R. Whitney (Amer) John Williams (D)
North Carolina	
Senators	**Representatives**
David S. Reid (D) Asa Biggs (D)	Lawrence O'B. Branch (D) Thomas L. Clingman (W) F. Burton Craige (D) Robert T. Paine (Amer) Richard C. Puryear (W) Edwin G. Reade (Amer) Thomas Ruffin (D) Warren Winslow (D)

Ohio	
Senators	**Representatives**
Benjamin F. Wade (W) George E. Pugh (D)	Charles J. Albright Edward Ball (W) John A. Bingham Philemon Bliss Lewis D. Campbell (W) Timothy C. Day Jonas R. Emrie Samuel Galloway Joshua R. Giddings (W) Aaron Harlan (W) John Scott Harrison (W) Valentine B. Horton (W) Benjamin F. Leiter Oscar F. Moore Richard Mott Matthias H. Nichols William R. Sapp (W) John Sherman Benjamin Stanton (W) Edward Wade (W) Cooper K. Watson (Free-Soiler)
Pennsylvania	
Senators	**Representatives**
Richard Brodhead (D) William Bigler (D) s. 1856	John Allison (W) David Barclay (D) Samuel C. Bradshaw (W) Jacob Broom John Cadwalader (D) James H. Campbell (W) John Covode (W) John Dick John R. Edie (W) Thomas B. Florence (D) Henry M. Fuller (W) Galusha A. Grow (D) John Hickman (D) J. Glancy Jones (D) Jonathan Knight (W) John C. Kunkel (W) William Millward (W) Asa Packer (D) John J. Pearce (W) Samuel A. Purviance (W) David Ritchie Anthony E. Roberts (W) David F. Robison (W) Lemuel Todd Job R. Tyson (W)
Rhode Island	
Senators	**Representatives**
Charles T. James (D) Philip Allen (D)	Nathaniel B. Durfee (Amer) Benjamin B. Thurston (D)
South Carolina	
Senators	**Representatives**
Andrew P. Butler (SRD) Josiah J. Evans (SRD)	William Aiken (D) William W. Boyce (SRD) Preston S. Brooks (SRD) d. Jan. 1857 Laurence M. Keitt (D) John McQueen (D) James L. Orr (D)

Tennessee	
Senators	**Representatives**
John Bell (W) James C. Jones (W)	Emerson Etheridge (W) George W. Jones (D) Charles Ready (W) Thomas Rivers (Amer) John H. Savage Samuel A. Smith (D) William H. Sneed (Amer) Albert G. Watkins (D) John V. Wright (D) Felix K. Zollicoffer (SRW)
Texas	
Senators	**Representatives**
Sam Houston (D) Thomas J. Rusk (D)	Lemuel D. Evans (Amer) Peter H. Bell (D)
Vermont	
Senators	**Representatives**
Solomon Foot (R) Jacob Collamer (R)	George T. Hodges James Meacham (W) d. Aug. 1856 Justin S. Morrill (W) Alvah Sabin (W)
Virginia	
Senators	**Representatives**
James M. Mason (D) Robert M.T. Hunter (D)	Thomas H. Bayly (SRD) d. June 1856 Thomas S. Bocock (D) John S. Carlile (Amer.) John S. Caskie (D) Henry A. Edmundson (D) Charles J. Faulkner Muscoe R. H. Garnett (D) s. 1856 William O. Goode (D) Zedekiah Kidwell (D) John Letcher (D) Fayette McMullen (D) John S. Millson (D) Paulus Powell (D) William Smith (D)
Wisconsin	
Senators	**Representatives**
Henry Dodge (D) Charles Durkee	Charles Billingshurst Cadwallader C. Washburn Daniel Wells, Jr. (D)

Note: * D, Democrat; W, Whig; SRD, States Right Democrat; SRW, States Right Whig; R, Republican (after 1856); Un, Union Party (Civil War only); Amer, American or "Know-Nothing" Party. Some members did not serve a full term, usually because somebody died in office or resigned. Where that occurred: r, resigned; d, died in office.; s, started.
Source: Notable Names in American History: A Tabular Register, 3d ed. (Clifton, N.J.: James T. White, 1973), 92–120.

TABLE 9.6 THIRTY-FIFTH CONGRESS, MARCH 4, 1857, TO MARCH 3, 1859

President of the Senate	Presidents Pro Tempore of the Senate	Speaker of the House of Representatives
John C. Breckinridge	James M. Mason Thomas J. Rusk Benjamin Fitzpatrick	James L. Orr

Alabama	
Senators	**Representatives**
Benjamin Fitzpatrick (SRD) Clement Claiborne Clay (D)	Williamson R. W. Cobb (D) Jabez L. M. Curry (SRD) James F. Dowdell (SRD) George S. Houston (D) Sydenham Moore (D) Eli S. Shorter (D) James A. Stallworth (D)
Arkansas	
Senators	**Representatives**
William K. Sebastian (D) Robert W. Johnson (D)	Alfred B. Greenwood (D) Edward A. Warren (D)
California	
Senators	**Representatives**
William M. Gwin (D) David C. Broderick (D)	Joseph C. McKibbin (D) Charles L. Scott (D)
Connecticut	
Senators	**Representatives**
Lafayette S. Foster (R) James Dixon (R)	Samuel Arnold (D) William D. Bishop (D) Ezra Clark, Jr. (R) Sidney Dean (R)
Delaware	
Senators	**Representative**
James A. Bayard (D) Martin W. Bates (D)	William G. Whiteley (D)
Florida	
Senators	**Representative**
Stephen R. Mallory (D) David Levy Yulee (D)	George S. Hawkins (D)
Georgia	
Senators	**Representatives**
Robert Toombs (SRD) Alfred Iverson (D)	Martin J. Crawford (D) Lucius J. Gartrell (D) Joshua Hill (Amer) James Jackson (D) James L. Seward (D) Alexander H. Stephens (D) Robert P. Trippe (W) Augustus R. Wright (D)

(continued)

TABLE 9.6 (continued)

Illinois	
Senators	Representatives
Stephen A. Douglas (D) Lyman Trumbull (R)	John F. Farnsworth (R) Thomas L. Harris (D) d. Nov. 1858 Charles D. Hodges (D) s. 1859 William Kellogg (R) Owen Lovejoy (R) Samuel S. Marshall (D) Isaac N. Morris (D) Aaron Shaw (D) Robert Smith (D) Elihu B. Washburne (W)
Indiana	
Senators	Representatives
Jesse D. Bright (D) Graham N. Fitch (D)	Samuel Brenton (W) d. Mar. 1857 Charles Case (D) Schuyler Colfax (R) John G. Davis (D) William H. English James B. Foley (D) James M. Gregg (D) James Hughes (D) David Kilgore (R) James Lockhart (D) d. Sept. 1857 William E. Niblack (D) John U. Pettit (R) James Wilson (R)
Iowa	
Senators	Representatives
George W. Jones (D) James Harlan (R)	Samuel R. Curtis (R) Timothy Davis (W)
Kentucky	
Senators	Representatives
John B. Thompson (W) John J. Crittenden (Un)	Henry C. Burnett (D) James B. Clay (D) John M. Elliott (D) Joshua H. Jewett (D) Humphrey Marshall (Amer) John C. Mason (D) Samuel O. Peyton (D) John W. Stevenson (D) Albert G. Talbott (D) Warner L. Underwood (Amer)
Louisiana	
Senators	Representatives
Judah P. Benjamin (W) John Slidell (SRD)	Thomas G. Davison (D) George Eustis, Jr. (Amer) John M. Sandidge (D) Miles Taylor (D)
Maine	
Senators	Representatives
William P. Fessenden (W) Hannibal Hamlin (D)	Nehemiah Abbott (R) Stephen C. Foster (R) Charles J. Gillman (R) Freeman H. Morse (R) Israel Washburn, Jr. (R) John M. Wood (R)

Maryland	
Senators	Representatives
James A. Pearce (W) Anthony Kennedy (Un.)	Thomas F. Bowie (D) H. Winter Davis (R) J. Morrison Harris (Amer) Jacob M. Kunkel (D) James B. Ricaud (Amer) James A. Stewart (D)
Massachusetts	
Senators	Representatives
Charles Sumner (R) Henry Wilson (Free-Soiler)	Nathaniel P. Banks (R) r. Dec. 1857 James Buffinton (R) Anson Burlingame (Amer) Calvin C. Chaffee (Amer) Linus B. Comins (R) William S. Damrell (R) Timothy Davis (R) Henry L. Dawes Daniel W. Gooch (R) s. 1858 Robert B. Hall (R) Chauncey L. Knapp Eli Thayer (R)
Michigan	
Senators	Representatives
Charles E. Stuart (D) Zachariah Chandler (R)	William A. Howard (R) DeWitt C. Leach (R) David S. Walbridge (R) Henry Waldron (R)
Minnesota	
Senators	Representatives
Henry M. Rice (D) s. 1858 James Shields s. 1858	James M. Cavanaugh (D) William W. Phelps (D)
Mississippi	
Senators	Representatives
Albert G. Brown (D) Jefferson Davis (D)	William Barksdale (SRD) Reuben Davis (D) Lucius Q. C. Lamar (D) John J. McRae (SRD) s. 1858 John A. Quitman (D) d. July 1858 Otho R. Singleton
Missouri	
Senators	Representatives
James S. Green (D) Trusten Polk (D)	Thomas L. Anderson (Amer) Francis P. Blair, Jr. (Free-Soiler) Samuel Caruthers (D) John B. Clark (D) James Craig (D) John S. Phelps (D) Samuel H. Woodson (Amer)
New Hampshire	
Senators	Representatives
James Bell (W) d. May 1857 Daniel Clark (R) John P. Hale	Aaron H. Cragin (R) James Pike (Amer.) Mason W. Tappan (R)

New Jersey	
Senators	**Representatives**
John R. Thomson (D) William Wright (D)	Garnett B. Adrain (D) Isaiah D. Clawson (W) John Huyler (D) George R. Robbins (W) Jacob R. Wortendyke (D)

New York	
Senators	**Representatives**
William H. Seward (R) Preston King (R)	Samuel G. Andrews (R) Thomas J. Barr (D) s. 1859 Henry Bennett (W) Silas M. Burroughs (R) Horace F. Clark (D) Clark B. Cochrane (R) John Cochrane (SRD) Erastus Corning (D) Edward Dodd (W) Reuben E. Genton (R) Henry C. Goodwin (R) Amos P. Granger (W) John B. Haskin (D) Israel T. Hatch (D) Charles B. Hoard (R) John Kelly (D) r. Dec. 1858 William H. Kelsey (W) William B. Maclay (D) Orsamus B. Matteson (W) Edwin B. Morgan (R) Oliver A. Morse (R) Ambrose S. Murray (R) Abram B. Olin (R) George W. Palmer (R) John M. Parker (W) Emory P. Pottle (R) William F. Russell (D) John A. Searing (D) Judson W. Sherman (R) Daniel E. Sickles (D) Francis E. Spinner (R) George Taylor (D) John Thompson (R) Elijah Ward (D)

North Carolina	
Senators	**Representatives**
David S. Reid (D) Asa Biggs (D) r. May 1858 Thomas L. Clingman (D) s. 1858	Lawrence O.B. Branch (D) Thomas L. Clingman (W) r. May 1858 F. Burton Craige (D) John A. Gilmer (Amer) Thomas Ruffin (D) Alfred M. Scales (D) Henry M. Shaw (D) Zebulon B. Vance (D) s. Dec. 1858 Warren Winslow (D)

Ohio	
Senators	**Representatives**
Benjamin F. Wade (R) George E. Pugh (D)	John A. Bingham (R) Philemon Bliss (R) Joseph Burns (D) Lewis D. Campbell (W) r. May 1858 Joseph R. Cockerill (D) Samuel S. Cox (D) Joshua R. Giddings (W) William S. Groesbeck (D) Lawrence W. Hall (D) Aaron Harlan (W) Valentine B. Horton (W) William Lawrence (D) Benjamin F. Leiter (R) Joseph Miller (D) Richard Mott (R) Matthias H. Nichols (R) George H. Pendleton (D) John Sherman (R) Benjamin Stanton (W) Cydnor B. Tompkins (R) Clement L. Vallandigham (D) s. 1858 Edward Wade (R)

Oregon	
Senators	**Representative**
Joseph Lane (D) s. 1859 Delazon Smith (D) s. 1859	La Fayette Grover (D) s. 1859

Pennsylvania	
Senators	**Representatives**
William Bigler (D) Simon Cameron (D)	John A. Ahl (D) Henry Chapman (D) John Covode (R) William L. Dewart (D) John Dick (R) William H. Dimmick (D) John R. Edie (W) Thomas B. Florence (D) James L. Gillis (D) Galusha A. Grow (R) John Hickman (D) J. Glancy Jones (D) r. Oct. 1858 Owen Jones (D) William H. Keim (D) s. 1858 John C. Kunkel (W) James Landy (D) Paul Leidy (D) William Montgomery (D) Edward Joy Morris (W) Henry M. Phillips (D) Samuel A. Purviance (W) Wilson Reilly (D) David Ritchie (R) Anthony E. Roberts (W) William Stewart (R) Allison White (D)

Rhode Island	
Senators	**Representatives**
Philip Allen (D) James F. Simmons	William D. Brayton (R) Nathaniel B. Durfee (R)

(continued)

TABLE 9.6 (continued)

South Carolina	
Senators	**Representatives**
Andrew P. Butler (SRD) d. May 1857 James H. Hammond (SRD) s. 1857 Josiah J. Evans (SRD) d. May 1858 Arthur P. Hayne (D) ta. 1858 James Chesnut, Jr. (SRD) s. 1859	Milledge L. Bonham (SRD) William W. Boyce (SRD) Laurence M. Keitt (D) W. Porcher Miles (D) John McQueen (D) James L. Orr (D)
Tennessee	
Senators	**Representatives**
John Bell (W) Andrew Johnson (D)	John D. C. Atkins (D) William T. Avery (D) George W. Jones (D) Horace Maynard (Amer) Charles Ready (W) John H. Savage (D) Samuel A. Smith (D) Albert G. Watkins (D) John V. Wright (D) Felix K. Zollicoffer (SRW)
Texas	
Senators	**Representatives**
Sam Houston (D) Thomas J. Rusk (D) d. July 1857 J. Pinckney Henderson ta. 1857 Matthias Ward (D) s. 1858	Guy M. Bryan (D) John H. Reagan (D)
Vermont	
Senators	**Representatives**
Solomon Foot (R) Jacob Collamer (R)	Justin S. Morrill (W) Homer E. Royce (R) Eliakim P. Walton (R)
Virginia	
Senators	**Representatives**
James M. Mason (D) Robert M. T. Hunter (D)	Thomas S. Bocock (D) John S. Caskie (D) Sherrard Clemens (D) Henry A. Edmundson (D) Charles J. Faulkner Muscoe R. H. Garnett (D) William O. Goode (D) George W. Hopkins (D) Albert G. Jenkins (D) John Letcher (D) John S. Millson (D) Paulus Powell (D) William Smith (D)
Wisconsin	
Senators	**Representatives**
Charles Durkee (R) James R. Doolittle (R)	Charles Billinghurst (R) John F. Potter (R) Cadwallader C. Washburn (R)

Note: * D, Democrat; W, Whig; SRD, States Right Democrat; SRW, States Right Whig; R, Republican (after 1856); Un, Union Party (Civil War only); Amer, American or "Know-Nothing" Party. Some members did not serve a full term, usually because somebody died in office or resigned. Where that occurred: r, resigned; d, died in office.; s, started.

Source: Notable Names in American History: A Tabular Register, 3d ed. (Clifton, N.J.: James T. White, 1973), 92–120.

TABLE 9.7 THIRTY-SIXTH CONGRESS, MARCH 4, 1859, TO MARCH 3, 1861

President of the Senate	Presidents Pro Tempore of the Senate	Speaker of the House of Representatives
John C. Breckinridge	Benjamin Fitzpatrick Jesse D. Bright Solomon Foot	William Pennington

Alabama	
Senators	**Representatives**
Benjamin Fitzpatrick (SRD) Clement Claiborne Clay (D)	David Clopton (SRD) Williamson R. W. Cobb (D) r. Jan. 1861 Jabez L. M. Curry (SRD) George S. Houston (D) Sydenham Moore (D) James L. Pugh (D) James A. Stallworth (D)
Arkansas	
Senators	**Representatives**
William K. Sebastian (D) Robert W. Johnson (D)	Thomas C. Hindman (D) Albert Rust (D)
California	
Senators	**Representatives**
William M. Gwin (D) David C. Broderick (D) d. Sept. 1859 Henry P. Haun (D) ta. 1859 Milton S. Latham (D) s. 1860	John C. Burch (D) Charles L. Scott (D)
Connecticut	
Senators	**Representatives**
Lafayette S. Foster (R) James Dixon (R)	Alfred A. Burnham (R) Orris S. Ferry (R) Dwight Loomis (R) John Woodruff (Amer)
Delaware	
Senators	**Representative**
James A. Bayard (D) Willard Saulsbury (D)	William G. Whitely (D)
Florida	
Senators	**Representative**
Stephen R. Mallory (D) David Levy Yulee (D)	George S. Hawkins (D)
Georgia	
Senators	**Representatives**
Robert Toombs, (SRD) r. Feb. 1861 Alfred Iverson (D) r. Jan. 1861	Martin J. Crawford (D) Lucius J. Gartrell (D) Thomas Hardeman, Jr. (D) Joshua Hill (Amer.) r. Jan. 1861 James Jackson (D) John J. Jones (D) Peter E. Love (D) John W. H. Underwood (D)

Illinois	
Senators	**Representatives**
Stephen A. Douglas (D) Lyman Trumbull (R)	John F. Farnsworth (R) Philip B. Fouke (D) William Kellogg (R) John A. Logan (D) Owen Lovejoy (R) John A. McClernand (D) Isaac N. Morris (D) James C. Robinson (D) Elihu B. Washburne (W)

Indiana	
Senators	**Representatives**
Jesse D. Bright (D) Graham N. Fitch (D)	Charles Case (D) Schuyler Colfax (R) John G. Davis (D) William McK. Dunn (R) William H. English (D) William S. Holman (D) David Kilgore (R) William E. Niblack (D) John U. Pettit (R) Albert G. Porter (R) James Wilson (R)

Iowa	
Senators	**Representatives**
James Harlan (F) James W. Grimes (R)	Samuel R. Curtis (R) William Vandever (R)

Kansas	
Senators	**Representative**
Vacant Vacant	Martin F. Conway (R)

Kentucky	
Senators	**Representatives**
John J. Crittenden (Un) Lazarus W. Powell (D)	Green Adams (Amer) William C. Anderson (Amer) Francis M. Bristow (W) John Y. Brown (D) Henry C. Burnett (D) Robert Mallory (D) Laban T. Moore (Amer) Samuel O. Peyton (D) William E. Simms (D) John W. Stevenson (D)

Louisiana	
Senators	**Representatives**
Judah P. Benjamin (W) John Slidell (SRD)	John E. Bouligny (Amer) Thomas G. Davidson (D) John M. Landrum (D) Miles Taylor (D)

Maine	
Senators	**Representatives**
William P. Fessenden (W) Hannibal Hamlin (D) r. Jan. 1861 Lot M. Morrill (R) s. 1861	Stephen Coburn (R) s. 1861 Stephen C. Foster (R) Ezra B. French (R) Freeman H. Morse (R) John J. Perry (R) Daniel E. Somes (R) Israel Washburn, Jr. (R) r. Jan. 1861

Maryland	
Senators	**Representatives**
James A. Pearce (W) Anthony Kennedy (Un.)	H. Winter Davis (R) J. Morrison Harris (Amer) George W. Hughes (D) Jacob M. Kunkel (D) James A. Stewart (D) Edwin H. Webster (R)

Massachusetts	
Senators	**Representatives**
Charles Sumner (R) Henry Wilson	Charles Francis Adams (R) John B. Alley (R) James Buffinton (R) Anson Burlingame (R) Henry L. Dawes Charles Delano (R) Thomas D. Eliot (R) Daniel W. Gooch (R) Alexander H. Rice (R) Eli Thayer (R) Charles R. Train (R)

Michigan	
Senators	**Representatives**
Zachariah Chandler (R) Kinsley S. Bingham (R)	George B. Cooper (D) r. May 1860 William A. Howard (R) s. 1860 Francis W. Kellogg (R) De Witt C. Leach (R) Henry Waldron (R)

Minnesota	
Senators	**Representatives**
Henry M. Rice (D) Morton S. Wilkinson (R)	Cyrus Aldrich (R) William Windom (R)

Mississippi	
Senators	**Representatives**
Albert G. Brown (D) Jefferson Davis (D)	William Barksdale (SRD) Reuben Davis (D) Lucius Q. C. Lamar (D) r. Dec. 1860 John J. McRae (SRD) Otho R. Singleton (D)

Missouri	
Senators	**Representatives**
James S. Green (D) Trusten Polk (D)	Thomas L. Anderson (D) John R. Barret (D) Francis P. Blair (Free-Soiler) John B. Clark (D) James Craig (D) John W. Noell (D) John S. Phelps (D) Samuel H. Woodson (Amer)

New Hampshire	
Senators	**Representatives**
John P. Hale Daniel Clark (R)	Thomas M. Edwards (R) Gilman Marston (R) Mason W. Tappan (R)

(continued)

TABLE 9.7 (continued)

New Jersey	
Senators	**Representatives**
John R. Thomson (D) John C. Ten Eyck (R)	Garnett B. Adrain (D) John T. Nixon (R) William Pennington (W) Jetur R. Riggs (D) John L. N. Stratton (R)
New York	
Senators	**Representatives**
William H. Seward (R) Preston King (R)	Thomas J. Barr (D) Charles L. Beale (R) George Briggs (Amer) Silas M. Burroughs (R) d. June 1860 Martin Butterfield (R) Luther C. Carter (R) Horace F. Clark (D) Clark B. Cochrane (R) John Cochrane (SRD) Roscoe Conkling R. Holland Duell (R) Alfred Ely (R) Reuben E. Fenton (R) Augustus Frank (R) James H. Graham (R) John B. Haskin (D) Charles B. Hoard (R) James Humphrey (R) William Irvine (R) William S. Kenyon (R) M. Lindley Lee (R) James B. McKean (R) William B. Maclay (D) Abram B. Olin (R) George W. Palmer (R) Emory B. Pottle (R) Edwin R. Reynolds (R) s. 1860 John H. Reynolds (R) Charles B. Sedgwick (R) Daniel E. Sickles (D) Elbridge G. Spaulding (Un) Francis E. Spinner (R) Charles H. Van Wyck (R) Alfred Wells (R)
North Carolina	
Senators	**Representatives**
Thomas L. Clingman (D) Thomas Bragg (D)	Lawrence O'B. Branch (D) F. Burton Craige (D) John A. Gilmer (Amer) James M. Leach (W) Thomas Ruffin (D) William N. H. Smith (D) Zebulon B. Vance (D) Warren Winslow (D)

Ohio	
Senators	**Representatives**
Benjamin F. Wade (R) George E. Pugh (D)	William Allen (D) James M. Ashley (R) John A. Bingham (R) Harrison G. O. Blake (R) John Carey (R) Thomas Corwin (R) Samuel S. Cox (D) Sidney Edgerton (R) John A. Gurley (R) William Helmick (R) William Howard (D) John Hutchins (R) Charles D. Martin (D) George H. Pendleton (D) John Sherman (R) Benjamin Stanton (R) Thomas C. Theaker (R) Cydnor B. Tompkins (R) Carey A. Trimble (R) Clement L. Vallandigham (D) Edward Wade (R)
Oregon	
Senators	**Representative**
Joseph Lane (D) Edward D. Baker (R)	Lansing Stout (D)
Pennsylvania	
Senators	**Representatives**
William Bigler (D) Simon Cameron (D)	Elijah Babbitt (Un) Samuel S. Blair (R) James H. Campbell (W) John Covode (R) William H. Dimmick (D) Thomas B. Florence (D) Galusha A. Grow (R) James T. Hale (R) Chapin Hall (R) John Hickman (D) Benjamin F. Junkin (R) John W. Killinger (R) Henry C. Longnecker (R) Jacob K. McKenty (D) s. 1860 Robert McKnight (R) Edward McPherson (R) William Millward (W) William Montgomery (D) James K. Moorhead (R) Edward Joy Morris (W) John Schwartz (D) d. June 1860 George W. Scranton (R) Thaddeus Stevens (R) William Stewart (R) John P. Verree (R) John Wood (R)
Rhode Island	
Senators	**Representatives**
James F. Simmons (W) Henry B. Anthony (R)	Christopher Robinson (Amer.) William D. Brayton (R)

South Carolina	
Senators	Representatives
James H. Hammond (SRD) James Chesnut, Jr. (SRD)	John D. Ashmore (D) Milledge L. Bonham (SRD) William W. Boyce (SRD) Laurence M. Keitt (D) W. Porcher Miles (D) John McQueen (D)
Tennessee	
Senators	Representatives
Andrew Johnson (D) Alfred O. P. Nicholson (D) r. Mar. 1861	William T. Avery (D) Reese B. Brabson (D) Emerson Etheridge (W) Robert H. Hatton (Amer) Horace Maynard (Amer) Thomas A. R. Nelson (Un) James M. Quarles (W) William B. Stokes (W) James H. Thomas (D) John V. Wright (D)
Texas	
Senators	Representatives
Matthias Ward (D) Louis T. Wigfall (D) s. 1859 John Hemphill (SRD)	Andrew J. Hamilton (D) John H. Reagan (D)
Vermont	
Senators	Representatives
Solomon Foot (R) Jacob Collamer (R)	Justin S. Morrill (W) Homer E. Royce (R) Eliakim P. Walton (R)
Virginia	
Senators	Representatives
James M. Mason (D) Robert M. T. Hunter (D)	Thomas S. Bocock (D) Alexander R. Boteler (Amer) Sherrard Clemens (D) Daniel C. De Jarnette (D) Henry A. Edmundson (D) Muscoe R. H. Garnett (D) William O. Goode (D) d. July 1859 John T. Harris (D) Albert G. Jenkins (D) Shelton F. Leake (D) Elbert S. Martin (Amer) John S. Millson (D) Roger A. Pryor (D) William Smith (D)
Wisconsin	
Senators	Representatives
Charles Durkee (R) James R. Doolittle (R)	Charles H. Larrabee (D) John F. Potter (R) Cadwallader C. Washburn (R)

Note: * D, Democrat; W, Whig; SRD, States Right Democrat; SRW, States Right Whig; R, Republican (after 1856); Un, Union Party (Civil War only); Amer, American or "Know-Nothing" Party. Some members did not serve a full term, usually because somebody died in office or resigned. Where that occurred: r, resigned; d, died in office.; s, started.

Source: Notable Names in American History: A Tabular Register, 3d ed. (Clifton, N.J.: James T. White, 1973), 92–120.

TABLE 9.8 THIRTY-SEVENTH CONGRESS, MARCH 4, 1861, TO MARCH 3, 1863

President of the Senate	President Pro Tempore of the Senate	Speaker of the House of Representatives
Hannibal Hamlin	Solomon Foot	Galusha A. Grow

Alabama	
Senators	Representatives
Clement Claiborne Clay (D) r. Mar. 1861 Vacant	Vacant
Arkansas	
Senators	Representatives
William K. Sebastian (D) r. July 1861 Charles B. Mitchel (D) r. July 1861	Vacant
California	
Senators	Representatives
Milton S. Latham (D) James A. McDougall (D)	Frederick F. Low (R) Timothy G. Phelps (R) Aaron A. Sargent (R)
Connecticut	
Senators	Representatives
Lafayette S. Foster (R) James Dixon (R)	Alfred A. Burnham (R) James E. English (D) Dwight Loomis (R) George C. Woodruff (D)
Delaware	
Senators	Representative
James A. Bayard (D) Willard Saulsbury (D)	George P. Fisher (R)
Florida	
Senators	Representative
Stephen R. Mallory (D) r. Mar. 1861 Vacant	Vacant
Georgia	
Senators	Representatives
Vacant	Vacant
Illinois	
Senators	Representatives
Stephen A. Douglas (D) d. June 1861 Orville H. Browning (R) ta. 1861 William A. Richardson (D) s. 1863 Lyman Trumbull (R)	William J. Allen (D) s. 1862 Isaac N. Arnold (R) Philip B. Fouke (D) William Kellogg (R) Anthony L. Knapp (D) John A. Logan (D) r. Apr. 1862 Owen Lovejoy (R) John A. McClernand (D) r. Oct. 1861 William A. Richardson (D) r. Jan. 1863 James C. Robinson (D) Elihu B. Washburne (W) Joseph A. Wright (D) s. 1862

(continued)

TABLE 9.8 (continued)

Indiana	
Senators	Representatives
Jesse D. Bright (D) r. Feb. 1862 David Turpie (D) ta. 1862 Joseph A. Wright (D) s. 1862 Henry S. Lane (R)	Schuyler Colfax (R) James A. Cravens (D) William McK. Dunn (R) William S. Holman (D) George W. Julian (R) John Law (D) William Mitchell (R) Albert G. Porter (R) John P. C. Shanks (R) Daniel W. Voorhees (D) Albert S. White (R)

Iowa	
Senators	Representatives
James Harlan (R) James W. Grimes (R)	Samuel R. Curtis (R) r. Aug. 1861 William Vandever (R) James F. Wilson (R)

Kansas	
Senators	Representative
Samuel C. Pomeroy (R) James H. Lane (R)	Martin F. Conway (R)

Kentucky	
Senators	Representatives
Lazarus W. Powell (R) John C. Breckinridge (D) r. Dec. 1861 Garrett Davis (W) s. 1861	Henry C. Burnett (D) r. Dec. 1861 Samuel L. Casey (R) s. 1862 John J. Crittenden (Un) George W. Dunlap (Un) Henry Grider (W) Aaron Harding(Un) James S. Jackson (Un) r. Dec. 1861 Robert Mallory (D) John W. Menzies (Un) William H. Wadsworth (Un) Charles A. Wickliffe (Un) George H. Yeaman (Un) s. 1862

Louisiana	
Senators	Representatives
Judah P. Benjamin (W) r. Mar. 1861 Vacant	Benjamin F. Flanders (Un) s. 1862 Michael Hahn (Un) s. 1863

Maine	
Senators	Representatives
William P. Fessenden (W) Lot M. Morrill (R)	Thomas A. D. Fessenden (R) s. 1862 Samuel C. Fessenden (R) John N. Goodwin (R) Anson P. Morrill (R) Frederick A. Pike (R) John H. Rice (R) Charles W. Walton (R) r. May 1862

Maryland	
Senators	Representatives
James A. Pearce (W) d. Dec. 1862 Thomas H. Hicks (R) s. 1863 Anthony Kennedy (Un)	Charles B. Calvert (D) John W. Crisfield (Un) Cornelius L. L. Leary (Un) Henry May (D) Francis Thomas (R) Edwin H. Webster (R)

Massachusetts	
Senators	Representatives
Charles Sumner (R) Henry Wilson	Charles Francis Adams (R) r. May 1861 John B. Alley (R) William Appleton (W) r. Sept. 1861 Goldsmith F. Bailey (R) d. May 1862 James Buffinton (R) Henry L. Dawes Charles Delano (R) Thomas D. Eliot (R) Daniel W. Gooch (R) Samuel Hooper (R) Alexander H. Rice (R) Benjamin F. Thomas (Un) Charles R. Train Amasa Walker (R) s. 1862

Michigan	
Senators	Representatives
Zachariah Chandler (R) Kinsley S. Bingham (R) d. Oct. 1861 Jacob M. Howard (R) s. 1862	Fernando C. Beaman (R) Bradley F. Granger (D) Francis W. Kellogg (R) Rowland E. Trowbridge (R)

Minnesota	
Senators	Representatives
Henry M. Rice (D) Morton S. Wilkinson (R)	Cyrus Aldrich (R) William Windom

Mississippi	
Senators	Representatives
Vacant	Vacant

Missouri	
Senators	Representatives
Trusten Polk (D) r. Jan. 1862 John B. Henderson (D) s. 1862 Waldo P. Johnson (D) r. Jan. 1862 Robert Wilson (Un) ta. 1862	Francis P. Blair, Jr. (Free-Soiler) r. July 1862 John B. Clark (D) r. July 1861 William A. Hall (D) s. 1862 John W. Noell (D) Elijah H. Norton (D) John S. Phelps (D) Thomas L. Price s. 1862 John W. Reid (D) r. Dec. 1862 James S. Rollins

New Hampshire	
Senators	Representatives
John P. Hale (R) Daniel Clark (R)	Thomas M. Edwards (R) Gilman Marston (R) Edward H. Rollins (R)

New Jersey	
Senators	Representatives
John R. Thomson (D) d. Sept. 1862 Richard S. Field (R) ta. 1862 James W. Wall (D) s. 1863 John C. Ten Eyck (R)	George T. Cobb (D) John T. Nixon (R) Nehemiah Perry (Un) William G. Steele (D) John L. N. Stratton (R)

New York	
Senators	Representatives
Preston King (R) Ira Harris (R)	Stephen Baker Jacob P. Chamberlain (R) Ambrose W. Clark (R) Frederick A. Conkling (R) Roscoe Conkling (R) Erastus Corning (D) Isaac C. Delaplaine Alexander S. Diven (R) R. Holland Duell (R) Alfred Ely (R) Reuben E. Fenton (R) Richard Franchot (R) Augustus Frank (R) Edward Haight (D) James E. Kerrigan (D) William E. Lansing (R) James B. McKean (R) Moses F. Odell (D) Abram B. Olin (R) Theodore M. Pomeroy (R) Charles B. Sedgwick (R) Socrates N. Sherman (R) Edward H. Smith (D) Elbridge G. Spaulding (Un) John B. Steele (D) Burt Van Horn (R) Robert B. Van Valkenburg (R) Charles H. Van Wyck (R) Chauncey Vibbard (D) William Wall (R) Elijah Ward (D) William A. Wheeler (R) Benjamin Wood (D)

North Carolina	
Senators	Representatives
Thomas L. Clingman (D) r. Mar. 1861 Thomas Bragg (D) r. Mar. 1861	Vacant

Ohio	
Senators	Representatives
Benjamin F. Wade (R) Salmon P. Chase (D) r. Mar. 1861 John Sherman (R) s. 1861	William Allen (D) James M. Ashley (R) John A. Bingham (R) Harrison G. O. Blake (R) Thomas Corwin (R) r. Mar. 1861 Samuel S. Cox (D) William P. Cutler (R) Sidney Edgerton (R) John A. Gurley (R) Richard A. Harrison (D) s. 1861 Valentine B. Horton (R) John Hutchins (R) James R. Morris (D) Warren P. Noble (D) Robert H. Nugen (D) George H. Pendleton (D) Albert G. Riddle (R) Samuel Shellabarger (R) John Sherman (R) r. Mar. 1861 Carey A. Trimble (R) Clement L. Vallandigham (D) Chilton A. White (D) Samuel T. Worcester (R) s. 1861

Oregon	
Senators	Representatives
Edward D. Baker (R) d. Oct. 1861 Benjamin Stark (D) ta. 1862 Benjamin F. Harding (R) s. 1862 James W. Nesmith (D)	George K. Shiel (D) Andrew J. Thayer (D) r. July 1861

Pennsylvania	
Senators	Representatives
Simon Cameron (R) r. Mar. 1861 David Wilmot (R) s. 1861 Edgar Cowan (R)	Sydenham E. Ancona (D) Elijah Babbitt (R) Joseph Bailey (D) Charles J. Biddle (D) Samuel S. Blair (R) James H. Campbell Thomas B. Cooper (D) d. Apr. 1862 John Covode (R) William M. Davis (R) Galusha A. Grow (R) James T. Hale (R) John Hickman (R) Philip Johnson (R) William D. Kelley (R) John W. Killinger (R) Jesse Lazear (D) William E. Lehman (D) Robert McKnight (R) Edward McPherson (R) James K. Moorhead (R) Edward J. Morris (W) r. June 1861 John Patton (R) George W. Scranton (R) d. Mar. 1861 John D. Stiles (D) s. 1862 Thaddeus Stevens (R) John P. Verree (R) John W. Wallace (R) Hendrick B. Wright (D)

Rhode Island	
Senators	Representatives
James F. Simmons (W) r. Aug. 1862 Samuel G. Arnold (R) s. 1862 Henry B. Anthony (R)	George H. Browne (D) William P. Sheffield (R)

South Carolina	
Senators	Representatives
James Chesnut, Jr. (SRD) r. July 1861 Vacant	Vacant

Tennessee	
Senators	Representatives
Andrew Johnson (D) r. Mar. 1862 Alfred O. P. Nicholson r. July 1861	George W. Bridges (Un) s. 1863 Andrew J. Clements (Un) s. 1862 Horace Maynard (Amer)

(continued)

TABLE 9.8 (continued)

Texas	
Senators	Representatives
John Hemphill (SRD) r. Mar. 1861 Louis Wigfall (D) r. Mar. 1861	Vacant

Vermont	
Senators	Representatives
Solomon Foot (R) Jacob Collamer (R)	Portus Baxter (R) Justin S. Morrill (W) Eliakim P. Walton (R)

Virginia	
Senators	Representatives
James M. Mason (D) r. Mar. 1861 Waitman T. Willey Robert M. T. Hunter r. Mar. 1861 John S. Carlile (Un)	Jacob B. Blair (Un) William G. Brown (Un) John S. Carlile (Amer) r. July 1861 Lewis McKenzie (Un) s. 1863 Joseph E. Segar (Un) Charles H. Upton (R) Kellian V. Whaley (R)

Wisconsin	
Senators	Representatives
James R. Doolittle (R) Timothy O. Howe (R)	Luther Hanchett (R) d. Nov. 1862 Walter D. Mclndoe (R) s. 1863 John F. Potter (R) A. Scott Sloan (R)

Note: * D, Democrat; W, Whig; SRD, States Right Democrat; SRW, States Right Whig; R, Republican (after 1856); Un, Union Party (Civil War only); Amer, American or "Know-Nothing" Party. Some members did not serve a full term, usually because somebody died in office or resigned. Where that occurred: r, resigned; d, died in office.; s, started.
Source: Notable Names in American History: A Tabular Register, 3d ed. (Clifton, N.J.: James T. White, 1973), 92–120.

TABLE 9.9 THIRTY-EIGHTH CONGRESS, MARCH 4, 1863, TO MARCH 3, 1865

President of the Senate	President Pro Tempore of the Senate	Speaker of the House of Representatives
Hannibal Hamlin	Solomon Foot Daniel Clark	Schuyler Colfax

Alabama	
Senators	Representatives
Vacant	Vacant

Arkansas	
Senators	Representatives
Vacant	Vacant

California	
Senators	Representatives
James A. McDougall (D) John Conness (D)	Cornelius Cole (R) William Higby (R) Thomas B. Shannon (R)

Connecticut	
Senators	Representatives
Lafayette S. Foster (R) James Dixon (R)	Augustus Brandegee (R) Henry C. Deming (R) James E. English (D) John H. Hubbard (R)

Delaware	
Senators	Representative
James A. Bayard (D) r. Jan. 1864 George R. Riddle (D) s. 1864 Willard Saulsbury (D)	Nathaniel B. Smithers (R)

Florida	
Senators	Representative
Vacant	Vacant

Georgia	
Senators	Representatives
Vacant	Vacant

Illinois	
Senators	Representatives
Lyman Trumbull (R) William A. Richardson (D)	James C. Allen (D) William J. Allen (D) Isaac N. Arnold (R) John R. Eden (D) John F. Farnsworth (R) Charles M. Harris (D) Ebon C. Ingersoll (R) s. 1864 Anthony L. Knapp (D) Owen Lovejoy (R) d. Mar. 1864 William R. Morrison (D) Jesse O. Norton (R) James C. Robinson (D) Lewis W. Ross (D) John T. Stuart (D) Elihu B. Washburne (W)

Indiana	
Senators	Representatives
Henry S. Lane (R) Thomas A. Hendricks (D)	Schuyler Colfax (R) James A. Cravens (D) Ebenezer Dumont (Un) Joseph K. Edgerton (D) Henry W. Harrington (D) William S. Holman (D) George W. Julian (R) John Law (D) James F. McDowell (D) Godlove S. Orth (R) Daniel W. Voorhees (D)

Iowa	
Senators	Representatives
James Harlan (R) James W. Grimes (R)	William B. Allison (R) Josiah B. Grinnell (R) Asahel W. Hubbard (R) John A. Kasson (R) Hiram Price (R) James F. Wilson (R)

Kansas	
Senators	Representative
Samuel C. Pomeroy (R) James H. Lane (R)	A. Carter Wilder

Kentucky	
Senators	Representatives
Lazarus W. Powell (D) Garrett Davis (W)	Lucien Anderson (Un) Brutus J. Clay (Un) Henry Grider (W) Aaron Harding (Un) Robert Mallory (D) William H. Randall (R) Green C. Smith William H. Wadsworth (Un) George H. Yeaman (Un)

Louisiana	
Senators	Representatives
Vacant	Vacant

Maine	
Senators	Representatives
William P. Fessenden (W) r. July 1864 Nathan A. Farwell (R) s. 1864 Lot M. Morrill (R)	James G. Blaine (R) Sidney Perham (R) Frederick A. Pike (R) John H. Rice (R) Lorenzo D. M. Sweat (D)

Maryland	
Senators	Representatives
Thomas H. Hicks (R) d. Feb. 1865 Reverdy Johnson (D)	John A. J. Creswell (R) H. Winter Davis (Un.) Benjamin G. Harris (D) Francis Thomas (Un) Edwin H. Webster (R)

Massachusetts	
Senators	Representatives
Charles Sumner (R) Henry Wilson	John B. Alley (R) Oakes Ames (R) John D. Baldwin (R) George S. Boutwell (R) Henry L. Dawes Thomas D. Eliot (R) Daniel W. Gooch (R) Samuel Hooper (R) Alexander H. Rice (R) William B. Washburn (R)

Michigan	
Senators	Representatives
Zachariah Chandler (R) Jacob M. Howard (R)	Augustus C. Baldwin (D) Fernando C. Beaman (R) John F. Driggs (R) Francis W. Kellogg (R) John W. Longyear (R) Charles Upson (R)

Minnesota	
Senators	Representatives
Morton S. Wilkinson (R) Alexander Ramsey (R)	Ignatius Donnelly (R) William Windom (R)

Mississippi	
Senators	Representatives
Vacant	Vacant

Missouri	
Senators	Representatives
John B. Henderson (D) Robert Wilson (Un) r. 1863 B. Gratz Brown (D) s. 1863	Francis P. Blair (Free-Soiler) r. June 1864 Henry T. Blow (R) Sempronius H. Boyd (Emancipationist) William A. H. Hall (D) Austin A. King (D) Samuel Knox (R) s. 1864 Benjamin F. Loan (Emancipationist) Joseph W. McClurg (Emancipationist) John W. Noell (D) d. Mar. 1863 James S. Rollins (Con) John G. Scott (D)

Nevada	
Senators	Representative
William M. Stewart (R) s. 1865 James W. Nye (R) s. 1865	Henry G. Worthington (R) s. 1864

New Hampshire	
Senators	Representatives
John P. Hale (R) Daniel Clark (R)	Daniel Marcy (D) James W. Patterson (R) Edward H. Rollins (R)

New Jersey	
Senators	Representatives
John C. Ten Eyck (R) William Wright (D)	George Middleton (D) Nehemiah Perry (Un) Andrew J. Rogers (D) John F. Starr William G. Steele (D)

New York	
Senators	Representatives
Ira Harris (R) Edwin D. Morgan (R)	James Brooks (D) John W. Chanler (D) Ambrose W. Clark (R) Freeman Clarke (R) Thomas T. Davis (Un) Reuben E. Fenton (R) r. Dec. 1864 Augustus Frank (R) John Ganson (D) John A. Griswold (D) Anson Herrick (D) Giles W. Hotchkiss (R) Calvin T. Hulburd (R) Martin Kalbfleisch (D) Orlando Kellogg (R) Francis Kernan (D) De Witt C. Littlejohn (R) James M. Marvin (Un) Samuel F. Miller (R) Daniel Morris (R) Homer A. Nelson (D) Moses F. Odell (D) Theodore M. Pomeroy (R) John V. L. Pruyn (D)

(continued)

TABLE 9.9 (continued)

	William Radford (D) Henry G. Stebbins (D) r. Oct. 1864 John B. Steele (D) Dwight Townsend (D) s. 1864 Robert B. Van Valkenburg (R) Elijah Ward (D) Charles H. Winfield (D) Benjamin Wood (D) Fernando Wood (D)
North Carolina	
Senators	Representatives
Vacant	Vacant
Ohio	
Senators	Representatives
Benjamin F. Wade (R) John Sherman (R)	James M. Ashley (R) George Bliss (D) Samuel S. Cox (D) Ephraim R. Eckley (R) William E. Finck (D) James A. Garfield (R) Wells A. Hutchins (D) William Johnston (D) Francis C. Le Blond (D) Alexander Long (D) John F. McKinney (D) James R. Morris (D) Warren P. Noble (D) John O'Neill (D) George H. Pendleton (D) Robert C. Schenck (R) Rufus P. Spalding (D) Chilton A. White (D) Joseph W. White (D)
Oregon	
Senators	Representative
James W. Nesmith (D) Benjamin F. Harding (R)	John R. McBride (R)
Pennsylvania	
Senators	Representatives
Edgar Cowan (R) Charles R. Buckalew (D)	Sydenham E. Ancona (D) Joseph Bailey (D) John M. Broomall (R) Alexander H. Coffroth (D) John L. Dawson (D) Charles Dension (D) James T. Hale (R) Philip Johnson (R) William D. Kelley (R) Jesse Lazear (D) Archibald McAllister (D) William H. Miller (D) James K. Moorhead (R) Amos Myers (R) Leonard Myers (R) Charles O'Neill (R) Samuel J. Randall (D) Glenni W. Scofield (R) Thaddeus Stevens (R) John D. Stiles (D) Myer Strouse (D) M. Russell Thayer (R) Henry W. Tracy (R) Thomas Williams (R)
Rhode Island	
Senators	Representatives
Henry B. Anthony (R) William Sprague	Nathan F. Dixon (R) Thomas A. Jenckes (R)
South Carolina	
Senators	Representatives
Vacant	Vacant
Tennessee	
Senators	Representatives
Vacant	Vacant
Texas	
Senators	Representatives
Vacant	Vacant
Vermont	
Senators	Representatives
Solomon Foot (R) Jacob Collamer (R)	Portus Baxter (R) Justin S. Morrill Frederick E. Woodbridge (R)
Virginia	
Senators	Representatives
John S. Carlile (Un) Lemuel J. Bowden (R) d. Jan. 1864	Vacant
West Virginia	
Senators	Representatives
Peter G. Van Winkle (Un) Waitman T. Willey (R)	Jacob B.Blair William G. Brown (Un) Kellian V. Whaley (R)
Wisconsin	
Senators	Representatives
James R. Doolittle (R) Timothy O. Howe (R)	James S. Brown (D) Amasa Cobb (R) Charles A. Eldridge (D) Walter D. Mclndoe (R) Ithamar C. Sloan (R) Ezra Wheeler (D)

Note: * D, Democrat; W, Whig; SRD, States Right Democrat; SRW, States Right Whig; R, Republican (after 1856); Un, Union Party (Civil War only); Amer, American or "Know-Nothing" Party. Some members did not serve a full term, usually because somebody died in office or resigned. Where that occurred: r, resigned; d, died in office.; s, started.

Source: Notable Names in American History: A Tabular Register, 3d ed. (Clifton, N.J.: James T. White, 1973), 92–120.

TABLE 9.10 THIRTY-NINTH CONGRESS, MARCH 4, 1865, TO MARCH 3, 1867

President of the Senate	Presidents Pro Tempore of the Senate	Speaker of the House of Representatives
Andrew Johnson	Lafayette S. Foster Benjamin F. Wade	Schuyler Colfax

Senators	Representatives
Alabama	
Vacant	Vacant
Arkansas	
Vacant	Vacant
California	
James A. McDougall (D) John Conness (R)	John Bidwell (Un) William Higby (R) Donald C. McRuer (R)
Connecticut	
Lafayette S. Foster (R) James Dixon (R)	Augustus Brandegee (R) Henry C. Deming (R) John H. Hubbard (R) Samuel L. Warner (R)
Delaware	
Senators	Representative
Willard Saulsbury (D) George R. Riddle (D)	John A. Nicholson (D)
Florida	
Senators	Representative
Vacant	Vacant
Georgia	
Vacant	Vacant
Illinois	
Lyman Trumbull (R) Richard Yates (R)	Jehu Baker (R) Henry P. H. Bromwell (R) Burton C. Cook (R) Shelby M. Cullom (R) John F. Farnsworth (R) Abner C. Harding (R) Ebon C. Ingeroll (R) Andrew J. Kuykendall (R) Samuel S. Marshall (D) Samuel W. Moulton (D) Lewis W. Ross (D) Anthony Thornton (D) Elihu B. Washburne (W) John Wentworth (R)
Indiana	
Henry S. Lane (R) Thomas A. Hendricks (D)	Schuyler Colfax (R) Joseph H. Defrees (R) Ebenezer Dumont (Un) John H. Farquhar (R) Ralph Hill (R) George W. Julian (R) Michael C. Kerr (D) William E. Niblack (D) Godlove S. Orth (R) Thomas N. Stillwell (R) Daniel W. Voorhees (D) r. Feb. 1866 Henry D. Washburn (R) s. 1866
Iowa	
James Harlan (R) r. May 1865 Samuel J. Kirkwood (R) s. 1866 James W. Grimes (R)	William B. Allison (R) Josiah B. Grinnell (R) Asahel W. Hubbard (R) John A. Kasson (R) Hiram Price (R) James F. Wilson (R)
Kansas	
Senators	Representative
Samuel C. Pomeroy (R) James H. Lane (R) d. July 1866 Edmund G. Ross (R) s. 1866	Sidney Clarke (R)
Kentucky	
Senators	Representatives
Garrett Davis (W) James Guthrie (D)	Henry Grider (W) d. Sept. 1866 Aaron Harding (D) Elijah Hise (D) s. 1866 Samuel McKee (R) William H. Randall (R) Burwell C. Ritter (Con) Lovell H. Rousseau (R) George S. Shanklin (D) Green C. Smith (Un) r. 1866 Lawrence S. Trimble (D) Andrew H. Ward s. 1866
Louisiana	
Vacant	Vacant
Maine	
Lot M. Morrill (R) William P. Fessenden (W)	James G. Blaine (R) John Lynch (R) Sidney Perham (R) Frederick A. Pike (R) John H. Rice (R)
Maryland	
Reverdy Johnson (D) John A. J. Creswell (R)	Benjamin G. Harris (D) Hiram McCullough (D) Charles E. Phelps (Con) Francis Thomas (R) John L. Thomas, Jr. (R) Edwin H. Webster r. July 1865

(continued)

TABLE 9.10 (continued)

Massachusetts	
Senators	Representatives
Charles Sumner (R) Henry Wilson	John B. Alley (R) Oakes Ames (R) John D. Baldwin (R) Nathaniel P. Banks (R) George S. Boutwell (R) Henry L. Dawes (R) Thomas D. Eliot (R) Samuel Hooper (R) Alexander H. Rice (R) William B. Washburn (R)
Michigan	
Senators	Representatives
Zachariah Chandler (R) Jacob M. Howard (R)	Fernando C. Beaman (R) John F. Driggs (R) Thomas W. Ferry (R) John W. Longyear (R) Rowland E. Trowbridge (R) Charles Upson (R)
Minnesota	
Senators	Representatives
Alexander Ramsey (R) Daniel S. Norton (Con)	Ignatius Donnelly (R) William Windom (R)
Mississippi	
Senators	Representatives
Vacant	Vacant
Missouri	
Senators	Representatives
John B. Henderson (D) B. Gratz Brown (D)	George W. Anderson (R) John F. Benjamin (R) Henry T. Blow (R) John Hogan (D) John R. Kelso (Radical) Benjamin F. Loan (Emancipation) Joseph W. McClurg (Radical) Thomas E. Noel (D) Robert T. Van Horn (R)
Nebraska	
Senators	Representative
John M. Thayer (R) s. 1867 Thomas W. Tipton (R) s. 1867	Turner M. Marquette (R) s. 1867
Nevada	
Senators	Representative
William M. Stewart (R) James W. Mye (R)	Delos R. Ashley (R)
New Hampshire	
Senators	Representatives
Daniel Clark (R) r. July 1866 George G. Fogg (R) s. 1866 Aaron H. Cragin (Amer)	Gilman Marston (R) James W. Patterson (R) Edward H. Rollins (R)

New Jersey	
Senators	Representatives
William Wright (D) d. Nov. 1866 Frederick T. Frelinghuysen (R) s. 1866 John P. Stockton (D) r. 1866 Alexander G. Cattell (R) s. 1866	William A. Newell (R) Andrew J. Rogers (D) r. Mar. 1866 Charles Sitgreaves (D) John F. Starr (R) Edwin R. V. Wright (D) s. 1866
New York	
Senators	Representatives
Ira Harris (R) Edwin D. Morgan (R)	Teunis G. Bergen (D) James Brooks (D) r. Apr. 1866 John W. Chanler (D) Roscoe Conkling (R) r. Mar. 1867 William A. Darling (R) Thomas T. Davis (Un) William E. Dodge (R) s. 1866 Charles Goodyear (D) John A. Griswold (R) Robert S. Hale (R) s. 1866 Roswell Hart (R) Sidney T. Holmes (R) Giles W. Hotchkiss (R) Demas Hubbard, Jr. (R) Edwin N. Hubbell (R) Calvin T. Hulburd (R) James Humphrey (R) d. June 1866 James M. Humphrey (D) John W. Hunter s. 1866 Morgan Jones (D) Orlando Kellogg (R) d. Aug. 1865 John H. Ketcham (R) Addison H. Laflin (R) James M. Marvin (Un) Daniel Morris (R) Theodore M. Pomeroy (R) William Radford (D) Henry J. Raymond (R) Stephen Taber (D) Nelson Taylor (D) Henry Van Aernam (R) Burt Van Horn (R) Hamilton Ward (R) Charles H. Winfield (D)
North Carolina	
Senators	Representatives
Vacant	Vacant
Ohio	
Senators	Representatives
Benjamin F. Wade (R) John Sherman (R)	James M. Ashley (R) John A. Bingham (R) Ralph P. Buckland (R) Hezekiah S. Bundy (R) Reader W. Clarke (R) Columbus Delano (R) Ephraim R. Eckley (R) Benjamin Eggleston (R) William E. Finck (D) James A. Garfield (R) Rutherford B. Hayes (R) James R. Hubbell.(R) William Lawrence (R) Francis C. Le Blond (D) Tobias A. Plants (R) Robert C. Schenck (R) Samuel Shellabarger (R) Rufus P. Spalding (D) Martin Welker (R)

Oregon	
Senators	Representative
James W. Nesmith (D) George H. Williams (R)	James H. Henderson (R)

Pennsylvania	
Senators	Representatives
Edgar Cowan (R) Charles R. Buckalew (D)	Sydenham E. Ancona (D) Abraham A. Barker (R) Benjamin M. Boyer (D) John M, Broomall (R) Alexander H. Coffroth (D) r. July 1866 Charles V. Culver John L. Dawson (D) Charles Denison (D) Adam J. Glossbrenner (D) Philip Johnson (R) d. Jan. 1867 William D. Kelley (R) William H. Koontz (R) s. 1866 George V. Lawrence (W) Ulysses Mercur (R) George F. Miller (R) James K. Moorhead (R) Leonard Myers (R) Charles O'Neill (R) Samuel J. Randall (D) Glenni W. Scofield (R) Thaddeus Stevens (R) Myer Strouse (D) M. Russell Thayer (R) Thomas Williams (R) Stephen F. Wilson (R)

Rhode Island	
Senators	Representatives
Henry B. Anthony (R) William Sprague (R)	Nathan F. Dixon (R) Thomas A. Jenckes (R)

South Carolina	
Senators	Representatives
Vacant	Vacant

Tennessee	
Senators	Representatives
Joseph S. Fowler (R) s. 1866 David T. Patterson (D) s. 1866	Samuel M. Arnell (R) s. 1866 William B. Campbell (D) s. 1866 Edmund Cooper (Con) s. 1866 Isaac R. Hawkins (R) s. 1866 John W. Leftwich (D) s. 1866 Horace Maynard (R) s. 1866 William B. Stokes (R) s. 1866 Nathaniel G. Taylor s. 1866

Texas	
Senators	Representatives
Vacant	Vacant

Vermont	
Senators	Representatives
Solomon Foot (R) d. Mar. 1866 George F. Edmunds (R) s. 1866 Jacob Collamer (R) d. Nov. 1865 Luke P. Poland (R) s. 1865	Portus Baxter (R) Justin S. Morrill Frederick E. Woodbridge (R)

Virginia	
Senators	Representatives
Vacant	Vacant

West Virginia	
Senators	Representatives
Peter G. Van Winkle (Un) Waitman T. Willey (R)	Chester D. Hubbard (R) George R. Latham (R) Kellian V. Whaley (R)

Wisconsin	
Senators	Representatives
James R. Dottlittle (R) Timothy O. Howe (R)	Amasa Cobb (R) Charles A. Eldridge (D) Walter D. McIndoe (R) Halbert E. Paine (R) Philetus Sawyer (R) Ithamar C. Sloan (R)

Note: * D, Democrat; W, Whig; SRD, States Right Democrat; SRW, States Right Whig; R, Republican (after 1856); Un, Union Party (Civil War only); Amer, American or "Know-Nothing" Party. Some members did not serve a full term, usually because somebody died in office or resigned. Where that occurred: r, resigned; d, died in office.; s, started.
Source: Notable Names in American History: A Tabular Register, 3d ed. (Clifton, N.J.: James T. White, 1973), 92–120.

TABLE 9.11 FORTIETH CONGRESS, MARCH 4, 1867, TO MARCH 3, 1869

President of the Senate	President Pro Tempore of the Senate	Speakers of the House of Representatives
Vacant	Benjamin F. Wade	Schuyler Colfax Theodore M. Pomeroy

Alabama	
Senators	Representatives
George E. Spencer (R) s. 1868 Willard Warner (R) s. 1868	Charles W. Buckley (R) s. 1868 John B. Callis (R) s. 1868 Thomas Haughey (R) s. 1868 Francis W. Kellogg (R) s. 1868 Benjamin W. Norris (R) s. 1868

Arkansas	
Senators	Representatives
Alexander McDonald (R) s. 1868 Benjamin F. Rice (R) s. 1868	Thomas Boles (R) s. 1868 James T. Elliott (R) s. 1868 James Hinds (R) s. 1868 Logan H. Roots (R) s. 1868

California	
Senators	Representatives
John Conness (R) Cornelius Cole (R)	Samuel B. Axtell (D) s. 1867 William Higby (R) s. 1867 James A. Johnson (D) s. 1867

Connecticut	
Senators	Representatives
James Dixon (R) Orris S. Ferry (R)	William H. Barnum (D) Julius Hotchkiss (R) Richard D. Hubbard (D) Henry H. Starkweather (R)

(continued)

TABLE 9.11 (continued)

Delaware	
Senators	**Representative**
George R. Riddle (D) d. Mar. 1867 James A. Bayard (D) Willard Saulsbury (D)	John A. Nicholson (D)

Florida	
Senators	**Representative**
Thomas W. Osborn (R) s. 1868 Adonijah S. Welch (R) s. 1868	Charles M. Hamilton (R) s. 1868

Georgia	
Senators	**Representatives**
Vacant	Joseph W. Clift (R) s. 1868 William P. Edwards (R) s. 1868 Samuel F. Gove (R) s. 1868 Charles H. Prince (R) s. 1868 Nelson Tift (D) s. 1868 Pierce M. B. Young (D) s. 1868

Illinois	
Senators	**Representatives**
Lyman Trumbull (R) Richard Yates (R)	Jehu Baker (R) Henry P. H. Bromwell (R) Albert G. Burr (D) Burton C. Cook (R) Shelby M. Cullom (R) John F. Farnsworth (R) Abner C. Harding (R) Ebon C. Ingersoll (R) Norman B. Judd (R) Samuel S. Marshall (D) Green B. Raum (R) Lewis W. Ross (D) Elihu B. Washburne (W)

Indiana	
Senators	**Representatives**
Thomas A. Hendricks (D) Oliver H. P. T. Morton (R)	John Coburn (R) Schuyler Colfax (R) William S. Holman (D) Morton C. Hunter (R) George W. Julian (R) Michael C. Kerr (D) William E. Niblack (D) Godlove S. Orth (R) John P. C. Shanks (R) Henry D. Washburn (R) William Williams (R)

Iowa	
Senators	**Representatives**
James W. Grimes (R) James Harlan (R)	William B. Allison (R) Grenville M. Dodge (R) Asahel W. Hubbard (R) William Loughridge (R) Hiram P. Rice (R) James F. Wilson (R)

Kansas	
Senators	**Representative**
Samuel C. Pomeroy (R) Edmund G. Ross (D)	Sidney Clarke (R)

Kentucky	
Senators	**Representatives**
Garrett Davis (W) James Guthrie (D) r. Feb. 1868 Thomas C. McCreery (D) s. 1868	George M. Adams (D) James B. Beck (D) Jacob S. Golladay (D) Asa P. Grover (D) Thomas L. Jones (D) J. Proctor Knott (D) Samuel McKee (R) s. 1868 Lawrence S. Trimble (D) s. 1868

Louisiana	
Senators	**Representatives**
John S. Harris (R) s. 1868 William P. Kellogg (R)	W. Jasper Blackburn (R) s. 1868 James Mann (D) d. 1868 Joseph P. Newsham (R) s. 1868 J. Hale Sypher (R) s. 1868 Michel Vidal (R) s. 1868

Maine	
Senators	**Representatives**
Lot M. Morrill (R) William P. Fessenden (W)	James G. Blaine (R) John Lynch (R) Sidney Perham (R) John A. Peters (R) Frederick A. Pike (R)

Maryland	
Senators	**Representatives**
Reverdy Johnson (D) r. July 1868 William P. Whyte (D) s. 1868 George Vickers (D) s. 1868	Stevenson Archer (D) Hiram McCullough (D) Charles E. Phelps (Con) Frederick Stone (D) Francis Thomas (R)

Massachusetts	
Senators	**Representatives**
Charles Sumner (R) Henry Wilson (Free-Soiler)	Oakes Ames John D. Baldwin (R) Nathaniel P. Banks (R) George S. Boutwell (R) Benjamin F. Butler (R) Henry L. Dawes Thomas D. Eliot (R) Samuel Hooper (R) Ginery Twichell (R) William B. Washburn (R)

Michigan	
Senators	**Representatives**
Zachariah Chandler (R) Jacob M. Howard (R)	Fernando C. Beaman (R) Austin Blair (R) John F. Driggs (R) Thomas W. Ferry (R) Rowland E. Trowbridge (R) Charles Upson (R)

Minnesota	
Senators	**Representatives**
Alexander Ramsey (R) Daniel S. Norton (Con)	William Windom (R) Ignatius Donnelly (R)

Mississippi	
Senators	**Representatives**
Vacant	Vacant

Missouri

Senators	Representatives
John B. Henderson (D) Charles D. Drake (R)	George W. Anderson (R) John F. Benjamin (R) Joseph J. Gravely (R) Joseph W. McClurg (Radical) r. 1868 Benjamin F. Loan (Radical) James R. McCormick (D) Carman A. Newcomb (R) Thomas E. Noell (Radical) d. Oct. 1867 William A. Pile (R) John H. Stover s. 1868 Robert T. Van Horn (R)

Nebraska

Senators	Representative
John M. Thayer (R) Thomas W. Tipton (R)	John Taffe (R)

Nevada

Senators	Representative
William M. Stewart (R) James W. Nye (R)	Delos R. Ashley (R)

New Hampshire

Senators	Representatives
Aaron H. Cragin (Amer) James W. Patterson (R)	Jacob Benton (R) Jacob H. Ela (R) Aaron F. Stevens (R)

New Jersey

Senators	Representatives
Alexander G. Cattell (R) Frederick T. Frelinghuysen (R)	Charles Haight (D) George A. Halsey (R) John Hill (R) William Moore (R) Charles Sitgreaves (D)

New York

Senators	Representatives
Edwin D. Morgan (R) Roscoe Conkling (R)	Alexander H. Bailey (R) Demas Barnes (D) James Brooks (D) John W. Chanler (D) John C. Churchill (R) Thomas Cornell (R) Orange Ferriss (R) William C. Fields (R) John Fox (D) John A. Griswold (R) Calvin T. Hulburd (R) James M. Humphrey (D) William H. Kelsey (R) John H. Ketcham (R) Addison H. Laflin (R) William S. Lincoln (R) Dennis McCarthy (R) James M. Marvin (Un) John Morrissey (D) Theodore M. Pomeroy (R) John V. L. Pruyn (D) William H. Robertson (R) William E. Robinson (D) Lewis Selye Thomas E. Stewart Stephen Taber (D) Henry Van Aernam (R) Burt Van Horn (R) Charles H. Van Wyck (R) Hamilton Ward (R) Fernando Wood (D)

North Carolina

Senators	Representatives
Joseph C. Abbott (R) s. 1868 John Pools. 1868	Nathaniel Boyden (R) s. 1868 John T. Deweese (D) s. 1868 Oliver H. Dockery (R) s. 1868 John R. French (R) s. 1868 David Heaton (R) s. 1868 Alexander H. Jones (R) s. 1868 Israel G. Lash (R) s. 1868

Ohio

Senators	Representatives
Benjamin F. Wade (R) John Sherman (R)	James M. Ashley (R) John Beatty (R) s. 1868 John A. Bingham (R) Ralph P. Buckland (R) Samuel F. Cary (R) Reader W. Clarke (R) Columbus Delano (R) s. 1868 Ephraim R. Eckley (R) Benjamin Eggleston (R) James A. Garfield (R) Cornelius S. Hamilton (R) d. Dec. 1867 Rutherford B. Hayes (R) r. July 1867 William Lawrence (R) George W. Morgan (D) r. Jun. 1868 William Mungen (D) Tobias A. Plants (R) Robert C. Schenck (R) Samuel Shellabarger (R) Rufus P. Spalding (D) Philadelph Van Trump (D) Martin Welker (R) John T. Wilson (R)

Oregon

Senators	Representative
George H. Williams (R) Henry W. Corbett (R)	Rufus Mallory (R)

Pennsylvania

Senators	Representatives
Charles R. Buckalew (D) Simon Cameron (R)	Benjamin M. Boyer (D) John M. Broomall (R) Henry L. Cake (R) John Covode (R) Charles Denison (D) d. June 1867 Oliver J. Dickey (R) s. 1868 Darwin A. Finney (R) d. Aug. 1868 J. Lawrence Getz (D) Adam J. Glossbrenner (D) William D. Kelley (R) William H. Koontz (R) George V. Lawrence (W) Ulysses Mercur (R) George F. Miller (R) James K. Moorhead Daniel J. Morrell (R) Leonard Myers (R) Charles O'Neill (R) S. Newton Pettis (R) s. 1868 Samuel J. Randall (D) Glenni W. Scofield (R) Thaddeus Stevens (R) d. Aug. 1868 Caleb N. Taylor (R) Daniel M. Van Auken (D)

(continued)

TABLE 9.11 (continued)

Senators	Representatives
	Thomas Williams (R) Stephen F. Wilson (R) George W. Woodward (D)
Rhode Island	
Senators	Representatives
Henry B. Athony (R) William Sprague (R)	Thomas A. Jenckes (R) Nathan F. Dixon (R)
South Carolina	
Senators	Representatives
Thomas J. Robertson (R) s. 1868 Frederick A. Sawyer (R) s. 1868	Christopher C. Bowen (R) s. 1868 M. Simeon Corley (R) s. 1868 James H. Goss (R) s. 1868 B. Frank Whittemore (R) s. 1868
Tennessee	
Senators	Representatives
Joseph S. Fowler (R) David T. Patterson (D)	Samuel M. Arnell (R) s. 1868 Roderick R. Butler (R) s. 1868 Isaac R. Hawkins (R) s. 1868 Horace Maynard (R) s. 1868 James Mullins (R) s. 1868 David A. Nunn (R) s. 1868 William B. Stokes (R) s. 1868 John Trimble (R) s. 1868
Texas	
Senators	Representatives
Vacant	Vacant
Vermont	
Senators	Representatives
George F. Edmunds (R) Justin S. Morrill (R)	Luke P. Poland (R) Worthington C. Smith (R) Frederick E. Woodbridge (R)
Virginia	
Senators	Representatives
Vacant	Vacant
West Virginia	
Senators	Representatives
Peter G. Van Winkle (Un) Waitman T. Willey (R)	Chester D. Hubbard (R) Bethuel M. Kitchen (R) Daniel H. Polsley (R)
Wisconsin	
Senators	Representatives
James R. Doolittle (R) Timothy O. Howe (R)	Charles A. Eldredge (D) Amasa Cobb (R) Benjamin F. Hopkins (R) Halbert E. Paine (R) Philetus Sawyer (R) Cadwallader C. Washburn (R)

Note: * D, Democrat; W, Whig; SRD, States Right Democrat; SRW, States Right Whig; R, Republican (after 1856); Un, Union Party (Civil War only); Amer, American or "Know-Nothing" Party. Some members did not serve a full term, usually because somebody died in office or resigned. Where that occurred: r, resigned; d, died in office.; s, started.

Source: Notable Names in American History: A Tabular Register, 3d ed. (Clifton, N.J.: James T. White, 1973), 92–120.

TABLE 9.12 FORTY-FIRST CONGRESS, MARCH 4, 1869, TO MARCH 3, 1871

President of the Senate	President Pro Tempore of the Senate	Speaker of the House of Representatives
Schuyler Colfax	Henry B. Anthony	James G. Blaine

Senators	Representatives
Alabama	
Senators	Representatives
George E. Spencer (R) Willard Warner (R)	Alfred E. Buck (R) Charles W. Buckley (R) Peter M. Dox (D) Charles Hays (R) Robert S. Heflin (R) William C. Sherrod (D)
Arkansas	
Senators	Representatives
Alexander McDonald (R) Benjamin F. Rice (R)	Thomas Boles (R) Anthony A. C. Rogers (D) Logan H. Roots (R)
California	
Senators	Representatives
Cornelius Cole (R) Eugene Casserly (D)	Samuel B. Axtell (D) James A. Johnson (D) Aaron A. Sargent (R)
Connecticut	
Senators	Representatives
Orris S. Ferry (R) William A. Buckingham (R)	William H. Barnum (D) Stephen W. Kellogg (R) Henry H. Starkweather (R) Julius L. Strong (R)
Delaware	
Senators	Representative
Willard Saulsbury (D) Thomas F. Bayard (D)	Benjamin T. Biggs (D)
Florida	
Senators	Representative
Thomas W. Osborn (R) Abijah Gilbert (R)	Charles M. Hamilton (R)
Georgia	
Senators	Representatives
Joshua Hill (R) s. 1871 Homer V. M. Miller (D) s. 1871	Marion Bethune (R) s. 1871 Stephen A. Corker (D) s. 1871 Jefferson F. Long (R) s. 1871 William W. Paine (D) s. 1871 William P. Price (D) s. 1871 Richard H. Whiteley (R) s. 1871 Pierce M. B. Young (D) s. 1871
Illinois	
Senators	Representatives
Lyman Trumbull (R) Richard Yates (R)	Horatio C. Burchard (R) Albert G. Burr (D) Burton C. Cook (R) John M. Crebs (D) Shelby M. Cullom (R) John F. Farnsworth (R)

	John B. Hawley (R) John B. Hay (R) Ebon C. Ingersoll (R) Norman B. Judd (R) Thompson W. McNeely (D) Samuel S. Marshall (D) Jesse H. Moore (R)

Indiana	
Senators	Representatives
Oliver H. P. T. Morton (R) Daniel D. Pratt (R)	John Coburn (R) William S. Holman (R) George W. Julian (R) Michael C. Kerr (D) William E. Niblack (D) Godlove S. Orth (R) Jasper Packard (R) John P. C. Shanks (R) James N. Tyner (R) Daniel W. Voorhees (D) William Williams (R)

Iowa	
Senators	Representatives
James W. Grimes (R) r. Dec. 1869 James B. Howell (R) s. 1870 James Harlan (R)	William B. Allison (R) William Loughridge (R) George W. McCrary (R) Frank W. Palmer (R) Charles Pomeroy (R) William Smyth (R) d. Sept. 1870 William P. Wolf (R) s. 1870

Kansas	
Senators	Representative
Samuel C. Pomeroy (R) Edmund G. Ross (D)	Sidney Clarke (R)

Kentucky	
Senators	Representatives
Garrett Davis (D) Thomas C. McCreery (D)	George M. Adams (D) James B. Beck (D) Jacob S. Golladay (D) r. Feb. 1870 Thomas L. Jones (D) J. Proctor Knott (D) Joseph H. Lewis (D) s. 1870 John M. Rice (D) William N. Sweeney (D) Lawrence S. Trimble (D) Boyd Winchester (D)

Louisiana	
Senators	Representatives
John S. Harris (R) William P. Kellogg (R)	Chester B. Darrall (R) s. 1870 Frank Morey (R) s. 1870 Joseph P. Newsham (R) s. 1870 Lionel A. Sheldon (R) J. Hale Sypher (R) s. 1870

Maine	
Senators	Representatives
William P. Fessenden d. Sept. 1869 Lot M. Morrill (R) s. Dec. 1869 Hannibal Hamlin (R)	James G. Blaine (R) Eugene Hale (R) John Lynch (R) Samuel P. Morrill (R) John A. Peters (R)

Maryland	
Senators	Representatives
George Vickers (D) William T. Hamilton (D)	Stevenson Archer (D) Samuel Hambleton (D) Patrick Hamill (D) Frederick Stone (D) Thomas Swann (D)

Massachusetts	
Senators	Representatives
Charles Sumner (R) Henry Wilson	Oakes Ames (R) Nathaniel P. Banks (R) George S. Boutwell (R) r. Mar. 1869 George M. Brooks (R) James Buffinton (R) Benjamin F. Butler (R) Henry L. Dawes George F. Hoar (R) Samuel Hooper (R) Ginery Twichell (R) William B. Wahsburn (R)

Michigan	
Senators	Representatives
Zachariah Chandler (R) Jacob M. Howard (R)	Fernado C. Beaman (R) Austin Blair (R) Omar D. Conger (R) Thomas W. Ferry (R) Randolph Strickland (R) William L. Stoughton (R)

Minnesota	
Senators	Representatives
Alexander Ramsey (R) Daniel S. Norton (Con) d. July 1870 William Windom (R) ta. 1870 Ozora P. Stearns (R) s. 1871	Morton S. Wilkinson (R) Eugene M. Wilson (D)

Mississippi	
Senators	Representatives
Hiram R. Revels (R) s. 1870 Adelbert Ames (R) s. 1870	Henry W. Barry (R) s. 1870 George E. Harris (R) s. 1870 George C. McKee (R) s. 1870 Joseph L. Morphis (R) s. 1870 Legrand W. Perce (R) s. 1870

Missouri	
Senators	Representatives
Charles D. Drake (R) r. Dec. 1870 Daniel T. Jewett (R) ta. 1870 Francis P. Blair, Jr. (D) s. 1871 Carl Schurz (R)	Joel F. Asper (R) John F. Benjamin (R) Sempronius H. Boyd Samuel S. Burdett (R) David P. Dyer (R) Gustavus A. Finkelnburg (R) James R. McCormick (D) Robert T. Van Horn (R) Erastus Wells (D)

(continued)

TABLE 9.12 (continued)

Nebraska

Senators	Representative
John M. Thayer (R) Thomas W. Tipton (D)	John Taffe (R)

Nevada

Senators	Representative
William M. Stewart (R) James W. Nye (R)	Thomas Fitch (R)

New Hampshire

Senators	Representatives
Aaron H. Cragin (Amer) James W. Patterson (R)	Jacob Benton (R) Jacob H. Ela (R) Aaron F. Stevens (R)

New Jersey

Senators	Representatives
Alexander G. Catell (R) John P. Stockton (D)	John T. Bird (D) Orestes Cleveland (D) Charles Haight (D) John Hill (R) William Moore (R)

New York

Senators	Representatives
Roscoe Conkling (R) Reuben E. Fenton (R)	Alexander H. Bailey (R) David S. Bennett (R) James Brooks (D) Hervey C. Calkin (D) John C. Churchill (R) George W. Cowles (R) Samuel S. Cox (D) Noah Davis (R) r. July 1870 Orange Ferriss (R) John Fisher (R) John Fox (D) George W. Greene (D) r. Feb. 1870 John A. Griswold (D) Charles H. Holmes (R) s. 1870 Giles W. Hotchkiss (R) William H. Kelsey (R) John H. Ketcham (R) Charles Knapp (R) Addison H. Laflin (R) Stephen L. Mayham (D) Dennis McCarthy (R) John Morrissey (D) Clarkson N. Potter (D) Henry A. Reeves (D) Stephen Sanford (R) John G. Schumaker (D) Porter Sheldon (R) Henry W. Slocum (D) Adolphus H. Tanner (R) Charles H. Van Wyck (R) s. 1870 Hamilton Ward (R) William A. Wheeler (R) Fernando Wood (D)

North Carolina

Senators	Representatives
Joseph C. Abbott (R) John Pool	Clinton L. Cobb (R) John T. Deweese (D) r. Feb. 1870 Joseph Dixon (R) s. 1870 Oliver H. Dockery (R) David Heaton (R) d. June 1870 Alexander H. Jones (R) Israel G. Lash (R) John Manning, Jr. (D) s. 1870 Francis E. Shober (D)

Ohio

Senators	Representatives
John Sherman (R) Allen G. Thurman (D)	Jacob A. Ambler (R) John Beatty (R) John A. Bingham (R) Edward F. Dickinson (D) James A. Garfield (R) Truman H. Hoag (D) d. Feb. 1870 William Lawrence (R) Eliakim H. Moore (R) George W. Morgan (D) William Mungen (D) Erasmus D. Peck (R) s. 1870 Robert C. Schenck (R) r. Jan. 1871 John A. Smith (R) Job E. Stevenson (R) Peter W. Strader (D) William H. Upson (R) Philadelph Van Trump (D) Martin Welker (R) John T. Wilson (R) James J. Winans (R)

Oregon

Senators	Representative
George H. Williams (R) Henry W. Corbett (R)	Joseph S. Smith (D)

Pennsylvania

Senators	Representatives
Simon Cameron (R) John Scott (R)	William H. Armstrong (R) Henry L. Cake (R) John Cessna (R) John Covode (R) s. 1870 d. Jan. 1871 Oliver J. Dickey (R) Joseph B. Donley (R) J. Lawrence Getz (D) Calvin W. Gilfillan (R) Richard J. Haldeman (D) William D. Kelley (R) Ulysses Mercur (R) John Moffet (D) r. Apr. 1869 Daniel J. Morrell (R) Leonard Myers (R) James S. Negley (R) Charles O'Neill (R) John R. Packer (R) Darwin Phelps (R) Samuel J. Randall (D) John R. Reading (R) r. Apr. 1870 Glenni W. Scofield (R) John D. Stiles (D) Caleb N. Taylor (R) s. 1870 Washington Townsend (R) Daniel M. Van Auken (D) George W. Woodward (D)

Rhode Island	
Senators	Representatives
Henry B. Anthony (R) William Sprague (R)	Thomas A. Jenckes (R) Nathan F. Fixon (R)

South Carolina	
Senators	Representatives
Thomas J. Robertson (R) Frederick A. Sawyer (R)	Christopher C. Bowen (R) Solomon L. Hoge (R) Joseph H. Rainey (R) s. 1870 Alexander S. Wallace (R) s. 1870 B. Frank Whittemore (R) r. Feb. 1870

Tennessee	
Senators	Representatives
Joseph S. Fowler (R) William G. Brownlow (R)	Samuel M. Arnell (R) Roderick R. Butler (R) Isaac R. Hawkins (R) Horace Maynard (R) William F. Prosser (R) William J. Smith (R) William B. Stokes (R) Lewis Tillman (R)

Texas	
Senators	Representatives
Morgan C. Hamilton (R) s. 1870 James W. Flanagan (R) s. 1870	William T. Clark (R) s. 1870 John C. Conner (D) s. 1870 Edward Degener (R) s. 1870 George W. Whitmore (R) s. 1870

Vermont	
Senators	Representatives
George F. Edmunds (R) Justin S. Morrill (R)	Luke P. Poland (R) Worthington C. Smith (R) Charles W. Willard (R)

Virginia	
Senators	Representatives
John W. Johnston (Con) s. 1870 John F. Lewis (R) s. 1870	Richard S. Ayer (R) s. 1870 George W. Booker (Con) s. 1870 Richard T. W. Duke (Con) s. 1870 James King Gibson (D) s. 1870 Lewis McKenzie (Un) s. 1870 William Milnes, Jr. (Con) s. 1870 James H. Platt, Jr. (R) s. 1870 Charles H. Porter (R) s. 1870 Robert Ridgway (Con) d. 1870

West Virginia	
Senators	Representatives
Waitman T. Willey (R) Arthur I. Boreman (R)	Isaac H. Duval (R) James C. McGrew (R) John S. Witcher (R)

Wisconsin	
Senators	Representatives
Timothy O. Howe (R) Matthew H. Carpenter (R)	David Atwood (R) s. 1870 Amasa Cobb (R) Charles A. Eldredge (D) Benjamin F. Hopkins (R) d. 1870 Halbert E. Paine (R) Philetus Sawyer (R) Cadwallader C. Washburn (R)

Note: * D, Democrat; W, Whig; SRD, States Right Democrat; SRW, States Right Whig; R, Republican (after 1856); Un, Union Party (Civil War only); Amer, American or "Know-Nothing" Party. Some members did not serve a full term, usually because somebody died in office or resigned. Where that occurred: r, resigned; d, died in office.; s, started.

Source: Notable Names in American History: A Tabular Register, 3d ed. (Clifton, N.J.: James T. White, 1973), 92–120.

TABLE 9.13 FORTY-SECOND CONGRESS, MARCH 4, 1871, TO MARCH 3, 1873

President of the Senate	President Pro Tempore of the Senate	Speaker of the House of Representatives
Schuyler Colfax	Henry B. Anthony	James G. Blaine

Alabama	
Senators	Representatives
George E. Spencer (R) George T. Goldthwaite (D) s. 1872	Charles W. Buckley (R) Peter M. Dox (D) William A. Handley s. 1872 Charles Hays (R) Joseph H. Stloss (D) Benjamin S. Turner (R)

Arkansas	
Senators	Representatives
Benjamin F. Rice (R) Powell Clayton (R)	Thomas Boles (R) s. 1872 John Edwards (R) r. Feb. 1872 James M. Hanks (D) Oliver P. Snyder (R)

California	
Senators	Representatives
Cornelius Cole (R) Eugene Casserly (D)	John M. Coghlan (R) Sherman O. Houghton (R) Aaron A. Sargent (R)

Connecticut	
Senators	Representatives
Orris S. Ferry (R) William A. Buckingham (R)	William H. Barnum (D) Joseph R. Hawley (R) s. Dec. 1872 Stephen W. Kellogg (R) Henry H. Starkweather (R) Julius L. Strong (R) d. Sept. 1872

Delaware	
Senators	Representative
Thomas F. Bayard (D) Eli Saulsbury (D)	Benjamin T. Biggs (D)

Florida	
Senators	Representatives
Thomas W. Osborn (R) Abijah Gilbert (R)	Silas L. Niblack (D) s. 1873 Josiah T. Walls (R) r. Jan. 1873

Georgia	
Senators	Representatives
Joshua Hill (R) Thomas M. Norwood (D)	Erasmus W. Beck (D) s. 1872 John S. Bigby (R) Dudley M. DuBose (D) Archibald T. MacIntyre (D) William P. Price (D) Thomas J. Speer (R) d. Aug. 1872 Richard H. Whiteley (R) Pierce M. B. Young

(continued)

TABLE 9.13 (continued)

Illinois	
Senators	**Representatives**
Lyman Trumbull (R) John A. Logan (R)	John L. Beveridge (R) r. Jan. 1873 Horatio C. Burchard (R) Burton C. Cook (R) r. Aug. 1871 John M. Crebs (D) John F. Farnsworth (R) Charles B. Farwell (R) John B. Hawley (R) John B. Hay (R) Thompson W. McNeeley (D) Samuel S. Marshall (D) Jesse H. Moore (D) Edward Y. Rice (R) James C. Robinson (D) Henry Snapp (R) Bradford N. Stevens (D)
Indiana	
Senators	**Representatives**
Oliver H. P. T. Morton (R) Daniel D. Pratt (D)	John Coburn (R) William S. Holman (D) Michael C. Kerr (D) Mahlon D. Manson (D) William E. Niblack (D) Jasper Packard (R) John P. C. Shanks (R) James N. Tyner (R) Daniel W. Voorhees (D) William Williams (R) Jeremiah M. Wilson (R)
Iowa	
Senators	**Representatives**
James Harlan (R) George G. Wright (R)	Aylett R. Cotton (R) William G. Donnan (R) George W. McCrary (R) Jackson Orr (R) Frank W. Palmer (R) Madison M. Walden (R)
Kansas	
Senators	**Representative**
Samuel C. Pomeroy (R) Alexander Caldwell (R)	David P. Lowe (R)
Kentucky	
Senators	**Representatives**
Garrett Davis (D) d. Sept. 1872 Willis B. Machen (D) s. 1872 John W. Stevenson (D)	George M. Adams (D) William E. Arthur (D) James B. Beck (D) Edward Crossland (D) Joseph H. Lewis (D) Henry D. McHenry (D) William B. Read (D) John M. Rice (D) Boyd Winchester (D)
Louisiana	
Senators	**Representatives**
William P. Kellogg (R) r. Nov. 1872 J. Rodman West (R)	Aleck Boarman (Lib) s. 1872 Chester B. Darrall (R) James McCleery (D) d. Nov. 1871 Frank Morey (R) Lionel A. Sheldon (R) J. Hale Sypher (R)
Maine	
Senators	**Representatives**
Hannibal Hamlin (R) Lot M. Morrill (R)	James G. Blaine (R) William P. Frye (R) Eugene Hale (R) John Lynch (R) John A. Peters (R)
Maryland	
Senators	**Representatives**
George Vickers (D) William T. Hamilton (D)	Stevenson Archer (D) Samuel Hambleton (D) William M. Merrick (D) John Ritchie (D) Thomas Swann (D)
Massachusetts	
Senators	**Representatives**
Charles Sumner (R) Henry Wilson r. Mar. 1873	Oakes Ames (R) Nathaniel P. Banks (R) George M. Brooks (R) r. May 1872 James Buffinton (R) Benjamin F. Butler (R) Alvah Crocker (R) s. 1872 Henry L. Dawes Constantine C. Esty (R) s. 1872 George F. Hoar (R) Samuel Hooper (R) Ginery Twichell (R) William B. Washburn (R) r. Dec. 1871
Michigan	
Senators	**Representatives**
Zachariah Chandler (R) Thomas W. Ferry (R)	Austin Blair (R) Omar D. Conger (R) Wilder D. Foster (R) William L. Stoughton (R) Jabez G. Sutherland (D) Henry Waldron (R)
Minnesota	
Senators	**Representatives**
Alexander Ramsey (R) William Windom (R)	John T. Averill (R) Mark H. Dunnell (R)
Mississippi	
Senators	**Representatives**
Adelbert Ames (R) James L. Alcorn (R)	Henry W. Barry (R) George E. Harris (R) George C. McKee (R) Joseph L. Morphis (R Legrand W. Perce (R)
Missouri	
Senators	**Representatives**
Carl Schurz (R) Francis P. Blair, Jr. (D)	James G. Blair (D) Samuel S. Burdett (R) Abram Comingo (D) Gustavus A. Finkelnburg (R) Harrison E. Havens (R) Andrew King (D) James R. McCormick (D) Isaac C. Parker (R) Erastus Wells (D)

Nebraska	
Senators	Representative
Thomas W. Tipton (D) Phineas W. Hitchcock (R)	John Taffee (R)

Nevada	
Senators	Representative
William M. Stewart (R) James W. Nye (R)	Charles W. Kendall (D)

New Hampshire	
Senators	Representatives
Aaron H. Cragin (Amer) James W. Patterson (R)	Samuel N. Bell (D) Ellery A. Hibbard (D) Hosea W. Parker (D)

New Jersey	
Senators	Representatives
John P. Stockton (D) Frederick T. Frelinghuysen (R)	John T. Bird (D) Samuel C. Forker (D) George A. Halsey (R) John W. Hazelton (R) John Hill (R)

New York	
Senators	Representatives
Roscoe Conkling (R) Reuben E. Fenton (R)	James Brooks (D) John M. Carroll (D) Freeman Clarke (R) Samuel S. Cox (D) R. Holland Duell (R) Smith Ely, Jr. (D) Milo Goodrich (R) John H. Ketcham (R) Thomas Kinsella (D) William H. Lamport (R) William E. Lansing (R) Clinton L. Merriam (R) Eli Perry (D) Clarkson N. Potter (D) Elizur H. Prindle (R) Ellis H. Roberts (R) William R. Roberts (D) John Rogers (D) Robert B. Roosevelt (D) Charles St. John (R) John E. Seeley (R) Walter L. Sessions (R) Henry W. Slocum (D) H. Boardman Smith (R) Dwight Townsend (D) Joseph H. Tuthill (D) Seth Wakeman (R) Joseph M. Warren (D) William A. Wheeler (R) William Williams (D) Fernando Wood (D)

North Carolina	
Senators	Representatives
John Pool Matt W. Ransom (D) s. 1872	Clinton L. Cobb (R) James C. Harper (Con) James M. Leach (Con) Sion H. Rogers (D) s. 1872 Francis E. Shober (D) Charles R. Thomas (R) Alfred M. Waddell (D)

Ohio	
Senators	Representatives
John Sherman (R) Allen G. Thurman (D)	Jacob A. Ambler (R) John Beatty (R) John A. Bingham (R) Lewis D. Campbell (D) Ozro J. Dodds (D) s. 1872 Charles Foster (R) James A. Garfield (R) Charles N. Lamison (D) John F. McKinney (D) James Monroe (R) George W. Morgan (D) Erasmus D. Peck (R) Aaron F. Perry (R) r. 1872 Samuel Shellabarger John A. Smith (R) William P. Sprague (R) Job E. Stevenson (R) William H. Upson (R) Philadelph Van Trump (D) John T. Wilson (R)

Oregon	
Senators	Representative
Henry W. Corbett (R) James K. Kelly (D)	James H. Slater (D)

Pennsylvania	
Senators	Representatives
Simon Cameron (R) John Scott (R)	Ephraim L. Acker (R) Frank C. Bunnell s. 1873 John V. Creely (R) Oliver J. Dickey (R) Henry D. Foster (D) J. Lawrence Getz (D) Samuel Griffith (D) Richard J. Haldeman (D) Alfred C. Harmer (R) William D. Kelley (R) John W. Killinger (R) William McClelland (D) Ebenezer McJunkin (R) Ulysses Mercur (R) r. Dec. 1872 Benjamin F. Meyers (D) Leonard Myers (R) James S. Negley (R) John B. Packer (R) Samuel J. Randall (D) Glenni W. Scofield (R) Henry Sherwood (D) Lazarus D. Schoemaker (R) R. Milton Speer (D) John B. Storm (D) Washington Townsend (R)

Rhode Island	
Senators	Representatives
Henry B. Anthony (R) William Sprague (R)	Benjamin T. Eames (R) James M. Pendleton (R)

South Carolina	
Senators	Representatives
Thomas J. Robertson (R) Frederick A. Sawyer (R)	Robert C. De Large (R) r. Jan. 1873 Robert B. Elliott (R) Joseph H. Rainey (R) Alexander S. Wallace (R)

(continued)

TABLE 9.13 (continued)

Tennessee	
Senators	**Representatives**
William G. Brownlow (R) Henry Cooper (D)	John M. Bright (D) Roderick R. Butler (R) Robert P. Caldwell (D) Abraham E. Garrett Edward I. Golladay (D) Horace Maynard (R) William W. Vaughan (D) Washington C. Whitthorne (D)
Texas	
Senators	**Representatives**
Morgan C. Hamilton (R) James W. Flanagan (R)	William T. Clark (R) s. 1872 John C. Conner (D) De Witt C. Giddings (D) s. 1872 John Hancock (D) William S. Herndon (D)
Vermont	
Senators	**Representatives**
George F. Edmunds (R) Justin S. Morrill (R)	Luke P. Poland (R) Worthington C. Smith (R) Charles W. Willard (R)
Virginia	
Senators	**Representatives**
John W. Johnston (Con) John F. Lewis (R)	Elliott M. Braxton (D) John Critcher (Con) Richard T. W. Duke (Con) John T. Harris (D) James H. Platt, Jr. (R) Charles H. Porter (R) William H. H. Stowell (R) William Terry (Con)
West Virginia	
Senators	**Representatives**
Arthur I. Boreman (R) Henry G. Davis (D)	John J. Davis (D) Frank Hereford (D) James C. McGrew (R)
Wisconsin	
Senators	**Representatives**
Timothy O. Howe (R) Matthew H. Carpenter (R)	J. Allen Barber (R) Charles A. Eldredge (D) Gerry W. Hazelton (R) Alexander Mitchell (D) Jeremiah M. Rusk (R) Philetus Sawyer (R)

TABLE 9.14 FORTY-THIRD CONGRESS, MARCH 4, 1873, TO MARCH 3, 1875

President of the Senate	Presidents Pro Tempore of the Senate	Speaker of the House of Representatives
Henry Wilson	Matthew H. Carpenter Henry B. Anthony	James G. Blaine

Alabama	
Senators	**Representatives**
George E. Spencer (R) George T. Goldthwaite (D)	Frederick G. Bromberg (D) John H. Caldwell (D) Charles Hays (R) Charles Pelham (R) James T. Rapier (R) Joseph H. Sloss (D)
Arkansas	
Senators	**Representatives**
Powell Clayton (R) Stephen W. Dorsey (R)	Thomas M. Gunter (D) s. 1874 Asa Hodges (R) s. 1874 Oliver P. Snyder (R) William W. Wilshire (R) r. June 1874
California	
Senators	**Representatives**
Eugene Casserly (D) r. Nov. 1873 John S. Hager (D) s. 1874 Aaron A. Sargent (R)	Charles Clayton (R) Sherman O. Hougton (R) John K. Luttrell (D) Horace F. Page (R)
Connecticut	
Senators	**Representatives**
Orris S. Ferry (R) William A. Buckingham (R) d. 1875 William W. Eaton (D) s. 1875	William H. Barnum (D) Joseph R. Hawley (R) Stephen W. Kellogg (R) Henry H. Starkweather (R)
Delaware	
Senators	**Representative**
Thomas F. Bayard (D) Eli Saulsbury (D)	James R. Lofland (R)
Florida	
Senators	**Representatives**
Abijah Gilbert (R) Simon B. Conover (R)	William J. Purman (R) r. Jan. 1875 Josiah T. Walls (R)
Georgia	
Senators	**Representatives**
Thomas M. Norwood (D) John B. Gordon (D)	Hiram P. Bell (D) James H. Blount (D) Philip Cook (D) James C. Freeman (D) Henry R. Harris (D) Morgan Rawls (D) r. Mar. 1874 Andrew Sloan (R) s. 1874 Alexander H. Stephens (D) s. 1874 Richard H. Whiteley (R) Pierce M. B. Young (D)

Illinois	
Senators	**Representatives**
John A. Logan (R) Richard J. Oglesby (R)	Granville Barrere (R) Horatio C. Burchard (R) Joseph G. Cannon (R) Bernard G. Caulfield (D) s. 1875 Isaac Clements (R) Franklin Corwin (R) John R. Eden (D) Charles B. Farwell (R) Greenbury L. Fort (R) John B. Hawley (R) Stephen A. Hurlbut (R) Robert M. Knapp (D) John McNulta (R) Samuel S. Marshall (D) James S. Martin (D) William R. Morrison (D) William H. Ray (R) John B. Rice (D) d. 1874 James C. Robinson (D) Jasper D. Ward (D)

Indiana	
Senators	**Representatives**
Oliver H. P. T. Morton (R) Daniel D. Pratt (R)	Thomas J. Cason (D) John Coburn (D) William S. Holman (D) Morton C. Hunter (R) William E. Niblack (D) Godlove S. Orth (R) Jasper Packard (R) John P. C. Shanks (R) Henry B. Sayler (R) James N. Tyner (R) Jeremiah M. Wilson (R) William Williams (R) Simeon K. Wolfe (D)

Iowa	
Senators	**Representatives**
George G. Wright (R) William B. Allison (R)	Aylett R. Cotton (R) William G. Donnan (R) John A. Kasson (R) William Loughridge (R) George W. McCrary (R) James W. McDill (R) Henry O. Pratt (R) Jackson Orr (R) James Wilson (R)

Kansas	
Senators	**Representatives**
Alexander Caldwell (R) r. Mar. 1873 Robert Crozier (R) ta. 1873 James M. Harvey (R) s. 1874 John J. Ingalls (R)	Stephen A. Cobb (R) David P. Lowe (R) William A. Phillips (R)

Kentucky	
Senators	**Representatives**
John W. Stevenson (D) Thomas C. McCreery (D)	George M. Adams (D) William E. Arthur (D) James B. Beck (D) John Y. Brown (D) Edward Crossland (D) Milton J. Durham (D) Charles W. Milliken (D) William B. Read (D) Elisha D. Standiford (D) John D. Young (D)

Louisiana	
Senators	**Representatives**
J. Rodman West (R) Vacant	Chester B. Darrall (R) Effingham Lawrence (D) s. 1875 Frank Morey (R) Lionel A. Sheldon (R) George A. Sheridan (Lib) s. 1875 George L. Smith (R) J. Hale Sypher (R)

Maine	
Senators	**Representatives**
Hannibal Hamlin (R) Lot M. Morrill (R)	James G. Blaine (R) John H. Burleigh (R) William P. Frye (R) Eugene Hale (R) Samuel Hersey (R) d. Feb. 1875

Maryland	
Senators	**Representatives**
William T. Hamilton (D) George R. Dennis (D)	William J. Albert (R) Stevenson Archer (D) Lloyd Lowndes, Jr. (R) William J. O'Brien (D) Thomas Swann (D) Ephraim K. Wilson (D)

Massachusetts	
Senators	**Representatives**
Charles Sumner (R) d. Mar. 1874 William B. Washburn (R) s. 1874 George S. Boutwell (R)	James Buffinton (R) Benjamin F. Butler (R) Alvah Crocker (R) d. Dec. 1874 Henry L. Dawes Daniel W. Gooch (R) Benjamin W. Harris (R) Ebenezer R. Hoar (R) George F. Hoar (R) Samuel Hooper (R) d. Feb. 1875 Henry L. Pierce (R) Charles A. Stevens William Whiting (R) d. June 1873 John M. S. Williams (R)

Michigan	
Senators	**Representatives**
Zachariah Chandler (R) Thomas W. Ferry (R)	Josiah W. Begole (R) Nathan B. Bradley (R) Julius C. Burrows (R) Omar D. Conger (R) Moses W. Field (R) Jay A. Hubbell (R) Henry Waldron (R) George Willard (R) William B. Williams (R)

Minnesota	
Senators	**Representatives**
Alexander Ramsey (R) William Windom (R)	John T. Averill (R) Mark H. Dunnell (R) Horace B. Strait (R)

(continued)

TABLE 9.14 (continued)

Mississippi	
Senators	**Representatives**
Adelbert Ames (R) r. Jan. 1874 Henry R. Pease (R) s. 1874 James L. Alcorn (R)	Henry W. Barry (R) Albert R. Howe (R) Lucius Q. C. Lamar (D) John R. Lynch (R) George C. McKee (R) Jason Niles (R)

Missouri	
Senators	**Representatives**
Carl Schurz (R) Lewis V. Bogy (D)	Richard P. Bland (D) Aylett H. Buckner (D) John B. Clark, Jr. (D) Abram Comingo (D) Thomas T. Crittenden (D) John M. Glover (D) Robert A. Hatcher (D) Harrison E. Havens (R) Ira B. Hyde (R) Isaac C. Parker (R) Edwin O. Stanard (R) William H. Stone (D) Erastus Wells (D)

Nebraska	
Senators	**Representative**
Thomas W. Tipton (D) Phileas W. Hitchcock (R)	Lorenzo Crounse (R)

Nevada	
Senators	**Representative**
William M. Stewart (R) John P. Jones (R)	Charles W. Kendall (D)

New Hampshire	
Senators	**Representatives**
Aaron H. Cragin (Amer) Bainbridge Wadleigh (R)	Hosea W. Parker (D) Austin F. Pike (R) William B. Small (R)

New Jersey	
Senators	**Representatives**
John P. Stockton (D) Frederick T. Frelinghuysen (R)	Amos Clark, Jr. (R) Samuel A. Dobbins (R) Robert Hamilton (D) John W. Hazelton (R) William W. Phelps (R) Isaac W. Scudder (R) Marcus L. Ward (R)

New York	
Senators	**Representatives**
Roscoe Conkling (R) Reuben E. Fenton (R)	Lyman K. Bass (R) James Brooks (D) d. Apr. 1873 Simeon B. Chittenden (R) s. 1874 Freeman Clarke (R) Samuel S. Cox (D) Thomas J. Creamer (D) Philip S. Crooke (R) David M. De Witt (D) R. Holland Duell (R) Robert S. Hale (R) Henry H. Hathorn (R) George G. Hoskins (R) William H. Lamport (R) William E. Lansing (R) John D. Lawson (R) Clinton MacDougall (R) David B. Mellish (R) d. May 1874 Clinton L. Merriam (R) Eli Perry (D) Thomas C. Platt (R) Clarkson N. Potter (D) Ellis H. Roberts (R) William R. Roberts (D) Charles St. John (R) Richard Schell (D) s. 1874 John G. Schumaker (D) Henry J. Scudder (R) Walter L. Sessions James S. Smart (R) H. Boardman Smith (R) Lyman Tremain (R) William A. Wheeler (R) John O. Whitehouse (D) David Wilber (R) Fernando Wood (D) Stewart L. Woodford (R) r. 1874

North Carolina	
Senators	**Representatives**
Matt W. Ransom (D) Augustus S. Merrimon	Thomas S. Ashe (Con) Clinton L. Cobb (R) James M. Leach (Con) William M. Robbins (D) William A. Smith (R) Charles R. Thomas (R) Robert B. Vance (D) Alfred M. Waddell (D)

Ohio	
Senators	**Representatives**
John Sherman Allen G. Thurman (D)	Henry B. Banning (D) John Berry (D) Hezekiah S. Bundy (R) Lorenzo Danford (R) William E. Finck (D) s. 1874 Charles Foster (R) James A. Garfield (R) Lewis B. Gunckel (R) Hugh J. Jewett (D) r. June 1874 Charles N. Lamison (D) William Lawrence (R) James Monroe (R) Lawrence T. Neal (D) Richard C. Parsons (R) James W. Robinson (R) Milton Sayler (D) Isaac R. Sherwood (R) John Q. Smith (R) Milton I. Southard (D) William P. Sprague (R) Laurin D. Woodworth (D)

Oregon	
Senators	**Representatives**
James K. Kelly (D) John H. Mitchell (R)	James W. Nesmith (D) Joseph G. Wilson (R) d. July 1873

Pennsylvania	
Senators	**Representatives**
Simon Cameron (R) John Scott (R)	Charles Albright (R) James S. Biery (R) John Cessna (R)

	Hiester Clymer (D) Carlton B. Curtis (R) Alfred C. Harmer (R) William D. Kelley (R) John W. Killinger (D) Ebenezer McJunkin (R) r. Jan. 1875 John A. Magee (D) William S. Moore (R) Leonard Myers (R) James S. Negley (R) Charles O'Neill (R) John B. Packer (R) Samuel J. Randall (D) Hiram L. Richmond (R) Sobieski Ross (R) Glenni W. Scofield (R) Lazarus D. Shoemaker (R) A. Herr Smith (R) R. Milton Speer (D) John B. Storm (D) James D. Strawbridge (R) Alexander W. Taylor (R) John M. Thompson (R) s. 1875 Lemuel Todd (R) Washington Townsend (R)
Rhode Island	
Senators	Representatives
Henry B. Anthony (R) William Sprague (R)	Benjamin T. Eames (R) James M. Pendleton (R)
South Carolina	
Senators	Representatives
Thomas J. Robertson (R) John J. Patterson (R)	Richard H. Cain (R) Lewis C. Carpenter (R) s. 1874 Robert B. Elliott (R) r. Nov. 1874 Joseph H. Rainey (R) Alonzo J. Ransier (R) Alexander S. Wallace (R)
Tennessee	
Senators	Representatives
William G. Brownlow (R) Henry Cooper (D)	John D. C. Atlins (D) John M. Bright (D) Roderick R. Butler (R) William Crutchfield (R) Horace H. Harrison (R) Barbour Lewis (R) Horace Maynard (R) David A. Nunn (R) Jacob M. Thornburgh (R) Washington C. Whitthorne (D)
Texas	
Senators	Representatives
Morgan C. Hamilton (R) James W. Flanagan (R)	De Witt C. Giddings (D) John Hancock (D) William S. Herndon (D) William P. McLean (D) Roger Q. Mills (D) Asa H. Willie (D)
Vermont	
Senators	Representatives
George F. Edmunds (R) Justin S. Morrill (R)	George W. Hendee (R) Luke P. Poland (R) Charles W. Willard (R)

Virginia	
Senators	Representatives
John W. Johnston (Con) John F. Lewis (R)	Rees T. Bowen (Con) Alexander M. Davis r. Mar. 1874 John T. Harris (D) Eppa Hunton (D) James H. Platt, Jr. (R) James B. Sener (R) J. Amber Smith (R) William H. H. Stowell (R) Christoper Y. Thomas (R) s. 1874 Thomas Whitehead (Con)
West Virginia	
Senators	Representatives
Arthur I. Boreman (R) Henry G. Davis (D)	John J. Davis (D) s. 1874 John M. Hagans (R) s. 1874 Frank Hereford (D)
Wisconsin	
Senators	Representatives
Timothy O. Howe (R) Matthew H. Carpenter (R)	J. Allen Barber (R) Charles A. Eldredge (D) Gerry W. Hazelton (R) Alexander S. McDill (R) Alexander Mitchell (R) Jeremiah M. Rusk (R) Philetus Sawyer (R) Charles G. Williams (R)

Note: * D, Democrat; W, Whig; SRD, States Right Democrat; SRW, States Right Whig; R, Republican (after 1856); Un, Union Party (Civil War only); Amer, American or "Know-Nothing" Party. Some members did not serve a full term, usually because somebody died in office or resigned. Where that occurred: r, resigned; d, died in office.; s, started.

Source: Notable Names in American History: A Tabular Register, 3d ed. (Clifton, N.J.: James T. White, 1973), 92–120.

TABLE 9.15 FORTY-FOURTH CONGRESS, MARCH 4, 1875, TO MARCH 3, 1877

President of the Senate	President Pro Tempore of the Senate	Speakers of the House of Representatives
Henry Wilson	Thomas W. Ferry	Michael C. Kerr Samuel J. Randall

Alabama	
Senators	Representatives
George E. Spencer (R) George T. Goldthwaite (D)	Taul Bradford (D) John H. Caldwell (D) William H. Forney (D) Jeremiah Haralson (R) Charles Hays (R) Goldsmith W. Hewitt (D) Burwell B. Lewis (D) Jeremiah N. Williams (D)
Arkansas	
Senators	Representatives
Powell Clayton (R) Stephen W. Dorsey (R)	Lucien C. Gause (D) Thomas M. Gunter (D) William F. Slemons (D) William W. Wilshire (R)
California	
Senators	Representatives
Aaron A. Sargent (R) Newton Booth (Anti-Monopolist)	John K. Luttrell (D) Horace F. Page (R) William A. Piper (D) Peter D. Wigginton (D)
Colorado	
Senators	Representative
Jerome B. Chaffee (R) s. 1876 Henry M. Teller (R) s. 1876	James B. Belford (R) s. 1877
Connecticut	
Senators	Representatives
Orris S. Ferry (R, D) d. Nov. 1875 James E. English (D) ta. 1875 William H. Barnum (D) s. 1876 William W. Eaton (D)	William H. Barnum (D) r. May 1876 George M. Landers (D) James Phelps (D) Henry H. Starkweather (R) d. Jan. 1876 John T. Wait (R) s. 1876 Levi Warner (D) s. 1876
Delaware	
Senators	Representative
Thomas F. Bayard (D) Eli Saulsbury (D)	James Williams (D)
Florida	
Senators	Representatives
Simon B. Conover (R) Charles W. Jones (D)	Jesse J. Finley (D) s. 1876 William J. Purman (R) Josiah T. Walls (R) r. Apr. 1876
Georgia	
Senators	Representatives
Thomas M. Norwood (D) John B. Gordon (D)	James H. Blount (D) Milton A. Candler (D) Philip Cook (D) William H. Felton (D) Henry R. Harris (D) Julian Hartridge (D) Benjamin H. Hill (D) William E. Smith (D) Alexander H. Stephens (D)
Illinois	
Senators	Representatives
John A. Logan (R) Richard J. Oglesby (R)	William B. Anderson (D) John C. Bagby (R) Horatio C. Burchard (R) Alexander Campbell Joseph G. Cannon (R) Bernard G. Caulfield (D) John R. Eden (D) Charles B. Farwell (R) r. May 1876 Greenbury L. Fort (R) Carter H. Harrison (D) William Hartzell (D) Thomas J. Henderson (R) Stephen A. Hurlbut (R) John V. Le Moyne (R) s. 1876 William R. Morrison (D) William A. J. Sparks (D) William M. Springer (D) Adlai E. Stevenson (D) Richard H. Whiting (R) Scott Wike (D)
Indiana	
Senators	Representatives
Oliver H. P. T. Morton (R) Joseph E. McDonald (D)	John H. Baker (R) Nathan T. Carr (D) s. 1876 Thomas J. Cason (R) James L. Evans (R) Benoni S. Fuller (D) Andrew H. Hamilton (D) William S. Haymond (D) William S. Holman (D) Andrew Humphreys (D) s. 1876 Morton C. Hunter (R) Michael C. Kerr (D) d. Aug. 1876 Franklin Landers (D) Jeptha D. New (D) Milton S. Robinson (R) James D. Williams (D) r. Dec. 1876
Iowa	
Senators	Representatives
George G. Wright (R) William B. Allison (R)	Lucien L. Ainsworth (Anti-Monopolist) John A. Kasson (R) George W. McCrary (R) James W. McDill (R) S. Addison Oliver (R) Henry O. Pratt (R) Ezekiel S. Sampson (R) John Q. Tufts (R) James Wilson (R)
Kansas	
Senators	Representatives
John J. Ingalls (R) James M. Harvey (R)	William R. Brown (R) John R. Goodin (D) William A. Phillips (R)
Kentucky	
Senators	Representatives
John W. Stevenson (D) Thomas C. McCreery (D)	Joseph C. S. Blackburn (D) Andrew R. Boone (D) John Y. Brown (D)

	John B. Clarke (D) Milton J. Durham (D) Thomas L. Jones (D) J. Proctor Knott (D) Charles W. Milliken (D) Edward Y. Parsons (D) d. July 1876 Henry Watterson (D) s. 1876 John D. White (R)

Louisiana	
Senators	**Representatives**
J. Rodman West (R) James B. Eustis (D) s. 1876	Chester B. Darrall (R) E. John Ellis (D) Randall L. Gibson (D) William M. Levy (D) Frank Morey (R) r. June 1876 Charles E. Nash (R) William B. Spencer (D) s. 1876 r. Jan. 1877

Maine	
Senators	**Representatives**
Hannibal Hamlin (R) Lot M. Morrill (R) r. July 1876 James G. Blaine (R) s. 1876	James G. Blaine (R) r. July 1876 John H. Burleigh (R) Edwin Flye (R) s. 1876 William P. Frye (R) Eugene Hale (R) Harris M. Plaisted (R)

Maryland	
Senators	**Representatives**
George R. Dennis (D) William P. Whyte (D)	Eli J. Henkle (D) William J. O'Brien (D) Charles B. Roberts (D) Thomas Swann (D) Philip F. Thomas (D) William Walsh (D)

Massachusetts	
Senators	**Representatives**
George S. Boutwell (R) Henry L. Dawes (R)	Josiah G. Abbott (D) s. 1876 Nathaniel P. Banks (R) Chester W. Chapin (D) William W. Crapo (R) Rufus S. Frost (R) r. July 1876 Benjamin W. Harris (R) George F. Hoar (R) Henry L. Pierce (R) Julius H. Seelye John K. Tarbox (D) Charles P. Thompson (D) William W. Warren (D)

Michigan	
Senators	**Representatives**
Thomas W. Ferry (R) Isaac P. Christiancy (R)	Nathan B. Bradley (R) Omar D. Conger (R) George H. Durand (D) Jay A. Hubbell (R) Allen Potter Henry Waldron (R) George Willard (R) Alpheus S. Williams (D) William B. Williams (R)

Minnesota	
Senators	**Representatives**
William Windom (R) Samuel J. R. McMillan (R)	Mark H. Dunnell (R) William S. King (R) Horace B. Strait (R)

Mississippi	
Senators	**Representatives**
James L. Alcorn (R) Blanche K. Bruce (R)	Charles E. Hooker (D) Lucius Q. C. Lamar (D) John R. Lynch (R) Hernando D. Money (D) Otho R. Singleton (D) G. Wiley Wells (R)

Missouri	
Senators	**Representatives**
Lewis V. Bogy (D) Francis M. Cockrell (D)	Richard P. Bland (D) Aylett H. Buckner (D) John B. Clark, Jr. (D) Rezin A. De Bolt (D) Benjamin J. Franklin (D) John M. Glover (D) Robert A. Hatcher (D) Edward C. Kehr (D) Charles H. Morgan (D) John F. Philips (D) David Rea (D) William H. Stone (D) Erastus Wells (D)

Nebraska	
Senators	**Representative**
Phineas W. Hitchock Algernon S. Paddock (R)	Lorenzo Crounse (R)

Nevada	
Senators	**Representative**
John P. Jones (R) William Sharon (R)	William Woodburn (R)

New Hampshire	
Senators	**Representatives**
Aaron H. Cragin (Amer) Bainbridge Wadleigh (R)	Samuel N. Bell (D) Henry W. Blair (R) Frank Jones (D)

New Jersey	
Senators	**Representatives**
Frederick T. Frelinghuysen (R) Theodore F. Randolph (D)	Samuel A. Dobbins (R) Augustus W. Cutler (D) Robert Hamilton (D) Augustus A. Hardenbergh (D) Miles Ross (D) Clement H. Sinnickson (R) Frederick H. Teese (D)

New York	
Senators	**Representatives**
Roscoe Conkling (R) Francis Kernan (D)	Charles H. Adams (R) George A. Bagley (R) John H. Bagley, Jr. (D) William H. Baker (R) Lyman K. Bass (R) George M. Beebe (D) Archibald M. Bliss (D) Simeon B. Chittendin (R) Samuel S. Cox (D) John M. Davy (R) Smith Ely, Jr., (D) r. Dec. 1876 David Dudley Field (D) s. 1877

(continued)

TABLE 9.15 (continued)

Senators	Representatives
	Henry H. Hathorn (R) Abram S. Hewitt (D) George G. Hoskins (R) Elbridge G. Lapham (R) Elias W. Leavenworth (R) Scott Lord (D) Clinton D. MacDougall (R) Edwin R. Meade (D) Henry B. Metcalfe (D) Samuel F. Miller (R) Nelson I. Norton (R) N. Holmes Odell (D) Thomas C. Platt (R) John G. Schumaker (D) Martin I. Townsend (R) Charles C. B. Walker (D) Elijah Ward (D) William A. Wheeler (R) John O. Whitehouse (D) Andrew Williams (R) Benjamin A. Willis Fernando Wood (D)
North Carolina	
Senators	Representatives
Matt W. Ransom (D) Augustus S. Merrimon (D)	Thomas S. Ashe (D) Joseph J. Davis (D) John A. Hyman (R) William M. Robbins (D) Alfred M. Scales (D) Robert B. Vance (D) Alfred M. Waddell (D) Jesse J. Yeates (D)
Ohio	
Senators	Representatives
John Sherman (R) Allen G. Thurman (D)	Henry B. Banning (D) Jacob P. Cowan Lorenzo Danford (R) Charles Foster (R) James Garfield (R) Frank H. Hurd (D) William Lawrence (R) John A. McMahon (D) James Monroe (R) Lawrence T. Neal (D) Henry B. Payne (D) Earley F. Poppleton (D) Americus V. Rice (D) John S. Savage (D) Milton Sayler (D) Milton I. Southard (D) John L. Vance (D) Nelson H. Van Vorhes (R) Ansel T. Walling (D) Laurin D. Woodworth (R)
Oregon	
Senators	Representatives
James K. Kelly (D) John H. Mitchell (R)	George A. La Dow (D) d. May 1875 La Fayette Lane (D)
Pennsylvania	
Senators	Representatives
Simon Cameron (R) William A. Wallace (D)	Hiester Clymer (D) Alexander G. Cochran (D) Francis D. Collins (D) Albert G. Egbert (D) Chapman Freeman (R) James H. Hopkins (D) George A. Jenks (D) William D. Kelley (R) Winthrop W. Ketchum (R) r. July 1876 Levi A. Mackey (D) Levi Maish (D) William Mutchler (D) Charles O'Neill (R) John B. Packer (R) Joseph Powell (D) Samuel J. Randall (D) James B. Reilly (D) John Reilly (D) John Robbins (R) Sobieski Ross (R) James Sheakley (D) A. Herr Smith (R) William H. Stanton (D) s. 1876 William S. Stenger (D) Washington Townsend (R) Jacob Turney (D) John W. Wallace (R) Alan Wood, Jr. (R)
Rhode Island	
Senators	Representatives
Henry B. Anthony (R) Ambrose E. Burnside (R)	Latimer W. Ballou (R) Benjamin T. Eames (R)
South Carolina	
Senators	Representatives
Thomas J. Robertson (R) John J. Patterson (R)	Charles W. Buttz (R) s. 1877 Solomon L. Hoge (R) Edmund W. M. Mackey (R) r. July 1876 Joseph H. Rainey (R) Robert Smalls (R) Alexander S. Wallace (R)
Tennessee	
Senators	Representatives
Henry Cooper (D) Andrew Johnson (D) d. July 1875 David M. Key (D) ta. 1875 James E. Bailey (D) s. 1877	John D. C. Atkins (D) John M. Bright (D) William P. Caldwell (D) George G. Dibrell (D) John F. House (D) William McFarland (D) Haywood Y. Riddle (D) s. 1876 Jacob M. Thornburgh (R) Washington C. Whitthorne (D) H. Casey Young (D)
Texas	
Senators	Representatives
Morgan C. Hamilton (R) Samuel B. Maxey (D)	David B. Culberson (D) John Hancock (D) Roger Q. Mills (D) John H. Reagan (D) Gustave Schleicher (D) James W. Throckmorton (D)
Vermont	
Senators	Representatives
George F. Edmunds (R) Justin S. Morrill (R)	Dudley C. Denison (R) George W. Hendee (R) Charles H. Joyce (R)

Virginia	
Senators	Representatives
John W. Johnston (Con) Robert E. Withers (Con)	George C. Cabell (D) Beverly B. Douglas (Con) John Goode, Jr. (D) John T. Harris (D) Eppa Hunton (D) William H. H. Stowell (R) William Terry (Con) John R. Tucker (D) Gilbert C. Walker (Con)
West Virginia	
Senators	Representatives
Henry G. Davis (D) Allen T. Caperton (D) d. July 1876 Samuel Price ta. 1876 Frank Hereford (D) s. 1877	Charles J. Faulkner (D) Frank Hereford (D) r. Jan. 1877 Benjamin Wilson (D)
Wisconsin	
Senators	Representatives
Timothy O. Howe (R) Angus Cameron (R)	Samuel D. Burchard (D) Lucien B. Caswell (R) George W. Cate Alanson M. Kimball (R) William P. Lynde (D) Henry S. Magoon (R) Jeremiah M. Rusk (R) Charles G. Williams (R)

Note: * D, Democrat; W, Whig; SRD, States Right Democrat; SRW, States Right Whig; R, Republican (after 1856); Un, Union Party (Civil War only); Amer, American or "Know-Nothing" Party. Some members did not serve a full term, usually because somebody died in office or resigned. Where that occurred: r, resigned; d, died in office.; s, started.
Source: Notable Names in American History: A Tabular Register, 3d ed. (Clifton, N.J.: James T. White, 1973), 92–120.

Party Realignment

A major reordering of the established two-party system occurred in the 1850s. The stage was set in the 1844 presidential election when the Southern plantation aristocracy cemented its control of the Democratic Party. Henceforward it would be known as the party of the South, motivated by the twin principles of states' rights and slavery, no longer a truly national party. Urban political machines in Northern cities—built on immigrants and industrial workers—battled the Southerners for control, but they only succeeded in causing a deep split that threatened to destroy the party of Andrew Jackson for good. The rise of the Republicans as the "opposition party" in the 1850s was a natural outgrowth of these developments.

The Whigs, who had held down the opposition role in the two-party system since 1832, began a swift decline after they opposed the U.S.-Mexican War (1846–48) and dragged their feet on western expansion. They also failed to forge a distinctive identity on any issue or rally around any single national leader.

In the key election year of 1852 voters punished their representatives for the hated Compromise of 1850, heaping most of their wrath on the Whigs. The party split into "Conscience Whigs" and "Cotton Whigs," tried to reprise their successful campaign strategy of 1840 and 1848 by backing a military hero (Winfield Scott) for president but found themselves permanently out of favor with the electorate.

The Whigs were replaced briefly as No. 2 party by the American Party, better known to history as the "Know-Nothings" because of their cryptic answer to questions about their platform. They were a single-issue party based on nativism and never became a permanent force in national politics. The flood of immigration that had been washing onto American shores for several years had crystallized xenophobic fears into a loose political organization that had its strongest support in the big cities of the East.

Seldom in U.S. history have the issues dividing the parties been so clear-cut as during the 1850s. There was no middle of the road. Whether the issue was slavery, immigration restriction, or religion, the battle lines were clearly drawn. And the issues even lent themselves readily to sloganeering: The Democrats were sneeringly referred to by their opponents as the party of "Slavery, rum, and Romanism," while the Know-Nothings became the champions of "Freedom, temperance, and Protestantism."

The short-lived American or Know-Nothing Party was soon superseded as the "other" major party in national politics by the Republicans, who progressed from a grass-roots movement to national status in record time. Founded in 1854 in the Midwest, they ran a candidate in the 1856 presidential election, John C. Frémont, who won 33 percent of the popular vote. Four years later the Republican Abraham Lincoln captured the presidency with 40 percent of the popular vote in a four-way race. After 1860 the third and final realignment of the U.S. two-party system into Democrats and Republicans was set in stone. A process that had begun with the death of the Whigs and the temporary ascendancy of the American Party was now complete.

The Rise and Fall of Third Parties

America was a hodgepodge of political parties and factions in this era. The end of party unity opened the door to a host of third-party movements that sprang up like weeds amid the rubble of the second two-party system. The general contrariness of Americans coupled with the explosive political situation led angry groups to break away from the major parties and create new organizations composed of "true believers." Jumping parties, either as a form of protest or just out of political expediency, became a common practice. William H. Hoppin of Rhode Island was elected governor in three successive elections in the 1850s by running on three different tickets (Whig, Know-Nothing, Republican). Indeed, the fluidity of the party structure was one of the most notable features of this period. The historian J. David Gillespie has called the 19th century "the third-party golden age" in U.S. history, and the middle years were the most active period. Among the splinter groups that rose and fell during these years, most staying around no more than one or two election cycles, were the Liberty Party, Union Democrats, Liberal Republicans, Conservative Democrats, Free-Soilers, Prohibitionists, and Know-Nothings. Each was organized around a single issue and driven by a sense that the leaders of the major parties were all apostates.

The Liberty Party arrived on the scene in 1840, the Free-Soil Party in 1847, then the American Party or "Know-Nothings" at the end of the decade. The first two were antislavery movements; the third was a nativist movement. All three drew their strength from both major parties but hurt the Whigs more than the Democrats. The Free-Soil Party won 10 percent of the popular vote in 1848; the Know-Nothings, 21 percent in 1856.

After the explosive Kansas-Nebraska Act of 1854, new partisan groups sprang up with names such as "Anti-Nebraska Men, "the "People's Party," or the "Anti-Slavery Party." None of these could claim a galvanizing leader like a Thomas Jefferson or an Andrew Jackson; they were grassroots movements with little organization or structure, just a strong antipathy toward the two major parties. Third parties tended to rise and fall rapidly, appearing on the scene in a burst of passion, then fading as rapidly as the passions that gave birth to them. Most of these movements were doomed from the start, but they propelled certain issues to the forefront and shaped national debate while trying to push their way into the mainstream. Some represented protest movements; others, reform movements; others were simply fringe groups with a particular grievance. To their credit all attempted to play by the established electoral rules of U.S. politics. Only the Republicans and the Know-Nothings successfully made the leap from third-party to major-party status, and only the Republicans became a permanent fixture on the political scene. It is fair to say no single-issue local movement ever reached the big leagues and stayed competitive.

TABLE 9.16 THIRD-PARTY MOVEMENTS IN U.S. POLITICS, 1850–1875

Group/Party	Organized	Major Issue(s) and Platform	Leadership (Source of Political Support)	Largest Number of Votes (or Percentage) in Any Presidential Election	Fate
Free Soil	1848	Opposed expansion of slavery into territories	Martin Van Buren; John P. Hale; George W. Julian ("Barnburner" Democrats, Northern abolitionists, former Liberty Party members and antislavery Whigs)	10.12% (1848)	Absorbed by Republican Party after mid-1850s
American Party (Know-Nothings)[a]	1849	Exclusion of foreigners and Catholics from public office; raising of residency requirement for naturalization from five to 21 years; complete immigration ban on "paupers, criminals, idiots, lunatics, insane and blind persons."	Millard Fillmore; George D. Prentice of Ky.; Henry J. Gardner of Mass. (nativists, xenophobes, anti-Catholics)	21.53% (1856)	Split after 1856 over slavery issue, with antislavery element's joining of Republican Party
"Silver Grays"	1850	Anti–Compromise of 1850; pro-Union; moderate on slavery	Disaffected Whigs; significant only in New York State	None	Could not break through on national level; joined Know-Nothings in 1856, then absorbed by Constitutional Union Party in 1860
Unionist	1851	Preserve Union with guarantees for slavery	Alexander H. Stephens, Robert Toombs, and Howell Cobb, all of Ga.	None (limited to Southern state and local elections)	Southern faction in Congress that disappeared after 1851–53 term
States Rights	1851	Secession-minded faction of Democratic Party	Robert Barnwell Rhett, John A. Quitman, and William L. Yancey	None (limited to Southern state and local elections)	Southern faction in Congress that disappeared after one congressional election
Constitutional Union	1860	Preservation of federal union with constitutional guarantees for slavery	John Bell of Tenn. (Former Whigs and Know-Nothings)	12.61% (1860)	One-shot party; elected members to Congress but collapsed as national party after election of Lincoln

Group/Party	Organized	Major Issue(s) and Platform	Leadership (Source of Political Support)	Largest Number of Votes (or Percentage) in Any Presidential Election	Fate
Southern Democratic	1860	Protection of slavery with constitutional amendment or secession	John Breckinridge of Ky. (plantation aristocracy, Southern nationalist; states' righters)	18.09% (1860)	Died when Southern states seceded after election of Lincoln
National Union	Mid-1863 (first national convention, June 1864)	Bipartisan support for war aims of Lincoln administration: preservation of Union, emancipation of slaves, and mild reconstruction	Abraham Lincoln (1864–65); Govs. John Brough (Ohio), Oliver P. Morton (Ind.) Andrew Johnson (Tenn.)	55% of popular vote for Lincoln–Johnson ticket in 1864	Second national convention in 1866 victim of centrifugal pull of two major parties and traditional loyalties
Independent Republican	1864	Opposed reelection of Lincoln	John C. Frémont	N/A	Died after reelection of Lincoln
National Prohibition	1869 (Sep. 1)	End manufacture and sale of alcoholic beverages	James Black (moral fundamentalists; conservative Protestants); 500 founders from 20 states	5,607 Popular votes, no electoral votes (1872)	Still in existence; third oldest national U.S. party
The Readjusters	1870	Taxation and debt relief, education	William Mahone (Va. poor blacks and white farmers)	N/A (state-centered)	Reached high tide in 1879 state elections; faded in 1880s
Liberal Republican	1872	Opposed reelection of U.S. Grant, domination of party by commercial interests, and widespread corruption	Horace Greeley, B. Gratz Brown	N/A	One-shot party, buried by majority wing of Republican Party
National Labor and Reform	1872	Anticorruption, workers' rights	Urban working class	N/A	Absorbed into two major parties
"Straight Democratic Party"	1872 (Only national convention Sep. 3)	Opposed "fusion" with Liberal Republicans; favored ending congressional Reconstruction and returning home rule to South	Charles O'Connor (N.Y.) and John Quincy Adams II (Mass.) conservative, old-style ("Bourbon") Democrats	N/A	Reunited with "Alliance Democrats," continued to oppose Republicans as other half of two-party system

[a] The party was first dubbed the Native American Party when it was formed in 1853, then renamed the American Party at its national convention in 1855. But it was more commonly known by its unofficial nickname, "Know-Nothings," which was based on its secretiveness about its political agenda and principles.
Sources: J. David Gillespie, *Politics at the Periphery* (Columbia: University of South Carolina Press, 1993), passim; Chris Cook and David Waller, *The Longman Handbook of Modern American History* (New York: Addison Wesley Longman, 1998), 99; Samuel Eliot Morison, Henry Steele Commager, and William E. Leuchtenburg, *The Growth of the American Republic,* vol. 1, 6th ed. (New York: Oxford University Press, 1969), passim; Edward L Ayers, *The Promise of the New South* (New York: Oxford University Press, 1992), passim.

The Politics of Violence

In addition to breaking up political parties, the slave debate had another unfortunate result: It drove reason and decorum out of the national discourse. Violent passions replaced calm deliberations, abetted by two facts: First, elections were public in those days; Second, there were no gun control laws to keep guns off the streets and out of public assemblies. At election time each party printed its own distinctive ballots and handed them out to voters, who then went to the polling places, marked the ballots, and handed them to election officers sitting at their party's table. Such an open process, in which everyone knew how everyone else voted, made it easy to intimidate voters and even take over polling places. The fact that poll watchers were often armed, drunk, and/or belligerent heightened the likelihood of confrontation.

Even the hallowed halls of Congress were not immune to the climate of violence. Behavior usually associated with frontier saloons occurred in the chamber of the U.S. Senate. In 1850 Mississippi senator Henry Foote pulled a pistol on Missouri senator Thomas Hart Benton during debates over the Compromise of 1850. Six years later in a more famous incident known as the "Sumner-Brooks affair," the South Carolina representative Preston Brooks took a cane to Senator Charles Sumner of Massachusetts while Sumner was sitting at his desk on the Senate floor. Afterward, it was said, all members began to go around armed. But the most spectacular brouhaha in the history of the Congress occurred in the early morning hours of February 6, 1858, after another round of angry debate over the issue of slavery. The Republican Galusha Grow of Pennsylvania made the mistake of walking through the Democratic side of the House, where he was cursed and attacked by a Democrat, Lawrence Keitt. Other representatives quickly joined in, producing a full-scale brawl in the chamber before participants disengaged themselves.

After Southern Democrats withdrew from Congress in late 1860 and early 1861, conflict among the nation's representatives simmered down to the more traditional verbal invective salted with occasional sarcasm. The truce continued through Reconstruction, although with some close calls.

In this fanciful depiction a Northern magazine ridicules Southern "Arguments of Chivalry." The image characterizes the 1856 incident when Representative Preston Brooks of South Carolina took a cane to Massachusetts senator Charles Sumner on the floor of the Senate, putting him out of commission for months. The illustration's caption gives Henry Ward Beecher's words: "The symbol of the North is the pen; the symbol of the South is the bludgeon." (Library of Congress, Prints and Photographs Division [LC-USZ62-38851])

The Issues

Slavery in the Territories

The slavery debate before the Civil War was not couched in terms of whether to continue slavery or do away with it where it already existed, but whether to allow its extension into the new western territories. The Missouri Compromise had seemed to settle that issue in 1820 by designating those territories open to slavery versus those closed to it. But the Mexican Cession reopened the question by expanding the boundaries of the United States all the way to the Pacific Ocean. After California entered the Union as a free state in 1850, attention turned to the Great Plains, particularly the Nebraska Territory. This area was not only projected to become the home for tens of thousands of Americans, but the likeliest route for building a transcontinental railroad. Whether it eventually entered the Union as one state or several, its elected representatives would sit in Congress and vote on the great national issues. The question was, Would they vote with the North or the South?

On January 4, 1854, Congress took up the issue of the Nebraska Territory bill. When the debate stalled, Northern and Southern negotiators agreed to divide the area into two separate territories, Kansas and Nebraska, and leave the slave question to the voters of each territory (popular sovereignty). In May the Kansas-Nebraska bill was passed into law, setting the stage for the long-running tragedy known as "Bleeding Kansas," when the two sides battled for control of the territory in a dress rehearsal for the Civil War.

General Zachary Taylor, as he appeared while commanding U.S. forces during the 1847 drive on Mexico City. Success in Mexico catapulted Taylor into the White House in 1848, and his premature death in 1850 sparked the beginning of a decade-long sectional crisis. (Lithograph from portrait by Alonzo Chappel print from author's collection)

The women's rights pioneer Lucretia Mott (1793–1880), looking stern and very proper in her bonnet from an unidentified 1849 illustration. Mott was described as "The Impersonation of Righteousness and sympathy with the victims of wrong." (Tennessee State Library and Archives)

Temperance and Women's Rights

While slavery practically monopolized national politics, some other issues sought to push their way to center stage. The flame of social and political reform first fanned during the Jacksonian period generated more heat than light in the 1850s. The broad spirit of reform waned, to be replaced by more narrowly focused movements with firm agendas. Leading the list of noble causes that motivated large numbers of Americans were abolitionism, temperance, and women's rights. To outsiders the temperance movement seemed as mild as milquetoast compared to abolitionism. After a rousing start in Maine, the movement picked up speed during the 1850s. Thirteen more states followed Maine's example by enacting laws that prohibited the manufacture and sale of liquor.

The celebrated "age of the common man" before the Civil War owed much of the progress it achieved to the "common woman." Yet women's rights was an issue that barely registered for the majority of Americans at this time. It seemed a tempest in a teapot compared to the more "manly" political issues of the day. Not even all reform-minded women rushed to join the crusade for women's rights. Although outspoken and progressive women were at the forefront of every major reform movement, a surprising lack of unity prevailed among women in to respect to their own interests. There was broad support among women for the practical objectives of legal equality and the twin rights to vote and hold office. But in regard to social equality or equality in the workplace, the consensus evaporated along with whatever support they had among the menfolk.

This era opened with the first women's right convention (1848 at Seneca Falls, New York), still a topic of conversation because the attendees issued the first public call for universal woman suffrage. The movement sputtered in the 1850s, but after 1848 a national gathering was held every year to inspire the troops, map out strategies, and focus on new objectives. These conventions sparked much lobbying on the state level, which led to more favorable property laws and divorce laws and raised the consciousness of legislators on the twin issues of voting and holding office. The first success on the voting front finally occurred in 1869 in the Wyoming Territory.

Immigration and Manifest Destiny

As abolition, temperance, and women's rights did, the issue of immigration stirred up strong feelings, but the so-called reformers were more xenophobic than visionary. Immigration restriction was such an emotional issue that, as with slavery, there could be no rational debate on it; one was either for it or against it. A significant and highly vocal segment of the polity, believing that immigration was the greatest problem facing the nation, formed the "Know-Nothing" Party in 1854, actually more of a secret society than a national party. They were anti-immigration in general but were especially hostile to Catholics, whom they believed to be traitors and conspirators. The Know-Nothings were raucous and violence-prone but nonetheless enjoyed a rowdy sort of popularity that was more evident in riots and rallies than at the ballot box. Still, they exercised power on the municipal level in Washington, D.C.; Baltimore, Maryland; and St. Louis, Missouri, among other cities; they were the majority party in the Massachusetts legislature in 1854 and that same year gained control over the Washington National Monument Association and used it to block construction of the monument to the nation's first president. In 1856 they held their first and last national convention, nominating the former Whig president Millard Fillmore as their candidate for president. Fillmore placed a poor third in the November balloting, but the party could still take pride in winning 20 percent of the popular vote. That was their high-water mark. In 1858 the party split irrevocably between pro- and antislavery factions and disbanded.

Manifest Destiny was the last major issue driving the nationalist sentiment in politics in the antebellum period. As articulated by the newspaper editor John L. O'Sullivan in 1845, it was the belief that "no nation on earth should be allowed to interfere with America's manifest destiny to overspread the continent allotted by Providence for the free development of our yearly multiplying millions." With the oratorical bombast wrung out of it, it was nothing more than good old-fashioned imperialism, but it had a profound effect on both foreign policy and domestic politics. Americans cast covetous eyes on Mexico, Cuba, and much of Central America. In particular, the Southern plantation aristocracy saw territorial expansion into the Caribbean and south of the Rio Grande as a good way to draw in new slaveholding states.

The intellectual wing of the manifest destiny movement was led by a vague, "romantically" inclined group who called themselves Young America. They were an element within the Democratic Party who espoused the cause of liberty, democracy (white man's), commercial development, and territorial expansion, all without seeing any contradiction in their beliefs. Ralph Waldo Emerson in 1844 had first given wide currency to the name. They represented something more than a slogan but less than an organized movement: the "young, overpowering spirit of the country," as one Boston editor described it. Their chosen name suggested a progressive new generation who would lead the country to new heights of power and prosperity. They dismissed the despotism of the Old World and spoke of expanding markets and the march of progress. Although they were a part of the Democratic Party, unlike old-fashioned Democrats, they were sympathetic to the development of commerce and industry and new technology such as the railroad and the telegraph. This put them in the forefront of economic developments at mid-century, but the growing sectional crisis muted their message and took the steam out of their movement.

Filibustering

Manifest Destiny and slavery merged to create the filibustering phenomenon of the 1850s. Filibusters were armed expeditions, privately mounted, that aimed to seize territory in neighboring countries through naked conquest. The individuals who led such groups were called filibusterers, from the Spanish word *filibustero,* meaning "adventurer" or "pirate." British officials denounced U.S. filibusterers as "the advance guard of Manifest Destiny" and criticized the U.S. government for routinely looking the other way. The practice enjoyed support in Washington, D.C., from Presidents Pierce and Buchanan, Secretary of War Jefferson Davis, Senator John Slidell of Louisiana, and the diplomat Pierre Soulé, among others. Apart from dubious moral justification, armed invasion of foreign territory was contrary to U.S. neutrality laws, but this did not deter such demagogues as John A. Quitman and William Walker, who openly recruited their private armies from among Southern gentlemen, unprincipled adventurers, and fugitives from justice. New Orleans was the unofficial capital of the filibustering movement. These early-day "freedom fighters" hurt America's democratic image abroad and seriouly damaged relations with Spain and Britain in particular. A series of bloody failures in Cuba in 1851 and Central America later in the decade took a lot of the steam out of the movement, then the Civil War came along to provide employment for would-be soldiers. By the end of the war public opinion had soured on Manifest Destiny, Reconstruction dominated national politics, and filibustering ceased to be a problem. But for more than a decade filibustering was practically an instrument of U.S. policy, albeit a covert one.

TABLE 9.17 FILIBUSTERERS AND WOULD-BE FILIBUSTERERS, 1840–1873

Name(s)	Background	Takeover Target	Political Objective	Date(s)	Results
Col. Joseph A. White and the American Volunteers Regiment	Former captain of 13th Infantry Regiment during U.S.-Mexican War	Yucatán (Mexico)	Land and adventure	1848–49	Wiped out in fighting with local Indian tribes
Narciso López	Venezuelan adventurer and former general	Cuba	Liberatation of Cuba from Spain and annexation to United States	1849	Prevented from leaving New York City by federal authorities
Jane McManus Cazneau (Cora Montgomery)	Author, newspaperwoman, wife of Gen. William. L. Cazneau, U.S. government agent	Mexico, Cuba, and Dominican Republic (Santo Domingo)	Expansion of U.S. territory and spread of democracy in Latin America through forceful annexation	1850–70	Working largely undercover as agent provocateur with husband, intrigues that produced nothing of substance
José Mariá Jesús Carvajal	Mexican expatriate adventurer	Mexico	Seize northern Mexico and set up independent republic	1851–53	Gave up after two failed attempts and two arrests by U.S. authorities

Name(s)	Background	Takeover Target	Political Objective	Date(s)	Results
Gen. Juan José Flores ("the Father of Ecuador") and Captain Aleck Bell	Flores was one of Simón Bolívar's top generals during wars of liberation versus Spain, then president of Ecuador; Bell, an Alabamian, was a veteran of U.S.-Mexican War	Ecuador	Regain presidency and power in Republic of Ecuador	1851	Americans betrayed by their native allies, turned over to authorities, disarmed,and deported to Panama
Gaston Raoux de Raousset-Boulbon	Aristocratic French adventurer	Northern Mexico (state of Sonora)	Carve out colony in Sonora; annex it to France	1852–53	Became sick; returned to California in failure
William Walker	Flamboyant Tenn. soldier of fortune; champion of slavery and Manifest Destiny	Baja California and Mexican state of Sonora Nicaragua	Create republic with himself as president Form Central American federation of slave states allied to United States Restore his personal rule	Fall 1853 1855–57 1860	Failed; fled back to U.S. territory; tried for violating 1838 U.S. neutrality law; acquitted Victorious initially; rules as dictator; overthrown by regional coalition; exiled Captured and executed by Honduran firing squad
John A. Quitman	Career soldier known as Mississippi Hotspur; Mexican War general; government of Missi.	Cuba	Liberate Cuba by force and transform it into new slave state; ultimately to ensure "safety to the South and its institutions"	1851 1853–54	Forced to resign as government when indicted by federal grand jury for conspiracy Plans doomed by threat of legal prosecution and lack of funds
Henry L. Kinney	Self-styled "colonel"; Tex. land speculator, rancher, and trader	Nicaragua (the Mosquito Coast)	Establish personal fief on 30-million-acre land grant	Aug.–Sep. 1855	Financial ruin; returned to Tex. in disgrace
Henry A. Crabb	U.S. adventurer	Northern Mexico (state of Sonora)	Carve out independent republic in Sonora	1857	Betrayed by Mexican associate, captured, and executed, Apr. 1857
Chatham Roberdeau Wheat	Colonel; New Orleans lawyer and soldier of fortune, never more than second in command	Cuba, Nicaragua, northern Mexico	Expand Southern slave system in the name of "liberty"	1852–55	Survived several failed expeditions to fight in Civil War for Confederate States of America
George Washington Lafayette Beckley	U.S. general and leader of Knights of the Golden Circle	Mexico	Create "Americanized and Southernized empire" on Caribbean littoral	1860–61	Reached planning stage only; derailed by Civil War
Sterling Price and Joseph O. Shelby	Confederate generals who refused to surrender in 1865	Mexico	Establish colony of former Confederates in Mexico ("Carlota") under Emperor Maximillian	1865–67	Returned to United States after Maximillian overthrown by Juaristas
Charles Fry	U.S. sea captain (the *Virginius*)	Cuba	Liberation from Spain followed by United States annexation	Oct.–Nov. 1873	*Virginius* captured at sea by Spain; 53 executed, deported; war scare with Spain ended by Protocol of Nov. 28, 1873

Sources: Charles H. Brown, *Agents of Manifest Destiny* (New York and Chapel Hill: University of North Carolina Press, 1980); Edward S. Wallace, *Destiny and Glory* (New York: Coward-McCann, 1957), passim.

Presidential Elections

If overheated passions and fractured parties made conducting normal business in Congress difficult, they made choosing a president almost impossible. The national nominating conventions, which had done the job effectively for two decades, were by the 1850s political brawls in which old-fashioned wheeling and dealing were replaced by endless argument and frequent walkouts. Nominating a candidate under such circumstances took the Democrats 49 ballots in 1852. Then in 1860 they split into two groups and convened in different cities, where each proceeded to nominate its own candidate. Even "Abraham Lincoln" was a third-ballot selection of the Republicans in 1860. The Civil War settled many questions but not how to maintain party unity at election time. The Democrats in 1872 tried to avoid the problem and sneak back into the White House through the back door by endorsing the candidate of the third-party Liberal Republicans, Horace Greeley. That did not work either.

All six of the presidential elections during this era revolved around the sectional crisis and/or festering racial issues. The debate over the Compromise of 1850 and the Kansas-Nebraska Act of 1854 drove the elections of 1852 and 1856, respectively. Abolitionist outrage over the 1857 *Dred Scott* decision was a major impetus to Lincoln's election in 1860, and the status of the freedmen was an issue in both 1868 and 1872. Only after 1876 did the twin demons of race and sectionalism fade from presidential politics.

Presidential candidates in that day and age were at least spared the necessity of making endless campaign appearances on the hustings. They left those up to their lieutenants. It was not only impractical to go gallivanting around the country but unnecessary, because elections were determined in smoke-filled rooms by party leaders. Public campaigning among the common people was also considered undignified for anyone who would be president, however much candidates might pay lip service to that ideal. This is why the Lincoln-Douglas debates of 1858 were such an event; people were not accustomed to seeing their candidates for national office in person. But when it came time to run for president in 1860, Lincoln, the man lauded as "the Great Rail-Splitter," stayed at home in Springfield, Illinois, while state party organizers conducted a spirited campaign in his name organized around the usual rallies, barbecues, and parades.

The election of 1860 was one of only a handful of genuine four-way races in U.S. history. Others were in 1824, 1912, and 1948.) The four candidates—Abraham Lincoln, Stephen Douglas, John C. Breckenridge, and John Bell—split the popular vote so hopelessly that the winner (Lincoln) entered the White House as a "minority president" after garnering only 40 percent of the total. This election result dangerously weakened his mandate in responding to the twin crises of secession and civil war that faced the nation.

During just four years Lincoln did much to create the modern "imperial presidency" with all its enormous unwritten powers. He made the office more powerful than anyone before him had by suspending habeas corpus without congressional approval, dismissing representative assemblies by force, ordering the incarceration of citizens who criticized government policy, and allowing trials of civilians by military tribunals in areas where the civil courts were still functioning. The fact that he got away with it says much about Lincoln's hard-won popularity with the electorate and the dire threat to the Union posed by his opponents.

A peculiar characteristic of U.S. politics that stands out during this period is a fondness for elevating military heroes to the White House, in the mistaken belief that anyone who can run a military operation successfully can also master the political system. The erstwhile general Zachary Taylor, elected in 1848, died in office, with no chance to prove or disprove the theory convincingly. Another U.S.-Mexican War hero, Winfield Scott, was the choice of the Republicans in 1856; the failed Union general George B. McClellan was tapped by the Democrats in 1864; and the fabulously successful Union general Ulysses Grant was entrusted with the nation's highest office twice (1868, 1872). In the course of eight incompetent years Grant did more to lay to rest the myth that military talent translates into political success than any other president in U.S. history before or since. He proved a disaster in the White House, ranked by most scholars as one of the worst presidents ever.

This portrait of Senator Stephen A. Douglas of Illinois was taken by Mathew Brady or one of his assistants, probably at his Washington, D.C., studio, sometime between 1844 and 1860. Known as the Little Giant, Douglas's presidential ambitions were thwarted by sectionalism and his fellow Illinoisan Abe Lincoln. (Library of Congress, Prints and Photographs Division [LC-USZ62-110141])

With the exception of Lincoln, the six presidents between 1850 and 1875 are, likewise, among the weakest in U.S. history. The record shows that they were not equal to the task of governing the nation at this critical juncture. Three of them, Fillmore, Pierce, and Buchanan, are virtual nonentities, and two, Johnson and Grant, are remembered for their failures in office: Johnson never had a handle on Reconstruction, and Grant presided over the most corrupt administration in U.S. history until Warren G. Harding's. Two of these presidents, Fillmore and Johnson, were "accidental presidents," a status that helps explain their lack of solid accomplishment: The people never elected them, and they were not chosen for the second place on the ticket for their presidential qualities.

The un-Lincolnesque five were as unpopular with the electorate as they have been with historians. Among the five 19th-century presidents who as incumbents sought their party's nomination for another term but were denied, three were from this group: Fillmore, Pierce, and Johnson. When a political party turns its back on its own president, preferring to take their chances with an unknown, both the president and the party are in serious trouble.

TABLE 9.18 PRESIDENTIAL ELECTIONS, 1848–1876

Year	Number of States in Union	Percentage of Voter Turnout[a]	Candidates[b]	Party	Popular Vote	Percentage of Popular Vote[c]	Electoral Votes	Percentage of Electoral Vote
1848	30	72.7	**Zachary Taylor**	Whig	1,360,967	47.4	163	56.10
			Lewis Cass	Democrat	1,222,342	42.5	127	43.90
			Martin Van Buren	Free Soil	291,263	10.1	0	N/A
1852	31	69.6	**Franklin Pierce**	Democrat	1,601,117	50.9	254	85.80
			Winfield Scott	Whig	1,385,453	44.1	42	14.20
			John P. Hale	Free Soil	155,825	N/A	0	N/A
1856	31	78.9	**James Buchanan**	Democrat	1,832,955	45.3	174	58.80
			John C. Frémont	Republican	1,339,932	33.1	114	38.50
			Millard Fillmore	American (Know-Nothing)	871,731	21.6	8	2.70
1860	33	81.2	**Abraham Lincoln**	Republican	1,865,593	39.8	180	59.52
			Stephen A. Douglas	Democrat	1,382,713	29.5	12	3.95
			John C. Breckinridge	Southern Democrat	848,356	18.1	72[d]	23.76
			John Bell	Constitutional Union	592,906	12.6	39	12.87
1864	36	73.8	**Abraham Lincoln**	Unionist	2,206,938	55.0	212	90.99
			George B. McClellan	Democrat	1,803,787	45.0	21	9.01
			John C. Frémont	Radical Republican	Unknown	N/A	0	N/A
			(Not voted)	N/A	N/A	N/A	81	N/A
1868	37	78.1	**Ulysses S. Grant**	Republican	3,013,421	52.7	214	72.99
			Horatio Seymour	Democrat	2,706,829	47.3	80	27.01
			(Not voted)	N/A	N/A	N/A	23	N/A
1872	37	71.3	**Ulysses S. Grant**	Republican	3,596,745	55.6	286	71.94
			Horace Greeley (B. Gratz Brown)[e]	Democrat	2,834,761	43.83	66 (18)[f]	16.6 (4.53)[g]
			Horace Greeley (B. Gratz Brown)[e]	Liberal Republican	Same[h]	Same	Same	Same
			Charles O'Connor	Straight Democrat	29,489	0.46	0	N/A
			Thomas A. Hendricks	Independent-Democrat	N/A	N/A	42	10.58
			Charles J. Jenkins	Democrat	N/A	N/A	2	0.50
			David Davis	Democrat	N/A	N/A	1	0.25
			James Black	Prohibition Party	5,607	0.09	0	N/A
			(Not voted)	N/A	N/A	N/A	17	N/A
1876	38	81.8	**Rutherford B. Hayes**	Republican	4,036,572	48.0	185	50.25
			Samuel J. Tilden	Democrat	4,284,020	51.0	184	49.75
			Peter Cooper	Greenback	81,737	N/A	0	N/A

[a] Winners' names are in **boldface** type.
[b] Candidates receiving less than 1% of the popular vote are not included; therefore, total popular vote may not add up to 100 percent.
[c] Percentage of eligible voters who actually voted.
[d] Includes all the cotton states.
[e] Horace Greeley was a "fusion party" candidate in 1872: nominated by both the Liberal Republican and the Democratic Parties, with B. Gratz Brown of Missouri as his vice-presidential running mate.
[f] Greeley died shortly after the November election and before the electoral count, throwing the normal procedure into turmoil. He was entitled to 66 electoral votes if he had lived. As it was, 63 of his electors scattered, casting their votes for other candidates, but three from Georgia cast their votes for him anyway, knowing they would be disallowed by Congress. They were.
[g] Eighteen of the electors originally pledged to Greeley cast their votes for his running mate, Gratz, on the basis of some sort of informal succession principle. Congress duly counted those votes for Gratz as the "fusion" party candidate.
[h] There was no distinction made between the votes cast for Greeley as the Democratic candidate versus Greeley as the Liberal Republican candidate; all of his popular votes were lumped together.
Sources: Charles Van Doren and Robert McHenry, *Webster's Guide to American History* (Springfield, Mass.: G. C. Merriam, 1971), 768; J. David Gillespie, *Politics at the Periphery* (Columbia: University of South Carolina Press, 1993), 295.

Presidential Administrations

A president is seldom known for his cabinet, although his place in history is at least partly determined by how well they do their jobs. Two presidents during this era were overshadowed by their cabinets: Franklin Pierce and James Buchanan. They were completely outclassed by the men they named to run daily affairs. Pierce, it was reported, put every policy of his administration to a cabinet vote and meekly accepted the majority's opinion. That sort of pusillanimity changed with Lincoln, who selected mostly first-rate men, then listened to their opinions, but set his own course on everything from emancipation to Reconstruction policies. Andrew Johnson, who inherited Lincoln's cabinet, found himself unable ever to put his own stamp on the group, and Grant's cabinet, full of Radical Republicans and venal cronies, rewrote the book on political scandals, in the process adding colorful new language to the American political lexicon to describe their escapades: "Black Friday," "Whiskey Ring," and "Crédit Mobilier" were just the most infamous. During his two terms, 26 men went through the revolving door of Grant's cabinet, 20 of whom proved to be incompetent, unprincipled, or both. As an institution, the cabinet sank to its lowest level in the history of the Republic up to that date. Not until the 20th century would another presidential administration be so notorious and so corrupt.

TABLE 9.19 PRESIDENTIAL ADMINISTRATIONS FROM ZACHARY TAYLOR THROUGH ULYSSES GRANT, 1849–1877

The Taylor Administration		1849–50
Position	Officeholder	Year
President	Zachary Taylor	1849–50
Vice president	Millard Fillmore	1849–50
Secretary of state	John M. Clayton	1849–50
Secretary of treasury	William Meredith	1849–50
Secretary of war	George Crawford	1849–50
Attorney general	Reverdy Johnson	1849–50
Secretary general	Jacob Collamer	1849–50
Secretary of navy	William Preston	1849–50
Secretary of interior[a]	Thomas Ewing	1849–50
The Fillmore Administration[b]		**1850–53**
Position	Officeholder	Years
President	Millard Fillmore	
Vice president	None	
Secretary of state	Daniel Webster	1850–52
	Edward Everett	1852–53
Secretary of treasury	Thomas Corwin	1850–53
Secretary of war	Charles Conrad	1850–53
Attorney general	John J. Crittenden	1850–53
Postmaster general	Nathan Hall	1850–52
	Sam D. Hubbard	1852–53
Secretary of navy	William A. Graham	1850–52
	John P. Kennedy	1852–53
Secretary of interior	Thomas McKennan	1850
	Alexander Stuart	1850–53
The Pierce Administration		**1853–57**
Position	Officeholder	Years
President	Franklin Pierce	
Vice president	William R. King	1853–57
Secretary of state	William L. Marcy	1853–57
Secretary of treasury	James Guthrie	1853–57
Secretary of war	Jefferson Davis	1853–57
Attorney general	Caleb Cushing	1853–57
Postmaster general	James Campbell	1853–57
Secretary of navy	James C. Dobbin	1853–57
Secretary of interior	Robert McClelland	1853–57
The Buchanan Administration		**1857–61**
Position	Officeholder	Years
President	James Buchanan	
Vice president	John C. Breckinridge	1857–61
Secretary of state	Lewis Cass	1857–60
	Jeremiah S. Black	1860–61
Secretary of treasury	Howell Cobb	1857–60
	Philip Thomas	1860–61
	John A. Dix	1861
Secretary of war	John B. Floyd	1857–61
	Joseph Holt	1861
Attorney general	Jeremiah S. Black	1857–60
	Edwin M. Stanton	1860–61
Postmaster general	Aaron V. Brown	1857–59
	Joseph Holt	1859–61
	Horatio King	1861
Secretary of navy	Isaac Toucey	1857–61
Secretary of interior	Jacob Thompson	1857–61
The Lincoln Administration		**1861–65**
Position	Officeholder	Years
President	Abraham Lincoln	
Vice president	Hannibal Hamlin	1861–65
	Andrew Johnson	1865
Secretary of state	William H. Seward	1861–65
Secretary of treasury	Samuel P. Chase	1861–64
	William P. Fessenden	1864–65
	Hugh McCulloch	1865
Secretary of war	Simon Cameron	1861–62
	Edwin M. Stanton	1862–65
Attorney general	Edward Bates	1861–63
	Titian J. Coffey	1863–64
	James Speed	1864–65
Postmaster general	Horatio King	1861
	Montgomery Blair	1861–64
	William Dennison	1864–65
Secretary of navy	Gideon Welles	1861–65
Secretary of interior	Caleb B. Smith	1861–63
	John P. Usher	1863–65
The Johnson Administration		**1865–69**
Position	Officeholder	Years
President	Andrew Johnson	
Vice pesident	None	
Secretary of state	William H. Seward	1865–69
Secretary of treasury	Hugh McCulloch	1865–69
Secretary of war	Edwin M. Stanton	1865–67
	Ulysses S. Grant	1867–68
	Lorenzo Thomas	1868
	John M. Schofield	1868–69
Attorney general	James Speed	1865–66
	Henry Stanbery	1866–68
	William M. Evarts	1868–69
Postmaster general	William Dennison	1865–66
	Alexander Randall	1866–69
Secretary of navy	Gideon Welles	1865–69
Secretary of interior	John P. Usher	1865
	James Harlan	1865–66
	Orville H. Browning	1866–69

The Grant Administration		1869–77
Position	**Officeholder**	**Years**
President	Ulysses S. Grant	
Vice president	Schuyler Colfax	1869–73
	Henry Wilson	1873–77
Secretary of state	Elihu B. Washburne	1869
	Hamilton Fish	1869–77
Secretary of treasury	George S. Boutwell	1869–73
	William Richardson	1873–74
	Benjamin Bristow	1874–76
	Lot M. Morrill	1876–77
Secretary of war	John A. Rawlins	1869
	William T. Sherman	1869
	William W. Belknap	1869–76
	Alphonso Taft	1876
	James D. Cameron	1876–77
Attorney general	Ebenezer Hoar	1869–70
	Amos T. Akerman[c]	1870–71
	George H. Williams	1871–75
	Edwards Pierrepont	1875–76
	Alphonso Taft	1876
Postmaster general	John A. J. Creswell	1869–74
	James W. Marshall	1874
	Marshall Jewell	1874–76
	James N. Tyner	1876–77
Secretary of navy	Adolph E. Borie	1869
	George M. Robeson	1869–77
Secretary of interior	Jacob D. Cox	1869–70
	Columbus Delano	1870–75
	Zachariah Chandler	1875–77

[a] Taylor's was the first administration to have a secretary of the interior because Congress only created the cabinet-level department in 1849.
[b] The cabinet that Fillmore inherited from Zachary Taylor resigned en masse on his first day in office, Jul. 10, 1850, partly as a bow to British tradition, more as a sign of their contempt for the new president.
[c] The first attorney general also to administer the Justice Department, newly created by act of Congress in 1870.
Source: Carol Berkin et al., *Making America: A History of the United States* (Boston: Houghton Mifflin, 1995), A-38–A-39.

Politics during the Civil War

The political breakdown that occurred in 1861 affected government operations from top to bottom. Army and navy officers chose sides, and those who went south resigned their commission. Members of Congress also resigned and returned to their home state, most of them to take a seat in the Confederate Congress almost as soon as they unpacked. Other federal government departments, such as the Treasury, Interior, and Customs Departments, had to cease operations south of the Potomac River. The U.S. Post Office made the smoothest transition, probably because it was the least politicized department before the war and because it was in everyone's best interest to keep the mail moving. For four months after the formation of the Confederacy in February 1861, the U.S. Post Office continued to deliver the mail across the South. Only in June, six weeks after the firing on Fort Sumter, did the Confederate Postal Department take over mail delivery. On May 30 Southern postal workers conducted business as usual for the U.S. government, completing and forwarding all necessary paperwork before they called it a day. The next morning, on June 1, they went to work as Confederate government employees performing the same duties at precisely the same rank and salary.

In most other respect, the bureaucratic breakdown caused by secession and war has generally been overlooked by historians. The Confederacy was faced with the daunting task in 1861 of creating a mirror image of the federal bureaucracy if it hoped to make its new nation a fully functioning entity. Creating an army and navy to fight the war was only part of the problem, although the part that received the most attention. Meanwhile the U.S. government continued with business as usual, even expanding the bureaucracy during the war. In 1862 Congress created the new subcabinet-level Department of Agriculture. Previously agricultural affairs had been overseen by the Patent Office, and earlier attempts to create a separate agency had been rebuffed. The new department's mission, according to the legislation that created it, was "to acquire and to diffuse among the people of the United States useful information on subjects connected with agriculture in the most general and comprehensive sense of that word, and to procure, propagate, and distribute among the people new and valuable seeds and plants."

Partisan politics was not adjourned during the conflict but required the respective national governments to drum up popular support for the war effort and stamp out opposition whenever and wherever it flared. In the North the Lincoln administration had to keep the antiwar "Copperheads" and the Radical Republicans in check while trying carefully to balance individual civil rights with national interests. Lincoln suspended the right of habeas corpus in April 1861, and some 13,000 citizens were arrested and imprisoned without due process during the next four years. On the local level the Democratic Party enjoyed a resurgence in the North as the war dragged on, even though it was the party that had led the South out of the Union. The revival of the Democrats in the North was in inverse proportion to the popularity of the war; the less popular the war became, the more support the antiwar Democrats gained. And after the Lincoln administration introduced new taxes and conscription, the two most popular issues with voters in local elections were opposition to the draft and to taxation, both of which worked against the Republicans. To keep the War Democrats happy, Lincoln had to appoint men such as Nathaniel Banks and Benjamin Butler of Massachusetts to high command and accept Tennessee's Andrew Johnson as his running mate in 1864.

In the South the Davis administration never faced an organized political opposition and never suspended the right of habeas corpus, but it did order harsh reprisals against die-hard Unionists in distant corners of the Confederacy. And Davis was constantly beset by independent-minded state officials such as Governor Joe Brown of Georgia, who refused to put Confederate interests ahead of state interests. The politics of states' rights dictated that Richmond defend every inch of Southern soil and every mile of coastline. Political considerations were also at work in the appointments of men such as the former governor Henry A. Wise of Virginia and the hypercritical Robert Toombs of Georgia to high command. Politics dictated strategy even when the resulting strategy was self-defeating. Ideals of individual liberty and states' rights also had to be compromised when as early as April 1862 it became necessary to enact conscription to fill the ranks. Starting from opposite ends of the political spectrum on so many principles, Davis and Lincoln were pushed closer and closer together in practice by the demands of war as the fight dragged on.

Democratic politics and military strategy were inseparably intertwined, too. It was victories on the battlefield that allowed Lincoln to issue the Emancipation Proclamation in 1862 (after the Battle of Antietam) and win reelection two years later (after the fall of Mobile and the capture of Atlanta). In Grant's titanic struggle against Lee in northern Virginia in the summer of 1864, every reverse suffered by the Union army was felt by Lincoln. The *New York Herald* astutely observed that the president's "political fortunes, not less than the Great Cause of the country, are in the hands of General Grant, and the failure of the General will be the overthrow of the President."

Politics during Reconstruction

Reconstruction began with a debate between President Lincoln and Congress over policy toward the defeated Confederate states. Lincoln's lenient "Ten Percent Plan" (December 1863) and Radical Republicans' vindictive Wade-Davis bill (1864) canceled each other out and left the determination of how the Union was to be reconstructed still unresolved at the war's end. The basic issue was whether the president should control the treatment of the South through his pardoning power or whether Congress should have that right through its control of matters of admission (or in this case, readmission) to the Union. The issue became first a political then a constitutional fight. The Command of the Army Act, the Tenure of Office Act, and the Civil Rights Act, all in 1866, sought to curtail presidential power in one way or another and eventually led to the impeachment battle of 1868, when Andrew Johnson became the first president in U.S. history to be impeached. The tissue-thin acquittal that resulted from Johnson's trial before the Senate preserved the principle of separation of powers but left the presidency in a weakened state for the rest of the century.

Three amendments to the Constitution were created in the period, the so-called Reconstruction Amendments. They represent a flurry of constitutional adjustments second only to the four amendments of the Progressive period (1900–20). The Thirteenth, Fourteenth, and Fifteenth Amendments all were provoked by the problem of defining the status of the nation's African-American population: The Thirteenth extended personal freedom to all slaves everywhere in the United States; the Fourteenth defined the principle of national citizenship and guaranteed "equal protection" under the law to all citizens; and the Fifteenth guaranteed the right to vote to the freedmen to go along with their freedom.

Tammany Hall, in New York City, is decorated for the Democratic National Convention on July 4, 1868, awaiting only the arrival of the delegates. The Democrats met here to escape the taint of treason and rebellion. They nominated the former governor of New York Horatio Seymour. (Library of Congress)

On May 19, 1870, a parade was held in Baltimore to celebrate adoption of the Fifteenth Amendment and the progress of African Americans. Heroes of the struggle for emancipation can be seen around the edge of this commemorative picture. That Baltimore had a large black population who would pay for copies of this print influenced its publishers. (The Maryland Historical Society, Baltimore, Maryland)

TABLE 9.20 THE RECONSTRUCTION AMENDMENTS, 1865–1869

Amendment	Date Passed by Congress[a]	Date Ratified[b]	Major Provisions
XIII	Jan. 1865	Dec. 6, 1865	All "involuntary servitude" (i.e., slavery) abolished except as punishment for a duly convicted crime
XIV	Jun. 1866	Jul. 9, 1868	1) All persons born in the United States or naturalized are citizens of the United States and of their state of residence 2) No state may deny rights of citizenship, especially "due process of law" and "equal protection of the laws" to any citizen
XV	Feb. 1869	Feb. 3, 1870	No state may deny any citizen the right to vote "on account of race, color, or previous condition of servitude"

[a] Passage requires a two-thirds majority in both houses of Congress, plus the president's signature.
[b] Ratification requires approval by three-fourths of all states, including former Confederate states. At the time of these amendments, that meant 27 states.
Source: Robert A. Divine et al., *America Past and Present,* vol. 1: *To 1876,* 6th ed. (New York: Addison-Wesley Educational, 2002), 462.

Between 1867 and 1877 the South made the transition from military rule to "redemption" as the traditional elite recaptured control of their section, ending "carpetbag government." The traditional elite in the South meant the so-called Bourbon Democrats (the conservative, white aristocracy), who had controlled politics and society before the war. For them, regaining power represented redemption. Reconstruction ended not because the South was truly remade in the Northern image or full equality was achieved for blacks, but because the North chose to walk away. This retreat from Reconstruction began as early as 1870 in North Carolina and was completed when conservatives regained control in Louisiana in 1877. Despite subsequent mythology about the "long night" of carpetbag rule, no Southern state had to endure postwar occupation longer than eight and a half years, and it was benign by the standards of their time.

In the South opposition to Reconstruction took two forms: creation of a "lost cause" mythology that explained the war in terms of a heroic resistance to Northern aggression and a tyrannical federal government, and, second, stubborn obstructionism to the outcome of the war through black codes, Jim Crow laws, and organizations such as the Ku Klux Klan. The last-named was the most insidious and shocking expression of Southern defiance. It was formed in Pulaski, Tennessee, in 1866 as a fraternal society of Confederate war veterans, led by former officers such as Nathan Bedford Forrest and (later) John B. Gordon. The name was derived from the Greek word for "circle"

TABLE 9.21 CONGRESSIONAL (REPUBLICAN) RECONSTRUCTION OF FORMER CONFEDERATE STATES, 1868–1876

Former Confederate State	Readmitted to Union under Congressional Reconstruction	"Bourbon Democrats" Regain Control[a]	Duration of Republican Rule (in years)
Ala.	Jun. 25, 1868	Nov. 14, 1874	6½
Ark.	Jun. 22, 1868	Nov. 10, 1874	6½
Fla.	Jun. 25, 1868	Jan. 2, 1877	8½
Ga.	Jul. 15, 1870	Nov. 1, 1871	1
La.	Jun. 25, 1868	Jan. 2, 1877	8½
Miss.	Feb. 23, 1870	Nov. 3, 1875	5½
N.C.	Jun. 25, 1868	Nov. 3, 1870	2
S.C.	Jun. 25, 1868	Nov. 12, 1876	8
Tenn.	Jul. 24, 1866[b]	Oct. 4, 1869	3
Tex.	Mar. 30, 1870	Jan. 14, 1873	3
Va.	Jan.26, 1870	Oct. 5, 1869[c]	0

[a] Southern white conservatives, from the name given by history to the French aristocracy who stubbornly resisted all liberal reform when restored to power after Napoléon's overthrow.

[b] Admitted by President Andrew Johnson, before Congress took control of Reconstruction.

[c] Democrats regained control before formal readmission occurred.

Source: John Hope Franklin, *Reconstruction after the Civil War* (Chicago: University of Chicago Press, 1962), 231.

This sketch by Cora R. Jones shows the Pulaski, Tennessee, law office of Judge Thomas M. Jones in which the Ku Klux Klan (KKK) was founded in 1866. (Alabama Department of Archives and History, Montgomery, Alabama)

This 1871 lithograph shows a Ku Klux Klan gathering, in full regalia, to terrorize another poor victim, this one white, seen here kneeling with a rope around his neck. (Library of Congress)

(kuklos). Within a year it had evolved into a neo-Confederate, paramilitary guerrilla band, whose objective was to perpetuate white supremacy and drive carpetbag rule completely out of the South.

The Klan and its imitators were responsible for beating and murdering hundreds of blacks and whites alike between 1868 and 1871. Intervention by Congress in the form of the three Enforcement Acts finally broke the power of the Klan in the South. Those acts put federal courts and troops in the front lines against vigilantism and terrorism and finally restored some semblance of law and order.

Tradition dies hard, and racial prejudice dies harder. Participation by African Americans in the political process had been routinely denied during the first seven decades of the nation's history. That legacy could not be overcome by federal legislation or even presidential pronouncement. The record shows the first black man to hold public office in the United States was John Mercer Langston, elected town clerk of Brownhelm Township, Ohio, in 1855. After the Civil War, blacks began to take their rightful place in U.S. politics with a number of notable trailblazers showing the way. Principal among these were Robert Smalls of South Carolina; Pinckney Benton Stewart Pinchback and John R. Lynch, both of Louisiana; and a handful of others in Southern states where there was a sufficient black constituency to put them in office—at least until Jim Crow laws severely curtailed the African Americans' right to vote. Reconstruction was the heyday of 19th-century black political activism, when Joseph Hayne Rainey became the first black to serve in the House of Representatives (1870–79) and Hiram Rhoades Revels the first in the U.S. Senate (1870–71).

Reconstruction left its own legacy of enormous problems to be solved by future U.S. generations, what one historian has called "America's unfinished revolution." But in retrospect it also hastened the healing between North and South. It left Radical Republicans in the ascendancy in the North and Bourbon Democrats in the South. The so-called Solid South of the Democratic Party would not be cracked until 1928 and not shattered until the 1960s.

On the positive side the era of the Civil War and Reconstruction repudiated for all time the destructive doctrines of secession and states' rights. Never again would they pose a serious threat to the Union.

The Politics of Race, Gender, and Ethics

The prewar issue of slavery was succeeded by the postwar issue of race in national politics; the chief difference was that black men were now included in the debate. Beginning with the adoption of the Thirteenth Amendment in 1865, freedmen had the right to vote, although in the event, that right was not as clear-cut as it seemed. The politicization of the former slaves began with the arrival of the Freedman's Bureau in the South. A Republican-dominated Congress originally set up the Bureau of Freedmen, Refugees and Abandoned Lands on March 3, 1865, as a temporary agency to feed and care for destitute whites and blacks in the devastated South. In the immediate aftermath of the war it was the only organization doing large-scale relief work across the South, under the conscientious guidance of Major General Oliver Otis Howard. In the next five years it distributed more than 21 million rations out of surplus army stores, 15.5 million of those rations to blacks and the rest to needy whites, including former Confederates. It was despised by those very same Southerners, and Andrew Johnson, always a Southerner at heart, was determined to kill it when he became president. He had his chance when it came up for renewal in February 1866 and used his veto power, branding it an unconstitutional abuse of federal power.

Congress passed the Freedman's Bureau bill again, this time over Johnson's veto. It was the beginning of the end of his effectiveness as president. For the next six years, until it went out of business in 1872, the agency fulfilled its mandate albeit not without controversy. The bureau was political dynamite that represented the best and the worst of Reconstruction. On the one hand, it was the champion and protector of the former slave, negotiating better working conditions, establishing schools, and providing legal defense for a virtually helpless population. On the other hand, it was a tool of the Republican Party in the South, notoriously corrupt, and a humiliating reminder of defeat. An examination of the bureau's accomplishments in just one state (South Carolina) shows its impressive impact on every aspect of black life. By the end of its tenure, the bureau's mandate had been so circumscribed that it could do little more than operate schools and process black veterans' claims. Bureau record-keeping also provided a valuable service by assembling a statistical profile of Reconstrcution.

Black political participation tended to peak early in Reconstruction and then taper off as time passed and Northern commitment to reform weakened. Their best hope for changing the system were the constitutional conventions that were held in every former Confederate state except one (Tennessee) during winter and spring 1867–68. Those conventions, under federal oversight, were charged with rewriting antebellum state constitutions to reflect the new political reality of the end of slavery and diminution of states' rights. Many whites dismissed them as "bones and banjoes conventions" because large numbers of freedmen participated. The racial breakdown of these state conventions as a whole was 30 percent black and 70 percent white, a significant minority participation considering that there had not been a single black in an elected position in the South up to just two years before.

TABLE 9.22 THE WORK OF THE FREEDMAN'S BUREAU IN SOUTH CAROLINA, 1865–1870

Service Provided	Particulars	Period
Ration distribution	3,000,000 (approximate)	Summer 1865–Dec. 1868
Medical treatment	175,000 patient-cases	Summer 1865–Dec. 1868
Transportation	4,500 persons	Summer 1865–Dec. 1868
Funding for black education	$25,000	1866–67
School creation for blacks (student enrollment)	54 (8,000)	1866
	73 (8,000)	1867
	49(7,000)	1868
	54(5,500)	1869
	86 (9,000)	1870
Black banking	$300,000 deposited	1866

Source: Martin Abbot, *The Freedman's Bureau in South Carolina, 1865–1872* (Chapel Hill: University of North Carolina Press, 1967), 51, 87–88.

TABLE 9.23 COMPLAINTS FILED WITH THE FREEDMAN'S BUREAU IN SOUTH CAROLINA (AGAINST BLACKS), MAY 1866

Category of Complaint	Number of Complaints
Claims for money	97
Disorderly conduct	22
Unlawful entry	16
Property disputes	14
Labor questions	15
Other (family quarrels, disturbing of the peace, etc.)	50
Total	214

Source: Martin Abbott, *The Freedman's Bureau in South Carolina, 1865–1872* (Chapel Hill: University of North Carolina Press, 1967), 17.

TABLE 9.24 PARTICIPATION OF SOUTHERNERS BY RACE IN THEIR STATE CONSTITUTIONAL CONVENTIONS, 1867–1868

State[a]	Black Delegates as a Percentage of Convention	White Delegates as a Percentage of Convention
Ala.	17	83
Ark.	13	87
Fla.	40	60
Ga.	19	81
La.	50	50
Miss.	17	83
N.C.	11	89
S.C.	61	39
Tex.	10	90
Va.	24	76

[a] Of the 11 former Confederate states, Tennessee did not participate in the new constitution writing because it had already been "reconstructed" (i.e., restored to the Union) in 1866.

Source: John M. Murrin et al., *Liberty, Equality, Power: A History of the American People* (Fort Worth Tex.: Harcourt, Brace, 1996), 566.

The real political power in these conventions lay not with the freedmen or even the white planter class, but with Republicans, as at least 25 percent of those delegates were Northern transplants ("carpetbaggers"). The constitutions that the conventions produced were remarkably progressive, with universal male suffrage, mandated public schools, and at least a tip of the hat to social welfare in their provisions. But they were all opposed by the majority of white Southerners, and none survived the end of Reconstruction.

The national elections of 1872 saw a three-way race for president, and a strong Democratic Party challenge to regain control of Congress for the first time in more than a decade. The Republicans split into reform and conservative factions, but the black voting bloc in the South represented by the freedmen was more than enough to ensure Grant another four years. But Democrats recaptured control of the House of Representatives.

With Radical Republicans in full retreat in 1872, Congress passed the Amnesty Act restoring full political rights to 160,000 former Confederates. Reformers rallied long enough to push one more Civil Rights Act through Congress in 1875, the capstone of a legislative program that began with the Civil Rights Act of 1866 and the last legislation of its kind until 1965.

Other major political developments of Reconstruction were the decline of public ethics and the acceleration of the women's rights movement. The ethical bankruptcy of the period was laid at Ulysses Grant's feet ("Grantism"). Grant was elected president in 1868, solely on the basis of his record as a war hero in the North, capturing the electoral votes of 26 of 34 states and 53 percent of the popular vote. Personally honest, Grant had poor judgment and blind loyalty to subordinates, which allowed high appointed officials to feather their own nests, in the process embarrassing both the general and the Republican Party. And the corruption and venality were not limited to the party that held the White House. Democrats also indulged in what one critic called the Great Barbecue. The result was a flood of scandals and chicanery during Grant's two terms in office unequaled until the 20th century.

Working on the fringes of the political system were the reformers of the women's rights movement. Their cause had formerly been tied to the abolitionists' cause, but after the Civil War they sought to forge their own identity and fight against the complacency that followed national emancipation of slaves. In the persons of a handful of willful women, they became more aggressive in demanding action. The predominant focus of the movement in these years was equality before the law and in society rather than the specific rights to vote and hold office, which were considered to be more extremist demands.

TABLE 9.25 COMPARING THE TWO CIVIL RIGHTS ACTS OF RECONSTRUCTION, 1866 AND 1875

Comparative Elements	Civil Rights Act of 1866	Civil Rights Act of 1875
Support by the president	No	Yes
Sponsor	Senator Lyman Trumball of (Ill.)	Senator Charles Sumner (Mass.)
Passage	Apr. 1866 (over President Johnson's veto)	Feb. 1875
Major provisions	Protected freedmen's civil rights against discrimination *by states;* defined citizenship without reference to race	Equal accommodations in inns, theaters, and public transportation (but *not* schools or cemeteries); no discrimination in jury selection
Charged with enforcement	Federal officials and courts	Federal courts up to the Supreme Court
Aftermath	Major provisions incorporated into Fourteenth Amendment (1868)	Most provisions declared unconstitutional by Supreme Court (1883)

Source: Hans L. Trefousse, *Historical Dictionary of Reconstruction* (Westport, Conn.: Greenwood Press. 1991), 42–43; Harold M. Hyman, *A More Perfect Union* (New York: Knopf, 1973), passim.

Belva Ann Lockwood is shown in a photo taken by Matthew Brady or one of his assistants between 1880 and 1890. Even her 1884 run for the presidency as the candidate for the National Equal Rights Party could not move her out of the shadow of her "sister" in the women's rights movement, Elizabeth Cady Stanton. (Library of Congress, Prints and Photographs Division [LC-BH834])

Women became increasingly assertive in fighting for their political rights after the Civil War. Many had worked for the abolition of slavery and considered it time to secure their voting rights. In this engraving from *Frank Leslie's Illustrated Newspaper,* February 4, 1871, a delegation of female suffragists present their case (based on the Fourteenth and Fifteenth Amendments) to the House Judiciary Committee of the U.S. Congress on January 11, 1871. For their efforts, they received publicity but no concessions on the right to vote. (Library of Congress)

The Growing Institution of Government

Up until the middle of the 19th century national life was small-scale and localized, and so was government. Citizens thought of themselves as Virginians, Pennsylvanians, and so on, first, and as Americans second. They turned to family, friends, or church to provide what they needed. State governments granted charters to cities, banks, and universities; issued marriage licenses; and patented (i.e., registered claims to) public lands. Going to a government bureaucrat and filling out reams of paperwork would have been practically incomprehensible before the Civil War, and even after the 1860s introduced the Homestead Act and military conscription with all their requirements for enrollment and registration, the hand of government still rested lightly on most Americans.

Lightest of all was the hand of the federal government. Most Americans only dealt with Uncle Sam when they went to the post office or applied for pensions as veterans. There were a grand total of 18,417 post offices in the country in 1850. No other federal agency, including the U.S. mint, the military, and the customs service, touched Americans' lives so directly. Very few citizens, unless they lived in a major city or near the national capital, ever actually saw their president or representatives in the flesh. Likewise, the burden of supporting the national government was light on the pocketbook, costing the average citizen just $2.85 per year out of pocket. There was no such thing as an income tax before 1862, and the modern concepts of long-term federal planning and direct aid to citizens were still unknown. It was not until the need for a transcontinental railroad that long-range planning and large-scale public works projects became part of U.S. government.

About the only time government and citizens came together on a large scale was during elections. A majority of the citizenry tended to do their civic duty when it came to voting, as more than 50 percent participation was the norm in national elections, and there was a high of 73 percent voter turnout for the presidential election of 1848. But after elections they left the running of government to their elected and appointed officials with little or no oversight by watchdog groups. As a rule the parties kept an eye on each other, periodically turning out the old "scoundrels" and replacing them with new scoundrels. The political system operated on the principle of patronage, also known as the spoils system, according to the old saw, "To the victor go the spoils." After every major election appointive offices were used to reward supporters and to strengthen the party's hold on power. The system worked so well that nobody was very eager to change it, and the two major parties alternated extended stretches in the driver's seat. To grease the wheels of patronage, parties assessed the salaries of federal appointees at a rate of 2–3 percent. This collected enough money to fund essential activities, especially around election time. The practice of assessment was not seriously challenged until 1865, when the first civil service reform bill was introduced in Congress, and it was defeated handily. The spoils system was at its worst immediately after a presidential election, when office seekers swarmed the White House demanding a comfortable position as a federal marshal, customs collector, postmaster, or clerk in the Census or Pension Bureau.

In its entirety the federal workforce consisted of elected representatives, appointees (i.e., the bureaucracy), and active duty military personnel (army and navy). There were 26,274 federal workers in 1850 and another 20,824 military personnel constituting the bulk of the federal employee rolls. Even in 1871, at the dawn of the modern industrial age, the federal government still employed only 51,000 civilians, of whom 37,000 were postal workers. The remaining 14,000 constituted the entire national bureaucracy of a country with a population of roughly 41 million people, or one federal employee per 2,900 citizens versus one for every 100 citizens by the late 20th century. A majority of those 51,000 depended on the patronage system for their job.

Gradually during these years the peacetime federal bureaucracy grew. New agencies were created to keep track of weather, resources, and schools, reflecting the growing complexity of American life and the increasing responsibilities of government at all levels. Congress started the ball rolling in 1849 when it created the Home Department, soon to be named Interior, as the sixth cabinet level department in the executive branch, with Thomas Ewing as the first secretary. In the years that followed, Congress created various additional offices and agencies, placing them within existing cabinet departments.

Below the cabinet level the federal government grew even more rapidly, becoming increasingly involved in the life of private citizens. Not all of this was intrusive or even resisted. For instance, the government expanded its protection of intellectual property by registering patents, copyrights, and trademarks. The advent of new technology (e.g., the camera) coupled with powerful business interests pushed Congress to enact legislation protecting the creations of inventors, authors, and artists. Responsibility was first placed under the patent office until the size of the job and the diversity of intellectual property required other arrangements. (See the discussion of patent activity in chapter 17.) The results were not just a truly impressive outpouring of Yankee ingenuity across the board but a larger federal bureaucracy to register and protect the fruits of that ingenuity.

TABLE 9.26 GROWTH OF THE FEDERAL BUREAUCRACY, 1849–1875

Agency	Date Established	Background
Department of the Interior	Mar. 3, 1849	Combined the General Land Office (from Treasury Dept.), the Office of Indian Affairs (from War Dept.), the Pensions Office (from War and Navy Depts.), and the Census Bureau(from Treasury Dept.)
Department of Agriculture	May 5, 1862	Headed by commissioner until raised to cabinet rank in 1889, when replaced by Secretary
Department of Education	Mar. 2, 1867	Reduced to bureau status within the Interior Dept. in 1869
U.S. Weather Bureau	Feb. 9, 1870	Placed within U.S. Army Signal Service (later Signal Corps) under War Dept. aegis until moved to Dept. of Agriculture in 1891
Commission of Fish and Fisheries	1871	Placed under Treasury Dept., emphasizing its revenue-generating potential rather than ecological concerns
Department of Justice	Jun. 22, 1870	Given authority over all U.S. attorneys and marshals; under direction of attorney general

Sources: Gorton Carruth, *The Encyclopedia of American Facts and Dates,* 8th ed. (New York: Harper & Row, 1987), passim; Calvin D. Linton, ed., *A Diary of America: The American Almanac,* rev. ed. (Nashville: Thomas Nelson, 1977), passim; Thomas H. Johnson, *Oxford Companion to American History* (New York: Oxford University Press, 1966), passim.

TABLE 9.27 GROWTH OF U.S. GOVERNMENT PROTECTION OF INTELLECTUAL PROPERTY, 1831–1897

Type of Legislation	Date	What Was Covered
Copyright law[a]	1831	Musical compositions
Patent law[b]	Jul. 4, 1836	Tightened application process and emphasized criterion of "novelty"; introduced new numbering system for applications
Patent law	1842	Made designs as well as material items patentable
Copyright law	1856	Dramatic compositions with the right of public performance
Patent law	1861	Abolished discriminatory fees paid by foreign applicants
Copyright law	1865	Photographs
Copyright law	1870	Paintings, drawings, sculpture, and models or designs for works of the fine arts
Trademark law[c]	1870	Any picture, word, or phrase used by a manufacturer or merchant to distinguish goods from others'
Copyright law	Jun. 18, 1874	Commercial prints and labels
Trademark law	1881	Protected only marks used in foreign commerce, not domestic
Copyright law	1897	Performance rights in music

[a] The first U.S. copyright law in 1790 protected only books, charts, and maps. Subsequent legislation expanded that protection.
[b] The first U.S. patent law was passed in 1790 for any "new and useful" invention, process, *or* improvement thereof.
[c] This was the first trademark law in U.S. history. It was declared unconstitutional in 1879 because Congress attempted to slip it in under the patent and copyright clause of the Constitution.
Source: U.S. Dept. of Commerce, *Historical Statistics of the United States, Colonial Times to 1970,* part 2, Bicentennial ed. (Washington, D.C.: Department of Commerce, 1975), 954–56.

The Civil War forced the federal government to take a greatly expanded role in the life of its citizens, especially those recently in rebellion. Here, the Commissary Department of the U.S. Army distributes rations to the destitute residents of Richmond, Virginia, both black and white, in 1866. (Library of Congress)

The creeping federal bureaucracy exploded during the Civil War in order to meet the crush of wartime emergencies. Afterward, there was some cutback, but many agencies simply refused to go away, or as was the Pension Office, were even more important than before the war. The excesses of the spoils system also became more and more deplorable. Because the Republican Party controlled the national machinery of government, they became the biggest target for criticism from gadflies such as Mark Twain and Horace Greeley. A small company of early civil service reform advocates within the Republican Party included Jacob Cox, E. Rockwood Hoar, Charles Sumner, John Lothrop Motley, and Carl Schurz. But they were opposed by powerful politicians such as Benjamin Butler, Roscoe Conkling, and James G. Blaine, who preferred the status quo. Although civil service reform was an urgent issue, it would have to wait until after the 1870s to be legislated.

Concerns over the growing cost of the federal government became a political hot potato between the two major parties. In 1874 Democrats in Congress issued a study of the "miscellaneous expenditures" of the government that compared the last Democratic administration (James Buchanan's) with that of the Republican Ulysses Grant for fiscal 1873, showing the cost spread out over the general population. Intending to show that the Republicans were more spendthrift than the Democrats, the figures mainly illustrate the extent to which the obligations of government had grown in 15 years, especially when the Civil War is factored in.

Because the federal payroll and federal obligations were relatively small by modern standards, the government's expenditures were fairly modest during these years. (The Civil War was an aberration.) The army, navy, and post office were the largest peacetime budget items, followed by Indian affairs and pension benefits. Federal receipts were from customs duties (i.e., the tariff), internal revenue (e.g., liquor taxes), and the sale of public lands, with the largest proportion by far coming from customs duties. During normal years receipts covered annual expenses. During wartime or national economic crisis, however, the public debt could mount dramatically, requiring years to pay it off. During the decade preceding the Civil War a lingering recession aggravated by the sectional crisis caused the federal government to run a deficit in four consecutive years (1857–60), something that had not occurred since the War of 1812. Even in that era of small government and modest commitments, Uncle Sam had trouble keeping within his budget.

Unlike in modern times, neither the annual budget nor the debt grew steadily; both fluctuated, being up some years and dropping in other years. The federal government's annual budgets in the last decade before the Civil War averaged less than 2 percent of the gross national product (versus more than 20 percent today). The Civil War caused a temporary spike up to about 15 percent during the war years, but after that, annual budgets fell sharply, though never back to prewar levels. Uncle Sam was generally a model citizen in terms of living within his means, the Civil War notwithstanding. To fiscal conservatives, the worst sin of the federal government was not the income tax enacted during the Civil War but the issuance of $447 million in paper money (i.e., greenbacks) beginning in 1862.

TABLE 9.28 PARTIAL COST OF RUNNING THE U.S. GOVERNMENT UNDER JAMES BUCHANAN (DEMOCRAT) COMPARED TO THE COST UNDER ULYSSES S. GRANT (REPUBLICAN), 1858–1873

Fiscal Year[a] (administration)	Miscellaneous Expenditures[b]	Population (approximate)	Expenses per Capita (approximate)
1858 (Buchanan)	$26,400,000	28,000,000	$0.94
1859 (Buchanan)	$23,797,000	29,000,000	$0.80
1860 (Buchanan)	$27,977,000	30,000,000	$0.90
1861 (Buchanan/Lincoln)	$23,327,000	31,000,000	$0.74
1873 (Grant)	$73,327,804	40,000,000	$1.32

Note: The figures are *not* adjusted for inflation to current dollars.
[a] The fiscal year, as opposed to calendar year, is Jul. 1–Jun. 30. Therefore, fiscal 1858, for instance, is Jul. 1, 1858, through Jun. 30, 1859.
[b] The given figures include the "cost of supporting the President and his Cabinet, Congress, and all the office-holders." They do not include "the costs of war, navy, pension, Indian, interest and debt" payments.
Source: World Almanac and Book of Facts, 1868–1875 (Washington, D.C.: U.S. Government Printing Office, 1876), 14.

TABLE 9.29 FEDERAL SPENDING, 1850–1880

Year	Gross Receipts	Gross Expenditures[a]	Public Debt[b]
1850	$ 47,649,388	$ 44,604,718	$ 3,656,335
1851	$ 52,702,704	$ 48,476,104	$ 654,912
1852	$ 49,893,115	$ 46,712,608	$ 2,152,293
1853	$ 61,603,404	$ 54,577,061	$ 6,412,574
1854	$ 73,802,343	$ 75,473,170	$ 17,556,806
1855	$ 65,351,374	$ 66,164,775	$ 6,662,065
1856	$ 74,056,899	$ 72,726,341	$ 3,614,618
1857	$ 68,969,212	$ 71,274,587	$ 3,276,606
1858	$ 70,372,665	$ 82,062,186	$ 7,505,250
1859	$ 81,773,965	$ 83,678,642	$ 14,685,043
1860	$ 76,841,407	$ 77,055,125	$ 13,854,250
1861	$ 83,371,640	$ 85,387,313	$ 18,737,100
1862	$ 581,680,121[c]	$ 565,667,563	$ 96,097,322
1863	$ 889,379,652	$ 899,815,911	$ 181,081,635
1864	$ 1,393,461,017	$ 1,295,541,114	$ 430,572,610
1865	$ 1,805,939,345	$ 1,906,433,331	$ 609,616,141
1866[d]	$ 1,270,884,173	$ 1,139,344,081	$ 620,263,249
1867	$ 1,131,060,920	$ 1,093,979,655	$ 735,536,980
1868	$ 1,030,749,516	$ 1,069,889,970	$ 692,549,685
1869	$ 609,621,828	$ 584,777,996	$ 261,912,718
1870	$ 696,729,973	$ 702,907,842	$ 393,254,282
1871	$ 534,234,240	$ 424,316,763	$ 132,139,575
1875[e]	$ 288,000,000	$ 274,000,000	$ 2,156,300
1880[e]	$ 267,600,000	$ 333,500,000	$ 2,090,900

Note: Calculated by fiscal year (i.e., Jul. 1–Jun. 30), not by calendar year, and *not* adjusted for inflation to current dollars.
[a] Includes, in addition to regular government operations, interest payment on the public debt.
[b] The debt is a product of current year's deficit plus outstanding debt from previous years.
[c] A Federal income tax (3 percent on income greater than $ 600 per year), enacted by Congress in Aug. 1861 and signed by Lincoln in Jul. 1862, was first collected at the beginning of 1863 (fiscal 1862), and it is reflected in the inflated receipts for this year.
[d] Debt and expenditure figures for 1866 do not include more than $4 million in "outstanding warrants" unpaid by the federal government.
[e] Figures for 1875 and 1880 are approximate, calculated to the nearest 100,000.
Sources: World Almanac and Book of Facts, 1868–1875 (Washington, D. C.: U.S. Government Printing Office, 1876), 34–35; Joseph Conlin, *The American Past,* part 2: *Since 1865* (San Diego: Harcourt Brace Jovanovich, 1984), 511.

The Supreme Court

The Supreme Court in these years was far less authoritative and esteemed than it is today. In fact, it was frequently slighted, ignored, or manipulated by both Congress and the president. In 1857 President James Buchanan tried to pass off the slave issue to the Court, promising he would "cheerfully submit " to its considered opinion, but the resulting *Dred Scott* decision set off a firestorm in national politics that ultimately pushed the country into civil war, along the way making Buchanan one of the most hated men in America. This was not the first, nor would it be the last time the nation's highest court entered a political minefield. As a result the Court was subjected to such opprobrium and abuse as it has seldom experienced during its history.

Buchanan's ploy was as surprising as it was unsuccessful. The Supreme Court was not regarded as the all-powerful institution, whose decisions are the final word on every issue, that it has become. Judicial activism had been at low ebb ever since John Marshall retired in 1837. Nor did Court appointments and related confirmation hearings provoke the media-fueled political donnybrooks they do today. There were fewer earth-shaking decisions that affected the average citizen, *Dred Scott* the notable exception, because few cases of note were argued before the Court. Of the historic decisions that emerged from this era, almost all dealt with presidential authority and separation of powers. Hot-button issues were settled by legislatures or political caucuses. The rights of minorities and women and the expansion of the Bill of Rights were matters that would have to wait for later courts.

When the constitutional battle over Reconstruction heated up, the Court was a minor player. When it did try to challenge Congress's historic ironclad rule against "meddling" in serious political matters, it was forced to the sidelines. Radical Republicans put the Court in its place by defining down its jurisdiction and manipulating the number of justices—up to 10 in 1863, down to seven in 1866, then back up to nine in 1869.

Justices were not expected to be paragons of virtue as they are today, nor extraordinary legal scholars. They were expected to be "good party men." They also worked in more solitude than today because they did not have retinues of law clerks to do their research

TABLE 9.30 HISTORIC SUPREME COURT DECISIONS, 1850–1875

Case	Reference	Date of Decision	How Justices Voted[a]	Majority Opinion Written by	Issue or Constitutional Principle
Strader v. Graham	51 U.S. 82	1851	5-4	Mr. Chief Justice Roger B. Taney	Left it to each state to determine status of persons (e.g., slaves) within its jurisdiction without federal court interference; anticipates *Dred Scott* decision
Cooley v. Board of Wardens of the Port of Philadelphia	12 Howard 299; 13 L. Ed. 996	Mar. 2, 1852	7-2	Mr. Justice Benjamin R. Curtis	Defined commerce clause in terms of national versus local jurisdiction
Dred Scott v. John F.A. Sandford [sic.][b]	19 How. (60 U.S.) 393	Mar. 1857	7-2	Mr. Chief Justice Roger B. Taney	Negroes not citizens; United States slaves property protected by the Consitution; Congress unable to forbid/abolish slavery in any territory
Ableman v. Booth and *United States v. Booth*	21 How. (62 U.S.) 506	Mar. 7, 1859	9-0	Mr. Chief Justice Roger B. Taney	Established supremacy of federal over state authority in matters of habeas corpus
Ex parte Merryman	17 Fed. Case No. 9487 (144)	1861	N/A[c]	Mr. Chief Justice Roger B. Taney	Denied president's right to suspend writ of habeas corpus without due process and related right of military to arrest civilians in areas where civil law still operative.
Kentucky v. Dennison	24 How. (65 U.S.) 66	Mar. 14 1861	8-0	Mr. Chief Justice Roger B. Taney	Allowed some discretion to state governors in complying with art. IV, sec. 2, cl. 2 of Constitution (criminal extradition clause)
The Prize Cases[d]	2 Black (67 U.S.) 635; and 17 L. Ed. 459	Mar. 10, 1863	5-4	Mr. Justice Robert C. Grier	Upheld constitutionality of Lincoln's theory of Civil War as domestic insurrection with some attributes of international war
Ex parte Milligan	4 Wallace (71 U.S.) 2	Apr. 3, 1866[e]	9-0	Mr. Justice David Davis	Denied authority of military courts in areas where civil courts still functioning.
Cummings v. Missouri and *Ex parte Garland*	4 Wallace (71 U.S.) 277 and 4 Wallace (71 U.S.) 333	Jan. 14, 1867 (both cases)	5-4 (both cases)	Mr. Justice Stephen J. Field	Declared loyalty oaths unconstitutional for layers and clergy[f]
Mississippi v. Johnson	4 Wallace, 475; 18 L. Ed. 437	Apr. 15, 1867	9-0	Mr. Chief Justice Salmon P. Chase	Said courts cannot enjoin president from executing laws as he sees fit, in this case, Reconstruction Acts of 1867
Georgia v. Stanton	6 Wallace, 50	1867	9-0	Mr. Chief Justice Salmon P. Chase	Bookend decision with *Mississippi v. Johnson,* upholding enforcement of Reconstruction Acts
Ex parte McCardle	7 Wallace 506; 19 L. Ed. 264	Apr. 12, 1869	9-0	Mr. Chief Justice Salmon P. Chase	Challenged constitutionality of congressional Reconstruction; affirmed Congress's authority over Court's jurisdiction
Texas v. White	7 Wallace (74 U.S.), 700	Apr. 12, 1869	5-3	Mr. Chief Justice Salmon P. Chase	Union is indissoluble; therefore; secession legally impossible, but Reconstruction as practical matter is constitutional[g]
Veazie Bank v. Fenno	8 Wallace, 533; 19 L. Ed. 482	1869	5-2	Mr. Chief Justice Salmon P. Chase	Asserted Congress has power to "restrain the circulation [of] money" issued by private persons, state banks, others
Hepburn v Griswold	8 Wallace (75 U.S.), 603	Feb. 7, 1870	5-3	Mr. Chief Justice Salmon P. Chase	Declared Legal Tender Act of 1862 which tried to force citizens to accept "greenbacks" as legal tender unconstitutional
Legal tender cases[h]	12 Wallace 457; 20 L. Ed. 287	May 1, 1871	5-4	Mr. Justice William Strong	Overruled *Hepburn* case; upheld constitutionality of Legal Tender Act, thereby endorsing absolute congressional power over currency

Case	Reference	Date of Decision	How Justices Voted[a]	Majority Opinion Written by	Issue or Constitutional Principle
The Collector v. Day (Buffington v. Day)	11 Wallace 113; 20 L. Ed. 122	1871	8-1	Mr. Justice Samuel Nelson	Said Congress has no power to impose tax on salary of a state official, a usurpation of state authority[i]
The Slaughter-House Cases[j]	16 Wallace 36; 21 L. Ed. 394	Apr. 14, 1873	5-4	Mr. Justice Samuel F. Miller	Said Fourteenth Amendment not a limitation on states' economic regulatory powers; laid out doctrine of "dual citizenship" (i.e., state vs. U.S.).
Bradwell v. Illinois	16 Wallace (83 U.S.) 130	Apr. 15, 1873	8-1	Mr. Chief Justice Salmon P. Chase	Denied sex discrimination a justiciable issue under Fourteenth Amendment
Citizen's Savings & Loan Assoc. v. Topeka	20 Wallace 655; 22 L. Ed. 455	1874	8-1	Mr. Justice Samuel F. Miller	Denied right of any political authority to lay tax for nonpublic purposes
Minor v. Happersett	21 Wallace 162; 22 L. Ed. 627	Mar. 30, 1875	9-0	Mr. Chief Justice Morrison R. Waite	Denied women's suffrage protection under provisions of Fourteenth Amendment ("privileges and immunities" clause)
Shuey, Executor, v. United States	92 Wallace (U.S. 73)	1875	9-0	Mr. Justice William Strong	Enabled businesses to change product prices and terms of offers without notifying all potential customers individually

Note: The tenure of the (Roger B.) Taney court was Mar. 15, 1836, through Dec. 5, 1864. That of the (Salmon P.) Chase court was Dec. 6, 1864, through Jan. 20, 1874; that of the (Morrison R) Waite court was Jan. 21, 1874, through Jul. 19, 1888.

[a] In some cases the votes do not add up to nine because during the Civil War–Reconstruction era, Congress changed the size of the Court three times for political reasons.

[b] Through a clerical error Sanford's name is misspelled as *Sandford* in court records, so the case has gone down in history as *Dred Scott v. Sandford [sic.]*.

[c] This was not a case heard by the full Court, but rather an opinion handed down by the chief justice while on circuit court duty, supporting his writ of habeas corpus. (The chief justice's writ was refused on the authority of President Lincoln, thereby nullifying the opinion.)

[d] Specifically the wartime cases of the ships *Amy Warwick, Hiawatha, Brilliante,* and *Crenshaw.*

[e] Decision not released until Dec. 17, 1866, for political reasons. (This is another example of a case in which the Court's considered opinion was ignored because of the exigencies of wartime.)

[f] This was the first time an act of Congress was held unconstitutional by such a margin (5-4).

[g] *Texas v. White* was a landmark case in Supreme Court history: the only time the Court ever took up the explosive issue of the constitutionality of secession.

[h] The so-called "Legal Tender" cases are, specifically, *Knox v. Lee* and *Parker v. Davis.*

[i] This case was subsequently overruled by *Graves v. New York ex. rel. O'Keefe,* 306 U.S. 466 (1939).

[j] Specifically *Butchers' Benevolent Association v. Crescent City Live-Stock Landing and Slaughter-House Co.*

Sources: Lee Epstein et al., eds., *The Supreme Court Compendium: Data, Decisions, and Developments* (Washington, D.C.: Congressional Quarterly, 1994), passim; Kermit L. Hall, ed., *The Oxford Companion to the Supreme Court of the United States* (New York: Oxford University Press, 1992), passim; Paul C. Bartholomew, *Summaries of Leading Cases on the Constitution* (Totowa, N.J.: Littlefield, Adams, 1967), passim.

and polish their decisions. Although they heard far fewer cases, they were still more overworked than today's justices.

Three men occupied the chief justice's seat between 1850 and 1875: Roger Taney (March 15, 1836–December 5, 1864), Salmon Chase (December 6, 1864–January 20, 1874), and Morrison R. Waite (January 21, 1874–July 19, 1888). They were not the sort of men to leave an enduring stamp on the Court, such as John Marshall or Earl Warren. Taney is remembered for the *Dred Scott* decision (which he wrote) and as the chief justice who moved Court fashion into the modern age by wearing long trousers instead of the traditional knee breeches. During his tenure the Court handed down numerous decisions touching on slavery and economics, frequently tying the two together by ignoring the humanity of the slaves. Taney championed local rule, states' rights, and laissez-faire capitalism.

Taney's successor, appointed by Lincoln for political reasons, was just as staunchly antislavery as Taney had been proslavery. As a lawyer before the war, Salmon P. Chase had been known as "the Attorney-General for runaway slaves" because of his battles against the 1850 Fugitive Slave Law. He wore his "Radical" politics on his sleeve but was still able to preside with calmness and good judgment over the 1868 impeachment trial of Andrew Johnson. While Chase was on the bench, the high court clashed on several occasions with the other branches of the government over such issues as test oaths and military tribunals.

Morrison Waite was appointed chief justice by Ulysses Grant because of his faithful service to the Republican Party and his fundamental conservatism. He proved to be only a mediocre jurist, who favored strict construction of the Constitution and was a lukewarm supporter of freedmen's rights. He did pull the Court back from the extreme laissez-faire positions of his two immediate predecessors but without seriously reining in the freedom of large corporations. The Morrison court was busy if not outstanding, hearing 3,470 cases in 14 years.

TABLE 9.31 JUSTICES OF THE U.S. SUPREME COURT, 1850–1875

Name	Home State	Appointed by	Position at Time of Appointment	Age at Time of Appointment	Party Affiliation	Term of Service	Length of Service
John McLean	Ohio	Andrew Jackson	U.S. postmaster general	43	Democrat	1829–61	32 yr., 2 mo.
James M. Wayne	Ga.	Andrew Jackson	U.S. representative	45	Democrat	1835–67	32 yr., 5 mo.
Roger B. Taney	Md.	Andrew Jackson	Lawyer	57	Democrat	1836–64	28 yr., 6 mo.
John Catron	Tenn.	Martin Van Buren	Lawyer	51	Democrat	1837–65	28 yr., 2 mo.
John McKinley	Ala.	Martin Van Buren	U.S. senator	57	Democrat	1837–52	14 yr., 9 mo.
Peter V. Daniel	Va.	Martin Van Buren	U.S. district court judge	56	Democrat	1841–60	19 yr., 2 mo.
Samuel Nelson	N.Y.	John Tyler	N.Y. supreme court judge	52	Democrat	1845–72	27 yr., 9 mo.
Levi Woodbury	N.H.	James K. Polk	U.S. senator	56	Democrat	1845–51	5 yr., 8 mo.
Robert C. Grier	Pa.	James K. Polk	U.S. district court judge	52	Democrat	1846–70	23 yr., 6 mo.
Benjamin R. Curtis	Mass.	Millard Fillmore	Mass. state representative	42	Whig	1851–57	5 yr., 11 mo.
John A. Campbell	Ala.	Franklin Pierce	Lawyer	41	Democrat	1853–61	8 yr., 1 mo.
Nathan Clifford	Maine	James Buchanan	Lawyer	54	Democrat	1858–81	23 yr., 6 mo.
Noah H. Swayne	Ohio	Abraham Lincoln	Lawyer	56	Republican	1862–81	19 yr.
Samuel F. Miller	Iowa	Abraham Lincoln	Lawyer	46	Republican	1862–90	28 yr., 2 mo.
David Davis	Ill.	Abraham Lincoln	Ill. circuit court judge	47	Republican	1862–77	14 yr., 2 mo.
Stephen J. Field	Calif.	Abraham Lincoln	Calif. supreme court judge	46	Democrat	1863–97	34 yr., 8 mo.[a]
Salmon P. Chase	Ohio	Abraham Lincoln	U.S. secretary of the treasury[b]	56	Republican	1864–73	8 yr., 5 mo.
William Strong	Pa.	Ulysses S. Grant	Lawyer	61	Republican	1870–80	10 yr., 9 mo.
Joseph P. Bradley	N.J.	Ulysses S. Grant	Lawyer	56	Republican	1870–92	21 yr., 10 mo.
Ward Hunt	N.Y.	Ulysses S. Grant	N.Y. commissioner of appeals	62	Republican	1873–82	9 yr., 1 mo.
Morrison R. Waite	Ohio	Ulysses S. Grant	President of state constitutional convention lawyer	57	Republican	1874–88	14 yr., 2 mo.

Note: Names of chief justices are in **boldface** type.

[a] At 34 years, eight months, Field had the second-longest tenure on the high court bench after William O. Douglas (36 years, seven months), and just three months longer than Supreme Court legend John Marshall.

[b] More precisely Chase was in retirement at the time, having resigned from Lincoln's cabinet in Jun. 1864 over political differences. He waited six months before the president sent his name to the Senate for the vacant chief justice seat.

Sources: John M. Murrin et al. *Liberty, Equality, Power: A History of the American People* (Fort Worth, Tex.: Harcourt Brace, 1996) 1,086–88; Lee Epstein et al., *The Supreme Court Compendium* (Washington, D.C.: Congressional Quarterly, 1994), 266–68, 275–77.

Foreign Affairs

Foreign affairs during these years either took a back seat to the sectional crisis or became entangled with sectional issues. Relations with Great Britain, still considered the major threat to U.S. interests, and various Latin American republics dominated policy. Expanding the national domain at the expense of foreign nations was much on the mind of some men who dreamed of Americanizing the world. Targets of the expansionists included Cuba, Santo Domingo (i.e., the Dominican Republic), Nicaragua, Mexico, Hawaii, and Canada. The vague philosophy of Manifest Destiny drove the fevered ambitions of those who dreamed of a Greater United States, but slaveholders were also a powerful constituency. Cooler heads and partisan politics checked most of these ambitions, but U.S.-style jingoism still caused strained relations with a number of nations whose lands were coveted by Americans.

Quietly the United States inaugurated diplomatic relations with several foreign states, signaling a turn away from isolationism and a more aggressive stance in world affairs. Economics as well as politics drove the decisions to open formal relations with distant countries. Most of the new relations were with the recently independent nations of Latin America. Extending recognition to such states as Bolivia and Uruguay gave them much-needed international credibility but also reaffirmed the Monroe Doctrine, which warned Europe's imperialist powers away from the Western Hemisphere.

Diplomatic recognition, unfortunately, was not the same as an official presence in a foreign country, that is, an embassy or consul. By law, once the United States extended diplomatic recognition, a "chief

TABLE 9.32 CHIEF U.S. DIPLOMATIC OFFICIALS AND FOREIGN MINISTERS (SERVING IN MAJOR OVERSEAS POSTS), 1850–1875

President	Secretary of State	Chairman, Senate Foreign Relations Committee	Minister to Great Britain	Minister to France	Minister to Other Major Nations
Zachary Taylor (1849–50)	James M. Clayton (1849–50)	William R. King (1849–50)	Abbott Lawrence (1849–52)	William C. Rives (1849–53)	George P. Marsh Turkey (1849–53)
Millard Fillmore (1850–53)	Daniel Webster (1850–52) Edward Everett (1852–53)	Henry S. Foote (1850–51) James M. Mason (1851–61)	Abbott Lawrence (1849–52) Joseph R. Ingersoll (1852–53)	William C. Rives (1849–53)	Daniel D. Barnard Prussia (1850–53)
Franklin Pierce (1853–57)	William Marcy (1853–57)	James M. Mason (1851–61)	James Buchanan (1853–56) George M. Dallas (1856–61)	John Y. Mason (1854–59)	James Gadsden Mexico (1853–56) August Belmont Netherlands (1854–57) Pierre Soulé Spain (1853–55)
James Buchanan (1857–61)	Lewis Cass (1857–60) Jeremiah S. Black (1860–61)	James M. Mason (1851–61)	George M. Dallas (1856–61)	John Y. Mason (1854–59) Charles J. Faulkner (1860–61)	Joseph A. Wright Prussia (1857–61) Townsend Harris Japan (1859–62)
Abraham Lincoln (1861–65)	William H. Seward (1861–65)	Charles Sumner (1861–71)	Charles F. Adams (1861–68)	William L. Dayton (1861–64)	Cassius M. Clay Russia (1861–62; 1863–69) Thomas Corwin Mexico (1861–64) Norman B. Judd Prussia (1861–65) George P. Marsh Italy (1861–82)
Andrew Johnson (1865–69)	William H. Seward (1865–69)	Charles Sumner (1861–71)	Charles F. Adams (1861–68)	John Bigelow (1865–66) John A. Dix (1866–69)	Cassius M. Clay Russia (1865–69) William S. Rosecrans Mexico (1868–69)
Ulysses S. Grant (1869–77)	Elihu B. Washburne (1869) Hamilton Fish (1869–77)	Charles Sumner (1861–71) Simon Cameron (1871–77)	John Lothrop Motley 1869–70) Robert C. Schenck (1870–76) Edwards Pierrepont (1876–77)	Elihu B. Washburne (1869–77)	Daniel E. Sickles Spain (1869–74) John W. Foster Mexico (1873–80) J. Milton Turner Liberia (1871–78)[a] John A. Bingham Japan (1873–85)

Note: Term of office is below each name. Some terms are shortened because of political circumstances or death. This means that some offices were filled by more than one man during a given presidential administration.
[a] Turner was an African American appointed to the U.S. diplomatic service.
Source: John E. Findling, *Dictionary of American Diplomatic History,* 2d ed., rev. (Westport, Conn.: Greenwood Press, 1989), 584–86.

of mission" (ambassador) had to be appointed by the president and confirmed by the Senate, then he or she had to be accredited to (accepted by) the foreign government. During this period there was considerable delay on several occasions in sealing formal diplomatic relations with an exchange of ambassadors. For example, the State Department commissioned diplomatic officials to Costa Rica, El Salvador, and Honduras in 1853, but no U.S. representative presented credentials to those governments until years later.

The language and workings of the diplomatic community were different in the 19th century. The senior official representing U.S. interests in a foreign country carried the generic title of *minister,* while European governments used a more formal nomenclature dating from the 1814 Congress of Vienna that included ambassadors, envoys, ministers-resident, and chargés d'affaires. Not until 1893 did the U.S. government begin to use the formal title *ambassador* for the chief of mission in a foreign capital. And U.S. diplomatic agents abroad were under strict State Department orders after 1853 to perform all their official duties "in [the] simple dress of an American citizen," eschewing the knee breeches, cut-away coat, and tails favored by European diplomats.

Even in this heyday of U.S. isolationism, the United States participated in international events to a surprising degree. In 1851 60 U.S. delegates attended a peace conference in London; in 1871 the Grant administration agreed to submit an old dispute with Great Britain to international arbitration; and in 1874 the United States was a participant in the first International Postal Congress in Bern, Switzerland. (That same year the United States joined the General Postal Union, subsequently known as the Universal Postal Union.)

This was a formative period in U.S. foreign relations, highlighted by more than a score of bilateral agreements covering such diverse matters as commerce, extradition, navigation, neutrals' rights, reciprocity, and friendship. (None dealt specifically with international peace or human rights, the two chief topics of international agreements today.) Among the nations with whom the United States reached agreements on one or more of these matters were Borneo (1850), Peru (1851), Costa Rica (1851), France (1852), Netherlands (1852 and 1855), Argentina (1853), Bavaria (1853), Russia (1854), the Kingdom of the Two Sicilies (1855), Persia (1856), Siam (1856), Belgium (1858), Mexico (1859), Paraguay (1859), and Venezuela (1859 and 1860). The series of treaties signed between 1850 and 1875 had the cumulative effect of broadening American involvement in the world at the same time as they defended U.S. interests abroad.

Members of the U.S. State Department gather to sign the Russian treaty for the purchase of Alaska in 1867. Seated on the left is Secretary of State William H. Seward. His son, Fred W. Seward (assistant secretary), and Senator Charles Sumner are seated on far right and right, respectively. (Library of Congress, Prints and Photographs Division [LC-USZ62-12505])

TABLE 9.33 MAJOR INTERNATIONAL AGREEMENTS NEGOTIATED BY U.S. GOVERNMENT, 1850–1875

Name of Treaty	Treaty Signatories	Date of Signing	Provisions
Treaty of Amity	United States and El Salvador	Jan. 2, 1850	Inaugurates formal diplomatic relations; deals with commerce, navigation, and general matters of friendship
Clayton-Bulwer Treaty	United States and Great Britain	Apr. 19, 1850	Pledge of both nations to cooperate in building a canal across isthmus of Central America, keeping it neutral and not trying to colonize in the region[a]
Treaty of Amity	United States and Swiss Confederation	Nov. 25, 1850	Deals with general matters of friendship and commerce
Gadsden Treaty	United States and Mexico	1853 (Dec. 30)	Purchases a strip of 29, 640 sq. m. from Mexico for $10 million.
Treaty of Kanagawa	United States and Japan	1854 (Mar. 31)	Grants the United States a consulate in Japan, use of two Japanese ports for supplies and trade; guarantees humane treatment for future shipwrecked Americans
Canadian Reciprocity Treaty	United States and Great Britain	1854 (Jun. 5)	Opens U.S. market to Canadian agriculture products, timber, and fish; grants fishing rights to U.S. fishermen in Canadian waters[b]
Marcy-Elgin Treaty	United States and Great Britain	Jun. 5, 1854	Settled several U.S.-Canadian fishing and trade disputes
Hawaiian Annexation Treaty	United States and Hawaiian monarchy	Nov. 11, 1854	U.S. possession of Hawaiian Islands, which become a state immediately, in return for $300,000 annual payment to monarchy[c]
Diplomatic Convention	United States and Japan	1857	Established diplomatic relations on ministerial level between the two governments
China Treaty	United States and China	Jun. 18, 1858	Established "peace, amity and commerce"
Shimoda Convention	United States and Japan	Jul. 29, 1858	Commercial treaty opening trade relations between the two nations[d]
Two Tientsin (Tianjin) treaties (aka, Shanghai Conventions)	United States, Great Britain, France, Russia, and China	Nov. 8, 1858	Settled claims of U.S. citizens against China; gives United States access to certain Chinese ports, and other privileges include diplomatic representation in Peking (now Beijing)
West Indies Treaty	United States and Denmark	1867	U.S. negotiation of purchase of Danish West Indies; Senate refusal to ratify
Alaska Purchase Treaty	United States and Russia	Mar. 30, 1867	U.S. purchase of vast territory of "Russian America" for $7.2 million[e]
African Slave Trade Treaty	United State and Great Britain	Apr. 7, 1862	Two-country agreement to cooperate in suppressing African slave trade
Burlingame Treaty	United States and China	Jul. 20, 1868	Clarifies U.S. rights in China and reaffirms Chinese sovereignty
Santo Domingo Treaty	United States and Santo Domingo (Dominican Republic)	1869	Negotiation by U.S. representatives of purchase of West Indies republic; voted down by Senate in Jun. 1870
Treaty of Washington	United States and Great Britain	May 8, 1871	Sets up four major arbitrations of issues between United States and Great Britain, including *Alabama* claims and fishing rights
Hawaiian Reciprocity Treaty	United States and Hawaiian monarchy	Jan. 30, 1875 (Ratified by Senate, Mar. 18)	Opens U.S. market to Hawaiian sugar in return for Hawaiian concessions

[a] Abrogated by Hay-Pauncefote Treaty in 1901.
[b] The treaty was legally abrogated by the United States in 1866.
[c] The treaty was rejected by Secretary of State William Marcy out of hand without ever being submitted it to the Senate.
[d] This was the first commercial treaty ever signed by Japan with a Western government. It was confirmed by the U.S. Senate on Dec. 15.
[e] The name *Alaska* was given to the territory by Senator Charles Sumner, whose influence as chairman of the Senate Foreign Relations Committee was vital in inducing the Senate to approve the treaty.

Sources: John E. Findling, *Dictionary of American Diplomatic History,* 2d ed. rev. (Westport, Conn.: Greenwood Press, 1989), 567–68; Hans L. Trefousse, *Historical Dictionary of Reconstruction* (Westport, Conn.: Greenwood Press, 1991), 80–82; Calvin D. Linton, ed. *A Diary of America: The American Almanac* (Nashville: Thomas Nelson, 1977), passim; Thomas A. Bailey, *A Diplomatic History of the American People,* 8th ed. (New York: Appleton-Century-Crofts, 1969), 159, 265–66, 275–78, 280, 306–08, 310–13, 361, 366–68, 376, 382, 373–74, 384–85, 391–92, 428–29.

Although domestic sectionalism and partisanship severely hurt U.S. foreign affairs during this period, it was still an extremely active and important period that belies the 19th century's undeserved reputation as a time of complete isolationism in U.S. history. The nation welcomed foreign statesmen who honored democracy, reached out to forge ties with Asia, and even dreamed of an overseas empire modeled on Great Britain's. Most such dreams and ambitions were preempted by the Civil War and Reconstruction.

When the Americans of Commodore Perry's squadron first landed in Japan, the Japanese were as amazed by their visitors as the Americans were by the locals. This 1854 print shows, Captain Joel Adams as he appeared to the eye of a Japanese artist. (Library of Congress, Prints and Photographs Division [LC-USZ62-7834])

Politically, the Civil War–Reconstruction era forever changed the relationship between the American people and their government and between the state and the national governments. In essence nationalism and centralized government triumphed over sectionalism and states' rights. Never again would a state threaten to secede, and after the Fourteenth Amendment, the federal government would become the principal guarantor of due process and equal protection under the law for all citizens. Through the wartime income tax, conscription, martial law, and the Freedman's Bureau, Washington intruded more into the local and private spheres than could ever have been imagined in the early years of the Republic. The powers of the federal government expanded exponentially under wartime pressure, never to return to anything like their modest antebellum levels. All of these factors reflect the influence of the 16th president of the United States and what the historian George P. Fletcher calls the "Lincolnian moment" in U.S. constitutional history. That moment produced a radical reinterpretation of the original Constitution created in 1787. That document enshrined states' rights, individual liberty, and rule by sociopolitical elites. The "new Constitution" subtly shifted the emphasis to nationhood, equality, and popular democracy, all very different concepts from what the founding fathers intended.

The familiar U.S. two-party system received its final form at this time, with Democrats and Republicans staking out their turfs on the national and local levels. The Civil War destroyed the South's near-stranglehold on national politics dating back to the beginnings of the Republic. Eight presidents of the 15 before Lincoln were Southern-born, and two of the Northerners, Pierce and Buchanan, were Southern sympathizers ("Dough-Faced Presidents"). After the war, there would not be another Southern-born resident of the White House until Lyndon B. Johnson in 1963.

Southerners were also able to dominate Congress during the antebellum period through a combination of political skills, economic clout, agrarian alliance with western farmers, and ultimately the threat of secession if they did not get their way. After Southerners returned to Washington, D.C., in 1865, they never again possessed the same political power as a section that they had had before the Civil War.

Among the various components of the U.S. political system, the presidency was changed the most by events during these 25 years. Lincoln materially strengthened the presidency by his bold actions in preserving the Union and ending slavery. The constitutional line between the presidency and Congress was reinforced by the outcome of the 1868 impeachment crisis, although in the process it destroyed the career of a sitting president.

This era included one of the greatest presidents, if not the greatest president of all time, Abraham Lincoln, but it also included four of the worst presidents by most rankings, including the man who was arguably the worst of all, Millard Fillmore. Between Fillmore and Lincoln is a gulf so great it is amazing both men could have been elevated to the nation's highest office in such a short span of time.

Finally the central government's primacy over the states was established by war, legislation, and constitutional amendments. This federal supremacy included the right to manage the economy and promote an agenda of "national interests." Such a right was forcefully asserted via measures such as the Homestead Act, the National Banking Act, and subsidies for the transcontinental railroad, thus setting the stage for big government in the 20th century.

CHAPTER 10 The Civil War

The Civil War has been anointed by historians "America's supreme historical experience," meaning the defining moment in the nation's history. Reflecting the intensely partisan feelings that have existed about the war since the beginning, it has also been referred to by many other names, some from a Southern perspective and some from a Northern perspective, but very few neutral. Not surprisingly because Southerners lost the war, they have been the most creative in coining alternate names for the conflict, always with the intention of justifying their actions and thereby avoiding the taint of treason and rebellion. Northern names tend to focus on preserving the Union, freeing the slaves, and putting down a rebellion. Southern names tend to focus on Southern nationality, constitutional rights, and Northern aggression.

Partisan Names for the Civil War throughout U.S. History

Alternate Name	Perspective/Bias
The War between the States	Southern
The Civil War between the States	Southern
The War for Southern Independence	Southern
The War for Nationality	Southern
The War for Southern Nationality	Southern
The War against Northern Aggression	Southern
The War to Suppress Yankee Aggression	Southern
The Yankee Invasion	Southern
The War for the Union	Northern
The War for Separation	Southern
The War of Secession	Southern
The War for Abolition	Either
The War against Slavery	Northern
The Second [American] War for Independence	Southern
The Great Rebellion	Northern
The Southern Rebellion	Northern
The War of the Rebellion	Northern
Mr. Lincoln's War	Southern
The War for Constitutional Liberty	Southern
The War for States' Rights	Southern
The War for Southern Rights	Southern
The War of the Southern Planters	Northern
The Brothers' War	Either
The War for Nationality	Southern
The War of the Sixties	Either
The Confederate War	Southern
The War of the Southrons [sic]	Northern
The War for Southern Freedom	Southern
The War of the North and the South	Either
The Lost Cause	Southern
The Late Unpleasantness	Either

Source: Burke Davis, *Our Incredible Civil War* (New York: Holt, Rinehart & Winston, 1960), 79–80.

A "Modern" and "Total" War

The Civil War represented a complete breakdown in the democratic process, a contradiction of the basic principles of democracy, union, and constitutionalism on which the nation was founded. When the war ended, the Union was preserved and slavery was abolished but at a huge cost. The American Civil War was the single most destructive conflict in Western history until World War I, exceeding any of Napoleon's wars, the imperial wars of the 18th century, and the wars of the Reformation. Along with the institution of slavery, the entire socioeconomic system of the South was destroyed, as well as the long-standing dominance of the South in national politics.

Its significance does not stop there. In terms of technology, the Civil War was the first modern war in history because it was the first to incorporate all of the following in a systematic and significant way: the telegraph, armored ships, submarines, mine warfare, repeating weapons, and aerial observation. This is not to say that any of these was invented by Americans between 1861 and 1865, but all were effectively employed in determining the outcome of the conflict.

The basic rules and assumptions of warfare also changed between 1861 and 1865. In the beginning, both sides tried to fight a limited, or "gentleman's," war. For the North, this meant safeguarding enemy property (including slaves) and making the seizure of territory rather than the annihilation of armies the military objective. It also meant exchanging prisoners, relaying personal messages between the lines, and especially being willing to compromise all other issues except the right of secession. This easygoing attitude changed dramatically over the next four years on both sides as war began to include the destruction and confiscation of civilian property, emancipation of slaves, and suspension of basic civil rights of citizens, North and South. General William T. Sherman said late in the war, "We are not only fighting hostile armies, but a hostile people, and must make old and young, rich and poor, feel the hard hand of war." What had started out as a conventional civil war by the end had become arguably the first "total war" in history with both sides mobilizing all their resources and population for victory. Yet even at that it was not the sort of totalitarian war known today with ethnic cleansing, concentration camps, mass killing, indiscriminate bombardments, and torture; those were still in the future. When Sherman's "March to the Sea" ended at Savannah, he generously extended his official protection to the families of Confederate (enemy) general officers. He never even considered *not* doing so.

The Civil War was also an ideological war, settling the central question of whether the United States would be a federal or confederation form of government, tolerating slavery or championing human liberty. And it guaranteed the triumph of industrial capitalism over agrarianism and the plantation aristocracy.

The Causes of the War

The Civil War has been the most quantified, calibrated, and statistically analyzed event in U.S. history. Every aspect of the conflict has been broken down into its numerical components for study. Fortunately for scientific historians the U.S. government kept excellent records of even the most trivial aspects for posterity. Unfortunately, those records are much poorer for the South than for the North. But the wealth of data makes it relatively easy to profile the war statistically.

Some aspects of the Civil War cannot be quantified, however. Its causes, in particular, have long been argued. Certainly slavery played a central role, and the issue of states' rights is often cited by Southern apologists. The North and South had differing views of the Constitution and sovereignty. Their economies, social systems, and cultures were all at odds long before 1861. These differences have led some to argue that the country was split into two "nations" and that what started at Fort Sumter in April 1861 was an irrepressible conflict. No one, however, disagrees that the proximate causes of the great conflict were the election of Abraham Lincoln in November 1860 and the firing on Fort Sumter in April 1861. The former started the stampede to

TABLE 10.1 THE CONFEDERATE STATES OF AMERICA—SECESSION AND READMISSION, 1861–1870

State	Date of Secession	Date of Readmission	State	Date of Secession	Date of Readmission
S.C.	Dec. 20, 1861	Jul. 9, 1868	Tex.	Mar. 2, 1861[a]	Mar. 30, 1870
Miss.	Jan. 9, 1861	Feb. 23, 1861	Va.	Apr. 17, 1861	Jan. 26, 1870
Fla.	Jan. 10, 1861	Jun. 25, 1861	Ark.	May 6, 1861	Jun. 22, 1868
Ala.	Jan. 11, 1861	Jul. 13, 1868	N.C.	May 20, 1861	Jul. 4, 1868
Ga.	Jan. 19, 1861	Jul. 15, 1870	Tenn.	Jun. 8, 1861	Jul. 24, 1866
La.	Jan. 26, 1861	Jul. 9, 1868			

[a] Of all the Confederate states, Texas went through the most convoluted process to leave the Union. A specially called convention adopted a secession ordinance by a vote of 166 to 8 on Feb. 1. The issue was then submitted to popular vote in a statewide referendum on Feb. 23, which confirmed the convention's vote. On Mar. 2 the decision was officially announced as a fait accompli, a symbolic date already commemorated in Texas history as Independence Day (since 1836). Historians ever since have been divided over whether to use Feb. 1 or Mar. 2 as the official date of secession. Because Texans considered Mar. 2 as the "official date" at the time, that is the date used here.

Sources: The Civil War Book of Lists (Conshohocken, Pa.: Combined Books, 1993) 196; Hans L. Trefousse, *Historical Dictionary of Reconstruction* (Westport, Conn.: Greenwood Press, 1991), ix–xii.

secession, which began with South Carolina on December 20, 1860, and soon turned what had been a war of words into a shooting war after 10 additional states followed South Carolina's lead.

In February 1861, while the border states were still sitting on the fence, the seven states of the Deep South met in Montgomery, Alabama, to form the Confederate States of America. It would be eight long years of war and Reconstruction before any of them returned, and in winter 1861 none of them had any intention of returning to the Union. They had committed themselves to forming a new nation, much as their forebears had in 1776.

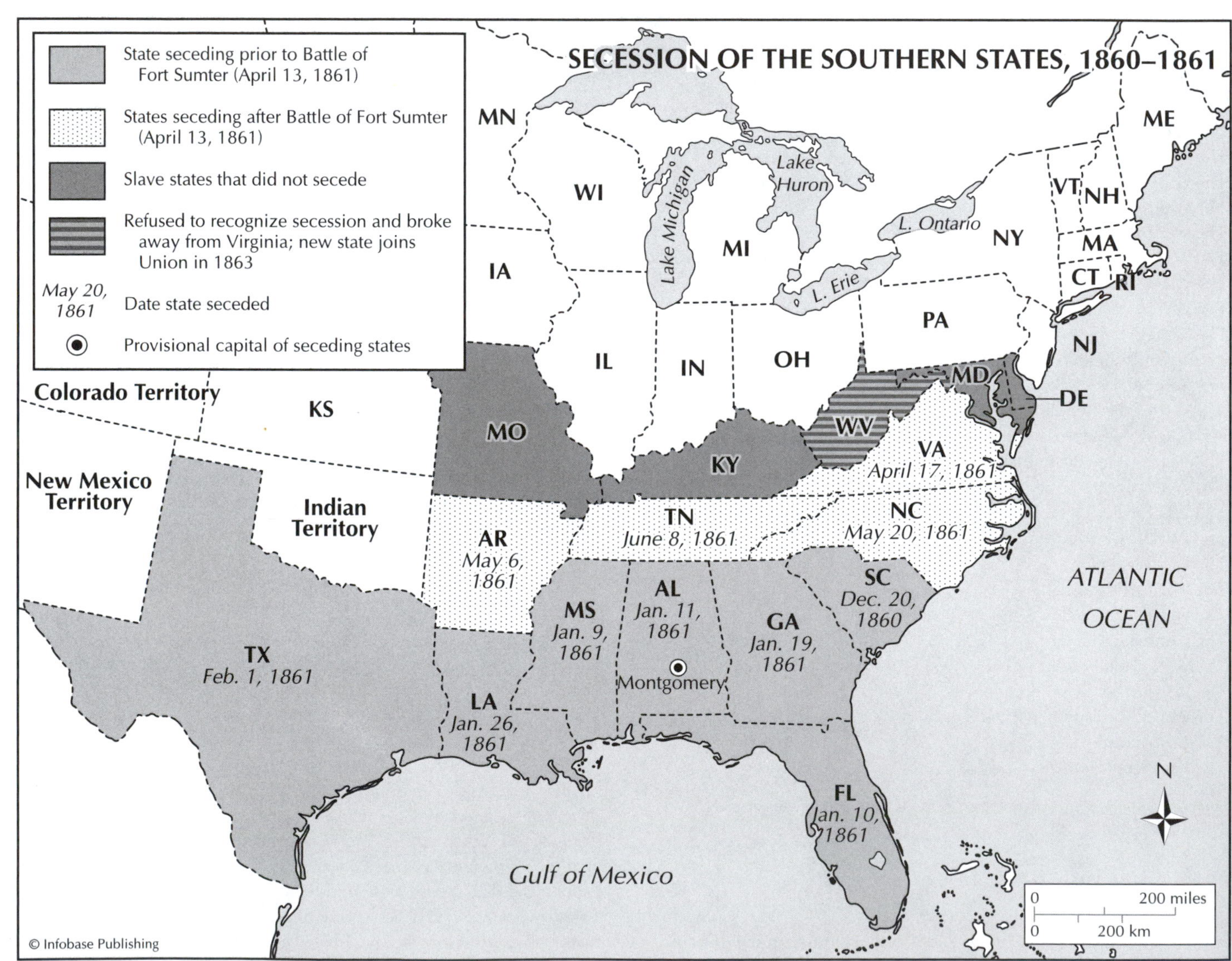

Four key states—Virginia, Arkansas, Tennessee, and North Carolina—did not secede until after the fall of Fort Sumter. The border slave states of Maryland, Delaware, Kentucky, and Missouri stayed in the Union.

Source: Paul S. Boyer, Clifford E. Clark, Jr., et al. *The Enduring Vision: A History of American People,* 2d ed. Lexington, Mass.: D.C. Heath and Co., 1993, 472, *Historical Maps On File,* New York: Facts On File, 2001.

TABLE 10.2 PROFILE OF THE CONFEDERATE STATES OF AMERICA, 1861–1865

State	Total Population	White Population	Black Population	Percentage of Blacks in Total Population
S.C	703,620	291,300	412,320	58.6
Miss.	791,303	353,899	437,404	55.3
Fla.	140,423	77,746	62,677	44.6
Ala.	964,041	526,271	437,770	45.4
Ga.	1,057,248	591,550	465,698	44.0
La.	707,829	357,492	350,337	49.5
Tex.	603,812	420,891	182,921	30.3
Va.	1,596,206	1,047,299	548,907	34.4
Ark.	434,402	323,143	111,259	25.6
N.C.	991,464	629,942	361,522	36.5
Tenn.	1,109,741	826,722	283,019	25.5

Source: The Civil War Book of Lists (Conshohocken, Pa.: Combined Books, 1993), 187–91, 197–98.

Two Wartime Governments

In 1861 Americans became one people divided by a common form of government. Both Southerners and Northerners claimed to be true believers in the Constitution, and this attitude was reflected in the fact that the two governments were mirror images of each other. But at the head of those two governments were two men as opposite as night and day.

Representatives of the new Confederate States of America, meeting in Montgomery, Alabama, in February, elected Jefferson Davis of Mississippi, the former U.S. secretary of war, as their chief executive. He would be the Confederacy's only president during its four years of existence. Then on March 4, Abraham Lincoln took the oath of office to commence his duties as president of the United States. The whole country held its breath to see what the two leaders would do. They tried to surround themselves with the most qualified men they could find while also recognizing the political reality that certain important constituencies had to be served.

Lincoln and Davis faced their daunting jobs aided by two very different groups of advisers. Lincoln's cabinet was made up of recent refugees from other political parties (e.g., Whigs, and Free Soilers). The 13 men who served under him during the course of the war were on the whole able, ambitious, and experienced politicians. They were chosen to represent a broad spectrum of political and ideological interests, forming a coalition who were as willing to fight among themselves as against the Confederates. Lincoln gave them a great deal of latitude in running their departments. In December 1862, a small cabal of Republican senators provoked a constitutional crisis when they conspired with one member of the cabinet (Secretary of Treasury Salmon P. Chase) to challenge Lincoln for control of the cabinet. Lincoln triumphed, asserting his control over the executive department, but he suffered back-stabbing, scheming cabinet officers to stay on so long as they ran their departments effectively. Because Jefferson Davis, by contrast, hand-picked every member of his cabinet, their generally poor performance reflects badly on the president's judgment. The Confederate Congress pressured Davis throughout the war to reform the cabinet to make it more to their liking, but he successfully resisted. Generally the principal qualification for membership in Davis's cabinet was a demonstrated ability to get along with the prickly president. Fourteen men served in the Confederate cabinet during the war.

TABLE 10.3 TOP UNION AND CONFEDERATE GOVERNMENT OFFICIALS, 1861–1865

Official	Union Government	Confederate Government
President	Abraham Lincoln, Ill. (1861–65)	Jefferson Davis, Miss. (1861–65)
Vice president	Hannibal Hamlin, Maine (1861–64)[a] Andrew Johnson, Tenn. (1864–65)[b]	Alexander H. Stephens, Ga. (1861–65)
Secretary of state	William H. Seward, N.Y. (1861–65)[c]	Robert Toombs, Ga. (Feb. 21, 1861–Jul. 24, 1861) R. M. T. Hunter, Va. (Jul. 25, 1861–Mar. 17, 1862) Judah P. Benjamin, La. (Mar. 18, 1862–Apr. 1865)
Attorney general	Edward Bates, Mo. (1861–Nov. 1864)[d] James Speed, Ky. (Dec. 1864–65)	Judah P. Benjamin, La. (Feb. 25, 1861–Nov. 20, 1861) Thomas Bragg, N.C. (Nov. 21, 1861–Mar. 17, 1862) Thomas H. Watts, Al. (Mar. 18, 1862–Jan. 1, 1864) George Davis, N.C. (Jan. 2, 1864–Apr. 1865)
Secretary of war	Simon Cameron, Pa. (1861–Jan. 1862) Edwin M. Stanton, Ohio (Jan. 1862–65)[e]	Leroy Pope Walker, Ala. (Feb. 21, 1861–Nov. 20, 1861) Judah P. Benjamin (Nov. 21, 1861–Mar. 17, 1862) George W. Randolph, Va. (Mar. 18, 1862–Nov. 16, 1862) Gen. Gustavus W. Smith, Ky. (Nov. 17, 1862–Nov. 20, 1862)[f] James A. Sedden, Va. (Nov. 21, 1862–Feb. 5, 1865) Gen. John C. Breckenridge, Ky. (Feb. 6, 1865–Apr. 1865)
Secretary of the treasury	Salmon P. Chase, Ohio (1861–Jun. 1864) William P. Fessenden, Maine (Jul. 1864–Mar. 1865) Hugh McCulloch, Ind. (Mar.–Apr. 1865)	Charles G. Memminger, S.C. (Feb. 21, 1861–Jul. 17, 1864) George A. Trenholm, S.C. (Jul. 18, 1864–Apr. 1865)

(continued)

TABLE 10.3 (continued)

Official	Union Government	Confederate Government
Secretary of the navy	Gideon Welles, Conn. (1861–65)	Stephen D. Mallory, Fla. (Mar. 4, 1861–Apr. 1865)
Postmaster general	Montgomery Blair, Md. (1861–Sep. 1864) William Dennison, Ohio (Sep. 1864–Apr. 1865)	Henry T. Ellet, Miss. (Feb. 25, 1861–Mar. 5, 1861) James Reagan, Tex. (Mar. 6, 1861–Apr. 1865)
Secretary of the interior	Caleb B. Smith, Ind. (1861–Dec. 1862) John P. Usher, Ind. (Dec. 1862–Apr. 1865)	N/A

[a] The only U.S. vice president to have concurrent military and political careers in office, Hamlin served as a private in the Maine Coast Guard during the Civil War.
[b] Assumed presidency after Lincoln assassinated in Apr. 1865; voted out of office in Nov. 1868.
[c] One of only two officers to serve in Lincoln's cabinet throughout the entire war; the other was the secretary of the navy, Gideon Welles.
[d] The first cabinet officer in U.S. history from a state west of the Mississippi River.
[e] Served in Andrew Johnson's cabinet until May 26, 1868, when he quit in a power struggle over Reconstruction.
[f] Had the shortest tenure of any cabinet officer in either administration, and one of only two to hold an officer's commission while serving in a cabinet post; the other was Confederate secretary of war, John C. Breckenridge.
Sources: Robert C. Wood, *Confederate Handbook* (privately printed, 1900), passim; *The Civil War Book of Lists* (Conshohocken, Pa.: Combined Books, 1993), 203–06; Stewart Sifakis, *Who Was Who in the Civil War* (New York: Facts On File, 1988), passim.

In the early days of 1861, officers of the U.S. Army and Navy were resigning their commissions en masse daily to join the Confederacy: 313 of 1,098 army officers on active duty went south, and 322 naval officers (about one-fourth of the total) likewise switched loyalties. Together they formed the core of the Confederate military. The brotherhood of West Point alumni was hit especially hard. With partisan feelings riding high, all attempts at compromise failed, including the two most promising proposals, those of Senator John Crittenden and of the Virginia Peace Convention. Across the South, patriotic citizens flocked to the colors, determined to eject all "enemy" forces and seize all U.S. property within their borders.

The war of words turned into a shooting war at half past 4:00 A.M. on Friday, April 12, 1861, when Confederate forces surrounding Charleston harbor, South Carolina, opened fire on Fort Sumter. The first shot in defense of the Union was fired by Captain Abner Doubleday at 7:00 A.M. The Confederate bombardment continued for 34 hours before the garrison surrendered. Only one man, Private Daniel Hough, a federal soldier, was killed, but the war was truly joined.

News of Fort Sumter galvanized the nation as Pearl Harbor, Lexington and Concord, the sinking of the USS *Maine,* and the attacks of September 11, 2001, would at the beginning of other wars in U.S. history. Among other results, it branded the South as the aggressor, the breaker of the peace, in the conflict that followed. President Lincoln promptly seized the moral high ground, calling for 75,000 volunteers to put down the rebellion, an action that pushed the border states to choose sides. Virginia, Arkansas, Tennessee, and North Carolina, after much agonizing and political maneuvering, cast their lot with the Confederacy. Kentucky, Missouri, Maryland, Delaware, and the northwestern counties of Virginia chose to stay with the Union.

The Two Sides Compared

At the outset the Northern states clearly had all the advantages. The South lacked material and economic resources but possessed such intangible advantages as a strong martial spirit, capable leadership dedicated to the cause of states' rights, defensible territory, and the economic trump card of cotton. The two sides split over the claim to moral rectitude, with the North fighting for preservation of the Union ("the best government on Earth" and "the last hope for democracy") and the South painting itself as the champion of the Constitution and the right to be left alone. Neither side talked about slavery, neither defending it or abolishing it.

The material advantages all lay on the Northern side in terms of both population and economic resources. The South's major asset was "King Cotton," which could be used as both a diplomatic and an economic weapon. The South also possessed certain intangibles, such as a strong military tradition, a fiercely independent spirit, and the incentive to defend their own invaded lands. But by all quantifiable measures, the North clearly had the upper hand.

TABLE 10.4 COMPARISON OF RESOURCES NORTH AND SOUTH, 1860

Areas of Comparison	North (Free States)	South (Slave States)	United States
Number of states	23 (and seven territories)[a]	11	34
Population	20,700,000	9,105,000 (including 3,654,000 slaves)	31,443,321
"Military population" (ages 18–45)[b]	3,904,647	898,184	5,318,916
Banking capital (deposits)	$189 million	$47 million	$233 million
Gold specie	$56 million	$27 million	$83 million
Property values	$11 billion	$5½ billion	$16.5 billion
Railroad mileage	21,973 miles	9,283 miles	31,256 miles
Locomotives built in 1860	451	19	470
Naval forces[c]	42 ships	0 ship	84 ships
Land area	2,219,640 sq. miles	750,000 sq. mi.	2,969,640 sq. mi[d]
Value of farmland per acre	$25.67	$10.40	N/A
Value of farm machinery and implements per acre	$.89	$0.42	N/A

Areas of Comparison	North (Free States)	South (Slave States)	United States
Value of farm machinery and implements per worker	$52.00	$30.00	N/A
Horses and mules	4,600,000	2,600,000	7,200,000
Capital invested in manufacturing per capita	$43.73	$13.25	N/A
Number of manufacturing establishments (factories)	110,000	18,000	128,000
Number of manufacturing workers[e]	1,300,000	110,000	1,410,000
Average number of school days per year	135 days	80 days	N/A
Per capita wealth of free population	$2,040	$3,978 (including slaves)	N/A
Per capita income of total population	$141	$103	N/A
Number of newspapers[f]	N/A	N/A	3,300

Note: Based on 1860 census statistics.
[a] Includes the three border states of Mo., Ky., and Md., which, though supporting the South in principle, remained in the Union during the war.
[b] Does not include the three border states of Ky., Md., and Mo., which had a combined military population of 516,085 and furnished substantial numbers of troops to both sides.
[c] The 42 ships of the North accounts for usable warships; the 84 ships of the U.S. Navy in 1860 includes all vessels of every class and condition.
[d] Based on 1860 U.S. Census, but not including territories.
[e] Counting both slave and free manufacturing workers.
[f] The regional distribution of newspapers is unknown, although the North had overwhelming numerical superiority.
Sources: James M. McPherson, *Ordeal by Fire: The Civil War and Reconstruction* (New York: Alfred A. Knopf, 1982), 24; Carol Berkin et al., *Making America: A History of the United States* (Boston: Houghton Mifflin, 1995), 410; Joseph R. Conlin, *The American Past,* Part 1, *A Survey of American History to 1877* (San Diego: Harcourt Brace Jovanovich, 1984), 367, 389; Kenneth C. Davis, *Don't Know Much about History* (New York: Crown, 1990), 166; Robert C. Wood, *Confederate Hand-book* (privately printed, 1900), 23.

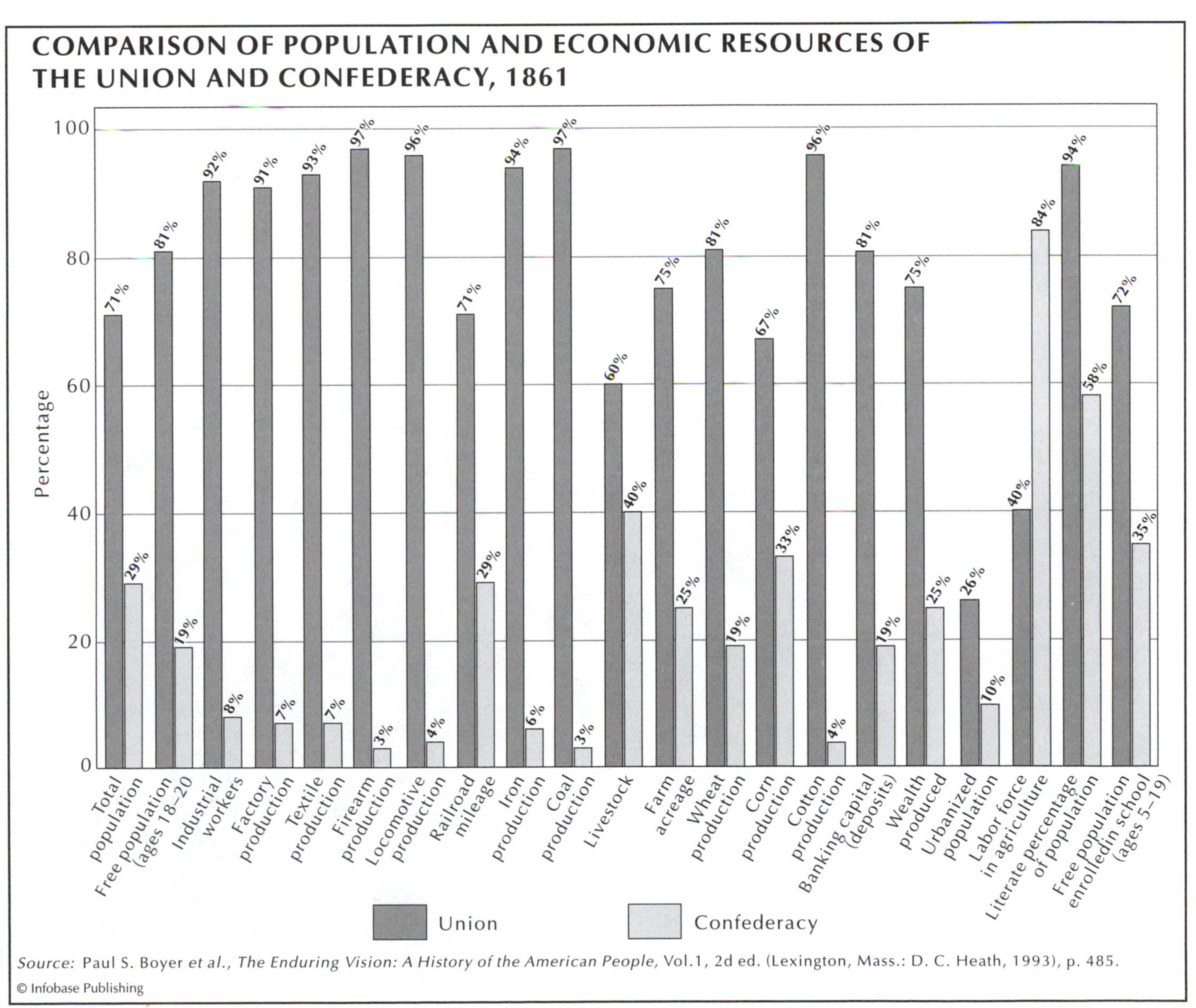

Source: Paul S. Boyer et al., *The Enduring Vision: A History of the American People,* Vol.1, 2d ed. (Lexington, Mass.: D. C. Heath, 1993), p. 485.

The Soldiers

In the first flush of patriotism during the opening weeks of the war, men flocked to the colors to fight for cause and country in such numbers that they could not be processed by their respective government. Neither side anticipated a long war, so the initial calls that went out were for three-month enlistments. The early enlisted units had a certain homogeneity, as men signed up en masse from the same county, town, or university. Many of the soldiers were little more than boys, 19 or 20 years old. Men in their 30s were considered "graybeards." Most were farm boys: 50 percent on the Northern side, 90 percent on the Southern. Many were less than five feet nine inches in height and weighed no more than 140 pounds.

Every state and territory of the old United States furnished troops to its respective cause, although some—such as Virginia and North Carolina for the Confederacy, and Pennsylvania and Illinois for the Union—contributed far more than others. Some states, most notably Maryland, Kentucky, and Tennessee, contributed substantial numbers of troops to both sides. Despite the Civil War's characterization as a "citizen's war," the average percentage of the population from any state serving in the military was around 12 percent, meaning that some 88 percent of the nation did not take up arms in the war.

The war was still new and hopes were high as Confederate troops march past Pulaski Monument in Savannah, Georgia, on August 7, 1861, before heading off to the front in Virginia. (Courtesy of the Georgia Historical Society)

TABLE 10.5 NUMBERS OF MEN FURNISHED BY EACH STATE DURING THE CIVIL WAR

State	North or South[a]	Number of Men Furnished[b]	As Percentage of State's Population	As Percentage of Total Union/ Confederate Army
N.Y.	North	448,850	11.6	11.7
Va.	South	192,924	12.1	15.0
Del.	North	12,284	10.9	0.3
Pa.	North	337,936	14.3	8.8
N.J.	North	76,814	11.4	2.0
Ga.	South	133,486	12.6	3.5
Conn.	North	55,864	12.1	1.5
Mass.	North	146,730	11.9	3.8
Md.	Both	66,638	9.7	1.7
S.C.	South	65,462	9.3	1.7
N.C.	South	135,191	13.6	3.5
N.H.	North	33,937	10.4	0.9
R.I.	North	23,236	13.3	0.6
Vt.	North	33,288	10.6	0.9
Ky.	Both	100,760	8.7	2.6
Tenn.	South	166,227	15.0	4.3
Ohio	North	313,180	13.4	8.2
La.	South	82,276	11.6	2.1
Ind.	North	196,363	14.5	5.1
Miss.	South	103,414	13.1	2.7
Ill.	North	259,092	15.1	6.8
Ala.	South	107,547	11.2	2.8
Maine	North	70,107	11.2	1.8
Mo.	Both	149,111	12.6	3.9
Ark.	South	58,815	13.5	1.5
Mich.	North	87,364	11.8	2.3
Fla.	South	17,334	12.3	0.5
Tex.	South	60,012	9.9	1.6
Iowa	North	76,242	11.3	2.0
Wis.	North	91,194	11.8	2.4
Calif.	North	15,725	4.8	0.4
Minn.	North	24,020	14.2	0.6
Oreg.	North	1,810	3.5	0.0
Kans.	North	20,149	18.8	0.5
W.Va.[c]	North	N/A	N/A	N/A
Nev.[d]	North	1,080	15.8	0.0
District of Columbia	North	16,534	22.0	0.4

Note: Does not include organized territories (i.e., Utah, Colorado, Nebraska, New Mexico, Washington, Dakota, or Indian Territory).
[a] States that contributed significant numbers of troops to both sides are so indicated, with no distinction made for the numbers they contributed to each side. Because this was a civil war, practically every state had its citizens serving in both armies.
[b] These numbers represent all men furnished by the state regardless of side.
[c] W.Va. split off from Va. after Va. seceded, and it joined the Union as a separate state on June 20, 1863. No figures are available for its contributions to the war as a separate political entity.
[d] Nev. was a territory until it was formally admitted into the Union on Oct. 31, 1864. No distinction is made between its troop contribution as a territory versus as a state.
Source: The Civil War Book of Lists (Conshohocken, Pa.: Combined Books, 1993), 16–19.

In both armies foreign-born men formed a significant portion of the troops. Here the flood of immigrants landing on U.S. shores in the 10–15 years before the war was reaping unforeseen fruits. The North had become the home to far more of those immigrants than the South for reasons both economic and social. Among Confederate states, only about 1 percent of the population in 1860 had been foreign-born. But regardless of background, on both sides, they tended to join the fight along with their native-born neighbors, although the Germans in the Texas hill country represented an exception to this rule. In the Northern army a much larger percentage, about 25 percent, were foreign-born, whereas in the Southern army no more than 5–10 percent were. On the Northern side, most were Germans and Irish; on the Southern side, Scots and Scotch-Irish predominated. Many of the foreign-born troops padding the Southern numbers were from New Orleans, which was the second-most cosmopolitan city in the country after New York. The upper officers' ranks on both sides welcomed foreign-born men of ability. General officers such as Sigel, Schurz, Spinola, and Stahel in the Northern army and Cleburne and De Polignac in the Southern army fought with distinction that reflected well on their countrymen. In one respect, at least, this was a North American war: significant numbers of Mexicans and Canadians fought on the two sides, although for personal reasons, not as representatives of their people. The armies of both sides were "melting pots" of different ethnic and national groups that defy easy stereotyping.

TABLE 10.6 FOREIGN-BORN SOLDIERS IN THE ARMIES OF THE NORTH AND THE SOUTH

National Background	Union Army	Confederate Army
British[a]	60,000	10,000
Canadian[b]	53,500	10,000
French	1,000	1,000
German[c]	200,000	10,000
Hungarian	800	N/A
Irish	144,200	20,000
Italian	2,000	500
Mexican[d]	4,500	7,500
Dutch	100	N/A
Norwegian	6,500	N/A
Polish	4,000	1,000
Spanish[e]	300	N/A
Swedish	3,000	N/A
Swiss	500	N/A
Total	**478,700**	**92,800**

[a] Includes Welsh- and Scottish- as well as English-born persons.
[b] Estimates of the numbers of Canadians who fought on the two sides vary widely, ranging as high as 40,000 in gray according to some sources, and as low as 40,000 in blue.
[c] Figures for Germans are also imprecise, because Germany only became a unified nation state in 1871, so "Germans" before that date could include Austrians and even ethnic Poles, Czechs, and Hungarians living under Teutonic rulers.
[d] Most of these were not Mexican nationals but descendants of Hispanics living in the Southwest on lands annexed by the United States in the 1840s and 1850s, so their status as "foreign-born" is questionable.
[e] *Spanish* here includes, besides European-born, those from Cuba and Puerto Rico.
Source: Albert A. Nofi, "Knapsack: A Civil War Digest," *North & South Magazine* 2, no. 5 (June 1999), 8.

Blurring all ethnic differences, the two armies were quickly dubbed "Billy Yank" and "Johnny Reb," reflecting the U.S. fondness for wartime nicknames (similar to 20th-century examples "doughboys" of World War I and "G.I.s" of World War II). After 1862, large numbers of African Americans were enlisted in the Union army, most of them free blacks from the North. In Southern and border states, runaway slaves attached themselves to the Union army, but the overwhelming majority were assigned to menial tasks rather than actual soldiering. Early in the war there was some debate whether they should be returned to their Southern masters or treated as captured contraband and employed in the Northern war effort.

After considerable agonizing, the Lincoln government decided to enlist blacks as soldiers, an experiment that was fraught with political as well as military risks, not the least of which was a white backlash in the loyal border states. By the end of the war, some 200,000 African Americans were fighting on the Northern side, a number that represents a remarkable advance over the estimated 5,000 who fought in the American Revolution and 3,000 who fought in the War of 1812. (A small but significant number of blacks, it seems, also chose to fight for the South.) Regardless of which side they fought on, or whether they were runaway slaves or free blacks, when given the chance, African Americans fought with distinction and, in several notable cases, with heroism on a par with that of their better-paid and better-trained white comrades. In three years of fighting, 68,000 blacks died in the service and 21 (13 army, eight navy) received the Medal of Honor for conduct "above and beyond the call of duty."

A Northern wartime recruiting poster aimed at African Americans invited them to join the great cause and fight for emancipation. The poster reveals that all black units were commanded by white commissioned officers. (Library of Congress, Prints and Photographs Division [LC -USZ62 2048])

The Armies

In January 1861 there were 16,400 men and officers in the U.S. Regular Army. In the next four years that number increased exponentially as both sides rushed to fill the ranks through appeals to patriotism, levies on state militias, and ultimately conscription. By the end of the war there were more than 3,217,000 men in uniform. The rapid military expansion began by calling out tens of thousands of trained militia, which every state possessed by constitutional guarantee. On top of that, the military *potential* for each side has been calculated at 2,486,000 for

Lincoln and His Generals depicts the president in an imaginary wartime conference with (*left* to *right*) Admirals David Porter and David Farragut and Generals William Sherman, George Thomas, U.S. Grant, and Phillip Sheridan. This sort of patriotic print sold very well after the war. (Lithograph by Peter Kramer, print from author's collection)

the North and 692,000 for the South. It is impossible to calculate accurately the number of men who served in the respective armed forces because many men enlisted more than once and because of poor record keeping. But it is fair to say that from the beginning, Union forces consistently outnumbered Confederate, and by an ever-growing margin as the war dragged on. At the beginning of 1862 it was a two-to-one advantage; by the end of 1864, it had risen to a three-to-one edge. The manpower pool for the North, in the all-important age group 18–45 (from 1860 Census figures), was more than four times that of the South. The Southern boast that one Reb could whip 10 Yankees was a necessary self-delusion. Not only were Northern armies larger, they were also more ethnically and racially diverse, counting large numbers of blacks and foreign-born. Southern armies were drawn almost 100 percent from native-born whites of Anglo-Saxon heritage.

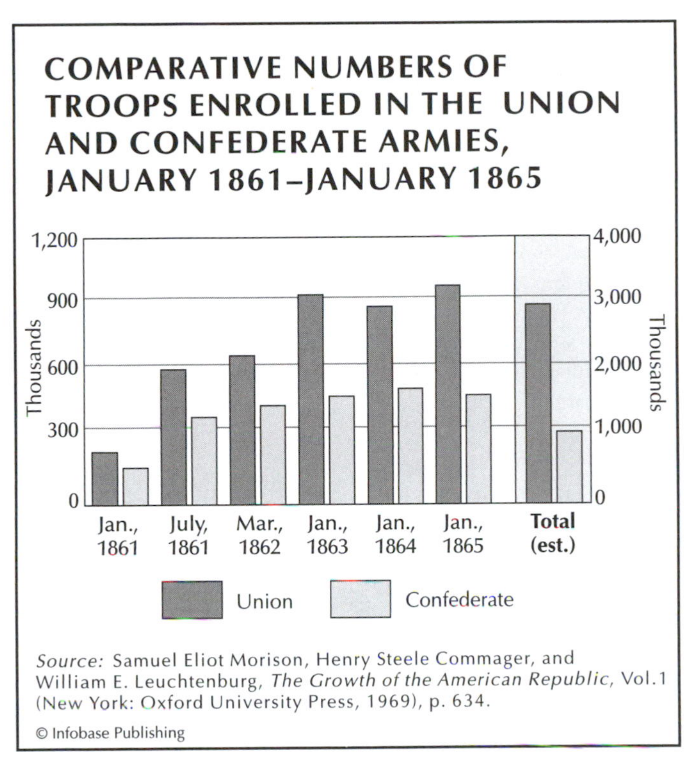

TABLE 10.7 DEMOGRAPHIC ANALYSIS OF UNITED STATES AND CONFEDERATE STATES FORCES

Forces	Total Enlisted Personnel[a]	African Americans	African Americans as Percentage of Total	Foreign-Born	Foreign-Born as Percentage of Total	Northern-Born/ Southern-Born	Native Americans	Jewish
U.S. Army	2,129,000	178,975	9.0	500,000	24	Unknown	Unknown	6,000–8,500
U.S. Navy	60,000	18,000	14.0	3,000	2.3	8,500 (North) 6,500 (South)	Unknown	Unknown
U.S. Marines	4,167	Unknown	Unknown	Unknown	Unknown	Unknown	Unknown	Unknown
C.S. Army	882,000	Unknown	Unknown	98,135	9.0–10.0	Unknown	4,000 (Nov. 1861)	1,800–2,000
C.S. Navy	3,674[b]	Unknown	Unknown	Unknown	Unknown	Unknown	Unknown	Unknown
C.S. Marines	753[b]	Unknown	Unknown	Unknown	Unknown	Unknown	Unknown	Unknown

Note: Returns for Confederate forces are incomplete and inexact because many of the records did not survive the war; therefore, they can only be taken as educated guesses.
[a] Includes both officers and enlisted men.
[b] Numbers are for peak year of 1864 only, rather than total wartime numbers.
Sources: William H. Price, *The Civil War Handbook* (Fairfax, Va.: Prince Lithograph, 1961), 31, 38, 43; Patricia L. Faust, ed., *Historical Times Illustrated Encyclopedia of the Civil War* (New York: Harper & Row, 1986), passim; James M. McPherson, *Ordeal by Fire: The Civil War and Reconstruction* (New York: Alfred A. Knopf. 1982), 358; Philip Katcher, *The American Civil War Source Book* (London: Arms and Armour, 1992), 226, 233, 235; Raimondo Luraghi, *A History of the Confederate Navy* (Annapolis, Md.: Naval Institute Press, 1996), 27; Thomas L. Livermore, *Numbers and Losses in the Civil War in America, 1861–1865* (Boston: Houghton Mifflin, 1900), passim; Albert A. Nofi, "Foreigners in the Armies," *North & South Magazine* 2, no. 5 (June 1999): 8; Joseph P. Reidy, "Black Civil War Sailors Project," *Columbiad Quarterly* 3, no. 2 (Summer 1999): 17–20.

The Fighting

Strategy on the two sides was fairly simple. In order to win, the North had to wage an offensive war of conquest by invading and subduing the South. This involved destroying Confederate armies wherever they arose, crushing the South's will to rebel, and isolating it from outside support by blockading the coastline. By contrast, the South in order to win had only to prevent the North from being victorious, to outlast the North much as the 13 colonies had outlasted the British in the American Revolution.

The tactics of fighting would be shaped by the use of railroads, rifled muskets, and long-range artillery, making defense the king of the battlefield and turning attack into a risky and bloody proposition at best. Before the war was over, the traditional massed frontal attack perfected by Napoléon had been thoroughly discredited at such places as Gaines Mill (1862), Gettysburg (1863), and Cold Harbor (1864). Unfortunately these lessons were learned slowly and painfully with the expenditure of tens of thousands of lives in heroic if hopeless charges.

According to the best estimate, some 10,455 clashes of arms were fought between 1861 and 1865. These can be broken down from the largest, campaigns lasting months and producing tens of thousands of casualties, to inconsequential "affairs" and "scouts." In between are the major battles and actions that mark the progress of the war toward victory for one side and defeat for the other. Unfortunately there is no handy guide to Civil War field operations that carefully defines every clash of arms in terms of numbers engaged, duration, casualties, and other details. Contemporary usage is the only guideline that exists. Although campaigns, sieges, and scouts are easy to define, the differences between, say, a "combat" and an "engagement" is much more subtle and arbitrary. In many cases the classification depends on the terminology favored by the participants. Major battles require no such fine parsing of terminology, because most people understand in a vague sort of way what a "battle" is.

TABLE 10.8 10,455 CLASHES OF ARMS DESIGNATED BY CATEGORY

Type of Action	Number	Type of Action	Number
Campaigns	29	Sieges	26
Battles	76	Raids	64
Engagements	310	Expeditions	727
Combats	46	Reconnaissances	252
Actions	1,026	Scouts	434
Assaults	29	Affairs	639
Skirmishes	6,337	Occupations	82
Operations	299	Captures	79

Note: According to contemporary 19th-century usage.
Source: E. B. Long, *The Civil War Day by Day* (Garden City, N.Y.: Doubleday, 1971), 718–19.

The Civil War produced its share of atrocities. One of the most notorious was the Fort Pillow Massacre of April 12, 1864, when troops of the Confederate general Nathan B. Forrest overran the Union garrison and killed some 231 men, mostly blacks. In this artist's rendering, the Southerners have driven their opponents down the bluff to bank of the Mississippi, where they are bayoneting and clubbing men and women alike. (Library of Congress)

TABLE 10.9 THE MAJOR BATTLES OF THE CIVIL WAR, 1861–1865

Battle (Theater)	Date	Casualties[a]	Confederate Commander	Union Commander	Victor	Significance
Fort Sumter (Eastern)	Apr. 12–14, 1861	3 Federals 0 Confederates	General P. G. T. Beauregard	Major Robert Anderson	Confederates	Opening shots of Civil War are fired.
First Bull Run (Eastern)	Jul. 21, 1861	2,645 Federals 1,981 Confederates	Generals J. E. Johnson and P. G. T. Beauregard	General Irvin McDowell	Confederates	Both sides prepare for long war.
Forts Henry and Donelson (Western)	Feb. 6, 16, 1862	2,879 Federals 16,702 Confederates[b]	Generals, S. B. Buckner, J. Floyd, G. Pillow	General U. S. Grant	Federals	North gains control of Tennessee and Cumberland Rivers; begins campaign to open Mississippi River.
Shiloh/Pittsburgh Landing (Western)	Apr. 6–7, 1862	10,162 Federals 9,735 Confederates	General A. S. Johnston	General U. S. Grant	Federals	First important battle in the West occurs.
New Orleans (Western)	Apr. 29, 1862	171 Federals 50 Confederates	General Mansfield Lovell	Captain David Farragut, U.S. Navy General Ben Butler, U.S. Army	Federals	North gains control of mouth of Mississippi River.
Fair Oaks/Seven Pines (Eastern)	May 31, 1862	5,031 Federals 6,134 Confederates	General J. E. Johnston	General George B. McClellan	Federals	North tries unsuccessfully to capture Richmond.
Seven Days' Battles (Eastern)[c]	Jun. 25–Jul. 1, 1862	15,849 Federals 20,141 Confederates	General R. E. Lee	General George B. McClellan	Confederates	North fails to capture capital of the Confederacy; Lee takes command of Confederate army.
Second Bull Run (Eastern)	Aug. 29–30, 1862	16,000 Federals 9,108 Confederates	General R. E. Lee	General John Pope	Confederates	North again fails to capture Richmond.
Antietam/Sharpsburg (Eastern)	Sep. 16–17, 1862	11,657 Federals 11,724 Confederates	General R. E. Lee	General George B. McClellan	Federals	South fails in first invasion of the North.
Perryville, Ky. (Western)	Oct. 8, 1862	4,211 Federals 3,396 Confederates	General Braxton Bragg	General Don Carlos Buell	Confederates	South fails to wrest Ky. from the Union.
Fredericksburg (Eastern)	Dec. 13, 1862	12,700 Federals 5,300 Confederates	General R. E. Lee	General Ambrose E. Burnside	Confederates	North again fails to capture Richmond.
Murfreesboro/Stones River, Tenn. (Western)	Dec. 31, 1862	12,906 Federals 9,239 Confederates	General Braxton Bragg	General William S. Rosecrans	Federals	North gains control of middle Tenn.
Chancellorsville (Eastern)	May 5, 1863	11,116 Federals 10,746 Confederates	General R. E. Lee	General Joseph Hooker	Confederates	North fails fifth time to capture Richmond.
Gettysburg (Eastern)	Jul. 1–3, 1863	17,684 Federals 22,638 Confederates	General R. E. Lee	General George G. Meade	Federals	South fails in second invasion of the North.
Vicksburg, Miss.[d] (Western)	May 18–Jul. 4, 1863	4,536 Federals 31,277 Confederates[e]	General John C. Pemberton	General U. S. Grant	Federals	North gains control of the Mississippi River.
Chickamauga, Ga. (Western)	Sep. 20–22, 1863	11,413 Federals 16,986 Confederates	General Braxton Bragg	General William S. Rosecrans	Confederates	South gains last great victory.
Chattanooga, Tenn. (Western)[f]	Nov. 23–25, 1863	5,616 Federals 8,684 Confederates	General Braxton Bragg	General U. S. Grant and General William T. Sherman	Federals	North opens way for invasion of Ga.
Wilderness (Eastern)	May 5–7, 1864	14,283 Federals 10,887 Confederates[g]	General R. E. Lee	General U. S. Grant	Indecisive	North starts final drive toward Richmond.
Spotsylvania Court House (Eastern)	May 10–19, 1864	12,632 Federals 11,999 Confederates[g]	General R. E. Lee	General U. S. Grant	Confederates	North continues drive toward Richmond.
Cold Harbor (Eastern)	Jun. 1–3, 1864	7,000 Federals 5,227 Confederates[g]	General R. E. Lee	General U. S. Grant	Confederates	North continues drive toward Richmond.
Petersburg (Eastern)[h]	Jun. 15–19, 1864	11,386 Federals Unknown Confederates	General R. E. Lee	General U. S. Grant	Indecisive	North closes in on Richmond.
Atlanta (Western)	Sep. 2, 1864	10,528 Federals 9,187 Confederates	General John B. Hood General J. E. Johnston	General William T. Sherman	Federals	Sherman begins famous March to the Sea.
Ft. Fisher, N.C. (Eastern)	Jan. 13–15, 1865	1,641 Federals[i] 2,483 Confederates	Colonel W. Lanb	General Alfred H. Terry	Federals	Confederacy's last blockade-running port (Wilmington) closed.
Sayler's Creek, Va. (Eastern)	Apr. 6, 1865	1,180 Federals 7,000 Confederates[j]	General R. E. Lee	General U. S. Grant	Federals	Last significant battle between Grant and Lee before surrender. at Appomattox (Apr. 9, 1865)

(continued)

TABLE 10.9 (continued)

Battle (Theater)	Date	Casualties[a]	Confederate Commander	Union Commander	Victor	Significance
Palmito Ranch, Tex. (Trans-Mississippi)	May 12–13, 1865	30 Federals 5 Confederates	Colonel John S. "Rip" Ford	Colonel Theodore H. Barrett	Confederates	Last battle of the war occurs.

[a] Includes killed, wounded, and missing, but not captured.
[b] Includes many who escaped and disappeared into surrounding country.
[c] Includes the following battles: Oak Grove (Jun. 25), Mechanicsville (Jun. 26), Gaines' Mill (Jun. 27–28), Savage's Station and Allen's Farm (Jun. 29), White Oak Swamp/Frayser's Farm (Jun. 30), and Malvern Hill (Jul. 1).
[d] Properly speaking, a siege, not a battle.
[e] Includes large number of surrendered troops, subsequently paroled.
[f] Includes Battles of Orchard Knob, Lookout Mountain, and Missionary Ridge.
[g] The latest research in the records revises Confederate casualties sharply upward from the traditional numbers. See Alfred C. Young, "Numbers and Losses in the Army of Northern Virginia [May–Jun., 1864]," *North & South Magazine,* no. 3 (March 2000), 26–27.
[h] Includes only the initial battle, not the subsequent siege and related actions.
[i] Includes 955 army and 686 navy casualties.
[j] Overwhelming majority were captured, but surviving records do not distinguish between casualties and captives.
Sources: Patricia L. Faust, ed., *Historical Times Illustrated Encyclopedia of the Civil War* (New York: Harper & Row, 1986), passim; Mark M. Boatner III, *The Civil War Dictionary* (New York: David McKay, 1959), passim; Alfred C. Young III, "Numbers and Losses in the Army of Northern Virginia [May–June, 1864]," *North & South Magazine,* no. 3 (March 2000): 26–27.

By far the two bloodiest battles of the Civil War were Antietam/Sharpsburg and Gettysburg. Antietam was the single bloodiest day for U.S. soldiers in history. Killing on such a scale was new to Americans, whose experience to date had been relatively small wars against the British, Mexicans, and American Indians. None of those prepared them for the shock of the killing fields of the Civil War. Europeans might have enlightened them about modern warfare. The Napoleonic Wars (1800–15), the Crimean War (1854–56), and the

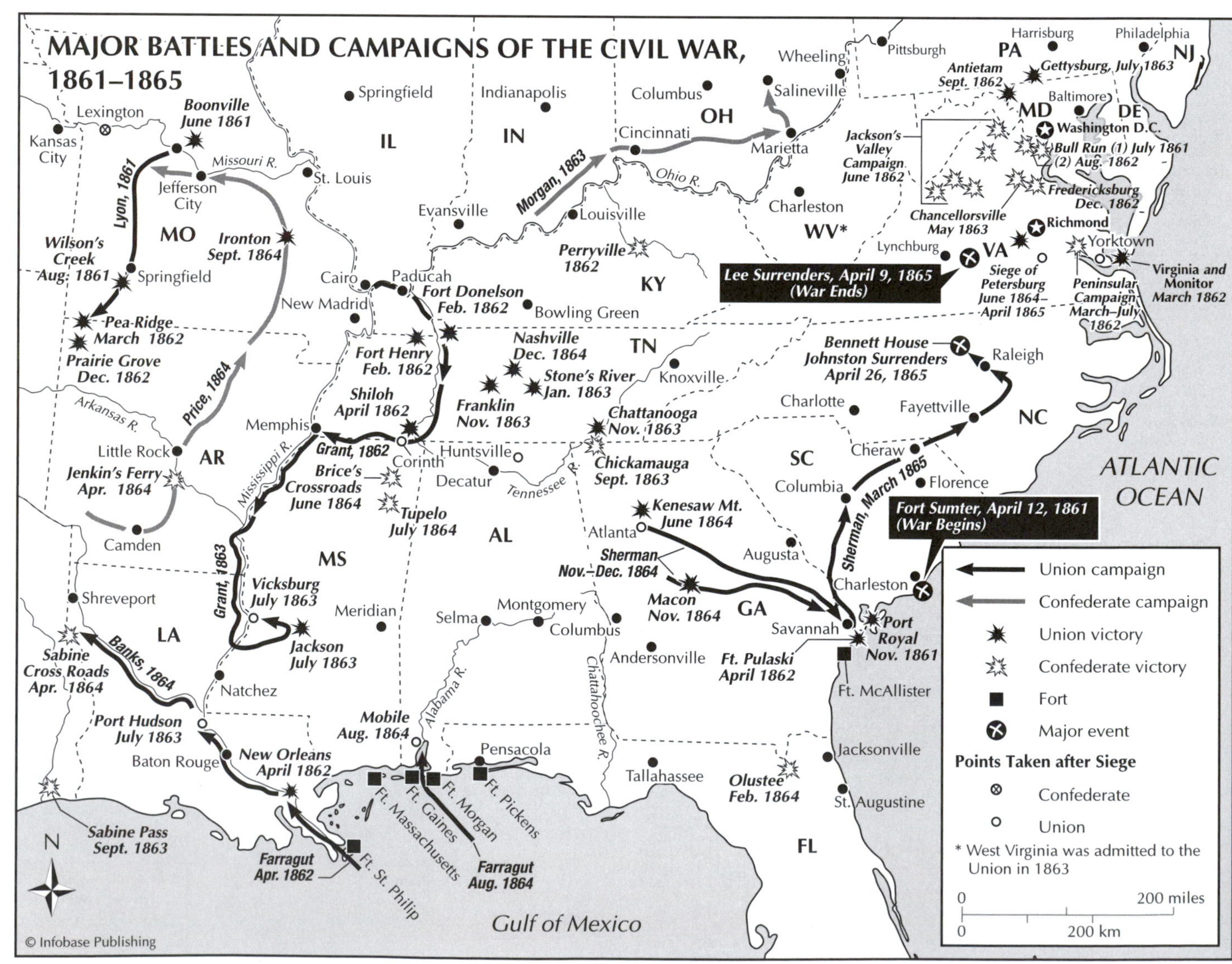

Source: Samuel Eliot Morison, Henry Steele Commager, and William Leuchtenburg, *The Growth of the American Republic* (New York: Oxford University Press), 1: 640–41.

TABLE 10.10 COMPARISON OF GETTYSBURG AND ANTIETAM/SHARPSBURG TO THE BLOODIEST BATTLES IN EUROPE'S WARS IN THE 19TH CENTURY, 1800–1870

Battle	Year	Combatants[a]		Size of Armies[b]		Casualties (as percentage of Total)[c]	
		Winner	Loser	Winner	Loser	Winner	Loser
Moscow	1812	French	Russians	120,000	125,000	23,000 (19)	51,000 (40)
Marengo	1800	French	Austrians	28,000	40,000	7,000 (25)	12,000 (30)
Gettysburg	1863	Federals	Confederates	117,000	68,000	17,000 (14)	27,000 (40)
Leipzig[d]	1813	Germans	French	300,000	171,000	47,000 (16)	60,000 (36)
Wagram	1809	French	Austrians	140,000	90,000	32,000 (22)	25,000 (28)
Jena	1806	French	Prussians	40,000	70,000	4,000 (10)	27,000 (39)
Austerlitz	1805	French	Austrians	70,000	84,000	12,000 (17)	26,000 (31)
Waterloo	1815	British	French	101,000	120,000	22,000 (22)	29,000 (24)
Bautzen	1813	French	Prussians	150,000	110,000	28,000 (18)	24,000 (21)
Sedan	1870	Prussians	French	190,000	124,000	9,000 (5)	38,000 (31)
Gravelotte	1870	Germans	French	270,000	126,000	35,000 (13)	27,000 (22)
Antietam (Sharpsburg)	1862	Federals	Confederates	87,000	97,000	11,000 (13)	20,000 (20)

Note: Table is based on cumulative percentage losses for the two sides.
[a] In every battle involving the French up through 1815, Napoleon was the commanding general against a variety of opponents. In battles involving Americans, Lee was the losing commander at both Antietam and Gettysburg, the first time against George McClellan, the second time against George Gordon Meade.
[b] Figures represent the best estimates of the time, based on numbers of troops on the field on the day(s) of battle, not support troops and reserves in the rear.
[c] Includes killed, wounded, and missing.
[d] Also known as "the Battle of Nations."
Source: Michael G. Mulhall, *The Dictionary of Statistics* (London: George Routledge and Sons, 1899), 89.

Franco-Prussian War (1870–71) set new standards for death and destruction in their employment of mass armies and modern weapons coupled with the desire to annihilate instead of outmaneuvering the enemy. By this measure, Austria suffered higher losses, both absolutely and relatively, than any other Western nation in the 19th century, and Napoléon-led France inflicted greater losses on their enemies than any other nation. Only Gettysburg, among all battles involving Americans, ranked in the top five in terms of bloodiness, even with the qualifier that it was a three-day battle. Still, Confederates suffered a higher single-battle loss at Gettysburg than any other nation save Russia at Moscow, but what is incredible is that the French, Austrians, and others, as opposed to the Americans, experienced this level of casualties repeatedly during the century. Killing on the scale of Gettysburg or Antietam occurred no fewer than 10 times in Europe between 1800 and 1870.

The major fear of most soldiers, aside from showing cowardice in front of their fellows, was being wounded and then dying a slow, agonizing death. It was a very reasonable fear. The chance of being killed in combat for Union army and navy personnel was one in 65, but the odds rose dramatically if a man was wounded. The chance of surviving a combat wound was only one in seven. Some 43,000 Northerners were wounded in battle and died subsequently. Another 275,000 were wounded and lived to tell about it. The latter were said to have earned their "red badge of courage," and for the lucky ones who were only slightly wounded, that meant a one-way trip home. In the Confederate army some 40,000 received battlefield wounds that proved fatal, and another 226,000 were wounded and survived. Many of the wounded on both sides were able to return to duty after a period of convalescence. Others were maimed or crippled for life.

Under the chaotic conditions of a battlefield, a wound could result from something as ordinary as being kicked by a horse or struck by a recoiling cannon. These injuries did not qualify as a red badge of courage. Combat caused the overwhelming majority of wounds, by shot, shell, or bayonet. A breakdown of battlefield casualties from a typical Union unit after combat shows that the most lethal instrument in any Civil War clash of arms was the simple minié ball (conoidal rifle bullet).

TABLE 10.11 CAUSES OF WOUNDS FOR SAMPLE GROUP OF 144,000 UNION CIVIL WAR CASUALTIES

Wound Caused by	Number of Wounded
Conoidal rifle bullet	108,000
Smooth-bore musket, round ball	16,000
Shell fragments	12,500
Canister, grape, and cannonball	359
Explosive bullets	139
Edged weapons (mostly sabers)	7,002
Total	**144,000**

The Geography of War

The fighting was compartmentalized into three regional theaters of war: (1) the East, which included all territory east of the Appalachian Mountains, but mostly concentrated in the area between Washington, D.C., and Richmond, Virginia; (2) the West, which included the area between the Appalachian Mountains and the Mississippi River; and (3) the Trans-Mississippi, which included all land on the western side of the river and was commonly regarded as the backwater of the war, the end of the line for supplies, and the burying ground for military careers. Additionally a fourth theater can be identified in retrospect: the Atlantic coast and the Gulf Coast. Union combined-arms operations against the Southern coast constituted a distinct albeit unrecognized theater of war, featuring a new and different kind of warfare and a different set of problems than encountered in any other area. Most of these operations were on the Atlantic coast between the James River and the Florida-Georgia border; Mobile, New Orleans, and Galveston on the Gulf Coast were also scenes of major fighting. The administrative compartmentalization of the war does not follow strict geographic lines. For instance, Georgia is clearly on the Atlantic coast and east of the Appalachian Mountains, yet it was regarded as part of the western theater.

Geographic location, the political situation, and luck determined the level of fighting in any given area, with military strategy a factor of the first two. More battles and engagements were fought in Virginia than in any other state. Tennessee ranks second, and Missouri was the third most fought-over state. Generally, the more combat that occurred in a state (or territory), the more destruction and the more suffering the people endured. The notable exception to this rule was Confederate Georgia. Although it was down the list in terms of sheer numbers of engagements fought within its borders, it suffered some of the heaviest destruction thanks to General Sherman's "March to the Sea" in late 1864. No other state not on the front lines suffered such devastation, and for that reason William T. Sherman is reviled in the South. Among the four major theaters of war (the East, the West, the Trans-Mississippi, and the Coast), the East saw the most combat and therefore suffered the most destruction of both human life and property. The West was second, with the Coast and Trans-Mississippi bringing up the rear; that is not to say that violence and killing were less severe in Texas or around Charleston than in Virginia, just that Texas and Charleston were less fought over and marched over than Virginia. The East was always considered the "main show" in terms of both strategic importance and caliber of fighting. The best of the Union commanders (e.g., Ulysses Grant and Phillip Sheridan) were promoted to the East after proving themselves in the West. The worst of the Confederate general officers (e.g., Theophilus Holmes and Alfred Iverson) were transferred to the West or Trans-Mississippi after failing in the East.

The Civil War on the western frontier could be brutal and merciless to innocent civilians. These refugees were forced to flee their homes in the Ozarks during guerrilla fighting in northwestern Arkansas. (Arkansas History Commission)

TABLE 10.12 CLASHES OF ARMS ("MILITARY EVENTS") BY STATE AND THEATER

State (Theater)	Number of "Military Events"
Va. (E/C)	2,154
Tenn. (W)	1,462
Mo. (W)	1,162
Miss. (W)	772
Ark. (T)	771
W.Va.[a] (E)	632
La. (W/C/T)	566
Ga. (W/C)	549
Ky. (W)	453
Ala. (W/C)	336
N.C. (E/C)	313
S.C. (E/C)	239
Md. (E)	203
Fla. (E/C)	168
Tex. (T/C)	90
Indian Territory (T)	89
Calif. (T)[b]	88
New Mexico Territory (T)	75

Note: Refers to one of the four major theaters: E, Eastern; W, Western; C, Coastal; T, Trans-Mississippi. Some states fit into more than one category, for instance, Eastern and Coastal (E/C).

[a] The state of West Virginia after 1863.

[b] Largely against Indians who were not fighting for one side of the other, but for their own motives.

Source: E. B. Long, *The Civil War Day by Day* (Garden City, New York: Doubleday, 1971), 719.

Principal Campaigns

In the middle of the 19th century war was still fought as much as possible only during campaign season when weather conditions were most conducive to fighting and marching. The military campaigning season was generally understood to be from early spring through late fall. Armies tried to disengage in November and spend the next three or four months in winter quarters, resting and recuperating and planning for the forthcoming spring campaign. With a few notable exceptions, most of the important fighting during the Civil War occurred during one of the five campaign seasons (1861–65). The Battles of Fredericksburg, Virginia (December 1862), and Stones River, Tennessee (December 1862–January 1863), and the attacks on Fort Fisher, North Carolina (December 1864 and January 1865), represent exceptions to the general rule caused by special circumstances.

The most strategically important campaigns were those in the Eastern Theater, focused on Richmond—defending it for the Confederates and taking it for the Federals. Union armies launched a total of nine "On to Richmond" drives between 1861 and 1865, all of them starting somewhere north of the Potomac River. The first four ground to a halt in northern Virginia, and another one fizzled on the James River, before the last one finally captured the prize on April 2, 1865.

With a couple of notable exceptions—the Vicksburg and Atlanta campaigns—the war west of the Appalachian Mountains was always secondary to the war in the East. Although some historians dispute this thesis today, there was no doubt among the leadership on either side at the time which theater was primary and which was secondary: Virginia was always

The siege of Vicksburg, May 19–July 4, 1863, saw U.S. Grant's Union forces surround the Mississippi River fortress and starve out the defenders. Grant in the lower right corner observes the enemy through his spy glass while his staff await him. (Library of Congress)

primary. That is why the Civil War was virtually over after Robert E. Lee surrendered the Army of Northern Virginia at Appomattox.

The Civil War on Water

The Civil War represented a revolution in warfare, not just on land but on the water. The old days of wood and sail gave way to new technology. Pushed by the desire to gain a telling advantage, North and South both became pioneers in a new kind of warfare that combined the steam engine, armor, and rifled cannon all on a single naval platform. That same kind of creativity and experimentation also produced mines, submarines, and torpedoes that were primitive but effective. In all of these developments the South, driven by a greater sense of urgency, proved to be more proactive than the North in trying new methods.

The war on water divided into four phases: the blockade, commerce raiding on the high seas, amphibious operations on the Southern coast, and control of the inland waterways. The closest equivalent the North had to a comprehensive war strategy, the Anaconda Plan, was predicated on the Union's overwhelming naval superiority. Yet that naval superiority in the beginning was largely on paper. The U.S. Navy began the war with just 84 vessels, counting both steam- and sail-powered units. With this meager fleet, they had to enforce a blockade of 3,550 miles of shoreline stretching from the Potomac River to the Rio Grande River. The Southern coastline contained 189 harbors, inlets, bays, and coves, including 10 fortified ports on the Gulf and Atlantic coasts, that wily blockade runners could use.

In September 1861 the fleet was divided into four major commands or "Departments": The Atlantic coast from Virginia to Key West, Florida, was covered by the North and South Atlantic Blockading Squadrons, while the Gulf coastline from Key West to Brownsville, Texas, was watched by the East and West Gulf Blockading Squadrons. Thanks to a crash construction program and aggressive purchasing in the private sector, the navy was rapidly expanded to fight a war for which there were no contingency plans and no experience to draw from when it began.

The first new ships to enter service were the whimsically named "90-day gunboats," so called because they were built in roughly three months, between July 1861 and February 1862. There were 23 such vessels, and on them largely rested the burden of making Lincoln's blockade work during the first year of the war. They were built of unseasoned timber, displaced less than 700 tons, were schooner-rigged with auxiliary steam engines, and carried just four guns when they first took to sea. They did yeoman service in every theater of the naval war: blockade duty, coastal operations, even high-seas pursuit of commerce raiders.

What began as a paper blockade was ultimately transformed into an amazingly efficient operation that strangled the South, but in the beginning it was as leaky as a sieve. About 800 blockade runners slipped through the net during the first year, a 90 percent success rate. By 1865, however, the success rate had fallen to one of every two getting through. Over the course of four years about 8,500 successful runs through the blockade were chalked up, but that statistic is deceiving because there were nearly 60,000 "callings", or visits to ports, in Southern states in 1860; that means that shipping into the South was down more than 70 percent as a result of the blockade.

The growing efficiency of the Union blockade was largely attributable to the highly innovative strategy of combined army-navy attacks on the South's principal ports and harbors. In four years of war all the important ports except Charleston, which was effectively corked until captured by land forces at the very end of the war, were taken by seaborne attack. In these operations the two oft-bickering services learned to cooperate well enough to seize virtually every point they targeted on the Southern coast. In the process a whole new form of military operation was born—amphibious warfare, or as they were called in those days combined operations.

The U.S. Navy concentrated most of its resources and effort on patrolling the oceans, with special attention to the south Atlantic and Gulf Coast areas. Those areas were the responsibility of the so-called blue-water navy as opposed to the "brown-water navy," which operated exclusively on inland waters. Complicating this simple distinction was the fact that some ships operated on both coastal and inland waters. Despite the strategic importance attached to the Mississippi River, it was the blue-water navy that received most of the Navy Department's attention.

The South found itself at a greater disadvantage on water than on land, forced to fight with a patchwork navy, trying to make up what it lacked in materièl with large measures of ingenuity and chutzpah. The first Confederate warships to put to sea were the privateers, private vessels chartered by either Richmond or the state governments with letters of marque (i.e., legal authorization) to attack the U.S. merchant fleet. They operated out of Confederate ports, prowling coastal waters, where they looked for easy marks. Richmond commissioned at least 51 such ships, most of them in the first year, before the U.S. Navy tightened the blockade and unarmed merchant ships became hard to find. Only 23, led by the *Calhoun,* the *Ivy,* and the *Webb,* enjoyed any success. The rest were more of an irritant than a threat to Union maritime power.

Far more dangerous and much more effective were the commerce raiders, which were genuine warships that stayed at sea for months sinking anything flying a U.S. flag that they could find. Almost all of the eight successful Confederate cruisers, most notably the CSS *Florida* and CSS *Alabama,* were built or purchased abroad and never saw home during their lifetime. Despite their small numbers, however, they succeeded in driving the American flag from the high seas between 1861 and 1865, to such an extent that the U.S. merchant marine never recovered its former glory after peace resumed.

The most numerous Confederate vessels were not warships but sleek, fast merchantmen. An estimated 8,500 blockade runners kept the South supplied with the essentials of war—and more than a few highly profitable luxuries—for four years. Almost all were privately owned and operated, their ownership motivated by a combination of patriotism and greed. Not until 1864 did the Confederate government jump into the blockade-running business, purchasing and outfitting 42 vessels that proved immensely successful but too late to affect the outcome of the war.

In four years of war the Confederate States Navy (CSN) commissioned some 175 warships, while hundreds of other vessels were pressed into service by the Southern states or private interests. This hodgepodge of anonymous craft included "cotton-clads," transports, small tugs, towboats, and tenders. They showed the flag and performed valuable service but were not decisive in determining the outcome of the war.

The most important class of vessels on either side was the ironclads, the "queens" of the two fleets. They were the product of frantic programs to develop superwarships. The South started the race with the slope-shouldered CSS *Virginia* (originally the *Merrimack*), which it launched in March 1862. It set the pattern for virtually every other Confederate ironclad that followed: an elongated, armored casemate mounted on a cut-down hull, with a ram attached to the bow. It displaced 3,200 tons fully loaded and therefore was confined to deeper waters. The U.S. government countered with three prototypes based on three different designs. The cheese-box-on-a-raft USS *Monitor* proved the most successful and revolutionized future warship design. It carried just two guns in its revolving turret, but that turret was armored with eight-inch-thick iron. Monitor-class boats displaced less than 1,000 tons but because of their extremely low freeboard were not stable in open waters. By the end of the war the U.S. Navy had built and commissioned 22 Monitor-class boats, 17 with single turrets and five with double turrets. As a class, Monitors remained part of the U.S Navy for the next 30 years. Altogether the North started construction on some 60 ironclads, 33 of which actually saw service in coastal or inland waters. In addition, the U.S. Navy captured from the Confederates three more ironclads, which were reflagged and employed in blockade duty and shore bombardment; none was satisfactory. Union ironclads proved invaluable in bottling up the South's shipping, reducing its heavily defended ports, and opening its rivers. Only one U.S.-built ironclad from either side, the USS *New Ironsides,* was a true seagoing vessel.

Meanwhile, the Confederacy's ironclad program was much less successful, although it did produce some remarkable accomplishments. The Confederate Congress appropriated $2 million in 1861 to build or buy ironclad warships. Most of those that were subsequently in service were makeshift juggernauts built of whatever was available in terms of engines, armor, and platform. With a couple of exceptions, they were all built according to the same simple, casemate design, created by the naval architect John L. Porter. In four years determined Southerners contracted for some 60 ironclads, but only 21 were actually commissioned (the final step before a ship enters service). Most of the home-grown ironclads were converted from existing vessels rather than built from the keel up; they were underpowered and completely unseaworthy. Another five were ordered from British or French shipyards, only one of which (CSS *Stonewall*) ever went to sea. The Confederate ironclads as a group had a mixed record: Three or four fought well, but most of them in the end had to be destroyed by their own crews to prevent capture, some before they ever saw combat. One was sunk by worms in the wood!

Even at the end of the war the Southerners were still trying frantically to complete new ironclads, using green wood, railroad rails, and whatever else they could scrounge. No fewer than 10 were in some stage of construction when the war ended. Meanwhile the North had a number of even more powerful ironclads under construction; after the war they were scrapped or sold abroad. These included four Kalamazoo-class double-turreted Monitors, which were laid down but became "war surplus" after April 1865.

Unlike those of modern U.S. Navy ships, the names given to ironclads by both sides were based on no system. The North favored Indian names and also used names of cities and states, geographically based names, and a few that did not fit into any normal category (e.g., *Monitor* and *Dictator*). The South was almost as eclectic, assigning the names of towns, rivers, states, and one beloved general (i.e. *Stonewall*).

The best measure of the U.S. Navy's success against its counterpart in the Civil War can be found in the numbers of Confederate vessels captured and destroyed during the four years of combat. Some 1,500 vessels of all classes and types from harbor defense ironclads to seagoing blockade runners were either sent to the bottom or seized, and that total does not take into account the vessels destroyed by the Southerners themselves to prevent them from falling into Yankee hands.

The war on inland waters was a struggle for control over the Mississippi River and its tributaries—the Tennessee, Cumberland, Arkansas, and Red Rivers. The South hoped to use them for internal commerce and communications; the North desired them as highways into the vulnerable Confederate heartland. Here again Northern industrial superiority and maritime skills triumphed over Southern pluck and ingenuity. The Union created an inland fleet of rams, armor-clad gunboats, and mortar, which were ideally suited to the special conditions of river warfare. After the fall of Vicksburg in the summer of 1863, President Lincoln paid tribute to "Uncle Sam's web-feet."

TABLE 10.13 TOTAL NUMBER OF CONFEDERATE VESSELS CAPTURED OR DESTROYED BY THE U.S. NAVY DURING THE CIVIL WAR

Type of Ship or Boat	Captured	Destroyed
Steamers	210	85
Schooners	569	114
Sloops	139	32
Ships	13	2
Brigs	29	2
Barks	25	4
Yachts	2	0
Small boats	139	96
Rams	6	5
Gunboats	10	11
Others	7	0
Total	1,149	351

Source: Secretary of the Navy Gideon Welles's Annual Report to the President, dated Dec. 31, 1865, cited in Paul H. Silverstone, *Warships of the Civil War Navies* (Annapolis, Md.: Naval Institute Press, 1989), passim.

At the end of the Civil War the U.S. Navy was the largest in the world, with some 700 ships of all types, many of them also among the most modern in the world. Between 1861 and 1865, the U.S. Navy had performed the prodigious feat of constructing more than 200 vessels from the keel up and purchasing another 418 on the open market. Personnel at the end consisted of 6,759 officers and 51,537 enlisted men, the equal of any seagoing fighting force in the world at the time. In fact, the navy was limited only by its mission, which was still understood to be coastal defense first, last, and always. As a result of demobilization, the U.S. Navy would not be so large again in numbers of ships or men until World War I.

The Politics of War

Sometimes politics was as important as military operations. This could affect decisions on firing and promoting general officers, organizing the war effort, or keeping up morale on the home front. Or it could mean redirecting the entire focus of the war, as occurred with the issuance of the Emancipation Proclamation in late 1862. For the first year and a half of fighting, independence or union was the stated war aim of the South and the North, respectively. Yet even as Lee moved north into Maryland in September 1862, forces were at work in the North to transform the conflict into a war to free the slaves. Abolitionists had been pressuring Lincoln to take a stand since the beginning, but he had resisted for a variety of reasons, some philosophical and some practical. After the Battle of Antietam revealed that Lee was not invincible and that the war was far from over, Lincoln made his move. He issued the remarkable proclamation, one of the shrewdest and at the same time most idealistic documents in U.S. history. This simple presidential pronouncement, issued under Lincoln's authority as commander in chief, held out the promise of freedom to all slaves in the states under Confederate control. The pronouncement was more of a public relations and diplomatic coup than an effective policy at this time, but it would make abolition of slavery a coequal war aim of the North along with preservation of the Union. It placed the South on the wrong side of the central moral issue in the world's eyes and greatly complicated the Southern objective of winning European recognition for the Confederate States of America.

The proclamation also contained a provision for enlisting former slaves in the Union army, thereby putting them squarely on the front lines in the fight for their own freedom, but also reassuring nervous whites that some kind of official control would be maintained over the great mass of freedmen. Even that reassurance left many skeptical or downright hostile toward the new war policy. The London *Times* gloomily anticipated that military employment of former slaves against their former masters would produce a spiraling series of atrocities—"horrible massacres of white women and children, to be followed by the extermination of the black race." Many thoughtful people on both sides believed that no good would result from the president's proclamation. Nevertheless Lincoln considered it "a new birth of freedom" for the entire nation.

The politics of war also included such thorny issues as retribution and punishment because the loser in any war for independence can be punished as a traitor. On this issue the North was surprisingly lenient toward Southern leaders. Only two men were ever prosecuted by Federal authorities, the Confederate president, Jefferson Davis, and the prison camp commandant Henri Wirz. Davis's offenses were of a purely political nature; Wirz's crimes had a more outrageous and inhumane character. Davis, without even the formality of a trial, was imprisoned in Fortress Monroe, Virginia, in solitary confinement for two years before he was released. Captain Henri Wirz, the infamous commander of Andersonville prison camp (Georgia), was arrested and indicted for "impairing the health and destroying the lives of prisoners." He was convicted by a military tribunal and hanged on November 10, 1865. There the reprisals might have ended but for the assassination of Abraham Lincoln on April 15, 1865, by the actor John Wilkes Booth in a last, desperate act of madness. Booth was killed resisting arrest, but his fellow conspirators were tried by military tribunal and either executed (July 7, 1865) or sentenced to long prison terms. The legacy of bitterness and hatred of these final acts in the great drama after four years of bloody combat, would haunt the nation until very nearly the end of the century. It would take another war (Spanish-American, 1898) to reunite the nation in common purpose.

Women at War

The "Petticoat War" was carried on by a small but significant number of women on both sides who broke out of their traditional roles to serve the national cause. Some 400, by historical estimates, even fought in the ranks. Countless others traveled with loved ones in the armies, doing domestic chores, thereby earning the fond title "daughter of the regiment." Only a few are known to have lived in the field or served in high government posts; many more contributed to their respective cause in other valuable ways. Nurse or spy seemed to be the principal wartime service of women. In 1864 President Lincoln told a large audience, "If all that has been said by orators and poets since the creation of the world in praise of woman applied to the women of America, it would not do them justice for their conduct during this war." Although he had in mind specifically the women of the North, the characterization applied equally to those on both sides. After the war a surprising number published their memoirs, but neither their wartime contributions nor their writings did much to change traditional gender roles in the late 19th century.

This image shows the historic moment on April 19, 1865, when Lee *(left)* and Grant *(right)* sat down in Wilmer McLean's parlor at Appomattox Court House, Virginia, to negotiate the surrender of the Army of Northern Virginia. General George Meade stands at Grant's left shoulder and the Seneca Indian Ely Parker, Grant' military secretary, stands just to the left of Meade. (Library of Congress)

TABLE 10.14 NOTABLE WOMEN OF THE CIVIL WAR—UNION AND CONFEDERATE

Name	Life Dates	Union/Confederate	Civil War–Themed Writings	Role/Career
Maria Isabella "Belle" Boyd	(1844–1900)	Confederate	*Belle Boyd in Camp and Prison* (1865)	South's most notorious and colorful spy
Pauline Cushman	(1833–93)	Union	*The Thrilling Adventures of Pauline Cushman* (1864), ghostwritten	Actress-turned-spy in western theater; arrested and sentenced to hang; rescued by Union troops
Kate Cumming	(1835–1909)	Confederate	*A Journal of Hospital Life in the Confederate Army of Tennessee* (1866); *Gleanings from the Southland* (1895)	Scottish-born Confederate patriot and most famous nurse in western Confederacy
Elizabeth Van Lew	(1818–1900)	Union	none known	Notoriously eccentric spy who lived in Richmond; gathered information to aid Yankees escaping Libby Prison
Anna Elizabeth Dickinson	(1832–1932)	Union	*What Answer* (novel, 1868)	Lecturer on causes of women's rights, Union, and abolitionism; Republican Party representative; Quaker
Mary Bowser	Unknown	Union	None known	African-American former slave of Van Lew family; aided Elizabeth Van Lew; worked inside Confederate White House
Louisa May Alcott	(1832–88)	Union	*Hospital Sketches* (1863)	Tireless nurse and hospital reformer; retired to become author in 1862
Phoebe Yates Pember	(1823–1913)	Confederate	*A Southern Woman's Story* (memoir, 1879; "the best first person account of Confederate hospitals")	Iron-willed matron of Richmond's Chimborazo Hospital No.2, 1862–65
Susan B. Anthony	(1820–1906)	Union	None known	Teacher, women's rights and suffrage advocate; temperance crusader; organized Women's Loyal League
Mary Boykin Chestnut	(1823–86)	Confederate	*A Diary from Dixie* (1905)	Most famous and observant diarist of Civil War on either side
Mary Anne Ball Bickerdyke	(1817–1901)	Union	None known	Nurse in western hospitals; agent for U.S. Sanitary Commission (USSC)
Clara Barton	(1821–1912)	Union	None known	Patent Office clerk who became self-taught nurse and lifetime philanthropist
Dr. Elizabeth Blackwell	(1821–1910)	Union	None known	First female M.D. graduated in United States; worked with sister, Emily; helped organize USSC
Mary Ashton Rice Livermore	(1820–1905)	Union	*My Story of the War; A Woman's Narrative of Four Years Personal Experience* (1889)	Prewar reformer; cofounder of USSC; national director 1862–65
Rose O'Neal Greenhow	(ca. 1815–64)	Confederate	*My Imprisonment and the First Year of the Abolition Rule in Washington*	Spy who delivered Union plans for First Bull Run; unmasked and exiled to South, where received as heroine
Dorothea Lynde Dix	(1802–87)	Union	None known	Prewar reformer for the cause of prisoners and mentally ill; wartime superintendent of Women Nurses Corps
Sarah Emma Edmonds	(1841–98)	Union	*Nurse and Spy in the Union Army* (1865)	Served as soldier under alias Frank Thompson; also served as spy and nurse during war
Loreta Velasquez	Unknown	Union	*The Woman in Battle* (1876); denounced by Jubal Early as a fraud	Served as soldier under alias Harry T. Buford
Jennie Hodgers	Unknown	Union	None known	Served as soldier under alias Albert D. J. Cashier
Mary Scaberry	Unknown	Union	None known	Served as soldier under alias Charles Freeman
Sarah Rosetta Wakeman	Unknown	Union	None known	Served as soldier under alias Lyons Wakeman
Julia Ward Howe	(1819–1910)	Union	"Battle Hymn of the Republic" (1861)	Patriotic poet; also leader in abolitionist and women's suffrage movements
Harriet Beecher Stowe	(1811–96)	Union	*Uncle Tom's Cabin* (1852)	Unremarkable novelist who produced one political blockbuster
Dr. Mary Edwards Walker	(1832–1919)	Union	None known	Only woman doctor in the army on either side and only female recipient of the Medal of Honor in U.S. history to date[a]

[a] Mary Walker's Medal of Honor was revoked upon review in 1916 because she was a noncombatant, but in 1977 President Jimmy Carter restored it.

Sources: Elizabeth D. Leonard, *All the Daring of the Soldier: Women of the Civil War Armies* (New York: W. W. Norton, 1999), passim; *The Civil War Book of Lists* (Conshohocken, Pa.: Combined Books, 1993), 208–10.

Treatment of Prisoners of War

Two names, Henri Wirz and Andersonville, symbolize one of the darkest chapters of the war—the prisoner of war (POW) camps maintained by both sides. Andersonville (Camp Sumter) was not necessarily the worst, merely the most notorious. On the Northern side, places such as Camp Douglas and Fort Delaware were scarcely better and had far less excuse for the shameful way they treated helpless men. When the war began, neither side was prepared to handle the tens of thousands of prisoners who would fall into their hands beginning with First Bull Run. They never did handle the problem better. During the next four years facilities built hurriedly to handle a few thousand were soon crammed with many times that number. The results were predictable: of some 674,000 soldiers captured during the war, more than 56,000 died in confinement, a death rate of nearly 13 percent, or twice the death rate from combat. The causes were overcrowded facilities, inadequate food and clothing, lack of good hygiene, plus apathy and sheer incompetence of those charged with taking care of the POWs. Whereas other supply and organization problems were generally handled better as the war advanced, the POW problem only became worse, reaching tragic proportions after 1863, when the two governments agreed to halt the convention of prisoner exchanges. That cold-blooded decision condemned thousands of men to slow death from disease and starvation. How many thousands died is the question that provokes the arguments. Defenders of the North and the South after the war tried to seize the high ground by claiming that the other side killed, directly or indirectly, more of their prisoners. Because most of the statistics were gathered and published by the federal government, the numbers naturally favored the North. In 1866 the War Department laboriously calculated the number of prisoners who were held by each side during the war and how many of those men died in captivity. Their published figures raised an immediate howl of protest. Colonel Robert C. Wood, formerly of the Confederate army, produced a different set of numbers in the late 1800s, which proved kinder to the Southerners. In 1906 the historian James Ford Rhodes made his own calculations and produced a different set of numbers. The argument continues today.

TABLE 10.15 DUELING STATISTICS ON PRISONER OF WAR NUMBERS AND DEATHS

Source	North			South		
	Prisoner of War Held	Deaths in Captivity	Rate of Death, Percentage	Prisoners of War Held	Deaths in Captivity	Rate of Death, Percentage
U.S. War Department	220,000	26,436	12.0	126,000	22,576	17.9
Colonel Robert C. Wood	170,136	22,878	12.9	270,000	22,570	8.4
James Ford Rhodes	215,000	25,800	12.0	194,000	30,070	15.5

Source: Robert E. Denney, *Civil War Prisons and Escapes: A Day-by-Day Chronicle* (New York: Sterling, 1993), 12, 381.

The camps were located in vacant warehouses, in isolated rural areas, and on unpopulated islands, inadequately funded, poorly staffed, and scarcely supervised. When the war ended their pitiful populations were turned free and told to go home. Most of the camps did not keep records, and even their existence was quickly forgotten after the war, so gathering complete statistics is impossible. Such statistics as have been gathered show a sorry record of negligence and abuse by both blue and gray that would be branded war crimes today. Yet only one man among all those from the top officials down to the lowliest guards ever paid for what was done. Because there were no heroes and the story did not reflect well on the leadership of either side, there was almost a conspiracy of silence about the matter after the war. Memorials and myths were created about the soldiers and civilians, but nobody talked about the prisoners until historians began to reconstruct the story a generation or two later.

This 1877 lithograph shows Camp Sumter (Andersonville Prison Camp), Georgia, in 1864. The "dead wagon" stands near the front gate. The 26-acre Andersonville, encircled by a stockade, was the most notorious prisoner-of-war camp of the Civil War and as such was immortalized in highly stylized pictures such as this one. (Courtesy of the Georgia Historical Society)

TABLE 10.16 MAJOR CIVIL WAR PRISON CAMPS, NORTH AND SOUTH, 1861–1865

Name	Operated by	Location	In Existence	Maximum Inmate Population at Any Time[a]	Known Escapes[a]	Known Deaths[a]
Alton	United States	Ill.	1862–65	1,891	120	1,508
Camp Butler	United States	Ill.	1862–63	2,186	203	866
Camp Chase	United States	Ohio	1861–65	9,423	37	2,260
Camp Douglas	United States	Ill.	1862–65	12,082	317+[b]	4,454
Camp Morton	United States	Ind.	1862–65	5,000	150+[b]	1,763
Camp Randall	United States	Wis.	1862	1,260	N/A	142
Carroll Prison	United States	District of Columbia	1862–65	2,763[c]	16[c]	457[c]
Elmira	United States	N.Y.	1864–65	9,441	17	2,933
Fort Delaware	United States	Del.	1861–65	12,600	52	2,460
Fort McHenry	United States	Md.	1861–65	6,957	37	33
Fort Mifflin	United States	Pa.	1863–64	215	42	3
Fort Pulaski	United States	Ga.	1864–65	558	0	0
Fort Warren	United States	Mass.	1861–65	394	4	12
Gratiot Street	United States	Mo.	1861–65	1,800	109+[b]	1,140
Hart Island	United States	N.Y.	1865	3,446	4	235
Johnson's Island	United States	Ohio	1862–65	3,256	12	235
Lafayette	United States	Ind.	1862–63	500	N/A	28
Little Rock	United States	Ark.	1864–65	718	3	217
Louisville	United States	Ky.	1863–65	6,737	25	343
Memphis	United States	Tenn.	1864–65	582	1	3
Morris Island	United States	S.C.	1864	558	0	3
Nashville	United States	Tenn.	1863–65	7,460	36	359
Newport News	United States	Va.	1865	3,490	17	168
Old Capitol	United States	District of Columbia	1861–65	2,763[c]	16[c]	457+[b,c]
Parish Prison	United States	La.	1863–65	1,856	226	213
Point Lookout	United States	La.	1863–65	22,000	50	3,584
Rock Island	United States	Ill.	1863–65	8,607	41	1,960
Ship Island	United States	Miss.	1864–65	4,430	5	103
Wheeling	United States	W. Va.	1863–65	497	12	2
Camp Sumter (Andersonville)	CSA[d]	Ga.	1864–65	33,000	N/A	13,000
Castle Thunder[e]	CSA	Richmond, Va.	1862–65	3,000+[b]	N/A	N/A
Charleston	CSA	S.C.	1861–65	1,100	N/A	N/A
Charlotte	CSA	N.C.	1865	1,200	30+[b]	N/A
Danville	CSA	Va.	1863–65	4,000	70+[b]	1,297
Florence	CSA	S.C.	1864–65	1,500+[b]	N/A	N/A
Greensboro	CSA	N.C.	1865	1,800	N/A	N/A
Libby Warehouse	CSA	Va.	1862–65	4,221	60+[b]	20+[b]
Ligon's Warehouse	CSA	Va.	1861–62	600	N/A	N/A
Lynchburg	CSA	Va.	1862–64	500+[b]	N/A	N/A
Macon	CSA	Ga.	1861–64	1,900	N/A	N/A
Mayo's Factory	CSA	Va.	1861–63	500	N/A	N/A
Meridian	CSA	Miss.	1863–65	700	N/A	N/A
Millen	CSA	Ga.	1864	10,299	N/A	488+[b]
Raleigh	CSA	N.C.	1861–65	500	600+[b]	N/A
Richmond	CSA	Va.	1861–65	13,500	N/A	200+[b]
Salisbury	CSA	N.C.	1861–65	10,321	500+[b]	3,963[f]
San Antonio	CSA	Tex.	1861	360+[b]	N/A	N/A
San Pedro Springs	CSA	Tex.	1862	350	12	N/A
Savannah	CSA	Ga.	1864	6,000+[b]	0	2+[b]

Note: N/A indicates either that the numbers are not available or that they are unknown.

[a] All figures given here are approximations or educated guesses because record keeping by prison officials on both sides was very poor and haphazard, worse on the Southern side than on the Northern.

[b] Some sources give a larger number; here the sign (+) means the given number of inmates or more.

[c] Combined totals of both Old Capitol and Carroll Prisons.

[d] Confederate States of America.

[e] There was another prison camp named Castle Thunder in Petersburg, Va., for which statistics are unknown.

[f] In the five months between Oct. 1864 and Feb. 1865, one in three of Salisbury's POWs (3,708 men) died from sickness or starvation, a figure representing nearly 94 percent of the prison's total deaths during its existence. Brigadier General John H. Winder, commissary general of prisoners east of the Mississippi, wrote in Dec. 1864, "The ratio of mortality at Salisbury . . . exceeds, I think, that at Andersonville."

Source: Lonnie R. Speer, *Portals to Hell: Military Prisons of the Civil War* (Mechanicsburg, Pa.: Stackpole Books, 1997), 323–40.

The Cost of the War

Setting aside the political and social dilemmas spawned by the war, the physical and human costs were truly staggering. The national debt of the United States, which stood at a modest $64.8 million in 1860, soared to $2.7 billion in the next five years. The reason is not hard to understand: Fighting wars is the most expensive activity of any government. In 1863 that cost for the Union ran to $2.5 million per day and rose to $4 million per day by 1865. The cost for the Confederacy, which was comparable, is impossible to quantify as precisely because of poor record keeping and runaway inflation on the Southern side. The best estimate is that the Confederacy spent $2.1 billion to finance its unsuccessful struggle for independence. Of that amount the Southern states owed some $712 million in war debts. (By comparison, it cost the United States $156 billion to fight World War II, and fighting the Vietnam War at its height cost almost $2 billion a month. At the end the Confederacy had nothing to show for four years of war but destruction and bitterness. Livestock, crops, industrial plants, and the transportation system were all in shambles. The economic write-off in terms of lost property value for freeing nearly 4 million slaves without compensation was roughly $2 billion. Emancipation was the right thing to do morally but an economic disaster nonetheless. Southerners who had invested in Confederate war bonds were also not compensated under the provisions of the Fourteenth Amendment, and a special cotton tax that took an additional $68 million out of Southern pockets during Reconstruction was imposed by Congress.

The South lost twice in terms of the human cost: once for the casualties that took away so many of its menfolk and again after the war when thousands fled abroad rather than live under Yankee rule. The historian Wilmer Jones has estimated that more than 10,000 took part in "the largest movement of expatriates in American history." Canada, Mexico, Egypt, and the West Indies were favorite destinations. A colony of 4,000 expatriates also settled in Brazil, where slavery was still legal and the climate was conducive to raising cotton. Hundreds of these exiles to foreign land swallowed their pride and returned home by 1870, but thousands of brilliant and talented people never returned.

TABLE 10.17 PHYSICAL AND HUMAN COSTS OF THE CIVIL WAR

Costs	North	South	Total for the Nation
Killed or mortally wounded in combat	111,904	94,000	205,904
Died of disease	197,388	140,000	337,388
Died in prison	30,192	26,000	56,192
Accidental or unspecified deaths	24,881	No estimates	24,881
Wounded (not mortally)	277,401	195,000	472,401
Amount raised by taxes and loans	$3 billion	$2 billion (loans)	N/A
Increase/decrease in wealth, 1860–70	50% increase	60% decrease (30% not counting slaves)	
Percentage of war costs paid by taxation	20% includes 8% from income tax, 1863–65	5%	N/A
Percentage of war costs financed by borrowing	65%	35%	N/A
Percentage of war financed by issuing paper money	15%	60%	N/A
Number of merchant ships sunk by Confederate raiders	250	N/A	N/A
Value of merchant ships sunk by Confederate raiders	$15.5 million	N/A	N/A
Loss of 4 million freed slaves from economy	N/A	$2+ billion	N/A
Government spending as percentage of gross national product, 1860 (1865)	2% (15%)	N/A	N/A
Interest paid on Civil War debt	N/A	N/A	$2.8 billion
Government pensions paid to veterans	N/A	Confederate veterans paid by states, if at all	$8 billion
Total cost of Civil War (estimate)	N/A	N/A	$20 billion

Sources: John M. Murrin et al., *Liberty, Equality, Power: A History of the American People* (Fort Worth, Tex.: Harcourt Brace, 1996), 552 ff.; Phillip Shaw Paludan, *A People's Contest: The Union and Civil War, 1861–1865,* 2d ed. (Lawrence, Kans.: University Press of Kansas, 1996), 45, 121; James A. Henretta, David Brody, and Lynn Dumenil, *America: A Concise History,* vol. 1, *To 1877* (Boston: Bedford/St. Martin's, 1999), 405; James M. McPherson, *Ordeal by Fire: The Civil War and Reconstruction* (New York: Alfred A. Knopf, 1982), 476 ff.

TABLE 10.18 FINANCIAL COST OF THE CIVIL WAR COMPARED TO THAT OF OTHER U.S. WARS

Conflict	Net Military Cost	Debt Interest	Veterans' Benefits	Total Cost
Revolutionary War	$101,000,000	$84,000,000	$70,000,000	$255,000,000
War of 1812	$90,000,000	$50,000,000	$49,000,000	$189,000,000
U.S.-Mexican War	$71,000,000	$35,000,000	$64,000,000	$170,000,000
Civil War				
1) Union	1) $3,183,000,000	1) $2,593,000	1) $8,541,000,000	1) $14,317,000,000
2) Confederacy	2) $1,520,000	2) N/A	2) N/A	2) $1,520,000,000
Spanish-American War	$283,000,000	$83,000,000	$4,117,000,000	$4,483,000,000
World War I	$24,269,000,000	$20,468,000,000	$20,294,000,000	$65,031,000,000
World War II	$315,227,000,000	$62,278,000,000	$46,800,000,000	$425,305,000,000
Korean conflict	$18,000,000,000	$338,000,000	$2,825,000,000	$21,163,000,000

Note: Because data for this table were assembled in 1962, before the Vietnam War became a major conflict, statistics on that war are not included.
Source: Thomas C. Cochran, ed., *Concise Dictionary of American History* (New York: Charles Scribner's Sons, 1962), 996.

TABLE 10.19 CASUALTIES OF THE CIVIL WAR COMPARED TO THOSE OF OTHER U.S. WARS

War	Duration	Total Who Served[a]	Battle Deaths	Deaths of Other Causes	Average Daily Combat Deaths	Nonmortaly Wounded	Total Casualties
Revolutionary War	1775–83	(50,000)	4,435	N/A	1.8	6,188	N/A
War of 1812	1812–15	286,730	2,260	N/A	2.5	4,505	N/A
U.S.-Mexican War	1846–48	78,718	1,733	11,550	2.9	4,152	17,373
Civil War	1861–65						
1) Union		1) 2,213,363	1) 140,414	1) 224,097	1) 76.4	1) 281,851	1) 646,392
2) Confederate		2) (900,000)	2) 95,000	2) 165,000	2) 51.1	2) 194,000	2) 454,000
3) Combined		3) 3,113,363	3) 235,414	3) 389,097	3) 128.2	3) 475,851	3) 1,100,392
Spanish-American War	1898	306,760	385	2,061	6.4	1,662	4,108
World War I	1917–18[b]	4,734,991	53,402	63,114	198.2	204,002	320,518
World War II	1941–45	14,903,213	291,557	113,842	221.3	670,846	1,076,245
Korean conflict	1950–53	5,720,000	33,629	20,617	30.3	103,284	157,530
Vietnam War[c]	1954–73	2,600,000–2,800,000	47,366	10,801	17.5[d]	153,303	211,470

Note: In some cases the figures are not available (N/A).

[a] Numbers in parentheses represent the best available estimate in cases in which accurate records are lacking.

[b] WWI fighting lasted from 1914 to 1918, but the United States only fought from 1917 to 1918, less than two years in all.

[c] Also known in U.S. history as the Southeast Asia War and the Second Indochina War. U.S. military involvement in a long-running conflict officially began in 1954 with the committing of U.S. advisers to the South Vietnamese government and ended in 1973 with the signing of the Paris Peace Accords.

[d] For the years 1959–75.

Sources: Frank Burd, ed., *Civil War Book of Facts* (Gettysburg, Pa.: Americana Souvenirs & Gifts, n.d.), 14; James F. Dunnigan and Albert A. Nofi, *Dirty Little Secrets of the Vietnam War* (New York: St. Martin's Press, Thomas Dunne Books, 1999), 15, 240–42; Thomas C. Cochran, ed., *Concise Dictionary of American History* (New York: Charles Scribner's Sons, 1962), 997.

In terms of sheer human destruction, the Civil War took more American lives than any other war in the nation's history, including all 20th-century conflicts. Although the conflict was comparable in length to other major wars in U.S. history (about four years), the scale of death was of a much greater order of magnitude—for the simple reason that it was the only war in which Americans were killing Americans. If the combatants had been using the weapons of mass destruction available in the 20th century, the death toll would have increased exponentially.

The Civil War is the most statistically analyzed period in U.S. history before the 20th century. This is true for several reasons. For one, armies of clerks in the adjutant general's office on both sides kept detailed records of military operations, and a great many of their reports were collected after the war in the monumental *Official Records (OR)* series. The *OR* represents an inexhaustible gold mine for modern researchers. Add to the exceptionally quantifiable nature of the conflict the immense popular interest attending the Civil War among modern researchers, and the result is a war that has been measured, studied, broken down, and added up ad infinitum.

As to the question of why the Civil War was more quantified than other U.S. wars of the 19th century (of which there were five altogether, including the Indian Wars), it was particularly vast and at the same time personal to Americans. Also, it occurred at a time when statistics gathering was just coming into its own as a governmental duty. Bureaucrats are by nature number crunchers, and the Civil War produced an army of pencil-pushing bureaucrats as large as many of its marching armies.

CHAPTER 11 States and Territories

Territorial Additions to the National Domain

The years 1850–75 saw significant additions to the national domain as the United States rounded out its continental boundaries and for the first time expanded beyond its contiguous landmass. Not only were new lands acquired but some territories already under U.S. sovereignty were formally organized according to a process set up by Congress in the 18th century.

The additions of the Gadsden Territory (1853) and Alaska (1867) followed in the tradition of Louisiana and Florida, being acquired by business transactions rather than war or forcible annexation. Alaska, bought from czarist Russia, was the first noncontiguous territory added by the United States; the Gadsden Purchase, bought from Mexico, was a direct outgrowth of several factors: the U.S.-Mexican War (1846–48), sectionalism, and the drive to build a transcontinental railroad. Alaska, acquired at a time when the United States already had more territory than it could readily occupy, was a monument to the foresight of Secretary of State William Seward and to the fading dreams of imperial Russia.

Of all the new territories added to the United States in more than 200 years of history, the Gadsden Purchase (1853) is surely the oddest acquisition. It was never organized as a territory, never had a territorial governor, nor experienced a surge of settlement propelling it toward statehood. Eventually the territory would be divided between the states of New Mexico and Arizona. The U.S. government negotiated the deal with the Mexican president, Antonio López de Santa Anna, the same ruler who had earlier lost the Mexican Cession to the United States as a consequence of the U.S.-Mexican War. The Americans hoped to obtain Baja (Lower) California at the same time as the Gadsden Teritory, but Mexican pride prevented them from selling off additional territory to the hated gringo. Instead the United States got a barren border strip for some $10 million, or more than three times the price paid in 1803 for the Louisiana Purchase. The ill-starred Gadsden Purchase Treaty increased sectional tensions, led to the overthrow of Santa Anna by his own people in 1855, and did not yield the desired transcontinental railroad route for many years. The Gadsden legacy includes the city of Tucson, Arizona, as its only significant population center, and El Paso, Texas, as its gateway city.

Second only to the Louisiana Purchase, Alaska—its vast storehouse of natural resources, beautiful scenery, and strategic location—was the slickest land deal ever pulled off by the United States. For $7 million the United States acquired some 591,000 square miles at a price of roughly two cents per acre. At the time the territory was vaguely seen as a stepping stone to the China trade and a potential route for a trans-Pacific telegraph. Neither idea ever crystallized. For its first 10 years the territory was occupied by only a handful of U.S. Army troops because few settlers wanted to make the difficult move to such a remote clime. Mostly it attracted fur traders and missionaries. Home rule and economic development occurred much later, leading some to charge Washington, D.C., with mismanagement and neglect in its policies toward Alaska.

The international treaties signed with Mexico and Russia were only the first step to incorporating these two new territories. Both had to be formally annexed by act of Congress, which not only completed the process but put them on track for eventual statehood under the terms of the Northwest Ordinance of 1787 (providing for orderly admission of new states into the Union according to a specific formula). At this time in U.S. history, eventual statehood was virtually a forgone conclusion for every new acquisition.

Meanwhile within the vast geographic expanse of the United States the march of western expansion continued with the creation of new territorial governments in regions already under U.S. jurisdiction. According to the Northwest Ordinance residents of the territories gained citizenship and Constitutional protections as soon as Congress bestowed statehood. This system prevented the assigning of some sort of "colonial" or second-class status to later additions to the Union, guaranteeing instead that all states would have equal rights under the laws of the country.

Using *territory* in this narrow, political sense avoided use of the hated term *colony* to describe U.S. possessions and the accompanying word *colonist* to describe the inhabitants of those possessions. By law western territories were distinguished as either "organized" or "unorganized." A territory had to be organized under congressional mandate before it could be admitted to the Union as a state. In the 170 years between 1789 and 1959, only Texas bypassed this process because it was a republic before joining the Union in 1845. At this time there was no legal distinction made between incorporated and unincorporated territories; that would only occur later (the Supreme Court's so-called Insular Cases [1901–1904]: *Delima v. Bidwell* [1901], *Downes v. Bidwell* [1901], *Hawaii v. Mankichi* [1903], *Dorr v. United States* [1904]). But the distinction is a convenient way to describe the different *types* of territory claimed by the United States.

Seven states entered the Union between 1850 and 1875, all but one (West Virginia) carved out of the lands beyond the western frontier. There were 30 states when California entered in 1850; 36, when Nebraska joined in 1867. The admission of California, Minnesota, and Oregon was driven by westward expansion and the vague philosophy of manifest destiny. Kansas, West Virginia, and Nevada came in under the shadow of sectional politics and wartime passions. By the time Nebraska entered the Union in 1867, settlement, not sectionalism, was again the driving force behind westward expansion.

A turning point in westward expansion occurred in 1848, when gold was discovered on the American River in California. Up to that time the westward march of the frontier and the orderly admission of new states had generally followed a predictable pattern, but admission of the bear state leapfrogged settlement of the Plains and Rocky Mountains, and California elbowed its way into the Union without the preliminary step of territorial status. The rules of the game changed forever after the admission of California, and the "frontier" became more of a concept than a line on a map. That U.S. map took on the appearance of a patchwork with large empty areas of the West broken up by new states, each following its own logic of development.

TABLE 11.1 INCORPORATED TERRITORIES OF THE UNITED STATES, MID-NINETEENTH CENTURY

Territory	How Acquired	Territorial Government Organized	First Territorial Governor	Principal Economic Activity	Earliest Settlers	Early Problems	Admitted to Union
Utah	Part of Mexico Cession (1848)	Sep. 9, 1850	Brigham Young	Agriculture	Mormons, from 1847	Popular hostility to Mormon religious practices	1896
N. Mex.	Part of Mexico Cession (1848)	Sep. 9, 1850	Charles Bent, military governor (1846)	Sheep and cattle rasing; gold after 1875	Spanish descendants	Indian hostilities	1912
Wash.	Treaty with Great Britain (1846)	Mar. 2, 1853	Isaac Ingals Stevens	Agriculture	Fur trappers and missionaries	Rival sovereignty claims by Britain and Americans until 1846[a]	1889
Kans.	Part of Louisiana Purchase (1803)	May 30, 1854	Andrew H. Reeder	Trade routes and immigrant trails	Ohio River valley immigrants	Indians relocated from East; "Bleeding Kansas"[b]	Jan. 29, 1861
Nev.	Part of Mexico Cession (1848)	Mar. 2, 1861	James W. Nye	Silver mining	Miners	Indian-white relations	Oct. 31, 1864
Colo.	Part of Mexico Cession (1848)	Feb. 28, 1861	William Gilpin	Gold mining	Impresario "colonies"	Lawless boomtowns and hostile Indians	Aug. 1, 1876
Dakota	Part of Louisiana Purchase (1803)	Mar. 2, 1861	William Jayne (1861–63)	Agriculture ("king wheat")	Induced by railroad routes and land promoters	Attracting settlers	Nov. 2, 1889 as N. Dak. and S. Dak.
Nebr.	Part of Louisiana Purchase (1803)	May 30, 1854	Francis Burt[c]	Agriculture	Homesteaders; immigrants on westward trails	Perceived as a "great desert"; slavery	Mar. 1, 1867
Alaska	Purchased from Russia (1867)	Organic Act of Aug. 24, 1912[d]	John H. Kinkead (1884–85)[e]	Fur seal hunting; mining	Hunters, miners, missionaries	Official apathy; Indian unrest; isolation	Jan. 3, 1959

[a] The Oregon Treaty between the United States and Britain settled the ownership dispute.
[b] The Indians were relocated to Kansas from eastern areas under the Indian Removal Act of 1830. The sectional conflict between slave-owning and "free" settlers in the 1850s led to the characterization "Bleeding Kansas."
[c] Died two days after taking office; succeeded by Thomas B. Cuming.
[d] Administered first by U.S. Army, then by Customs Service of until Organic Act of 1884; officially referred to as an "Outlying Area" previously.
[e] Kinkead and those who followed him from 1884 to 1913 were "district governors"; the title *territorial governor* was first used in 1913. Between 1867 and 1884 Alaska was under the Departments of the Army, Treasury, and Navy successively.
Sources: Erik W. Austin, *Political Facts of the United States Since 1789* (New York: Columbia University Press, 1986), 68–69; Howard R. Lamar, ed., *The Reader's Encyclopedia of the American West* (New York: Thomas Y. Crowell, 1977), passim.

The statehood process set up by Congress in 1787 began with the subdivision of unincorporated lands into specific political units called territories. For instance, Nebraska was divided into the territories of Kansas and Nebraska in 1854 by congressional action. Once the status of organized territory was conferred, the remaining steps were a natural progression: when the population reached 50,000 free, white, adult males, local autonomy, including a legislative assembly, would be granted. Congress, however, retained the right to appoint territorial governors, judges, and marshals, thereby keeping the agents of law and order firmly in its hands. When the population reached 60,000 free inhabitants, the territory could apply for admission into the Union. Congress was under no obligation to accept the petition or to grant statehood according to a certain timetable. But it was inconceivable that any territory might be left standing outside forever. It was simply a matter of timing.

TABLE 11.2 NEW STATES ADDED TO THE UNION, 1850–1875

State[a]	Date of Admission
Calif. (31)	Sep. 9, 1850
Minn. (32)	May 11, 1858
Oreg. (33)	Feb. 14, 1859
Kans. (34)	Jan. 29, 1861
W. Va. (35)	Jun. 20, 1863
Nev. (36)	Oct. 31, 1864
Nebr. (37)	Mar. 1, 1867

[a] Numbers in parentheses are the chronological order of admission; e.g., California was the 31st state to enter the Union.
Source: Carol Berkin et al., *Making America* (Boston: Houghton Mifflin, 1995), A-30.

TABLE 11.3 TERRITORIES ADDED TO THE UNITED STATES, 1850–1875

Territory	How Acquired	Date Acquired	Size of Territory (in square miles)
Gadsden Territory	Purchased from Mexico	1853	29,640 sq. mi.
Johnson and Sand Islands	Annexed[a]	1858	Less than 1 sq. mi.
Swan Islands	Annexed[a]	1863	1 sq. mi.
Navassa Island	Annexed[a]	1865	2 sq. mi.
Alaska	Purchased from Russia	1867	589,757 sq. mi.
Midway Islands	Annexed[a]	1867	2 sq. mi.

[a] Johnson and Sand Islands in the Pacific and Swan and Navassa Islands in the Caribbean were all unilaterally annexed by the United States under the dubious authority of the Guano Island Act, passed by Congress in 1856. Guano, mined from seabird droppings, is rich in nitrate and therefore was considered prime agricultural fertilizer in the 19th century. Appropriation of these distant spots where it was found provoked several international incidents.
Source: Charles Van Doren and Robert McHenry, eds., *Webster's Guide to American History* (Springfield, Mass.: G. & C. Merriam, 1971), 671.

State Profiles

Numbers that follow may be slightly different from those cited in similar reference works; this is the result not of carelessness but of discrepancies in the original sources used by different authors. The reader is advised to beware of trying to be too precise in matters of population, elevation, land area, and the like.

Notes: * Indicates state capitals. The various governors' political affiliations are denoted as follows: by (D) for Democrat; (W) for Whig; (K) for Know-Nothing, or American; (R) for Republican; (U) for National Union or Union Democrat; (C) for Conservative; (CR) for Conservative Republican; (FS) for Free-Soil; (FSD) for Free-Soil Democrat, as opposed to Slave Democrat; (L) for Liberal Republican; (I) for Independent; (G) for Greenback; (NP) for "no party," where a man was appointed governor rather than elected through the normal electoral process. (CSA) by a governor's name indicates that he was a governor under the Confederate States of America during the Civil War (1861–65); (T) beside a name means he was territorial governor before statehood. N/A (not available) is used for western states and territories where population figures are unknown or too insignificant to be counted; this is particularly true of the black population in those areas during this era.

Rank represents current ranking in geographic size among the 50 states, not its ranking in the 19th century.

Famous Natives are people whose claim to fame at least began during the given era (1850–75). They are called natives of the state with which they were primarily identified, not their place of birth. In the western states in particular (e.g., Missouri, Nebraska) their most famous people were usually born elsewhere but made a name for themselves in their adopted state. In some cases, the birth state is only of interest because someone important had lived there before achieving fame.

For African-American population figures the numbers include both slaves and free blacks without distinction as to status.

Alabama

Land

Area: 50,750 sq. mi. (land); 52,423 sq. mi. (total). Rank: 30th. Principal rivers: Alabama, Tombigbee, Mobile, Tennessee, Perdido, Chattahoochie. Mountains (or high point): Appalachians, Cumberland (Cheaha Mt.). Major cities: Mobile, Montgomery,* Tuscaloosa.

People

Population: 771,677 (1850), 964,201 (1860), 996,992 (1870). Population by race: 427,000 (W) 345,000 (B) (1850); 526,000 (W) 438,000 (B) (1860); 521,000 (W) 476,000 (B) (1870).

Famous Natives

William Rufus DeVane King (1786–1853), U.S. senator, minister to France, vice president under Franklin Pierce; John A. Campbell (1811–89), U.S. Supreme Court justice, assistant secretary of war, (CSA); William Lowndes Yancey (1814–63), leader of Southern "fire-eaters" before the Civil War, defender of slavery, states' rights, and secession; Booker T. Washington (1856–1915), African-American educator and spokesman.

Governors

Henry W. Collier (D)	1849–53
John A. Winston (D)	1853–57
Andrew B. More (D)	1857–61
John G. Shorter (D)	1861–63
Thomas H. Watts (D)	1863–65
Lewis E. Parsons (D)	1865 (provisional governor)
Robert M. Patton (R)	1865–67
Wager Swayne (NP)	1867–68 (Reconstruction military governor)
William H. Smith (R)	1868–70
Robert B. Lindsay (D)	1870–72
David P. Lewis (R)	1872–74
George S. Houston (D)	1874–78

Memorable Events in State History

January 11, 1861	Delegates to secession convention vote to secede from Union by majority of 61 to 39.
February 4, 1861	Provisional Congress of Confederate States of America meets for first time in Montgomery.
August 5, 1864	U.S. naval forces under Admiral David Farragut win Battle of Mobile Bay, closing last major Confederate port on Gulf of Mexico.
December 15, 1864	Union forces invade Alabama from Tennessee and Georgia.
April 12, 1865	Mobile and Montgomery surrender to Union forces three days after Robert E. Lee surrenders at Appomattox.
September 30, 1865	New state constitution is adopted in place of Confederate constitution.
December 9, 1873	State's first "normal" (i.e., teacher education) school for blacks opens in Huntsville.

Year Admitted

1819.

Arkansas

Land

Area: 52,075 sq.mi (land); 53,182 sq. mi. (total). Rank: 29th. Principal rivers: Mississippi, Arkansas, Ouachita, White. Mountains (or high point): Ozarks (Magazine Mountain, near Logan City). Major cities: Fort Smith, Little Rock,* Hot Springs.

People

Population: 209,897 (1850); 435,450 (1860); 484,471 (1870). Population by race: 162,000 (W) 48,000 (B) (1850); 324,000 (W) 111,000 (B) (1860); 362,000 (W) 122,000 (B) (1870).

Famous Natives

Thomas C. Hindman, Confederate general and antebellum U.S. congressman; Albert Pike, antebellum lawyer, Confederate general and emissary to the Five Civilized Tribes, Freemason leader; Sanford C. Faulkner (1803–74), planter and Confederate colonel, best known for writing words and music of well-known fiddle tune "The Arkansas Traveler."

Governors

John S. Roane (D)	1849–52
Elias N. Conway (D)	1852–60
Henry M. Rector (D)	1860–62
Harris Flanagin (D)	1862–64
Isaac Murphy (U)	1864–68
Powell Clayton (R)	1868–71
Ozra A. Hadley (R)	1871–73 (acting)
Elisha Baxter (R)	1873–74
Augustus H. Garland (D)	1874–77

Memorable Events in State History

May 6, 1861	State convention votes to secede from Union and join Confederacy.
1864	Unionist convention abolishes slavery and adopts new state constitution.
March 2, 1867	Martial law is imposed by Republican-controlled Congress.

The "Arkansas Traveler" of folk song fame is a local legend that first appeared as the subject of a tall tale. This particular version is from a later painting by Edward Payson Washburn (1858). The legend and song underscore the remote backwoods image of the state. (Arkansas History Commission)

June 22, 1868	Congress readmits Arkansas to Union.
October 13, 1874	Reconstruction era ends with ratification of new state constitution restoring franchise to all whites and guaranteeing civil rights to all black citizens.

Year Admitted

1836.

California

Land

Area: 155,973 sq. mi. (land); 163,707 sq. mi. (total.) Rank: 3rd. Principal rivers: Sacramento, San Joaquin, Klamath. Tidal shoreline: 3,427 mi. Mountains (or high point): Sierra Nevada range of Rockies (Mt. Whitney, in Tulare Co.). Major cities: San Diego, San Francisco, Sacramento.*

People

Population: 92,597 (1850); 379,994 (1860); 560,247 (1870). Population by race: 92,000 (W) 1,000 (B) (1850); 323,000 (W) 4,000 (B) (1860); 499,000 (W) 4,000 (B) (1870).

Famous Natives

Stephen J. Field (1816–99), U.S. Supreme Court justice (1863–97) and chief justice (1859–63); John Charles Frémont (1813–1890), known as "the Pathfinder" for his pioneering expeditions to the West, served as civil governor of state before statehood, became one of the state's first two U.S. senators, newly formed Republican Party's first presidential candidate in 1856; John Muir (1838–1914), naturalist who fought successfully for establishment of Yosemite National Park; Charles Crocker (1822–88), Mark Hopkins (1813–78), Collis P. Huntington (1821–1900), and Leland Stanford (1824–93), known collectively as the "Big Four" railroad barons; John Sutter (1803–80), owner of the mill where California gold rush began in 1848.

Governors

Peter H. Burnett (D)	1849–51
John McDougal (D)	1851–52 (acting)
John Bigler (D)	1852–56
John N. Johnson (K)	1856–58
John B. Weller (D)	1858–60
Milton S. Latham (D)	1860
John G. Downey (D)	1860–62 (acting)
Leland Stanford (R)	1862–63
Frederick F. Low (U)	1863–67
Henry H. Haight (D)	1867–71
Newton Booth (R)	1871–75
Romualdo Pacheco (R)	1875 (acting)
William Irwin (D)	1875–80

Memorable Events in State History

September 9, 1850	Congress admits California to Union as free state, thus ending long-standing delicate balance between slave and free states in the federal government. Population at the time was approximately 96,000, most of whom had entered during the preceding two years.
1852	San Quentin prison founded.
1852	Gold production peaks from the great 1849 rush.
April 30, 1855	College of California is established as the first institution of higher learning in the state.
April 3, 1860	Brief experiment of Pony Express mail delivery begins at Saint Joseph, Missouri, headed for Sacramento. Soon to be superseded by telegraph.

In *View of the Procession,* Californians at the new state capital of Sacramento celebrate the admission of their state into the Union on September 9, 1850. (Library of Congress)

March 23, 1868	University of California at Berkeley is chartered by the legislature.
1869	California's Central Pacific Railroad, building east, joins the Union Pacific, building west, at Promontory Point, Utah.

Year Admitted

1850.

Connecticut

Land

Area: 4,845 sq. mi. (land); 5,544 sq. mi. (total). Rank: 48th. Principal rivers: Connecticut, Housatonic, Thames. Mountains (or high point): Berkshires (Mt. Frissell in Litchfield Co.). Major cities: Hartford,* New Haven,* Waterbury.

People

Population: 370,792 (1850); 460,147 (1860); 537,454 (1870). Population by race: 363,000 (W) 8,000 (B) (1850); 452,000 (W) 9,000 (B) (1860); 528,000 (W) 10,000 (B) (1870).

Famous Natives

Morrison R. Waite (1816–88), U.S. Supreme Court justice; Gideon Welles (1802–78), Lincoln's secretary of the navy; Frederick Law Olmsted (1822–1903), first American landscape architect; Harriet Beecher Stowe (1811–96), writer of *Uncle Tom's Cabin* (1852); Horace Bushnell (1802–76), father of the U.S. Sunday school movement; Lyman Beecher (1775–1863), Protestant theologian and outspoken reformer; Henry Ward Beecher (1813–87), son of Lyman Beecher, religious leader, abolitionist; Charles Goodyear (1800–60), inventor; Samuel Colt (1814–62), inventor; Phineas Taylor "P. T." Barnum (1810–91), legendary showman and impresario; John Pierpont Morgan (1837–1913), industrial mogul and financier; William Graham Sumner (1840–1910), social scientist, champion of Social Darwinism.

Governors

Thomas H. Seymour (D)	1850–53
Charles H. Pond (D)	1853–54
Henry Dutton (W)	1854–55
William T. Minor (K)	1855–57
Alexander H. Holley (W)	1857–58
William A. Buckingham (R)	1858–66
Joseph R. Hawley (R)	1866–67
James E. English (D)	1867–69, 1870–71
Marshall Jewell (R)	1869–70, 1871–73
Charles R. Ingersoll (D)	1873–77

Memorable Events in State History

1855	A branch of the new Republican Party is founded in the state.
1855	Progressive educator Henry Barnard founds the first national educational journal, the *American Journal of Education,* in Hartford.
1861	Yale University awards its first Ph.D.
September 10, 1862	Famed inventor and manufacturer Samuel Colt dies in Hartford.
1865	State's white voters reject a proposal to enfranchise its black residents
1873	Legendary Colt "Peacemaker" revolver enters production at the Colt Patent Firearms Manufacturing Company in Hartford.
1875	After 172 years of two official capital cities (Hartford and New Haven), Hartford is designated the sole capital.

Year Admitted

1788.

Delaware

Land

Area: 1,955 sq. mi. (land); 2,489 sq. mi. (total). Rank: 49th. Principal rivers: Delaware, Christina, Nanticoke, Pocomoke. Tidal shoreline: 8,426 miles. Mountains (or high point): Appalachians (foothills). Major cities: Dover,* Newark, Wilmington.

People

Population: 91,532 (1850); 112,216 (1860); 125,015 (1870). Population by race: 71,000 (W) 20,000 (B) (1850); 91,000 (W) 22,000 (B) (1860); 102,000 (W) 23,000 (B) (1870).

Famous Natives

Louis McLane (1786–1857), U.S. secretary of state; John M. Clayton (1796–1856), U.S. secretary of state; Thomas F. Bayard (1828–98), U.S. secretary of state; Du Pont (du Pont) family, including Samuel F. Du Pont (1803–65), Civil War naval officer; the industrialists Éleuthère I. du Pont (1771–1834), founder of namesake company, and Pierre S. Du Pont (1870–1954), architect of modern corporation.

Governors

William Tharp (D)	1847–51
William H. Ross (D)	1851–55
Peter Causey (K)	1855–59
William Burton (D)	1859–63
William Cannon (U)	1863–65
Gove Saulsbury (D)	1865–67 (acting)
Gove Saulsbury (D)	1867–71
James Ponder (D)	1871–75

Memorable Events in State History

1855	Statewide prohibition law enacted; it was repealed in 1857.
December, 1865	State finally frees its slaves when forced to by adoption of the Thirteenth Amendment.
1867	A branch of the Freedman's Bureau is set up in the state, though Delaware did not secede during the Civil War.
1875	Legislature for the first time appropriates money for black schools.

Year Admitted

1787.

Florida

Land

Area: 53,997 sq. mi. (land); 65,758 sq. mi. (total). Rank: 22nd. Principal rivers: Saint Johns, Apalachicola, Suwanee. Tidal shoreline: 2,344 miles. Mountains (or high point): (Walton County near Florida-Alabama border). Major cities: Tallahassee,* Jacksonville, Fort Lauderdale, Gainesville, Tampa.

People

Population: 87,445 (1850); 140,424 (1860); 187,748 (1870). Population by race: 47,000 (W) 40,000 (B) (1850); 78,000 (W) 63,000 (B) (1860); 96,000 (W) 92,000 (B) (1870).

Famous Natives

David Levy Yulee (1810–86), first Jew in U.S. Senate, congressman, railroad builder; Edmund Kirby Smith (1824–93), Confederate commander of Trans-Mississippi West; Stephen R. Mallory (1811–73), U.S. senator and Confederate secretary of the navy (one of only two Cabinet officers to retain his office throughout the life of the CSA); John F. Gorrie (1802–55), developer of air-conditioning and prototype ice-making machine; Henry M. Flagler (1830–1913), railroad and hotel builder; developer of Florida's east coast; Henry B. Plant (1819–99), railroad and hotel magnate, developer of Florida's west coast.

Governors

Thomas Brown (W)	1849–53
James E. Broome (D)	1853–57
Madison S. Perry (D)	1857–61
John Milton (D)	1861–65
Abraham K. Allison (NP)	1865 (acting)
William Marvin (NP)	1865 (provisional)
David Shelby Walker (D)	1865–68
Harrison Reed (R)	1868–73
Ossian B. Hart (R)	1873–74
Marcellus L. Stearns (R)	1874–77 (acting)

Memorable Events in State History

1858	Legislation encourages free blacks to return to slavery by promising right to choose their own master.
January 10, 1861	Florida becomes third state to secede from Union and join CSA.
February 20, 1864	Battle of Olustee (won by Confederates) is the largest Civil War engagement in the state.
November 1865	New state constitution is written for readmission to Union.
December 22, 1867	Ku Klux Klan organizes in Florida.
July 4, 1868	Florida formally readmitted to Union.

Year Admitted

1845.

Georgia

Land

Area: 57,919 sq. mi. (land); 59,441 sq. mi. (total). Rank: 24th. Principal rivers: Altamaha, Chattahoochee, Savannah. Mountains (or high point): Blue Ridge range of Appalachians (Brasstown Bold in Towns Union Co.). Major cities: Albany, Atlanta,* Columbus, Macon, Savannah.

People

Population: 906,185 (1850); 1,057,286 (1860); 1,184,109 (1870). Population by race: 522,000 (W) 285,000 (B) (1850); 592,000 (W) 466,000 (B) (1860); 639,000 (W) 545,000 (B) (1870).

Famous Natives

Cobb brothers: Howell (1815–68), U.S congressman, speaker of the House, U.S. secretary of treasury, state governor, and Thomas R. R. (1823–62), CSA congressman and Confederate general officer; Robert Toombs (1810–85), U.S. congressman, CSA secretary of state and Confederate general officer; Alexander H. Stephens (1812–83), vice president CSA, U.S. congressman, state governor; Joseph Wheeler (1836–1906), CSA general, U.S. congressman, and major general, U.S. Volunteers in Spanish-American War; John B. Gordon (1832–1904), CSA general, U.S. senator, state governor, commander-in-chief United Confederate Veterans after war; Joseph E. Brown (1821–94), state governor, chief justice state supreme court, U.S. senator; Sidney Lanier (1842–81), literary critic, poet ("the Keats of the Confederacy"); Joel Chandler Harris (1848–1908), Southern folklorist, children's author.

Governors

George W.B. Towns (D)	1847–51
Howell Cobb (D)	1851–53
Herschel V. Johnson (D)	1853–57
Joseph E. Brown (D)	1857–65
James Johnson (D)	1865 (provisional)
Charles J. Jenkins (D)	1865–68
Thomas H. Ruger (NP)	1868 (military governor)
Rufus B. Bullock (R)	1868–71
Benjamin Conley (R)	1871–72 (acting)
James M. Smith (D)	1872–77

Memorable Events in State History

January 19, 1861	Georgia secedes from Union to join CSA.
September 20, 1863	Great Confederate victory at Battle of Chickamauga.
November 15, 1864	General Sherman begins infamous "March to the Sea" from Atlanta.
April 1, 1867	Georgia placed under martial law by Congress.
July 21, 1868	Legislature ratifies Fourteenth Amendment and civil government is restored.
July 15, 1870	Legislature ratifies Fifteenth Amendment to be readmitted to Union.

Year Admitted

1788.

State Constitutions

1777, 1789, 1798, 1861, 1865, 1868.

Illinois

Land

Area: 55,593 sq. mi. (land); 57,918 sq. mi. (total). Rank: 25th. Principal rivers: Ohio (boundary), Mississippi (boundary), Illinois, Wabash (boundary), Rock, Kaskaskia. Mountains (or high point): (Charles Mound in northwest corner of state). Major cities: Springfield,* Chicago, Peoria, Decatur, DeKalb.

People

Population: 851,470 (1850); 1,711,951 (1860); 2,539,891 (1870). Population by race: 846,034 (W) 5,436 (B) (1850); 1,704,000 (W) 8,000 (B) (1860); 2,511,000 (W) 29,000 (B) (1870).

Famous Natives

Abraham Lincoln (1809–65), 16th president and "The Great Emancipator"; Stephen A. Douglas (1813–61), Vermont-born U.S. senator, Democratic Party leader, unsuccessful presidential candidate; Dwight Moody (1837–99) politically powerful religious leader and reformer; John Deere (1804–86), Vermont-born manufacturer, inventor, entrepreneur; Cyrus Hall McCormick (1809–84), inventor of the reaping machine; George Pullman (1831–97), industrialist and inventory; Philip Armour (1832–1901), meat packer and industrialist; Marshall Field (1834–1906), businessman and merchandiser, philanthropist; Aaron Montgomery Ward (1843–1913), businessman, pioneer of mail order catalog; James Butler "Wild Bill" Hickock (1837–76), frontiersman, lawman, gunfighter.

Governors

Augustus C. French (D)	1846–53
Joel A. Matteson (D)	1853–57
William H. Bissell (R)	1857–60
John Wood (R)	1860–61
Richard Yates (R)	1861–65
Richard J. Oglesby (R)	1865–69
John M. Palmer (R)	1869–73
Richard J. Oglesby (R)	1873
John L. Beveridge (R)	1873–77

Memorable Events in State History

1856	Illinois Central Railroad is completed from, Chicago to Cairo becoming the longest railroad in the world at the time and carrying the river trade from both the Ohio and Mississippi Rivers directly into Chicago.
1858	Series of seven historic debates between Abraham Lincoln and Stephen Douglas on the nature and future of the Union during their race for one of the state's Senate seats.
1860	Favorite son Abraham Lincoln receives Republican presidential nomination in Chicago and is elected president in November.
February 1, 1865	First state to ratify Thirteenth Amendment.
1865	Union Stock Yards open in Chicago, soon the largest and most important in the country.
1867	University of Illinois is founded.
October 8, 1871	Great Chicago Fire levels most of the city, leaving 90,000 homeless.
November 1, 1873	Joseph Glidden begins manufacturing his version of barbed wire, which soon outsells all others.

Year Admitted

1818.

Indiana

Land

Area: 35,870 sq. mi. (land); 36,420 sq. mi. (total). Rank: 38th. Principal rivers: Wabash, Ohio, White. Mountains (or high point): (Franklin Township in Wayne Co.). Major cities: Indianapolis,* Fort Wayne, Evansville.

People

Population: 988,416 (1850); 1,350,428 (1860); 1,680,637 (1870). Population by race: 977,000 (W) 11,000 (B) (1850); 1,339,000 (W) 11,000 (B) (1860); 1,656,000 (W) 25,000 (B) (1870).

Famous Natives ("Hoosiers")

Benjamin Harrison (1833–1901), U.S. senator, 23rd U.S. president; Schuyler Colfax (1823–85), speaker of the House of Representatives, vice president; Hugh McCulloch (1808–95), twice secretary of the treasury, under Andrew Johnson and Grover Cleveland; Walter Q. Gresham (1832–95) postmaster general, secretary of the treasury, and secretary of state; Ambrose Burnside (1824–81), commanding general, Army of the Potomac, governor of Rhode Island; Lew Wallace (1827–1905), Union general, novelist *(Ben-Hur);* James Whitcomb Riley (1849–1916), romantic poet, virtual poet laureate of Indiana.

Governors

Joseph A. Wright (D)	1849–57
Ashbel P. Willard (D)	1857–60
Abram A. Hammond (D)	1860–61
Henry S. Lane (R)	1861
Oliver P. Morton (R)	1861–67
Conrad Baker (R)	1867–73
Thomas A. Hendricks (D)	1873–77

Memorable Events in State History

1851	New state constitution bars blacks from settling in Indiana.
1853	Opening of Wabash & Erie Canal links Toledo on Lake Erie with Evansville on the Ohio River.
July 8–13, 1863	Confederate cavalryman John Hunt Morgan's raid into southern Indiana marks the farthest northern penetration of Southern forces in the West.

Year Admitted

1816.

Iowa

Land

Area: 55,875 sq. mi. (land); 56,276 sq. mi. (total). Rank: 26th. Principal rivers: Des Moines, Missouri, Big Sioux. Mountains (or high point): (Osceloa Co.). Major cities: Des Moines,* Iowa City (capital until 1857), Sioux City, Cedar Rapids.

People

Population: 192,214 (1850); 674,913 (1860); 1,194,020 (1870). Population by race: 977,000 (W) 11,000 (B) (1850); 1,339,000 (W) 11,000 (B) (1860); 1,656,000 (W) 25,000 (B) (1870).

Famous Natives

Samuel F. Miller (1816–90), U.S. Supreme Court justice; James W. Grimes (1816–72), state governor, U.S. senator, abolitionist leader; Asa Turner (1799–1885), abolitionist leader; William F. "Buffalo Bill" Cody (1846–1917), legendary frontiersman and showman.

Governors

Ansel Briggs (D)	1846–50
Stephen Hempstead (D)	1850–54
James Wilson Grimes (W, FSD)	1854–58
Ralph P. Lowe (R)	1858–60
Samuel J. Kirkwood (R)	1860–64
William M. Stone (R)	1864–68
Samuel Merrill (R)	1868–72
Cyrus C. Carpenter (R)	1872–76

Memorable Events in State History

1851	Last Indian lands in Iowa ceded by Sioux for cash settlement.
April 14, 1856	First train across Mississippi River crosses bridge at Davenport.

1857	New constitution (the 2nd) written and state capital moved from Iowa City to Des Moines.
1862	Iowa becomes first state to accept terms of Morrill Land-Grant College Act.
1868	1857 constitution amended to extend to blacks the right to vote and hold office.
1872	Iowa has the strongest Grange organization in the country: more than half the local chapters of the movement.

Year Admitted

1846.

Kansas

Land

Area: 81,823 sq. mi. (land); 82,282 sq. mi. (total). Rank: 15th. Principal rivers: Arkansas, Missouri, Kansas. Mountains (or high point): (Mt. Sunflower in Wallace Co.). Major cities: Topeka,* Wichita, Overland Park, Dodge City, Ellsworth.

People

Population: N/A (1850); 107,206 (1860); 364,399 (1870). Population by race: N/A (1850); 106,000 (W) 1,000 (B) (1860); 346,000 (W) 17,000 (B) (1870).

Famous Natives

Edmund G. Ross (1826–1907), U.S. senator, major figure in Andrew Johnson impeachment trial; John L. Ingalls (1833–1900), U.S. senator, noted literary figure; Carry Nation (1846–1911), colorful leader of temperance movement; John Brown (1800–59), abolitionist martyr and adopted Kansan.

Governors**

Andrew H. Reeder (T)	1854–55
Wilson Shannon (T)	1855–56
John W. Geary (T)	1856–57
Robert J. Walker (T)	1857
James W. Denver (T)	1857–58
Samuel Medary (T)	1858–60
George M. Beebe (T)	1860–61 (acting)

Statehood

Charles Robinson (R)	1861–63
Thomas Carney (R)	1863–65
Samuel J. Crawford (R)	1865–68
Nehemiah Green (R)	1868–69 (acting)
James M. Marvey (R)	1869–73
Thomas A. Osborn (R)	1873–77

Memorable Events in State History

May 30, 1854	Territory of Kansas established by Kansas-Nebraska Act.
July 2, 1855	First territorial legislature meets in Pawnee.
October 23–November 11, 1855	Free-Soil convention meeting in Topeka adopts antislavery constitution.
May 21, 1856	Antislavery town of Lawrence sacked by proslavery raiders.
May 23–24, 1856	John Brown retaliates for sack of Lawrence with murderous raid against settlers on Pottawatomie Creek.
April 1860	Pony Express mail service to California established.
1860	First railroad reaches the state.
January 29, 1861	Congress admits Kansas to Union as 34th state.
November 5, 1861	Topeka chosen as permanent state capital.
1863	Congress provides for removal of all Native Americans from Kansas.
1863	Confederate guerrillas under William Quantrill loot and burn Lawrence again.
September 1866	Grasshopper plague hits northern Kansas.
1874	Mennonites from Russia introduce new strain of wheat ("Turkey Red").

**Includes both territorial (T) governors (1854–61) and state governors from 1861 on.

Year Admitted

1861.

Kentucky

Land

Area: 39,732 sq. mi. (land); 40,411 sq. mi. (total). Rank: 37th. Principal rivers: Ohio, Kentucky. Mountains (or high point): Appalachians (Black Mountain in Harlan Co.). Major cities: Frankfort,* Lexington, Louisville.

People

Population: 982,405 (1850); 1,155,684 (1860); 1,321,011 (1870). Population by race: 761,000 (W) 221,000 (B) (1850); 919,000 (W) 236,000 (B) (1860); 1,099,000 (W) 222,000 (B) (1870).

Famous Natives

Abraham Lincoln (1809–65), born in Hodgenville, before moving to Indiana; Mary Todd Lincoln (1818–82), wife of Abraham Lincoln; Jefferson Davis (1808–89), CSA's only president, U.S. senator, and secretary of war; John C. Breckenridge (1821–75), youngest man ever to hold office of vice president, CSA general and secretary of war; Henry Clay (1777–1852), speaker of U.S. House of Representatives, secretary of state, U.S. senator, three-time presidential candidate, "The Great Compromiser"; Kit Carson (1809–68), legendary frontiersman; Carry Nation (1846–1911), temperance warrior born Cary Amelia Moore; Francis P. Blair, Sr. (1791–1876), newspaper editor, adviser to presidents from Andrew Jackson to Andrew Johnson.

Governors

John L. Helm (W)	1850–51
Lazarus W. Powell (D)	1851–55
Charles S. Morehead (K)	1855–59
Beriah Magoffin (D)	1859–62
James F. Robinson (U)	1862–63
Thomas E. Bramlette (U)	1863–67
John L. Helm (D)	1867
John W. Stevenson (D)	1867–71
Preston H. Leslie (D)	1871–75

Memorable Events in State History

August 6, 1855	During "Bloody Monday" riots 22 people die.
April 15, 1861	Lincoln guarantees state's neutrality at beginning of the Civil War.
September 3, 1861	Confederates violate Kentucky's neutrality by invading.
October 4, 1862	Provisional Confederate government briefly set up at Frankfort.

July 1864	President Lincoln places the state under martial law.
March 20, 1868	Jesse James and gang commit their first bank robbery at Russellville.
May 17, 1875	First Kentucky Derby is held in Louisville (winning horse is Aristides).

Year Admitted

1792.

Louisiana

Land

Area: 43,566 sq. mi. (land); 51,843 sq. mi. (total). Rank: 31st. Principal rivers: Mississippi, Atchafalya, Red, Ouachita. Tidal shoreline: 7,721 miles. Mountains (or high point): (Driskill Mt. in Bienville Parish). Major cities: New Orleans (capital until 1850), Baton Rouge*, Shreveport.

People

Population: 517,762 (1850); 708,002 (1860); 726,915 (1870). Population by race: 255,491 (W) 262,271 (B)** (1850); 357,456 (W) 350,373 (B)** (1860); 362,065 (W) 364,210 (B) (1870).

Famous Natives

Zachary Taylor (1784–1850), 12th U.S. president, U.S.-Mexican War hero; Judah P. Benjamin (1811–84), U.S senator, first American Jew to serve in a presidential Cabinet (Jefferson Davis's); Leonidas Polk (1806–64), State's first Episcopal bishop, lieutenant general, CSA; Pierre Gustave Toutant Beauregard (1818–93), CSA general, director of Louisiana state lottery; Norbert Rillieux (1806–94), African-American inventor of new sugar refining process; George Washington Cable (1844–1925), influential regional author; Louis Gottschalk (1829–69), composer, concert pianist.

Governors

Joseph Marshall Walker (D)	1850–53
Paul Octave Hebert (D)	1853–56
Robert Charles Wickliffe (D)	1856–60
Thomas Overton Moore (D)	1860–64
Henry Watkins Allen (D)	1864–65 (CSA)
George F. Shepley (NP)	1862–64 (Union military governor)
George Michael Hahn (NP)	1864–65 (Free State)
James Madison Wells (NP)	1865–67 (Free State)
Benjamin Flanders (NP)	1867 (Reconstruction military governor)
Joshua Baker (NP)	1867–68 (Reconstruction military governor)
Henry Clay Warmoth (R)	1868–73
P. B. S. Pinchback (R)	1873
William Pitt Kellogg (R)	1873–77

Memorable Events in State History

1850	Baton Rouge becomes state capital.
1853	Yellow fever epidemic kills thousands across the state.
December 1, 1859	First U.S. opera house devoted to French opera opens in New Orleans.
January 26, 1861	Louisiana secedes from the Union.
March 21, 1861	State officially joins the Confederate States of America.
April 25, 1862	Federal land and naval forces capture New Orleans.
June 23, 1864	Republican convention in occupied Louisiana revises state constitution, abolishing slavery.
March 11, 1868	New constitution grants full social and civil rights to freedmen.
June 25, 1868	Louisiana readmitted to Union.
September 14, 1874	White League takes control of city and its government after bloody street battle.

**Includes slave and free black population.

Year Admitted

1812.

Maine

Land

Area: 30,865 sq. mi./35,387 sq. mi. Rank: 39th. Principal rivers: Androscoggin, Kennebec, Penobscot, St. Croix. Tidal shoreline: 3,478 miles. Mountains (or high point): Appalachians (Mt. Katahdin in Piscataquis Co.). Major cities: Augusta,* Portland.

People

Population: 583,169 (1850); 628,279 (1860); 626,915 (1870). Population by race: 582,000 (W) 1,000 (B) (1850); 627,000 (W) 1,000 (B) (1860); 625,000 (W) 2,000 (B) (1870).

Famous Natives

Hannibal Hamlin (1809–91), state governor, vice president under Abraham Lincoln; James G. Blaine (1830–93), U.S. congressman and senator, secretary of state, unsuccessful presidential candidate, known as "Mr. Republican"; Dorothea Lynde Dix (1802–87), social reformer and humanitarian; Neal Dow (1804–97), prohibition crusader, Union general, unsuccessful presidential candidate; Henry Wadsworth Longfellow (1807–82), beloved national poet; Winslow Homer (1836–1910), trendsetting artist; Joshua Chamberlain (1828–1914), Union general, "Hero of Gettysburg," governor.

Governors

John Hubbard (D)	1850–53
William G. Crosby (W, FS)	1853–55
Anson P. Morrill (R)	1855–56
Samuel Wells (D)	1856–57
Hannibal Hamlin (R)	1857
Joseph H. William (R)	1857–58 (acting)
Lot M. Morrill (R)	1858–61
Israel Washburn (R)	1861–63
Abner Coburn (R)	1863–64
Samuel Cony (D)	1864–67
Joshua L. Chamberlain (R)	1867–71
Sidney Perham (R)	1871–74
Nelson Dingley (R)	1874–76

Memorable Events in State History

1851	State legislature passes "the Maine law" prohibiting sale of liquor anywhere in state; it becomes a model for many other states.
1861	Hannibal Hamlin, native son, becomes first Republican vice president.
1862	State College of Agriculture and the Mechanic Arts is established at Orono, later (1897) the University of Maine.

Year Admitted

1820.

Maryland

Land

Area: 9,775 sq. mi. (land); 12,407 sq. mi. (total). Rank: 42nd. Principal rivers: Potomac, Susquehanna, Patuxent. Tidal shoreline: 3,190 miles. Mountains (or high point): (Backbone Mountain in Garrett Co.). Major cities: Annapolis,* Baltimore, Silver Spring.

People

Population: 583,034 (1850); 687,049 (1860); 780,894 (1870). Population by race: 418,000 (W) 165,000 (B) (1850); 516,000 (W) 171,000 (B) (1860); 605,000 (W) 175,000 (B) (1870).

Famous Natives

Frederick Douglass, born Frederick Augustus Washington Bailey (ca. 1817–95), African-American abolitionist spokesman, lecturer, and writer; Harriet Tubman (ca. 1821–1913), African-American abolitionist leader, lecturer, and "conductor" on the Underground Railroad; George Peabody (1795–1869), founder of Peabody Conservatory of Music (Institute); Johns Hopkins (1795–1873), financier, philanthropist (Johns Hopkins University); Booth family of stage actors: Edwin Booth (1833–93), brother of John Wilkes Booth (1838–65), Lincoln's assassin.

Governors

Enoch Louis Lowe (D)	1850–53
Thomas Watkins Ligon (D)	1853–58
Thomas Holliday Hicks (K)	1858–62
Augustus W. Bradford (U)	1862–65
Thomas Swann (U, D)	1865–68
Oden Bowie (D)	1868–72
William Pinkney Whyte (D)	1872–74
James Black Brome (D)	1874–76

Memorable Events in State History

April 19, 1861	Baltimore mob attacks 6th Massachusetts Regiment en route to Washington, D.C., leading to 16 deaths.
September 16–17, 1862	Battle of Sharpsburg (Antietam) produces bloodiest single day of the war and ends Lee's first invasion of the North.
1870	Pimlico Race Track (horses) opens near Baltimore.

Year Admitted

1788.

Massachusetts

Land

Area: 7,838 sq. mi. (land); 10,555 sq. mi. (total). Rank: 44th. Principal rivers: Connecticut, Merrimack, Charles, Housatonic. Tidal shoreline: 1,519 miles. Mountains (or high point): Appalachians (Mt. Greylock in Berkshire Co.). Major cities: Boston,* Cambridge, Springfield.

People

Population: 994,514 (1850); 1,231,066 (1860); 1,457,351 (1870). Population by race: 985,000 (W) 9,000 (B) (1850); 1,221,000 (W) 10,000 (B) (1860); 1,443,000 (W) 14,000 (B) (1870).

Famous Natives

Daniel Webster (1782–1852), U.S. senator and representative, secretary of state under three presidents, legendary orator ("the Godlike Daniel"); Charles Sumner (1811–74), U.S. senator, abolitionist, leader of Radical Republicans; Charles Francis Adams (1807–86), scion of famous family, U.S. representative, diplomat; Nathaniel Hawthorne (1804–64), author, literary and social critic, "Father of the American psychological novel"; Louisa May Alcott (1832–88), novelist, lecturer on women's rights and temperance; Horatio Alger (1832–99), author of "rags to riches" novels for boys, philanthropist; William James (1842–1910), philosopher and psychologist, brother of Henry James (see New York entry); Ralph Waldo Emerson (1803–82), essayist, poet, philosopher ("the Sage of Concord"); Henry David Thoreau (1817–62), poet, philosopher, naturalist; John Greenleaf Whittier (1807–92), poet ("the Bard of Freedom"), a founder of the Republican Party; Oliver Wendell Holmes, Sr. (1809–94), author, lecturer, physician; James Russell Lowell (1819–91), poet, educator, diplomat, editor, and literary critic; Emily Dickinson (1830–86), Romantic poet; Henry B. Adams (1838–1918), magisterial historian and biographer; Mary Baker Eddy (1821–1910), founder of Christian Science and the Church of Christ, Scientist; William Lloyd Garrison (1805–79), abolitionist spokesman and newspaper editor; Lucretia Coffin Mott (1793–1880), representative of women's rights movement; Lucy Stone (1818–93), advocate for women's rights movement; Horace Mann (1796–1859), education reformer, U.S. representative, college president; Dorothea Lynde Dix (1802–87), crusader for humane care of mentally ill; Clara Barton (1821–1912), reformer, social activist, founder of American Red Cross; James Abbott McNeil Whistler (1834–1903), pioneering impressionist artist; Winslow Homer (1836–1910), artist who specialized in seascapes; Samuel F. B. Morse (1791–1872), portrait artist, inventor of telegraph; Benjamin Butler (1818–93), U.S. congressman, governor, unsuccessful presidential candidate, Union general ("Beast Butler").

Governors

George N. Briggs (W)	1844–51
George S. Boutwell (D, FS)	1851–53
John H. Clifford (W)	1853–54
Emory Washburn (W)	1854–55
Henry J. Gardner (K)	1855–58
Nathaniel P. Banks (R)	1858–61
John A. Andrews (R)	1861–66
Alex H. Bullock (R)	1866–69
William Claflin (R)	1869–72
William B. Washburn (R)	1872–74
Thomas Talbot (R)	1874–75 (acting)

Memorable Events in State History

1852	Massachusetts establishes compulsory school attendance for all children between the ages of eight and 14.
April 26, 1854	Massachusetts Emigrant Aid Society is founded.
1859	Massachusetts Institute of Technology is founded.
1863	Massachusetts Agricultural College is founded at Amherst; the first classes are held in 1867, and the name is changed to University of Massachusetts in 1947.
1866	Massachusetts Institute of Technology offers the first architecture course in the United States.

Year Admitted

1788.

Michigan[**]

Land

Area: 56,809 sq. mi. (land); 96,810 sq. mi. (total). Rank: 11th. Principal rivers: Clinton, Huron, Raisin, Detroit, Saginaw. Mountains (or high point): Porcupine Mts., Huron Mts. (Mt. Curwood in Barago Co.). Major cities: Lansing,* Dearborn, Detroit.

People

Population: 397,854 (1850); 749,113 (1860); 1,184,059 (1870). Population by race: 395,000 (W) 3,000 (B) (1850); 736,000 (W) 7,000 (B) (1860); 1,167,000 (W) 12,000 (B) (1870).

Famous Natives

Lewis Cass (1782–1866), U.S. senator, U.S. secretary of war and of state, diplomat, unsuccessful candidate for president; Zachariah Chandler (1813–79), U.S. secretary of the interior, U.S. senator, leader of Radical Republicans; James E. Scripps (1835–1906), newspaper publisher, businessman, philanthropist; George A. Custer (1839–76), Union general, celebrated Indian fighter.

Governors

Epaphroditus Ransom (D)	1848–50
John S. Barry (D)	1850–51
Robert McClelland (D)	1852–53
Andrew Parsons (D)	1853–54 (acting)
Kinsley S. Bingham (R)	1855–58
Moses Wisner (R)	1859–60
Austin Blair (R)	1861–64
Henry H. Crapo (R)	1865–68
Henry P. Baldwin (R)	1869–72
John J. Bagley (R)	1873–76

Memorable Events in State History

May 31, 1855	Soo Canal opens, linking Lake Superior with Lake Huron.
May 16, 1861	A Michigan regiment is the first western troops to reach Washington, D.C., in response to Lincoln's call for volunteers.
July 3, 1863	Michigan Cavalry Brigade ("the Wolverines") under George A. Custer defeats Jeb Stuart's Confederate cavalry on the climactic day at Gettysburg.

Year Admitted

1837.

Minnesota

Land

Area: 79,617 sq. mi. (land); 86,943 sq. mi. (total). Rank: 12th. Principal rivers: Mississippi, Red River of the North, Minnesota, St. Croix, Rainy. Mountains (or high point): (Eagle Mt. in Cook Co.). Major cities: St. Paul,* St. Anthony (present-day Minneapolis), Duluth.

People

Population: 6,077 (1850); 172,023 (1860); 439,706 (1870). Population by race: 6,000 (W) N/A (B) (1850); 169,000 (W) N/A (B) (1860); 438,000 (W) 1,000 (B) (1870).

[**]The state's name itself means "large river" from a Chippewa Indian word, a reference to the four Great Lakes surrounding it.

Famous Natives

John S. Pillsbury (1828–1901) flour-milling entrepreneur, three-time governor; William W. Mayo (1819–1911), physician and founder of famous namesake clinic; Ignatius Donnelly (1831–1901), quirky writer, editor, orator, U.S. congressman, unsuccessful vice presidential candidate, political reformer ("the Prince of Cranks"); James J. Hill (1838–1916), railroad magnate and corporate tycoon; Oliver H. Kelley (1826–1913), organizer of the first National Grange.

Governors

Alexander Ramsey (T)	1849–53
Willis A. Gorman (T)	1853–57
Samuel Medary (T)	1857–58
Henry H. Sibley (D)	1858–60
Alexander Ramsey (R)	1860–63
Henry A. Swift (R)	1863–64
Stephen Miller (R)	1864–66
William R. Marshall (R)	1866–70
Horace Austin (R)	1870–74
Cushman K. Davis (R)	1874–76

Memorable Events in State History

1851	Dakota Sioux Indians cede most of southern Minnesota by treaty.
1856	Chippewa (Ojibway) Indians cede most of northern Minnesota.
July 13, 1857	Delegates meeting in St. Paul draw up a state constitution.
May 11, 1858	Minnesota is formally admitted to the Union as the 32nd state.
1858	The first load of commercial wheat is shipped out of the state, beginning the long reign of wheat as "king" of the state's economy.
January 22, 1861	By resolution of state legislature Minnesota becomes first state to offer money and soldiers to President Lincoln to put down the rebellion.
August 17–September 23, 1862	Uprising by Santee Sioux under Little Crow ends in defeat at the Battle of Wood Lake, but not before 500–800 of both sides are killed.
December 26, 1862	Largest mass hanging in U.S. history: 38 Dakota Sioux publicly hanged in retaliation.
1867	St. Paul and Minneapolis linked to Chicago by rail.
1867	Board of Immigration is established to lure settlers to the state, particularly from Europe.
1873	Beginning of four-year grasshopper plague that devastates crops.

Year Admitted

1858.

Mississippi

Land

Area: 46,914 sq. mi. (land); 48,434 sq. mi. (total). Rank: 32nd. Principal rivers: Mississippi, Yazoo, Pearl, Big Black. Mountains (or high point): (Woodall Mt. in Tishomingo Co.). Tidal shoreline: 359 miles. Major cities: Jackson,* Greenville, Biloxi.

People

Population: 606,526 (1850); 791,305 (1860); 827,922 (1870). Population by race:** 296,000 (W) 311,000 (B) (1850); 354,000 (W) 437,000 (B) (1860); 383,000 (W) 444,000 (B) (1870).

Famous Natives

Jefferson Davis (1808–89), Kentucky-born but spent most of his life in Mississippi, U.S.-Mexican War hero, U.S. congressman, U.S. secretary of war, U.S. senator, CSA president; Lucius Quintus Cincinnatus Lamar (1825–93), U.S. congressman, Confederate minister to Russia, U.S. senator, U.S. secretary of the interior, U.S. Supreme Court associate justice.

Governors

John A. Quitman (D)	1850–51
John I. Guion (D)	1851
James Whitfield (D)	1851–52
Henry S. Foote (U)	1852–54
John J. Pettus (D)	1854
John H. McRae (D)	1854–57
William McWillie (D)	1857–59
John J. Pettus (D)	1859–63
Charles Clark (D)	1863–65
William L. Sharkey (NP)	1865 (provisional)
Benjamin G. Humphrey (D)	1865–68
Adelbert Ames (NP)	1868–70 (provisional military governor)
James L. Alcorn (R)	1870–71
Adelbert Ames (R)	1874–76

Memorable Events in State History

January 9, 1861	Mississippi is second state to secede from the Union.
February 22, 1862	Jefferson Davis, favorite son, inaugurated as CSA president.
July 4, 1863	Union forces capture fortress of Vicksburg after 47-day siege. Lincoln proclaims, "The Father of Waters now flows unvexed to the sea."
1867	Reconstruction Act places Mississippi under martial law.
February 23, 1870	Mississippi readmitted to Union, ending Reconstruction in the state.
1871	First Mississippi monument to Confederate war dead is dedicated at Liberty.
December 7, 1874	Race riots near Vicksburg result in deaths of 70 blacks.

Year Admitted

1817.

Missouri

Land

Area: 68,898 sq. mi. (land); 69,709 sq. mi. (total). Rank: 21st. Principal rivers: Missouri, Mississippi, Osage, Grand. Mountains (or high point): (Taum Sauk Mt. in Iron Co.). Major cities: Jefferson City,* Independence, Kansas City, St. Louis.

**Mississippi was the only state in the Union where blacks outnumbered whites for all three mid-century censuses, 1850, 1860, and 1870.

People

Population: 682,044 (1850); 1,182,012 (1860); 1,721,295 (1870). Population by race: 592,000 (W) 90,000 (B) (1850); 1,063,000 (W) 119,000 (B) (1860); 1,603,000 (W) 118,000 (B) (1870).

Famous Natives

Hiram Ulysses "U.S." Grant (1822–85), 18th U.S. president, Union general, general-in-chief of U.S. Army, one of the "Great Captains" of military history, memoirist, Ohio-born; Blair family: Montgomery Blair (1813–83), mayor of St. Louis, U.S. postmaster general, Republican Party leader; Francis P. Blair, Jr. (1821–75), U.S. congressman, U.S. senator, Union general, unsuccessful candidate for vice president; Carl Schurz (1829–1906), German-born politician, Union general, U.S. minister to Spain, U.S. senator, U.S. secretary of the interior, champion of civil service reform; Thomas Hart Benton (1782–1858), North Carolina–born U.S. senator and congressman, champion of manifest destiny, newspaper editor and author, known as "Old Bullion" for his opposition to paper currency; Richard P. Bland (1835–99), Kentucky-born U.S. congressman, "Free Silver" spokesman ("Silver Dick Bland"); Dred Scott (1795–1858), Virginia-born slave owned by a Missourian who became the defendant in the infamous *Dred Scott v. Sandford* Supreme Court case. James brothers: Jesse James (1847–82), outlaw and bank robber, and Frank James (1843–1915), outlaw and bank robber who eventually reformed; Younger brothers: Thomas Coleman "Cole" Younger (1844–1916), John Younger (1846–74), James Younger (1850–1902), Robert Younger (1853–89), all murderers and outlaws who robbed banks, trains, and stage coaches until the law caught up with them; William Torrey Harris (1835–1909), noted educator, U.S. commissioner of education; Susan Elizabeth Blow (1843–16), cofounder with William Harris of first U.S. public kindergarten (St. Louis, 1873); Adolphus Busch (1839–1913), German-born brewmaster; Mark Twain, born Samuel Langhorne Clemens (1835–1910), immensely popular author, humorist, and lecturer, known as "the Great American Humorist"; George Caleb Bingham (1811–79), Virginia-born genre and portrait artist, politician.

Governors

Austin A. King (D)	1848–52
Sterling Price (D)	1852–56
Trusten Polk (D)	1856–57
Hancock Jackson (D)	1857 (acting)
Robert M. Stewart (D)	1857–61
Claiborne F. Jackson (D)	1861
Hamilton R. Gamble (U)	1861–64
Willard P. Hall (U)	1864–65 (acting)
Thomas C. Fletcher (R)	1865–69
Joseph W. McClurg (R)	1869–71
B. Gratz Brown (L)	1871–73
Silas Woodson (D)	1873–75

Memorable Events in State History

1856	Long-running guerrilla war begins in the state over slavery question.
1857	U.S. Supreme Court hands down infamous *Dred Scott* decision in the case of a Missouri slave.
April 3, 1860	First Pony Express rider starts from St. Joseph, Missouri, for Sacramento, California.
March 6, 1861	State convention on eve of Civil War sends secessionists down to defeat, ensures Missouri will stay in the Union.

August 10, 1861	Battle of Wilson's Creek prevents Confederates from seizing control of state by main force.
November 7, 1861	An unknown Ulysses Grant loses his first battle attacking Belmont.
September 27, 1864	Centralia massacre when Confederate guerrillas stop a train and murder 25 unarmed Federal soldiers, then later that same day ambush and kill 116 men of the 39th Missouri (Union) Infantry who were pursuing them.
January 11, 1865	Slavery abolished in Missouri by decree.
1870	First stockyards built in Kansas City, making it a major beef transport center.

Year Admitted

1821.

Nebraska

Land

Area: 76,878 sq. mi. (land); 77,359 sq. mi. (total). Rank: 16th. Principal rivers: Platte, Missouri, Loup, Nebraska, Elkhorn. Mountains (or high point): Sand Hills (Chimney Rock). Major cities: Lincoln (known as Lancaster until 1867),* Omaha (territorial capital until 1867), Nebraska City, Columbus.

People

Population: N/A (1850); 28,841 (1860); 122,993 (1870). Population by race: N/A(W) N/A(B) (1850); 28,696 (W) 82 (B) (1860); 122,117 (W) 789 (B) (1870).

Famous Natives

J. Sterling Morton (1832–1902), U.S. secretary of agriculture, founder of annual Arbor Day celebration; Red Cloud (Makhpiya-Luta) (ca. 1822–1909), Oglala Sioux war leader and headman; Crazy Horse (Tashunca-uitco) (ca. 1841–77), Oglala Sioux military leader.

Governors

Francis Burt (Territorial Governor-Democrat)	1854
Thomas B. Cuming (Territorial Governor-Democrat)	1854–55 (acting)
Mark W. Izard (Territorial Governor-Democrat)	1855–57
Thomas B. Cuming (Territorial Governor-Democrat)	1857–58 (acting)
William A. Richardson (Territorial Governor-Democrat)	1858
Julius Sterling Morton (Territorial Governor-Democrat)	1858–59 (acting)
Samuel W. Black (Territorial Governor-Democrat)	1859–61
Algernon S. Paddock (Territorial Governor-Republican)	1861 (acting)
Alvin Saunders (Territorial Governor-Republican)	1861–67

Statehood

David Butler (Republican)	1867–71
William H. James (Republican)	1871–73
Robert W. Furnas (Republican)	1873–75

Memorable Events in State History

1851	Territory's first newspaper is published at Bellevue (until 1855).
March 15–16, 1854	Territory's principal tribes cede all lands west of the Missouri River in return for two protected reservations.
May 30, 1854	Kansas-Nebraska Act creates Nebraska Territory, comprising all the land north of Kansas between the Missouri River and the Continental Divide.
July 10, 1865	Union Pacific Railroad begins laying rails westward from Omaha for its portion of the transcontinental railroad.
March 1, 1867	Nebraska is admitted to the Union as the 37th state, with the capital at Lancaster (renamed Lincoln in honor of the recently slain president).
1871	David Butler, Nebraska's first state governor, is impeached and removed from office for misappropriating state funds.
1872	Completion of the first railroad bridge across the Missouri River links Nebraska and Iowa.
1873	Ogallala becomes Nebraska's "cowboy capital," serving for more than a decade as an important depot for cattle drives up from Texas.
1874–1877	A plague of grasshoppers descends on the state, causing great economic and personal distress.
1875	New constitution adopted to replace the original state charter.

Year Admitted

1867.

Nevada

Land

Area: 109,800 sq. mi. (land); 110,567 sq. mi. (total). Rank: 7th. Principal rivers: Humboldt, Truckee, Carson, Walker. Mountains (or high point): Sierra Nevada range of the Rockies (Boundary Peak in Esmeraida Co.). Major cities: Carson City,* Reno.

People

Population: N/A (1850); 6,857 (1860); 42,491 (1870). Population by race: N/A (W) N/A (B) (1850); 7,000 (W) N/A (B) (1860); 39,000 (W) N/A (B) (1870).

Famous Natives

James W. Nye (1815–76), governor who led Nevada Territory into statehood; William M. Stewart (1827–1909), U.S. senator, author of Fifteenth Amendment to Constitution; John McKay (1831–1902), one of "Big Four" of Comstock Lode, philanthropist; Wovoka (1856–1932), Paiute mystic who launched Ghost Dance Indian movement.

Governors

James W. Nye (T)	1861–64
Henry G. Blasdel (R)	1864–71
L. R. Bradley (D)	1871–79

Memorable Events in State History

1851	Mormon Station (later renamed Genoa) becomes first permanent settlement in Nevada Territory.

1854	Norwegian-born John A. Thompson introduces skiing to Nevada when he incorporates the practice into his speedy mail delivery service.
1858	Nevada's first newspaper is published in Genoa.
1859	The Comstock Lode, richest mineral strike in U.S. history, is discovered 30 miles north of Genoa. In the next 23 years it produces $293 million worth of silver and gold. Virginia City is founded.
1860	Ten thousand prospectors from California rush to the Comstock area to grab a piece of the bonanza.
1861	Congress creates Nevada Territory, with Carson City as the capital.
October 31, 1864	Nevada joins the Union as the 36th state during the Civil War.
1867	The Gold Hill and Virginia City miners' union forces the establishment of a closed shop and four-dollar-a-day wage for underground workers.
1868	The Central Pacific Railroad, constructed from the West, reaches Nevada.
1869	The legislature legalizes gambling, and it remains legal until 1910.
1874	First two American Indian reservations in Nevada established around Pyramid Lake and Walker Lake (for Northern Paiute [Numu] Indians).
1875	University of Nevada is founded at Elko.

Year Admitted

1864.

New Hampshire

Land

Area: 8,968 sq. mi. (land); 9,351 sq. mi. (total). Rank: 46th. Principal rivers: Connecticut, Merrimack, Androscoggin. Tidal shoreline: 131 miles. Mountains (or high point): White Mts. range of the Appalachians (Mt. Washington in Coos Co.). Major cities: Concord,* Portsmouth, Manchester, Nashua.

People

Population: 317,976 (1850); 326,073 (1860); 318,300 (1870). Population by race: 317,000 (W) 1,000 (B) (1850); 326,000 (W) 494 (B) (1860); 318,000 (W) 1,000 (B) (1870).

Famous Natives

Franklin Pierce (1804–69), 14th president, U.S. congressman and senator, U.S. attorney general; Henry Wilson (1812–75), U.S. senator, vice president, abolitionist, and advocate of racial justice for African Americans; John Parker Hale (1806–73), U.S. senator, unsuccessful presidential candidate, diplomat; Hosea Ballou (1796–1861), leader of Universalist Church, educator, theologian; Mary Baker Eddy (1821–1910) founder of Church of Christ, Scientist; Sarah Josepha Hale (1788–1879), magazine editor, author, social and political activist; Horace Greeley (1811–72), newspaper editor, gadfly, unsuccessful presidential candidate; Thomas Bailey Aldrich (1836–1907), novelist, editor; Augustus Saint-Gaudens (1848–1907), sculptor.

Governors

Samuel Dinsmoor (D)	1849–52
Noah Martin (D)	1852–54
Nathaniel B. Baker (D)	1854–55
Ralph Metcalf (K)	1855–57
William Haile (R)	1857–59
Ichabod Goodwin (R)	1859–61
Nathaniel S. Berry (R)	1861–63
Joseph A. Gilmore (R)	1863–65
Frederick Smyth (R)	1865–67
Walter Harriman (R)	1867–69
Onslow Stearns (R)	1869–71
Ezekiel A. Straw (R)	1872–74
James A. Weston (D)	1874–75

Memorable Events in State History

March 4, 1853	Franklin Pierce, native son, inaugurated as 14th president.
1866	Future University of New Hampshire is chartered as the New Hampshire College of Agriculture and Mechanic Arts.
1870	The state's first normal school (i.e., teachers' college) opens at Plymouth.
1871	Compulsory school attendance is mandated by state law.

Year Admitted

1788.

New Jersey

Land

Area: 7,419 sq. mi. (land); 8,722 sq. mi. (total). Rank: 47th. Principal rivers: Raritan, Delaware, Hudson, Passaic. Tidal shoreline: 1,792 miles. Mountains (or high point): Appalachian Ridge, the Highlands, Watchung, Palisades (Kittatinny Mt. in Sussex Co.). Major cities: Trenton,* Camden, Newark.

People

Population: 489,555 (1850); 672,035 (1860); 906,096 (1870). Population by race: 466,000 (W) 24,000 (B) (1850); 647,000 (W) 25,000 (B) (1860); 875,000 (W) 31,000 (B) (1870).

Famous Natives

Grover Cleveland (1837–1908), two-time president, Democratic Party leader; Joseph P. Bradley (1813–92), U.S. Supreme Court justice, legal scholar, member of Electoral Commission of 1877; Thomas Alva Edison (1847–1931), genius inventor, industrialist; Asher B. Durand (1796–1886), artist, founder of Hudson River School of landscape painting; Walter Whitman (1819–92), New York–born poet, literary icon (spent his latter years in Camden).

Governors

Daniel Haines (D)	1848–51
George F. Fort (D)	1851–54
Rodman M. Price (D)	1854–57
William A. Newell (R)	1857–60
Charles S. Olden (R)	1860–63
Joel Parker (D)	1863–66
Marcus L. Ward (R)	1866–69
Theodore F. Randolph (D)	1869–72
Joel Parker (D)	1872–75

Memorable Events in State History

1858	First transatlantic cable message arrives from Queen Victoria of England to President James Buchanan; received by John Wright at Trenton.
1870	First boardwalk (tourist promenade) is completed in Atlantic City.
1871	Free public school system is established in the state.
1873	Legislature passes a General Railroad Act ending the Pennsylvania Railroad's monopoly in New Jersey.
1874	Legislature passes compulsory school attendance law.

Year Admitted

1787.

New York

Land

Area: 47,224 sq. mi. (land); 54,475 sq. mi. (total). Rank: 27th. Principal rivers: Hudson, East, Niagara, St. Lawrence, Mohawk, Susquehanna, Delaware. Shoreline: (Great Lakes and Atlantic Ocean) 192 miles. Mountains (or high point): Adirondacks, Catskills (Mt. Marcy). Major cities: Albany,* Buffalo, New York City.

People

Population: 3,097,394 (1850); 3,880,735 (1860); 4,382,759 (1870). Population by race: 3,048,000 (W) 49,000 (B) (1850); 3,832,000 (W) 49,000 (B) (1860); 4,330,000 (W) 52,000 (B) (1870).

Famous Natives

Martin Van Buren (1782–1862), vice president, eighth U.S. president; Millard Fillmore (1800–74), vice president, 13th U.S. president ("Accidental President"); William Henry Seward (1801–72), governor, U.S. senator, U.S. secretary of state under two presidents; Hamilton Fish (1808–93), governor, U.S. senator, secretary of state; Brigham Young (1801–77), Vermont-born leader of Mormon Church, governor of Utah; Asa Gray (1810–88), botanist, author, champion of ideas of Darwin; George Westinghouse (1846–1914), inventor; Washington Irving (1783–1859), author, folklorist; Walter Whitman (1819–92), avant garde poet, journalist, essayist ("the Good Gray Poet"); Henry James (1843–1916), expatriate author, pioneer of American realism, dramatist; James Fenimore Cooper (1789–1851), first important U.S. novelist, New Jersey–born; Peter Cooper (1791–1883), industrialist, inventor, railroad pioneer, founder of Cooper Union College, unsuccessful candidate for president.

Governors

Hamilton Fish (W)	1849–50
Washington Hunt (W)	1851–52
Horatio Seymour (D)	1853–54
Myron H. Clark (W)	1855–56
John A. King (R)	1857–58
Edwin D. Morgan (R)	1859–62
Horatio Seymour (D)	1863–64
Reuben E. Fenton (R)	1865–68
John T. Hoffman (D)	1869–72
John Adams Dix (R)	1873–74
Samuel J. Tilden (D)	1875–76

Memorable Events in State History

1848	State legislature passes the Married Women's Property Act.
1853	College of the City of New York is incorporated.
1853	The chain of rail lines that began with a line from Albany to Schenectady in 1831 is combined to form the New York Central Company.
February 14, 1854	Elizabeth Cady Stanton becomes the first woman to address the legislature of New York, demanding that the state constitution be amended to include women.
1857	Frederick Law Olmsted and Calvert Vaux begin designs for Central Park.
July 13–16, 1863	New York antidraft riots result in 1,000 casualties.
November 25, 1864	Confederate scheme to burn important buildings in the city fails.
November 11, 1868	The influential New York Athletic Club is founded.
1870	New York City runs the first elevated train along Greenwich Street and Ninth Avenue in Manhattan.
1871	The Tweed Ring, a circle of corrupt city officials, is broken. Tweed himself is convicted at a trial on November 19, 1873.
September 20, 1873	Panic closes New York Stock Exchange for 10 days.

Year Admitted

1788.

North Carolina

Land

Area: 48,718 sq. mi. (land); 53,821 sq. mi. (total). Rank: 28th Principal rivers: Yadkin, Pee Dee, Cape Fear, Neuse, Roanoke. Tidal shoreline: 3,375 miles. Mountains (or high point): The Blue Ridge, Unaka and Smoky ranges of the Appalachians (Mt. Mitchell in Yancey Co.). Major cities: Raleigh,* Charlotte, Winston-Salem.

People

Population: 869,039 (1850); 992,622 (1860); 1,071,361 (1870). Population by race: 553,000 (W) 316,000 (B) (1850); 630,000 (W) 362,000 (B) (1860); 678,000 (W) 392,000 (B) (1870).

Famous Natives

Andrew Johnson (1808–75), vice president, 17th U.S. president, U.S. senator and congressman, governor of Tennessee, first president in U.S. history to be impeached; William Rufus King (1786–1853), vice president, U.S. senator, diplomat; Hiram Revels (1827–1901), U.S. senator, Methodist clergyman, educator; Hinton Rowan Helper (1829–1909), author, Southern apologist; Zebulon B. Vance (1830–94), wartime governor, U.S. senator and representative; William W. Holden (1818–92), editor, political leader, first state governor in U.S. history to be impeached; Richard J. Gatling (1818–1903), inventor, manufacturer.

Governors

Charles Manly (W)	1849–51
David S. Reid (D)	1851–54
Warren Winslow (D)	1854–55
Thomas Bragg (D)	1855–59

John W. Ellis (D)	1859–61
Henry T. Clark (D)	1861–62
Zebulon B. Vance (C)	1862–65
William W. Holden (NP)	1865 (provisional)
Jonathan Worth (C)	1865–68
William W. Holden (R)	1868–71
Tod R. Caldwell (R)	1871–74
Curtis H. Brogden (R)	1874–75

Memorable Events in State History

May 20, 1861	Secedes from the Union, the last border state to join the Confederacy.
November 9, 1865	Legislature votes to overturn the secession ordinance approved in 1861 and formally abolish slavery.
June 25, 1868	Resumes its place in Congress.
December 1, 1870	Republican governor, William Holden, is impeached.

Year Admitted

1789.

Ohio

Land

Area: 40,953 sq. mi. (land); 44,828 sq. mi. (total). Rank: 34th. Principal rivers: Ohio, Miami, Muskingum, Scioto. Mountains (or high point): (Campbell Hill in Logan Co.). Major cities: Columbus,* Cincinnati, Dayton, Akron.

People

Population: 1,980,329 (1850); 2,339,511 (1860); 8,865,260 (1870). Population by race: 1,955,000 (W) 25,000 (B) (1850); 2,303,000 (W) 37,000 (B) (1860); 2,602,000 (W) 63,000 (B) (1870).

Famous Natives

Rutherford B. Hayes (1822–93), 19th U.S. president, governor, Union general, U.S. congressman; James A. Garfield (1831–81), 20th U.S. president, Union general, U.S. congressman; Benjamin Harrison (1833–1901), 23rd U.S. president, Union general, U.S. senator; Salmon P. Chase (1808–73), U.S. secretary of the treasury, chief justice of Supreme Court, U.S. senator, governor, a founder of Republican Party ("Attorney General for Runaway Negroes"); Morrison R. Waite (1816–88), chief justice of U.S. Supreme Court; Sherman brothers: John Sherman (1823–1900), U.S. senator, U.S. congressman, U.S. secretary of the treasury and secretary of state, and William Tecumseh Sherman (1820–91), Union general, general-in-chief of the U.S. Army; Edwin M. Stanton (1814–69), U.S. attorney general, secretary of war under two presidents; William Dean Howells (1837–1920), novelist, magazine editor, literary mentor; Whitelaw Reid (1837–1912), journalist, publisher, editor, unsuccessful candidate for vice president; Ambrose Bierce (1842–ca.1914), journalist, author, social commentator ("Bitter Bierce"); Clement Laird Vallandigham (1820–71), U.S. congressman, Northern antiwar activist during Civil War, only American ever banished from his country; John D. Rockefeller, Sr. (1839–1937), industrialist who created Standard Oil monopoly, philanthropist, at one time the world's wealthiest man.

Governors

Reuben Wood (D)	1850–53
William Medill (D)	1853–56
Salmon P. Chase (R)	1856–60
William Dennison (R)	1860–62
David Tod (U)	1862–64
John Brough (U)	1864–65
Charles Anderson (U)	1865–66
Jacob D. Cox (U)	1866–68
Rutherford B. Hayes (R)	1868–72
Edward F. Noyes (R)	1872–74
William Allen (D)	1874–76

Memorable Events in State History

1856	Rudolph Wurlitzer founds music house in Cincinnati.
July 1863	Confederate cavalry under General John Morgan raid the state and are captured July 26 near Salineville.
1863	The exiled Peace Democrat Clement Vallandigham runs unsuccessfully for governor as antiwar candidate, receiving about 40 percent of the popular vote.
1870	John D. Rockefeller organizes Standard Oil Company in Cleveland, capitalized at $1 million.

Year Admitted

1803.

Oregon

Land

Area: 96,003 sq. mi. (land); 98,386 sq. mi. (total). Rank: ninth. Principal rivers: Columbia, Snake, Willamette, Rouge. Tidal shoreline: 1,410 miles. Mountains (or high point): Coast, Klamath, Cascade, and Blue-Wallowa Ranges of the Rockies (Mt. Hood in Clackamas-Hood River Co.). Major cities: Eugene, Portland, Salem.*

People

Population: 12,093 (1850); 52,465 (1860); 90,923 (1870). Population by race: 13,000 (W) N/A (B) (1850); 52,000 (W) 128 (B) (1860); 87,000 (W) N/A (B) (1870).

Famous Natives

Robert Gray (1755–1806), first white man to explore Columbia River; Chief Joseph (ca. 1840–1904) Nez Perce chief and personification of "noble Indian" myth; Abigail Scott Duniway (1834–1915), journalist, women's suffrage leader; Henry Villard (1835–1900), venture capitalist, president of Northern Pacific Red River, started first news syndicate, created General Electric; Joaquin Miller (ca. 1839–1913), popular poet of frontier life.

Governors

Joseph Lane (T)	1849–50
Kintzing Pritchett (T)	1850 (acting)
John P. Gaines (T)	1850–53
Joseph Lane (T)	1853
George L. Curry (T)	1854–59 (acting)

Statehood

John Whiteaker (D)	1859–62
Addison C. Gibbs (R)	1862–66
George L. Woods (R)	1866–70
La Fayette Grover (D)	1870–77

Memorable Events in State History

1851	Salem replaces Oregon City as the seat of government.
1853	Gold is discovered in the Rogue River Valley, drawing miners from California. A brief but bloody war is fought with Rogue River Indians.
1853	Steamboats begin plying the Columbia and Willamette Rivers as far inland from Astoria as Salem. In 1857 they reach Eugene.
1855	Umatilla Reservation created in northeastern Oregon for Umatilla, Walla Walla, and Cayuse Indians; Warm Springs Reservation established in the northwest for Wasco, Walla Walla, and (after 1868) Paiute.
1857	Voters approve a constitution rejecting slavery *and* barring free blacks from entering the territory.
February 14, 1859	Oregon is admitted to the Union as the 33rd state.
1868	John West establishes the first salmon cannery in Oregon at a site between Astoria and Portland that he names Westport.

Year Admitted

1859.

Pennsylvania

Land

Area: 44,820 sq. mi. (land) 46,058 sq. mi. (total). Rank: 33rd. Principal rivers: Delaware, Ohio, Allegheny, Susquehanna. Tidal shoreline: 89 miles. Mountains (or high point): Allegheny range of Appalachians (Mt. Davis in Somerset Co.). Major cities: Harrisburg, Philadelphia,* Pittsburgh.

People

Population: 2,311,786 (1850); 2,906,215 (1860); 3,521,951 (1870). Population by race: 2,258,000 (W) 54,000 (B) (1850); 2,849,000 (W) 57,000 (B) (1860); 2,738,000 (W) 1,017,000 (B) (1870).

Famous Natives

James Buchanan (1791–1868), 15th president, diplomat, U.S. secretary of state; Jeremiah Sullivan Black (1810–83), U.S. attorney general, U.S. secretary of state, constitutional scholar, highest-paid lawyer of his day; John Wanamaker (1838–1922), merchant, merchandising pioneer; Simon Cameron (1799–1889), U.S. secretary of war, diplomat, U.S. senator; George B. McClellan (1826–85), Union general-in-chief, unsuccessful presidential candidate, governor of New Jersey; Winfield Scott Hancock (1824–86), Union general, unsuccessful presidential candidate; Nathaniel Chapman (1780–1853), physician, medical authority, first president of American Medical Association (1848); Anthony J. Drexel (1826–93), investment banker, philanthropist; Andrew Carnegie (1835–1919), Scottish-born iron and steel magnate, philanthropist; Thomas Eakins (1844–1916), avant garde realist painter.

Governors

William F. Johnston (W)	1848–52
William Bigler (D)	1852–55
James Pollock (W, K)	1855–58
William Fisher Packer (D)	1858–61
Andrew Gregg Curtin (R)	1861–67
John White Geary (R)	1867–73
John F. Hartranft (R)	1873–79

Memorable Events in State History

1855	Horse-drawn streetcars begin operation in Philadelphia.
1856	Republican Party holds its first national nominating convention in Philadelphia.
August 2, 1859	The nation's first commercial oil well is drilled by Edwin Drake and crew at Titusville.
1862	Bethlehem Iron Company, forerunner of Bethlehem Steel, is founded.
July 1–3, 1863	Union forces win the pivotal Battle of Gettysburg.
November 19, 1863	President Abraham Lincoln delivers his Gettysburg Address.
1867	The first practical U.S. production of Bessemer steel occurs at Steeltown.
1873	Widespread financial panic sweeps the nation after the Philadelphia banking house of Jay Cooke fails.

Year Admitted

1787.

Rhode Island

Land

Area: 1,045 sq. mi. (land); 1,545 sq. mi. (total). Rank: 50th. Principal rivers: Pawtuxet, Sakonnet, Blackstone/Seekonk, Pawcatuck, Woonasquatucket. Tidal shoreline: 384 miles. Mountains (or high point): (Jerimoth Hill near Providence). Major cities: Portsmouth, Newport, Providence,* Cranston, Warwick.

People

Population: 147,545 (1850); 174,620 (1860); 217,353 (1870). Population by race: 144,000 (W) 4,000 (B) (1850); 171,000 (W) 4,000 (B) (1860); 212,000 (W) 5,000 (B) (1870).

Famous Natives

Nelson W. Aldrich (1841–1915), U.S. senator and congressman, businessman; Henry Bowen Anthony (1815–84), newspaper editor, U.S. senator, governor; Matthew C. Perry (1794–1858), U.S. Navy commodore.

Governors

Henry B. Anthony (W)	1849–51
Philip Allen (D)	1851–53
Francis M. Dimond (D)	1853–54 (acting)
William H. Hoppin (W, K, R)	1854–57
Elisha Dyer (R)	1857–59
Thomas G. Turner (R)	1859–60
William Sprague (U)	1860–63
William C. Cozzens (U)	1863 (acting)
James Y. Smith (R)	1863–66
Ambrose E. Burnside (R)	1866–69
Seth Padelford (R)	1869–73
Henry Howard (R)	1873–75
Henry Lippitt (R)	1875–77

Memorable Events in State History

1852	State legislature abolishes capital punishment.
1857	William H. Hoppin, elected governor in 1854 as a Whig, jumps to the Know-Nothing Party for his second term, then to the Republican

	for his third term in office, an unprecedented example of tacking to meet the political winds in U.S. history.
1861	The first Rhode Island troops join the Union army in the Civil War. More than 24,000 Rhode Islanders eventually march off to war.
1870	State legislature abolishes imprisonment for debts.

Year Admitted

1790.

South Carolina

Land

Area: 30,111 sq. mi. (land); 32,007 sq. mi. (total). Rank: 40th. Principal rivers: Pee Dee, Santee, Edisto, Savannah, Cooper, Black. Tidal shoreline: 2,876 miles. Mountains (or high point): Blue Ridge Range of Appalachians (Sassafras Mountain in Pickens Co.). Major cities: Columbia,* Charleston.

People

Population: 668,507 (1850); 703,708 (1860); 705,606 (1870). Population by race: 275,000 (W) 394,000 (B) (1850); 291,000 (W) 412,000 (B) (1860); 290,000 (W) 416,000 (B) (1870).

Famous Natives

Joel R. Poinsett (1779–1851), diplomat, statesman, U.S. secretary of war, proponent of manifest destiny; James Longstreet (1821–1904), Confederate general, memoirist; Francis Lieber (1800–72), educator, political writer, reformer, expert on international law; Robert Mills (1781–1855), architect, designer of Washington Monument; William Gilmore Simms (1806–70), poet, novelist, historian.

Governors

Whitemarsh B. Seabrook (D)	1848–50
John H. Means (D)	1850–52
John L. Manning (D)	1852–54
James H. Adams (D)	1854–56
Robert F. W. Allstop (D)	1856–58
William H. Gist (D)	1858–60
Francis W. Pickens (D)	1860–62
Milledge L. Bonham (D)	1862–64
Andrew G. Magrath (D)	1864–65
Benjamin F. Perry (D)	1865
James L. Orr (NP)	1865–68 (provisional)
Robert K. Scott (C)	1868–72
Franklin J. Moses, Jr. (R)	1872–74
Daniel H. Chamberlain (R)	1874–76

Memorable Events in State History

December 20, 1860	South Carolina is the first state to secede from the Union.
April 12, 1861	Confederate troops fire on Fort Sumter, beginning the Civil War.
February 17, 1865	William T. Sherman burns Columbia at the end of his "March to the Sea."
June 25, 1868	The state is readmitted to the Union, and a revised state constitution is adopted abolishing slavery.
1868	The state's first free public school system is established.

Year Admitted

1788.

Tennessee

Land

Area: 41,220 sq. mi. (land); 42,146 sq. mi. (total). Rank: 36th. Principal rivers: Mississippi, Tennessee, Cumberland. Mountains (or high point): Great Smoky Range of Unaka Mountains (Clingman's Dome in Sevier Co.). Major cities: Nashville,* Memphis, Knoxville, Chattanooga.

People

Population: 1,002,717 (1850); 1,109,801 (1860); 1,256,520 (1870). Population by race: 757,000 (W) 246,000 (B) (1850); 827,000 (W) 283,000 (B) (1860); 936,000 (W) 322,000 (B) (1870).

Famous Natives

Andrew Johnson (1808–75), North Carolina-born, wartime governor, U.S. vice president and president; John Eaton (1790–1856), North Carolina-born, U.S. senator, secretary of war, Florida governor, minister to Spain; John Bell (1797–1869), U.S. representative, secretary of war, U.S. senator, presidential candidate (1860); Sam Houston (1793–1863), U.S. representative, governor of Tennessee, founding father of Texas, U.S. senator, governor of Texas; Nathan Bedford Forrest (1821–77), Confederate cavalryman ("the Wizard of the Saddle"); William G. "Parson" Brownlow (1805–1877), Virginia-born, Methodist preacher, newspaper editor, unionist, governor, U.S. senator; Cave Johnson (1793–1866), Democratic Party leader, U.S. postmaster general, Confederate supporter.

Governors

William Trousdale (D)	1849–51
William B. Campbell (W)	1851–53
Andrew Johnson (D)	1853–57
Isham G. Harris (D)	1857–62
Andrew Johnson (NP)	1862–65 (military occupation gov.)
William G. Brownlow (R)	1865–69
DeWitt C. Senter (CR)	1869–71
John C. Brown (D)	1871–75

Memorable Events in State History

June 3–12, 1850	The Southern Convention of states' rights defenders meets in Nashville to oppose the Compromise of 1850.
June 8, 1861	Tennessee is the last of 11 Southern states to secede from the Union and join the CSA.
February 1862	General Ulysses S. Grant captures Fort Henry and Fort Donelson, launching him on the road to military immortality.
April 6–7, 1862	Grant wins at the Battle of Shiloh, the bloodiest battle on U.S. soil to that date.
June 6, 1862	Memphis falls to Union forces traveling down the Mississippi River, completing the task of clearing the upper Mississippi of Confederate forces.
November 24–25, 1863	Northern victory at Chattanooga opens the way for Union forces to advance to Atlanta.
April 12, 1864	Confederates under Nathan Bedford Forrest capture Fort Pillow, in the process raising questions about a massacre of black troops.

April 6, 1865	Radical Reconstruction begins in the state when the Republican William G. "Parson" Brownlow is inaugurated as governor.
1866	Tennessee is the first former Confederate state to be restored to the Union.
February 25, 1869	Radical Reconstruction ends in the state when DeWitt C. Senter succeeds "Parson" Brownlow as governor.

Year Admitted

1796.

Texas

Land

Area: 261,914 sq. mi. (land); 268,601 sq. mi. (total). Rank: 2d. Principal rivers: Rio Grande (boundary), Red (boundary), Brazos, Colorado, Trinity, Sabine (boundary). Tidal shoreline: 3,359 miles. Mountains (or high point): Davis Mountains of Rocky Mt. chain (Guadalupe Peak in Culberson Co.). Major cities: Brownsville, Austin,* San Antonio, Galveston.

People

Population: 212,592 (1850); 604,215 (1860); 818,579 (1870). Population by race: 154,000 (W) 59,000 (B) (1850); 421,000 (W) 183,000 (B) (1860); 565,000 (W) 253,000 (B) (1870).

Famous Natives

Sam Houston (1793–1863), Tennessee-born hero of Texas Revolution, first president of Republic of Texas, U.S. senator, governor; John H. Reagan (1818–1905), political leader, Confederate postmaster general, U.S. representative and senator; Roy Bean (ca. 1825–1903), legendary judge of Pecos County; John Wesley Hardin (1853–95), legendary gunfighter; Richard King (1825–85), steamboat entrepreneur, livestock capitalist, founder of a worldwide ranch empire; Charles Goodnight (1836–1929), pioneer rancher, cattleman, amateur botanist ("Burbank of the Range"), frontier legend; Gail Borden (1801–74), publisher, dairy industry pioneer; Quanah Parker (ca. 1845–1911), mixed-blood Comanche chief, peacemaker with whites.

Governors

P. Hansborough Bell (D)	1849–53
James W. Henderson (D)	1853 (acting)
Elisha M. Pease (D)	1853–56
Hardin R. Runnels (D)	1857–59
Sam Houston (I)**	1859–61
Edward Clark (D)	1861 (acting)
Francis R. Lubbock (D)	1861–63
Pendleton Murrah (D)	1863–65
Andrew J. Hamilton (C)	1865–66
James W. Throckmorton (C)	1866–67
Elisha M. Pease (R)	1867–69
Edmund J. Davis (R)	1870–74
Richard Coke (D)	1874–76

Memorable Events in State History

1851	Construction of first railroad in Texas begins.
1853	King Ranch, eventually the largest in the United States, is established.
February 1, 1861	Texas secedes from the Union and joins the Confederate States of America.
March 16, 1861	Sam Houston is deposed as governor for refusing to take oath of allegiance to the Confederacy.
May 12–13, 1865	Last battle of Civil War is fought at Palmito Ranch near the mouth of the Rio Grande River. (Soldiers in Texas had not heard of the war's end.)
1866	Jesse Chisholm leads the first cattle drive from Texas to Kansas, opening the era of the "long drives."
March 30, 1870	Texas is officially readmitted to the Union.

**When the state Democratic Party began talking about taking Texas out of the Union, Houston announced he was an "Independent" or "Unionist," to which Texans responded by throwing him out of office.

This 1862 or 1863 daguerreotype is the best known likeness of Sam Houston as governor of Texas. It is one of only two images of Houston known to exist today. (Tennessee State Library and Archives)

Year Admitted

1845.

Vermont

Land

Area: 9,249 sq. mi. (land); 9,615 sq. mi. (total). Rank: 45th. Principal rivers: Connecticut (boundary), Winooski, Lamoille, White. Mountains (or high point): Green Mountain, Worcester, and Hoosac Ranges of the Appalachians (Mount Mansfield in Lamoille Co.). Major cities: Monpelier,* Burlington.

People

Population: 314,120 (1850); 315,098 (1860); 330,551 (1870). Population by race: 313,000 (W) 1,000 (B) (1850); 314,000 (W) 1,000 (B) (1860); 330,000 (W) 1,000 (B) (1870).

Famous Natives

Chester Alan Arthur (1829–86), 21st president, vice president (though he spent most of his career in New York); Justin Smith Morrill (1810–98), businessman, U.S. representative and senator; Erastus Fairbanks (1792–1864), governor, businessman, antislavery and temperance leader; Hunt brothers: Richard Morris (1827–95), architect and William Morris (1824–79), painter.

Governors

Charles K. Williams (W)	1850–52
Erastus Fairbanks (W)	1852–53
John S. Robinson (D)	1853–54
Stephen Royce (R)	1854–56
Ryland Fletcher (R)	1856–58
Hiland Hall (R)	1858–60
Erastus Fairbanks (R)	1860–61
Frederick Holbrook (R)	1861–63
John Gregory Smith (R)	1863–65
Paul Dillingham (R)	1865–67
John B. Page (R)	1867–69
Peter T. Washburn (R)	1869–70
George W. Hendee (R)	1870 (acting)
John W. Stewart (R)	1870–72
Julius Converse (R)	1872–74
Asahel Peck (R)	1874–76

Memorable Events in State History

1850	State legislature nullifies the U.S. Fugitive Slave Law; ironically, the only state to nullify an act of Congress after South Carolina in 1832.
October 1864	Confederate raiders hit St. Albans, robbing banks and shooting up the town.
1865	Vermont ratifies the Thirteenth Amendment, abolishing slavery.

Year Admitted

1791.

Virginia

Land

Area: 39,598 sq. mi. (land); 42,769 sq. mi. (total). Rank: 35th. Principal rivers: James, Potomac, Rappahannock, Shenandoah, Roanoke. Mountains (or high point): Blue Ridge and Cumberland Ranges of Appalachians (Mt. Rogers in Grayson Smyth Co.). Major cities: Richmond,* Alexandria, Norfolk, Roanoke.

People

Population: 1,119,348(1850); 1,219,630(1860); 1,225,163 (1870). Population by race: 895,000 (W) 527,000 (B) (1850); 1,047,000 (W) 549,000 (B) (1860); 712,000 (W) 513,000 (B) (1870).

Famous Natives

John Tyler (1790–1862), 10th president, U.S. senator, vice president, Southern apologist; John Y. Mason (1799–1859), U.S. congressman, U.S. secretary of the navy, U.S. attorney general, diplomat; James M. Mason (1798–1871), U.S. senator and representative, Confederate diplomat, Southern spokesman; Winfield Scott (1786–1866), general-in-chief of U.S. Army, war hero, unsuccessful presidential candidate; Robert E. Lee (1807–70), Confederate general, educator, Southern icon; Thomas Jonathan "Stonewall" Jackson (1824–63), Confederate general; John Esten Cooke (1830–86), poet, novelist, biographer, Southern apologist.

Governors

John B. Floyd (D)	1849–52
Joseph Johnson (D)	1852–56
Henry A. Wise (D)	1856–60
John Letcher (D)	1860–64
William Smith (D)	1864–65
Francis H. Pierpont (R)	1865–68
Henry H. Wells (R)	1868–69
Gilbert G. Walker (R)	1869–74
James L. Kemper (D)	1874–78

Memorable Events in State History

October 25, 1851	New state constitution that includes universal white male suffrage is ratified.
October 16, 1859	John Brown seizes the U.S. arsenal at Harper's (later, Harpers) Ferry.
February 4, 1861	The Virginia legislature calls for a "peace conference" to avert impending civil war; 21 states attend but cannot resolve anything.
April 25, 1861	Virginia joins the Confederacy.
May 21, 1861	Richmond becomes the capital of the Confederacy.
July 21, 1861	First Battle of Manassas.
March 9, 1862	The CSS *Virginia* (originally the *Merrimack*) fights the USS *Monitor* in history's first engagement between armored ships.
May 2, 1863	Stonewall Jackson is mortally wounded at the Battle of Chancellorsville.
April 2–3, 1865	Confederate government flees Richmond and the city is burned.
April 9, 1865	General Lee surrenders to General Grant at Appomattox.
March 2, 1867	The Reconstruction Act places Virginia under martial law as "Military District No. 1."
May 13, 1867	The former Confederate president, Jefferson Davis, is indicted for treason in Richmond.
January 26, 1870	Virginia is readmitted to the Union.

Year Admitted

1788.

West Virginia

Land

Area: 24,087 sq. mi. (land); 24,231 sq.mi. (total). Rank: 41st. Principal rivers: Ohio (boundary), Shenandoah, Kanawha, Potomac, Monongahela. Mountains (or high point): Appalachians (Spruce Knob in Pendleton Co.). Major cities: Charleston,* Wheeling, Huntington.

People

Population: 302,313 (1850); 376,688 (1860); 442,014 (1870). Population by race: N/A (W) N/A (B) (1850); N/A (W) N/A (B) (1860); 424,000 (W) 18,000 (B) (1870).

Famous Natives

Alexander Campbell (1788–1866), Irish-born leader of U.S. "Restoration" movement, founder of Disciples of Christ; Belle Boyd (1843–1900), Confederate spy, actress, author.

Governors

Arthur I. Boreman (R)	1863–69
Daniel D.T. Farnsworth (R)	1869 (acting)
William E. Stevenson (R)	1869–1871
John J. Jacob (D)	1871–77

Memorable Events in State History

October 16, 1859	The abolitionist John Brown seizes the arsenal at Harper's Ferry but is soon captured.
December 2, 1859	After his trial for treason John Brown is hanged in Charles Town.
April 20, 1863	President Lincoln issues a proclamation that West Virginia will be admitted to the Union after a 60-day waiting period.
June 20, 1863	West Virginia admitted to the Union as 35th state.
May 24, 1866	Voters ratify an amendment to the state constitution denying citizenship to anyone who aided the Confederacy during the recent war.
February 10, 1869	Charleston is named the seat of the new state government beginning on April 1, 1870.
April 27, 1871	Citizenship (including right to vote) is restored to all former Confederates.

Year Admitted

1863.

Wisconsin

Land

Area: 54,314 sq. mi. (land); 65,503 sq. mi. (total). Rank: 23rd. Principal rivers: Mississippi (boundary), Wisconsin, Chippewa. Mountains (or high point): (Timms Hill in Price Co.). Major cities: Madison,* Kenosha, Milwaukee.

People

Population: 305,391 (1850); 775,881 (1860); 1,054,670 (1870). Population by race: 305,000 (W) 1,000 (B) (1850); 774,000 (W) 1,000 (B) (1860); 1,051,000 (W) 2,000 (B) (1870).

Famous Natives

Jeremiah Rusk (1830–93), U.S. representative, U.S secretary of agriculture, governor, career politician; William F. Vilas (1840–1908), U.S. postmaster general, U.S. secretary of the interior, Democratic Party leader, legal scholar, educator; Philetus Sawyer (1816–1900), U.S. senator and representative, "lumber king," entrepreneur; Edward P. Allis (1824–89), industrial pioneer; Christopher L. Sholes (1819–90), journalist, inventor of typewriter.

Governors

Nelson Dewey (D)	1848–52
Leonard J. Farwell (W)	1852–54
William A. Barstow (D)	1854–56
Arthur MacArthur (NP)	1856 (acting)
Coles Bashford (R)	1856–58
Alexander W. Randall (R)	1858–62
Louis P. Harvey (R)	1862
Edward P. Salomon (R)	1862–64
James T. Lewis (R)	1864–66
Lucius Fairchild (R)	1866–72
Cadwallader C. Washburn (R)	1872–74
William R. Taylor (D,G)	1874–76

Memorable Events in State History

1853	Railroad links Milwaukee and Madison.
1854	According to popular lore, the Republican Party is founded at Ripon, Wisconsin.
1854	First great wave of German immigration into the area reaches crest.
October 8–10, 1871	More than 1,000 people perish, including 600 at Peshtigo alone, when a devastating forest fire sweeps through six counties.
1872	The dairy promoter and future governor William Dempster Hoard forms a powerful lobby, the Wisconsin Dairy Men's Association.

Year Admitted

1848.

CHAPTER 12 Major Cities

Cities are the nexus of civilization.
— Robert A. Caro, historian

The "Second Wave" of American Cities

Americans did not create a significant urban population until a couple of generations after independence. The first wave of U.S. cities had been founded in the colonial era as compact communities that were small enough to be termed walking cities by urban historians. Businesses and residences, rich and poor, all coexisted in close proximity. Public services, such as fire and police protection, were in the hands of private citizen groups, such as the legendary volunteer firemen who went running when the big bell sounded. In the early national period those same cities continued to fulfill their primary role, which was as trading centers for the collection of goods sent abroad and entrepôts for goods imported from abroad. Only a small fraction of the nation's population lived in urban areas in those years, so cities played an insignificant role in national life. This even included the nation's capital, Washington, D.C., which was a national embarrassment whenever visitors arrived from Europe. It was small, dirty, still unfinished some 80 years after the nation was born. The District, or "Washington City" as it was usually called, did not really occupy a central place in national life until the beginning of the Civil War in 1861. Even then, filled with thousands of soldiers and politicians and directing the great civil conflict that would determine the lives of millions of people, it remained a laughingstock. The writer Louisa May Alcott, who worked as a volunteer nurse in the city during the war, noted primly that "one-half of the city's male population seemed to be taking the other half to the guard house," and the officers and their ladies "dressed in the worst possible taste and walked like ducks." Washington, D.C.'s, lack of sophistication and greatness was more the rule than the exception for U.S. cities.

As a clearinghouse for trade, the average U.S. city served a hinterland of no more than a 150-mile radius. All of that began to change, however, with the development of canals and railroads in the second quarter of the 19th century, allowing cities to extend their influence into vast unopened regions.

By mid-century, the map of the United States showed a number of large and growing interior cities that were part of a "second wave" of urbanization, although the largest population centers were still the old Atlantic ports founded in colonial times. The beginnings of the transformation can be seen in 1820, at which time only 7 percent of the population lived in cities. In the next 40 years, driven by a powerful combination of market forces and population growth, there occurred a faster rate of urban growth than during any other time in U.S. history. While the national population increased by 35 percent in the decade before 1850, urban population in the same period grew by an astounding 92 percent, a rate never again seen in the United States or any other country in the world. By 1860 the number of Americans living in cities had soared to 20 percent.

Detroit was a 150-year-old sleepy river town on the Detroit River until 1825, when the Erie Canal opened the Great Lakes region to commerce. Then its economy took off. Pictured here in 1860 on the eve of the Civil War, it was a major rail center and shipping port for the Midwest—although it still did not rank in the top 10 cities (print from original woodcut in author's collection)

In 1820 only two American cities, New York and Philadelphia, ranked with the great cities of Europe, and neither had even 200,000 residents. No U.S. city, not even New York City, possessed the kind of economic and political clout of Paris, London, or Madrid. But something extraordinary happened in the next 30-years. The four major Atlantic seaports (New York, Boston, Baltimore, and Philadelphia) grew at a rate of 25 percent or more per decade. Other U.S. cities followed a similar trajectory. Ironically Washington, D.C., remained the smallest of the nation's major cities, a paradox among the world's capitals.

U.S urbanization gathered momentum every decade, as the census records show. From 1790 until the middle of the 20th century the Census Bureau defined an *urban area* as any place having at least 2,500 people, or what would be good-size town to most people. There were 26 urban areas in 1830 with a population in excess of 8,000. In the next three decades urban growth took off, thanks to a flood of foreign immigrants, westward migration, and economic expansion. By 1860 the number of urban communities that had more than 8,000 had quadrupled to 141. Cincinnati, Buffalo, Cleveland, and Chicago were the fastest-growing of the new wave of cities. One common denominator among these four, as well as other rapidly growing communities, was strategic location on a major waterway (lake or river) that served as a highway for the movement of both people and goods.

Some towns that did not even exist when the 1850 Census count was taken seemed to appear Brigadoon-like out of nowhere on the 1860 or 1870 records. St. Paul, Minnesota, experienced more than 10,000 percent growth between 1850 and 1860, calling itself "the commercial emporium of the [Old] Northwest." And although no other U.S city could match those numbers, some other humble hamlets experienced their own explosive growth. Evolving trade patterns, military importance, or the presence of some valuable natural resource nearby were three of the myriad factors that could spark such explosive growth.

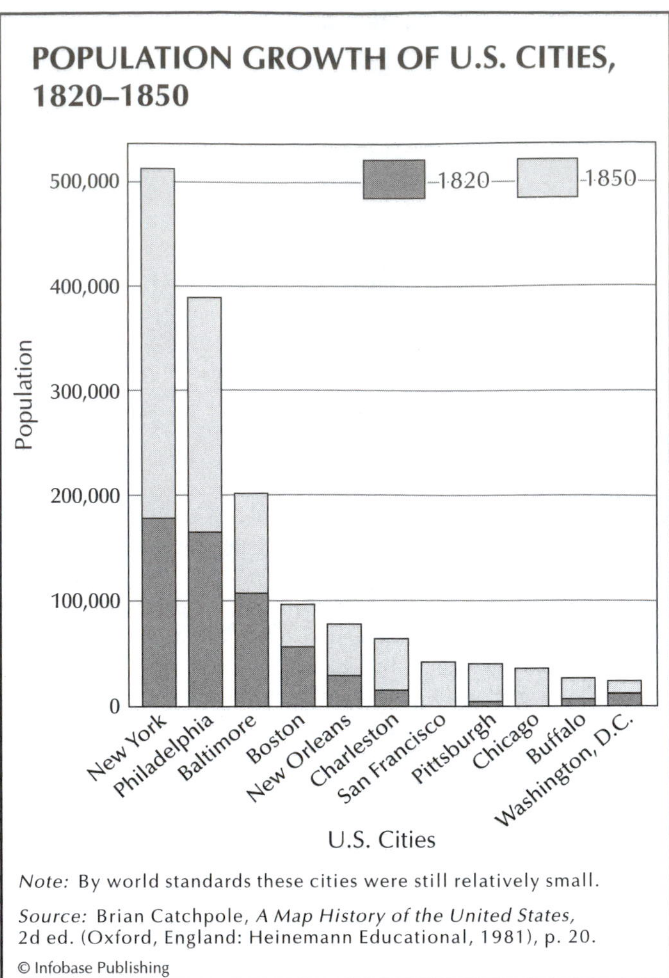

Note: By world standards these cities were still relatively small.

Source: Brian Catchpole, *A Map History of the United States*, 2d ed. (Oxford, England: Heinemann Educational, 1981), p. 20.

TABLE 12.1 TOWNS AND CITIES ESTABLISHED 1850–1870

Town or City	Population in 1850	Population in 1860	Population in 1870	Principal Cause of Rapid Growth
Corpus Christi, Tex.	Less than 1,000	Less than 1,600	3,000	Shipping center, transportation hub, immigrant entry port
Denver, Colo.	Less than 1,000	Less than 1,000	5,000	Discovery of gold, regional gateway, capital city
Des Moines, Iowa	1,000	4,000	12,000	Military post, state capital, transportation hub, foreign immigrants
Minneapolis, Minn.	Less than 1,000	3,000	13,000	Water power for manufacturing, commercial gateway, transportation hub
Portland, Oreg.	1,000	3,000	8,000	Emporium for regional export–import trade, transportation hub
St. Paul, Minn.	1,000	10,000	20,000	Port of call for Mississippi River traffic, rail hub, territorial capital
San Diego, Calif.	Less than 1,000	1,000	2,000	Gateway city to both Mexican and Pacific trade, good rail and river connections, salubrious climate

Sources: B. R. Mitchell, *International Historical Statistics: The Americas and Australasia* (Detroit: Gale Research, 1983), 97–100; Howard R. Lamar, ed., *The Reader's Encyclopedia of the American West* (New York: Thomas Y. Crowell, 1977), passim.

Although common themes can be detected in the stories of many cities, trying to fit all of them to a single model is a mistake. Each had its own combination of circumstances and conditions that contributed to its growth. Urbanization was a complex nationwide phenomenon that defies easy generalization, although some factors stand out. Certainly a flood tide of European immigrants (and to a lesser extent, Asian immigrants) played a major role. Untold numbers of urban dwellers also entered from rural areas within the United States itself. Mechanization on the farm and the lure of bright city lights also caused many a country dweller to strike out for the city. Not so well known is the demographic fact that rural birth rates in the United States were consistently high during these years, and rural death rates were lower than urban. The agrarian economy could not support such numbers, so much of the "surplus population" found new homes in the cities, attracted by the promise of more opportunity and an easier life than down on the farm.

However, all the stories of rapid urban growth from this period did not have happy endings. Some towns charged ahead for a few years before falling back in the pack. For instance, Fall River, Massachusetts, grew steadily in the second half of the 19th-century, from 12,000 in 1850 to 74,000 in 1900, but still it faded in the long run. By 1900, settling in among those whose best years were behind them, Fall River was no longer considered a major city. Spring Garden, Pennsylvania, had a population of 58,894 people in 1850, sufficient to rank ninth among all major cities in the United States that year. Four years later it was being swallowed up by a rapidly expanding Philadelphia, becoming nothing more than a suburb of its larger neighbor.

Some cities that were thriving communities at one census count actually contracted in population in the years following. Memphis, Tennessee, had 40,000 people in 1870 but dropped down to only 34,000 10 years later, the result of epidemics and changing trade patterns. Tampa, Florida, and San Jose, California, had 1,000 and 4,000 people, respectively, in 1850; neither could count even 1,000 residents in 1860.

The capital of unfulfilled promise in the 19th century was Hartford, Connecticut. Around the time of the Civil War it seemed on the verge of making the leap to greatness as the cradle of the U.S. insurance and arms industries. It was also home to such luminaries as Mark Twain, Noah Webster, and Harriet Beecher Stowe during these years. But it ultimately fell back into the pack of midsize cities.

The Shifting U.S. Population Center

The U.S. population was expanding explosively but not uniformly, during these years, across the width and breadth of the country. Population grew faster in the North than in the South, and in the West than in the East. One way of tracking the population growth of the nation is by calculating the precise location of the mean population center over the course of several decades. This produces a statistical construct, expressed in terms of latitude and longitude, that is quite useful as a demographic tool. The mean center of population is that point at which the United States would balance perfectly if the distribution of the population were plotted on a map assigning identical weight values to every man, woman, and child. For the 1800s these points are calculated by the Census Bureau using only the contiguous states and territories, what is termed "the lower 48." They reveal important trends in settlement, westward migration, and urbanization during this time period.

Up to 1850 the population center of the United States was still east of the Appalachian Mountains. Four of the country's 10 largest cities were located in the state of New York—New York City (1), Brooklyn (7), Albany (8), and Buffalo (10). Five of the top 10 (New York City, Philadelphia, Boston, Brooklyn, Baltimore) and eight of the top 13 (add Washington, D.C.; Newark, New Jersey; and Charleston, South Carolina) were Atlantic coast cities, and they had occupied the top spots since colonial times. Four of the five largest cities in 1800 still held that distinction in 1850. Only Charleston had dropped out of the top five, to be replaced by another Southern city, New Orleans, which had not even been a U.S. city in 1800.

In the next 25 years after 1850 as steady European immigration and the lure of the frontier did their work, the population center of the country shifted steadily westward. Not coincidentally, Buffalo and Albany dropped out of the top 10, to be replaced by Chicago and San Francisco, which were the new metropolises of the Midwest and Far West, respectively. Yet even as the urban demographic of the nation was changing, the United States remained largely a rural and small-town country, sneered at by the elite of the Old World, yet still regarded as the Promised Land by the European masses.

TABLE 12.2 THE MEAN CENTER OF POPULATION OF THE UNITED STATES, 1840–1880

Census Year	North Latitude	West Longitude	Approximate Location
1840	39°02′00″	80°18′00″	Modern Upshur County, W.Va., 16 miles south of Clarksburg
1850	38°59′00″	81°19′00″	Wirt County, W.Va., 23 miles south/east of Parkersburg
1860	39°00′24″	82°48′48″	Pike County, Ohio, 20 miles south by east of Chillicothe
1870	39°12′00″	83°35′42″	Highland County, Ohio, 48 miles east by north of Cincinnati
1880	39°04′08″	84°39′40″	Boone County, Ky., 8 miles west by south of Cincinnati, Ohio.

Note: Expressed in terms of degrees, feet, and inches of latitude/longitude.
Source: United States Department of Commerce, Bureau of the Census, Statistical Information Office, Population Division (Washington, D.C.), "Population and Geographic Centers" Geography Div., U.S. Bureau of the Census, Washington., D.C. Available online as Table A: Mean Ctr. of Pop. of the United States: 1790–1990. URL: http://www.census.gov/population/censusdata/popctr.pdf.

TABLE 12.3 U.S. CITIES GROUPED INTO STANDARDIZED CATEGORIES, 1850, 1860, 1870

Year	Number of Cities with Population above 2,500	Number of Cities with Population of 2,500–24,999	Number of Cities with Population of 25,000–249,999	Number of Cities with Population of 250,000 and Higher
1850	236	210	25	1
1860	392	357	32	3
1870	663	611	45	7

Source: Glenn Porter, ed., *Encyclopedia of American Economic History,* vol. 3 (New York: Charles Scribner's Sons, 1980), 1030.

TABLE 12.4 REPRESENTATIVE U.S. CITIES

(ranked by Standardized Demographic Categories, 1860)

Population Range	Some Cities within the Given Range
800,000–1,500,000	New York City, N.Y.
250,000–799,999	Philadelphia, Pa.
125,000–249,999	New Orleans, La.; St. Louis, Mo.; Cincinnati, Ohio.; Baltimore, Md.; Boston, Mass.
100,000–124,999	Chicago, Ill.
30,000–99,999	Louisville, Ky.; San Francisco, Calif.; Charleston, S.C.; Richmond, Va.; Montgomery, Ala.; Buffalo, N.Y.; Albany, N.Y.; Washington, D.C.
Less than 30,000	Salem, Mass.; Norfolk, Va.

Source: John Mack Faragher et al., eds., *Out of Many: A History of the American People,* 2d ed. (Upper Saddle River, N.J.: Prentice-Hall, 1997), 381.

The Emergence of the Modern City

In the 50 years after 1860, the American city emerged in its modern form, complete with suburbs, municipal services, and mass public transportation. One of the major steps occurred in the 1870s, when the suburb first appeared as the preferred residential area for the rising urban middle class. Suburbs offered privacy, aesthetic advantages, and home ownership at a reasonable price. But suburbs were adjuncts to cities, not replacements. On the contrary, they contributed to the rapid growth of American cities. By the end of the 19th century the benchmark for large urban centers was 100,000 residents. By that time 50 cities met that criterion. In 1830 the benchmark for being considered a "big city" had been a mere 8,000 population. That benchmark had to be reconsidered by the mid-century mark and discarded entirely within another decade after that. In the 10 years from 1860 to 1870, the urban population of the country grew by 59.3 percent, and between 1870 and 1880 by 42.7 percent.

As villages grew into towns and towns into cities, modern urban problems inevitably appeared, in particular crime, sanitation, and the 19th-century bugaboo of "pauperism." These characteristics led some Americans to view the city with deeply ambivalent feelings. The author George Foster in *New York by Gas-Light* (1850) described the "fearful mysteries of darkness in the metropolis," and he did not mean merely the darkness of night. Foster and many others believed in the "dark soul of the city." Josiah Strong *(Our Country),* another critic, saw only danger in urbanization, considering cities "a serious menace to [American] civilization." But such voices of gloom and doom were more akin to Luddism than to thoughtful critique, and they were definitely in the minority. Most Americans saw cities as a natural by-product of progress.

By the mid-19th century, American cities were already beginning to display the ethnic diversity so characteristic of the nation's later industrial metropolises. After the English, Irish, and Scotch (generally lumped together under the heading of "British"), Germans were the single largest ethnic minority. The French ranked a distant third in sheer numbers. Swiss and Bohemians constituted a small but significant proportion of the foreign-born urban U.S. population. In the decades to follow the ethnic melting pot that was American cities would be filled by many ethnic streams, both European and non-European.

TABLE 12.5 ETHNIC AND RACIAL COMPARISONS OF SOME MAJOR CITIES IN THE UNITED STATES, 1850

Largest Foreign-Born Population		Smallest Foreign-Born Population		Largest Local-Born Population		Smallest Local-Born Population		Largest Black Population		Smallest Black Population	
City	Percentage	City	Percentage	City	Percentage	City	Percentage	City	Percentage	City	Percentage
Milwaukee, Wis.	63.7	Portland, Maine	12.1	Portsmouth, N.H.	72.6	St. Louis, Mo.	27.1	Charleston, S.C.	53.4	Boston, Mass.	1.5
Chicago, Ill.	52.3	Manchester, N.H.	12.1	Portland, Maine	72.6	Mobile, Ala.	26.8	Wilmington, N.C.	50.7	Chicago, Ill.	1.1
St. Louis, Mo.	51.6	Washington, D.C.	10.7	Manchester, N.H.	68.6	Memphis, Tenn.	24.1	St. Augustine, Fla.	50.1	Milwaukee, Wis.	0.5
Cincinnati, Ohio	47.2	Nashville, Tenn.	9.0	New Haven, Conn.	67.7	Chicago, Ill.	19.5	Savannah, Ga.	45.2	Portsmouth, N.H.	0.5
Detroit, Mich.	47.2	Richmond, Va.	7.6	Baltimore, Md.	67.2	Milwaukee, Wis.	13.2	Richmond, Va.	44.6	Manchester, N.H.	0.3

Source: Glenn Porter, ed., *Encyclopedia of American Economic History,* Vol. 3 (New York: Charles Scribner's Sons, 1980), 1033.

These two views of Harpers Ferry show the immense changes many American towns were going through in the mid-19th century: from its bucolic days as a river crossing at the confluence of the Potomac and Shenandoah Rivers, 1833 *(top)*, to its emergence as a booming industrial town with a canal, railroad roundhouse, trestle, musket factory, and arsenal within four decades, 1870 *(bottom)*. (Harpers Ferry National Historical Park)

TABLE 12.6 FOREIGN-BORN POPULATION OF 20 LARGEST CITIES, WITH PRINCIPAL COUNTRIES OF ORIGIN, 1870

City	Total Foreign-Born Population	Four Largest Contributing Emigrant Countries			
New York, N.Y.	419,094	234,594 Great Britain and Ireland	151,216 Germany	8,265 France	2,794 Italy
Philadelphia, Pa.	183,624	123,408 Great Britain and Ireland	50,746 Germany	2,479 France	1,791 Switzerland
Brooklyn, N.Y.	144,718	97,475 Great Britain and Ireland	36,771 Germany	1,894 France	1,105 Sweden
St. Louis, Mo.	112,249	50,040 Germany	38,961 Great Britain and Ireland	2,902 Switzerland	2,788 France
Chicago, Ill.	144,557	54,800 Great Britain and Ireland	52,318 Germany	6,277 Bohemia[a]	6,154 Sweden
Baltimore, Md.	56,484	18,051 Great Britian and Ireland	35,276 Germany	766 Bohemia[a]	437 France
Boston, Mass.	87,986	64,787 Great Britian and Ireland	5,606 Germany	647 Sweden	615 France
Cincinnati, Ohio	79,612	49,448 Germany	23,447 Great Britian and Ireland	2,093 France	995 Switzerland
New Orleans, La.	48,475	17,361 Great Britain and Ireland	15,239 Germany	8,845 France	1,571 Italy
San Francisco, Calif.	73,719	32,998 Great Britain and Ireland	13,602 Germany	11,729 China	3,547 France
Buffalo, N.Y.	46,237	22,249 Germany	15,917 Great Britain and Ireland	2,232 France	612 Switzerland
Washington, D.C.	13,757	8,505 Great Britain and Ireland	4,133 Germany	193 France	175 Italy
Newark, N.J.	35,884	17,457 Great Britain and Ireland	15,873 Germany	710 France	613 Switzerland
Louisville, Ky.	25,668	14,380 Germany	8,888 Great Britain and Ireland	860 France	560 Switzerland

Note: Not counting Britain's American possessions, e.g., Canada.
[a]Bohemia is modern-day Czech Republic.
Source: Compendium of Ninth United States Census, 1870 (reprint, New York: Arno Press, 1976), 448–49.

Over time cities began to be seen as something more than merely masses of people living in close proximity. Now they were organic entities whose whole was greater than the sum of the parts. This was still a far cry from the ancient Greek city-state model but a vast improvement over the almost instinctual distrust and aversion felt by earlier generations to cities. The new attitude expressed itself as a kind of civic pride in one's city—an entirely different sort of loyalty from the familiar loyalty to one's state or region or even to the Union as a whole. Urban dwellers expected their cities to provide, not only jobs and a safe place to live, but also cultural opportunities in the form of theaters, art galleries, opera houses, and museums. New criteria were considered for ranking "great cities," beyond traditional measurements such as manufacturing output and transportation links. One of those new yardsticks was public libraries. The first ones were in the Puritan bastion of New England: 1833 in Peterboro, New Hampshire, and 1854 in Boston. The same year that Boston established its first public library, New York City built the Astor Library. Three years later Baltimore built the Peabody Library. The rush was on. During the decade of the 1850s, the number of U.S. public libraries increased eightfold to more than 1,000, and library holdings increased fivefold to nearly 8 million volumes.

Civilizing the City

Some urban communities that had large populations obviously ranked higher on the cultural scale than others. Cultural amenities tended to diminish as one traveled west, although economic opportunity tended to remain a constant. Frederick Law Olmsted, America's first landscape architect and city planner, turned New York City into his personal laboratory to prove his theories that the city should serve the needs not only of commerce but of "humanity, religion, art, science and scholarship." Unfortunately politicians did not share his vision. His greatest triumph was in the 1860s, when he turned Central Park into a sylvan oasis for New York City's masses. He was also far ahead of his time in advocating a regional system of parks and roads running from the Atlantic Ocean to the Hudson Valley.

Farther west, town builders were less concerned with urban parks and athletic fields. They were more interested in new buildings, streets, and sewers. This era saw a whole new wave of cities established in the West. Starting with San Francisco and Chicago, this third wave of U.S. cities grew up along western trade and immigration routes. Eventually they would achieve equality with the older, seaboard cities of the East and the second generation of interior cities across the Appalachians. More than anything, they were living proof of America's westering impulse. Urban population, as did the frontier itself, moved inexorably from east to west. Among the new western cities destined for greatness were San Francisco, Chicago, Denver, and Kansas City, all of which first appeared on the scene in the mid-19th century.

The Expanding American City

This was a time of tremendous growth for U.S. cities, not in terms of just population, but also of land area. Because major cities tended to be surrounded by large hinterlands, there was plenty of room for urban expansion. In the years between 1850 and 1870 practically every city annexed large areas of land. Only a handful of cities hemmed in by water or political constraints, such as New York and Washington, D.C., did not add measurably to their territory. And among those who did aggressively annex surrounding territory, Philadelphia and Pittsburgh outdistanced all others in both absolute and relative terms.

TABLE 12.7 TERRITORIAL GROWTH OF 20 MAJOR U.S. CITIES, 1850–1870

City	Area Size in 1850[a]	Area Size in 1870
New York City, N.Y.	22 sq. mi.	22 sq. mi.
Chicago, Ill.	10 sq. mi.	36 sq. mi.
Philadelphia, Pa.	2 sq. mi.	130 sq. mi.
Detroit, Mich.	6 sq. mi.	13 sq. mi.
Baltimore, Md.	13 sq. mi.	13 sq. mi.
Washington, D.C.	60 sq. mi.	60 sq. mi.
Cleveland, Ohio	5 sq. mi.	12 sq. mi.
San Francisco, Calif.	5 sq. mi.	42 sq. mi.
Boston, Mass.	5 sq. mi.	13 sq. mi.
St. Louis, Mo.	14 sq. mi.	61 sq. mi.
Pittsburgh, Pa.	2 sq. mi.	23 sq. mi.
Minneapolis, Minn.	N/A	8 sq. mi.
Buffalo, N.Y.	39 sq. mi.	39 sq. mi.
Cincinnati, Ohio.	6 sq. mi.	20 sq. mi.
Newark, N.J.	15 sq. mi.	16 sq. mi.
Louisville, Ky.	5 sq. mi.	12 sq. mi.
Oakland, Calif.	5 sq. mi.	5 sq. mi.
Birmingham, Ala.	N/A	1 sq. mi.
Rochester, N.Y.	8 sq. mi.	8 sq. mi.
St. Paul, Minn.	5 sq. mi.	6 sq. mi.
Total	**235 sq. mi.**	**540 sq. mi.**

[a] N/A (not available) indicates that the area size of the town is unknown.
Source: Kenneth T. Jackson and Stanley K. Schultz, *Cities in American History* (New York: Alfred A. Knopf, 1972), 445.

The rapid growth of American cities only slowly changed traditional governing patterns. City government in the 19th century was firmly in the hands of the upper classes, who made their homes, ran their businesses, and enjoyed the cultural amenities of urban life. The middle and working classes might share the urban space, but they were hardly equals in the municipal power structure. Until industrialization and immigration changed everything, the wealthy, patrician classes ran the cities more as their personal fiefs than for the masses of people who lived there. The growth of political machines and suburban flight, toward the end of the 19th century, would produce a profound power shift in urban America, but that shift was not visible from the vantage point of 1850 or even 1875.

Ten Largest Cities in the United States

This is a somewhat subjective ranking of major cities, according to population and economic influence, rather than the 10 largest cities in the United States during this time, because the rankings changed from 1850 to 1875. For instance, Chicago was the 13th-largest city in the United States in 1850 and San Francisco was unranked; by 1870 Chicago had jumped to fifth largest and San Francisco to 10th. Baltimore had also dropped out of the top five by 1870, while St. Louis had risen to that exalted status.* Statistical weather data are not available for every city on the decennial years, either because record keeping was poor because no data were gathered at that location at that time. In those cases the nearest data year is used instead to provide a general weather picture. The final ranking among U.S. cities is factored by economy and population.

New York, New York

Profile

Founded: 1613; incorporated: 1898

Total population: 696,115 (1850) U.S. ranking: 1 (1850)
1,174,779 (1860) 1 (1860)
1,478,103 (1870) 1 (1870)

Black Population: 13,073 (1870)

Area: 22 sq. mi. (1850); 22 sq. mi. (1870)

Elevation: 55 ft. above sea level

Annual mean temperature: 51°F (1850); 52°F (1860); 53°F (1870)

Annual total precipitation: 44.6 inches (1850); 31.1 inches (1860); 37.8 inches (1870)

Average annual precipitation (today): 43.0 inches

Capital invested in manufacturing, 1860: $61,212,757

Ranking among U.S. cities: 1

History

Before 1664 this little settlement on the Hudson River was Dutch-owned and known as New Amsterdam. In that year an English fleet captured the place and possession was given to the king's brother, the duke of York. From its colonial beginnings New York City prospered, although it lagged behind both Boston and Philadelphia until the Erie Canal was completed in 1825. It always had a cosmopolitan population and an outward-looking, trade-based economy that gave birth to the first home-grown U.S. millionaire, John Jacob Astor, who made his first fortune in the fur trade and a second in the city's booming real estate market. By 1850 New York City was home to the largest and busiest port in the nation, measured either by the volume of freight *or* by the number of passengers who passed through every year. It was also the nation's leading industrial center at that time and the arbiter of national taste, in theater, fashion, and so on. The author George Foster described it as the "centre and brain" of the country. New York was a highly politicized city, too, where national political careers of men such as Dan Sickles and William Seward could be made or broken. During the Civil War the working-class masses and profit-driven merchants found common cause in resisting Union war policies. Conscription provoked the infamous draft riots in the summer of 1863, which caused President Lincoln to send federal troops into the city to restore order. New York was the chief port of entry during the 19th century for European immigrants entering the United States, first at Castle Garden then at Ellis Island. The immigrants swelled the city's population until New York became the largest urban center in the United States. Population also caused the city's boundaries to be pushed constantly outward, taking over neighboring communities that had been historically distinct until in 1898 five boroughs were all incorporated into the modern New York City. Population growth and expansion also caused social tensions and chronic political squabbling. To run the sprawling, ethnically diverse city, the nation's first major political machine, the Democratic-controlled Tammany Hall, emerged in mid-century. It worked but at a heavy cost to the city's public image and reputation. Still, New York was the first U.S. city seen by tens of thousands of newcomers after crossing the Atlantic, and it symbolized much about the "Land of Liberty," both good and bad.

Miscellaneous Facts

- Todt Hill is the highest point in the greater metropolitan area, at 409 ft.
- In 1856 New York City had 10,384 indoor flush toilets for a population more than 630,000 people.
- In 1860 New York City was the largest "Irish city" in the world, with almost half of its population foreign-born and the largest number of those from the Emerald Isle.
- In 1860 New York City was twice the size of the next largest city, Philadelphia.

*Linda Schmittroth, ed., *Cities of the United States,* 2d ed. (Detroit: Gale Research, Inc., 1994), Vol. I: *The South;* Vol II: *The West;* Vol. III: *The Midwest;* Vol. IV: *The Northeast,* passim.

One of the most famous landmarks of New York City was the Great East River Suspension Bridge, better known as the Brooklyn Bridge. This 1874 artistic representation imagines the way it will look when the soaring span finally connects Brooklyn and Manhattan in 1883. (Library of Congress)

- The New York City draft riots of July 1863 were the most serious domestic disturbance in the United States in the 19th century.
- From 1861 until the 1930s Tammany Hall (the city's Democratic Party headquarters) became synonymous with big city political machines.

Philadelphia, Pennsylvania

Profile

Founded: 1682; incorporated: 1701

Total population:	121,376 (1850)	U.S. ranking:	4 (1850)
	565,529 (1860)		2 (1860)
	674,022 (1870)		2 (1870)

Black population: 22,147 (1870)

Area: 2 sq. mi. (1850); 129 sq. mi.* (1870)

Elevation: 0 to 431 ft. above sea level

Annual mean temperature: 54°F (1850); 54°F (1860); 57°F (1870)

Annual total precipitation: 54.55 inches (1850); 44.17 inches (1860); 44.11 inches (1870)

Capital invested in manufacturing, 1860: $73,318,885

Ranking among U.S. cities: 2

History

The first European settlement on this site was Swedish, in the 17th century, but it did not last long. It soon became English, part of the proprietary colony of Pennsylvania. Philadelphia was a leading shaper of colonial opinion during the 18th century, and when the American Revolution began, it vied with Boston for leadership of the 13 colonies. Both the First and Second Continental Congresses met there, and in 1787 the Constitutional Convention was held there. Philadelphia was the U.S. capital, from 1790 to 1800, when the new District of Columbia became the capital. It was the largest and most important city in the country in the early 19th century, served as the nation's financial center until 1836 because of the presence of the headquarters of the Bank of the United States, and was the leader of the antislavery movement before the Civil War. Philadelphia was home to one of the largest and most influential African-American communities in the nation during the antebellum period. In 1854 the city aggressively extended its boundaries to take in the entire surrounding county, thereby ensuring plenty of space for future growth. During the Civil War its industrial strength was a crucial component of the Union war machine, and the threat posed by Robert E. Lee's second invasion of the North in the summer of 1863 was true cause for alarm. After the war the city maintained its industrial and financial leadership. The national financial panic of 1873 and resulting depression began there with the failure of Philadelphia's two major banking houses. But the city recovered from that disaster and continued to combine prosperity with culture, perhaps more than any other city in the United States.

Miscellaneous Facts

- The city's highest point is Chestnut Hill (431 ft.).
- The city of Philadelphia is virtually synonymous with the county of Philadelphia.
- Sometimes known as "the Nation's Birthplace," also as "the City of Brotherly Love" and "the Quaker City."

* By the Consolidation Act of 1854 the state legislature set Philadelphia's boundaries at roughly 129 sq. mi., almost the same as they are today.

- When the city's 29 political divisions were consolidated in 1854, only London, Paris, and New York City could boast larger populations in the Western world.
- In 1850 greater Philadelphia had a greater metropolitan population of 371,860 and a city population of 121,376 (metropolitan = city + surrounding area [suburbs and undeveloped area]).

Brooklyn, New York

Profile

Founded: 1645; incorporated: 1834

Total population:	96,838 (1850)	U.S. ranking:	7 (1850)
	266,661 (1860)		3 (1860)
	396,099 (1870)		3 (1870)

Black population: 4,944 (1870)

Area: 70.2 sq. mi. (1850)

Elevation: 0 to 55 ft. above sea level

Annual mean temperature*: 52.01°F (1850); 49.9°F (1863)**; 54.67°F (1870)

Annual total precipitation: 45.89 inches (1850); 41.62 inches (1863); 50.01 inches (1870)

Capital invested in manufacturing, 1860: $12,320,876

Ranking among U.S. cities: 5

History

Brooklyn is located on the southwestern extremity of Long Island. The first European settlement on this site dated from the mid-1630s, when the Dutch claimed the area. Ten years later a town was established and given the name Breuckelen after a village of the same name back in the Netherlands. The little town struggled through the colonial and early national periods showing little growth or economic initiative. The U.S. Navy moved in in 1801, establishing the Brooklyn Navy Yard, which was one of the navy's most important installations up through the Civil War. The introduction of steam-powered transportation in the early 19th century created regular ferry service across the East River to New York City, and only then did the town really begin to grow. Irish and German immigrants were a major factor in boosting the town's population up to respectable numbers. Brooklyn Village was chartered in 1816, when the population reached 4,000, and in 1836 it was incorporated as a city after annexing several small neighboring towns in King's County. Until 1854 there was a strong rivalry between Brooklyn and Williamsburg (incorporated 1851) to be the dominant city in King's County. Brooklyn won by absorbing Williamsburg as well as Bushwick in 1855, thereby following a familiar pattern of growth by annexation. From that point on Brooklyn City achieved prominence and a certain degree of independence as a manufacturing and port facility in the shadow of New York City. Ferry service acted as both a social line and a political shackle for the smaller community. New Yorkers as early as 1820 regarded Brooklyn as a "suburb" for its rapidly growing population. In the antebellum period Brooklyn's Plymouth Church was a center of the Northern abolitionist movement. During the Civil War tens of thousands of patriotic Brooklynites served in the Union Army, although back home dissidents rioted and burned government supply houses. After the Civil War improvements to the docking facilities drew more traffic through the port and led to rapid change in the city. In the grand optimism of the industrial age, it was only natural for someone to propose the construction of a great bridge spanning the space between Brooklyn and Manhattan Island. The result of that idea, the legendary Brooklyn Bridge, was a technological marvel when completed (1883), but also the beginning of the end of Brooklyn as an independent city.

*Weather conditions, including temperature and rainfall, are calculated from the nearest reporting weather station, which in 1850 were military posts, practically the only places regularly gathering weather data. For Brooklyn the nearest reporting stations are Fort Hamilton and Fort Columbus; information is based on data from Fort Hamilton.

**Weather records from the middle of the 19th century are incomplete; the nearest reporting year to 1860 is 1863, the date used here.

Miscellaneous Facts

- The USS *Monitor,* first U.S. Navy ironclad constructed, was launched at Brooklyn (Greenpoint) in 1862.
- Brooklyn was long known as the "Borough of Churches" because of their numbers, including such famous churches as Plymouth Church, where Henry Ward Beecher had his pulpit for 40 years, and Saint John's Church, where R. E. Lee and Thomas J. Jackson (in his pre-"Stonewall" days) worshipped.
- Brooklyn grew over the years by annexation, adding, for instance, the small neighboring villages of Williamsburg and Bushwick in 1854.
- Brooklyn consolidated with New York City in 1898, losing its city status and becoming one of New York's boroughs.

St. Louis, Missouri

Profile

Founded: 1763; incorporated: 1822

Total population:	77,860 (1850)	U.S. ranking:	7 (1850)
	160,773 (1860)		8 (1860)
	310,864 (1870)		4 (1870)

Black population: 22,088 (1870)

Area: 14 sq. mi. (1850); 61 sq. mi. (1870)

Elevation: 535 ft. above sea level

Annual mean temperature: 55°F (1850); 56°F (1860); 56°F (1870)

Annual total precipitation: 50.5 inches (1850); 29.8 inches (1860); 27.1 inches (1870)

Capital invested in manufacturing, 1860: $9,205,205

Ranking among U.S. cities: 7

History

St. Louis is located on the Mississippi River, 10 miles below its confluence with the Missouri River, a strategic location in geopolitical terms to take advantage of both north-south and east-west movements of people and goods. A city that literally outgrew its past, it was built originally on the fur trade and transportation (both river and rail) but transformed itself into an industrial city by the end of the 19th century. The first settlement on the site was a French settlement in the 17th century; the French were soon superseded by the Spanish as colonial masters. By the middle of the 19th century, the predominant national/ethnic group was the Germans. After the United States purchased the Louisiana Territory in 1803, it became the "Crossroad of Westward Expansion" for the next 40 years, where immigrants, travelers, and explorers like Lewis and Clark started their westward journeys. It also achieved a dubious reputation as a wild river-port town. A disastrous riverfront fire in 1849 was followed by a major cholera epidemic. These twin disasters threatened to kill the town, and many residents actually did leave. But it rose phoenixlike out of the ashes and rebuilt itself in the 1850s as a city of brick and public health initiatives. St. Louis's rebirth was greatly aided by the railroads that entered in the 1850s, but its long-term economic revival was delayed again by the Civil War. The city suffered from divided wartime sympathies as both sides fought for control of Missouri and its most important city. Unionists triumphed and the city became the staging area for the three-year federal campaign to secure the Mississippi River. Confederate sympathizers were forced underground or out of the city entirely. Amid all the political turmoil, St. Louis actually profited from the war, as manufacturing increased 296 percent between 1860 and 1870. The federal government purchased some $180 million worth of goods from the city's manufacturers during the war. After the war, the city's economy reoriented itself from its antebellum north-south axis as a river-port town to an east-west axis as a railroad town. The Eads railroad bridge, completed in 1874, was the first to span the Mississippi River, as well as the world's first arched steel truss bridge. St. Louis's modern German flavor was sealed when more than 30,000 German immigrants arrived between 1832 and 1850.

Miscellaneous Facts

- Local bartenders before the Civil War are credited with inventing the "highball," Southern comfort, and planter's punch—drinks that are cocktail standards today.
- The modern upscale suburban phenomenon of private streets and gated communities may have been invented in St. Louis, where they existed as early as the 1850s.
- Slaves were still sold on the front steps of the Old Courthouse up to the Civil War. The same courthouse was the site of the appeal proceedings in the famous *Dred Scott v. Sandford* case in 1857.
- The Basilica of Saint Louis the King is the oldest cathedral in the United States west of the Mississippi River (1834).
- St. Louis in 1850 had a greater metropolitan population of 77,860.

Chicago, Illinois

Profile

Founded: 1830; incorporated: 1837

Total population:	29,963 (1850)	U.S. ranking:	13 (1850)
	112,172 (1860)		9 (1860)
	298,977 (1870)		5 (1870)

Black population: 3,691 (1870)
Area: 10 sq. mi. (1850); 36 sq. mi. (1870)
Elevation: 595 ft. above sea level
Annual mean temperature: 43.57°F (1850)*; 44.5°F (1863)**; 52.9°F (1870)
Annual total precipitation: N/A (1850); N/A (1863); 23.4 inches (1870)
Average annual precipitation (today): 33.0 inches
Capital invested in manufacturing, 1860: $5,422,225
Ranking among U.S. cities: 16

History

Strategically situated on the Chicago River and Lake Michigan, the site began as a trading post and fort. Only a whim of boundary drawing in 1818 prevented Chicago from becoming a Wisconsin city. It was settled by squatters who anticipated the arrival of the Illinois & Michigan Canal. The surrounding territory was bought or taken from American Indians over the years that followed. From the beginning Chicago was a great market center, serving Lake Michigan, the canal, and later the railroads. Along the way the population grew in leaps and bounds, with the city limits constantly pushed outward onto the prairies to absorb its people. By 1856 the city incorporated 18 sq. mi., most of it swampland unfortunately. Chicago literally had to raise itself from the mud by moving in landfill to lift the street level 12 ft. starting in 1855. The Panic of 1857 hit the city especially hard, closing one-tenth of its business houses. Chicago was saved in the 1860s by a combination of events: the first national convention of the new Republican Party and the beginning of the Civil War. The latter required enormous quantities of meat and grain, drawn from the region served by Chicago. In 1864 Union Stock Yards was built on a one-square-mile parcel of land. This was followed by the McCormick Reaper factory, Pullman Palace Car factory, and Chicago Clearing House (1865). After the Civil War a rich industrial class rose to power, running the city's politics and economy while living uncomfortably side by side with the foul slums of the old city. The great fire of 1871 destroyed three and a third acres in the heart of the city, causing great anguish and loss of life but presenting a golden opportunity to rebuild a more modern, permanent city. The city could never die, no matter what the disaster: Chicago's future was assured by its position as the most important port on the Great Lakes. After 1869 it was the eastern terminus of the transcontinental railroad, connecting it directly to the Pacific coast. By the late 19th century Chicago had leaped ahead of St. Louis as the "Capital City of the West."

Miscellaneous Facts

- In the 1850s Chicago had the highest per capita annual death rate of any city in the United States, a combination of poor working conditions, low public health standards, and a frontier mind-set about law and order.
- In 1855 Chicago became the first U.S. city to build a comprehensive sewerage system.
- In 1867 the historian James Parton wrote a paean to Chicago for the *Atlantic Monthly* celebrating the combination of commerce, large population, and human intellect in creating such great urban center.
- Chicago harbor on Lake Michigan did more business in 1869 (13,730 shipping arrivals) than did New York City, Philadelphia, Baltimore, or Charleston.
- Chicago was the terminus for 15 rail lines in the 1850s; after 1869 it was the hub of the nation's transcontinental rail network
- In 1860 Chicago was the site of the Republican Party's first national nominating convention.
- In 1871 the Great Chicago Fire destroyed $200 million in property, killed 250, and left 100,000 people homeless.
- Chicago is popularly known as "the Windy City" due to its blustery weather.

*The nearest reporting station for Chicago in 1850 was Fort Howard at Green Bay, Wisconsin.
**The nearest reporting year to 1860 is 1863, the date used here. Figures are only available for the first seven months of the year 1863, however, so the temperature given represents the mean temperature only for January–July.

Baltimore, Maryland

Profile

Founded: 1696; incorporated: 1797

Total population:	169,054 (1850)	U.S. ranking:	2 (1850)
	212,418 (1860)		4 (1860)
	267,354 (1870)		6 (1870)

Black population: 39,558 (1870)
Area: 13 sq. mi. (1850); 13 sq. mi. (1870)
Elevation: 0 to 148 ft. above sea level
Annual mean temperature: 58°F (1850); 54°F (1860); 58°F (1870)

Annual total precipitation: 44.8 inches (1850); 37.5 inches (1860); 22.4 inches (1870)
Capital invested in manufacturing, 1860: $9,009,107
Ranking among U.S. cities: 8

History

Located on the Patapsco River at the upper end of Chesapeake Bay, Baltimore has always had a split personality, either the most Northern of Southern cities or the most Southern of Northern cities. The city jumped aboard the railroad boom early when local merchants organized the Baltimore & Ohio Railroad in 1827 as a response to the commercial threat posed by New York's Erie Canal. Popular sympathies were with the South when the Civil War broke out in 1861, sparking riots in April, when federal troops marched through on their way to Washington, D.C. For the duration of the war Baltimore remained a city pulled in both directions, a city of sometimes "violent contradictions," and a city often described as "ugly" where mob action was never unlikely. It was a port city from its colonial beginnings, home to clipper ships before the Civil War and a leading port of entry for both European immigrants and African slaves. Not surprisingly it developed several significant ethnic communities, not as numerous but almost as diverse as New York City's. It was the scene of numerous political conventions by Democrats, Whigs, and Republicans over the years, all seeking the approval of a local populace quick to take to the streets. The nativist Know-Nothing Party gained control of the city in the 1850s. At the beginning of the Civil War Abraham Lincoln placed the city under martial law because he could ill afford to lose control to Southern sympathizers, thus isolating the national capital from the rest of the North. The four-year conflict not only imposed political burdens but also disrupted long-established trade and cultural ties to the South. On the positive side it also provided rich opportunities for illegal trade across the lines. The city emerged from the war economically strong but stagnated during Reconstruction until it could develop more railroad connections to the interior and find new markets in Europe. The 1873 Panic and resulting depression hit Baltimore especially hard, leading to riots and labor strikes before the economy began improving. Historically Baltimore was a city built on fishing and maritime trade, but the maritime trade never recovered from the Civil War, and the fishing industry declined steadily in the late 19th century as Chesapeake Bay suffered the effects of pollution and overcrowding.

Miscellaneous Facts

- When it opened for business in 1828, the Baltimore & Ohio was the nation's first public railroad and also the first steam-operated railway.
- In 1867 Johns Hopkins University opened as the first graduate education and research institution based on the German model in the United States.
- Baltimore was a notorious political hotbed, with Know-Nothing riots in the 1850s and an antifederal riot in April, 1861.
- Even in the 19th century Baltimore was famous for its crab cakes, cobblestone streets, and lack of sewers.

Boston, Massachusetts

Profile

Founded: 1630; incorporated: 1822

Total population:	136,881 (1850)	U.S. ranking:	3 (1850)
	177,840 (1860)		5 (1860)
	250,526 (1870)		7 (1870)
Black population:	3,496 (1870)		

Area: 5 sq. mi. (1850); 13 sq. mi. (1870)
Elevation: 15 to 29 ft. above sea level
Annual mean temperature: 50.34°F (1850); N/A (1860); 52.13°F (1870)*
Annual total precipitation: 54.14 inches (1850); 45.08 inches (1860); 43.53 inches (1870)
Capital invested in manufacturing, 1860: $13,927,230
Ranking among U.S. cities: 4

History

Boston began life as a Puritan Commonwealth in the 17th century and never strayed far from those roots for the next two centuries. It enjoyed a well-deserved reputation as a strongly moralistic and highly educated community. From 1830 to 1865 it was the center of the Northern antislavery movement, thanks to men like Charles Sumner, William Lloyd Garrison, Frederick Douglass, and the "Secret Six" who backed John Brown's cause. It was a whaling and trade center before the Civil War in addition to being the capital of New England culture. When war began, Boston played a surprisingly prominent role, although overshadowed in the public mind by other cities such as Washington, D.C., and New York City. It has been called "the intellectual capital of the North" and "the moral engine of the Union."** No battles were fought in the area, but the Union army recruited its first regiment of Northern blacks there, the famed 54th Massachusetts led by Colonel Robert Gould Shaw. Ironically Boston could not meet its government quota for voluntary enlistments from its white population, and had to resort to a draft in 1863, which sparked bloody riots. Nonetheless during the war Boston provided 26,000 soldiers and sailors to the Union cause and functioned as an important military seaport. After the Civil War the local economy underwent wrenching change. The comings and goings of the graceful clipper ships of the antebellum period had marked the last golden age of U.S. shipping. Now smoke-belching steamers under European registration were most of the ships lining the same docks where once English colonists dumped tea into the harbor. Maritime trade was replaced by the new shoe and textile mills manufacturing as the principal financial activity. Outside money flowed into the city, causing a wave of new factory construction and also creating a new class of urban industrial workers to operate those factories. This trend also allowed Boston to survive for a few more years as a leading Atlantic coastal port thanks to raw materials taken in for the city's factories. Meanwhile the laboring and rich socialite classes grew further and further apart. In what proved to be their last great service to America in the 19th century, Boston intellectuals such as James Russell Lowell, Henry W. Longfellow, Oliver Wendell Holmes, Ralph Waldo Emerson, and John Greenleaf Whittier helped reunite the divided nation and heal the wounds of war. Economic tides might ebb and flow, but Boston would remain the nation's undisputed intellectual capital.

Miscellaneous Facts

- Boston was known in the 19th century as "the Athens of America" for its intellectual and cultural accomplishments. Locals referred to it proudly as "the hub of the universe."
- The "Flowering of New England" in the antebellum period reflects the tremendous intellectual ferment, literary output, prosperity, and self-confidence that characterized the city.
- In 1872 the worst fire in the city's history destroyed 60 acres, including 800 buildings, and caused $75 million in property damage.

*The nearest reporting station for Boston in 1870 is Cambridge, which is used here.
**Dara Horn, "The Northern Front: Civil War Boston," *American Heritage Magazine* 49, no. 2 (April 1998): 48–61.

Still the third largest city in the United States in 1850 (after New York City and Baltimore), Boston was living largely on past glories when it had been an intellectual and political center and major whaling port. Pictured here is old Faneuil Hall *(center, right),* "Cradle of American Liberty" and of the New England town meeting, "where the meanest citizen . . . may deliver his sentiments and give his suffrage in very important matters, as freely as the greatest Lord in the Land!" (from original 1850 woodcut engraving by A. H. Payne, print from author's collection)

- Boston is the home of the nation's oldest institution of higher learning, Harvard College (founded in 1636).
- Donald McKay's shipyard in East Boston turned out the finest clipper ships in the world before the Civil War.
- In 1860 with a population of almost 178,000 Boston had about 5,000 flush toilets, a far higher ratio of toilets per capita than in any other U.S. city.

Cincinnati, Ohio

Profile

Founded: 1789; Incorporated: 1802 as a town; 1819 as a city

Total Population:	115,435 (1850)	U.S. Ranking:	6 (1850)
	161,044 (1860)		7 (1860)
	216,239 (1870)		8 (1870)

Black Population: 5,900 (1870)

Area: 6 sq. mi. (1850); 20 sq. mi. (1870)

Elevation 550 ft. above sea level

Annual mean temperature: N/A (1850); 53.98°F (1863); 55.53°F (1870)

Annual total precipitation: N/A (1850); 38.69 inches (1863); 29.38 inches (1870)

Capital invested in manufacturing, 1860: $17,855,753

Ranking among U.S. cities: 3

History

Located on the Ohio side of the Ohio River, Cincinnati began life as so many other early western cities did, as a river crossing. But it did not really grow until it became an agricultural processing point on the Miami and Erie Canal in 1832. From that time it grew steadily and its reputation as a city on the go attracted large numbers of European immigrants, especially Germans and Irish, who influenced the local culture as well as the economy. The city became a grape culture center and wine market with the influence of the Germans. In a few short years it was being referred to as the "Queen City of the West," serving as a regional capital for the Old Northwest Territory. Before 1850 Cincinnati was already the world's greatest pork-packing and pork-shipping capital. The center of the city was its public landing, with a riverfront six miles long devoted to moving the commerce of a western empire to eastern markets. The golden years were short-lived, however, by 1860 Cincinnati had been supplanted by Chicago as the meat-packing center of the United States. The Civil War tore the city apart as economics and politics pulled the citizens in two different directions. On the one hand were the strong trading ties to the South, being strangled by the Union blockade; on the other were the strong abolitionist sentiments of many leading citizens. Fortunately rich federal government contracts saved the economy and eased political tensions at the same time, at least until after the war. The river trade that had been the lifeblood of the city for so many years finally dried up in the 1870s, killed by the spread of the railroads in all directions, and Cincinnati had to reorient itself to rail-carried commerce rather than the river variety. During all these years Cincinnati was known as a liberal city. African American males were allowed to vote locally in 1855, 18 years before the adoption of the Fifteenth Amendment, and Harriet Beecher Stowe lived in the city from 1832 to 1850, writing much of *Uncle Tom's Cabin* there.

Miscellaneous Facts

- The English author Charles Dickens visited Cincinnati in 1842 and was much impressed by what he saw.
- Cincinnati had the nation's first *free* public high school, founded in 1847.
- Cincinnati was one of the nation's major rail terminals by 1850.
- In 1867 the city was connected by (suspension) bridge for the first time with Kentucky on the other side of the Ohio River; heretofore all connection had been by boat.
- Cincinnati was known as "the Queen City of the West" before the Civil War.

New Orleans, Louisiana

Profile

Founded: 1718; incorporated: 1805

Total population:	116,375 (1850)	U.S. ranking:	5 (1850)
	168,675 (1860)		6 (1860)
	191,418 (1870)		9 (1870)

Black population: 50,546 (1870)

Area: 16 sq. mi. (1850); 16 sq. mi. (1870)

Elevation: from 5 ft. below to 15 ft. above above sea level

Annual mean temperature: ca. 66.0°F (1850)*; 71.07°F (1859); 68.4°F (1871)

Annual total precipitation: 51.13 inches (1850); 39.22 inches (1860); 48.36 inches (1870)

Average annual precipitation (today): 57.0 inches

Capital invested in manufacturing, 1860: $2,693,746

Ranking among U.S. cities: 17

History

This most cosmopolitan of American cities was part of the Spanish and French empires for some two centuries before it was acquired by the United States as part of the Louisiana Purchase (1803). Subsequently it became the first capital of the state of Louisiana (1812–49). But its most important role was not as a political capital but as the commercial gateway to the Mississippi River. Because of its strategic location throughout its history the city was threatened with invasion by one great power or another: the Spanish, the British, and the French. In April 1862 Confederate New Orleans fell to Union forces and for the rest of the war the Stars and Stripes flew over it and the hated Yankees ruled. It was a natural target for the North, as the largest and richest city south of the Mason-Dixon line in the mid-19th century. Its exotic nature was reflected by its French-based legal system, its large European and black populations, its Old World culture, and its semitropical climate. New Orleans was an urban oasis amid the swampland of southern Louisiana. Creoles (Spanish heritage) mixed with Cajuns (French heritage) and Anglos to produce a multicultural population unique among American cities of the period. The late-coming Americans laid a thin veneer of Yankee enterprise on the city's Old World culture. New Orleans grew fat and rich off the Mississippi River boat trade, especially in cotton and slaves. It also vied with New York City for the title of "First American Port" during the antebellum period. It was the fourth-ranking city in terms of population. Only recurrent fever epidemics and seasonal flooding held the city back; one or the other was an almost annual occurrence. The Civil War hit New Orleans especially hard because the Union occupation put a damper on its Creole culture and rich trade. During the Reconstruction period racial and political strife plagued the city, limiting its growth and civic improvements as blacks battled whites and Republicans battled Democrats until martial law had to be proclaimed in 1874. Its postwar renaissance was thus delayed longer than that in some other areas of the South.

*Mean annual temperature for this year is a very rough estimate because two of the reporting months (August and September) are missing from the U.S. Army Signal Corps records, New Orleans station.

Miscellaneous Facts

- New Orleans was the first U.S. city west of the Alleghenies to be served by a railroad.
- When the Civil War began, New Orleans was the South's premier city in terms of size and wealth, and the nation's second leading port after New York City.
- Before the Civil War New Orleans had more free blacks who owned slaves than any other city in the South.
- New Orleans the only city in the United States to be the subject of a military order directing its women to show proper respect to officers of the U.S. Army or suffer the consequences of being treated as prostitutes (General Benjamin Butler's General Order No. 28, May 15, 1862).
- It is known variously as "the Crescent City" (because it curves around a bend in the Mississippi River 107 mi. upriver from the Gulf of Mexico) and the "Yellow Fever Capital of the South."
- The city endured regular outbreaks of deadly cholera and yellow fever during the 19th century, including the worst yellow fever epidemic on record in 1853.
- The longstanding celebration of Mardi Gras became regularized as an event in 1857 with the annual parade of the Mistick Krewe (club) of Comus.

San Francisco, California

Profile

Founded: 1776; incorporated: 1850

Total population:	34,770 (1850)	U.S. ranking:	unranked (1850)
	56,802 (1860)		15 (1860)
	149,473 (1870)		10 (1870)

Black population: 1,330 (1870)

Area: 5 sq. mi. (1850); 42 sq. mi. (1870)

Elevation: 0 to 925 ft. (Mt. Davidson) above sea level

Annual mean temperature: N/A (1850); N/A (1860); N/A (1870); 58.6°F (today)

Annual total precipitation: 17.41 inches (1850); 21.18 inches (1860); 16.24 inches (1870)

Average annual precipitation (today): 22.0 inches

Capital invested in manufacturing, 1860: $2,221,300

Ranking among U.S. cities: 9

History

On July 9, 1846, San Francisco was occupied by the U.S. Navy during the U.S.-Mexican War (1846–48). The small mission town received its current name in 1847 and took off after gold was discovered nearby the next year. The influx of forty-niners caused the population to jump from 1,000 in 1849 to 50,000 in the next seven years. Overnight, it seemed, what had been a sleepy little mission town was transformed into what John W. Audubon called "a pandemonium of a city." During the next decade the gold played out, but the local economy survived, now based on new iron foundries and flour mills. In the 1860s it developed as a commercial and fishing port, although remaining vulnerable to financial panics and crashes. It became the western terminus of the first transcontinental railroad in 1869. It was the most cosmopolitan city in the western half of the United States and the first great western metropolis. Already before the Civil War more than 20 nationalities and races were represented in the city's population. No other U.S. city contained more people from different parts of the world, and only two (St. Louis and Milwaukee) had a higher proportion of foreign-born residents in 1860. It continued to be the largest metropolis west of the Mississippi River until well into the 20th century. The dark side of San Francisco was its legendary violence, which led outraged citizens to organize the first Committee of Vigilance in 1851 to take over the work of the ineffective police force; it would not be the last such committee. They patrolled the streets, drove undesirables out of town, and carried out summary executions of thieves and murderers. San Francisco thus became the classic "boom town" during its early years, with vigilante justice, shocking inflation, rampant vice, and an indomitable "can-do" spirit. The Civil War introduced political debate over whether to support the Union or declare unilateral independence as the "Pacific Republic." The Unionists won, and California gold continued to flow into federal coffers without interruption. San Francisco's wild and woolly reputation drew famous writers such as Bret Harte and Mark Twain to see the "City on the Bay." The city produced vast fortunes for its resident tycoons as well as a strong labor union movement in the years after the Civil War. The city continued to grow outward without rhyme, reason, or urban planning of any sort. It had a second boom from the 1859 silver strike in Nevada and the completion of the first transcontinental railroad in 1869. The railroad opened up a limitless interior hinterland to match the already established seagoing trade. In the years ahead San Francisco would be unchallenged as the commercial, financial, and banking capital for the entire region west of the Rocky Mountains.

Miscellaneous Facts

- The small village that grew up to be San Francisco was known as Yerba Buena until 1847, when the name was officially changed to the present name.
- San Francisco's population increased from roughly 800 in 1848 to nearly 35,000 in 1850, an increase of more than 4,000 percent, which was due to the California gold rush.
- Six great fires devastated San Francisco within four years after it was incorporated in 1850, preludes to the greatest fire of all, caused by the earthquake of 1906.
- By the 1850s San Francisco's Irish population outnumbered every other foreign-born group in the city.
- In the early years of the gold rush the city had six to 10 times as many men as women.
- In the 1860s the notorious lawless district around Pacific Avenue and Kearny Street was dubbed the "Barbary Coast."
- The first railroad from the East reached the city in 1869 with the completion of the transcontinental railroad.

CHAPTER 13 Representative Americans

Phineas T. Barnum (1810–1891)

He was America's first great showman, a person who was every bit as flamboyant and bizarre as the exhibits he put on display. P. T. Barnum, as he preferred to be called, was bigger than life and willing to use any trick he could think of to make a buck or attract a crowd. In his day he was the preeminent brash American stereotype. It was his dream to make the public pay for the honor of being hoodwinked, and he fulfilled that dream for more than half a century. He once told an acquaintance he was in the "brand-new business . . . called advertising." When asked to explain the unfamiliar term, he replied that it was "selling the public on the idea of throwing away the things they need and buying the things they don't need." "And so far," he added, "it's made me a rich man."

Barnum assembled the oddest people and things he could find in exotic exhibits that were dubbed sideshows because at first they were not considered to be main-event caliber. No creature was too strange and no item too unbelievable for him to put on display. In fact, the more bizarre, the better. And when he could not secure the real thing, he created a copy and displayed it without a second thought. Ironically the original was often as phony as his copy, but that did not bother him either. The show was the thing. This is what he did with the famous "Cardiff Giant" petrified man: When its English owners refused to sell the fake relic, he went home and created his own mummy, which he dubbed "Colorado Man." When exposed on this occasion and others, Barnum laughed it off and convinced his victims that they had really enjoyed being tricked after all. Over the decades millions gladly bought tickets and stood in line to be duped by the master, known as the "Prince of Humbugs."

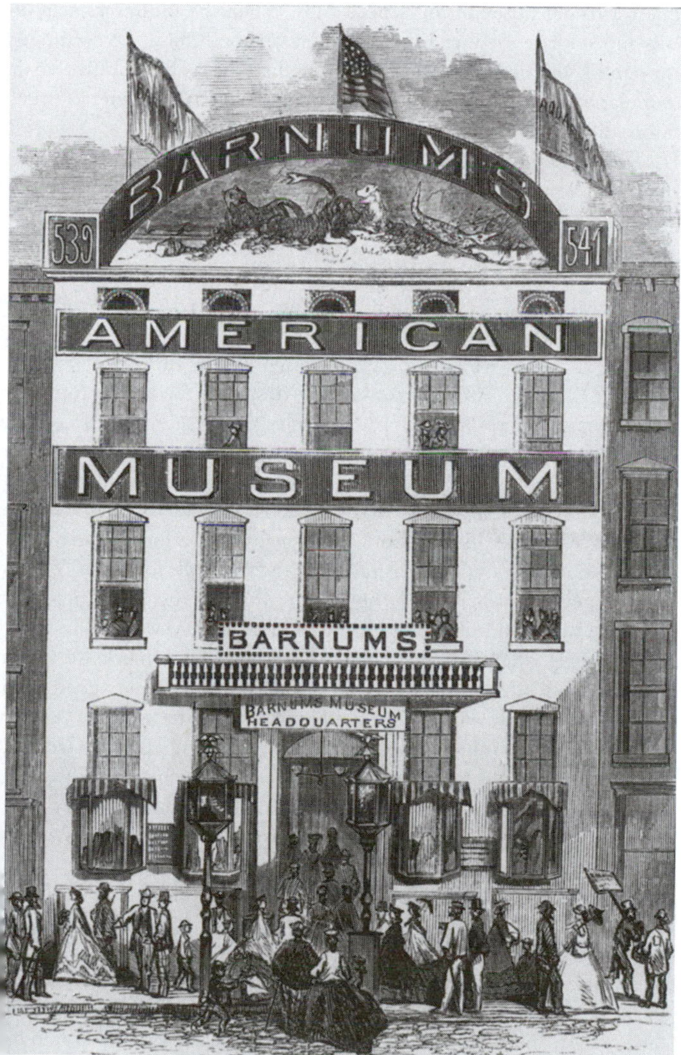

P. T. Barnum first made a name for himself as a "purveyor of humbug" at his American Museum in New York City (on Broadway between Prince and Spring Streets). Opened in 1842, Barnum's museum is pictured here as it looked before it burned down on July 13, 1865. He rebuilt it bigger and better than ever, kept it running, and eventually sold some 82 million tickets at 25 cents each. (Library of Congress, Prints and Photographs Division [LC-USZ62-072719])

The only trait stronger than chicanery in his character was cheapness. He hated paying fair market value for anything, but if forced to in order to bag a unique exhibit, he would outspend all competitors without blinking. The only thing he did not stint on was advertising; it was the lifeblood of his business, and he spent money lavishly to promoted his latest exhibits. A few genuine acts even got into his shows. Among his best was the midget General Tom Thumb and the giant African elephant Jumbo. Both served him well for many years.

Barnum "arrived" on the national scene after he opened the Great American Museum in New York City. As he saw it, it was the greatest museum in the country located appropriately in the greatest city in the country. It definitely stretched the classical definition of *museum,* but he liked the name because it added a certain aura of authenticity to his exhibits. With an endless supply of visitors keeping the turnstiles turning, he was on top of the world. As a master wordsmith and advertising genius, he added new words to the American lexicon: *jumbo, egress, sucker,* and *white elephant* as synonyms for *giant, exit, dumb,* and *useless,* respectively.

Barnum had a cozy relationship with the press: They publicized his exhibits while trying mightily to expose the fakes behind the advertising. Meanwhile Barnum used the gentlemen of the press shamelessly for his own purposes, often making them his accomplices. In the process he treated his frauds as a game and cheerfully owned up when caught in one of his whopper lies.

His greatest skill was self-promotion, and he showed that there was a third path to fame and success besides genuine talent or hard work; it was simple chutzpah.

Henry Ward Beecher (1813–1887)

The most famous and perhaps the most unconventional pulpit minister of the 19th century, Beecher spoke out on a variety of social and political issues with mesmerizing oratorical style. He championed a variety of controversial causes, along the way causing an uproar in both his public and private lives.

Henry Ward Beecher was born into one of the most intellectually gifted families of the day. His father was Lyman Beecher, also a high-profile preacher; one sister was the educator Catharine Beecher, and another was the famed author Harriet Beecher Stowe. He was on the path toward higher education from the beginning and graduated from Amherst College in 1834. He spent the next three years at Lane Theological Seminary in Cincinnati. In addition to his studies, he first started preaching there, as an Independent Presbyterian. In 1837 he married Eunice Bullard and started his ministerial career in Indianapolis, Indiana, with the Presbyterian Church. Ten years and two congregations later, with a rapidly growing family, he "heard the call" to move to Brooklyn, New York, to become pastor of the Plymouth

Congregational Church. There he finally began making a national reputation for himself, speaking to overflow crowds and publishing his sermons in pamphlet form for wide distribution. He understood the power of the dramatic gesture and used it to good effect. In 1848 he briefly turned his church building into a mock slave market. Flocking to see and hear the next Beecher performance, his audiences sometimes numbered 2,500 or more in a week. Those who could squeeze into the Plymouth church building heard him speak on a variety of social and political issues, including temperance, but his favorite topic was abolition, which he urged Southerners to adopt voluntarily. Because he advocated voluntary emancipation rather than government action, he was considered a moderate in the abolitionist crusade. He was more forceful, however, in his opposition to extending slavery into the western territories. When slave owners and Free-Soilers began fighting it out in Kansas in the mid-1850s, he advised abolitionists back East to ship rifles rather than Bibles to the Free-Soilers. Boxes of rifles labeled "Bibles" and dubbed "Beecher's Bibles" by grateful recipients soon began arriving in Kansas.

During the Civil War he preached the Union cause from the pulpit and even made a speaking tour of England to promote it. When complete emancipation was achieved at the end of the war, he moved on to women's suffrage and civil service reform as the objects of his righteous indignation. He had already written two books of denominational interest in the antebellum period, but during the war years he expanded his audience by editing a Congregational journal called the *Independent.* In 1870 he moved on to editorship of the nondenominational *Christian Union,* but he had left a brewing scandal behind him. In 1874 his successor as editor of the *Independent,* Theodore Tilton, filed adultery charges against him for his long-running affair with Tilton's wife, Elizabeth. The affair made a big splash in the newspapers despite the best efforts of church leaders to hush it up. A sensational civil trial on the adultery charge resulted in acquittal thanks to a hung jury, all of them men. A chastened Beecher returned to his Brooklyn pulpit, but his career as a minister and moral spokesman was irreparably damaged. Many of his faithful followers did not return, although he continued to preach, write, and edit almost to the end of his life. At his death on November 8, 1887, he had found a new cause in denouncing evolution and left unfinished one book *(The Life of Jesus Christ),* which his sons completed in his name.

It is hard to say how great his influence might have been if not for the scandal. Victorian Americans took those matters more seriously than people do today, especially when marital infidelity was involved. The fact that he was forgiven at all and allowed to resume his public preaching was a sign of his great popularity with the masses. He continued to enjoy an enormous though diminished following through his sermons and writings. All his life he had preached a gospel of love and joy, which was comforting, but his appeal derived as much from the show he put on as the message he delivered. With his silver tongue and flair for the dramatic he prefigured the flashy evangelist preachers of the next century such as Billy Sunday and J. Frank Norris.

Amelia Bloomer (1818–1894)

Amelia Bloomer, a women's rights pioneer and journalist, is better known as a style setter whose name was applied to a type of women's wear. As a result, she is remembered more as a feminist caricature than as the intelligent and articulate reformer she was.

Amelia Jenks was born into a humble family in Homer (Cortland County), New York, and gave no sign early in life that she would become anything other than a typical 19th-century homemaker or perhaps never marry. She attended the local public school for a few terms, just enough that at 17 she could herself begin teaching. Leaving the classroom, she worked as a tutor and governess and lived with her married sister in Waterloo, New York. Her life took a dramatic turn when at the age of 22 she married a Seneca Falls Quaker, Dexter C. Bloomer, who also happened to be editor and part owner of a Whig newspaper. Dexter Bloomer had a lot of liberal ideas by the standards of the day, which included mentoring his wife as a writer and editor. For her part Amelia soon blossomed into an outspoken social and political activist. In 1848 she attended the first women's rights meeting in Seneca Falls, New York, where she met Lucretia Mott and Elizabeth Cady Stanton. But Bloomer was not yet ready to become a frontline soldier in the suffrage movement. Instead she made her primary cause temperance and joined the Ladies' Temperance Society. She found her public voice and put what she had learned from her husband to work in 1849 when she started her own newspaper, the twice-weekly *Lily.* She was its publisher, editor, and chief writer for the next six years, addressing a variety of reform causes in its pages but devoting it principally to "the interests of women," as the masthead read. It was her work at the helm of the *Lily* that transformed her into a pioneer of the women's rights movement. She also proved herself to be a capable publisher, increasing her readership steadily from 200 or 300 for the inaugural issue to more than 4,000 by 1853. At the same time she became deputy postmaster to her husband for Seneca Falls. When the Bloomers eventually moved from Seneca Falls to Mount Vernon, Ohio, she continued to publish the newspaper, although the long distance from the main population centers and established readership made doing so much more difficult.

If she had done nothing but publish and write for the *Lily,* Amelia Bloomer would have remained a minor figure in a nascent movement, but she suddenly achieved celebrity status when in the pages of the *Lily* she publicly advocated a revolution in women's dress style that would allow them more freedom to pursue an active life in the real world. This defining moment occurred in the winter of 1850–51, when she was visited by Elizabeth Smith Miller, who was wearing a strange-looking garb highlighted by Turkish-style pantaloons. Although Amelia was not the first to wear it, she immediately began championing it in the pages of the *Lily* as a practical, even liberating style for the modern, active woman. What quickly became known as the "Bloomer Costume" consisted of an ordinary bodice and short skirt, but with ruffled trousers worn under the skirt. When other newspapers published illustrations of the odd-looking outfit, hoots of derision from the menfolk followed. Taking it as a personal challenge, she began wearing the new "bloomer dress" in her own public appearances. The result was to draw overflow crowds wherever she spoke, not to hear her remarks so much as to see her strange outfit. But having arrived, they listened, and what they heard was a confident and articulate woman. Other notable reformers, including Susan B. Anthony and Horace Greeley, began appearing on the platform with her, and even the traditional, male-dominated newspapers began to give her favorable reviews. After several years the fascination with "bloomers," which had defined her in the public mind, died down.

Dexter Bloomer quietly continued his own career as editor and postmaster, although he now lived in the shadow of his wife's notoriety. To their credit they maintained a strong marriage despite all the public attention and demands on Amelia's time. In 1854 they decided to move to Council Bluffs, Iowa, which was still considered part of the frontier. She sold the *Lily* in 1856 and thereafter assisted him in his work. She maintained her interest in reform causes but mainly through correspondence. She also did some lecturing and made their home a gathering place for visitors of a like mind on the issues of the day. During the Civil War she organized the local Soldiers' Aid Society, then returned to her favorite causes after the war. One of her last accomplishments was to lobby the state legislature for greater protec tion of married women's property rights. Dexter Bloomer died before Amelia, and she stayed on in Council Bluffs until her own death on December 30, 1894.

Her place in U.S. history is assured because of the short-lived revolution she stirred up in women's dress. The "bloomer" style never caught on, but the name did, and so she has been remembered in history. Style aside, Amelia Bloomer's real contribution to U.S. history was to make a successful career and marriage for herself at a time when women had very few options open to them, and she accomplished it all with limited preparation and no training except what she received on the job.

Mathew Brady (1823–1896)

One biographer has called him "a historian with a camera." Brady came along at a propitious time, when Americans were just discovering the exciting new technology of picture taking and the greatest war in U.S. history provided a wealth of images for the lens. No photographer since has ever achieved the level of fame and respect as Mathew B. Brady. He recorded the nation's living history and most famous figures on wet plates for posterity. Mathew Brady did not invent photography—that credit goes to the Frenchman Louis Daguerre in 1839—but he introduced it to the masses. He was born in Warren County, New York, in 1823 and left the family farm as soon as he could escape. He first read about Daguerre's work in the New York *Observer,* but the turning point in his life occurred when he met the artist and future inventor Samuel F. B. Morse, who also happened to be tinkering with the photographic process at the time in his own studio. Brady set himself up in New York City in 1844 (Brady of Broadway) and began to win prizes in competitive photographic exhibitions. He quickly made himself an acknowledged expert in the daguerreotype process, perfecting his skills and padding his bank account along the way with a plentitude of commissions. The rich and famous paid him visits to have their portrait made.

In 1849 Brady took his equipment to Washington, D.C., to photograph President Zachary Taylor and his Cabinet, the first photographic portrait of a chief executive in the nation's history. He set himself a goal of assembling an "album of illustrious Americans," including scientists, writers, artists, stage performers, politicians, and soldiers. By 1860 he was not the only photographer in America, but he was by far the most famous, and well on the way to being the richest. Among his other customers were *Harper's Weekly* and *Frank Leslie's Illustrated Newspaper,* for whom he was the principal supplier of the photographs that filled their pages.

Tragically for a man whose life was devoted to capturing visual images, his eyesight began to fail when he was young, and by his third decade he was wearing thick spectacles but nevertheless could barely see the subjects in front of his camera. He virtually retreated to his studio to devote himself to the management and promotion end of the business, leaving the field work to others. His health was also chronically poor. In his 40s he married Juliet Handy of Maryland, and they moved into the National Hotel in Washington, D.C., which became their permanent home for the next 40 years. He had already opened a Washington, D.C., gallery to be closer to the most powerful men of the land, while still operating his New York gallery.

He smoothly moved from daguerreotypes to glass-plate photographs in the 1850s, staying one step ahead of most of his competitors, and oversaw the transition of photography from an exotic art form for the rich to a big business accessible to the masses. After 1857, when the *carte de visite* craze swept the country, he was in a position to cash in on that trend by turning out tens of thousands of the small calling-card pictures.

When the Civil War began in 1861, Brady was presented with the photographic opportunity of a lifetime. He received official permission from the Lincoln government to capture the war on plates, then lost no time in sending his "operators" far and wide to do their work. He himself made a rare foray into the field in order to record the first major clash of the war at Manassas, Virginia, on July 20, 1861. Later he would make very few field expeditions; in April 1865 he visited Richmond and Appomattox to see where the war ended. Confining himself mostly to the studio, he stayed busy recording the images of enlisted men and officers who wanted to show off their new uniform or have a memento to send home to their family in case they did not return from the war. Some men, such as George Custer, made a second career of posing for the camera. Mostly Brady planned photographic expeditions for his excellent staff with all the care of a commanding general and dispatched them to various fields in teams

At the Battle of First Bull Run, July 21, 1861, the photographer Mathew Brady was almost killed, then caught up in the rout of Union forces, and wandered around lost for three days. He finally dragged himself back to his Washington, D.C., studio, gaunt and hungry and still wearing the linen duster, straw hat, and borrowed sword that he wore on the battlefield. Undaunted, however, he packed up new supplies and rushed back to the front. This photo is erroneously labeled July 22, 1861. (Library of Congress, Prints and Photographs Division [LC-BH 827701-550])

to record events. While Brady stayed close to home, the men on both sides who snapped the shutters were mostly his disciples, men trained and nurtured by him in earlier years. The wartime images of people such as Alexander Gardner (North) and George Cook (South) would not have been possible without the trailblazing efforts of Mathew Brady, and the soldiers themselves dubbed him "that grand picture-maker."

In his zeal to capture history, he sacrificed both his health and his fortune during the war. Afterward he tried to recoup his losses by selling his magnificent collections to the U.S. government, but Congress was in a shortsighted, budget-minded mood, so he was forced to declare bankruptcy in 1871. He first lost control, then knowledge, of even the whereabouts of his thousands of wartime plates. Three years later many of the images were auctioned off in bankruptcy proceedings. Ironically the principal buyer was the U.S. government. In 1875 Congress finally appropriated $25,000 as belated reimbursement for his selfless services to the country as the photographic historian of the Civil War. But even with that endowment, he remained almost a pauper the rest of his life. Brady was too broken in health and spirit to try to capture the western movement. He preferred to stay in the East and let others brave the wild frontier while he took portrait photos of the great men and women of the age, so long as they were willing to go for a sitting in his studio.

He died on January 15, 1896, alone and forgotten in the alms ward of a New York City hospital. He was buried in Arlington Cemetery, to be celebrated by later generations far more than his own.

A man who began life as a farm boy but went on to become a pioneer of the industrial age and the first "historian with a camera," he had stood at the dawn of the photography age and made the Civil War the most visually accessible war in history up to that date. Although he did not actually take most of the famous battlefield images of the Civil War credited to his studio, he was the guiding spirit behind all of them. Brady saw history through his assistants' eyes.

Tunis G. Campbell (1812–1891)

Tunis Campbell was born a free black but still had to overcome the disadvantage of his race in the mid-19th-century United States to become one of the leading post–Civil War political figures in Georgia. Tragically his fall followed just as quickly.

Tunis Gulic Campbell was born in Middlebrook, New Jersey, on the eve of the War of 1812. His father was a blacksmith whose customers included both blacks and whites, and a wealthy white friend of the family financed Campbell's education at an otherwise all-white Episcopal boarding school in New York. The idea was that Campbell would graduate and become a missionary in Liberia, but Tunis had other ideas for his future that did not include foreign mission work. He saw himself as "a moral reformer and temperance lecturer" called to the pulpit in his own country. At the age of 20 he joined the abolitionist movement and was soon appearing on the lecture platform with Frederick Douglass. For the next 29 years he devoted his heart and mind to helping the cause of abolition while earning a living in a variety of jobs and writing a book, *Hotel Keepers, Head Waiters, and Housekeepers' Guide,* which was the first book written in the United States on the subject of hotel management. He also married and began to raise a family.

When the Civil War began, he volunteered for the Union army but was rejected because of his race. After the Emancipation Proclamation the government sought out Campbell to help resettle runaway slaves in Georgia and South Carolina. This was more than a year before Congress established the Freedman's Bureau. Campbell threw himself into the work, transporting black settlers to the Georgia Sea Islands, where he helped them create self-contained communities with their own farms, schools, and local government. By 1865 he had successfully settled more than 1,000 freedmen. When Andrew Johnson took over the presidency, the progressive programs such as the Sea Islands settlements were cut adrift and white planters reclaimed their power over local affairs. Campbell moved his operation to McIntosh County on the Georgia mainland and invited free blacks to join him there in establishing a freedmen's community. The agricultural enterprise did not prosper but at the same time Campbell was registering freedmen as voters, thus creating a south Georgia political machine that frightened the conservative whites in the area. It did not hurt his high visibility that, on top of everything else, he was also a minister of the African Methodist Episcopal Church and used his pulpit to advance his cherished causes, as well as his own political ambitions. With federal troops ensuring peace and an open political system, a coalition of black and carpetbag votes gave Campbell the second highest post in the local Republican Party, sent him to the state constitutional convention, elected him a member of the state Senate, and made him a justice of the peace in just three years' time.

Campbell became a spokesman for blacks and for liberal Reconstruction policies. His principal causes were land ownership and access to education. He testified before Congress for the anti–Ku Klux Klan laws and the Fifteenth Amendment, and he lobbied the Georgia legislature for fairer treatment of blacks. His message was the same for all audiences: He advocated harmony between the races but advised blacks not to compromise on the principle of equality. When white conservatives returned to power in Georgia in 1872, they targeted Campbell as an "uppity" black man and political threat. He was, successively, stripped of his Senate seat, expelled from the state legislature by the white majority, and indicted on trumped-up charges for actions taken as justice of the peace. He was convicted and spent the next 21 months behind bars, despite repeated appeals for his release by respected public figures. Perhaps worst of all, at the age of 64, having spent all his life a free man, he suffered the humiliation of being hired out as "convict labor" to a white plantation owner. When he was released at the end of his sentence he moved to Washington, D.C., and did not return to Georgia for five years. When he did return briefly in 1882 to attend the state Republican convention in Atlanta, the authorities proved to have long memories and jailed him again for a few days "as a warning." He left Georgia for the last time on December 30, 1882, and dropped out of public sight. Ten years later he died in Boston on December 4, 1891.

His legacy as a black activist is difficult to gauge because unlike Frederick Douglass, he was broken by the racist power structure in the Deep South and ultimately banished from his home. He never lost his popularity among local blacks in Georgia, but his usefulness as a spokesman for them ended after 1875. After that he became a martyr to the cause of black civil rights. His conviction and the time he served in prison also left a stain on his reputation that all the revisionist historians since have never been able to remove. In the end his abbreviated political career was a tragic testimonial to what might have been for African Americans after the Civil War. He was a moderate willing to work with former while masters to create a just society for both races in the South. He failed because there was no empowered civil rights movement to back him in these years as there was a century later.

Henry Carter (Frank Leslie) (1821–1880)

Better known as Frank Leslie, Carter was the first publishin tycoon in American history. Born in England, he got his start at young age making drawings for the *Illustrated News* of London. Whe his father opposed this line of work, he continued to submit his draw ings under the nom de plume Frank Leslie. He became part of the immigration flood into the United States in the late 1840s and in 1854 started his first magazine, *Frank Leslie's Ladies' Gazette of Fashion and Fancy Needlework,* to cash in on the new focus on the "women's sphere." He started up a dozen or more magazines in the next 23 years, most of them proudly bearing his new name in the title. Among those bearing his brand but not his name were the *Illustrated Zeitung* (for Germans speakers), the *Budget of Fun* (whimsical fiction), the *Ten Cent Monthly,* and the *Ladies' Illustrated Almanac.* He quickly showed himself a genius at plugging into the nation's hunger for information in such emerging areas as homemaking, national news, leisure, and romantic fiction. More than anything, however, he longed to create a U.S version of the London *Illustrated News;* he did that in 1855 under the name *Frank Leslie's Illustrated Newspaper.* Carter showed himself to be technologically savvy by utilizing the new lithograph technology to produce text-and-picture stories for his publications. Although he called it a newspaper, *Leslie's* was really an "underweight" magazine of 16 pages selling for 10 cents and published on a weekly schedule. The American reading public had never seen anything like it in the United States: a general interest magazine with popularly written stories on politics, society, music, theater, art, and sports, all interspersed with eye-catching illustrations. He printed the news, usually no more than two weeks after the event, and he was not above using a sensational tone to attract the interest of the average reader. Reporting murders and sex scandals as well as serious news such as the events in "Bleeding Kansas" attracted readers who had never picked up a magazine before because they considered them too highbrow. By its third year *Frank Leslie's Illustrated's* circulation was up to 100,000. When competition arrived in the form of *Harper's Weekly* in 1857, he responded by cutting his price to six cents per issue (or two dollar for a year's subscription) and beefing up the sensationalism.

The Civil War proved a godsend by boosting circulation among a public hungry for news *and pictures* of the war. He beat the drum for the Union in his pages, but it was a business decision as much as a matter of conscience: The majority of his readers were in the North. After 1865 he continued to add new titles to his stable of publications, creating a genuine publishing empire in a nation of highly literate people that most European intellectuals still denigrated as "the colonies." Belying their reputation for being provincial, Americans eagerly read *Leslie's Weekly,* as he recast his flagship publication, for news of David Livingstone's explorations in Africa, Commodore Perry's historic visit to Japan, and the latest European wars. Leslie also served Americans stories of adventures and disasters closer to home—in the West, which was already being mythologized at mid-century. He never let facts or editorial consistency stand in the way of a good story, showing the way for the later "yellow journalists." His magazines also pioneered in other ways, such as being the first to focus attention on the fad of billiards and other new sporting activities and using the terse, journalese writing style familiar to newspaper readers today. Leslie found that crusading journalism mixed well with a sensational tone and took out after such corrupt enterprises as the "swill milk" industry in New York in a series of hard-hitting editorials that prefigured the later muckraking journals of the 20th century. And the best part was, his major stories were always accompanied by dramatic pictures, a format unequaled until photojournalism began. Along the way circulation of *Leslie's* rose to 200,000 and even hit 347,000 for an issue reporting an important prizefight.

Carter's persona was almost as big as his publishing empire. He was a handsome man, short and broad-beamed, with a full black beard that thrust out in front of him. As do most successful people, he had boundless energy and a constantly churning mind. As a Horatio Alger story, his rise from poor immigrant to business tycoon was as inspiring as that of any contemporary captain of industry. In addition, Carter's personal life was as sensational as his best stories. After achieving success, he divorced his English wife to marry one of his female editors, who proved to be as high-profile as he. After he died, leaving a bankrupt shell of an empire, she kept the presses rolling until forced to sell out in 1889. Their flagship publication survived in name until 1922.

Henry Carter, Known as Frank Leslie, was the first celebrity in the staid old publishing business. Before there could be a Henry Luce or a Conde Nast, there had to be Frank Leslie. He built a wealthy and influential publishing empire on one simple idea: "Never shoot over the heads of people," a precept that set the stage for such magazines as *Life, People,* and *Entertainment Weekly* in the next century. It was his insight that the reading public really wanted to be amused and entertained more than informed or instructed, and he cashed in on it in a way that was possible only in America.

Dorothea Dix (1802–1887)

Dorothea Lynde Dix single-handedly changed the treatment accorded to society's outcasts through a 46-year crusade for reform. The fact that she was a woman in an age when women's activities were routinely limited to the home makes her accomplishments all the more remarkable.

Dix did not set out to be a crusader. She was born into an unremarkable family in Hampden, Maine, and at 10 went to live with her grandmother in Boston. Her health was never very good: She had weak lungs and suffered from a chronic nervous condition. Her first career was as a teacher. At 14 years of age she was teaching school in Worcester, Massachusetts, and at 19 she started the Dix Mansion School for girls. Even then she emphasized morality in her teaching along with the natural sciences. She might easily have joined the women's rights movement at this point, but she found a different calling for her strong social conscience—helping a group even more oppressed than women. The spark did not catch, however, for another 14 years. During the time from 1821 to 1841 she worked as a tutor to a minister's family, wrote uplifting books for children, and traveled abroad. A small inheritance in 1830 allowed her just enough financial independence not to have to marry or work herself to death in menial jobs.

In 1841 her life, which had been undistinguished to that date, arrived at a crossroads when she began teaching a Sunday school class in a women's prison in East Cambridge, Massachusetts. Observing the harsh treatment meted out to the inmates, she set herself the task of studying the problem on a larger scale. She toured every jail, asylum, and poorhouse in the state and then expanded her investigation beyond Massachusetts in a three-year, fact-finding tour that took over her 10,000 miles and into hundreds of institutions for the incarceration of the criminal, the insane, and the impoverished. Her persistent and well-reasoned arguments had already led to improvements in the asylum at Worcester, Massachusetts. Now she raised her sights, aiming at a national crusade for a cause that most Americans did not even recognize as a problem. She enlisted political allegiances with men such as Senator Charles Sumner and wrote erudite reports on her observations, not stopping there but including recommendations for improvements as well. She sent a model investigative report to the state legislature ("Memorial to the Legislature of Massachusetts," 1843), then followed that up with petitions to the U.S. Congress.

Her message was always the same: The asylums and institutions where society dumped its unwanted were hellholes of neglect and abuse. She denounced the conventional wisdom that the insane and feebleminded were moral degenerates who did not deserve humane treatment. She recommended the separation of criminals from the mentally deficient, arguing that the two groups were not the same. In her petition to Congress in 1848 she identified some 9,000 "idiots," lunatics, epileptics, and paupers locked away in dungeonlike conditions.

Her lonely crusade attracted supporters and paid off in visible improvements within 10 years. By 1852 15 states and two cities in Canada had established better facilities for the mentally ill, with public funding and enlightened treatment. In the years that followed she took her work to Europe, winning reforms in Scotland, Austria, France, Germany, Italy, Russia, and a dozen other countries. Unfortunately she was less successful in the United States than she wished, although not for lack of persistence or of thinking big. She lobbied Congress successfully in 1852–53 to pass a bill with the breathtaking proposal to set aside public lands to raise money for the care of the insane, thus placing the federal government squarely behind a social program more than 75 years before such liberal thinking was considered good government policy. But the 1854 bill was vetoed by President Franklin Pierce, himself ironically the husband of a woman who had severe mental problems.

Returning to the States in 1857 from her European tour, she launched the second phase of her national crusade, aimed at raising funds for construction of new institutions and advising on their design and staffing. All of this came to an end when the Civil War broke out in 1861 and national attention was focused on winning the war to the exclusion of all other issues. But she shifted gears and devoted her attentions to the physical victims of the conflict, accepting an appointment as superintendent of nurses for all Union hospitals. Thus she passed another milestone, holding the highest government post held by a woman to that time.

She continued her humanitarian service after the war for another 16 years, then retired in 1881 to Trenton, New Jersey, where she took up residence in one of the first institutions built through her efforts, the New Jersey State Hospital. She left a legacy that included two books on her life's work, *Conversations about Common Things* (1824) and *Prisons and Prison Discipline* (1845). More important were the 32 or more enlightened mental institutions that were opened as a direct result of her efforts during her lifetime in North America, Europe, and even Japan, and the revolution in thinking with regard to the treatment of mental illness that she inspired. Because her star has been eclipsed by her contemporaries Susan B. Anthony and Elizabeth Cady Stanton, she has been called the "Forgotten Samaritan."

Frederick Douglass (1817–1895)

The most influential and universally respected African American of the 19th-century, Frederick August Washington Bailey, better known as Frederick Douglass, was an opponent of slavery, a mesmerizing orator, and an accomplished author. His life began on a slave plantation at Tuckahoe, Maryland, as the son of a black slave woman and a white master. He grew up in the gray world between whites and blacks as many mixed-race Americans did in that century, not recognized by the white side of his family and not trusted by the black side. At an early age he was taught the rudiments of reading and writing by the plantation mistress, and he subsequently learned a trade on the Baltimore docks. On September 3, 1838, he used a black sailor's papers to escape to the North, where he settled in New Bedford, Massachusetts, and adopted the new name Douglass to make it hard for the slave catchers to track him down. His first work as a common laborer was harder than what he had endured as a house servant back on the plantation, but he found even the most menial job preferable to a life of slavery. Desiring to become an activist in the antislavery fight rather than hiding out, he joined the Massachusetts Anti-Slavery Society and made his first speech at a Nantucket convention in 1841. He was an immediate sensation thanks to his natural oratorical gifts and the heart-tugging story he had to tell. The society put him on the payroll and sent him out as a lecturer to spread the gospel of abolition. He became a lightning rod for the cause, addressing both sympathetic audiences and jeering mobs who sometimes assaulted him. In 1845 he decided to put his story on paper, writing and publishing his memoirs, *The Narrative of the Life of Frederick Douglass: An American Slave.*

Fearing recapture as much as death, he traveled to England that same year, letting the heat die down back home while he earned lecture fees telling British audiences about his life and the great cause. Even after nine years he was still legally a fugitive in Maryland. There was no statute of limitations for runaway slaves. He returned from England in 1847 with enough money to purchase his freedom and did so through the good offices of friends. He moved to New York City and began editing an abolitionist newspaper, the *North Star,* which he continued publishing until 1864, when it became clear that emancipation was on the horizon for all the nation's slaves. During the run-up to the Civil War he continued to place himself in harm's way, lecturing publicly and becoming a not-so-secret adviser to John Brown. When Brown's 1859 raid on Harper's Ferry, Virginia, failed, followed by his arrest and conviction for treason, Douglass fled to Canada and then back to Britain. He did not return to the United States until after the war had begun, but he maintained a high profile for the next four years. He became the adviser and confidante of Lincoln and assisted in recruiting black soldiers for the Union army.

When the war ended and he no longer had to be constantly looking over his shoulder, he finally received the accolades he deserved for his role in abolishing slavery. He was appointed to a succession of federal posts: secretary of the Santo Domingo Commission (1871), U.S. marshal (1877–81), recorder of deeds for the District of Columbia (1881–86); he capped his public service career as U.S. consul general to Haiti (1889–91). He retired in the United States, where he spent his final years as something of an elder statesman. He also found time during his busy life to marry twice (his first wife died), father four children, and write two more books of memoirs, *My Bondage and My Freedom* (1855) and *Life and Times of Frederick Douglass* (1882).

When he died in Washington, D.C., on February 20, 1895, he was mourned by blacks and whites alike because during a long life he had fought not just for his personal cause of black freedom but also for educational opportunity and women's suffrage. He had fought injustice in many guises. Because of his extraordinary speaking and writing talents, he would have been recognized by his contemporaries even if he had not been a celebrated former slave and even if he had not used those talents to talk about the cause nearest and dearest to his heart. For countless members of his race he was a living testament to the fact that a black man and former slave could succeed in the white man's world, on his wits and character, not just his muscles.

George Fitzhugh (1806–1881)

Southern intellectual, author, and apologist, George Fitzhugh was born in Prince William County, Virginia, to Lucy and George Stuart. His father was a country physician and small-scale planter who eventually settled his family near Alexandria, Virginia. Young George grew up with little formal schooling and was forced to assume responsibility for his own education. He read for the law and gained admission to the Virginia bar in 1829. That same year he married into the prominent Brockenbrough family and through his wife acquired a plantation of his own near Port Royal, Virginia. He was an indifferent planter and bored by the law profession. He had a real gift for fathering children, however, siring nine in the years that followed. He finally found his calling as an apologist for slavery. Whereas other Southern apologists reacted to Northern criticism defensively, Fitzhugh went on the attack, justifying slavery as a positive institution that benefited all concerned and was certainly much more humanitarian than the factory system Northern wage earners endured.

From the late 1840s on Fitzhugh devoted himself almost entirely to defending the South's "peculiar institution" both on the lecture circuit and with his pen. He found that despite his weak educational background, he was an eloquent writer and a persuasive speaker. He produced his first work, a pamphlet titled *Slavery Justified,* in 1849 and in the next 30 years churned out two books (1854 and 1857) and dozens of articles and editorials on the subjects of the South and white agrarian supremacy. He also ventured north to do battle with abolition advocates such as Wendell Phillips on the lecture platform. He supported the Democrat James Buchanan for president in 1856 and was rewarded the next year with an appointment in the attorney general's office despite highly dubious qualifications.

When civil war loomed, he at first opposed secession, instead urging peaceful resolution, but when it appeared inevitable he came to view it as a purifying ordeal that the South must experience to achieve righteousness. Once the shooting started in 1861, he removed himself to his Port Royal plantation, but when Union forces threatened the region, he relocated his family to Richmond and went to work for the Confederate Treasury Department as a clerk. After Appomattox Court House he adapted his politics to the new reality if not his principles. He had lost the plantation during the war, so he went to work for the Freedmen's Bureau as a judge until Radical Reconstruction was imposed. Then, unable to stomach the new carpetbag regime, he returned to the life of the gentleman writer, publishing in *DeBow's Review, Lippincott's Magazine,* and other periodicals until his eyesight began to fail. Unable to support himself, he moved in first with his son in Kentucky, then in 1880 with his daughter in Huntsville, Texas. He died in Texas on July 30, 1881, largely forgotten by a South he had defended well if not wisely for many years.

In the body of writings he left behind, Fitzhugh showed himself to be eminently quotable although not intellectually profound. His rhetorical prowess was not on a par with that of such slavery opponents as Abraham Lincoln, Horace Greeley, or Frederick Douglass, but he made up in passion what he lacked in erudition. He won recognition largely because he was one of the very few moderate Southerners willing to offer a rational defense of slavery as a good and to do so loudly and proudly. He was never embarrassed by the conclusions to which his arguments led him in terms of undemocratic racial and class attitudes. Today he mostly serves as the perfect foil for historians eager to caricature all Southern plantation owners as narrow-minded, provincial bigots bound to an indefensible ideology. Separated from its racist elements, however, his brand of old-fashioned conservatism recognized a "natural elite" who preserved law and order in society, placed community ahead of individual rights, and criticized unfettered liberty as license.

John Charles Frémont (1813–1890)

John Frémont first made a name for himself as an intrepid continental explorer, then ruined it as a failed general and would-be politician. A self-promoter extraordinaire, he was driven equally by wanderlust and the siren call of ambition.

John Fremon was born out of wedlock and lived a footloose life as a boy with his unconventional mother. He showed a natural affinity for math and science, which got him admitted to the College of Charleston, but he was dismissed for "incorrigible negligence" before he could graduate. While living in Charleston he found the first of several mentors in his life, Joel R. Poinsett, future secretary of war, who helped him get his first job as surveyor for a railroad. In 1838 he followed Poinsett to Washington, D.C., and received a commission as a second lieutenant in the Corps of Topographical Engineers. His first survey expedition was with the French scientist Joseph Nicollet, who made such an impression on John Charles that he Gallicized his name to Frémont. Two years with Nicollet exploring the upper Midwest gave him not only invaluable training but the public recognition that he craved.

Back in Washington, D.C., Frémont picked up another mentor, the Missouri senator Thomas Hart Benton, who bestowed both his expansionist dreams and his beautiful daughter on the young officer. Sixteen-year-old Jesse Anne Benton was a remarkable creature even before she and Frémont eloped. She and her father would become the twin pillars of Frémont's public career. Through Benton's influence, Frémont received his first major command—another exploratory expedition to the Far West to trace the route of the Platte River across the Rockies. When he submitted his report to Congress, they quickly authorized a second expedition, which took him on a 14-month journey up to Oregon, down through California, and back to Missouri via the Old Spanish Trail. His official report was accompanied by excellent maps that exponentially increased geographic knowledge of the Far West. Frémont was now being celebrated as a great national hero, in the tradition of Lewis and Clark. But he was not around to receive the accolades, having already set out in the summer of 1845 on his third expedition, this time to follow the Arkansas and Red Rivers across the Rockies into California. There was also an implicit military objective to his instructions, prompted by a looming war with Mexico.

When he reached California in winter 1846 he impulsively involved himself in the Bear Flag revolt of American settlers against Mexican rule. After Californios won independence, Frémont anticipated being named U.S. territorial governor, but he became enmeshed in the middle of a power struggle between two U.S. military officers. He was ordered to Washington to face court-martial charges of mutiny, disobedience, and conduct prejudicial to military discipline. The court found him guilty on all counts, but President James Polk set aside the verdict. Still, Frémont preferred to resign his commission.

He took up exploring again, leading his fourth expedition (1848–49) to find a suitable route through the Rockies for the proposed transcontinental railroad. When he reached California he stayed to look after a vast estate he had been given but ultimately lost the property through his own mismanagement. In the meantime he had entered politics as a U.S. senator from California (1850–51).

His fame as the self-proclaimed "Pathfinder of the West" and his brief tenure in the Senate attracted the interest of the newly formed Republican Party, who made him their first presidential candidate in 1856. He lost to the Democrat James Buchanan but was not out of the spotlight for long. When the Civil War began, his antislavery credentials led to his appointment as a major general in the U.S. Volunteer forces, commanding the Army's Western Department with headquarters in St. Louis. He promptly alienated the residents of his department by unilaterally declaring all slaves emancipated and imposing martial law. After only 100 days in his new post, he was removed from command and sent off to the Shenandoah Valley, where his military incompetence was exposed by General Stonewall Jackson.

Resigning yet again, he effectively ended his military career, but his political career had one last gasp: He opposed Lincoln for the Republican nomination in 1864 as the standard bearer for the party's Radical wing, withdrawing only at the last minute to avoid a humiliating defeat.

He took another stab at business after the war, trying to join the ranks of railroad promoters, but his usual poor judgment led him to back the wrong iron horse, and he was bankrupted by 1870, living off Jessie's writing income. The Republican-controlled Congress took pity and in 1878 appointed him territorial governor of Arizona, where he used his office to try to rebuild his finances. His administrative record was poor enough that he was forced to resign in 1881. He spent his last six years writing his memoirs while Jessie became the family's breadwinner. Broken and bitter he died in New York City on July 13, 1890.

John C. Frémont was given two talents in life: exploring and self-promotion. As an explorer he carried on the fine tradition of Daniel Boone. Even if he did not open up new trails, he certainly publicized little-known routes and distant territories. He was also blessed in his marriage to Jessie Benton Frémont, who was not only his wife but his partner and publicity agent. For nearly 40 years he was never out of the public eye. He was part of that generation of Americans who pushed the frontier all the way to the Pacific Ocean. Fortune often put him in the right place at the right time, but he routinely misplayed the hand he had been dealt.

William Lloyd Garrison (1805–1879)

As was that of many of the men and women of the era, William Lloyd Garrison's career was essentially shaped by the slavery question. Until he latched onto that issue and made it his own, he was a moderately successful but unknown newspaper editor.

Garrison was born in Newburyport, Massachusetts, and grew up in its strong Puritan reformist tradition, although neither his father nor his mother was a crusader. At the age of 12 he apprenticed to the Newburyport *Herald.* For the next 10 years he split time between the *Herald* and the town's other newspaper, the *Free Press.* In 1828 he went to work for a temperance journal, launching his career as a reformer. The following year he made his first public antislavery speech and went to work as editor for a Baltimore antislavery weekly. His intemperate words yielded an acquaintance with the inside of a Baltimore jail but also attracted several prominent supporters, including John Greenleaf Whittier and Henry Clay. With their support and financial backing he launched his life's work, the *Liberator,* in Boston in 1831. He was the founder, editor, and principal writer of this weekly journal of opinion. For the next 34 years it would be the principal voice of the antislavery community in the United States and the main object of Southern hatred. An uncompromising abolitionist, Garrison was fearless in denouncing slavery as an abomination and calling for immediate emancipation. In the first issue of the *Liberator,* he declared, "I am in earnest—I will not equivocate—I will not excuse—I will not retreat a single inch—and I will be heard!" He was more than an editor. He helped organize protests, establish antislavery societies, arrange lectures, and lobby government officials. As a liberal reformer he also advocated women's rights at a time when the two causes found common purpose. He paid a price for his outspokenness: In 1835 he was almost killed by mobs in Boston and New York City at different times, and his newspaper offices were destroyed on more than one occasion. More moderate abolitionists distanced themselves from him, but this reaction did not slow him down. He denounced the Compromise of 1850, the Kansas-Nebraska Act of 1854, the *Dred Scott v. Sandford* decision of 1857, and even the U.S. Constitution, which provided legal protection for slavery. He was one of the very few publicly to defend the actions of the fanatic John Brown, even after the abortive raid on Harper's Ferry in 1859.

When the Civil War began, Garrison became both an adviser to and a thorn in the side of President Lincoln. He was completely in favor of the Emancipation Proclamation; his only question was why Lincoln had not written it sooner. When the end of the war effected the abolition of slavery everywhere in the nation, Garrison folded the *Liberator* and retired from crusading. In 1868 his admirers presented him with a gift of $33,000 to cushion his retirement. In his twilight years he traveled at home and abroad and was usually feted as a hero. He also watched his children grow up and saw two of them take up the crusader's cross, carrying on the Garrison legacy by battling for minorities and against U.S. imperialism. He died before Jim Crow was locked in, believing that the major battle for the equality of African Americans had been won with the abolition of slavery, and that their future was full of promise. His life as a white liberal champion of racial equality set a standard for a new generation of civil rights activists in the 1960s.

Ben Holladay (1819–1887)

He was known as the "Stagecoach King" and the "Napoleon of the Plains," but he was far more than either of those titles indicates. He was a transportation entrepreneur par excellence. While some better known men such as Daniel Drew and Jay Gould made fortunes in railroads, and Cornelius Vanderbilt ("the Commodore") controlled both railroads and steamships, only Holladay juggled stagecoaches, railroads, and steamship lines.

Ben Holladay was born in Nicholas County, Kentucky, but at an early age moved out to the frontier in Missouri. His first entry into business was as a hotel and store operator in Weston. As did many on the frontier, he lacked formal schooling, but he was energetic and a quick study with a head for business. After the U.S.-Mexican War he shrewdly purchased surplus wagons, oxen, and other equipment from the U.S. Army and opened a freighting business between Missouri and Salt Lake City, Utah. He also drove livestock to California to sell to the miners, and it was in California that he first got into the stagecoach business in the midst of the Civil War. Since 1858 he had been supplying goods to the freighting firm of Russell, Majors and Waddell, known as the Central Overland California and Pike's Peak Express Company. In 1860 when they launched the Pony Express to provide regular mail service to California, he was there with the cash and guarantees to back the venture. Two years later when Russell & Co. went bankrupt, Holladay was there again to step in and purchase the company's properties for a bargain $100,000. Deciding there was more money to be made in delivering mail and passengers than freight, he turned the company into the Overland Stage Line. He soon had a going concern, thanks largely to securing a contract with the government to deliver the U.S. mail, which he in turn subcontracted to his own Overland Mail Company. He expanded his branch and feeder lines into Colorado and Nebraska, Idaho, Montana, Oregon, and Washington Territories until he ultimately controlled a 5,000-mile route system. He also won fatter and fatter government mail contracts and used them to subsidize his passenger service. The latter was a chronic problem of the business that caused him to begin looking for other opportunities. In 1863 he began to investigate the West Coast steamship business and to plan for the day he would get out of the stagecoach business.

When Indian attacks caused mounting losses to his Overland holdings, he sold out in 1866 to Wells Fargo & Co. and promptly sank the money from that deal into the Northern Pacific Transportation Company, which operated steamships between Alaska and Mexico. Two years later he shifted gears again to become chief owner of the Oregon Central Railroad Company. He sold the steamship company and used the profits to build hundreds of miles of track through the Northwest. Along the way he became the first bicoastal tycoon, running his businesses on the West Coast while his family dwelled in a fabulous mansion near White Plains, New York. He also spent a great deal of time in Washington, D.C., keeping his political fences mended.

He seemed to have the Midas touch until 1873. That was the year the worst financial panic in U.S. history occurred, and his first wife, of some 30 years, died. The panic hit the transportation industry especially hard. Holladay's fragile paper empire collapsed, and he found himself stripped of his power by angry bondholders. By 1876 the major mover and shaker in the American transportation industry had been forced into premature retirement. His former bicoastal interests withered to a home in Portland, Oregon, where he died On July 8, 1887.

During a career that spanned four decades, he was one of the most important figures in pushing back the frontier and linking the far corners of the country with his ships and trains and stagecoaches. His "robber baron" methods of doing business were not altogether admirable, and he wielded unscrupulous influence in the nation's capital, but he built a transportation empire that advanced the nation's interests along with his own.

Bridget "Biddy" Mason (1818–1891)

Biddy Mason was a woman who was caught up in several of the historic movements of the mid-19th century: abolitionism, Mormonism, and the California gold rush. Her journey from slavery to wealth and respect is a truly remarkable one.

She was born a slave on the plantation of John Smithson in Hancock County, Mississippi, on August 5, 1818. When she reached age 18 she was given as a wedding gift to Robert and Rebecca Smith. The Smiths converted to Mormonism in 1847 and decided to move to Utah to be with others of their faith. They took Mason and their other slaves with them. Mason's particular skills as a nurse and a midwife were valuable to any family, so when they moved again after just four years in Utah, they took Mason with them. The alternatives would have been either to sell her or to manumit her. This time the Smith family settled down in San Bernadino, which, as was all of California, was experiencing boom times because of the gold rush. But California was also at the center of the sectional conflict over slavery, and that fact worked to Mason's favor. In 1850 California had been declared a "free state" by act of Congress, so Robert Smith was faced with the choice of either manumitting his 14 slaves or leaving the state immediately. He made plans to go to Texas, but Mason was unwilling to be dragged around the country in bondage any longer. She made contact with free blacks in the area, who helped her escape. The law, especially the Fugitive Slave Act, usually worked against slaves, but Mason was able to make it work for her. She filed charges against Smith for owning slaves in a free state, and a court date was set. Smith chose to flee the state, leaving Mason behind, so California officially manumitted her on January 1, 1856.

She was now a free woman with the skills and ambition to make something of herself. She moved to Los Angeles and set herself up as a nurse and midwife, administering folk medicine learned on the plantation in Mississippi and assisting in the delivery of hundreds of babies of every race in the city. Over the course of 35 years she made enough money to survive and even managed to set a little aside. But from the start she had greater ambitions than to be a midwife always at the call of others. By November 1866 she had saved \$250 and used it to purchase a piece of property just beyond the city limits. There she established her residence and made it a sort of rescue mission for people of color with nowhere else to go. In time, as the city grew out to her, 331 South Street became known as a haven for the flotsam and jetsam of society. The South Street property was also her first foray into the real estate market and established her as one of the first African-American property owners in the city's history. As the real estate market in Los Angeles took off, her property became quite valuable. She sold off a portion of it in 1884 for \$1,500 and used the profits to build a two-story commercial building, part of it as her headquarters and the rest rented out to provide a steady source of income. The building eventually housed a nursery, bakeries, a restaurant, and furniture and carpet stores. She had no business training and no formal education, but she was showing herself to be a natural businesswoman and continued to invest her income in city property

She also had a strong religious faith all her life. In 1872 she helped found the city's first African Methodist Episcopal Church, which still existed in modern times. Her faith and her big heart merged in her philanthropic work. At a time when philanthropy was identified as practically the private preserve of white business tycoons such as Carnegie and Rockefeller, Biddy Mason used the return on her real estate deals and commercial enterprises to operate a free nursery for orphans and poor children, supply food to needy families, and help stranded settlers passing through the city on the way to their new homes. She also donated generously out of her own pocket to established charities whenever the hat was passed. Although her giving was not on the scale of Carnegie's and Rockefeller's, she was as much a philanthropist as any rich businessman who gave libraries or endowed universities.

Mason died in 1891 at the age of 72 and, despite all her contributions to the city over the years, was buried in an unmarked grave in the "Colored Cemetery." Ninety-seven years later the city belatedly honored her as a woman who pulled herself up from slavery and carried many others with her.

Cyrus H. McCormick (1809–1884)

Inventor, manufacturer, and promoter, Cyrus McCormick combined the rare talents of the scientist and the business person in one, a capacity that made his contemporaries Thomas Edison and Alexander Graham Bell household names in U.S. history but somehow failed to place him in their exalted company.

He was born in Rockbridge County, Virginia, and as most Americans of his day received very little formal schooling. But he was apparently blessed with good genes because his father was a successful inventor. McCormick senior was also a farmer, so young Cyrus grew up on the land and in the workshop and, as his father did, directed his inventive mind toward agricultural machines. McCormick's father spent two decades of his life trying to invent a practical reaper—without success—but Cyrus by the time he was 22 had solved the basic problems in constructing a working reaper. It became the archetype of all later reapers perfected by McCormick and his competitors. He demonstrated the machine in 1832 and two years later took out a patent on the basic design while continuing to add improvements, driven as much by financial considerations as by scientific curiosity. By 1840 he was producing them for sale out of the family workshop at Walnut Grove, Illinois. That year he sold 50. But while sales looked rosy, patent problems cropped up. When his original patent ran out in 1848, a host of competitors jumped in and began selling rival machines based on his designs. He refused to relinquish proprietary control meekly and spent the rest of his life and a considerable chunk of his fortune in legal battles trying to protect his interests. It became an obsession.

In the meantime he moved his production facilities to Chicago in 1847 and focused his energies on the production and marketing of his invention. As a businessman McCormick proved himself even more astute than he was as an inventor. He adopted cutting-edge practices of mass production, creative advertising, field demonstrations, warranties, and consumer financing, in the process outmaneuvering his competitors. One of his best ideas was sending out traveling salesmen, who visited farmers and sold the McCormick reaper on commission. It was a marketing method that benefited everybody concerned. By 1860 he was selling 5,000 machines a year, despite the competition from more than 100 rival companies.

One of the greatest advantages he had over his rivals was international recognition for the McCormick reaper. He signed up as an exhibitor at the Crystal Palace Exhibition in London in 1851, the first modern world's fair, and took home the top exhibitor's prize awarded at the exhibition. During the next 25 years the McCormick reaper won prizes at more than half a dozen subsequent world's fairs from Europe to Australia. Overseas sales started slowly but eventually took off just as they had back home in the States. All the while he was adding further refinements to the basic machine and new machines to his product line, including a self-raking device and a wire binder. His McCormick Reaper Company became a mainstay of Chicago's economy, employing 1,400 workers at peak production. When the Great

Chicago Fire of 1871 destroyed the plant, he rebuilt even bigger and better than before. The spread of farming on the Great Plains produced boom times for the business until by the mid-1880s the company was selling 50,000 machines a year.

In his later years success allowed McCormick to devote time to his other two loves—the Presbyterian Church and the Democratic Party. His support of a struggling Presbyterian seminary was substantial and regular enough that they changed its name to the McCormick Theological Seminary and moved it to Chicago. He played an active role as a layman in church affairs for many years, and because of his great wealth and power, his opinions always carried great weight in church councils. He exercised only slightly less influence in Democratic Party affairs. He mounted an unsuccessful run for Congress in 1864 and was a serious candidate for the vice-presidential spot on the Tilden ticket. He also accepted the responsibilities of noblesse oblige by becoming a philanthropist. Before his death he had given away some $500,000, most to the Presbyterian Church.

When Cyrus McCormick died on May 13, 1884, he left a fortune estimated at $10 million, which was not a bad ending for a Virginia farm boy. He also left a solid company to his heirs and a world-famous name synonymous with the mechanical reaper.

With his invention he had revolutionized not just agricultural production but U.S. society, adding impetus to the homesteaders' rush out west and making farming a more efficient enterprise, thereby freeing up more of the nation's workforce for the industrial expansion that occurred in the late 19th century. The quantum leap in grain production also fueled the nation's export-driven economy while furnishing enough cheap food for the incoming immigrant multitudes. His impact was best summarized in the testimonial to his accomplishments that accompanied his 1879 election to the French Academy of Sciences, which declared that he had "done more for the cause of agriculture than any other living man," a fitting epitaph to his 62-year career.

Samuel F. B. Morse (1791–1872)

Samuel Finley Breese Morse was that rarest of individuals deserving of a place in the select company of Renaissance men who combined the insights of the artist with the precise mind of the inventor in one person. He was recognized in his day for both, although today he is only remembered as the inventor of the telegraph.

Finley Morse, as his family called him, was born in Charlestown, Massachusetts, into a family who could trace their roots back to the earliest Puritan colonists. Eight of his 11 siblings died either at birth or in childhood, so his parents doted on him more than they might have otherwise. From them also he got an enterprising mind, a strong will, and a good dose of common sense. He received a good education, which included Yale University. While at Yale he first began to reveal his artistic talents, but his father disapproved of his trying to make a career in art. But his work was good enough to attract the attention of professional artists, and in 1811 he went to England to do advanced studies under Benjamin West, among others. He spent four happy years there developing a Romantic style, then returned in summer 1815 to open his own studio in Boston. But there was little market in the United States for classical subjects such as *The Dying Hercules,* so commissions and paying students were rare. He closed his studio and took to the road, ending up in New York City in 1823. There he settled down and achieved his greatest success as an artist, especially of portraits. He enjoyed enough respect among his peers to become one of the founders and the first president of the National Academy of Design in 1826. In that capacity he was able to utilize his magnetic personality, superior verbal skills, and smooth manners to promote both the academy and himself. In his own art he liked to exercise his inventive turn of mind by trying out new color formulations and combinations. But his professional recognition yielded no financial success. In 1829 he fled back to Europe, where he spent the next three years traveling and painting. He returned home in 1832 a confirmed anti-Catholic and chauvinistic American. When his art career continued to struggle, he made an unsuccessful run for public office as mayor of New York City.

He might have become completely misanthropic but for a chance encounter on his voyage home from the Continent. He had met a man named Charles Thomas Jackson, who sparked in him an interest in the practical uses of electricity. He had always had a curious mind that led him to read in many fields, including technical literature, and even attend lectures on esoteric subjects. But those other subjects had always been just an avocation next to his art. He also had some affinity for the mechanical, having helped invent a successful piston pump and a marble-cutting machine in his younger days. He now made the fateful decision to turn his back on art and apply himself to inventing the first electrical communication system. He piggybacked his own concepts for the way such a system should operate on the trailblazing scientific work of others. His own unique contribution to the technology of the system was the development of a relay device that transformed a laboratory toy into a genuine long-distance communication system. By January 1836 he had a working model of the telegraph, which he showed to a professor friend at the University of the City of New York and then incorporated the man's suggested improvements. Next he took on partners, Alfred Vail and Francis O. J. Smith, and filed a patent with the U.S. Patent Office in 1837. Leaving Vail and Smith to look after matters in the United States, Morse stormed Europe to defend his proprietary rights. Seven years of legal battles followed on both sides of the Atlantic because other inventors had been thinking along the same lines for some time, and some had even built their own working models.

Finally in 1843 he received a $30,000 grant from a skeptical Congress to demonstrate the "Morse telegraphic system." Part of his invention had been the development of a practical code for sending messages (Morse code). On May 24, 1844, using an experimental line strung from Washington, D.C., to Baltimore, he sent the historic message "What hath God wrought!" When it was received at the other end, he knew he was vindicated. He and Vail offered to sell their invention to the U.S. government for a lump sum of $100,000, but Congress refused to move, so they began exploring private financing. Morse had a trusting nature and no business sense whatsoever, so the inventor was easily taken advantage of by both his partners and his rivals. For years, he found himself tied up in litigation, which cost him time and money and at least one dear friend. The U.S. Supreme Court finally upheld his patent rights in 1854. The upside of the whole matter was all the honors and acclaim that were showered on him both in the United States and in Europe. Except in the matter of exclusive ownership of his invention, the world was willing to recognize his remarkable accomplishment with emoluments, decorations, and honorariums. Those did not pay the bills, however, and he continued to struggle financially for many years. Had the telegraph not taken up all his time and energy, he might have become another Mathew Brady. He was one of the pioneers in daguerreotype photography in the 1840s and 1850s.

It was his work in telegraphic communications that put his name before the world and opened new doors. He made unsuccessful run for Congress on the Democratic ticket in 1854, then was appointed to the board of Cyrus Field's transatlantic cable company (which was unsuccessful) and served another term as president of the National Academy of Design. In 1861 he joined a group who founded Vassar College. In his last years he finally achieved the level of material wealth that he had always thought he deserved for his accomplishments—which included a 200-acre estate on the Hudson River and a winter residence in New York City. He also had a much, much younger wife and eight children to comfort him in his old age. He tried to return to his art in 1864 but found that the muse had deserted him; his talent had been dulled by the years away from his easel. He died in his New York City brownstone at 5 West 22nd Street on April 2, 1872.

Samuel Morse's double-barreled career should have made him one of the most honored and admired people of his lifetime. Instead he experienced twice the grief and frustration of the normal working person. Only after his death did Congress finally commemorate him, and the posthumous memorials held around the country were for "The Father of the Telegraph." Then, as today, the artistic phase of his career was scarcely recognized, although it dominated the first 46 years of his life and at one time he was one of the most promising U.S. artists. As an artist and inventor he had much to be proud of; by contrast, his few forays into politics did great harm to his reputation. They were ill advised and embarrassing. One can only speculate what he might have accomplished had he devoted himself to one or the other career, or if he had not spent the most productive years of his life tied up in litigation for his single, great invention. On its basis alone, he was elected to the Inventors Hall of Fame 28 years after his death. In truth he was a Renaissance man born three centuries too late.

Frederick Law Olmsted (1822–1903)

America's foremost landscape architect even before there was such a profession and father of the urban park movement were just two of Olmsted's claims to fame. He, as were many of his mid-19th-century contemporaries, was a self-invented man who carved out a unique career in the land of opportunity.

Frederick Law Olmsted was born in Hartford, Connecticut, into the middle class and received most of his early education outside the public school system. Just before entering Yale University in 1837 he ingested some poison sumac, which left him half-dead and with permanently weakened eyesight. It also derailed his plans for traditional higher education. He only attended Yale for one semester. For the next decade he was tutored by various people and took a year-long trip to China. In 1848 he settled down to the life of a gentleman farmer on Staten Island, where he taught himself scientific agriculture and read widely among British nature writers.

He published his first work in 1850 after a six-month walking tour of the British Isles and the Continent. *Walks and Talks of an American Farmer in England* showed that he already had a bent toward observing nature. During the rest of the decade he made three more tours of Europe studying every aspects of parks. He also applied his powers of observation to social matters with two tours of the South in 1852 and 1853–54 on assignment from the *New York Times*. From these trips he produced three works, *A Journey in the Seaboard States, A Journey through Texas,* and *A Journey in the Back Country,* which offered a stinging criticism of slavery. He blamed the system for retarding social and economic development in the South, including its lack of urban centers, and warned that its extension into the western territories would only create the same conditions in that region. He was a firm believer in the benefits of the free-labor system, both morally and culturally. For Olmsted *back country* was a pejorative term as compared to the more civilized urbanism of the North. Widely read, these works provided intellectual arguments for the Free-Soil movement in the 1850s, and Olmsted backed his arguments with his money by supporting Free-Soil immigration into Kansas and Texas. In 1861 he combined the three titles into one two-volume work, *The Cotton Kingdom*.

In addition to his writing and traveling, Olmsted found time to marry in the 1850s and embark on a second career as a publisher-editor. He spent two years at the helm of *Putnam's Monthly Magazine,* which kept him in New York City and provided the contacts that launched the next phase of his career: In 1857 he was appointed superintendent of Central Park, which was then under study for a comprehensive redesign. What it had become over the years was a tangled jungle that served as a refuge for hoboes and criminals. Olmsted and a partner, Calvin Vaux, submitted the winning design with their heavily European-influenced landscaping plan, and from 1859 to 1861 Olmsted was the chief architect directing some 4,000 men in completely reinventing the park with open spaces, artificial lakes, bridle paths, and all the other elements that known today.

Olmsted's skills as an administrator attracted so much favorable attention that when the Civil War began in 1861 he was appointed chief executive officer of the U.S. Sanitary Commission. In that capacity he created a comprehensive and efficient relief system that supplied tons of medical supplies and clothing to Union troops, but he also ruffled bureaucratic feathers with his brusque steamrolling style. In summer 1863 he resigned, but he had already begun funneling his energies into the war effort in other ways, such as writing legislation and drumming up public support for emancipation. Still not sufficiently challenged or satisfied, he took off to California in late 1863 to run a vast gold mining operation in the Sierra Nevada. That venture went under, but he used his time in California to pursue his principal interest in landscapes and public parks. Over the short span of two years he launched the movement that ultimately led to the creation of Yosemite and Mariposa, as inalienable public trusts to be managed by the state of California, and designed a college campus, a cemetery, and a public park. Then he returned to New York, where, with the war over, attention was again focused on urban improvements. He resumed his partnership with Calvin Vaux and together they completed Central Park, created Prospect Park in Brooklyn, and laid out the nation's first "comprehensive and unified" park system in Buffalo. Olmsted would devote the next 20 years of his life to the Buffalo work. He also built parks for Boston and Chicago.

Olmsted's thinking was also evolving. He began using the title *landscape architect* to describe himself and characterized his work in terms of taming the urban frontier, that is, combining the best elements of nature and city life in a single synthesis. He saw parks as works of art to restore the human spirit and provide large democratic spaces for urban dwellers. In his writings and lectures he virtually created the philosophy of landscaping and focused public attention on the spaces that expressed that philosophy. His ideas led him naturally to thinking about urban living spaces that harmonized with his parks. Beginning in 1868 he designed the nation's first residential suburban community in Riverside, Illinois, with gracefully curving streets, homes set well back from the street, sidewalks for pedestrians, scenic vistas, green spaces, and integrated municipal services. With Riverside he had become more than just a landscaper; he had become an urban planner. It was arguably the high point of his career, although less well known than Central Park.

By the 1870s Olmsted had become a national treasure, in demand for many more jobs than even his boundless energy could complete. But he still managed to add substantially to his résumé. Before the end of the century he planned campuses for Stanford University and Lawrenceville School; laid out the grounds for such residential institutions as the McLean Asylum in Belmont, Massachusetts; led the movement to create a scenic reservation at Niagara Falls; designed the U.S. Capitol grounds; and planned the site of the 1893 World's Columbian Exposition in Chicago. His fingerprints or influence was to be found in public works projects all over the nation. By the time of his death in 1903 he had personally designed almost 80 parks and 13 college campuses, not to mention his other grand projects. But something else happened during the last few decades of his life: He became disillusioned with the slow acceptance of his revolutionary theories about urban planning and turned away from great social projects to accept aesthetic commissions working for the superwealthy. He laid out the grounds or served as the consultant for some 200 private estates. This phase of his career is best represented by the Biltmore estate, which he designed for George W. Vanderbilt near Asheville, North Carolina. It proved to be his last major project, as he retired in 1895.

During a 37-year career, Frederick Law Olmsted founded U.S. landscape architecture and had more impact on the way Americans live than did Louis Sullivan or Frank Lloyd Wright or any of a host of later urban architects and designers. He created ecological sensitivity before there was such a concept, and he invented urban planning even before the end of the American frontier had closed off easy access to open lands in the West. On top of all that, he was a prolific writer and a first-rate administrator, talents that he could have parlayed into careers just as successful as his chosen field had he been so inclined. He was a true visionary and genius who changed the course of U.S. history without ever holding elective office or wearing a uniform, with the pure force of his intellect.

Miguel Antonio Otero, Sr. (1829–1882)

Miguel Otero is a rare example of a 19th-century Hispanic American who is not remembered by Anglos as either a bandit or a revolutionary but as a prominent citizen. During his long career in New Mexico politics he helped bridge the gap between Hispanics and Anglos, between colonial and territorial status, and between Washington, D.C., and Santa Fe.

Miguel Otero was born in New Mexico at Valencia during the time the territory was still part of Mexico. He was a member of a distinguished family, who gave him many advantages in education and political connections that most of his fellow Hispanics did not enjoy. He made the most of this head start. He spent his first 12 years in Valencia being educated in private and parochial schools, then his father sent him to St. Louis University in St. Louis, Missouri, one of the "most Spanish" cities in the United States at the time. There the young Otero could continue his formal education while receiving his first immersion in Anglo culture. Six years later he attended Pingree's College in Fishkill, New York, where after graduation he was on the faculty for a while. His parents wanted him to become a priest, but he preferred to return to St. Louis and study law. He completed his studies and returned home in 1852 to begin a law career. In his 11-year absence the U.S.-Mexican War had occurred and New Mexico had become part of the United States. His knowledge of the U.S. legal system and familiarity with American culture stood him in good stead in the years ahead. He also had political ambitions, which he was not long in testing. He ran for and won a seat in the territorial legislature in 1852. Three years later he was elected a territorial delegate to Washington, D.C., after winning a fiercely contested election; he was reelected in 1857 and 1859. During his six years in Congress he was an outspoken advocate of New Mexico's interests, especially protection from Indian depredations.

In Washington, he continued his Anglo aculturization, by aligning himself with the Democratic Party and marrying a prominent South Carolina woman. These actions placed him squarely in the Southern camp at the time the ongoing sectional debate was coming to a boil. By the terms of the Compromise of 1850, New Mexico was administered under the "popular sovereignty" principle, and Otero worked to make it a slave state aligned with the plantation aristocracy of the Deep South. He successfully lobbied the territorial legislature to pass a "slave code" in the hope that slaveholders would settle the territory in large numbers. When that dream died a-borning, he began advocating the creation of an independent Western Confederation of states that would serve as a balance wheel between North and South. He attended the 1860 Democratic Party convention in Charleston and supported the moderate Stephen A. Douglas to become the party's presidential nominee. At the same time his political base back home was being eroded by Republican Party gains.

When the South seceded en masse to start the Civil War in the winter of 1860–61, Otero stayed with the Union, even though he could have pushed New Mexico down the same path its next-door neighbor Texas took. Lincoln sought to reward him by offering him the post of U.S. minister to Spain, but he declined it, so the president attempted to appoint him as territorial secretary, a position that would also have made him ex officio governor of the territory. The Republican-controlled Senate distrusted his politics, however, and refused to confirm the appointment. He left Washington and went to Kansas, where he entered the mercantile business. He also kept a hand in politics, working to extend one or more railroads into New Mexico to end its isolation and boost the territorial economy. He helped organize the New Mexico and Southern Pacific Railroad, but he did not live long enough to see a southern transcontinental railroad run through the territory. Relocating his mercantile business to Las Vegas, New Mexico, in 1879, he aggressively expanded his interests into banking, ranching, and other related ventures, working both sides of the United States-Mexico border. He was one of the richest and most powerful men in the entire Southwest. He purchased the immense Maxwell land grant, founded the San Miguel National Bank of Las Vegas, and sat on the board of the Atchison, Topeka, and Santa Fe Railroad.

In 1880 at 51 years of age, he decided to jump back into electoral politics by running on the Democratic ticket for his old office of territorial delegate to Congress. But Republicans controlled the state now, and his failing health prevented him from campaigning as intensely as he had some 20 years earlier. He lost the race, and the next year he saw his great mercantile company, Otero, Sellar & Co., break up in a dispute with his partner, John Sellar. He was forced by poor health virtually to withdraw from public affairs during the last year of his life, and he died at home in Las Vegas on May 30, 1882. He left behind a business empire, a sizable fortune, and a bright son to sustain the family influence in political and economic affairs.

Miguel Otero was a major political figure in early New Mexico politics and one of the first Hispanic Americans to represent his people in Washington, D.C. Ethnic influence aside, he was also a shrewd and successful businessman who did a great deal to help develop the Southwest and ultimately, through his family legacy, make New Mexico part of the Union in 1912.

Ely S. Parker (1828–1895)

One of the first American Indians to receive a formal education and serve in a high government post, Ely (pronounced "ee-LEE") Parker was present at some of the great moments in U.S. history, probably the most dramatic of which was the surrender of Lee to Grant at Appomattox in 1865.

He was born into a prominent Seneca Indian family, part of the Iroquois confederacy of New York. He was given the name Do-Ne-Ho-Ga-Wa ("Leading Name") by his parents and grew up on the Tonawanda Reservation. But he attended a Baptist mission school, took the Anglo name Ely, and early on made the decision to succeed in the white man's world, seemingly rejecting his Indian heritage. He left the reservation to enroll in Yates and Cayuga Academies in western New York. He then read law but was refused admission to the New York bar on the narrowly based reasoning that as an Indian, he was not a "citizen" of the state. Undeterred, he turned his considerable intellect and energy to engineering, learning on the job with the New York canal system.

But he did not forget his Indian roots completely. He frequently represented the Seneca tribe's interests in both Albany and Washington, D.C., even negotiating a treaty that saved the Tonawanda Reservation from being taken over for white settlement. And he ably assisted white scholars in their research on the culture and history of the Iroquois. In the course of his dealing, Parker had occasion to meet and get to know three presidents: Polk, Pierce, and Buchanan. His tribespeople were impressed enough with his contributions to elect him a sachem (leader) of the Iroquois Confederacy and to use him as their intermediary with whites.

His obvious intelligence and practical talents impressed whites as much as Indians. He was hired as an engineer by the New York State Canal Board and by the Chesapeake and Albemarle Ship Canal company. Then he went to work with the U.S. Treasury, in which capacity he first met Ulysses Grant in Galena, Illinois. Parker was a powerfully built man who found his heft to be an advantage in breaking into a highly bigoted society in which Indians were still considered second-class humans, if not savages. He usually maintained the stereotype of an Indian's stoic silence, carefully measuring his words whenever he chose to speak. But he also had an occasional drinking problem, which made him a soul mate with his mentor Grant. Both men battled demon alcohol most of their lives.

When the Civil War began, Grant remembered Parker and appointed him to his military staff. Parker stayed with Grant throughout the war and beyond, rising to the rank of brevet brigadier general. As the general's personal secretary, he accompanied Grant to the surrender negotiations with Lee at the McLean home at Appomattox on April 9, 1865. There he wrote out the official copy of the terms of surrender that the two generals signed. The story has been told that when Lee was introduced to Parker, he remarked, "I am glad to see at least one real American here."

Once peace returned, Parker went to work with the Office of Indian Affairs; he rose to commissioner of Indian Affairs in 1869. He became the point man in Grant's cherished "Peace Policy" after the latter became president. The policy proved to be a failure in practice, but Parker performed his duties capably as usual. During his two years as commissioner there were no major conflicts with the western tribes, but partisan politics clouded his service, as charges of corruption leveled against Parker led to a congressional investigation. The commissioner was cleared of any wrongdoing, but his judgment was questioned in several matters and the authority of the office was reduced. Parker resigned and left Washington, D.C. He and Grant drifted apart after he returned to private life and attempted to launch a business career, only to discover that his talents did not lie in business. Swallowing his pride he took a clerical job with the New York City Police Department, which he held for the next 19 years. During that time he was active in Freemasonry and Union veterans' organizations. He also continued to serve as a spokesman and legal representative for the Iroquois up until his death on August 30, 1895, at the age of 67.

During his lifetime Ely Parker had lived successfully in two worlds. He forged a career in the white man's world as a soldier and public servant and he married a white woman, Minnie Orton Sackett, who outlived him by 37 years. Toward the end of his life he expressed some remorse that he had turned his back on his Indian heritage, but those feelings were more an expression of self-conscious guilt than a reflection of reality. He never denied his Indian blood and was always on call to represent his people using the skills and influence he had acquired in the white man's world.

Red Cloud (1822–1909)

Red Cloud (Makhpiya) was not only well known but was highly successful in moving back and forth between the white world and the Indian world. Moreover, he was perhaps the only 19th-century Native American leader to leave an account of his life written by himself. As they are for most Native Americans of the time, the details of his early life before fame found him are obscure. He was born into the powerful Snake clan of the Oglala Lakota Sioux near the forks of the Platte River in modern-day Nebraska. Lacking any hereditary claim to chieftainship, he rose to prominence through his fighting prowess and eloquence. As a young warrior he was known as a cruel enemy of the Ute and Pawnee tribes. When the Plains Indians Wars erupted after 1865 he made himself the leader of an aggressive band of Lakota. His most notable accomplishment was forcing the U.S. Army to abandon the Bozeman Trail between the North Platte River and the goldfields of Montana. He did this by stopping virtually all civilian travel over the trail, isolating Forts Reno, Phil Kearny, and C. F. Smith, and on December 21, 1866, massacring a troop of 80 cavalrymen led by Lt. Col. W. J. Fetterman, the worst defeat suffered by the U.S. Army in the Indian wars to that date.

The Fetterman Fight, as it is known, confirmed Red Cloud's standing among both whites and Indians, and after another two years of bloody war, the U.S. government was persuaded to resume serious peace negotiations with the Lakota. Red Cloud entered Fort Laramie and after heated negotiations put his mark on the Treaty of Laramie in November 1868. The following spring he brought in 1,000 of his followers to the reservation without incident. It is doubtful whether he understood all the ramifications of the Fort Laramie Treaty, which committed his people to resettling on land located north of the Platte Valley and west of the Missouri River in return for government annuities and other gifts. It is just as doubtful that he intended to abide by it any longer than he needed to regroup and resume fighting. For the next decade the treaty was frequently bent by both sides but never completely broken. The Fort Laramie Treaty marked the end of Red Cloud's days as a warrior chief and the beginning of those as a diplomat and peacemaker, a role in which he was never entirely comfortable.

In this photograph by William Gardner the Oglala Lakota Sioux war chief Red Cloud shakes hands with William Blackmore, during a visit to Washington, D.C., in May 1872. Red Cloud's warlike days were behind him by this time, though he was still an impassioned spokesman for his people. (Library of Congress)

His new role took him to Washington, D.C., in 1870 on the first of seven trips back east representing his people. Unfortunately although he was always treated with respect by the government, he was never the only spokesman for the Sioux, much less all the other Plains Indians. Even his own group of Lakota was divided on whether to follow him or not. As the reluctant intermediary between the government and the Sioux, he became the chief instrument of the government's "Peace Policy," which aimed at nothing less than the extinguishing of traditional tribal life. He stubbornly if hopelessly resisted permanent assignment of the Sioux to reservation status, all the while suffering removal from one location to another, ultimately to the Pine Ridge Reservation in South Dakota. During his trips to the East he was always feted by white crowds whose knowledge of Indians was obtained mostly through dime novels and artists' renderings. He looked every inch the "noble red man" and possessed a gravitas that was unmistakable even when filtered through interpreters' halting translations. He enjoyed the public expressions of honor but also saw how hopeless it would be to continue the struggle against creeping white civilization. It was irresistible, and this was the message he took back to his people. He did not join in the Sioux uprising of 1876 that massacred George Custer on the Little Bighorn, and the next year he turned in one of the leaders of that uprising, Crazy Horse. When the Ghost Dance movement appeared in 1890 he also opposed that as likely to provoke another army crackdown, but many members of the tribe ignored the old man, whom they considered nothing but a pawn of the whites, and the result was another massacre (Wounded Knee).

He never completely lost his famous fighting spirit, but he fought now with words instead of guns and tomahawks. His major battle was against the assigned Indian agent at the Pine Ridge Reservation, whom he considered a crook and a scoundrel. He carried on the fight until the man left in 1886, but even after that he maintained barely civil relations with the agents who followed. Yet he continued to be treated as chief of his tribe by the uneasy Pine Ridge community until he passed on the reigns of power to his son in 1903. During those years it became his sad duty to preside over the transition of the Plains Indians from proud and independent warriors to wards of the government, in a role that won him the hatred and resentment of the young men always eager to resume their traditional ways and violently resist assimilation. The irony of his position is that he was never as respected by his own people as he was by the whites, who credited him with far more authority than he ever possessed in the Sioux tribal structure.

Near the end of his life he followed another white practice by writing his autobiography, which was regarded suspiciously by scholars until 1994, when it was finally authenticated. In it he apologized for his mistakes while trying to justify his actions. It covers the majority of the 19th century from the perspective of one who was at the center of the action, making it an extremely valuable document in Native American history. Red Cloud died on December 10, 1909, at the advanced age of 87 or 88, a tragic yet noble figure forced to live in two worlds for most of his life. To his eternal credit, having agreed to cease violent resistance in 1868, he honored his word for the next 40 years.

Carl Schurz (1829–1906)

Often lost in the shadow of more famous 19th-century immigrant business and labor leaders the German-born Carl Schurz made his mark in politics and the military. He became a lifelong champion of liberty and democracy.

He was born in north Germany into a strongly Protestant middle-class family and attended university, where he was bitten early by the liberal and nationalist bugs. He enthusiastically joined the liberal revolution of 1848 against the Prussian monarchy, and when that failed he fled abroad. In an incident that revealed both his bravery and his loyalty, he returned just long enough to free a friend and mentor from prison. He spent the next three years roaming Europe as an exile until two decisions in 1852 changed his life forever: He married a wealthy German heiress and emigrated to the United States. The former set him up financially in his new country, and the latter gave him a new stage on which to display his liberal reform convictions. In the United States he tried his hand first at business, but failing in that he became a journalist, an occupation he had first practiced in Europe. It did not hurt that he had become fluent, even eloquent, in English, and for the rest of his life he spoke and wrote English with a facility that most native speakers could only envy. Journalism became not just a way to earn a living but his ticket into politics, the field in which his true interest lay. When he settled in Wisconsin in 1856, he quickly made himself the spokesman for the state's large German community. He made a public stand against slavery, which violated his convictions about liberty and free enterprise, and joined the nascent Republican Party. He quickly established himself as such a strong party man and effective campaigner that he was vetted for the state's highest offices and then installed as chairman of the Wisconsin delegation to the Republican National Convention in 1860. He went to Chicago as a William Seward supporter but soon switched to Abraham Lincoln and was rewarded after the latter became president by an appointment as minister to Spain.

Schurz was too much a man of action to remain out of the arena for long. In early 1862 he returned to the United States to become a liaison for German Americans in the North and an unofficial adviser to the Lincoln administration. He did not hurt his own cause by becoming an early convert to emancipation as a war aim. Trading his frock coat for a uniform, he accepted an appointment as a brigadier general attached to the XI Corps in the Army of the Potomac. He fought well enough in the summer and fall of 1862 to be promoted to major general, but his military career suffered after that. He was first tarred with some of the command errors at Chancellorsville and Gettysburg, then shipped to the Western Theater, where he was unjustly accused of incompetence and removed from field command. He finished the war as General Henry Slocum's chief of staff in North Carolina. While his military career seemed stuck in reverse, he kept his political fences mended, working for Lincoln's reelection in 1864.

When Lincoln was assassinated in April 1865, Schurz tried to transfer his loyalty to Andrew Johnson, even making a tour of inspection of the defeated South for the new president. His subsequent report warned of Southern intransigence to Reconstruction and led to a complete break with Johnson. He left government service and returned to work as a newspaperman in 1866. Because of his influence in the large ethnic German community, he was not out of politics long; he was elected chairman and keynote speaker of the 1868 Republican National Convention, which nominated Ulysses Grant for president. He campaigned for Grant and for a U.S. Senate seat for himself. The state legislature bestowed the seat on him in 1869, and he entered Congress as the "Dutch Senator." Although he had been a Republican almost since the beginning, he broke with his party over the corruption of the Grant administration and helped organize the Liberal Republican splinter group dedicated to civil service reform and reconciliation with the South. Their cause failed at the polls, taking Schurz down with it. He lost his Senate seat in 1875 but returned to Washington, D.C., with Rutherford B. Hayes after the election of 1876. He was appointed secretary of the interior, in which position he at last had leverage to effect some of the reforms he cherished: fair treatment for the Indians, merit promotions (as opposed to the spoils system), and conservation of natural resources. He also managed to ruffle many feathers among conservative Republicans, and in 1881 he returned to private life, taking over the editor's chair at the *New York Evening Post*. In the last two decades of his life he continued to speak out for political reform, leading national organizations for civil service reform and even supporting the Democrat Grover Cleveland for president in 1884 and William Jennings Bryan for president in 1900. He found new causes late in life, opposing imperialism in the 1890s and Jim Crow practices after the turn of the century, both of which characteristically put him at odds with large numbers of his fellow Americans. (He had become a naturalized citizen in 1857.) He put his pen to work opposing the Spanish-American War and the annexation of overseas territories, writing editorials in *Harper's Weekly* and speaking out publicly. He continued to act as a political independent, supporting Democrats or Republicans on the basis of their stands on the issues Schurz considered important.

Between politics and journalism he also found time in his later years to write extensively, focusing on essays, biography, and his own *Reminiscences.* This gave him the chance to tell his version of history and cast himself in the role of lonely paladin of liberty. He died in New York City on May 19, 1906, at the dawn of the Progressive era, which brought many of the reforms that he had championed for so many years.

Unlike many men, he lived long enough to see some of his ideals realized: a strong, ethnically diverse nation dedicated to achieving a more equitable society. Carl Schurz was more than an idealist; he was equal parts patriot and politician. But even more than as a reformer or idealist, Schurz's principal importance was as an openly ethnic representative in 19th-century American politics. At a time when German Americans were either demeaned or despised, Schurz was a respected spokesman and a model of success. The fact that his liberalism was of the elitist, Old World variety that cared little for the individual victim of oppression did not detract from his stature as a genuine reformer who worked diligently to improve the U.S. system and achieve the melting pot ideal.

Sojourner Truth (ca. 1797–1883)

A self-educated African-American woman, Sojourner Truth was a combination of religious mystic and crusading reformer who became a legend in her own lifetime.

Sojourner Truth was born Isabella Baumfree in Ulster County, New York, in either 1797 or 1799 (sources are unclear.) A slave, she was passed around as a child among several abusive masters. At the age of 13 she had her first child, and in the next 17 years she had four more, all with the same father, a slave named Thomas. In 1827 she ran away from her master and was sheltered by Isaac Van Wagener, a Quaker, who purchased her freedom for her. In return she took his name as a free woman. Her first battle with the system occurred when she filed suit to recover her small son, who had been sold illegally into slavery in the South. In her ensuing legal battle she was assisted by newfound Quaker friends. Two years after gaining her freedom she settled in New York City with her two youngest children, supporting the family by working as a domestic servant. There is no record that Thomas, the father of her children, was a part of the family.

She was already hearing voices and seeing visions when she began street preaching with a fellow mystic, Elijah Pierson. She preached a nondenominational message and led gospel songs in a strong voice. Her close association with Pierson and some other unsavory religious cult leaders tarnished her reputation and led her to withdraw from public preaching for several years, but in 1843 she received a vision to change her name to Sojourner Truth (literal translation: "itinerant preacher") and resume her itinerant preaching. She was a striking woman: tall, gaunt, and muscular as a result of her years as a slave laborer, with eyes that flashed fire when she spoke about God in her heavily Dutch-inflected African English. She was illiterate but spoke with a simple eloquence that was mesmerizing whether in debates or in camp meetings. She described her speeches and sermons as "testifyin'," and she did resemble in many ways an Old Testament prophet. One of her modern biographers has called her "God's Faithful Pilgrim." Her travels through New England in 1843 put her in contact with the abolitionist movement for the first time, and she became an eager convert. By the time she turned her face westward around 1850, she had become a celebrity, and as she toured Ohio, Indiana, Missouri, and Kansas, great crowds turned out to hear the famous preacher woman. Some came to ridicule and malign her, and she was even physically assaulted on more than occasion. Because of her hard features and masculine build, she was accused of being a man in women's clothing. In answer to her critics she once bared her breasts on stage in a famous episode that did not hush the critics but won her even more fame. About this same time she also dictated her autobiography to Olive Gilbert, and it was published in 1850 as the *Narrative of Sojourner Truth.* She sold copies at every stop in her travels. In the following years it would have numerous reprintings, plus a second, expanded edition in 1878. It was also in 1850 that she became a convert to the nascent women's rights movement. She now had three great causes to preach: God's love, abolitionism, and women's rights. With her revival meetings and issue-oriented conventions she maintained a full schedule of speaking appearances.

In the mid-1850s she moved her family to Battle Creek, Michigan, which she called home for the rest of her life. When the Civil War began in 1861 she went on the road again to raise support for black regiments being enlisted for service in the Union Army. Her efforts caught the eye of Abraham Lincoln, and the Republicans, as a result, paid her train fare east to meet the president and to assume the role of unofficial adviser to the Freedmen's Relief Association. After the war she advocated the migration of African Americans to the West, where there were greater opportunity and plenty of public land for freed men to begin a new life. She continued to travel across the length and breadth of the country to deliver her message, which had grown again when she added temperance to her portfolio of causes. Paradoxically most of her audiences were whites rather than members of her own race, because whites still had the power to effect change and the sheer numbers to pack the house at every appearance on her schedule.

In 1875 she retired to Battle Creek, nearing 80 years old, her once tough constitution failing the demands of her fiery spirit. Even in retirement she did not drop out of sight but continued to attract admirers and the curious, who traveled to her home to see her. Long before she died on November 26, 1883, she had become an icon and a heroine to the causes she had so long fought for. Her legacy is difficult to assess. She was certainly one of a kind, even among the numerous eccentric utopians and single-minded reformers of the mid-19th century. As an agent for change she was not significant. Her solid accomplishments were far outshone by her colorful personality and celebrity status. She was a romantic figure in a romantic age that was equally fascinated by other visionaries such as John Brown and Joseph Smith. She is also a prime example of the transforming power of myth: In the 20th century feminists and black civil rights activists would make her a patron saint of their causes, filling in the many gaps in her story with fables and pointed allegories. Long after her death the modest facts of her life became blended with legends, many of which she created herself in her public speeches, for instance, claiming a biblical span of 40 years of her life spent in slavery, which was actually 30 years. But the hold of this simple 19th-century evangelist on the 20th-century mind is undeniable. Her dramatic battle cry "And a'n't I a woman?" is often included in the same exalted category as Martin Luther King, Jr.'s, "I have a dream" declaration. As another of her numerous biographers has said, "The ex-slave . . . has become the emblematic nineteenth-century black woman and the symbol of the conjunction of sex and race."

William Marcy Tweed (1823–1878)

William Tweed was the 19th century's most notorious example of the corrupt big-city politician. As the "boss" of Tammany Hall he virtually ran New York City, in the process proving that white-collar crime was less dangerous and a lot more lucrative than bank or stagecoach robbery.

Tweed was a native New Yorker, the son of a chair maker, who had only an elementary school education. At the age of 11 he was apprenticed to a saddle maker, but his intelligence and ambition made him restless. He studied bookkeeping and went to work as a clerk. He also organized his own volunteer fire company, an act that was often the first step into urban politics in the 19th century. The tiger head that he had painted on his fire engine later became the symbol of the Tammany Hall machine. His first political office was as an alderman on the city council, which he won on his second try with a little typical chicanery. He was in his element because the New York City Council was known as "The Forty Thieves." His subsequent career in state and local politics veered up and down. He began assembling the so-called Tweed Ring in 1857, when he maneuvered three friends into the district attorney's, recorder's, and county clerk's offices while he himself was school commissioner. In the years that followed he built up his power base even while moving back and forth between the public and private sectors. Along the way he opened a law office without ever having studied law, earned a fortune through his various schemes, and spent a fortune paying off friends and opponents alike.

His power base was founded on the control of four offices that he held personally throughout most of his career: Democratic county chairman, school commissioner, assistant street commissioner, and president of the Board of Supervisors. Individually none of these offices was as important as mayor or alderman, but together they placed him at the center of city politics. His power was always exercised behind the scenes. The highest elective office he held at the height of his power was chief of the Department of Public Works. It did not hurt that he also had most of the big railroads on his side. The final piece of the puzzle fell into place in 1868, when he took over control of the local Democratic Party machine as "Grand Sachem" of Tammany Hall. It was an unelected position, but the most powerful position in New York politics because it controlled the party that controlled city government.

Over the span of 15 years the Tweed legend was created. He stitched together a coalition of immigrants, factory workers, and urban poor to create an effective voting bloc that was able to frustrate reformers and political opponents. The Tweed Ring bestowed selective favors in return for votes and financial considerations. His political reach extended all the way to Albany and the state government. He used kickbacks, patronage, graft, and bribery as his tools of the trade. His objective was a simple power grab undisguised by noble rhetoric or high political principles. He could as easily have been a Whig or a Know-Nothing as a Democrat. The major boondoggle of his reign was the building of the new county courthouse, which finally cost $12 million, $8 million of that in outright graft. One workman crony of Tweed's was paid $50,000 a day for 30 days for plastering! In 1869 his power was so secure that he decreed that all state billings to New York City include a 50 percent surcharge for graft—which he later upped to 85 percent! It was the brazen pronouncement of a man who was untouchable.

He was eventually taken down not by a rival politician or a crime-busting district attorney but by a newspaper cartoonist, Thomas Nast, and that too is part of the legend. Nast skewered the Tweed Ring in a series of editorial cartoons that were simple enough for the masses to understand but revealing enough to embarrass "the Boss." Tweed first tried to buy off the cartoonist, then to intimidate him into silence. None of it worked as public outrage toward the corrupt politicians mounted.

In 1872 Tweed's luck ran out when he was caught in a scandal that exposed his dealings. Even hardened New Yorkers could not ignore. Indicted and convicted, he was sentenced to prison for 12 years. Rather than do hard time, he fled the country to Cuba and thence to Spain, where the Spanish government agreed to extradite him back to the United States. Locked up behind bars finally, he tried to made a deal with the authorities to name names and reveal where the skeletons were hidden, but his star had set. He died in prison, a broken man at 55. Justice had triumphed, however belatedly.

CHAPTER 14 Education

Literacy

During this period education became widely available for the mass of American people and for the first time became a national issue. The change can be tracked statistically. Literacy rates were one of the statistics that the U.S. government carefully gathered, and those figures painted a very rosy picture of U.S. schooling, with the qualification that the literacy rate was higher in free states than in slave states if slaves were included in the count. (If free blacks were counted, the literacy rate would have been only about 1 percent lower.) But inclusive or exclusive of slaves, U.S. literacy was indeed something to be proud of, as even the lowest-ranked state in 1840 (South Carolina) still had a higher literacy rate than that of European nations that were accustomed to bragging about their superior civilization.

The national "rate of illiteracy" among Americans, which is the way the government preferred to count it, peaked in 1840 at 11 percent. Thereafter, it fell steadily until 1860, despite the massive influx of European immigrants with little or no education in those years. In the decade from 1860 to 1870 illiteracy actually increased; the increase was attributable to the Civil War coupled with changes in the Census Bureau's statistical methodology. Specifically the bureau in 1870 began differentiating between adults (21 and older) and juveniles (younger than age 21) in determining literacy. That same year also saw a distinction for the first time between writing versus reading literacy; formerly, the two had been lumped together. The new distinctions were a sign of the importance the government attached to the issue of literacy. Much of that concern can be directly attributable to official thinking that a modern industrial society required an educated people to run it. High literacy therefore was more important than rivalries among "civilized" nations; it was a basic measure of national economic well-being.

TABLE 14.1 LITERACY RATES BY STATE, RANKED FROM LOWEST TO HIGHEST LITERACY, 1840

State	Percentage of Literate Residents
N.C.	72
Tenn.	76
Ark.	78
Ga.	80
S.C.	81
Va.	81
Del.	82
Ala.	82
Ky.	83
Mo.	85
Ind.	85
Ill.	86
Miss.	88
Fla.	90
Md.	92
La.	94
Iowa	94
Ohio	94
Pa.	95
N.Y.	96
N.J.	96
R.I.	97
Mich.	98
Vt.	98
Maine	99
Mass.	99
N.H.	99.4
Conn.	99.7

Note: The Census Bureau counted both slave and free, male and female, in this statistic, making no distinctions. The effect of this statistical methodology was to lower the literacy rate significantly in southern states with large slave populations and to lower it across the board in every state since females were typically less educated than males at this time in U.S. history.
Source: Harvey J. Graff, *The Legacies of Literacy* (Bloomington: Indiana University Press, 1987), 343.

TABLE 14.2 ILLITERACY IN THE UNITED STATES, 1850

State or Territory	Total Illiterate Population	Native-Born Illiterate Population	Foreign-Born Illiterate Population	White Illiterate Population		Black Illiterate Population	
				Male	Female	Male	Female
Ala.	33,992	33,853	139	13,163	20,594	108	127
Ark.	16,935	16,908	27	6,810	10,000	61	55
Calif.	5,235	2,318	2,917	4,237	881	88	29
Conn.	5,306	1,293	4,013	2,037	2,702	292	275
Del.	10,181	9,777	404	2,012	2,524	2,724	2,921
Fla.	4,129	3,834	295	1,736	2,123	116	154
Ga.	41,667	41,261	406	16,552	24,648	208	259
Ill.	41,283	35,336	5,947	16,633	23,421	605	624
Ind.	72,710	69,445	3,265	26,132	44,408	1,024	1,146
Iowa	8,153	7,076	1,077	2,928	5,192	15	18
Ky.	69,706	67,359	2,347	27,754	38,933	1,431	1,588
La.	24,610	18,339	6,271	9,842	11,379	1,038	2,351
Maine	6,282	2,154	4,148	3,259	2,888	77	58
Md.	41,877	38,426	3,451	8,557	12,258	9,422	11,640
Mass.	28,345	1,861	26,484	11,578	15,961	375	431
Mich.	8,281	5,272	3,009	4,037	3,875	201	168
Miss.	13,528	13,447	81	5,522	7,883	75	48
Mo.	36,778	34,917	1,861	14,458	21,823	271	226
N.H.	3,009	945	2,064	1,662	1,295	26	26
N.J.	18,665	12,787	5,878	6,007	8,241	2,167	2,250
N.Y.	98,722	30,670	68,052	39,178	52,115	3,387	4,042
N.C.	80,423	80,083	340	26,239	47,327	3,099	3,758
Ohio	66,020	56,958	9,062	22,994	38,036	2,366	2,624
Pa.	76,272	51,283	24,989	24,380	42,548	4,115	5,229
R.I.	3,607	1,248	2,359	1,330	2,010	130	137
S.C.	16,564	16,460	104	5,897	9,787	421	459
Tenn.	78,619	78,114	505	28,469	49,053	506	591
Tex.	10,583	8,095	2,488	4,988	5,537	34	24
Vt.	6,242	616	5,624	3,601	2,588	32	19
Va.	88,520	87,383	1,137	30,244	46,761	5,141	6,374
Wis.	6,453	1,551	4,902	2,930	3,431	55	37
Washington, D.C.	4,671	4,349	322	601	856	1,106	2,108
Arizona Territory	N/A	N/A	N/A	N/A	N/A	N/A	N/A
Colorado Territory	N/A	N/A	N/A	N/A	N/A	N/A	N/A
Dakota Territory	N/A	N/A	N/A	N/A	N/A	N/A	N/A
Idaho Territory	N/A	N/A	N/A	N/A	N/A	N/A	N/A
Kansas Territory	N/A	N/A	N/A	N/A	N/A	N/A	N/A
Minnesota Territory	649	259	390	389	260	N/A	N/A
Montana Territory	N/A	N/A	N/A	N/A	N/A	N/A	N/A
Nebraska Territory	N/A	N/A	N/A	N/A	N/A	N/A	N/A
Nevada Territory	N/A	N/A	N/A	N/A	N/A	N/A	N/A
New Mexico Territory	25,089	24,429	660	13,334	11,751	2	2
Oregon Territory	162	99	63	86	71	3	2
Utah Territory	154	121	33	88	65	1	N/A
Washington Territory	N/A	N/A	N/A	N/A	N/A	N/A	N/A
Wyoming Territory	N/A	N/A	N/A	N/A	N/A	N/A	N/A
United States (Total)	1,053,420	858,306	195,114	389,664	573,234	40,722	49,800

Note: Figures are for both reading- and writing-deficient, by race, national origin, and gender, for all states and territories reporting. No distinction is made in this count between adults and juveniles, nor between any races but white and black. N/A (not available) indicates territories that did not report illiteracy rates in general or in a specific category as indicated.
Source U.S. Census Office, *A Compendium of the Ninth Census (1870)* (Washington, D.C.: U.S. Government Printing Office, 1872), 459.

TABLE 14.3 ILLITERACY IN THE UNITED STATES, 1860

State or Territory	Total Illiterate Population	Native-Born Illiterate Population	Foreign-Born Illiterate Population	White Illiterate Population		Black Illiterate Population	
				Male	Female	Male	Female
Ala.	38,060	37,302	758	14,517	23,088	192	263
Ark.	23,665	23,587	78	9,379	14,263	10	13
Calif.	19,693	11,509	8,184	11,835	7,154	497	207
Conn.	8,833	925	7,908	3,405	5,083	181	164
Del.	13,169	11,503	1,666	2,838	3,823	3,056	3,452
Fla.	5,461	5,150	311	2,378	2,963	48	72
Ga.	44,257	43,550	707	16,900	26,784	255	318
Ill.	59,364	39,748	19,616	24,786	33,251	632	695
Ind.	62,716	55,903	6,813	24,297	36,646	869	904
Iowa	19,951	12,903	7,048	7,806	11,976	92	77
Ky.	70,040	65,749	4,291	28,742	38,835	1,113	1,350
La.	19,010	15,679	3,331	8,051	9,757	485	717
Maine	8,598	2,386	6,212	4,282	3,270	25	21
Md.	37,518	33,780	3,738	7,290	8,529	9,904	11,795
Mass.	46,921	2,004	44,917	16,969	29,293	291	368
Mich.	18,485	8,171	10,315	8,596	8,845	558	486
Minn.	4,763	1,055	3,708	2,382	2,369	6	6
Miss.	15,636	15,136	500	6,256	9,270	50	60
Mo.	60,545	51,173	9,372	24,255	35,405	371	514
N.H.	4,717	1,093	3,624	2,023	2,660	15	19
N.J.	23,081	12,937	10,144	8,436	10,840	1,720	2,085
N.Y.	121,878	26,163	95,715	47,703	68,262	2,653	3,260
N.C.	74,977	74,877	100	26,024	42,104	3,067	3,782
Ohio	64,828	48,015	16,813	23,297	35,345	2,995	3,190
Oreg.	1,511	1,200	311	762	737	7	5
Pa.	81,515	44,930	36,585	27,560	44,596	3,893	5,466
R.I.	6,112	1,202	4,910	2,057	3,795	119	141
S.C.	16,208	15,792	416	5,811	8,981	633	783
Tenn.	72,054	69,262	2,792	27,358	43,001	743	952
Tex.	18,476	11,832	6,644	8,514	9,900	25	37
Vt.	8,916	933	7,983	4,467	4,402	27	20
Va.	86,452	83,300	3,152	31,178	42,877	5,489	6,908
Wis.	16,546	2,663	13,883	7,465	8,983	53	45
Washington, D.C.	6,881	4,860	2,021	1,258	2,248	1,151	2,224
Arizona Territory	N/A	N/A	N/A	N/A	N/A	N/A	N/A
Colorado Territory	N/A	N/A	N/A	N/A	N/A	N/A	N/A
Dakota Territory	77	60	17	62	15	N/A	N/A
Idaho Territory	N/A	N/A	N/A	N/A	N/A	N/A	N/A
Kansas Territory	3,067	2,695	372	1,228	1,776	25	38
Montana Territory	N/A	N/A	N/A	N/A	N/A	N/A	N/A
Nebraska Territory	634	357	277	317	304	6	7
Nevada Territory	150	40	110	138	5	6	1
New Mexico Territory	32,785	31,626	1,159	16,008	16,750	12	15
Utah Territory	323	162	161	98	225	N/A	N/A
Washington Territory	438	207	231	295	142	1	N/A
Wyoming Territory	N/A	N/A	N/A	N/A	N/A	N/A	N/A
United States (Total)	1,218,311	871,418	346,893	467,023	659,552	41,275	50,461

Note: Figures are for both reading- and writing-deficient, by race, national origin, and gender, for all states and territories reporting. No distinction is made in this count between adults and juveniles, nor between any races except white and black. N/A (not available) indicates territories that did not report illiteracy rates in general or in a specific category, as indicated.
Source: U.S. Census Office, *A Compendium of the Ninth Census (1870)* (Washington, D.C.: U.S. Government Printing Office, 1872), 458.

TABLE 14.4 ILLITERACY IN THE UNITED STATES, 1870

State or Territory	Total Illiterate Population	Native-Born Illiterate Population	Foreign-Born Illiterate Population	White Illiterate Population		Black Illiterate Population		Chinese Illiterate Population		Indian Illiterate Population[a]	
				Male	Female	Male	Female	Male	Female	Male	Female
Ala.	383,012	382,142	870	40,285	51,774	141,024	149,874	N/A	N/A	23	32
Ark.	133,339	133,043	296	28,298	35,797	34,896	34,326	4	N/A	8	10
Calif.	31,716	9,520	22,196	14,633	11,525	522	394	2,331	522	957	832
Conn.	29,616	5,678	23,938	11,595	16,318	779	896	N/A	N/A	9	19
Del.	23,100	20,631	2,469	5,229	6,051	5,744	6,076	N/A	N/A	N/A	N/A
Fla.	71,803	63,090	8,713	8,713	10,191	25,953	26,941	N/A	N/A	5	N/A
Ga.	468,593	467,503	1,090	54,843	70,096	165,210	178,427	N/A	N/A	7	10
Ill.	133,584	90,595	42,989	54,571	69,053	4,924	5,026	N/A	N/A	5	5
Ind.	127,124	113,185	13,939	49,238	69,523	4,079	4,179	N/A	N/A	42	63
Iowa	45,671	24,979	20,692	20,227	23,918	738	786	N/A	N/A	N/A	2
Kans.	24,550	20,449	4,101	8,796	8,182	3,563	3,650	N/A	N/A	146	213
Ky.	332,176	324,945	7,231	94,302	106,775	62,937	68,113	N/A	N/A	6	37
La.	276,158	268,773	7,385	23,888	26,861	109,463	115,530	41	1	194	180
Maine	19,052	7,986	11,066	9,545	9,329	99	74	N/A	N/A	2	3
Md.	135,499	126,907	8,592	20,640	26,152	41,341	47,362	1	N/A	1	2
Mass.	97,742	7,912	89,830	36,148	59,428	927	1,221	2	N/A	8	8
Mich.	53,127	22,547	30,580	25,244	23,405	1,354	1,301	N/A	N/A	791	1,032
Minn.	24,413	5,558	18,855	11,177	12,764	57	45	N/A	N/A	178	192
Miss.	313,310	312,483	827	22,978	25,050	128,102	136,800	16	N/A	169	195
Mo.	222,411	206,827	15,584	77,044	84,719	28,721	31,901	N/A	N/A	10	16
Nebr.	4,861	3,552	1,309	2,440	2,190	124	81	N/A	N/A	10	16
Nev.	872	98	774	502	151	15	6	185	13	N/A	N/A
N.H.	9,926	1,992	7,934	4,529	5,362	52	43	N/A	N/A	N/A	N/A
N.J.	54,687	29,726	24,961	19,615	26,771	3,794	4,503	N/A	N/A	2	2
N.Y.	239,271	70,702	168,569	92,118	136,306	4,868	5,862	13	2	45	57
N.C.	397,690	397,573	117	68,735	97,662	111,323	119,283	N/A	N/A	284	403
Ohio	173,172	134,102	39,070	65,071	87,312	10,177	10,589	N/A	N/A	9	14
Oreg.	4,427	3,003	1,424	1,818	1,653	55	35	775	33	39	79
Pa.	222,356	126,803	95,553	75,589	130,869	6,878	9,015	N/A	N/A	2	3
R.I.	21,921	4,444	17,477	8,901	12,730	380	490	N/A	N/A	6	14
S.C.	290,379	289,726	653	25,200	29,967	112,046	123,115	N/A	N/A	20	28
Tenn.	364,697	362,955	1,742	74,562	104,165	88,644	97,308	N/A	N/A	9	9
Tex.	221,703	203,334	18,369	35,820	35,075	74,628	75,989	N/A	N/A	114	77
Vt.	17,706	3,902	13,804	9,219	8,365	64	52	N/A	N/A	3	3
Va.	445,893	444,623	1,270	57,486	6,052	153,792	168,444	1	N/A	51	67
W.Va.	81,490	78,389	3,101	31,693	39,800	4,891	5,106	N/A	N/A	N/A	N/A
Wis.	55,441	14,113	41,328	25,444	29,401	222	138	N/A	N/A	98	135
Washington, D.C.	28,719	26,501	2,218	1,730	3,146	9,688	14,155	N/A	N/A	N/A	N/A
Arizona Territory	2,753	262	2,491	1,586	1,143	1	N/A	N/A	5	7	11
Colorado Territory	6,823	6,568	255	3,286	3,278	80	66	N/A	N/A	34	79
Dakota Territory	1563	758	805	463	411	10	21	N/A	N/A	269	349
Idaho Territory	3,388	138	3,250	341	145	6	10	2,792	80	9	5
Montana Territory	918	394	524	497	146	38	30	119	10	19	59
New Mexico Territory	52,220	49,311	2,909	23,378	27,762	70	36	N/A	N/A	331	640
Utah Territory	7,363	3,334	4,029	3199	3,898	10	12	209	6	13	16

State or Territory	Total Illiterate Population	Native-Born Illiterate Population	Foreign-Born Illiterate Population	White Illiterate Population		Black Illiterate Population		Chinese Illiterate Population		Indian Illiterate Population[a]	
				Male	Female	Male	Female	Male	Female	Male	Female
Washington Territory	1,307	804	503	512	271	37	12	N/A	N/A	92	358
Wyoming Territory	602	266	336	362	119	37	12	33	1	8	30
United States (Total)	5,658,144	4,880,271	777,873	1,250,970	1,600,941	1,342,347	1,447,351	6,527	668	4,044	5,305

Note: Figures are for writing-deficient only by race, national origin, and gender, for all states and territories reporting. No distinction is made in this count between adults and juveniles; the figures given include everyone 10 years of age and older. N/A (not available) is used in place of zero (0) when a state or territory does not report an illiteracy rate in a particular category because we cannot determine today whether there were no resident members of that group living there, there was no (0) illiteracy in the group, or the group was considered too insignificant to be counted. In the case of such hard-to-count populations as African Americans and Native Americans, it is more likely that there was not a full accounting than that there were no members of that group in the population or there was a zero illiteracy rate.

[a] The Native American count includes only those living on reservations, which in many areas of the West was only a small percentage of the total Native American population.

Source: U.S. Census Office, *A Compendium of the Ninth Census (1870)* (Washington, D.C.: U.S. Government Printing Office, 1872), 456–57.

Primary and Secondary Education

The spirit of Jacksonian democracy, which had flourished since the 1820s, caused an educational "awakening" similar to what occurred in U.S. religious life. In the North and the West at least, the right to a "free" public education was seen as a civil right second only to the right to vote, and Southerners gradually came to accept this point of view before the end of the era. As in so many matters, slavery had been the stumbling block.

Compared to other Western nations, the United States already had a highly educated people by 1850, although most Americans stopped with the "three Rs" ("readin', writin', and 'rithmetic"). The little red schoolhouse was a cherished institution for primary schooling. The primary grades, one through eight, were widely regarded as the only essential education a boy needed to make his way in the world, and girls needed even less according to conventional wisdom. Secondary education started with the ninth grade and progressed through 12th grade, representing four years of "advanced" education. Since the 1820s Americans had used the term *high school* for those years, borrowing the terminology from the Scots. Gradually over the next three decades high school was incorporated into the U.S. educational system, replacing the elite "academy" as the preferred form of secondary schooling. But it was not until 1874, after a Michigan Supreme Court decision, that tax-supported high schools were recognized as legitimate public enterprises.

Even with legal recognition secondary schooling was still seen as unnecessary or a luxury for most students, who tended to go to work on the farm or in the factory or apprentice themselves to one of the trades after the eighth grade anyway. In 1860 with a population of 31.4 million people there were only about 300 secondary schools in the entire country, and only a third of those were publicly supported.

The first figures available for the numbers of students and teachers in U.S. public schools are from the 1870 Census, with enumeration of students carried over to the next year. U.S. officials were decades behind their British counterparts in gathering such statistics. Between 1870 and 1875 figures on the number of teachers, but not the numbers of students, were gathered annually, so it is necessary to go to 1880 to have an idea of the amount of growth in the U.S. public school system.

TABLE 14.5 NUMBERS OF PUPILS AND TEACHERS IN U.S. PUBLIC SCHOOLS, 1870–1880

Year	Primary School Pupils	Secondary School Pupils	Teachers (All Schools)
1870	N/A	N/A	201,000
1871	7,481,000	80,000	220,000
1872	N/A	N/A	230,000
1873	N/A	N/A	238,000
1874	N/A	N/A	248,000
1875	N/A	N/A	258,000
1880	9,757,000	110,000	287,000

Source: B. R. Mitchell, *International Historical Statistics: The Americas and Australasia* (Detroit: Gale Research, 1983), J1.

Colleges and Universities

Colleges and universities were even more rare than secondary schools and generally regarded as either elitist institutions for the privileged classes or sectarian training academies for soul savers. This attitude began to change after the Civil War as agricultural and mechanical colleges and technical institutes multiplied alongside the older liberal arts and church schools. Higher education was not even a viable option for 98 percent of Americans in the 19th century. Before the Civil War no more than 2 percent of the 17 to 22-year-old population attended college, and this percentage would remain constant until the 1880s. Apart from the expense of additional schooling beyond the secondary level, one reason higher education had so little appeal is that it was seen as superfluous, focusing as it did on the antiquated liberal arts curriculum of Latin, philosophy, mathematics, and history. The only exception were the schools devoted to religious instruction, both the venerable institutions from colonial times and the new wave of evangelical training schools that appeared in the first half of the 19th century. For many years higher education as a practical course of study was seen as relevant only for would-be ministers of the church, that is, advanced theological studies. Harvard College was founded on that concept in 1636. By 1860 some 200 colleges had been founded by various denominations to train preachers and missionaries; church-affiliated institutions continued to attract their share of both students and financial support in the second half of the century, including such outstanding institutions as Boston College, for Catholics (1863) and Hebrew Union College, for Jews (1875).

Surprisingly in relation to such a small pool of college-bound students, there were many colleges and universities around the country in the mid-19th century, most with no more than a few dozen students, tenuous funding, and complete lack of visibility outside their local community. For instance, Catholics alone opened 88 new colleges and universities between 1850 and 1875 in such places as Ellicott's Mills, Maryland; Elizabethtown, Kentucky; and Pass Christian, Mississippi. Only 24 of those schools are still in operation today, not including the three just mentioned. For the rest, the year of founding has long since been forgotten in some cases, and in others even the exact name of the institution is lost. Methodists and Presbyterians were also busy opening colleges, believing "If you build it, they will come." So many colleges came and went, it is impossible to compile a comprehensive list. They sprang up and after a few years withered and died, but they proliferated because college was not an option for most students, and because a combination of provincialism and local boost-

The University of Alabama's first home was the four-story Woods Hall, shown here as it appeared when it opened in 1868. The all-male student body lived, dined, studied, and attended classes all in the same building. Crowding was hardly a problem because there were only 180 students. (This lithograph was made more to record the rare snowfall than to picture the school.) (Alabama Department of Archives and History, Montgomery, Alabama)

erism made countless small communities want to have their own college just as they had their own public schools. If a college education was an impossible dream for most Americans, having a hometown college was no more daunting for a little town than having a one-room schoolhouse and scarcely required more of an investment. Modern concerns such as accreditation and endowment were non-issues. One tends to think of the venerable Ivy League schools when one thinks of early colleges and universities in the United States, but there were few budding Harvards and Yales in the ranks of start-ups at this time. Many schools had a faculty of two or three and a political or sectarian agenda that completely overshadowed their academic mission. Wheaton College was a station on the underground railroad in the antebellum years, and both Oberlin College (Oberlin, Ohio) and Lane College (Galesburg, Illinois) had strong abolitionist ties. The attrition rate among such institution tended to be high, as changing political climate or flagging religious zeal caused their support to dry up. State universities and nationally recognized institutions were new at this time and represented only a fraction of the new colleges. Even with the shake-out that followed, there were still a remarkable number of additions to the ranks of institutions of higher education in these years.

As for U.S. primary and secondary schools, statistical records for institutions of higher education are fragmentary for these years. The best source (virtually the *only* source) is the census, but that gives a clear picture only at decennial intervals. To derive some idea of the growth in U.S. higher education during these years, it is necessary to include the 1840 and 1880 census figures.

TABLE 14.6 STATISTICAL PROFILE OF HIGHER EDUCATION IN THE UNITED STATES, 1840–1880

Year	Number of Institutions	Number of Professors/ Instructors	Number of Students Enrolled
1840	173	N/A	16,233
1850	234	1,651	27,159
1860	467	2,895	56,120
1870	N/A	N/A	52,000
1871	426	4,125	53,130
1880	N/A	N/A	116,000

Note: N/A (not available) indicates that the numbers of institutions, professors, or students is unknown.
Sources: Joseph R. Conlin, *The American Past,* vol. 2 (New York: Harcourt Brace Jovanovich, 1984), 581; B. R. Mitchell, *International Historical Statistics: The Americas and Australasia* (Detroit: Gale Research, 1983), J2.

TABLE 14.7 MAJOR PUBLIC AND PRIVATE COLLEGES AND UNIVERSITIES FOUNDED IN THE UNITED STATES, 1850–1875

College or University	Date(s) Founded/Existence	Location	Founder(s) and/or First President
Urbana University	1850	Urbana, Ohio	Milo G. Williams, first dean
University of Rochester	1850	Rochester, N.Y.	Baptist Church; M. B. Anderson, first president
Carroll College	1850	Waukesha, Wis.	John A. Savage, first president
College of the Pacific	1851	Santa Clara, Calif.	Methodist Church
Hope College	1851	Holland, Mich.	Dutch Reform Church (Reformed Church in America)
Wisconsin University	1851	Madison, Wis.	Henry Barnard, first chancellor
Racine College	1852	Racine, Wis.	Episcopalian Church; Roswell Park, first president
Milwaukee Female College	1852	Milwaukee, Wis.	I. A. Lapham, first president
Antioch College[a]	1852	Yellow Springs, Ohio	Christian institution; Horace Mann, first president (1852–59)
Paducah College	1852	Paducah, Ky.	M. H. Fisk, first president
Willamette University	1853	Salem, Oreg.	Methodist Church
Polytechnic College	1853	Philadelphia, Pa.	Dr. A. L. Kennedy, M.D., first president
Ohio Wesleyan University	1854	Delaware, Ohio	Methodist Church; Edward Thomson, first president
Pacific University	1854	Forest Grove, Oreg.	Presbyterian Church
Tufts College	1854	Medford, Mass.	Universalist Church; Hosea Ballou II, first president
The College of California	1855	Berkeley, Calif.	Presbyterian Church
Iowa State University	1855	Iowa City, Iowa	Amos Dean, first president
Iowa Wesleyan University	1855	Mt. Pleasant, Iowa	Methodist Church; Lucien W. Berry, first president
Santa Clara College	1855	Near San Jose, Calif.	Catholic Church; the Reverend Felix Cicaterri, first president
Berea College	1859[b]	Berea, Ky.	The Reverend John G. Fee and wealthy landowner-abolitionist Cassius M. Clay

(continued)

TABLE 14.7 (continued)

College or University	Date(s) Founded/Existence	Location	Founder(s) and/or First President
Wilberforce University	1856	Wilberforce, Ohio	African Methodist Episcopal Church[c]
Semple Broaddus	1856	Centre Hill, Miss.	Baptist Church; the Reverend William C. Crane, first president
Baker University	1858	Baldwin City, Kans.	Methodist Church
Cooper Union (for the Advancement of Science & Arts)	1859	New York, N.Y.	Peter Cooper, merchant-philanthropist
Massachusetts Institute of Technology	1861[d]	Boston, Mass.[e]	Chartered by the General Court of Commonwealth of Mass.; William Barton Rogers, first president
Vassar College for Women	1861	Poughkeepsie, N.Y.	Matthew Vassar, rich N.Y. brewer[f]
Boston College for Catholics	1863	Chestnut Hill, Mass.	Jesuit Order of Catholic Church
University of Kansas	1864[g]	Lawrence, Kans.	Amos Lawrence, philanthropist-abolitionist
Swarthmore College	May 5, 1864	Swarthmore, Pa.	Society of Friends (Quakers)
Columbia Institute for the Deaf and Blind[h]	1864	Washington, D.C.	Chartered by U.S. Congress
Fisk University	1866	Nashville, Tenn.	Union general Clinton Fisk
Augusta Institute[i]	1867	Augusta, Ga. (Springfield Baptist Church)	The Reverend William Jefferson White (with Richard C. Coulter and the Reverend Edmund Turney)
Howard Theological Seminary[j]	1867	Washington, D.C.	Union general Oliver Otis Howard (also first president)
Storer College	1867–56	Harpers Ferry, W.Va.	John Storer, philanthropist and lawyer
Hampton Institute	1868	Hampton, Va.	Union general Samuel Armstrong
Cornell University	1868	Ithaca, N.Y.	Andrew D. White, philanthropist, and Ezra Cornell, statesman-scholar
Clark College[k]	1869	Atlanta, Ga.	Methodist African-American Church
Wellesley Women's College	1870[l]	Wellesley, Mass.	Henry Fowle Durant, philanthropist
Hunter College (for Women)	1870	New York, N.Y.	Thomas Hunter, Irish immigrant and social reformer
Smith College (for women)	1871[l]	Northampton, Mass.	Sophia Smith, heiress (with the Reverend John M. Greene)
Atlanta University[m]	1865	Atlanta, Ga.	Two former slaves, who turned it over to the American Missionary Association (AMA) in 1867; AMA appointed first president, Edmund Ware
Paul Quinn College	1872	Waco, Tex.	Methodist African Episcopal Church
Brigham Young University	1875	Provo, Utah	Mormon institution
Hebrew Union College	1875	Cincinnati, Ohio	Rabbi Isaac M. Wise

Note: Trying to determine founding dates is a somewhat arbitrary exercise because different sources cite different dates, which are based on when a particular institution was chartered, when it dedicated its first building, when it opened its doors, when its first class graduated. There is also some rivalry among the partisans of various schools to be the first, second, and so on, in some significant category. Further complicating the issue is that some schools changed hands in their early years, so they cannot claim "continuous existence" since one date. The date of charter is used, here whenever that is available.

[a] The first fully coeducational college or university in the United States.

[b] Berea College began life as a grammar school in 1855 before being incorporated as a college by the Presbyterian Church in 1859. It did not have its actual first academic year until 1869.

[c] The African Methodist Episcopal (AME) Church acquired the school from its previous owners.

[d] This is the date the charter of incorporation was granted; the opening was delayed by the Civil War until 1865.

[e] The campus moved to its current location at Cambridge, Mass., in 1916.

[f] For years the students honored his memory with this irreverent song: "And so you see, to old V.C. / Our love shall never fail / Full well we know that all we owe / To Matthew Vassar's ale."

[g] First classes, 1866.

[h] Now Gallaudet University.

[i] In 1906 the name was changed to its current form, Morehouse College.

[j] Later became Howard University.

[k] Combined with Atlanta University in 1988.

[l] Both Wellesley and Smith opened their doors in 1875.

[m] Chartered by the state of Ga., Oct. 16, 1867. In 1929 Atlanta University joined Spelman University and Morehouse College in a consortium with all three maintaining their historical identity. In 1988 Atlanta University combined with Clark College to form Clark-Atlanta University.

Sources: The American Almanac and Repository of Useful Knowledge for the Year 1860, vol. 2. (Boston: Crosby, Nichols, and Company, 1860), 204–07; Gorton Carruth, *The Encyclopedia of American Facts and Dates,* 8th ed. (New York: Harper & Row, 1987), *passim;* Samuel Eliot Morrison, Henry Steele Commager, and William E. Leuchtenburg, *The Growth of the American Republic,* 6th ed., 2 vols. (New York: Oxford University Press, 1969), 806–08.

For those who had an interest in higher education but no interest in the ministry, there were the handful of great public universities. The oldest state universities were in Virginia, Georgia, and Vermont, but publicly supported schools were most numerous in the Far West and Midwest, where commitment to public education was strong and private financing weak. Michigan and Iowa (1855) set the standard, and by 1860 more than 60 percent of U.S. colleges and universities were located in the western states.

Federal Support for Higher Education

Federal support for higher education took two forms; the first was a policy of land grants to the states dating back to the Northwest Ordinance of 1787. Under this long-standing policy, two "townships" or 72 sections (46,080 acres total) were set aside for the endowment of a university in each new territory as it was organized. Originally set up just for the Old Northwest Territory, this subsequently became the standard procedure used by Congress whenever new states were admitted to the Union, and several western states benefited. Entirely separate from the "two-township" grants were the better known Morrill land grants, named for the congressman Justin Morrill of Vermont. The Morrill Act of 1862, initiated at the time of the rise of industrial America, shook up the traditional education system. It granted federal land (30,000 acres for each senator and representative) to the states to build colleges where "the industrial classes" (as opposed to the "professional classes") could learn "the agricultural and mechanical arts," but not to the exclusion of "other scientific and classical studies." This was the beginning of advanced technical schools (the famous agricultural and mechanical or "A&M" universities) in the United States. Many of the great state universities of the West and Midwest owe their existence to the Morrill Act. Some incoming states were even able to get land grants under both the Morrill Act and the two-township policy. The Morrill Act not only created a nationwide network of publicly sponsored colleges and universities, but by stipulating that academic studies be taught alongside practical subjects, guaranteed that American higher education would not follow the European model whereby the two were segregated in different schools. Thus, the college and university system was forever linked to the productive economy. Only one state school completely bypassed the entire federal land grant program: the University of Texas at Austin, founded and supported purely under state aegis in 1881.

Philanthropy

The number of colleges and universities in the United States also grew by means other than federal largesse. Industrialization was producing a new class of supermillionaires who saw both practical benefits and personal fulfillment to be gained from endowing institutions of higher learning, which repaid their philanthropy by taking the name of their benefactor. Among the more prominent, and successful, philanthropist-school connections were Cornell (1865), Drew (1866), Johns Hopkins (1867), and Vanderbilt (1872) Universities, named, respectively, for Ezra Cornell, Daniel Drew, Johns Hopkins, and Cornelius Vanderbilt.

A very unusual institution in that day and age because of both its location and the gender of its student body, the Fayetteville Female Seminary at Fayetteville, Arkansas, is shown as it appeared on November 16, 1852. Founded by Sophie Sawyer in 1839, it was dependent on philanthropic donations thereafter. (Arkansas History Commission)

Higher Education for Women

Educational opportunity was strictly divided along race and gender lines. Traditionally women were considered sufficiently educated after they had finished the primary grades. It was the rare girl who was allowed to advance into secondary school. The specious reasoning behind this was that women were by nature inferior to men both physically and intellectually. The handful of women who advanced to higher education before the Civil War were likely to attend one of the "female seminaries" or perhaps Mount Holyoke (1837) in Massachusetts. Among major universities, Iowa in 1858 became the first to open its doors to women. In the East, however, a select group of women's colleges opened with the support of wealthy benefactors—Elmira Female College (1855), Vassar College (1865)*, Smith College (1871), and Wellesley College (1870)—catered to those who intended to become professional women.

By 1870 women's opportunities in higher education had improved sufficiently to merit statistical measurement. At that time more than one in five of all students enrolled was a woman, and in the next 10 years that figure increased to more than one in three.

The first college devoted exclusively to training women for the medical profession was the Woman's Medical College of Pennsylvania, founded in 1850 and thereafter doing remarkable work at a time when most men were still going to Europe for advanced medical training. One of its prize alumnae was Dr. Mary Putnam Jacobi, who graduated in 1864 and had postgraduate studies in France, where in 1871 she became the first woman in the history of the École de Médicine to sit for regular examinations and finish with honors. She returned to the United States and built a fine medical career in the ensuing decades. In the meantime Elizabeth Blackwell, the United States's first accredited female doctor, had established a second women's medical college in 1868 in New York City.

John Crouse Memorial College for Women, part of Syracuse University, Syracuse, New York, was built in the popular neo-Gothic style of the day. (The architect was Archimedes Russell of Syracuse.) This college was part of the wave of women's colleges established during the mid-19th century. Many were started up, but many also failed, mostly for financial reasons. (sketch from *Scientific American, Architects and Builders Edition,* 1887, print from author's collection)

* Vassar was actually founded by Matthew Vassar in 1861 but because of the Civil War, did not begin operations until 1865.

TABLE 14.8 WOMEN ENROLLED IN INSTITUTIONS OF HIGHER LEARNING, 1870, 1880

Year	Women's Colleges	Coed Institutions	Total Enrollment of Women's Institutions	Women as a Percentage of All Students Enrolled
1870	6,500	4,600	11,100	21.0
1880	15,700	23,900	39,600	33.4

Source: Mabel Newcomer, *A Century of Higher Education for American Women* (New York: Harper & Row, 1959), 46.

Advanced schooling for female lawyers or ministers was even more rare because women themselves were not considered equal to men before the law or in the eyes of the church. Among older colleges and universities coeducation was practically anathema. Antioch College in Ohio was the second to admit both women and men (1853) after Oberlin Collegiate Institute, also in Ohio, had blazed the trail (1833). Most established schools, with rare exceptions, held the line against women, believing with the U.S. Supreme Court that "the paramount mission and destiny of women are to fulfill the noble and benign offices of wife and mother."

Schooling for African Americans

African Americans were even more excluded from the nation's educational system than women, and, unlike women, they were excluded on all levels. In most Southern states during the antebellum period slaves were prohibited by law from learning. This meant that reading and writing among African Americans were almost entirely limited to the minuscule free black population living in a few cities, mostly Northern. Among those cities Baltimore, New York, and Philadelphia stood out as having the largest free black populations and therefore the largest numbers of blacks in schools.

TABLE 14.9 SCHOOL ATTENDANCE AND ADULT ILLITERACY AMONG BLACKS IN 16 MAJOR CITIES, 1850

City	Total Free Black Population	Free Blacks in School	Illiterate Free Blacks
Boston, Mass.	2,038	1,439	205
Providence, R.I.	1,499	292	55
New Haven, Conn.	989	360	167
Brooklyn, N.Y.	2,424	507	788
New York, N.Y.	13,815	1,418	1,667
Philadelphia, Pa.	10,736	2,176	3,498
Cincinnati, Ohio	3,237	291	620
Louisville, Ky.	1,538	141	567
Baltimore, Md.	25,442	1,453	9,318
Washington, D.C.	8,158	420	2,674
Richmond, Va.	2,369	0	1,594
Petersburg, Va.	2,616	0	1,155
Charleston, S.C.	3,441	68	45
Savannah, Ga.	686	0	185
Mobile, Ala.	715	53	12
New Orleans, La.	9,905	1,008	2,279

Source: Peter Bergman, *The Chronological History of the Negro in America* (New York: Harper & Row, 1969), 195.

In 1860 the census showed only 32,629 blacks in school, or 0.73 percent of the total black population of 4,441,830. The situation improved only slowly after the Civil War. At the time slavery was abolished nationally (1865), only one in 10 slaves was capable of either reading or writing. Setting up primary and secondary schools for former slaves was a priority for the Freedman's Bureau when it arrived in the South. Because the students were former slaves and most of their teachers were carpetbaggers, the schools were not popular with white Southerners. The end of Reconstruction led to Jim Crow segregation, and public investment in black education was willfully slighted in the states of the former Confederacy. As the historian Otto Bettmann has said, "Negro education meant compulsory ignorance." Meanwhile in the nation at large black literacy climbed to 18.6 percent by 1870 and would rise to 30 percent in the next decade.

Access to higher education for African Americans was limited, not just by racist laws and custom, but by the fact that most African Americans could not even read and write, much less perform on a university level. Although access was extremely limited by several factors, it was still available during these years for men of color (not women). The first white college to open its doors to blacks was Oberlin College (Ohio), which began its enlightened admissions policy in 1835. Between 1850 and 1875 a few dozen black colleges and universities were founded in two waves. The first wave occurred during the antebellum period and was largely focused on producing leaders for the abolitionist movement. The second wave was immediately after the Civil War, its goal to produce an educated professional class to lead the freedmen on the upward path to equality. Both waves were largely financed and even operated by white Northerners, either evangelically oriented churches or private philanthropists. Even the most enlightened of those white philanthropists did not intend that their efforts should produce a class of independent businessmen, scientists, or political leaders. Rather, they had the much more modest goal of training men for the ministry, so the schools they founded emphasized theology over either the sciences or liberal arts. Saving black souls was less threatening than raising blacks to social, political, and economic equality.

Most of these institutions were obscure, underfunded, and short-lived. As a result they are scarcely remembered today except as a footnote in African-American history. They included Tougaloo College, Bennett College, Claflin College, Morgan College, Benedict College, Shaw University, Biddle University, and Leland University. The chief difference between those calling themselves colleges and those calling themselves universities was the scale of their ambition.

The first *dedicated* black college was Ashmun Institute, chartered in 1854 by the Presbyterian Church at the urging of one of its abolitionist ministers, for the purpose of educating "colored youth of the male sex." Ashmun, as did others in this first wave, had to struggle mightily to keeps its doors open during the Civil War; then after the war it had to begin admitting white students to stay solvent. Schools in the second wave of black institutions often owed their existence to white former Union officers who had led black troops in the Civil War and been impressed with their courage and determination. Second-wave black institutions named for former Union generals included Howard University and Fisk University. Howard benefited from the unique advantage of receiving substantial U.S. government funding, thanks to the lobbying efforts of General Oliver Otis Howard, head of the Freedman's Bureau in the South after the Civil War. As the home of more black schools than any other city in the country, Atlanta, Georgia, became the Oxford or Athens of the South. Black colleges founded after the Civil War had several common denominators: Most were focused on training teachers (normal schools) and preachers (seminaries), they suffered from chronically poor finances, and those that survived very many years went through numerous name changes and mergers. The graduates of these institutions formed the basis of a small but significant African-American professional class who have only recently received just recognition from historians.

TABLE 14.10 FUNDING BLACK EDUCATION IN SOUTH CAROLINA, 1866–1867

Source	Amount of Money
Benevolent societies (mostly Northern)	$65,000
Freedman's Bureau	$25,000
Freedmen (former slaves)	$17,000
Total	**$107,000**

Source: Martin Abbott, *The Freedman's Bureau in South Carolina, 1865–1872* (Chapel Hill: University of North Carolina Press, 1967), 88.

TABLE 14.11 BLACK SCHOOLS IN SOUTH CAROLINA, 1866–1870

School Information	1866	1867	1868	1869	1870
Number of schools	54	73	49	54	86
Teaching staff	130	140	123	N/A	200
Enrollment	8,000	8,000	7,000	5,500	9,000

Source: Martin Abbott, *The Freedman's Bureau in South Carolina, 1865–1872* (Chapel Hill: University of North Carolina Press, 1967), 88.

TABLE 14.12 HISTORICALLY BLACK COLLEGES AND UNIVERSITIES FOUNDED, 1850–1875

Institution	Date(s) of Founding/Existence[a]	Location	Founder(s)
Ashmun Institute[b]	1854–66	Near Oxford, Pa.	John Miller Dickey with funding by Presbyterian Church
Wilberforce College	1856[c]	Wilberforce, Ohio	Methodist Episcopal Church
Berea College	1859[d]	Berea, Ky.	The Reverend John G. Fee with financing by Cassius M. Clay, wealthy landowner-abolitionist
LeMoyne-Owen College[e]	1862	Memphis, Tenn.	Dr. Francis J. LeMoyne
Bluefield Colored Institute[f]	1865	Bluefield, W. Va.	Philanthropic reformers
Baltimore Normal School[g]	1865	Baltimore, Md.	Baltimore Association for the Moral and Educational Improvement of Colored People
Richmond Theological Institute[h]	1865	Richmond, Va.	Philanthropic reformers
Avery Institute	1865 (Oct.)	Charleston, S.C.	Charles Avery, white philanthropist
Lincoln Normal School[i]	1866	Marion, Ala.	Philanthropic reformers
Brown Theological Institution[j]	1866	Jacksonville, Fla.	African Methodist Episcopal Church
Shaw School[k]	1866	Holly Springs, Miss.	Freedman's Aid Society of the Methodist Episcopal Church
Fisk College (University)	1866 (Jan. 9)	Nashville, Tenn.	White Union general Clinton Fisk[l]
Augusta Institute[m]	1867–1906	Augusta, Ga.	The Reverend William Jefferson White with Richard C. Coulter and Edmund Turney
Howard Normal and Theological Institue[n]	1867 (May 1)	Washington, D.C.	White Union general Oliver Otis Howard (also first president)
Howard School[o]	1867	Fayeteville, Ark.	Seven black philanthropists
Centenary Biblical Institute[p]	1867	Baltimore, Md.	Religious-minded philanthropists
Saint Augustine's College	1867	Raleigh, N.C.	Protestant Episcopal Church with the Episcopal Diocese of N.C.
Scotia (Women's) Seminary[q]	1867	Concord, N.C.	Presbyterian Church
Talladega College	1867	Talladega, Ala.	Group of former slaves, assisted by the American Missionary Association
Storer College	1867–1956	Harpers Ferry, W. Va.	John Storer, philanthropist-lawyer
Atlanta University[r]	1867–1988	Atlanta, Ga.	Founded by two former slaves who turned it over in 1867 to American Missionary Association (AMA), who appointed first president, Edmund Ware
Hampton Normal & Agricltural Institute[s]	1868 (Apr.)	Hampton, Va.	White Union general Samuel C. Armstrong
Straight University[t]	1869–1930	New Orleans, La.	Freedman's Bureau (taken over by American Missionary Association)
Clark University[u]	1869–1988	Atlanta, Ga.	Freedman's Aid Society of the Methodist (African) Episcopal Church
Alcorn Agricultural & Mining College	1871	Alcorn, Miss.	Congress as a land-grant college
Union Normal School[v]	1869	New Orleans, La.	Methodist Episcopal Church
Tougaloo College	1869	Tougaloo, Miss.	American Missionary Association of New York
Payne Institute[w]	1870	Columbia, S.C.	African Methodist Episcopal Church
Benedict Institute	1870	Columbia, S.C.	Philanthropic reformers
Alcorn University	1871	Lorman, Miss.	State of Mississippi (first president, Hiram Revels)
Claflin College	1871	Orangeburg, S.C.	Boards of Baker Biblical Institute and Claflin University
Paul Quinn College[x]	1872	Austin, Tex.	Group of black circuit-riding African Methodist Episcopal ministers

Institution	Date(s) of Founding/Existence[a]	Location	Founder(s)
South Carolina Agricultural & Mechanical Institute[y]	1872	Orangeburg, S.C.	Founders of Claflin College
Bennett (Women's) Seminary[z]	1873	Greensboro, S.C.	United Methodist Church
Wiley College	1873	Marshall, Tex.	Freedman's Aid Society of (African) Methodist Church
Huntsville Normal School[aa]	1875	Huntsville, Ala.	Philanthropic reformers
Tillotson College[bb]	1875	Austin, Tex.	Philanthropic reformers
Knoxville College	1875	Knoxville, Tenn.	Presbyterian missionaries

[a] Trying to determine founding dates is a somewhat arbitrary exercise because different sources cite different dates, which are based on when a particular institution was chartered, when it dedicated its first building, when it opened its doors, when its first class graduated. There is also some rivalry among the partisans of various schools to be the first, second, and so on, in some significant category. Further complicating the issue is that some schools changed hands in their early years, so they cannot claim "continuous existence" since one date. The date of charter whenever that is available is used here.
[b] Renamed Lincoln University in 1866; taken over by the state of Pennsylvania in 1972.
[c] The Civil War forced Wilberforce to close its doors in 1862, but it was purchased the following year and reopened by the African Methodist Episcopal Church.
[d] Berea began life as a grammar school in 1855 before it was incorporated as a college in 1859; its first academic year was 1869. As the first racially integrated college in the Old South, it experienced no end of problems and local hostility during the Jim Crow era from the late 19th century.
[e] Originally founded as Lincoln (elementary) School for Negroes; renamed LeMoyne College, then merged with Owen College in 1868; name changed to LeMoyne Normal and Commercial School in 1871.
[f] Bluefield Colored Institute became Bluefield State College in 1943.
[g] After several name changes Baltimore Normal School became Bowie State University in 1988.
[h] The Richmond Theological Institute became Virginia Union University in 1899 when it merged with Wayland Seminary; in the 20th century it merged with other traditionally black colleges but retained its name.
[i] Lincoln Normal School moved to Montgomery, Ala., in 1887 and became Alabama State University in 1969. It is notable as the first state-supported U.S. college for training African-American teachers.
[j] Brown Theological Institution became Edward Waters College in later years.
[k] Shaw School became Rust College in later years.
[l] Fisk was the trailblazer and the most famous of the second wave of black institutions of higher learning founded after the Civil War specifically to provide educational opportunities for the freedmen.
[m] In 1879 Augusta Institute moved to Atlanta, Georgia; it changed its name to Morehouse College (its current name) in 1913.
[n] Howard Normal and Theological Institute became Howard University the same year as its founding, and the first comprehensive institution of higher learning for blacks anywhere in the world.
[o] Howard School became Fayetteville State University in 1969.
[p] Centenary Biblical Institute became Morgan State University in later years.
[q] Scotia Seminary merged with Barber Memorial College in 1930 and became Barber-Scotia College in 1932.
[r] Atlanta University was chartered by the state of Georgia on Oct. 16, 1867. In 1929 the university joined with Spelman University and Morehouse College in a consortium in which all retained their historic identity. In 1988 Atlanta University combined with Clark College to form Clark-Atlanta University.
[s] Hampton Institute began life as a "contraband camp" for runaway slaves during the Civil War before becoming an agricultural and industrial college after the war.
[t] Straight merged with New Orleans University in 1930 to form Dillard University.
[u] Clark University was chartered by the state as Clark College in 1877; it merged with Atlanta University in 1988.
[v] Union Normal School became New Orleans University before the end of the century, then merged with Straight College in 1930 to form Dillard University.
[w] Payne Institute closed for a period, then reopened in 1880 as Allen University.
[x] Paul Quinn is the oldest traditionally black college west of the Mississippi River; it moved to Waco in 1887, then to Dallas in 1990.
[y] South Carolina Agricultural & Mechanical Institute became South Carolina State University in 1896.
[z] Bennett Seminary became Bennett (Women's) College in 1889.
[aa] Huntsville Normal School became Alabama Agricultural & Mechanical College in 1890, and Alabama A&M University in 1969.
[bb] Tillotson College merged with Samuel Houston College in 1952 and became Houston-Tillotson College.
Sources: Jack Salzman, David L. Smith, and Cornel West, eds., *Encyclopedia of African-American Culture and History* (New York: Simon & Schuster Macmillan, 1996, 2001), en passant; Robert L. Gale, *A Cultural Encyclopedia of the 1850s in America* (Westport, Conn.: Greenwood Press, 1993), xv–xvi, 10–11; Alton Hornsby, Jr., *Chronology of African American History* (Detroit: Gale Research, 1997), 55–86.

Schooling for American Indians

Schooling for American Indians lagged even behind what was available for African Americans. Part of the reason for this was a basic philosophical problem: As long as Indians were considered sovereign peoples, education was purely a tribal matter. Not until the Congress began treating Indians as wards of the state did schooling become a government matter. Even then, it ranked far below administration, annuities, and law and order as a priority (in terms of budget allotments and personnel). The Office of Indian Affairs (the 19th-century name for the Bureau of Indian Affairs) first began budgeting for and collecting data on education in 1865. The system of Indian education operated by the government consisted of agency schools, in which rudimentary reading, writing, and arithmetic skills were taught to all grades together by, usually, a single poorly trained and underpaid teacher. In 1865, the first year records were kept, there were 71 agency teachers for 59 agencies; eight years later there were 91 teachers for 77 agencies.

TABLE 14.13 EXPENDITURES AND PERSONNEL OF U.S. GOVERNMENT FOR AMERICAN INDIAN EDUCATION, 1873–1876

(*government* refers to the Office of Indian Affairs; figures given in constant dollars)

Fiscal Year	Total Budget for Indian Affairs	Budget for Schools	Schools as a Percentage of Total Indian Affairs Budget	Increase in School Budget over Previous Year	Number of Teachers in the Field	Teachers as a Percentage of Total Indian Affairs Employment
1873–74	$4,676,222.60	$37,597.31	0.81	N/A[a]	91[b]	8.8
1874–75	$5,544,122.10	$99,036.29	1.79	163.4	N/A[a]	N/A[a]
1875–76	$5,538,864.50	$140,129.01	2.53	41.49	117	16.6

[a] Data not available.
[b] For 63 agencies reporting of 77.
Source: Paul Stuart, *The Indian Office* (Ann Arbor, Mich.: UMI Research Press, 1979), 127–31.

Apart from the agency school, the only formal education available to Native Americans was at mission schools run by the Baptists and member of other denominations. This is how Ely Parker, who eventually became commissioner of Indian Affairs, received his formal education in the antebellum period.

Only three schools offered what might be called higher education tailored to American Indians specifically, and all three were on an extremely limited basis: the Choctaw Academy in Kentucky (founded 1825) and the Cherokee Male and Female Seminaries in Oklahoma (founded ca. 1851). They reflected the progressive, assimilationist thinking of the Five Civilized Tribes, but they did not welcome members of other tribes. Excepting these three institutions, higher education for Native Americans during this era was virtually not an option. Not until Hampton Institute in Virginia threw open its doors to Indians in 1878, and Carlisle Indian Industrial School (Carlisle, Pennsylvania) opened in 1879 did all American Indians have genuine options in higher education.

Growth of U.S. Higher Education

The major change in the higher education movement after the Civil War was the introduction of professional and elective studies alongside the traditional liberal arts curriculum. The new curriculum was aimed at preparing students for a career, a very important objective to the rising middle class. The elective system, whereby students shaped their own course of study, was pioneered by President Charles W. Eliot of Harvard University (1869–1909), starting in 1869. Harvard men were allowed to pursue majors in such new disciplines as the social sciences, engineering, and business administration.

Above the basic college education elite U.S. schools starting with Yale University in 1847 began offering instruction in studies beyond the normal undergraduate curriculum, with an emphasis on research and scholarship. That first graduate program enrolled 11 students, eight of them concentrating in the sciences, and granted only master's degrees. The teaching methodology was seminars, an approach borrowed from Germany, as was the whole idea of graduate studies as a middle-class alternative to the ancient apprentice system for training of lawyers, physicians, and other professionals. Other schools followed Yale's lead in the next decade, including the first state university to offer a master's degree, the University of Michigan. Graduate curriculums tended to consist of "philosophy, literature, history, the moral sciences other than law and theology, and natural sciences excepting medicine." Yale raised the bar again when it launched doctoral studies, awarding the nation's first Ph.D. (actually, three Ph.D.'s) in 1861. It was followed by the University of Pennsylvania in 1870, Harvard in 1872, and Princeton in 1879. All graduate programs at this time tilted heavily toward the sciences, a sharp contrast from earlier emphasis on law and theological studies in higher education. The new science of physical chemistry was introduced in the 1860s, and doctoral studies in physics made their appearance in the early 1870s.

In 1867 only 400 students had graduate study under their belts (almost all done in Europe) when Johns Hopkins opened the first thoroughgoing postgraduate program in the United States. U.S. higher education in the latter decades of the 19th century was controlled by what one contemporary called "the great American universities," an exclusive club of 14 institutions that enrolled one of every five graduate and undergraduate students.

Specialized Higher Education

Aside from schools based on race or gender, U.S. institutions of higher education during these years began specializing by offering advanced instruction in fields such as medicine, music, law, theology (seminaries), and teacher training (normal schools). These fields were much in demand for professional-minded adults and reflected the growing complexity of U.S. higher education, as well as the increasingly technical nature of knowledge. For instance, New York City's Bellevue Hospital opened the first school of nursing in the United States in 1873. Schools devoted to religious study by far outnumbered all others; their number reflected popular interest as well as the capacity of affiliated churches to provide substantial and steady financial support.

Pedagogical standards were not high at the seminaries and "Bible institutes"; nor were they much better at the medical and law schools. Most of them had no more than two or three professors and some were one-man operations. Qualified faculty were hard to find, and low teaching ratios were not a selling point in the 19th century as they are today. It was a truly unusual institution that had as many as six professors on the faculty, as did the Theological Seminary at Andover, Massachusetts.

TABLE 14.14 MEDICAL SCHOOLS IN THE UNITED STATES, 1852

Institution	Location	Date of Opening	Size of Student Body	Size of Faculty (Professors)	Number of Graduates to 1852
Maine Medical School	Brunswick, Maine	1820	51	5	634
New Hampshire Medical School	Hanover, N.H.	1797	50	6	800
Castleton Medical College	Castleton, Vt.	1818	104	7	555
Vermont Medical College	Woodstock, Vt.	1835	90	7	332
Harvard University Medical School	Cambridge, Mass.	1782	117	6	575
Berkshire Medical School	Pittsfield, Mass.	1823	103	5	473
Yale College Medical Institute	New Haven, Conn.	1813	38	6	595
New York College of Physicians and Surgeons	New York, N.Y.	1807	219	6	862
Geneva College Medical Institute	Geneva, N.Y.	1835	60	6	98
University of New York Medical Faculty	New York, N.Y.	1837	421	6	597
Albany Medical College	Albany, N.Y.	1839	114	8	58
University of Pennsylvania Medical Department	Philadelphia, Pa.	1765	450	7	5,316
Jefferson Medical College	Philadelphia, Pa.	1824	514	7	2,036
Pennsylvania College Medical Department	Philadelphia, Pa.	1838	176	7	73
Philadelphia College of Medicine	Philadelphia, Pa.	N/A	75	7	250
University of Maryland Medical School	Baltimore, Md.	1807	100	6	909
Washington Medical College	Baltimore, Md.	1827	25	6	N/A
Columbia College Medical School	Washington, D.C.	1825	40	6	81
University of Virginia Medical School	Charlottesville, Va.	1825	95	3	N/A
Hampton Sidney College Medical Department	Richmond, Va.	1838	90	7	40
Winchester Medical College	Winchester, Va.	N/A	N/A	5	N/A
State of South Carolina Medical College	Charleston, S.C.	1833	158	8	N/A
Medical College of Georgia	Augusta, Ga.	1830	115	7	194
University of Louisiana Medical Department	New Orleans, La.	1835	188	7	N/A
University of Nashville Medical Department	Nashville, Tenn.	1850	N/A	7	N/A
University of Transylvania Medical Department	Lexington, Ky.	1818	214	7	1,351
University of Louisville Medical Department	Louisville, Ky.	1837	376	7	53
Western Reserve Medical College	Cleveland, Ohio	1844	202	6	411
Medical College of Ohio	Cincinnati, Ohio	1819	130	8	331
Western College of Homeopathic Medicine	Cleveland, Ohio	1850	62	8	17
Starling Medical College	Columbus, Ohio	1847	194	8	53
Indiana Medical College	Laporte, Ind.	N/A	104	7	19
Indiana Central Medical College	Indianapolis, Ind.	1849	50	8	28
Rush Medical College	Chicago, Ill.	1842	70	6	16
University of Michigan	Ann Arbor, Mich.	1837	95	5	N/A
St. Louis University Medical Department	St. Louis, Mo.	1836	107	9	87
Missouri University Medical Department	Columbia, Mo.	1840	92	7	N/A

Note: N/A (not available) indicates that the opening date, size of student body, or size of faculty is not known.
Source: The American Almanac and Repository of Useful Knowledge, for the Year 1852, Part 2 (Boston: Charles C. Little and James Brown, 1851), 207.

TABLE 14.15 LAW SCHOOLS IN THE UNITED STATES, 1852

Institution	Location	Size of Student Body	Size of Faculty (Professors)
Harvard University	Cambridge, Mass.	98	3
Yale College	New Haven, Conn.	26	2
University of Albany	Albany, N.Y.	N/A	3
College of New Jersey	Princeton, N.J.	8	3
Dickinson College	Carlisle, Pa.	9	1
William & Mary College	Williamsburg, Va.	32	1
University of Virginia	Charlottesville, Va.	70	1
North Carolina University	Chapel Hill, N.C.	10	1
Alabama University	Tuscaloosa, Ala.	N/A	1
University of Louisiana	New Orleans, La.	N/A	3
Transylvania University	Lexington, Ky.	75	3
University of Louisville	Louisville, Ky.	50	3
Cumberland University	Lebanon, Tenn.	56	3
Cincinnati College	Cincinnati, Ohio	25	3
Indiana State University	Bloomington, Ind.	29	2
Indiana Asby University	Greencastle, Ind.	N/A	1

Note: N/A (not available) indicates that the opening date, size of student body, or size of faculty is not known.
Source: The American Almanac and Repository of Useful Knowledge, for the Year 1852, Part 2 (Boston: Charles C. Little and James Brown, 1851), 206.

The Cost of Higher Education

The cost of a college education in the mid-19th century was not nearly as exorbitant as it is today. Although it represented a substantial investment in terms of the contemporary cost of living, it did not require massive loans and government grants. In fact, it was a bargain. One reason is that there was a limited market for a college degree; the masses of Americans certainly had no need for it. Second, most colleges of the day were closer to one-room schoolhouses than to the sprawling suburban campuses of today. They also taught a very basic curriculum and employed a handful of faculty, so they had very little overhead. In the more prestigious universities resident students paid for their tuition plus room and board, just as they do today, but they also paid for some additional expenses out of pocket that were a sign of the times: fuel (wood) for their stoves, lamp oil, and washing, which were whatever the local market would bear. The school year was typically 39 or 40 weeks, though terms at some schools (e.g., Dartmouth College) were as short as 38 weeks and at others (e.g., University of Virginia) were as long as 44 weeks, a marked departure from the current U.S. typical 30- to 32-week academic calendar. For many reasons a college education at mid-century was a rare and extravagant commodity.

TABLE 14.16 ANNUAL COLLEGE EXPENSES AT SOME LEADING U.S. SCHOOLS, MID-1800s

Institution	Tuition	Room Rent and School Fees	Board	Weeks in Academic year	Cost of Wood, Light, and Washing
Bowdoin	$24.00	$22	$56.50	39 weeks	$35
Dartmouth	$27.00	$13.24	$57	38 weeks	$9
Harvard	$75.00	$15	$70–90	40 weeks	N/A
Williams	$30.00	$9	$65	39 weeks	N/A
Amherst	$33.00	$15	$60	40 weeks	$17
Brown	$40.00	$23	$60	39 weeks	N/A
Yale	$33.00	$21	$60–90	40 weeks	$20
Wesleyan	$36.00	$11.25	$58.50	39 weeks	$20
Hamilton	$26.00	$14	$58	38 or 39 weeks	N/A
New Jersey	$50.00	$28.14	$80	40 weeks	$28
Dickinson	$33.00	$14	$76.25	43 weeks	$22.75
University of Virginia	$75.00	$23	$110	44 weeks	$20
North Carolina University	$50.00	$11	$90	40 weeks	$20
Transylvania	$40.00	$12	$100	40 weeks	$25
Western Reserve	$30.00	$11	$50	42 weeks	$12

Note: N/A (not available) indicates that cost is not known.
Source: The American Almanac and Repository of Useful Knowledge, for the Year 1852, Part 2 (Boston: Charles C. Little and James Brown, 1851), 205.

Reforming U.S. Public Education

The proper role of public education in a democratic society was a hot topic, as demonstrated by the fact that one of the public heroes of the age was the educator Horace Mann. Many reformers besides Mann believed that education had a higher purpose than just to teach the traditional three Rs. Public education, it was argued, was one of the principal tools for Americanizing a nation of immigrants. As the flood of immigration rose around mid-century, so did fears for the future of the country. What better place to begin acculturating the newcomers into the U.S. mainstream than in the classroom, with a properly structured curriculum and instructional materials. Schools therefore taught Protestant morality, capitalist values, and Christianity as much as the basics, and the greatest vehicle for that instruction was the venerable series of *McGuffey's Readers,* named for William Holmes McGuffey, which sold some 50 million copies between 1836 and 1870. U.S. public schools in the second half of the 19th century made assimilation and character building their primary missions. This new philosophy rode in on the coattails of earlier reform movements to broaden and upgrade the educational system.

The need to reform the U.S. educational system from top to bottom had long been recognized. The 19th-century schoolroom could be a stultifying and even dangerous place. Children were force-fed a steady diet of trivial facts, "noble" precepts, and harsh discipline. The traditional curriculum included arithmetic, U.S. history (with a strong patriotic flavor), geography, reading, grammar, and spelling. Science, higher mathematics, and world history were practically unknown. Corporal punishment enshrined the birch rod as the principal teaching tool. Great emphasis was placed on learning how to spell properly and "do sums," and the system often lumped pupils from ages five through 16 together in a single classroom with one harried teacher—usually a male who had failed at everything else and had no training. For most American children schooling did not start until they were six or seven or even older. Kindergarten schooling, a progressive German concept, did not arrive on U.S. shores until 1856 and remained an exotic branch of education for the next two decades. Despite some modest improvements on the front end of children's education, formal schooling still tended to end by age 16, at which time the students were pushed out into the working world.

Teaching was not an honored job, in terms of either pay or respect. It meant low pay even by the standards of the day, low prestige, and a personal life subject to constant scrutiny by the school board. Teachers were expected to be disciplinarians first, educators second. The dangers of teaching unruly, ill-mannered children coupled with prevailing ideas about feminine frailty had long kept women out of the classroom and intimidated those who braved it. Etta Barstow, a Canton, Massachusetts, schoolteacher, on October 8, 1870, was stoned to death by some of her pupils after she punished them for some trivial infraction. But that tradition was changing, and New England led the way as it did in most other educational reforms. By the 1850, nearly three-fourths of public school teachers in New England were women, a trend that was also visible in other sections of the country as well, as attested by anecdotal not statistical evidence.

Rural schools had their own set of problems, beginning with a small tax base and difficulty in attracting qualified teachers. In rural areas, the so-called district schools handled educational needs with an informal, penny-pinching pragmatism. They taught farmers' children reading, writing, and counting but little more. The typical country school was characterized by heavy doses of discipline, lack of books and other materials, and substandard facilities.

City schools were no better than the rural variety. They were often victims of corrupt political machines who withheld approved funding and were in cahoots with the local school board. They suffered the additional handicap of serving children who had many different national and ethnic backgrounds. In 1871 the New York commissioner of education admitted that "thousands of children [were leaving] school without being able to read and write." Schools were located in abandoned, ramshackle buildings, next door to saloons, factories, and slaughterhouses. Most had no playground, indoor plumbing, or even desks for students.

School reform before the Civil War started with Horace Mann, who argued that an educated citizenry was essential for democracy. Moreover education would create a more orderly and efficient workforce. His ideas made little headway in the South but rapidly caught on in the North, where the Puritan legacy was still strong and the new industrialists saw the dollars and cents wisdom of his logic. His tireless advocacy as the first secretary of Massachusetts's state board of education persuaded the Massachusetts legislature to enact the nation's first compulsory school law (1852). Elsewhere, however, the idea of a tax-supported public school system still had many doubters, including farmers, Catholic Church leaders, even industrial laborers, who wanted their children to go to work rather than "waste time" sitting in school. Even after three decades of reform in the Five Points section of New York City, only nine of 600 school-age children there attended school in 1870. The rest either worked or ran the streets.

Southern elites flatly rejected the idea of compulsory education even while it was gaining ground in the North during the 1850s. They feared education of blacks and the underclass as well as the expense of maintaining tax-supported schools. High-quality education remained the province of the upper classes, and that meant private schools and tutors. At the beginning of the Civil War 60 percent of North Carolinians who enlisted in the army of the Confederacy were illiterate, versus about 30 percent of the enlistees from Northern states.

The modern elementary grade school building with multiple classes divided by age was a product of 1870s urban reforms. One-room schoolhouses had become totally inadequate for the needs of big cities. A system of progressive grades was more of an ideal than a reality, however, as a result of inadequate financing, lack of teacher training, and the practice of social promotion. Drill and recitation were still the norm.

Education reformers wrought a profound change when they introduced the kindergarten, thereby starting the learning process at an earlier age. As was advanced graduate study, it was an idea borrowed from the Germans. The first kindergarten on U.S. soil was set up by Mrs. Carl Schurz in 1856 in Watertown, Wisconsin, for recently arrived German immigrant children. The idea spread, and the first publically supported kindergarten was opened in St. Louis, Missouri, in 1873 by Susan Blow with the full support of the progressive superintendent, William Torrey Harris.

Reforming secondary education meant establishing broad-based and publicly supported high schools, as opposed to the older system of private, narrowly focused academies (e.g., music, military). The tax-supported concept was challenged in court by the more traditional-minded folks but was upheld in 1874 in a Kalamazoo, Michigan, decision. Subsequently high school—free, public, and comprehensive in curriculum—became the standard path followed by U.S. schoolchildren after primary grades.

At the same time high school was being recognized as the next logical step after the primary grades, there was a movement afoot to upgrade the high school curriculum. By 1860 all schools offered mathematics, English, and science in some form. U.S. history, by contrast, was offered to only 15 percent of high school students. In English the emphasis shifted from teaching grammar and rhetoric to introducing students to "good literature." According to the limited data available, this seems to have meant a heavy emphasis on Shakespeare plus inspirational poetry by both U.S. and English authors. The result was a good grounding in the received "classics." In the years that followed English (both grammar *and* literature) became the only subject universally required by all U.S. high schools.

TABLE 14.17 REQUIRED READING LIST IN HIGH SCHOOLS IN THE NORTH-CENTRAL STATES, 1860

Ranking on the List	Works That Appeared on 25 Percent or More of the Lists	Type and Date of Work	Author of Work
1	*Merchant of Venice*	Play (comedy), ca. 1596	William Shakespeare
2	*Julius Caesar*	Play (tragedy), ca. 1599	William Shakespeare
3	*Bunker Hill Oration*	Patriotic poem, 1837	Ralph Waldo Emerson
4	*Evangeline*	Narrative poem, 1847	Henry Wadsworth Longfellow
5	*Vision of Sir Launfal*	Epic poem (long verse parable), 1848	James Russell Lowell
6	*Snow-Bound*	Nostalgic pastoral poem, 1866	John Greenleaf Whittier
7	*Macbeth*	Play (tragedy), ca. 1605	William Shakespeare
8	*Hamlet*	Play (tragedy), ca. 1600	William Shakespeare
9	*Deserted Village*	Pastoral elegy poem, 1770	Oliver Goldsmith
10[a]	*Gray's Elegy* (i.e., *An Elegy Written in a Country Church Yard*)	Lyric poem (meditative), 1751	Thomas Gray
10	*Thanatopsis*	Lyric poem (meditative), first published., 1817; revised, 1821	William Cullen Bryant
10	*As You Like It*	Play (comedy), ca. 1599	William Shakespeare

Note: Based on the number of lists it appeared on; this ranking shows the popularity of various works among high school educators of the day.
[a] There was a tie among three books for 10th place on the list.
Source: Gladys A. Wiggin, *Education and Nationalism* (New York: McGraw-Hill, 1962), 163.

A Military Education

One traditional element of the U.S. educational system that continued to flourish throughout all the reforms of the 19th century was the old-fashioned military academy, which had its roots in the militia tradition and the Second Amendment to the Constitution. Every eastern state had one or more, although the greatest number were located in the Deep South. Most were mere preparatory schools with uniforms and military drill, but a few actually aspired to challenge West Point as a training ground for future officers. The largest and best known in the South were the Virginia Military Institute in Lexingon, Virginia; the Citadel in Charleston, South Carolina; the Georgia Military Institute (founded 1851) in Marietta, Georgia; the University of Alabama (converted to a military school in 1860) in Tuscaloosa, Alabama; the West Florida Seminary (now Florida State University) in Tallahassee, Florida; and the Louisiana Military Academy (founded 1860) in Baton Rouge, Louisiana. Most of these proud Southern institutions were forced to shut their doors when the Civil War began because their students and faculty left to join the Confederate army, but there was a small revival after the war. The North also had its share of military academies established in the antebellum years, two of the most prominent of which were the Mount Pleasant Military Academy in Sing Sing, New York (founded 1854), and the Highland Military Academy in Worcester, Massachusetts (founded 1857). While competing with the United States Military Academy for students and reputation, they still maintained a close connection to West Point, especially in the matter of hiring West Point graduates as faculty. Their primary role was not education but feeding of the martial spirit in a supposedly peace-loving nation.

New Concepts in Education

The field of education was expanded by a number of new concepts during the 19th century. One of these was adult education, a particularly American concept that appealed to reformers and moral uplifters. It first appeared in the United States in the form of the lyceum and chautauqua movements. The postwar lyceum circuit, reviving a movement first launched in 1821 by Josiah Holbrook, emerged in 1868, when James Redpath started recruiting well-known speakers to tour rural areas delivering lectures on timely topics. Ministers and statesmen earned fat fees for filling small-town auditoriums and big-tops. Out of this arose the chautauqua movement, named for a town in upstate New York, which began as an eight-week summer training institute for Sunday school teachers. The first of these was held in 1874 under the leadership of Bishop John H. Vincent, and in the years that followed, the spread of railroads and the thirst for new knowledge led organizers to take their show on the road. Lyceum lectures and chautauqua meetings were a combination of religious instruction, mass entertainment, and adult education.

The proliferation of libraries in cities across the nation also reflected the interest in adult education. George Ticknor, the publisher and editor, saw free public libraries as "the crowning glory of our public schools," where "the whole people" could have access to books "tending to moral and intellectual improvement." Education, seen in this light, was not a matter of just acquiring knowledge but also of strengthening morals, and this was a lifetime job.

For the obvious reasons education was an idea more acceptable to middle-class adults than to the nation's schoolchildren. At the end of this era education of the young was still commonly regarded as a joyless, dreary, noncreative, and regimented activity that had to be endured as part of the growing up experience. Thomas Jefferson's visionary dream of creating a "national university" would not even be attempted for many years. But education had arrived as a national issue, a fact marked by the appointment of Henry Barnard as the first U.S. commissioner of education (1867–70).

The heightened interest in organized sports resonated in U.S. education as the connection between mind and body began to show up in curriculum planning for the first time. Starting in 1870 what were then called physical education courses were introduced on the grammar school level in some urban systems. Most of the focus was on boys, and most of the interest was from the middle class, but there was some awareness that exercise was healthy as well as tiring. The wealthy classes even began to build private gymnasiums (in the classic sense of the word) in their home, outfitted with primitive exercise equipment. The fad for physical fitness and exercise did not really make a splash, however, until the end of the century.

Among the more progressive steps taken by American educators was the creation of special schools for the handicapped, such as the Boston School for the Deaf. Here, the faculty and pupils pose for their class picture in 1871. Alexander Graham Bell, a patron of the school, can be seen on the left at the top of the steps; the school's first principal, Sarah Fuller, is second from the left halfway down the steps. (Library of Congress)

The Little Red Schoolhouse on the Hill

The Puritans had once dreamed that America would be a "city on a hill" to be emulated by the rest of the world. That dream had persisted even after the weakening of the Puritan hold on the nation's consciousness and had been expanded to include not just faith and political institutions but also the educational system. Despite what seems to be a mixed report card for U.S. education during these years, the U.S. system still shone as the model for the rest of the world. In 1854 the British Parliament sent a special commission to the United States to study manufacturing methods with the hope of learning practices they could use to make British industry more competitive. The commission expanded their study far beyond factories and mills. They looked especially closely at U.S. schools and decided that the nation's educational system provided a major advantage to U.S. manufacturers. U.S. students were being "educated up to a far higher standard" than their counterparts across the Atlantic. As one result U.S. inventiveness was not confined to the upper classes but spread throughout society even down to the lowest laborer. Six years later the American educational system was still outperforming its nearest European rivals: In 1860 almost 95 percent of American adults *in Northern states* were literate versus a national rate of people considered literate of 65 percent in Britain and 55 percent in France. This was a ringing endorsement of the U.S. educational system that not even the virtual exclusion of American Indians and African Americans could negate.

U.S. education during the 25 years from 1850 to 1873 would look quite familiar to a modern American transported to the mid-19th century. It was locally controlled, concerned with quality of teaching and curriculum issues, and largely segregated by race, gender, and religious orientation. In 1850 it stood poised with one foot in the past and the other in the future. A certain quaint innocence was apparent in the emphasis placed on patriotism and moral values more than on rigorous intellectual training. There were still important differences between city and rural schools and between upper-class and lower-class educational opportunities. Religious influence continued to be strong on all levels of schooling.

True to the nation's democratic roots, American education was very diverse, with public and private schools, a multiplicity of denominational schools, and state supported colleges and universities. There was a debate over the constitutionality of publicly supported schools. At the same time more and more states were funding institutions of higher education, and with federal encouragement after 1862. Anybody could still open a school and operate it without worrying about certification or public oversight. And "book learning" was still seen as less important than work and learning a trade. This was most apparent in the difference between city and rural schools. In the cities children attended school from 180 to 200 days per year on average; in rural areas farm chores and harvesting kept attendance to fewer than 100 days per year on average.

Looking to the future, such thorny subjects as oversight (boards of education), elective studies, professional development, kindergarten schooling, and the relative merits of a science versus humanities curriculum were all being debated during these years. The importance of education to the nation's future was recognized, but how best to achieve educational excellence was the question. One group of reformers pushed for such radical ideas as a national educational policy and universal standards. The beginnings of this movement could be seen in the publication of the *American Journal of Education* (1855–82) and the creation of the U.S. Commission of Education as a federal agency.

American education was being broadened, sometimes painfully, with the admission of women, blacks, and American Indians to the system, even though opportunities remained quite limited for these groups for many years. Antioch College (Yellow Springs, Ohio), founded in 1853, carried the torch for nonsectarian, coeducational schooling.

A reform movement, spearheaded by Horace Mann, known as the "father of American public education," was just getting under way in the United States when the period opened. It put emphasis on raising of educational standards, tax-supported schools, and better teachers. The latter led to the establishment of numerous teacher training institutions (normal schools). Professional education, beginning in the sciences (Massachusetts Institute of Technology, 1861) and medicine (the American Medical Association, 1847) soon spread to other fields. Adult education, beginning with the antebellum lyceums and expanding with the chautauqua movement after 1874, became part of the mix.

All in all the U.S. education system as it exists today, with all its problems and accomplishments, can be seen in outline in the mid-19th century: better than what most people in the world enjoyed, but not yet good enough to satisfy Americans.

CHAPTER 15 Arts, Letters, Music, and Theater

I must study politics and war, that my sons may have liberty to study mathematics and philosophy, geography, natural history and naval architecture, navigation, commerce and agriculture, in order to give their children a right to study painting, poetry, music, architecture, statuary, tapestry and porcelain.

—John Adams (1735–1826),
second president of the United States

Literature

American artists and authors of the mid-19th century seemed determined to put as much distance between themselves and Europe as possible, at the same time nurturing a lingering inferiority complex in regard to all things European. Indeed establishing a national art, music, and literature that reflected the so-called American genius is the main theme of the period. The American genius was defined by the traits of individualism, self-sufficiency, and a passionate love of liberty. Before 1850 such sentiments had not won much respect on the eastern shores of the Atlantic, particularly for American literature. In 1820 the British author Sidney Smith wrote in the *Edinburgh Review,* "In the four quarters of the globe, who reads an American book?" Or for that matter, sang an American song or admired an American painting? After mid-century such a question sounded not only supercilious but ignorant, such was the growth of American literature in the intervening years. In the fine arts, recognition and respect were slower in coming.

American literature was in transition in the mid-19th century. Four distinct types or genres had dominated the early 1800s: sentimental, satirical, Gothic, and historical romance. Those basic types evolved and became more nuanced until by the third quarter of the century, half a dozen distinct types could be identified. Among the changes satire, as represented by Bret Harte and Mark Twain, was still flourishing, while gothic stories, as represented by Nathaniel Hawthorne and Edgar Allan Poe, were fading. Sentimental novels and historical romances were threatening to take over American prose while poetry enjoyed an Indian summer that would never be seen again. Poets were lionized, and their latest works, particularly on epic and patriotic themes, were eagerly snapped up by the reading public. Schoolchildren routinely memorized the "great American poems" as part of their education, and poetry was so popular with the masses that antebellum newspapers often carried verses on page one.

The single most important piece of literature for 19th-century Americans was the Bible. It was a publishing phenomenon in terms of sheer numbers of readers and influence on the publishing industry. At least 760,900 Bibles were published in 1848, the last year of the period for which reliable figures are available. A continuous stream of reprints, new translations, and new editions (19 between 1850 and 1876) indicated that the faithful frequently had to replace their old Bible with the latest version. As a cultural touchstone and source of reference the "Good Book" was the nation's chief written text. All other books were second.

Several new literary subgenres now demanded space on the shelf, among them, sectional writings, women's literature, travel literature, and slave narratives. As this era ended, American Indian stories, urban literature, and true-crime tales were just starting to appear.

Sectional Literature

Regional- or sectional-themed literature begins with the New England circle of writers Henry Wadsworth Longfellow, Ralph Waldo Emerson, Nathaniel Hawthorne, Henry David Thoreau, William Cullen Bryant, John Greenleaf Whittier, and Herman Melville who represent a who's who of American literature. Not all of them wrote about New England specifically, but they all reflected its values and intellectual climate and are therefore dubbed "the New England Renaissance." Among the elite circle of authors and poets Whittier and Hawthorne were probably the most provincial in their choice of

WALDEN;

OR,

LIFE IN THE WOODS.

BY HENRY D. THOREAU,

AUTHOR OF "A WEEK ON THE CONCORD AND MERRIMACK RIVERS."

I do not propose to write an ode to dejection, but to brag as lustily as chanticleer in the morning, standing on his roost, if only to wake my neighbors up. — Page 92.

BOSTON:

TICKNOR AND FIELDS.

M DCCC LIV.

The title page for the 1854 edition of Henry David Thoreau's *Walden; or, Life in the Woods,* shows a cozy cabin nestled in trees. (Library of Congress, Prints and Photographs Division [LC-US262-90560])

themes. Whittier, in fact, has been called the poet-laureate of New England.

As a group the New Englanders wrote in an elevated, genteel, romantic spirit that came to be identified as the national style although it really was not. Their subject matter were rural scenes and the beauties of nature, human struggle, and natural order. Above all, perhaps, their work was marked by an unflagging optimism in humankind and in the American nation in particular. They championed the great movements of their day, such as abolitionism and transcendentalism.

The New Englanders' reign as the nation's literary aristocracy lasted roughly from 1830 through the Civil War, a period known as the Golden Age in American literature. Its fullest flowering could be seen in the 1850s when its leading lights were at the peak of their creative power. They made Boston the literary capital of America, with its extensions in nearby Concord and Cambridge, where Ralph Waldo Emerson lived and Harvard stood, respectively. Many of them outlived the Civil War, but by then their best work was behind them; the nation and its literary tastes had moved on. By the late 1850s they were already in the autumn of their reign over American letters. But for more than three decades through books and literary periodicals such as *The Atlantic Monthly* the New England light shone forth over all of the United States, withering the literature in all other regions of the country. After the Civil War the voice of New England was not its literary geniuses but its politicians, hucksters, and financiers. But even today those antebellum writers form the core of the traditional American literary canon.

As the great sectional conflict drew nearer, the divisive spirit of sectionalism infused every aspect of American life, including its literature. This split produced dueling literary traditions in the North and the South. Sectional pride and partisan politics stoked the literary fires. Northern literature still reflected its Puritan heritage, but it was now defined by the antislavery screeds of such authors as William Lloyd Garrison, John Greenleaf Whittier, and Harriet Beecher Stowe. Other reformist writers took their cue from the abolitionists. Southern literature, by contrast, was more derivative, idealizing romantic European authors such as Sir Walter Scott rather than home-grown talent, the most successful of whom were those chauvinistic authors who proudly wore the label "Sons of the South." The most consistent theme was the proslavery apologia, which ranged from commentary by Edgar Allan Poe to pseudoscholarly critiques such as *The Impending Crisis* by Hinton Helper. Not surprisingly, agriculture and plantation life played a major role in the works of Southern writers, giving rise to a subgenre known as plantation romances. Southern poetry was even less distinguished than the region's prose. As the South became increasingly insular and defensive in the antebellum period, it gradually ceded cultural leadership to the North.

The Civil War sparked an outburst of patriotic prose and poetry on both sides, little of which, outside Julia Ward Howe's inspiring "Battle Hymn of the Republic," is remembered today. Southern poets, even more than their Northern counterparts, were long on sentimental themes and short on style and technique. The popularity of Southerners such as Theodore O'Hara ("The Bivouac of the Dead," 1866) was a product more of their times than of their literary merit.

The third major section of the country, the West, inspired more writers back East than it actually produced on the local scene and in the long term had a greater impact on U.S. reading tastes than either New England or the South. The Western genre actually began with James Fenimore Cooper's *Leatherstocking Tales* (1823–41), which introduced the first genuine American fictional hero, Natty Bumpo: a "natural man," a "man of action" who was almost anti-intellectual. From that beginning it followed several diverse trails that included the dime novels of Ned Buntline, the reality-grounded short stories of Bret Harte (e.g., *The Luck of Roaring Camp and Other Sketches,* 1870), and the self-conscious poetry of Joaquin Miller (e.g., *Songs of the Sierras,* 1871). It burst into the public consciousness after the Civil War with stories of cow towns and cattle drives, mining camps and boom towns, outlaws and lawmen. Bret Harte invented the stereotypes of all later Western stories: the pretty New England schoolmarm, the flinty sheriff, the bad man, the slick gambler, the heroic stagecoach-driver, the harlot with the heart of gold. They all appeared in one or more of Harte's stories and helped make him by the early 1870s the best-known and highest-paid writer in America.

TABLE 15.1 THE "NEW ENGLAND FLOWERING" OR GOLDEN AGE OF AMERICAN LITERATURE, 1850–1860

Work	Author	Type of Literature	Date of Publication
The Scarlet Letter	Nathaniel Hawthorne	Novel	1850
Representative Men	Ralph Waldo Emerson	Biographical essays	1850
Songs of Labor	John Greenleaf Whittier	Poetry anthology	1850
White-Jacket	Herman Melville	Novel	1850
Conspiracy of Pontiac	Francis Parkman	History	1851
The House of the Seven Gables	Nathaniel Hawthorne	Novel	1851
Moby-Dick	Herman Melville	Novel	1851
The Golden Legend	Henry Wadsworth Longfellow	(Narrative) poetry	1851
Pierre	Herman Melville	Novel	1852
Uncle Tom's Cabin	Harriet Beecher Stowe	Novel	1852
Walden, or Life in the Woods	Henry David Thoreau	Memoir	1854
Maud Muller	John Greenleaf Whittier	Poetry anthology	1854
Leaves of Grass	Walt Whitman	Poetry anthology	1855
Song of Hiawatha	Henry Wadsworth Longfellow	(Narrative) poetry	1855
My Bondage and My Freedom	Frederick Douglass	Autobiography	1855
The Barefoot Boy	John Greenleaf Whittier	Poetry anthology	1855
Life of George Washington	Washington Irving	Historical biography	1855–59
The Piazza Tales	Herman Melville	Short stories	1856
English Traits	Ralph Waldo Emerson	Essays	1856
The Courtship of Miles Standish	Henry Wadsworth Longfellow	(Narrative) poetry	1858
Autocrat of the Breakfast Table	Oliver Wendell Holmes, Sr.	Collection of essays	1858

Sources: Merriam-Webster's Encyclopedia of Literature, Kathleen Kuiper, *et al.,* eds. (Springfield, Mass.: Merriam-Webster, 1995) 342, 376, 523, 553, 589, 693, 748, 1,072, 1,111, 1,199; *Benét's Reader's Encyclopedia,* 3d ed. (New York: Harper & Row, 1987), 273, 300–01, 429–30, 456,486, 579–80, 637, 737, 937, 975, 1,061–62.

TABLE 15.2 LEADING DIME NOVEL PUBLISHERS, NINETEENTH CENTURY

Firm	Address	Most Popular Titles (Series Number and Authors Where Known)
Beadle & Adams	98 William Street, New York City	*Seth Jones, or The Captives of the Frontier* (no. 1, E. S. Ellis) *Deadly-Eye* (no. 24, Buffalo Bill) *Fancy Frank, or Colorado, or The Trapper's Trust* (no. 158, Buffalo Bill) *Kansas King, or The Red Right Hand* (no. 1,038, Buffalo Bill) *The Dread Shot Four, or My Pards of the Plains* (no. 973, Buffalo Bill) *Adventures of Wild Bill, the Pistol Prince* (no. 354, P. Ingraham) *Night Hawk George, and His Daring Deeds and Adventures in the Wilds of the South and the West* (no. 39, P. Ingraham) *Bowie Knife Ben, The Little Hunter of the Nor'west* (no. 29, Oll Coomes) *Buffalo Bill, the King of Border Men* (Ned Buntline) *Theyendangea, the Scourge, or The War Eagle of the Mohawks* (no. 14, Ned Buntline) *Deadwood Dick's Dream; or, The Rivals of the Road* (Edward L. Wheeler) *The Mustang-Hunters; or, The Beautiful Amazon of the Hidden Valley* (Frederick Whittaker)
Frank Tousey Publisher	34–36 North Moore Street, New York City	*The Life and Trial of Frank James* ("Special") The Wide Awake Library
John W. Morrison, Publisher	13–15 Vandewater Street, New York City	Morrison's Sensational Series
Street and Smith	29 Rose Street, New York City	The Diamond Dick Library

Sources: Denis McLoughlin, *Wild and Woolly: An Encyclopedia of the Old West* (New York: Barnes & Noble Books, 1975), 37–38, 134–35; Howard R. Lamar, ed., *The Reader's Encyclopedia of the American West* (New York: Thomas Y. Crowell, 1977), 303–04.

Bret Harte was an original, but he inspired a host of imitators who created a new form of literature in the "dime novel." The success of this legendary genre depended less on authors than on editors and publishers, who turned the work of hack writers into best sellers. The New York firm of Beadle & Adams and their editor, Orville J. Victor, were the major players in the game, churning out so many dime novels a year the volumes had to be numbered serially. In the process they practically invented the "celebrity author" (e.g., Buffalo Bill Cody), the "ghost writer" (e.g., Edward Z. C. Judson), and the formulaic plot. The typical dime novel was roughly 30,000 words (about 160 pages), printed on cheap paper in magazine-size format (about 8½ by 11 inches), and sold for a nickel ("Special Issues" cost 10 cents). (Though mass-market novels originally cost 5 cents, they soon went up to 10 cents, and all were dubbed by the generic name "dime novels.") New titles were issued weekly by upstart publishing houses eager to cash in on the craze before the bubble burst.

Nationalist Literature

Despite all the emphasis on sectional themes, a truly nationalist literature did begin to develop during these years. Its beginnings could be seen in 1833, when the first *Encyclopedia Americana,* modeled after the *Encyclopaedia Britannica,* was published. By the 1850s it was a steady seller to middle-class families as well as schools and libraries. Between 1834 and 1874 the historian George Bancroft published his magisterial 10-volume *History of the United States,* which would remain the standard national history for many years.

It was the "age of the common man," and American writers began exploring national subjects such as slavery, manifest destiny, and the West. Additionally the themes of self-discovery and the "natural man" were quite popular. By the time of the Civil War a distinctive national literary tradition that could stand beside the best of Europe had been created.

The end of that war led to a new phase in American literature: more realistic, less regional in appeal, more grounded in everyday life. Scholars have applied the labels *realistic* and *naturalistic* to it because it veered away from the romantic spirit and idealism of pre–Civil War literature.

Sentimental Literature

The remaining genres of American 19th-century literature were less colored by politics. Sentimental literature was driven by emotion, specifically, feminine emotions, of both its readers and its writers. These were works of a melodramatic nature that limned the conflict of good versus evil, with good always triumphant. The poet John Greenleaf Whittier was the finest representative of this type of writing, but the genre is primarily notable for the extraordinary numbers of women writers it attracted. They wrote for a vast, mostly feminine audience that crossed all state and sectional boundaries. Sentimental novels, also known as parlor literature, were partly a reaction to the cult of rugged individualism and issue-oriented subject matter that occupied contemporary male writers. They were disdained by the male literary fraternity but proved immensely profitable for publishers, drawing in $12.5 million in 1850 alone. The sentimental genre, however, in a few years degenerated into a formulaic style built on the rigid social codes and proper manners favored by the rising middle class.

Women Writers

The most important accomplishment of the sentimentalist genre was to provide entry into the world of letters for a significant number of women for the first time in U.S. history. Writers such as Fanny

Fern (the pseudonym of Sara Payson Willis Parton), Lydia Maria Child, and Lydia Howard Huntley Sigourney for the first time challenged the historically male-dominated literary fraternity. Their ranks included both poets and prose writers, but novelists were at the forefront of this literary insurgency.

What these women lacked when compared to the men was not so much sheer literary talent as the knack of self-promotion possessed by such individuals as Walt Whitman and Nathaniel Hawthorne. Often their very success was held against them. They faced obstacles the men did not have to face, not the least of which was being expected to write on "feminine" topics in a "ladylike" way. Despite these obstacles, women writers flourished during this period as never before, making a significant impact on any list of best sellers. In fact, the highest-selling group of authors in this era were the women. This point is often forgotten because of the focus on the enduring masterpieces of men such as Melville, Hawthorne, and Emerson. Yet, Elizabeth Wetherell's 1851 work *The Wide, Wide World,* a typical "women's novel," sold 300,000 copies, numbers no publisher could ignore. And two of the highest sellers of 1868 were Louisa May Alcott's novel *Little Women* and W. R. Alger's nonfiction study *The Friendship of Women.* These and similarly themed books put the publishing world on notice that women readers were a market to be reckoned with, and no one could serve that market better than women writers.

Travel Literature

Another favorite genre among American readers was travel literature. It was only natural that books about exotic places would sell to a restless people always looking for a better place to live or a new adventure. Writers famous and not so famous hopped on stage coaches, joined exploring expeditions, and sailed to distant ports with pen always in hand to record their impressions. Not surprisingly, Europe was a favorite destination for literary wanderers, and American authors, as well as their artistic compatriots, did not consider themselves complete until they had made the Old World pilgrimage. Unlike the artistic elite, however, native authors invariably returned home confirmed in their "Americanness" by their travels and content to write about what they knew best.

Most U.S. writers, determined to "see the elephant," turned their feet westward toward the frontier rather than eastward toward the Old World. Such celebrated writers as Bret Harte, Mark Twain, and Horace Greeley found more to inspire them in the western reaches of the United States than in all the cosmopolitan capitals of Europe. Together they helped create a booming market for tales of the Wild West and thus beget what is known today as Western literature.

Urban Literature

Western literature even in these years bordered on quaint mythology because the West it described was fast disappearing, if such a place ever existed at all. More avant garde at this time was an emerging literature about city life and industrial America. One scholar has counted only 38 "urban novels" published in the United States up to 1839, compared to nearly 340 published in the 20 years after 1840. Between 1840 and 1870 works in urban literature outnumbered those on Western subjects by more than three to one. The trend was led by the beloved "rags-to-riches" novels of Horatio Alger, which were more than children's literature, although they were written for boys. They created a sort of urban mythology comparable to that created by the famous dime novels for the West. In this version of city life street urchins could through hard work and perseverence rise to be business executives. The bootstrap literature that Alger and others produced hammered home the themes of self-improvement and personal reformation. The best example was *Ten Nights on a Bar-room Floor* (1855), which painted the evils of strong drink in such grim terms that every reader should have wanted to hop "on the wagon." Theodore Dreiser, the greatest critic of industrialization's dehumanizing effects, was born only at the end of this period (1871); most writers still saw America in Jeffersonian (i.e., agrarian) terms.

African-American Literature

A small but significant black literature appeared during these years, most of it centered around slave narratives, so named because they chronicled the lives of African Americans trapped in bondage. Typically such works described life on a plantation and the author's struggles to reach freedom. To be a genuine slave narrative, the story must be autobiographical; for that *Uncle Tom's Cabin* was not, strictly speaking, a slave narrative. The best were published by English or Northern presses; some were even privately printed when all other outlets were closed. They were universally praised by abolitionists as honest and real while being roundly damned by Southerners as scurrilous attacks on their "peculiar institution." Most of the authors were still classified as runaways when they wrote their memoirs, so they were forced to write either anonymously or under a pseudonym because of very real fears of being recaptured if they drew attention to themselves.

The first slave narrative was published in Boston in 1760, and in the next 100 years they became almost a subgenre of American literature. There is some suspicion that many were ghost-written and sensa-

Twelve Years A Slave: Narrative of Solomon Northrup was of the most remarkable examples of the popular 19th-century literary genre, the slave memoir. Unlike *Uncle Tom's Cabin,* this account is authentic. (The Gilder Lehrman Collection at the Pierpont Morgan Library, New York. GLC 5840)

tionalized for polemical purposes. Some other entries in the genre were outright frauds, such as Mattie Griffith's *The Autobiography of a Female Slave* (1856). Because few blacks could read and fewer still had access to books, the readership for this kind of literature consisted almost exclusively of white abolitionists and those who had a burning curiosity about how the "other half" lived (what one scholar calls "a black message inside a white envelope"). The heyday of the genre occurred between 1830 and 1860. The Civil War shifted the focus of the abolition struggle from the lecture platform and the publishing house to the battlefield and the halls of Congress.

After the Civil War slave narratives fell out of favor because curiosity and outrage had both been sated. Furthermore the battle for emancipation had been won and other issues were demanding the nation's attention. After the turn of the century many slave narratives were gathered in anthologies as part of oral history projects, but these lacked the literary impact of the original monographs. Today examples of the genre are virtually ignored except by scholars of African-American history and professors of 19th-century literature. And because they remain virtually the only source for early African-American literature, they are sometimes lauded beyond their actual literary merits.

TABLE 15.3 NOTABLE FIRST-PERSON SLAVE NARRATIVES, MID-1800s

Name of Work	Author (Pseudonym)	Date Published	Significance
Narrative of the Life of Frederick Douglass, an American Slave	Frederick Douglass	1845 (revised, 1882)	Sold 30,000+ copies in first five years; made its author the first international black celebrity of abolitionist movement
The Fugitive Blacksmith	James Pembroke (James William Charles Pennington)	1849	Pembroke also authored of the first textbook by an African American, *The Origin and History of Colored People* (1841)
Narrative of the Life and Adventures of Henry Bibb, an American Slave. Written by Himself	Henry Walton Bibb	1849 ("By the Author")	Pushed the author to forefront of abolitionist movement as spokesman for emigration and black autonomy
Narrative of the Life of Henry Box Brown	Henry B. Brown	1851	Published in England because the author (and supporters) could not find U.S. publisher
Twelve Years a Slave, Narrative of Solomon Northrup, A Citizen of New York, Kidnaped in Washington in 1841, and Rescued in 1853, from a Cotton Plantation Near the Red River in Louisiana	Solomon Northrup	1853 (Summer) (reprinted, 1965)	Sold more than 30,000 copies in its first printing, rivaling in popularity *Narrative of the Life of Frederick Douglass*
My Bondage and My Freedom	Frederick Douglass	1855	More carefully crafted telling of his famous memoir with an eye on history
Autobiography of a Fugitive Negro: His Anti-Slavery Labours in the United States, Canada, and England	Samuel Ringgold Ward	1855	First published in London because it found no U.S. publisher.
The Life of John Thompson, A Fugitive Slave; Containing His History of 25 Years in Bondage, and His Providential Escape. Written by Himself	John Thompson	1856	. . .
Twenty-Two Years a Slave, and Forty Years a Freeman	Austin Steward	1857	. . .
Our Nig; or, Sketches from the Life of a Free Black, in a Two-Story White House, North. Showing That Slavery's Shadows Fall Even There	Harriet E. Adams Wilson ("Our Nig")[a]	Sep. 5, 1859 (republished 1983)	"Probably the first woman of African descent to publish a novel in any language"; attracted little attention at the time
Incidents in the Life of a Slave Girl: Written by Herself	Harriet A. Jacobs (Linda Brent)	1861	"Most comprehensive antebellum autobiography by an African-American woman"; first to discuss sexual side of slavery
Narrative of the Live of Jacob D. Green, a Runaway Slave, From Kentucky, Containing an Account of His Three Escapes, in 1839, 1846, and 1848	Jacob D. Green	1864	8,000 copies printed for first run

Name of Work	Author (Pseudonym)	Date Published	Significance
Behind the Scenes, or, Thirty Years a Slave, and Four Years in the White House	Elizabeth Keckley	1868 (reprinted, 1988)	Unique view of the Lincoln White House
Scenes in the Life of Harriet Tubman	Harriet Tubman[b]	1869	No political impact; primarily interesting as first-person account of woman called "the Moses of her people"
The Underground Railroad. A Record of Facts, Authentic Narratives, Letters, etc. . . .	William Still	1871 (revised, second edition, 1879)	"Narrating the hardships, hair-breadth escapes and death struggles of the Slaves in their efforts for Freedom, as related by Themselves and others, or witnessed by the author."

[a]Almost nothing is known of the author's life either before or after the book, and there is still some doubt that Adams was "Our Nig."
[b]As told to Sarah H. Bradford.
Sources: Yuval Taylor, ed., *I was Born a Slave: An Anthology of Classic Slave Narratives,* vol. 2: *1849–1866* (Chicago: Lawrence Hill Books, 1999), passim; Jack Salzman, David L. Smith, and Cornel West, eds., *Encyclopedia of African-American Culture and History,* 5 vols. (New York: Simon & Schuster/Macmillan, 1996), passim; *Merriam-Webster's Encyclopedia of Literature,* Kathleen Kuiper et al., eds., (Springfield, Mass.: Merriam-Webster, 1995), passim; Marion Wilson Starling, *The Slave Narrative: Its Place in American History* (Washington, D.C.: Howard University Press, 1988), passim.

American Indian Literature

This period also saw the first serious treatment of American Indians in American literature, as opposed to the dime-novel tales of bloodthirsty savages. James Fenimore Cooper introduced the theme with his sympathetic treatment of Native Americans in the "Leatherstocking" series of novels. He was to American literature what George Catlin (1796–1872) was to American art as a sympathetic interpreter of Indian life. Cooper was the first popular U.S. author to recognize the injustices done to the Indians by white settlers. His most interesting characterization in *Last of the Mohicans* is not the supposed hero, Hawkeye (Natty Bumpo), but the noble chief, Uncas. Picking up on that same theme, Longfellow's *The Song of Hiawatha* was factually grounded on the work of the Indian ethnologist Henry Rowe Schoolcraft, who declared it the first literary work to treat Native Americans "seriously and respectfully." A further breakthrough occurred with the publication in 1854 of the first novel by a Native American, *The Life and Adventures of Joaquin Murieta,* by the Cherokee author John Rollin Ridge (Yellow Bird). These beginnings were modest, but they represented a significant advance over previously unenlightened treatment of the Indian as a cartoonish literary subject.

True Crime Tales

The appearance of several new forms made this an age of ferment in American literature. Perhaps the most notable were the sentimental novels and slave narratives because these represented the emergence of new voices, namely, those of women and African Americans. A lesser genre appearing at this time were true-crime stories, gothic tales of murder and lust that titillated Victorian sensibilities used to the high-toned literature of the New England Brahmins. The popularity of the form even inspired a subgenre, fictionalized biographies of the murderers and their victims. Their titles were lurid come-ons, the authors were invariably hacks, and the books were rushed into print to cash in on public curiosity while the crime was still fresh in the news.

TABLE 15.4 A SELECTION OF TRUE-CRIME TALES, MID-1800s

Title	Author[a]	Date (Publisher)
Horrible Murder of Mrs. Ellen Lynch, and Her Sister, Mrs. Hannah Shaw	A. Winch	1853 (Philadelphia: privately printed)
Tragedies on the Land, Containing an Authentic Account of the Most Awful Murders	A. Winch	1853 (Philadelphia: privately printed)
Trial of Professor John W. Webster for the Murder of Dr. George Parkman	John A. French	1850 (Boston: privately printed)
Life and Confession of Mrs. Henrietta Robinson, the Veiled Murderess!	Dr. H. P. Skinner	1855 (Boston: privately printed)
Trial of Reuben Dunbar, for the Murder of Stephen V. Lester and David L. Lester	P. L. Gilbert	1850 (Albany, N.Y.: privately printed)
The Fyler Murder Case	Unknown	1855 (Syracuse, N.Y.: Smith & Hough)
The Burdell Murder Case	Unknown	1857 (New York: Stearns & Co.)
The Conspirators' Victims, or, the Life and Adventures of J. V. Craine	Unknown	1855 (Sacramento, Calif.: Gardiner & Kirk)
A Sketch of the Life and Adventures of Henry Leander Foote	Henry Leander Foote	1850 (New Haven, Conn.: T. J. Stafford)
The Trial for Murder of James E. Eldredge	Unknown	1857 (Ogdensburgh, N.Y.: Hitchock, Tillotson Y Stilwell's Steam Presses)

[a] Many of these books were churned out quickly by anonymous contract writers in almost formulaic fashion in order to rush them into print. Authorship was not important.
Source: Karen Halttunen, *Murder Most Foul* (Cambridge, Mass.: Harvard University Press, 1998), xi–xiv.

Civil War Literature

The Civil War produced a tremendous outpouring of literature, especially in the North, where publishing was easier and the literary tradition ran deeper. Almost 4,000 titles were published by Northern houses in 1862 alone. Typical titles were *The Quadroon of Louisiana* and *Scar Chief the Wild Halfbreed*. Most Civil War literature had a patriotic theme, but it included everything from war romances and spy novels to children's stories. The authors for the most part were not members of the antebellum literary pantheon, and few were heard from in later years. Furthermore many of their subjects and titles were politically incorrect by the standards of today, and for that reason the entire field of Civil War popular literature has often been dismissed by scholars as "low literature." But it was much more.

The most popular reading matter among soldiers was still the Bible. More than 1 million were distributed to Union troops by the U.S. Christian Commission during the war. The same group also created the first "bookmobiles" by outfitting wagons as portable libraries, each with 75 to 125 volumes, and making the rounds of the Union army camps.

The Publishing Industry

Book publishing underwent a transformation during these years that saw it become big business. The industry grew from offering approximately 100 titles every year with revenues of some $2.5 million up to 1850, to producing 1,092 titles in 1855 with revenues of $16 million. Total annual production reached 12 million volumes in 1850, a fivefold increase over that of 1820. The increase was partly due to the introduction of new technology, such as the steam press and stereotyping, and partly to the growing appetite of Americans for reading matter of all kinds.

The center of the publishing industry was in the New York–Philadelphia–Boston triangle, cities that were already the media centers of the nation. Harper and Brothers, a New York City firm, moved their operations into a pair of seven-story buildings in 1853. The transformation of the publishing industry into big business also changed the relationship between authors and the reading public, with the biggest change being the aggressive marketing of "best sellers" to a reading-hungry public. Traditionally authors assumed the financial risk of publishing their own works, as books were presold by subscription before the presses ever rolled. Adding to the chaotic and insecure nature of publishing for authors, there was no international copyright law, so the English in particular routinely published the most popular U.S. works (and vice versa) without paying a penny in royalties. Charles Dickens, who had a huge U.S. readership, railed against the situation, calling himself "the greatest loser by it" and labeling U.S. firms who routinely reprinted his works "American robbers." (The situation did not change until 1891, when the United States and Great Britain signed an international copyright agreement.)

Heretofore no one had thought much about best sellers because the world of literature had always belonged to "gentlemen of elegant leisure" (Edgar Allan Poe's words), who were expected to read for education and edification, not pleasure. Most U.S. authors, it seemed, were either New Englanders or Virginians and the product of genteel backgrounds. They tended to write of serious matters for thoughtful readers. Patriotism and moral dilemmas were favorite subjects. Adventure tales, lusty or sensual topics, frivolous matters, and low humor were all considered unseemly.

All that was already changing before mid-century, but the change began to accelerate after 1850, when the U.S. book trade began to reorganize itself along more commercial and populist lines. One of the major changes was that publishers gained more control over the business at the expense of authors, by taking on a greater share of the financial risks. This gave them motivation to promote their books aggressively to the public, but it also allowed them to dictate the sort of works authors should write. It was publishing considerations that persuaded Nathaniel Hawthorne to switch from writing short stories to novels because the latter sold better. Before anyone could say "best seller," the publisher became as important as the author in the world of literature, and powerful publishers such as James T. Fields of Boston's Ticknor, Reed & Fields used this power to decide what Americans read. For the author this meant that henceforward critical acceptance must be weighed against commercial success.

The Lost Trail was a typical dime novel from the "fiction factory" of Beadle and Adams of New York. Starting in 1860 B&A became the most successful publishers of this most popular form of "literature" in American history. This 1864 volume was number 71 in a series that eventually reached thousands. Soldiers on both sides during the Civil War eagerly read the books when they could get them. Lithograph, 1864. (Library of Congress, Prints and Photographs Divisions [LC-USZ62-075779])

Prose and poetry, fiction and nonfiction—there were best sellers in all of these categories. The measure of a best seller was quite different in the middle of the 19th century. Selling books by subscription meant that agents were sent out to take orders; only after sufficient orders were in hand were the books printed. Few bookshops existed outside the Northeast, and the capsule book review that readers rely on today was not yet a staple of newspapers and magazines. Books became best sellers largely through word of mouth, a process that could be very slow, so a book that sold 200,000 copies or went through multiple editions was truly a phenomenon. The best-selling English-language author of the day was not even an American; he was the Englishman Charles Dickens. The author of *David Copperfield* (1850), *Bleak House* (1853), and a dozen other classics put seven books on the best-seller list between 1850 and 1875, selling a combined total of more than 1,725,000 volumes. It is no wonder that in 1842 this most English of authors made a triumphal five-month tour of the United States—an occasion that he used to criticize U.S. copyright law and pirating practices.

In fact, Dickens would have had seven books on the best-seller lists if there had been best-seller lists in the mid-19th century. There were not because such figures were not even tabulated until 1895, when *The Bookman* first began gathering sales figures. For earlier years historians have had to try to assemble lists from the available information. In the mid-20th century, the literary historian Frank Luther Mott compiled his own list of U.S. best sellers for the 19th century, based on the benchmark of total sales "equal to one per cent of the population of the continental United States for the decade in which it was published." That meant, for the decade 1850–59, sales of 225,000; for 1860–69, sales of 300,000; and for 1870–1879, 375,000. This benchmark provides an arbitrary but useful standard of measurement to gauge popularity.

Not every important book was a best seller. The impact of a literary work is not based only on its popularity. In the 19th century with no competition from television or radio people had to get most of their knowledge from the printed page. That is why books played an even more crucial role in shaping public opinion than they do today. *Uncle Tom's Cabin* (1852) influenced so many Americans' attitudes about slavery that when Abraham Lincoln met Harriet Beecher Stowe during the Civil War, he remarked, "So you're the little woman that wrote the book that started this great war!" Similarly influential, *The Gilded Age* (1872) gave its name to the entire post–Civil War era. *Uncle Tom's Cabin* is one book that met both criteria: i.e., historical significance and huge popularity. In many other cases works that are considered significant or influential in hindsight were not best sellers at the time. And historical significance is not limited to fiction or even to prose. The epic poetry of Henry Wordsworth Longfellow or John Greenleaf Whittier helped shape Americans' vision of their country in heroic terms. A short story, a memoir, or even an essay could have great impact on the national consciousness even without selling 100,000 copies.

The Grolier Club of New York City has assembled a list of "The 100 Most Influential American Books" based on its own criteria. It is interesting to compare that listing to Luther Mott's calculation of best-sellers for the years 1850 through 1875.

TABLE 15.5 TOP SELLERS ACCORDING TO THE GROLIER CLUB'S "100 MOST INFLUENTIAL AMERICAN BOOKS," 1850–1875

Year	Book	Author
1850	*The Scarlet Letter*	Nathaniel Hawthorne
1851	*Moby-Dick*	Herman Melville
1852	*Uncle Tom's Cabin*	Harriet Beecher Stowe
1854	*Ten Nights in a Bar-Room*	T. S. Arthur
1854	*Walden*	Henry David Thoreau
1855	*The Song of Hiawatha* (poem)	Henry Wadsworth Longfellow
1855	*Leaves of Grass*	Walt Whitman
1855	*Familiar Quotations*	John Bartlett
1855	*The Age of Fable*	Thomas Bulfinch
1857	*Dred Scott v. Sandford* (Supreme Court decision)	Chief Justice Roger Taney and others
1858	*The Autocrat of the Breakfast Table*	Oliver Wendell Holmes
1860	*Malaeska*	Ann S. Stephens
1862	Emancipation Proclamation (presidential announcement)	Abraham Lincoln
1863	Gettysburg Address (speech)	Abraham Lincoln
1866	*Snow-Bound*	John Greenleaf Whittier
1868	*Ragged Dick*	Horatio Alger, Jr.
1868	*Little Women*	Louisa May Alcott
1870	*The Luck of Roaring Camp* (short story)	Bret Harte
1872	First mail-order catalog	Sears & Roebuck
1875	Science and Health	Mary Baker Eddy

Note: The Grolier Club listing does not include the Bible, omits some years (e.g., 1853), and includes several books from other years (e.g., 1855).
Source: Rancy F. Nelson, *The Almanac of American Letters* (Los Altos, Calif.: William Kaufmann, 1981), 16–20.

Art

American art during the middle years was primarily defined by painting, and American painting was in the midst of a transition from the romantic style to the realistic, and from the European "grand manner" to the less affected genre form. Concurrent with this stylistic and generic evolution was a profound struggle to find a national identity—American as opposed to European, nationalist as opposed to regional, and distinctive as opposed to derivative. For centuries European art had been dominated by court artists painting either heroic battlefield victories or wealthy patrons surrounded by the symbols of their wealth and power. In America art, as did society, took on a more populist tone, although not all at once nor as a result of orders from on high.

Before 1850 the two most popular European schools of painting, historic and portraiture, had received only a lukewarm reception on the American side of the Atlantic. In fact there was little market for it. Historic painting failed to catch on perhaps because the United States had so little history at this point to celebrate; there was a dearth of those dramatic, myth-shrouded moments of national crisis that Europeans cherished. And portraiture languished because there was no self-obsessed noble class wealthy enough and numerous enough to provide a steady stream of commissions to would-be Rembrandts.

Three names stand out in American portraiture, two at the beginning of the period and one just emerging at the very end. At the front end were William Page (1811–85) and George Healy (1813–94). Page was a largely self-taught artist who painted psychologically profound likenesses of such celebrities as John Quincy Adams, William Lloyd Garrison, and Robert Gould Shaw (the hero of the 54th Massachusetts Colored Regiment during the Civil War). Although dubbed the American Titian for his creative use of color, Page had a career that faded in his later years. Healy also painted contemporary U.S. statesmen, presidents, and generals as well as figures from U.S. history, taking on 100 commissions a year. Despite his prolific output, Healy, as is Page, is largely forgotten today.

John Singer Sargent (1856–1925), the third notable portraiture artist, was at the end of this era on his way to becoming the portrait painter of choice for the privileged classes on both sides of the

Atlantic. He was the last great portraiturist of the 19th century. In painting America's nouveau riche in the old larger-than-life court style, his style represented a throwback to an earlier time.

The Romantic Style

The historic and portraiture artists emerged from a romantic tradition that still reigned supreme at the beginning of this period. The romantic artists produced work unrelated to romantic love; its focus was on natural beauty and emotive images, dreamlike scenes and shameless sentimentalism. The works conveyed no sense of the sweat, blood, and dirt that are intrinsic parts of real life. U.S. painters in the romantic tradition tended to emphasize two subjects, nature and the so-called Natural Man, finding the former in landscapes and the latter in genre studies. The subjects were realistic; it was the style that was romantic.

The Landscape and Genre Schools of Painting

U.S. artists were most drawn to the landscape and genre schools of the several schools that arose out of the romantic tradition. Landscape painting was an understandable choice in a country with so many sweeping vistas and breathtaking natural wonders wherever a person looked. Any discussion of American landscape painting must begin with the Hudson River School, which was America's first native school of painting. It was named for the area of New York State where it was born and whose wild, natural beauty furnished the favorite subject matter for most of its artists. The artists represented a true "school" because most of them lived and worked in the same locale, knew each other at least casually, and used the same techniques. As their work became more popular, they also included printmakers who were able to multiply the impact of the Hudson River School by reaching out to the masses.

The romantic classical style with its godlike figures and swirling clouds was alive and well in Constantino Brumidi's 1865 fresco *The Apotheosis of George Washington* on the dome of the Rotunda in the national Capitol building. The artist, who was paid only eight dollars a day for his work, could still state: "I have no longer any desire for fame or fortune. My one ambition and my daily prayer is that I may live long enough to make beautiful the Capitol of the one country on earth in which there is liberty." (Library of Congress, Prints and Photographs Division [230240])

The Hudson River artists represented a rebellion against the older neoclassical tradition of heroic, toga-bedecked subjects. Whereas the neoclassicists focused on portraiture, the Hudson River artists derived their inspiration from landscapes, combining realistic detail with idealized composition. Their landscapes, for all their detail, still had that picture-postcard-perfect look of the Old Masters. The Hudson River School was not a revolution in art, but a statement of American independence.

Their heyday lasted more than half a century, beginning in 1825 and divided into three distinctive periods or "generations." The first generation, led by Thomas Cole, originated in New York's Catskill Mountains in the 1820s, and their work was characterized by "dark-hued, meticulous compositions." After Cole's death in 1848 a second generation took their cues from Asher B. Durand and Frederic E. Church, seeking to introduce more subtle technique and greater realism into their work. Because of their distinct fondness for light-diffused scenes, they are sometimes known as the luminists. This was the high period of what could now be described as the Hudson River style, when its influence reached far beyond New York. The second generation lasted through the 1860s. The third generation emerged in the 1870s and represented both a decline and an evolution. It was less vigorous, less optimistic, but more natural than its predecessors. It was also strongly influenced by the latest import from Europe, French impressionism.

TABLE 15.6 THE SECOND AND THIRD GENERATIONS OF THE HUDSON RIVER SCHOOL

Artist (Life Dates)	Generation	Major Work(s)	Date of Work	Notable Features
Albert Bierstadt (1830–1902)	Second	1) *Buffalo Trail: The Impending Storm*[a] 2) *Evening on the Prairie* 3) *El Capitan, Yosemite Valley* 4) *Discovery of the Hudson*	1) 1869 2) ca. 1870 3) 1875 4) 1875	More a beneficiary than an exemplar of the Hudson River School; *Discovery of the Hudson* only claim to fame as member of the school
Ralph A. Blakelock (1847–1919)	Third	1) *Moonlight* 2) *Moonlight Indian Encampment*	1) ca. 1870s 2) ca. 1870s[b]	Landscapes imbued with "dark, brooding intensity" or melancholy
Frederic E. Church (1826–1900)	Second	1) *Niagara* 2) *Cayambe* 3) *Rainy Season in the Tropics*	1) 1857 2) 1858 3) 1866	Championed realistic style; preferred heroic-size geographic subjects
Jasper F. Cropsey (1823–1900)	Second	*Autumn on the Hudson River*	1860	Known for autumnal scenes
Asher B. Durand (1796–1886)	Second	1) *Kindred Spirits* 2) *In the Woods*	1) 1849 2) 1855	Unofficial group mentor and theorist
Sanford Robinson Gifford (1823–80)	Second	1) *Summer Afternoon* 2) *Kauterskill Cove*	1) 1853 2) 1862	Pioneer in luminist style; major member of second generation, with 739 known paintings
Martin Johnson Heade (1819–1904)	Third	*Storm Approaching Narragansett Bay*	1868	"Lost" work until discovered in antique store in 1940; sparked reevaluation of artist; leading representative of luminist style, who specialized in seascapes
George Inness (1825–94)	Third	1) *Lackawanna Valley* 2) *Peace and Plenty*	1) 1854 2) 1875	1) "A fine feeling for the new industrial landscape" with "rich harmonies of tone and color" 2) Represents a break with Hudson River style
John F. Kensett (1816–72)	Second	1) *Niagara Falls* 2) *A Woodland Waterfall* 3) *Storm over Lake George*	1) 1851 (1852?) 2) ca. 1855 3) 1870	Established school's basic compositions, sensation for its minute color gradations
Fitz Hugh Lane (1804–1865)	Second	*Owl's Head, Penobscot Bay, Maine*	1862	"Minor master of luminist mode"; spare, meticulous style
Homer Martin (1836–97)	Third	1) *Upper Ausable Lake* 2) *Lake Sanford*	1) 1868 2) 1870	Favored realistic wilderness scenes without intruding presence of humans
Thomas Worthington Whittredge (1820–1910)	Third	1) *Scene Near Hawk's Nest* 2) *Summer Pastorale* 3) *View of West Point* 4) *Old Hunting Ground* 5) *Camp Meeting*	1) 1845 2) 1853 3) 1860 4) 1864 5) 1874	"A sense of deep tranquility"; also representative of luminist style; several changes before mature style of *Old Hunting Ground*
Alexander Helwig Wyant (1836–92)	Third	*Tennessee* (formerly *The Mohawk Valley*)	1866	Heavily influenced by study in Europe; foreshadowed tonal impressionism

[a] Also known as *The Last of the Buffalo,* this work was rejected as "too old-fashioned" by the American selection committee for the Paris Universal Exposition in 1889.
[b] Most of Blakelock's works cannot be accurately dated.
Sources: The Britannica Encyclopedia of American Art (Chicago: Encyclopaedia Britannica Educational, 1973), 290–91; Matthew Baigwell, *Dictionary of American Art* (New York: Harper & Row, 1979), 174–75; Jane Turner, ed., *The Dictionary of Art,* vol. 14 New York: Grove's Dictionaries, 1996), 843–44.

The Hudson River School gave rise to another group of landscape artists, the luminists, who found their inspiration in the Far West. The beauties and the vastness of the wilderness beyond the frontier seemed to hold special fascination for artists such as George Caleb Bingham, George Catlin, Thomas Moran, and Alfred Jacob Miller. Some, such as Frederic Church and Albert Bierstadt, considered themselves explorers as well as artists, choosing to devote their career to discovering and recording America's natural wonders. Their landscapes usually had a panoramic perspective that dwarfed any human or animal in the scene and conveyed a sense of the vastness and silence of the West. The works of these men, displayed in the East, heightened popular interest in the country's western reaches. They also gave expression to the growing mythology of the West. Despite the best efforts of the Hudson River School and the luminists, by the end of the era, U.S. landscape painting was dying. Its passing might have been marked in 1889 by the refusal of the selection committee to accept Albert Bierstadt's epic canvas *The Last of the Buffalo* as one of the American entries at the Paris Universal Exposition later that year. The committee rejected it as "not representative" of contemporary American art.

The other major school to take root in the American artist community was genre painting, the depiction of men and women as social creatures at work and play. Its practitioners rejected the traditional European "grand manner" of art (an elevated form of historical or mythic narrative, full of heroes and demigods) in favor of more mundane subject matter. Scenes of common people engaged in everyday pursuits had a populist appeal that dovetailed nicely with the Jacksonian spirit of democracy and egalitarianism. This was an example of art's imitating society.

Although invented by Europeans, genre painting seemed to be truly "American." It had existed in the United States on a modest scale since the early 1820s, but only around mid-century did it come into its own, with archetypical "American" scenes (no fox hunts or religious pilgrimages) depicting strong masculine subjects and rugged settings. Genre artists also preferred a naturalism that had not heretofore been seen and so set the stage for the next big movement, realism.

The ever-present West exercised just as strong a pull on the genre painters as on the landscape painters. In fact, genre stylist George Caleb Bingham (1811–79) is often considered to be the first notable painter of the great American West, sharing Bierstadt's fascination with the frontier but working on the human rather than the landscape scale. Genre works about the West are full of colorful representative characters and violent confrontations—what later generations considered "real" Western art.

What did not seem to interest the genre painters much was Native American life. Earlier George Catlin had built an impressive career painting scenes of "noble savages," but Catlin fell out of favor, and Indians whether at war or peace were passé as a subject by 1850. The only artist still making a living painting Indians in this era was the illustrator Seth Eastman, who has never been considered in the front ranks of American painters.

Stump Speaking (1856) shows a favorite campaign tactic in 19th-century American politics. This work by the lithographer Louis-Adolphe Gautier is from a painting by the famous genre artist George Caleb Bingham, who here celebrates old-fashioned politics at a time when Kansas was "bleeding" and the sectional crisis was white hot. (The Gilder Lehrman Collection at the Pierpont Morgan Library, New York. GLC 4075)

Home Again (1866), an oil painting by Trevor McClurg, was a sentimental scene of a wounded Union veteran reunited with his family, portrayed in the old-fashioned romantic style. Such works were part of the national healing process after the Civil War, and the public snapped them up as fast as artists could paint, draw, or engrave them. *Home Again* was turned into an extremely popular engraving. (Library of Congress)

The Realistic Style

For all their chasing after nature and the natural man, America's genre and landscape artists were still firmly grounded in the romantic style. It took a new generation of artists to carry American art into its next period, realism. The realists strove for carbon-copy reproductions of their subjects on canvas and tried to show the real world, even with all its warts. They not only strove for accurate detail but stuck with subjects on a human, even mundane, scale. Their rise to prominence coincided with the rise of the industrial age, which impacted American art as much as it did American society and the economic system. The realists rejected what the historian Carol Strickland calls "Neoclassicism's anachronisms and Romanticism's escapism."The successor style to romanticism only emerged in America after mid-century, but before the end of the 19th-century it had displaced every genre that preceded it. The most influential American realist was Winslow Homer (1836–1910), who started as a commercial illustrator, blossomed during the Civil War, and pioneered a new medium, watercolor, at the same time that he was popularizing a new genre.

Rivaling Homer in importance as both an American artist and a representative of the realistic genre was Thomas Eakins (1844–1916). Eakins too aimed for photolike images of real-life scenes, but he moved his subject indoors and made the action more intimate. Eakins was something of a radical, marginalized in his day, but today he is widely considered America's finest 19th-century painter, perhaps even the greatest painter the nation ever produced.

Civil War Art

Although the Civil War exerted a powerful influence on music and only slightly less on literature, it scarcely touched art, or at least "serious" art. This was not due to a lack of effort. Patriotically inclined artists produced a multitude of powerful wartime images, but the nation's most gifted painters and sculptors seemed to sit out the war. Most men who earned a living as artists during the war did so by hiring themselves out as illustrators to such popular periodicals as *Frank Leslie's Illustrated Newspaper* and *Harper's Weekly*. Their ranks included the brothers William and Alfred R. Waud and the cartoonist Thomas Nast. Illustrators were considered the poor man's artists because they painted for a mass audience, and because although they possessed impressive technical skills, their artistic vision and individual styles were obscured by the limitations of wood-block engraving. Illustrating paid piecework wages, anywhere from five dollars to $25 per picture upon acceptance by an editor. As a result of the primitive state of reproductive technology, the true artistry of the original works was only approximated in the end product. Every illustration first had to be transferred to either stone or wood block by engravers, a grueling process that required up to four weeks for a single reproduction, and then inked onto newsprint. What the public eventually saw was a second- or third-generation copy of an original work, and even the original work was usually thrown away after it was reproduced.

As a genre Civil War art continued long after the guns fell silent, and some of the most moving and well-executed works appeared decades later. By that time nostalgia and romantic imagery had taken over, so that much of what was produced was burdened with strong messages of healing, hero worship, and other popular sentiments. The "best" of Civil War art in terms of authenticity and immediacy was produced between 1861 and about 1865.

Civil War art after 1865 included the primitive works of amateur soldier-artists such as the Confederate Conrad Chapman and the vast canvases known as battle cycloramas. The intended audience for these was as diverse as the artistic quality. The soldier-artists painted and drew more for personal satisfaction than for critical approval, and with rare exception their works were not displayed publicly during the artist's lifetime. What they sketched and painted served a therapeutic function by helping them cope with the grim memories of war. In Chapman's case his art therapy left a legacy of more than 600 oils, watercolors, and drawings of Confederate life. The cycloramas were enormous (400 by 50 feet typically) epic paintings that depicted entire battles in minute and realistic detail. They were conceived by such talented artists as Paul Philippoteaux and based on exhaustive research to ensure authenticity but executed by armies of semiskilled hirelings, a tradition at least as old as the Renaissance. Cycloramas were made for public display. They were exhibited around the country in specially constructed round buildings that allowed paying customers to enjoy an experience that could not be surpassed until moviemaking began decades later.

Notable Contemporary Artists and Their Works

One problem created by categorizing artists is that many move back and forth between genres and mediums during their lifetime, and some begin in one style then evolve into another, different style. For instance, Winslow Homer began his long career making realistic illustrations of Civil War scenes, then years later concentrated on impressionist-like marine studies. Albert Bierstadt began his career in the Hudson River School before expanding his horizons quite literally and becoming one of the foremost historians of the Far West. At any given time certain pioneers or trendsetters stand out from the group by showing a different way to look at the surrounding world.

TABLE 15.7 PIONEERS AND TRENDSETTERS IN AMERICAN ART, MID-1800s

Artist	Life Dates	School/Genre/Style (Medium)	Most Famous Work(s)
George Peter Alexander Healy	1813–94	Portraiture (oil)	*The Peacemakers* (1868) *Abraham Lincoln* (1864)[a]
George Catlin	1796–1872	Portraiture Genre studies (oil)	The Indian Gallery (1837*f*) The Cartoon Collection (1870*f*)
Albert Bierstadt	1830–1902	Landscape painting Romanticism (oil)	*The Rocky Mountains, Lander's Peak* (1863) *Domes of Yosemite* (1867) *Evening on the Prairie* (1870)
George Caleb Bingham	1811–79	Portraiture Genre painting Landscapes (oil)	*Emigration of Daniel Boone* (1851) *County Election* (1851, 1852) *Stump Speaking* (1854)
Edgar Degas[b]	1834–1917	French impressionism (oil)	*Woman with Bandage* (1872–73) *A Cotton Office in New Orleans* (1873)
Thomas Eakins	1844–1915	Realism Genre Portraiture (watercolor; oil) Sculpture	*Max Schmitt in a Single Scull* (1871) *Clinic of Dr. Gross* (1875) *Chess Players* (1875)
Seth Eastman	1808–75	Illustrations Genre scenes of American Indians (watercolor; oil)	Illustrations for Mary Eastman's *The Iris* (1852) and Henry Rowe Schoolcraft's *Information Regarding the History, Conditions, and Prospects of the Indian Tribes of the United States* (1851–57)[c]
Winslow Homer	1836–1910	Illustrations Landscape Genre (Civil War scenes) Marine subjects (watercolor; oil)	*Sharpshooter* (1863) *Prisoners from the Front* (1865) *Morning Bell* (1866) *High Tide at Long Branch* (1869) *Snap-the-Whip* (1872) *The Carnival* (1875)
William Morris Hunt	1824–79	Portraiture (oil)	*Self-Portrait* (1866)
Jonathan Eastman Johnson	1824–1906	Genre Portraiture (oil)	*Old Kentucky Home—Life in the South* (1859) *The Boyhood of Abraham Lincoln* (1868) *The Family Group* (1871) *Self Portrait* (1899) Portraits of Daniel Webster, Henry Wadsworth Longfellow, Ralph Waldo Emerson

Artist	Life Dates	School/Genre/Style (Medium)	Most Famous Work(s)
John La Farge	1835–1910	Murals (oil)	Interior walls of Trinity Church, Boston, Mass.
Emanuel Leutze	1816–68	Historical (allegory) Portraiture Murals (oil)	*Washington Crossing the Delaware* (1850)[d] *Westward the Course of Empire Takes Its Way* (1862, mural) Portraits of Generals Grant and Burnside
Thomas Moran	1837–1926	Landscapes (particularly of the West) (oil; watercolor)[e]	*The Grand Canyon of the Yellowstone* (1875) *The Teton Range* (1897) *Summit of the Sierras* (ca. 1872–75)
William Sidney Mount	1807–68	Genre (oil)[f]	*Farmers Nooning* (1836) *The Painter's Triumph* (1838) *Eel Spearing at Setauket* (1845) *The Bone Player* (1856)
Albert Pinkham Ryder	1847–1917	Marine subjects, pastoral landscapes, allegorical and literary subjects (oil mixtures)	*Moonlight Marine* (ca. 1870s)
James McNeill Whistler[g]	1834–1903	Realism English aesthetic movement (oil, watercolor, pastel, etchings, lithographs)	*At the Piano* (1858) *The White Girl (Symphony in White)* (1861, 1867–72) *Arrangement in Grey and Black no. 1, Portrait of the Painter's Mother* (1872)

Note: This listing includes both native-born and naturalized American citizens; the only qualification is not where they were born or even lived most of their life, but whether they are identified as "American" artists.

[a] A large part of Healy's work was lost in the Great Chicago Fire of 1871.

[b] Although 100 percent French, Degas deserves inclusion on this list as the only 19th-century French impressionist to visit America and paint U.S. scenes. He spent five months in the Crescent City in 1872 and thereafter considered himself "almost a child of New Orleans," painting some 40 scenes of the city, all of them either interiors or portraits.

[c] Eastman is regarded today as "the foremost pictorial historian of the American Indian" in the 19th century.

[d] Leutze's *Washington Crossing the Delaware* is probably the single most famous U.S. painting to the average American citizen, not because of its technical aspects or even the artist, but because of its subject matter and heroic style.

[e] Moran has been dubbed the "Dean of American Landscape Painters" and "Artist of the Mountains" by art historians.

[f] Mount was the first identifiable genre painter among American artists and the first to paint the Yankee as a type.

[g] Whistler was an expatriate American artist who spent almost none of his professional career in the United States, yet is nonetheless identified as an "American artist" by scholars.

Sources: Jane Turner, ed., *The Dictionary of Art* (New York: Grove's Dictionaries, 1996), passim; *The Britannica Encyclopedia of American Art* (Chicago: Encyclopedia Britannica Educational, 1973), passim.; Matthew Baigell, *Dictionary of American Art* (New York: Harper & Row, 1979), passim.

The Bird's-Eye View Fad

One of the most curious and underappreciated byways of 19th-century American art was the bird's-eye view, which first became popular just before mid-century and turned into a craze after the Civil War. Bird's-eye view pictures were detailed aerial perspectives of towns, cities, and the occasional battlefield, seen as if from on high. Also known as aeronautical or balloon views, they did not actually require the artist to leave terra firma; all that they required were a good eye for detail, good technique, and a vivid imagination. In fact, although showing photographic-like detail, they were not scrupulously realistic; instead they were idealized representations that tended to show scenes as those paying for them wanted them shown, not as they really were. But in the days before controlled flight and sophisticated photography, this kind of artwork captured all the distinctive features of a locale with photolike realism that impressed the residents. A number of firms went into business to meet the demand, sending their artists crisscrossing the country to sign up such towns as Hannibal, Missouri, or Davenport, Iowa, for these urban portraits. Most of the artists were unknown journeymen who worked fast and efficiently. Their employers made a fat fee from the city fathers, and the artist earned a modest commission for a few weeks' work. A handful of large firms dominated the business, producing the artwork then paying engravers/lithographers such as Currier & Ives or L. Prang & Co. to turn the original art into prints. Some of the larger firms did all the processing in-house.

View of Washington by Eugene Sachse, 1852, showing the national Capitol building looking toward the Potomac River. Note the close-in residential neighborhoods and the fanciful rendering of the Washington Monument, which was still not complete in reality. As in all bird's-eye views, the perspective is compressed and slightly distorted to show the panoramic view. (Library of Congress, Prints and Photographs Division [230240])

Bird's-eye views had a mechanistic, almost photographic appearance. This feature is not surprising because they were popular at the dawn of the age of photography. Bird's-eye views represented an attempt to combine the best of photography and art but were not entirely satisfactory as either.

TABLE 15.8 LEADING ARTISTS AND FIRMS PRODUCING BIRD'S-EYE VIEWS, NINETEENTH CENTURY

Artist or Firm	No. of Bird's-Eye Views Produced	Details of Career
Edwin Whitefield	Unknown	One-man operation from the 1840s
Edward Sachse & Co.	73+	Former German printmaker
James T. Palmatary	Unknown	Formerly associated with Sachse; on his own from mid-1850s
John Bachmann & Co.	53+	Former German printmaker
Albert Ruger	250+	Began in 1866
Thaddeus Mortimer Fowler	426+	Active until 1922
Oakley Hoopes Bailey	374+	Active until 1926

Sources: Jane Turner, ed., *The Dictionary of Art,* vol. 4 (New York: Grove's Dictionaries, 1996), 80–82; John W. Reps, *Bird's Eye Views* (New York: Princeton Architectural Press, 1998) 7–11, 116.

Photography as Art

Many quite capable U.S. artists of the late 19th-century failed to make a splash for reasons that were unrelated to their talent or critical acceptance. What happened was that artistic representation had been eclipsed by the new technology of the camera. Photographs were not only cheaper and faster than artistic images but widely accepted as 100 percent realistic in their detail. Always in love with the new and the modern, Americans embraced photography as did no other people on Earth, claiming it as their own. The decline of traditional art forms as a medium of expression was well under way by the end of this period.

Photography in one form or another had been around since the 1830s; because it was only slowly recognized as an art form, it is also discussed in chapter 17. Viewed in hindsight as an art form, however, photography began at just the right time to cash in on two things Americans had in abundance during these years: war images and unspoiled natural vistas. It was the wartime photos of Mathew Brady and a few others that made the Civil War real to the average American in all its horrors as no previous war in history had been recorded. And it was the travel photographs of such men as St. Louis's J. H. Fitzgibbon that helped persuade Congress to appropriate funds for creating the first national park, Yellowstone.

These artists of the camera had to deal with composition, perspective, lighting, and other technical matters just as brush artists such as Albert Bierstadt and Frederic Church did. And they represented the vanguard of a viable landscape school in American photography. Even with the primitive technology of the day, photography could rightfully boast of being a "mirror with a memory," as one contemporary described it. The photograph, as did the painting, had the ability to extend human vision beyond the immediately observable. If anything, photography could do that even better than paint and brush, and this characteristic has been called by photo historian Robert Taft "its greatest aesthetic function."

The most tradition-bound of camera artists concentrated on portraiture in the mid-19th century, represented by the popular *cartes de visite* (small photographs used as calling cards) starting in 1861. This technique for the first time in history spread portraiture to the masses, who could purchase portraits as cheap as six for a dollar from most photographers. They were not only passed out as calling cards, but zealously collected in photo albums by the middle class. After the Civil War the same item in a larger size, known as the cabinet photograph, was introduced, and a new fad was off and running. The brush artist and the aristocrat no longer enjoyed a monopoly of the visual image.

Meanwhile the line between art and photography was being blurred by such techniques as lithographing and retouching negatives, the latter a practice common in Europe long before it came into vogue in the United States about 1867. It also seemed as if the expert photographer, like the talented artist, could peer into the soul of his subject. Both Mathew Brady's careful posing of Lieutenant General Ulysses S. Grant standing outside his tent during the siege of Petersburg in 1865 and Alexander Gardner's seated portrait of Abraham Lincoln in 1865 not only captured a human form but revealed something of the subject's character just as traditional oil portraits did, but in a single take. Brady and Gardner were photographers who had an artist's sensibilities. They even took artistic license by altering reality, as Gardner did when he placed a dead Rebel sharpshooter and his rifle in a picturesque spot on the field of Gettysburg after the battle. Of course brush artists had always altered reality in their works to suit the demands of patrons or public opinion.

Camera artists were not above borrowing both technique and jargon (e.g., "landscape photography") from their more traditional brethren. As brush artists did, they published their own journals (e.g., *Philadelphia Photographer*) and mounted public exhibitions in galleries. There were numerous photographic competitions during this era, and ambitious photographers such as Mathew Brady entered every one to which they could gain admission. These competitions routinely conferred awards and citations that were regarded as badges of merit by their recipients. The most prestigious competitions awarded jury prizes for aesthetic merit, thus helping transform a technological process into another medium of artistic expression. Not everyone, however, was enamored with the idea of photography as art. The noted author and social critic George G. Foster grumbled about the state of the arts in 1850, noting that "every muddy Daguerreotype is [considered] a 'magnificent specimen of the fine arts.'"

Some 19th-century celebrities who would never have thought of sitting for a traditional oil portrait willingly posed for dozens of photo portraits. Practical as well as philosophical considerations influenced the decision. Not only was a photograph the poor man's portrait, but a photo image could be captured on wet plate in about 20 seconds, whereas an oil portrait could require numerous sittings over the course of weeks or even months.

Ultimately photography turned out the lights on the slavishly realistic style of painting. One of the oldest schools of painting, historic or patriotic, no longer conveyed the same immediacy it once did, nor did it still possess the ability to mesmerize the public. The principal representative of this form, who used U.S. history as his inspiration, was Emanuel Leutze (1816–68) whose works were practically a throwback to the drum-and-trumpet canvases of imperial Europe. The last gasp of

Mathew Brady's spacious and plush photographic gallery in New York City (corner of Broadway and 10th Street) helped put the relatively new technology on a par with traditional art. A steady stream of visitors flocked to see his handiwork displayed. This engraving by A. Berghaus is from *Frank Leslie's Illustrated Newspaper,* January 5, 1861. (Library of Congress)

patriotic painting in the grand style on the U.S. side of the Atlantic was Erasmus Field's *Historic Monument of the American Republic* (ca. 1875). This 13-foot canvas was produced very late in the artist's career as a tribute to American civilization, intended for display at the 1876 Centennial. It was already passé when it was completed.

The Professionalization of Art

The professionalization of art, as in medicine, engineering, and other fields, proceeded rapidly during these years. It began with the founding of several associations to protect the interests and advance the careers of professional artists. The same organizations also aimed to further the studies of young artists so that they would not always have to travel to Europe for the best academic training. The most important of these by the 1850s was the National Academy of Design, which despite its rather limited-sounding name, was an umbrella organization for painters, sculptors, engravers, and architects. Artists who were identified as having "arrived" received the honor of being voted into the academy, first as an "associate" then as an "academician." Among the most notable students of the academy was Winslow Homer. The academy's primary public service was to hold annual exhibitions to display "the best" of American art in all fields. Over the years these became virtual "coming-out parties" for the best and brightest among young American artists so that selection to participate in the event became very competitive. By 1877 the selection process had become so contentious that a group of artists broke off from the academy and founded a rival organization, the Society of American Artists.

Art training took several forms. More than a few artists were self-taught, including such worthies as Worthington Whittredge and Homer Martin. In fact most of the esteemed Hudson River School were self-taught at the beginning, though most of them later made the pilgrimage to Europe to hone their skills. In the United States, being self-taught was not necessarily dishonorable. In the democratic American climate, people whose art flowed from natural talent and instinct could wear their lack of training as a badge of honor.

However, there were other possible avenues to professional recognition. Many novices preferred a more rigorous approach, apprenticing themselves to established artists in the "master's" studio. But for artists who had ambitions to reach the pinnacle of their profession, there was nowhere else but Europe. There they could acquire advanced technical training and rub elbows with the masters, and so a steady stream of American artists made the pilgrimage to Europe, maintaining a practice that began back in colonial times and would go on until the end of the 19th century. Old World artistry cast a spell over New World artists, so much so that art sometimes seemed to have begun and ended with the Renaissance. Some American artists, most notably John Singer Sargent and James McNeill Whistler, spent virtually their entire career in Europe. These expatriates exercised a much greater influence in American art than their like-minded brethren did in American literature. But they all paid a high personal price for their artistic snobbery.

Patriotic issues aside, training in Europe was almost a requirement for professional success in America. Before the Civil War the principal training grounds were Düsseldorf, Munich, and Antwerp. After the war the spotlight shifted to France, especially Paris, where the École des Beaux-Arts was located. (Thomas Eakins spent three years studying there.) At the same time Munich continued to be a primary destination for aspiring U.S. artists. Each center, Germany and France, contributed a specific influence on American art. From the Germans came drama and panorama; from the French, mood and intimacy.

Americans, in what almost amounted to a mass inferiority complex, saw Europe as the fount of artistic excellence. European masters dictated the standards in both technique and subject matter. Some U.S. artists became so enamored with the cultural richness of the European art capitals that they chose to become expatriates, living out most of their career in Britain, France, Germany, or Italy. For this group of Americans nationalism had little allure. Their ranks included Frank Duveneck (1848–1919), William Page (1811–1885), and James McNeill Whistler (1834–1903).

For those who desired formal training but preferred to study in the United States, there were a handful of well-regarded U.S. art schools and academies. The oldest, in Philadelphia, dated from the early years of the century. Others followed, and New York replaced Philadelphia as the art center of the nation. The arbiter of American style for many years was the National Academy of Design in New York. But artists always kept one eye on what was happening on the eastern side of the Atlantic. American schools everywhere slavishly followed European traditions, beginning with the romantic style before the Civil War and switching to the French-inspired naturalism and "direct painting" in the 1870s. The academic side of the arts was first endorsed by Harvard College, which hired Charles Eliot Norton in 1873 as the first professor of fine arts in the United States. Now it was possible for an aspiring U.S. art student to pursue a complete program of study, both practical and academic, without traveling to Europe.

By the end of this period academically trained U.S. artists were beginning to rival their European counterparts in the quality of work they were producing. This advance was at least partly attributable to the rising quality of U.S. art schools and academies. But the improved training was not available in all fields. Sculptors, for example, had much less opportunity for professional education than painters; schools offering formal instruction in sculpture were extremely rare in the United States until late in the century, and more sculptors than painters remained self-taught.

Then as now art was the life's work of the artist but the plaything of the connoisseur. Art collecting had come into its own early in the 19th century as a wealthy class sought to establish its cultural superiority. In a tradition at least as old as the Renaissance, America's professional artists were supported by wealthy patrons who financed those they deemed worthy. By mid-century the dominance of this art elite had faded to be replaced by a rising middle class with more democratically grounded aesthetic tastes.

With their patronage and private collections the patrician elite were also the arbiters of American taste in art. Historically artists had to cater to these patrons if they hoped to have a long career. However, the spirit of Jacksonian democracy in the United States made it possible for another arbiter to appear on the scene, the American Art Union, founded in New York City in 1839 to purchase and display works by American artists. Until its demise in 1852 the Art Union was a major counterforce to traditional elitism in shaping U.S. taste. At its peak there were approximately 19,000 dues-paying members. They adopted a practical method of popularizing the works of American artists: The annual five-dollar dues were used to make judicious purchases, which were auctioned off, but only after they were turned into steel engravings to be "given away" as membership bonuses. In 13 years of existence the Art Union distributed some 150,000 engravings of some 2,400 paintings. Even the efforts of the Art Union could not influence the practice of most U.S. collectors of primarily collecting European works, only turning to American works to round out their collections. Not until the second half of the 19th century did the European bias begin to fade as a new generation of collectors and institutions began acquiring American art widely.

The formal exhibition of art is a natural outgrowth of its collection. Yet art exhibitions traditionally were neither regular nor public events. They were dependent upon the whims of the wealthy connoisseurs and the occasional special event. Connoisseurs such as New York's Luman Reed and Philadelphia's John G. Johnson displayed their acquisitions in their homes for friends and families. Occasionally

TABLE 15.9 LEADING U.S. ART SCHOOLS AND INSTITUTES, NINETEENTH CENTURY

School	Location	Founding Date	Founder(s)
New York Academy of the Fine Arts[a]	New York, N.Y.	1801 (or 1802)	A group of businessmen and amateur painters
New York Academy of Art	New York, N.Y.	1870	William Merritt Chase
Boston Museum of Fine Arts (School)	Boston, Mass.	1877	Museum trustees, including Charles Eliot Norton (president of Harvard College)
Boston Academy of Art[b]	Boston, Mass.	1870	Unknown
Cooper Union School for the Advancement of Science and Art	New York, N.Y.	1859	Peter Cooper
National Academy of Design	New York, N.Y.	Nov. 1825[c]	Thomas Cole Henry Inman John Frazee Ithiel Town Peter Maverick Samuel F. B. Morse
Lowell Institute[d]	Boston, Mass.	1836	John Lowell, Jr.
Society of American Artists	New York, N.Y.	1877	Walter Shirlaw Augustus Saint-Gaudens John La Farge and others[e]
The American Painters in Watercolor[f]	New York, N.Y.	Dec. 5, 1866	Samuel Colman (first president) Gilbert Burling
Pennsylvania Academy of the Fine Arts[g]	Philadelphia, Pa.	1805	Charles Wilson Peale Rembrandt Peale (son) William Rush
Chicago Academy of Design[h]	Chicago, Ill.	1866	The lithographer Louis Kurz ("Father of Chicago Art") and others[i]
Art Students League[j]	New York, N.Y.	1875	Walter Shirlaw

[a] The New York Academy became the American Academy of the Arts in 1808 and constructed its own exhibit space in 1831.
[b] Founded in conjunction with the Boston Museum of Fine Arts.
[c] Originally founded on this date as the New York Drawing Association, it changed its name the next year to the National Academy of the Arts of Design, then in 1828 was incorporated as the National Academy of Design.
[d] Named for John Lowell, Sr. (1799–1836), a wealthy globe-trotting art collector who took the first Egyptian antiquities into the United States.
[e] Founded by disenchanted members of the National Academy of Design as a rival organization to the National Academy of Design. The two organizations merged in 1906.
[f] The name was changed in 1878 to The American Water Color Society, by which it is known today.
[g] The oldest U.S. art school although at the time of its founding there was no provision for either public exhibitions or a school. The first exhibitions were held in 1811. Most of its founders were not in the artistic but in the city's business and legal community. The school was an on-again, off-again affair for its first 50 years. Thomas Eakins became dean of the faculty and its most distinguished instructor in the 1870s (and for many years thereafter). In 1876 the academy moved into magnificent neo-Gothic quarters (the Furness-Hewitt Building), which it still occupies today.
[h] The name was changed in 1882 to the Art Institute of Chicago, by which the institution is currently known.
[i] The financially troubled academy was taken over in 1871 by a group of Chicago philanthropists, who included Edward E. Ayer, Marshall Field, Potter Palmer, and Martin A. Ryerson.
[j] Organized after the National Academy of Design (NAD) closed (temporarily); it continued in operation after the academy reopened, winning kudos for its "liberal" education policies and modern sensibilities.
Sources: Jane Turner, ed., *The Dictionary of Art* (New York: Grove's Dictionaries, 1996), 212, vol. 3; 476–77, vol 4; 843–44, vol. 14; 575, vol. 6; 46–47, vol. 23; 600–01, vol. 24; Macmillan Library Reference, eds., *American Life: A Social History* (New York: Macmillan Library Reference USA, 1993), 532.

paintings were hung in prominent public buildings, usually on temporary loan. The idea of institutions open to the public, dedicated to the permanent display of high-quality artwork, gained ground only slowly during the century. In 1832 Luman Reed set up a gallery in his mansion in lower Manhattan, the first in the United States granting full public access. Thereafter New York, Boston, and Philadelphia were the homes of most public galleries, which were usually associated with groups of prominent local citizens and artists.

The art clubs and associations preceded the public galleries, and some, for example, the Boston Art Club, were so munificent as to have their own buildings complete with exhibition spaces. Their absolute numbers were relatively small by European standards and

TABLE 15.10 MAJOR PRIVATE GALLERIES AND COLLECTIONS FOUNDED IN THE NINETEENTH CENTURY

Gallery	Location	Date	Founders
New York Historical Society	New York, N.Y.	1804	Thomas Jefferson Bryant Luman Reed
Boston Athenaeum	Boston, Mass.	1807[a]	Unknown
Reed Gallery	New York, N.Y.	1832	Luman Reed
Trumball Gallery	New Haven, Conn.	1832	Yale University
Apollo Gallery[b]	New York, N.Y.	1838	James Herring, painter
Brooklyn Institute[c]	Brooklyn, N.Y.	1843	Unknown
Boston Art Club	Boston, Mass.	1854 (alt. 1855)[d]	Frederick D. Williams Joseph Ames (first president) Benjamin Champney Alfred Ordway Horace H. Moses with 15 associates
Corcoran Gallery of Art	Washington, D.C.	1869	William Wilson Corcoran, banker
Metropolitan Museum of Art	New York, N.Y.	1870 (alt. 1874)	Group of businessmen and artists led by Frederic Church
Museum of Fine Arts	Boston, Mass.	Feb. 1870[e]	Board of 12 founders, including Charles Eliot Norton Martin Brimmer (first president)
Philadelphia Museum of Art[f]	Philadelphia, Pa.	May 10, 1877	Coleman Sellers (first president) William Pepper John Sartain Thomas Cochran James L. Claghorn Samuel Wagner, Jr.
Society of American Artists	New York, N.Y.	1877	Thomas Eakins Winslow Homer Charles Yardley Turner Kenyon Cox Edward Emerson Simmons and others
Detroit Museum of Art[g]	Detroit, Mich.	Apr. 16, 1885	Thomas W. Palmer (president) James McMillan Miss Jennie M. Smith William A. Moore and others

[a] The Boston Athenaeum did not hold its first public exhibition until 1827; thereafter it remained a major force in Boston art society until it shut down in 1874.
[b] Herring's gallery, the forerunner of the American Art Union, invented the annual art lottery scheme.
[c] The Brooklyn Institute began life as the Brooklyn Apprentices Library in 1823 before relocating and changing its name in 1843. In the 20th century it relocated again and became the Brooklyn Museum.
[d] The Boston Art Club incorporated in 1871; it died in the early 1950s as a result of lack of interest.
[e] The collection was launched in 1870, but the museum's building did not open to the public until 1876. Today the Boston Museum of Fine Arts has the finest collection of 19th-century American art anywhere.
[f] The Philadelphia Museum grew out of the 1876 Centennial Exhibition; it became permanent institution the following year as the Pennsylvania Museum and School of Industrial Art.
[g] The name was changed in 1927 to Detroit Institute of Art.
Sources: Stephen Koja, ed., *America: The New World in 19th-Century Painting* (New York: Prestel Verlag, 1999), 198; Jane Turner, ed., *The Dictionary of Art* (New York: Grove's Dictionaries, 1996), 212, vol. 3; 476–77, vol. 4; 843–44, vol. 14; 575, vol. 6; 46–47, vol. 23; 600–601, vol. 24.

confined to a few major cities, but nonetheless they played an important role in introducing the U.S. public to the world of fine art.

The Commercialization of Art

Commercialization went hand in hand with the professionalization of art. Albert Bierstadt found a new way for the practical-minded artist to make money—not just by selling off his works but by keeping them at least for a time and charging admission to view them: 25 cents per person. Just as he had predicted, crowds lined up to see his grandiose paintings of the West. He even placed his paintings in an elegant setting, surrounding them with potted plants and draperies and furnishing magnifying glasses for viewers to study the richly detailed canvases up close.

Another step in the process of commercialization was the issuing of cheap prints and lithographs of popular works. This broadened the market for art by making it available to the masses and even inspired original works. Some of these mass-produced prints by such companies as Currier & Ives (C&I) (founded in 1835) and Kurz & Allison (K&A) (founded in 1880) cost as little as 25 cents at the time, but they later became prized as collectibles in their own right. Both C&I and K&A first made a name for themselves by introducing the evocative image of the Civil War into the parlors of tens of thousands of Americans who purchased their prints.

The lithograph industry was almost single-handedly created by the Civil War. Before the events of 1861–65 mass-marketed art had little appeal to the average American. One of the country's most famous historical artists, John Trumball, had once attempted to turn a series of paintings on the Revolution into engravings and sell them by subscription, but the effort went nowhere. The tide began to turn in the 1850s, when a few artists such as Eastman Johnson and Arthur Fitzwilliam Tait began routinely selling their works to lithographic firms. George Caleb Bingham took the next step by retaining complete control of his works in his own hands, personally supervising their transformation into colorized lithographs and engravings, and turning a tidy profit in the process. Most artists still preferred to entrust their works to firms such as William Smith of New York, who made William Washington's *The Burial of Latané* a best seller on both sides of the Mason-Dixon Line in 1868. Four years earlier another version of the *Latané* print had been rushed into production in the midst of the war and marketed to Southerners as a fund-raiser for the Confederate cause.

The production of art for the masses required the involvement of at least two collaborators: The artist of record, whose vision produced an original work, and the copy artist, who transformed the original work into a woodcut engraving or a lithograph. Though the public saw only a pale imitation of the original artist's work, the consumer-friendly pricing and the increased availability of art formerly not seen outside museums proved a winning combination.

One of the biggest examples of selling art to the masses was the annual lottery of the American Art Union (AAU) held between 1844 and 1851. The organization bought original works of art not to keep and exhibit but to auction off to one of its 19,000+ members at the end of the year. Before auctioning off the prize, however, they also produced a nice steel engraving of it for the general membership. As a moneymaker for the organization and free publicity for the lucky artist, the annual AAU auction was brilliant. It also helped the AAU hold a virtual monopoly over the art market in the United States until the lottery was declared illegal and shut down by the state of New York in 1851.

Murals and Sculpture

All of the artists discussed up to this point were known for their easel painting. Even grand-scale artists such as Albert Bierstadt, whose landscape paintings were almost as large as their subjects, still confined themselves to painting on canvas. A completely different category of artists at work during this era concentrated on mural painting. Men such as John La Farge (1835–1910) and William Morris Hunt (1824–79) preferred to use walls as their "canvas" and Renaissance Venetians as their role models. The style lent itself mostly to neoclassicism, with abundant gods and Greek heroes in evidence. The muralists represented a very small group within the American artistic community. Their efforts to revive the nearly lost art of mural painting met with mixed success, though some of the leading beaux-arts architects of the day did hire them to decorate a few buildings. Their work was much more popular among church officials steeped in biblical imagery (e.g., *Assumption of the Virgin*) than among commercial architects. La Farge was best known for his wall paintings in Boston's Trinity Church and New York City's Church of the Ascension, but he had to produce more conventional easel art in order to avoid being a true starving artist.

One reason mural artists did not prosper was that they were heavily dependent on government commissions, and even in the most flush of times, elected officials were reluctant to spend the public treasury for artworks. William Morris Hunt created two murals for the New York State capitol in Albany, which brought him neither fame nor fortune. The leading mural artist of the day was the Italian American Constantino Brumidi, who arrived in the United States in 1849 and spent the rest of his career there. He started painting murals on the walls of the U.S. Capitol in the mid-1850s, making only laborer's wages at first (eight dollar per day), but before his death in 1880 he attained the position of unofficial artist laureate of the federal government. His largest work was *The Apotheosis of George Washington*, a fresco on the dome of the Rotunda, for which he was paid $40,000. Emanuel Leutze, painter of grand "historyscapes," received a commission from Congress in 1862 to paint his allegorical *Westward the Course of Empire Takes Its Way* on one of the Capitol's walls; it was a subject much on Congress's mind in this, the year that saw the passage of the Homestead Act. Apart from these few artists and some of their masterpieces, mural painting did not make an easy transition from the Old World to the New.

An only slightly less select company of U.S. artists were the sculptors. As were the mural painters, they were more obsessed with classical themes and the European tradition than their easel brethren. Most chose to relocate to Europe at the first opportunity. Among the expatriates were Horatio Greenough (1805–52) and Hiram Powers (1805–73). Those who stayed in the United States and attempted to succeed there included William Rush, Erastus Dow Palmer, John Frazee, and William Rimmer. Few American sculptors achieved much success in their chosen medium for two crucial reasons. First, they could not be formally trained in the United States, and therefore even those with natural talent often felt a sense of inadequacy. William Rush always referred to himself with undue modesty as "a carver."

The young sculptor Vinnie Ream at work on a marble bust of her most famous subject, President Lincoln. She became famous in 1866, when she won a commission from Congress to create a heroic-sized statue of Lincoln. At the time she was not only the youngest person (18 years) ever awarded such a federal commission but the first woman so honored. (Library of Congress, Prints and Photographs Division [LC-USZ62-10284])

Second, and probably a consequence of the first problem, their works were even more derivative and insipid than those of American painters. For the generation of sculptors before the Civil War, everything was measured by the standard of Greek or Italianate classicism. Greenough at least argued for "Greek principles, not Greek things," and became part of the vanguard of American artists who strove to create a truly American artistic heritage.

A second generation of American sculptors after the Civil War finally began to break the shackles of Italianate classicism by carving more realistic and contemporary works. John Q. A. Ward, Daniel Chester French, and Frederick MacMonnies were leading representatives of this generation. But it was Augustus Saint-Gaudens (1848–1907), who attracted public attention only after 1872, who took American sculpture in an entirely new direction, in the process establishing himself as the foremost American sculptor of the 19th century. His work possessed a distinctively nationalistic character and a robustness that had been lacking in the antebellum generation's work. Saint-Gaudens and the other sculptors of his generation showed that Americans could genuinely appreciate three-dimensional artwork when the subject was something other than minor Greek gods in classical pose.

The Intersection of American Art and Science

Americans, with their notorious practical bent and suspiciousness of Old World culture, looked favorably on art that was realistic and historically grounded. One of the most famous works of the 19th century was Christian Schussele's masterpiece *Men of Progress,* which first appeared as a steel engraving in 1851 and then as an oil portrait in 1862. It depicted 19 of the greatest inventors and innovators of the age in formal tableau, with the painting measuring an impressive four by six feet. *Men of Progress* was an American classic whose artistic merit was highly dubious. But that was not the point. These were the "gods" of American technology, who easily outshone the Greek and Roman gods of antiquity—men such as Samuel Colt, Cyrus McCormick, Peter Cooper, Elias Howe, and John Ericsson, whom more Americans recognized than they did the likes of Apollo, Poseidon, or Ares. Reproductions of Schussele's only claim to fame eventually hung on countless walls of U.S. homes, school rooms, and public buildings; it was a union of art, science, and jingoism that captured the national character more than half a dozen academic tomes.

New Directions in American Art

At the end of this period American art was moving in two new directions: impressionism and "art for art's sake," the former represented by Winslow Homer and the latter by James McNeill Whistler. Impressionism had its origins in France, and Americans were first introduced to this new style when the Frenchman Edgar Degas visited New Orleans in 1872 and created some 40 drawings and paintings of local scenes. Yet they scarcely caused a ripple in the art establishment at the time. Even in the mid-1870s American art still had not fully weaned itself off the European tradition. Just when the obsession with classical European style was fading, French impressionism landed on U.S. shores. Not only did impressionism restore Europe to its former place of honor, but it displaced both romanticism and realism.

The artistic climax of this period (1850–75) occurred with the appointment of a Painting Committee in 1875 to select works to be displayed at the following year's Centennial Exhibition. It was headed by Worthington Whittredge and acted as a virtual high commission of excellence for the nation's artists during its brief existence.

Music

If you wish to find the hearts of the people you will hear it in their songs.

—H. M. Wharton, former private in Lee's army (1904)

America in the mid-19th century was a music-loving nation, although little of that music was either original or substantial by classical standards. Early music scholars were contemptuous of U.S. musical traditions, finding no homespun Mozarts or Beethovens creating joyous noise on the western side of the Atlantic. One of the earliest music historians, Frédéric Louis Ritter, sniffed, "The American farmer, mechanic, journeyman, stage-driver, shepherd, etc., does not sing unless he happens to belong to a church-choir or a singing society," an observation that led Ritter to conclude that in musical terms the national "landscape" was "silent and monotonous."

Actually nothing could have been further from the truth. Americans embraced all kinds of music although they showed a preference for vocal over instrumental and folk music over formal concert performances. Within these broad parameters four distinct types of music competed for attention: patriotic or martial, sentimental, humorous, and religious.

The Vocal Tradition

In the first half of the 19th century the emphasis in all forms of music was on the vocal, whether patriotic, religious, or another type. Both composition and performance celebrated the human voice, as illustrated by the popularity of the impromptu sing-along, practically a U.S. invention. More often than not, instrumentation served merely as necessary backing for the singers. From roughly 1840 to 1860 singing families were among the most popular performers with audiences, who enjoyed their complex harmonizing on ballads and folk songs. Often the family members were multitalented, accompanying themselves on a variety of musical instruments. Some families such as the four Hutchinson siblings were popular enough to tour Europe. They also sold a ton of sheet music over the years.

The human voice ruled in American music. Even music education in public schools, such as it was during the first half of the century, was limited to vocal instruction. The reasons for this state of affairs derived from a combination of factors: Words could better express deeply held sentiments than musical notation, musical instruments were rare and precious commodities, and musical training was practically unknown. Not surprisingly, therefore, the most popular songs of the century were not dance numbers, show tunes, or even piano solos, but vocal ballads, with their appealing melodies, simple chord progressions, and emotional lyrics. These were the songs that Americans knew at church, sang during the Civil War, and performed at home in the parlor gathered around the piano. Before the end of the century there were more than 400 choral groups or vocal societies, in 135 cities.

Instrumental Music

In the second half of the century the overwhelming attention given to vocal music began to shift as Americans took more interest in purely instrumental music. That was in part the result of town bands, orchestras, and symphonies that were being formed all over the country, coupled with the rise of a new generation of classically trained composers and visits by European performing groups who demonstrated what beautiful sounds could be produced by instruments alone. Patrick Gilmore, John Philip Sousa, and Theodore Thomas helped win over American audiences to instrumental performances whether band, orchestra, or symphony.

This awakening of interest in instrumental music began slowly. It was heralded by the founding in 1842 of the private New York Symphony Society, a semiprofessional group more adept at talking than at performing. Americans heard their first full-fledged symphony orchestra in 1853 when 100 trained musicians led by a professional conductor performed a concert in New York's Castle Garden. More than a decade after that historic moment New York became the first city in the nation to be home to a full-time professional orchestra with the launching of the Theodore Thomas Orchestra. Thomas put on endless concerts in the city and took his group on a grueling series of winter and summer tours. For the remainder of the century he was the personification of the U.S. symphony orchestra, setting standards that were admired on both sides of the Atlantic. Theodore Thomas did more to "cultivate the public taste for instrumental music" (his own words) than any other American of his time.

Thus New York City grabbed the initiative in making a symphony orchestra part of the civic fabric, as were museums and public libraries. Other cities followed slowly, first in the East, and gradually the idea moved westward. Cities found it easy to organize a symphony orchestra once they had made the financial commitment. Every town had a number of local bands that performed for special occasions or just for the fun of it. A brass band was easily converted into an orchestra by adding a string section and piano, changing from band uniforms to formal attire, and replacing the drum major with an orchestra con-

TABLE 15.11 OLDEST PROFESSIONAL SYMPHONY ORCHESTRAS IN THE UNITED STATES, 1842–1900

City (Official Name of Group)	Date of Founding
New York, N.Y. (New York Philharmonic)	1842
New York, N.Y. (New York Symphony)[a]	1878
St. Louis, Mo.	1880
Boston, Mass. (Boston Symphony)	1881
Boston, Mass. (Boston Pops Orchestra)	1885
Chicago, Ill.	1891
Cincinnati, Ohio	1895
Pittsburgh, Pa.	1895[b]
Los Angeles, Calif.	1897[c]
Philadelphia, Pa.	1900

[a] The second rival to the Philharmonic; the first was the Theodore Thomas Orchestra (1864). The New York Philharmonic was launched by Leopold Damrosch.
[b] Disbanded in 1910 because of financial problems and later reorganized.
[c] Became the Los Angeles Philharmonic in 1919.
Sources: Wayne Andrews, *Concise Dictionary of American History* (New York: Charles Scribner's Sons, 1962), 636; Paul Henry Lang, ed., *One Hundred Years of Music in America* (New York: G. Schirmer, 1961), 39.

ductor. The two cultural centers of the nation, New York and Boston, had two professional orchestras before most other cities in the country had one.

The concert programs of these symphony orchestras were dominated by the works of European masters, to the virtual exclusion of anything by any American composer. In 1854 the composer William Henry Fry complained bitterly that the New York Philharmonic was "consecrated to foreign music," and his friend and colleague George F. Bristow went even further, by accusing them of desiring nothing less than "the extinction of American music." Ironically it was Bristow who became the first American composer to break the Old World monopoly when the New York Philharmonic performed some of his works in 1847. Few other American composers, however, were able to get a fair hearing for their music from the public during these years because of the deeply held biases of the musical establishment in the United States.

In a different category were the so-called community orchestras formed of nonprofessionals who represented their community and played for special civic occasions but were not publicly maintained. Some of the community orchestras were quite good, only a notch or two below the best of the professional groups. By the end of the century there were 10 of these. It was on the community level that the first all-female orchestra in the United States was formed by a group of Whittier, California, women. A third tier of symphony orchestras were the college orchestras that filled both an instructional and a performing niche in many communities, which might otherwise have been denied high-quality musical performances. Altogether there were 37 symphony orchestras founded before 1900 on the college, community, and professional levels.

In so-called serious music (i.e., classical) this was the age of romantic nationalism, which celebrated American themes but in a manner highly derivative of the grand European style. The leading avatar of this style was Louis Moreau Gottschalk, born in Louisiana but trained and first recognized as a major concert pianist in Europe. Gottschalk, who incorporated African-American melodies and rhythms in his music, has been called the quintessential American Romantic composer.

TABLE 15.12 EARLIEST U.S. MUNICIPAL ORCHESTRAS, 1855–1899

City (Official Name of Group)	Date of Founding
Columbus, Ga.	1855
St. Louis, Mo. (Philharmonic)	1860
San Jose, Calif. (Civic Symphony)	1860
Belleville, Ill. (Philharmonic)	1866
Sheboygan, Wis. (Civic Symphony)	1889
Whittier, Calif. (California Women's Symphony)	1893
New Haven, Conn.	1894
Bangor, Maine	1896
Peoria, Ill.	1897
Battle Creek, Mich.	1899

Note: All groups are symphony orchestras unless otherwise designated.
Source: Paul Henry Lang, ed., *One Hundred Years of Music in America* (New York: G. Schirmer, 1961), 39–40.

Popular Music

But symphonies and concerts by virtuoso performers were still foreign to the majority of Americans. The music of the people, "popular music," was not defined by formal performances on the concert stage but by participation around a piano or campfire. In fact music making was the most popular form of home entertainment for U.S. families, who often gathered after dinner in the evenings for sing-alongs. This was particularly prevalent among middle-class families who could afford a piano or a modest reed organ and a parlor to put it in. The popularity of the simple piano on both sides of the Atlantic spurred an impromptu cultural exchange program with concert pianists from the Old World and the New embarking on nonstop international tours. It was the age of the virtuoso composer and the pianist as celebrity, characterizations that fit men such as Franz Liszt and Sigismond Thalberg. Both made triumphal tours of the United States, the former from 1845 through 1847, and the latter from 1856 through 1857, performing night after night to critical acclaim and a full house.

Part of the popularity of the piano on all levels of society was due to the fact that it was equally accessible to the concert master and to the parlor putterer. "Piano mania" also created an insatiable thirst for new music suitable for the nonprofessional. To quench that thirst, a new subgenre of music known as parlor music appeared. Although the melodies were kept basic, even simplistic, the verses were often complicated and seemingly endless by modern standards. Songs were popularized, not as today by continuous play on radio, concerts, and music videos, but by sheet music sales. The two most important composers of parlor music were Stephen Foster (1826–64), who practically invented it, and George Frederick Root (1820–95), who arrived late to the genre but still managed to write some of the most popular songs of the era and make a very nice income in the process. Every middle-class home had a piano, and people played the day's most popular songs on piano while family and friends gathered around to sing.

The popularity of this particular form of musical activity produced its own distinctive oeuvre. Parlor music became a major subgenre of American music during these years. It generally included a young woman who sang current tunes and accompanied herself on the piano, while other family members and guests joined in on the rousing numbers. Learning to play and sing thus became part of a young woman's education. It should be added, however, that such training was not intended to produce professional performers.

Parlor music was just one form of popular music, but it staked out its territory before the Civil War and eventually dominated all American music, displacing religious, patriotic, and "serious" or classical.

Minstrelsy

Minstrelsy was an important if somewhat awkward subgenre of 19th-century American popular music. Unlike other 19th-century forms, it is completely passé today because of its racist origins. It can be placed under the general category of "humorous" because it was typically jocular and mocking of African-American culture, but it also had roots in the popular singing families who made the rounds in the 1840s. Even at its best, minstrel music was patronizing and bigoted, written in "Uncle Remus"–style dialect and full of "pickaninny" stereotypes. It was usually performed on the stage by white actors and singers in blackface. Daniel Decatur Emmett, who wore two hats as both a composer and a performer, wore such makeup on stage. Mid-19th century white audiences in every section of the country loved it. Although Stephen Foster and Daniel Emmett were the best known composers of minstrel music, their prominence did not indicate that their songs were either accurate or fair to black culture. Early in his career Foster considered such music beneath him, calling what he wrote in that genre "Ethiopian music" and "plantation music."

Among the musical competitors to Foster and Emmett were Henry Clay Work and James Bland. The musical authorities Willard A. Heaps and Porter W. Heaps consider Work's "Songs of the Negro" to be the "best written by a [white] Northerner," perhaps because he had a strong abolitionist background. Then there is James Bland, called "the Negro Stephen Foster" by *The Cambridge History of American Theater.* He entered the field of minstrelsy only at the end of the era, but he quickly made a name for himself with songs like "The Bright Light" (1875), "Carry Me Back to Old Virginny" (1878), and "Oh, Dem Golden Slippers" (1879).

Minstrel music could be performed and sung by anyone—in a parlor, on the stage of a concert saloon, or even in a camp of soldiers. During the Civil War to lighten the mood of camp, the Confederate general J. E. B. Stuart organized a group of his troopers into "a band of Aethiopian [sic.] minstrels, ten or twelve in number, who on Saturday nights discoursed very eloquent music [that] elicited rapturous applause." And Stephen Foster's sheet music was at the center of many a family sing-along. When performed in a parlor setting, the music tended to be "cleaned up" and simplified from its stage origins.

TABLE 15.13 POPULAR MUSICAL PERFORMING GROUPS, MID-1800s

Name	Type of Performing Group	Notable Characteristics
Virginia Minstrels	White minstrel group	Dan Emmett's quartet; launched minstrelsy phenomenon of 19th century in 1843; leader, a versatile composer, singer, and banjo player; wrote "Dixie" and other popular songs of the day
Ethiopian Serenaders	White minstrel group	Performed entirely in blackface
Virginia Serenaders	White minstrel group	. . .
Christy's Minstrels	White minstrel group	Edwin P. Christy leader of the prototypical group; introduced black ministrelsy in Europe; widely imitated; tradition carried on by sons after his early death
Buckley's New Orleans Serenaders	White minstrel group	. . .
Kentucky Minstrels	White minstrel group	. . .
White's Minstrels	White minstrel group	. . .
Kitchen Minstrels	White minstrel group	. . .
Bryant's Minstrels	White minstrel group	Bucked formulaic trend of minstrel shows, rejuvenated the form, and had huge financial success even during Civil War
Harmonium Troupe	White minstrel group	. . .
Buckeye Minstrels	White minstrel group	. . .
Sable Harmonists	White minstrel group	Performed entirely in blackface
Sanford's Opera Troupe	White minstrel group	Performed opera as well as popular tunes.
Kentucky Rattlers	White minstrel group	. . .
Brooker and Clayton's Georgia Minstrels	Black minstrel group	. . .
Harvey's Colored Minstrels	Black minstrel group	. . .
Callender's Original Georgia Minstrels	Black minstrel group	. . .
Haverly's Colored Minstrels	Black minstrel group	. . .
The Alleghanies	Singing family	Beautiful harmonies and performances of their own ballads
The Bakers	Singing family	. . .
The Hutchinsons	Singing family	Quartet formed by three brothers and sister; promoted abolition, temperance, and other reform movements; disbanded in 1873; most famous family group of 19th century
The Moravians	Singing family	Specialized in German folk songs

Sources: Marc McCutcheon, *The Writer's Guide to Everyday Life in the 1800s* (Cincinnati: Writer's Digest Books, 1993) 196–97; William Mahar, *Behind the Burnt Cork Mask Early Blackface Minstrelsy and Antebellum American Popular Culture* (Urbana: University of Illinois Press, 1999), passim; Robert C. Toll, *Blacking Up: The Minstrel Show in Nineteenth-Century America* (New York: Oxford University Press, 1974) 275–79.

When such music was a part of elaborate stage productions it is properly included in the discussion of American theater. Popular music performers at the beginning of the period included both family singers (becoming less popular) and minstrel groups (growing in popularity).

Patriotic Music and the Civil War

Patriotic music, which is often lumped together with martial music, has a strong American heritage. Indeed, one scholar of 19th-century music has identified the distinguishing characteristic of American music as its "very spirit of patriotism." Martial or patriotic music was firmly established as an American genre thanks to the great songfest known as the Civil War. Because of all the music that was created during the war, one sometimes wonders whether the participants spent as much time singing as shooting. The music covered the emotional spectrum from joyous ("The Battle Cry of Freedom") to sentimental ("Aura Lee") to dirgelike ("The Vacant Chair"). Almost all of it had a strong patriotic theme. Fanfares, marches, and the like, rallied the folks on the home front and raised the spirits of the men in the field. In truth no other event in U.S. history inspired so much music. In the South alone more than 600 separate pieces of music were published during the lifetime of the Confederacy. In the North, where the publishing business was much bigger, the number of songs inspired by the war was even higher.

The sheer volume of Civil War music was due to a combination of factors, including that patriotic fervor on both sides was white-hot, that an extraordinary number of talented popular composers were inspired by the conflict, and that the technology to listen to recorded music was not yet available. So the soldiers sang as they marched off to war, while their loved ones sang many of the same songs back home, each expressing some deep sentiment or emotion. It would be impossible to overestimate the importance of music to the Civil War. Abraham Lincoln took time out from his presidential duties to write to the composer George Root, author of several patriotic classics, "You have done more than a hundred generals and a thousand orators." Gen. Robert E. Lee once mused to some of his officers, "I don't believe we can have an army without music."

There is no complete accounting of the music written during the Civil War. Composers on both sides worked overtime to produce patriotic music, some of it aimed at the soldiers in the ranks and some of it at the home front. One chronicler of that day estimated that 2,000 brand-new songs were published in the first 12 months of the war alone, and that number increased in the following three years. No other war or event in U.S. history has produced such an outpouring of popular music. Every notable event of the war—victories and defeats, advances and retreats—seemed to inspire some musical tribute, and sometimes several songs about the same event.

Billy Yank and Johnny Reb sang a wide selection of patriotic, martial, and sentimental songs to comfort and motivate themselves. Nothing could be more telling of the musical nature of this war than that each side had its unofficial national anthem: "Battle Hymn of the Republic" for the North and "Dixie" for the South. Ironically neither song began as a wartime song, nor even as the exclusive property of one particular section. They were merely appropriated by opposing sides for the cause(s). Compounding the irony, the Northern anthem was written by a Southerner and the Southern anthem by a Northerner! Thousands of other songs were inspired directly by the passions of war. In fact the history of the four-year conflict can practically be told just by using the titles of the many wartime compositions.

Many of the songs consisted of new, partisan lyrics shamelessly grafted onto popular prewar melodies. R. B. Buckley's antebellum favorite "Wait for the Wagon" is a good example of new wine in old skins. Other songs started as wartime compositions on one side, then proved so catchy that they were soon appropriated by the other with new lyrics. Harry Macarthy's "The Bonnie Blue Flag," first used by South Carolina troops, was an example. Many unknowns during this musical Civil War produced one or two songs that proved briefly or locally popular; the most enduring songs were from the pens of a handful of talented professionals. Premier among them was George Frederick Root, who was the most prolific if not necessarily the greatest Northern composer. He had an extensive background in church music and was an ardent abolitionist. Sometimes writing under the pseudonym "G. Friedrich Wurzel" (German for "root"), he churned out upward of 40 wartime songs of various types. Even without counting Root, the North seemed to possess the best songwriters, judging from the quality of the rival musical streams that poured forth from the two sides. The closest the South had to George Root, in terms of patriotic-driven output if not talent, were the composers Hermann L. Schreiner of Atlanta, Georgia, and Will S. Hays of Memphis, Tennessee. Root, Schreiner, and Hays were united by one idea: All preferred to write their own words and music.

Other composers besides George Root found it easy—and profitable—to shift from prewar themes in their music to patriotic themes. Stephen Foster wrote classic minstrel and nostalgia songs before the war; William B. Bradbury and Philip P. Bliss were well-known gospel hymn writers. The threesome shifted smoothly into wartime mode after 1861, though their patriotic efforts were far from memorable. Henry Clay Work, one of the finest Northern wartime composers, on the other hand, proved as adept at patriotic melodies as he had been at prewar temperance songs ("Come Home, Father") and pop tunes ("Grandfather's Clock"). The Connecticut-born Charles Carroll Sawyer staked his claim to fame on sentimental ballads that appealed to both sides, with the result that his treacly songs sold more than 1 million copies during the war, a record for the time.

The positive side of the tragedy was that the Civil War produced unprecedented opportunity for women composers to break into the mainstream. Many of the thousands of popular wartime songs were written by women and snapped up by publishers eager to feed the voracious appetite for patriotic music and therefore less concerned than heretofore for the gender of the composer. Julia Ward Howe was the most notable but was hardly unique.

Religious Music

Religious music was arguably the most significant contribution of native-born composers to 19th-century American music. It was certainly the freshest and most enduring popular music of this era, and it all started with the creation of a new type of church hymn, eventually dubbed the gospel song, which was a simple tune in verse and chorus format that emphasized Christ and the New Testament "Good News." Gospel songs were perfect for congregational singing, with or without accompaniment. Many of the hymns and spirituals created in these years are still sung regularly today across all denominational lines.

The burst of religious songwriting was a direct result of the Second Great Awakening 20 years earlier (ca. 1800–30), and given added impetus by the Third Great Awakening that began in 1857. The spirit of evangelicalism made hymns as important a component of worship as the sermon. Congregational singing and the faddish popularity of church organs came together to inspire a new generation of songwriters such as Fanny Crosby and Isaac Watts. Writers adapted old tunes or put new music to old verses, and they turned out a wide variety of fresh music that included camp-meeting spirituals, slave spirituals, Sunday school songs, and devotional hymns.

The new writers were characterized as much by their professionalism as by their spiritual devotion. They treated songwriting not just as a divine gift but as their craft. They also changed the focus of church music, emphasizing the person of a loving Jesus rather than the fearsome image of an Almighty God. Protestant believers monopolized songwriting with pop-flavored tunes that could be sung a capella, unlike in days of old, when Catholic hymns composed for organ and choir were the dominant form of religious music. Many of the new songs were collaborative efforts of composer, lyricist, arranger, and choral writer. The process was sometimes spread out over several years before words and music finally melded. For instance, "We'll Work til Jesus Comes" had lyrics attributed to Elizabeth K. Mills, first appearing in Wakefield's *Christian Harp* in 1836. The melody was attributed to William Miller, first appearing in Jenks's *Devotional Melodies* in 1859. Even then it was still a work in progress. "We'll Work til Jesus Comes" was given its modern arrangement by William J. Kirkpatrick in 1876.

Religious music provided the entrée for women into the music publishing business in the United States. A surprising number of the lyricists of church hymns were female. Most composers of mid-19th century music, whether religious or secular, were male.

Many religious songwriters, regardless of gender, took familiar old tunes and matched them up with appropriately themed sentimental poetry. Also, religious songwriters were not above borrowing liberally from classical composers such as Bach, Mendelssohn, even Mozart for their melodies, a practice that almost guaranteed instant hymn classics, much as the *William Tell Overture* was later co-opted for the Lone Ranger's theme. Lyricists, too, derived their inspiration from a variety of sources, including personal experience and the rhythms of daily life in rural America. Psalms from the Old Testament were also a rich source of lyrical content; all that lyricists had to do was attach a melody.

The chief way of spreading the new songs among the public was not the tried-and-true method of sheet music but the revival meetings being held all over the country during these years. Music was integral to these revivals, as the evangelists worked in teams with one "preaching the gospel and one singing the gospel." Thus Ira D. Sankey filled the role of official song leader for Dwight L. Moody, and Philip P. Bliss filled the same role for Daniel Webster Whittle. Only after gospel songs, as they were now called, were introduced to the faithful on tour were they collected and subsequently published.

Among the many writers of U.S. church music, most of whom have long since been forgotten, some are remembered more for their contributions to literature than to music, most notably Harriet Beecher Stowe and John Greenleaf Whittier. Three songwriters stand out in both the quantity of music they produced and the quality of that music. Fanny J. Crosby (1820–1915), Philip P. Bliss (1838–76), and Ira D. Sankey (1840–1908) among them wrote literally thousands of songs. Indeed they produced a disproportionate share of the most beloved church music in American history. It drew from, yet was also different from, both the exuberant spirituals and the more solemn hymns with which Americans were already familiar in their worship services. What they created was a new style of church music, eminently memorable and peculiarly American.

American Composers

American composers produced both popular and "serious" (or classical) music in these years. In the latter category, however, they were completely overshadowed by their European counterparts.

TABLE 15.14 BELOVED GOSPEL HYMNS, MID-1800s

Title	Words By (Original Title)	Lyrics Composed	Music by/Original Source	Music Composed
"O How I Love Jesus"	Unknown	1855	William B. Bradbury	1864
"I Gave My Life for Thee"	Frances R. Havergal	1858 1860	Philip P. Bliss	1873
"What a Friend We Have in Jesus"	Joseph Scriven	1858	Charles C. Converse	1868
"The Great Physician"	William Hunter	1859	John H. Stockton	1869
"Jesus Loves Me"	Anna B. Warner	1860	William B. Bradbury	1862
"Shall We Gather at the River"	Robert Lowry	1864	Robert Lowry	1864
"Jesus Paid It All"	Elvina M. Hall ("All to Christ I Owe")	1865	John T. Grape	1868
"There's a Church in the Valley"	William S. Pitts ("The Church in the Wildwood")	1865	William S. Pitts	1865
"I Love to Tell the Story"	A. Catherine Hankey Chorus: William G. Fischer	1866	William G. Fischer	1869
"Tell Me the Old, Old Story"	A. Catherine Hankey	1866	William H. Doane	1867
"Sweet By and By"	Sanford F. Bennett	1867	Joseph P. Webster	1867
"O Little Town of Bethlehem"	Philips Brooks	1868	Lewis H. Redner	1868
"Whispering Hope"	Septimus Winner	1868	Septimus Winner	1868
"Jesus, Keep Me near the Cross"	Fanny J. Crosby	1869	William H. Doane	1869
"Whosoever Heareth"	Philip P. Bliss ("Whosoever Will")	1869	Philip P. Bliss	1869
"Take the Name of Jesus with You"	Lydia Baxter	1870	William H. Doane	1871
"Footprints of Jesus"	Mary B. C. Slade	1871	Asa B. Everett	1871
"Nearer the Cross"	Fanny J. Crosby	1873	Phoebe Palmer Knapp	1873
"Hark! The Gentle Voice"	Mary B. C. Slade	1873	Asa B. Everett	1873
"I Am Thine, O Lord"	Fanny J. Crosby	1875	William H. Doane	1875

Note: All of these songs were written, both words and music, by Americans between 1850 and 1875. Many other popular gospel hymns of this era take their words or music from works created before 1850, including some based on tunes by Felix Mendelssohn or Johann S. Bach. They were not less popular or less revered than the songs on this list, but the titles listed here are all contemporary compositions with both words and music by Americans.
Source: John P. Wiegand, ed., *Praise for the Lord Hymnal,* rev. ed. (Nashville: Mark M. McInteer, 1997), passim.

A nostalgia-soaked illustration for Stephen Foster's beloved tune "Old Folks at Home" (1851), with its haunting opening, "Way Down Upon the Swanee Ribber [sic.]" rendered in faux black dialect. First made famous by Christy's Minstrels, "Old Folks at Home" went on to become an anthem of the Old South rivaling "Dixie" in popularity. (Library of Congress, Prints and Photographs Division [LC-USZ62-062593])

American classical music during this period can charitably be described as derivative. Most composers had studied in Germany or Austria and were heavily influenced by the German romantic style. The most influential group of composers have been called by historians "the Boston Classicists" because of their connection to that city and their emulation of such Old World masters as Liszt, Wagner, and Tchaikovsky. They were almost slavishly devoted to the romantic style, although the best of them, such as George W. Chadwick (1854–1931), tried to Americanize it and dreamed of creating a "national school" of classical music in the United States.

The favorite classical forms were the cantata and the symphonic poem. Cantatas were elaborate vocal show pieces without orchestral scoring, intended to be sung rather than acted out à la opera, and having either religious or secular themes. Piously inclined Americans who thought that operas were decadent and immoral liked cantatas because they did not have the theatrical stigma. The first publicly performed secular cantata by an American was George Root's *The Flower Queen, or The Coronation of the Rose* (with text by Fanny Crosby) in 1852. Other popular cantatas that followed were *The Pilgrim Fathers* (1854) and the critically acclaimed *The Haymakers* (1857).

Most of these classical compositions survive today only in archives and music libraries. Almost no classical works in the repertoires of modern musicians are by 19th-century American composers. Although the Americans' technical expertise and talent were undeniable, their works lacked inspiration and originality compared to those of the European masters.

Then there was the small group of American composers who worked in the popular idiom yet still managed to receive a certain level of respect from the classical establishment, of whom Stephen Foster and John Philip Sousa are the most recognized. John Hill Hewitt (1801–90) also made a substantial if less recognized contribution to the popular music oeuvre as the "Father of the American ballad." He composed nearly 300 pieces, including patriotic music during the Civil War.

In addition to the critical darlings such as Foster and Hewitt, the United States had its share of gifted native-born composers creating

TABLE 15.15 FIRST SCHOOL OF AMERICAN COMPOSERS, 1800–1875

Name	Life Dates	Notable For/Favorite Form(s)
Anthony Philip Heinrich	1781–1861	Described by contemporaries as "the American Beethoven"; composed in almost every major musical form; first American composer to find musical themes in the American wilderness
John Hill Hewitt	1801–90	Ballads and sentimental songs
William Henry Fry	1813–64	Orchestral works and operas; "militant champion of musical Americanism"
George F. Root	1820–95	Known as "the layman's composer" because of work accessible to amateur musicians
George Frederick Bristow	1825–98	Symphonies and operas influenced by popular-music idioms; first U.S.-born composer whose works were performed in concert in America
Stephen Foster	1826–64	Minstrel tunes and other popular songs
Louis Moreau Gottschalk	1829–69	"Romantic nationalism," which mined folk and popular music; virtuoso piano pieces and orchestral works
William Mason	1829–1908	Member of foremost U.S. musical family of 19th century; virtuoso piano pieces in "overrefined style"
Richard Hoffman	1831–1909	Romantic piano opuses
Henry Clay Work	1832–84	Best known for Civil War and popular songs
John Knowles Paine	1839–1906	Orchestral music in late romantic style; first American to "demonstrate complete grasp of symphonic idiom"; mentor and patriarch to second school of American composers
Dudley Buck	1839–1909	Church music and large-scale secular cantatas for organ
Sidney Lanier	1842–81	Better known as academician and poet than composer; music for flute
John Philip Sousa	1854–1932	America's "March King"; marches and martial airs; more a taste setter than composer
Arthur H. Bird	1856–1923	Piano pieces; late romantic style
George Templeton Strong	1856–1948	Classicist; German-influenced choral, orchestral, and chamber pieces
Edgar Stillman Kelley	1857–1944	Organ pieces and light musical theater
Edward MacDowell	1860–1908	Best-known U.S. composer before 20th century; one of first to receive international recognition; romantic style, piano pieces; highly derivative of German style

Note: This listing has been expanded to include both "serious" and "popular" composers of the first three-quarters of the 19th century, although the conventional understanding of this "school" is limited to serious or classical composers.
Sources: Karl Krueger, *The Musical Heritage of the United States* (New York: Society for the Preservation of the American Musical Heritage, 1973), 23–24; Stanley Sadie, ed., *The New Grove Dictionary of Music and Musicians,* 20 vols. (London: Macmillan Publishers, 1980), passim.

works with broad popular appeal. Their ranks included men and women who have been praised by the historian Karl Krueger as "a highly productive group" and credited with creating "interesting music" (faint praise by any standard). They are sometimes categorized as the first school of American composers. All were active in the period from 1800 to 1875. Most were ethnic Anglo-Saxons, New England–rooted and European-trained, who combined a strong academic background with a performing career.

Music Advocacy and Musical Instruction

Before the middle of the century music advocacy, as well as financial support for performers, was left to a small handful of musical societies, the most notable of which were the Boston Handel and Haydn Society (founded 1815) and the New York Philharmonic Society (founded 1842). Music education was also left to the private sector. Americans of that generation did not consider music a suitable subject for serious academic study (i.e., of its history, theory, and composition). The music spark was left to be fanned by an unsung and unorganized army of private teachers aided by the class-conscious musical societies. For the highest levels of music study, Americans went to Europe, just as they did in the fields of medicine and art. This national indifference did not begin to dissipate until Harvard University added musical instruction to its curriculum in 1856 with the following announcement in its catalog:

> Instruction in Music, with special reference to the devotional services in the Chapel, is open to all Undergraduates. The course will extend to the higher branches of part-singing. Separate classes for graduates will be formed if desired.

Other institutions of higher learning followed Harvard's lead, albeit slowly, placing music instruction under the traditional liberal arts umbrella.

The musical talent of Americans was nurtured in a handful of music conservatories, schools that trained performing artists. The earliest of these schools was not established until the 1850s, and then there was a lull until after the Civil War. From the beginning they faced resistance from both aesthetes, who considered any music created outside Europe second-rate, and democrats, who accused them of putting on European airs. One critic said, "It would be no more possible to establish a conservatory in this country than to make a whistle out of a pig's ear." But such men as the New England Conservatory's Eben Tourneé persisted and eventually succeeded in establishing a respected music training network in the United States.

TABLE 15.16 OLDEST CONSERVATORIES AND UNIVERSITY-LEVEL MUSIC PROGRAMS IN THE UNITED STATES

Conservatory (Location)	Founding Date
Peabody Conservatory/Institute (Baltimore, Md.)	1857[a]
New England Conservatory (Boston, Mass.)	1867
Chicago Musical College (Chicago, Ill.)	1867
Cincinnati Conservatory of Music (Lawrence, Kans.)	1867
Oberlin College Conservatory of Music (Oberlin, Ohio)[b]	1865
Philadelphia Conservatory of Music (Philadelphia, Pa.)	1877
National Conservatory of Music of America (New York, N.Y.)[c]	1885

Academic Program Date (Location)	Founding Date
Harvard College (Boston, Mass.)	1856/1862[d]
Northwestern University (Evanston, Ill.)	1865
Illinois Wesleyan University (Bloomington, Ill.)	1871
University of Kansas (Cincinnati, Ohio)	1877
University of Wisconsin (Madison, Wis.)	1880

[a] The Civil War delayed its opening until 1868.
[b] Oberlin College already had a Chair of Sacred Music, established in 1835.
[c] Unique because it held two charters: one from the state of New York and another from the U.S. Congress. It was tuition-free until 1915, thanks to a trust fund set up by its founder, Jeannette Thurber.
[d] Harvard offered musical instruction to its undergraduates as early as 1856 but did not hire a full-time faculty member and offer theoretical courses until the 1862–63 academic year, when John Knowles Paine joined the faculty as the first professor of music at a U.S. university.
Source: Karl Krueger, *The Musical Heritage of the United States* (New York: Society for the Preservation of the American Musical Heritage, 1973), 24–26.

As a result of the work of the music societies and conservatories, a new generation of trained, professional American musicians came along in the second half of the 19th century who were able to compete on more equal terms with their European counterparts. It would be a few more years before advanced degrees in music were awarded, but in the meantime the musical flame was kept burning in the hinterlands of civilization.

Americans had slightly better success in introducing music to the public school curriculum. In fact, the historian Karl Krueger has argued that in no other nation "does public-school music hold so honored a place and enjoy such assiduous cultivation."

The Music Publishing Business

Music, as was its close cousin art, was a moneymaking business, and most of the money went into the pocket of the publisher, not the composer or performer. It became big business as soon as the popular-music publishers realized they did not have to wait for lightning to strike in order to have hit songs; hit songs could be manufactured as any other product could. As a result of this epiphany they shifted their focus from song marketing to "song manufacturing." By the end of this era publishers had composers writing on demand, cranking out customized music, some of which turned out to be hugely popular, even timeless. There

TABLE 15.17 MOST POPULAR MUSIC HITS OF THE NINETEENTH CENTURY, 1800–1875

Song	First Appeared
"Home, Sweet Home!"	1823
"Woodman! Spare That Tree!"	1837
"She Wore a Yellow Ribbon"	1838
"Skip to My Lou"	1844
"Oh! Susanna"	1848
"Camptown Races"	1850
"I Gave My Love a Cherry"	1850
"Old Folks at Home," or "Way Down upon the Swanee River"	1851
"Rosalie, the Prairie Flower"	1851
"My Old Kentucky Home"	1852
"Pop Goes the Weasel"[a]	1853
"Old Dog Tray"[b]	1853
"Jeanie with the Light Brown Hair"	1854
"Listen to the Mocking Bird"	1855
"Wait for the Wagon"	ca. 1850s
"Lorena"	1857[c]
"The Yellow Rose of Texas"	1858
"I Wish I Was in Dixie's Land" ("Dixie")	1859
"The Flying Trapeze"	1868
"Little Brown Jug"	1869
"Sweet Genevieve"	1869
"Put Me in My Little Bed"	1869
"Silver Threads among the Gold"	1872
"Over the Hills to the Poor House"	1874
"Frankie and Johnny Were Lovers"	1875
"I'll Take You Home Again, Kathleen"	1875
"Grandfather's Clock"	1875
"Oh, Dem Golden Slippers"[d]	1879
"My Bonnie Lies over the Ocean"	1881
"When Strolling through the Park One Day"	1884
"Oh My Darling Clementine"	1884
"After the Ball"[e]	1892

Note: As opposed to patriotic/martial music or church music. See table 15.14 for those church songs.
[a] A popular tune in 1853, *"Pop Goes the Weasel"* was originally a children's song in the 1600s.
[b] A Stephen Foster chestnut that represented a sharp departure from his earlier dialect songs; more than 125,000 copies sold within first 18 months of publication.
[c] "Lorena" was reborn as a favorite soldiers' song during the Civil War, and its popularity from that point on led thousands of parents to christen their girl babies with this name.
[d] "Slippers" was a favorite with saloon crowds in the West; every piano player knew it.
[e] "After the Ball" was the first certified million-seller in U.S. music history.
Sources: Marc McCutcheon, *The Writer's Guide to Everyday Life in the 1800s* (Cincinnati: Writer's Digest Books, 1993), 300–01; Charles Panati, *Panati's Parade of Fads, Follies, and Manias* (New York: HarperCollins, 1991), 44–45; Daniel Kingman, *American Music* (New York: Schirmer Books, 1998), 314–25.

were no certified million-sellers in this era; the first of those was Charles Harris's "After the Ball" in 1892. But there were any number of songs popular enough to become musical standards transcending geography, class, even ethnic group. "Grandfather's Clock" by Henry C. Work (1876), sold more than 800,000 copies, generating for its composer more than $4,000 in royalties over the latter years of his life, a remarkable return in those days of no royalties. Publishers typically bought songs outright, and any payment of subsequent royalties if they became hits was purely a courtesy. The first commercial hit of the century was John Howard Payne's "Home, Sweet Home!" in 1823. Most of the hits that followed were similar sentimental and/or nostalgic songs; few upbeat tunes created a big splash (e.g., "The Yellow Rose of Texas").

By the time of the Civil War the U.S. publishing industry for popular music was firmly established and ringing up the sales. It was able to get new songs to the public with an amazing rapidity that owed much to lessons learned during the war. A number of music houses dotted the country, mostly in the North, and played almost as important a role in shaping public opinion as the national press. Countless obscure publishing houses—practically every town of any size had one or more—served local markets, and the major firms controlled the industry by deploying battalions of agents and dealers across the country to market the latest songs. The two most powerful firms in the nation were Firth & Pond of New York, who owned the golden goose with most of Stephen Foster's music under copyright, and Oliver Ditson of Boston, who consolidated more than 50 independent firms under their banner. Those two were the "media giants" of their day.

The influence of music publishers on 19th-century musical tastes is comparable to that of radio and television today. The currency was sheet music, and they controlled it absolutely. Hit songs were judged by the number of copies of the sheet music sold. That is the way new hits were introduced and made their way from the cities to the hinterlands. Typically sheet music could be purchased for 10 cents a copy, and in those prephotocopying days, publishers possessed an ironclad monopoly of their product. During the Civil War most publishers in a combination of shrewdness and patriotism distributed their music free to the soldiers in the field. This helped create some hugely popular tunes (e.g., "Rally 'round the Flag, Boys") but skewed sales records because nobody kept track of what was given away versus what was sold.

The popular music business in a few short years developed its own publishing rules and practices. After the Civil War the distinction between serious and popular music hardened as the publishers of the latter focused their efforts not just on publishing good-quality music but on discovering the next popular tune. The first "manufactured" hit song was Henry Clay Work's "Kingdom Coming" in 1862. Root & Cady Publishers of Chicago launched a prepublication promotion blitz that papered the city with advertisements trumpeting the premier public performance of the song by Christy's Minstrels on April 23, 1862. Sure enough, the song became an immediate hit in the city and spread from there. The big-city publishing houses, with their assembly-line production and mass-marketing methods, ruled the music industry for the next 100 + years.

Additions to the Family of U.S. Musical Instruments

Americans also made a small but significant contribution to musical instrumentation during these years. Simplicity and portability defined the instruments Americans preferred, that is why the lowly harmonica and tambourine were favorites. Musical instruments, as everything else in those days, also seemed to be gender-specific. Men tended to join brass bands; "ladies" were pointed to the piano, organ, harp, or guitar.

Americans invented the reed (or pipe) organ and steam organ, popularized the African banjo and Spanish guitar, and turned the venerable violin into the "fiddle." It was the reed organ (also known as the melodeon or harmonium), not the piano, that went West with the pioneers because of its small size and big voice, and Europeans called it the "American organ." The steam organ or calliope was invented in 1856, and it was quickly embraced by the circus business. The German immigrant Heinrich Steinweg (1797–1871) began manufacturing Steinway pianos in the United States in 1853 and introduced the last fundamental structural improvement (the cast-iron frame) to this venerable instrument. By the Civil War American companies led by Steinway were producing 20,000 pianos a year and exporting to Europe. On average 30 instruments were being sold in the United States every day. The tuneful and easily portable fiddle (the "people's violin") held a place of honor on the American frontier enjoyed by no other instrument. Meanwhile the popularity of minstrel music, thanks in part to composer-performers such as Dan Emmett and Joel Walker Sweeney, made the banjo a standard instrument on the musical stage. Often combined with the fiddle, the banjo created an Americanized form of the chamber music ensemble that evolved into the familiar New Orleans jazz combo around the turn of the century.

The U.S. Musical Heritage

Whether in the saloon, the concert hall, or the parlor, Americans embraced music of all sorts. A remarkable number of people could play some instrument, and many more were willing to add vocal support whenever a well-known tune was played. Every cowtown and mining camp formed a local band of the available talent almost as soon as it formed a government. The historian Robert Haywood calls these local bands "an essential tool in organizing society" in the new communities. The talent level was not always inferior; even in a frontier joint such as Bearry & Kelley's saloon in Dodge City in 1873, customers could enjoy a classically trained Italian gentleman playing harp and violin to earn his supper! And countless German immigrants after 1848 had an enormous impact on the U.S. musical heritage by founding musical societies, filling out the ranks of civic orchestras, and entering the music publishing business.

The strong musical streak in Americans meant that sheet music and instruments of all sorts enjoyed brisk sales throughout the 19th century. The outlets for musical talent were numerous, from variety theaters to church choirs, and from the formal recital to the hoedown. Everywhere musical talent was honored and encouraged. Even the quaint term *professor* acquired a new meaning in these years outside academe; in its musical application it was applied with due respect to concert pianists, honky-tonk piano players, and private music teachers. Americans were slightly in awe of a person who had musical talent, especially anyone who could boast of musical training. Without radios and stereos to gather around, Americans were always ready to form an impromptu audience if someone would perform music.

At the end of this period two trends were apparent on the musical scene: the freeing of American music from its European roots and the emergence of a centralized industry for publishing and promoting American popular songs. Both trends saw a widening gulf between classical music, which still looked to the European masters, and popular music, which drew on home-grown sources. The latter was increasingly commercialized, causing the classicists to denigrate it further, but set the stage for the rise of Tin-pan Alley at the end of the century. Perhaps for the mass of Americans, popular music's most important quality was that it could be performed by amateur musicians with little or no formal training and modest technique.

Theater

A Taste for Drama

The mid-19th century was a golden age in American theater when public interest was higher than at any other time in history. Some the ater historians, such as Arthur Hornblow and Margaret Mayorga, also believe that the quality of U.S. stagecraft was also at its peak during those years. What is sure is that as a form of public entertainment, the theater had no rivals in an age before movies and major league sports. Unlike live theater today, with its well-heeled audiences, 19th-century theater was a form of mass-entertainment, closer in spirit to the original performances of Shakespeare than to the Broadway experience.

Americans' taste in the dramatic arts in the mid-19th century ran toward historical drama, light romance, and unsophisticated comedy. Earlier in the century U.S. theater companies had presented foreign plays, melodramas, and tragedies. By 1860 history plays were all the rage. Between 1825 and 1860 at least 190 historically themed plays were staged in the United States, no fewer than 50 involving major Indian characters. In fact the "noble savage" became a stock character in American theater at this time.

The immense popularity of U.S. history themes took nothing away from the eternal appeal of Shakespeare. The Bard of Avon's works remained the meat and potatoes of every repertory company in America, with *Richard III, Macbeth, Hamlet,* and *Romeo and Juliet* enacted somewhere on any given night of the year. Shakespeare's themes were universal, his characters classic, and there were no troubling copyright issues for his plays.

Drama American-style often crossed the line into broad melodrama, characterized by spectacular staging, laughable overacting, simplistic conflicts between good and evil, and stock characters (e.g., the noble hero, the helpless heroine, the hard-hearted villain). The most popular melodramas of the era were those of Dion Boucicault, who was the most important figure in American theater before the Civil War. It was Boucicault who pioneered the modern practice of sending out multiple touring companies to perform beloved plays in small-town America and who changed the entire focus of the theater from the actor to the play itself. Two of his works, *The Poor of New* York (1857) and *The Octaroon* (1859), along with Augustin Daly's *Under the Gaslight* (1867), were the most important *original* U.S. stage shows of the era. All three were melodramas, as was *Uncle Tom's Cabin.* When Harriet Beecher Stowe's novel was turned into a stage play in 1852, it proved readily adaptable to the conventional melodrama form and went on to become the most popular pre-Broadway American play. Meanwhile Augustin Daly was the most important American playwright after the Civil War, when realism and burlesque began to replace the old melodramas and historical plays.

The majority of American playwrights were content to write standard three-act dramas and comedies for the proscenium stage. They borrowed shamelessly from each other and from classical sources. Copyright was not a concern for either playwrights or producers. Numerous variations of the same play might be staged with no thought to the integrity of the original work. "Rip Van Winkle," the old Washington Irving folk tale, was adapted to the stage by Charles Burke (1850), J. H. Wainwright (1855), Dion Boucicault (1865), and Joseph Jefferson (1866) and even turned into grand opera! None of its adapters had any particular legal rights or artistic monopoly of the story. And Harriet Beecher Stowe's novel *Uncle Tom's Cabin* proved so popular (read that, profitable) with Northern audiences after it was published in 1852 that the showman P. T. Barnum produced a "pro-Southern" version in 1853 without even bothering to ask Stowe's permission.

Just as today, most stage plays opened in New York City, but Philadelphia was a close second, and even boomtown San Francisco became a surprising oasis of culture in the Far West. As urbanization spread and civilization took root, small towns aspired to leaven rural society with a little high culture. By 1850 there were an estimated 50 stock companies performing somewhere in the United States on a regular basis. Texas had the most theaters and the biggest audiences of any area between the Mississippi and San Francisco. Galveston and Houston each had several theaters, each with its own stock company, before the Civil War. For those western towns too small or too poor to afford a resident acting company, there were the touring companies from the East that traveled one of the regular circuits, letting the locals see the same shows being seen back in New York City or Boston. As the frontier moved steadily westward, new stops were added to these circuits, boosting both receipts and audiences for any given production. In January 1850 the first professional actors' troupe reached San Francisco to entertain the Forty-niners. By the end of that same year four theaters had been built there to entice more troupes to visit the City by the Bay. Although conditions remained primitive and the journey long, the pay was good in a region of culture-starved miners.

When acting troupes hit the road in the mid-19th century, that road was much more arduous and even dangerous than today. Touring companies performed on primitive saloon stages on the frontier where rowdy patrons might be as likely to take potshots at them as to watch the show. If there was no public stage available at a stop, the company set up tents for their performances. All Easterners were considered dandies until proved otherwise, and actors were considered the greatest dandies of all. Sometimes they were run out of town; sometimes they were forced to pay their expenses out of pocket. In San Francisco in 1851 the French actor Amedee Fayolle was beaten and shot by the local bully just for sport. Still there was no shortage of determined thespians ever ready to take a show on the road. In 1851 the first big-time touring circuses were launched.

American Playwrights

There were many more working playwrights in those days than there are now, and although few of them were able to earn a living at it, nonetheless they churned out a steady stream of works that actually went before the stage lights. The first American playwright of the 19th century who was actually able to earn a living at his craft was Bronson Howard, who saw his first work produced in 1870. Most of the rest considered themselves lucky to see their works performed on stage and to pocket a modest return on their time. A good run was 100 performances. When Augustin Daly's *Divorce* ran for 200 consecutive performances in 1871–72, it set an American theater record. In a category all by itself was Charles Barras's *The Black Crook; An Original Magical and Spectacular Drama in Four Acts,* which opened in 1866 and ran an amazing 475 performances before closing in 1867. The potential returns were so good for playwrights that even a few literary lights of the day, including Julia Ward Howe, Harriet Beecher Stowe, and Henry Wadsworth Longfellow, tried their hand at original drama and were successful in having their works produced.

Stage Actors

The large number of stages and the effusion of new works being produced meant steady work for many actors in the 19th century. The acting ranks even opened up to admit women in significant numbers for the first time, the most notable being Louisa Lane Drew (1820–97) and Laura Keene (ca. 1820–73). Drew was a member of one of the "royal families" of the U.S. stage, along with her husband, John Drew (1827–62), and their children, John Drew, Jr., and Georgiana Drew. Another trend started in 1852 when the first child star made her debut. Four-year-old Cornelia Howard was a phenomenon playing Little Eva in an adaptation of *Uncle Tom's Cabin.* She had an advantage in that her father, George C. Howard, wrote the adaptation with her in mind. Little Cornelia's sweetness helped break down some of the traditional prejudice against stage actors as immoral performing gypsies.

Among the ranks of male actors, most were forgettable minor-leaguers who would have had to find other work in a tighter acting market. Instead they found no shortage of jobs, if not on a big-city

Edwin Booth (1833–93), elder brother of the presidential assassin John Wilkes Booth and a member of the first family of the American stage, strikes a Napoleonic pose for the camera. (Tennessee State Library and Archives)

stage, then on the circuit through the backcountry. Some fortunate few latched onto a dream role and reprised it for practically an entire career. For instance, Frank Mayo played the title character in Frank Murdoch's *Davy Crockett* for a quarter-century.

The great actors of the day are still honored even 150 years later. They performed under trying conditions, breathing life into hoary characters and creaky vehicles that would have tried the talents of a Barrymore. Some of them enjoyed celebrity status on a par with that of the today's major Hollywood stars. The roll call of great 19th-century U.S. actors begins with the Booth family, particularly Edwin Booth (1833–93), then John Howard Payne (1791–1852), Edwin Forrest (1806–72), Charlotte Cushman (1816–72), Joseph Jefferson (1829–1905), and E. L. Davenport (1816–77). Even John Wilkes Booth was known as a great actor before he achieved immortality as a presidential assassin.

The highest-paid performer of the day was not a conventional stage actor nor a trained musician. He was a man who dressed up in an American flag suit, performed with a trained pig named Lord Byron, and told jokes. He was Daniel McLaren Rice (1823–1900), a tall, lanky, bearded character who broke into show business as a circus clown in 1845 and was still entertaining crowds into his seventh decade in the 1880s. He was loved by Abraham Lincoln and turned into a character in one of Mark Twain's novels. Rice combined singing, dancing, exchanging jokes with the audience, trick riding, reciting his own poetry, and several other talents into a one-man show that amazed and delighted audiences on both sides of the Atlantic. He invented the popular image of Uncle Sam known today. During his long career he ran his own circus and worked for other impresarios. Most impressive, perhaps, he was making the phenomenal salary of $1,000 a week during the 1840s and 1850s. During the Civil War he was an unabashed Unionist, though much of his prewar fame had originated south of the Mason-Dixon line. In 1869 he took his act out on a riverboat tour, which netted him $125,000 pure profit. Unfortunately, although he had the talent and stage presence of Mickey Rooney, Milton Berle, and Will Rogers, he had the business sense of Bozo the Clown. By the mid-1870s his career was on the skids and for the rest of his life he was in and out of bankruptcy. He was the greatest entertainer of the 19th century, but today he is completely forgotten or else dismissed as merely a circus performer.

Theater Venues

The middle years of the 19th century saw a boom in the construction of all types of performance venues. More new theaters went up during this time than during any other comparable span of U.S. history. The majority were built in New York and other large eastern cities, such as the Front Street Theater in Baltimore, Lent's New National Theater in Philadelphia, and Niblo's Garden in New York City. But the Midwest and Far West also witnessed their share of theater construction. Some of the new gold and silver boom towns in the Rocky Mountain area went hog-wild in using some of their sudden wealth to create instant culture. Virginia City, Nevada, for instance, built five opera theaters and six variety houses in two years (1862–65). Many of the new places were grandiloquently named opera houses when, the truth be told, they were really only variety theaters. Some of the venues would be considered very strange by modern standards. For instance, P. T. Barnum's American Museum in New York was a popular place to see all sorts of live performances. The museum's "Lecture Hall" could hold 3,000, and more than that number jammed the hall for every performance when Jenny Lind ("the Swedish Nightingale") appeared in 1850. The Boston Museum and George Wood's Museum and Metropolitan Theatre (New York) were other similarly misnamed venues that attracted far more patrons to their stage shows than to their exhibits.

Most of the new theaters and performing halls were built not with public monies but by deep-pocketed individuals who as a result were able to see their name written over the door. And most of those names over the door belonged to either successful impresarios or well-known actors who decided to work on both sides of the lights. James W. Wallack (Wallack's Theater in New York) and George L. Fox (National Theater, New York) were two of the most popular stage performers in America before they moved to the business side of their profession. Wallack was a dramatic actor, and Fox, a comedian and pantomime artist. Fox went on to become one of the pioneers in American burlesque along with his highly successful careers as a performer, producer, impresario, and theater owner. Members of the legendary Booth family of actors, Edwin and Junius, Jr., opened their own theater in New York four years after their brother, John Wilkes Booth, shot Lincoln.

A new venue that first made its appearance during these years was the so-called concert saloon, early home to burlesque. The first opened in New York City in 1850. These were a cut or two below the traditionally highbrow concert halls and had greater appeal to the masses. As the name suggests, they were basically bars with midsize performing stages that offered popular entertainments, such as minstrel shows, burlesque, and even a genuine concert occasionally. The Santa Claus Concert Saloon on Broadway (New York) introduced a hugely popular "variety" program in 1857 that quickly became the standard for such places. Aiming to expand beyond their normal, boisterous male clientele, several of New York's concert saloons in 1866 began closing the

TABLE 15.18 LEADING U.S. THEATERS, STAGES, AND PERFORMANCE HALLS, 1850–1870

Theater	Location	Date of Opening	Owner/Management
Purdy's National Theater[a]	New York, N.Y.	1850	A. H. Purdy
American Theater	San Francisco, Calif.	1850	N/A
Wallack's Lyceum Theater[b]	New York, N.Y.	Sep. 8, 1851	James W. Wallack
First Chinese Theater	San Francisco, Calif.	1852	N/A
Boston Music Hall[c]	Boston, Mass.	1852	N/A
Metropolitan Theater[d]	San Francisco, Calif.	Dec. 24, 1853	Catherine Sinclair
Philadelphia Minstrel Theater	Philadelphia, Pa.	1853	Sam Sanford
Boston Theater	Boston, Mass. (Washington Street)	1853	N/A
Stadt Theater[e]	New York, N.Y.	1854	N/A
Laura Keene's Varieties Theater	New York, N.Y.	1855	Laura Keene (actress-manager)
New Theater	New York, N.Y.	1856	Laura Keene
New Bowery Theater	New York, N.Y.	1859	George L. Fox and James W. Lingard
The Melodeon (concert saloon)	New York, N.Y.	1859	N/A
The New Wallack's Theater[f]	New York, N.Y.	Sep. 25, 1860	James W. Wallack
Pastor's Variety Theater	New York, N.Y.	1861	Tony Pastor
Salt Lake Theater	Salt Lake City, Utah	1861 (or 1862)	Brigham Young
Brooklyn Academy of Music Theater	Montague Street, Brooklyn, N.Y.	1861	Brooklyn Academy of Music
Ford's Theater	Washington, D.C.	1861	John T. Ford
Yesler Hall[g]	Seattle, Wash.	1861	N/A
Piper's Opera House	Virginia City, Nev.	1863	N/A
Haverly's Theater	Toledo, Ohio	1864	Col. Jack H. Haverly
Tony Pastor's Opera House (i.e., variety theater)	New York, N.Y.	Aug. 14, 1865	Tony Pastor
Crosby Opera House	Chicago, Ill.	Apr. 20, 1865	N/A
Fifth Avenue Theater	New York, N.Y.	1865	N/A
Théâtre Française[h]	New York N.Y.	1866	N/A
Pence Opera House	Minneapolis, Minn.	Jun., 1867	N/A
Booth's Theater	Sixth Avenue and Twenty-third Street, New York, N.Y.	Feb. 3, 1869	Edwin Booth and Junius Booth, Jr.
California Theater	Bush Street, San Francisco, Calif.	Jan. 18, 1869	John McCullough and Lawrence Barrett (managers)
Merced Theater	Los Angeles, Calif.	1870	N/A

[a] Formerly Chatham's Theater, 1839–50.
[b] Originally John Brougham's Broadway Theater, 1850–51.
[c] Still in operation at the same location today.
[d] San Francisco's leading theater until 1869.
[e] Home to the first successful German-language company in the United States.
[f] A brilliant stock theater, renamed the Star in 1881.
[g] The first permanent performance space in Seattle.
[h] Later the Fourteenth Street Theater.
Source: Don B. Wilmeth and Christopher Bigsby, eds., *The Cambridge History of American Theater,* vol. 1, *Beginnings to 1870* (New York: Cambridge University Press, 1999), 88–109.

bar twice a week, when they would offer matinees for women and children, both of whom were excluded from nightly performances.

The most successful venues, such as Niblo's Garden or Wallack's Lyceum Theater, were multipurpose facilities. They could stage a circus one week, a dramatic production the next, and a lyceum lectureship the third. This sort of versatility allowed for the most economical use of performing halls, guaranteeing that they were seldom darkened.

Minstrelsy on Stage

Minstrel shows were one of the oddest forms of stage entertainment ever to become popular; in them white actors performed in blackface, caricaturing Southern slaves for all-white audiences. Ironically the shows began as the most racist of all U.S. performing arts but before they faded from the scene gave African Americans their first large-scale entrance into show business. A black veteran of the minstrel stage, W. C. Handy, recalled many years later, "All the best black talent of that generation" gravitated to minstrelsy; "composers, singers, musicians, speakers, and stage performers—the minstrel show got them all." But in the beginning it was all-white entertainment for all-white audiences.

Minstrelsy, as opposed to legitimate theater, was a cross between a musical performance and a variety show; it required elements of both the dramatic arts and musicianship and therefore did not fit neatly into either category. As the historian William Pierce Randel has observed, (white) Americans loved minstrel shows almost as much as they loved "warmed-over English plays and the freaks in Barnum's Museum." Members of both genders and every class flocked to the performances, making minstrel acts some of the highest-paid performers of their day.

Minstrelsy became almost a subgenre of the American performing arts, with its own booking network, full-time theaters and touring companies, and favorite stars. The British, who had been introduced to U.S. minstrel performers as early as the 1830s, considered it a purely American form of musical theater. In truth its origins can be found in African culture and British music halls, but that did not prevent Americans from embracing it as home-grown.

The first complete minstrel show was probably staged by Edwin P. Christy and his Christy Minstrels in Buffalo, New York, in 1842. Six years later they began a hugely successful 10-year run at Mechanic's Hall in New York City. Other groups were quickly organized to cash in on the craze for these "Negro Extravaganzas."

The typical program included popular songs such as "Dixie," simple skits, and ribald jokes. The most popular stereotypes in minstrel shows were "Jim Crow" and "Zip Coon," representing the slow rural black

TABLE 15.19 LEADING MINSTREL COMPANIES, 1859

Company	Hometown (Management)
Sanford's Opera Troop	Philadelphia, Pa.
Ordway's Aeolians	Boston, Mass.
Woods' Minstrels	New York, N.Y.
Campbell's Minstrels	Touring Company (Mat Peel, manager)
Christy Minstrels	Touring company (a part of original company)
Campbell's Minstrels	Touring company (Rumsey and Newcombe managers)
San Francisco Minstrels	California-based
Buckley's Serenaders	Touring company; hometown unknown
Bryant's Minstrel's	New York, N.Y.
George Christy and Hooley's Minstrels	Touring company; hometown unknown
Morris, Pell and Trowbridge's Minstrels	Boston, Mass.

Source: The New York Clipper, 23 April 1859, cited in Richard Moody, *America Takes the Stage* (Millwood, N.Y.: Kraus Reprint, 1977), 46.

and the conniving city black, respectively. The show was divided into two acts, with the first devoted to jokes and singing by the company both collectively and individually, often while seated. The second act was more of the same but with more farce and knock-about, climaxed by a "walk-around" grand finale in which everyone presented his specialty while the other members of the company sang and clapped in unison in the background. The talent level varied greatly from one company to the next, but the form was practically cast in concrete.

By mid-century minstrel shows were the most popular form of American theater, filling stages from New York's Bowery to San Francisco's Barbary Coast. There were at least 75 separate companies putting on minstrel shows around the United States in 1850 (with untold numbers additionally touring overseas). New York City was home to "six companies of Minstrels in full blast" in 1853 by one contemporary reckoning. In 1860 the number of companies had doubled from that 10 years earlier, but after 1870 their popularity began a slow decline as musical tastes changed and the big names retired.

In 1859, 11 companies dominated bookings on the minstrel circuit, most of them with East Coast roots. Some had permanent theater homes; others were traveling companies, as they were known in that day, who spent more time on trains and stagecoaches than on the stage. The Christy and Campbell organizations were big enough to maintain resident companies and touring companies at the same time.

Blacks on the American Stage

The heyday of blackface minstrelsy was roughly 1840–70. After the Civil War emancipation opened the door to black minstrel performers, who quickly proved themselves the best interpreters of "Negro culture." The curiosity of performances of African Americans on the stage in front of white audiences probably prolonged the minstrelsy era a few more years, but even talented black acts could not prevent the slow decline of this unique American art form. Tastes changed and some forms of racism were too uncomfortable even for audiences of that day to support. Today it is hard to explain the immense popularity of blackface minstrel shows, unless it was the appeal of the exotic (most white audiences understood little or nothing of black culture), coupled with the bigoted desire to laugh at those who were different.

Outside minstrelsy, blacks' presence in American theater in these years was small but significant. The so-called stage negro was a favorite comedy type on the antebellum stage and had been since at least 1795. For many years black actors were limited to these "Sambo" roles. Ironically, however, outside the Deep South, blacks were often present in theater audiences. Their dollars were as good as any white person's, although just as in churches and other public places, they had segregated seating. This same logic later would be applied to movie theaters.

Opera

Opera represented an amalgam between music and theater that did not do well in the translation from the Old World to the New. Grand opera in the Old World tradition first made its appearance in the United States in New Orleans at the end of the 18th century, and from there it spread to New York, Philadelphia, Baltimore, and other cosmopolitan eastern cities. Its modest spurt of growth in the mid-19th century was due largely to the efforts of a few professional traveling companies and the wonders of the U.S. rail network. The formation of resident opera companies in major cities lagged along with commitment to constructing true opera houses. The first dedicated opera house was the French Opera in New Orleans, which represented a bastion of *haute culture* for Crescent City society. For years that was the only permanent venue for grand opera in the United States. Finally in 1854 New Yorkers built the Academy of Music, which provided the only full-time venue for opera in the nation's largest city for the next 29 years. Chicago inaugurated Crosby's Opera House in April 1865, with a performance of *Il Trovatore* that drew the prairie aristocracy out in full force.

In the early years, aficionados could hear classical opera in Italian, French, and German, but not until 1855 could they hear an English-language opera on an American subject (the folk tale "Rip Van Winkle"), marking a milestone in the public acceptance of this peculiarly European art form. Even then visits by some of the leading divas of the day, including Jenny Lind, Maria Malibran, and Adelina Patti, were required to attract the large, enthusiastic crowds that other performing arts had attracted for years. Whereas some equated European opera with sophistication and refined tastes, others considered the theater a den of iniquity because of the quantity of overwrought and amorous women as featured performers. American composers such as George F. Bristow and William Henry Fry did their best to put an American patina on this basically non-American art form, but most of their countrypeople continued to think of opera as snobbish entertainment for the wealthy class. Even the staging of hybrid "ballad operas" and "Ethiopian operas" with more populist appeal failed to pull in audiences. Then, as now, part of its appeal truly was snob appeal. Not only was opera suspect morally, it was expensive to stage, requiring large orchestras and choruses, accomplished soloists, and often elaborate sets. Not until after 1875 did grand opera really gain a foothold on the western shores of the Atlantic.

Largely unimpressed by opera, Americans took to the dramatic cantata as their preferred form of extended vocal composition. A pair of antebellum landmarks in this musical form were George F. Root's *The Pilgrim Fathers* (1854) and B. F. Baker's *The Burning Ship* (1858), both of which benefited from historical subjects familiar to most Americans and performance in English. They also benefited from the influx of German musical talent that followed the failed revolutions of 1848. Many U.S. choirs and choral societies were started by those German refugees, who performed publicly to great acclaim and thereby inspired other similar groups.

The zenith of the U.S. infatuation with dramatic cantatas occurred with the two "peace jubilees," held in New York City in 1869 and Boston in 1872. The first was called the National Peace Jubilee and Great Musical Festival, for which were assembled a chorus of 10,000 and an orchestra of 1,000 in a specially built coliseum seating 50,000. The music scholar Irving Sablosky has described the five-day event as a "brash mixture of art and commerce, education and showmanship lofty rhetoric and ballyhoo." It was also the inspiration for a series o similar musical extravaganzas that followed. Three years after the first jubilee a group of Boston sponsors topped the New Yorkers by putting on the World Peace Jubilee of 1872, which had a chorus of 20,000 and an orchestra of 1,000 and even added a military band of 1,000. Enormous crowds from all over the East poured into Boston to witness the historic performances. It is likely that more Americans were present for either of these events than attended all the operas performed around the country the same year.

New Directions

American theater was another part of the national trend toward popular mass entertainment. By the postwar period American theater was branching out into exciting new directions—specifically, vaudeville and burlesque. Burlesque developed first as an impudent satire of conventional stage and literary forms, starting in New York City. Its favorite targets were the grand opera and romantic melodrama favored by the middle classes. The English performers Lydia Thompson and her British Blondes took their farcical act to the United States in 1868. Soon thereafter the English immigrant actor John Brougham became burlesque's first star, writing and acting in shows that lampooned Pocahontas, Columbus, and Yankees, among other subjects.

Burlesques consisted of music and humor that included plenty of double-entendres and raunchy behavior, which shocked stuffy theatergoers. After 1860 burlesque shows also began to feature bevies of scantily dressed women dancers, who did not necessarily have to be able either to sing or to act, thus earning burlesques the name, "leg shows." This development was created by such producers as M. B. Leavitt and the actress-manager Laura Keene, both New York–based. By the 1870s burlesque had evolved into a standardized form that included comedy routines, musical numbers, and healthy doses of lasciviousness, particularly in the form of the French-imported can-can dance. Burlesque's regular venue was the saloon, and its regular audience was all-male.

The stage genre known as vaudeville (variety theater) was a loosely structured pastiche of song and dance, comedy, and hard-to-categorize acts that owed much to the old minstrel shows. But whereas minstrelsy was rural, Southern, and ethnically distinctive (black), vaudeville was urban, Northern, and ethnically diverse. The variety form emerged from the shadows in the 1870s after fermenting for a couple of decades. The music and structure of vaudeville also borrowed heavily from the antebellum singing family acts, but those all-singing shows of yore did not evolve into vaudeville until impresarios began filling out the play bill with various novelty acts. In time the stage was filled with dancers, magicians, jugglers, and comics, even animal acts, all of which eventually overshadowed the singers. The idea was to serve up continuous and fast action.

The next step was to package the singers, dancers, comedians, and others, into touring shows that could play many venues. (New York had 60 performance halls and four "summer gardens" in 1850, in addition to legitimate theaters.) In variety theater plot, character, and sustained drama were unknown, leaving legitimate theater to carry on the older traditions of the stage. A new form of entertainment had been invented, very plebeian in spirit, and as a result the afcionados of so-called legitimate theater sneered at it. Audiences of course flocked to it.

The typical vaudeville/variety show included 12 to 15 separate acts—thus its early name *variety theater*—and paid widely varying rates to performers, slotted on the daily program according to their popularity with customers. (The most popular act was last.) Acts tended to be added or dropped on short notice according to the reaction of the audience. A polite or tepid response could be the kiss of death. That is why vaudeville performers were said to be the hardest workers in show business. Vaudeville proved highly profitable for management because as many as six performances might be given in a single day. The shows were fast-paced and undemanding intellectually and contained something for everybody, whether it was singing, juggling, magic, or even poetry readings. If one did not like one act, the next would begin in about 15 minutes. The usual entry fee was 25 cents. And unlike burlesque, vaudeville did not seem out of place in polite theaters.

Vaudeville's first home was the same stages where minstrel and burlesque shows had been performed. The first venue dedicated to vaudeville performance was Tony Pastor's Opera House, which began at one New York City location in 1865 and eventually settled at 14th Street 16 years later. Pastor had a nose for talent and for business, recognizing early on that a clean show would attract families and therefore make him more money than a bawdy show for a strictly male audience. Pastor is considered the "Father of Vaudeville."

Many other vaudeville halls followed Pastor's lead by appropriating and Americanizing the term *opera house* for a type of entertainment scarcely related to the high European art form long patronized by the upper classes. The opera houses that sprang up across the Midwest and Far West after the Civil War likely never staged a performance of Verdi or Wagner for the local citizens. But they did a booming business and created an outlet for American performing talent that launched the careers of George M. Cohen, Eddie Foy, Maurice Barrymore, Lillian Russell, and Sophie Tucker. The first major stars of vaudeville were the musical and comedy team of Ned Harrigan and Tony Hart, starting in the early 1870s. Vaudeville circuits crisscrossed the West giving even whistle-stops and cowtowns the latest in eastern entertainment. A rising form of entertainment at the end of this era, vaudeville by the turn of the century would replace minstrelsy and burlesque as the dominant form of live entertainment in the nation.

The fact that vaudeville and burlesque superseded minstrelsy reflected a shift in national demographics as much as in taste among American audiences. The crucial demographic shift was from a rural to an urban society, an accelerating process in the late 19th century, which was not completed until 1920. The simple slave-based minstrel show appealed to unsophisticated, rural-dwelling audiences of males, whereas the bawdier, faster-paced vaudeville and burlesque shows found their audiences in the cities and offered entertainment for both men and women. And whereas minstrelsy had been race-based, as was much of U.S. society, the new forms of theater were class-based. They often poked fun at the "swells," mocking behavior and sensibilities. Plus, the growing acceptance of women alongside men in the audience was one of the more significant changes produced by the new forms of theater.

Together vaudeville and burlesque set the stage for the modern American musical, a distinctive form and unique American contribution to theater. In form the musical comedy is characterized by extravagant production values, a simple plot advanced through music and dialogue, catchy "show tunes" that the audience can hum on the way home, and a happy ending. With roots in European light opera and English music halls the musical was thoroughly americanized through the influence of vaudeville and burlesque in the years after the Civil War. From vaudeville it took its quick pace and mass appeal; from burlesque it took the concept of big musical production numbers. At the end of this era the parts had not all blended yet, but the cake was baking. According to most authorities, the first modern American musical, containing all the characteristic elements, was Charles M. Barras's *The Black Crook* (1866). It gave Americans the first hit show tune to make the crossover from stage to popular music, "You Naughty, Naughty Men."

Musical comedy, vaudeville, and burlesque were the wave of the future in 1875. Melodrama and minstrels were on their way out, although they were far from dead, and the new era of mass entertainment had arrived, its object to appeal to a wide audience, which now included women, children, blacks, and whites. Whichever form(s) of American theater were best able to do that would triumph over all others.

CHAPTER 16 Architecture and Design

Every great building is a history in stone . . . shedding light on the styles of past ages.

— Sir Jocelyn Stevens

Architectural Styles

American architecture in the mid-19th century was a mishmash of cribbed styles and warmed-over European forms. Not until nearly the end of the century did U.S. architecture come into its own by blazing new trails and setting new standards for the rest of the world to emulate. Behind it was more than a century of aping European styles, especially the English Palladian and Greek revival (also known as Classical Greek and neo-Greek). American architecture depended for its sources on influential English design books, on a handful of prestigious technical schools on the Continent, and on a few master builders who immigrated from the Old World to the New. Most of the significant buildings were either churches (e.g., Christ Church in Cambridge, Massachusetts, or King's Chapel, Boston) or private residences of the wealthy (e.g., George Mason's Gunston Hall in Fairfax, Virginia). It is fair to say that there was nothing particularly original or inspiring about architecture in the United States in the colonial and early national periods.

This is not to say that Americans were not building impressive buildings or creating cityscapes. Buildings must be designed, and the builder's personality becomes part of the final structure, but this process is not the same as an overarching vision. Architecture as a fine art entails more than the simple functional forms used for homes and businesses; it also entails the grand designs of great buildings that make a statement. Truly important buildings are as readily identifiable by their designers as by their appearance and function.

The third quarter of the 19th century spans two historical periods in U.S. architecture, the romantic period (ca. 1820–60) and a transitional or eclectic period (ca. 1861–76). Of the two, the former is much more important. Architectural romanticism derived its inspiration from the ancient world, mainly from republican Rome and democratic Greece, less from Egyptian, Asian, and medieval sources. It was also a revolt against Renaissance styles typified by the English Georgian school.

The romantic period in architecture gave the United States the first great American national style. It was a self-conscious style that aimed to capture the glory and the idealism of ancient Rome and Greece and graft them onto the U.S. scene. The effect of building classical Greek temples in the American wilderness was sometimes comparable to the wearing of a powdered wig by a dirt farmer. But classicism was considered the architectural style of "the important." Only three elements of U.S. society seemed really to care anything about creating buildings that made a statement: Northern merchants, Southern planters, and public officials. Naturally most of the attention focused on public buildings because they were larger and more visible and were financed with public monies. The dominant image for a public building was the classical temple, usually Greek-inspired but sometimes, in the fascination with large domes, Roman-influenced (as in the case of the Thomas Jefferson–designed Virginia state capitol in Richmond). The classical was scrupulously copied for everything from county courthouses to the Bank of the United States in Philadelphia and the great structures of the national capital. Building them required a lot of money, skilled craftsmen, quarried stone, and time, but most Americans thought that a nation as great as the United States of America needed a similarly great architecture, and nobody could deny the feelings of awe inspired by viewing classical Greek structures. They also made a strong statement about civic and public purpose, which appealed to U.S. populist tastes. Greek classicism represented the first continentwide style in U.S. history, and examples had already appeared in Monterey, California, as early as the 1850s.

But nowhere was it more whole-heartedly embraced than south of the Mason-Dixon line. Southerners seemed to be so smitten with the Greek revival style that it completely dominated most of the region's state capitals, in particular Richmond and Charleston. It was also favored by the wealthy plantation owners for their mansions, the finest example of which was John Andrews's home at White Castle, Louisiana, built in 1857. Robert Mills (1781–1855), the first thoroughly home-grown American architect, created a national reputation as more than a designer of government monuments by creating elegant, classic revival homes across the South. The great plantation mansions with their tall white-columned porticos and broad verandas made a statement: They were the most powerful symbol in the national consciousness of the antebellum slave aristocracy, particularly when contrasted with the rough-hewn log cabins of the slaves' quarters. A century later the magic name of the fictional "Tara" could still evoke images of gentility and breeding, of magnolias and mint juleps.

At odds with the neoclassical Greek style, and a rival for dominance on the American scene, was a medieval style influenced by both the Romanesque and the Gothic, with the two styles often being (inaccurately) lumped together under the generic name *neo-Gothic.* The medieval was certainly more dramatic and massive-looking than the Greek temple style, distinguished by castlelike turrets rising from a crenelated roof line and fortresslike walls with small windows admitting little light. The whole was covered by rich ornamentation and decorative scrollwork. Medievalists rejected the symmetry and restraint of Greek classicism. Irregularity, informality, and mood-elevating quirkiness were the hallmarks of their preferred style.

The two men who popularized the Gothic revival in the United States in the early 1840s were Richard Upjohn (e.g., his Trinity Church) and James Renwick, Jr. (e.g., his Grace Episcopal Church). But both turned to other styles—Upjohn to Renaissance and Renwick to Romanesque and Second Empire—in their later works. The person who embraced the neo-Gothic and put his stamp on it more than any other was Boston's Henry Hobson Richardson (1838–86), whose professional influence was so powerful that the derivative medievalist style he popularized was dubbed "Richardsonian Romanesque." Richardson's interpretation included such features as squat columns, rounded arches for doorways, and elaborate interiors.

Neo-Gothic found a receptive audience in the American public. In some ways it was better suited to the national character than rigid classicism because it allowed for more individuality and personal taste in its design. The private house, for instance, could become an extension of its owner. To the untrained eye of later generations the pure Gothic conjured up images of the dark, brooding works of Nathaniel Hawthorne and Edgar Allan Poe. Purely apart from a setting for horror stories, however, it seemed particularly suited to formal military structures. The original buildings of the Virginia Military Institute were designed in the Gothic style by Alexander Jackson Davis (1803–92) of New York in 1851, and the magnificent Saint Patrick's Cathedral in New York City, designed by James Renwick, Jr., adopted the same style. Although Renwick was the champion of the Gothic revival, he chose to follow the neo-Romanesque route for the design of the Smithsonian Institution (1846–55), which is today probably the best-known example of the medieval architectural style in the United States. Its 500-foot-long red-stone exterior and central location in the nation's capital among all the classical Greek and federal style buildings of the District of Columbia make it stand out even more than it would otherwise.

Not just public buildings but the homes of the wealthy were also built on the imposing Gothic/Romanesque style, albeit on a smaller scale than the Smithsonian and Saint Patrick's. For instance, H. H. Richardson's towered and turreted country homes were highly prized among New England's merchant princes.

U.S. builders were influenced toward the Gothic not just by what they saw in stone but what they read in architectural textbooks. Congressman Robert Dale Owen, who served as head of the Smithsonian building committee, published *Hints on Public Architecture* three years after construction began, advocating the medieval revival over the Greek style for public buildings because, he argued, the Gothic and Romanesque were more religious and individualistic in their appearance. Greek classicism, on the other hand, bespoke civic virtue and egalitarianism.

The neo-Gothic never displaced Greek revival in the American heart because classical Greek architecture was a metaphor for classical Greek democracy, and nothing was more dear to Americans than that. But the Gothic style in churches persisted long after the Greek style in public buildings had faded, harking back to the great piety and devotion of its medieval builders.

The neo-Gothic and Greek revival styles, strikingly different in appearance, shared several common elements: (1) their appeal to distant times and exotic places; (2) their emphasis on thematic style rather than convenience or function; and (3) their English origin, dating from the mid- to late 18th century. Further, both styles, as the architectural historian Daniel M. Mendelowitz has said, "tended toward the grand manner" in striving for high concept and profundity. They rejected the new scientific rationalism and spreading industrial technology, preferring to look to the distant past for inspiration.

Both neo-Gothic and Greek revival styles were well represented in the standard texts of the day. U.S. texts seemed to follow almost slavishly the lead of their European counterparts, first beating the drum for classicism, then trumpeting the Gothic when the allure of Greek revival faded. Only in home design and construction did Americans contribute anything fresh or original to the field. For reasons cultural as well as economic, American architects had that field almost to themselves.

With their eyes on exterior appearance and the grand statement, Americans scarcely noticed the quiet revolution in building materials that occurred at this time—the use of iron for framing. In the short

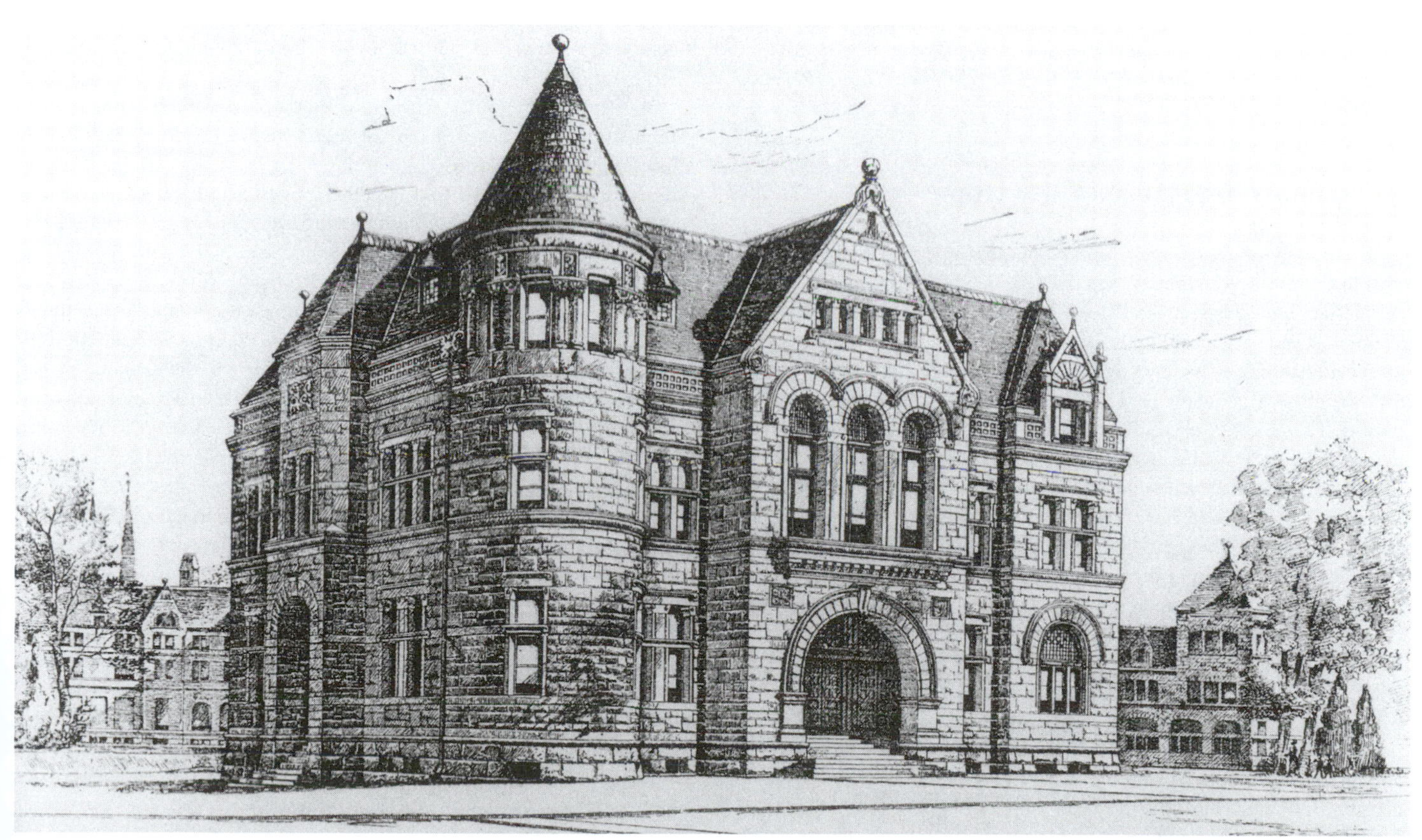

By mid-century the brooding neo-Gothic style, characterized by towers, turrets, and massive stone construction, was all the rage for public buildings. Here, the new post office in Springfield, Ohio, was described by *Scientific American* magazine as "a substantial structure, effective and satisfactory in appearance." (sketch from *Scientific American, Architects and Builders Edition* [1887], print from author's collection)

TABLE 16.1 MAJOR ARCHITECTURAL BOOKS THAT SHAPED AMERICAN TASTE, MID-1800s

Name of Work	Date of Publication	Author	Significance
A Home for All; or, A New, Cheap, Convenient, and Superior Mode of Building	1848 (revised and enlarged, 1853)	Orson Squire Fowler	Recommended the octagonal shape as the optimal for domestic dwellings; 1853 edition endorsed gravel-wall method of construction; "a pioneering architectural treatise"
Hints on Public Architecture	1849	Robert Dale Owen	Powerful American voice for the switch from Greek revival to neo-Gothic
The Architecture of Country Houses	1850	Andrew Jackson Downing	Aimed squarely at the Southern aristocracy with its elegant designs for stately mansions surrounded by acres of land
Stones of Venice	1851	John Ruskin (English)	Redirected Gothic revival style toward Venetian Gothic, which particularly appealed to Americans
Upjohn's Rural Architecture	1852	Richard Upjohn, Sr.	Contained numerous designs for Gothic-style cottages, churches, and schools for those too poor to afford the author's professional services

Source: American National Biography, John A. Garraty et al., eds. (New York: Oxford University Press, 1999), passim.

term it did nothing either to detract from or to increase the popular fondness for Greek and Gothic design styles. But it heralded a sea change in architectural thinking about the form and function of public buildings that coincided with the arrival of the industrial age in the second half of the 19th century. Adaptable for both framing and facades, iron as a structural material gave us what one expert calls "the first identifiable commercial vernacular architecture" in history. Increasingly the great public buildings of the future would not be banks, capitols, and churches, but office buildings and factories, and for these the sturdiness, strength, and durability of iron were perfect.

The Architecture of the Home

Perhaps the most remarkable development in the field of architecture in the mid-19th century was the sudden awakening of interest in the design and construction of private dwellings. Architects lavished as much attention on building residential housing as on erecting large public edifices. They were driven by the same force that drove American society—a growing middle-class population demanding to be served. That middle class cherished home life and had the financial wherewithal to hire the best architects to design their homes. Some architects, such as Alexander J. Davis, practically built their career by catering to the demand for well-designed private homes. The new residential housing fell somewhere between the dreary row houses of the city and the outsized country estates of the very rich. Popular styles included American log cabin, English cottage, manor house, collegiate Gothic, Lombard Italian, and something called "suburban Greek." One style that captured middle-class fancy up north was the Tuscan villa, which satisfied romantic tastes without being overdone. More traditional was the small frame cottage with high-pitched gabled roof and front porch. These houses, which proliferated all over the North and Midwest, became an icon of American home life by the end of the century. Individual tastes also ran to the unconventional, such as the octagonal house championed by Orson S. Fowler in his popular house-patterns book, *A Home for All* (1848, six subsequent printings). Hundreds of such structures were constructed all over the country, including one 60-room behemoth at Fishkill, New York. The octagon house was easily the most radical housing concept of the 19th century, and for a time it was lauded as the wave of the future—a spacious and inexpensive home for the common people. It let in plenty of light and fresh air and provided open living spaces, but, though it had its vocal defenders, it proved too quirky for most Americans' taste. Other home styles across the country were more indigenous to their regions, such as Spanish style in the Southwest.

The biggest breakthrough in home architecture, however, was not some exotic new style but the construction technique known as balloon framing, whereby lightweight, precut studs and laths (two-by-four-pieces) were joined with nails and the whole solidly attached to a foundation, then covered with wooden or brick siding. Traditionally houses were laboriously assembled from heavy frame timbers dressed, jointed, and fitted together, all by hand, on site. The new technique was cheaper and quicker and allowed for much more flexibility of design. It was also dependent upon another product of the Industrial Revolution—cheap, mass-produced iron nails, which cost only a few cents per pound. Balloon-frame construction first made its appearance in 1833 in Chicago, where impatient town builders were throwing up houses almost overnight to meet the demand, and it was quickly dubbed "Chicago construction." The inherent superiority of this method of construction was so obvious that by the 1850s it had become the preferred method all over the country, as it remains today. The historian Daniel Mendelowitz quotes one contemporary, who said that "if it had not been for the knowledge of the balloon frame, Chicago and San Francisco could never have arisen as they did, from little villages to great cities in a single year."

Urban living would also be profoundly affected in the long run by the appearance of the first multifamily apartment houses on the American scene during this period. Not surprisingly they were built in New York City: the Stuyvesant Apartments, built between 1869 and 1870, and Stevens House, built between 1870 and 1872. These were the brainchild of Richard Morris Hunt, modeled on the cramped multifamily dwellings he had seen in Paris while studying at the École des Beaux-Arts. They proved equally suited to the lifestyle and the tighter urban spaces of growing U.S. cities.

The rich, as always, had grand estates, which were as much monuments to status as homes for their owners. What was new at this time was the creation by the Industrial Revolution of a nouveau riche class, who were able to choose from a variety of exotic styles for their huge

"Dorsey's Gothic Mansion" in Philadelphia is shown as it appeared before the Civil War. The Gothic revival style of architecture, imported from Europe, was popular not just for large public institutions but for the homes of the very wealthy. It never caught on with the mass of Americans, however. (Tennessee State Library and Archives)

urban mansions. George Pullman, the father of American train travel, built his Chicago mansion in 1873 to resemble the Paris grand opera theater. His fellow railroad magnate Perry Smith wanted something equally opulent and overwhelming but preferred the style of a Greek renaissance palace. Apart from their size such mansions were most notable for the immense sums of money sunk into their construction.

Books on home building became an important subgenre within architectural literature. In 1850 Andrew Jackson Downing published *The Architecture of Country Houses,* which went on to sell 16,000 copies during the next 15 years, a remarkable number of sales for a work that had no heroine, no villain, and no plot. In 1852 Lewis F. Allen published *Rural Architecture,* in which he recommended that the home harmonize with the lifestyle of its residents. In 1869 the abolitionist author Harriet Beecher Stowe with her sister Catherine jumped into the booming field as coauthors of *The American Woman's Home,* which saw in the simple residential house a higher purpose: to permit each member of the family to realize his or her full potential. Some of their suggestions, such as a central kitchen area and a family room that could be partitioned off for different activities, have become standard features of middle-class homes in modern times.

Notable American Architects

It is arguable whether the first half of the 19th century produced any American architects of the stature of the previous generation's Benjamin Latrobe (1764–1820), Charles Bulfinch (1763–1844), or even Thomas Jefferson (1743–1826), who only dabbled in the subject. Those three worthies had put their stamp on American architecture during the colonial and early national periods, working in the neoclassical and neo-Gothic styles. Latrobe, besides his native genius, had the benefit of being appointed by Jefferson while the latter was president, to serve as both architect of the Capitol and surveyor of the District's public buildings, thus putting him in the perfect position to help create the look and feel of a great city almost from scratch. But early 19th-century U.S. architects as a group were dismissed as second-rate imitators and "contrivers," even by their celebrated compatriot Benjamin Latrobe. The next "great" period in American architecture would not occur until the late 19th century, when Stanford White (1853–1906), Louis Sullivan (1856–1924), and the legendary Chicago School would remake the U.S. urban skyline.

TABLE 16.2 MOST INFLUENTIAL AMERICAN ARCHITECTS, MID-1800s

Name	Life Dates	Leading Examples of His Work	Principal Claim to Fame
Andrew Jackson Downing	1815–52	Inspired Olmsted and Vaux's design for N.Y.C.'s Central Park; Roche home in New Bedford, Mass. (1845); started landscaping of District of Columbia's public grounds.	Most influential advocate for romantic style of architecture in early 19th century; emphasized landscaping as much as building architecture; published first book of house patterns
Richard Upjohn, Sr.	1802–78	Boston's Trinity Church (1841–46); Christ Church, Raleigh, N.C. (1846–61); Lindenwald estate of Martin Van Buren, in Newport, R.I. (1852); Bowdoin College (Maine) chapel and library (1845–55); Baltimore's Saint Paul's Church (1854–56); New York's Saint Thomas Church (1868–70)	Leading interpreter of neo-Gothic style in 19th century; favorite architect of U.S. Episcopal Church; a founder of American Institute of Architects (1857)
Alexander Jackson Davis	1803–92	New York Customs House (1832); U.S. Patent Office (1832); House of Mansions (N.Y.C. 1858–59); William Paulding's "Lyndhurst" (Tarrytown, N.Y., 1838)	Designed more buildings than any other 19th-century U.S. architect, principally rural estates and villas; invented "American bracketed" style by adding projections in all directions to standard boxlike house.
Robert Mills	1781–55	Washington Monument (1845–55); U.S. Treasury Building (1836); U.S. Patent Office expansion (1836); (Old) U.S. Post Office (1839)	Chief U.S. government architect, 1836–51; first important U.S.-trained architect
James Renwick, Jr.	1818–95	N.Y.C. Grace Episcopal Church (1843); Smithsonian Institution (1846–55); N.Y.C. Saint Patrick's Cathedral (1853); Washington, D.C., Corcoran Gallery (1859–71)	Helped launch United States Gothic revival; later helped introduce United States Second Empire style; helped "shape the nation's cultural identity" with his public buildings
Henry Hobson Richardson	1838–86	Unity Church, Springfield, Mass. (1866–69); Marshall Field Wholesale Store (1885–87);[a] Boston Trinity Church (1872–77); Boston Brattle Street Church (1870); Harvard's Sever Hall (1878); New York State Hospital/Asylum at Buffalo (1869–80); Western Railroad Offices, Springfield, Ill. (1867–69)	Virtually invented the neo-Romanesque style; "brought order out of chaos" in U.S. architecture; mentored young architects, including Charles McKim and Stanford White; 1885 listing of the "10 best buildings in America" by his peers included five of his designs, most influential architect of his day
William Le Baron Jenney	1832–1907	Chicago Home Insurance Company Building (1883)	First architect to use steel-beam skeleton as basic element of construction; introduced passenger elevator
Thomas Ustick Walter	1804–87	Philadelphia Jayne Building (1849–51); Library of Congress reconstruction (1852–53); U.S. Capitol dome and extensions (1855–63); U.S. Patent Office extension (1851); completion of U.S. Treasury Building (1855); U.S. Post Office extension (1855); Baltimore Eutaw Place Baptist Church (1868–71)	One of first Americans to combine professions of architect and engineer; more than any other architect of the 19th century, "transformed the Federal city" with his work

[a]This seven-story granite and red sandstone building is considered Richardson's masterpiece. It was demolished in 1893.
Sources: American National Biography, John A. Garraty et al., eds., (New York: Oxford University Press, 1999), passim; William H. Pierson, Jr., *American Buildings and Their Architects,* Garden City, N.Y.: Doubleday, 1970), vol. 1: *The Colonial and Neoclassical Styles,* 373–94, 415–16, 419–24, 437–39, 444, vol. 2: *Technology and the Picturesque,* passim; Daniel M. Mendelowitz, *A History of American Art* (New York: Holt, Rinehart Winston, 1960), 219–26.

Whereas center ring for U.S. architects at the beginning of the century had been the District of Columbia, followed by Boston and Philadelphia, the changing urban scene in the second half of the century put New York City and Chicago in the spotlight. The greatest architects hoped to showcase one of their creations in one of those cities. Boston had increasingly become a quaint urban backwater, and Washington, D.C.'s, architectural style was already, quite literally, cast in stone.

The new industrial age also changed the focus of American architectural design. No longer did architects save their grandest and most ambitious designs for churches and government buildings. Although faith and politics might still drive inspiration, more and more the most magnificent edifices were devoted to commerce and business. Office buildings and retail stores were the most important structures in the late 19th century. They also yielded the most lucrative commissions. Government architecture was practically frozen in the classical Greek style, and church architecture seemed stuck in the Gothic period. Such straitjacket thinking discouraged the most brilliant and creative architects from trying to make their mark in either of those two areas. Henry Hobson Richardson's last two major commissions would be the John Ames Office Building in Boston and the Marshall Field department store in Chicago. The new "business-building" style broke away from the older flourishes of classical cornices, arches, and entablature that earlier generations routinely added to their buildings. The underlying idea was eventually summed up by Louis Sullivan in his dictum "Form should follow function."

The New York Tribune Building on Printing House Square, (Nassau, Chatham, Spruce, and Frankfort Streets) was designed by the architect Richard Morris Hunt in the beaux arts style and built in 1873–75. A forerunner of the following decade's skyscrapers, it symbolized the rising power of the mass communications industry. (Library of Congress, Prints and Photographs Division [LC-USZ62-100900])

This 1861 picture shows a design for a sprawling Moorish-style villa, with a beautifully landscaped lawn, suitable for suburb dwellers. Such houses were far beyond the means of most American families. (Library of Congress, Prints and Photographs Division [LC-USZ62-053305])

The Suburb

As urbanization proceeded apace, a small group of avant-garde American architects began to dream of creating a middle ground between city and country life. Thus was born the concept of the modern suburb, aimed squarely at the middle class and separating workplace from residence. The mid-century leader of this movement was Andrew Jackson Downing, who believed that suburban living allowed the genteel citizen to enjoy the peace and quiet of the country without giving up the cultural benefits of the city. In the 1850s Downing first proposed what he called "country villages" to describe the communities of spacious single-dwelling lots and gently curving roadways that he believed were the wave of the future. Unfortunately he died in a steamboat accident in 1852 and was not able to translate his dreams into wood and brick reality. But his progressive ideas were carried forward and refined by Frederick Law Olmsted, Llewellyn S. Haskell, Alexander Jackson Davis, and William Le Baron Jenney, among others. The first modern suburb was Riverside, Illinois, laid out by Olmsted and Jenney between 1869 and 1870. It was quickly followed by Llewellyn Park near West Orange, New Jersey, designed by Davis and Haskell, which began selling lots in the 1870s. But the suburb would remain mostly a dream until the introduction of streetcars and light rail systems to move masses of people cheaply and efficiently between city centers and suburban communities.

Monuments to American Architecture

In the city, suburb, or country, in private home or "civic temple," American architects for all their copycat ways produced some magnificent structures during the mid-19th century. Most were government buildings or churches, reflecting the traditional bias of monumental architecture. Still, it was a sign of the changing times that at least two train stations should be included on a list of great U.S. buildings before 1875. No single style ruled; styles ran the gamut from classical Egyptian to Beaux Arts.

One of the most recognizable structures in the United States is the Capitol building in Washington, D.C. Begun during the presidency of George Washington in 1792 and modeled on an English Palladian-style country estate, it was not completed until 1830. Expansion, begun in 1851, was capped off by the new dome, pictured here under construction on December 31, 1851. (Library of Congress)

TABLE 16.3 GEMS OF AMERICAN ARCHITECTURE, 1850–1875

Building/Structure	Location	Construction Date(s)	Style	Architect(s)
Washington Monument	Washington, D.C.	1848–84	Classical Egyptian obelisk, 555.5 ft. high[a]	Robert Mills; Thomas Casey
U.S. Treasury building	Washington, D.C.	1) 1836–55 2) 1855–79	Classical Greek	1) Robert Mills 2) Thomas U. Walter
Smithsonian Institution	Washington, D.C.	1846–55	Lombard Romanesque	James Renwick, Jr.
President Street Station of Philadelphia, Wilmington and Baltimore Railroad	Baltimore, Md.	1849–50	Classic railroad station design	Unknown
Virginia Military Institute	Lexington, Va.	1848–61	Neo-Gothic	Alexander Jackson Davis
Jayne Building	Philadelphia, Pa.	1848–51	Neo-Gothic[b]	Started by William L. Johnston; completed by Thomas U. Walter
Expansion of U.S. Capitol Building (dome plus two wings)	Washington, D.C.	1851–63	Classical revival (Greek and Roman)	Thomas U. Walter
Crystal Palace Exposition[c]	New York, N.Y. (corner of 42nd Street and Fifth Avenue)	1853	An "Aladdin's Palace" of cast iron and glass, topped by neoclassical dome	Firm of Carstensen & Gildemiester of New York
Home of E. C. Litchfield	Brooklyn, N.Y.	1854	Italian villa	Alexander Jackson Davis

Building/Structure	Location	Construction Date(s)	Style	Architect(s)
Tennessee state capitol building	Nashville, Tenn.	1845–59	Classical Greek	William Strickland
Harper Bros. Building (publishing)	New York, N.Y.	1854	Italian palazzo	James Bogardus
"Belle Grove" (plantation mansion)	White Castle, La.	1857	Classical Greek	Henry Howard
Saint Patrick's Cathedral	New York, N.Y.	1858–79	Neo-Gothic	James Renwick, Jr.
A. T. Stewart Store	New York, N.Y.	1862	"Commercial Vernacular"[d]	John Kellum
(First) Vassar College Building	Poughkeepsie, N.Y.	1865	Neo-Gothic	James Renwick, Jr.
(First) Grand Central Station	New York, N.Y.	1871	Iron and glass functionalism	John B. Snook
Pennsylvania Academy of the Fine Arts	Philadelphia, Pa.	1871–76	"Victorian Gothic"	Frank Furness[e]
Philadelphia City Hall	Philadelphia, Pa.	1871–1901	Second (French) Empire (neo-Baroque)	John McArthur, Jr.
State, War, and Navy Building (now Old Executive Office Building)	Washington, D.C.	1871–88	Second (French) Empire (neo-Baroque)	Alfred B. Mullett
Trinity Episcopal Church	Boston, Mass.	1) 1841–46 2) 1872–77	1) Gothic revival 2) Neo-Romanesque	1) Richard Upjohn 2) Henry H. Richardson
Tribune Building	New York, N.Y.	1873–75	Beaux Arts	Richard Morris Hunt
Mark Twain house	Hartford, Conn. (351 Farmington Avenue)	1873–74	Combination of neo-Gothic and Mansard[f]	Edward Tuckerman Potter (of N.Y.)
Home of Watts Sherman	Newport, R.I.	1874–76	English Queen Anne (with Vernacular details)	H. H. Richardson

[a]Mills won the design competition in 1845; construction began in 1848 then was halted in 1854 because of political and financial considerations. The original design called for a Greek-style temple encircling the base of the Egyptian-style obelisk, but this design proved too ambitious and costly. The design was reworked and the project was finally completed in 1884 under the supervision of the architect and engineer Thomas L. Casey.
[b]An eight-story building using structural cast iron with a granite exterior. It was one of the first U.S. buildings on record to use iron in the framing and therefore a forerunner of the later steel-beam-and-curtain-wall skyscrapers.
[c]Considered a white elephant even at the time, the Crystal Palace, for all its technical accomplishment, had virtually no influence on the architectural profession of the day.
[d]Built entirely of cast iron in columns, beams, and facade, it had a central rotunda surrounded by galleries and topped by a plate-glass skylight.
[e]Furness's, masterpiece, establishing him as one of the major architects of his generation, though his professional reputation dropped precipitously before his death in 1912.
[f]In Mar. 1874 the Hartford *Daily Times* described it as "one of the oddest looking buildings in the State ever designed for a dwelling."
Sources: Leland M. Roth, *A Concise History of American Architecture* (New York: Harper & Row, 1979), 128, 130–31, 135–36; *American National Biography,* John A. Garraty et al., eds. (New York: Oxford University Press, 1999), passim; John Burchard and Albert Bush-Brown, *The Architecture of America* (Boston: Little, Brown, 1966); Daniel M. Mendelowitz, *A History of American Art* (New York: Holt, Rinehart and Winston, 1960), 218–30, 357–66; William H. Pierson, Jr., *American Buildings and Their Architects,* vol. 1, *The Colonial and Neoclassical Styles,* 395–97, 404–17, 481, vol. 2, *Technology and the Picturesque,* 4, 205–24, 228–70 (Garden City, N.Y.: Doubleday, 1970); "Architecture," in *Dictionary of American History,* vol. 1, Louise Bilebofketz et al., eds., (New York: Charles Scribner's Sons, 1976), 162–64.

Design and Interior Decoration

In the relatively new fields of design and interior decoration, as in architecture, Americans were heavily influenced by European tastes. The English writer Sir Charles Locke Eastlake's *Hints on Household Taste* (1868) was only a middling success in his home country, but became a trendsetter in the United States. He argued for some higher, transcendent plane of furniture making, stressing "the moral necessity that furniture should show the grain of the wood and the cut of the joint."

The opulent and bejeweled look that characterized Victorian interiors was just coming into vogue at the end of this period. In the years after 1875 a new decorative age known as "the American Renaissance" would take over, led by such notables as Louis C. Tiffany, Edward Chandler Moore, and John La Farge, but the movement had not yet meshed before 1875. Most interior decorators were classically trained artists who branched out, offering their services as arbiters of good taste for the status-conscious wealthy. Tiffany and many others studied at New York City's National Academy of the Arts of Design, founded in 1826 by Samuel F. B. Morse and friends. Not content to be merely painters or sculptors, the new breed of artists handed down definitive judgments on the whole gamut of decorative arts, including tiles, wall hangings, portieres, murals, and stained glass (Tiffany's specialty). Their job was to finish what the architects had begun by giving personality and character to Victorian mansions, churches, and theaters, and they received fat commissions for their expertise.

To many, the biggest name in design and decoration was Tiffany, both the father, Charles Lewis Tiffany (1812–1902), and the son, Louis Comfort Tiffany (1848–1933). The father's firm (Tiffany & Co.) produced exquisite jewelry, silverware, timepieces, and novelty items that were known for their style and quality. In 1852 Tiffany, Sr., introduced sterling silver into the United States from Europe. The son perfected his own artistic talents until 1876, when he and three friends formed L. C. Tiffany & Associated Artists as one of the first complete interior decorating firms in the United States. Tiffany products, from father and son, eventually defined the decorative arts in the United States, achieving the status of being considered collectibles because of their pedigree alone. Charles Tiffany produced miniature jeweled items for several P. T. Barnum extravaganzas, such as the marriage of "General Tom Thumb" in 1863. Some years later Louis Tiffany got the commissions to decorate Mark Twain's house in Hartford, Connecticut, and to redecorate Chester A. Arthur's White House. His work tended to be heavy on mosaic, glasswork, tapestries, and wall sconces.

One of Tiffany, Jr.'s chief rivals for major commissions such as the White House or the Vanderbilt mansion in New York City was John La Farge (1835–1910), who also had a studio and offices in Manhattan. La Farge had a traditional art background. In the 1870s he decided to combine interior decorating with architecture to design "complete" structures. He contributed beautiful murals to Boston's Trinity Church and New York's Church of the Ascension, and he pioneered new methods of stained glass making ("the American School"). He often teamed with the architect Henry Hobson Richardson, carrying out the latter's neo-Romanesque themes in the building's interior spaces.

For public buildings interior decoration in the Victorian era aimed for the grand statement. Often this meant sweeping murals on entire walls. The more important the public building, the more majestic and evocative the mural. It was a populist form of artwork that told history in epic-sized chunks. The foremost mural painter of the day practicing his art in the United States was Constantino Brumidi (1805–80), who immigrated to the United States from his native Italy in 1852 and was subsequently hired in the midst of the Civil War to decorate the national Capitol.

Interior decorating appealed to a key element in romantic thinking—the desire to express the owner's individuality and uniqueness in every building. On the outside of period buildings this approach produced neo-Gothic asymmetry and flourishes. On the inside, builders could arrange interior spaces in new and unique ways, then decorate those spaces, giving free rein to their imagination. This resulted in the "busyness" so associated with Victorian interiors.

The wealthy such as Commodore Vanderbilt and Mark Twain enjoyed other uncommon features in their custom-built houses besides exquisite Tiffany decorations. Twain filled his home with the latest technological marvels, which were unavailable to the masses until the 20th century, such as central heating, hot running water, and even a burglar alarm system. When the telephone became available, he was among the first to install one. Such conveniences coupled with the rise of interior decorating as an art signaled a new attitude about the American home. For middle-class Victorians it was a refuge from the world, a nesting place where the family spent a great deal of time. It had to be spacious and comfortable because it was the center of Victorian life. The Victorians practically made their residence an extension of the family, imbuing it with human character traits and even personal names. Mark Twain wrote about his place that "it had a heart, and a soul, and eyes to see us with; and approvals and solicitudes, and deep sympathies; it was of us, and we were in its confidence, and lived in its grace and in the peace of its benediction."

The Professionalization of Architecture

Before the mid-19th century architecture was widely regarded as a craft rather than a profession. Traditionally it had been the preserve of master builders and carpenters who learned their craft through apprenticeships and worked almost intuitively. This quaint system changed only slowly as the handful of art academies in the United States began to include architecture in their curriculum. The transformation from mere builder into architect of men such as Thomas Ustick Walter (1804–87), a transitional figure, was accomplished without fanfare in the antebellum period. In 1824 Walter was apprenticing on the Second Bank of the United States (Philadelphia); in 1831 he was architect of record on the Philadelphia County Prison. The professional transformation of American architecture gained momentum in the 1850s after Richard Morris Hunt (1827–95) opened his atelier in New York City modeled after the École des Beaux-Arts in Paris, where he had studied. At that time the premier French schools, the École des Beaux Arts and the École Centrale des Arts et Manufactures, were the Mecca for American architects. The rising stars, or at least those with sufficient financial resources, went there to complete their studies for the same reasons that the most promising American doctors traveled to Europe to study medicine: It was the best academic training ground. Hunt was the first notable American architect to study in Europe, and he returned home to introduce a variety of École-inspired designs based on French, English Gothic, and Renaissance styles. He designed New York City's Tribune building, but his real fame arose as architect to the wealthy, who called on him to provide ever bigger and more opulent Gilded Age estates.

Hunt's most important contribution to American architecture may not have been his private residences and public buildings but the atelier that he opened in New York City after returning from Paris. Historians credit his studio as the birthplace of American professional architecture in the 19th century.

Hunt's pilgrimage to Paris was imitated by Henry Hobson Richardson, William Le Baron Jenney, and Louis H. Sullivan, all of whom went on to become torchbearers for American architectural achievement. It was Richardson who turned tradition on its head by becoming the first American to create a distinctively American style ("Richardsonian Romanesque"), which then conquered the Continent. Historically, new styles began in Europe then were imported to the United States. His masterpiece was Trinity Church in Boston. He went on to design libraries, railroad stations, and government buildings all over the country. Jenney designed Chicago's Home Insurance Building, arguably the first skyscraper in the United States, and was a pioneer in the use of structural steel. Sullivan did not really make his mark until after this period as the leading light of the Chicago School, but he also was a product of the École.

Sullivan had another distinction, that of being the first star pupil of the Massachusetts Institute of Technology's (MIT) architectural school (1872–73; he did not graduate). For years U.S. students unwilling or unable to make the pilgrimage to Paris prepared for a career in architecture by studying engineering at Harvard or Columbia or one of the other prestigious eastern universities, or attended a trade school, such as the Franklin Institute of Philadelphia (opened 1824), whose limited architectural program was taught by the respected architect John Haviland. All that changed in 1865, however, when MIT established the first U.S. school of architecture, a two-year program under the direction of William Robert Ware and Eugene Letang. No longer would aspiring architects have to go to Europe for their advanced studies.

The professionalization of architecture was also advanced by the creation of both a professional literature and a professional organization to set standards and grade achievement. Professional literature took the form not just of books but also of periodical literature. The leading architectural journal before the Civil War was the *Journal of the Franklin Institute,* published in Philadelphia from 1824. Following the Civil War, trade journals multiplied, starting with *American Builder,* launched by Charles D. Lakey in Chicago in 1873, to be followed by *Carpenter Trade* (1875), *American Contractor* (1879), and *American Building Association News* (1880). Chicago became the unofficial headquarters of the architectural and building publication trades after post–Great Fire reconstruction was under way in 1871.

Interior decoration also inspired its share of trade literature, starting with *American Cabinet Maker and Upholsterer* and the *Carpet (and Upholstery) Trade Review,* both in 1870. They were followed by *Carpet Trade* in 1875.

Meanwhile popular magazines devoted to the architectural and building arts had caught the public's fancy, with several start-ups during this period. Chief among those was *American Architect and Building*

News, a weekly founded in Boston in 1876 under the editorship of William P. Longfellow, followed by *Carpentry and Building* (1879) and *Building* (1882). A spate of regional architectural magazines sprang up in the 1880s, led by *California Architect* (1880), *Northwestern Architect* (1882), *Western Architect and Builder* (1883), and *Inland Architect and Builder* (1883). Home design and building had become almost a required subject for the rising urban middle class as they sought to distance themselves from the poorer classes and emulate the traditional privilege of the upper class to create stately, personalized residences. And publishers were more than willing to feed that interest with an assortment of consumer and trade publications.

The American Institute of Architects was founded in 1857 by Alexander Jackson Davis and others who wanted to create a homegrown architectural fraternity that could stand alongside its European counterparts. It was regarded as an upstart and treated with appropriate disdain by the art establishment, particularly as represented by the New York National Academy of the Arts of Design.

The growth of professionalism was also marked by a transition from individual architects working virtually solo to extended partnerships of architects, draftsmen, and even engineers combining their talents, energies, and connections to win huge contracts. An efficient partnership divided responsibilities so that different members handled the administrative and business side versus the design side. It also put expertise in more than one style under the same roof so that potential clients were not bound by a single architectural vision. The arrangement guaranteed long-term work because established firms constantly introduced new blood in the form of young, rising stars, thus echoing a practice established in the legal profession for many years. One of the most successful of the early firms was that of Henry Hobson Richardson and Charles Dexter Gambrill in New York, formed in 1867 and amicably dissolved in 1878. Other leading lights of this period were Daniel Burnham and John Wellborn Root of Chicago, who formed their partnership in 1873, and Charles McKim, William Meade, and Stanford White of New York, who joined forces in 1879 to become the first "superstar" firm of architects in U.S. history.

Landscape Architecture

A new breed of architects appeared on the scene in the 19th century, dubbed environmental engineers by later historians. Their appearance coincided with the spread of urbanization, and their mission was to try to preserve some shred of natural surroundings in the heart of the country's sprawling cities. To do this they favored setting aside public land for city parks and beautifying institutional landscapes (i.e., hospitals, government buildings). The architect Thomas Story Kirkbride argued that the grounds surrounding an institution should be "highly improved, and tastefully ornamented; a variety of objects of interest should be collected around it . . . trees and shrubs, flowering plants, summer-houses, and other pleasing objects should add to its attractiveness."

The point man of this movement was Andrew Jackson Downing, the iconoclastic architect who combined his taste for neo-Gothic architecture with fondness for naturalistic and simplistic designs. Downing was the first champion of his profession to argue forcefully for creating city parks to break up the joyless urban grid. He started the fight for a "central park" in New York City that was eventually completed by his pupil Calvert Vaux working with Frederick Law Olmsted. It was Downing who first articulated the philosophy of landscape gardening to "retain the feeling of nature refined and softened by art." The more flamboyant and voluble Olmsted took that idea and ran with it, along the way coining the name *landscape architect* to describe himself and his fellow parks-minded professionals.

Olmsted, the self-taught architect, assured his place in U.S. history by completing the design and supervising the construction of New York City's Central Park. Olmsted and Vaux won a design competition over 33 other entries in 1857 to turn 843 acres of undeveloped wilderness in the middle of Manhattan Island into a permanent green space. A year later Olmsted was appointed chief architect for the project. He and his partner laid out a park that simultaneously shaped and celebrated nature. Construction began in 1858, took time off for the Civil War, and was completed in 1875. During those years they relocated some 1,600 residents from the property, blasted out huge boulders, and carted off more than 10 million cartloads of debris, replacing it with 500,000 cubic feet of New Jersey topsoil to stabilize the swampy land.

The result was a pastoral urban oasis stretching from 59th Street to 110th and from Fifth Avenue to Central Park West, within a 15-minute walk for hundreds of thousands of people. The park has been continuously expanded and reconfigured since 1875. Its characteristic features of gently curving walkways and carriage paths sunk below ground level, informal groupings of trees and shrubs, quiet pools of water, and well-manicured lawns became standard elements of every great urban park of the 19th century, more than a few of which were Olmsted commissions.

New York's Central Park was not just Olmsted's masterpiece and the urban pastoral space par excellence; it became the benchmark for all 19th-century city parks. Other cities large and small created their own green spaces and filled them with groves, artificial lakes, bridle paths, aviaries, and pagodas. One of the finest was in Chicago, conceived even before the Great Chicago Fire and designed by William Jenney. Another early midwestern jewel was the Milwaukee city park. In July 1869, even before the park was finished, the city's *Weekly Wisconsin* boasted that the "great Central Park of New York is, of course, the pride and envy of Gotham, but we doubt if the Park contains so many beauties of such variety of scenery and so much of nature's romance in all acres as are to be found in Milwaukee Park."

Olmsted spent the next quarter-century after completing his Central Park commission creating more than 60 parks and planned neighborhoods throughout the country, including Buffalo, New York's public parks system; Cornell University; Morningside Park in New York; the Biltmore estate in North Carolina; and the Stanford University campus in California.

During these same years other landscape architects besides Olmsted, Vaux, and Downing found common cause with the rising conservation movement, in particular fighting to set aside parcels of western land as national parks. Both groups hoped to preserve some the beauty and tranquility of nature in U.S. life against the advance of civilization. In 1851 Olmsted's partner in the Central Park project, along with Andrew Downing, carried out the long overdue landscape design of the U.S. Capitol grounds. It was to be Downing's last major commission.

The Civil War scarcely interrupted the budding landscape movement. In 1864 Arlington National Cemetery was established by Congress as a properly dignified final resting place for the nation's war dead, on land formerly belonging to Robert E. Lee. When Lee joined the Confederacy in 1861 his estate in Arlington, Virginia, was confiscated by the U.S. government, and thus was created the nation's most revered burial ground for those who have served it loyally. Following the Civil War the landscape and conservation movements strengthened their alliance and at the same time increased public awareness. Thanks to the efforts of J. Sterling Morton in 1872, April 10 was officially designated as Arbor Day. Then in 1874 the first zoological garden in the United States was created in Philadelphia, and the following year the American Forestry Association was founded. Americans were slowly learning that having respect for nature was not the same as being a Luddite or being antidevelopment.

This 1862 engraving, *Central Park, The Drive,* shows people strolling and riding through New York's Central Park before it was even completed. It is a highly stylized representation of the nation's first large city park. As soon as it opened, Central Park became a bucolic refuge in the heart of the city, beloved by citizens of all classes. (The Gilder Lehrman Collection at the Pierpont Morgan Library, New York. GLC 3566)

New Directions in Architecture

The later years of this period, from the Civil War through the mid-1870s, have often been characterized as a period of chaos and indecision in American architecture. The simplest explanation for this situation is the same one used to explain every disruption in national life that occurred in the second half of the 19th century: the Civil War. Whether that explanation is the full story or not is arguable, but what is true is that U.S. architectural styles seemed to be adrift and uninspired. A mansard style, heavily influenced, as were fashion and military science, by France's Second Empire, was briefly popular. And Gothic was extended to Venetian Gothic and other variations, again following European trends, in this case the influence of the Englishman John Ruskin. The only saving architectural grace may have been Richardson's neo-Romanesque, discussed earlier. But even that failed to inspire the masses. It was simply too "Old World" and had insufficient reference to the American people.

In the meantime public architecture was evolving along two different lines: First, what might be called the new commercial architecture favored by the business culture was definitely committed to the "office box" look with less and less ornamentation. The stale neo-Gothic and Greek revival styles were unsuitable to both the functional demands and the mood of the new industrial–commercial age. Their decline was hastened by the coming proliferation of skyscrapers on the urban skyline. Second, the more orthodox public buildings such as courthouses and churches still followed traditional medieval and classical Greek forms.

The end of this period would witness a transition to an "age of elegance" in American architecture on the smaller scale than skyscrapers, not entirely divorced from but less tied to trends in Europe. The new pluralistic styles would include colonial American revival, Italian Renaissance, and the austere "office box" form. As are most transitions from an old period to a new, it would be driven by a combination of new technology, fresh ideas, and general weariness with old forms and old styles.

CHAPTER 17 Science and Technology

These were wonderful years for American science and technology. Advances made on all fronts reflected well on the vaunted "American genius." The nation's intellectual climate was percolating with original ideas and new inventions. Every day seemed to have news of some new industrial process or agricultural machine until the public became almost blasé about such ideas as soaring through the air (balloon), racing over the Earth at 30 miles per hour or faster (via the railroad), and having iced drinks on even the hottest summer day (John Gorrie's ice-making machine). In December 1852 President Millard Fillmore in his third annual State of the Union address proudly proclaimed, "We live in an age of progress. . . . The numerous applications for patents and for valuable improvements distinguish this age and its people from all others [before]. . . . The whole country is full of enterprise."

Agricultural Technology

Much of the focus was on the agricultural-machine revolution, which had begun earlier with John Deere's invention of the steel plow (1837) and Cyrus McCormick's invention of the mechanical reaper (1841). The former demonstrated the innovations possible even with a relatively simple device such as a plow. The older cast-iron Eagle plow still sold at the rate of 25,000 a year in the 1850s, mainly to eastern farmers. It was unsuitable for the heavy, densely packed soil of the Great Plains. Enter the 125-pound Prairie Breaker, which suffered from its requirement for up to seven yoke of oxen to break up the prairie grassland. Initially Deere's improved steel plow was too expensive to be really successful, but when mass-produced steel became available in the mid-1850s, the Deere plow became the plow of choice on the Great Plains. McCormick's reaper was an even greater marvel of its time: the early models allowed two men to do the work formerly performed by 10; later models even improved on that by allowing one farmer to do the work of 14 field hands. Its primary application was in wheat farming. Formerly a single laborer with a hand-held scythe and cradle could harvest two acres of wheat in a day. Using the McCormick reaper and a team of horses, a person could harvest two acres an hour. In fact the only real drawback was that one of the brand-new machines cost about $130 in the 1850s, a prohibitive amount of money by the standards of the day, but McCormick allowed, even encouraged farmers to buy on installment. In 1854 McCormick's Chicago factory produced 4,000 reapers. By the end of this era they were producing 14,000 machines a year and shipping all over the country. The Civil War was a huge stimulus to production because it created a scarcity of men in the workforce, making mechanization on the farm a necessity, not just a luxury.

The synergy of the agricultural-machine revolution, as did the earlier revolution in the English textile industry, meant that advances in one area of farm machinery fostered advances in related areas. Thus improved plows and reapers led to improved harrows, seed drills, and cultivators. Design changes and improved materials in one type of machinery inspired would-be inventors to begin tinkering with other implements. Mechanical cultivators largely replaced the hand-held hoe for removing weeds in the 1850s, improved seed drills were on the market by the 1860s, and better harrows became available after the Civil War. If word of mouth or the traveling salesman did not keep the farmer up on the latest piece of machinery he needed, then he could always turn to *Scientific American*. In the 19th century the magazine served as a kind of *Consumer Reports* on the best of the latest technology, and in 1857 it even included a few tips for its rural readers.

Essential Farm Machinery, 1857

This list includes machinery every progressive farmer needs who hopes to produce for the market, according to *Scientific American* magazine.

One combination reaper-mower
One horse rake
One seed planter and sower
One hand-operated thresher and grain cleaner
One portable gristmill
One corn sheller
One two-horse plow (+ 3 other smaller plows)
Three harrows
One roller
One cultivator

Source: John W. Oliver, History of American Technology (New York: Ronald Press, 1956), 234.

It was no accident that the earliest breakthroughs in American technology were in agriculture. America was still, after all, a nation of farmers who shared an almost mystical faith in the land. It was relatively easy to arouse interest in and secure investment for improved agricultural implements. Everybody wanted machinery that would cut down on back-breaking toil, reduce the expensive need for hired help, and produce bumper crops. The result was a succession of plows, drills, cultivators, and harvesters turned out by Yankee ingenuity. American farmers proved not the least hesitant in adopting the latest invention, and the use of the most up-to-date machinery, more than anything else, came to define the American farmer. One result was that the value of farm machinery increased from less than $7 million in 1850 to more than $20 million in 1860.

And the American farmer also proved to be brand-conscious even at this early date. According to the historian Howard Segal, the farmer was strongly influenced in his choice of equipment by "who manufactured it and how it was supposedly manufactured." Thus names like "John Deere" and "McCormick," once they were established, had a virtually captive market, indeed, a monopoly, for every new piece of machinery they put out with their name on it. And the high quality of U.S. farm machinery seemingly more than repaid the farmer's loyalty to the biggest companies.

The revolution down on the farm that began in the antebellum period picked up speed in the 1860s. The Civil War increased the demand for the farmer's product and as a result sent farm prices soaring. Even the most conservative farmer could see the advantage of mechanized farming to the bottom line; suddenly the race was on to invest in new equipment. Only cotton and tobacco cultivation seemed immune to all the new technology. The momentum continued after the war as improved harvesters and binders entered the marketplace. The latest machines did more than mere harvesting or reaping of grain; they prepared the soil (harrows) and planted the seed (seed drills). Specifically seed drills and harvesters reached the virtual apex of their technological evolution at this time and led directly to the development of the American "wheat belt." Still in the future when this era closed were the threshing machine (to strip the grain from the stalks) and the giant combine (combination thresher and harvester), which took production to still higher levels. But by 1875 there was no going back; American farmers were wholeheartedly committed to technology, and the more, the better. This trend led Horace Greeley to observe (1871), "We use far better implements than did our grandfathers with corresponding increase in effi-

"Scientific agriculture" was widely influential in the 1850s. This 1854 lithograph from *The American Farmer* magazine shows the award-winning farm buildings of the Maryland farmer Charles B. Calvert. The octagonal barn has a glass door to admit light for the livestock, and the barnyard has an innovative drainage system. (The Maryland Historical Society, Baltimore, Maryland)

ciency." He added that although Americans might learn much from the farmers of Britain, Belgium, Holland, and France, "in selection of implements and average efficiency of labor our best farmers are ahead of them all."

In fact it was the chronic labor shortage in the farm belt (and the related problem of lack of money to hire workers) as much as anything else that drove the American farmer to embrace technology. To the average overworked and hard-pressed farmer, all the new machinery represented more than just a technological revolution; it was a heaven-sent blessing. With the help of technology it was possible drastically to reduce both the number of laborers and the hours required to produce the same yield of crops. And technology made American farmers major players in the world grain market. Before better reapers and plows were invented, American farmers simply could not harvest enough, even with the best of weather conditions, to satisfy the potential market for their crops. By mid-century agricultural production depended as much upon technology as on the farmers' hard labor.

As with computers today, the new technology was not static; machinery such as reapers and binders underwent continuous redesign and improvement, not the least of which was the substitution of steam power for horse and oxen power, beginning with plows and reapers in the late 1850s. The application of steam power to farm machinery marked the outer limits of the agricultural machine revolution in the mid-19th century. Hundreds of patent applications for steam-driven reapers and threshers were submitted from the late 1860s, but none produced an efficient, reliable machine at this point. All proved to be both too expensive and too complex for practical use. And the more advanced British imports failed both the simplicity and "made in America" tests. The horse and oxen teams would not be completely replaced until the application of the internal combustion engine to farm machinery.

TABLE 17.1 IMPORTANT U.S. INVENTIONS, MID-1800s

Invention	Inventor(s)	Patented/First Introduced	Description
McCormick reaper	Cyrus Hall McCormick	1831 (1834)[a]	Contained seven innovative features; operated by horse power; could cut up to 12 acres of wheat per day
Hussey reaper	Obed Hussey	1833[b]	Superior machine to McCormick's, but not marketed as well
Corn planter	Henry Blair[c]	1834	Simple horse-drawn machine that required the farmer to walk behind it, planting one row at a time
Mechanical thresher	John and Hiram Pitts	1837	Combined separating and fanning of stalks into one operation; replaced old-fashioned hand flail

Invention	Inventor(s)	Patented/First Introduced	Description
Sulky rake	Calvin Delano	1849	Cultivator that allowed farmer to ride while weeding instead of walking behind horse-drawn machine
Wire binder	John H. Heath, S.D. Locke, and others	1850–	Evolutionary descendant of the reaper; automatically tied harvested grain into sheaves and bound each sheaf with wire bands
Improved corn planter	George Brown	1853	Horse-drawn machine that allowed farmer to plant two rows at a time, in hilly or flat fields
Mowing machine (cf. the reaper)	Cyremus Wheeler	1856	Two-wheeled machine with flexible cutter bar for cutting hay or wheat
Harvester(s)	Charles W. and William W. Marsh, and others	1858, 1870–	Descendant of reaper but better in that it had an attachment to carry cut grain to a platform where workers could bind sheaves
Twine binder (self-binder; aka "Appleby Knotter")	John Francis Appleby	1859	Bound sheaves with twine instead of wire and then tied ("knotted") each bundle; drove wire binder off the market
Gang plow (i.e., riding plow)	J. C. Pfeil	1865	Plow with attached seat to allow operator to ride instead of walk
Post driver	John Anderson	1866	"A device for driving fence posts . . . to greatly reduce the labor and facilitate the operation"
Chilled iron plow	James Oliver	1868	Method of cooling iron during production to make harder, smoother finished product
Disk plow	J. S. Godfrey	1868	Used a concave moldboard with revolving scrapers
Steam plow	Henry Burden Obed Hussey J. W. Fawkes P. H. Standish	Late 1840s 1856 1858 1868	Impractical for most farms; too balky and expensive; not marketed until 1873 and never perfected
Improved plow	Various	1869	"Holy grail" of farm technology; more than 250 patents issued in 1869 alone
Spring-toothed harrow	Various	Late 1860s	Pulverized and turned over soil for planting; used steel teeth with adjustable settings
Disk harrow	Various	1870s	Used variously shaped and sized disks to turn over soil, with automatic scraper to clean disks
Seed drill	Various	Mid-1870s	Controlled the amount of grain sown and injected it directly into furrows
Straddle-row cultivator	Various	1870s	Replaced hand-held hoe for turning over ground and chopping weeds; two-wheeled, double-shovel machine drawn by two horses with seat for operator

[a] McCormick perfected his reaper in 1831, applied for a patent, and received it in 1834. That original patent ran out in 1848, but he continued to introduce improvements, file for new patents, and battle his competitors in court for many years.

[b] Hussey first introduced his version of the mechanical reaper in Jul. 1833 and patented it that same year (a year before McCormick). His patent ran out in 1847, and he succeeded in renewing it only after a spiteful legal battle with McCormick.

[c] Henry Blair was an African American, but not the first of his race to apply for and receive a patent from the U.S. Patent Office. The first was Thomas L. Jennings, a free black tailor in New York City who invented "a method for dry cleaning clothes" in 1821.

Sources: John W. Oliver, *History of American Technology* (New York: Ronald Press, 1956), 222–35, 362–76; Alan I. Marcus and Howard P. Segal, *Technology in America: A Brief History* (San Diego: Harcourt Brace Jovanovich, 1989), passim; Joseph and Frances Gies, *The Ingenious Yankees: The Men, Ideas, and Machines that Transformed a Nation, 1776–1876* (New York: Thomas Y. Crowell, 1976), passim; David Freeman Hawke, *Nuts and Bolts of the Past: A History of American Technology, 1776–1860* (New York: Harper & Row, 1988), passim.

Industrial Technology

In U.S. industry, as in agriculture, labor-saving machinery was the name of the game. Looking back on these years from the vantage point of 1884, Senator Orville H. Platt praised American inventiveness by declaring that "the American hand fashioned labor saving machines . . . made this nation throb with new energy and new life." It was true that his countrypeople showed few reservations about investing in the latest technology if it would lighten their workload, particularly if it increased profits at the same time. After a tour of

U.S. factories in 1853, a British engineer observed, "Wherever [machinery] can be introduced as a substitute for manual labor, it is universally and willingly resorted to."

The rapid evolution of the factory system illustrated the truism that production is more efficient when centralized under one roof. The early days of the Industrial Revolution began in home workshops and cottage industries, but when it leaped the Atlantic, American-style industrialism quickly adopted the factory model, with the emphasis on technology and labor conservation. Americans took industrialism to the next level and added their own refinements. The ideal, of course, was mass production at the lowest possible cost. A factory required a central power source, a ready supply of labor, and easy access to the distribution network. By mid-century U.S. factories were being largely driven by steam power from Pennsylvania coal; the labor supply problem was solved by locating on the outskirts of cities, where large numbers of recent immigrants lived; and the distribution was taken care of by tying into the spreading railroad network.

It was in the use of power that American industrialists made their most important contribution. The English system used a rigid system of gears and drive shafts to distribute power to all the machines throughout a factory. The Americans preferred to use leather belts joined in endless loops and connected to pulleys to carry power because they performed more quietly and smoothly, were easier to install, and were cheaper to replace than metal gears. Belt drives provided a much more flexible power train than the English system. The disadvantages were loss of efficiency from slippage, frequent breaks in the leather belts, and overheating caused by friction. Both the English and Americans claimed superiority for their system.

Possibly because of the lack of an entrenched cottage industry and entrenched economic interests, the factory system spread much more rapidly in the United States than in Britain or the rest of Europe. U.S. manufacturers also worshiped at the shrine of uniformity, elevating standardization practically to a secular religion. This was particularly evident in the shoe- and boot-making industry, which quickly relegated cobblers to repair work in the mass market.

The "American System": Rifles and Sewing Machines

The quest for uniformity led U.S. companies to develop manufacturing processes that produced truly the first interchangeable mechanical parts, albeit on a very small scale. Historically machine production turned out parts that had to be filed down and "finished" by hand before they could be assembled. That process required skilled craftsmen, who were always at a premium. Furthermore even with hand finishing, the best that could be hoped for was uniformity, not true interchangeability. But Americans pushed the boundaries of manufacturing, striving for greater and greater exactitude. As a result they were able to make precision machine tools (i.e., machines that shape metal products), which turned out more nearly identical parts than any other industrial nation in the world.

Guns

The first industry in which these methods were applied on a large scale was the nascent U.S. arms industry. No technology was nearer and dearer to U.S. hearts than gun making, and this era saw the United States claim both quantitative and qualitative leadership among the world's leading arms manufacturers. (France was the world leader in arms making in the 18th century, replaced by Britain in the early 19th century.) In the first three decades of the 19th cen-

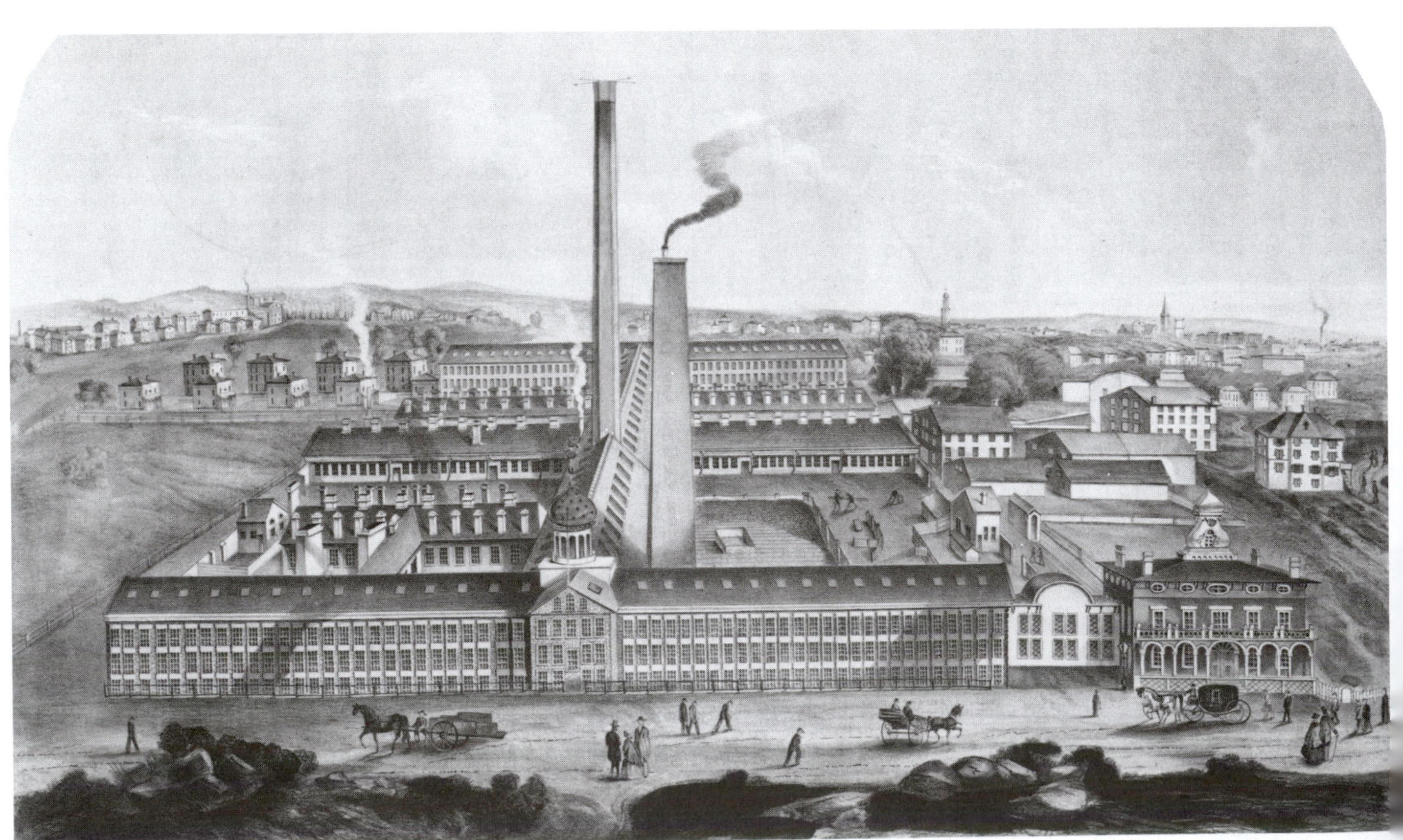

Samuel Colt's Patent Fire Arms Manufactory in Hartford, Connecticut, opened in 1849. It became the largest private armory in the world within a few years. (Library of Congress, Prints and Photographs Division [LC-USZ62-18103])

tury government armories produced enough weapons for the military, leaving the civilian market for high-quality personal arms to European firms, who enjoyed a lucrative export business across the Atlantic. America's rise to prominence in the arms industry started slowly in the 1840s and took off in the following decade. The 1850s saw the emergence of some of the most famous brand names in the business: Colt, Sharps, Remington, Robbins and Lawrence, Smith & Wesson, and Winchester. They led a host of smaller firms who sprang up to fill the insatiable U.S. demand for guns of all kinds to use in fighting Indians, guarding homesteads, and defending (and breaking) the law. It was an industry centered on the East Coast, with no arms manufacturing plants south of Virginia or west of the Appalachians. The nine largest firms were all located in Connecticut.

The arms industry helped produce a generation of technologically savvy American workers while making the United States the most heavily armed in the Western world. From 11 factories in 1833 (capitalized at $207,550), the U.S. gun-making industry grew to 317 facilities in 1858 (capitalized at $577,509), employing a total of 1,547 workers.

The federal government was more than an interested observer, forging a historic partnership with the gun-making industry that preceded and presaged the more famous public-private partnership with U.S. railroads later. Uncle Sam provided capital, patent and tariff protection, technological expertise, and a ready market for the product in its armed forces. The government was both a patron and a competitor to private arms makers, operating its own armories at Harper's Ferry, Virginia, and Springfield, Massachusetts.

Still, lack of foresight and years of penny-pinching budgets prevented the nation from exploiting its full arms-making capacity when the Civil War began. In January 1860 the U.S. government had on hand just 610,000 small arms of all types, most of them antiquated flintlock muskets modified for percussion use. A little over a year later the Confederate government offered to buy up every spare musket the Europeans would sell, while making plans to arm thousands of its troops with medieval-style pikes in the interim! By 1865 both sides were turning out thousands of serviceable weapons for their fighting forces, giving further impetus to a burgeoning home-grown industry and helping to ensure America's position as a premier military power for decades.

The arms industry played a central role in the rapid march of American technology. It was Samuel Colt who pioneered the "American system" in the private sector when he applied it to making small arms under military contract. He was the quintessential entrepreneur, recognizing a need, applying new technology to that need, then shrewdly marketing the resulting product, which in Colt's case were revolvers and rifles that proved to be both innovative and high in quality. Colt refined the new manufacturing processes at his Hartford, Connecticut, factory, turning out weapons that were among the finest in the world and putting an American stamp on a very old and honored industry.

So impressive was his brand of precision-based manufacturing that it was initially dubbed the "armory system" by admiring Englishmen, and only later the "American system." The main advantage was that it required fewer skilled craftsmen in the workforce. The downside was that in the mid-19th century precision manufacturing was actually more expensive and time-consuming than normal manufacturing methods, but it clearly represented the wave of the future, and it had American fingerprints all over it. The philosophical implications of the assembly line and interchangeable parts for individualism, for labor relations, and for aesthetic value did not seem to bother 19th-century Americans much, especially when balanced against the economies of mass production and lower labor costs.

As impressive as the Colt revolver itself was its ammunition. The mass-produced metal cartridge that fit both the Colt revolver and the Model 1873 Winchester rifle proved to be the single most important interchangeable part in the whole firearm. Without a cheap and ready supply of cartridges, the best gun in the world is useless. Rollin White, a onetime Colt employee, knew this when he patented his own cartridge in 1855, but neither he nor his new employer, Smith & Wesson, could successfully exploit it. Samuel Colt died before he could grasp this profound insight, but his company realized it after his death and began to make up for lost time in 1873. The result was what the historian Phil Patton calls "the cartridge that won the West," enthusiastically adopted by both the U.S. Army and a multitude of western outlaws and lawmen.

As Samuel Colt did, Christian Sharps learned gunsmithing as an apprentice before opening his own factory, the Sharps Rifle Manufacturing Company, in 1851. For the next two decades he turned out a variety of military and sporting rifles, carbines, and even some pistols in his factory, selling some 89,653 breechloaders to the federal government during the Civil War alone. Together Colt and Sharps made Hartford, Connecticut, the "Gun-Making Capital of the World."

Sewing Machines

But the most important success story in U.S. industry was Isaac Singer's sewing machine. It also happened to be the perfect marriage of technology and mass marketing techniques. Singer applied the principles pioneered by the armaments industry to the home consumer market, and the market composed of wives, mothers, and tailors was just as open to new technology as that of soldiers, outlaws, and lawmen. By any standard Isaac Merritt Singer accomplished some amazing achievements, starting with the first practical sewing machine in 1850. The Americans Walter Hunt and Elias Howe and the Frenchman Barthelemy Thimonnier had already developed similar machines, but they were frustrated by the technical details, poor marketing, and moral doubts about putting thousands of tailors and seamstresses out of work. After Singer's machine became a huge success, the other unsuccessful inventors of the sewing machine began trying to enter the market, resulting in a flurry of lawsuits and countersuits in the 1850s known as "the Great Sewing Machine War." One of the lessons of Singer's experience was that technology did not exist in a vacuum but had to contend with fears of automation and legal questions of proprietorship. These two issues, and the parallel concern with the best way to market new technologies, were never far from center stage in the flowering of U.S. technology. The year after he unveiled his sewing machine, Isaac Singer set up a company to mass produce it. He proved a master of marketing, selling his machines all over the world, launching the first multinational company in the United States, and virtually inventing installment buying for the consumer. Singer also bluntly summed up the driving force behind many inventions, and it was not curiosity or the burning desire to build a better mousetrap. As Singer once said, "I don't care a damn for the invention. The dimes are what I'm after." In the end he got both the "dimes" and credit for his creation. Thanks also to his wonderful invention, ready-made uniforms clothed hundreds of thousands of soldiers during the Civil War and revolutionized American dress habits when peace returned to the nation after Appomattox.

Ironically the astounding success stories of Singer's sewing machine and McCormick's reaper demonstrated a breakdown in the transfer of American inventiveness to the free market economy: Neither product represented the best technology of the time. Singer's sewing machine was not intrinsically superior to its rivals; it was simply marketed better, driving the competition out of business. McCormick's reaper, truth be told, mowed poorly and broke down frequently, and the production techniques in his Chicago plant were not the most modern, being more dependent upon skilled craftsmen than upon an efficient assembly line. But he still managed to achieve a stranglehold in the manufacture of reapers by shrewd advertising and

The American-invented sewing machine was such a marvelous piece of technology that it created intense interest all over the world. Here, a group of Japanese officials on a visit to Washington, D.C., in 1860 intently observe an employee of Willard's Hotel working a Wheeler and Wilson sewing machine. It may have been idle curiosity or a desire to copy it when they returned home that caused them to watch so closely. (Library of Congress, Prints and Photographs Division [LC-USZ62-02020])

aggressive marketing. He simply did a better job creating a sales network than anybody else in the business. He also wooed agricultural societies and trade newspapers and exhibited his machines at every agricultural fair that he heard about. Two things he did that won his customers' loyalty were to issue a warranty with every reaper sold and maintain a full stock of replacement parts that his salesmen were trained to install. Thus the marriage between American technology and marketing was established from the beginning.

Every American inventor of this era did not have the smashing success Samuel Colt and Cyrus McCormick had: Even the most brilliant inventors had their share of miscalculations and blunders. This happened to the Swedish-American genius John Ericsson, who immigrated to the United States in 1839 and subsequently perfected the screw propeller, pioneered the manufacturing of scientific instruments, and designed and built the revolutionary *Monitor* type of ironclad. Unfortunately he was also the inventor of the embarrassing "caloric engine" in 1851. Supposedly using renewable heat rather than conventional steam to produce power, he put on a public demonstration the next year that was heralded before the event as the dawn of "the Age of Caloric." The demonstration failed miserably and the inventor shelved his creation, leading to its being dubbed "the nine-days' wonder." Ericsson went on to further brilliant successes, and his caloric engine (the "regenerator") was quickly forgotten.

Steel Production

The sewing machine, the revolver, and the reaper are all inspiring American success stories and testimonials to Yankee ingenuity. But the single most important industrial advance of these years was the development of an efficient process for the manufacture of structural steel, which was stronger and more durable than simple iron. The story involved dueling processes developed independently on both sides of the Atlantic. In the United States William Kelly received a patent in 1851 for his process of purifying iron by blowing air through it while it was in its molten state. Meanwhile on the other side of the Atlantic the Englishman Henry Bessemer perfected an almost identical steelmaking technique in 1856, and it is Bessemer who is remembered as "the Father of the Steel Age."

Kelly, an iron maker at Eddyville, Kentucky, made his discovery while making large sugar-boiling kettles for his Southern planter customers. He discovered through practical experimentation that a steady blast of air during the refining process would convert pig iron into high-quality steel, but his "newfangled" methods drew nothing but skepticism and ridicule from his customers and investors. He persisted in true American fashion and built a converter at Johnstown, Pennsylvania's, Cambria Iron Works in 1851. He patented his converter in 1857, but that same year, the financial panic drove him out of business, and his patent passed into the hands of other family members.

Meanwhile a third contributor entered the picture, Alexander Lyman Holley, an American engineer who held a license to use the Bessemer process in the United States. He acquired the rights to the Kelly process and, combining it with the Bessemer process, sold the whole package to investors, becoming the first American to turn steelmaking technology into a moneymaking business. The first Bessemer-style converter in the United States was built in Troy, New York, in 1864, the same year that a Kelly-style converter was built in Wyandotte, Michigan.

Holley's technological contribution was the so-called American plan of steelmaking, which transformed a heretofore small-scale, arcane process into a mass-production process. Holley became the leading engineer of U.S. steel plants, designing practically all the large-scale works. In 1868 the open-hearth process, which efficiently removed sulfur and phosphorus from molten iron, was introduced into the U.S. steel industry from Britain by Abraham S. Hewitt. The first working model was built in Trenton, New Jersey, and its obvious advantages caused it to spread quickly to other steelmaking plants. By the end of the 1870s thanks to all the new technologies and rapid expansion, the United States rivaled Britain in steel production.

However, the technological breakthrough was almost overshadowed by a legal battle over rights to the process. Patent holders for the Kelly and Bessemer process battled for years to stake out their respective legal claims and thereby reap the attendant financial rewards. The fighting dragged through the courts for years until it was finally resolved in 1866, but history was the ultimate judge of who got the credit, identifying Bessemer's not Kelly's name with the process of purifying iron into steel.

Timing as well as genius and persistence were needed to create the giant U.S. steel industry. Mass-produced steel became available just as the U.S. railway industry was taking off. Here was an immediate and ravenous market for all the steel the industry could produce. Economic boom times and western expansion had created a demand for rapid rail construction to tie the nation and its markets together. The early wooden and wrought-iron rails were clearly inadequate for the vast distances and heavy carrying being placed on them. Steel rails were the solution, and the railroad industry was able to proceed full-throttle with expansion. After the railroads, farm machinery makers represented the second biggest user of the new steel. The widespread use of steel in building construction and naval warships occurred later.

The railroad was the greatest advance in transportation since the horse; in fact, it was sometimes known as the iron horse. It provided the complete package in terms of speed and power. It also represented the culmination of a thousand separate technological advances, some large and some small. From a curiosity to an industry, the growth of the railroad in the 19th century is an amazing story. No industry depended more on a steady stream of technical breakthroughs. The obvious need for safer, more comfortable, more efficient service called forth one innovation after another. Some were the brainchild of inventive geniuses; others were the work of ordinary tinkerers who saw a problem and solved it. Fortunately the industry was still in its "wildcatting" days and therefore receptive to new ideas, so the latest technology could be readily adopted, and the time lag from invention to general use was brief.

The United States and Britain: Rivals or Partners?

Thanks in large part to steel production, the United States was, before the end of this era, the second greatest industrial nation in the world after Great Britain. The relationship between the two industrial giants was a combination of rivalry and cooperation. The United States was the clear leader in one area: mass production of interchangeable parts. This was a revolutionary concept that originated with the manufacture of firearms and spread to locks, clocks, furniture, sewing machines, and all sorts of mechanical goods. American ingenuity perfected methods of turning out special-purpose machine tools that could in turn be used to produce an endless stream of identical parts that could be fitted together to make brand-new copies of the original design. The results were inferior in quality, but also cheaper and more readily available on demand. Mass-produced U.S. goods so impressed British competitors that it was they who characterized the process as the "American system [of manufactures]." The British government sent two commissioners across the Atlantic to study the U.S. methods and imported American experts to advise British companies on how to set up the same system in Britain.

The synergy between U.S. and British industry produced the strange case of the Enfield rifle. The Americans first developed a superior rifled musket at the Harper's Ferry, Virginia, arsenal (U.S. Rifle Model 1841), which the British copied and produced at their Enfield, England, arsenal. The nine-pound Enfield musket was adopted by the British army in 1855 and was widely considered one of the best shoulder arms in the world. When the Civil War began and the governments on both sides were caught short of weapons for their armies, they looked to the Enfield factory, which began reexporting the weapon to America—almost half a million to the North and several hundred thousand to the South, where it quickly won the hearts of Confederate infantrymen. It was a situation full of irony with a U.S. design manufactured in Britain and then sold back to the Americans, but this is what happened when the Industrial Revolution met international capitalism.

Advances in Communication

Advances in communication during this era begin with the telegraph. After years of development and legal wrangling, the worth of the telegraph was decisively demonstrated in 1844. It produced a rippling effect throughout technology, communications, society, economics, and politics. It was the first practical use of electricity, carried the latest news faster than ever before in human history, tied even the most distant parts of the country to the rest, became the first of the "natural monopolies," revolutionized business, and changed the way wars were fought—and those were just for starters. It was rightly hailed at the time as "the greatest invention of the age." Not until the middle of the 20th century would wireless communications make serious inroads into the almost universal use of cable for long-distance communications.

In its early years telegraphy demonstrated the "dynamics of industrialism" by sparking related advances in printing and the transmission of information, such as R. H. Hoe's rotary printing press (the "lightning press," 1847) and Stephen Tucker's gathering and delivery cylinder. The Hoe press fed a continuous stream of newsprint into the inking machinery, and the Tucker cylinder collected the finished pages. In tandem the two machines allowed the New York *Tribune* to print 18,000 newspapers an hour, getting out the latest news to the public in a fraction of the time required by the older technology. And the news was coming in faster thanks to the telegraph. New York City newspapers could now be apprised of current developments in Charleston or St. Louis or even San Francisco within hours of an event. The first transcontinental telegram was received by President Lincoln from the chief justice of California on October 24, 1861.

In 1865 William Bullock's web press took printing to the next level. It combined a continuous "web," or roll, of paper with curved stereotype plates to print a page on both sides and even cut the paper either before or after printing. Each invention that streamlined the printing process helped the public learn the news that much faster.

In the process newspapering changed even in its basic assumptions: With the rapid transmission of news and opinion, U.S. newspapers were transformed from news reporting to news making, transmitting their version of events to thousands of readers. Between 1830 and 1850 the number of newspapers in the United States jumped by more than 300 percent, at least partly in response to the ready availability of regional and even national news to fill the pages of a daily edition. More than ever before newspapers occupied the crucial role of intermediary between the events and the public.

By 1850 the ubiquitous "singing wires" connected all the states east of the Mississippi and were spreading out over the West inexorably. Railroad and telegraph forged a natural alliance so that in a few short years telegraph lines strung up along the railroad's right-of-way were commonplace. North America became the first continent "wired" by technology. The difference between so-called rapid communications before and those after the telegraph is encapsulated in the story of the Pony Express. When the Pony Express went into service in April 1860, it was the fastest way to send a message across the western half of the continent, but sending it from Saint Joseph, Missouri, to Sacramento, California, still took 10 days and cost five dollars per ounce. Twenty months later, after the telegraph went into operation, in a matter of seconds one could transmit a message, and the cost was a dollar per word from San Francisco to the Missouri River. Not long after that the cost dropped to six dollars for 10 words between San Francisco and New York City and 75 cents for each additional word.

Behind the communications marvel were a pair of scientific breakthroughs: the development of a reliable electric battery and of an improved electromagnet, which permitted the conversion of electrical impulses into mechanical energy. Samuel F. B. Morse received credit for the invention, but his most original contribution was the ingenious code system of dots and dashes that made it possible to

The laying of the first transatlantic telegraph cable was accomplished in 1857 after several false starts. The 1,950-mile-long insulated line was completed August 5, from Trinity Bay, Newfoundland, to Valencia, Ireland, with the western half laid by the U.S. steamer *Niagara*, pictured here at the end of the job in an engraving from *The Illustrated News,* August 22, 1857. (Library of Congress)

transmit complicated messages and created a universal language for operators. In the years that followed, refinements in the basic technology, which included boosting weak signals over long distances and sending multiple messages simultaneously in both directions over the same wire (first the duplex key, then the quadriplex key in 1874), were made.

After connecting the major regions of the United States, the next step was connecting as many cities as quickly as possible into the national network. Fortunately the technology was ridiculously simple and cheap to put in place. All that was required were a local telegraph office, some sturdy poles, and miles of copper wire. And beginning in the 1850s, some big-city fire and police departments linked their scattered stations with their own systems. The nation's biggest financial houses soon followed with their own private systems to transmit stock information quickly and discreetly. The telegraph itself made history by carrying history-making news. When the Civil War began in April 1861, the telegraph quickly flashed the news of Fort Sumter across the nation, drawing soldiers on distant posts and civilians out West back to the East to join the colors. During the next four years the frontiers of telegraphic communications were pushed outward beyond what anyone had dreamed of just a few short years before. Jury-rigged telegraph lines kept generals in touch, destroying those lines became a major campaign objective, and, combining two new advances, telegraph wires were connected from the ground to observation balloons so that military observers could instantly report what they saw to headquarters. With the end of the war and the return of peace, new uses were found for communication by wire. In 1872 telegraph "call boxes" were introduced in some larger cities, allowing any citizen to send or receive a message across the city or across the country.

Meanwhile the communications industry was born when Western Union Telegraph Company was founded in 1856. It promptly set about gobbling up competitors (more than 500 local companies), until in a few short years it possessed a near-monopoly with the blessing of both business and government. Unfortunately Western Union did not start keeping records of telegraph communications until 1867. By that date there were already nearly 6 million telegrams being sent annually by U.S. customers. Telegraph communications would nearly triple in the eight years after 1867, and nearly double again in the six years after that.

TABLE 17.2 GROWTH OF WESTERN UNION TELEGRAPH COMPANY, 1866–1875

Year[a]	Number of Telegraph Offices	Number of Miles of Wire	Number of Messages Sent[b]
1866	2,250	76	N/A
1867	2,565	85	5,879,000
1868	3,219	98	6,405,000
1869	3,607	105	7,935,000
1870	3,972	112	9,158,000
1871	4,606	121	10,646,000
1872	5,237	137	12,444,000
1873	5,740	154	14,457,000
1874	6,188	176	16,329,000
1875	6,565	179	17,154,000

[a] The company's accounting year ended Jun. 30.
[b] N/A (not available) indicates that figures are unknown for a given year.
Sources: U.S. Department of Commerce, *Historical Statistics of the United States, Colonial Times to 1970,* Bicentennial Edition, Part 2 (Washington, D.C.: Dept of Commerce, 1975), 788; B. R. Mitchell, *International Historical Statistics: The Americas and Australasia* (Detroit: Gale Research, 1983), 735.

The telegraph had a social as well as a technological dimension. The same wires that transmitted news also transmitted cultural attitudes and values, thereby creating a shared sense of nationalism between, say, New England fishermen and California gold miners. Good communication meant good information, and that was as useful to the businessperson as to the soldier. With the growth of international markets U.S. merchants needed to know conditions in Europe, and vice versa. Fortunately even the great oceans were no barrier to the telegraph.

In 1858 after several false starts, telegraph cable was laid across the Atlantic linking the United States with Britain via Newfoundland and Ireland. That first transatlantic cable, only five-eighths of an inch in diameter and insulated with gutta percha, transmitted the first international message, on August 17, from Queen Victoria to President James Buchanan, taking 16½ hours; in a relatively brisk 10 hours the president's reply was received by the British monarch. Even at upward of 10 hours of transit time, this still represented an enormous advance over the usual 12 days required for communications by fast steamer. Despite the exhilarating success of this official test, the technology was far from perfected. After just 271 messages, the cable went dead on September 18, plagued by flaws in the copper core and insulation, coupled with poor electrical management. The beginning of the Civil War along with the enormous expenses involved prevented another cable from being laid until 1866. By 1868 not one but two cables were in service, the original one having been repaired, and in 1869 a third was laid between the United States and France.

The laying of the Atlantic cable is one of the great technological success stories of the 19th century, ranking with the building of the Suez Canal and the transcontinental railroad. Everything about it was bigger than life, including the steamship that laid the cable, the *Great Eastern,* which, when completed in 1858, was five times larger than anything else afloat at the time. Not only did undersea telegraphy require creation of new science and advances in marine engineering; it also necessitated the forging of unprecedented partnerships between government and industry and between two often hostile great powers, the United States and Britain. More than a century would pass before the next stage in transatlantic communications, satellite communications, would supersede undersea cable transmission.

Meanwhile landlocked communications underwent a different sort of revolution at the very end of this era. The new technology that challenged the communications monopoly of the telegraph industry was the telephone, which could provide not only near-instant communication but actual voice communication. In the early 1870s Elisha Gray, an Oberlin College professor, and Alexander Graham Bell, a Scottish-born tinkerer living in Boston, began doing experiments with the electrical transmission of the human voice via an "annunciator." They could never have achieved anything if the groundwork had not been done by the invention of telegraph communications. At the very end of this period, on June 2, 1875, Bell finally made a breakthrough, transmitting his own voice to an assistant sitting in another room of his laboratory. Bell named his machine a "harmonic telegraph" and began making improvements immediately, but the world would not learn of his marvelous machine until 1876 at the Philadelphia Centennial Exposition.

The final phase of the communications revolution of the mid-19th century was the invention of a swift and uniform way to produce written messages. It began with the telegraph, naturally. A telegraph ticker that printed stock reports was invented by David Edward Hughes in 1856 and quickly snapped up by a commercial company for $100,000. The first operational typesetting machine was invented by Timothy Alden in 1857. But it required Christopher Sholes's 1868 invention of the typewriter to take the twin ideals of speed and uniformity in written communication to the public at large. The advantage of the new machine over old-fashioned handwritten communication was obvious immediately. E. Remington & Sons signed a contract with the inventor in 1873 to mass produce the "typewriter" (Sholes also invented the name). And a revolution in American office work was launched.

The man soon to be America's most beloved author, Mark Twain, did much to popularize the machine by using it to produce two full-length book manuscripts in the same year. *The Adventures of Tom Sawyer* became the first typewritten book manuscript when it was typed on a Remington machine in 1875. Later that same year Twain also used his new machine to write *Life on the Mississippi,* and though he hated being a shill for the business world, his fame and that of Sholes's invention were soon inseparably linked.

Photography

One new area of technology that particularly enchanted Americans was photography, which took the nation by storm in the 1840s using a primitive process developed by L. J. M. Daguerre of France. "Daguerrotypes," as they were called, used copper plates coated in silver and exposed to light to produce their image. Only a single picture could be made from an exposed plate, eliminating the mass market for daguerrotypes. Because of its limitations the process was originally suited only for landscape pictures, but this is where the Americans took over. Americans such as Alexander Wolcott, Samuel F. B. Morse, and John William Draper improved the process enough to do portraiture. Still far from efficient, the process required from 40 seconds to two minutes to create a daguerreotype of a posed subject. Candid photography or action pictures were out of the question. By the early 1850s there were an estimated 2,000 daguerrotypists at work in the United States, working out of both back rooms and elegant studios. The largest number and the most skilled were in New York City. Customers were charged one to two dollars for a sitting, a substantial sum of money for such a mere trifle.

The enormous popularity of daguerreotypes and subsequent forms of photography in the United States is at least partially explained by Americans' fascination with every kind of new technology. But it also derived from the national penchant for self-examination. Americans believed that photographs revealed the subject's inner character and therefore were a sort of window to the soul. They saw photography in the same terms as phrenology and physiognomy, that is, as tools to understanding themselves individually and collectively.

By the 1850s the rapid advance of technology had produced several new forms of photography, including ambrotypes and tintypes. But the most promising was the collodion process, which used glass plates coated with "collodion," rather than sliver-coated copper plates, to capture the image. One advantage of the new process was that it produced a glass negative that could be used to create any number of albumen-coated paper prints.

Americans quickly fell in love with making—and giving away—pictures of themselves (*cartes de visite*); the Civil War gave the still-infant technology its greatest boost. The work of Mathew Brady, Alexander Gardner, and a few others, in conveying scenes of war to the average American safely back home revolutionized war reporting and the way the public viewed war in general. Photography took most of the romance out of war as it had been written about and painted previously.

Brady's name and reputation overshadow all others in Civil War photography, although his reputation is largely based on myth and misinformation. After July 1861 the master seldom ventured far from the safe confines of his Washington, D.C., studio. He did not personally take more than a small fraction of the thousands of battlefield photos attributed to him. Not only was he not by temperament a field man, but he was practically blind by the 1860s, forced to wear dark glasses to protect his eyes from the sunlight. It was his often-anonymous assistants who took the photographs of most of the front-line scenes that were published under his name. One of those assistants, Alexander Gardner, who struck out on his own during the war, probably took 75 percent of the "Brady photos" of the Army of the Potomac. In fact by the end of the war Gardner, not Brady, was considered the preeminent professional U.S. photographer, although not the official photographer of the Army of the Potomac. That honor went to Timothy O'Sullivan, who was the only photographer permitted by Ulysses Grant to accompany the army on its last campaign, 1864–65. Demonstrating how public opinion as much as science drove technology, O'Sullivan eschewed pictures of Union dead in his combat photographs; he specialized in Confederate dead. Meanwhile George N. Bernard, who also had his start as a Brady assistant, became the official photographer of the Military Department of the Mississippi late in the war.

The artist Constantino Brumidi was captured in a working pose by the celebrated photographer Mathew Brady. The Italian-born painter was known as "the Michelangelo of the Capitol" for his ornate frescoes on the building. This stark photograph does not really do justice to the five-foot-five artist with gray-blue eyes, brown hair, and dark complexion but was included in Brady's "Great Americans" series. (Library of Congress, Prints and Photographs Division [230240])

Southerners who photographed the war from the opposite side of the lines included George S. Cook, J. D. Edwards, and A. D. Lytle, who were constrained by lack of equipment and facilities, and less visionary in terms of trying to create a photographic history of the conflict.

The technology of reproducing photographs for mass circulation did not yet exist, so the collections of Brady, Gardner, and the others, could not be widely viewed in their original form until many years later. (Nor could photographic images be enlarged for closer study or use as broadsides.) Instead, the mid-19th-century technology for reproducing pictures was limited to artistic renditions of photographs in the form of woodcuts and lithographs. Both methods were primitive, inexact, and laborious.

One of the most remarkable technical advances in 19th-century photography were stereoscopic views, which presented two images of the same subject from different angles side by side; when looked at through a special binocular viewer, what appeared was a rough approximation of a three-dimensional view. Stereotype images had been produced as early as 1838, and they had undergone continuous improvement since then. They became a genuine fad among the middle class on both sides of the Atlantic after Queen Victoria and Prince Albert were presented with a stereoscopic viewer as a gift at the Crystal Palace Exhibition in 1851. The favorite subjects for stereoscopic treatment became landscapes, quaint genre scenes, architectural studies, and sweeping city views. They did have the power to make viewers feel they were part of some distant scene, not just viewers of a representation of it. Carleton Watkins, one of the 19th century's greatest photographers, practically made a career of creating three-dimensional pictures of natural wonders such as the Yosemite Falls or the giant redwood trees.

With the Civil War, "stereographs," as they were called, became more than just a minor fad. These three-dimensional images of the war brought the terrible conflict home to Americans as no visual medium ever had. Thousands paid 50 cents each for three-dimensional photographs and purchased fancy stereoscopic viewers to look at their pictures for hours on end. The technology inevitably was transformed into a very profitable business, which marketed stereoscopic views in catalogs, even offering some that had been hand-colored.

After the Civil War the fad gathered steam, and an evening of stereoscopic home viewing became the equivalent to an evening of television watching today. Well into the 20th century, this pastime, according to the historian Bob Zeller, was the most popular form of commercial home entertainment in the United States.

Stereo photography for all its technical limitations and relatively high costs (four dollars for a dozen images, five dollars if colorized) nonetheless begat other advances in photographic technology that foreshadowed the 20th century. In 1863 Samuel D. Goodale of Cincinnati received a patent for a stereoscopic device that could be operated by hand to show scenes in motion, a primitive forerunner of the peep show.

Another form of "trick photography" was the zoetrope, which consisted of a revolving drum with numerous slits to let in light and a series of sequential pictures. When the drum was rapidly rotated, the viewer saw what appeared to be a moving picture. The zoetrope was popular primarily as a parlor amusement.

The American consumer embraced the new imaging technology more enthusiastically than any other single form. From a handful of professional technicians in the 1840s, photography became next a fad, then eventually an art form. By 1850 every large city in the country had several professional photographers doing business. In the years that followed, mass demand for photo images led to constant improving and simplifying of cameras until picture taking became something the average American could do with little technical expertise.

TABLE 17.3 NUMBER OF PROFESSIONAL PHOTOGRAPHERS/DAGUERROTYPISTS IN U.S. POPULATION, 1840–1880

Year	Total United States Population	Photographers[a]
1840	17,069,453	N/A[b]
1850	23,191,876	938
1860	31,000,000	3,154[c]
1870	39,000,000	7,558
1880	50,000,000	9,990

Note: One of the leading historians of photography, Robert Taft, believes it is "reasonable to assume" that the number of professional photographers was at least double the number stated in the census reports because enumerators counted only those who listed it as their "leading" line of work.

[a] Up through the 1850s many photographers preferred to be called daguerreotypists, a name derived from the earliest commercial photographic process. By 1860 both *photographer* and *daguerreotypist* were in wide use, but 10 years later the census recognized no distinction and listed only the occupation "daguerreotypist/photographer." These statistics were based on questions asked by census takers of citizens about their line of work.

[b] The profession of photography is not listed in the 1840 Census at all because it was still too new, so there is no way of knowing how many were in the business.

[c] In the 1860 Census 2,650 daguerreotypists were identified and 504 photographers.

Sources: Statistical View of the United States, (Washington, D.C.: a Compendium of the Seventh Census, J. D. B. De Bow, 1854), 126; *U.S. Decennial Reports, 1840–1880,* cited in Robert Taft, *Photography and the American Scene* (New York: Macmillan, 1942), 61.

Oceanography and Marine Technology

Historically Americans were dependent upon seaborne trade to drive the economy, and this fact explains the high level of interest in the allied sciences of ship construction and oceanography. U.S. shipbuilders made one huge advance in naval construction, the clipper ship, but although it was undeniably swift and beautiful, it proved to be a technological dead end. The clipper ship, which is discussed in greater detail in chapter 6, proudly carried the flag to the four corners of the globe, but it was a less efficient cargo vessel than the plodding, smoke-belching steamship. While the Americans sank their time and expertise into building a fleet of the labor-intensive sailing ships, the British developed increasingly better marine steam engines. Americans compounded their error when they finally began changing to steam power by staying with wooden hulls and investing in paddle-wheel technology, while the British pioneered iron-hull construction and screw propellers. It was the Civil War that revolutionized U.S. naval technology, but all efforts went into warship construction, and while the North and South were busy sinking each other's ships as fast as they could, the British managed to capture the world's carrying trade. The combination of war and backing of the wrong technological horse produced a disaster, and naval technology proved the only area of technology in the 19th century in which the United States clearly came in a poor second.

Americans almost made up for their failures in seagoing technology by doing remarkable work in oceanography. In fact it was an

American, Matthew Fontaine Maury, who almost single-handedly invented the scientific study of the world's ocean currents, weather, and marine life. Maury did most of his work before the Civil War diverted his efforts into war making for the Confederacy. The U.S. naval officer Charles Davis of Massachusetts published a welcome volume for U.S. sea captains in 1853, the first *American Nautical Almanac,* which contained a wealth of valuable practical information. In 1873 Harvard College's Louis Agassiz built on his legacy by establishing the Anderson School of Natural History in Massachusetts, the first U.S. institution to have an oceanography studies program.

Balloon Flight and Other Exotic Transportation Technology

The relatively new science of aeronautics lay somewhere between the practical and the visionary in the 19th century. Balloon flight had first been demonstrated by pioneering Frenchmen toward the end of the 18th century. Using heated air for lift, they managed to reach heights of 5,000 feet and above. Balloon ascensions were the purview of scientists and daredevils before the French army found a more practical use for them as a form of military reconnaissance.

It was the American professor Thaddeus Sobieski Coulincourt Lowe of New Hampshire who demonstrated their real potential as more than a curiosity. He entered the field of ballooning in 1856, and soon any number of intrepid U.S. aeronauts were fearlessly soaring through the clouds. Some of their accomplishments far exceeded mere carnival demonstrations. On July 1, 1859, John Wise ascended at St. Louis, Missouri, with three companions in a craft he named the *Airship Atlantic.* They safely landed in Jefferson County, New York, 19 hours later, having traveled 1,200 miles in the air. But without an obvious practical application on the horizon, Wise's feat was quickly forgotten. Then came the Civil War.

Soon after the outbreak of that conflict Professor Lowe was back in the spotlight demonstrating the military potential for this new technology by making a test flight that covered 900 miles of Confederate territory in nine hours. A cavalry reconnaissance under optimal conditions could not cover a fraction of that distance in the same span of time. Now doors were opened and funding provided for his research. Two months later he was a federal government employee attached to the Army of the Potomac. As chief of the Aeronautic Corps he established a balloon force that employed seven inflatables designed and constructed by him. The largest had a capacity of 32,000 cubic feet and cost $1,500 to construct. During the next two years he was able to provide valuable information by locating enemy positions, monitoring troop movements, and even directing artillery fire. His success provoked the Confederate general Joseph Johnston to rant about "those infernal balloons." But in 1863 science and the military parted company when Lowe resigned in a fit of pique and returned home. Other aeronauts continued to work for the Union, however, including the aforementioned John Wise of Lancaster, Pennsylvania, and John LaMountain of Troy, New York.

After the Civil War the future of lighter-than-air craft remained in private hands. When the government turned its back on aerial research, the showmen rushed in to transform a revolutionary new technology into another form of mass entertainment. All further progress in developing practical air travel came to a halt for decades while showmanship took over. In lieu of dedicated scientists daredevil balloonists such as the colorful W. H. Donaldson sold their services to P. T. Barnum and other impresarios, staging events and taking up intrepid customers for short flights. Donaldson disappeared somewhere over Lake Michigan in 1875 on his 139th ascension, while performing at Barnum's Great Roman Hippodrome in New York City. His remains were never found, but the dream lived on. What Lowe, Donaldson, and others accomplished was science at its most amateurish, and even with their contributions, ballooning was still a far cry from controlled flight, but at least humans had burst the bonds of Earth and the United States was at the forefront of the new science.

All flights of fancy in transportation technology did not involve leaving terra firma. Steam had been successfully applied to rail travel for more than 30 years when W. W. Austen of Detroit invented a working steam-powered automobile in 1864. To say he perfected it is to give him too much credit, but he did develop, in the words of a Detroit newspaper, a "light buggy capable of carrying two persons . . . propelled by a little engine of three horse power, which is arranged behind the seat in such a way as to be ornamental as well as useful." The *Detroit Daily Advertiser* of August 30, 1864, hailed it as "Professor Austen's Marvel of the Age," noting that it attained speeds of 30 miles per hour "noiselessly [and] unwarily" in test drives. The same account also reported that this first-generation "horseless carriage" was rugged enough to function on rural roads: "It runs with ease, avoids obstacles on the road and seems to be in complete control of the driver." But Austen's invention failed to catch on for a variety of reasons, practical as well as financial. These included lack of backers and the intrinsically dangerous and unwieldy nature of steam propulsion. Instead of a revolution in transportation, the "Self-Propelling Road Carriage" became a circus attraction and nothing more until the 20th century, by which time Europeans, not Americans, were the trailblazers in this new technology.

Better Living through Technology

Part of the American fascination with scientific subjects arose from the fact that scientists were inventing practical devices that made everyday life better. Most of the esoteric creations turned out by modern-day research laboratories do not have the obvious and immediate practical benefits of the things turned out in the workshops and kitchens of 19th-century tinkerers. America's preeminent scientific genius, Thomas Alva Edison, was personally responsible for more than 1,000 inventions in his time, including the ticker tape machine that helped create the modern stock market (1870) and an electric voting machine (1868), which promised to save time and remove the likelihood of vote-counting fraud. The latter was a rare Edison failure: a technical success but a commercial flop that was rejected by the voting public. Other inventors with much less intelligence than Edison nonetheless managed to make useful contributions to daily life. In 1856 H. L. Lipman improved the basic lead pencil by attaching an eraser and received a patent for his inspiration. (But it was Eberhard Faber, a German-American manufacturer, who cashed in on the idea by opening a factory in New York City five years later to mass produce the Lipman pencil.) In 1869 Ives W. Gaffey of Chicago received a patent for the suction vacuum cleaner, which would have to wait until the 20th century to revolutionize house cleaning. Labor-saving technology for the home was also the goal of inventors filing patents for a "washing machine." A number of competing patents were issued until by 1860 there were 29 factories producing some version of the latest home improvement. There were seemingly endless areas of daily life that needed improvement, and thousands of inventors willing to meet that need. Tolbert Lanston of Ohio in 1870 patented the padlock, one of the earliest and simplest security measures available to the general public. And a wave of bank robberies during Reconstruction years by the likes of the James brothers inspired James Sargent and Halvert Greenleaf to invent a time lock for bank vaults (1875) that would discourage would-be robbers from trying to intimidate bank employees to open the safe for them. Andrew Hallidie, a California engineer, invented the cable car to get up and down the famous hills of San Francisco.

Supposedly, a woman's life was improved by the new household appliances, such as this "home washing machine and wringer," the very latest in benign technology shown in a magazine advertisement, 1869. (Library of Congress)

Creating More Efficient Killing Machines

Wars are always a big boost to scientific progress, and the Civil War was no different from others. In fact, it marked a turning point in the application of technology to the art of war because never before had science changed warfare so greatly in such a short span of time. The four years of the Civil War marked the transition from sail and wood to steam and ironclad warships, from muskets to rifles, from single-shot to repeating weapons, from land-bound warfare to aerial, and from horse-drawn transportation to rail. The nature of the Civil War—"total war"—meant that the contributions of the artisan and the mechanic were as important as those of the soldier and the farmer.

Among the new and more efficient weapons developed during the war were rapid-fire guns, turreted warships, and underwater mines. It is incorrect to say that the American Civil War was the first to be photographed, or the first to use observation balloons, telegraphy, rifled muskets, repeating weapons, and railroads. All those things were introduced in European wars earlier. What is true is that these things were *extensively* used for the first time in the Civil War and that they made a *difference,* or at least that is the considered opinion of the vast majority of historians. Lonely dissenting voices are those of Joseph and Frances Gies, who believe that the new military technology of the Civil War was more "spectacular" and prophetic than it was decisive.

Some of the most remarkable of the new technology was pioneered by the Confederacy, desperate to offset the enormous advantages the North had in numbers and resources. A man named Van Houten received the first Confederate patent on August 1, 1861, for his "breech-loading gun," although nothing ever came of that particular design. While trying to win the technology war, the South was forced to resort to some ancient expedients along the way. In 1861 the Richmond government, short of all types of shoulder arms, ordered the manufacture of thousands of pikes to arm its soldiers. Fortunately for the Southern men in the ranks, they were never forced to face musket-toting Yankees with nothing more than spears in their hands!

The North was fortunate to have someone as president who was himself something of an amateur inventor and, therefore, deeply interested in the practical application of science to the art of war. Lincoln enjoyed personally testing the latest repeating rifle or examining design specs for new ironclad warships. He was greatly influenced by a letter from the respected inventor John Ericsson in August 1862, advising that "our cause will have to be sustained not by numbers, but by superior weapons." The letter went on to say, "By a proper application of mechanical devices alone will you be able with absolute certainly to destroy the enemies of the Union . . . without enlisting another man." The inventor's faith in technology proved to be overstated in terms of replacing manpower, but he had identified one of the decisive elements in ultimate Union victory. For the rest of the war Lincoln consistently placed the weight of his office behind the development of new technology.

Southerners proved conclusively during the war that "Yankee ingenuity" was not confined to Northerners. Demonstrating that "necessity is the mother of invention," Southerners could be equally creative in defending their homes against Union invaders. Private John Gilleland of Athens, Georgia, saw up close what every Confederate knew, namely, that they were heavily outgunned by their enemies. But Gilleland decided to do something about it, inventing the world's first and so far only double-barreled cannon in 1863. A local foundry produced the exotic-looking weapon, but it never advanced past the field-testing stage. There was neither the time nor the expertise to work out the practical problems, so the prototype was retired to storage and became a memorial on the lawn in front of city hall after the war.

One of the major success stories of Confederate science (specifically, the Torpedo Bureau and Naval Submarine Battery Service) were submersible mines, known as torpedoes in the vernacular of the day. Confederate torpedoes sank or disabled 32 Union vessels during four years of war, including the USS *Cairo* (December 12, 1862) and the USS *Tecumseh* (August 5, 1864). The South even developed electrically detonated torpedoes but were unable to exploit the weapon because of a shortage of copper wire.

Other Confederate "superweapons," such as the submarine *H. L. Hunley* and the spar torpedo boat *David,* not only became fully operational, but proved their worth in combat against the enemy. The *David* launched three attacks against major Union warships beginning with the USS *New Ironsides* off Charleston on October 5, 1863. The CSS *Hunley* sank the USS *Housatonic* in Charleston harbor on the night of February 17, 1864. Together these two little vessels helped revolutionize naval warfare, and when coupled with the submersible mine, signaled the world that in the future combat at sea would occur both above and below the surface.

In the long run the Confederates lacked the basic know-how, the raw materials, facilities, and mechanical skills, to win the technological war against the North. After the war the former Confederate general Jubal Early blamed the death of the Confederacy on "steam power, railroads, [and] mechanism." It was a simplistic but accurate assessment by one who was in a position to know. Even when the South succeeded in producing spectacular technological breakthroughs such as the CSS *Virginia* in 1862, it could not subsequently exploit them. The casemated ironclad had the potential to break the Northern blockade and win the war on the water, but the South could not replicate the prototype in either sufficient numbers or to the necessary performance standards. As a result Confederate ironclads were always delayed for lack of parts, breaking down at critical moments, or of such inferior quality that they became sitting ducks when facing northern Monitor-type ironclads.

Ironically another reason why the South lost the technology war is that although they could produce spectacular weapons such as the submarine and torpedo mine, they could not furnish their armies with the basics such as gunpowder, shoes and uniforms, and rolling stock for their railroads. The result was that Southern soldiers, dressed in rags, going barefoot, and armed with smoothbore muskets, often faced well-outfitted Northerners armed with repeating rifles.

The U.S. Patent Office and Government Support for Science

The U.S. government proved to be a willing ally of science in peacetime as well as war. In 1872 Congress funded a series of experiments by an Englishman, Eadweard Muybridge, in the photography of moving objects. But that was hardly the first foray by Uncle Sam into the world of science. Long before the Civil War the U.S. government had made a major commitment to fostering home-grown science and technology. In 1836 Congress passed the revised Patent Act, which set up a review process and register system for all future patent applications, plus authorized a building to house the Patent Office. In the years that followed, thousands of new applications were filed annually, each accompanied by a demonstration model and a $40 application fee. The work became so overwhelming that in 1842 Congress took the Patent Office out of the Department of State, where it had resided since 1790, and set it up as a separate agency within the government—the first independent patent office established by any country in the world. (In subsequent years it would be placed under the Department of the Interior, and ultimately under the Department of Commerce, as it remains today.)

Right from the beginning the U.S. patent system became the model for other countries in recognizing by law the basic right of an inventor to legal protection of his or her intellectual property and in systematically evaluating the worth of patent applications. Lincoln called the system "the fuel of interest to the fire of genius." Mark Twain, a patent holder himself, had one of his characters in *A Connecticut Yankee in King Arthur's Court* say, "A Country without a patent office and good patent laws is just a crab and can't travel anyway but sideways and backways."

The U.S. Patent Office did not merely award patents to deserving inventors; it often had to judge among competing claims for the same or almost the same technology. In the early years it was Cyrus McCormick's and Obed Hussey's rival reapers. In the 1850s it was between Bessemer's and Kelly's steelmaking processes, and after 1873 it was Joseph Glidden's barbed wire design versus Michael Kelly's (or Jacob Haish's). By bestowing official approval on one or another patent application, the office guaranteed that inventors could profit from their creations and kept a lot of unsound technology off the market. There was also some politics involved in the decision-making process, as rival applicants enlisted both the courts and their congressmen in their battles for fame and fortune. U.S. patents ran for 14 years, then the holder/inventor could file for a renewal if he or she had made improvements in the original design. But a highly successful patent drew imitators swarming out of the woodwork with rival designs and petitions to deny renewal, all of which had to be passed on by the Patent Office all over again.

Americans were a remarkably curious and inventive people, judging by the enormous number of patent applications during these years. Even the humblest farmer, it seemed, had an idea for a surefire invention rattling around in his head. Not all inventions were practical, however, and some were downright bizarre. Among the new mechanical devices proposed to the Patent Office in the 1850s and 1860s were a dog-powered butter churn, a mechanical apple peeler, and a rocking chair rigged up so that its motion would shoo the flies from the dinner table and rock an infant's cradle at the same time. Design drawings and miniature models for all these and thousands more were duly submitted to the office in Washington, D.C.

Indeed, Americans proved to be so invention-happy that by 1850 the Patent Office held more than 17,000 models in storage and had already outgrown the expanded quarters it had occupied for the past 13 years. That same year, 2,183 new patents were issued, adding an equal number of working models to the department's eclectic collections.

Some of the most famous names in U.S. history are on the official register as patent holders, including the 16th president of the United States himself, from his prepresidential days, whereas other inventors are virtually unknown by name, though their inventions would change the world.

As every Tom, Dick, and Abe was dreaming of inventing a better mousetrap, the number of applications threatened to overwhelm the Patent Office. The technical staff after 1848 consisted of only the commissioner, four examiners, and four assistant examiners—one of the smallest bureaucracies of any office in the federal government. The number of applications they had to evaluate carefully and pass on more than tripled between 1850 and 1869, and that number nearly doubled again between 1870 and 1879.

As did every other aspect of the patent process, the understanding of what was patentable expanded over the years. In 1842 Congress enacted legislation making it possible to patent "any new and original

TABLE 17.4 SOME FAMOUS AND NOT-SO FAMOUS PEOPLE AND THE U.S. PATENTS THEY RECEIVED UNDER THE NEW PATENT ACT OF 1836

Inventor	Device or Machine	Patent Number	Date of Patent
John Ruggles[a] (senator, Maine)	"A locomotive steam engine for rail and other roads, designed to give a multiple tractive power to locomotives, and prevent the evil of the sliding of the wheel"	1	1836
George Bruce	Printing types	1 (revised numeration system)	Nov. 9, 1842
Abraham Lincoln (representative, Illinois)	"A device buoying vessels over shoals"	6,469	May 22, 1849
John Gorrie	Ice-making machine ("improved process for the artificial production of ice")	8,080	May 6, 1851
Horace Smith and Daniel B. Wesson	An improved revolver[b]	10,535	Feb. 14, 1854
J. C. Stoddard	"A new musical instrument to be played by the agency of steam or highly compressed air" (i.e., a steam calliope)	13,668	Oct. 9, 1855
Gail Borden	Condensed milk	15,553	Aug. 19, 1856
John Mason	The screw-neck bottle/jar	22,186	Nov. 30, 1858
J. E. B. Stewart	"A method of attaching sabers to belts"	25,684	Oct. 4, 1859
Richard J. Gatling	"Improvement in revolving battery guns" (i.e., a machine gun)	36,836	Nov. 4, 1862
Christopher L. Sholes	Typewriter	79,265	Jun. 23, 1868
George Westinghouse, Jr.	"Improvement in steam-power brake devices"	88,929	Apr. 13, 1869
Thomas Alva Edison	Electronic vote recorder	90,649	Jun. 1, 1869
O. B. Brown	"Moving picture projector"	93,594	Aug. 10, 1869
John H. Hyatt, Jr., and Isaiah S. Hyatt	"Improvements in treating and molding Pyroxyline" (basic material of celluloid)	105,338	Jul. 12, 1870
Samuel L. Clemens (Mark Twain)[c]	"An improvement in adjustable and detachable straps for garments" (suspenders)	121,992	Dec.19, 1871
Louis Pasteur (French)	"Improvements in the process of making beer"	135,245	Jan. 28, 1873
Louis Pasteur	"Improvements in the manufacture and preservation of beer and in the treatment of yeast and wort together with apparatus for the same"	141,072	Jul. 22, 1873
Eli H. Janney	"Car couplings" (i.e., an automatic car coupler for trains)	138,405	Apr. 29, 1873
Joseph F. Glidden	"Improvement in wire fences" (barbed wire)[d]	157,124	Nov. 24, 1874
Alexander Graham Bell	"An apparatus for transmitting vocal or other sounds telegraphically . . . by causing electrical undulation." (i.e., the telephone)	174,465	Mar. 7, 1876

[a]Ruggles was the author of the New Patent Act, so it was only fitting that the senator and amateur inventor also receive patent number 1.
[b]The beginnings of the Smith & Wesson Arms Company lie in this "Valentine's Day" patent.
[c]This is the first of three patents that Twain received: The second (1873) was for "Mark Twain's Self Pasting Scrapbook," and the third (1885) was for a game to help players remember important historical dates.
[d]Glidden was not the first to design "barbed wire" fencing, nor the only inventor to get a patent on the idea (some 400 others also), but he modestly named his design "the Winner."
Source: U.S. Department of Commerce, *The Story of the United States Patent Office* (Washington, D.C.: U.S. Government Printing Office, 1972), 7–16.

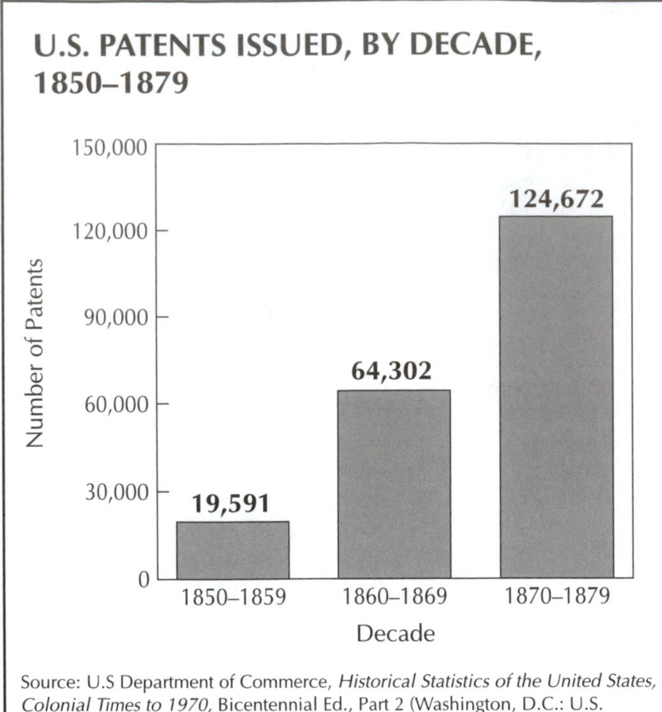

Source: U.S Department of Commerce, *Historical Statistics of the United States, Colonial Times to 1970,* Bicentennial Ed., Part 2 (Washington, D.C.: U.S. Department of Commerce, 1975), p. 959.

TABLE 17.5 U.S. PATENT APPLICATIONS AND GRANTS, 1850–1875

(issued by type)

Year	Patent Applications	Patents Granted: For Inventions	Patents Granted: For Designs	Patents Granted: To Foreign Residents
1850	2,193	883	83	20
1851	2,258	752	90	17
1852	2,639	885	109	20
1853	2,673	846	86	26
1854	3,324	1,755	57	35
1855	4,435	1,881	70	41
1856	4,960	2,302	107	31
1857	4,771	2,674	113	45
1858	5,364	3,455	102	28
1859	6,225	4,160	108	47
1860	7,653	4,357	183	49
1861	4,643	3,020	142	83
1862	5,038	3,214	195	80
1863	6,014	3,773	176	125
1864	6,932	4,638	139	181
1865	10,664	6,088	221	181
1866	15,269	8,863	294	244
1867	21,276	12,277	325	275
1868	20,420	12,526	446	337
1869	19,271	12,931	506	377
1870	19,171	12,137	737	644
1871	19,472	11,659	905	522
1872	18,246	12,180	884	581
1873	20,414	11,616	747	493
1874	21,602	12,230	886	547
1875	21,638	13,291	915	563

Sources: U.S. Department of Commerce, *The Story of the U.S. Patent and Trademark Office* (Washington, D.C.: U.S. Government Printing Office, 1988), 44; U.S. Patent and Trademark Office, *Technology Assessment and Forecast Program, Seventh Report.* U.S. Patent and Trademark Office Internet Research: http://www.uspto.gov/web/offices/ac/ido/oeip/taf/tafp.html; U.S. Patent Activity, 1790–1998 viewable report file: h_counts.pdf (updated annually) for this Table, updated 12/'98.

design" (a design patent) for a period of seven years. This was an addition to the original legislation, which covered only mechanical inventions ("utility patents"), protecting their creators for 14 years. In later years Congress also provided protection for foreign citizens wishing to secure U.S. patent rights for their inventions or designs. The result of all this legislation was a very complex and technical process for granting patents in the United States which was nevertheless affordable for the average citizen.

The Patent Office was recognized as such an important part of government that one of the first acts of the new Confederate government when it organized in 1861 was to create its own office (May 21). The first Confederate patent was issued in August, and before the end of the war four years later, 266 patents had been issued, most for machines of war.

The great powers of Europe also followed Uncle Sam's lead in extending official government protection over the intellectual property of their citizens, but the groundwork was already being laid for future U.S. technological dominance over all the world. In 1857 the United States, with a smaller population, smaller economy, and no overseas empire, still issued about 35 percent more patents than Great Britain (2,910 versus 2,155), and for all their military might and long histories, Prussia with 48 patents and Russia with 24 were not even in the race. The rate at which the United States was creating new technology, even in the mid-19th century, was an early indicator of the shift in global power that would take place in the 20th century.

The U.S. Patent Office grew steadily over the years, both in the amount of space required for its operations and in its personnel needed to perform its myriad functions. Among other duties it was

TABLE 17.6 COMPARATIVE PATENT ACTIVITY IN THE UNITED STATES, GREAT BRITAIN, AND FRANCE, 1850–1880

Period	Great Britain		France		United States		Fees Paid by U.S. Applicants[a]
	Number of Applications	Number Granted	Number of Applications	Number Granted	Number of Applications	Number Granted	
1850	N/A	N/A	N/A	1,687	2,193	993	$87,597
1860	N/A	N/A	N/A	4,606	7,653	4,778	$281,430
1860–69	34,870	21,910	N/A	N/A	N/A	N/A	N/A
1870	N/A	N/A	N/A	3,029	19,171	13,333	$638,400
1870–79	44,950	30,360	N/A	N/A	203,234	137,662	N/A
1880	N/A	N/A	N/A	6,057	23,021	13,917	$752,856

Note: Unfortunately for comparison's sake, the measuring periods for the three countries do not exactly match. For instance, the British count is not broken down by year for the period 1850–80, unlike the French and U.S. counts, and the number of applications for French patents is nowhere given, just the number actually granted. Therefore the picture is incomplete but nonetheless enlightening for the big picture.

[a]Only the U.S. government charged fees at this time. Converted to U.S. dollars from British pounds sterling at an "exchange par" of $4.8665 per British pound for 1850; $5.31 per pound, 1860; $5.32 per pound, 1870; and $4.826 per pound, 1880. For 1850 see L. E. Davis and J. R. T. Hughes, "A Dollar–Sterling Exchange, 1809–1895," *Economic History Review,* 13, no. 1 (August 1960): 54–55. For 1860, 1870, and 1880, see B. R. Mitchell, *British Historical Statistics* (Cambridge: Cambridge University Press, 1988), 702.

Sources: Michael G. Mulhall, *The Dictionary of Statistics,* 4th ed., rev. (London: George Routledge and Sons, Ltd., 1899), 438–39; U.S. Department of Commerce, *The Story of the U.S. Patent and Trademark Office* (Washington, D.C.: U.S. Government Printing Office, 1988), 44.

charged with collecting and publishing agricultural statistics until the newly created Department of Agriculture took over that task in 1862. In 1870 Congress gave the office responsibility for registering trademarks, and in 1872 the office began issuing its own publication, the *Official Gazette of the United States Patent Office,* to keep the public up to date on the latest creative advances. It was headed by a succession of very capable commissioners, paid $3,000 dollars a year, who possessed the necessary political skills and vision to make the agency a respected part of the national government.

Men were not the only Americans who had an inventive and inquiring mind; women also found time in the midst of their traditional roles to invent things, and not just household goods. Women gave birth to their share of mechanical inventions, and they demanded the same official recognition men received. The U.S. Patent Office did not consider gender one of the requirements for receiving a patent and approved 28 for women in the 1850s, 441 in the 1860s, and more than 2,000 in the 1870s. It was a truly remarkable accomplishment in the era when women's lives were circumscribed by the concept of the "women's sphere."

The U.S. Patent Office was just one example of the government's commitment to fostering science and technology. In 1846 Congress took the belated if highly admirable step of creating the Smithsonian Institution "for the increase and diffusion of knowledge among men." Quickly dubbed "America's attic" for its vast collections of historical

TABLE 17.7 COMMISSIONERS OF THE U.S. PATENT OFFICE, 1850–1875

Name	Tenure
Thomas Ewbank[a]	May 10, 1849–Nov. 8, 1852
Silas Henry Hodges	Nov. 8, 1852–Mar. 25, 1853
Joseph Holt	Sep. 10, 1857–Mar. 14, 1859
William Darius Bishop	May 23, 1859–Feb. 15, 1860
Philip Francis Thomas	Feb. 16, 1860–Dec. 10, 1860
David P. Holloway	Mar. 28, 1861–Aug. 16, 1865
Thomas C. Theaker	Aug. 16, 1865–Jan. 20, 1868
Elisha Foote	Aug. 1, 1868–Apr. 25, 1869
Samuel Sparks Fisher	Apr. 26, 1869–Nov. 10, 1870
Gen. Mortimer D. Leggett	Jan. 16, 1871–Oct. 31, 1874
John Marshall Thacher	Nov. 1, 1874–Sep. 30, 1875
Robert Holland Duell	Oct. 1, 1875–Dec. 31, 1876

[a] Ewbank was the third commissioner of patents since the office was created in 1842, after Henry L. Ellsworth and Edmund Burke.

Source: U.S. Department of Commerce, *The Story of the United States Patent and Trademark Office* (Washington, D.C.: U.S. Government Printing Office, 1988), 50.

TABLE 17.8 SELECTED CATEGORIES OF U.S. PATENTS GRANTED TO WOMEN, 1850–1875

Patent Type	Number Granted
Railroad	34[a]
Agricultural and dairy	28
Pest control	3
Stoves	15
Food processing	13
Patient care	8
Sewing machines	33
Dishwashers	7
Washing machines	15
Total	156

[a] Sixteen of these inventions were created by a single woman, Eliza Dexter Murfey.

Source: Anne L. Macdonald, *Feminine Ingenuity* (New York: Ballantine Books, 1992), 383–94.

TABLE 17.9 SOME SIGNIFICANT WOMEN INVENTORS, 1850–1875

Name(s)	Invention(s)	Date(s)
Jane Wells	The "baby jumper"[a]	1872
Margaret Knight[b]	a) Improvement in paper-feeding machines b) Machine for making brown paper bags	a) Nov. 15, 1870 b) Jul. 11, 1871
Ebenezer and Eleanor Butterick, William and Ellen Demorest[c]	Paper dress patterns that allow ordinary women to sew their own fashions at home	1860s
Elizabeth Miller	Women's "bloomer" pants[d]	1851
Amanda Theodosia Jones	a) Fruit jars b) Improved vacuum canning process[e]	a) Jun. 3, 1873 b) 1873
Susan Bidwell (and copatentees)	Improved toothbrush	1875
Sarah Ruth	a) "Horse bonnet" b) Sun shade for horses	a) Aug. 25, 1868 b) Jan. 7, 1873
Harriet Morrison Irwin	Design for hexagonal building[f]	Aug. 24, 1869
Martha Coston	"Pyrotechnic night signals" (maritime signal flare, later known as the "Very pistol") and subsequent improvements[g]	Apr. 5, 1859; Jun. 13,1871
Sara Mather	"Submarine telescope" for studying the ocean depths	Jul. 5, 1864
Anna Baldwin	a) Milk treating process b) Improved milk separator and milk cooler	a) Jun. 9, 1868 b) Aug. 10, 1869
Helen Blanchard	Sewing machine improvements	Aug. 19, 1873; Jul. 7, 1874; Mar. 30, 1875; Apr. 13, 1875
Mary Jane Montgomery	a) Improved war vessel b) Improved locomotive wheels c) Improved hospital table d) Improved metal hole-punching device	a) Jan. 5, 1864 b) May 31, 1864 c) May 23, 1865 d) May 8, 1866
Temperance P. Edson	Self-inflating device for raising sunken vessels	Jul. 4, 1865
Clarisa Britain	a) Improved ambulance b) Improved boiler c) Floor warmer d) Improved "lantern dinner pail" e) Improved vegetable boiler f) Improved dish drainer g) Improved lamp burner	a) Aug. 11, 1863 b) Oct. 5, 1863 c) Mar. 10, 1863 d) Jan. 19, 1864 e) Jun. 14, 1864 f) Jun. 1, 1864 g) Sep. 27, 1864
Rebecca Sherwood	a) Reducing hemp, etcetera, to "fibrous substances" b) Improved process for manufacturing paper pulp from straw, etcetera	a) Nov. 10, 1863 b) Dec. 13, 1863
Thiphena Hornbrook	Design for a better bee hive	May 21, 1861
Emeline Brigham	Improved "pessary" (i.e., contraceptive device)[h]	Dec. 3, 1867
Mary Evard	Improved cooking stove ("The Reliable Cook Stove")	Apr. 7, 1868
Elizabeth Hawks	Improvements in cooking stove	Apr. 23, 1867; Apr. 6, 1875
Elizabeth Burns	Improved mining process (removal of sulfur from ores)	Mar. 8, 1870
Maria L. Ghirardini	Rails for street railways	Jul. 29, 1873
Mary Hooper	Improvements in sewing machine	Jan. 25, 1870; Feb. 21, 1871; Oct. 1, 1872; Jan. 4, 1876
Augusta Rodgers	a) Car heater b) Improved exhaust for smoke and cinders from locomotives c) Improved conveyor mechanism	a) Apr. 4, 1871 b) May 9, 1871 c) Oct. 10, 1871
Lydia Bonney	Improved undergarments (women's)	Dec. 28, 1875
Laura Chapman	Improved lap table	May 19, 1874
Clara Clark	a) Improved corset b) Improved "skirt supporter"	a) Oct. 27, 1874 b) Jun. 29, 1875
Henrietta Cole	Fluting machine	Jun. 12, 1866
Margaret Colvin	Improved washing machine	Nov. 7, 1871
Ellen Fitz	Globes	Jan. 1, 1875
Lavinia Foy	Improved "corset skirt-supporter"	Jul. 22, 1862
Elizabeth French	Improved electrotherapeutic appliances	Aug. 31, 1875
Eliza Harding	Improved "abdominal supporter"	Jul. 15, 1873
Celine Laumonier	Improvement in "combined traveling bag and chair"	Oct. 5, 1875
Sarah Mossman	Improved military cap	Aug. 25, 1863

Name(s)	Invention(s)	Date(s)
Hannah Mountain	Improved "life-saving mattress"	Mar. 1, 1873
Elizabeth Perry	Design for fans	May 1, 1875
Charlotte Sterling	Improved dishwasher	Aug. 20, 1872
Elizabeth Stigale	a) Method of preserving flowers b) Rail for ornamental fences c) Improved floral bracket	a) Apr. 27, 1869 b) Dec. 14, 1869 c) Mar. 14, 1871
Elizabeth Stiles	Improved reading and writing desk	Sep. 7, 1875
Hannah Suplee	Sewing machine needle	Sep. 14, 1869
Mary Whitner	Improved stereoscope (i.e., photographic viewer)	Jan. 5, 1875

[a]Lets a baby play alone in complete safety; basic design still in use today.
[b]During her lifetime Margaret Knight (1838–1914) patented more than 22 inventions, defending her rights against all comers and making quite a bit of money in the process.
[c]Rival husband-wife teams battled for years for the patent rights to the cutout paper dress pattern before the Buttericks finally won.
[d]Named for the feminist Amelia Bloomer, but created and patented by Elizabeth Miller.
[e]Consisted of six separate patents, all granted the same year, and known collectively as "the Jones process." Subsequently she started the Women's Canning and Preserving Company and incorporated it to launch a vacuum canning business.
[f]The first woman to receive a patent in architecture. She built a model hexagonal house that stood until 1962.
[g]Although Coston received the patent for the invention, the U.S. Navy named it the "Very pistol" after Lt. E. W. Very, who made some slight improvements to it.
[h]Eventually banned by the U.S. government from being either advertised or sold through the mail.
Source: Anne L. Macdonald, *Feminine Ingenuity* (New York: Ballantine Books, 1992), 383–94.

artifacts and memorabilia, the institution performed equally important duties in such scientific areas as gathering weather data and sponsoring scientific expeditions to the four corners of the world. Named for James Smithson, who left a $550,000 bequest to get it started, it eventually symbolized Yankee ingenuity and scientific endeavor at their best. The Smithsonian also emphasized the utilitarian aspects of science in its exhibits, its publications, and the expeditions it underwrote.

The Pursuit of Pure Research

Pure research in the 19th century generally took a back seat to practical application. The majority of working scientists proceeded with definite objectives in mind. The American people seemed to support science in direct proportion to its perceived usefulness. Whatever could not be seen to have immediate or practical application was therefore considered useless. Advances in pure science during this period must begin with Charles Darwin's pioneering work on evolutionary development. His masterpiece, *On the Origin of Species by Means of Natural Selection or the Preservation of Favoured Races in the Struggle for Life,* was published in England in 1859 and by the next year was the subject of hot debate in the United States. Harvard University brilliant resident naturalist Louis Agassiz argued against species evolution while his equally brilliant Harvard colleague, the botanist Asa Gray, became the chief defender of Darwin's theories in U.S. academia.

Darwin's scientific expedition around the world on the HMS *Beagle* (1831–36) and natural American curiosity inspired a number of similar United States–sponsored scientific expeditions to the far corners of the globe. In 1851 the U.S. Coast Survey dispatched Agassiz on a 10-week exploration of the Florida Reefs, for scientific as well as for navigational information. In 1853–54 a U.S. Navy expedition surveyed the North Pacific. Starting in the spring of 1865 Professor Agassiz led a 19-month expedition into the jungles of Brazil, collecting a wealth of fauna and flora. And in 1871–72 the Charles F. Hall Scientific Expedition to the Arctic penetrated farther into the icecap than any previous vessel. Even the normally penny-pinching Congress supported these ventures, regularly appropriating funds for the U.S. Coast Survey and taking special interest in Hall's expedition by giving him $50,000 and the use of a U.S. naval vessel. Only his untimely death during the trip ended further Arctic exploration for many years. In 1875 Alexander Agassiz, son of the famous naturalist, explored the west coast of South America, gathering all sorts of scientific data.

Despite Darwin's higher public profile, the era's leading devoté of pure science was the Yale University professor Josiah Willard Gibbs, who developed the theory of thermodynamics, the basis for all modern physical chemistry and chemical engineering. His major works were not published until after this period, but the groundwork for works like "On the Equilibrium of Heterogeneous Substances" was done in the years before. He also did pioneering work in his Yale laboratory in statistical mechanics, vector analysis, crystallography, and electromagnetic theory.

The observation of nature produced a number of other scientific breakthroughs besides Darwin's work, not all of them by trained professionals. This was still the age of the "gentleman scientist"—the amateur who puttered away in a laboratory or workshop or even garden, producing sometimes remarkable results. The botanist/horticulturalist Luther Burbank (1849–1926) was one such amateur, who was inspired by reading Charles Darwin's *Variation of Animals and Plants under Domestication* in 1868. Burbank launched a career as a scientific plant breeder that in 1871 produced the hybrid Russet potato (subsequently known as the Burbank or Idaho potato), which went on to become a staple of U.S. agriculture and a gift of U.S. agriculture to the world. He sold the rights for his creation for $150 and moved to California to continue his ground-breaking experiments, which eventually produced more than 800 new strains and varieties of plants, helping to lay the foundation for the modern science of genetics.

Henry Draper (1837–82) was another gentleman scientist, who began his career in medicine in 1858, switched to natural science two years later, then discovered his true love in astronomy. He built an observatory on his family estate in Virginia and began grinding his own telescope mirrors. He made his greatest contribution to science in stellar spectroscopy, or photographing the stars and the planets, gathering invaluable data on thousands of heavenly bodies, which are still used today. By the mid-1870s he was the official astronomer of the U.S. government and a member of the National Academy of Sciences and the American Philosophical Society. Late in life he generously permitted the use of his masterful 11-inch reflecting telescope and provided funds to start Harvard University's astronomy program.

Burbank and Draper were two examples of upstart Americans who made a profound impact on the world of science. They and others like them represented a national trend of young people's choosing to devote their life to the observation and exploration of the physical world. Their accomplishments opened the door to the older European scientific community, which in turn inspired other young Americans to follow in their footsteps. Already by the 1870s Americans were taking a greater interest in science for the sake of science, and Europeans were taking notice of that interest. In 1872 the noted British scientist John Tyndall crossed the Atlantic to give a series of lectures, "The Physics of Light," to standing-room-only crowds in New York, Boston, and Philadelphia. The New York *Tribune* declared in banner headlines, "The People Have a Wonderful Appetite for Science Just Now." Four years later another famed British scientist, Thomas Huxley, made his own successful lecture tour of the United States. In the aftermath of their visits several major universities, including Columbia University and the University of Pennsylvania, set up advanced science departments and began offering scholarships for study in Europe.

Popularizing Science

The enthusiastic response of the U.S. public to the visits of Tyndale and Huxley demonstrated that scientific discussion did not have to be confined to the laboratory or the fusty professional conference. Americans were becoming truly interested in the advances that their scientists and inventors were producing. All that was needed was a connection between the technical folks and John Q. Public. That connection took two forms: a burgeoning new scientific literature and a variety of adult education programs, both aimed at keeping the public knowledgeable about the latest advances. The popularization of science was in full swing even before mid-century. Convincing the public of the value and need for scientific inquiry involved more than just informing them of advances. It also meant establishing professional standards in the scientific community, defending intellectual freedom, and raising funds to support basic research. Before 1850 the small U.S. community of scientists benefited from the infusion of accomplished European scientists—the original "brain drain" in a sense. The endorsement of respected institutions of higher education, such as Harvard and Yale Universities, and the support of the federal government also helped enormously. A handful of men played key roles in popularizing science in the United States. Besides the Agassizes, father and son, there was the geologist Edward Hitchcock (1793–1864) a Congregational clergyman who successfully mixed faith, scientific curiosity, and pedagogical talents all together to reach a large, heterogeneous audience. He helped found the Association of American Geologists, which became the American Association for the Advancement of Science (1847). It did not hurt that he was a prolific writer, who produced 14 volumes, five tracts, and 75 technical papers on botanical, mineralogical, geological, and physical subjects, in addition to works in religion and drama. His text *Elementary Geology* (1840) went through 30 editions.

Even more important to the popularization of science was Frank Hamilton, a Vermont physician, who began publishing *Popular Science* as a monthly magazine in 1872. It was such an immediate and enduring success that it is still published today, one of only two or three periodicals that have been published without interruption since the middle quarter of the 19th century. Meanwhile a different type of literary light, the Frenchman Jules Verne, began publishing his series of hugely popular science fiction novels beginning with *Journey to the Center of the Earth* in 1864. Verne's fanciful tales proved as popular in translation in the United States as in his native country. This literary love affair was mutual, as Verne predicted that America would lead in the eventual conquest of space, which he foresaw in humankind's future.

Another type of popularization was accomplished by Professor Louis Agassiz, taking his cue from the popular chatauqua movement: He opened the Anderson School of Natural History in July 1873 at Buzzard's Bay, Massachusetts, as a kind of summer academy of science where teachers and others could receive rudimentary training in science so that they could return home and instruct others in the proper study of nature. In this way he hoped to influence U.S. education from the bottom up. He secured philanthropic funding and accepted 50 students from hundreds of applicants that first summer. Unfortunately his dream of field laboratory studies for laypeople did not long outlive its creator, who died in December 1873. Agassiz's son, Alexander, was less committed to it, and a wonderful opportunity to do some scientific evangelizing among the masses died aborning.

A much more dramatic display of native brains and talent took place in New York City in 1853 on the occasion of the Crystal Palace Exposition. Modeled after the identically named extravaganza in London two years earlier, it had the purpose of showing off U.S. technology, although ostensibly it was for the "Industry of All Nations." The London exhibition had showed the way by awarding prizes for the best technology in various categories. In 1851 U.S. exhibitors walked away with five Great Council Awards of 170 given out by the royal judges: (1) Cyrus McCormick's reaper, (2) Charles Goodyear's rubber vulcanizing process, (3) William C. and George P. Bond's astronomical clock, (4) David Dick's antifriction press for the manufacture of heavy tools and machine parts, and (5) Gail Borden's preserved meat biscuit. Americans planned to do a lot better at the next "science and technology fair," especially when it would be in their own house.

Thousands of private citizens helped raise the projected $200,000 cost through subscriptions, New York State chartered it, and more than 1 million visitors arrived to gawk during its run. It was equal parts entertainment and education. President Franklin Pierce gave the opening speech, in which he noted science's contribution to every aspect of life. The exhibits, from both sides of the Atlantic, included the latest in agricultural machinery, printing presses, stereoscopic photography, quick-firing firearms, the first working elevator, and an array of labor-saving household products. They were all on display day or night thanks to the wonder of modern gas lighting. Toward the end there was talk of turning it into something between a museum and a school "that would spread abroad knowledge of America's great scientific, industrial development." Instead the directors declared bankruptcy and closed the doors in November after a six-month run. As only the second "World's Fair" of the century, it had been a proper showcase for U.S. science and technology, even if a financial disaster. In subsequent world's fairs (e.g., Paris, 1867) U.S. inventors and manufacturers would show up en masse to match the pride of U.S. technology with Europe's best.

Popularizing science also fell under the purview of several new organizations dedicated to that purpose. The National Academy of Science was founded as a private, nonprofit organization in 1863 to promote science but also to scrutinize carefully the new technology being offered to the federal government during wartime. A rival organization for scientists and the promotion of science was the American Academy of Arts and Sciences. It differed chiefly from its rival by being more broadly based and less closely tied to the federal government. The U.S. Agricultural Society, founded in 1851, functioned as both a publicity organization and a lobbying group to gain more government support for farmers.

As great as the popular fascination was with science (and its partner technology), it was still not universal. The most passionate criticism came from two directions: Die-hard Southerners believed that technology and all its attendant materialist trappings were a threat to destroy the traditional gentility and "civilization" of the South. They saw the devil himself in Northern machinery and incorporated that view into the Lost Cause mythology that grew up to explain away Southern defeat in the war. Another passionate critic who also saw Satan in the things of science was Mary Baker Eddy, founder of the Christian Science movement in the 1870s. This new religion was anything but scientific. In her seminal work, *Science and Health* (1875), she attacked the ascendancy of science over spiritual faith, aiming to

Art and science join together in Christian Schussele's 1862 masterpiece *Men of Progress.* This heroic four-by-six-foot canvas depicts 19 great inventors and technology pioneers of the age in tableau. It has been reproduced countless times in photos and prints. The original work belongs to Cooper Union College. Schussele's galaxy of stars are *(from left to right)* William Morton, James Bogardus, Samuel Colt, Cyrus McCormick, Joseph Saxton, Charles Goodyear (sitting at table front center), Peter Cooper, Jordan Mott, Joseph Henry, Eliphalet Nott, John Ericsson, Frederick Sickels, Samuel Morse (sitting at table front center), Henry Burden, Richard Hoe, Erastus Bigelow, Isaiah Jennings, Thomas Blanchard, and Elias Howe. (Library of Congress)

"re-instate primitive Christianity and its lost element of healing" in place of medical science. Although her movement gained a loyal following, it did not appreciably detract from the steady advance of science and technology in the United States.

Publications such as *Popular Science* magazine and Jules Verne's science-grounded tales helped inspire a generation of younger Americans to pursue scientific studies. Fortunately an alliance of educators and philanthropists were busy establishing institutions of higher learning devoted to such studies. The industrialist-cum-philanthropist Peter Cooper founded Cooper Union in New York in 1858 as an adult education institute emphasizing technical and art courses. The following year, the Massachusetts Institute of Technology was founded at Cambridge, although the first classes were not offered until 1865. The Stevens Institute of Technology opened its doors in Hoboken, New Jersey, in 1871. Three years later Robert Thurston, a successful Rhode Island engineer, established the nation's finest mechanical engineering program at Stevens Institute. And when Congress passed the Morrill Act in 1862, the intention was to establish agricultural and mechanical arts colleges to advance the frontiers of learning on a broad front. Even the classic liberal arts universities jumped on the science bandwagon. In 1871 Yale administrators for the first time incorporated laboratory science classes in the curriculum after a university self-study, *The Needs of the University,* endorsed the idea.

In 1859 after a breathtaking ride through his land on a American-made locomotive, the pasha of Egypt exclaimed, "God is great, but those Yankees are very near perfection!" Most Americans would have agreed heartily with him then, and in the next 26 years, nothing would happen to change that opinion.

CHAPTER 18 Medicine and Psychiatry

Medicine

Medicine in the 19th century had not changed much since the Middle Ages: The germ theory was still unknown, antibiotics had yet to be discovered, and treatment was more an art than a science. The impressive advances made in the mechanical sciences during these years did not extend to medical science. As the historian Richard Shyrock has noted, there were no medical equivalents of the steam engine or the telegraph. The biggest breakthrough in preventive medicine, the Englishman Edward Jenner's discovery of vaccination in 1796, was still regarded with suspicion by the public. The truth of the matter was that medical science could not cure the simplest ailments or relieve ordinary aches and pain, much less prevent disease. As a result, life expectancy for the average American in the 1850s was about 40 years. The child mortality rate ran from 30 to 50 percent, and more than one in 30 mothers died in childbirth.

Certain facts of U.S life exacerbated the primitive state of medicine, beginning with a tendency to overeat among the middle and upper classes and disdain for bathing among all classes. Furthermore egalitarian thinking of the day allowed any quack with a medical bag and a knowledgeable air about him to set up as a physician. The medical profession was unregulated by either the government or a broad-based professional society. One perfectly acceptable path to becoming a physician was to apprentice oneself to a working member of the profession in the same way many aspiring lawyers got their start.

But although medicine still had one foot in the Dark Ages, there were a number of modern trends just emerging that were noteworthy. To begin with, the field of medicine was being separated into male and female divisions. Women doctors and female medical colleges coincided with the development of obstetric medicine, replacing the ancient practice of midwifery. But women's medicine and women practitioners were relegated in this new order to second-class status. As the medical field became increasingly professionalized, it also became totally male-dominated. The female was thought to be not only constitutionally different from the male both physically and mentally but also intellectually unsuited to the rigors of medical science. It would be many years before this bias would be overcome.

Another modern trend was the development of criminal medicine, or what contemporaries called criminal anthropology, which focused on the physical traits of the "criminal class." Criminals were considered to be constitutionally different from "normal" people in the same way that females were different from males. Law and medicine even joined forces in the courtroom with the use of the postmortem report in homicide cases.

Medicine also became more specialized, sometimes in bizarre ways, such as the pseudosciences of phrenology and physiognomy, which taught that specific body types, the shape of the head, and facial features were all definitive guides to moral character.

Finally this era saw the emergence of a new science of the mind that was the forerunner of modern psychiatry. It was based on the theory that all mental aberrations are somatic (i.e., diseases of the brain), replacing an older theory that the insane were moral degenerates, separated from God. In this new scheme of things a doctor of the mind was termed an *alienist* because he investigated "mental diseases," and any person so afflicted was known as a mental alien, that is, someone separated from normal people. Among other ideas this new thinking promoted the concept of the "criminal mind."

Diseases and Epidemics

Epidemics were a familiar part of life, caused not just by ever-present germs, but by poor hygiene, overcrowded living conditions, and underfunded public health care. Although there was some awareness that good sanitation could prevent sickness and alleviate its impact after it began, the exact connection was not understood. The modern germ theory of disease was yet to be discovered. Out of ignorance diseases were attributed to "miasma" (poisonous air), commonly associated with swamps, slums, and low-lying areas; "bad humors" (imbalances in the body fluids); or the vaguely frightening and completely unhealthy "night air." Certain areas were known to be more unhealthy than others, but wherever they lived, every family had lost loved ones to disease, and many had lost multiple family members to the epidemics that descended unannounced on communities. America was better off than the Old World only because of the relatively sparse population and widely dispersed communities, which tended to keep disease outbreaks localized.

Epidemics were also commonly blamed on "outsiders" so that strangers arriving in a community were regarded with suspicion because they might be carriers of diseases. This was particularly true in port cities, which had more than their share of foreign visitors and epidemic outbreaks. Advances in transportation as the century progressed had the unforeseen effect of spreading local epidemics to previously uninfected areas. Diseases were carried far and wide by travelers via rail and boat so that major transportation centers such as New Orleans, St. Louis, and Nashville suffered one epidemic after another.

And epidemics were more than just a public health problem; they were also a drag on the economy that was not apparent among the usual business indicators. They struck the working, contributing members of society, removing them from their normal pursuits. As a result an epidemic striking a major city such as New York or Philadelphia could paralyze business and commerce.

The least healthy parts of the country in terms of climate were in the South because it was semitropical and the Midwest because the humid river valleys of the Mississippi, Missouri, and Tennessee were conducive to chronic malaria and pulmonary ailments. The healthiest section was the Far West because the dry, cool climate was less hospitable to disease-causing conditions. Nonetheless disease killed more people than either Indians or starvation on the emigrant trails taking people out West. In the year 1849 there were 5,000 deaths caused by cholera on the California Trail alone. As people went west at least in part for the supposedly healthy and epidemic-free environment, they took their diseases with them and suffered the additional burden of being farther from good medical care than those who lived back in the eastern cities.

Among major U.S. cities, New Orleans had the reputation of being "the most unhealthy city on Earth," but many other U.S. cities were not much better. The lack of knowledge about public health was only exceeded by the lack of accountability by public officials and private industries. Boston dairymen knowingly sold milk from diseased cows in 1864, and neither the city nor the courts were willing to do anything about it until an exposé in the newspapers raised a public outcry. The first U.S. city to filter its municipal drinking water was Poughkeepsie, New York, in 1871. New York City, which was in a category by itself because of its population, wealth, and culture, also was the most vulnerable to all sorts of disease epidemics. The same immense size that made it a great city also made it a public health nightmare, and the fact that it was the primary gateway for foreign immigrants entering the United States only added to the problems. Not surprisingly New York created the first board of health of any U.S. city, in 1867. (Louisiana created the first state board of health in 1855.)

Among the most deadly diseases in the 19th century were cholera, smallpox, typhoid fever, measles, typhus, and tuberculosis. Today none of these poses the kind of threat in the Western world that it once did, so people tend to forget how terrifying those diseases were in the days before antibiotics and antivirals. Cholera, caused by a bacterium that attacks the human intestines, routinely claimed more than one-half of its victims during an outbreak. It regularly struck 19th-century urban communities, attacking through the water supply and spreading like wildfire.

Another living terror was yellow fever, which was variously known as "the scourge of American cities" and "the American plague." A modern medical historian calls it "the single most dreaded disease" of that day. It typically arrived with warm weather in spring or summer and persisted until the first frost. Devastating yellow fever epidemics struck port cities on the south Atlantic and Gulf Coasts, killing an estimated 100,000 during the century, 41,000 in New Orleans alone. No one knew where it began or how it spread, so when yellow fever season began, those who could, fled to safer climes. Because there was no known cure, victims either got well on their own or died a horrible death.

Other diseases acquired their own lethal reputations among the vulnerable masses. Measles arrived in North America with the first European immigrants and then traveled west with the wagon trains in the 19th century, sometimes wiping out whole parties on the trail. Eventually it became endemic, never entirely absent from the population but erupting in epidemics only at intervals. Smallpox, one of the chief killers of the 19th century, sparked a more fearful reaction than any other disease, even after the Boston Board of Health first introduced immunization through vaccination in 1801. Typhus first appeared in the United States in the early 19th century, and there were no major outbreaks after 1837, although in its various forms, such as Rocky Mountain spotted fever, it continued to be a threat. Puerperal fever took its toll among women who had recently given birth and ironically was spread primarily by medical personnel assisting the new mothers.

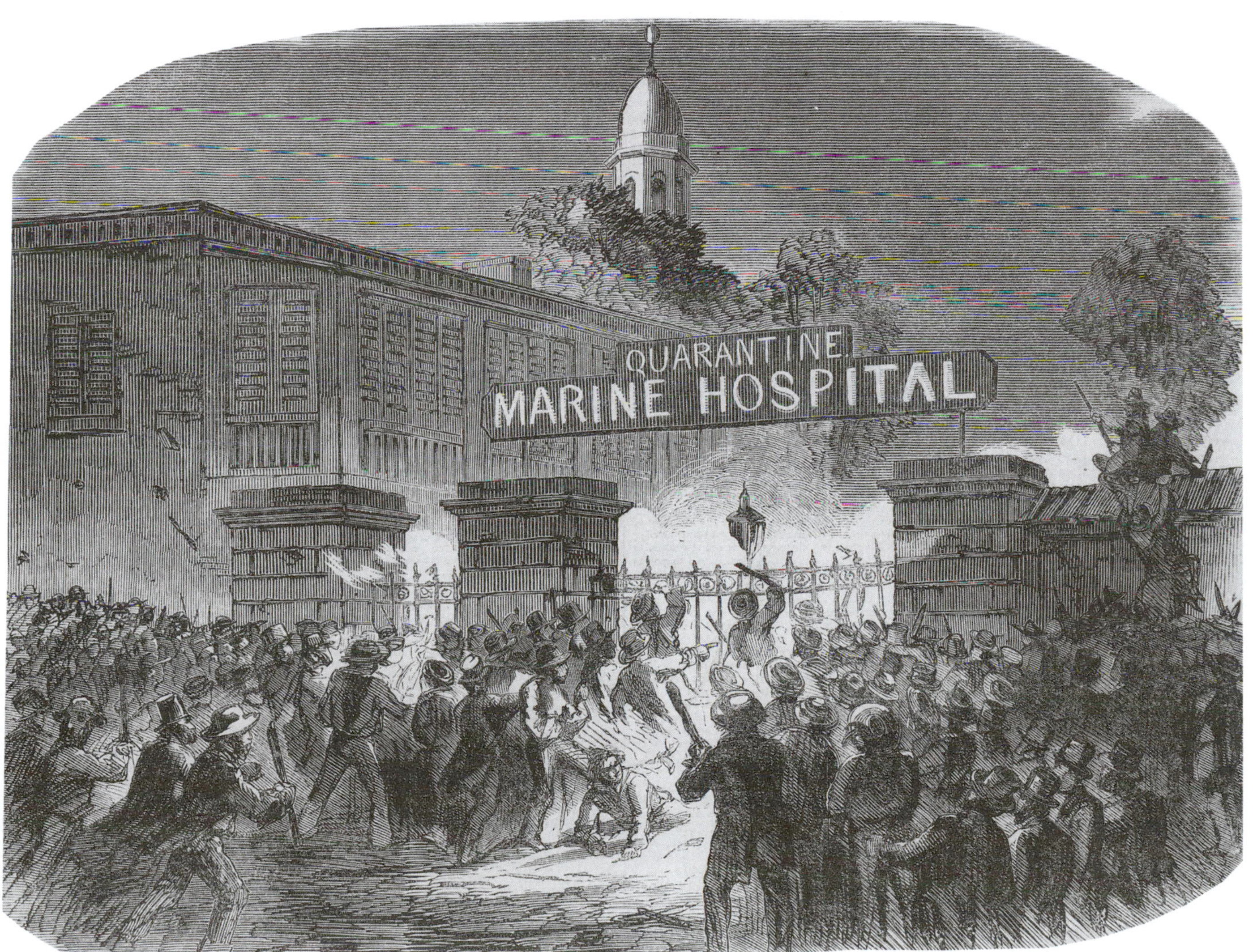

The usual way to address epidemic outbreaks was to quarantine the victims and, if necessary, even the area. Fear of the disease victims sometimes caused mobs to attack the hospitals in an effort to drive the patients away. A New York mob attacked the Marine Quarantine Hospital on September 1, 1858, during one of the city's periodic epidemics. (Library of Congress)

Many terrifying diseases had colorful descriptive names such as "childbed fever" for puerperal fever, "breakbone fever" for dengue fever, "ague" for malaria, "consumption" or "the white plague" for tuberculosis, "the grippe" for influenza, and "yellow jack" or "the American plague" for yellow fever.* And having no understanding of the concept of microorganisms, people simply described all contagious diseases as "pestilence."

If rampant disease was hard on the poor, the youngest, and the oldest, it was truly devastating to the Native American population. Because American Indians had no resistance to European diseases, the periodic epidemics that swept through the tribes became a form of "genocide" that virtually exterminated the Mandan, Hidatsa, Coeur d'Alene, and Arikara tribes and almost wiped out the Cree and Blackfeet. Although measles and typhus also took their toll, the Indians proved especially vulnerable to smallpox, which swept through one tribe after another in periodic epidemics that broke out in widely scattered locales almost annually with no rhyme or reason. Death rates of 60 percent to 70 percent were common and exceeded 98 percent among some tribes. Two smallpox epidemics before 1850 were estimated to have killed more than 300,000 alone; recurring epidemics in 1861–62, 1865, 1867, 1869–70, and 1872–73 killed untold thousands more. Medical historians suspect non-Indians of being the carriers in every case, but this idea cannot be proved. Adding a shameful moral element to the problem, white authorities made only halfhearted efforts to introduce smallpox inoculation to the tribes under their control, although its benefits were widely known as early as 1832.

By the second half of the 19th century the state of medical knowledge and conventional wisdom had both advanced to the stage at which disease epidemics were no longer viewed as moral issues so much as public health problems to be addressed by better sanitation measures, tighter quarantines, and expanded hospital facilities. Improved living conditions coupled with rising public health standards led to a huge decline in cholera outbreaks in the United States after 1874.

Certain diseases were more closely associated with urban society, principal among these being tuberculosis, influenza, rickets, and cancer. All of these were worsened by the living conditions found in industrial cities: overcrowding, lack of sunlight and fresh air, and high concentrations of industrial pollutants. Though all these conditions had been recognized as unhealthy long before industrialization, they came to be identified with modern urban life. The United States witnessed a much higher incidence of these diseases in the late 19th century. A truly unique industrial age illness, however, was "the bends" or "caisson disease," first encountered during foundation work on the Brooklyn Bridge in the 1870s, when workers were forced to work in high-pressure chambers under water. Not a disease but a disorder caused by too much nitrogen in the blood, it was not preventable or even understood until the 20th century.

*The etymology of many disease names was only slowly taken out of the public domain and appropriated by the medical profession over the course of the 19th century; for instance, *consumption* became *tuberculosis* after the mid-1830s thanks to the work of Dr. J. L. Schönlein.

TABLE 18.1 MAJOR EPIDEMIC OUTBREAKS IN AMERICA 1850–1875

Disease	Date/Length of Outbreak	Locality	Number of Victims
Cholera[a]	1850[b]	Midwest, especially Chicago, Ill.	416 deaths in Chicago, Jul. 18–Aug. 21
Smallpox	Winter 1850 ("the Big Small Pox Winter" in Sioux lore)	Upper Midwest Sioux encampments	Unknown
Smallpox	1850	Northern Plains and Alaska	Unknown, but virtually wiped out Coeur d'Alene, Dakota, and Aleut Indian tribes
Dengue fever	Jul. 1850–early 1851	Major Southern port cities beginning with Charleston, S.C.	Unknown
Cholera	1852	Chicago, Ill.	630 deaths; morbidity rate of 1,626 per 100,000
Smallpox	1852	Southwest	Hundreds of Pueblo Indians (exact number unknown)
Smallpox	1852–54	Pacific Northwest along Columbia, Yakima, and Klikitat Rivers	Nitinat, Nootka, and Makah Indian tribes reduced from 6,000 to 500 members
Yellow fever	1853	New Orleans	7,848 dead
Smallpox	Feb. 1853–Jan. 1854	California and Hawaiian Islands	9,082 cases, 5,748 deaths in Hawaii, or more than 8% of native population; no statistics for California, where it started
Dengue fever	1854	Mobile, Ala.	Unknown
Cholera	1854	Chicago, Ill.	1,424 deaths; morbidity rate of 2,162 per 100,000
"National Hotel disease"[c]	Jan.–Mar. 1857	Washington, D.C.	Unknown
Smallpox	1857	Kansas and Washington Territories	Unknown numbers of Kickapoo (Kans.), Yankton Dakota Sioux, Winnebago, and Squaksin (Wash.)
Yellow fever	1858	Mobile, Ala.	Unknown
Measles	Fall 1861	Confederate army in western Va.	Unknown ("Those on the sick list would form an army."—R. E. Lee)

Disease	Date/Length of Outbreak	Locality	Number of Victims
Smallpox	1861–62 (Fall and winter)	Va. and Washington, D.C.	Unkown (Abraham Lincoln among the infected)
Smallpox	Feb. 1862–Jun. 1865	Camp Douglas, Ill. (Prisoner of War camp)	2,000 cases, 618 deaths
Infectious hepatitis	Spring 1862	Union army camps on James Peninsula, Va.	3,400 reported cases
Smallpox	Winter 1863–64	Army of Northern Virginia, Chancellorsville, Va.	2,513 cases recorded, Oct. 1, 1862–Jan. 31, 1864, with 1,020 fatalities
Yellow fever	Apr.1864	Bermuda	Unknown but threatened to halt Confederate blockade running
Cholera	Apr. 1866–end of 1867	True pandemic that first appeared in New York City, then spread to South and Midwest; concentrated in cities and army posts	1,200 dead in New York City; 834 in Philadelphia; 1,200 in Cincinnati; 3,500 in St. Louis; 1,350 in New Orleans; 510 in Vicksburg (including 100 + blacks); 500 in San Antonio; 990 in Chicago; total deaths estimated at 40,000–60,000.
Yellow fever	Sep. 1867	Galveston, Tex.	Unknown number of military and civilian dead, including U.S. Army Major General Charles Griffin (Sep. 16)
Smallpox	Series of outbreaks beginning in winter 1868–69, 1872, 1874–75	New York, N.Y.[d]	3,084 cases reported in New York City in 1868–69, including 805 dead; another 929 dead in 1872, 484 in 1874, and 1,280 in 1875
Smallpox	1869	Northern Montana (the Gros Ventre Indian tribe)	About 800 deaths out of tribal population of 1,500
Puerperal fever	1873	Cincinnati, Ohio	130 women
Dengue fever	1873	New Orleans, La.	40,000 reported ill
Cholera	1873	Starting in New Orleans, spreading through South and Midwest	259 in New Orleans; in Memphis, 1,000 infected, 275 dead; 1,000 dead in Nashville; 700 dead in St. Louis
Yellow fever	Fall 1873	Shreveport, La., and other Southern cities	More than 400 in Shreveport alone

[a]First reported cases in North America were in 1832, in New York City; by 1834 it had reached the Pacific shores of the continent.
[b]A continuation of the pandemic that hit North America in 1848–49 and did not subside until 1856–58. During that time various intense outbreaks can be singled out.
[c]This disease sounds suspiciously like the modern "Legionnaire's disease," which was only diagnosed by doctors in 1976. Back in 1857 a medical commission created to investigate and report on the "National Hotel disease" attributed its cause to "fetid air escaping into the building from sewers," a cause almost identical to that of Legionnaire's disease!
[d]Other cities, e.g., Philadelphia, also reported smallpox outbreaks in this same period, although on a smaller scale.
Sources: H. H. Cunningham, *Doctors in Gray,* 2d ed. (Baton Rouge: Louisiana State University Press, 1960), 184–217; George Worthington Adams, *Doctors in Blue* (reprint, Dayton, Ohio: Morningside Press, 1985), 222–30; George C. Kohn, ed., *Plague and Pestilence* (New York: Facts On File, 1995), 123–24, 130–31, 336–41, 400; "Chronology," *The American Almanac and Repository of Useful Knowledge,* vols. 22–32 (Boston: David H. Williams, 1851–62); *The American Almanac and Repository of Useful Knowledge for the Years 1850-1861,* Part II (Boston: Chas. C. Little & Jas. Brown, 1849 [sic], 1850, 1851; Boston: Crosby, Nichols & Co., 1860, 1861, 1875); pages for each edition: 1849: 344–52, 137–39; 1851: 344–52; 1875: 364–76; 1860: 383–91; 1861: 407–13; R. S. Bray, *Armies of Pestilence* (New York: Barnes & Noble Books, 1996), 133.

The Medical Profession

In 1850 for the first time the U.S. government began to make a count of practicing physicians in the United States. That count included everyone who called himself (or herself) a physician without regard to training or licensing. Medical doctor was just another occupation to the census counters. During the next 30 years the number of doctors in the population more than doubled, although there was still no attempt to judge the qualifications of the persons who listed themselves as "physicians."

A vast gulf existed between rural and urban medicine. Even with the deplorable standards of public health that existed in most cities, the level of professionalism among urban doctors was several times removed from that of their country colleagues. Many rural areas had no resident doctor, and even small towns often had to make do with a drunken quack who received his training through reading a book or serving as an army steward. On the positive side country doctors when they were available charged much less than their city counterparts—sometimes half as much. Physicians were guided in setting their fees by their local medical societies, which distributed copies of what were variously called a "Fee Bill," "Fee Table," or "Table of Charges." These were not binding, but a maverick doctor broke with his fellows at his own professional risk.

TABLE 18.2 NUMBER OF PHYSICIANS IN THE U.S. POPULATION, 1850–1880

Decennial Year	Census Count
1850	40,755
1860	55,055
1870	64,414
1880	85,671

Sources: United States Bureau of the Census, *Historical Statistics of the United States* (Washington, D.C.: U.S. Government Printing Office, 1960), 34; R. G. Leland, *Distribution of Physicians in the United States* (Chicago: American Medical Association, 1935), 2.

The Civil War opened the door for women to enter the medical profession in large numbers for the first time. Thousands of women, such as those pictured here ca. 1863, served without pay or training in nursing roles, either as private citizens or for various organizations, especially the U.S. Sanitary Commission. In the decades following the Civil War, women began to dominate the previously all-male nursing field while doctoring continued in its hidebound ways. (Print from author's collection)

The medical profession was only slowly opening up to women at this time, and even at that, only allowed them to deal with women's disorders and women patients. In this engraving from *Frank Leslie's Illustrated Newspaper,* April 16, 1870, a properly attired female doctor instructs her students in the anatomical lecture room of the New York City Medical College for Women. (Library of Congress)

TABLE 18.3 COMPARATIVE MEDICAL FEES CHARGED BY DOCTORS IN NEW YORK CITY (1860) VERSUS DOCTORS IN KNIGHTSTOWN, INDIANA, 1862

Service Provided	Urban New York[a]	Rural Indiana[b]
Visit to doctor's office for verbal advice	$1.00–$2.00	$0.50
Charge for written advice (including prescriptions)	$5.00–$15.00	Unknown
Ordinary house call	$1.50–$3.00	$0.75–$1.00
Extra for travel more than one mile (per mile rate)	$0.50–$1.00	$0.75–$1.00
Night house call	$5.00–$10.00	$1.10–$1.50
Vaccination	$1.50–$3.00	$0.50
Catheterization—urethral	$3.00–$10.00	Unknown
Maternity—natural labor	$10.00–$50.00	$5.00
Reduction of fractures	$10.00–$50.00	$5.00–$30.00
Removal of stones from bladder	$100.00–$500.00	Unknown
Hernia—reduction by operation	$50.00–$500.00	$50.00
Operation for cataract	$100.00–$500.00	$40.00–$75.00
Excision of tonsils	$25.00–$50.00	$5.00

[a]As adopted by the Medical Society of Washington County, N.Y., in 1860.
[b]As adopted by the Union Medcial Soceity of Knightstown, Ind., in 1862.
Source: James Bordley III and A. McGehee Harvey, *Two Centuries of American Medicine* (Philadelphia: W. B. Saunders, 1976), 75.

Conventional Medical Treatment

Nobody in the medical profession knew much about treating the most common ailments afflicting society. Physicians were not trained to treat or even recognize infectious diseases. Quite often they attributed epidemic outbreaks to ridiculous causes, such as "malarial miasma," "Mephitic effluvia," "crowd poisoning," "choleric temperament," or "poisonous fungi in the atmosphere." Baffled by the onslaught of diseases, they turned to perfecting surgical technique, and the 19th century witnessed amazing advances in that field.

Meanwhile the usual treatment for serious illness was either to wait it out or to administer some folk remedy that was useless at best and many times made the condition worse. Truth be told, there were few weapons in the medical bag for doctors to use against killer diseases: quinine for malaria (available since 1822) and inoculation for smallpox (accepted since 1798). Those were effective, but nobody really knew why or how. Emetics were a popular form of treatment for a variety of illnesses, including typhoid, and the favorite emetic of the medical profession was calomel or mercurous chloride, which was administered in massive dosages. Unfortunately mercury is toxic even in minute doses, leading to a slow and painful death. The author Louisa May Alcott's health was ruined after she was heavily dosed with calomel during a stint as a nurse in Washington, D.C., during the Civil War. Her teeth fell out and she suffered from rheumaticlike pain for the rest of her life.

For cholera and some other diseases the liberal application of quicklime or other disinfectant was thought to prevent the spread of contagions. City authorities sprang into action and doused the site of the outbreak with carbolic acid, chlorine mixture, creosote, zinc

A doctor vaccinates a baby for smallpox during a home visit. Vaccinations were a relatively recent development in medicine. This engraving from a sketch by Sol Ettinge ran in *Harper's Weekly,* February 19, 1870. (Library of Congress)

One of the most feared diseases in history, cholera was caused by foul water and was highly contagious, requiring quarantine whenever it broke out. The nation's last major Asiatic cholera epidemic struck several Southern cities in 1873, leading to widespread death and suffering. (Library of Congress)

chloride, or just old-fashioned lye soap and water. This practice did not actually alleviate the disease, but it did give the appearance that the authorities were doing something, and it had the positive side effect of covering up the filth and the sickening stench of death. When all else failed, the response of last resort was quarantine, which was also useless as a curative but at least slowed the spread of the disease. Ironically the quarantine response reinforced racial segregation in Southern cities, where the same methods used to contain disease could be applied to containing blacks.

As for hospitalization coupled with treatment, the concept was practically unknown in the 19th century except for soldiers during wartime and those who were receiving charity at any other time. Hospitals were widely considered to be places where poor people with diseases went to die. For true healing the middle and upper classes made pilgrimages to natural springs and health spas in pleasant pastoral settings. Belatedly during this period the popular image of hospitals began to improve: From traditionally being considered charitable refuges for the indigent sick, they began to be regarded as the headquarters of medicine. It was a welcome change but only a small part of the monumental task of dragging medicine into the modern era.

Preventive medicine, for instance, was still virtually unknown until the Union army began to give dosages of quinine to many of its soldiers in summer 1861 on the recommendation of the U.S. Sanitary Commission.

As a rule conventional medical treatment consisted of about equal parts folk remedies and esoteric natural extracts, all heavily laced with alcohol. Among the most popular medicinal ingredients were camphor, cayenne pepper, herb teas, onions, garlic, and tobacco smoke, none of which was particularly dangerous to the patient, although they could make him extremely ill. The more pungent, spicy, or bitter the medicine tasted, the better it was thought to work. These ingredients could be mixed with rum, brandy, or whiskey to make them more tolerable and to achieve the desired kick. Every doctor's medical bag also contained some truly dangerous drugs, which had potentially addictive if not lethal side effects. Calomel was not just for typhoid; it was the first medicine most doctors reached for when their patients were feeling "puny," and it had the reputation of being something of a wonder drug. Other dangerous drugs favored by doctors included opium, morphine, strychnine, turpentine, laudanum, blue mass (mercury and chalk mixture), belladonna, silver nitrate, sulfuric acid, and potassium iodide. Any of these might be nonchalantly administered alone or in combination. Nor were creative physicians limited in treatment to what they could pour into the patient. There were a number of more intrusive procedures, too. Bleeding, cupping, blistering, leeching, binding, chafing, and purging all enjoyed near-sacrosanct standing among members of the medical profession, although their patients were more likely to consider them tortures than treatments.

TABLE 18.4 CONVENTIONAL MEDICAL TREATMENTS PRESCRIBED BY PHYSICIANS, 1800s

Condition or Ailment	Prescribed Treatment
Alcoholism	"Slowly suck an orange"
Earache	Pour water into ear "as hot as it can be borne"
Insomnia	Drink a cup of coffee
Attack of hysteria	Electric shocks
Bronchitis	"Bleed" patient from jugular vien
Vomiting during pregnancy	Morphine suppositories
Acne	Apply arsenic to affected area

Source: Merck Research Laboratories, *The Merck Manual of Diagnosis and Therapy* (Rahway, N.J.: Merck, 1899), en passant. (This was the first edition of the classic physician's reference work.)

Civil War Medicine

The Civil War provided the greatest living laboratory for the practice of medicine in the United States before the 20th century and not just for the enormous numbers of combat wounds. As one historian has pointed out, "Germs, not bullets were the soldiers' deadliest foes." The vast numbers of people massed together in close proximity as either soldiers or refugees fleeing the war created ideal conditions for the spread of disease. New recruits and rural inhabitants were the most likely to fall victim, and they did so in the tens of thousands. This situation in turn made it incumbent upon the authorities on both sides to find the most efficient ways to treat the ill and prevent the further spread of disease—and this on top of treating the tens of thousands of wounded from combat.

A statistical profile of Civil War medicine can be only half drawn. The Union kept excellent and very detailed records, while the Confederacy kept poor records, many of those lost at the end of the war. As a result much of Confederate medical history had to be gleaned from fragmentary records and physicians' recollections long after the event. For instance Dr. Joseph Jones, one of the Confederacy's most respected doctors, calculated that of the roughly 600,000 soldiers who served in Southern armies from 1861 to 1865, each one on the average was lost to the service as a result of either wounding or sickness six times during the war. Jones's statistical method does not stand close examination, but it does provide a starting point for understanding the scope of the medical situation on the Confederate side. Fortunately because both sides were fighting under the same conditions, had roughly the same backgrounds, and were treated by doctors with the same level of knowledge, it is possible to extrapolate for Confederate forces from Union figures.

The medical system of the country in 1861 was totally inadequate to the demands of total war. There were only about 55,000 trained doctors in the entire United States, no corps of professional nurses, and no more than 150 general hospitals. From this beginning the Union and the Confederacy had to create and staff facilities to treat more than a half million sick and wounded men during the next four years. What the North was able to do that the South was not was to organize a regular medical corps early in the war and provide an uninterrupted flow of medicines to its doctors. At the end of 1862 the Union had 151 general hospitals in operation, with 58,715 beds. Two years later those numbers had risen to 190 hospitals and 120,521 beds. Throughout the war large numbers of sick and wounded were also treated in regimental, camp, and field hospitals or by their family at home, but those numbers are not quantifiable.

Early in the war the treatment of both the wounded and the diseased was haphazard and inadequate, but gradually over the course of the conflict the situation improved on both sides, although much less on the Confederate side. Extensive U.S. government records show some 300,000 Union military deaths during the war (two-thirds of disease), and nearly 6 million cases of sickness. Southern sources estimate some 200,000 Confederates died of either wounds or sickness during the war. (The modern estimate is 350,000 deaths to disease on both sides, of nearly 10 million cases of reported sickness.) By contrast in the entire U.S. Army of 16,000 men before the war, only 30,300 cases of sickness were treated during the two-year period 1859–60. A detailed breakdown by specific cause of death or illness was also made by Union doctors. Confederate figures for the official medical history of the war had to be estimated by the Adjutant General's Office in 1885.

Types and rate of sickness are determined from records by Union army doctors of "sick call," a morning routine in both hospitals and the field when the doctor examined patients and prescribed appropriate medication(s) to match the diagnosis. The thousands of sick call reports accumulated during four years of war were carefully compiled into a comprehensive analysis of illness in the Union army after the war. Those figures show an annual average of 2,435 cases of sickness per thousand among white troops (some reported sick more than once), with an annual death rate of 53.4 per thousand. This compared favorably with a death rate of 11 percent among U.S. forces during the U.S.-Mexican War.

The records also reveal the shameful fact that black soldiers were much more likely to contract disease and much more likely to die of it than white soldiers. The reasons for this are complex, but undeniably racism in the matter of living conditions and medical treatment played a part. In the Union army the mortality rate for disease was 55 per thousand per year among white volunteer troops (32 per thousand for Regulars), but 133 per thousand among black troops. This indicates that a black soldier who had cholera or smallpox or one of the other prevalent camp diseases was more than twice as likely to die as his white compatriot.

The most common ailment among Civil War soldiers—and the major single killer—was diarrhea (or dysentery in its most serious form). It affected approximately 54 percent of all Union soldiers and 99 percent of all Confederates and killed more men than bullets did. One of every 10 military deaths could be directly attributed to intestinal disorders, or as many as 100,000 according to some sources. Chronic diarrhea in the Northern ranks claimed 37,794 white victims and 6,764 black soldiers. The poet Walt Whitman, who worked as a nurse in a Northern hospital, wrote that the war was "about 999 parts diarrhea and one part glory." Second and third on the official list of killer diseases were "continued fevers" and pneumonia, which were usually associated with typhoid fever and malaria.

TABLE 18.5 SICK REPORT IN THE U.S. ARMY: THE MOST COMMON ILLNESSES AND THEIR USUAL PRESCRIBED TREATMENT, 1861–1865

Disease[a]	Number of Reported Cases	Number of Reported Deaths	Rate of Attack (Morbidity per Thousand)	Rate of Death among Afflicted (Mortality in Percentage)	Standard Treatment[b]
Typhoid fever	79,462	29,336	1/1,000	37	Saline purgatives followed by stimulants; also oil of turpentine applied externally
Malaria (or typhomalarial fever)	1,315,955	10,063	1/1,000	0.95	Quinine sulfate dissolved in whiskey; or tree-bark derivative from either dogwoods or poplars; alternatively, turpentine applied externally
Smallpox	12,190 (whites) 6,7 16 (blacks)	4, 717 (whites) 2,341 (blacks)	5/1,000 (whites)	38.76 (whites)	Quarantine; plenty of fresh air, plus saline purgatives, cooling drinks, and enemas
Measles[c]	67,763 (whites)	4,246 (whites)	Unknown	6.37	Quarantine and plenty of fresh air; sassafras herb tea
Typhus	2,501	850	Unknown	3.40	Isolation and fresh air
"Continued fever"[d]	11,898	147	Unknown	22.28	Isolation and fresh air
Acute diarrhea	1,155,266	2,923	Unknown	0.25	Plug of opium *or* tree bark substitute from willows or sweet gums, plus calomel, ipecac, opium, epsom salts, or castor oil administered internally[e]
Chronic diarrhea	170,488	27,558	Unknown	0.01.	Same
Acute dysentery	233,812	4,084	Unknown	1.75	Same
Chronic dysentery	25,670	3,229	Unknown	12.58	Same
All dysentery and diarrhea[f]	1,739,135	44,558	37/1,000	1.25	Same
"Inflammation of the lungs" (i.e., pneumonia)	61,202	14,738	Unknown	0.10	Tartar emetic, preparations of antimony, "bleeding"(all traditional); dosage of opium/quinine, mustard plasters (wartime)
Syphilis	73,382	123	3/1,000	0.17	Mercury and potassium iodide; also arsenical compounds, elder, wild sarsaparilla, sassafras, jessamine
Gonorrhea	95,833	6	Unknown	0.006	Same as for syphillis
Scurvy (including incipient scurvy or scorbutic diathesis)	30,714	383	Unknown	1.25	Diet of green vegetables and/or fruit; also wine vinegar
Delirium tremens[g]	3,744	450	Unknown	12.02	Strong stimulants and strictly enforced sobriety

Disease[a]	Number of Reported Cases	Number of Reported Deaths	Rate of Attack (Morbidity per Thousand)	Rate of Death among Afflicted (Mortality in Percentage)	Standard Treatment[b]
"Mania and dementia" (i.e., insanity)[h]	2,410	80	1/1,000	3.32	Confinement in an asylum
Paralysis	2,837	231	6/1,000	8.14	None

[a]All names are based on the diagnoses of the Union army doctors at the time and therefore reflect the state of medical knowledge at mid-century.
Note: Includes all troops, black and white, unless otherwise indicated.
[b]Included alcohol in "medicinal doses" in all cases.
[c]Many of the deaths attributed to measles were probably the result of pulmonary complications, especially pneumonia.
[d]This broad 19th-century term included typhoid fever, typhus fever, and other unspecified but persistent fevers. It was usually used for typhoidlike fevers that could not be specifically diagnosed as typhoid.
[e]By comparison, constipation was treated with dosage of "blue mass" (mercury and chalk mixture) or a vegetable cathartic but was not listed as a serious medical problem because it was not potentially fatal as diarrhea was.
[f]*Diarrhea* and *dysentery* are both generic descriptive terms when used in Civil War medical reports, meaning loose bowels. The problem as described by Civil War doctors could have been symptoms of other diseases or a result of dietary or climatic conditions. A true technical diagnosis of either bacillary or amebic dysentery was not possible with the medical knowledge of the time.
[g]Strictly associated with alcoholism. Chronic drunks could be cashiered or "suspended from service" under military law.
[h]In Civil War medical parlance, not the same as "nostalgia," which was the generic name for the condition known today as depression or posttraumatic stress disorder.
Sources: Compiled from official records by Francis R. Packard, *History of Medicine in the United States* (New York: Hafner, 1963), 646; *Medicine of the Civil War,* National Library of Medicine (Washington, D.C.: U.S. Government Printing Office, n.d.) 9; *Medical and Surgical History of the Civil War,* vol. 1 (Wilmington, N.C.: Broadfoot, 1990–1991), 146–47, 296–97, 452–53, 604–5, 630–31; George Worthington Adams, *Doctors in Blue* (Dayton, Ohio.: Morningside Press, 1985), 239–44; George C. Kohn, ed., *Encyclopedia of Plagues and Pestilence* (New York: Facts On File, 1995), 340–41; Lawrence J. Bopp, "Medicine," in *Historical Times Illustrated Encyclopedia of the Civil War* ed. Patricia L. Faust (New York: Harper & Row, 1986), 484–85.

TABLE 18.6 CASUALTIES OF WAR, 1861–1865

Category	Union	Confederate
Deaths		
In battle	110,070	94,000
Of battle wounds (later)	43,012	Unknown
Of disease	224,586	164,000
Of accident, suicide, other	24,872	Unknown
Total	359,528	258,000
Black troops (all causes)[a]	33,380	N/A
Number of Wounded[b]		
Gunshot	245,790	Unknown
Saber or bayonet	922	Unknown
Total	246,712	Unknown
Number of Reported Sick	5,825,480	Unknown

[a]The records only cover the period from Sep. 1862 to Dec. 1866.
[b]Number of wounded by weapons of war only.
Sources: National Library of Medicine *Medicine of the Civil War* (Washington, D.C.: U.S. Government Printing Office, n.d). 8; Francis R. Packard, *History of Medicine in the United States* (New York: Hafner, 1963), 645–46.

A Civil War soldier was eight times more likely to die of a battle wound than his modern counterpart in the U.S. Army, but he was 10 times more likely to die of disease. A combined mortality rate from disease of 71 soldiers per thousand in Civil War armies, three times the number who died in battle, provoked a belated revolution in public health measures. In addition to the familiar diseases of typhoid, malaria, and measles, wartime conditions caused venereal diseases and dysentery to become much worse problems than they had been in peacetime. This was because the assembling of large armies of young males, their subsequent rootlessness, and the lack of hygiene changed the equation. The shameful treatment of black soldiers in the Union army also produced a mortality rate more than twice as high as that of white soldiers (133/1,000 versus 55/1,000). Medical treatment in the Civil War for Northern armies was the responsibility of the U.S. Army Medical Corps when the war began; it was joined in June 1861 by the civilian-led U.S. Sanitary Commission.

The busiest members of the medical profession during the war were the knife-happy surgeons, who were often more interested in speed than in need. They had to be fast because there were never enough surgeons to handle all the work after a major battle. An experienced surgeon could amputate a leg in less than three minutes even under battlefield conditions. The Union army averaged one surgeon for every 100 men; the Confederates, one for every 324 men. The surgeons in both armies became, by necessity, amputation artists. Amputations accounted for 75 percent of wartime surgical procedures. Fractured and lacerated limbs were routinely lopped off by battlefield surgeons without a second thought, and piles of arms and legs wherever the doctors worked became legendary. Conventional wisdom dictated that amputations had to be performed within 48 hours to have any chance of success. A shortage of trained doctors coupled with filthy operating conditions further aggravated the situation. Although U.S. doctors had some knowledge of antiseptic procedure, pioneered in Europe by Ignaz Semmelweiss and others, it was largely ignored—a Civil War scandal that has never been adequately explored. Surgeries were done in field tents, confiscated barns, and under trees, using doors laid across boxes as operating tables. Doctors used the same instruments over and over again, wiping them off on their apron or a dirty rag between surgeries. If the patient survived the surgery he was laid out on the ground in the shade and left to recover or die as luck or the strength of his constitution dictated.

Surviving the wounding itself and the surgery that inevitably followed did not mean the patient was out of the woods. Even more lethal than the other two were the variety of postoperative infections that were endemic. Pyemia, or "pus in the blood," had a mortality rate of 97.4 percent. Tetanus was another killer, which affected the brain at the end. "Hospital gangrene" struck the lightly wounded as well as the badly wounded. This highly contagious condition—recognizable because it produced rotting flesh in rainbow hues of blue, black, and green—plagued even well-run hospitals on both sides. Even the best-trained physicians did not understand the bacterial origins of the invisible killers. Yet, despite the odds against them, an amazing percentage of soldiers who had amputation did survive to spend the rest of their life stumping around their hometown, the countless handicapped veterans to remind the nation of the awful conflict.

Civil War advances in medical science were limited to orthopedic surgical techniques and anesthesia, not the treatment of disease or organ surgery. Through frequent "clinical" practice on real patients, surgeons became very proficient at amputations, joint resections, and ligations. On the other hand, Civil War surgeons tended to stay away from the "great cavities" and viscera. Likewise, antisepsis (i.e., germ-fighting) procedures had to wait until after the Civil War to be advanced into the modern age.

Each side's army had a medical corps, which consisted in the field of a few trained doctors, assisted by stewards, orderlies, and local civilians. (Most of the treatment of the sick and injured during the Civil War was done by civilian volunteers rather than military personnel, in private homes and appropriated public buildings.) In the field they had to take care of the transportation and treatment of the sick and wounded. Transportation from the battlefield to field hospitals and then from field hospitals to rear areas was happenstance, dependent on whatever wagons could be rounded up on the spot. The Union army finally created an ambulance corps in fall 1862. The Confederates continued to rely on conventional wagons, two-wheel and four-wheel, which were unsprung and filthy, for the duration of the war. Medical supplies were transported as part of an army's regular baggage train, and they included quantities of standard medicaments such as quinine, morphia, opium, iodine, and calomel. Chloroform was a relatively new addition to the medicine chest; whiskey had been used by soldiers as a medicinal aid since time immemorial. Some other products in the Civil War medicine chest are practically unknown today outside medical museums.

TABLE 18.7 PROFILE OF AMPUTATION CASES IN THE UNION ARMY DURING THE BATTLE OF THE WILDERNESS, MAY 5–7, 1864

Amputated Part	Cases	Deaths	Percentage of Fatalities
Finger(s)	7,902	198	2.5
Forearm	1,761	245	13.9
Upper arm	5,540	1,273	23.0
Toe(s)	1,519	81	5.3
Shin	5,523	1,790	32.4
Thigh	6,369	3,411	53.6
Knee joint	195	111	56.9
Hip joint	66	55	83.3
Ankle joint	161	119	73.9

Note: During this three-day battle between the Army of the Potomac and the Army of Northern Virginia, the Federals suffered 17,500 of 115,000 effectives (a standard military term for soldiers present and fighting), or about a 15 percent casualty rate.
Source: Compiled by Stephen T. Foster, Library of Congress, from *Medical and Surgical History of the Civil War,* vols. 9–12 (Wilmington, N.C.: Broadfoot, 1990–91), passim.

When the Hicks U.S. General Hospital at Baltimore opened in June 1865, it had the latest pavilion style. But its large airy wards never held more than a few patients because the war had ended in April. (The Maryland Historical Society, Baltimore, Maryland)

Typical "Articles of Medical and Hospital Property" Carried by the Army of the Potomac on Its last Campaign, 1864–1865

Acacia	Collodion
Sulfuric acid	Ferric chloride
Tannic acid	Mercury pills
Tartaric acid	Morphine
Ether	Olive oil
Alcohol	Castor oil
Alum	Turpentine
Ammonium carbonate	Opium
Ammonia water	Whiskey
Spirits of ammonia	Brandy
Silver nitrate	Lead acetate
Camphor	Potassium arsenite
Cantharides	Potassium iodide
Chloroform (35 quarts)	Quinine
Liquid soap	Squill

Source: Compiled from *Official Records* by National Library of Medicine, *Medicine of the Civil War* (Washington, D.C.: U.S. Government Printing Office, n.d.), 9.

Contents of a Typical Confederate Medicine Wagon

Acetic acid	Columbo
Adhesive plaster	Copaiba
Alcohol	Creosote
Aloes	Digitalis
Ammonia water	Ether
Arsenic oxide	Hydrochloric acid
Asafetida	Hyoscyamus
Morphine sulfate	Rhubarb
Opium	Senna
Quinine sulfate	Sugar
Whiskey	Sulfuric acid

Source: Compiled from *Official Records* by National Library of Medicine, *Medicine of the Civil War* (Washington, D.C.: U.S. Government Printing Office, n.d.), 10.

Dueling Medical Theories

The medical profession of the day was a fractious group, much less monolithic than today. One historian has described the state of the medical arts in the United States at the time as "a galaxy of therapeutic measures touted in the laissez-faire shopping-mall [that was] American medicine." Rival schools or theories competed in the marketplace just as in politics or religion. The practitioners called M.D.'s today were commonly known as the "medical regulars" or "allopaths." Their opponents, the "irregulars," advocated a broad range of unorthodox therapies organized into several major groupings, all competing for a public following. The most important were the Thomsonians, the Eclectics ("Reform Medicine"), the homeopaths, and the hydropaths. Generally all the antiestablishment schools shared some common beliefs, which included an aversion to formal training, opposition to surgery and pharmaceutical drugs, and faith in "natural" cures or "folk medicine." In their laissez-faire attitude toward the practice of medicine, they regarded the idea of government regulation, licensing, and the like, with the same horror that classical economists did. The leading 19th-century branches of U.S. medicine have been described by one historian as follows: "The homeopaths administered their tiny doses; the allopaths purged their patients drastically; the hydropaths bathed and dunked; and the eclectics borrowed a little from each." The reality was more complicated, but because M.D.'s did not enjoy the virtual monopoly they have today, all groups competed more or less equally for patients and scientific credibility. In the long run, however, many proved more faddish than effective, and after the antebellum period, only homeopathy and eclecticism maintained both scientific credibility *and* a respectable following all the way to the end of the century.

All of the mid-19th-century alternative schools of medicine had a faith in the "natural" precepts of good hygiene and preventive medicine, which they promoted as reforms of traditional medical practice. They preached the health benefits of exercise, fresh air, bathing, nutritious eating, and sexual abstinence. One of the more progressive of the lot was the Harvard Medical School graduate George Winship, who began to preach on "physical culture" in the 1860s with the battle cry "Strength is health!" The five-foot-seven-inch, 143-pound advocate made his most lasting impact by introducing Americans to the benefits of weight lifting. He also favored an exclusively vegetarian diet. Some other men who made names for themselves around this time with unusual ideas on diet reform were the temperance preacher Sylvester Graham (who popularized Graham flour, which gave rise to "Graham crackers"), Dr. John Kellogg (the future cereal king of Battle Creek, Michigan), and the physician-educator William Alcott (opposed to meat eating). Most of these men were ridiculed as health fanatics or worse by cynical contemporaries such as Mark Twain. But their ideas still flourished, particularly among the health-conscious middle classes. One eccentricity of all of them was that they saw a direct connection between good digestion and sexual purity, advocating better diet as a way to controlling man's "animal desires." As a group they had a tremendous influence on Victorian sexual attitudes. But the supposed connections among morality, nutrition, and medicine that they perceived led most of their ideas to be ultimately consigned to the trash heap of quackery.

To compete better with the regular practitioners, some of the alternative groups established their own medical schools around the country, but none before 1850. Among the lot, the homeopaths and Eclectics were the most determined to raise standards and introduce some form of licensing. This bow toward regularization was strongly opposed by elements within both sects and as a result did not really become established until after 1875.

Growing professionalization scarcely slowed the proliferation of unconventional medical beliefs and outright charlatanism. Among the more bizarre systems were phrenology, physiognomy, "moral therapy," and "nature's way" (or Grahamism, named after Sylvester Graham), all of which had their passionate advocates and loyal patients. Even the watchdog American Medical Association could not quash every new theory or radical treatment that came down the pike. In 1864 Dr. Weir Mitchell, the respected Philadelphia neurologist, announced his theory of "causalgia" for neurological disorders. During the next 10 years he developed his theories further, until in 1875 he introduced the "rest cure" for treatment of various nervous conditions. His theories, some of which were highly sexist, had a profound effect on the subsequent development of modern psychology, influencing even Sigmund Freud. Weir, with his studies in toxicology, immunology, and the use of drugs, was precisely the kind of doctor whom the "irregular" prectitioners loved to hate.

TABLE 18.8 POPULAR ALTERNATIVE SYSTEMS OF MEDICINE, 1800s

Alternative Systems	Principal Concept(s)	Founder/ Spokesman	Origins	Centers	Followers	Definitive Writings	Opposed to	Peak Years of U.S. Popularity
Thomsonianism	Self-doctoring; botanical/vegetable-based medicines; classical theory of bodily "humors"	Samuel A. Thomson (1769–1843)[a]	1813[e]	Botanico-Medical College of Ohio (Cincinnati) and Family Botanic Societies in New England	Rural folks	*New Guide to Health* (Thomson, 1822); *The Thomsonian Recorder* (journal)	"Book doctors"; state licensing laws; pharmaceutical drugs	1830s (split after 1838)
Hydropathy	Good hygiene and purity; water-cure treatment, both internal and external	Vincent Priessnitz (1799–1851)[b]	1830s	Graefenberg, Austria; Malvern, Worcestshire, England; various U.S. water-cure spas	Middle and upper classes especially women	*The Water Cure in Chronic Disease* (Dr. James Gully, 1848); *Water-Cure Journal*	Conventional drugs, bleeding, purging	Second half of 19th century
Homeopathy	First law: Law of Similars ("Like cures like"); second law: "infinitesimals" (highly diluted drug dosages); third law: "with a little help, the body can cure itself"	Samuel Hahnemann (1755–1833); U.S. introduced by Johannis B. Gram (1825)[c]	Beginning of 19th century	Homeopathic clinics drugstores, dispensaries and hospitals	Fashionable among middle and upper classes	*Organon of the Art of Healing* (Hahnemann, 1810) *Handbook of Rational Healing* (Hahnemann, 1810)	"Heroic therapies" (bleeding, purging) and "heroic dosing" (heavy use of chemical drugs)	1830s to present
Eclecticism	Borrowing of "the best" of other on indigenous plants therapies; botanic medicine based	Constantine Smaltz Rafinesque (1784–1841); Wooster Beach (1794–1859)[d]	1830s	Reformed Medical College of New York; Reformed Medical College at Worthington, Ky.; Eclectic Medical Institute of Cincinnati (after 1845)	Schismatics from Thomsonian sect	*Medical Flora; or Manual of Medical Botany of the United States of North America* (Rafinesque, 1828–32); *The American Practice of Medicine* (Beach, 1833); *New Guide to Health; or Botanic Family Physician* (Thomson, 1835)	Heroic dosing; chemical-based medications; Thomsonian training and all traditional schools of medicine	Post–Civil War period

[a]An uneducated New England farmer.
[b]A Silesian (Austria) farmer.
[c]Hahnemann was a German physician; Gram was a Boston physician.
[d]The Connecticut-born Beach is considered the founder of the Eclectic school, which he called the "Reformed System" of medicine.
[e]In 1813 Thomson received a U.S. patent on his "medical system." He received a second patent on "Thomsonianism" in 1823.
Sources: James H. Cassedy, *Medicine in America: A Short History* (Baltimore: Johns Hopkins University Press, 1991), 33–39; Roy Porter, *The Greatest Benefit to Mankind* (New York: W. W. Norton, 1997), 389–94; Francis R. Packard, *History of Medicine in the United States,* vol. 2 (New York: Hafner, 1963), 1,227–39.

TABLE 18.9 ALTERNATIVE MEDICAL SCHOOLS IN THE UNITED STATES, 1850–1880

Year	Homeopathic			Eclectic			Other		
	Schools	Students	Graduates	Schools	Students	Graduates	Schools	Students	Graduates
1850	3	N/A	N/A	4	N/A	N/A	1	N/A	N/A
1860	6	N/A	N/A	4	N/A	N/A	2	N/A	N/A
1870	8	N/A	N/A	5	N/A	N/A	2	N/A	N/A
1880	14	1,220	380	8	830	188	2	N/A	N/A

Source: William G. Rothstein, *American Physicians in the Nineteenth Century* (Baltimore: Johns Hopkins University Press, 1972), 287.

In 1874 Dr. Andrew T. Still of Kansas pioneered a new branch of medicine that proved to be more permanent and mainstream than most of the contemporary unconventional theories. He called his system osteopathy because it stressed the importance of healthy bones and muscles to overall good health. His most radical contribution to the body of medical knowledge was the idea of "manipulations" to the muscular-skeletal structure to achieve a healthy physiological balance. Eventually doctors of osteopathy would be accepted as the principal rivals if not complete equals of M.D.'s.

Regardless of which school they followed, U.S. doctors as a group were far behind their European counterparts. Training on the American side of the Atlantic was indifferent, and general practice was backward, even fraudulent, in what it promised versus what it could deliver. While the best and the brightest gravitated toward law or theology when they went on to higher education, medicine tended to attract mediocrities, or worse. Coupled with ignorance and provincialism was a strong streak of male chauvinism that was only gradually overcome.

Incompetence extended from top to bottom throughout the medical profession. Nurses, the foot soldiers of the profession, were not regarded as genuine professionals but as menials. Until the Civil War the nursing field was closed to women because the work was considered unfit for them. Clara Barton, Dorothea Dix, Mary Ann ("Mother") Bickerdyke, Sally Tompkins, and a group of similarly determined women on both sides broke down the gender barrier during the war. Most were upper-class matrons; Harriet Tubman, a former slave, was the exception to both class and race stereotypes. From zero women nurses at the beginning of the war, the Union army was employing some 600 volunteers within a few months. After a while the government grudgingly paid them—about $12.00 per month plus rations and housing versus $20.50 per month plus better benefits for male nurses. On the Confederate side they were not put on the payroll, but Sally Tompkins was given a captain's commission in the army by President Jefferson Davis. Their main reward was the love and respect they received from the soldiers they served so selflessly. They became folk heroes, and the Florence Nightingale image of caring, angelic nurses gradually entered American popular culture. There was still no professional training required, only a strong stomach and a strong constitution, until 1873, when Bellevue (New York) Nursing School opened. That event marked the beginning of professional nursing in the United States, as well as the transformation of the title *nurse* into a gender-specific one in the public mind.

Women aiming to break down the sexist barriers at the upper levels of the medical profession were led by a group of pioneering female physicians, who included Emeline Horton Cleveland, Mary Putnam Jacobi, Hannah Myers Longshore, and Clara A. Swain. They had to take their training in one of two institutions: either the Woman's Medical College of Pennsylvania or the Woman's Medical College of the New York Infirmary. They established a remarkable record, in particular considering the odds against them. Dr. Cleveland performed the earliest instance of major surgery by a woman in 1875 (an ovariotomy). Dr. Jacobi was admitted to the prestigious École de Médicine in France and graduated with the highest honors in 1871. Dr. Longshore became the first woman faculty member of a medical school in the United States as a "demonstrator" at the Woman's Medical College of Pennsylvania in 1852. Dr. Swain became the first woman physician from the United States to work as a missionary in Asia when she went to Bareilly, India, in 1870. In time they advanced beyond the male chauvinist advice given by Mary Jacobi's father when she decided she wanted to go to medical school: "If you must be a doctor and a philosopher, be an attractive and agreeable one."

The Professionalization of Medicine

The professionalization or institutionalization of medicine with standardized procedures and practices was just getting under way in the mid-19th century. Physician training, like legal training, was based more on an antiquated apprenticeship system than on advanced schooling, and professionalization was still feared by most Americans because of its elitist, undemocratic image. Still, common sense dictated that a *trained* physician was better than an untrained or self-taught physician. By 1850 every large city in the country had at least one medical school, and every state had chartered one or more. But the best and the brightest of U.S. medical students still traveled to Europe to study at schools in Vienna, Paris, Edinburgh, or some other venerable medical center. For those less fortunate or with fewer financial resources, there were 85 medical schools in the United States at the beginning of this period, the majority of them located in the East, close to big cities and other institutions of higher learning. Those 85 included a lower tier of 28 rural medical schools, which constituted a distinctive national quirk of U.S. medical education. They offered cheaper tuition, lower living expenses, and less rigorous standards than their big-city counterparts. Of necessity they were also forced to depend on visiting faculty to conduct classes and to do without normal facilities for clinical instruction. Yet it is estimated that they trained almost one-third of all U.S. physicians educated in medical schools before the Civil War. The number of U.S. medical schools of all persuasions had risen to 108 by 1875.

U.S. medical schools were chartered by the states or other governing bodies; that was where oversight of their operations began and ended. Chartering was usually a mere formality, and financing was always problematical. As a result more than a few opened and closed quickly. When the Civil War increased the demand for doctors exponentially, a wave of "instant medical schools" sprang up turning out "instant doctors." Most of the established big-city schools were departments of major universities, and the number of those even before the Civil War was growing as the professionalization of medicine gained momentum. The best U.S. schools were based on the European model but still allowed for a strong dose of American populism and market forces: admission of almost anybody who showed up at the door with tuition in hand.

TABLE 18.10 NUMBERS OF DEGREE-GRANTING "REGULAR" MEDICAL SCHOOLS IN THE UNITED STATES, 1840–1880

Year	Total of All Schools	Number of Schools in Northeast[a]	Total Number of Students Enrolled[b]
1840	30	16	N/A
1850	44	17	N/A
1860	53	16	N/A
1870	60	N/A	N/A
1880	76	N/A	9,776

[a]The New England states, New York state, and Philadelphia, Pa.
[b]N.A. (not available) indicates that there was no official count of the exact numbers of medical students and graduates from U.S. schools before 1880.
Source: William G. Rothstein, *American Physicians in the Nineteenth Century* (Baltimore: The Johns Hopkins University Press, 1972), 93, 287.

Most physicians could best be described as country doctors who received training more in the manner of members of a trade than members of a profession. Those who chose to attend one of the numerous medical schools in the country found the course of study none too rigorous. The typical program of study at mid-century lasted only a year; it consisted of two four- to six-month terms for which $60 tuition was charged per term. The second term was usually a verbatim repetition of the first both because the faculty's knowledge was limited and because many students could not master it the first time around. Some textbooks were 50 or even 75 years old. By 1875 the situation had improved, and 95 percent of the schools now required a two-year program of study. However, some conditions did not improve: Laboratories and libraries were still inadequate, and exit exams were still a rarity. When Dr. Charles Eliot of Harvard Medical School had attempted to introduce written exams in 1869, he was rebuffed by the dean because "a majority of the students cannot write well enough [to pass]." After sitting through a year or two at most of medical school, the newly minted doctor was ready to hang out the shingle.

TABLE 18.11 NUMBER OF GRADUATES FROM U.S. MEDICAL SCHOOLS, 1840–1876

Years	Number of Graduates
1840–49	11,828
1850–59	17,213
1860–69	16,717
1870–76	14,704

Sources: John S. Billings, "Literature and Institutions," in *A Century of American Medicine,* Edward H. Clarke et al., eds. (Philadelphia: Lea, 1876), 359; Francis R. Packard, *History of Medicine in the United States,* vol. 2 (New York: Hafner, 1963), 1,213.

The overwhelming majority of physicians were general practitioners, but as professionalism spread, so did licensing and specialization. The trend toward professionalization that occurred during this period began with the establishment of the American Medical Association (AMA) in 1847. This organization of "regular" doctors filled the need for a national body of reputable physicians to set educational standards, evaluate innovations, and give the profession "a sense of concerted action." Within a few years the AMA was followed by various specialized medical societies, a development that was encouraged by the increasingly complex nature of the field as well as by the demands for expert faculty in the teaching schools. It began with the separation of dentistry from general surgery in 1840 and grew from there. The American Ophthalmological Society (1864), the American Otological Society (1868), and the American Neurological Association (1875) all followed after mid-century. The establishment of such specialized medical organizations would accelerate after 1875.

Professionalization was also aided by the growth of a professional literature written by doctors for doctors. By 1850 there were 24 U.S. medical journals in circulation, supplemented by a number of imported European journals that were avidly read by the top U.S. doctors.

Psychiatry

Psychiatric Medicine—the Early Years

In the entire field of medicine no discipline has been more controversial or less understood than psychiatry. In its early years it was the preserve of quacks and zealots with little true scientific basis. Until the end of the 18th century there had been no such field as psychiatry; it was not an acknowledged medical discipline. The study of the mind had its origins in the field of philosophy, only slowly separating itself from philosophical inquiry. In the mid-19th-century it was closely associated with such pseudosciences as phrenology, craniometry, and neurasthenia as Victorian humbugs. Its slow acceptance by the public was impeded by the fact that its subjects were the outcasts of society. In the small rural communities that composed the majority of the nation, those who were "mental aliens" or "queer" (i.e., odd) were shunned, confined, or banished. The usual solution was to lock them away at home or in one of the asylums maintained "for the support and maintenance of Ideots, Lunatics, and other persons of unsound minds," as these places were described in the bureaucratese of the day. The alternative to confinement, at least for those with enough money, was to seek out one of the high-society "nerve doctors" who dabbled in pseudotreatments for such vague ailments as melancholia, hysteria, nostalgia, and vapors.

U.S. medical thinking tended to follow the European lead, slavishly adopting whatever treatment model was in vogue across the Atlantic. The concept of "psychic medicine" as science was new and quite revolutionary when it first reached the American shores. But Americans quickly adapted it to New World attitudes.

According to the experts mental disorders in the 19th century were somatic, hereditary in nature, localized to specific areas of the brain ("faculties"), and accompanied by clear physical signs (e.g., a receding forehead). Most psychiatric disorders were blamed on "poisoned heredity," which meant that the mentally ill were a disgrace to their family as well as being social outcasts. For the mildly troubled with adequate financial means, there were numerous health spas around the country whose treatment methods rested on the benefits of "therapeutic water" and plenty of rest. For those without money or families to care for them, there were the asylums, both publicly and privately operated. Genuine hospitalization, as opposed to "institutionalization," under qualified doctors' care was not a realistic option until the 20th century. Nineteenth-century asylums were mostly hell-holes of abuse and neglect, a well-known fact that was dramatized in sensational form by Charles Read's novel *Hard Cash* in 1863.

Early in the 19th century most asylums were based on the relatively enlightened therapeutic model, offering their patients some kind of treatment that was usually as useless as it was well intentioned. But with the spread of reformism and growing attention to mental illness, institutionalization became a growth industry from the 1820s on. Mental hospitals sprang up all over the country, both public and private institutions. They were regarded as a tremendous leap forward in treatment of the mentally ill; they also provided a wealth of jobs for the new "mental doctors" and their allied staffs charged with treating the "chaotic darkness of the disordered soul." In addition to running their institutions, the experts were kept busy "certifying" the insane and serving as expert witnesses in criminal cases.

The practical demands of a frontier society soon overwhelmed the efforts of reformers and the abilities of the mental doctors to uplift others. The Civil War also diverted the medical profession and soaked up funds that had formerly gone to reformist causes. By the postwar period the therapeutic ideals of treatment and recovery were being abandoned everywhere as too utopian, not to mention too expensive. The new way in psychiatric care was the barbarous custodial model under which the mentally ill were locked up without any hope of release. New York's Willard State Hospital, opened in 1869, was the first U.S. institution to abandon all pretense of curing patients, opting instead to simply confining them for the protection of society. For the rest of the 19th century involuntary lockups became the norm as courts and "sane" family members held complete power over the poor unfortunates who were caught in the system. Patients lived out their life and died in these institutions, and when they were dead, they were even buried on the hospital grounds in small private cemeteries, their identity hidden behind a veil of legally imposed silence. Today tens of thousands of unmarked graves can still be seen in these now-abandoned cemeteries, mute testimony to the treatment meted out in the 19th century to powerless groups such as orphans, the physically disabled, and the mentally ill. Heroic reformers such as Dorothea Dix and Horace Mann, who preached that "unproductive" members of society should be protected as "wards of the state," were lonely voices. Entrenched social attitudes would not change for many years.

Counting the Mentally Ill

The 1850 census was only the second (1840 was the first) to attempt an enumeration of the nation's mentally ill. There was heated debate after the first census over the need for such a statistical accounting of a "useless" segment of the population. One government report stated that "idiots" as a class were "so utterly helpless that it is a waste of time even to collect any statistics concerning them." Even when such statistics were collected, they were highly suspect because of the lack of standardized terminology and methodology. But the raw data that were collected give at least some idea of the scope of the problem.

For the roughly 70 psychiatric institutions that existed during this period, it is possible to use hospital archives and government records to derive a profile of the patient population between 1850 and 1870. The figures show average annual admissions at the reporting hospitals to be fewer than 150 patients in most cases. The same historical sources also indicate the average number of patients treated in U.S. mental hospitals per year. The remarkably low numbers show not so much that the United States was a mentally healthy nation as that most mental patients were still hidden away at home or that their care assumed by charitable groups, as distinct from institutions.

The immature medical science of psychiatry did receive one helpful boost from the Civil War: The large numbers of mental breakdowns caused by combat (today termed posttraumatic stress disorder) and the damage wrought by four years of war on the national psyche encouraged greater scientific inquiry into the origins of mental illness. A growing segment of the nation's medical establishment began to focus attention on neurological medicine, led by men such as S. Weir Mitchell and William A. Hammond.

By the end of this period the professional organization of medicine was advancing steadily. Training and licensing for physicians had become the norm and were gaining acceptance for nurses. Nursing had even come to be accepted as a respectable occupation for women and an honest profession for either gender. Meanwhile as the senior members of the medical profession most physicians were still general practitioners, but regularization was proceeding as M.D.'s asserted control over their profession. Scientific advances in the field, however, did not translate to social advances. Medicine was still basically a white, Anglo-Saxon, Protestant, and male profession. Women doctors were not admitted to the American Medical Association until the 20th century. The profession was even more hostile to people of color. African Americans, barred from hospital staffs and medical societies, were forced to create a parallel medical establishment to serve their race. Catholics, who likewise found it advantageous to train their own doctors and operate their own hospitals, were only slightly better off in terms of medical treatment.

Three-quarters of the way through the century much medical care was still given at home and by family members, but increasing specialization and institutionalization were transforming medicine into more of a science than an art. Before the Civil War the only specializations within the field were surgery and dentistry. The postwar period witnessed the emergence of pharmacology, pathology, and neurology as major branches of medicine. Asepsis and anesthesia, however, were still lagging far behind in 1875.

TABLE 18.12 DEMOGRAPHICS OF THE MENTALLY ILL POPULATION OF THE UNITED STATES, 1858 AND 1868

(according to U.S. government studies)

Demographic Profile	1858	1868
Living in asylums	4,420	6,032
Living with families	2,055	2,208
Total	**6,475**	**8,240**
Less than 30 years old	1,313	1,660
30–50 Years old	2,658	3,382
More than 50 years old	2,504	3,198
Total	**6,475**	**8,240**
Married men	499	639
Married women	468	685
Unmarried men	2,809	3,453
Unmarried women	2,184	2,806
Widowers	173	195
Widows	342	462
Total	**6,475**	**8,240**
Deaths (as a percentage of total)	503 (7.7%)	557 (6.7%)
Certified cured*	520	626

Note: Probably the least reliable statistic. During the heyday of the mid-century "cult of curability," institutions and doctors frequently inflated their success rate by treating the same patients repeatedly and each time, after a brief treatment, declaring them "cured."
Source: Michael G. Mulhall, *The Dictionary of Statistics,* 4th ed., rev. (1899, reprint, Gale, 1969), 329.

TABLE 18.13 AVERAGE ANNUAL ADMISSIONS AND TOTAL NUMBER OF PATIENTS TREATED IN U.S. MENTAL HOSPITALS, 1850–1870

Year	Average Annual Admissions	Average Total Number of Patients Treated
1850	140	333
1851	136	323
1852	139	332
1853	156	354
1854	157	371
1855	129	313
1856	130	309
1857	134	337
1858	141	354
1859	137	351
1860	142	369
1861	131	368
1862	131	378
1863	127	375
1864	140	399
1865	154	417
1866	151	416
1867	162	432
1868	172	449
1869	183	480
1870	182	473

Source: Gerald N. Grob, *Mental Institutions in America* (New York: The Free Press, 1972), 371–72.

TABLE 18.14 NUMBERS OF INSANE PATIENTS IN THE UNITED STATES, 1850, 1860, 1870

(by medical determination, as reported in U.S. Census)

Year	Lunatics	Idiots	Total	Per 100,000 Inhabitants	Sex Ratio (Percentage of Males)		
					Lunatics	Idiots	Total
1850	15,610	15,790	31,400	136	51	60	55
1860	24,040	18,930	42,970	139	49	58	53
1870	37,430	24,530	61,960	161	47	60	53

Note: In the 19th century a pseudoscientific distinction was made between so-called idiots (the "feeble-minded") and "lunatics." The former category was understood to include the mentally deficient, or "those in whom the intellectual faculties have never been manifested," whereas the latter were those who were judged certifiably insane, whose mind was "diseased." Both groups were commonly confined in the same institutions and considered the same in the eyes of the law.
Source: Michael G. Mulhall, *The Dictionary of Statistics,* 4th ed., rev. (1899, reprint, Gale, 1969), 329.

The most important postwar change was the wave of dedicated hospitals constructed to replace the older multipurpose poorhouses and health spas that had long served only the two extremes of society. The historian James Cassedy calls the proliferation of hospitals after 1870 a true revolution in American medicine, representing a sea change in both thinking and treatment.

As in so much else the Civil War represented a watershed in the nation's medical history. The boom in hospital construction, the growth in specialized medicine, the collection of vital statistics, all gained immeasurably from the experience of wartime. The Civil War was the single most important factor in transforming medicine from a private and personal matter into a public and official matter with government on all levels taking an active part.

CHAPTER 19 Popular Culture

They want [lack] taste, and they want grace.

—Frances Trollope after traveling to the United States from England, 1832

"Popular culture" is everyday life, with the focus on work and leisure, entertainment, food, fashion, and the mass media. It is also their impact an people's values, their behavior, and their views of society and of the world at large.

As U.S. society in general was during this period, the nation's popular culture was transformed by industrialization, immigration, and war. Industrialization was directly related to the growth of a distinctive urban lifestyle. Immigration patterns began to dilute the early English-Scottish-Irish flavor of American culture. And the Civil War caused upheaval in every segment of American society but hit the South hardest: There a way of life was "gone with the wind" when the war ended.

Significant cultural changes occurred across the board in gender roles, lifestyles, artistic expression, and popular entertainment. But also like American society in general, popular culture was still largely shaped by agrarian, middle-class, Anglo-Saxon tastes at the end of the period, as at the beginning.

Family Life and Domesticity

Until mid-century the lives of rural people were still determined largely by their families and local communities, although the spread of democratic politics (Jacksonian democracy) and the ready availability of newspapers and magazines increased their exposure to the wider world beyond farm and village.

The family was the basic unit of American life; more than 3.5 million "households"—all the family members and servants or slaves living under one roof—were counted in 1850. On the average, households and families tended to be larger then; six or more generally constituted a household until about 1870 when the number started to drop. The reasons for the larger numbers are that having many children was considered a blessing on a farm and that even poorer families could afford to keep a servant or two, paid with room and board. The result was a whole different concept of the "nuclear family" from that of today—more than two generations lived under one roof, and live-in servants were considered part of the basic family unit.

The rise of urban industrial society put new stresses on the U.S. family, making something as basic as family size an issue. Middle-class couples consciously decided to limit the number of offspring, either through watching the calendar, adopting artificial birth control methods, or using abortion. Testimony to their success was the dramatic drop of 50 percent in birth rate during the 19th century.

Roles within the family were also changing, and again the middle class was at the forefront of the change. The last half of the 19th century represented the high tide of domesticity in the United States, a

TABLE 19.1 PROFILE OF U.S. HOUSEHOLDS, 1850–1870

Household	1850	1860	1870
U.S. population (total)	23,191,876	31,443,321	39,818,449
Households (total)[a]	3,600,000	5,200,000	7,600,000
Individuals per household[b]	6.4	6.0	5.1
Domestic servants (total)[c]	350,000	600,000	1,000,000
Domestic servants per 10 households[d]	1.0	1.2	1.3
Children younger than 5 per 10 white women[e]	8.92	9.05	8.14
Children older than 5 per 10 black women[e]	10.87	10.72	9.97

[a] These numbers are rounded off to the nearest 100,000.
[b] Includes both servants and slaves, along with family members.
[c] Does not include slaves.
[d] Includes those 10 years and older.
[e] Includes only women 20–44 years of age.
Source: Glenna Matthews, *"Just a Housewife": The Rise and Fall of Domesticity in America* (New York: Oxford University Press, 1987), 263–66.

An idealized Victorian family Christmas: Gathering around the tree and giving presents in the parlor were rituals available only to middle- and upper-class Americans. For the poor, Christmas was usually just another day. (Courtesy of the Georgia Historical Society)

movement encapsulated in the concept of the "separate spheres," which assigned men and women rigidly circumscribed roles in the family. The man was the breadwinner, money manager, and master of the family. The woman was the homemaker, nurturer, spiritual center, and guardian of purity in the home. The home became the "temple" of American family life. Industrialization contributed to the movement by providing the machinery, such as the stove and the sewing machine, that helped define home life.

Domesticity was a theme expounded in journals, advice books, popular novels, sermons, and even the legal system. It augmented the influence of women in a traditionally patriarchal society while severely limiting their opportunities outside the home. As a cultural ideology, domesticity helped define the United States as a middle-class nation.

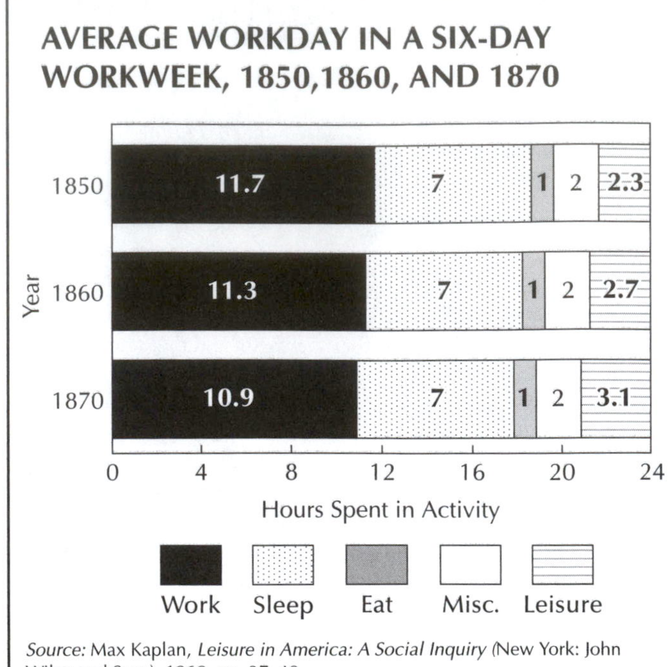

Source: Max Kaplan, *Leisure in America: A Social Inquiry* (New York: John Wiley and Sons), 1960, pp. 37–40.

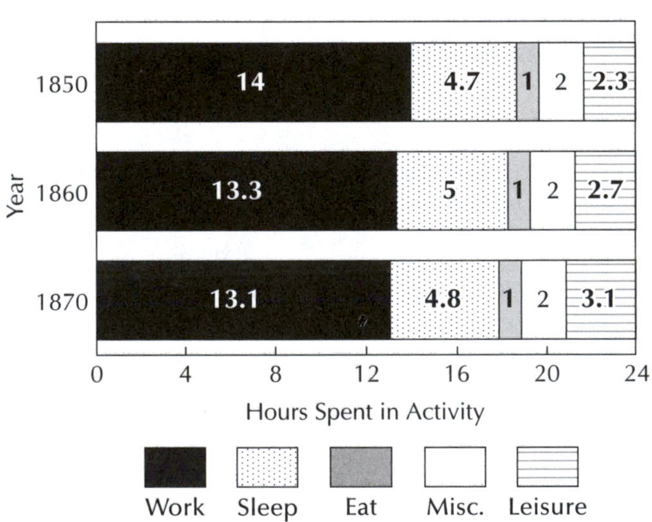

Source: Max Kaplan, *Leisure in America: A Social Inquiry* (New York: John Wiley and Sons, 1960), pp. 37–40.

The Rhythms of Life

The rhythms of U.S. life were shaped by race, work, and nature. These three elements merged most visibly in the South, which was also the most insular section of the country. Even after the abolition of slavery African Americans continued to be segregated both as a people and as a culture from white society. Southern blacks found that freedom did not produce equality. There were unspoken taboos and unwritten rules governing the relationship between races. Woe to anyone who broke those rules or violated those taboos. Many blacks preferred to pull up roots and head west in the hope of finding genuine freedom on the frontier. Known as "Exodusters" after the mid-1870s, their ranks produced thousands of black cowboys, miners, and homesteaders. Those who remained in "the land of cotton" were forced to create their own churches, schools, business districts, and other social institutions in order to live alongside but separately from their white neighbors. This situation produced two distinctive communities in every Southern town and city. During the years of Reconstruction at least, whites and blacks lived in uneasy concordance, overseen by federal troops and carpetbag governments. At the end of Reconstruction, however, African Americans seemed destined to remain a permanent underclass in the South.

For the white majority of Americans there was a certain sameness to life in the mid-19th century. The United States was still a preindustrial society, with a traditional social hierarchy that placed great importance on rank and status, distinguishable by dress and manner. Standards in taste and style were set by the rich and powerful, whom Thomas Jefferson had called "a natural aristocracy."

Life in a preindustrial society was generally slower and more flexible because it was shaped by the rhythms of the seasons, not by the clock. Rural Americans were still driven by the Puritan work ethic, which saw work as part of the natural order as well as an activity that consumed their daily lives. Work and leisure blended together; home and workplace were usually one and the same.

The typical workweek at mid-century was six days but was evolving slowly toward the modern concept of a five-day workweek. In a six-day week characteristic of agricultural America, work normally consumed 11 hours of the day. But while eating, sleeping, and miscellaneous duties remained constant from 1850 to 1870, the time allotted for leisure pursuits grew by nearly 35 percent. In a five-day workweek more characteristic of an industrialized, middle-class society, the hours taken up by work every day actually declined by about 6 percent between 1850 and 1870, and the time devoted to leisure increased by about the same 35 percent. Clearly whether they worked a five-day week or a six-day week, Americans were spending more time on fun and relaxation as the century progressed.

Leisure Time and Public Entertainments

Leisure time and organized entertainment were largely the provinc of the new middle class. They turned "play" into something as importan as work, yet playtime was not a complete repudiation of the old Purita work ethic so long as it was both fun and uplifting. Members of the mid dle class were quick to embrace the latest cultural fad if that contribute to the twin ideals of self-improvement and intellectual growth. Compara ble to a good dose of castor oil, museums, art galleries, libraries, lectures, and church were all seen as uplifting and therefore to be patronized. P. T. Barnum's eclectic American Museum in New York City (opened, 1841) set the early standard. It continued through the 1850s and the Civil War to be the most popular public museum in the United States, helping to make its owner a household name. Barnum proved that the average American would pay an admission fee (25 cents per person) and even stand in line to view examples of the strange and the exotic. When it burned down in 1865, he wasted no time reopening at a new location in New York City. (It also burned in 1868).

For the lower levels of society life continued to revolve around work, and they were known as the working class. What little time was left over from working and securing the basic necessities of life was spent in rowdy amusements within the ethnic group or the neighborhood.

Traditionally people made their own entertainment when the opportunity presented itself, and, therefore, leisure time was unstructured and unplanned. Indeed the whole concept of leisure time was new in American life, a by-product of industrialization that had made the workday inviolable, and any time off from work a precious commodity. Industrial wage earners were too tired to invest much energy or creativity in play, and white-collar workers who led nonphysical lives preferred the pleasures of spectator sports.

Public entertainment in the United States had always meant either holidays such as the Fourth of July or communitywide gatherings such as church picnics. As urbanization transformed work schedules and communal relationships, however, leisure became a more important element of daily life and, coupled with the rise of a money economy, produced the phenomenon of spectator sports.

A genuine sports mania swept the country in the 1850s as people discovered the joys of athletic competition. Most of the new games and sports that Americans took up were British imports, distinguished by their emphasis on rules and formal play as opposed to the more traditional American amusements, such as hunting, foot races, and log rolling. This era saw the rise of organized ("mass") sports, which crossed social and ethnic lines. Mass sports created the "fan" as distinct from the player and new community loyalties, channeled the pent-up physical energies of an increasingly sedentary urban population, and provided acceptable outlets for male aggression. On top of all that, they were highly profitable. In time ballparks and racetracks became the new arenas of public spectacle, and organized sports was on its way to becoming big business.

Entertainment was much more gender-specific than today. Historically the most popular male entertainments were drinking, gambling, and any sort of physical contest involving speed and/or strength. Gambling, for instance, was an honorable pursuit, and cock-fighting and bare-knuckle boxing always drew good crowds. Women, by contrast, were expected to find their entertainments at home, in small groups with other women or centered around the family. As the century progressed, several changes occurred. The traditional male entertainments received increasing criticism from the womenfolk as well as from social reformers, and the number of people watching spectator sports increased dramatically over the number personally involved.

A jubilant gentleman at Booth's Theater in 1873 springs up to show off his winning poker hand. In this, the dawn of organized sports, gambling was still the favorite pastime of the American male. (Arkansas History Commission)

The Rise of Spectator Sports

Horse Racing

A more civilized concept of "sports" began to replace traditionally brutal spectacles in the 19th century. The new sports combined the old bloodfests and contests of speed and strength with more enlightened concepts of teamwork and formal rules of play. Jingoism was an important part of the popular appeal, with international contests in sailing, boxing, and the like, serving as the World Series and Super Bowl of the day.

The three most important spectator sports were horse racing, prizefighting, and baseball. Horse racing, although known as "the sport of kings," proved just as popular with the masses of Americans, who held horses in such high regard that horse theft was widely considered a capital offense. Racing became a mass spectator sport when oval tracks were laid out, grandstands built, and betting formalized. The first organized stakes race in U.S. history (The Travers) was held at Saratoga Springs, New York, in 1864 on a track specially built for that purpose. Both the track and the regularly scheduled stakes meets proved immensely popular, as well as profitable for the organizers. In the years that followed, other deep-pocketed horse owners built public racetracks in the East, where the big populations and big money were. Baltimore's Pimlico Racetrack, built in 1870, aimed to steal away some of Saratoga's business with one of the finest courses in the country and the annual classic known as the Preakness stakes. In 1873 a group of Louisiana racing enthusiasts built the Fair Grounds racecourse at New Orleans to introduce Saratoga Springs–style racing to the South, and it too was a hit.

The big three (Triple Crown) of modern U.S. stakes races—the Belmont, the Preakness, and the Kentucky Derby—all started in these years, deriving their names from some distinguishing characteristic that fans could recognize instantly as representing the best in U.S. thoroughbred horse racing. The first running of the Belmont Stakes was in 1867, of the Preakness in 1873, and of the Kentucky Derby in 1875. After the inaugural race each became a regular event on the racing calendar every season.

Horse racing was America's first national sport, and the nation's first professional athletes were jockeys. Horse racing was also the first integrated sport, as black jockeys competed equally with white jockeys. The names of the African Americans Abe Hawkins and Ed "Brown Dick" Brown were well known to followers of the Kentucky Derby in these years, and their talents with horses were respected without regard to their color.

Two years after its first horse race, Pimlico Race Course at Baltimore, shown here 1875, could boast of a grandstand, a clubhouse, and a full slate of races every season. It was a rich man's sport, but the common folks would always watch and wager a few dollars. (The Maryland Historical Society, Baltimore, Maryland)

TABLE 19.2 THE BIG THREE STAKES RACES (TRIPLE CROWN) IN U.S. HORSE RACING, 1867–1875

Race	In Series	Date	Distance	Winning Horse	Winning Time	Winning Jockey
Belmont Stakes[a]	First annual	Jun. 19, 1867	1⅝ mi.	Ruthless	3:05 min.	J. Gilpatrick
Belmont Stakes	Second annual	Jun. 10, 1868	Same	General Duke	3:02 min.	Robert Swim
Belmont Stakes	Third annual	Jun. 5, 1869	Same	Fenian	3:04¼ min.	C. Miller
Belmont Stakes	Fourth annual	Jun. 4, 1870	Same	Kingfisher	2:59½ min.	W. Dick
Belmont Stakes	Fifth annual	Jun. 10, 1871	Same	Harry Bassett	2:56 min.	W. Miller
Belmont Stakes	Sixth annual	Jun. 1, 1872	Same	Joe Daniels	2:58¼ min.	James Rowe
Belmont Stakes	Seventh annual	Jun. 7, 1873	Same	Springbok	3:01¾ min.	James Rowe
Belmont Stakes	Eighth annual	Jun. 13, 1874	1½ mi.	Saxon	2:39½ min.	G. Barbee
Belmont Stakes	Ninth annual	Jun. 12, 1875	Same	Calvin	2:42¼ min.	Robert Swim
Preakness Stakes[b]	First annual	May 27, 1873	Unknown (varying distances over the years)	Survivor	2:43 min.	G. Barbee
Preakness Stakes	Second annual	May 26, 1874	Same	Culpepper	2:56½ min.	W. Donohue
Preakness Stakes	Third annual	May 28, 1875	Same	Tom Ochiltree	2:43½ min.	L. Hughes
Kentucky Derby[c]	First annual	May 17, 1875	Unknown	Aristides	2:37¼ min.	Oliver Lewis

[a] The race site was Jerome Park, New York, until 1889.
[b] The race site was Pimlico Track at Baltimore, Maryland.
[c] The site was Churchill Downs, Kentucky.
Source: Gordon Carruth, ed., *The Encyclopedia of American Facts and Dates,* 8th ed. (New York: Harper & Row, 1987), passim.

Boxing (Prizefighting)

Boxing in this era was more an organized brawl than a true sport, but that did not hurt its popularity; in fact it probably enhanced it among the male population. American boxing's roots were in Britain, but the American version seemed little more than an excuse for tough men to pummel each other into insensibility—or worse. Fights were bare-knuckle affairs, with no limit to the number of rounds and the marquis of Queensbury rules ignored if they were even known. Prize-fighting, with dueling and cock-fighting, was illegal in most states but was widely tolerated as part of male culture. It also suffered from an unsavory association with slavery: Southern plantation owners often pitted their toughest slaves against each other and wagered on the outcome. This aspect plus the savage violence were enough to raise a hue and cry against it by polite society. Enthusiasts attempted to clean up their sport's image by formulating rules, reporting major bouts as sporting events in respectable publications such as the *Police Gazette,* and, in 1849, publishing the first history of boxing in this country, *The American Fistiana.* But the "manly art" remained condemned and criminalized virtually everywhere.

One major problem was that the sport lacked a pantheon of identifiable heroes for whom fans could root. The world-class boxers were all British (either English or Irish), and the most successful American practitioners seemed to be little more than brawlers and "plug-uglies." The most renowned American pugilists of the day were Tom Hyer (unknown–1864) and John Carmel Heenan (1813–73).

After operating in the shadows for decades, U.S. boxing took off after 1849, thanks to a series of major matches, beginning with a bout between the New Yorker Tom Hyer, whose ring name was "Young America" or "The Chief," and the sport's unofficial reigning champion, the Irishman James Ambrose "Yankee" Sullivan. When Hyer won by a knockout, it was the first time an American had ever beaten a British champ in a match that meant anything. Hyer was promptly hailed as the U.S. champion, sans crown, and suddenly Americans had something else to brag about being better at than their British cousins. Hyer retired and U.S. boxing suffered without a recognized champion until 1853, when the immigrant Irishman John C. "Old Smoke" Morrissey beat Sullivan on a technicality.

Boxing was virtually an underground sport, with no official governing body, no rankings, and most fights staged in out-of-the-way places where the law was less likely to intervene. Some of the most celebrated fights were for national bragging rights rather than a purse or title.

The first sanctioned world heavyweight championship bout, in 1873, was between an American and an Englishman meeting in St. Louis, Missouri. This time the Englishman won, and the next official U.S.-British championship bout did not occur until 1892, after the Americans had found another worthy to send against Britain's best.

TABLE 19.3 MAJOR U.S. BOXING MATCHES, 1841–1876

Opponents (Nationality)[a]	Date	Site	Length of Fight[b]	Winner	Size of the Crowd	Prize Money	Notable for
James Ambrose "Yankee" Sullivan (I) v. Vincent Hammond (E)	1841	Philadelphia	Unknown	Sullivan	Unknown	$100	. . .
J. A. Sullivan (I) v. Tom Secor (A)	1842	New York Narrows	65 rounds	Sullivan	2,000 spectators	$300	. . .
J. A. Sullivan (I) v. William Bell (E)	1842	Hart Island, N.Y.	24 rounds	Sullivan	6,000 spectators	$300	. . .
Christopher Lilly (E) v. Thomas McCoy (I)	1842	Hastings, N.Y.	119 rounds	Lilly	12 boatloads of people	Unknown	McCoy killed, first ring death in U.S. boxing

(continued)

TABLE 19.3 (continued)

Opponents (Nationality)[a]	Date	Site	Length of Fight[b]	Winner	Size of the Crowd	Prize Money	Notable for
J. A. Sullivan (I) v. Robert Caunt (E)	1847	Harper's Ferry, Va.	Unknown	Sullivan	700 spectators	$1,000	Revived interest after McCoy scandal
J. A. Sullivan (I) v. Tom "Young America" Hyer (A)	1849	Still Ponds Heights, Md.	16 rounds	Hyer	Little more than 100 spectators	$5,000	First "modern" prizefight in United States, Hyer crowned unofficial U.S. champion
John "Old Smoke" Morrissey (I) v. George Thompson (E)	1852	Mare's Island, Calif.	Unknown	Morrissey	Unknown	$2,000	Supporters of both boxers brandished pistols during fight; Thompson took a dive
John Morrissey (I) v. J. A. Sullivan (I)	1853	Boston Corners, between New York and Massachusetts Streets	37 rounds	Morrissey	3,000–6,000 spectators	$1,000	Sullivan unable to answer bell for 38th round; his last professional fight
John Morrissey (I) v. John "Benicia Boy" Heenan (A)	1858	Island in St. Lawrence River, 80 miles from Buffalo, N.Y.	Unknown	Morrissey	Unknown	Unknown	Morrissey retired permanently after fight; Heenan assumed title "National Champion"
John Heenan (A) v. Tom Sayers (E)	Apr. 17, 1860	Farnborough, Hampshire, England	42 rounds (2 hr., 40 min.)	Draw	Unknown	Unknown	Sayers was undisputed British champion at the time; fought under marquis of Queensbury rules
John Heenan (A) v. Tom King (E)	1863	Wadhurst, Sussex, England	25 rounds	King	Unknown	Unknown	King was British champion at the time; Heenan's last challenge match
Joe Coburn (E) v. Mike McCoole (A)	May 5, 1863	Charleston, Md.	63 rounds	Coburn	Unknown	Unknown	Coburn proclaimed U.S. heavyweight boxing champion; retired in 1865
Tom Allen (E) v. Mike McCoole (A)	Jun. 15, 1869	St. Louis, Mo.	9 rounds	Allen (foul charged to McCoole)	Unknown	Unknown	Allen claimed U.S. championship
Jem Mace (E) v. Tom Allen (E)	May 10, 1870	Near Kennersville, La.	10 rounds	Mace	Unknown	Unknown	Mace claimed world heavy-weight title
Allen v. McCoole (rematch)	Sep. 23, 1873	Near St. Louis, Mo.	7 rounds	Allen	Unknown	Unknown	McCoole retired; Allen claimed world heavyweight title (bare-knuckle)
Tom Allen (E) v. Joe Goss (E)	1876	Ky.	37 rounds	Goss	Unknown	Unknown	Goss claimed world championship

[a] Nationality here is country of origin: (A), American; (E), English; (I), Irish.
[b] Then, as now, fights were measured in rounds; the fight time per round in those days was about 30 sec.
Sources: Gorton Carruth, *The Encyclopedia of American Facts and Dates,* 8th ed. (New York: Harper & Row, 1987), passim (see note on pp. 1,061/1,278); Robert L. Gale, *A Cultural Encyclopedia of the 1850s in America* (Westport, Conn.: Greenwood Press, 1993), 40–43.

Baseball

Although it had been around in one form or another for a long time, baseball became an organized sport in 1845 when the New York Knickerbockers were formed. The Knickerbockers and other teams established in the Northeast in subsequent years followed the "club" model, whereby all the players were expected to be amateurs, playing for the sheer love of the game while holding down a regular job. Professionals were denounced in these years for trying to "degrade our great National Game and make it a business." The darker side of this system was that it also contained a built-in class bias toward "gentlemen" players, who possessed both the leisure time and the money to join a team. In 1857 the gentlemen from 25 New York clubs formed the National Base Ball Players, and the next season 60 local teams took the field as members of the association. Despite the founders' best efforts, in the years that followed professionalism gradually crept into the sport; they were more successful in holding the line against vulgar behavior and crass commercialism.

Baseball's popularity soared in the Northeast and spread across the country from there. By 1867 there were 300 clubs in the nation, 10[illegible] of them in the Midwest, rising to 400 the following year in 18 states

TABLE 19.4 ORIGINAL RULES OF THE KNICKERBOCKER BASE BALL CLUB, 1845

(adopted by the club on September 23, 1845, and issued over the names of William R. Wheaton and William H. Tucker, Committee on By-laws)

Rule	Explanation
1st Rule	Members must strictly observe the time agreed upon for exercise, and be punctual in their attendance.
2nd Rule	When assembled for exercise, the President, or in his absence the Vice-President, shall appoint an Umpire, who shall keep the game in a book provided for that purpose, and note all violations of the By-laws and Rules during the time of exercise.
3rd Rule	The presiding officer shall designate two members as Captains, who shall retire and make the match to be played, observing at the same time that the players put opposite to each other should be as nearly equal as possible; the choice of sides to be then tossed for, and the *first in hand* to be decided in like manner.
4th Rule	The bases shall be from "home" to second base, forty-two paces; from first to third base, forty-two paces, equidistant.
5th Rule	No stump match shall be played on a regular day of exercise.
6th Rule	If there should not be a sufficient number of members of the Club present at the time agreed upon to commence exercise, gentlemen not members may be chosen in to make up the match, which *shall not be broken up* to take in members that may afterwards appear; but, in all cases, members shall have the preference, when present, at the making of a match.
7th Rule	If members appear after the game is commenced they may be chosen in if mutually agreed upon.
8th Rule	The game to consist of twenty one counts, or aces [i.e., runs]; but at the conclusion an equal number of hands must be played.
9th Rule	The ball must be pitched, and not thrown, for the bat.
10th Rule	A ball knocked out of the field, or outside the range of the first or third base, is foul.
11th Rule	Three balls being struck at and missed and the last one caught, is a hand out; if not caught is considered fair, and the striker bound to run.
12th Rule	If a ball be struck, or tipped, and caught, either flying or on the first bound, it is a hand out.
13th Rule	A player running the bases shall be out, if the ball is in the hands of an adversary on the base, or the runner is touched with it before he makes his base; it being understood, however, that in no instance is a ball to be thrown at him.
14th Rule	A player running who shall prevent an adversary from catching or getting the ball before making his base, is a hand out.
15th Rule	Three hands out, all out.
16th Rule	Players must take their strike in regular turn.
17th Rule	All disputes and differences relative to the game, to be decided by the Umpire, from which there is no appeal.
18th Rule	No ace or base can be made on a foul strike.
19th Rule	A runner cannot be put out in making one base, when a balk is made by the pitcher.
20th Rule	But one base allowed when a ball bounds out of the field when struck.

Source: Charles Peverelly, *The Book of American Pastimes* (New York: privately printed, 1866), 341–42.

and territories from New York to California. It was already being hailed as "the national game" in 1856, with box scores and team reports in major newspapers. Rivals for the title of "the national game" included cricket, foot ball [sic.], and racquets (tennis). Of them cricket was the strongest contender. Baseball and cricket were closely related in both rules and play, and the sporting press seemed to prefer the more gentlemanly game of cricket, but the U.S. public lined up behind baseball. At a time when many forces were pulling the country apart, baseball was one of the few national unifiers, leading one New Orleans newspaper in 1869 to inquire, "Would it not be pleasant to see the hatchet buried in the great national game [in] spite of the efforts of politicians to keep up ill feeling between the sections?"

Rules and play varied from city to city and region to region for many years before the Knickerbocker model captured control of the game. In 1845 the New Yorkers began to print up the rules or "by-laws" for their particular form of play and distribute them to all players and interested parties. Their basics included a diamond-shaped field and a batter's box ("the striker's point"), nine-man teams, and three strikes and three outs per side. Some of their ideas seem charmingly quaint today: Games were "exercise," at bats were "hands," and outs were "hands out." Deep hits were ruled "fouls," not home runs.

What began as the Knickerbocker club by-laws ultimately became known as the "New York Game," beating out the rival "Massachusetts Game" favored by New England clubs. By the Civil War virtually every club in the Northeast was playing the New York Game. The differences between the two versions were significant, causing one to wonder how the "national pastime" might have developed if it had followed the road less traveled.

TABLE 19.5 DIFFERENCES BETWEEN THE NEW YORK GAME AND THE MASSACHUSETTS GAME OF BASEBALL, 1850s

Point of Reference	New York Game	New England Game
Distance between bases	90 feet	60 feet
Type of base	Bags	Wooden stakes hammered into ground
Distance between "pitcher's point" and "striker's point"	15 yards	Unknown
Size and weight of ball	5½- to 6-oz. with diameter of 2¾–3½ in. (from 1854)	Smaller, and not standardized
Number of players to a side	9	10–14
Length of game	21-run limit until 1857; 9 innings after 1857	100-run limit
To get a runner out	Tag the runner or the base with the ball	Tag runner or base *or* hit the runner with the ball

Sources: Jonathan Fraser Light, *The Cultural Encyclopedia of Baseball* (Jefferson, N.C.: McFarland, 1997), 445, 491–92; George B. Kirsch, "Bats, Balls and Bullets: Baseball and the Civil War," *Civil War Times* Magazine, May 1998, 30–37.

The game spread to the college level in 1859, when Ivy League players took it up in intercollegiate competition, and it reached the West Coast in 1860, when the first clubs organized and began playing in San Francisco. Next to prospecting for gold, baseball proved to be the most popular outdoor activity among the overwhelmingly male population of that city.

Even the Civil War could not slow the irresistible spread of the game. On the contrary the conflict fostered expansion. Northeastern players introduced it to their midwestern compatriots in training camps and garrisons, and many Southern boys picked it up while incarcerated in Northern prisoner of war camps.

After the war as the practice of charging admission spread, unofficial championship matches were held, and city rivalries heated up, it was no longer possible to ignore the enormous money-making potential of the game. It had ceased to be a leisurely hobby for well-to-do gentlemen; it was fast becoming a business with skilled "employees" and expensive operations. In 1869 the Cincinnati Red Stockings broke with tradition and began to pay their players a regular salary tied to performance and popularity. Amateurism in big-time baseball was dead. Two years later the National Association of Base Ball Players gave way to the National Association of Professional Baseball Players with more than 1,000 teams represented. Baseball had changed a lot in the years between 1850 and 1875: from clubs and amateur players dressed in any old clothes to professional teams, uniforms, and paying spectators.

The popularity of baseball grew rapidly after the Civil War. One of the earliest professional clubs and a charter member of the National League was the Cincinnati Red Stockings, with their starting nine pictured here in 1869. (Library of Congress, LC-USZ62-844)

TABLE 19.6 EVOLUTION OF ORGANIZED BASEBALL, 1850–1875

Rule or Practice	Date Introduced	Significance
Team uniforms are worn.[a]	ca. 1851	Early step toward professionalization
Regular baseball coverage appears in newspapers.[b]	1853	Growing public interest in the game in general, and scores and players in particular
Size and weight of baseball are standardized for the first time.	1854	. . .
Twenty-five amateur clubs meet to form the National Association of Base Ball [sic.] Players, which is launched the following season.	1857–58	Rapid growth of the association, in membership and geographic distribution, reflecting broad popularity of the game
A new rule fixes the length of the game at nine innings.	1857	. . .
Admission to a game (50 cents at the gate) is charged.[c]	Jul. 20, 1858	Game not only fun but profitable
The first intercollegiate game is played.	Jul. 1, 1859	Game popular among all classes
The tradition of the "seventh inning stretch" begins.	1860	Fan ritual ever since
The first trophy is awarded (by the *New York Clipper* newspaper).	1861	Adds incentive to playing besides money and love of competition.
The first enclosed field (Union Grounds at Brooklyn, N.Y.) is used.	1862	Both introduces the challenge for "swinging for the fences" and makes it easier to charge admission
A new rule states that both balls *and* strikes are to be called by umpires.	1863	Shortens playing time; formerly only strikes called
Base stealing is introduced.[d]	1863	Innovation not covered in the rules
The rule against paying players rescinded.	1864	Recognition that most clubs are already "compensating" their best players in some form: birth of professionalism
The first intentional curve ball is thrown in a regular game (by William A. "Candy" Cummings of Brooklyn).	1864	Thought to be an optical illusion until Aug. 16, 1870, pitching demonstration by Fred Goldsmith

Rule or Practice	Date Introduced	Significance
The first gambling scandal occurs.[e]	1865	Association of game of skill and/or chance with, gambling; with gambling, eventual scandal
The first championship game (unofficial) is played.	1866	Not officially recognized by association, but highly popular with fans
The first history of the (U.S.) game is written by Harry Chadwick.	1867	Baseball becoming an institution
Cincinnati Red Stockings are the first to turn professional by paying all players a salary.	Mar. 15, 1869	Professional baseball
The National Association of Base Ball Players splits into two groups: professionals and "others."	1869	Contrast to earlier Knickerbocker refusal to play socially inferior or professional teams.
A new rule permits the batter to call for a high or low pitch.[f]	1871	Victory for batters in constant seesaw battle with pitchers
The National Association of *Professional* Baseball Players is organized.[g]	1871	Old amateur clubs no longer competitive against professionals
A new rule permits the pitcher to snap his delivery, though he still has to pitch underhand style.	1872	Advantage: pitcher
The size and weight of the ball are changed to their modern dimensions.	1872	Most significant change until 20th-century introduction of "designated hitter"
A baseball glove is first used in the field.[h]	1875	Soon a standard tool of the trade

[a] The New York Knickerbockers.
[b] The first newspaper to offer baseball stories was the *New York Mercury;* the stories were written by it editor, William Cauldwell.
[c] Fifteen hundred spectators pay to see Brooklyn play a team of New York All Stars. New York wins, 22–18.
[d] Eddie Cuthbert of the Philadelphia Keystones is the first player in the record books to have stolen a base successfully, in a game against the Brooklyn Atlantics this season.
[e] After a game between the New York Mutuals and the Brooklyn Eckfords on Sep. 28, 1865, won by Brooklyn, three of the Mutuals are accused of throwing the game for pay.
[f] This rule is rescinded in 1887.
[g] This replaces the old National Association of Base Ball Players (1857–71).
[h] Introduced by the Boston first baseman Charles G. Waite, whose glove is unpadded.
Sources: Gorton Carruth, ed., *Encyclopedia of American Facts and Dates,* 8th ed. (New York: Harper & Row, 1987), passim; Jonathan Fraser Light, *The Cultural Encyclopedia of Baseball* (Jefferson, N.C.: McFarland, 1997), various pages, 49, 171, 293, 475, 506, 662, 693, 765; John Thorn, Pete Palmer, et al., *Total Baseball: The Official Encyclopedia of Major League Baseball,* 5th ed. Appendix 1 ("Rules and Scoring"), 2,377–2,385.

Yachting

In the marketplace of sporting activities, even sports that could not lay claim to being "the national sport" attracted their share of fans and managed to carve out a respectable niche in popular culture. Among these niche sports was yachting, which lacked an "Everyman" appeal because of its expense and snobbishness. If horse racing was the sport of kings, then yachting's image made it the sport of gentlemen. Racing of small, expensive sailing vessels according to strictly formalized rules had occurred in Europe for years but did not make its debut in the United States until 1844 when the New York Yacht Club was organized. With its limited appeal and elitist aura, the sport did not take off immediately. The first dozen or so annual regattas were small club affairs. A second club was not organized until 12 years after the first, and only seven clubs were up and running by 1866.

TABLE 19.7 GROWTH OF AMERICAN YACHTING, 1844–1866

Name of Club	Location	Date Organized
New York Yacht Club	New York, N.Y.	Jul. 30, 1844
Hoboken Yacht Club	Hoboken, N.J.	Sep. 1, 1856
Brooklyn Yacht Club	Brooklyn, N.Y.	Fall 1857
Jersey City Yacht Club	Jersey City, N.J.	Jul. 23, 1858
Union Yacht Club	New York, N.Y.	Jan. 7, 1864
Ioni Yacht Club	New York, N.Y.	Sep. 12, 1865
Atlantic Yacht Club	New York, N.Y.	1866

Source: Charles A. Peverelly, *The Book of American Pastimes* (New York: Author, 1866), passim.

Yachting gained its major boost by beating the drum of nationalism, specifically by tweaking the nose of John Bull. In 1850 the New York yachtsman John Cox Stevens contracted for the construction of a 101-foot schooner to challenge British dominance of yachting, investing $20,000 of his own money. It would carry the colors of the New York Yacht Club, but he christened it *America* because it represented the nation. He threw down the gauntlet to the venerable Royal Yacht Squadron, and in October of the following year *America* bested a field of 14 British vessels in a 53-mile race in the English Channel, crossing the finish line seven miles ahead of the first English boat. For his efforts and expense Stevens and the New Yorkers won an unpretentious silver ewer known as the Royal Yacht Squadron Hundred Guinea Cup and ascendancy in the aristocratic world of yachting. In 1857 the cup was deeded to the New York Yacht Club as "a perpetual Challenge Cup for friendly competition between foreign countries," although the famous series of races did not begin until 12 years later. In 1869 the annual America's Cup Challenge was born (the race was the following year). There were eight more races before the end of the century and all were won by the cocky Yanks, a fact that eventually led to the prize's being named the America's Cup. Today it is the oldest trophy awarded for a regular championship match in any sport in the world. (In the 20th century the Americans won every race until 1984, the longest victory string in modern sports competition.)

Other Sports

A wide variety of other sports blossomed in the fertile U.S. soil, with varying degrees of popular appeal. Trotting and rowing, for instance, attracted a small but well-heeled following. Trotting never rivaled thoroughbred racing in popularity, but it grew enough to have its own race tracks and stakes races, whereas rowing initially seemed destined to be nothing more than an intramural event in the Ivy League. Most of the attention focused on the traditional Harvard–Yale boat races, which were interrupted by the Civil War in 1861 but resumed in 1864 with Northern victory in sight. By the 1870s rowing had produced some of the major sports heroes in the country, and collegiate sculling contests on the Hudson River could attract 60,000 spectators to line the banks.

Sculling was small peanuts, however, compared to croquet, another English import, which was introduced in America before the Civil War and slowly won a following, which was due to its cross-gender appeal and leisurely pace. The level of physical exertion allowed it to be played by men and women at the same time, in ordinary clothes, and required only slightly more skill than a party game. The veritable craze for croquet that peaked in the 1870s owed more to its compatibility with Victorian courting ideas than to its competitive challenge.

Skating, whether on blades or wheels, was the next sporting fad to catch the Victorian fancy. It was the sort of genteel but healthy activity that the middle class liked, and it had the same sort of coeducational appeal as croquet. Skating also demonstrated that technology played an important role in the new popularity of sports: Only after the introduction of steel-bladed skates (coupled with competitive meets) in the 1850s did ice skating become a major winter pastime. And roller skating captured the popular fancy only after the invention of a safe and efficient four-wheeled shoe. Beginning in New York City in 1863, roller skating spread across the urban America, catching on wherever public rinks could be profitably built.

The sports of "racquets" and lawn tennis were also English imports, the former arriving on the East Coast during the Civil War, and the latter imported to the United States in 1874 by an American woman returning from a holiday in Bermuda. Both flourished in the years following in direct proportion to the likelihood of beating the Brits at their own games, an attraction they shared with boxing, yachting, and cricket, although only boxing truly had the American rags-to-riches spirit. Velocipeding, the forerunner of bicycling, reached U.S. shores from France toward the end of the 1860s and quickly became another activity both sexes could do together.

In contrast to such games as croquet and lawn tennis, football was an all-male, red-blooded sport that, like so many other sports, was borrowed from the British, who called it rugby. Like American football the imported game quickly acquired a reputation as being brutal and dangerous, which only served to win a loyal following among young college lads looking for some way to test their mettle short of fighting Indians or dueling. The principal source of fans and players alike in these years were eastern colleges, until the presidents and trustees began banning the sport as too violent and barbaric. In an effort to clean up the game, the first code of football rules was drawn up by representatives of the Ivy League schools in 1873, patterning the game more on the soccer model than on the so-called Boston game played at Harvard.

Sports, as a term for athletic contests rather than for gentlemen gamblers, represented a major shift in American thinking and the new "sporting life" became a much-discussed topic in the public print. In former days that term denoted a life of gambling and debauchery, but

Badminton was a new sport in these years, recently arrived from England and very "civilized" because both men *and* women could play at the same time. (Library o[f] Congress)

now it meant a life of healthy physical activity—the "gospel of exercise." Large numbers of Americans who formerly would have shunned gratuitous physical activity when not on the job now took up hiking, bicycle riding, and calisthenics. This was particularly true of the middle class, who were always first to embrace the "new" in entertainment, fashion, and other lifestyle matters.

Less physical games were also a part of the new mix of leisure activities; of them chess and billiards made the biggest splash. U.S. chess players organized their own association in 1857 and sent their champion, Paul C. Morphy of New Orleans, to Europe to challenge the world's greatest masters. Morphy upheld U.S. honor for the next two years, beating all the Old World players he faced on the way to becoming the first identifiable American hero for a rather fusty and sedate game and helping to spark a chess boom in the United States. Around this same time billiards moved from the smoky saloon to the public hall, where challenge competitions were held. In 1858 the first national billiards championship was held at Fireman's Hall in Detroit, Michigan. Michael J. Phelan won the top prize after a championship match lasting nine and a half hours. Two years later the game entered intercollegiate competition when Harvard and Yale players squared off.

Entertainment for the Classes and the Masses

For the nonsporting members of society, stage plays, operas, minstrel shows, concerts, and circuses were important forms of mass entertainment. A trend in entertainment well under way by 1850 was commercialization: admission fees for more events, heavier promotion of those events, and more spacious venues. Whereas some public entertainments, such as the theater, had appeal across all social lines, others were definitely class oriented. Parades, boxing, dancing, and ninepins (bowling) were all working-class amusements; operas, balls, and symphony concerts were upper class. In sports, yachting, polo, lawn tennis, rowing, golf, and croquet were all pretty much limited to the upper classes, who could afford the equipment, the specially built playing fields, and the investment of time necessary to develop the specialized skills.

The spread of mass entertainment was accompanied by a drop in general admission prices. Theater tickets fell steadily between 1820 and 1850 until, by 1850, 50 cents represented an unofficial ceiling for everything except opera. Lowbrow entertainment such as variety and minstrel shows charged as little as five cents a head. Having large audiences were expected to compensate for cheaper ticket prices.

Grand Centennial Gala Day !

AT

Van Buren, SATURDAY, Nov. 4th.

W. W. COLE'S

The Mammoth, Model Show.

FAMOUS EVERYWHERE !

Larger than Ever. The Largest of all Zoological Collections ! Great Hippodrome, Museum and Circus ! Coming by Rail altogether. Thirty-six Railroad Cars. Its Leading Features are

A School of LIVING SEA LIONS, cost $20,000. The largest one, Neptune. weighing 9,000 pounds; eats forty lbs fresh fish daily; as large as a horse. The monster, KOODOO, he first one ever seen, weighs 3200 lbs. The giant KYLGHAN, only one in America. The Largest ASIATIC LIONS ever captured, as large as full grown cows. ROYAL BENGAL TIGERS!

AUSTRALIAN KANGAROOS, *MANATEES*, SEA COWS, SACRED CATTLE, GORRILLAS, BABOONS. *OSTRICHES*, JAGUARS, LEOPARDS, CAGES OF SINGING BIRDS, Beasts from all parts. In fact, the most varied and comprehensive collection LIVING ANIMALS ever seen South

W. W. Coles Grand Traveling Zoological Circus was one of many traveling shows that carried excitement and exotic entertainment to even small rural communities in the mid-1870s. This announcement would have appeared in the newspaper just a few days before the circus arrived in town to build anticipation. (Arkansas History Commission)

Here Comes the Circus!

As a result of the spread of Jacksonian democracy in the antebellum period, the formerly privileged worlds of culture and show business were thrown open to the common people. This not only had a refining effect on the masses but also had a democratizing effect on the performing arts. No form of show business symbolized the new democratic spirit in entertainment more than the circus. Actually a very old form of popular entertainment, it experienced a major revival during this period that eventually made the circus part of American national folklore. In its 19th-century incarnation the circus became a combination of acrobatic troupes, menageries, and horse shows, staged both in indoor halls and "under the big top." The tent shows took over the business as the years passed, partly because as the performances grew, large indoor spaces were harder to secure and scheduling of performance halls on tour was a logistical nightmare.

Traveling circuses became a familiar sight in the 1830s, and by the 1850s they were big business, thanks to the network of rail and steamboat connections across the country. By road, rail, and river boat the circus took big-time entertainment to small-town America. Some 40 major companies and numerous smaller outfits were on tour, making it possible for every village and hamlet to enjoy a visit at some point. The business was fiercely competitive, producing frequent mergers and bitter breakups. The classic case of this merger mania produced the last great touring circus of today out of the old P. T. Barnum, James A. Bailey, and Ringling Brothers Circuses.

That grand showman P. T. Barnum sent out his first touring show in 1851, calling it "the Grand Colossal Museum and Menagerie." It toured for four years before he shut it down to concentrate on his New York operations. In 1871 the 60-year-old Barnum joined forces with two other men to send his famous circus out on tour again. "Barnum's Great Traveling Museum, Menagerie, Caravan, Hippodrome, and Circus" was bigger and even more spectacular than before. His troupe included the Tom Thumb–like midget Admiral Dot, Essau the Bearded Boy, and a group of "Fijian cannibals," all performing under the world's largest tent (seating 5,000) with simultaneous action in three rings. The 1872 season launched the "golden age of circuses" that would last until the 1930s.

Virtually every circus included both human acts and a menagerie, the latter because people were fascinated by exotic creatures such as giraffes, elephants, and gorillas. The circus was the premier international form of entertainment also. Whereas European operas and concerts had a limited appeal on the American side of the Atlantic and American-style minstrel shows were less popular in nations that had abolished slavery, the circus had universal appeal. English circuses regularly toured the United States, and U.S. circuses returned the favor.

The most popular circuses of the day took their names from their owners (e.g., P. T. Barnum, Dan Rice), then added some thoroughly unsupportable claim to fame, such as "The Greatest Show on Earth." Business ethics and scruples were rare in the circus business. Frequent name changes were normal as partnerships were formed and dissolved and owners tried various creative variations in their advertising. A new union was usually announced by adding the word *United* or *Combined* to the title after the majority partner's name. In 1850 there were no fewer than 71 American circuses doing business in the United States, not counting visiting European companies. Twenty-five years later most of those circuses had been reorganized or bought out, but the numbers had scarcely changed, and at least 75 independent companies were identifiable, according to the circus historian George L. Chindahl.

The most powerful circus ownership was a New York cartel that called itself "the Syndicate" or sometimes simply "the Flatfoots." Before they were superseded by Barnum's "Greatest Show on Earth," these men enjoyed a virtual monopoly for the better part of five decades (ca. 1835–80), defining the mass entertainment business with their stable of stage shows, circuses, and menageries.

TABLE 19.8 LEADING U.S. CIRCUSES, 1800s

Name	Hometown/Venue	Years of Operation	Founder(s) and Operator(s)
Robinson Family Circus	Touring company (mostly in the South)	ca. 1824–1938	John Robinson, Sr. James M. Fitzgerald (Robinson)
Lafayette Amphitheater (Circus)	New York City (Canal Street)	1825–26	Charles Sandford
Mount Pitt Circus	New York City (Broome Street)[a]	1826–29	Charles Sandford
The New York Circus	New York City	1826–	James W. Bancker[b]
The Syndicate family of circuses and menageries	Westchester County, N.Y.	1835–75[c]	Shareholders group of 128 headed by board of five directors: James Raymond Hiram Waring Caleb S. Angevine Lewis B. Titus William Howe, Jr. ("the Flatfoots")
Howes' Circus (Howes' Great London Circus and Sanger's Royal British Menagerie)	Touring (United States and Europe)	1836–	Nathan Howes Seth B. Howes (brother) "Colonel" Joseph Cushing[d]
Bowery Amphitheater	New York City	1838–	A. J. Purdy Daniel Drew Isaac Van Amburgh
Dan Rice's Own Circus (Dan Rice's Great Show)	New Orleans (French Quarter)	1849–65	Dan Rice
Spalding & Rogers' Amphitheater	New Orleans	ca. 1857–58	Dr. George R. Spalding Charles J. Rogers
Spalding & Rogers Circus (including the Amburgh and Raymond Menagerie after 1854)	*The Floating Palace* (barge with paddleboat)[e]	Mar. 1852–62	Dr. Glibert R. Spalding Charles J. Rogers
The Mabie Brothers Circus	Touring	ca. 1840–64	Edmund Foster Mabie Jeremiah Mabie[f]
P. T. Barnum's Great Asiatic Caravan, Museum and Menagerie	Touring	1851–55	P. T. Barnum Seth B. Howes Sherwood Stratton
The Hippodrome	New York City (Broadway and 23rd Street)	May 2, 1853–	Richard B. Sands Seth B. Howes Henri Franconi
Rowe's Circus	San Francisco, (Kearney Street)	ca. 1849–54 1856–57	Joseph Andrew Rowe
Orton Circus	Touring	1854–71	Hiram Orton Miles Orton R. Z. Orton (after 1852)
Stokes' Circus	Touring (Midwest)	1849–63	Spencer Q. Stokes
"Yankee" Robinson's Great Show	Touring (mostly Midwest and Northeast)	ca. 1856–73	Fayette Lodawick Robinson[g]
George F. Bailey's Circus	Touring	1850s–75	George F. Bailey[h]
The Winter Circus (the Lent Circus or the Equescurriculum)	New York City (14th Street)	1850s–Aug. 1872	Lewis B. Lent[i]
Sands' Multiserial Combination Circus & Homophipocal Amphitheater Combined	New York City	ca. 1850–	Richard B. Sands
Lent's National Circus (New York Circus, Traveling World's Fair, Equescurriculum)	Touring	ca. 1857–74	Lewis B. Lent

Name	Hometown/Venue	Years of Operation	Founder(s) and Operator(s)
O'Brien's Great World's Fair/Six Consolidated Shows	Touring	1873–83	John V. O'Brien James L. Spalding Patrick Ryan
Castello's Circus	Touring	Antebellum years–1870	Dan Castello James Nixon and others
Van Amburgh's Circus	Touring	ca. 1821–65	Isaac A. Van Amburgh and others
Forepaugh's Circus & Menagerie[j]	Touring	1866–90	Adam Forepaugh Pogey O'Brien (with Dan Rice)
Grand National Circus (formerly Tom King Show)	Touring	1864–	John V. O'Brien
Thayer's Circus/New Circus	Touring	1870–86	Dr. J. L. Thayer
The Great Eastern Circus	Touring	ca. 1871–74	Miles Anthony (Andrew) Haight
Robinson & Howes Champion Circus	New York City (Winter Pavilion)	1863–64	John Robinson Seth B. Howes
The Hippotheatron	New York City (Broadway and 14th Street)[k]	1864–Dec. 24, 1872	James Cooke Lewis Lent
Barnum's Great Roman Hippodrome (Barnum's Hippodrome, Gilmore's Garden, Madison Square Garden)[l]	New York City (on Madison Square, between Fourth and Madison Avenues)	Apr. 1874–89	P. T. Barnum
Sell's Brothers Circus	Touring	1873–87; 1892–95	Willie Sells
Barnum's Great Traveling Museum, Menagerie, Caravan, Hippodrome, and Circus	Touring (opened in Brooklyn, N.Y.)	Apr. 10,1870–present[m]	Phineas T. Barnum William C. Coup Dan Costello
Ringling Brothers Classic & Comic Concert Company (later Ringling Brothers Carnival of Novelties)	Touring	1882–present[m]	German immigrant family: Al, Charles, Otto, John, Alf T., Gus, and Henry Rungeling [sic.] "Yankee" Robinson
Wallace Circus[n]	Touring	1884–1923	Ben Wallace

[a] The Broome Street address was said to be the biggest U.S. entertainment hall in at the time, seating 3,500 people.
[b] The first U.S. proprietor of a circus in the United States.
[c] George F. Bailey's Circus, the last of the legendary "Flatfoot" shows, closes this year, marking the end of an era in U.S. show business.
[d] Nathan Howes partnered with several men over the years, but he was always the dominant partner.
[e] The first river craft built specifically as a traveling circus venue, *The Floating Palace* was built at Cincinnati for $42,000, consisting of a stern-wheel paddleboat and a barge. The barge was 250 by 60 ft., had gas lighting, and could accommodate 3,400 spectators at a time. The boat was destroyed by fire in spring 1865.
[f] The Mabie Brothers Circus was bought out by Adam Forepaugh and Pogey O'Brien in 1866 or 1867 and thereafter toured as the Dan Rice Circus and Menagerie.
[g] F. L. Robinson was no relation to the John Robinson circus family, a fact that explains his chosen nickname, "Yankee."
[h] George F. Bailey went into business on his own after inheriting the Aaron Turner Circus in the 1850s. When he retired in 1875 he was the last of the old "Flatfooters."
[i] Lent sold out in 1872 to P. T. Barnum, who turned it into a "Museum."
[j] Adam Forepaugh first entered the business in 1863, added a menagerie in 1865, and began to tour under his own name in 1866 or 1867. In the early 1870s his was the largest circus touring by wagon, as most other major circuses had switched to rail transportation by that time. In 1881 Forepaugh invented the classic U.S. beauty pageant.
[k] America's only permanent circus venue at the time, its home was also known to New Yorkers as "Lent's Iron Building" because it was an architectural monstrosity of ugly sheet-iron construction.
[l] Barnum sold the property at the end of the 1874 season to take his show on the road. As Gilmore's Gardens it continued to host circuses through 1879, when its name was changed again, this time to Madison Square Garden, until it was demolished in 1889 to make way for a new Madison Square Garden.
[m] In its present incarnation it is Ringling Bros. and Barnum & Bailey's Circus.
[n] After 1906 the Hagenbeck-Wallace Circus.

Sources: George Chindahl, *History of the Circus in America* (Caldwell, Idaho: Caxton Printers, 1959), 240–72; Howard Loxton, *The Golden Age of the Circus* (New York: Smithmark, 1997), 20–31; John Culhane, *The American Circus* (New York: Henry Holt, 1990), 19, 104–5, 169–70; Marian Murray, *Circus!* (Westport, Conn.: Greenwood Press, 1956), 141.

Zoos (Menageries)

Zoological gardens have a very long tradition in European history, but most U.S. zoos in the 19th century were affiliated with circuses and called menageries. Two of the most famous zoo-circus combinations of the era were Dan Castello's Overland Circus and Menagerie and Raymond & Van Amburgh's Combined Circus & Menagerie. The menageries satisfied the public's curiosity and relative ignorance about exotic animals, particularly African species. The major crowd pleasers were the giraffes, the hippopotamuses, and the mighty elephants, all displayed in cramped cages with signs hung on the front that often as not displayed the exhibitor's own ignorance about the creatures by misspelling the name. At a time when there was considerable moral opposition to circuses and minstrel shows as crass, degrading spectacles, menageries were considered educational, comparable to museums. In truth they offered virtually no science, just old-fashioned showmanship, particularly with their trained wild animal shows, which blurred the distinction with circuses. By 1850 all the leading circuses included menageries, which were featured prominently in their advertising. Only a handful of menageries still toured independently, and whenever they arrived in small rural communities, they were always careful to emphasize that "no circus nor negro variety acts [i.e., minstrel performers]" were part of the show.

TABLE 19.9 MOST POPULAR MENAGERIES, 1830s–1880s

Name	Owner/ Proprietor	Known Years of Operation
Barnum's Asiatic Caravan, Museum & Menagerie	P. T. Barnum	1849–53
Raymond & Company's Menagerie	James R. Raymond	1840s–50s[a]
New York Zoological Institute	Group of 128 stockholders of the "Syndicate"	1835–70s
Central Park Menagerie, International Circus and Iroquois Indian Troupe	Denison W. Stone (proprietor)	ca. 1872–73
Castello's Overland Circus & Menagerie	James Nixon, Seth B. Howes, and Dan Castello (proprietors)	1868–69
Driesbach & Company's Menagerie	Johann Driesbach of Germany	ca. 1853–59
Mabie's Great Show, Circus, and Menagerie	Edmund Foster Mabie and Jeremiah Mabie (brothers)	1862–67
Sanger's Menagerie	H. F. Sanger	1871–78
Jones' Menagerie	Edmond Jones	ca. 1845
New York & New England Circus, Museum & Menagerie	O. J. Ferguson (proprietor) Charles F. Cooper (manager)	ca. 1880s
Older's Museum, Circus & Menagerie	Older	ca. 1870
Van Amburgh & Company's Menagerie	Isaac A. Van Amburgh	1840s–50s[a]
Waring, Raymond, & Weeks Menagerie	Noell E. Waring James Raymond Chauncey R. Weeks	1840s

[a] Raymond and Van Amburgh combined operations in 1852, under the convoluted name Raymond & Co.'s and Van Amburgh & Co.'s Combined Menageries. Van Amburgh's principal claim to fame was as the first U.S. "lion tamer" of note.
Source: George L. Chindahl, *A History of the Circus in America* (Caldwell, Idaho: Caxton Printers, 1959), 240–72.

TABLE 19.10 FAVORITE LYCEUM SPEAKERS, MID-19TH CENTURY

Speaker	Topics/Expertise
Daniel Webster	Politics and law
Caroline Beecher	Women's affairs and morality
Theodore Dwight	Social commentary, political affairs
Ralph Waldo Emerson	Literature, poetry readings, philosophy (i.e. transcendentalism)
Henry David Thoreau	Literature, philosophy
Oliver Wendell Holmes	Literary criticism, science, poetry readings, social commentary, law and politics
Theodore Parker	Politics, religion, reform, philosophy, abolition (e.g., "The Political Destiny of America")
Edgar Allan Poe	Poetry readings and literary criticism (e.g., "Selections from English Poetry with Critical Remarks")
Professor Louis Agassiz	Science, natural history (e.g., "Glaciers")
Edwin P. Whipple	Literary criticism
Starr King	Social commentary, humor (e.g., "The Ludicrous Side of Life")
Henry Ward Beecher	Religion, temperance, phrenology (e.g., "Sic Warnings" and "Popular Amusements")
Nellie Ames	Women's subjects, literature, social commentary
Josh Billings	Humor, social commentary
Professor W. D. Gunning	Geology and other scientific subjects
Colonel T. W. Higginson	Politics, economics, social commentary
Henry James	Literature, social commentary
The Honorable Charles Sumner (senator)	Politics
Mark Twain	Humor, travelogues

Sources: Macmillan Library Reference USA, *American Life, a Social History* (New York: Charles Scribner's Sons, 1993), 533; "Lyceums and Their Wants" (1869), in *Readings in American History*, ed. Oscar Handlin (New York: Alfred A. Knopf, 1957), 308–10.

Lectureships

A much more elevated form of mass entertainment was the lectureship, which appealed to both the populist and educational sensibilities of Americans. It was democratic without being too lowbrow and educational without being "highfalutin.'" In an age before radio and television and at a time when many people were barely literate, lectures filled an important role in the spread of knowledge. Moreover, Americans seemed to have a thirst for new knowledge even on such arcane subjects as geology and literary criticism. The old-fashioned educational lecture or demonstration had long been a New England staple, but in the 1830s a national lecture circuit of "lyceums" was organized to bring together noted public figures and audiences for both profit and edification. By the 1850s the lyceum movement was sending out a who's who of entertainers and educational speakers, always of "high moral character." One of the most popular speakers, Ralph Waldo Emerson, said, "The lyceum is my pulpit," and a lucrative pulpit it was. A popular speaker might be paid $75 or even $100 a night. For the lesser lights on the circuit and for appearances in "villages" as opposed to cities, $30 to $40 was the usual fee. Groups of 10 or more speakers could be packaged together for between $400 and $700 for the bunch. In 1869 the humorist Mark Twain was paid $100 an appearance plus expenses, whereas the more serious author Henry James was available for $50.

The lyceum movement flourished for more than 40 years (1820–60s) before giving way to less intellectual and more exciting rivals for the public's entertainment dollar. In 1869 it tried to reinvent itself when James Redpath founded the Boston Lyceum Bureau as "an intermediate agency between lyceums and lecturers." Even with a more businesslike approach and centralized management the movement continued to fade, but the intellectuals and puritans refused to admit defeat. The lectureship was reborn in the late 1870s in the guise of the chautauqua movement, with a more religious orientation. But during its heyday the lyceum movement symbolized the U.S. fondness for knowledge as entertainment, a phenomenon that reemerged in the 20th century as television's Public Broadcasting System (PBS).

Fairs and Expositions

Some of the more old-fashioned forms of entertainment continued to exercise a powerful hold on the masses at this time. Fairs and expositions as far back as the Middle Ages had been popular among tradesmen and farmers to display their goods in the most advantageous setting. These events also gave a certain holiday atmosphere to the mundane life of ordinary people. The growth of cities with their urban entertainments was a profound development but did not sweep away all that had come before. Rural residents still formed the majority of the nation's populace, so their interests had to be catered to by organizers. A series of agricultural fairs were held in the East and Midwest starting in the 1850s and continuing until 1876. Most were regional events, but a few were national. In both cases they attracted large numbers of both exhibitors and spectators. The largest were the

U.S. Agricultural Exhibitions held at Philadelphia (1856); Louisville, Kentucky (1857); and Richmond, Virginia (1859). Regional fairs were held at Syracuse, New York (1857), and Rochester, New York (1868). The regional events typically were glorified county fairs that attracted rural residents to see displays of giant watermelons, plump hogs, and new farm machinery. For farmers and stockmen they combined work and pleasure, and many men took their family. Some 50,000 visitors attended the fair at Rochester. By 1876, when Philadelphia held the Centennial Exposition, agricultural fairs had faded into the background of national life as attention shifted to the themes of technology and industrial progress. The farmer, interested in crop yields and animal husbandry, was rapidly becoming outmoded.

The great age of industrial expositions in America, focusing on progress and technology, was kicked off by the Crystal Palace Exhibition of the Industry of All Nations in New York City in 1853. The building that housed the exhibits itself was worth the visit with its soaring iron skeleton and glasswork that caused reporters to dub it "Aladdin's Palace." Billed as the first American world's fair, it shamelessly copied the British exhibition of the same name of two years earlier and prepared the way for the Centennial Exposition in Philadelphia in 1876. By 1867, nine years before the event, planning was already under way for the Philadelphia extravaganza. When not holding their own expositions, Americans were exhibiting the products of U.S. technology and factories in world's fairs overseas. It was the first exposure to "Yankee ingenuity" and "American know-how" for many Europeans.

Expositions such as the Rochester Fair and the Crystal Palace drew visitors streaming to see them from all over the country. But entertainment during these years also hit the road. It has been said that mass entertainment American-style had its birth when eastern agencies began to organize entertainers into traveling troupes and sending them out to the hinterlands to perform. Traveling across country was nothing new; booking agencies were the key to the new system in the Gilded Age. They could send top-quality actors and musicians into distant corners of the country, such as Maurice Barrymore to East Texas; Eddie Foy to Dodge City, Kansas; and Lilly Langtry to whistle-stops all across the Southwest.

"American know-how" was first exhibited to the world at London's Crystal Palace Exposition in 1851. (Library of Congress, Prints and Photographs Division [LC-USZ62-24803])

London's Crystal Palace Exposition was so successful that Americans copied it with the New York Crystal Palace for the Exhibition of the Industry of All Nations in 1853. The New York version, built by the firm of Carstensen & Gildemeister, was destroyed by fire in 1858 but not before launching the age of expositions in the United States. (Library of Congress, Prints and Photographs Division [LC-USZ62-421])

TABLE 19.11 WORLD'S FAIRS AND EXPOSITIONS, 1850–1870

Name	Date	Location
Pubblica Esposizione dei prodotti naturali e industrali della Toscana	1850	Florence, Italy
Great Exhibition of the Works of Industry of All Nations (the original "Crystal Palace")	1851	London, England
Exposition d'art industriel	1853	Brussels, Belgium
Exhibition of Art and Art-Industry	1853	Dublin, Ireland
Exhibition of the Industry of All Nations (the Crystal Palace)	1853–54	New York, N.Y.
New York Business Fair[a]	1853	New York, N.Y.
Exposition Universelle	1855	Paris, France
Esposizione Italiana	1861	Florence, Italy
International Exhibition	1862	London, England
Exhibition of Manufacture, Machines, and Fine Arts	1864	Dublin, Ireland
Metropolitan Fair in Aid of the U.S. Sanitary Commission	1864	New York, N.Y.
International Exposition	1865	Dunedin, Scotland
International Exhibition of Australia	1866–67	Melbourne, Australia
Exposition Retrospective	1866	Paris, France
Exposition Universalle	1867	Paris, France
Annual Exhibition of the American Institute	1869	New York, N.Y.

[a] A would-be World's Fair organized by Horace Greeley; it proved to be a financial disaster and killed enthusiasm for more U.S. fairs until after the Civil War.
Source: Smithsonian Institution, *The Books of the Fairs: Materials about* World's *Fairs, 1834–1916* (Chicago: American Library Association, 1992), passim.

The Public Parks Movement

As leisure time became a communal concept, cities began to set aside public land for the enjoyment of their residents who longed for an occasional taste of wide-open spaces or unspoiled nature. New York City's Central Park was the first large metropolitan green area, and it offered a variety of leisure activities, including ice skating from 1858. Other large cities soon followed with their own green areas. These parks served as social gathering places, urban oases where middle and working classes might escape, if only for a few hours, from the stresses and squalor of modern life. But working- and middle-class tastes diverged over the best ways to use the precious park areas: for flower gardens and band shells or picnickers and ball games?

The Culture of Drinking

Despite the growing organization of play and the proliferation of theaters and public halls, most red-blooded American males still preferred to spend their leisure time down at the tavern soaking up something other than high culture. In America, the tavern (or its western equivalent, the saloon) enjoyed special status as a social institution. It was a center of male drinking and socializing but also of riots and brawls. It was the favorite after-work spot of the laborer and the cowboy, respectively, and in any given community, taverns outnumbered churches, a fact often cited by reformers calling for their regulation.

The subculture of tavern and saloon revealed the shockingly permissive attitudes of the general population toward drinking and drunkenness. Nineteenth-century Americans were a hard-drinking lot, much more so than they are today, as a result of cultural influences as well as the tough environment in which they lived. According to the most credible studies, per capita consumption of distilled spirits rose gradually from about 2.5 gallons per person in the closing years of the 18th century to an all-time high of 3.25 gallons per person in 1860. That figure subsequently dropped as temperance reformers gained ascendancy and the cultural climate changed, until it was down to 1.45 gallons per capita by the end of the 19th century. One English visitor declared, "I am sure Americans can do nothing without a drink." The unofficial national beverage was whiskey (known by a variety of colorful names in different locales), replacing the two 18th-century favorites, rum and ale. Whiskey was cheap, easy to make, readily stored, and immune to spoilage, plus it packed a bigger kick per ounce than any other libation. It was used as a social stimulant, a medication, a comforter, and even a lubricant for the wheels of U.S. politics. By the middle of the 19th century rum and ale did not even register on the surveys of American drinking habits.

Although Americans were big-time imbibers by any measure, they were still choosy about what they drank, much preferring beer to either wine or hard liquor. Despite this bias they were not in the same league with certain European nations in terms of production capacity because they produced strictly for the home market. In sheer numbers of breweries the United States ranked third behind Britain and Germany, but ahead of France. (The French have always preferred wine to beer.) And in annual production U.S. breweries not only ranked behind those of the United Kingdom and Germany but also of France, Austria, and tiny Belgium. Still U.S. production more than doubled every decade after 1850, the result not just of population increase but of the fact that a large percentage of that population increase were immigrants from heavy beer-drinking countries (i.e., Ireland and Germany).

TABLE 19.12 AMERICAN ALCOHOL CONSUMPTION, 1850–1875

(per capita for every man, woman, child [in U.S. gallons])

Year	Spirits[a]	Wine[b]	Beer[c]	Total
1850	2.1	0.2	1.6	3.9
1855	2.2	0.2	2.7	5.1
1860	2.3	0.3	3.8	6.4
1865	2.1	0.3	3.5	5.9
1870	1.9	0.3	5.2	7.4
1875	1.7	0.5	6.2	8.4

Note: By necessity these figures represent general guidelines, not sophisticated statistical computations. They simply show patterns of drinking based on the best available numbers for three types of alcoholic beverage. Cider was no longer a factor in American alcohol consumption after 1830 because of changing tastes.
[a] Made from grain or fruit. Absolute alcohol content for 1850, 1865, and 1870 was 0.9; for 1855 and 1860, 1.0; for 1875, 0.8.
[b] Absolute alcohol content for 1850 and 1855 was less than 0.05; for 1860–75, 0.1.
[c] Absolute alcohol content for 1850 and 1855 was 0.1; for 1860 and 1865, 0.2; for 1870 and 1875, 0.3.
Source: W. J. Rorabaugh, *The Alcoholic Republic: An American Tradition* (New York: Oxford University Press, 1979), 232–33.

TABLE 19.13 CONSUMPTION OF ALCOHOL COMPARED TO THAT IN SELECTED EUROPEAN NATIONS 1851–1870

(per capita of total population [in U.S. gallons])

Country	1851–1860				1861–1870			
	Distilled Spirits	Wine	Beer	Total	Distilled Spirits	Wine	Beer	Total
United States	2.2	0.2	2.7	5.1	2.1	0.3	4.2	6.6
United Kingdom[a]	1.4	0.3	28.3	30.0	1.3	0.5	32.0	2.6
France	1.1	15.9	4.1	21.1	1.3	26.4	5.0	3.8
Holland	1.9	0.5	N/A[b]	2.4	2.0	0.5	N/A	2.5
Sweden	3.3	0.1	2.8	6.2	2.6	0.1	2.9	5.6

[a] Includes England, Scotland, and Ireland.
[b] N/A, not available.
Source: W. J. Rorabaugh, *The Alcoholic Republic: An American Tradition* (New York: Oxford University Press, 1979), 238–39.

TABLE 19.14 ANNUAL PRODUCTION OF U.S. BREWERIES COMPARED TO THOSE IN LEADING EUROPEAN COUNTRIES, 1840–1880

Year	United Kingdom	France	Germany	Austria	Belgium	United States
1840	650	92	500	160	100	23
1850	710	106	600	180	120	36
1860	770	140	700	200	140	100
1870	980	150	800	220	153	204
1880	1,020	180	815	240	200	413

Note: All figures are in millions of gallons.
Source: Michael G. Mulhall, *The Dictionary of Statistics,* 4th ed., rev. (London: George Routledge and Sons, 1899), 89.

Statistics on production and consumption furnished the ammunition that reformers needed to launch a broad-front assault on the drinking culture. With the exception of the abolition of slavery, no reform crusade of the mid-19th century stirred up as much passion as the temperance crusade. From pulpits, street corners, and the halls of state legislatures, reformers called for an organized effort to curb the use of intoxicants.

The movement really took off after Maine passed the nation's first statewide prohibition law in 1851 (an earlier New York law had been repealed after only two years). The ranks of reformers grew steadily until in 1869 delegates from 20 states met in Chicago to form the Prohibition Party, which ran candidates in every presidential election after 1872. Working against the temperance crusaders were a number of factors: Most Americans were not convinced of the evils of "demon rum" and all its relatives; Americans as a people, whatever their moral persuasion, do not like to be told how to live; and government on every level made good money from liquor and beer sales in the form of taxes and licenses. In fact the U.S. Internal Revenue Service during these years derived most of its regular receipts from sales of distilled spirits, fermented liquors, and tobacco.

TABLE 19.15 RECEIPTS OF THE U.S. INTERNAL REVENUE SERVICE, 1863–1875
(for fiscal years)

Fiscal Year[a]	Receipts from Distilled Spirits	Receipts from Fermented Liquors	Receipts from Tobacco	Aggregate Receipts (from All Sources)
1863	$5,176,530.50	$1,628,933.82	$3,097,620.47	$41,003,192.93
1864	$30,329,149.53	$2,290,009.14	$8,592,098.98	$116,965,578.26
1865	$18,731,422.45	$3,734,928.06	$11,401,373.10	$210,855,864.53
1866	$33,268,171.82	$5,220,552.72	$16,531,007.83	$310,120,448.13
1867	$33,542,951.72	$6,057,500.63	$19,765,148.41	$265,064,938.43
1868	$18,655,630.90	$5,955,868.92	$18,730,095.32	$190,374,925.59
1869	$45,071,230.86	$6,099,879.54	$23,430,707.88	$184,302,828.34
1870	$55,606,094.15	$6,319,126.90	$31,350,707.88	$184,302,828.34
1871	$46,281,848.10	$7,389,501.82	$33,578,907.18	$143,198,322.10
1872	$49,475,516.36	$8,258,498.46	$33,736,170.52	$130,890,096.90
1873	$52,099,371.78	$9,324,937.84	$34,386,303.09	$113,504,012.80
1874	$49,444,089.85	$9,304,679.72	$33,242,875.62	$102,191,016.98
1875	$52,081,991.12	$9,144,004.41	$37,303,461.88	$110,071,515.00
Total	$489,763,979.14	$80,728,431.98	$305,077,378.16	$2,102,845,488.33

Note: Congress passed the law collecting taxes on distilled spirits, fermented liquors, and tobacco on Jul. 1, 1862.
[a] The fiscal year is an accounting device used by the government. It covers the period from Sep. 1 of one year to Jun. 30 of the next year.
Source: The Cyclopaedia of Temperance and Prohibition (New York: Funk & Wagnalls, 1891), 254.

Food

Food is one of the most important defining elements of a culture. U.S. eating habits were notoriously bad up and down the social spectrum. Food quality was poor, cooking was an onerous job, and table manners were atrocious. Salt beef, corn, beans, and coarse bread, mixed together in various combinations, were the staples of the middle and lower classes. Fruits and vegetables were rare, and even had they been more available, they were not a normal part of the diet of most Americans. The Civil War veterans who had regular servings of fruit at the National Home in 1875 considered themselves privileged. The typical American's diet, where standards of living permitted choice, was remarkably heavy. People ate heartily—three square meals a day—if not healthfully. Already in the mid-19th century, observers noted a tendency of Americans to gain excessive weight as they grew older—and more prosperous. This trend was measured by the old-fashioned device of watching people regularly outgrow their clothes. The weekly menu of the Civil War soldiers' National Home in 1875 is indicative. The aging "boys in blue" packed away the victuals in proportions that suggest they were trying to compensate for going hungry or having to eat hardtack so often during the war. And although many complained about the services and facilities otherwise, by all accounts, they were more than pleased with the Home's rations.

The Fannie Farmer or Betty Crocker of her day was "Miss Beecher," and her *Domestic Recipe Book* was the standard reference work for homemakers. Cooking was considered part of the woman's sphere of responsibilities, unless none was around, when it fell on the unluckiest or least useful member of a male group. Dining out was rare except when traveling far from home, so the few restaurants there were did not make much effort to cater to their customers. There was not much chance of return business. Many restaurants were sidelines of the saloon business. Food quality standards and health inspections were matters of conscience, not law.

Three developments made a profound impact on American eating habits after the Civil War: refrigeration, rapid transportation by rail, and industrialization of food processing. The icebox, which *Godey's* called a "necessity of life" in 1850, made it possible to keep butter and milk longer. The railroad made it possible for midwestern farmers to eat fresh oysters and salmon and for Easterners to eat fresh beef. More efficient canning by companies such as Van Camp and Borden's introduced such culinary delights as canned peaches, beans in tomato sauce, and condensed milk to even the most isolated settlements.

In 1863 the Great Atlantic Tea Company (forerunner of the A&P grocery store chain) first began to sell a full line of canned foods to the public. Together all these technological advances made it possible to add variety to traditional diets and keep foods fresh much longer. The cookbook as a standard adjunct to the home kitchen was still decades away. American food remained depressingly plain and unhealthily heavy throughout this period.

TABLE 19.16 TYPICAL WEEK'S MENU AT THE NATIONAL HOME FOR CIVIL WAR VETERANS, 1875

Meal[a]	Sunday	Monday	Tuesday	Wednesday	Thursday	Friday	Saturday
Breakfast	Boiled ham Potatoes Brown bread and butter Coffee	Corned beef Potatoes Bread and butter Coffee	Irish stew Potatoes Bread and butter Coffee	Beef Stewed onions Potatoes Bread and butter Coffee	Shoulders Potatoes Bread and butter Coffee	Mackerel Stewed onions Potatoes Bread and butter Coffee	Beef fricassee Bread and butter Coffee
Dinner	Roast mutton Potatoes Beets Bread and butter Pie Coffee	Vegetable soup Boiled beef Potatoes Bread Crackers	Pork loins Peas or green beans Cucumbers Bread and butter Coffee	Roast mutton Tomatoes Brown and white bread Coffee	Roast beef Potatoes Bread and Butter Pie Coffee	Corned beef Cabbage Potatoes Bread and butter Coffee	Pork or bacon Beans Cucumbers Potatoes Bread and butter Coffee
Supper	Bread and butter Cookies Fruit Tomatoes Tea	Mush and "sirup" Warm biscuit and butter Cheese Tea	Bread and butter Cake Fruit Tea	Cold beef or tongue Beets Bread and butter Tea	Warm biscuit Bread and butter Fruit Tea	Bread and butter Cake Fruit Tea	Rice and "sirup" Bread Biscuit Cheese Tea

Note: This is the menu for the week Jun. 19–25, 1875.
[a] Typically in the 19th century the main meal was served in the middle of the day (dinner) and a lighter meal in the evening (supper). Today most Americans prefer a lighter meal at midday (lunch) and their main meal in the evening (dinner).
Source: Patrick J. Kelly, *Creating a National Home* (Cambridge, Mass.: Harvard University Press, 1997), 151.

Fashion

Fashion is another defining element of culture. American clothing fashions of the day were conservative, gender-specific, and far from comfortable. What Americans wore was heavily influenced by the Victorian style prevalent in England at the time. The clothing of both genders was heavy and quite complicated to put on and take off. When going out for business or social occasions, men wore somber black suits with waistcoats (vests), starched shirts, and ties. Women wore full, long dresses, high-necked, in one of several basic colors or Scottish plaid. Hoops, petticoats, corsets, and bustles were added for more formal occasions. The crinoline or hoop skirt grew in both popularity and bulk from mid-century until the 1870s. Bonnets and cloaks or shawls completed the standard woman's attire in public. The frilled trousers known as bloomers (worn under a skirt) were a brief fad among women who were more independent-minded than fashion-conscious. Women's fashions closely followed the European lead, as interpreted for Americans by a handful of fashion magazines, the most influential of which was *Godey's Lady's Book* (1830–98).

For home and work, men and women both wore homespun clothing. After mid-century denim jeans became the preferred pants for miners, farmers, and cowboys. Ready-made clothes, bought in a store, were just coming into vogue at mid-century, and they received a major boost with wartime production of uniforms for the soldiers during the Civil War. All men wore a hat of one style or another: Stove-pipe hats starting around mid-century, bowlers from the 1860s on, "cowboy hats" out West. In 1865 John B. Stetson, a small-time Philadelphia hatmaker, introduced the trendsetting hat named after its creator. The Stetson was instantly recognizable by its broad brim and tall crown decorated with ornamental braids known as galloons. An English visitor to the United States in 1850 noted that "all classes of people are well-dressed and the cast-off clothes of one class are never worn by another."

While women's fashions would continue to change and evolve throughout the 19th century, men's dress by the 1860s had reached a fashion dead end. The business suit consisting of coat, vest, and trousers was permanently entrenched in the male wardrobe. At least two of the three pieces were expected to match in color and

The curious attire known as "bloomers" (after Amelia Bloomer) consisted of frilled trousers gathered about the ankles and worn under a short skirt, thus preserving modesty while increasing freedom of movement. In this 1851 lithograph by N. Currier, the 18-year-old daughter of "a well-known West End [Boston] citizen" is seen on a stroll through town dressed to the nines in "pink satin bloomers and a round hat." (Library of Congress)

fabric. Trousers had changed most since grandfather's time: Knee-breeches were out, replaced by stove-pipe legs extending all the way to the shoe tops. The knotted, four-in-hand tie was standard attire for refined men, and it was the only article of male clothing for which bright colors were acceptable in fashionable society. Otherwise men's clothing tended to be somber, dominated by blacks, browns, and blues. Hats were still de rigeur, although the derby and porkpie had largely replaced the top hat for the upper classes. Working-class males might wear a suit once a year; the rest of the time they favored coveralls with caps as the essential headgear. The choice in footwear for all classes of men was either high-top, lace-up shoes or boots.

All infant children were attired in dresses. Boys graduated to short pants as soon as they could walk. The Victorian middle class also forced their boys to endure years of wearing Fauntleroy suits of velvet with lace collars until they were finally allowed as teenagers to adopt the attire of their father. Among the middle class in the second half of the 19th century variations were possible, of course, but a modern time traveler who suddenly appeared in any of these would not appear to be out of place either on the street or in the parlor during the years from 1850 to 1875.

TABLE 19.17 CONVENTIONAL FASHION FOR THE MIDDLE-CLASS AMERICAN MALE, 1850–1875

Article of Clothing	Usually Worn by	Worn during or for	Preferred Color(s)	Preferred Fabric(s)	Other Identifying Characteristics
Dress Coat					
Prince Albert	Conservative and older men	Formal occasions (nighttime)	Black or brown	Broadcloth	Knee-length, snug-fitting
Sack coat	Young and more liberal-minded men	Daytime	White or dark brown	Tweed	Box-shaped
Cutaway	Professionals and businessmen	Sport Morning coat	Solid colors	Tweed	Midthigh length
Tails	Conservatives, dandies, high society	Daytime	Black	Broadcloth	Waist length in front; tails to just above knees
Vest	Middle and upper classes	Formal and causal occasions	Plaids, checks, embroidered, quilted	Whatever matches coat	Worn more for fashion than necessity; single- or double-breasted
Shirt	All men[a]	All occasions	White	Cotton	Great collar style variation; detachable collars and cuffs; frilly fronts unacceptable
Trousers	All men	All occasions	Quite subdued colors; checks, plaids, or stripes for casual wear; always black for formal wear	Wool Denim (jeans) in West	Fitted waist, stove-pipe legs; button-up fly; no cuffs or creases
Ties					
Cravat	Upper and middle classes	Casual or more formal occasions	Any color	Silk	Four to six inches wide; typically 24 to 30 in. long
Bow	Westerners	All occasions	Black, plaid, or striped	String or ribbon	None
Four-in-hand	Most fashionable men	All occasions	Usually brilliant colors	Silk	Conveyed somber, neat image befitting Victorian ideals
Hat					
Derby	Gentlemen	All but most formal occasions	Black, brown, or tan	Felt with silk trim and/or liner	Modeled on English bowler hat
Cap	Working class	All occasions	Any	Wool	Some with visors
Porkpie or slouch	Lower middle class; Southern planters before Civil War	All occasions	Beige or white	Felt	Broad brim, low corwn
10-Gallon	Westerners	Work; protection from Sun	Beige, black, or white	Felt	Broad brim, high crown; assumed classic form with Stetson
Underwear ("Drawers" or "Union Suit")	All respectable men	All occasions	Blue or red	Wool, cotton, or flannel depending on season and availability	Tended to be heavy, bulky, and uncomfortable; shorter briefs or boxers unknown

[a] Up until about 1865 some men still wore stiffly starched false front shirts or "dickeys."
Source: William Harlan Shaw, *American Men's Wear, 1861–1982* (Baton Rouge, La.: Oracle Press, 1982), 6–10.

Urban Culture

The growth and diversity of U.S. cities during this time created a new urban culture unlike town life in former days. Taverns were just one element of it. Another were theaters, which lost their patrician exclusiveness and began to stage melodramas, musical comedies, and minstrel shows, all aimed at working-class audiences. New theaters offering the new-style entertainment included New York's Lafayette Circus and Bowery Theater. Meanwhile the upper classes withdrew to more respectable venues to watch Shakespeare and other classic works.

Working-class entertainments, like the working class itself, made the middle and upper classes nervous. Rowdyism and lack of respect alarmed polite folks, causing them to create professional police forces (replacing the traditional night watchmen), withdraw into sheltered urban enclaves, form exclusive private clubs and fraternal organizations, create elaborate codes of etiquette, and launch temperance crusades. Even the words used to describe the working classes and urban poor were revealing: They were now "the dangerous classes." All of these developments signaled a breakdown in the traditional sense of community.

The growth of a distinctively urban society accelerated after the Civil War. It was accompanied by a rising standard of living (a peculiarly American concept), fed by such new institutions as the department store. A. T. Stewart's "Marble Palace" in New York City was the largest and fanciest emporium in the country, and several degrees removed from the typical small-town dry goods store where most Americans shopped.

Among the most prized benefits of urban living were regular bathing and indoor plumbing. For centuries bathing had been regarded as either a luxury or an eccentricity in the Old World. Its acceptance among the masses of Americans required a revolution in thinking about matters of hygiene, plus practical improvements in plumbing, including expanded municipal water works and extensive underground piping. Many Americans were introduced to the pleasures of gas lighting, steam heat, and indoor plumbing when they visited one of the major cities. The nation's first public bathrooms were in big-city hotels such as Boston's Tremont House, and they were tastefully separated into water closets (i.e., toilets) and bathing rooms (i.e., single-person bathtubs). As city governments recognized the health benefits of regular bathing, they began to build public baths for the poor, led by New York in 1852. By the Civil War public baths were still rare outside big cities, but bathing was considered such an important measure of public health that the U.S. Census included a count of the number of bathtubs. In 1860 Boston had 3,910 tubs, an impressive-sounding number until one remembers that the city's resident population was nearly 178,000, a ratio of about one tub per every 45 people. Even in New York City, where most of the hotels now offered bathing facilities for their guests, in the city at large there was only one bathtub for every 463 persons. Baltimore in 1860 had a ratio of one tub for every 84 citizens, making it one of the "cleanest" U.S. cities. Much more typical of the nation as a whole was Albany, New York, with only 19 tubs for a population of 62,367, or one tub for every 3,282 citizens.

The growing gap between rich and poor was more than a matter of bathrooms. The more egalitarian nature of agrarian society was being superseded by the extremes of wealth and poverty found in industrial societies. The new industrialism concentrated more and more of the nation's wealth in fewer and fewer hands. The new superwealthy nouveau riche were first castigated by Mark Twain and Charles Dudley Warner in their realistic novel *The Gilded Age* (1873). With incomes topping hundreds of thousands of dollars per year and no income tax, the nouveau riche were on the way to becoming a permanent aristocracy of wealth, built on investment and financial manipulation, most believed, rather than talent and hard work; they were the idle rich. They violated the sacred principles of the Puritan work ethic, enjoying a hedonistic pursuit of money and leisure that one critic called "conspicuous consumption." Meanwhile the poorer classes learned to subsist on as little as $5.25 per week for a family of four.

Callous disregard for the working poor was so ingrained in U.S. society that the presidential candidate James Buchanan could remark in 1856 that 10 cents a day was "wage enough for a workingman"—and be elected to the nation's highest office.

With the entry of large numbers of women and children into the workforce, the culture of work changed, blurring gender roles and family relationships. The urban poor lived much of their life on the streets, quite literally, because their small, poorly lighted and poorly ventilated private living quarters limited any sort of social interaction indoors. They gathered on the stoop or the street. In 1866 the New York City Board of Health found 400,000 people living in overcrowded tenements with no windows and another 20,000 living in cellars below the water table so that their apartment flooded at high tide every day. The city ordered the cellars closed and 46,000 windows cut in airless rooms, but this order did little to alleviate the situation.

TABLE 19.18 WORKING-CLASS COST OF LIVING, 1853

(for a typical urban working-class family of four, per week and per year [in 1853 prices])

Item	Per Week[a]	Per Year
Rent[b]	$1.92	$100.00
Clothing and bedding[c]	2.54	132.00
Furnishings ("kitchen and parlor, etc.")	0.38	20.00
Fuel[d]	0.35	18.00
Lights[e]	0.19	10.00
Physician's and druggist's bills[f]	0.19	10.00
Traveling (i.e., for family trips)	0.23	12.00
Taxes[g]	0.10	5.00
Newspapers, postage, and library fee	0.19	10.00
Church pew (rental)	0.19	10.00
Food[i]	$5.25	$273.00
Bread at $0.06 per loaf	. . .	. . .
Butter at $0.02¼ per pound	. . .	. . .
Beef ("good") at $0.08 per pound	. . .	. . .
Beef ("bad") at $0.12 per pound	. . .	. . .
Lamb at $0.12½ per pound	. . .	. . .
Veal at $0.08–at $0.14 per pound	. . .	. . .
Potatoes at $0.25 per peck	. . .	. . .
Apples at $0.75 per peck	. . .	. . .
Total Living Expenses	$11.54	$600.00

[a] The actual *Times* budget was calculated by the year. The weekly figures are extrapolated from the annual figures.
[b] For a three-room apartment on an upper floor.
[c] Estimating $33 per year per person.
[d] Including three tons of coal per year, pine wood, and charcoal.
[e] Including candles at $0.16 per pound and whale oil at $1.50 per gallon.
[f] Including doctor's house calls and prescribed medicines.
[g] Includes city and county taxes, plus water bill and "commutation" expenses.
[h] *Newspaper* refers to the *Times,* of course.
[i] The *Times* did not calculate the cost of various food items by the week or year; it gave only a total amount for the food bill.
Source: New York Daily Times, 8 November 1853, 4.

The social link between the poorest and the richest Americans was the servant class—people who for almost no wages maintained the houses and performed the chores for their "betters." More than a million women alone were in domestic service in the last half of the century. In return for their labor, loyalty, and discretion, the servant class were provided with a roof over their head, food, clothing (livery), and social status above that of the industrial worker. Hired help was so cheap that even lower-middle-class families could afford a live-in servant or two, while the wealthiest might employ dozens. It was an arrangement that was made possible by the one-sided labor market and social attitudes of the day.

As American society became more citified, it also became more regulated. The frontier was still available to nonconformists, but urban dwellers increasingly had to tolerate such restrictions on their freedom as blue laws and zoning ordinances. The days of the unfettered pioneer were numbered.

Those regulations and other aspects of the new urban-industrial culture produced a backlash that took various forms. One was sentimentalism, a nostalgia for an older, simpler way of life that became a strong theme in American culture even before the Civil War thanks to such spokesmen as Henry David Thoreau and Ralph Waldo Emerson.

Another response to the rapidly changing world could be found in the rigid codes of etiquette imposed on such defining events as death, marriage, and childbirth. The "professional widow," such as LaSalle Corbell Pickett and Elizabeth Bacon Custer, were the most prominent examples of Americans' creation of a culture of mourning. They literally earned a living from their widowhood through writing and speeches about their famous husband. Such codes of etiquette were strongly embraced by the middle class, dictating what was respectable and proper in public life. Although named for Queen Victoria of England, Victorian morality proved to be as American as goober peas and shoo-fly pie.

As the perceived need for codes of etiquette suggests, the relationship between the sexes was changing, as men increasingly concentrated on their career and occupation while women's focus remained child rearing and homemaking and increasingly on "churching." Social roles followed work roles, and because women were considered the "gentler sex," their "sphere" was the home. Clearly defined gender roles became the norm for the middle and upper classes, while working-class women were forced to leave the home and take a job in the industrial economy to help support the family. In general "working girls" were still looked down upon, so much so that the term was often used as a euphemism for prostitutes.

A Nation of Joiners and Followers

Another characteristic of Americans was that they were joiners, as first observed by the French visitor Alexis de Tocqueville. Clubs, political parties, fraternal organizations, granges, athletic teams, and such, were entrenched in the national life. Perhaps because success was not a simple matter of individual effort and hard work, these organizations sprang up to provide support and an early form of networking. Sociologists call them voluntary associations and attribute their popularity to the heterogeneous nature of U.S. society: there were so many "others" that like-minded people felt forced to form such associations for their own protection. This tendency was strongest in but not exclusive to the middle class. Long before the Civil War there had been Freemasons and Odd Fellows. After the war the number multiplied to include such groups as the Independent Order of Gophers, the United Order of Druids, and the Tribes of Ben Hur. Among the most important groups formed during this period were the Knights of Pythias (1864), the Ku Klux Klan (1866), and the Benevolent and Protective Order of Elks (1868). None of these could compare to the membership and influence of the postwar veterans' groups, the Grand Army of the Republic (1866) in the North and the various state organizations of Confederate Veterans. Meanwhile the women participated as either auxiliaries to the group or formed their own literary societies, art clubs, and sewing circles.

Americans were also quick to follow the latest fad or popular movement. Several crazes swept the nation in the prewar period, each attracting its share of enthusiastic followers. At opposite ends of the spectrum were the celibacy and free love movements. Much more popular with the U.S. masses were the pseudoscience of phrenology and the pseudoreligion of spiritualism. The former claimed that it is possible to read a person's character by the shape and "topography" of the cranium. Though advocated by the respected Dr. Samuel Morton of Philadelphia among others, phrenology was nevertheless a disreputable forerunner of psychology.

Even more disreputable was the cult of charlatans calling themselves spiritualists who claimed that spirits from the next world were constantly trying to communicate with the living in this world. They make their presence known through physical manifestations such as knocking, wailing, and moving furniture. Unlike phrenology, spiritualism was a native movement, which first appeared in Rochester, New York, in the late 1840s. Believers included the newspaperman Horace Greeley and the first lady Mary Todd Lincoln. The spiritualist movement introduced such terms as *séance, medium, mesmerism,* and *clairvoyance* into the U.S. idiom.

The Popular Press

Newspapers

As a whole Americans were an amazingly literate people, and slaves were the only group systematically excluded from acquiring the skills to read and write. Otherwise, rich and poor, immigrant and native-born, men and women—almost all possessed at least a modicum of literacy. One clear sign of this state of affairs was the healthy newspaper industry that flourished during the first half of the 19th century. By 1840 there were 138 dailies in the United States with a cumulative annual circulation in excess of 147 million.

TABLE 19.19 NEWSPAPER PUBLISHING IN THE UNITED STATES, 1840

Demographic Profile	1840
U.S. population	17,120,000
Newspapers published	1,404
Newspaper editions per week	2,281
Daily newspapers	138
Annual circulation	147,500,000
Annual newspaper copies per capita	8.6

Source: Harvey J. Graff, *The Legacies of Literacy* (Bloomington: Indiana University Press, 1987), 353.

That number grew fourfold in the years that followed, until by 1870 there were 574 newspapers with a total daily circulation of a little less than 3 million. These figures suggest it was a wonderful era for the business of newspaper (and magazine) publishing. A U.S. newspaper, the *New York Herald,* even had the largest circulation in the world in 1860—77,000 copies sold daily. And not far behind was its great rival, the *New York Times,* launched in 1851 as a penny edition. A New York City newspaper also held the circulation record among the world's weeklies—the *New York Ledger* with a circulation of 200,000 per issue. Boston and Philadelphia were also major newspaper markets with multiple dailies and weeklies competing for the steadily expanding readership.

The U.S. people supported more newspapers than any other people in the world. A multiplicity of reasons explain that fact: The success of U.S. public education in producing a nation of readers, the abiding interest in political affairs of a democratic people, the cheap per-issue cost of U.S. newspaper compared to that of other goods and services, and the broad appeal of U.S. papers. As the editor of the *New York Times* observed in 1852, "American women read the papers as much as their men, a situation not found in other civilized countries." Informed opinion considered newspapers to be the popular educators of the day.

In the world of mid-19th-century journalism newspapers were expected to be partisan advocates of their favorite causes or political parties. However, the most remarkable phenomenon of U.S. journalism in the mid-19th century was not its partisanship but its democratization, symbolized by the penny press. The introduction of the one-cent newspaper enlarged the regular readership to include the heretofore ignored lower classes, producing an "information revolution" that had profound consequences for the nation's social, political, and economic life. The penny papers changed the way news was reported, putting a premium on sensational stories involving crime and sex and placing heavy emphasis on human interest pieces, thereby opening the door for publications such as Richard K. Fox's *Police Gazette.*

Publications such as the *Police Gazette* or *Frank Leslie's Weekly* also blurred the lines between magazines and newspapers of the day. Both forms were printed on cheap newsprint stock, often with 16 or fewer pages, and in a newspaper-style layout. A new literary wall between magazines and newspapers was erected when Frank Leslie began to use numerous woodcut engravings in his publications, something that traditional newspapers, with their tighter schedules and smaller budgets, could not match.

Still, any survey of the newspapers of the day is imperfect because of the sometimes arbitrary use of the term *newspaper* versus *magazine* and because many were short-lived, small-time operations. It would be easier and less problematical to lump everything together under the generic heading *periodicals.*

TABLE 19.20 LITERARY AND MISCELLANEOUS NEWSPAPERS AND PERIODICALS PUBLISHED IN THE STATES AND TERRITORIES, 1860

State or Territory	Literary Publications					Miscellaneous Publications						
	Daily	Weekly	Monthly	Quarterly	Annual	Daily	Biweekly	Triweekly	Weekly	Monthly	Quarterly	Annual
Ala.	0	2	2	0	0	0	0	0	0	1	0	0
Ark.	0	1	0	0	0	0	0	0	0	0	0	0
Calif.	0	9	1	0	0	0	0	0	8	1	0	0
Conn.	0	2	1	2	0	0	0	0	2	0	0	0
Del.	0	1	0	0	0	0	0	0	0	0	0	0
Fla.	0	2	0	0	0	0	0	0	0	0	0	0
Ga.	0	13	8	1	0	0	0	0	2	2	0	0
Ill.	0	3	5	0	0	0	1	0	2	5	0	0
Ind.	0	3	2	0	0	0	0	0	0	3	0	0
Iowa	0	0	1	0	0	0	0	0	6	3	0	0
Kans.	0	0	0	0	0	0	0	0	3	0	0	0
Ky.	0	3	1	0	0	0	0	0	0	3	0	0
La.	0	2	0	0	0	4	1	0	4	0	0	0
Maine	0	4	3	0	0	1	0	0	5	3	0	0
Md.	0	0	0	0	0	0	0	0	0	0	0	0
Mass.	0	31	18	2	0	0	1	0	18	7	1	1
Mich.	0	3	0	0	0	0	0	0	1	1	0	0
Miss.	0	1	0	0	0	0	0	0	1	0	0	0
Mo.	0	5	4	0	0	1	0	0	1	0	0	0
N.H.	0	2	0	0	0	0	0	0	7	4	0	0
N.J.	0	6	0	0	1	0	0	0	0	2	0	0
N.Y.	1	33	24	5	0	5	2	2	29	18	0	2
N.C.	0	5	2	0	0	0	0	0	0	1	0	0
Ohio	1	6	17	0	0	1	0	0	8	13	0	1
Oreg.	0	0	0	0	0	0	0	0	0	0	1	1
Pa.	0	17	6	1	1	1	0	0	18	2	1	0
R.I.	0	5	1	0	0	0	0	0	2	0	0	0
S.C.	0	4	1	0	0	0	0	0	3	1	0	0
Tenn.	0	2	1	1	1	0	0	0	1	1	0	0
Tex.	0	9	3	0	0	0	0	0	1	1	0	0
Vt.	0	0	1	0	0	0	0	0	0	0	0	0
Va.	0	2	1	0	0	0	0	0	5	1	0	0
Wis.	0	1	1	0	0	0	0	0	2	1	0	0
District of Columbia	0	0	0	0	0	0	0	0	0	0	0	0

(continued)

TABLE 19.20 (continued)

State or Territory	Literary Publications					Miscellaneous Publications						
	Daily	Weekly	Monthly	Quarterly	Annual	Daily	Biweekly	Triweekly	Weekly	Monthly	Quarterly	Annual
Nebraska Territory	0	0	0	0	0	0	0	0	0	1	0	0
New Mexico Territory	0	0	0	0	0	0	0	0	0	0	0	0
Utah Territory	0	0	0	0	0	0	0	0	2	0	0	0
Washington Territory	0	0	0	0	0	0	0	0	0	0	0	0
United States (Total)	2	177	104	12	3	13	5	2	131	75	3	5

Source: U.S. Census Bureau, *Preliminary Census Report for the Year Ending June 1, 1860* (Washington, D.C.: U.S. Government Printing Office, 1860), table 37.

Many frontier communities acquired their first newspaper when someone set up a used press in a tent and began to turn out single-sheet publications. Even newspapers in larger towns were quite provincial, sticking with the local news, current gossip, and comings and goings through town. Yet towns small and large alike often had two or more newspapers because there was a definite political slant to every paper's editorial policy that made no pretense of objectivity. Because of this variety and easy access to newspapers, Americans tended to be well informed in public affairs, even in the slow-paced days of telegraph communications and horse travel.

Although literacy was widespread, the choice of reading matter varied greatly across the socioeconomic spectrum. Among the lower classes, the penny papers were the most popular source of news and information. The New York *Morning Post,* the New York *Sun,* and the *Police Gazette* were the tabloids of their day, feeding an appetite for scandal, sensationalism, and crime stories. They also represented a way for "the great unwashed masses" to thumb their nose at their betters. "No narrative of human depravity or crime can shock or horrify an American reader" of such publications, claimed one man of letters, referring to the tabloid press. But alarmists could take some comfort from the fact that there was also a surprising number of sophisticated literary journals out there, still holding the line against the philistines.

Between New York City's penny press and the New England literary reviews were myriad newspapers, magazines, and journals for every taste and opinion. Americans in general and the middle class in particular devoured periodical literature in their desire to keep up with current events, follow the latest trends, and commune with the like-minded.

Magazines

The magazine was the last element of the print media to appear on the scene, after books and newspapers. Traditionally books had been regarded as a necessity and newspapers as a luxury because most people received news by word of mouth, from travelers or friends. Magazines filled an important niche in-between by offering timely news plus more substantial literary fare than newspapers but were less intellectually daunting than books. The development of practical methods of producing mass illustrations completed the package, launching a "golden age of magazines." What one historian calls the "great magazine explosion" occurred between 1825 and the end of the century, abating only briefly during the Civil War, then getting its second wind. From a mere handful at the beginning of the century, the number of magazines exploded to more than 600 by 1850, 700 in 1865, and 1,200 in 1870. That number doubled in the next decade and continued growing until the end of the century. There were magazines for farmers, for women's rights advocates, and for abolitionists; magazines for Christians and for atheists, for science junkies and for farmers; for free-traders and for protectionists. There was a magazine for practically every taste. Start-up costs for a new publication were not great: An office, a printing

This 1860 advertisement shows that even at that early date, African Americans were a part of the nation's emerging consumer culture, albeit always in subservient roles that amounted to caricature. Here, a magazine ad for Dixon's Stove Polish is apparently aimed at well-heeled families who can afford domestic servants (slaves). (Library of Congress, Prints and Photographs Division [LC-USZ62-39042])

press, and a publisher, who often filled the positions of editor and ace reporter, too, were all that were needed. Between 1850 and 1875 80 different magazines and journals that caused a splash can be identified, and another 1,200 that either fizzled quickly or else had a nice run but have long since been forgotten.

Some of those 80, such as *Popular Mechanics,* are still publishing today; others could not sustain themselves financially. In some cases, such as William Lloyd Garrison's *Liberator,* tastes changed or the times simply passed them by. But during the literary renaissance of the mid-19th century, mass circulation magazines such as *Harper's Weekly and Leslie's Illustrated* were significant arbiters of taste and shapers of public debate, while more specialized periodicals helped to popularize new fields such as photography, criminology, and organized sports. At the end of the era the leading magazines were still genteel and relatively expensive at 35 cents a copy. The most successful were still aimed at the upper end of the social scale.

The chief advance of the second half of the 19th century was the development of the pictorial magazine, modeled on the *Illustrated London News* and using woodcuts as illustrations. *Gleason's Pictorial Drawing-Room Companion* out of Boston started the trend in 1851 but was soon surpassed by *Harper's Weekly: A Journal of Civilization* and *Leslie's Illustrated Newspaper.* Not until the Civil War was the pictorial not just a publishing phenomenon but a national institution.

For reasons both economic and literary U.S. readers had a steady diet of English authors. But sectionalism also influenced U.S. reading habits. The antebellum South never developed much of a home-grown periodical literature; the *Southern Literary Messenger* (1834–64) and *De Bow's Review* (1846–80) were the principal exceptions. Otherwise Southerners pretty much read the same Boston- and New York–based magazines that Northerners read, after a slight delay in delivery. Attempts during the Civil War to establish a genuine regional periodical literature died aborning because of insurmountable obstacles to both printing and distributing.

In June 1858, *Harper's Magazine* chartered an entire Baltimore & Ohio (B&O) train to carry 20 artists, writers, and photographers on an excursion across Maryland and Virginia to record their impressions of the state of the nation. Perched here on the front of their train, they readily drew the conclusion that conditions were great. Even in the midst of the great sectional crisis there was a sense of optimism and confidence at work in the nation. (The Maryland Historical Society, Baltimore, Maryland)

TABLE 19.21 MOST POPULAR AND/OR INFLUENTIAL U.S. MAGAZINES, MID-1800s

Magazine	Magazine's Run	Periodicity/ Publishing Schedule	Purpose and/or Target Audience	Publisher/Founder and Important Editor(s)
The Boston Recorder[a]	?–1867	Weekly	Congregational Church journal	Nathaniel Parker Willis, editor
American Farmer	1819–97	Monthly	"Rural economy, internal improvements, news, prices current"	Samuel and William B. Sands, 1840–91
The Saturday Evening Post	1821–69	Weekly	Originally a "family newspaper," with news and serialized stories	Samuel C. Atkinson and Charles Alexander, founders; bought by George R. Graham and Charles J. Peterson; Henry Peterson, editor, 1846–73
The Albion	1822–75	Weekly	Eclectic literary magazine with strong Anglophile slant	Dr. John S. Bartlett, editor
New York Observer	1823–1912	Weekly	Presbyterian Church organ; literature, religion, and "general intelligence"	Sidney E. and Richard Morse (brothers of Samuel F. B. Morse), editors
African Repository	1825–92	Monthly	Antislavery; organ of American Colonization Society	Unknown
Graham's Magazine[b]	1841–58	Monthly	Digest of sensational fiction, poetry, travel, and book reviews from other periodicals; lavishly illustrated	George R. Graham, owner and chief editor, 1841–53; Edgar Allen Poe, literature edition 1841–42; Charles G. Leland, editor, 1857–58
The Friend[c]	1827–1955	Weekly	Oldest organ of Society of Friends; "an agreeable and instructive miscellany" for Quakers, with strong literary bent	Robert Smith, editor, advised by "20 Contributors"
Godey's Lady's Book	1830–98	Monthly	Leading fashion arbiter of its day for U.S. women; also printed serials, essays, poems, and craft projects; covered women's issues; nonpolitical	Louis Antoine Godey, publisher and coeditor with Sarah Josephine Hale; Lydia Sigourney also editor[d]

(continued)

TABLE 19.21 (continued)

Magazine	Magazine's Run	Periodicity/ Publishing Schedule	Purpose and/or Target Audience	Publisher/Founder and Important Editor(s)
The Liberator	1831–65	Weekly	Principal organ of antislavery movement	William Lloyd Garrison, publisher and editor
American Railroad Journal[e]	1832–86	Weekly/ semimonthly/ monthly	Trade journal of transportation field, heavily tilted towards Railroad Routes	D. Kimball Minor, founder and publisher, 1832–49; sold to John H. Schultz; John V. Poor, editor, 1849–62
Knickerbocker Magazine ("Old Knick")	1833–65	Monthly	First U.S. general monthly magazine; much beloved for its literary and humor pieces	Peabody & Co., publisher; Lewis Gaylord Clark, editor, 1834–60
The Albany Cultivator[f]	1834–65	Monthly	Farming, stock raising, and horticulture	State Agricultural Society of New York, publisher; Jesse Buel, Luther Tucker, editors
Southern Literary Messenger	1834–64	Monthly	Good literary magazine	Edgar Allan Poe once an editor
Pennsylvania Freeman	1838–54	Monthly	Abolitionist organ	Pennsylvania Anti-Slavery Society, publisher editors: John Greenleaf Whittier, 1838–39; James Russell Lowell, 1845–54
United States Magazine and Democratic Review[g]	1837–51 1856–59	Monthly	Literature and public affairs, with strongly partisan and nationalistic editorial policies; very influential	John L. O'Sullivan, founder and editor; S. D. Langtree, editor
Ballou's Dollar Monthly Magazine	1855–93	Monthly	General interest magazine featuring literature and miscellany	Maturin M. Ballou, founder and editor
Ladies' Repository	1841–76	Monthly	Methodist Church organ; devoted to literary and religious subjects	Editors: Benjamin F. Tefft, 1846–52; William C. Larabee, 1852–53; Davis W. Clark, 1853–63; Isaac Wiley, 1864–72
Peterson's Magazine	1842–98	Monthly	Illustrated women's magazine devoted to art, literature, and fashion; chief rival to *Godey's Lady's Book*	Charles J. Peterson, publisher and editor; Ann S. Stephens, associate editor
American Whig Review	1845–52	Monthly	Partisan journal devoted to politics and literature; national organ of Whig Party	George H. Colton, publisher and editor
National Police Gazette	1845–1932	Weekly	Men's magazine of sports and sensational crime reporting	Enoch E. Camp, publisher; George Wilkes, editor
Scientific American	1845–present	Weekly	Latest scientific discoveries and inventions, with sometimes futuristic slant	Rufus Porter, publisher and editor, 1845–47; Orson D. Munn, publisher and editor, 1847–1907
DeBow's Review[h]	1846–62 1866–80	Monthly	Politics, economics, and literature, with strong Southern bias	James D. B. DeBow
The Flag of Our Union	1846–70	Weekly	"Not very respectable" literary magazine	Frederick Gleason, founder and publisher; Maturin M. Ballou, publisher and editor, 1854–70
The Home Journal[i]	1846–20th century	Weekly	News, fashion, gossip, and reviews	Publishers and editors: George Pope Morris and Nathaniel Parker Willis, 1846–64; Willis and Morris Phillips, 1864–67; Phillips and George Perry, 1867–90
The National Era	1847–60	Monthly	Abolitionist and literary journal	Dr. Gamaliel Bailey, publisher and editor
The Independent	1848–1928	Weekly	Congregational Church organ and antislavery journal	Henry C. Bowen, publisher and editor; Henry Ward Beecher, editor, 1861–63; Theodore Tilton, editor, 1863–70
New England Farmer	1848–71	Semimonthly	"Agriculture and domestic economy"	Unknown
Moore's Rural New Yorker	1849–68	Weekly (?)	Well-loved journal of farm news, including new machines, methods, and rootstocks	D. D. T. Moore, publisher and editor
Lily	1849–56	Monthly (1849–52); semimonthly (1853–56)	"A ladies' journal devoted to temperance and literature"; focus on female suffrage and dress reform	Woman's Temperance Society of New York, publisher; Amelia Bloomer, editor.
The Daguerrean Journal[j]	1850–?	Monthly	First publication devoted to "the daguerrean and photogenic art"; full of latest scientific developments and gossip in photography	S. D. Humphrey, publisher and editor
Harper's Weekly / Monthly Magazine[k]	1850–present	Weekly/monthly	Self-described "Journal of Civilization," high-toned and informative, featuring woodcut illustrations and articles by distinguished European authors; on-the-scene Civil War news coverage	Fletcher Harper, publisher; Henry J. Raymond, first editor
Gleason's (or *Ballou's*) *Pictorial Drawing-Room Companion*	1851–59	Weekly	First of the great pictorials; copiously illustrated family magazine of miscellany	Frederick Gleason, publisher; Maturin M. Ballou, editor

Magazine	Magazine's Run	Periodicity/ Publishing Schedule	Purpose and/or Target Audience	Publisher/Founder and Important Editor(s)
Yankee Notions	1852–75	Monthly	Satire of Yankee culture; lowbrow humor	Editors: T. W. Strong, R. M. DeWitt
Young America[l]	1853–56	Weekly	Humor and satire	T. W. Strong, publisher; Charles Gayler, editor
Arthur's Home Magazine[m]	1853–98	Monthly	Literary works and practical domestic subjects for middle-class homemaker	Timothy Shay Arthur, editor and publisher (also author of *Ten Nights in a Bar-Room,* 1854)
The Country Gentleman	1853–1955	Weekly	"A [national] Journal for the Farm, the Garden, and the Fireside"; celebrated agrarian ideal	Luther Tucker, publisher and Editor; John Tucker, editor, 1853–73
Putnam's Monthly Magazine	1853–1910	Monthly	Literature, science, and art pieces; antislavery editorials; aimed to be high-class belles-lettres publication	G. P. Putnam and Co., publisher; editors: Charles F. Briggs, Frederick Law Olmsted, Parke Godwin, George W. Curtis
The New York Clipper	1853–1924	Weekly	Part newspaper and part magazine, devoted to sporting and theatrical news; absorbed by *Variety* in 1924	Frank Queen, publisher and editor
Frank Leslie's Ladies' Gazette of Fashion and Fancy Needlework	1854–57	Monthly	Trend-setting, illustrated fashion magazine for homemakers	Henry Carter (nom de plume Frank Leslie)
Criterion	1855–56	Weekly	Literary reviews, art and drama articles; high-class aspirations	Charles R. Rode, publisher and editor
American Journal of Education	1855–82	Monthly	Specialized topics for teachers and education reformers	Henry Barnard
Frank Leslie's Illustrated Newspaper[n]	Dec. 15, 1855–1922	Weekly	News and current events, often with sensational pictures; self-styled "crusading journal"	Henry Carter (nom de plume Frank Leslie)
Sybl	1856–64	Unknown	"A review of the tastes, errors, and fashions of Society"	Dr. Lydia Sayers, publisher and editor
New York Weekly[o]	1856–1914	Weekly	"General [interest] magazine"; lowbrow fiction	A. J. Williamson, publisher and editor
Frank Leslie's New Family Magazine	1857–82	Monthly	Sensationalist "digest" of unattributed articles from other periodicals	Henry Carter (Frank Leslie), publisher and editor
The Atlantic Monthly[p]	1857–20th century	Monthly	Elitest literary and reform-minded journal; called itself a "truly American magazine"; strong New England flavor	Francis H. Underwood, publisher; James Russell Lowell and James T. Fields, first editors
Harper's Weekly	1857–1916	Weekly	General readership; people who followed news	. . .
Douglass' Monthly	1858–63	Monthly	Political matters, especially as related to abolitionist movement	Frederick Douglass
Jolly Joker[q]	1862–77	Monthly; semimonthly	"Comic journalism"	. . .
Southern Illustrated News (of Richmond)	Sep. 13, 1862–Mar. 1865	Weekly	Southern loyalists and Yankee haters	E. W. Ayres and W. H. Wade, publishers; John R. Thompson, first editor
The United States Army and Navy Journal[r]	1863–20th century	Weekly	Unofficial spokesman of U.S.; military establishment to promote armed forces and patriotism	William Conant Church and Francis P. Church, publishers and editors *Note:* Partners also in publishing *The Galaxy*
Watson's Art Journal	1864–84	Weekly	Chiefly musical criticism, reviews, and trade news	Henry C. Watson, publisher and editor
American Journal of Conchology	1865–72	Monthly (?)	Study of shells and mollusks	Philadelphia Academy of Natural Sciences, publisher; George W. Tryon, Jr., editor
The Nation[s]	1865–81	Weekly	Review journal that championed blacks' rights; advocated free trade, civil service reform, and other liberal causes	Edwin L. Godkin and Wendell Phillips Garrison (with Frederick Law Olmsted)
New England Farmer[t]	1865–1913	Weekly	Eastern agriculture and horticulture	R. P. Eaton & Co., publisher
Saturday Night (of Philadelphia)	1865–1902	Weekly	"Story magazine" of fiction	James Elverson, publisher and editor
The Galaxy	1866–78	Monthly	"An illustrated magazine of entertaining reading"; "New York's *own* monthly"	William C. and Francis P. Church, publishers and editors
The Southern Review	1867–79	Quarterly	Southern apologia and literary review; "official exponent of the Lost Cause"	Albert T. Bledsoe and William Hand Browne, publishers and editors
Harper's Bazaar	1867–20th century	Weekly	"A repository of fashion, pleasure and instruction" for women	Fletcher Harper, publisher; Mary L. Booth, editor, 1867–89
McGee's Illustrated Weekly	1867–82	Weekly	One of several Catholic diocesan journals	Maurice Francis Egan, editor
Sporting Times (of Boston)	1867–72; 1884–86	Weekly	General sports periodical, especially baseball news	Unknown

(continued)

TABLE 19.21 (continued)

Magazine	Magazine's Run	Periodicity/ Publishing Schedule	Purpose and/or Target Audience	Publisher/Founder and Important Editor(s)
American Naturalist	1867–20th century	Monthly	"A popular illustrated magazine of natural history"	Essex Institute (lyceum), publisher; A. S. Packard, editor
Lippincott's Magazine	1868–1916	Monthly	Popular, high-quality journal of literature, science, and education; Conservative editorial policy	J. B. Lippincott & Co., publisher; John Foster Kird, editor, 1868–84
Our Dumb Animals[u]	1868–20th century	Monthly (?)	Crusading publication for prevention of cruelty to animals	George T. Angell, publisher and editor
Spectator	1868–20th century	Monthly (?)	"An American Review of Life Insurance" matters	Unknown
The Revolution	1868–72	Weekly	Women's rights issues, stories, and some literary miscellany	Susan B. Anthony, owner; Elizabeth Cady Stanton, editor, 1868–70
The Overland Monthly	1868–1923	Monthly	California boosterism and Western literature; "a Western *Atlantic Monthly*"	Anton Roman, publisher, 1868–69; Bret Harte, editor, 1868–70
Christian Union	1869–93	Weekly	Liberal religious publication; mouthpiece for Henry Ward Beecher, preacher, until 1881	Henry Ward Beecher, publisher, 1869–81
Appleton's Journal	1869–81	Weekly	"Information on all subjects of public importance," especially "contemporary scientific ideas" (literature, science, and art)	D. Appleton & Co., publishers; editors: Edward Livingston Youmans, 1869–70; Robert Carter, 1870–72; Oliver Bunce and Charles Henry Jones, 1872–81
Scribner's Monthly[v]	1870–81	Monthly	"An illustrated magazine for the people"; also called itself "a first-class magazine"; general interest and many fiction articles	Dr. Josiah Gilbert Holland, with Roswell Smith and Charles Scribner, founders; Scribner's Publishers, publisher; Dr. Holland, editor
New Remedies[w]	1871–20th century	Monthly	Druggists' trade journal	William Wood & Co., publishers and editor
Frank Leslie's Ladies' Journal[x]	1871–81	Weekly	"Devoted to fashion and choice literature"	Frank Leslie, publisher; Miriam F. Squier (Mrs. Frank Leslie), editor
Once a Week[y]	1871–72	Weekly	"The Young Lady's Own Journal"	Frank Leslie publisher; Miriam F. Squier, editor
Christian Union[z]	1871–92/93	Weekly	"Liberal," nondenominational religious periodical	American Tract Society, publisher; Lyman Abbott, editor
Popular Science	1872–94; 1900–present	Monthly	"An American journal to bring the world of science to laymen"	D. A. Appleton & Co., publishers, 1872–1900; Edward Livingston Youmans, first editor, 1872–87
Publishers Weekly	1872–present	Weekly	Book trade news for bibliophiles	Frederick Leypoldt, publisher and editor
The Delineator	1873–1937	Monthly	Magazine for women: "Illustrating European and American Fashions"; originally a compendium of sewing patterns	E. Butterick Co., publishers; Robert S. O'Loughlin, first editor, 1873–84
St. Nicholas	1873–1943	Monthly	Magazine for juvenile readers; colorful and upbeat stories and serials	Scribner & Co., publishers, 1873–80; Roswell Smith, founder and publisher (for Scribner); Mary Mapes Dodge, first editor, 1873–1905
Field and Stream[aa]	1874–present	Weekly	Covered racing, baseball, checkers, outdoor sports in general, especially kennels, guns, and game laws	George W. Strell, editor
Kentucky Livestock Record[bb]	1875–20th century	Monthly (?)	Horse racing and breeding	Unknown

Note: This listing does not even pretend to be exhaustive; there were too many short-lived magazines launched during this era that appeared briefly on the scene, had a short run, and then were promptly forgotten, leaving little or no trace of their passing. The magazines listed here had some kind of impact or left their mark on history. The names of many magazines evolved over the years. The names given here are the original names or the names by which they are remembered.

[a] Later *Boston Recorder.*

[b] Formed by the merger of two older magazines, *Casket* (1826–40) and *Burton's Gentleman's Magazine* (1837–40). The second of the great pictorials, after *Knickerbocker Magazine,* it published the greatest U.S. writers of the mid-19th century. Godey and Charles J. Peterson *(Peterson's Magazine)* were also coowners of the *Saturday Evening Post* in its early years.

[c] Later renamed *Friend's Journal.*

[d] While editor, Sarah Josephine Hale wages a successful seven-year campaign in the pages of the magazine to have Thanksgiving declared a national holiday (1863).

[e] Began life as the *Rail-Road Journal* in 1832, then in 1845 became the *American Railroad Journal and General Advertiser for Railroads, Canals, Machinery, Steam Boats and Mines;* in 1848 it became the *American Railroad Journal and Iron Manufacturer's and Mining Gazette* before taking its final form as the *American Railroad Journal* with various subtitles. The different ways of spelling *railroad* illustrate the evolving technical jargon of the industrial age.

[f] *The Albany Cultivator* merged with *Country Gentleman* in 1865.

[g] Also known as the *United States Democratic Review.*

[h] Known in the beginning as *The Commercial Review of the South and West.*

[i] Known as *Town & Country* after 1901.

[j] Later renamed *Humphrey's Journal.*

[k] Subsequently *Harper's New Monthly Magazine* and then *Harper's,* by which it is known today. An instant success with the U.S. reading public, it achieved a circulation of 200,000 monthly before the Civil War, surpassing every other contemporary magazine in the world.

[l] Also known as *Yankee Doodle* during part of its run. This is not the same publication as *Working Man's Advocate* (1829–44) which became *Young America* (1845–49)

[m] Originally *Arthur's Home Gazette: A Journal of Pure Literature for Home Reading* (1850–52). Both the *Home Gazette* and its successor reflected the puritanical zeal of its publisher/editor.

[n] Really a weekly magazine, it was renamed *Leslie's Weekly.*
[o] The *New York Weekly* was the publishing foundation for Street & Smith's profitable dime-novel business.
[p] Later simply *The Atlantic.*
[q] Reborn for a short run (1899–1900) in New Orleans.
[r] Later Known by various names: (1) *The Gazette of the Regular and Volunteer Forces* and (2) *Armed Forces Journal International.*
[s] *The Nation* merged with the New York *Evening Post* in 1881.
[t] This was the third magazine published under this name; the first was in 1848–71.
[u] Later *Animals.*
[v] Becomes *Century Magazine* in 1881 after the death of its guiding light, Dr. Holland, and a falling out with Scribner's Publishers. In its reincarnated form it really takes off with the reading public and continues publishing until 1930.
[w] Known after 1893 as *American Druggist & Pharmaceutical Record;* after 1927, as *American Druggist.*
[x] Successor to *Once a Week* in the Leslie family of magazines; known simply as *Frank Leslie's Journal* before the end of its run.
[y] Succeeded by *Frank Leslie's Ladies' Journal.*
[z] Also known as *Illustrated Christian Weekly,* this magazine was the medium of the popular preacher Henry Ward Beecher until 1881. After his death in 1887, it was reborn as *The Outlook* in 1893.
[aa] Name changed to *Field* in 1875, and to *American Field* in 1881.
[bb] Known as *Thoroughbred Record* after 1896.
Sources: Frank L. Mott, *A History of American Magazines,* vols. 2 and 3 (Cambridge, Mass.: Harvard University Press, 1938–68), passim; Amy Janello and Brennon Jones, *The American Magazine* (New York: Perry N. Abrams, 1991), 232–34.

The Magazine Publishing Industry

Then as now a handful of rich and powerful owners controlled the magazine publishing industry. The most influential of them was Henry Carter, better known to millions of readers of his magazines as Frank Leslie. He started his first magazine, *Frank Leslie's Ladies' Gazette of Fashion and Fancy Needlework,* in 1854 and ultimately established no fewer than nine magazines, most of them with his name in the title, during this period on the way to becoming the first U.S. publishing tycoon. Some of the greatest literary figures and artists in U.S. history had their start in popular magazines such as *Frank Leslie's Illustrated,* including Edgar Allen Poe, Henry Wadsworth Longfellow, Walt Whitman, and Winslow Homer. The great variety and diverse viewpoints of American periodicals were clear evidence that the United States had the "freest" press in the world.

The publishing business was also more progressive than most in recognizing women's accomplishments as professionals. A number of women made their mark during these years as writers and even editors for major magazines and newspapers. Among them were Jane Grey Swisshelm, the first female member of the Washington press corps, and Sarah J. Hale and Ann S. Stephens, editors of *Godey's Lady's Book* and *Peterson's Magazine,* respectively, pre–Civil War. Women's magazines made an impressive splash in U.S. publishing during these years. *Godey's,* the premier magazine for women, reached a circulation of 150,000 monthly by the late 1850s, with subscription priced at three dollars per year.

When this era, the years 1850–75, ended, what passed for American culture would have been scarcely recognizable to a person of the year 1800. It was broader and more diversified than it had been at the beginning of the century, or even in 1825. The influx of immigrants and the spread of Jacksonian democracy were at the root of much of the change. The immigrants' presence added greatly to the melting pot of national life, and contrary to popular fears, they were a positive influence. Jacksonian democracy had contributed to the transformation by elevating the common people and, by extension, their taste in political affairs, entertainment, reading matter, and a host of other areas.

Notions of what culture meant had also changed. Formerly considered the exclusive preserve of the upper classes, culture was now recognized as an integral part of daily life: Baseball was as much a part of American culture as grand opera. By the time of the Civil War the term was vying in the popular lexicon with *virtue* to describe the glue that held civilized society together.

After 1850 Americans had many more choices on their cultural plate, whether it was choosing between a county fair or a symphony concert, reading a dime novel or a Thoreau essay, or attending a lyceum lecture or a prizefight. American culture by 1875 was richer in many ways but also more fragmented and particularized than it had been before. And this was a long-term trend pointing toward the 20th century, when multiculturalism would become a defining facet of American society.

CHAPTER 20 Crime, Vice, and Violence

The 1960s radical H. Rap Brown said, "Violence is as American as cherry pie," an observation that surely applies to the mid-19th century. It was a violent time of civil conflict, Indian wars, lawlessness in the West, the oppression of slavery, and other forces. But the leading cause of the endemic violence that plagued the nation was racism. The racism began with the brutal control mechanisms and white paranoia of the slave system, but race was also a factor in the violence between whites and Indians, white and Mexicans, whites and Chinese.

Much of the antebellum violence was sparked by political passions in a dress rehearsal for the civil war that broke out in 1861. The center of the sectional conflict was Kansas, which earned the name "Bleeding Kansas" in the middle 1850s as proslavers battled antislavers for control of the territory. Both sides determined to settle the issue with bullets rather than ballots, and supporters back East were glad to ship crates of rifles ("Beecher Bibles") to swing the balance of power. Between 1855 and 1858, 52 people died in Kansas in the commission of murders. The breakdown of those figures shows that 36 free-state partisans were killed versus 14 proslave partisans, and two proslavery men died accidentally in the course of trying to murder their opponents.

A relatively new form of violence, urban violence, was also becoming a serious problem in this era. It took the form of riots, ethnic clashes, and mounting crime rates in U.S. cities. As the urban population grew, crime became much more visible than ever before. The U.S. crime rate far outpaced that of advanced European nations in the same period. In cities for which statistics are available, the rate of arrest was three times that of comparable cities in Western Europe. This difference has been attributed to various causes, including an excess of democracy, flagrant racism, and the frontier culture. The almost total absence of regular municipal police forces at the beginning of this period also must enter the equation. New York City had the first paid, uniformed force, beginning in 1845. Other cities followed slowly.

For reasons that are still unclear, the 25 years between 1850 and 1875 produced some of the most heinous crimes and bizarre criminal cases in U.S. history, including (1) the first insanity plea (Dan Sickles for murdering his wife's lover), (2) the first war criminal (Captain Henri Wirz for the horrors of Andersonville Prison Camp), (3) the first presidential assassination (John Wilkes Booth's murder of Abraham Lincoln), and (4) the first conviction for cannibalism (Alfred Packer for devouring five prospector companions). Add to this list the atrocities committed during the Civil War and the massacres on both sides during the Indian wars, and this period stands unsurpassed in its violence.

Violence Caused by Slavery and the Civil War

In the antebellum period a separate category of crime was that of slaves against whites. Particularly in the South, where the black population outnumbered the white in some areas, slave violence in any form was the citizens' worst nightmare. It was practically a primal fear. Authorities monitored their slaves carefully in order to keep control of the situation. Ironically statistics showed that violence among blacks was much lower than among whites, relatively speaking, which suggests that white fears of being murdered in their beds by their slaves were more alarmist or paranoid than real.

Even separating violence within the slave population from that in mainstream society, the Civil War and the anything-goes frontier culture still made this an especially violent era. The Civil War taught a generation of men to kill and destroy without compunction, while the absence of law and order on the frontier made it easy for the stronger to take what they wanted from the weaker. Add to this equation the easy availability of guns, and it becomes apparent why the United States was a dangerous place in which to live. The breakdown in law began during the Civil War. From 1861 to 1865 there was only the thinnest of lines drawn between military actions and criminal behavior. For instance it was often hard to see any distinction between so-called partisan rangers and bushwhackers in parts of Missouri, Tennessee, and northern Virginia. On the edges of the war men such as William Quantrill, Champ Ferguson, "Bloody Bill" Anderson, and even "Gray Ghost" John Mosby were a law unto themselves. But the Civil War eventually ended, thus closing the book on partisan rangers, whereas the frontier continued for another generation, providing both a haven and a training ground for outlaws.

TABLE 20.1 VICTIMS OF SLAVE MURDERS, 1780–1864

Type of Victim	Number of Victims
Master	56
Mistress	11
Overseer (whites only)	11
Other whites	120
Free blacks	7
Black children (by mother)	12
Not described	60
Total during 84 years	**362**

Note: As tabulated by the state of Virginia, only within Virginia.
Source: Carl Sifakis, *The Encyclopedia of American Crime* (New York: Facts On File, 1982), 665.

The whipping post was still a legal form of punishment in post–Civil War America, although no longer widely used. Public whippings, even more than public hangings, were offensive to many Americans by this time. Here a prisoner in Dover, Delaware, is punished by being whipped, while a well-dressed audience looks on nonchalantly. Note that the prisoner is a black man dressed in work clothes. The presence of a single black child in the front ranks of onlookers suggests a family connection. (Library of Congress)

Bank Robbers and Train Robbers

It is not without good reason that the era that followed the Civil War has been labeled by some historians the "gunfighter era" when speaking of the West. The period lasted roughly 30 years (1865–95) and produced some of the most famous names in U.S. history, including Wyatt Earp, Billy the Kid, and Wild Bill Hickock. There were as many as 225 men by one count who deserved the title *gunfighter,* and they engaged in almost 600 shootouts, although few at "high noon" on Main Street. Although there was plenty of gunplay from 1850 to 1875, the heyday of the gunfighter era would not be until the last quarter of the century.

In the "untamed" West criminality was a way of life for a broad segment of society, who included gamblers, gunmen, cattle rustlers, and "soiled doves" (prostitutes). Often the same men worked both sides of the law at different times, taking jobs as lawmen in one town and carrying on as outlaws in another—for example, Wyatt Earp, "Longhair Jim" Courtright, and Ben Thompson. In male-dominated frontier communities, nonviolent crimes such as gambling and prostitution were winked at, and "self-defense" was a one-size-fits-all justification for many homicides.

Many of the most notorious outlaws in the West received their training in the Civil War when they learned to plan lightning raids, elude pursuit, and assemble overwhelming firepower. They also learned contempt for law and order. In addition to all that, many Southern men who returned from the war found their homes and farms destroyed. With little hope of rebuilding their former life, they believed they could only make a living by stealing. Most of the big-time thieving during this era took the form of stock rustling, followed by bank and stage coach robberies. Only at the very end of the era would trains become a favorite target of outlaws.

Bank and stagecoach robberies were nothing new in history. But Civil War bushwhackers and partisans rewrote the book on both enterprises. They did it under the guise of military operations, and with the encouragement of their political leaders. It is not surprising therefore that after the Civil War the epidemic of bank robberies continued. Not only had the some of the restraints of civilization been permanently loosened, but banks were where the money was, and security measures were almost unknown. "Security" in those days meant organizing a posse and chasing down the robbers *after* the fact, hoping to catch up with them before they could return to their hideout or escape across jurisdictional lines. Bank robbers struck their targets in the same way that guerrilla raiders hit enemy towns during the Civil War—with guns blazing and everybody whooping it up to throw terror into the local citizenry. The tactics worked well at first. After 1875 bank robbing became tougher as paralyzing fear was replaced by stout resistance among the victims, and as the authorities became more watchful and their pursuit more determined. The result was not

The robbery of the Central Pacific No. 1 "sleeping train" at Verdi, Nevada, on November 4, 1871, by E. B. Parsons and Jack Davis, who made off with $40,000 of Wells Fargo's money. It was "the curtain-raiser for scores of similar robberies to come." Insert shows one of the robbers holding the train's engineer at bay while his confederates loot the express car. (Library of Congress)

so much that the number of robberies went down; rather that the bloodshed quotient went up, as both sides evinced more willingness to shoot it out.

The new breed of outlaws active during these years were not content merely to rob banks. They spread their net wider, and in the process they found stagecoaches to be a soft touch, especially out West, where their routes took them through desolate country far from the protection of the law, with only a driver and a "shotgun guard" to provide security. Stage robbing soon lost its thrill because there was bigger game to be had. Thus was born a new type of heist—the train robbery—and some of the sharpest, most ruthless of the new breed of outlaws put a distinctively American stamp on this new criminal enterprise. As in bank robbing, a Civil War apprenticeship under someone such as William Quantrill, John Hunt Morgan, or John Mosby proved invaluable. Starting with the Reconstruction years, train robbing became both big business and high adventure, and the odds of success were always in the robber's favor. It was during these years that the James gang became an outlaw legend, so much so that they are often credited with "inventing" train robbing. They were not the first, or necessarily the best, just the most famous. The true trailblazers in train robbing were the Reno brothers, Frank, John, William, and Simon, who plagued the Midwest for a little more than two years (October 1866 to December 1868).

But the most famous outlaw gang of all time was the James brothers and friends. The core of the gang was Frank and Jesse James, with their cousins Cole, Bob, Jim, and John Younger. For the better part of 16 years (1866–82) they alternately thrilled and terrorized the "Middle Frontier" (Midwest), developing a modus operandi that was dramatic and almost unfailingly successful, at least until they ran into a buzz saw in Northfield, Minnesota, on August 7, 1876.

Most gangs, including the Renos and the James-Youngers, alternated among bank, stagecoaches, and trains, depending on where the pickings were best and what kind of mood they were in. During these years many of the arrests were made not by the legally constituted authorities but by private enterprise in the form of the Pinkertons or some other detective agency. All the major express companies and railroads employed their own security forces, who were often little better than the outlaws they were chasing.

TABLE 20.2 MAJOR BANK ROBBERIES IN THE UNITED STATES, 1850–1875

Bank	Location	Date	Perpetrators	The Haul	Casualties
Malden Bank[a]	Malden Mass.	Dec. 15, 1863	Eddie Green	$5,000	One bank employee killed
Clay County Savings and Loan Association Bank[b]	Liberty, Mo.	Feb. 13, 1866	James Brothers (?) and eight or nine others	$60,000 in gold and nonnegotiable securities	One bystander (college student) killed
Hughes and Mason Bank	Richmond, Mo.	May 22, 1867	James-Younger gang and others	$4,000 in gold	Three citizens killed, including the mayor
County Bank	Daviess, Mo.	Spring 1867	Reno gang	$22,000	None
Harrison Bank	Magnolia, Iowa	Winter 1868	Reno gang	$14,000	None
Southern Bank of Kentucky	Russellville, Ky.	Mar. 20, 1868	James-Younger gang	$14,000	One wounded (a banker)
Alexander Mitchell Bank	Lexington, Mo.	Oct. 30, 1866	James gang	$2011.50 in cash	None
McClain's Bank	Savannah, Mo.	Mar. 2, 1867	James gang	Nothing (unsuccessful)	Bank's owner wounded
Deposit Bank	Columbia, Ky.	Apr. 29, 1872	James-Younger gang (Five men)	$1,500	One cashier killed; One citizen wounded
Davies County Savings Bank	Gallatin, Mo.	Dec. 7, 1869	James-Younger gang	$500	One killed (bank cashier)
Ocobock Brothers Bank	Corydon, Iowa	Jun. 3, 1871	James-Younger gang and others	$45,000	None
The Deposit Bank	Columbia, Ky.	Apr. 29, 1872	James-Younger gang and others	$600	One killed (bank cashier)
Savings Association Bank	St. Genevieve, Mo.	May 23, 1872	James-Younger gang and others	$4,000	None
Kansas City Fair	Kansas City, Mo.	Sep. 23, 1872	James-Younger gang	$978 (gate receipts)	One bystander wounded (young girl)
Ocean Bank	New York, N.Y.	1869	Bliss bank ring	$2.75 million	None

[a] The first daylight bank robbery in U.S. history, this was a spur-of-the-moment act by a lone gunman who shot the only witness, did not wear a mask, and did not even try to leave town with his loot.

[b] Famously, and incorrectly, known as the first bank robbery in U.S. history during peacetime (cf. the Civil War). It was, however, the first bank robbery by an *organized gang* of outlaws, and it included Frank but probably not Jesse James.

Sources: Carl Sifakis, *The Encyclopedia of American Crime* (New York: Facts On File, 1982), passim; Bill O'Neal, *The Encyclopedia of Western Gunfighters* (Norman: University of Oklahoma Press, 1979), passim.

TABLE 20.3 MAJOR TRAIN ROBBERIES IN THE UNITED STATES, 1850–1875

Site	Date	Perpetrator(s)	The Haul	Casualties	Perpetrators Caught
North Bend, Ohio[a]	May 9, 1865	Confederate guerrillas	Unknown	None	No
Between New York City and New Haven, Conn.	Jan. 6, 1866	Unknown	$700,000 (from Adams Express car)	None	No
Seymour, Ind.[b] (Ohio and Mississippi Railroad	Oct. 6, 1866	Reno gang	$10,000 in gold and cash (from Adams Express car)	None	No
Bristoe Station, Ky.	Oct. 11, 1866	John James, Newt Guy, Henry May, and Seaton May (?)	$8,000	None	No
Seymour, Ind.	Sep. 28, 1867	Walter Hammond and Michael Colleran	$8,000–$10,000	None	No
Marshfield, Ind. (Jefferson, Mo., and Indianaoplis, Ind., Railroad)	May 22, 1868	Reno gang (some 24 men)	$40,000–$96,000 in gold, cash, government bonds (from Adams Express car)	One guard fatally wounded	No
Brownstown, Ind.	Jul. 10, 1868	Reno gang (?)	None (foiled by Pinkerton trap)	Three wounded included two robbers	Yes
Verdi, Nev.[c]	Nov. 4, 1870	R. A. Jones John T. Chapman Jack Davis John Squires James Gilchrist Tilton Cockerell	$40,000	None	Yes

(continued)

TABLE 20.3 (continued)

Site	Date	Perpetrator(s)	The Haul	Casualties	Perpetrators Caught
Pequop, Nev.	Nov. 5, 1870	Army deserters from Camp Halleck	$4,500	None	Yes
Union City, Tenn. (Mobile and Ohio flyer)	1870	Levi and Hilary Farrington (brothers) William Barron William Taylor	$20,000 (from Southern Express car)	None	Yes
Meridian, Miss.	Jun. 18, 1871	Wash Crosby and Albert Grier	$12,000	None	No
Adair, Iowa (express train)[d]	Jul. 21, 1873	James-Younger gang	$1,700–$2,000	One killed (train's engineer)	No
Gadshill, Mo. (Iron Mountain Railroad express train)	Jan. 31, 1874	James-Younger gang and others	$22,000 in cash and gold	None	No
Muncie, Kans. (express train)	Dec. 12, 1874	James-Younger gang and others	$25,000–$32,000 in gold, cash, jewelry	None	No
Otterville, Mo. (Missouri-Pacific Express)	Jul. 7, 1875	James-Younger gang and others	$75,000	None	No

[a] Considered to be the last militarily justified train robbery of the Civil War, though it took place a month after Robert E. Lee surrendered the Army of Northern Virginia
[b] Generally acknowledged as the first peacetime train robbery in U.S. history, antedating the train-robbing career of the more famous James or Younger brothers.
[c] First train robbery west of the Mississippi River. Some sources place it at Independence, Nev.
[d] Contrary to Western lore, this was not the first train robbery, just the first by the James gang (and friends).
Sources: Richard Patterson, *The Train Robbery Era* (Boulder, Colo.: Pruitt, 1991), passim; Carl Sifakis, *The Encyclopedia of American Crime* (New York: Facts On File, 1982), passim; Bill O'Neal, *The Encyclopedia of Western Gunfighters* (Norman: University of Oklahoma Press, 1979), passim.

Labor Violence

Conflict between labor and capital, which involved both class and ethnic issues, ratcheted up the level of violence still further. This was the dawn of the industrial age in America, and workers increasingly resorted to violence to protect their rights. Nor was management averse to hiring strike-breakers in the form of goons and "private detectives" to win their points. Bloodshed on the strike line and even at the workplace became a common occurrence. In terms of the numbers of casualties and the duration of the fighting, the worst clash between workers and management in the 19th century occurred in the Pennsylvania coalfields when the Molly Maguires waged a decade-long campaign of terrorism and sabotage against the mine owners (1860s–70s). The organization, composed entirely of Irish immigrants, took their name from a notorious group of antilandlord agitators back in the old country who were led by a tough widow named Maguire. Transplanting the same class hatreds and violent methods to Pennsylvania, the Irish miners declared war on their tight-fisted bosses, leading to at least 16 murders and countless injuries, numerous arrests, and a series of sensational trials. Before the organization was finally crushed by the authorities, 20 men were convicted for the murders, and 19 of those were hanged (one was pardoned by the governor of Pennsylvania). The Molly Maguires lost not only the war in the coalfields and in the courts, but the war of public relations besides, as most Americans saw them as nothing more than a bunch of "foreign terrorists" who got what they deserved.

When Irish miners formed the secretive Molly Maguire Society in the Pennsylvania coal mines about 1865, they set up a confrontation with the owners that exploded into the "Long Strike" of 1874–75. In this engraving from a drawing by Frenzeny & Tavernier, in *Harpers Weekly,* January 31, 1874, strikers gather to discuss the situation during the Long Strike. (Library of Congress, [LC-USZ62 02016])

Crime Waves and Vice Districts

Making the problem of crime even worse than it was, law enforcement was haphazard and arbitrary. There were no police forces in most cities. Other cities followed slowly. Americans seemed adverse to any form of social control, as well as to the taxes necessary to support a professional police force. More often than not, the police were untrained bullies and gunmen who made more money from graft than from their pay. The public had little respect for and less faith in the average policeman. In New York City in 1858 the state legislature tried to clean house in the city's hopelessly corrupt police force, but they only made the situation worse when the state-hired replacements had a brawl with the existing municipal force that required calling out the state militia to restore order.

In one respect at least U.S. law enforcement was not still stuck in the Dark Ages: Americans eagerly embraced the latest technology, the telegraph and photography, in the war on crime. The telegraph made it harder for criminals to escape apprehension by fleeing to new territory, and photography made it easier to identify them by appearance rather than simply name or reputation, an advance signified by the opening of the first "rogue's gallery" of 450 wanted men in the New York City police headquarters in 1859.

Historically war, ethnic rivalry, and class conflict all can cause a notable rise in the crime rate, and there was no absence of any of these during this period. But adding to the breakdown in the system was collusion between lawbreakers and law enforcers whether it took the form of town marshals looking the other way for illegal card games in frontier towns or police officials blatantly extorting payoffs from businesses in eastern cities. Making law enforcement harder was the ease of escaping and dropping out of sight. The United States was a vast country with poor communications and little or no cooperation among various law enforcement agencies. An outlaw could rob a bank in one town and be across the county line and beyond apprehension before a posse could be organized.

Western outlaws were often romanticized, a fact that explains the enormous popularity of the dime novels. And because of ethnic and social tensions, one group's outlaws could be another group's heroes. The James gang were treated as heroes by their clannish Missouri neighbors, who were glad to hide them from the law. And the clash of Anglo versus Hispanic cultures in the Southwest produced two Mexican bandit-heroes who were considered outlaws by Anglo authorities but national liberators by their own people. Joaquin Murieta became a "Robin Hood" to oppressed Hispanic Californios (La Raza) during his brief outlaw career (1849–53) because he relieved hated gringos of their gold. When the California Rangers finally caught up with him, however, they treated him as a common bandit by summarily executing him. In Texas Juan Cortina began his outlaw career against Anglos in 1859 by capturing Brownsville and raising the Mexican flag. During the next few years his popularity soared, until he commanded a force of some 3,000 guerrilla fighters. Chased back across the Rio Grande border by the Texas Rangers and U.S. Army, he was arrested and imprisoned by the Mexican government in 1875 under pressure from U.S. authorities.

Regardless of their personal agenda or ethnic background, lawless types seemed to find the West an exceedingly tolerant place for their

TABLE 20.4 FELONY AND MISDEMEANOR CRIMES COMMITTED IN NEW YORK STATE, 1860

(of a total population of 805,651)

Criminal Charge[a]	Males (Arrested)	Females (Arrested)	Total Arrests
Assault and battery	6,077	1,667	7,744
Assault with intent to kill	197	1	198
Attempted rape	40	0	40
Abortion	2	2	4
Bastardy[b]	141	0	141
Bigamy	14	5	19
Disorderly conduct[c]	8,542	5,412	13,050
Intoxication	11,482	4,936	16,418
Juvenile delinquency	154	25	179
Kidnapping[d]	20	5	25
Acting suspiciously[e]	1,617	440	2,057
Vagrancy	978	838	1,816
Arson	35	0	35
Attempt to steal	236	9	245
Burglary	978	838	1,816
Forgery	151	3	154
Fraud	104	17	121
Grand larceny	1,675	946	2,621
Gambling	249	3	252
Highway robbery	199	6	205
Keeping a disorderly house[f]	177	165	342
Picking pockets	225	20	275
"Petit" (petty) larceny	3,380	1,860	5,240
Passing counterfeit money	414	46	460
Receiving stolen goods	166	51	217
Swindling	5	3	8
Violating Sunday (closing) laws	183	20	203

[a] Oddly enough, the categories do not include either rape or murder, although other felonies were included in the report, leading one to presume either that those two crimes were included in another, undiscovered report, or that they did not occur in New York in 1860.
[b] That is, giving birth to *or fathering* a child out of wedlock.
[c] Often a catch-all category for prostitutes actively soliciting business as well as for simple rowdy behavior that "breaks the peace," thus explaining the large numbers of those so charged.
[d] Kidnapping was a state crime, not a federal crime at this time.
[e] An archaic charge now considered unprovable in a court of law.
[f] That is, operating a bordello or other establishment where prostitution is practiced.
Source: New York State Census returns for 1860, reprinted in Marc McCutcheon, *The Writer's Guide to Everyday Life in the 1800s* (Cincinnati: Writer's Digest Books, 1993), 266.

violent ways. Gun-toting sociopaths robbed banks, held up stages, and shot down their fellow citizens, often with impunity. An excess of freedom and a shortage of law were at the root of what came to be known as the Wild West.

Back East major cities, with their dense populations and diverse cultures, produced a different set of social problems. Rapid population increase and urbanization broke down traditional family and village life and the ties that bound people. Crime was one of the results. In urban areas it was made worse by the absence of street lighting and social services for the poorest members of society, and by the flood of immigrants, especially from Ireland, Italy, and China, who introduced gang-controlled, organized crime to major U.S. cities.

Vice districts also flourished in every major city and many smaller towns. As a rule, it is safe to say, the farther west one went and the farther one moved from Victorian morality, the more blatant the vice activities became, although New York City took a back seat to no city in supporting the "oldest profession": In 1870 when its population was 950,000, more than 10,000 prostitutes plied their trade.

Perhaps the chief difference between crime on the frontier and crime in the big eastern cities was that in the cities crime statistics were routinely gathered and kept by authorities, and they allowed reformers and (later) historians to study the problem more thoroughly. Cities such as New York, Philadelphia, and Boston kept records of types of crimes, profiles of criminals, and other useful categories. The result was not a lower crime rate but at least a better understanding of the contributing factors.

Vigilantism

Violence could also be enlisted on the side of law and order in the form of vigilantism. Some crimes so outraged public opinion in small communities that the citizens short-circuited due process, going directly from accusation to punishment. Justice in such cases could be swift and brutal if not strictly by the book. Floggings, summary trials, and banishment were merely the least objectionable of the possible sentences meted out by vigilante groups. Calling it "vigilante justice" puts a better face on it than it deserved; it has also been called "popular justice with a vengeance." A wide variety of groups laid claim to being defenders of law and order in the 19th century, some 326 by one historian's count. That makes the 19th century the "heyday of American vigilantism," according to the historian Samuel Walker.

Of all the pseudo-law-and-order practices that arose during this time, none was more horrifying or repugnant to modern sensibilities than lynching. It was the quickest and cheapest form of "justice" for a society that had little patience for long, drawn-out legal proceedings. Hanging a man legally in Virginia in 1873 cost an estimated $358.80; by contrast, stringing him up from the nearest tree cost nothing. More than that, the traditional function of lynching was not retribution but intimidation: striking terror into a community perceived as a threat. Perhaps because lynching was more often than not directed against African Americans and Hispanics and involved the most barbaric tortures before the victim was finally allowed to die, it represents a particularly dark stain on U.S. justice.

A group of California vigilantes lynch a miscreant named Musgrove with the help of a rope and a railroad trestle. (Library of Congress, [LC-USZ62 050202])

Unfortunately only incomplete statistics were collected on lynchings during this time. A few newspapers occasionally reported statistics without specifying the source of the numbers, and in 1872 the Congressional Commission appointed to investigate the Ku Klux Klan issued its report citing numerous cases of "lynch law." The term *lynching* was used generically, being widely understood to mean not just hanging, but burning at the stake or any form of death at the hands of a mob. Quite often the lynching involved mutilation and torture before the victim was killed. Making the act of lynching a human being all the worse, these were not just criminal acts: They were public spectacles, routinely attended by women, children, and "respectable citizens."

When a mob constituted itself as a lawful authority, the result was vigilante justice, or justice administered by "committee," who were only slightly more humane and civilized than an ordinary bloodthirsty mob. The best documented examples of vigilante committees doing their work occurred in San Francisco in the 1850s and on the Montana cattle range in the 1860s. San Francisco gave birth to the two largest vigilante movements in all of U.S. history in 1851 and 1856 in response to the turmoil and lawlessness of the California gold rush. The city's self-appointed Committees of Vigilance banished troublemakers summarily and, when that did not work, resorted to more brutal methods to support their ideas of law and order. Even multiple hangings were carried out on more than one occasion.

A particularly bloody example of lynch law that had nothing to do with either claim jumpers or cattle rustlers occurred in July 1867 in Julesburg, Colorado. A Union Pacific construction crew who used the town for rest and recreation ordered vice operators to clear out or else, and after their warnings were ignored, they shot and hanged dozens of people as a lesson to the rest.

The historian Walter White and others agree that lynch law was a relatively minor occurrence early in the century but was increasingly resorted to as the decades passed, until it eventually reached epidemic proportions by the end of the 19th century. The first year that statistics

TABLE 20.5 DOCUMENTED LYNCHINGS IN THE UNITED STATES, MID-1800s

(with contemporary sources when identified)

Period	Location	Targeted Group	Perpetrators	Number of Victims
1836–Dec. 1856	Entire United States	Accused white criminals	Vigilante groups	"Over 300"[a]
1855–56	Calif.	Accused criminals	Vigilante groups	48 (cf. 19 legal executions)[b]
1850–60	The South	Black slaves who killed their master	White authorities	25 men and one woman: 17 by hanging, nine by burning
1850–60	The South	Black men accused of rape	White authorities	12: eight by hanging, four by burning
1868	The South	Freedmen	Unspecified	291
1869	The South	Freedmen	Unspecified	31
1870	The South	Freedmen	Unspecified	34
1871	The South	Freedmen	Unspecified	53
1870–72	Alabama	Freedmen	Ku Klux Klan and others	107[c]
1868	Bossier Parish, La.	Freedmen	Ku Klux Klan and others	120[c]
Apr. 1869–Apr. 1871	Miss.	Freedmen	Unspecified mobs	124[c]
Jan. 1866–Jul. 1867	N.C. and S.C.	Freedmen and others	Unspecified mobs	197[c]
End of Civil War to 1868	Tex.	Freedmen and others	Unspecified mobs	1,035[c]
Jul. 1867–Jun. 1868	Tenn.	Freedmen and others	Unspecified mobs	168[c]

Note: Figures were not gathered for the years 1872–79; all reports of lynchings during those years are therefore fragmentary or anecdotal.
[a] William Lloyd Garrison's *Liberator,* Dec. 19, 1856.
[b] *Frank Leslie's Illustrated Newspaper,* Mar. 1, 1856.
[c] 1872 Report of the Congressional Commission to investigate the Ku Klux Klan.
Sources: Walter White, *Rope & Faggot* (New York: Alfred A. Knopf, 1929), 91–96; Jack Salzman, David Lionel Smith, and Cornel West, eds., *Encyclopedia of African-American Culture and History,* vol. 5 (New York: Simon & Schuster/Macmillan, 1996), 2,954.

were gathered specifically on lynchings of blacks was 1882; in that year there were 49 recorded instances. In the next three years (1883–85) there were 53, 51, and 74 additional black victims, respectively.

Civil Disturbances (Rioting)

If vigilantism is what occurs when citizens take the law into their own hands, rioting is the result when law and order break down completely. There is a misconception that rioting in the United States is strictly a 20th-century phenomenon, sparked by black versus white issues. Both assumptions are wrong. Americans have always been suspicious of authority and not at all shy about taking to the streets when provoked. Rioting is, by definition, an urban phenomenon, and the 19th century United States was predominantly rural and agricultural. Still, a surprising number of incidents that can only be termed *riots* struck U.S. cities in the 19th century. They differed from earlier mob actions in U.S. history in that they were much bloodier and more lethal, producing scores of casualties. Historically mobs had relied on fists and clubs more than on guns and confined themselves to intimidation and property destruction, eschewing murder and arson. But conditions began to change after about 1830.

Between 1830 and 1860 at least 35 major civil disturbances occurred in Baltimore, Philadelphia, Boston, and New York City. And it was not just a problem in the large eastern cities. Cincinnati, Ohio, experienced one in 1829; Providence, Rhode Island, in 1831. Edward Z. C. Judson, better known by his pen name Ned Buntline, was personally culpable in fomenting riots in Nashville (1846), New York City (1849), and St. Louis (1852), possibly a record for any individual in any era. The group responsible for the most riots was the Know-Nothing Party, who were notorious for using thugs to intimidate their political opponents. Riots could be sparked by anti-immigrant speeches, election campaigns, even sporting events. The most common causes were religious beliefs and ethnic conflict, but class resentment was also sufficient provocation. And these civil disturbances were not minor in terms of either property damage or numbers of casualties. New York City and New Orleans were the most frequent sites of mob violence in the antebellum years, probably because they had the most heterogeneous populations and therefore the most social tensions.

Before the Civil War, riots were largely ethnic conflicts. The United States witnessed few race riots per se in the antebellum era (New York City, 1834; Philadelphia, 1834 and 1842) because in most Northern cities there was not a large enough population of free blacks to constitute a full-blown riot, and in the South, the urban slave population was kept on too tight a rein even to think of rising up en masse. There were, however, riots over the slavery issue when, after 1850, lawful authorities attempted to return fugitive slaves to the South. On several occasions state militias and even federal troops were called out to reinforce the local police in enforcing the hated Fugitive Slave Law in abolitionist communities such as Boston. Other antebellum riots that were unrelated to slavery were the product of political passions or rabid antiforeign and anti-Catholic prejudice. Rioting reached a crescendo in the 1850s, contributing to that decade's being remembered as the "Fiery Fifties." The situation in the East was sufficiently bad that even the press in the Far West commented on it. In 1857 when James Buchanan ordered federal troops into Utah, Mormon newspapers wondered why the president did not

Scenes in Memphis, Tennessee during the Riot of May 22, 1866 was probably from a sketch by A. R. Ward for *Frank Leslie's Illustrated Newspaper* (1866). The shocking reports of blacks being shot down on Southern streets by armed mobs of whites galvanized Congress to take control of Reconstruction. (Tennessee State Library and Archives)

deal with recent bloody riots in Baltimore, Washington, and New York instead of bothering the "Saints." The passions and prejudices that produced this wave of rioting mainly faded in the wake of the Civil War, although Catholics and Protestants could still work up a good civil disturbance as late as 1871. After 1870, says the historian Samuel Walker, "riots were more often industrial disputes" than religious and ethnic clashes. Racial issues, however, continued to be a prime cause.

The Civil War created a different kind of disturbance as Confederate and national governments attempted to enforce coercive wartime measures on populations not accustomed to such coercion. The worst riots in U.S. history up to the 20th century occurred in New York City in July 1863, the same month Union and Confederate armies were fighting the greatest battle of the war at Gettysburg, Pennsylvania. They were an outgrowth of the recently passed Conscription Act that began as an antidraft demonstration, then quickly escalated into a mass insurrection involving murder, looting, arson, and rampaging gangs. To restore peace, U.S. Regulars had to be sent into the city.

After the Civil War another racial group entered the picture—the Chinese—who, like Africans before them, were imported into the country in large numbers to do menial labor. By the 1870s thousands of Chinese were huddled in a handful of Chinatowns in cities such as San Francisco, Seattle, and Los Angeles. This decade witnessed the first outbreaks of mob violence in the West, pitting Anglos against Chinese and quickly escalating into as serious a problem as that of blacks versus whites. It derived from many of the same conditions that caused violence against the freedmen in the South: competition for jobs, fear of foreigners, and plain, old-fashioned bigotry. In 1869 the governor of California essentially announced open season on all Asians when he called them "a stream of filth and prostitution pouring in from Asia whose servile competition tends to cheapen and degrade [white] labor." The opening salvo in a race war against the Chinese followed in Los Angeles two years later.

TABLE 20.6 RIOTS IN U.S. CITIES, 1849–1875

Date	Location	Cause	Resolution	Casualties and/or Damage
May 10, 1849	New York, N.Y. (Astor Place Opera House)	A class conflict over a theater program, involving supporters of Britain versus U.S. stage actors	Troops are called out to quell it	Twenty deaths; many injuries
May 26, 1851	Hoboken, N.J.	Ethnic-based clash between local Germans and the "Rock Boys & Short Boys" of Hoboken and N.Y.C.	Police eventually quell it	Unknown
Aug. 21, 1851	New Orleans, La.	Execution of U.S. filibusterers in Cuba by Spanish authorities	Police finally quell riot; U.S. government pays indemnity to Spain government	No deaths; Spain Consulate destroyed, consul taken into protective custody by police; at least $25,000 in damage
Nov. 1852	St. Louis, Mo.	Bitter elections from recent election	Police intervention and exhaustion finally end it	One known killed plus multiple others unconfirmed
Mar. 1854	Washington, D.C.	Know-Nothing mob reacting to inclusion of memorial marble stone donated by the pope in construction of Washington Monument	Mob seizes stone and throws it into Potomac River; authorities do not intervene	No deaths; injuries, if any, unreported
Jun. 1854	Boston, Mass.	Runaway slave, Anthony Burns, seized by police for extradition to Va.; crowd of 50,000 jeers authorities escorting him through town	Several heads are cracked and at least one citizen, Theodore Parker, is arrested for "inciting a riot"	One policeman killed; cost of event estimated at $50,000 in personnel and damages
Apr. 1855 ("Bloody Monday")	Louisville, Ky.	Anti-Irish and anti-German violence organized by local Know-Nothing Party trying to prevent them from voting in election	Both sides arm themselves and fight spiritedly, but Know-Nothings win the Battle of the Polling Places	Best estimate of death is 22 (most German and Irish Americans); other estimates: 14 to 100 beaten or shot to death[a]
1855	New Orleans, La.	Nativists versus foreign-born residents	It is finally put down by police	Two killed, unknown numbers wounded
Oct. 8, 1856	Baltimore, Md.	Clash of Democrats and Know-Nothings sparked by election campaign	It is ended by local police	Four men killed initially; 88 wounded; five die later of wounds
Jun. 1, 1857	Washington, D.C.	Polling violence during municipal elections; initiated by Know-Nothing thugs ("plug-uglies")	Two companies of U.S. Marines called out from Washington Navy Yard disperse mob, using fixed bayonets[b]	Five men killed; 15 wounded

(continued)

TABLE 20.6 (continued)

Date	Location	Cause	Resolution	Casualties and/or Damage
Jun. 16, 1857	New York, N.Y.	Political feud between Mayor Fernando Wood and state authorities that turns bloody when Albany-controlled Metropolitan Police attempt to arrest Wood for assaulting the city's street commissioner, only to be opposed by mayor's loyal police force	Stand-off occurs	Unknown
Apr. 19, 1861	Baltimore, Md. ("the Pratt Street Riot")	Pro-Southern mob attacks 6th Massachusetts Regiment on its way to Washington, D.C.	The soldiers defend themselves and scatter the crowd before retreating	Four soldiers killed and 39 injured; at least nine and as many as 16 civilians killed (varying sources)
Apr. 2, 1863	Richmond, Va.	"Bread Riot" that began when mob demanded bread in Confederate capital; quickly turned into general looting rampage through the city	Police aided by militia dispersed the crowd and made several arrests	No significant bloodshed
Jul. 4, 1863	St. Louis, Mo. (Hyde Park)	Began as barroom brawl among Union soldiers; quickly escalated after police summoned and sputtered through the day	Troops of 2d Missouri Artillery arrived and opened fire "without sufficient provocation"	Four soldiers and two civilians killed; 12 people wounded
Jul. 13–16, 1863	New York, N.Y.	Antidraft riots, encouraged by Confederate agents and Peace Democrats; mob of large proportion of foreign laborers; blacks and federal officials the main targets	Police, firemen, and local troops are overwhelmed; veteran troops have to be rushed up from Gettysburg; first draft postponed until Aug. 10	1,000 killed and wounded (estimate); estimated $1,500,000 property damage
Jul. 12, 1871	New York, N.Y.	Irish Catholics versus Irish Protestants over the celebration of Orange Day	Troops are called out to quell it	At least 45 killed (52 in some sources); many injured
Oct. 24, 1871	Los Angeles, Calif. (Chinatown)	Police attempt to quell battle between rival Chinese gangs; white man killed; white mob gathered seeking vengeance	After rampaging for hours through Chinatown the mob finally disperses of its own accord	Six Chinese shot to death and 15 lynched, incuding 12-yr-old boy; Chinese "Quarter" ransacked
Summer 1873	Jacksonville, Tex.	Citizens of local community take exception to members of visiting Robinson Family Circus	After nine hours of fighting, authorities are unable to quell it; the riot winds down in exhaustion	Unknown
Jan. 1874	New York, N.Y. (Tompkins Square)	Demonstration for jobs by 7,000 unemployed laborers	Police are sent in to quell the riot	Many marchers arrested; unknown number of marchers and spectators injured

[a] This was the most violent of all antebellum political riots of the 19th century.
[b] This is the first time U.S. Marines ever intervened in a U.S. election.
Source: "Chronologies," in *The American Almanac and Repository of Useful Knowledge for the Years 1850–1861,* Part II (Boston: Chas. C. Little & James Brown; Crosby, Nichols, Lee and Company, 1849–75), 344–52; for 1856–57, 365–76; for 1858–59, 383–91; for 1860, 407–13; E. B. Long, *The Civil War Day by Day* (Garden City, N.Y.: Doubleday, 1971, passim; Gorton Carruth, *The Encyclopedia of American Facts and Dates,* 8th ed. (New York: Harper & Row, 1987), passim; Michael A. Bellesiles, *Arming America* (New York: Alfred A. Knopf, 2000), 367–70.

The Civil War created a new set of problems for both sides that stirred popular passions to the point that normally law-abiding citizens would take to the streets in an orgy of death and destruction. Lingering resentment over emancipation mixed with Reconstruction politics to produce all the ingredients necessary for violent urban clashes in Southern cities. On a half-dozen separate occasions the tension between whites and blacks turned into bloody clashes of an intensity and viciousness seldom seen in American society in any era. Race riots at Memphis and New Orleans scarcely a year after Appomattox left dozens dead and injured and provoked direct federal intervention in the form of military occupation. No one knew it at the time, but these were just the first outbreaks in an epidemic of race violence that struck Southern communities between 1866 and 1876.

TABLE 20.7 RACIAL VIOLENCE IN THE SOUTH DURING RECONSTRUCTION, 1866–1876

Event	Location	Date	Cause	Casualties	Consequences
Memphis Riot	Memphis, Tenn.	May 1–3, 1866	A white mob invades black section of town after white police and black veterans clash	Forty-six blacks and two whites killed; 75 people injured; five women raped	Congressional investigation recommends harsher Reconstruction policies
New Orleans Riot	New Orleans, La.	Jul. 30, 1866	A political rally by Unionists provokes attack by armed conservative mob.	At least 37 (48 in one source) blacks killed and three whites; more than 100 (mostly blacks) injured—"an absolute massacre"	President Johnson blames Republican agitators for provoking it; outraged Northern public turns against Johnson and his Reconstruction policies; event contributes to Republican victories in fall elections
Camilla Riot	Town in southwestern Ga.	Sep. 19, 1868	A black march on Camilla causes the sheriff to call out a posse of whites, who attack marchers	Nine blacks killed; 25–30 wounded; no deaths, unknown number of injuries among whites	Ga. legislature appoints investigating committee that absolves posse and blames Republican agitators
Louisiana Riots	New Orleans, Opelousas, St. Bernard Parish, La.	Sep. 22–Oct. 26, 1868	General unrest and political turmoil occur	Unknown	Further intimidation of black citizens results
Colfax Riot	Parish seat of Grant Parish, La.	Apr. 13, 1873 (Easter Sunday)	During political dispute, armed black Republicans take over courthouse; sheriff assembles white posse and orders attack	Fifty-nine blacks and two whites killed; unknown number wounded; some killed after they surrender	White leaders are indicted under provisions of 1870 Enforcement Act; freed x surrender order of U.S. Supreme Court (*U.S. v. Cruikshank*, 1876)
Coushatta Massacre	Red River Parish, La.	Ca. Aug. 31, 1874	Conservative "White League" arrests Republican officeholders, turns them over to murderous mob	Six white Republicans killed; two blacks killed days later; no White League casualties	Severely weakens Republicans carpetbag government in La.: hastens end of Reconstruction
The "Second Battle of Vicksburg"	Vicksburg, Miss.	Dec. 7, 1874	Mob of freedmen attack courthouse to protest ejection of popular carpetbag sheriff by local whites	About 70 blacks killed; unknown number of white casualties	Strong blow against carpetbag rule; city's black population more intimidated than ever
Battle of Liberty Place	New Orleans, La.	Sep. 1874	White League mob battles Metropolitan Police in support of rival claimants to statehouse	Eleven policemen and 21 White League members killed; 60 policemen and 19 White Leaguers wounded	Federal troops called in to restore order and defend Republican regime
Clinton Massacre	Clinton, La.	Sep. 4–6, 1875	White mob attempts to prevent black citizens from voting	More than 30 blacks killed	Federal troops deployed at governor's request; intimidation of black voters continues
Hamburg Massacre	Hamburg, S.C.	Jul. 8, 1876	White militia ("Red Shirts") besiege a black militia force in an armory and force them to surrender	One white militiaman killed; five captured black militiamen executed	Irreparable split between moderate Democrats and ruling Republican Party beginning of the end of Republican rule in state

Source: Hans L. Trefousse, *Historical Dictionary of Reconstruction* (Westport, Conn.: Greenwood Press, 1991), passim; E. L. Bute and H. J. P. Harmer, *The Black Handbook* (London: Cassell, 1997), 336–38; Alton Hornsby, Jr., *Chronology of African American History,* 2d ed. (Detroit: Gale Research, 1997), 75–82.

Juvenile Crime

Juvenile crime was as troublesome in the 19th century as it is today. Only the scale of the problem has changed. Youth was no guarantee against a life of crime, even when the home was still sacrosanct, values were still upheld, and justice was still relatively swift. And just as today, social critics pinned much of the blame on the nature of U.S. society: rapacious and brutal, they said. The social reformer Charles Loring Brace in 1872 wrote a best seller decrying the gratuitous meanness of young male lawbreakers.

Juvenile crime and urban life seemed to be related in those days too. Orphans and runaways roamed the streets of major cities in gangs as thoroughly ruthless as their elders, and the criminal justice system (police and courts) made no age distinction when it caught up with them. In fact juvenile criminals in the 19th century were processed through the judicial system in the same way as adults, partly because of lack of sentimentality and partly because of lack of agreement on the dividing line between children and adults. At a time when the age of consent for girls was as low as 10 years old in some states, and teenage boys could be strung up on the gallows as quickly as hardened criminals, the American people were somewhat hazy on the subtleties of child psychology. By mid-century juveniles were at least being confined in separate facilities or "houses of refuge" in major eastern cities. By the post–Civil War period what were now known as reform schools existed all over the country; at least 19 states had one or more such institutions, and sentencing guidelines had been established. Juvenile criminal law was on its way to becoming a separate branch of the legal system.

Baltimore's House of Refuge for juvenile delinquents was one of the first such institutions in the country when it opened in 1855. It housed young offenders four to 17 years old who were taught the three Rs and a useful trade during their incarceration. (The Maryland Historical Society, Baltimore, Maryland)

TABLE 20.8 PLACEMENT AND SENTENCING OF JUVENILE OFFENDERS IN REFORM SCHOOLS, 1868

State	Name and Type of School (If known)	Standard Sentencing Terms
Calif.	Industrial School	For duration of minority years
Conn.	State Reform School	For duration of minority years or for specific term
Ill.	Chicago Reform School	For duration of minority years
Ind.	House of Refuge	Minority years or until reformed
Ky.	House of Refuge	For duration of minority years
La.	House of Refuge	N/A
Maine	State Reform School	For duration of minority years or for specific term
Md.	House of Refuge	For duration of minority years
Mass.	State Reform School	For duration of minority years
Mass.	Nautical Reform School	For duration of minority years
Mass.	State Industrial Girls' School	Until 18 years of age with state option to incarcerate until 21 years
Mass.	House of Reformation	For duration of minority years or for specific term
Mich.	State Reform School	For duration of minority years
Mo.	House of Refuge	For duration of minority years
N.H.	State Reform School	For duration of minority years or for specific term
N.J.	State Reform School	For duration of minority years
N.Y.	Catholic Protectory	For duration of minority years
N.Y.	House of Refuge	For duration of minority years
N.Y.	Juvenile Asylum	Indefinite or for duration of minority years
N.Y.	Western House of Refuge	For duration of minority years
Ohio	House of Refuge	For duration of minority years
Ohio	State Reform School	For duration of minority years
Penn.	House of Refuge (Whites only)	For duration of minority years
Penn.	House of Refuge (Coloreds only)	For duration of minority years
Penn.	Western House of Refuge	For duration of minority years
R.I.	Providence Reform School	For duration of minority years or for specific term
Vt.	State Reform School	For duration of minority years
Wis.	State Reform School	For duration of minority years

Source: U.S. Office of Education, "Report on Reform Schools, 1868," cited in Margaret Werner Cahalan, *Historical Corrections Statistics in the United States 1850–1984* (Washington, D.C.: U.S. Department of Justice, 1987), 128.

The Prison System

The prevailing penal philosophy in the United States at mid-century was based on the Auburn system, named for the New York state prison in Auburn. Supposedly a humanitarian advance over older theories of incarceration, it kept prisoners in isolation, one to a cell, and imposed a rule of total silence even in communal areas. The idea was that this practice would foster self-reflection and repentance, thus ultimately leading to rehabilitation as solid citizens. The Auburn system was embraced by both federal and state officials, at least partly because it also promised to make prisons help pay for themselves by requiring the inmates to labor in prison industries. The penitentiary at Joliet, Illinois, and the Colorado territorial penitentiary at Canyon City were two of the most successful examples among the numerous prisons built on the Auburn model in the 19th century. Noble theories aside, however, most prisons remained custodial institutions dedicated to punishment, nor reformation.

The U.S. prison population leaped after mid-century and not only because of some newfound faith in the efficacy of bars and walls to protect society. The number of inmates tripled between 1850 and 1860 and then nearly doubled again in the next 10 years, driven by the massive influx of immigrants and the hostility that they tended to arouse among law enforcement officials, coupled with the lawlessness provoked by the Civil War. This era was a time of turmoil in U.S. life, and that fact is reflected in crime and punishment statistics.

Three black Mississippi state prison inmates, "an express robber, a poisoner and a cold-blooded murderer," await transportation to a work gang on a local plantation under the notorious convict lease system, in a lithograph from *Harper's Weekly,* September 16, 1871. (Courtesy of Mississippi Department of Archives and History)

TABLE 20.9 CRIMINAL CONVICTIONS AND INCARCERATIONS IN THE UNITED STATES IN DECENNIAL YEARS, 1850–1870

Decennial Year	Convictions	Prison Population on June 1	Convictions per 100,000 of Population	Prisoners per 100,000 of Population
1850	26,679	6,737	115.0	29.0
1860	19,086	19,086	314.3	60.7
1870	32,901	32,901	94.8	85.3

Source: Margaret Werner Cahalan, *Historical Corrections Statistics in the United States, 1850–1984* (Washington, D.C.: U.S. Department of Justice, 1987), 28.

TABLE 20.10 CRIMINAL POPULATION OF THE UNITED STATES BY NATIONAL ORIGIN, FOR ALL STATES AND TERRITORIES REPORTING, 1850

State or Territory	Total Population	Native-Born Population	Foreign-Born Population	Total Number of Convicted Criminals[a]	Native-Born in Prison	Foreign-Born in Prison
Ala.	771,623	763,089	7,509	122	69	1
Ark.	209,897	297,636	1,471	25	17	0
Calif.	92,597	70,340	21,802	1	35	27
Conn.	370,792	331,560	38,518	850	244	66
Del.	91,532	86,268	5,253	22	14	0
District of Columbia	54,687	46,720	4,918	132	26	20
Fla.	87,445	84,665	2,769	39	9	2
Ga.	906,185	899,132	6,488	80	36	7
Ill.	851,470	736,149	111,892	316	164	88
Ind.	988,416	930,458	55,572	175	41	18
Iowa	192,214	170,931	20,969	3	5	0
Ky.	982,405	949,652	31,420	160	41	11
La.	517,762	418,848	68,233	297	240	183
Maine	583,169	550,878	31,825	744	66	34
Md.	583,034	531,476	51,209	207	325	72
Mass.	994,514	827,430	164,024	7,250	653	583
Mich.	397,654	341,656	54,703	659	139	102
Minn.	6,077	4,097	1,977	2	0	1
Miss.	606,526	601,230	4,788	51	45	1
Mo.	682,044	604,522	76,592	908	55	125
N.H.	317,976	303,563	14,265	90	25	8
N.J.	489,555	429,176	59,948	603	198	92
N.Mex.	61,547	59,187	2,151	108	37	1
N.Y.	3,097,394	2,436,771	655,929	10,279	649	639
N.C.	869,039	866,241	2,581	647	43	1
Ohio	1,980,329	1,757,746	218,193	843	102	31
Oreg.	13,294	12,081	1,022	5	5	0
Pa.	2,311,786	2,006,207	303,417	857	296	115
R.I.	147,545	123,564	23,902	596	58	45
S.C.	668,507	659,743	8,707	46	21	15
Tenn.	1,002,717	995,478	5,653	81	276	12
Tex.	212,592	194,433	17,681	19	5	10
Utah	11,330	9,326	2,044	9	6	3
Vt.	314,120	280,055	33,715	79	64	41
Va.	1,421,661	1,398,205	22,985	107	291	22
Wis.	305,391	194,099	110,477	267	26	35
United States	23,191,876	20,912,612	2,244,602	26,679	4,326	2,411

Note: All dates are for the fiscal year (ending Jun. 1), not the calendar year. *Criminal population* is defined as anyone convicted of a crime, and *prison population* includes anyone incarcerated at any time during the (fiscal) year.

[a] Figures cover only persons convicted of crimes and incarcerated up to Jun. 1, 1850, end of the federal government fiscal year, not the calendar year.

Source: U.S. Census Office, *A Compendium of the 9th Census, June 1, 1870,* compiled by Frances Amasa Walker (Washington, D.C.: U.S. Govrnment Printing Office, 1872), 534–35.

TABLE 20.11 CRIMINAL POPULATION OF THE UNITED STATES BY NATIONAL ORIGIN, FOR ALL STATES AND TERRITORIES REPORTING, 1860

State or Territory	Total Population	Native-Born Population	Foreign-Born Population	Total Number of Convicted Criminals[a]	Native-Born in Prison	Foreign-Born in Prison
Ala.	964,201	951,849	12,352	179	183	43
Ark.	435,450	431,850	300,600	200	61	17
Calif.	379,994	233,466	146,528	915	336	546
Conn.	460,147	379,451	80,696	1,473	449	197
Del.	112,216	103,051	9,165	63	19	8
District of Columbia	75,080	62,596	12,484	264	163	47
Fla.	140,424	137,115	3,309	33	13	2
Ga.	1,057,286	1,045,615	11,671	251	77	34
Ill.	1,711,951	1,387,308	324,643	812	313	172
Ind.	1,350,428	1,232,144	118,284	1,184	129	155

State or Territory	Total Population	Native-Born Population	Foreign-Born Population	Total Number of Convicted Criminals[a]	Native-Born in Prison	Foreign-Born in Prison
Iowa	674,913	568,836	106,077	278	61	34
Kans.	107,206	94,515	12,691	24	22	9
Ky.	1,155,684	1,095,885	50,799	600	147	85
La.	708,002	627,027	80,975	3,197	359	490
Maine	628,279	590,826	37,453	1,215	107	58
Md.	687,049	609,520	77,529	283	99	17
Mass.	1,231,066	970,960	260,106	12,732	1,495	1,184
Mich.	749,113	600,020	149,093	871	505	252
Minn.	172,023	113,295	58,728	33	16	16
Miss.	791,305	782,747	8,558	219	35	18
Mo.	1,182,012	1,021,471	160,541	516	166	120
Nebr.	28,841	22,490	6,351	8	N/A	N/A
N.H.	326,073	305,135	20,938	795	138	55
N.J.	672,035	549,245	122,790	1,645	121	91
N. Mex.	93,516	86,793	6,723	23	8	2
N.Y.	3,880,735	2,879,455	1,001,280	58,067	2,861	4,021
N.C.	992,622	989,324	3,298	450	62	9
Ohio	2,339,511	2,011,262	328,249	6,830	265	358
Oreg.	52,465	47,342	5,123	29	6	7
Pa.	2,906,215	2,475,710	430,505	2,930	756	405
R.I.	174,620	137,226	37,394	718	100	81
S. C.	763,708	693,722	9,986	141	57	31
Tenn.	1,109,801	1,088,575	21,226	200	433	78
Tex.	604,215	560,793	43,422	214	40	. . .
Utah	40,273	27,519	12,754	24	5	3
Vt.	315,098	282,355	32,743	43	80	39
Va.	1,596,318	1,561,260	35,058	608	163	26
Wash.	11,594	8,450	3,144	15	3	12
Wis.	775,881	498,954	276,927	754	172	181
United States	31,443,321	27,304,624	4,138,697	98,836	10,143	8,943

Note: All dates are for the fiscal year (ending Jun. 1), not the calendar year. *Criminal population* is defined as anyone convicted of a crime, and *prison population* includes anyone incarcerated at any time during the (fiscal) year.
[a] Figures cover only persons convicted of crimes and incarcerated up to Jun. 1, 1860, end of the federal government's fiscal year.
Source: U.S. Census Office, *A Compendium of the 9th Census, June 1, 1870,* compiled by Frances Amasa Walker (Washington, D.C.: U.S. Government Printing Office, 1872), 532–33.

TABLE 20.12 CRIMINAL POPULATION OF THE UNITED STATES BY NATIONAL ORIGIN, FOR ALL STATES AND TERRITORIES REPORTING, 1870

State or Territory	Total Population	Native-Born Population	Foreign-Born Population	Total Number of Convicted Criminals[a]	Native-Born in Prison	Foreign-Born in Prison
Ala.	996,992	987,030	9,962	1,269	585	8
Ariz.	9,658	3,849	5,809	11	N/A	11
Ark.	484,471	479,445	5,026	343	322	40
Calif.	560,247	350,416	209,831	1,107	668	906
Colo.	39,864	33,265	6,599	32	15	3
Conn.	537,454	423,815	113,639	450	278	152
Dakota	14,181	9,366	4,815	2	1	2
Del.	125,015	115,879	9,136	145	57	9
District of Columbia	131,700	115,446	16,254	121	117	26
Fla.	187,748	182,781	4,967	335	176	3
Ga.	1,184,109	1,172982	11,127	1,775	723	14
Idaho	14,999	7,114	7,885	26	18	10
Ill.	2,539,891	2,024,693	515,198	1,552	1,372	423
Ind.	1,680,637	1,539,163	141,474	1,374	755	152
Iowa	1,194,020	989,328	204,692	615	287	110
Kans.	364,399	316,007	48,392	151	262	67
Ky.	1,321,011	1,257,613	63,308	603	968	99
La.	726,915	665,088	61,827	1,559	818	27
Maine	626,915	578,034	48,881	431	261	110
Md.	780,894	697,482	83,412	868	967	68

(continued)

TABLE 20.12 (continued)

State or Territory	Total Population	Native-Born Population	Foreign-Born Population	Total Number of Convicted Criminals	Native-Born in Prison	Foreign-Born in Prison
Mass.	1,457,351	1,104,032	353,319	1,593	1,291	1,235
Mich.	1,184,059	916,049	268,010	835	679	416
Minn.	439,706	279,009	160,697	214	73	56
Miss.	827,922	816,731	11,191	471	421	28
Mo.	1,721,295	1,499,028	22,267	1,503	1,217	406
Mont.	20,505	12,616	7,979	24	14	2
Nebr.	122,993	92,245	30,748	53	44	25
Nev.	42,491	23,690	18,801	132	40	59
N.H.	318,300	288,689	29,611	182	201	66
N.J.	906,096	717,153	188,943	1,040	640	439
N. Mex.	91,874	86,254	5,620	95	21	3
N.Y.	4,382,759	3,244,406	1,138,353	5,473	2,658	2,046
N.C.	1,071,361	1,068,332	3,029	1,311	462	6
Ohio	2,665,260	2,292,767	372,493	2,560	1,018	387
Oreg.	90,923	79,323	11,600	80	67	37
Pa.	3,521,951	2,976,642	545,309	3,327	2,532	699
R.I.	217,353	161,957	55,396	209	125	55
S.C.	705,606	697,532	8,074	1,390	714	18
Tenn.	1,258,520	1,239,204	19,316	722	902	79
Tex.	818,579	756,168	62,411	260	602	130
Utah	86,786	56,084	30,702	27	19	0
Vt.	330,551	283,396	47,155	139	145	48
Va.	1,225,163	1,211,409	13,754	1,090	1,232	12
Wash.	23,955	18,931	5,024	20	8	11
W.Va.	442,014	424,923	17,091	155	175	16
Wis.	1,054,670	690,171	364,449	837	215	203
Wyo.	9,118	5,605	3,513	24	7	6
United States	38,558,371	32,991,142	5,567,229	36,562	24,173	8,728

Note: All dates are for the fiscal year (ending Jun. 1), not the calendar year. *Criminal population* is defined as anyone convicted of a crime, and *prison population* includes anyone incarcerated at any time during the (fiscal) year.
Source: U.S. Census Office, *A Compendium of the 9th Census, June 1, 1870,* compiled by Frances Amasa Walker (Washington, D.C.: U.S. Government Printing Office, 1872), 530–31.

TABLE 20.13 CRIMINAL POPULATION OF THE UNITED STATES BY RACE, FOR ALL STATES AND TERRITORIES REPORTING, 1870

State or Territory	Total Population	White Population	Black Population	Total Number of Convicted Criminals[a]	Whites in Prison	Blacks in Prison
Ala.	996,992	521,384	475,510	1,269	149	436
Ariz.	9,658	9,581	26	29	N/A	N/A
Ark.	484,471	362,115	122,169	343	137	185*
Calif.	560,247	499,424	4,272	1,107	662	6
Colo.	39,864	39,221	456	32	11	5
Conn.	537,454	527,549	9,668	450	215	63
Dakota	14,181	12,887	94	2	1	N/A
Del.	125,015	102,221	22,794	145	13	44
District of Columbia	131,700	88,278	43,404	121	38	79
Fla.	187,748	96,057	91,689	335	20	156
Ga.	1,184,109	638,926	545,142	1,775	126	597
Idaho	14,999	10,618	60	26	17	1
Ill.	2,539,891	2,511,096	28,762	1,552	1,220	143
Ind.	1,680,637	1,655,837	24,560	1,374	691	64
Iowa	1,194,020	1,188,207	5,762	615	273	14
Kans.	364,399	346,377	17,108	151	202	60*
Ky.	1,321,011	1,098,692	222,210	603	525	443
La.	726,915	362,065	364,210	1,559	460	358
Maine	626,915	624,809	1,606	431	255	6
Md.	780,894	605,497	175,391	868	304	663
Mass.	1,457,351	1,443,156	13,947	1,593	1,152	139
Mich.	1,184,059	1,167,282	11,849	835	617	62#
Minn.	439,706	438,257	759	214	65	8
Miss.	827,922	382,896	44,201	471	128	293
Mo.	1,721,295	1,603,146	118,071	1,503	893	324

State or Territory	Total Population	White Population	Black Population	Total Number of Convicted Criminals[a]	Whites in Prison	Blacks in Prison
Mont.	20,595	18,306	183	24	13	1
Nebr.	122,993	122,117	789	53	35	9
Nev.	42,491	38,959	357	132	37	3
N.H.	318,300	317,697	580	182	199	2
N.J.	906,096	875,407	30,658	1,040	483	157
N. Mex.	91,874	90,393	172	95	18	3
N.Y.	4,382,759	4,330,210	52,081	5,473	2,323	335
N.C.	1,071,361	678,470	391,650	1,311	132	330
Ohio	2,665,260	2,601,946	63,213	2.,560	892	126
Oreg.	90,923	86,929	346	80	55	12[b]
Pa.	3,521,951	3,456,609	65,294	3,327	2,088	444
R.I.	217,353	212,219	4,980	209	113	12
S.C.	705,606	289,667	415,814	1,399	130	584
Tenn.	1,258,520	936,119	322,331	722	342	560
Tex.	818,579	564,700	253,475	260	237	365
Utah	86,786	86,044	118	27	19	N/A
Vt.	330,551	329,613	924	139	143	2
Va.	1,225,163	712,089	512,841	1,090	331	901
Wash.	23,955	22,195	207	20	7	1
W.V.	442,014	424,033	17,980	155	138	37
Wis.	1,054,670	1,051,351	2,113	837	192	23[c]
Wyo.	9,118	8,726	183	24	7	N/A
United States	38,558,371	33,589,377	4,880,009	36,562	16,117	8,056[d]

Note: All dates are for the fiscal year (ending Jun. 1), not the calendar year. *Criminal population* is defined as anyone convicted of a crime, and *prison population* includes anyone incarcerated at any time during the (fiscal) year.

[a] Figures cover only persons convicted of crimes and incarcerated up to Jun. 1, 1870, end of the federal government fiscal year.

[b] Includes three Indians.

[c] Includes two Indians.

[d] Includes 10 Indians.

Source: U.S. Census Office, *A Compendium of the 9th Census, June 1, 1870,* compiled by Frances Amasa Walker (Washington, D.C.: U.S. Government Printing Office, 1872), 530–31.

Penal Reform and Criminology

If violence and brutality seemed to be ingrained in the system, at least a group of reformers were making a determined effort to introduce change on the punishment side. The reformist zeal so characteristic of the Jacksonian age carried over to the mid-19th century. While alarmed citizens turned to their various governments to protect them from crime, reformers took the tack that criminals were not really as evil as their Puritan forebears had believed but were merely deluded or misguided; they needed kind but firm rehabilitation. Hard work, discipline, and a good dose of Christianity would put them on the right path to a productive life. The new breed of reformers focused less on the causes and prevention of criminal activity than on the conditions of incarceration in the belief that humane treatment could rehabilitate prison inmates. The concept of long-term imprisonment was still new to Americans. Historically, criminals had been either fined and released, physically mutilated (e.g., by branding), or, in extreme cases, hanged. Long-term imprisonment was an expensive and overindulgent option that had little public support before reformers took up the cause of penal reform.

Numerous jail and prison officials after the Civil War, particularly in the South, aimed to make incarceration pay for itself by leasing out convicts to the private sector to perform hard labor. This system, which flourished from 1866 until well into the 20th century, was almost as exploitative and cruel as slavery. It was a product of rising crime rates and bankrupt economies. It was also different from the notorious public road gangs of a later era. Contract prisoners worked on sugar and cotton plantations and in phosphate beds, coal mines, brickyards, and sawmills, all under the most brutal conditions for proceeds that went to others. The death rate for convict laborers across the South averaged 16–25 percent annually. It was a deplorable system of involuntary servitude plagued by corruption and racism but was highly profitable. One contractor in Georgia paid seven cents per man per working day into the state coffers for some 300 workers. As opposed to enlightened penology, this was merely the grafting of the free market enterprise onto the penal system. It would flourish despite laws and court decisions against it for more than six decades.

The new science of criminology, which started in Europe, found the United States a fascinating living laboratory. What early criminologists observed was that lawlessness was "an American phenomenon with no equal in the rest of the world," as one of them said. In the years after 1860 the crime rate rose more than 400 percent at the same time that the population was increasing only a little more than 100 percent.

A typical Southern prison of the post–Civil War period with white guards and black prisoners. Striped uniforms apparently were optional. The wooden fence is topped by (barbed?) wire. (Alabama Department of Archives and History, Montgomery, Alabama)

This engraving in *Harper's Weekly,* December 5, 1868, shows a chain gang making street repairs in Richmond, Virginia. The prisoners (black and white together) are probably part of the detestable convict lease program, prevented from escaping by their balls and chain and a single guard. (Library of Congress, [LC-USZ62 22083])

White-Collar Crime

In modern times people have used the term *white-collar crime* to describe nonviolent acts such as fraud and embezzlement, committed by members of the upper classes. The term did not exist in the 19th century, but the sort of criminal behavior it describes certainly did. The scandalous activities exposed by Mark Twain and Charles Dudley Warner in *The Gilded Age* (1873) did not involve either violent affrays or the guilty pleasures of the vice district. They involved malfeasance in high places. The social and political system of the day encouraged corruption on a scale never before seen in the United States. It reached into the highest offices of the land, including Congress and the White House. Much of the breakdown in morality is attributed to the legacy of the Civil War because the situation seemed to intensify in the years after 1865. Rapid industrialization created powerful business tycoons who felt no social responsibilities. Instead they sought and received favors from government officials for a price, and duly elected politicians shamelessly used public office as a source of private profit. The widespread political practice of patronage also rewarded personal loyalty more than civic responsibility, and Victorian morality placed a premium on public appearance rather than personal integrity. Because of the contradictory nature of Victorian morality, Congress could pass the so-called Comstock Law (1873) vaguely aimed at preventing obscene materials from being sent through the mail while at the same time lining its own pockets and help its influential friends. By the same token violent crimes against respectable citizens, particularly across class lines, and crimes against property even amounting to just a few dollars were usually punished severely, while grand larceny by the "malefactors of great wealth" went unpunished.

White-collar crime took the form of political machines on the municipal level, swindles on the federal level, and unregulated special interest groups on every level. New York City's notorious Tweed Ring stole more money from the city ($160 million) during its reign than the destruction caused by the Chicago Fire ($30 million). President Ulysses Grant's name became synonymous with political corruption ("Grantism"), although he himself was never accused of doing anything illegal. Among the most famous scandals of Grant's administration were the following:

1. The Credit Mobilier Affair, involving bribes of a congressman by railroad companies.
2. The Santo Domingo Affair, to annex Cuba unlawfully.
3. "Black Friday," when a pair of financiers attempted to corner the gold market.
4. The "Whiskey Ring" of distillers, who defrauded the government of millions in taxes.
5. The Belknap scandal, when the secretary of war sold frontier post traderships for payment under the table.
6. The Customs House Gang, who lined their pockets and took care of their friends.
7. The "Salary Grab of 1873," when Congress voted across-the-board increases for federal officials and then made them retroactive.

As a result of the widespread scandals in the government, much of Congress's time was taken up with investigations in a preview of the late 20th century.

In all of these scandals the public seemed to be either willfully ignorant or completely blasé. The superficial prosperity of the age, which concealed a host of ethical and social problems, led the authors Mark Twain and Charles Dudley Warner to label it the Gilded Age in their 1873 novel of the same title. They were not revealing anything new but simply putting a handle on a prevailing lifestyle characterized by ostentatious, vulgar, and immoral behavior. Respect for the law, the courts, and public officials reached an all-time low during these years. Honesty in public life was considered more of a hindrance than a virtue. Large corporations, political machines, and the wealthy classes were above the law.

An epidemic of crime and violence seemed to afflict the nation during these years. It can be blamed on war, or the frontier experience, or on general lawlessness, but there were deeper causes at work, too. There was a "gun culture" present in the United States, according to the historian Michael Bellesiles, that tolerated the unfettered possession and use of firearms on all levels of society. It was a culture encouraged by the government and excused by references to "dangerous times." For many Americans guns represented not a tool to be used and put away, but a constitutional right all wrapped up in their identity as a nation. The emphasis on personal freedom and the widespread tendency to resort to confrontation instead of compromise when problems arose only added to the violent culture. An American, when offended, could punch another American in the nose, challenge him to a duel, or cut him up with a bowie knife, usually with impunity. Not only society but also the law winked at such acts. Either authorities did not file charges, or, if they did, juries routinely sided with the aggressor.

Finally violence was encouraged by the great diversity of cultures, races, and ethnic groups who uneasily shared the nation. Ties of community and nationhood were very weak in the 19th-century United States because of mutual suspicions and animosities between groups such as American Indians and whites, Irish and English, Northerners and Southerners, homesteaders and ranchers, and countless others too numerous to mention. The vital sense of community or of nationalism that usually deflects such violence was missing. The results were civil war, Indian wars, range wars, race riots, and other forms of civil and military conflict. Americans were a fractious, quarrelsome, opinionated, and rowdy people for whom violence was often the first resort, not the last.

CHAPTER 21 Selected Documents

Excerpt from *Twelve Years a Slave. A Narrative of Solomon Northrup*, 1853

Most people are familiar with Uncle Tom's Cabin *and its dramatic depiction of slavery, but its author, Harriet Beecher Stowe, was writing merely a roman à clef with her account of the saintly Uncle Tom. Quite a different matter was Solomon Northrup's autobiographical story of life as a slave, which was published a year after* Uncle Tom's Cabin. *Solomon's real-life story seems even more incredible today than the fanciful tale of Uncle Tom, Little Eva, Simon Legree, and the rest of the characters in Stowe's novel.*

Northrup (ca. 1808–63) was a free black residing in upstate New York with his wife and children in March 1841 when he was shanghaied by a pair of nefarious slave traders, spirited down to New Orleans, and sold into slavery. His new master was a planter in the Bayou Boeuf country of Louisiana (near the Red River), who cared not a whit for Northrup's protestations. The black man spent the next 12 years in slavery, sold by one master to another, always under scrutiny, yet maintaining his dignity and still determined to escape one day.

Finally in 1852 Northrup was able to make contact with Northern abolitionists, one of whom went to Louisiana and made the legal arrangements for Northrup's release. It was not easy prying a $2,000 slave away from his legal owners in a slave state, but the evidence of chicanery was undeniable. Northrup finally was going back to his family. He reached his home in Glens Falls, New York, on January 20, 1853. Friends and would-be agents immediately pointed out the broad appeal of his amazing story about the odyssey of a free black man through the slave system of the Deep South. Uncle Tom's Cabin *had already demonstrated the marketability of this new literary genre known as slave narratives, and others were also coming off the presses. In fact, in an example of life's imitating fiction, Stowe used newspaper accounts of Northrup's adventure in her nonfiction sequel,* The Key to Uncle Tom's Cabin, *to help authenticate the basic facts of the novel. And Northrup dedicated his book to Stowe. Ironically if anything* Twelve Years a Slave *seemed more fictional than* Uncle Tom's Cabin *did.*

The major controversy around Twelve Years a Slave *was not its authenticity, but Northrup's decision to use a ghost writer, David Wilson, to put his story on paper. How much of the narrator's voice was Northrup's and how much was Wilson's posed a troubling question at the time, as it has ever since. The two men completed their task in three months, and the book was out by July 1853. It was an immediate success on very nearly the same scale as Harriet Beecher Stowe's work. It went through numerous reprints in the years that followed, was published in European editions, and sold more than 30,000 copies during the author's lifetime. Unfortunately Northrup made very little money on the book; he had sold his rights to the original publisher, Henry W. Derby, and was therefore cut out of the substantial profits.*

The story turned out to have an even more amazing ending than being turned into a literary best seller: Public interest aroused by the book helped bring the kidnappers to justice in 1854. A series of trials and appeals dragged on for years before the two men were ultimately released by a court order. Not long after, in 1863, the object of all the uproar died at home surrounded by his family.

Twelve Years a Slave *stands up well as both literature and history. The Northrup–Wilson style is just as lively as, and less syrupy than, Harriet Beecher Stowe's. It is also more valuable than* Uncle Tom's Cabin *as a first-person perspective on the institution of slavery. No other African American left such a detailed picture of slavery on a Deep South plantation, not even Frederick Douglass, who might have possessed more natural literary talent than Northrup but never experienced all the aspects of plantation life that Northrup did. The wonder is that the book is almost forgotten today and seldom appears on reading lists for either U.S. history or American literature classes. "Uncle Tom" has become a cultural touchstone; Solomon Northrup is a forgotten African American.*

In the chapter excerpted here (chapter XVI), Northrup has been sold to Mr. Epps and is still adjusting to life as a slave. He has chosen to keep his previous life a secret because to divulge it would cause his master(s) to regard him as a potential rabble-rouser or runaway and therefore treat him more harshly. So he keeps his mouth shut and does what he is told while still secretly trying to get word to his family and friends up north. As does his literary role model, Harriet Beecher Stowe, he describes the role of the overseer in the plantation system, but from personal experience, not with literary license.

With the exception of my trip to St. Mary's Parish, and my absence during the cane-cutting seasons, I was constantly employed on the plantation of Master Epps. He was considered but a small planter, not having a sufficient number of hands to require the services of an overseer, acting in the latter capacity himself. Not able to increase his force, it was his custom to hire during the hurry of cotton-picking.

On larger estates, employing fifty or a hundred, or perhaps two hundred hands, an overseer is deemed indispensable. These gentlemen ride into the field on horseback, without an exception, to my knowledge, armed with pistols, bowie knife, whip, and accompanied by several dogs. They follow, equipped in this fashion, in rear of the slaves, keeping a sharp lookout upon them all. The requisite qualifications in an overseer are utter heartlessness, brutality and cruelty. It is his business to produce large crops, and if that is accomplished, no matter what amount of suffering it may have cost. The presence of the dogs are necessary to overhaul a fugitive who may take to his heels, as is sometimes the case, when faint or sick, he is unable to maintain his row, and unable, also, to endure the whip. The pistols are reserved for any dangerous emergency, there having been instances when such weapons were necessary. Goaded into uncontrollable madness, even the slave will sometimes turn upon his oppressor. The gallows were standing at Marksville[1] last January, upon which one was executed a year ago for killing his overseer. It occurred not many miles from Epps' plantation on Red River. The slave was given his task at splitting rails. In the course of the day the overseer sent him on an errand, which occupied so much time that it was not possible for him to perform the task. The next day he was called to an account, but the loss of time occasioned by the errand was no excuse, and he was ordered to kneel and bare his back for the reception of the lash. They were in the woods alone—beyond the reach of sight or hearing. The boy submitted until maddened at such injustice, and insane with pain, he sprang to his feet, and seizing an axe, literally chopped the overseer in pieces. He made no attempt whatever at concealment, but hastening to his master, related the whole affair, and declared himself ready to expiate the wrong by the sacrifice of his life. He was led to the scaffold, and while the rope was around his neck, maintained an undismayed and fearless bearing, and with his last words justified the act.

Besides the overseer, there are drivers under him, the number being in proportion to the number of hands in the field. The drivers are black, who, in addition to the performance of their equal share of work, are compelled to do the whipping of their several gangs. Whips hang around their necks, and if they fail to use them thoroughly, are whipped themselves. They have a few privileges, however; for example, in cane-cutting the

[1] Founded by Marc Elisha around 1813, Marksville is the parish (county) seat of Avoyelles Parish.

hands are not allowed to sit down long enough to eat their dinners. Carts filled with corn cake, cooked at the kitchen, are driven into the fields at noon. The cake is distributed by the drivers, and must be eaten with the least possible delay.

When the slave ceases to perspire, as he often does when taxed beyond his strength, he falls to the ground and becomes entirely helpless. It is then the duty of the driver to drag him into the shade of the standing cotton or cane, or of a neighboring tree, where he dashes buckets of water upon him, and uses other means of bringing out perspiration again, when he is ordered to his place, and compelled to continue his labor.

At Huff Power, when I first came to Epps', Tom, one of Roberts' negroes, was driver. He was a burly fellow, and severe in the extreme. After Epps' removal to Bayou Boeuf, that distinguished honor was conferred upon myself. Up to the time of my departure I had to wear a whip about my neck in the field. If Epps was present, I dared not show any lenity, not having the Christian fortitude of a certain well-known Uncle Tom sufficiently to brave his wrath, by refusing to perform the office. In that way, only, I escaped the immediate martyrdom he suffered, and, withal, saved my companions much suffering, as it proved in the end. Epps, I soon found, whether actually in the field or not, had his eyes pretty generally upon us. From the piazza, from behind some adjacent tree, or other concealed point of observation, he was perpetually on the watch. If one of us had been backward or idle through the day, we were at to be told all about it on returning to the quarters, and as it was a matter of principle with him to reprove every offence of that kind that came within his knowledge, the offender not only was certain of receiving a castigation for his tardiness, but I likewise was punished for permitting it.

If, on the other hand, he had seen me use the lash freely, the man was satisfied. "Practice makes perfect," truly; and during my eight years' experience as a driver I learned to handle my whip with marvelous dexterity and precision, throwing the lash within a hair's breadth of the back, the ear, the nose, without, however, touching either of them. If Epps was observed at a distance, or we had reason to apprehend he was sneaking somewhere in the vicinity, I would commence plying the lash vigorously, when, according to arrangement, they would squirm and screech as if in agony, although not one of them had in fact been even grazed. Patsey would take occasion, if he made his appearance presently, to mumble in his hearing some complaints that Platt was lashing them the whole time, and Uncle Abram, with an appearance of honesty peculiar to himself, would declare roundly I had just whipped them worse than General Jackson whipped the enemy at New Orleans. If Epps was not drunk, and in one of his beastly humors, this was, in general, satisfactory. If he was, some one or more of us must suffer, as a matter of course. Sometimes his violence assumed a dangerous form, placing the lives of his human stock in jeopardy. On one occasion the drunken madman thought to amuse himself by cutting my throat.

He had been absent at Holmesville, in attendance at a shooting-match, and none of us were aware of his return. While hoeing by the side of Patsey, she exclaimed, in a low voice, suddenly, "Platt, d'ye see old Hog-Jaw beckoning me to come to him?"

Glancing sideways, I discovered him in the edge of the field motioning and grimacing, as was his habit when half-intoxicated. Aware of his lewd intentions, Patsey began to cry. I whispered to her not to look up, and to continue at her work, as if she had not observed him. Suspecting the truth of the matter, however, he soon staggered up to me in a great rage.

"What did you say to Pats?" he demanded, with an oath. I made him some evasive answer, which only had the effect of increasing his violence.

"How long have you owned this plantation, *say,* you d—d nigger?" he inquired, with a malicious sneer, at the same time taking hold of my shirt collar with one hand, and thrusting the other into his pocket. "Now I'll cut your black throat; that's what I'll do," drawing his knife from his pocket as he said it. But with one hand he was unable to open it, until finally seizing the blade in his teeth, I saw he was about to succeed, and felt the necessity of escaping from him, for in his present reckless state, it was evident he was not joking, by any means. My shirt was open in front, and as I turned round quickly and sprang from him, while he still retained his grip, it was stripped entirely from my back. There was no difficulty now in eluding him. He would chase me until out of breath, then stop until it was recovered, swear, and renew the chase again. Now he would command me to come to him, now endeavor to coax me, but I was careful to keep at a respectful distance. In this manner we made the circuit of the field several times, he making desperate plunges, and I always dodging them, more amused than frightened, well knowing that when his sober senses returned he would laugh at his own drunken folly. At length I observed the mistress standing by the yard fence, watching our half-serious, half-comical maneuvers. Shooting past him, I ran directly to her. Epps, on discovering her, did not follow. He remained about the field an hour or more, during which time I stood by the mistress, having related the particulars of what had taken place. Now, *she* was aroused again, denouncing her husband and Patsey about equally. Finally, Epps came towards the house, by this time nearly sober, 'walking demurely, with his hands behind his back, and attempting to look as innocent as a child.

As he approached, nevertheless, Mistress Epps began to berate him roundly, heaping upon him many rather disrespectful epithets, and demanding for what reason he had attempted to cut my throat. Epps made wondrous strange of it all, and to my surprise, swore by all the saints in the calendar he had not spoken to me that day.

"Platt, you lying nigger, *have* I?" was his brazen appeal to me.

It is not safe to contradict a master, even by the assertion of a truth. So I was silent, and when he entered the house I returned to the field, and the affair was never after alluded to.

Shortly after this time a circumstance occurred that came nigh divulging the secret of my real name and history, when I had so long and carefully concealed, and upon which I was convinced depended my final escape. Soon after he purchased me, Epps asked me if I could write and read, and on being informed that I had received some instruction in those branches of education, he assured me, with emphasis, if he ever caught me with a book, or with pen and ink, he would give me a hundred lashes. He said he wanted me to understand that he bought "niggers" to work and not to educate. He never inquired a word of my past life, or from whence I came. The mistress, however, cross-examined me frequently about Washington, which she supposed was my native city, and more than once remarked that I did not talk nor act like the other "niggers," and she was sure I had not seen more of the world than I admitted.

My great object always was to invent means of getting a letter secretly into the post-office, directed to some of my friends or family at the North. The difficulty of such an achievement cannot be comprehended by one unacquainted with the severe restrictions imposed upon me. In the first place, I was deprived of pen, ink, and paper. In the second place, a slave cannot leave his plantation without a pass, nor will a post-master mail a letter for one without written instructions from his owner. I was in slavery nine years, and always watchful and on the alert, before I met with the good fortune of obtaining a sheet of paper. While Epps was in New Orleans, one winter, disposing of his cotton, the mistress sent me to Holmesville, with an order for several articles, and among the rest a quantity of foolscap. I appropriated a sheet, concealing it in the cabin, under the board on which I slept.

After various experiments I succeeded in making ink, by boiling white maple bark, and with a feather plucked from the wing of a duck, manufactured a pen. When all were asleep in the cabin, by the light of the coals, lying upon my plank couch, I managed to complete a somewhat lengthy epistle. It was directed to an old acquaintance at Sandy Hill, stating my condition, and urging him to take measures to restore me to liberty. This letter I kept a long time, contriving measures by which it could safely be deposited in the post-office. At length, a low fellow, by the name of Armsby, hitherto a stranger, came into the neighborhood, seeking a situation as overseer. He applied to Epps, and was about the plantation for several days. He next went over to Shaw's, near by, and remained with him several weeks. Shaw was generally surrounded by such worthless characters, being himself noted as a gambler and unprincipled man.[2] He had made a wife of his slave Charlotte, and a brood of young mulattoes were growing up in his house. Armsby became so much reduced at last, that he was compelled to labor with the slaves. A white man working in the field is a rare and unusual spectacle on Bayou Boeuf. I improved every opportunity of cultivating his acquaintance privately, desiring to obtain his confidence so far as to be willing to intrust the letter to his keeping. He visited Marksville repeatedly, he informed me, a town some twenty miles distant, and there, I proposed to myself, the letter should be mailed.

Carefully deliberating on the most proper manner of approaching him on the subject, I concluded finally to ask him simply if he would deposit a letter for me in the Marksville post-office the next time he visited that place, without disclosing to him that the letter was written, or any of the particulars it contained; for I had fears that he might betray me, and knew that some inducement must be held out to him of a pecuniary nature, before it would be safe to confide in him. As late as one o'clock one night I stole noiselessly from my cabin, and, crossing the field to Shaw's, found him sleeping on the piazza. I had but a few picayunes—the proceeds of my fiddling performances, but all I had in the world I promised him if he would do me the favor required. I begged him not to expose me if he could not grant the request. He assured me, upon his honor, he would deposit it in the Marksville post-office, and that he would keep it an inviolable secret forever. Though the letter was in my pocket at the time, I dared not then deliver it to him, but stating I would have it written in a day or two, bade him good night, and returned to my cabin. It was impossible for me to expel the suspicions I entertained, and all night I lay awake, revolving in my mind the safest course to pursue. I was willing to risk a great deal to accomplish my purpose, but should the letter by any means fall into the hands of Epps, it would be a death-blow to my aspirations. I was "perplexed in the extreme."

My suspicions were well-founded, as the sequel demonstrated. The next day but one, while scraping cotton in the field, Epps seated himself on the line fence between Shaw's plantation and his own, in such a position as to overlook the scene of our labors. Presently Armsby made his appearance, and, mounting the fence, took a seat beside him. They remained two or three hours, all of which time I was in an agony of apprehension.

That night, while broiling my bacon, Epps entered the cabin with his rawhide in his hand.

"Well, boy," said he, "I understand I've got a larned nigger, that writes letters, and tries to get white fellows to mail 'em. Wonder if you know who he is?"

My worst fears were realized, and although it may not be considered entirely creditable, even under the circumstances, yet a resort to duplicity and downright falsehood was the only refuge that presented itself.

"Don't know nothing about it, Master Epps," I answered him, assuming an air of ignorance and surprise; "Don't know nothing at all about it, sir."

"Wan't you over to Shaw's night before last?" he inquired.

"No, master," was the reply.

"Hav'nt you asked that fellow, Armsby, to mail a letter for you at Marksville?"

"Why, Lord, master, I never spoke three words to him in all my life. I don't know what you mean."

"Well," he continued, "Armsby told me to-day the devil was among my niggers; that I had one that needed close watching or he would run away; and when I axed him why, he said you come over to Shaw's, and waked him up in the night, and wanted him to carry a letter to Marksville. What have you got to say to that, ha?"

"All I've got to say, master," I replied, "is, there is no truth in it. How could I write a letter without any ink or paper? There is nobody I want to write to, 'cause I haint got no friends living as I know of. That Armsby is a lying, drunken fellow, they say, and nobody believes him anyway. You know I always tell the truth, and that I never go off the plantation without a pass. Now, master, I can see what that Armsby is after, plain enough. Didn't he want you to hire him for an overseer?"

"Yes, he wanted me to hire him," answered Epps.

"That's it," said I, "he wants to make you believe we're all going to run away, and then he thinks you'll hire an overseer to watch us. He just made that story out of whole cloth, 'cause he wants to get a situation. It's all a lie, master, you may depend on't."

Epps mused awhile, evidently impressed with the plausibility of my theory, and exclaimed, "I'm d—d, Platt, if I don't believe you tell the truth. He must take me for a soft, to think he can come it over me with them kind of yarns, musn't he? Maybe he thinks he can fool me; maybe he thinks I don't know nothing—can't take care of my own niggers, eh! Soft soap old Epps, eh! Ha, ha, ha! D—n Armsby! Set the dogs on him, Platt," and with many other comments descriptive of Armsby's general character, and his capability of taking care of his own business, and attending to his own "niggers," Master Epps left the cabin. As soon as he was gone I threw the letter in the fire, and, with a desponding and despairing heart, beheld the epistle which had cost me so much anxiety and thought, and which I fondly hoped would have been my forerunner to the land of freedom, writhe and shrivel on its bed of coals, and dissolve into smoke and ashes. Armsby, the treacherous wretch, was driven from Shaw's plantation not long subsequently, much to my relief, for I feared he might renew his conversation, and perhaps induce Epps to credit him.

I knew not now whither to look for deliverance. Hopes sprang up in my heart only to be crushed and blighted. The summer of my life was passing away; I felt I was growing prematurely old; that a few years more, and toil, and grief, and the

[2] P. L. Shaw of Avoyelles Parish owned 48 slaves in 1840, while W. Shaw of Avoyelles owned six. Both are listed in the area where Epps resided, and Northup could have referred to either. *U.S. Census,* 1840.

poisonous miasmas of the swamps would accomplish their work upon me—would consign me to the grave's embrace, to moulder and be forgotten.[3] Repelled, betrayed, cut off from the hope of succor, I could only prostrate myself upon the earth and groan in unutterable anguish. The hope of rescue was the only light that cast a ray of comfort on my heart. That was now flickering, faint and low; another breath of disappointment would extinguish it altogether, leaving me to grope in midnight darkness to the end of life.

Source: Solomon Northrup, *Twelve Years a Slave. A Narrative of Solomon Northrup, A Citizen of New York, Kidnaped in Washington City in 1841, and Rescued in 1853, From a Cotton Plantation near the Red River, in Louisiana* (Auburn, N.Y.: Derby and Miller, 1853), 170–79.

Excerpt from *Ten Nights in a Bar-Room,* 1855

Timothy Shay Arthur's Ten Nights in a Bar-Room *is considered by many to be the most important temperance creed ever written and the best-selling novel of the 19th century after* Uncle Tom's Cabin. *Full of cardboard characters, preachy dialogue, and purple prose, it is written in romance or dime-novel style—a morality tale that beats the reader to death with the moral. Its popularity did not end with the book; in 1858 it was turned into a popular stage play, which was performed all over the country. Apart from* Ten Nights, *Arthur was a successful publisher and prolific writer (some 100 books to his name) with a strong moral streak. As do some modern figures, he managed to cash in on family values by combining his personal economy with deep-seated morality.*

It was first published in 1855 by two firms simultaneously, L. P. Brown & Co. of Boston and J. W. Bradley of Philadelphia, in an arrangement that would never be attempted today. The original 240-page work went through countless reprints and was republished to great fanfare on at least three occasions (1857, 1885, and 1904).

The excerpt here is from section 1 ("Night the First"), section 9 ("Night the Ninth"), and section 10 ("Night the Tenth"). In "Night the First" readers are introduced to the Sickle and Sheath Tavern in fictitious Cedarville; meet Simon Slade, the owner, and his family, Ann (wife), Flora, and Frank (children); they also meet Joe Morgan, the town drunk, and his daughter, Mary; Judge Hammond, his son, Willy, and his friend Harvey Green. By chapter 9 both Cedarville and Simon have fallen on hard times. Simon loses the tavern to Judge Lyman, he has a fight with his son and is killed, and Frank Slade is jailed. In the last section, all is made right in typical melodrama from: The good people of Cedarville embrace prohibition by destroying all liquor in the town and barring future sales in their reformed community. Reading this, one can see a likely influence if not the source for Frank Capra's classic film It's a Wonderful Life.

NIGHT THE FIRST

THE "SICKLE AND SHEAF"

TEN years ago, business required me to pass a day in Cedarville. It was late in the afternoon when the stage set me down at the "Sickle and Sheaf," a new tavern, just opened by a new landlord, in a new house, built with the special end of providing "accommodations for man and beast." As I stepped from the dusty old vehicle in which I had been jolted along a rough road for some thirty miles, feeling tired and hungry, the good-natured face of Simon Slade, the landlord, beaming as it did with a hearty welcome, was really a pleasant sight to see, and the grasp of his hand was like that of a true friend.

I felt, as I entered the new and neatly furnished sitting-room adjoining the bar, that I had indeed found a comfortable resting-place after my wearisome journey.

"All as nice as a new pin," said I, approvingly, as I glanced around the room, up to the ceiling—white as the driven snow—and over the handsomely carpeted floor. "Haven't seen any thing so inviting as this. How long have you been open?"

"Only a few months," answered the gratified landlord. "But we are not yet in good going order. It takes time, you know, to bring every thing into the right shape. Have you dined yet?"

"No. Every thing looked so dirty at the stage-house where we stopped to get dinner, that I couldn't venture upon the experiment of eating. How long before your supper will be ready?"

"In an hour," replied the landlord.

"That will do. Let me have a nice piece of tender steak, and the loss of dinner will soon be forgotten."

"You shall have that, cooked fit for an alderman," said the landlord. "I call my wife the best cook in Cedarville."

As he spoke, a neatly dressed girl, about sixteen years of age, with rather an attractive countenance, passed through the room.

"My daughter," said the landlord, as she vanished through the door. There was a sparkle of pride in the father's eyes, and a certain tenderness in the tones of his voice, as he said—"My daughter," that told me she was very dear to him.

"You are a happy man to have so fair a child," said I, speaking more in compliment than with a careful choice of words.

"I am a happy man," was the landlord's smiling answer; his fair, round face, unwrinkled by a line of care or trouble, beaming with self-satisfaction. "I have always been a happy man, and always expect to be. Simon Slade takes the world as it comes, and takes it easy. My son, sir"—he added, as a boy in his twelfth year, came in. "Speak to the gentleman."

The boy lifted to mine a pair of deep blue eyes, from which innocence beamed, as he offered me his hand, and said, respectfully—"How do you do, sir?" I could not but remark the girl-like beauty of his face, in which the hardier firmness of the boy's character was already visible.

"What is your name?" I asked.

"Frank, sir."

"Frank is his name," said the landlord—"we called him after his uncle. Frank and Flora—the names sound pleasant to our ears. But, you know, parents are apt to be a little partial and over fond."

"Better that extreme than its opposite," I remarked.

"Just what I always say. Frank, my son"—the landlord spoke to the boy, "there's some one in the bar. You can wait on him as well as I can."

The lad glided from the room, in ready obedience.

"A handy boy that, sir; a very handy boy. Almost as good in the bar as a man. He mixes a toddy or a punch just as well as I can."

"But," I suggested, "are you not a little afraid of placing one so young in the way of temptation."

"Temptation!" The open brows of Simon Slade contracted a little. "No, sir!" he replied, emphatically. "The till is safer under his care than it would be in that of one man in ten. The boy comes, sir, of honest parents. Simon Slade never wronged anybody out of a farthing."

"Oh," said I, quickly, "you altogether misapprehend me. I had no reference to the till, but to the bottle."

[3] Northup is not merely being dramatic. Charles David Bennett, writing from New York in the 1890s to his niece, Ezra Bennett's daughter, commented about the Boeuf country in the 1840s and 1850s: "Since the woods are cut away and the miasma washed and dried from the soil of the fields, I suppose the people run the risk of bilious fever and often stand a turn with the congestive. . . . I have never been in any other country where gray heads were so unfashionable as they were on Bayou Beuff *[sic]*." Charles David Bennett to Virginia Bennett, May 24, 1894, in Ezra Bennett Papers, LSU at Alexandria.

The landlord's brows were instantly unbent, and a broad smile circled over his good-humoured face.

"Is that all? Nothing to fear, I can assure you. Frank has no taste for liquor, and might pour it out for months without a drop finding its way to his lips. Nothing to apprehend there, sir—nothing."

I saw that further suggestions of danger would be useless, and so remained silent. The arrival of a traveller called away the landlord, and I was left alone for observation and reflection. The bar adjoined the neat sitting-room, and I could see, through the open door, the customer upon whom the lad was attending. He was a well-dressed young man—or rather boy, for he did not appear to be over nineteen years of age—with a fine, intelligent face, that was already slightly marred by sensual indulgence. He raised the glass to his lips, with a quick, almost eager motion, and drained it at a single draught.

"Just right," said he, tossing a sixpence to the young bar-tender. "You are first-rate at a brandy-toddy. Never drank a better in my life."

The lad's smiling face told that he was gratified by the compliment. To me the sight was painful, for I saw that this youthful tippler was on dangerous ground.

"Who is that young man in the bar?" I asked, a few minutes afterward, on being rejoined by the landlord.

Simon Slade stepped to the door and looked into the bar for a moment. Two or three men were there by this time; but he was at no loss in answering my question.

"Oh, that's a son of Judge Hammond, who lives in the large brick house just as you enter the village. Willy Hammond, as everybody familiarly calls him, is about the finest young man in our neighbourhood. There is nothing proud or put-on about him—nothing—even if his father is a judge, and rich into the bargain. Every one, gentle or simple, likes Willy Hammond. And then he is such good company. Always so cheerful, and always with a pleasant story on his tongue. And he's so high-spirited withal, and so honourable. Willy Hammond would lose his right hand rather than be guilty of a mean action."

"Landlord!" The voice came loud from the road in front of the house, and Simon Slade again left me to answer the demands of some new comer. I went into the bar-room, in order to take a closer observation of Willy Hammond, in whom an interest, not unmingled with concern, had already been awakened in my mind. I found him engaged in a pleasant conversation with a plain-looking farmer, whose homely, terse, common sense was quite as conspicuous as his fine play of words and lively fancy. The farmer was a substantial conservative, and young Hammond a warm admirer of new ideas and the quicker adaptation of means to ends. I soon saw that his mental powers were developed beyond his years, while his personal qualities were strongly attractive. I understood better, after being a silent listener and observer for ten minutes, why the landlord had spoken of him so warmly.

"Take a brandy-toddy, Mr. H——?" said Hammond, after the discussion closed, good humouredly. "Frank, our junior bar-keeper here, beats his father, in that line."

"I don't care if I do," returned the farmer; and the two passed up to the bar.

"Now, Frank, my boy, don't belie my praises," said the young man; "do your handsomest."

"Two brandy-toddies, did you say?" Frank made the inquiry with quite a professional air.

"Just what I did say; and let them be equal to Jove's nectar."

Pleased at this familiarity, the boy went briskly to his work of mixing the tempting compound, while Hammond looked on with an approving smile.

"There," said the latter, as Frank passed the glasses across the counter, "if you don't call that first-rate, you're no judge." And he handed one of them to the farmer, who tasted the agreeable draught, and praised its flavour. As before, I noticed that Hammond drank eagerly, like one athirst—emptying his glass without once taking it from his lips.

Soon after the bar-room was empty; and then I walked around the premises, in company with the landlord, and listened to his praise of every thing and his plans and purposes for the future. The house, yard, garden, and out-buildings were in the most perfect order; presenting, in the whole, a model of a village tavern.

"Whatever I do, sir," said the talkative Simon Slade, "I like to do well. I wasn't just raised to tavern-keeping, you must know; but I'm one who can turn his hand to almost any thing."

"What was your business?" I inquired.

"I'm a miller, sir, by trade," he answered—"and a better miller, though I say it myself, is not to be found in Bolton county. I've followed milling these twenty years, and made some little money. But I got tired of hard work, and determined to lead an easier life. So I sold my mill, and built this house with the money. I always thought I'd like tavern-keeping. It's an easy life; and, if rightly seen after, one in which a man is sure to make money."

"You were still doing a fair business with your mill?"

"Oh yes. Whatever I do, I do right. Last year, I put by a thousand dollars above all expenses, which is not bad, I can assure you, for a mere grist mill. If the present owner comes out even, he'll do well!"

"How is that?"

"Oh, he's no miller. Give him the best wheat that is grown, and he'll ruin it in grinding. He takes the life out of every grain. I don't believe he'll keep half the custom that I transferred with the mill."

"A thousand dollars, clear profit, in so useful a business, ought to have satisfied you," said I.

"There you and I differ," answered the landlord. "Every man desires to make as much money as possible, and with the least labour. I hope to make two or three thousand dollars a year, over and above all expenses, at tavern-keeping. My bar alone ought to yield me that sum. A man with a wife and children very naturally tries to do as well by them as possible."

"Very true; but," I ventured to suggest, "will this be doing as well by them as if you had kept on at the mill?"

"Two or three thousand dollars a year against one thousand! Where are your figures, man?"

"There may be something beyond the money to take into the account," said I.

"What?" inquired Slade, with a kind of half credulity.

"Consider the different influences of the two callings in life—that of a miller and a tavern-keeper."

"Well! say on."

"Will your children be as safe from temptation here as in their former home?"

"Just as safe," was the unhesitating answer. "Why not?"

I was about to speak of the alluring glass in the case of Frank, but remembering that I had already expressed a fear in that direction, felt that to do so again would be useless, and so kept silent.

"A tavern-keeper," said Slade, "is just as respectable as a miller—in fact, the very people who used to call me 'Simon,' or 'Neighbour Dustyeoat,' now say 'Landlord,' or Mr. Slade, and treat me in every way more as if I were an equal than ever they did before."

"The change," said I, "may be due to the fact of your giving evidence of possessing some means. Men are very apt to be courteous to those who have property. The building of the tavern has, without doubt, contributed to the new estimation in which you are held."

"That isn't all," replied the landlord. "It is because I am keeping a good tavern, and thus materially advancing the interests of Cedarville, that some of our best people look at me with different eyes."

"Advancing the interests of Cedarville! In what way?" I did not apprehend his meaning.

"A good tavern always draws people to a place, while a miserable old tumbledown of an affair, badly kept, such as we have had for years, as surely repels them. You can generally tell something about the condition of a town by looking at its taverns. If they are well kept, and doing a good business, you will hardly be wrong in the conclusion that the place is thriving. Why, already, since I built and opened the 'Sickle and Sheaf,' property has advanced over twenty per cent. along the whole street, and not less than five new houses have been commenced. . . ."

NIGHT THE NINTH

FEARFUL CONSUMMATION

It was after nine o'clock, and there was not half a dozen persons in the room, when I noticed Frank Slade go behind the bar for the third or fourth time. He was just lifting a decanter of brandy, when his father, who was considerably under the influence of drink, started forward, and laid his hand upon that of his son. Instantly a fierce light gleamed from the eyes of the young man.

"Let go of my hand," he exclaimed.

"No, I won't. Put up that brandy bottle,—you're drunk now."

"Don't meddle with me, old man!" angrily retorted Frank. "I'm not in the mood to bear any thing more from *you*."

"You're drunk as a fool now," returned Slade, who had seized the decanter. "Let go the bottle."

For only an instant did the young man hesitate. Then he drove his half-clenched hand against the breast of his father, who went staggering away several paces from the counter. Recovering himself, and now almost furious, the landlord rushed forward upon his son, his hand raised to strike him.

"Keep off!" cried Frank. "Keep off! If you touch me, I'll strike you down!" At the same time raising the half-filled bottle threateningly.

But his father was in too maddened a state to fear any consequences, and so pressed forward upon his son, striking him in the face the moment he came near enough to do so.

Instantly, the young man, infuriated by drink and evil passions, threw the bottle at his father's head. The dangerous missile fell, crashing upon one of his temples, shivering it into a hundred pieces. A heavy, jarring fall too surely marked the fearful consequences of the blow. When we gathered around the fallen man, and made an effort to lift him from the floor, a thrill of horror went through every heart. A mortal paleness was already on his marred face, and the death-gurgle in his throat! In three minutes from the time the blow was struck, his spirit had gone upward to give an account of the deeds done in the body.

"Frank Slade! you have murdered your father!"

Sternly were these terrible words uttered. It was some time before the young man seemed to comprehend their meaning. But the moment he realized the awful truth, he uttered an exclamation of horror. Almost at the same instant, a pistol-shot came sharply on the ear. But the meditated self-destruction was not accomplished. The aim was not surely taken; and the ball struck harmlessly against the ceiling.

Half an hour afterward, and Frank Slade was a lonely prisoner in the county jail!

Does the reader need a word of comment on this fearful consummation? No: and we will offer none.

NIGHT THE TENTH

THE CLOSING SCENE AT THE "SICKLE AND SHEAF"

On the day that succeeded the evening of this fearful tragedy, placards were to be seen all over the village, announcing a mass meeting at the "Sickle and Sheaf' that night.

By early twilight, the people commenced assembling. The bar, which had been closed all day, was now thrown open, and lighted; and in this room, where so much of evil had been originated, encouraged, and consummated, a crowd of earnest-looking men were soon gathered. Among them I saw the fine person of Mr. Hargrove. Joe Morgan—or rather Mr. Morgan—was also of the number. The latter I would scarcely have recognised, had not some one near me called him by name. He was well dressed, stood erect, and, though there were many deep lines on his thoughtful countenance, all traces of his former habits were gone. While I was observing him, he arose, and addressing a few words to the assemblage, nominated Mr. Hargrove as chairman of the meeting. To this a unanimous assent was given.

On taking the chair, Mr. Hargrove made a brief address, something to this effect.

"Ten years ago," said he, his voice evincing a slight unsteadiness as he began, but growing firmer as he proceeded, "there was not a happier spot in Bolton county than Cedarville. Now, the marks of ruin are every where. Ten years ago, there was a kind-hearted, industrious miller in Cedarville, liked by every one, and as harmless as a little child. Now, his bloated, disfigured body lies in that room. His death was violent, and by the hand of his own son!"

Mr. Hargrove's words fell slowly, distinctly, and marked by the most forcible emphasis. There was scarcely one present who did not feel a low shudder run along his nerves, as the last words were spoken in a husky whisper.

"Ten years ago," he proceeded, "the miller had a happy wife, and two innocent, glad-hearted children. Now, his wife, bereft of reason, is in a mad-house, and his son the occupant of a felon's cell, charged with the awful crime of parricide!"

Briefly he paused, while his audience stood gazing upon him with half suspended respiration.

"Ten years ago," he went on, "Judge Hammond was accounted the richest man in Cedarville. Yesterday he was carried, a friendless pauper, to the Almshouse; and to-day he is the unmourned occupant of a pauper's grave! Ten years ago, his wife was the proud, hopeful, loving mother of a most promising son. I need not describe what Willy Hammond was. All here knew him well. Ah! what shattered the fine intellect of that noble-minded woman? Why did her heart break? Where is she? Where is Willy Hammond?"

A low, half repressed groan answered the speaker,

"Ten years ago, you, sir," pointing to a sad-looking old man, and calling him by name, "had two sons—generous, promising, manly-hearted boys. What are they now? You need not answer the question. Too well is their history and your sorrow known. Ten years ago, I had a son,—amiable, kind, loving, but weak. Heaven knows how I sought to guard and protect him! But he fell also. The arrows of destruction darkened the very air of our once secure and happy village. And who was safe? Not mine, nor yours!

"Shall I go on? Shall I call up and pass in review before you, one after another, all the wretched victims who have fallen in Cedarville during the last ten years? Time does not permit. It would take hours for the enumeration! No: I will not throw additional darkness into the picture. Heaven knows it is black enough already! But what is the root of this great evil? Where lies the fearful secret? Who understands the disease? A direful pestilence is in the air—it walketh in darkness, and wasteth at noonday. It is slaying the first-born in our houses, and the cry of anguish is swelling on every gale. Is there no remedy?"

"Yes! yes! There is a remedy!" was the spontaneous answer from many voices.

"Be it our task, then, to find and apply it this night," answered the chairman, as he took his seat.

"And there is but one remedy," said Morgan, as Mr. Hargrove sat down. "The accursed traffic must cease among us. You must cut off the fountain, if you would dry up the stream. If you would save the young, the weak, and the innocent—on you God has laid the solemn duty of their protection—you must cover them from the tempter. Evil is strong, wily, fierce, and active in the pursuit of its ends. The young, the weak, and the innocent can no more resist its assaults, than the lamb can resist the wolf. They are helpless, if you abandon them to the powers of evil. Men and brethren! as one who has himself been wellnigh lost—as one who, daily, feels and trembles at the dangers that beset his path—I do conjure you to stay the fiery stream that is bearing every thing good and beautiful among you to destruction. Fathers! for the sake of your young children, be up now and doing. Think of Willy Hammond, Frank Slade, and a dozen more whose names I could repeat, and hesitate no longer! Let us resolve, this night, that from henceforth, the traffic shall cease in Cedarville. Is there not a large majority of citizens in favour of such a measure? And whose rights or interests can be affected by such a restriction? Who, in fact, has any right to sow disease and death in our community? The liberty, under sufferance, to do so, wrongs the individual who uses it, as well as those who become his victims. Do you want proof of this. Look at Simon Slade, the happy, kind-hearted miller; and at Simon Slade, the tavern-keeper. Was he benefited by the liberty to work harm to his neighbour? No! no! In heaven's name, then, let the traffic cease! To this end, I offer these resolutions: —

"Be it resolved by the inhabitants of Cedarville, That from this day henceforth, no more intoxicating drink shall be sold within the limits of the corporation.

"Resolved, further, That all the liquors in the Sickle and Sheaf be forthwith destroyed, and that a fund be raised to pay the creditors of Simon Slade therefor, should they demand compensation.

"Resolved, That in closing up all other places where liquor is sold, regard shall be had to the right of property which the law secures to every man.

"Resolved, That with the consent of the legal authorities, all the liquor for sale in Cedarville be destroyed; provided the owners thereof be paid its full value out of a fund specially raised for that purpose."

But for the calm, yet resolute opposition of one or two men, these resolutions would have passed by acclamation. A little sober argument showed the excited company that no good end is ever secured by the adoption of wrong means.

There were, in Cedarville, regularly constituted authorities, which alone had the power to determine public measures; or to say what business might or might not be pursued by individuals. And through these authorities they must act in an orderly way.

There was some little chafing at this view of the case. But good sense and reason prevailed. Somewhat modified, the resolutions passed, and the more ultra-inclined contented themselves with carrying out the second resolution, to destroy forthwith all the liquor to be found on the premises; which was immediately done. After which the people dispersed to their homes, each with a lighter heart, and better hopes for the future of their village.

On the next day, as I entered the stage that was to bear me from Cedarville, I saw a man strike his sharp axe into the worn, faded, and leaning post that had, for so many years, borne aloft the Sickle and Sheaf; and just as the driver gave word to his horses, the false emblem which had invited so many to enter the way of destruction, fell crashing to the earth.

Source: Timothy Shay Arthur, *Ten Nights in a Bar-Room, And What I Saw There,* edited by Donald A. Koch, 7–16, 232–34 (Cambridge, Mass.: Harvard University Press, the Belknap Press, 1964).

Excerpts from *Leaves of Grass,* 1855–1865

Walt Whitman first issued Leaves of Grass *as a collection of 12 poems published in 1855 sans author's name. During the remainder of his lifetime he continually expanded, polished, and reworked the collection into five revised and*

Walt Whitman in 1860, the distinguished curmudgeon known as "The Good Gray Poet," some felt that looked almost like a biblical patriarch in his later years. (Library of Congress, [LC-USZ62-089951])

reprinted editions (for a grand total of nine separate editions). The original collection was an immediate sensation when it appeared because of its unconventional verse form and shockingly frank subject matter (e.g., the human body, sexuality). The third edition (1860) contained 122 poems. After that the most important editions were the fourth (1867), containing his Civil War poems, which included "Drum-Taps and Sequel"; a "Centennial Edition" in 1876; one last revised edition in 1881–82; and a "Deathbed Edition" in 1891–92 crammed with more than 400 poems, the product of a lifetime. The classic "I Hear America Singing" was first published in the 1860 edition as no. 20 of "Chants Democratic" with a different opening line. By 1867 he had revised the opening line to its present form and given it the title it is known by today.

"Song of Myself" was first jotted down in the 1847–48 period and first appeared untitled and "unsectioned" in the 1855 edition, taking up more than half the volume. He did not give it its well-known title until 1881. It is an exuberant, self-confident celebration of life and the senses, of work and history. "Eighteen Sixty-One" first appeared in the third edition as "1861" as an independent poem rather than a canto. He offered it to the Atlantic Monthly, *but the editor, James Russell Lowell, rejected it with the curt comment that interest in the Civil War was temporary; therefore its subject "which is of the present—would have passed" before it could be published. "O Captain" became Whitman's best-known single poem after it was first published in the* Saturday Press *on November 4, 1865, as the author's first elegy to the assassinated President Lincoln. (Whitman wrote another poem later that same year, "When Lilacs Last in the Dooryard Bloom'd," his second heartfelt response to Lincoln's death, as well as a commentary on the evils of war. "Lilacs," too, was included in the 1867 edition of* Leaves of Grass.*) Ironically, although it was his most popular work with the public, it was Whitman's least favorite poem because of its conventional regularity in rhyme and meter. He once grumbled petulantly, "I'm almost sorry I ever wrote the poem."*

I Hear America Singing

I hear America singing, the varied carols I hear,
Those of mechanics, each one singing his as it should be blithe and strong,
The carpenter singing his as he measures his plank or beam,
The mason singing his as he makes ready for work, or leaves off work,
The boatman singing what belongs to him in his boat, the deck-hand singing on the steamboat deck,
The shoemaker singing as he sits on his bench, the hatter singing as he stands,
The wood-cutter's song, the ploughboy's on his way in the morning, or at noon intermission or at sundown,
The delicious singing of the mother, or of the young wife at work, or of the girl sewing or washing,

Each singing what belongs to him or her and to none else,
The day what belongs to the day—at night the party of young fellows, robust, friendly,
Singing with open mouths their strong melodious songs.

Excerpt from "Song of Myself"

1

I celebrate myself, and sing myself,
And what I assume you shall assume,
For every atom belonging to me as good belongs to you.

I loafe and invite my soul,
I lean and loafe at my ease observing a spear of summer grass.

My tongue, every atom of my blood, form'd from this soil, this air,
Born here of parents born here from parents the same, and their parents the same,
I, now thirty-seven years old in perfect health begin,
Hoping to cease not till death.

Creeds and schools in abeyance,
Retiring back a while sufficed at what they are, but never forgotten,
I harbor for good or bad, I permit to speak at every hazard,
Nature without check with original energy.

2

Houses and rooms are full of perfumes, the shelves are crowded with perfumes,
I breathe the fragrance myself and know it and like it,
The distillation would intoxicate me also, but I shall not let it.

The atmosphere is not a perfume, it has no taste of the distillation, it is odorless,
It is for my mouth forever, I am in love with it,
I will go to the bank by the wood and become undisguised and naked,
I am mad for it to be in contact with me.
The smoke of my own breath,
Echoes, ripples, buzz'd whispers, love-root, silk-thread, crotch and vine,
My respiration and inspiration, the beating of my heart, the passing of blood and air through my lungs,
My voice is the wife's voice, the screech by the rail of the stairs,
They fetch my man's body up dripping and drown'd.
I understand the large hearts of heroes,
The courage of present times and all times,
How the skipper saw the crowded and rudderless wreck of the steam-ship, and Death chasing it up and down the storm,
How he knuckled tight and gave not back an inch, and was faithful of days and faithful of nights,
And chalk'd in large letters on a board, *Be of good cheer, we will not desert you;*
How he follow'd with them and tack'd with them three days and would not give it up,
How he saved the drifting company at last,
How the lank loose-gown'd women look'd when boated from the side of their prepared graves,
How the silent old-faced infants and the lifted sick, and the sharplipp'd unshaved men;
All this I swallow, it tastes good, I like it well, it becomes mine,
I am the man, I suffer'd, I was there.

The disdain and calmness of martyrs,
The mother of old, condemn'd for a witch, burnt with dry wood, her children gazing on,
The hounded slave that flags in the race, leans by the fence, blowing, cover'd with sweat,
The twinges that sting like needles his legs and neck, the murderous buckshot and the bullets,
All these I feel or am.
I am the hounded slave, I wince at the bite of the dogs,
Hell and despair are upon me, crack and again crack the marksmen,
I clutch the rails of the fence, my gore dribs, thinn'd with the ooze of my skin,
I fall on the weeds and stones,

Source: Walt Whitman, *Leaves of Grass,* Comprehensive Reader's Edition, edited Harold W. Blodgett and Sculley Bradley, 28–29, 282–84, 337–38 (New York: New York University Press, 1965).

The riders spur their unwilling horses, haul close,
Taunt my dizzy ears and beat me violently over the head with
whip-stocks.

Agonies are one of my changes of garments,
I do not ask the wounded person how he feels, I myself become
the wounded person,
My hurts turn livid upon me as I lean on a cane and observe.

I am the mash'd fireman with breast-bone broken,
Tumbling walls buried me in their debris,
Heat and smoke I inspired, I heard the yelling shouts of my
comrades,
I heard the distant click of their picks and shovels,
They have clear'd the beams away, they tenderly lift me forth.

I lie in the night air in my red shirt, the pervading hush is for my
sake,
Painless after all I lie exhausted but not so unhappy,
White and beautiful are the faces around me, the heads are bared
of their fire-caps,
The kneeling crowd fades with the light of the torches.

Distant and dead resuscitate,
They show as the dial or move as the hands of me, I am the clock
myself.

I am an old artillerist, I tell of my fort's bombardment,
I am there again.

Again the long roll of the drummers,
Again the attacking cannon, mortars,
Again to my listening ears the cannon responsive.

I take part, I see and hear the whole,
The cries, curses, roar, the plaudits for well-aim'd shots,
The ambulanza slowly passing trailing its red drip,
Workmen searching after damages, making indispensable repairs,
The fall of grenades through the rent roof, the fan-shaped
explosion,
The whizz of limbs, heads, stone, wood, iron, high in the air.

Again gurgles the mouth of my dying general, he furiously waves
with his hand,
He gasps through the clot *Mind not me—mind—the entrenchments.*

34

Now I tell what I knew in Texas in my early youth,
(I tell not the fall of Alamo,
Not one escaped to tell the fall of Alamo,
The hundred and fifty are dumb yet at Alamo,)
'Tis the tale of the murder in cold blood of four hundred and
twelve young men.

Retreating they had form'd in a hollow square with their baggage
for breastworks,
Nine hundred lives out of the surrounding enemy's, nine times
their number, was the price they took in advance,
Their colonel was wounded and their ammunition gone,
They treated for an honorable capitulation, receiv'd writing and
seal, gave up their arms and march'd back prisoners of war.

They were the glory of the race of rangers,
Matchless with horse, rifle, song, supper, courtship,
Large, turbulent, generous, handsome, proud, and affectionate,
Bearded, sunburnt, drest in the free costume of hunters,
Not a single one over thirty years of age.

The second First-day morning they were brought out in squads
and massacred, it was beautiful early summer,
The work commenced about five o'clock and was over by eight.
None obey'd the command to kneel,
Some made a mad and helpless rush, some stood stark and
straight,
A few fell at once, shot in the temple or heart, the living and
dead lay together,
The maim'd and mangled dug in the dirt, the new-comers saw
them there,
Some half-kill'd attempted to crawl away,
These were despatch'd with bayonets or batter'd with the blunts
of muskets,
A youth not seventeen years old seiz'd his assassin till two more
came to release him,
The three were all torn and cover'd with the boy's blood.

At eleven o'clock began the burning of the bodies;
That is the tale of the murder of the four hundred and twelve
young men.

35

Would you hear of an old-time sea-fight?
Would you learn who won by the light of the moon and stars?
List to the yarn, as my grandmother's father the sailor told it to
me.

Our foe was no skulk in his ship I tell you, (said he,)
His was the surly English pluck, and there is no tougher or truer,
and never was, and never will be;
Along the lower'd eve he came horribly raking us.

We closed with him, the yards entangled, the cannon touch'd,
My captain lash'd fast with his own hands.

We had receiv'd some eighteen pound shots under the water,
On our lower-gun-deck two large pieces had burst at the first
fire, killing all around and blowing up overhead.
Fighting at sun-down, fighting at dark,
Ten o'clock at night, the full moon well up, our leaks on the gain,
and five feet of water reported,
The master-at-arms loosing the prisoners confined in the after-
hold to give them a chance for themselves.

The transit to and from the magazine is now stopt by the
sentinels,
They see so many strange faces they do not know whom to trust.

Our frigate takes fire,
The other asks if we demand quarter?
If our colors are struck and the fighting done?

Now I laugh content, for I hear the voice of my little captain,
We have not struck, he composedly cries, *we have just begun our part
of the fighting.*

Only three guns are in use,
One is directed by the captain himself against the enemy's
mainmast,

Two well serv'd with grape and canister silence his musketry and clear his decks.

The tops alone second the fire of this little battery, especially the main-top,
They hold out bravely during the whole of the action.

Not a moment's cease,
The leaks gain fast on the pumps, the fire eats toward the powder-magazine.

One of the pumps has been shot away, it is generally thought we are sinking.

Serene stands the little captain,
He is not hurried, his voice is neither high nor low,
His eyes give more light to us than our battle-lanterns.

Toward twelve there in the beams of the moon they surrender to us.

36
Stretch'd and still lies the midnight,
Two great hulls motionless on the breast of the darkness,
Our vessel riddled and slowly sinking, preparations to pass to the one we have conquer'd,
The captain on the quarter-deck coldly giving his orders through a countenance white as a sheet,
Near by the corpse of the child that serv'd in the cabin,
The dead face of an old salt with long white hair and carefully curl'd whiskers,
The flames spite of all that can be done flickering aloft and below,
The husky voices of the two or three officers yet fit for duty,
Formless stacks of bodies and bodies by themselves, dabs of flesh upon the masts and spars,
Cut of cordage, dangle of rigging, slight shock of the soothe of waves,
Black and impassive guns, litter of powder-parcels, strong scent,
A few large stars overhead, silent and mournful shining,
Delicate sniffs of sea-breeze, smells of sedgy grass and fields by the shore, death-messages given in charge to survivors,
The hiss of the surgeon's knife, the gnawing teeth of his saw,
Wheeze, cluck, swash of falling blood, short wild scream, and long, dull, tapering groan,
These so, these irretrievable.

Eighteen Sixty-One

Arm'd year—year of the struggle,
No dainty rhymes or sentimental love verses for you terrible year,
Not you as some pale poetling seated at a desk lisping cadenzas piano,
But as a strong man erect, clothed in blue clothes, advancing, carrying a rifle on your shoulder,
With well-gristled body and sunburnt face and hands, with a knife in the belt at your side,
As I heard you shouting loud, your sonorous voice ringing across the continent,
Your masculine voice O year, as rising amid the great cities,
Amid the men of Manhattan I saw you as one of the workmen, the dwellers in Manhattan,
Or with large steps crossing the prairies out of Illinois and Indiana,
Rapidly crossing the West with springy gait and descending the Alleghanies,

Or down from the great lakes or in Pennsylvania, or on deck along the Ohio river,
Or southward along the Tennessee or Cumberland rivers, or at Chattanooga on the mountain top,
Saw I your gait and saw I your sinewy limbs clothed in blue, bearing weapons, robust year,
Heard your determin'd voice launch'd forth again and again,
Year that suddenly sang by the mouths of the round-lipp'd cannon,
I repeat you, hurrying, crashing, sad, distracted year.

O Captain! My Captain!

O Captain! my Captain! our fearful trip is done,
The ship has weather'd every rack, the prize we sought is won,
The port is near, the bells I hear, the people all exulting,

While follow eyes the steady keel, the vessel grim and daring;
But O heart! heart! heart!
O the bleeding drops of red,
Where on the deck my Captain lies,
Fallen cold and dead.

O Captain! my Captain! rise up and hear the bells;
Rise up—for you the flag is flung—for you the bugle trills,
For you bouquets and ribbon'd wreaths—for you the shores a-crowding,
For you they call, the swaying mass, their eager faces turning;
Here Captain! dear father!
This arm beneath your head!
It is some dream that on the deck,
You've fallen cold and dead.

My Captain does not answer, his lips are pale and still,
My father does not feel my arm, he has no pulse nor will,
The ship is anchor'd safe and sound, its voyage closed and done,
From fearful trip the victor ship comes in with object won;
Exult O shores, and ring O bells!
But I with mournful tread,
Walk the deck my Captain lies,
Fallen cold and dead.

Excerpt from "Mary Chesnut's Civil War Diaries," July 1861

Mary Boykin Chesnut's Civil War diaries are generally regarded as "the finest firsthand account of the social world of the Confederacy." The fact that she was an educated woman, married to a highly placed Confederate official (James Chesnut, Jr.); a close friend of President Jefferson Davis and his wife and other Southern leaders; and spent most of the war in the Confederate capital certainly gave her a front-row seat to observe the life and death of the Confederate States of America during four years of war.

She began a private diary in February 1861, faithfully recording her thoughts, observations, impressions, and experiences in what eventually grew to 10 or more volumes. Unfortunately at least three were destroyed or lost by the author during the war. She also stopped making regular daily entries sometime after 1861 and did not resume until the beginning of 1865, when she was no longer living in Richmond. She stopped keeping a diary after June 26, 1865, because the war had ended, the South she had known was destroyed, and the Chesnuts were forced to make a new life for themselves.

But whether writing her observations while they were fresh on her mind or not, she was able to observe a great deal because the Chesnut home in Richmond was a gathering place for many of the major players in the wartime drama. That she was a first-rate eyewitness, there is no doubt. Her awareness that she was living in historic times and recording for posterity gives her observations a certain self-knowledge and depth that they would otherwise lack. But she was not so concerned with history that she did not indulge in chronic complaining about such matters as her physical ailments and her husband's lack of ambition or make insulting comments about people she did not like. She also loved to pass on the latest gossip and shamelessly drop names, so many names, in fact, that identifying all the people mentioned in passing is almost impossible. Her diaries were very much an unvarnished, stream-of-consciousness document with all the positives and negatives of that form of writing.

She always had in mind to publish the diaries, but she was long delayed in preparing them for publication. After a false start in the 1870s she began in 1881 to make major revisions of the original volumes by editing and expanding the entries until she had virtually created a new work. What she had produced was still a primary source document, but now more of a memoir than a diary with her original observations shaded by hindsight and long-term memory. The fact that she chose to maintain the diary format and incorporate additions and deletions into the original entries without any explanation is, to say the least, deceptive. But she never had to explain herself because in 1884, after producing some 2,500 pages of manuscript, she was forced to stop working on it. Her husband's death and her own poor health were the immediate causes of her hiatus. She fully intended to return to the work and complete it to publication, but she died in 1886.

The surviving seven journal volumes and the unfinished manuscript fell into the hands of a close friend, Isabella Martin, after Chesnut's death. Martin recognized the importance of what she had received but was intimidated by the massive project and so let it collect dust until she teamed with Myrta Lockett Avary, a New York journalist, in 1904. With Avary's prodding, the two women finally pushed the project to publication. It first saw the public light as serialized excerpts in the Saturday Evening Post *in 1904. It was there that the famously misleading title, "A Diary from Dixie," was first stuck on it. The entire "diary" appeared in book form the following year, published by D. Appleton under the verbose title* A Diary from Dixie, as Written by Mary Boykin Chesnut, Wife of James Chesnut, Jr., United States Senator from South Carolina, 1859–1861, and afterward an Aide to Jefferson Davis and a Brigadier-General in the Confederate Army. *The published edition credited Martin and Avary as "editors" and covered all four years of the war, as reconstructed by Chesnut a decade and more later. But that "minor detail" was glossed over. It was an immediate success, declared a classic, and republished in yet another "improved" edition in 1947.*

Meanwhile the original journal volumes languished first in private hands and then in a University of North Carolina archive until a pair of modern historians, C. Vann Woodward and Elisabeth Muhlenfeld, published the unexpurgated and incomplete diaries with minimal editing in 1984. For the first time the world could read Mary Chesnut's original entries as she had written them.

The excerpt here contains her entries around the time of the Battle of First Manassas (July 21, 1861) and reflect the confusion, uncertainty, and misinformation that were rampant at the time. Who ran and who fought, who was killed and who survived, and what were the army's plans were all burning questions of the moment with no ready answers—a situation reflected in her changes in tone between July 19 and 25. The one idea that comes through loud and clear is that "we think of nothing but Manassas." The reader should compare those timely impressions with the description of the same period as reconstructed by Chesnut, Martin, and Avary decades later. On the left side of the page are original diary entries from The Unpublished Civil War Diaries; *on the right side are excerpts from "A Diary from Dixie." It is immediately obvious that these are two different documents, a fact scarcely appreciated by fans of the 1905 book.*

[*July 19, 1861*]

Yesterday we little knew the truth. Beauregard telegraphed Joe Johnston "for god sake to come down & help," he was overwhelmed by numbers—& Davis telegraphed Johnston to come.[1]

Our forces fell back to Bull Run. Bonham's Brigade & Ewell's—& Longstreet's fought from twelve until five & repulsed the enemy three times. Our loss small, theirs great. We took six hundred prisoners. Last night I felt I was deceived, &c, by being shut up, & dressed & went down. There this *news* awaited me at the foot of the stairs by Mrs. Davis. Then Gen. Cooper, who has never spoken to me before, came rushing up & looked so bright & told me this news. Then Clingman.[2]

At tea we had a Col. Smith who was with McClellan & Garnett in Europe. Garnett is dead—killed—& his troops dispersed. *1,000* of our men taken—the cowardice or *treachery* of

July 19th.—Beauregard telegraphed yesterday (they say, to General Johnston), "Come down and help us, or we shall be crushed by numbers." The President telegraphed General Johnston to move down to Beauregard's aid. At Bull Run, Bonham's Brigade, Ewell's, and Longstreet's encountered the foe and repulsed him. Six hundred prisoners have been sent here.

I arose, as the Scriptures say, and washed my face and anointed my head and went down-stairs. At the foot of them stood General Cooper, radiant, one finger nervously arranging his shirt collar, or adjusting his neck to it after his fashion. He called out: "Your South Carolina man, Bonham, has done a capital thing at Bull Run—driven back the enemy, if not defeated him; with killed and prisoners," etc., etc. Clingman came to tell the particulars, and Colonel Smith (one of the trio with Garnett, McClellan, who were sent to Europe to inspect and report on military matters). Poor Garnett is killed. There was cowardice or treachery on the part of natives up there, or some of Governor Letcher's appointments to military posts. I hear all these things said. I do not understand, but it was a fatal business.

Mrs. McLane says she finds we do not believe a word of any news unless it comes in this guise: " A great battle fought. Not one Confederate killed. Enemy's loss in killed, wounded, and prisoners taken by us, immense." I was in hopes there would be no battle until Mr. Chesnut was forced to give up his amateur aideship to come and attend to his regular duties in the Congress.

[1] The Confederate generals P. G. T. Beauregard and Joseph Johnston, the former commanding at First Manassas, and the latter serving as his second-in-command for the the battle of July 21, 1861. The battle was known to Northerners as "First Bull Run" for the nearby creek; Southerners called it "the Battle of Manassas" for the nearby railroad junction. Jefferson Davis was president of the Confederate States of America, 1861–65.

[2] The reference to the fighting by Bonham's Brigade, and others, is properly to the Battle of Blackburn's Ford, a few miles from Bull Run Creek, which occurred on July 18. The officers are Luke Bonham, Richard S. Ewell, and James Longstreet. Cooper was General Samuel Cooper, the 63-year-old adjutant general of the Confederate army for the duration of the war.

Scott causing Garnett's death. Scott is one of the appointments of that horrid old Letcher. Last night Mrs. Davis sat with us until twelve & was *fascinating*. Old Waul is a fool with his nonsense.[3]

Mrs. Waul I shall treat differently. She has lost two children, both when she was away from home—the last burnt to death. Poor thing—Two Carolina regiments went by to day. The two *Carolinas* furnish men every day. So far no news today. Will Chesnut come up to the Congress—that is the question now to me. Mallory has sent to ask Mrs. Preston & me to go & see the *Patrick Henry*. We declined. He sent me *two* lovely peaches.[4]

Sat the morning with Mrs. McLean & Mrs. Johnston. Mrs. *Mc* is against us—seemed to enjoy the way I snapped up old Waul. Can't read. Too miserable. Mr. C dispatched me all was *well*.

Great disaffection in the legion. Wade Hampton in trouble. Told John C good b'ye. Mary H lent him twenty dollars. She gave me two hundred & eighty to keep for her.[5]

[July 20, 1861]

Stirring news. Still the cry is that a battle rages at Manassas. Keitt has come in. Says our great battle was a *skirmish*, to the disgust of every one. Last night Joe Davis wished some one with the genius of Napoleon would spring up. I said, "That would do no good. I did not think Walker would give him a commission."[6]

Last night I went down. Mrs. Carrington told me of a *fresh* fight & 140 killed. I was about to rush back in despair when Mr. Mallory came with Mr. Davis' contradiction. Went to tea with the President—then talked with Lieut. Col. Sumter who is a bridegroom, Mr. Mallory, Capt. Ingraham. Went for a sho[r]t time to Mrs. Davis' room. She came to Mrs. Preston's room. Stayed until 11.

Today had calls from Dr. LaBorde & Dr. Gibbes, Waul, &c. Read Jeff Davis' message. Keitt has come & Boyce. Dr. Gibbes at the opening of Congress sat in Mr. Chesnut's chair. Now try & sleep until dinner. Mrs. Davis' *own* niece of those Philadelphia Howells.

[July 21, 1861]

Troops pour in—every day several regiments pass. Tom Taylor & John Rhett bowed & laughed to us from their horses. Dined at Mrs. Davis' table—had a pass with Mrs. McLean. She said every body ought to be for their own section. I said yes, so much do I agree with you that I never see a northerner now that I do not doubt her.

Last night had a gay time with the two Tuckers—*Ran* & Beverley. I like *Ran*. *Bev* told us how he passed himself for [*illegible*

[3] "Col Smith" is actually the former-U.S. congressman Paul Thomas Delage Sumter, who is correctly identified in the 1880s manuscript. The Confederate general Robert S. Garnett is the first general officer on either side to die during the war, killed at First Manassas. Letcher is Governor John Letcher of Virginia. Mrs. Davis is Varina Howell Davis, wife of the Confederate president. Waul was the Texan Thomas N. Waul, Confederate congressman and later colonel in the Confederate army.

[4] Mallory is Secretary of the Confederate navy Stephen R. Mallory of Florida. The (C.S.S.) *Patrick Henry* is a Confederate gunboat, part of the James River squadron that guards Richmond. "Mr. C.," "JC," and "Col. Chesnut" throughout the text refer to her husband, James Chesnut.

[5] Wade Hampton was a colonel (later general) of cavalry in the Confederate army.

[6] Walker is the Confederate Secretary of war, Leroy Pope Walker of Alabama. Joe Davis is Leautinant Colonel Joseph Robert Davis of Mississippi, nephew of Jefferson Davis and soon to be the president's aide and ultimately a brigadier general in the Army of Northern Virginia.

Keitt has come in. He says Bonham's battle was a skirmish of outposts. Joe Davis, Jr., said: " Would Heaven only send us a Napoleon! " Not one bit of use. If Heaven did, Walker would not give him a commission. Mrs. Davis and Mrs. Joe Johnston, "her dear Lydia," were in fine spirits. The effect upon *nous autres* was evident; we rallied visibly. South Carolina troops pass every day. They go by with a gay step. Tom Taylor and John Rhett bowed to us from their horses as we leaned out of the windows. Such shaking of handkerchiefs. We are forever at the windows.

It was not such a mere skirmish. We took three rifled cannon and six hundred stands of arms. Mr. Davis has gone to Manassas. He did not let Wigfall know he was going. That ends the delusion of Wigfall's aideship. No mistake to-day. I was too ill to move out of my bed. So they all sat in my room.

July 22d.—Mrs. Davis came in/so softly that I did not know she was here until she leaned over me and said: " A great battle has been fought.[1] Joe Johnston led the right wing, and Beauregard the left wing of the army. Your husband is all right. Wade Hampton is wounded. Colonel Johnston of the Legion killed; so are Colonel Bee and Colonel Bartow. Kirby Smith[2] is wounded or killed."

I had no breath to speak; she went on in that desperate, calm way, to which people betake themselves under the greatest excitement: " Bartow, rallying his men, leading them into the hottest of the fight, died gallantly at the head' of his regiment. The President telegraphs me only that 'it is a great victory.' General Cooper has all the other telegrams."

Still I said nothing; I was stunned; then I was so grateful. Those nearest and dearest to me were safe still. She then began, in the same concentrated voice, to read from a paper she held in her hand: " Dead and dying cover the field. Sherman's battery taken. Lynchburg regiment cut to pieces. Three hundred of the Legion wounded."

That got me up. Times were too wild with excitement to stay in bed. We went into Mrs. Preston's room, and she made me lie down on her bed. Men, women, and children streamed in. Every living soul had a story to tell. "Complete victory," you heard everywhere. We had been such anxious wretches. The revulsion of feeling was almost too much to bear.

To-day I met my friend, Mr. Hunter. I was on my way to Mrs. Bartow's room and begged him to call at some other time. I was too tearful just then for a morning visit from even the most sympathetic person.

A woman from Mrs. Bartow's country was in a fury because they had stopped her as she rushed to be the first to tell Mrs. Bartow her husband was killed, it having been decided that Mrs. Davis should tell her. Poor thing! She was found lying on her bed when Mrs. Davis knocked. "Come in," she said. When she saw it was Mrs. Davis, she sat up, ready to spring to her feet, but then there was something in Mrs. Davis's pale face that took the life out of her. She stared at Mrs. Davis, then sank back, and covered her face as she asked: "Is it bad news for me!" Mrs. Davis did not speak. "Is he killed!" Afterward Mrs. Bartow said to me: "As soon as I saw Mrs. Davis's face I could not say one word. I knew it all in an instant. I knew it before I wrapped the shawl about my head."

(Footnotes have been renumbered for continuity.)

[1] The first battle of Bull Run, or Manassas, fought on July 21,1861, the Confederates being commanded by General Beauregard, and the federals by General McDowell. Bull Run is a small stream tributary to the Potomac.

[2] Edmund Kirby Smith, a native of Florida, who had graduated from West Point, served in the U.S. Mexican War, and been professor of mathematics at West Point. He resigned his commission in the United States Army after the secession of Florida.

name]—& so cheated old Giddings. Saw Mrs. Wigfall & Mrs. Bradley Johnson. We took six hundred stands of arms & three rifled cannon at Bull Run.[7]

President Davis has gone to Manassas—*left* Wigfall designedly. Poor Mrs. Wigfall. Mrs. Davis passed the morning with us. I feel really ill— no news—battle expected every day. Mrs. McLean came into my room with her sister's baby—quite humanized.

[July 22, 1861]

Yesterday after writing I laid so ill. Mrs. Davis came in, sat by me. Kissed me, said a great battle had been fought at Manassas—Jeff Davis led the centre—Beauregard the right wing—Johnston the left. Beauregard's staff safe. What a load from my heart. Wade Hampton wounded—Lieut. Col. Johnson killed—Gen. Bee killed—Kirby Smith killed *[following word added later:]* wounded. Poor Col. Bartow—killed gallantly leading his men into action. President telegraphs we have had a great victory—a thorough *rout*—dead & dying strewing the fields. Several batteries taken—Sherman's among others.—by the Lynchburg regiment which was cut to pieces in doing it.[8] Three hundred of the Legion killed—one U.S.A. flag. Then I lay upon Mrs. Preston's bed—one set of women & men coming in after another. Such miserable wretches, so glad of the victory, so sad for the dead. Those miserable beasts sent a flag of truce to bury their dead. Instead of burying them as they pretended, were throwing up entrenchments.

We are so frantic at this victory. Met Mr. Hunter to day; too busy crying over Mrs. Bartow to say much. Spent the morning with Mrs. Wigfall. She is nearly *mad* to see Louis Wigfall—he has not been here since Tuesday. *Drunk* somewhere—his troop ordered off tomorrow. Miserable woman.

The horrible accident maker, Mrs. Montmolin, is really mad with agitation at the report of her son wounded. She was so angry that she was not allowed to tell the bad news to Mrs. Bartow. Have not dared to face Mrs. Bartow. Met Trescot. Wonder what brings him here. Col. Meyers is so kind. George Deas will not know any thing.

Rain—rain—what is before us. Mrs. Davis has been so devoted to me since my trouble. Mrs. Preston's maid, when I read the papers, said no body talks in them of *S C*—but the number of our *dead* shows we were not backward. Telegraphed Col. Chesnut. Mrs. Johnston told me President Davis said he liked best to have me sit opposite *him;* he liked my style of *chat.* Mrs. McLean introduced her handsome brother in law & her sister—he is to take command somewhere in Western Virginia. Sydney Johnston is expected every day.[9]

We want to go & nurse the soldiers.

[July 23, 1861]

Yesterday dined at Mrs. Davis' table next to Mrs. Joe Johnston—had a merry time. So many witty things said. Came to my

[7] The Tuckers are John Randolph Tucker and Nathaniel Beverly Tucker of Virginia, members of a prominent family: John was attorney general of Virginia; Nathaniel was an officer in the Confederate army. Mrs. Wigfall was the wife of the Texan Louis T. Wigfall, Confederate officer and sometime congressman, who was a thorn in the side of Jefferson Davis during the war. Mrs. Bradley Johnson was the wife of the Confederate general Johnson of Maryland.

[8] Among the casualties at First Manassas were Brigadier General Barnard Bee of Texas, who reportedly christened "Stonewall" Jackson with his famous nickname, and Brigadier General Edmund Kirby Smith of Florida. Sherman is Colonel William T. Sherman of Ohio, later to become infamous for his "March through Georgia."

[9] Sydney Johnston is General Albert S. Johnston of Texas, expected to be the savior for the western Confederacy when he takes command of forces there.

Maria, Mrs. Preston's maid, furiously patriotic, came into my room. "These colored people say it is printed in the papers here that the Virginia people done it all. Now Mars Wade had so many of his men killed and he wounded, it stands to reason that South Carolina was no ways backward. If there was ever anything plain, that's plain."

Tuesday.—Witnessed for the first time a military funeral. As that march came wailing up, they say Mrs. Bartow fainted. The empty saddle and the led war-horse —we saw and heard it all, and now it seems we are never out of the sound of the Dead March in Saul. It comes and it comes, until I feel inclined to close my ears and scream.

Yesterday, Mrs. Singleton and ourselves sat on a bedside and mingled our tears for those noble spirits—John Darby, Theodore Barker, and James Lowndes. To-day we find we wasted our grief; they are not so much as wounded. I dare say all the rest is true about them—in the face of the enemy, with flags in their hands, leading their men. "But Dr. Darby is a surgeon." He is as likely to forget that as I am. He is grandson of Colonel Thomson of the Revolution, called, by way of pet name, by his soldiers, "Old Danger." Thank Heaven they are all quite alive. And we will not cry next time until officially notified.

July 24th.—Here Mr. Chesnut opened my door and walked in. Out of the fulness of the heart the mouth speaketh. I had to ask no questions. He gave me an account of the battle as he saw it (walking up and down my room, occasionally seating himself on a window sill, but too restless to remain still many moments); and told what regiments he was sent to bring up. He took the orders to Colonel Jackson, whose regiment stood so stock still under fire that they were called a "stone wall." Also, they call' Beauregard, Eugene, and Johnston, Marlboro. Mr. Chesnut rode with Lay's cavalry after the retreating enemy in the pursuit, they following them until midnight. Then there came such a fall of rain—rain such as is only known in semi-tropical lands.

In the drawing-room, Colonel Chesnut was the "belle of the ball"; they crowded him so for news. He was the first arrival that they could get at from the field of battle. But the women had to give way to the dignitaries of the land, who were as filled with curiosity as themselves—Mr. Barnwell, Mr. Hunter, Mr. Cobb, Captain Ingraham, etc.

Wilmot de Saussure says Wilson of Massachusetts, a Senator of the United States,[3] came to Manassas, *en route* to Richmond, with his dancing shoes ready for a festive scene which was to celebrate a triumph. The New York Tribune said: "In a few days we shall have Richmond, Memphis, and New Orleans. They must be taken and at once." For "a few days" maybe now they will modestly substitute "in a few years."

They brought me a Yankee soldier's portfolio from the battle-field. The letters had been franked by Senator Harlan.[4] One might shed tears over some of the letters. Women, wives and mothers, are the same everywhere. What a comfort the spelling was! We had been willing to admit that their universal free-school education had put them, rank and file, ahead of us *literarily,* but these letters do not attest that fact. The spelling is comically bad.

[3] Henry Wilson, son of a farm laborer and self-educated, who rose to much prominence in the antislavery contests before the war. He was elected United States senator from Massachusetts in 1855, he held the office until 1873, when he resigned, having been elected vice president of the United States on the ticket with Ulysses S. Grant.

[4] James Harlan, United States senator from Iowa from 1855 to 1865. In 1865 he was appointed secretary of the interior.

room & slept until nearly nine. Went down, had a long talk of poor Bartow with Judge Nisbet, Mrs. & Mr. Hill, &c. They told me he was an only son—devoted, good, clever, every thing. Was trying to rally his men. Said, "I wish to god as you disgrace me that a shot would go through my heart" & *it did.* His wife lies quiet. To day as a solemn touching military funeral went by, the first sound she heard of the dead march, she fainted!

Mrs. Sad Accident's son came—he was only hit by the butt end of a musket in the stomach. I found Mrs. Seddon in Mrs. Davis' room, a most agreeable room—had a long & most agreeable conversation— introduced the Hills, &c, then talked with Banks.[10] Left him because he ridiculed Mr. Hunter. There met Dr. Nott fresh from Manassas—he said they ran like dogs—lost three batteries of artillery, horses, men, ammunition, &c. John Cochrane & Ely came down to witness the fun & were taken prisoner—a *perfect* rout. He said he slept under a *tree* with General Johnston & Adèle said to Mrs. Johnston, "don't you wish it was you?" Every body giggled. *He* is very disagreeable. Met Trescot, went with him into Mrs. Davis' room. She treated him to a quantity of indirect abuse—& when we left the room he said she was the *vulgarest* woman he ever knew.

Came to Mrs. Preston's room, where all the Davises, Deas, & Dr. Nott met.[11] He made him self agreeable by saying that the President got there too late. Bledsoe wanted to turn a man out of office for saying so in the papers, but it is *true.* Then praised Beauregard & *not* Johnston which is the mode here—& then ridiculed John Preston & Mr. Chesnut, but he said Mr. Chesnut & the aides were in all the danger—& that Mr. C went with the foremost in the retreat. I mean pursuing the flying foe. Miles refused to recognize his *quondam foes* of the Congress—horrified the Mississippian by saying they ran. Said the Legion ran but Mrs. Preston made him take it back. She made a Mrs. Wynne write an apology for saying the same. Was introduced to a Mrs. Slocum who came to hear whether her husband was dead or alive—covered with diamonds. Saw *Chin* again. Mrs. McLean denouncing Mrs. Wigfall for saying she wished all the Yankee generals *dead.*

To day breakfasted with Mrs. Davis. Read a Baltimore *Sun* claiming the victory of last *Thursday,* but [in] a telegraph today they acknowledge more of a defeat than we claim. Why do not our Generals rush on to Washington? Davis still at Manassas—great jealousy of Beauregard. Mrs. Preston has just had a telegraph from her husband saying the enemy are flying through Washington. Mrs. Singleton came to day & mingled her tears with ours. We hear poor Today Barker & James Lowndes are killed. Darby shot down with the flag in his hand—Beauregard seized it & led on the men—not [a] handful of the men.

[July 24, 1861]

Lying down last night in a most dreary state at the loss of so many of my friends. Suddenly my husband came in the room. *Was* I not glad to see him!—safe & well. He was in all the fight—brought up regiments all day—heard shot whizzing round him—cannon & shell—carrying orders. Calls Beauregard "Eugene" and Johnston "Marlboro." Rode at the head of Lay's cavalry in the charge upon the retreating army—what a rout it was. I told him what Dr. Nott said & he wanted to cut his ears of[f]. So I talked something else. *None* of the young men we mourn so sincerely are even hurt.

(text continues in both columns on page 466)

July 27th.—Mrs. Davis's drawing-room last night was brilliant, and she was in great force. Outside a mob called for the President. He did speak—an old war-horse, who scents the battle-fields from afar. His enthusiasm was contagious. They called for Colonel Chesnut, and he gave them a capital speech, too. As public speakers say sometimes, "It was the proudest moment of my life." I did not hear a great deal of it, for always, when anything happens of any moment, my heart beats up in my ears, but the distinguished Carolinians who crowded round told me how good a speech he made. I was dazed. There goes the Dead March for some poor soul.

To-day, the President told us at dinner that Mr. Chesnut's eulogy of Bartow in the Congress was highly praised. Men liked it. Two eminently satisfactory speeches in twenty-four hours is doing pretty well. And now I could be happy, but this Cabinet of ours are in such bitter quarrels among themselves—everybody abusing everybody.

Last night, while those splendid descriptions of the battle were being given to the crowd below from our windows, I said: "Then, why do we not go on to Washington?" "You mean why did they not; the opportunity is lost." Mr. Barnwell said to me: "Silence, we want to listen to the speaker," and Mr. Hunter smiled compassionately, "Don't ask awkward questions."

Kirby Smith came down on the turnpike in the very nick of time. Still, the heroes who fought all day and held the Yankees in check deserve credit beyond words, or it would all have been over before the Joe Johnston contingent came. It is another case of the eleventh-hour scrape; the eleventh-hour men claim all the credit, and they who bore the heat and brunt and burden of the day do not like that.

Everybody said at first, "Pshaw! There will be no war." Those who foresaw evil were called ravens, ill-fore-' boders. Now the same sanguine people all cry, "The war is over"—the very same who were packing to leave Richmond a few days ago. Many were ready to move on at a moment's warning, when the good news came. There are such owls everywhere.

But, to revert to the other kind, the sage and circumspect, those who say very little, but that little shows they think the war barely begun. Mr. Rives and Mr. Seddon have just called. Arnoldus Van der Horst came to see me at the same time. He said there was no great show of victory on our side until two o'clock, but when we began to win, we did it in double-quick time. I mean, of course, the battle last Sunday.

Arnold Harris told Mr. Wigfall the news from Washington last Sunday. For hours the telegrams reported at rapid intervals, "Great victory," "Defeating them at all points." The couriers began to come in on horseback, and at last, after two or three o'clock, there was a sudden cessation of all news. About nine messengers with bulletins came on foot or on horseback—wounded, weary, draggled, footsore, panic-stricken—spreading in their path on every hand terror and dismay. That was our opportunity. Wigfall can see nothing that could have stopped us, and when they explain why we did not go to Washington I understand it all less than ever. Yet here we will dilly-dally, and Congress orate, and generals parade, until they in the North get up an army three times as large as McDowell's, which we have just defeated.

[10] Mrs. Seddon is wife of the Confederate congressman and future secretary of war James A. Seddon of Virginia.

[11] Mrs. Preston is the wife of 52-year-old Leautinant Colonel John Smith Preston of Virginia, serving as assistant adjutant general for the Confederate army.

(Continued from p. 465, left column)

We went to supper. A Carolina man, [*following name added later:*] Duncan, seemed so pleased that I bowed & [he] rushed up. Mr. C was the belle, a crowd round him all the time—Mr. Hunter, the Cobbs. Went to the drawing room, saw Wilmot DeSaussure & reassured him as to our loss. What a splendid victory.

All their cannon—ammunition—clothes—came near taking Wilson of Massachusetts. All had come here prepared for a ball in Richmond. The *Tribune* says they must have Charleston, Memphis, New Orleans & Richmond—perhaps Montgomery.[12]

Brought me a portfolio from the field of battle—filled with letters from *hard* Yankee women—*but women,* wives & mothers & I *cried.* One from a man to his sweetheart "thrilling with her last embrace." A bund[l]e of envelopes franked by *Harlan,* the villain.[13] Such spelling.

I have never seen a more brilliant drawing [room] than Mrs. Davis'. I went in with Mr. Robert Barnwell & Mr. Henry Marshall & Captain Ingraham. Sat between them while the president addressed the crowd— thousands. The President took all the credit to himself for the victory. Said the wounded roused & shouted for Jeff Davis—& the men rallied at the sight of him & rushed on & routed the enemy. The truth is Jeff Davis was not two miles from the battle field—but he is greedy for military fame. Mr. Chesnut was then called for & gave a capital speech. He gave the glory of the victory to Beauregard—& said if the President had not said so much for him self he would have praised him. Mrs. McLean left in disgust—& went off to write a note to one of the Prisoners.

To day she has had a row with Joe Davis who wishes all the Yankees *dead*—& Mrs. Davis has not taken it up, but consults with Mrs. Preston what she will do. Every body gives Mrs. McLean a fling.

I felt so proud of my husband last night—& so happy. To day we breakfasted with the president. They tell me my husband made another beautiful eulogy of Bartow. I sat with that poor woman hours last night & again to day. She seems so grateful for Mr. Chesnut's praise of her husband. She has neither father nor mother nor children—alone in the world. I wrote a long letter to my father in law today—& enclosed scraps from the papers. Then Mrs. Singleton came. Judge Nisbet & I had a long talk. How kind every body is to me. Then Waul. Then Mrs. Preston told me all the Cabinet quarrels.

Thousands of anecdotes of the war float round. Only 13 men killed in the Legion. Cut out the handsomest notice of Wade Hampton & gave it to Mrs. Preston. She loves him. Was so provoked when I found the *Dispatch* did not notice Mr. C's speech. Cut extracts from all the rest for the old gentleman.

Wigfall has come here to stay now—& his wife is jubilant, making a flag. The Davises go to their own house tomorrow. At least Mrs. Joe Davis begins it. What a reaction in Richmond when last week they were packing up for flight. Saw Mr. Seddon last night again—he's so pleasant. Then Mr. Rives.[14]

Men come in to Mrs. Davis' drawing room with their hats. The President swears vengeance against Dr. Nott for saying the Mississippians ran.

Adèle Auzé worse than ever—running out in a ragged old dressing gown to speak to a young officer. A beautiful Mrs. Slocum read aloud my Yankee letters. Must return some calls now—never read any thing.

[*July 25, 1861*]

Went down last night, found Brewster & Clingman. Mrs. Dubose, Mr. Toombs' daughter, wished she could scalp a man who went off for a tête à tête with Mrs. McLean, a surgeon U.S.A. on his parole. Went to supper with Mr. Trescot—he was as *insolent* as ever. Mrs. Reagan was as absurd with her damp mouth.[15] Arnoldus VanderHorst came—says we were whipped last Sunday until two o'clock.

Wigfall had been to see Arnold Harris, who says telegraphs came in until two in Washington announcing a great victory for *them.* Then there was no news until about nine or ten when the bulletins came in on foot—wounded, weary & terrified, spreading dismay & horror. Why did not our men push on. We wait until they prepare & fight us again.

They say a battle is raging now at Bethel. Wise has defeated them at Kanawha but we think of nothing but Manassas.[16] Mrs. McLean says this is no victory. It will not hurt the North. What a villain that woman is.

In Mrs. Davis' room saw some stupid women, Mrs. Allison among them. Then talked to John *Waties*—who described all the danger of the combat. Then *Mr. Shand*. Then Trescot & Mrs. Joe Johnston. Then a serenade & speech from the President & *then*—a call from the *mob* for *Chesnut*—South Carolina Chesnut. Today making visits all day— such stupid work. Venable says a Columbia Negro rushed in the midst of the fight & carried his Master a tin pan filled with rice & ham, screaming, "Make haste & *eat.* You must be *tired* & hungry, Massa."

We still find *cannon,* ammunition & rifles, every thing in the woods. The congressmen were having a *picnic* & had their luggage *ticketed* to Richmond. Saw a Mrs. Cole yesterday, cousin of Milledge Bonham, who was his confidante when he made love to me. Wadsie Ramsey was found killed, fighting against us. I said I was sorry—& Mr. Chesnut said, "What, sorry for your enemy?" I said, "*No,* sorry he fought against us." Mrs. Davis said I let Mr. C *bully* me. Cameron has issued a proclamation saying they are busier than ever getting ready to fight us—[17]

The Lord help us. Oh that England & France would help open a port.[18]

Sources: Mary Chesnut, *A Diary from Dixie,* edited by Isabella D. Martin and Myrta Lockett Avary (New York: D. Appleton & Co., 1905); C. Van Woodward and Elisabeth Muhlenfeld, eds., *The Private Mary Chesnut: The Unpublished Civil War Diaries* (New York: Oxford University Press, 1984), 98–105.

[12] Wilson is the despised abolitionist Henry Wilson of Massachusetts. The *Tribune* is the *New York Tribune,* which continued to be a major source of information for people on both sides during the war.

[13] Harlan is the Republican senator James Harlan of Iowa.

[14] Mr. Rives is the Confederate congressman William Cabell Rives of Virginia, who beat out James Seddon for the seat, whereupon Seddon secured the appointment as secretary of war.

[15] Mrs. Reagan is the wife of the Confederate postmaster general, John H. Reagan of Texas.

[16] Bethel, Virginia (Bethel Church or Big Bethel), was near Fortress Monroe and Newport News. It was the scene of an earlier battle, but nothing was happening there at this time; this is a false rumor. Kanawha is the Kanawha Valley in western Virginia, where Brigadier General Henry A. Wise, the former Virginia governor, commands. This is another false rumor because Wise has actually retreated in the face of a Northern advance on July 24.

[17] Cameron is the U.S. secretary of war, Simon Camerson of Pennsylvania. More false rumors here regarding any proclamation by the War Department; Lincoln on July 22 authorized another 500,000 volunteers for the Union army.

[18] Confederates desperately hoped throughout the war that England or France or both would intervene on the Southern side with diplomatic leverage if not military force, thus pressuring the North to cease its aggression and recognize Southern independence. Opening one of the South's blockaded ports, such as Charleston or New Orleans, would be the first step. That hope was never realized, although it was much more likely early in the war than during the last two years.

The Homestead Act, May 20, 1862

A comprehensive Homestead Bill was first passed by Congress in 1859, but it was vetoed by the president James Buchanan because it was clearly a slap at slave owners. Three years later, with the slaveocracy gone with the winds of secession, the legislation was proposed again and this time passed as one of the most important and popular measures ever effected by that body. It practically gave away public lands in the West to citizens, single or married, willing to take up the challenge of living on it and developing it for five years. The land had to be surveyed but unclaimed; the act recognized that "squatters" who arrived before the surveyors and homesteaders had legal rights, too. In addition to courage, stamina, and vision, all a person needed to sign up was the $34 registration fee, and even that was on a sliding scale. Lincoln signed the Homestead Act into law on May 20, 1862, even as the Union was fighting to survive. Although it did not throw open the entire West, contrary to myth, it did make available millions of acres in the upper Mississippi and Missouri valleys. The land was offered in 160-acre (or quarter-section) parcels. The first claim was registered by Daniel Freeman on January 1, 1863, for a parcel of land near present-day Beatrice, in Gage County, Nebraska. By the end of December 1865 some 2.5 million acres of western land had been claimed under the Homestead Act. Eventually 1,623,691 applications would be "carried to patent," indicating all conditions met and title assumed free and clear.

The Homestead Act marked a revolution in U.S. public land policy. Heretofore public lands had been looked upon either as free and open to anyone who claimed them or as federal largesse to be distributed at Congress's whim among the states and special interests such as the railroads. The Homestead Act bypassed state governments and special interests and gave land directly to citizens. In the long term it helped ensure that the rural West would be populated by individual landowners rather than by tenant farmers and/or slave owners. Speculators acquiring huge tracts of land and reselling them at exorbitant prices continued to be a problem in the settlement of the West, but thanks to the Homestead Act, a much smaller problem than it could have been.

AN ACT to secure homesteads to actual settlers on the public domain.

Be it enacted, That any person who is the head of a family, or who has arrived at the age of twenty-one years, and is a citizen of the United States, or who shall have filed his declaration of intention to become such, as required by the naturalization laws of the United States, and who has never borne arms against the United States Government or given aid and comfort to its enemies, shall, from and after the first of January, eighteen hundred and sixty-three, be entitled to enter one quarter-section or a less quantity of unappropriated public lands, upon which said person may have filed a pre-emption claim, or which may, at the time the application is made, be subject to pre-emption at one dollar and twenty-five cents, or less, per acre; or eighty acres or less of such unappropriated lands, at two dollars and fifty cents per acre, to be located in a body, in conformity to the legal subdivisions of the public lands, and after the same shall have been surveyed:

Provided, That any person owing or residing on land may, under the provisions of this act, enter other land lying contiguous to his or her said land, which shall not, with the land so already owned and occupied, exceed in the aggregate one hundred and sixty acres.

Section 2 That the person applying for the benefit of this act shall, upon application to the register of the land office in which he or she is about to make such entry, make affidavit before the said register or receiver that he or she is the head of a family, or is twenty-one or more years of age, or shall have performed service in the Army or Navy of the United States, and that he has never borne arms against the Government of the United States or given aid and comfort to its enemies, and that such application is made for his or her exclusive use and benefit, and that said entry is made for the purpose of actual settlement and cultivation, and not, either directly or indirectly, for the use or benefit of any other person or persons whomsoever, and upon filing the said affidavit with the register or receiver, and on payment of ten dollars, he or she shall thereupon be permitted to enter the quantity of land specified: *Provided, however,* That no certificate shall be given or patent issued therefor until the expiration of five years from the date of such entry; and if, at the expiration of such time or at any time within two years thereafter, the person making such entry—or if he be dead, his widow; or in case of her death, his heirs or devisee; or in case of a widow making such entry, her heirs or devisee, in case of her death—shall prove by two credible witnesses that he, she, or they have resided upon or cultivated the same for the term of five years immediately succeeding the time of filing the affidavit aforesaid, and shall make affidavit that no part of said land has been alienated, and that he has borne true allegiance to the Government of the United States; then, in such case, he, she, or they, if at that time a citizen of the United States, shall be entitled to a patent, as in other cases provided for by law: *And provided, further,* That in case of the death of both father and mother, leaving an infant child or children under twenty-one years of age, the right and fee shall inure to the benefit of said infant child or children; and the executor, administrator, or guardian may, at any time within two years after the death of the surviving parent, and in accordance with the laws of the State in which such children for the time being have their domicile, sell said land for the benefit of said infants, but for no other purpose; and the purchaser shall acquire the absolute title by the purchase, and be entitled to a patent from the United States, on payment of the office fees and sum of money herein specified. . . .

Source: United States Congress, *The Statutes at Large of the United States,* vol. 12 (Washington, D.C.: U.S. Government Printing Office, 1875–1936), 392–94.

The End of Slavery

Slavery had been a troubling national issue ever since the Continental Congress in 1776. It was no less troubling when the Southern states seceded in 1860–61. All slave owners did not live in the Confederacy, and many people of good character and loyalty to the Union saw nothing wrong with the enslavement of blacks. In 1862, when President Lincoln was moved to use his executive power to take the first step toward abolishing slavery, he did so with the knowledge that he was entering a political minefield. The so-called Emancipation Proclamation, issued in preliminary form in September 1862, then as an official act in January 1863, did not end slavery anywhere in the United States. It did not even try to do so in the North, where it was enforceable, and ironically it could not be enforced in the South as long as the Confederate government continued to exercise power. Nor was it intended as merely a long-overdue humanitarian gesture. It was, as Lincoln called it, "a fit and necessary war measure for suppressing rebellion."

The proclamation expanded the Northern objectives in the war from simply preserving the Union to preserving the Union and abolishing slavery; yet Lincoln had to word it carefully so that he did not increase antiblack sentiment in the North or encourage slaves anywhere to think they could attack their master with impunity. The proclamation did state that runaway slaves would be welcome in the U.S. armed forces.

The immediate effect of Lincoln's proclamation was to offer freedom only to slaves in secessionist Southern states, excepting West Virginia and parts of Virginia, and Louisiana that were under Union control. It did not apply to slaves in Northern states or in the border states of Delaware, Maryland, Kentucky, Tennessee, or Missouri. They were still bound by law to their master.

News of emancipation slowly made its way through the country; it did not reach Texas until June 19, 1865 (celebrated today as Juneteenth). Its main impact was to seize the moral high ground for the Union and win European support for the U.S. government on the diplomatic front.

Noble and courageous in hindsight, Lincoln's action did not please all his supporters, not even strong "Union men," at the time. Some of those Union men were residents of border states who also happened to be slave owners. Some, for example, Charles Jones of St. Louis, Missouri, expressed their displeasure in writing to the president. This was not the first time Jones had written to Lincoln about having his slaves "interfered with" by Union soldiers. So far as is known, Lincoln never responded either personally or officially to Charles Jones.

It is enlightening to compare the three Reconstruction Amendments to the Constitution that followed in 1865, 1868, and 1870. The first of these, the Thirteenth, actually abolished the institution of slavery, thereby for the first time freeing all slaves, everywhere in the country. The amendment had first been proposed in 1864 but at that time failed to muster a two-thirds vote in the House of Representatives. Taken up again in the new year, it was passed the second time around, on January 31, 1865, with two votes more than the necessary two-thirds majority, thanks to the bipartisan support of Republicans and Democrats. In the galleries that day black onlookers embraced each other and wept tears of joy. Ratification was won by December 18, 1865, when carpetbag governments and purged voting lists made the difference in some Southern states.

But the battle was not won. The Fourteenth Amendment aimed to guarantee all the rights of citizenship to the former slaves, using the key phrases "due process" and "equal protection of the laws" that echo down to today in U.S. constitutional law. The Fourteenth was also a catch-all amendment that repudiated the South's wartime debt (and therefore payment of that debt to Confederate creditors) and aimed to force the Southern states to enfranchise the freedmen by threatening loss of representation in Congress. It was passed by Congress on June 13, 1866, with the necessary two-thirds majority: 33 to 11 in the Senate and 138 to 36 in the House of Representatives. When it was submitted to the states for ratification, however, 12 Southern or border states rejected it, and it became a major issue in congressional elections that fall. When a more radicalized Congress returned to work in 1867, they passed the Reconstruction Act of March 2, 1867, making ratification a condition for readmission of Southern states to the Union. By July 20, 1868, North and South Carolina, Florida, Alabama, Louisiana, and Arkansas had fallen in line, but the process was complicated after New Jersey and Ohio rescinded their ratifications. Completely disregarding that awkward development, the secretary of state announced on July 28, 1868, that the Fourteenth Amendment was part of the law of the land.

Yet Southern states still resisted recognizing the full citizenship rights of the former slaves, in particular by doing everything possible to deny them the right to vote. In 1868, 16 of the 37 states, not all Southern, still denied suffrage to blacks. After much debate Congress passed the Fifteenth Amendment on February 26, 1869. By March 30, 1870, the necessary 28 states had ratified it, with some arm-twisting by the Republican-dominated Congress, and it too became part of the Constitution.

In the eyes of most Americans at the time, the basic work of Reconstruction in freeing the slaves and guaranteeing the constitutional rights of the freedmen had been done. A strong consensus existed that it was time to take up other national issues. "Let us have done with Reconstruction," said the New York Tribune *in April 1870. But the work of securing African-American rights had just begun.*

Abraham Lincoln's Emancipation Proclamation, 1863

UNITED STATES OF AMERICA:

A PROCLAMATION

WHEREAS on the 22d day of September, A.D. 1862, a proclamation was issued by the President of the United States, containing, among other things, the following, to wit:

That on the 1st day of January, A.D. 1863, all persons held as slaves within any State or designated part of a State the people whereof shall then be in rebellion against the United States shall be then, thenceforward, and forever free; and the executive government of the United States, including the military and naval authority thereof, will recognize and maintain the freedom of such persons and will do no act or acts to repress such persons, or any of them, in any efforts they may make for their actual freedom. . . .

Now, therefore, I, Abraham Lincoln, President of the United States, by virtue of the power in me vested as Commander in Chief of the Army and Navy of the United States in time of actual armed rebellion against the authority and government of the United States, and as a fit and necessary war measure for suppressing said rebellion, do, on this 1st day of January, A.D., 1863, and in accordance with my purpose so to do, publicly proclaimed for the full period of one hundred days from the first day above mentioned, order and designate as the States and parts of States wherein the people thereof, respectively, are this day in rebellion against the United States the following, to wit:

[The Confederate states, excepting designated Louisiana parishes, Virginia counties, and the state of Tennessee.]

And by virtue of the power and for the purpose aforesaid, I do order and declare that all persons held as slaves within said designated States and parts of States are, and henceforward shall be, free; and that the Executive Government of the United States, including the military and naval authorities thereof, will recognize and maintain the freedom of said persons.

And I hereby enjoin upon the people so declared to be free to abstain from all violence, unless in necessary self-defence; and I recommend to them that, in all cases when allowed, they labor faithfully for reasonable wages.

And I further declare and make known that such persons of suitable condition will be received into the armed service of the United States to garrison forts, positions, stations, and other places, and to man vessels of all sorts in said service.

And upon this act, sincerely believed to be an act of justice, warranted by the Constitution upon military necessity, I invoke the considerate judgment of mankind and the gracious favor of Almighty God.

Letter to Lincoln from a Missouri Slaveholder, March 24, 1863

St. Louis – March 24 1863

My Dear Sir,

You are aware that I have written to you several letters heretofore & in which I have shewn you that I have approved of your measures & especially do I refer to your suggestion or proposition to aid Missouri in emancipating slaves (which I fully indorse). That I have always I been a loyal man faithful to the Union and the constitution of the U. States, & know not how to be any thing but a devoted Union man. To be any thing else I would of course have to stultify myself.

Having more fully stated all these things to you in my previous communications, to you, & having more fully given my views., I now proceed to the matter for which this communication is more especially addressed. I live in Franklin County Mo, which I think is as loyal a county as perhaps any in the U. States, & most so of any in our State. It is the banner county for Loyalty & devotion to the Union. We were all getting along prosperously & unitedly until a few months ago, when by some construction of some order, the officers assigned us in our County came to the conclusion that all negroes who came into the camp then, & ever afterwards were free from their owners., & that no one could take them afterwards in the county without such person being arrested. Such being the case, the poor negro thought that he had nothing to do but to go to the camp & there be fed & clothed & do nothing & be free.

For a very long time under the operation of this construction of the order, my negroes remained quiet, until nearly evry other negro had left his owners & gone to Washington in Franklin County & took what they call free or Protection papers—

Mine having wives among some of those having free papers, of course would naturally become affected by it, & finally in my abscence at the hour of midnight when my wife & children were solitary & alone, nearly all of my negroes started off to Washington taking with them whatever they saw proper & are there now claiming to have free papers.

Even the nurse, that assisted in attending to my smallest child went off, a girl about 12 years old, leaving us without any one there to attend to the farm, or stock or any thing else. I have just passed through Washington & saw my negroes in a brick House, & they showed me what they call their free papers. The Capt intimated that he was sorry he could not do any thing—That he was under orders & would be removed, if he disobeyed. I told him that I did not wish him to disobey any order! but that I thought he was wrong in his construction of it. He said further that I could not get them, & that he would resist any & evry effort to retake them.

Evil by civil process. Now to be brief. Nearly all my negroes are there young & old, & nearly all of my best hands. My farm will go uncultivated, for there are no white men to get here. Is it right that I should be broken up. Last summer for being a Union man my horses were stolen from me & the only man in the neighborhood, who lost any thing that way was myself.

I have a large family, of helpless little children to support, & have got a farm to support them on, & if I cant cultivate it, it will be valueless to me. I make my appeal to you to grant me relief & that those professing to be agents of the Gov. should not destroy me.

Why cant Franklin Co be treated as well as Saline or Lafyette, where there are Southern sympathisers. Why cant the State Militia of Franklin Co attend to Franklin. Franklin is loyal to the backbone. Nearly all the slaves of Franklin County are now congregated at Washington. We can do nothing. And yet here there is no other earthly trouble. What shall I do? Were I a single man, & no family, I would not care, if my property was destroyed, And now if it was necessary to serve the interests of my country that I should sacrifice my property, I would submit without a murmur. I as a loyal man intending to stand by the Union & the Govermt of U. States, through evil as well as good report, I ask you to extend protection to me. My negroes are well treated well taken care of, & do less labor than any others in my county—A family of them that I purchased five or 6 years ago, who came to me to save them from being sold South, & whom I purchased more from sympathy than any other consideration, & who have never been taken to my residence, but lived on a farm near the County seat to themselves with evry comfort of life, they have taken up their abode in Washington.

I will not trouble you longer, but do again appeal to you to render me such assistance as may be proper; and command me for the Governmt in any way that I can be useful & I will give you any guantee that I will serve my country & Govt in any way in my power—I wish my rights to be protected in an open & substantial manner, that the people may see that there is propriety in being a loyal man, extending even to the protection of his property. I wish it to be effectual I tell my slaves, that I know they are misled, and if they return not a hair of their heads shall be Hurt & no violence used. And such shall be the case—I want protection that in the open day, like an honest transaction I can have my rights redressed. If it cant be done effectually & substantially I dont care to have it done. For as an honest man, making my living honestly & fairly in evry way, I desire protection as my Governmt always has protected her citizens fully, effectually & substantially. *I am a Loyal American Citizen.* Now having said this much, I deem it unnecessary to say more, but as we are now in a ruinous condition unable to cultivate our farms, implore your intervention, & you can accomplish it at once—

Permit me, My Dear Sir, to say that sinking or swimming, surviving or perishing, I will be found to [be] the last man standing if necessary solitary & alone *for the Union & the Constitution of the U. States.* With Sentiments of the very highest Consideration, I am Yours Most Truly

Charles Jones

I write hastily & hope you will excuse.

I again refer you to Hon. Ed. Bates, Att. Gen Our most excellent & worthy Gov. H.R. Gamble. Sam T. Glover, & John R. Shiply. Esqr. Our whole delegation in Congress, & to the County at large—

Amendments XIII–XV of the U.S. Constitution, 1865, 1868, 1870

AMENDMENT XIII

[ADOPTED 1865]

Section 1. Neither slavery nor involuntary servitude, except as a punishment for crime whereof the party shall have been duly convicted, shall exist within the United States, or any place subject to their jurisdiction.

Section 2. Congress shall have power to enforce this article by appropriate legislation.

AMENDMENT XIV

[ADOPTED 1868]

Section 1. All persons born or naturalized in the United States, and subject to the jurisdiction thereof, are citizens of the United States and of the State wherein they reside. No State shall make or enforce any law which shall abridge the privileges or immunities of citizens of the United States; nor shall any State deprive any person of life, liberty, or property, without due process of law; nor deny to any person within its jurisdiction the equal protection of the laws.

Section 2. Representatives shall be apportioned among the several States according to their respective numbers, counting the whole number of persons in each State, excluding Indians not taxed. But when the right to vote at any election for the choice of electors for President and Vice-President of the United States, Representatives in Congress, the Executive and Judicial officers of a State, or the members of the Legislature thereof, is denied to any of the male inhabitants of such State, being twenty-one years of age, and citizens of the United States, or in any way abridged, except for participation in rebellion, or other crime, the basis of representation therein shall be reduced in the proportion which the number of such male citizens shall bear to the whole number of male citizens twenty-one years of age in such State.

Section 3. No person shall be a Senator or Representative in Congress, or elector of President and Vice-President, or hold any office, civil or military, under the United States, or under any State, who, having previously taken an oath, as a member of Congress, or as an officer of the United States, or as a member of any State legislature, or as an executive or judicial officer of any State, to support the Constitution of the United States, shall have engaged in insurrection or rebellion against the same, or given aid or comfort to the enemies thereof. But Congress may by a vote of two-thirds of each House, remove such disability.

Section 4. The validity of the public debt of the United States, authorized by law, including debts incurred for payment of pensions and bounties for services in suppressing insurrection or rebellion, shall not be questioned. But neither the United States nor any State shall assume or pay any debt or obligation incurred in aid of insurrection or rebellion against the United States, or any claim for the loss or emancipation of any slave; but all such debts, obligations and claims shall be held illegal and void.

Section 5. The Congress shall have power to enforce, by appropriate legislation, the provisions of this article.

AMENDMENT XV

[ADOPTED 1870]

Section 1. The right of citizens of the United States to vote shall no be denied or abridged by the United States or by any State on account of race, color, or previous condition of servitude.

Section 2. The Congress shall have power to enforce this article by appropriate legislation.

Source: United States Congress, *The Statutes at Large of the United States,* vol. 12 (Washington, D.C.: U.S. Government Printing Office, 1875–1936), 1268–69; Ira Berlin et al., eds., *Freedom: A Documentary History of Emancipation 1861–1867,* series 1, vol. 1, *The Destruction of Slavery* (New York: Cambridge University Press, 1985), 450–53; United States Congress, *The Statutes at Large of the United States* (Washington, D.C.: U.S. Government Printing Office, 1875–1936), vol. 44, part 1, 1860 (XIII); vol. 15, Appendix, xiii (XIV); vol. 44, part 1, 1861 (XV).

Excerpt from *Ragged Dick,* 1868

First published serially in 1867, Ragged Dick *launched the career of one of the most popular U.S. authors of all time. Although his prose was not particularly memorable,* Horatio Alger *was more than the best-selling novelist of his day. He was enormously influential on the nation's morals and values. As ordainted minister with a shameful episode in his past, he launched his career in writing with this simple morality tale of a poor shoeshine boy who "pulls himself up by his boot-straps." More than 100 volumes using the same winning "rags-to-riches" formula followed. His message for his legions of youthful readers was that honesty, hard work, and perseverence would ultimately produce well-deserved success. The fact that good luck played as imortant a role in every hero's success story as hard work was glossed over.* Ragged Dick *was followed by the* Luck and Pluck *(1869) and* Tattered Tom *(1871). They were the Tom Swift and Hardy Boys of their day. Alger's personal life as a literary lothario would have shamed his pure-minded heroes but did not affect his popularity with his readers. In the end the author's name proved more enduring than any of his characters: It is widely identified today with the American ideal of rising from poverty to success through personal striving: the "Horatio Alger success story."*

In the chapter excerpted here the reader is introduced to Dick, who is not only industrious and honest but clever and self-confident enough to match wits with his elders. Dick's lack of education and his grammar prove not to be detrimental to rapid rise; nor are they indicative of his natural intelligence. All he needs is a little polishing, à la *Eliza Doolittle.*

CHAPTER 1

RAGGED DICK IS INTRODUCED TO THE READER

"WAKE UP there, youngster," said a rough voice.

Ragged Dick opened his eyes slowly, and stared stupidly in the face of the speaker, but did not offer to get up.

"Wake up, you young vagabond!" said the man, a little impatiently; "I suppose you'd lay there all day, if I hadn't called you."

"What time is it?" asked Dick.

"Seven o'clock."

"Seven o'clock! I oughter 've been up an hour ago. I know what 'twas made me so precious sleepy. I went to the Old Bowery last night, and didn't turn in till past twelve."

"You went to the Old Bowery? Where'd you get your money?" asked the man, who was a porter in the employ of a firm doing business on Spruce Street.

"Made it by shines, in course. My guardian don't allow me no money for theatres, so I have to earn it."

"Some boys get it easier than that," said the porter significantly.

"You don't catch me stealin', if that's what you mean," said Dick.

"Don't you ever steal, then?"

"No, and I wouldn't. Lots of boys does it, but I wouldn't."

"Well, I'm glad to hear you say that. I believe there's some good in you, Dick, after all."

"Oh, I'm a rough customer!" said Dick. "But I wouldn't steal. It's mean."

"I'm glad you think so, Dick," and the rough voice sounded gentler than at first. "Have you got any money to buy your breakfast?"

"No, but I'll soon get some."

While this conversation had been going on, Dick had got up. His bedchamber had been a wooden box half full of straw, on which the young bootblack had reposed his weary limbs, and slept as soundly as if it had been a bed of down. He dumped down into the straw without taking the trouble of undressing. Getting up too was an equally short process. He jumped out of the box, shook himself, picked out one or two straws that had found their way into the rents of his clothes, and, drawing a well-worn cap over his uncombed locks, he was all ready for the business of the day.

Dick's appearance as he stood beside the box was rather peculiar. His pants were torn in several places, and had apparently belonged in the first instance to a boy two sizes larger than himself. He wore a vest, all the bottons of which were gone except two, out of which peeped a shirt which looked as if it had been worn a month. To complete his costume he wore a coat too long for him, dating back, if one might judge from its general appearance, to a remote antiquity.

Washing the face and hands is usually considered proper in commencing the day, but Dick was above such refinement. He had no particular dislike to dirt, and did not think it necessary to remove several dark streaks on his face and hands. But in spite of his dirt and rags there was something about Dick that was attractive. It was easy to see that if he had been clean and well dressed he would have been decidedly good-looking. Some of his companions were sly, and their faces inspired distrust; but Dick had a frank, straight-forward manner that made him a favorite.

Dick's business hours had commenced. He had no office to open. His little blacking-box was ready for use, and he looked sharply in the faces of all who passed, addressing each with, "Shine yer boots, sir?"

"How much?" asked a gentleman on his way to his office.

"Ten cents," said Dick, dropping his box, and sinking upon his knees on the sidewalk, flourishing his brush with the air of one skilled in his profession.

"Ten cents! Isn't that a little steep?"

"Well, you know 'taint all clear profit," said Dick, who had already set to work. "There's the *blacking* costs something, and I have to get a new brush pretty often."

"And you have a large rent too," said the gentleman quizzically, with a glance at a large hole in Dick's coat.

"Yes, sir," said Dick, always ready to joke; "I have to pay such a big rent for my manshun up on Fifth Avenoo, that I can't afford to take less than ten cents a shine. I'll give you a bully shine, sir."

"Be quick about it, for I am in a hurry. So your house is on Fifth Avenue, is it?"

"It isn't anywhere else," said Dick, and Dick spoke the truth there.

"What tailor do you patronize?" asked the gentleman, surveying Dick's attire.

"Would you like to go to the same one?" asked Dick, shrewdly.

"Well, no; it strikes me that he didn't give you a very good fit."

"This coat once belonged to General Washington," said Dick comically. "He wore it all through the Revolution, and it got torn some, 'cause he fit so hard. When he died he told his widder to give it to some smart young feller that hadn't got none of his own; so she gave it to me. But if you'd like it, sir, to remember General Washington by, I'll let you have it reasonable."

"Thank you, but I wouldn't want to deprive you of it. And did your pants come from General Washington too?"

"No, they was a gift from Lewis Napoleon. Lewis had outgrown 'em and sent 'em to me,—he's bigger than me, and that's why they don't fit."

"It seems you have distinguished friends. Now, my lad, I suppose you would like your money."

"I shouldn't have any objection," said Dick.

"I believe," said the gentleman, examining his pocket-book, "I haven't got anything short of twenty-five cents. Have you got any change?"

"Not a cent," said Dick. "All my money's invested in the Erie Railroad."

"That's unfortunate."

"Shall I get the money changed, sir?"

"I can't wait; I've got to meet an appointment immediately. I'll hand you twenty-five cents, and you can leave the change at my office any time during the day."

"All right, sir. Where is it?"

"No. 125 Fulton Street. Shall you remember?"

"Yes, sir. What name?"

"Greyson,—office on second floor."

"All right, sir; I'll bring it."

"I wonder whether the little scamp will prove honest," said Mr. Greyson to himself, as he walked away. "If he does, I'll give him my custom regularly. If he don't, as is most likely, I shan't mind the loss of fifteen cents."

Mr. Greyson didn't understand Dick. Our ragged hero wasn't a model boy in all respects. I am afraid he swore sometimes, and now and then he played tricks upon unsophisticated boys from the country or gave a wrong direction to honest old gentlemen unused to the city. A clergyman in search of the Cooper Institute he once directed to the Tombs Prison, and, following him unobserved, was highly delighted when the unsuspicious stranger walked up the front steps of the great stone building on Centre Street, and tried to obtain admission.

"I guess he wouldn't want to stay long if he did get in," thought Ragged Dick, hitching up his pants. "Leastways I shouldn't. They're so precious glad to see you that they won't let you go, but board you gratooitous, and never send in no bills."

Another of Dick's faults was his extravagance. Being always wide-awake and ready for business, he earned enough to have supported him comfortably and respectably. There were not a few young clerks who employed Dick from time to time in his professional capacity, who scarcely earned as much as he, greatly as their style and dress exceeded his. Dick was careless of his earnings. Where they went he could hardly have told himself. However much he managed to earn during the day, all was generally spent before morning. He was fond of going to the Old Bowery Theatre, and to Tony Pastor's, and if he had any money left afterwards, he would invite some of his friends in somewhere to have an oyster stew; so it seldom happened that he commenced the day with a penny.

Then I am sorry to add that Dick had formed the habit of smoking. This cost him considerable, for Dick was rather fastidious about his cigars, and wouldn't smoke the cheapest. Besides, having a liberal nature, he was generally ready to treat his companions. But of course the expense was the smallest objection. No boy of fourteen can smoke without being affected injuriously. Men are frequently injured by smoking, and boys always. But large numbers of the newsboys and bootblacks form the habit. Exposed to the cold and wet they find that it warms them up, and the self-indulgence grows upon them. It is not uncommon to see a little boy, too young to be out of his mother's sight, smoking with all the apparent satisfaction of a veteran smoker.

There was another way in which Dick sometimes lost money. There was a noted gambling-house on Baxter Street, which in the evening was sometimes crowded with these juvenile gamesters, who staked their hard earnings, generally losing of course, and refreshing themselves from time to time with a vile mixture of liquor at two cents a glass. Sometimes Dick strayed in here, and played with the rest.

I have mentioned Dick's faults and defects, because I want it understood, to begin with, that I don't consider him a model boy. But there were some good points about him nevertheless. He was above doing anything mean or dishonorable. He would not steal, or cheat, or impose upon younger boys, but was frank and straight-forward, manly and self-reliant. His nature was a noble one, and had saved him from all mean faults. I hope my young readers will like him as I do, without being blind to his faults. Perhaps, although he was only a bootblack, they may find something in him to imitate.

And now, having fairly introduced Ragged Dick to my young readers, I must refer them to the next chapter for his further adventures.

Source: Horatio Alger, Jr., *Ragged Dick and Mark, The Match Boy,* ed. Richard Fink (New York: Collier Books, 1962), 39–44.

Excerpt from *My Life on the Plains,* 1874

After a brilliant Civil War career in which he became the youngest general in the Union army, George Armstrong Custer went west to assume command of the 7th Cavalry regiment. Now a lieutenant colonel, Custer made a new name for himself as an Indian fighter and flamboyant plainsman. Whatever qualities he had, prudence and mature judgment were not among them. Sometimes his recklessness caused him trouble, but on those occasions his courage, fortitude, and the famous "Custer Luck" extricated him from tight spots. In 1871 he was asked to write his memoirs by the editor of Galaxy Magazine. *The subsequent work appeared as a series of articles between January 1872 and October 1874, later collected and reissued as* My Life on the Plains *in late 1874 by Sheldon and Company of New York. Critics would quickly dub it, "My Lie on the Plains." In this excerpt Custer describes an impromptu one-man buffalo hunt that almost killed him. The story reveals both the best and the worst of the legendary Custer as he is caught up in the thrill of the chase, suffers a disaster, extricates himself, and lives to tell of it. Less than two years later, however, his luck would run out on the Little Bighorn River in Montana.*

When leaving our camp that morning I felt satisfied that the Indians, having travelled at least a portion of the night, were then many miles in advance of us, and there was neither danger nor probability of encountering any of them near the column. We were then in a magnificent game country, buffaloes, antelope, and smaller game being in abundance on all sides of us. Although an ardent sportsman, I had never hunted the buffalo up to this time, consequently was exceedingly desirous of tasting its excitement. I had several fine English greyhounds, whose speed I was anxious to test with that of the antelope, said to be—which I believe—the fleetest of animals. I was mounted on a fine large thoroughbred horse. Taking with me but one man, the chief bugler, and calling my dogs around me, I galloped ahead of the column as soon as it was daylight, for the purpose of having a chase after some antelope which could be seen grazing nearly two miles distant.

That such a course was rashly imprudent I am ready to admit. A stirring gallop of a few minutes brought me near enough to the antelope, of which there were a dozen or more, to enable the dogs to catch sight of them. Then the chase began, the antelope running in a direction which took us away from the command. By availing myself of the turns in the course, I was able to keep well in view of the exciting chase until it was evident that the antelope were in no danger of being caught by the dogs, which latter had become blown from want of proper exercise. I succeeded in calling them off, and was about to set out on my return to the column. The horse of the chief bugler, being a common-bred animal, failed early in the race and his rider wisely concluded to regain the command, so that I was alone. How far I had travelled from the troops I was trying to determine, when I discovered a large, dark-looking animal grazing nearly a mile distant. As yet I had never seen a wild buffalo, but I at once recognized this as not only a buffalo, but a very large one.

Here was my opportunity. A ravine near by would enable me to approach unseen until almost within pistol range of my game. Calling my dogs to follow me, I slowly pursued the course of the ravine, giving my horse opportunity to gather himself for the second run. When I emerged from the ravine I was still several hundred yards from the buffalo, which almost instantly discovered me and set off as fast as his legs could carry him. Had my horse been fresh the race would have been a short one, but the preceding long run had not been without effect. How long or how fast we flew in pursuit, the intense excitement of the chase prevented me from knowing. I only knew that even the greyhounds were left behind, until finally my good steed placed himself and me close alongside the game. It may be because this was the first I had seen, but surely of the hundreds of thousands of buffaloes which I have since seen, none have corresponded with him in size and lofty grandeur. My horse was above the average size, yet the buffalo towered even above him. I had carried my revolver in my hand from the moment the race began. Repeatedly could I have placed the muzzle against the shaggy body of the huge beast, by whose side I fairly yelled with wild excitement and delight, yet each time would I withdraw the weapon, as if to prolong the enjoyment of the race.

It was a race for life or death, yet how different the award from what could be imagined. Still we sped over the springy turf, the high breeding and mettle of my horse being plainly visible over that of the huge beast that struggled by his side. Mile after mile was traversed in this way, until the rate and distance began to tell perceptibly on the bison, whose protruding tongue and labored breathing plainly betrayed his distress. Determined to end the chase and bring down my game, I again placed the muzzle of the revolver close to the body of the buffalo, when, as if divining my intention, and feeling his inability to escape by flight, he suddenly determined to fight and at once wheeled, as only a buffalo can, to gore my horse. So sudden was this movement, and so sudden was the corresponding veering of my horse to avoid the attack, that to retain my control over him I hastily brought up my pistol hand to the assistance of the other. Unfortunately as I did so my finger, in the excitement of the occasion, pressed the trigger, discharged the pistol, and sent the fatal ball into the very brain of the noble animal I rode. Running at full speed he fell dead in the course of his leap. Quick as thought I disengaged myself from the stirrups and found myself whirling through the air over and beyond the head of my horse. My only thought, as I was describing this trajectory, and my first thought on reaching *terra firma,* was: "What will the buffalo do with me?" Although at first inclined to rush upon me, my strange procedure seemed to astonish him. Either that or pity for the utter helplessness of my condition inclined him to alter his course and leave me alone to my own bitter reflections.

In a moment the danger into which I had unluckily brought myself stood out in bold relief before me. Under ordinary circumstances the death of my horse would have been serious enough. I was strongly attached to him; had ridden him in battle during a portion of the late war; yet now his death, except in its consequences, was scarcely thought of. Here I was, alone in the heart of the Indian country, with warlike Indians known to be in the vicinity. I was not familiar with the country. How far I had travelled, or in what direction from the column, I was at a loss to know. In the excitement of the chase I had lost all reckoning. Indians were liable to pounce upon me at any moment. My command would not note my absence probably for hours. Two of my dogs overtook me, and with mute glances first at the dead steed, then at me, seemed to inquire the cause of this strange condition of affairs. Their instinct appeared to tell them that we were in misfortune.

While I was deliberating what to do, the dogs became uneasy, whined piteously, and seemed eager to leave the spot. In this desire I sympathized with them, but whither should I go? I observed that their eyes were generally turned in one particular direction; this I accepted as my cue, and with one parting look at my horse, and grasping a revolver in each hand, I set out on my uncertain journey. As long as the body of my horse was visible above the horizon I kept referring to it as my guiding point, and in this way contrived to preserve my direction. This resource soon failed me, and I then had recourse to weeds, buffalo skulls, or any two objects I could find on my line of march. Constantly my eyes kept scanning the horizon, each moment expecting, and with reason too, to find myself discovered by Indians.

I had travelled in this manner what seemed to me about three or four miles, when far ahead in the distance I saw a column of dust rising. A hasty examination soon convinced me that the dust was produced by one of three causes: white men, Indians, or buffaloes. Two to one in my favor at any rate. Selecting a ravine where I could crawl away undiscovered should the approaching body prove to be Indians, I called my dogs to my side and concealed myself as well as I could to await developments. The object of my anxious solicitude was still several miles distant. Whatever it was, it was approaching in my direction, as was plainly discernible from the increasing columns of dust. Fortunately I had my field-glass slung across my shoulder, and if Indians I could discover them before they could possibly discover me. Soon I was able to see the heads of mounted men running in irregular order. This discovery shut out the probability of their being buffaloes, and simplified the question to white men or Indians. Never during the war did I scan an enemy's battery or approaching column with half the anxious care with which I watched the party then approaching me. For a long time nothing satisfactory could be determined, until my eye caught sight of an object which, high above the heads of the approaching riders, told me in unmistakable terms that friends were approaching. It was the cavalry guidon, and never was the sight of stars and stripes more welcome. My comrades were greatly surprised to find me seated on the ground alone and without my horse. A few words explained all. A detachment of my men, following my direction, found my horse and returned with the saddle and other equipments. Another horse, and Richard was himself again, plus a little valuable experience and minus a valuable horse.

Source: George A. Custer, *My Life on the Plains,* ed Milo Milton Quaife (reprint, Chicago: R. R. Donnelley & Sons, The Lakeside Press, 1952), 80–85.

Pages from Montgomery Ward & Co. Mail-Order Catalogue No. 10, January 1874

In 1872 a young entrepreneur, Aaron Montgomery Ward, revolutionized U.S. retail sales in by launching the first mail-order house. Thus was born the catalog industry. His idea was to sell reasonably priced goods directly to the customer, cutting out both "drummers" (traveling salesmen who carried their catalogs and samples with them on the road) and traditional retail storekeepers. Instead his market would be the entire country, everywhere the U.S. mail went, and the consumer would buy what he or she wanted directly from the stock warehouse without the usual intermediaries. Thus he positioned his company to compete directly with the lower-priced wholesale distributors, a strategy reflected in his advertising: "Merchandise at Wholesale Prices." Ward knew his business from his years on the road as a traveling salesman himself, observing the high prices and shoddy goods that were foisted off on rural Americans who could not take their business elsewhere.

Ward knew from the beginning who his customers would be, farmers, so he approached the nation's largest organization of farmers, the Patrons of Husbandry, to form an informal partnership. Their relationship proved to be a long, lucrative, and happy one for both sides. Ward established his company in Chicago, which was ideally situated in the geographic heartland of the country with excellent rail connections in every direction, and that same year (1872) he issued his first catalog, a modest single sheet, listing 163 items, under the simple heading "Grangers Supplied by the Cheapest Cash house in America." All goods ordered by mail from the catalog were shipped by express, payment on delivery, and customers were entitled to examine their purchase and return it if displeased. This simple practice, introduced in the inaugural catalog, had become the famous "Satisfaction Guaranteed or Your Money Back" policy by the time the 1875 catalog appeared. Other retailers quickly fell in line with the same policy for their customers. In little more than a decade after he took his first order, Ward's catalogs had grown to include nearly 10,000 items in each issue.

The idea was so successful that Montgomery Ward & Company did not open their first free-standing retail store until 1926. Long before then its success had inspired a host of competitors, the most notable Sears, Roebuck, & Company, which was launched, also in Chicago, in 1886. Sears, Roebuck tried to separate itself from Ward's operation by offering the same services "but with more flair." Sear's was able to take over the number one spot by 1900, but Montgomery Ward's, a strong, multimillion-dollar business in its own right, would always be the granddaddy of all mail-order houses in the world, even if its catalogs in later years were less polished and "lively" than Sears's. Aaron Montgomery Ward had single-handedly invented a new way of selling. The success of his catalogs with rural Americans was indicated by the fact that they had become not just the standard marketing tool, but the preferred form of reading matter in countless outhouses across the land.

The catalog reproduced here is the January 1874 edition (No. 10). It had grown from one to four pages in the two years since the first was published and was organized by category for ease of shopping. It offered everything from dry goods and clothes to carpets, diapers, and diamond rings. And the company guaranteed to save buyers "from 40 to 100 per cent" on their purchases. Careful instructions on how to place an order were included at the back of every catalog, and "fast delivery" was promised. In two years also the company's "headquarters" had progressed from a post-office box to a street address in the city's business district (104 Michigan Street).

Source: Montgomery Ward's Catalogue No. 10 (January 1874) is reproduced here courtesy of the University of Wyoming American Heritage Center, Photo Archives, Laramie, Wyo.

CATALOGUE No. 10.

JANUARY 1874.

CHEAPEST CASH HOUSE
IN AMERICA!

MONTGOMERY WARD & CO.

(The Original Grange Supply House),

104 MICHIGAN STREET,
CHICAGO, ILL.

Grangers, Farmers, Mechanics,

SUPPLIED WITH A FULL LINE OF

DRY GOODS, CLOTHING,

Hats, Caps, Boots, Shoes, &c.,

AT THE

LOWEST WHOLESALE PRICES.

We give the following Reasons why we can sell Goods at the Prices quoted

We don't pay Forty Thousand a year Rent.
We don't employ high-priced Salesmen to sell our Goods.
We don't sell Goods to Country Retailers on six months' time.
We buy for Cash and sell for Cash.
Our Goods are bought direct from Manufacturers.
We make no Display, and keep no men to show Goods.

By purchasing of us you save from 40 to 100 per cent. which are the profits of middle men.

(*See 4th page for General Instructions.*)

MONTGOMERY WARD & CO.'S PRICE LIST.

COTTON GOODS.

No.

1 12 Yds. best quality Prints $1.00
2 8 " good " Bed Tick.... 1.00
3 9 " " " Gingham.... 1.00
4 10 " Fine Brown Cotton..... 1.00
5 9 " Extra Fine Yard Wide Cotton 1.00
6 10 " Heavy Standard Sheeting (Yard wide)............ 1.00
7 10 " Bleached Cotton yd. wide 1.00
8 7 " Blue or Brown Denim... 1.00
9 5 " Ex. qual., do. do. 1.00
10 5 " Best qual. Brown or Blue Check Shirting......... 1.00
11 7 " Blue Check Shirting.... 1.00
12 7 " Good quality Hickory Striped Shirting........ 1.00
13 5 " Best quality Hickory Striped Shirting........ 1.00
14 5 lbs. White Carpet Warp (5 lb. Bundles)... .... 1.65
15 5 " Cotton Yarn, (5 lb. bund.) 1.65
16 5 "American A" Seamless Bags.. 1.50
17 6 "Stark A" Seamless Bags 2.10
18 7 yds. Corset Jeans, (give color) 1.00
19 5 " Good qual. Brown Duck 1.00
20 10 " Paper Cambric, (give col) 1.00
21 11 " Flat Cambric, (give col). 1.00
22 Farmers' and Mechanics' Cottonade per Yard.......... .... .27½
23 5 yds. Plain Nankeen.......... 1.00
24 5 " Plaid do. 1.00
25 7 " Good qual. Cotton Flannel 1.00
26 10 lbs. Best qual. Cotton Batting 2.00
27 10 " Medium Cotton Batting. 1.60
28 2¾ yds. Great American Frost Killer (for Pants) 1.00
29 Amoskeag Feather Ticking pr. yd. .22½
30 One Yard Wide, Green or Buff Window Curtain Goods, pr. yd. .17½

FLANNELS.

40 Red Twilled Flannel, per yard.... .30
41 " " good quality " .... .37½
42 " " extra heavy " .... .42½
43 Good Plain Red, " .... .30
44 Medium Quality, plain red " .... .27
45 Extra Fine, " " .... .35
46 Plain White, " .... .27½
47 Good Quality White, " .... .32½
48 Extra " " " .... .37½
49 White Shaker (⅞ yd. wide) " .... .25
50 Cochico blk. & white plaid " .... .40
51 Wilson's Plaid, " .... .37½
52 All Wool Blue Twilled, " .... .40
53 Grey Twilled, " .... .35
54 Opera Flannels, red or blue " .... .45
55 Black and Red Plaid Flannel, manufactured by the Xenia, Clay Co., Ill. Woolen Mills,.......... .37½
56 Printed Opera Flannels, per yard. .37½
57 Fancy Plaid Wool Flannel, 1 yard wide............................ .33⅓
58 Grey Twilled Flannel, per yard.. .30

DRESS GOODS.

70 12 Yds. Empress Cloth, all Shades $4.50
71 10 " Japanese Striped Poplin. 1.75
72 10 " Fancy Poplin Dress Goods 1.50
73 10 " Colored Alpaca.......... 2.35
74 10 " Double Fold Imported Beaver Brand Black Alpaca, send for sample.... 3.25
75 10 " Double Fold Imported Alpaca, Garnet, Slate, Green and Brown,........ 3.25
76 1 Japanese (plain) Silk Pattern, in all shades, genuine goods, six yds. long and 1¼ yards wide, for...... 6.50
77 16 yards Irish Poplin, Green, Light Brown, Rose and Slate, for 15.00
78 Superfine Mohair, Alpaca Luster, Brilliantine, per yard.......... .50
79 5 yds. Marseilles or White Piques 1.00
80 6 " Medium Qual. Marseilles or White Piques......... 1.00
81 Ext. fine Heavy Quality Marseilles or White Piques, per yard...... .28½
82 6 yds. Pacific Lawns.......... 1.00
83 10 " Fancy Plaid Dress Goods 2.50
84 Organdies, per yard.............. .18
85 Percale, " .... .15
86 Belgian Cord Alpaca, per yard ... .25
87 3 yds. Black Silk Finished Velveteen................ 2.00
88 3 " Silk Finished Velveteen, Garnet, Blue, Purple or Brown................ 2.25

WHITE GOODS.

100 Victoria Lawn (good quality).... .20
101 " " (extra fine quality) .25
102 Plain Jaconet (good quality) .... .15
103 " " (extra fine quality) .22½
104 Striped or Checked do. (do. do.) .20
105 1 White Marseilles Quilt (10-4).. 1.50
106 1 " Honeycomb do. 1.00
107 8 Towels (Colored Border) 1.00
108 12 Bleached Linen Napkins..... 1.00
109 12 extra fine do. do. 1.50
110 1 piece Linen Diaper (10 yards).. 1.50
111 1 " fine Dice Diaper (10 yds.) 1.25
112 10 yards All Linen Russia Crash Towelling 1.00
113 8 yards Extra All Linen do. do... 1.00
114 2 Linen Table Cloths 1.25
115 2 Fine Damask Table Cloths.... 1.50
116 3 yards Table Damask.......... 1.00
117 1 Lady's Night Dress and 3 Hem-stitched Handkerchiefs 1.00
118 1 Pair Nottingham Lace Curtains 1.00
119 6 Yards fine Hamburg Edging .. 1.00
120 5 Linen Shirt Fronts........... 1.00
121 5 Yards Swiss Mull......... .... 1.00
122 12 Ruches for the Neck......... 1.00
123 6 Linen Damask Towels 1.00
124 5 Yards Valenciennes Lace 1.00
125 1 Chemise and 2 Hem-stitched Handkerchiefs 1.00
126 2 Ladies' White Six-tuck Skirts.. 1.00
127 12 Gents' Handkerchiefs 1.00
128 12 Ladies' Hem-stitched do...... 1.00
129 12 Gents' Linen Handkerchiefs.. 2.00
130 2 Gent's White Shirts........... 2.50
131 1 German Bed Quilt (5 lbs.)...... 2.50
132 12 Ladies' Fine Hem-stitched Handkerchiefs 1.50
133 12 Ladies' Extra Fine Linen do. 2.00
134 12 Gents' good quality Linen Handkerchiefs 1.50
135 12 Gents' Fine Linen Latest Style Collars....................... 1.50
136 12 Ladies' Linen Collars, assorted styles 1.00
137 6 Pairs Ladies' Fine Linen Cuffs, 1.50
138 6 Fine Lace Collars, for Ladies.. 1.00
139 4 Ladies' Embroidered Swiss Mull Ties 1.00
140 4 do. do. do. Bows, 1.00
141 2 Yards Irish Linen 1.00
142 1 Marseilles Colored Quilt....... 1.50

WOOLENS.

160 White Rose Blankets, each...... 1.50
161 Grey Colored do. " 1.25
162 1 Embossed Wool Table Cover.. 1.00
163 1 lb White Wool Yarn 1.00
164 1 lb Blue Mixed do .... .90
165 1 lb Scarlet Wool do............ 1.25
166 2 Wool Shawls, for Children, or Shoulder Shawls 1.00
167 1 Balmoral Skirt................ 1.00
168 1 Printed Felt do. 1.25
169 5 Yards Kentucky Jeans 1.00
170 Kentucky 10 oz. Jeans, ext. heavy, Western Manufacture, ₩ yard, .45
171 Doeskin Jeans............ " .35
172 2 Yds. Extra Fine West of England Black or Blue Broadcloth, Double Width............... 6.00
173 1 Josephine Striped Shawl 2.00
174 1 Heavy Double Plaid Shawl.... 3.50
175 1 All-Wool Henrietta, or 5th Ave. Ottoman Striped Shawl 2.50
176 2 Yards Best Quality Waterproof, Doub. Width, gold or black mix. 2.00
177 2 Yards Black Mixed Double-faced Waterproof 1.80
178 5 Yards Wool Linsey 1.00
179 Cassimere, All Wool, ex. fine, ₩ yd. 1.00
180 " " ....per yard .85
181 " " .... " .75
182 Tweeds, All Wool ...... " .60
183 Wool Cassimere........ " .50
184 Satinets .... " .30
185 Cassimeres............. " .60
186 Satinets, Plaids, or Stripes, ₩ yd. .40
187 1 Horse Blanket, with Buckles and Straps complete........... 2.35
188 Union Beaver Cloth, Black, Extra Fine, Double Width, per yard .. 1.75
189 Washington Mills Beaver Cloth, All Wool.............per yard 3.25
190 1 Extra Heavy Fine Ottoman Striped Shawl, both sides alike 4.50
191 Best Striped Hemp Carpet, ₩ yd. .25
192 Good Ingrain Carpet...... " .50
193 All-Wool Ingrain Carpet .. " .60
194 3 Yards Fancy Cloth, for Coat, Pants, or Vest 1.00
195 Ladies' Cloth, Double Width, only in New Shades of Sage Green................per yard 1.00

NOTIONS, FANCY GOODS, &c.

215 4 Yards Silk Fringe, Black, Brown, Slate, Blue and Green 1.00
216 2 Corsets, Beauty style, imported 1.25
217 2 Lotta Hoop Skirts 1.00
218 1 Gent's Toilet Set, containing Wostenholm Razor, Tooth-brush, Comb, Hair-brush, Lather-brush, Razor-strop, Shaving-box and Soap 1.00
219 1 Backgammon Board, with Dice Cup and Checkers, Book form.. 1.00
220 5 Boxes of Paper Collars, 3 Neck Ties and 1 Collar Button....... 1.00
221 6 Pairs Ladies' Col'd or White Merino Hose.................. 1.00
222 6 Prs. Men's British Cotton Socks 1.00
223 8 " Child'n's Balmoral Stockings 1.00
224 8 " Children's White Cotton do. .90
225 8 " Misses' do. do. do, 1.00
226 3 Ladies' Scarfs, 2 Lace Collars and 1 pair Sleeve Buttons 1.00
227 12 pairs Men's Cotton Socks..... 1.00
228 8 prs. Ladies' White Cotton Hose 1.00
229 6 " Ex. quality do. do. 1.00
230 6 " Gent's good quality Wool Socks 1.00
231 1 Hoop Skirt, 1 Bustle and 1 Hair Braid 1.00
232 1 pair Alexander's Kid Gloves, from 5½ to 8's, in all shades.... 1.00
233 2 pairs of Kid Gloves, Ladies.... 1.00
234 1 pair Gent's Kid Gloves 1.00
235 1 pr. Lady's Kid Mitts, Fur Tops 1.00
236 2 Oil-cloth Table Covers......... 1.00
237 10 Boxes Paper Collars, Cloth lined Button holes,........... 1.00

We SHIP GOODS by FREIGHT (if requested) to GRANGES, when the Seal is attached to Order, but require the money within 10 days from date of Shipment.

MONTGOMERY WARD & CO.'S PRICE LIST.

No.	Item	Price
238	6 fine Combs, 6 coarse Combs, Hair Brush, and 8 Papers Hair Pins	1.00
239	12 Yards, inch-wide Ribbon, all Shades (by the piece only)	1.00
240	12 Yards 2-inch-wide Ribbon, all shades (by the piece only	2.00
241	3 Ladies Silk Scarfs	1.00
242	5 Boxes Paper Collars and 1 pair Brace Suspenders	1.00
243	1 Ostrich Plume and 3 Bunches Fine French Flowers	1.00
244	15 Spools Belding Bros. 50 Yards Sewing Silk, Assorted Colors and Letters	1.00
245	2 Italian Lace Veils	1.00
246	12 Doz. Blk. Rubber Vest Buttons	.50
247	12 Doz. Blk. Rubber Coat Buttons	.85
248	12 Doz. Large do. do.	1.20
249	72 Doz. White Agate Shirt Buttons	.50
250	72 Doz. Lar. White Agate Buttons	.75
	(We don't sell less than the above amount of Buttons—don't break Packages.)	
251	4 Dozen Cakes Fine Toilet Soap	1.00
252	3 Dozen Cakes Fine Honey or Glycerine Soap	1.00
253	12 Cakes Honey Soap, 10 papers Sharp's Needles and 12 papers Pins	1.00
254	2 Wostenholm Razors, in Case	1.00
255	12 Pairs Men's Medium quality Wool Socks	1 50
256	1 Stereoscope and 6 Views, with Walnut Frame, good Glasses	1.25
257	1 Silk Fan and 3 Hem'd Handkerchiefs	1.00
258	1 Ivory Handle Silk Fan, with Spangles and Feathers, in Pink, Blue, Brown and White	1.00
259	2 Gingham Parasols	1.00
260	1 Silk Parasol	1.00
261	1 Silk Parasol, with Walking Stick Handle	1.50
262	1 Lined do. do. do.	3.00
263	1 Album, with Bevel Edges, Knobs, to hold 100 pictures	1.00
264	1 Album and Fancy Japanese Box	1.00
265	1 good Writing Desk, with Lock and Key, Paper, Pens and Envelopes complete	1.00
266	1 Portfolio, plain, 5 Pockets, Lock and Key, with Paper, Pens and Envelopes complete	1.00
267	Black Linen Thread, in lb. Boxes	.55
268	24 Spools Thread. 200 Yards each, in all numbers and colors	1.00

HATS, CAPS, UNDERCLOTHING, &c

No.	Item	Price
290	1 Gent's All Wool Cardigan Knit Jacket	$1.50
291	2 Orange Colored Undershirts	1 25
292	2 " " Drawers	1.25
293	1 Boy's Cap and 1 pr. Imt. Buck Gloves	1.00
294	1 Pair Buck Gloves and 1 pair Suspenders	1.25
295	2 White Undershirts	1.25
296	2 Pair White Drawers	1.25
297	2 Grey Undershirts	1.00
298	2 Pair Grey Drawers	1 00
299	1 Pair Buck Mitts	1.15
300	2 Boy's Cloth Caps	1.00
301	1 Gentleman's Black Hat	1.00
302	1 Gentleman's Stylish Hat	1.00
303	2 Pair Buck Gloves	1.25
304	2 Pair Gauntlets, Patney Hands.	1.50
305	1 Pair Genuine Buck Gloves	1.25
306	1 Pair Sheepskin Gauntlet Mitts, lined with Sheepskin, Leather [illegible]d hands	.90
307	1 Gent's Cloth Cap	.75
308	3 Pair Gent's Brace Suspenders.	1.00
309	1 Boy's Cap, 2 Pair Suspenders	1.00

CUTLERY, JEWELRY, Etc.

No.	Item	Price
320	1 Set White Handled Knives and Forks	1.00
321	1 Set Ebony Handled Knives and Forks	1.00
322	1 Set Cocoa Handled Knives and Forks	1.25
323	Carving Knife and Fork	.75
324	1 Six Bladed Pearl Handle Pocket Knife	.75
325	1 Four Bladed Pearl Handle Pocket Knife	.65
326	1 Three Bladed White Bone Handle Pocket Knife	.40
327	1 Heavy Two Bladed Farmer's Knife	.40
328	1 Silk Lined Case, containing one Plated Knife, Fork, Spoon and Napkin Ring	1.00
329	1 Oreide Hunting Case Watch	6.00
330	1 " " " Lady's Watch	8.00
331	1 Silver Plated Hunting Case Watch	6.00
332	1 Gent's Hunting Case Watch, Extra Nickel Silver Plate, good Time-Keeper, American Lever,	10.00
333	1 Solid Silver Hunting Case Lever Watch	12.00
334	1 Silver Hunting Case Imitation American Lever, Two Ounce Case Watch	15.00
335	12 Teaspoons, Nickel Silver Plate	1.00
336	12 Tablespoons, Nickel Silver Plate	2.00
337	12 Forks, Nickel Silver Plate	2.00
338	1 Extra Heavy Plated Butter Dish	1.50
339	1 Silver Plated Drinking Cup, Lined with Gold Plate	1.00
340	6 Plated Napkin Rings	1.00
341	1 Silver Plated Goblet, lined with Gold Plate	1.25
342	1 Pair of Extra Plated Flat or Oval Chased Bracelets	3.50
343	1 Plain Gold Ring, 14 k, all Sizes	2.00
344	1 Enameled Ring, 14 k, all sizes.	3.00
345	1 Lady's Seal Ring (20 patterns) 14 Karat	3.00
346	1 Lady's Seal Ring, Garnet and Pearl Settings	3.00
347	Gentlemen's and Ladies' Cluster, Alaska Diamonds, Rubies, Moss Agate, Onyx, Bloodstone. All of the above are genuine and Warranted	3.00
348	Gold Masonic Pins, Square and Compass, assorted styles	1.00
349	1 Granger's Solid Gold P. of H. Emblem	00
350	Odd Fellow's Flat, 3 links, assorted sizes	1.00
351	1 Ice Pitcher, extra plated	2.00
352	1 Extra fine Bracelets, with two tassels, solid gold	15.00
353	Jet Bracelets, with chased gold center	1.00
354	Plain Jet Bracelets	.50
355	1 Guard Watch Chain, fancy pattern, double plated	1.00
356	1 Silver Guard Chain	1.00
357	1 Lady's Set, Pin and Ear Rings, Etruscan gold	4.50
358	1 Lady's Set, Pin and Ear Rings, Medallion and Coral	5.00
359	1 Lady's Set, Pin and Ear Rings, Garnet, imported	4.50
360	1 Lady's Set, Pin and Ear Rings, Fine Onyx, set in gold	3.00
361	1 Lady's Gold Locket, plain	1.50
362	1 " " " chased	2.00
363	1 " " " enameled	2.00
364	1 Gold plated Opera Guard Chain, with 1 and 2 tassels	5.00
365	1 Lady's solid Gold Ear Drops	3.00
366	1 " " Pin	3.00

[All of the above which are marked gold you will find as represented. The others are equal to solid gold, and will wear for years.]

CLOTHING, BOOTS AND SHOES, Etc.

No.	Item	Price
400	2 Pair Cassimere Pants	3.00
401	1 " " "	2.00
402	1 " " "	3.00
403	1 " Pants and Vest	4.50
404	1 Gent's Cassimere Coat	3.50
405	1 Suit of Clothes	8.00
406	1 Gent's Cassimere Suit, Coat, Pants and Vest	10.00
407	1 Black Suit of Clothes, Coat, Pants and Vest	12.00
408	1 Fine Cassimere Suit	12.50
409	1 Extra fine all wool Cassimere suit	15.00
410	1 Cavalry Overcoat	5.50
411	1 Infantry Overcoat	4.25
412	1 Infantry Dress Coat	2.00
413	1 Lined Blouse	1.75
414	1 Unlined "	1.25
415	Chinchilla Overcoats	10.00
416	Black Beaver Overcoats from $8.00 to	12.00
417	1 Extra Fine all wool, Fur Beaver Overcoat	14.00
418	1 Cheap Overcoat	6.00
419	1 Rubber or Gum Coat	2.50
420	Gent's Calf Boots	4.50
421	Alaska Boots, Beaver Tops, leather trimmed	2.75
422	Ladies' Morocco Slippers	.75
423	Gent's Dressing Slippers	.75
424	1 Pair Sucker, custom made whole stock, Kip Boots	3.50
425	2 Pair Overalls, Blue Denim, for	1.25
426	2 " " Brown Duck, for	1.50
427	2 " Jumpers, " " for	1.50
440	Dark Striped (Imitation Mink) Muff and Collar, per set	4.00
441	Alaska Mink Muff and Collar, set	4.00
442	Genuine Striped Mink Muff and Collar, per set	13.50
443	Genuine Fitch Muff and Collar	15.00
444	Genuine Extra quality Mink Muff and Collar, per set	18.00
445	Imitation Seal Muff and Collar; looks like genuine. Takes a good judge to tell them from those worth $40.00. Per set	8.00
446	Imitation Ermine Muff and Collar, with black spots, for Children	1.50
447	Ladies' Morocco Shoes, High Polish Cut	2.00
448	Women's B Calf Shoes, High Polish Cut	1.75
449	Women's B Ext. heavy, High Cut	1.40
450	Ladies' Congress Gaiters	1.50
451	" Serge Lace Gaiters, High Cut	1.40
452	Ladies' Serge High Cut, Button	1.65
453	Ladies' Morocco Double Soles, Lace	1.75
454	Children's Shoes, from 50 cents to	1.50
455	Boys Boots from $2.00 to	2.50
456	U. S. Sewed Boots, made of Whole White Oak Stock. Cost the Government $5.00 a pair. We sell them for $2.75. Warranted sound. From 8's to 13's.	
	Packing Trunks from $2.00 to $5.00.	

Send your Orders for GROCERIES to Messrs. ROE BROTHERS, Wholesale Grocers, 148 and 150 South Water Street, Chicago. They will fill your orders at Wholesale Prices and give satisfaction.

MONTGOMERY WARD & CO.'S PRICE LIST.

To assist us in dispatching business, we request you to make out your order something after the following style, and if you have anything that requires answering, put it on another piece of paper.

SAMPLE OF ORDER.

Please send by Express to............ ...Town.................. ...

County.................State............as per Catalogue No.......

No. 1——12 *Yards Prints.*
" 2——9 " *Bed Ticking.*
" 42——16 " *Extra Heavy Twilled Flannel.*
" 70——12 " *Empress Cloth, (say what color.)*

And so on to the end. Order as much of anything as you want, and we will charge in proportion to our quotations. Write your name and address **Plain.** We can read anything else. In club orders we do each person's goods up by themselves, mark their names on the outside, and then pack them all to one address. All goods remaining over 10 days in the express office will be returned.

THE FOLLOWING ADVICE TO EXPRESS AGENTS IS SENT WITH EACH COLLECTION.

You are hereby requested to allow the Consignee or Agent to examine—if they so desire—all packages sent by our House for Delivery and Collection at your Station. If they refuse to take the goods, **Immediately notify us,** and we will order the disposal of them.

Respectfully,
MONTGOMERY WARD & CO.

By order of the Express Companies, we can allow only the individual to whom the goods are shipped to examine the goods at the Express Office. This is a privilege that should not be abused. Consider that the agent has no interest in the matter, and is responsible to us for the goods or the money. Do not detain him too long or scatter the goods.

Read the following from THE CHICAGO TRIBUNE, Dec. 24th, 1873:

MONTGOMERY WARD & CO.

On the 8th day of November there was published in the local columns of this paper an article purporting, and intended to be, an exposure of the business of the firm of Montgomery Ward & Co., of No. 104 Michigan Street. The article was based on what was supposed to be correct information, but a thorough investigation by this office satisfies us that the article was grossly unjust, and not warranted by the real facts. The firm of Montgomery Ward & Co., is a bona fide firm, composed of respectable persons, and doing a perfectly legitimate business in a perfectly legitimate manner. This business may be briefly described: They advertise, by circulars and otherwise, catalogues of a great variety of merchandise, including all manner of dry goods, cotton and woolen; plated ware, toilet goods, men's underclothing, carpets, blankets, hosiery and women's wear; quilts and other bed clothing; jewelery, watches, cutlery, boots and shoes, furs hats and caps, etc., including all the articles sold in a store of general trade. They profess, and we have no doubt truly, to purchase these articles for cash, direct from the manufacturers, and in large quantities, and, of course, at less cost than dealers who buy on credit. They also save all the cost and profits which are incidental to trade through several intermediary hands. They keep no large stores and warehouses, have no runners or salesmen, and thus avoid heavy rents and salaries. They do not retail goods. They sell upon written orders only, and for cash. They send these goods by express, and each consignee is, by express contract, authorized to open the package of goods, examine them, and, if not satisfied, can decline taking the things sent him. If the consignee is satisfied with the goods, he pays the bill to the express company, and in no event is he in any way obliged or compelled to take the goods, or pay therefor, except by his own volition. It is difficult to see how any person can be swindled or imposed upon by business thus transacted. We have taken pains to investigate this business, and have no question that Montgomery Ward & Co. are doing a legitimate trade.

This plan of doing business was suggested by the growing combinations of farmers and Grangers, to deal directly with first houses; and to meet this, manufacturers have already made arrangements in many cases to deal through agents with Granges or Clubs, at wholesale prices. Montgomery Ward & Co. are offering the same arrangements, but extend the advantage to all persons, clubs, or individuals.

We are obliged to say that we object to Visitors for the following reasons:

They require and are *entitled* to attention, which we have no time to give. They are in the way. We want all the space we have to work in. They want to purchase goods in the old way. We positively cannot and *will not* sell goods except on written orders—see form below, which must first be entered upon our books and follow the regular channel.

In order that our Customers may understand that we have nothing to hide, we will admit into our packing rooms (104 Michigan Street), any duly accredited representative of a neighborhood, who can remain until they are *perfectly satisfied* that we are doing a just and honorable business, and that we know how to do it in our way.

Please understand that we would be delighted to see you all, offer you suitable refreshments, and show you due attention, but we cannot afford it.

We are also prepared to make purchases of all kinds of Merchandise which we do not keep, for our Customers, charging them only five per cent. on the net cost. We do this simply as an accommodation.

All goods will be sent by express (Collect on delivery), subject to examination. In this way you can see just what you pay for. Any one sending us orders will please send the number opposite to the articles they wish sent. When convenient, as many as possible should club together, making one order. In this way the goods can be shipped at much less expense. Samples of piece goods sent on application by enclosing 10 cents to pay postage, &c. All Samples have numbers attached to correspond with the number on Catalogue.

We have the celebrated **"Murray" Wagons**, manufactured by one of the largest manufacturers in the State of Michigan. He has made special prices to us, in order to secure the Grange trade. Send for **Price List.** We also offer all the machinery and stock for sale.

Write your Names and make your Figures plain, and send Number of this Catalogue, No. 10, as Goods and Prices change with each issue.

We Employ No Agents and Pay No Commissions to Anyone. Don't ask.

Respectfully,

MONTGOMERY WARD & CO.,

104 MICHIGAN STREET.

Hindle & Jenkins, Printers, 166 Clark Street, Chicago.

Excerpt from *Science and Health*, 1875

Mary Baker Eddy is remarkable, not just as the founder of one of the five church denominations with U.S. origins in the 19th century (the others are Mormonism, Seventh-Day Adventism, Jehovah's Witnesses, and Pentacostalism), but also as the only woman ever to have founded one of the world's major religions. She set forth her theology for the Church of Christ, Scientist, in Science and Health, *first published in 1875. A victim all her life of poor health and depression, Eddy experienced an epiphany when she was 40 years old and was "miraculously" cured from a crippling, even mortal injury. She had discovered what she called the "science of divine metaphysical healing." She decided that mind and spirit control the body and that the power of autosuggestion can cure even the most hopeless diseases and injuries if a person has faith. She went to work proselytizing her newfound faith and at the age of 50 set out to record the principles of Christian Science. The resulting 456-page work combined some borrowed medical theories, numerous biblical illustrations, and her whimsical conjectures on the true nature of the universe in a surprisingly logical theology. She rushed the book into print with a church publishing house (Christian Scientist Publishing Company of Boston), and its lack of traditional institutional scrutiny showed: It was poorly bound and full of printing errors and embarrassing theological gaffes that had to be corrected in later editions with the help of a coauthor, James Henry Wiggin. Fortunately for her reputation this first run of what eventually became a publishing phenomenon consisted of only 1,000 copies. Curiously she chose to publish under her first married name, Mary Baker Glover, although George Washington Glover had been dead since 1844 and she had entered into a second marriage. In 1875 she was the (unhappy) wife of Dr. Daniel Patterson. (Not until 1877 did she marry Asa Gilbert Eddy, after divorcing Patterson, and establish the identity by which she is known in history, Mary Baker Eddy.)*

This photo shows Mary Baker Eddy, ca. 1852, some 14 years before the intensely spirited woman founded the Christian Science movement. (Library of Congress, [LC-US262-102788])

Despite laborious style and murky concepts, the book quickly became a bestseller. Several other editions followed in later years, but the 1875 edition was the only one completely attributable to Mary Baker Eddy. With the book to help spread her "gospel," she formed a Christian Science Association in 1876 and three years later founded the official Church of Christ (Scientist) in Boston. She was 58 years old and launching a new religion and a new phase in her own life. The Church of Christ (Scientist) was a work in progress, based on so-called scriptures contained in Science and Health *(in conjunction with the* Standard Christian Bible*).*

Despite widespread interest in the book, something strange happened soon after it appeared: Copies began to disappear mysteriously. There was a strong suspicion, vigorously denied by Eddy and her representatives, that the "Mother Church" in Boston was quietly removing the flawed volumes from circulation. The second and subsequent coauthored editions would prove much more durable. Today a first edition Science and Health *is one of the most rare of all U.S. literary works.*

The excerpt here from the 81st edition (1894) gives a glimpse of Eddy's theology after it was polished up by the author and her later collaborators. "The only reality of sin, sickness or death is the awful fact that unrealities seem real to human, erring belief, until God strips off their disguise," she explains. "They are not true, because they are not of God." Healing, therefore, is not miraculous but natural. Viruses and germs are false causes of sickness, and disease is a mental fabrication, nothing more than a delusion that can be eliminated through fervent prayer and full spiritual understanding. She intersperses her explanations with rhetorical question-and-answer sections, similar to those of a traditional Catholic catechism book. The text is set up as an extended outline, with major headings (e.g., "Theology," "Medicine") and smaller subheadings to help the lay reader follow along. Despite these reading aids the author's logic is not always clear, plus she is repetitious and rambling. The result is a book whose theological content far outweighs its literary content, as Mary Baker Eddy probably wanted it to be.

SCIENCE AND HEALTH

CHAPTER I

SCIENCE, THEOLOGY, MEDICINE

SCIENCE

But I certify you, brethren, that the Gospel which was preached of me is not after man; for I neither received it of man, neither was I taught it, but by the revelation of Jesus Christ.—Paul.

Another parable spake he unto them; The Kingdom of Heaven is like unto leaven, which a woman took and hid in three measures of meal, till the whole was leavened.—Matthew.

Christian Science discovered

In the year 1866 I discovered the Science of Metaphysical Healing, and named it Christian Science. God had been graciously fitting me, during many years, for the reception of a final revelation of the absolute Principle of Scientific Mind-healing.

Mission of Christian Science

This apodictical Principle points to the revelation of Immanuel, as "God with us." The sovereign Ever-presence, delivering the children of men from every ill "that flesh is heir to." Through Christian Science, religion and medicine are inspired with a diviner nature and essence, fresh pinion are given to faith and understanding, and thoughts acquaint themselves intelligently with God.

Demonstrable evidence

My conclusions were reached by allowing the evidence of this revelation to multiply with mathematical certainty, and the lesser demonstration to prove the greater; as the product of three multiplied by three, equaling nine, proves conclusively that three times three duodecillions will be, must be, nine duodecillions,—not a fraction more, not a unit less.

Light shining in darkness

When apparently near the confines of mortal existence, standing already within the shadow of the death-valley, I learned these truths in Divine Science: that all real Being is in the divine Mind and idea; that Life, Truth, and Love are all-powerful and ever-present; that the opposite of Truth—called error, sin, sickness, disease, death—is false testimony of false material sense; that this false sense evolves, in belief, a subjective state of mortal mind, which this same mind calls matter, thereby shutting out the true sense of Spirit.

Scientific evidence

Christian Science reveals incontrovertibly that Mind is All-in-all, that the only realities are the divine Mind and idea. This great fact is not, however, seen to be supported by sensible evidence, until its Principle is demonstrated by healing the sick, and thus proven absolute and divine. This proof once seen, no other conclusion can be reached.

God's allness learned

The three great verities of Spirit,—omnipotence, omnipresence, omniscience,—Spirit possessing all power, filling all space, constituting all Science,—these verities contradict forever the belief that matter can be actual. These eternal verities reveal primeval existence as the radiant reality of God's creation, wherein all that He has made is pronounced by His wisdom good.

Thus it was that I beheld, as never before, the awful unreality called evil. The equipollence of God brought to light another glorious proposition, concerning man's perfectibility, and the establishment of the Kingdom of Heaven on earth.

Scriptural foundations

In following these leadings of Scientific revelation, the Bible was my only textbook. The Scriptures were illumined, reason and revelation were reconciled; and afterwards the Truth of Christian Science was demonstrated. No human pen or tongue taught me the Science contained in this book, Science and Health, and neither tongue nor pen can ever overthrow it. This book may be distorted by shallow criticism, or by careless and mischievous students, and its ideas may be temporarily forced into wrong channels, but the Science and Truth therein will remain forever, to be discerned and demonstrated.

An optical illustration

Christian Science is natural, but not physical. The true Science of God and man is no more supernatural than is the science of numbers; though departing from the realm of the physical, as it must, some may deny its right to the name of Science. The Principle of Divine Metaphysics is God; its practice is the power of Truth over error; its rules demonstrate Science. It reverses all perverted and physical hypotheses concerning Deity, even as the science of optics rejects, while it explains, the incidental or inverted image, and shows what this inverted image is meant to represent.

Reversible propositions

The fundamental propositions of Christian Science are summarized in the four following, to me, self-evident propositions. Even if read backward, these propositions will be found to agree in statement and proof.

1. God is All.
2. God is Good. Good is Mind.
3. God, Spirit, being all, nothing is matter.
4. Life, God, omnipotent Good, deny death, evil, sin, disease.—Disease, sin, evil, death, deny Good, omnipotent God, Life.

Which of the denials in Proposition Four is true? Both are not, cannot be true. According to the Scripture, I find that God is true, "and every [mortal] man a liar."

Causation mental

Christian Science explains all cause and effects mental, not physical. It lifts the veil of mystery from Soul and body. It shows the Scientific relation of man to God, disentangles the interlaced ambiguities of Being, and sets free the imprisoned thought; so that we may know, in Divine Science, that the universe, including man and his divine Principle, is harmonious and eternal. Science shows that what is termed matter is but the subjective state of what is here termed mortal mind.

THEOLOGY

Churchly neglect

Must Christian Science come through the Christian churches, as some insist? This Science has come already, and come through the one whom God called. Jesus once said: "I thank Thee, oh Father, Lord of Heaven and earth, because Thou hast his these things from the wise and prudent, and hast revealed them unto babes." Even so, Father, for so it seemed good in Thy sight: As aforetime, the Spirit of the Christ, which taketh away the ceremonies and doctrines of men, is not accepted until the hearts of men are made ready for it.

St. John the Baptist, and the Messiah

The mission of Jesus confirmed prophecy, and explained the so-called miracles of olden time as natural demonstrations of the divine power, which were not understood. This established his claim to the Messiahship. In reply to John's inquiry, "Art thou he that should come?" he returned an affirmative reply,—recounting his works, instead of referring to his doctrine, confident that this exhibition of the divine power to heal would fully answer that question. Hence his reply: "Go and show John those things which ye do hear and see. The blind receive their sight and the lame walk. . . . And blessed is he whosoever shall not be offended in me." In other words, he gave his benediction to whomsoever should not deny that such effects, coming from Mind, prove the unity of God,—the divine Principle which brings out all harmony.

MEDICINE

Question of precedence

Which was first, Mind or medicine? If Mind was first, and self-existent, then Mind, not matter, must have been the first medicine. Mind being All, it made medicine; but that medicine was Mind. It could not have been that which departs from the nature and action of Mind, for Truth is God's remedy for error of every sort.

Methods rejected

It is plain that God does not employ drugs or hygiene, or provide them for human use; else Jesus also would have recommended and employed them in his healing. The sick are more deplorably lost than the sinful, if the sick cannot rely on God for help, and the sinful can. The divine Mind never called matter medicine; and matter required a material and human belief, before it could be considered as medicine.

Error and curative

The human mind uses one error as a medicine for another. It seeks, on the same principle, to appease malice with revenge, and to quiet pain with morphine. Of two evils, it chooses the greater in both cases. You admit that mind influences the body somewhat, but you conclude that the stomach, blood, nerves, bones, hold the preponderance of power. Controlled by this belief, you continue in the old routine. You lean on the inert and unintelligent, never discerning how this deprives you of the available superiority of Mind. The body is not controlled Scientifically by a negative mind.

Will-power

Will-power is not Science. It belongs to the senses, and its use is to be condemned. Willing the sick to recover is not the metaphysical practice of Christian Science, but sheer animal magnetism. Will-power may infringe the rights of man. It produces evil continually, and is not a factor in the Science of Being. Truth, and not corporeal will, is the divine power which says to disease, "Peace, be still."

Matter versus matter

Other methods undertake to oppose error with error, and thus they increase the antagonism of one form of matter towards other forms of matter. By so doing, mortal mind must continually weaken its own assumed power.

Healing lost

The theology of Christian Science includes healing the sick. Our master's first article of faith, propounded to his students, was healing, and he proved his faith be his works. The ancient Christians were healers. Why has this element of Christianity been lost? Because our systems of religion are governed more or less by our systems of medicine. The first idolatry was faith in matter. The schools have rendered in drugs the fashion, rather than faith in Deity. By trusting matter to destroy its own discord, harmony has been lost. Such systems are barren of the vitality of spiritual power, whereby material sense becomes the servant of Science.

Intoxicants

Drugs, cataplasms, and whiskey are stupid substitutes for the dignity and potency of divine Mind, and its power to heal. It is pitiful to lead men into temptation through the byways of physiology and material medica,—to victimize the race with intoxicating prescriptions for the sick, until mortal mind acquires an educated appetite for strong drinks, and men and women are made loathsome sots.

Selected Bibliography

Chapter 1: Climate, Natural History, and Historical Geography

Adams, James Truslow, ed. *Album of American History.* Vol. 2: *1783–1853;* Vol. 3: *1853–1893.* New York: Charles Scribner's Sons, 1981.

Bartlett, Richard. *Great Surveys of the American West.* Norman: University of Oklahoma Press, 1962.

Carlisle, Gene. "America's First Major Gold Rush . . . and the Twenty-Niners." *Wild West Magazine* (December 1999), pp. 18–22.

Dary, David. *The Santa Fe Trail: Its History, Legends, and Lore.* New York: Oxford University Press, 2000.

Drago, Harry Sinclair. *Great American Cattle Trails.* New York: Dodd, Mead, 1965.

Flanagan, Mike. *The Old West: Day by Day.* New York: Facts On File, 1995.

Flores, Dan. *The Natural West: Environmental History in the Great Plains and Rocky Mountains.* Norman: University of Oklahoma Press, 2001.

Galloway, John Debo. *The First Transcontinental Railroad.* New York: Dorset Press, 1989.

Goetzmann, William H. *Army Exploration in the American West, 1803–1863.* New Haven, Conn.: Yale University Press, 1959.

———. *Exploration and Empire: The Explorer and the Scientist in the Winning of the American West.* New York: Alfred A. Knopf, 1971.

———. *New Lands, New Men: America and the Second Great Age of Discovery.* Reprint, Austin: Texas State Historical Association, 2000.

Griswold, Wesley S. *A Work of Giants: Building the First Transcontinental Railroad.* New York: McGraw-Hill, 1962.

Hartigan, Francis X., ed. "Contributions of Medical Officers of the Regular Army to Natural History in the Pre–Civil War Era." In *Essays in Honor of Wilbur S. Shepperson,* 3–14. Reno: University of Nevada Press, 1989.

Hayden, Ferdinand Vandeveer. *Yellowstone and the Great West: Journals, Letters, and Images from the 1871 Hayden Expedition,* edited by Marlene Deahl. Lincoln: University of Nebraska Press, 1999.

Holford, Ingrid. *The Guinness Book of Weather Facts and Feats.* 2d ed. Enfield, England: Guinness Superlatives, 1982.

Jackson, John Brinckerhoff. *American Space, The Centennial Years: 1865–1876.* New York: W. W. Norton, 1972.

James, Preston E., and Geoffrey J. Martin. *All Possible Worlds: A History of Geographical Ideas.* 2d ed. New York: John Wiley, 1981.

Johnson, Otto, ed. *1996 Information Please Almanac.* 49th ed. Boston: Houghton Mifflin, 1996.

Lamar, Howard R., ed. *The Reader's Encyclopedia of the American West.* New York: Thomas Y. Crowell, 1977.

Lands and Peoples. Vol. 5: *North America.* Danbury, Conn.: Grolier, 1993.

Larkin, Robert P., and Gary L. Peters. *Biographical Dictionary of Geography.* Westport, Conn.: Greenwood Press, 1993.

Magill, Frank N., ed. *Great Events from History: North American Series.* Vol. 2: *1820–1895* Rev. ed. Pasadena, Calif.: Salem Press, 1997.

Meinig, D. W. *The Shaping of America.* Vol. 2: *Continental America, 1800–1867.* New Haven, Conn.: Yale University Press, 1993.

———. *The Shaping of America.* Vol. 3: *Transcontinental America, 1850–1915.* New Haven, Conn.: Yale University Press, 1998.

Mitchell, B. R. *International Historical Statistics: The Americas and Australasia.* Detroit: Gale Research, 1983.

Moulton, Candy. *The Writer's Guide to Everyday Life in the Wild West.* Cincinnati: Writer's Digest Books, 1999.

National Geographic Society. *Exploring Your World: The Adventure of Geography.* Washington, D.C.: National Geographic Society, 1989.

Reisner, Marc. *Cadillac Desert: The American West and Its Disappearing Water.* New York: Penguin Books, 1986.

Robbins, R. M. *Our Landed Heritage: The Public Domain, 1776–1936.* Princeton, N.J.: Princeton University Press, 1942.

Rybczynski, Witold. *A Clearing in the Distance: Frederick Law Olmsted and America in the Nineteenth Century.* New York: Scribner, 1999.

Schneider, Stephen H., ed. *Encyclopedia of Climate and Weather.* 2 vols. New York: Oxford University Press, 1996.

Skelton, William B. *An American Profession of Arms: The Army Officer Corps, 1784–1861.* Lawrence: University Press of Kansas, 1992.

Stansbury, Howard. *Exploration and Survey of the Valley of the Great Salt Lake of Utah.* Philadelphia: Lippincott, Grambo, 1852.

Tate, Michael L. *The Frontier Army in the Settlement of the West.* Norman: University of Oklahoma Press, 1999.

Thomas, Phillip Drennan. "The United States Army as an Early Patron of Naturalists in the Trans-Mississippi West," *Chronicles of Oklahoma* 56 (1978): 171–93.

U.S. Bureau of the Census. *Historical Statistics of the United States, Colonial Times to 1970.* 2 parts. Washington, D.C.: Government Printing Office, 1975.

U.S. Congress. *Reports of Explorations and Surveys to Ascertain the Most Practicable and Economical Route for a Railroad from the Mississippi River to the Pacific Ocean.* 13 vols. 33rd Cong., 2nd Session, Senate Exec. Doc. 78. Washington, D.C.: Beverly Tucker Printer, 1856.

Utley, Robert M., and Wilcomb E. Washburn. *The American Heritage History of the Indian Wars.* New York: Simon & Schuster in conjunction with American Heritage, 1977.

Wexler, Alan. *Atlas of Westward Expansion.* New York: Facts On File, 1995.

Winters, Harold A., et al. *Battling the Elements: Weather and Terrain in the Conduct of War.* Baltimore: Johns Hopkins University Press, 1998.

Wood, Richard A., ed. *The Weather Almanac: A Reference Guide to Weather, Climate, and Related Issues in the United States and Its Key Cities.* 9th ed. Farmington, Mich.: Gale Group, 1999.

Worcester, Donald. *A River Running West: The Life and Times of John Wesley Powell.* New York: Oxford University Press, 2000.

Chapter 2: Disasters, Natural and Human-Made

Adams, Charles Francis. *Notes on Railroad Accidents.* New York: Putnam's, 1879.

American Almanac and Repository of Useful Knowledge. 12 vols. Boston: Chas. C. Little and James Brown, 1849–51; Crosby, Nichols, Lee & Co., 1860–75.

Bixby, William. *Havoc: The Story of Natural Disasters.* New York: Longman's Green, 1961.

Bradford, Marlene. *Scanning the Skies: A History of Tornado Forecasting.* Norman: University of Oklahoma Press, 2001.

Cornell, James. *The Great International Disaster Book.* 3d ed. New York: Charles Scribner's Sons, 1982.

Cromie, Robert. *The Great Chicago Fire.* New York: McGraw-Hill, 1958.

Davis, Lee. *Man-Made Catastrophes: From the Burning of Rome to the Lockerbie Crash.* New York: Facts On File, 1993.

———. *Natural Disasters: From the Black Plague to the Eruption of Mt. Pinatubo.* New York: Facts On File, 1992.

DeQuille, Dan. *The Big Bonanza.* New York: Alfred A. Knopf, 1947.

Dunn, Gordon E., and Banner I. Miller. *Atlantic Hurricanes.* Baton Rouge: Louisiana State University Press, 1960.

Flanagan, Mike. *The Old West: Day by Day.* New York: Facts On File, 1995.

Flexner, Stuart Berg. *I Hear America Talking.* New York: Simon & Schuster, 1976.

Flexner, Stuart Berg, and Anne H. Soukhannov. *Speaking Freely: A Guided Tour of American English from Plymouth Rock to Silicon Valley.* New York: Oxford University Press, 1997.

Flora, Snowden D. *Tornadoes of the United States.* Norman: University of Oklahoma Press, 1953.

Hewitt, Ronald. *From Earthquake, Fire and Flood.* New York: Charles Scribner's Sons, 1957.

Hunter, Louis C. *Steamboats on the Western Rivers: An Economic and Technological History.* New York: Octagon Books, 1969.

Jensen, Oliver. *The American Heritage History of Railroads in America.* New York: American Heritage, 1981.

Kartman, Ben, and Leonard Brown, eds. *DISASTER!* New York: Berkley, 1960.

Keylin, Arleen, and Gene Brown, eds. *Disasters: From the Pages of the* New York Times. New York: Arno Press, 1976.

Kingston, Jeremy. *Catastrophe and Crisis.* New York: Facts On File, 1979.

Ludlum, David M. *Early American Hurricanes.* The History of American Weather Series. Boston: American Meteorological Society, 1963.

———. *Early American Tornadoes, 1586–1870.* The History of American Weather Series. Boston: American Meteorological Society, 1970.

———. *Early American Winters.* Vol. 2: *1821–1870.* The History of American Weather Series. Boston: American Meteorological Society, 1968.

Maloney, William E. *The Great Disasters.* New York: Grosset & Dunlap, 1976.

Miller, Denis. *Wild and Woolly: An Encyclopedia of the Old West.* New York: Barnes & Noble, 1975.

The Miners. The Old West Series. Alexandria, Va.: Time-Life Books, 1976.

Nock, Oswald S. *Historic Railway Disasters.* London: Allan, 1966.

Reed, Robert C. *Train Wrecks: A Pictorial History of Accidents on the Main Line.* Reprint, New York: Bonanza Books, 1968.

Rosenberg, Norman J., ed. *North American Droughts.* American Association for the Advancement of Science, Selected Symposia Series. Boulder, Colo.: Westview Press, 1978.

Shehan, James, and George Upton. *The Great Conflagration.* New York: Union Publishing, 1871.

Snow, Edward Rowe. *The Vengeful Sea.* New York: Dodd, Mead, 1956.

Stearns, Peter N., and John H. Hinshaw. *The ABC-CLIO World History Companion to the Industrial Revolution.* Santa Barbara, Calif.: ABC-CLIO, 1996.

Stover, John F. *American Railroads.* Chicago: University of Chicago Press, 1961.

The Townsmen. The Old West Series. Alexandria, Va.: Time-Life Books, 1975.

With, Emile. *Railroad Accidents.* Boston: Little, Brown, 1856.

Chapter 3: Native American Life

Axelrod, Alan. *Chronicle of the Indian Wars: From Colonial Times to Wounded Knee.* New York: Prentice Hall General Reference, 1993.

Chalfant, Harry. "Massacre at Old Fort Pueblo." *Wild West Magazine* (April 1999), pp. 56–59.

Crosby, David F. "Kickapoo Counterattack at Dove Creek." *Wild West Magazine* (December 1999), pp. 50–54.

Debo, Angie. *A History of the Indians of the United States.* Norman: University of Oklahoma Press, 1970.

Dockstader, Frederick J. *Great North American Indians: Profiles in Life and Leadership.* New York: Van Nostrand Reinhold, 1977.

Flanagan, Mike. *The Old West: Day by Day.* New York: Facts On File, 1995.

Hazen-Hammond, Susan. *Timelines of Native American History: Through the Centuries with Mother Earth and Father Sky.* New York: Berkley (Perigee Books), 1997.

Hirschfelder, Arlene, and Martha Kreipe de Montaño. *The Native American Almanac: A Portrait of Native America Today.* New York: Macmillan USA, 1993.

Johansen, Bruce E., and Donald A. Grinde, Jr. *The Encyclopedia of Native American Biography: Six Hundred Life Stories of Important People, from Powhatan to Wilma Mankiller.* New York: DaCapo Press, 1998.

Keenan, Jerry. *Encyclopedia of American Indian Wars, 1492–1890.* New York: W. W. Norton, 1999.

Kvasnicka, Robert M., and Herman J. Viola. *The Commissioners of Indian Affairs, 1824–1977.* Lincoln: University of Nebraska Press, 1979.

Langellier, John P. *American Indians in the U.S. Armed Forces, 1866–1945.* London: Greenhill Books, 2000.

Larson, Robert W. *Red Cloud: Warrior-Statesman of the Lakota Sioux.* Norman: University of Oklahoma Press, 2000.

LaVere, David. *Contrary Neighbors: Southern Plains and Removed Indians in Indian Territory.* Vol. 237, The Civilization of the American Indian Series. Norman: University of Oklahoma Press, 2000.

Marshall, S. L. A. *Crimsoned Prairie: The Indian Wars on the Great Plains.* New York: Charles Scribner's Sons, 1972.

Milner, Clyde A., II, Carol A. O'Connor, and Martha A. Sandweiss, eds. *The Oxford History of the American West.* New York: Oxford University Press, 1994

Moorehead, Warren K. *The American Indian in the United States, Period 1850–1914.* Andover, Mass.: The Andover Press, 1914.

Moulton, Candy. *The Writer's Guide to Everyday Life in the Wild West.* Cincinnati: Writer's Digest Books, 1999.

Myers, J. Jay. "The Notorious Fight at Sand Creek." *Wild West Magazine* (December 1998), pp. 42–47.

Pritzker, Barry M. *Native Americans: An Encyclopedia of History, Culture and Peoples.* 2 vols. Santa Barbara, Calif.: ABC-CLIO, 1998.

Prucha, Francis Paul. *American Indian Treaties: The History of a Political Anomaly.* Berkeley: University of California Press, 1994.

———. *The Great Father: The United States Government and the American Indians.* Lincoln: University of Nebraska Press, 1984.

Sajina, Mike. *Crazy Horse: The Life behind the Legend.* New York: John Wiley & Sons, 2000.

Schoolcraft, Henry Rowe. *Information Respecting the History, Conditions, and Prospects of the Indian Tribes of the United States.* 6 vols. Philadelphia: Lippincott, 1851–57.

Swanton, John R. *The Indian Tribes of North America.* Bureau of American Ethnology Bulletin Number 145. Washington, D.C.: Smithsonian Institution Press, 1952.

Tebbel, John, and Keith Jennison. *The American Indian Wars.* New York: Bonanza Books, 1960.

Utley, Robert M. *The Indian Frontier of the American West, 1846–1890.* Albuquerque: University of New Mexico Press, 1984.

———. *The Last Days of the Sioux.* Yale Western Americana Series No. 45. New Haven, Conn.: Yale University Press, 1966.

Utter, Jack. *American Indians: Answers to Today's Questions.* 2d rev. ed. Norman: University of Oklahoma Press, 2001.

Waldman, Carl. *Atlas of the North American Indian.* Rev. ed. New York: Facts On File, 2000.

Wallace, Ernest, and E. Adamson Hoebel. *The Comanches: Lords of the South Plains.* Reprint, Norman: University of Oklahoma Press, 1986.

Washburn, Wilcomb E, ed. *The American Indian and the United States.* 4 vols. New York: Random House, 1973.

Wilson, D. Ray. *Terror on the Plains, a Clash of Cultures.* Carpentersville, Ill.: Crossroads Communications, 1998.

Chapter 4: Chronology, 1850 to 1875

American Almanac and Repository of Useful Knowledge. 32 vols. Boston: David H. Williams; New York: Collins, Keese, and Co., 1830–61.

Anzovin, Steve, and Janet Podell. *Famous First Facts.* 5th ed. New York: H. W. Wilson, 1997.

Bain, David Haward. *Empire Express: Building the First Transcontinental Railroad.* New York: Viking Press, 1999.

Burrows, Edwin G. *Gotham: A History of New York City to 1898.* New York: Oxford University Press, 1999.

Bute, E. L., and H. I. P. Harmer. *The Black Handbook: The People, History and Politics of Africa and the African Diaspora.* London: Cassell, 1997.

Cerf, Christopher, and Victor Navasky. *The Experts Speak: The Definitive Compendium of Authoritative Misinformation.* New York: Random House (Pantheon Books), 1984.

Chase, Harold W., et al., eds. *Dictionary of American History.* Rev. ed. 10 vols. New York: Charles Scribner's Sons, 1976.

Cochran, Thomas C., and Wayne Andrews, eds. *Concise Dictionary of American History.* New York: Charles Scribner's Sons, 1962.

Commager, Henry Steele, and Milton Cantor, eds. *Documents of American History.* Vol. 1, *To 1898.* 10th ed. Englewood Cliffs, N.J.: Prentice Hall, 1988.

Culhane, John. *The American Circus, an Illustrated History.* New York: Henry Holt, 1990.

Davis, Kenneth C. *Don't Know Much about History: Everything You Need to Know about American History but Never Learned.* New York: Crown, 1990.

DeConde, Alexander. *A History of American Foreign Policy.* 2d ed. New York: Charles Scribner's Sons, 1971

1872–1972, a Century of Serving Consumers: The Story of Montgomery Ward. Chicago: Montgomery Ward, 1972.

Findling, John E. *Dictionary of American Diplomatic History.* 2d rev. ed. Westport, Conn.: Greenwood Press, 1989.

Flexner, Stuart Berg. *I Hear America Talking: An Illustrated History of American Words and Phrases.* New York: Simon & Schuster (Touchstone Books), 1976.

Gordon, Elizabeth P. *Women Torch Bearers.* Evanston, Ill.: National Woman's Christian Temperance Union, 1924.

Gross, Ernie. *This Day in American History.* New York: Neal-Schuman, 1990.

Hast, Adele, ed. *International Directory of Company Histories.* 29 vols. Detroit: St. James Press, 1992.

Holliday, J. S. *Rush for Riches: Gold Fever and the Making of California.* Berkeley: University of California Press, 1999.

Homberger, Eric. *The Historical Atlas of New York City: A Visual Celebration of Nearly 400 Years of New York City's History.* New York: Henry Holt, 1994.

Jackson, John Brinckerhoff. *American Space: The Centennial Years, 1865–1876.* New York: W. W. Norton, 1972.

Kaspi, André, ed. *Great Dates in United States History.* New York: Facts On File, 1994.

Kull, Irving S., and Nell M. Kull. *A Short Chronology of American History, 1492–1950.* New Brunswick, N.J.: Rutgers University Press, 1952.

Levins, Hoag. *American Sex Machines: The Hidden History of Sex at the U.S. Patent Office.* Boston: Adams, 1996.

Long, E. B. *The Civil War Day by Day; An Almanac 1861–1865.* Garden City, N.Y.: Doubleday, 1971.

Mack, William P., and Royal W. Connell. *Naval Ceremonies, Customs, and Traditions.* 5th ed. Annapolis, Md.: Naval Institute Press, 1980.

McPherson, James M. *Battle Cry of Freedom: The Civil War Era.* New York: Oxford University Press, 1988.

Moulton, Candy. *The Writer's Guide to Everyday Life in the Wild West from 1840–1900.* Cincinnati: Writer's Digest Books, 1999.

Nelson, Randy F. *The Almanac of American Letters.* Los Altos, Calif.: William Kaufmann, 1981.

Panati, Charles. *Extraordinary Origins of Everyday Things.* New York: Harper & Row, 1987.

Pease, Theodore Calvin, and Ashbel S. Roberts. *Selected Readings in American History.* New York: Harcourt Brace, 1928.

Sears, Stephen W. *George B. McClellan: The Young Napoleon.* New York: Ticknor & Fields, 1988.

Skelton, William B. *An American Profession of Arms: The Army Officer Corps, 1784–1861.* Lawrence: University Press of Kansas, 1992.

Volo, Dorothy Denneen, and James M. Volo. *Daily Life in Civil War America.* Westport, Conn.: Greenwood Press, 1998.

Wetterau, Bruce. *The New York Public Library Book of Chronologies.* New York: Prentice Hall Press (Stonesong Press Book), 1990.

Wilmeth, Don B., and Christopher Bigsby, eds. *The Cambridge History of American Theater.* Vol. 1: *Beginnings to 1870.* New York: Cambridge University Press, 1999.

Chapter 5: The Economy

Cochran, Thomas C., and Wayne Andrews, eds. *Concise Dictionary of American History.* New York: Charles Scribner's Sons, 1962.

Commager, Henry Steele, ed. *The Civil War Archive: The History of the Civil War in Documents,* rev. Erik Bruun. New York: Black Dog & Leventhal, 2000.

Commons, J. R., et al. *History of Labour in the United States.* 4 vols. New York: Macmillan, 1918–35.

Cook, Chris, and David Waller. *The Longman Handbook of Modern American History, 1763–1996.* New York: Addison Wesley Longman, 1998.

Derks, Scott, ed. *The Value of a Dollar: Prices and Incomes in the United States, 1860–1999.* 2d ed. Lakeville, Conn.: Grey House, 1999.

Dodd, Donald B., compiler. *Historical Statistics of the States of the United States: Two Centuries of the Census, 1790–1990.* Westport, Conn.: Greenwood Press, 1993.

Faragher, John Mack, et al., *Out of Many: A History of the American People.* 2d ed. Upper Saddle River, N.J.: Prentice Hall, 1997.

Fogel, Robert William. *Without Consent or Contract: The Rise and Fall of American Slavery.* New York: W. W. Norton, 1989.

Foner, Eric, and John A. Garraty, eds. *The Reader's Companion to American History.* Boston: Houghton Mifflin, 1991.

Foner, Philip S., and Brewster Chamberlin, eds. *Friedrich A. Sorge's Labor Movement in the United States: A History of the American Working Class from Colonial Times to 1890.* Translated by Brewster and Angela Chamberlin. Westport, Conn.: Greenwood Press, 1977.

Frank, Andrew K. *The Routledge Historical Atlas of the American South.* Routledge Atlases of American History, edited by Mark C. Carnes. New York: Routledge, 1999.

Friedman, Milton, and Anna J. Schwartz. *A Monetary History of the United States.* Princeton, N.J.: Princeton University Press, 1963.

Greever, William S. *Bonanza West: The Story of the Western Mining Rushes, 1848–1900.* Moscow: University of Idaho Press, 1991.

Groner, Alex. *The American Heritage History of American Business and Industry.* New York: American Heritage, 1972.

Holt, Michael F. *The Political Crisis of the 1850s.* New York: W. W. Norton, 1978.

Jordan, Winthrop D., et al. *The United States.* 5th ed., combined. Englewood Cliffs, N.J.: Prentice Hall, 1982.

Katcher, Philip. *The American Civil War Source Book.* London: Arms and Armour, 1992.

Klein, Maury. *The Flowering of the Third America: The Making of an Organizational Society, 1850–1920.* The American Ways Series. Chicago: Ivan R. Dee, 1993.

Klepper, Michael, and Robert Gunther. *The Wealthy 100, from Benjamin Franklin to Bill Gates—A Ranking of the Richest Americans Past and Present.* Secaucus, N.J.: Carol (Citadel Press), 1996.

Kurian, George Thomas. *Datapedia of the United States 1790–2000: America Year by Year.* Lanham, Md.: Bernan Press, 1994.

Levinson, E. *Labor on the March.* New York: Harper & Brothers, 1938.

Marvin, Winthrop. *The American Merchant Marine—Its History and Romance, from 1620–1902.* New York: Charles Scribner's Sons, 1902.

McCutcheon, Marc. *The Writer's Guide to Everyday Life in the 1800s.* Cincinnati: Writer's Digest Books, 1993.

McFaul, J. M. *The Politics of Jacksonian Finance.* Ithaca, N.Y.: Cornell University Press, 1972.

McNeill, George E., ed. *The Labor Movement: The Problem of Today.* 1887. Reprint, New York: Augustus M. Kelley, 1971.

McPherson, James M. *Ordeal by Fire: The Civil War and Reconstruction.* New York: Alfred A. Knopf, 1982.

Mitchell, B. R. *British Historical Statistics.* New York: Cambridge University Press, 1988.

———. *International Historical Statistics: The Americas and Australasia.* Detroit: Gale Research, 1983.

Mulhall, Michael G. *The Dictionary of Statistics.* 4th ed., rev. 1899. Reprint, Detroit: Gale Research, 1969.

Murrin, John M., et al. *Liberty, Equality, Power: A History of the American People.* Fort Worth, Tex.: Harcourt Brace, 1996.

Myers, Margaret. *Financial History of the United States.* New York: Columbia University Press, 1970.

Natkiel, Richard, and Anthony Preston. *Atlas of Maritime History.* New York: Facts On File, 1986.

Nelson, Daniel. *Shifting Fortunes: The Rise and Decline of American Labor, from the 1820s to the Present.* The American Ways Series. Chicago: Ivan R. Dee, 1997.

Nofi, Albert A. "Knapsack: A Civil War Digest, Profile: Money and Inflation," *North & South Magazine* 3, no. 2 (January, 2000): 12–15.

North, Douglass C., and Robert Paul Thomas, eds. *The Growth of the American Economy to 1860.* Columbia: University of South Carolina Press, 1968.

Olson, James S. *Dictionary of United States Economic History.* Westport, Conn.: Greenwood Press, 1992.

Panati, Charles. *Extraordinary Origins of Everyday Things.* New York: Harper & Row, 1987.

Patrick, Rembert W. *The Reconstruction of the Nation.* New York: Oxford University Press, 1967.

Pelling, Henry M. *American Labor.* The Chicago History of American Civilization Series, edited by Daniel J. Boorstin. Chicago: The University of Chicago Press, 1960.

Porter, Glenn, ed. *Encyclopedia of American Economic History.* 2 vols. New York: Charles Scribner's Sons, 1980.

Reader's Digest. *Stories behind Everyday Things.* Pleasantville, N.Y.: The Reader's Digest Association, 1980.

Rickard, T. A. *A History of American Mining.* New York: McGraw-Hill, 1932.

Rugoff, Milton. *America's Gilded Age: Intimate Portraits from an Era of Extravagance and Change, 1850–1890.* New York: Henry Holt, 1989.

Shannon, F. A. *The Farmer's Last Frontier: Agriculture 1860–1897.* New York: Farrar, Straus & Young, 1945.

Skelton, William B. *An American Profession of Arms: The Army Officer Crops, 1784–1861.* Lawrence: University Press of Kansas, 1992.

Stover, John F. *The Life and Decline of the American Railroad.* New York: Oxford University Press, 1970.

Taussig, F. W. *The Tariff History of the United States.* New York: Putnam, 1931.

Taylor, George R., and Irene D. Neu. *The American Railroad Network, 1861–1890.* Cambridge, Mass.: Harvard University Press, 1956.

Temin, Peter. *The Jacksonian Economy.* New York: W. W. Norton, 1969.

U.S. Bureau of the Census. *Historical Statistics of the United States, Colonial Times to 1970.* 2 parts. Washington, D.C.: Government Printing Office, 1975.

Walett, Francis G. *Economic History of the United States.* 2d ed. New York: Barnes & Noble, 1963.

Ware, N. J. *The Labor Movement in the United States.* New York: D. Appleton, 1929.

Weinstein, Allen. *Prelude to Populism: Origins of the Silver Issue.* New Haven, Conn.: Yale University Press, 1970.

Wetterau, Bruce. *The New York Public Library Book of Chronologies.* New York: Prentice Hall Press (A Stonesong Press Book), 1990.

White, Richard. *"It's Your Misfortune and None of My Own": A New History of the American West.* Norman: University of Oklahoma Press, 1991.

Wright, Gavin. *Old South, New South: Revolutions in the Southern Economy since the Civil War.* New York: Basic Books, 1986.

Chapter 6: Transportation

Ambrose, Stephen E. "The Big Road." *American Heritage Magazine* (October 2000), pp. 56–66.

———. *Nothing Like It in the World: The Men Who Built the Transcontinental Railroad, 1863–1869.* New York: Simon & Schuster, 2000.

Bain, David Haward. *Empire Express: Building the First Transcontinental Railroad.* New York: Viking Penguin, 1999.

Bettmann, Otto L. *The Good Old Days—They Were Terrible!* New York: Random House, 1974.

Chandler, Alfred D., Jr., ed. *The Railroads: The Nation's First Big Business: Sources and Readings.* The Sources in American Economic Growth Series. New York: Harcourt Brace & World, 1965.

Concise Dictionary of American History, edited by Wayne Andrews. New York: Charles Scribner's Sons, 1962.

Drago, Harry Sinclair. *The Steamboaters: From the Early Side-Wheelers to the Big Packets.* New York: Clarkson N. Potter (Bramhall House), 1967.

Dunbar, Seymour. *A History of Travel in America.* 4 vols. Indianapolis, Ind.: Bobbs-Merrill, 1915.

Galloway, John Debo. *The First Transcontinental Railroad.* New York: Dorset Press, 1989.

Griswold, Wesley S. *A Work of Giants: Building the First Transcontinental Railroad.* New York: McGraw-Hill, 1962.

Haites, Erik F., James Mak, and Gary M. Walton. *Western River Transportation: The Era of Early Internal Development, 1810–1860.* Baltimore, Md.: The Johns Hopkins University Press, 1975.

Hungerford, Edward. *Wells Fargo: Advancing the American Frontier.* New York: Random House, 1949.

Hunter, Louis C. *Steamboats on the Western Rivers: An Economic and Technological History.* New York: Octagon Books, 1969.

Kreiger, Michael. *Where Rails Meet the Sea: America's Connections between Ships and Trains.* New York: Friedman/Fairfax (Metro Books), 1998.

Lamar, Howard R., ed. *The Reader's Encyclopedia of the American West.* New York: Thomas Y. Crowell, 1977.

McLoughlin, Denis. *Wild and Woolly: An Encyclopedia of the Old West.* New York: Barnes & Noble Books, 1975.

Meinig, D. W. *The Shaping of America.* Vol. 3: *Transcontinental America, 1850–1915.* New Haven Conn.: Yale University Press, 1998.

Meyer, B. H., et al. *History of Transportation in the United States before 1860.* Washington, D.C.: Carnegie Institute of Washington, 1917.

Mitchell, B. R. *International Historical Statistics: The Americas and Australasia.* Detroit: Gale Research, 1983.

Moody, Ralph. *Stagecoach West: The Story of the Frontier Express Lines That Linked the Nation Together.* New York: Thomas Y. Crowell (Promontory Press), 1967.

Moulton, Candy. *The Writer's Guide to Everyday Life in the Wild West, from 1840–1900.* Cincinnati: Writer's Digest Books, 1999.

Oliver, John W. *History of American Technology.* New York: Ronald Press, 1956.

Pickenpaugh, Roger. *Rescue by Rail: Troop Transfer and the Civil War in the West, 1863.* Lincoln: University of Nebraska Press, 1999.

Porter, Glenn, ed. *Encyclopedia of American Economic History.* 5 vols. New York: Charles Scribner's Sons, 1980.

Stover, John F. *American Railroads.* 2d ed. The Chicago History of American Civilization Series. Chicago: University of Chicago Press, 1997.

———. *The Routledge Historical Atlas of the American Railroads.* Routledge Atlases of American History, edited by Mark C. Carnes. New York: Routledge, 1999.

Taylor, George Rogers. *The Transportation Revolution, 1815–1860.* Vol. 4: *The Economic History of the United States.* New York: Rinehart, 1957.

Taylor, George R, and Irene D. Neu. *The American Railroad Network, 1861–1890.* 1956. Reprint, Salem, N.H.: Arno, 1981.

Unruh, John D., Jr. *The Plains Across: The Overland Emigrants and the Trans-Mississippi West, 1840–1860.* Urbana: University of Illinois Press, 1979.

U.S. Bureau of the Census. *Historical Statistics of the United States.* 2 vols. Washington, D.C.: U.S. Government Printing Office, 1960.

Wright, Gavin. *Old South, New South: Revolutions in the Southern Economy since the Civil War.* New York: Basic Books, 1986.

Chapter 7: Population

Anderton, Douglas L., et al. *The Population of the United States.* 3d ed. New York: The Free Press, 1997.

Axlerod, Alan, Charles Phillips, and Kurt Kemper. *Cops, Crooks, and Criminologists: An International Biographical Dictionary of Law Enforcement.* New York: Facts On File, 1996.

Barth, Gunther. *Bitter Strength: A History of the Chinese in the United States, 1850–1870.* Cambridge, Mass.: Harvard University Press, 1964.

Bellesiles, Michael A. *Arming America: The Origins of a National Gun Culture.* New York: Alfred A. Knopf, 1999.

Bergman, Peter M. *The Chronological History of the Negro in America.* New York: Harper & Row, 1969.

Berlin, Ira. *Slaves without Masters: The Free Negro in the Antebellum South.* New York: Pantheon Books, 1974.

Bode, Carl. *Midcentury America: Life in the 1850s.* Carbondale: Southern Illinois University Press, 1972.

Boles, John B. *Black Southerners, 1619–1869.* Lexington: University Press of Kentucky, 1983.

Brace, Charles Loring. *The Dangerous Classes of New York and Twenty Years Work among Them.* New York: Wynkoop and Hallenbeck, 1872.

Brown, Richard M. *Violence in America: An Encyclopedia.* New York: Scribner's Sons, 1999.

Bute, E. L., and H. I. P. Harmer. *The Black Handbook: The People, History and Politics of Africa and the African Diaspora.* London: Casssell, 1997.

Cahalan, Margaret Werner. *Historical Corrections Statistics in the United States, 1850–1984.* Washington, D.C.: United States Department of Justice, 1987.

Carruth, Gorton. *The Encyclopedia of American Facts and Dates.* 8th ed. New York: Harper & Row, 1987.

Cayton, Mary Kupiec, Elliot J. Gorn, and Peter W. Williams, eds. *Encyclopedia of American Social History.* 3 vols. New York: Charles Scribner's Sons, 1993.

Christian, Charles M. *Black Saga: The African American Experience.* Boston: Houghton Mifflin, 1995.

Colbert, David, ed. *Eyewitness to the American West: 500 Years of Firsthand History.* New York: Penguin Books, 1998.

Collins, Bruce. *White Society in the Antebellum South.* New York: Longman, 1985.

Concise Dictionary of American History, edited by Thomas C. Cochran and Wayne Andrews. New York: Charles Scribner's Sons, 1962.

Cook, Chris, and David Waller. *The Longman Handbook of Modern American History, 1763–1996.* New York: Addison Wesley Longman, 1998.

Cott, Nancy F., ed. *No Small Courage: A History of Women in the United States.* New York: Oxford University Press, 1999.

Daniels, Roger. *Coming to America: A History of Immigration and Ethnicity in American Life.* New York: Harper Collins, 1990.

Davis, John P., ed. *The American Negro Reference Book.* Englewood Cliffs, N.J.: Prentice Hall, 1966.

Davis, William C. *The American Frontier: Pioneers, Settlers, and Cowboys.* Norman: University of Oklahoma Press, 2000.

DeBow, J. D. B. *Statistical View of the United States.* New York: Gordon and Breach, 1854.

Duane, Charles P. ("Dutch Charley"). *Against the Vigilantes: The Recollections of Dutch Charley Duane,* edited by John Boessenecker. Norman: University of Oklahoma Press, 1999.

Durham, Philip, and Everett L. Jones. *The Negro Cowboys.* Lincoln: University of Nebraska Press (Bison Books), 1983.

Earle, Jonathan. *The Routledge Atlas of African American History.* Routledge Atlases of American History Series, edited by Mark C. Carnes. New York: Routledge, 2000.

Frank, Andrew K. *The Routledge Historical Atlas of the American South.* Routledge Atlases of American History, edited by Mark C. Carnes. New York: Routledge, 1999.

Franklin, John Hope, and Loren Schweninger. *Runaway Slaves: Rebels on the Plantation, 1790–1860.* New York: Oxford University Press, 1999.

Gilje, Paul A. *Rioting in America.* Bloomington: Indiana University Press, 1996.

Gilmore, Donald L. "When the James Gang Ruled the Rails." *Wild West Magazine* (August 2000): 38–44.

Gross, Ernie. *This Day in American History.* New York: Neal-Schuman, 1990.

Holt, Marilyn. *Orphan Trains.* Lincoln: University of Nebraska Press, 1992.

Hornsby, Alton, Jr. *Chronology of African-American History: Significant Events and People from 1619 to the Present.* Detroit: Gale Research, 1991.

Jackson, Kenneth T., and Stanley K. Schultz, eds. *Cities in American History.* New York: Alfred A. Knopf, 1972.

Jacobson, Tim. *The Heritage of the South.* New York: Crescent Books, 1992.

Johnson, Susan Lee. *Roaring Camp: The Social World of the California Gold Rush.* New York: W. W. Norton, 1999.

Johnson, Walter. *Soul by Soul: Life inside the Antebellum Slave Market.* Cambridge, Mass.: Harvard University Press, 2000.

Katz, William Loren. *The Black West: A Documentary and Pictorial History.* Rev. ed. Garden City, N.Y.: Doubleday (Anchor Books), 1973.

Kenny, Kevin. *Making Sense of the Molly Maguires.* New York: Oxford University Press, 1998.

Kerber, Linda K. *No Constitutional Right to Be Ladies: Women and the Obligations of Citizenship.* New York: Hill & Wang, 1997.

Kolchin, Peter. *American Slavery, 1619–1877.* New York: Farrar, Straus & Giroux (Hill & Wang), 1993.

Litwack, Leon, and August Meier, eds. *Black Leaders of the Nineteenth Century.* Urbana: University of Illinois Press, 1988.

Long, E. B. *The Civil War Day by Day: An Almanac, 1861–1865.* Garden City, N.Y.: Doubleday, 1971.

Low, W. Augustus, and Virgil A. Clift, eds. *Encyclopedia of Black America.* New York: Da Capo Press, 1981.

Mancini, Matthew J. *One Dies, Get Another: Convict Leasing in the American South, 1866–1928.* Columbia: University of South Carolina Press, 1996.

Meier, Matt S. *Mexican American Biographies: A Historical Dictionary, 1836–1987.* Westport, Conn.: Greenwood Press, 1988.

Miller, Randall M., and John David Smith, eds. *Dictionary of Afro-American Slavery.* Rev. ed. Westport, Conn.: Praeger, 1997.

Miller, Stuart Creighton. *The Unwelcome Immigrant.* Berkeley: University of California Press, 1969.

Moody, Richard. *The Astor Place Riot.* Bloomington: University of Indiana Press, 1958.

Mulhall, Michael G., ed. *The Dictionary of Statistics.* 4th ed. 1899. Reprint, Detroit: Gale Research, 1969.

Nugent, Walter. *Into the West: The Story of Its People.* New York: Alfred A. Knopf, 1999.

Oakes, James. *The Ruling Race: A History of American Slaveholders.* New York: Alfred A. Knopf, 1982.

O'Neal, Bill. *Encyclopedia of Western Gunfighters.* Norman: University of Oklahoma Press, 1979.

Opdycke, Sandra. *The Routledge Historical Atlas of Women in America.* Routledge Atlases of American History Series, edited by Mark C. Carnes. New York: Routledge, 2000.

Orphan Train Heritage Society of America. *Orphan Train Riders: Their Own Stories,* compiled by Mary Ellen Johnson, edited by Kay B. Hall. 4 vols. Baltimore, Md.: Gateway Press, 1992–97.

Patterson, Richard. *The Train Robbery Era: An Encyclopedic History.* Boulder, Colo.: Pruett, 1991.

Peavy, Linda, and Ursula Smith. *Frontier Children.* Norman: University of Oklahoma Press, 1999.

Pritchard, James M. "Missouri Outlaws' Raid in West Virginia." *Wild West Magazine,* (December, 1998), pp. 48–52*ff.*

Reps, John W. *Bird's Eye Views: Historic Lithographs of North American Cities.* New York: Princeton Architectural Press, 1998.

Roberts, David. *A Newer World: Kit Carson, John C. Frémont, and the Claiming of the American West.* New York: Simon & Schuster, 2000.

Roller, David C., and Robert W. Twyman, eds. *The Encyclopedia of Southern History.* Baton Rouge: Louisiana State University Press, 1979.

Rugoff, Milton. *America's Gilded Age: Intimate Portraits from an Era of Extravagance and Change, 1850–1890.* New York: Henry Holt, 1989.

———. *Prudery & Passion.* London: Rupert Hart-Davis, 1972.

Russell, Paul. *The Gay 100: A Ranking of the Most Influential Gay Men and Lesbians, Past and Present.* New York: Citadel Press (Carol), 1995.

Salzman, Jack, David L. Smith, and Cornell West, eds. *Encyclopedia of African-American Culture and History.* 5 vols. New York: Simon & Schuster Macmillan, 2001.

Sifakis, Carl. *The Encyclopedia of American Crime.* New York: Facts On File, 1982.

Simmons, William J. *Men of Mark: Eminent, Progressive and Rising.* Cleveland: George M. Rewell, 1887.

Slatta, Richard W. *Cowboys of the Americas.* New Haven, Conn.: Yale University Press, 1960.

Smythe, Mabel M., ed. *The Black American Reference Book.* Englewood Cliffs, N.J.: Prentice Hall, 1976.

Sowell, Thomas. *Ethnic America: A History.* New York: Harper Collins (Basic Books), 1981.

Stampp, Kenneth M. *The Peculiar Institution: Slavery in the Ante-Bellum South.* New York: Alfred A. Knopf, 1956.

Streeter, Floyd Benjamin. *Prairie Trails and Cow Towns: The Opening of the American West.* New York: Dover Adair, 1963.

Sung, Betty Lee. *Mountain of Gold: The Chinese in America.* New York: Macmillan, 1967.

Teaford, Jon C. *The Unheralded Triumph.* Baltimore, Md.: Johns Hopkins University Press, 1984.

Thernstrom, Stephan. *A History of the American People.* San Diego, Calif.: Harcourt Brace Jovanovich, 1989.

Thernstrom, Stephan, et al., eds. *Harvard Encyclopedia of American Ethnic Groups.* Cambridge, Mass.: Harvard University Press (The Belknap Press), 1980.

Thomas, Hugh. *The Slave Trade: The Story of the Atlantic Slave Trade, 1440–1870.* New York: Simon & Schuster, 1997.

Thompson, Warren S., and P. K. Whelpton. *Population Trends in the United States.* 1933. Reprint, New York: McGraw-Hill, 1969.

Toll, Robert C. *Blacking Up: The Minstrel Show in Nineteenth-Century America.* New York: Oxford University Press, 1974.

Unruh, John D., Jr. *The Plains Across: The Overland Emigrants and the Trans-Mississippi West, 1840–60.* Urbana: University of Illinois Press, 1979.

U.S. Bureau of the Census. *A Century of Population Growth: From the First Census of the United States to the Twelfth, 1790–1900.* Washington, D.C.: Government Printing Office, 1909.

U.S. Census Office. *A Compendium of the 9th Census, June 1, 1870,* compiled by Frances Amasa Walker. Washington, D.C.: Government Printing Office. 1872. Reprinted, New York: Arno Press, 1976.

U.S. Civil Centennial Commission. *The United States on the Eve of the Civil War, as Described in the 1860 Census.* Washington, D.C.: Government Printing Office, 1963.

U.S. Department of Commerce. *Historical Statistics of the United States, Colonial Times to 1970.* Bicentennial edition. 2 parts. Washington, D.C.: Department of Commerce, 1975.

———. *Negro Population, 1790–1915.* Washington, D.C.: Government Printing Office, 1918.

Varhola, Michael J. *Everyday Life during the Civil War: A Guide for Writers, Students, and Historians.* Cincinnati: Writer's Digest Books, 1999.

Walch, Timothy. *Immigrant America: European Ethnicity in the United States.* New York: Garland, 1994.

Walker, Samuel. *Popular Justice: A History of American Criminal Justice.* New York: Oxford University Press, 1980.

Warren, James Perrin. *Culture of Eloquence: Oratory and Reform in Antebellum America.* University Park: Pennsylvania State University Press, 1999.

White, Richard. *"It's Your Misfortune and None of My Own": A New History of the American West.* Norman: University of Oklahoma Press, 1991.

White, Walter. *Rope and Faggot: A Biography of Judge Lynch.* New York: Alfred A. Knopf, 1929.

Woloch, Nancy. *Women and the American Experience.* 2d ed. New York: McGraw-Hill, 1994.

Wright, Gavin. *Old South, New South: Revolutions in the Southern Economy since the Civil War.* New York: Basic Books, 1986.

Chapter 8: Religion

Ahlstrom, Sydney E. *A Religious History of the American People.* New Haven, Conn.: Yale University Press, 1972.

The American Almanac and Repository of Useful Knowledge. 32 vols. Boston: David H. Williams; New York: Collins, Keese, and Co., 1830–61.

Auerbach, Susan. *Encyclopedia of Multiculturalism.* 6 vols. New York: Marshall Cavendish, 1994.

Baird, Robert. *Religion in America; or, An Account of the Origin, Relation to the State, and Present Condition of the Evangelical Churches in the United States.* Rev. ed. New York: Harper & Brothers, 1856.

Bar-Lev, Geoffrey, and Joyce Sakkal. *Jewish Americans Struggle for Equality.* Discrimination Series. Vero Beach, Fla.: Rourke, 1992.

"Bound for Canaan: The Spiritual Journey of Africans in America, 1619–1865." *Christian History Magazine* Special edition. 18, no. 2 (1999).

Finke, Roger, and Rodney Stark, "Turning Pews into People: Estimating Nineteenth Century Church Membership." *Journal for the Scientific Study of Religion* 25 (1986): 180–92.

Gaustad, Edwin Scott. *Historical Atlas of Religion in America* New York: Harper & Row, 1962.

Gilbert, Martin, ed. *The Illustrated Atlas of Jewish Civilization.* New York: Macmillan, 1990.

Handy, Robert T. *A History of the Churches in the United States and Canada.* New York: Oxford University Press, 1977.

Hudson, Winthrop S. *Religion in America.* New York: Charles Scribner's Sons, 1965.

Korn, Bertram W. *American Jewry and the Civil War.* Philadelphia: Jewish Publication Society, 2001.

Lippy, Charles H., and Peter W. Williams, eds. *Encyclopedia of the American Religious Experience.* 3 vols. New York: Charles Scribner's Sons, 1988.

Marshall, Peter, and David Manuel. *Sounding Forth the Trumpet: God's Plan for America in Peril, 1837–1860.* Grand Rapids, Mich.: Fleming H. Revel, 1997.

Miller, Kevin A., et al., eds. "The Untold Story of Christianity and the Civil War," *Christian History (Quarterly)* 11, no. 1 (n.d.).

Noll, Mark A. *A History of Christianity in the United States and Canada.* Grand Rapids, Mich.: William B. Eerdmans, 1992.

Queen, Edward L. II, Stephen R. Prothero, and Gardiner H. Shattuck, Jr. *The Encyclopedia of American Religious History.* 2 vols. New York: Facts On File, 1996.

Raboteau, Albert. *Slave Religion: The "Invisible Institution" in the Antebellum South.* New York: Oxford University Press, 1978.

Rosen, Robert N. *The Jewish Confederates.* Columbia: University of South Carolina Press, 2000.

Rosten, Leo, ed. *Religions of America: Ferment and Faith in an Age of Crisis, a New Guide and Almanac.* New York: Simon & Schuster, 1975.

Shamir, Ilana, and Shlomo Shavit, eds. *Encyclopedia of Jewish History.* New York: Facts On File, 1986.

Shattuck, Gardiner H. *A Shield and Hiding Place: The Religious Life of the Civil War Armies.* Macon, Ga.: Mercer University Press, 1987.

Shulman, Albert M. *The Religious Heritage of America.* New York: A. S. Barnes, 1981.

Stowell, Daniel W. *Rebuilding Zion: The Religious Reconstruction of the South, 1865–1877.* New York: Oxford University Press, 1998.

Sweet, William Warren. *The Story of Religion in America.* New York: Harper & Brothers, 1950.

"The Untold Story of the Church and the Civil War." *Christian History Magazine* Special edition. 11, no. 1 (1992).

U.S. Bureau of the Census. *Historical Statistics of the United States, Colonial Times to 1970.* 2 vols. Washington, D.C.: U.S. Government Printing Office, 1975.

Wigoder, Geoffrey, ed. *The New Standard Jewish Encyclopedia.* 7th ed. rev. New York: Facts On File, 1992.

Winebrenner, John. *History of All the Religious Denominations in the United States.* 3d ed. Harrisburg, Pa.: John Winebrenner, 1854.

Chapter 9: Government and Politics

Abbot, Martin. *The Freedman's Bureau in South Carolina, 1865–1872.* Chapel Hill: University of North Carolina Press, 1967.

The American Almanac and Repository of Useful Knowledge. 32 vols. Boston: David H. Williams; New York: Collins, Keese, and Co., 1830–1861.

Austin, Erik W. *Political Facts of the United States since 1789.* New York: Columbia University Press, 1986.

Ayers, Edward L. *The Promise of the New South: Life after Reconstruction.* New York: Oxford University Press, 1992.

Bacon, Donald C., Roger H. Davidson, and Morton Keller. *The Encyclopaedia of the United States Congress.* 4 vols. Paramus, N.J.: Prentice Hall, 1995.

Bailey, Thomas A. *Democrats vs. Republicans: The Continuing Clash.* New York: Meredith Press, 1968.

———. *A Diplomatic History of the American People.* 8th ed. New York: Appleton-Century-Crofts, 1969.

Ball, Durwood. *Army Regulars on the Western Frontier, 1848–1861.* Norman: University of Oklahoma Press, 2001.

Barney, William E. *The Road to Secession.* New York: Praeger, 1972.

Bartholomew, Paul C. *Summaries of Leading Cases on the Constitution.* Totowa, N.J.: Littlefield, Adams, 1967.

Bentley, George R. *A History of the Freedmen's Bureau.* Philadelphia: University of Pennsylvania, 1955.

Binkley, Wilfred E. *President and Congress.* 3d rev. ed. New York: Random House (Vintage Books), 1962.

Blue, Frederick J. *Salmon P. Chase: A Life in Politics.* Kent Ohio: Kent State University Press, 1987.

Breen, Robert A., et al. *America Past and Present.* 6th ed. New York: Addison-Wesley Educational (Longman Press), 2001.

Brown, Charles H. *Agents of Manifest Destiny: The Lives and Times of the Filibusterers.* Chapel Hill: University of North Carolina, 1980.

Bunch, Lonnie G. III, et al. *The American Presidency: A Glorious Burden.* Washington, D.C.: Smithsonian Press, 2000.

Camejo, Peter. *Racism, Revolution, Reaction, 1861–1877: The Rise and Fall of Radical Reconstruction.* New York: Pathfinder Press, 1976.

Campbell, James E. *The American Campaign: U.S. Presidential Campaigns and the National Vote.* College Station: Texas A&M University Press, 2000.

Capers, G. M. *Stephen A. Douglas: Defender of the Union.* Boston: Little, Brown, 1959.

Carruth, Gorton. *The Encyclopedia of American Facts and Dates.* 8th ed. New York: Harper & Row, 1987.

Chalmers, David. *Hooded Americanism: The History of the Ku Klux Klan.* 3d ed. Durham, N.C.: Duke University Press, 1987.

Commager, Henry Steele, ed. *Documents of American History.* 8th ed. New York: Appleton-Century-Crofts, 1968.

Conlin, Joseph. *The American Past.* 2 parts. San Diego, Calif.: Harcourt Brace Jovanovich, 1984.

Cook, Chris, and David Waller. *The Longman Handbook of Modern American History, 1763–1996.* New York: Addison Wesley Longman, 1998.

Cooper, William J., Jr. *Jefferson Davis, American.* New York: Alfred A. Knopf, 2000.

Craven, Avery. *Civil War in the Making.* Baton Rouge: Louisiana State University Press, 1959.

———. *The Coming of the Civil War.* Chicago: University of Chicago Press, 1970.

Cunliffe, Marcus. *Soldiers and Civilians: The Martial Spirit in America, 1775–1865.* Boston: Little, Brown, 1918.

Current, Richard N. *Those Terrible Carpetbaggers: A Reinterpretation.* New York: Oxford University Press, 1988.

Davis, Jefferson. *Messages and Papers of Jefferson Davis and the Confederacy, Including Diplomatic Correspondence, 1861–1865,* edited and compiled by James D. Richardson. 2 vols. New York: Chelsea House, 1966.

Del Castillo, Richard Griswold. *The Treaty of Guadalupe Hidalgo: A Legacy of Conflict.* Norman: University of Oklahoma Press, 1990.

Dobak, William A., and Thomas D. Phillips. *The Black Regulars, 1866–1898.* Norman: University of Oklahoma Press, 2000.

Dumond, Dwight L. *The Secession Movement, 1860–1861.* New York: Macmillan, 1931.

———. *Southern Editorials on Secession.* New York: Century, 1931.

Eaton, Clement. *A History of the Southern Confederacy.* Reprint, New York: Free Press, 1972.

Epstein, Lee, et al. *The Supreme Court Compendium: Data, Decisions, and Developments.* Washington, D.C.: Congressional Quarterly, 1994.

Faragher, John Mack, et al. *Out of Many: A History of the American People.* 2d ed. Upper Saddle River, N.J.: Prentice Hall, 1997.

Fehrenbacher, Don E., with Ward M. McAfee. *The Slaveholding Republic: An Account of the United States Government's Relation to Slavery.* New York: Oxford University Press, 2000.

Ferrell, Robert H. *American Diplomacy: A History.* 3d ed. New York: W. W. Norton, 1975.

Findling, John E. *Dictionary of American Diplomatic History.* 2d rev. ed. Westport, Conn.: Greenwood Press, 1989.

Flanders, Stephen A., and Carl N. Flanders. *Dictionary of American Foreign Affairs.* New York: Macmillan, 1993.

Fletcher, George P. *Our Secret Constitution.* New York: Oxford University Press, 2000.

Foner, Eric. *Free Soil, Free Labor, Free Men.* New York: Oxford University Press, 1970.

———. *Reconstruction: America's Unfinished Revolution, 1863–1877.* New York: Harper & Row, 1988.

Foner, Eric, and John A. Garraty, eds. *The Reader's Companion to American History.* Boston: Houghton Mifflin, 1991.

Fowler, Arlen L. *The Black Infantry in the West, 1869–1891.* 1971. Reprint, Norman: University of Oklahoma Press, 1996.

Gara, Larry. *The Presidency of Franklin Pierce.* Lawrence: University Press of Kansas, 1991.

Gillespie, J. David. *Politics at the Periphery: Third Parties in Two-Party America.* Columbia: University of South Carolina Press, 1993.

Goetzmann, William H. *When the Eagle Screamed: The Romantic Horizon in American Expansionism, 1800–1860.* Norman: University of Oklahoma Press, 2000.

Graebner, Norman A., ed. *Politics and the Crisis of 1860.* Urbana: University of Ilinois Press, 1961.

Grant, Susan-Mary. *North over South: Northern Nationalism and American Identity in the Antebellum Era.* Lawrence: University Press of Kansas, 2000.

Gray, Wood. *The Hidden Civil War: The Story of the Copperheads.* New York: Viking Press, 1942.

Hall, Kermit L., ed. *The Oxford Companion to the Supreme Court of the United States.* New York: Oxford University Press, 1993.

Hamilton, Holman. *Prologue to Conflict: The Crisis and Compromise of 1850.* New York: W. W. Norton, 1966.

Helper, Hinton Rowan. *The Impending Crisis of the South and How to Meet It.* 1860. Reprint, New York: A. B. Burdick, 1963.

Hesseltine, William B., ed. *Three against Lincoln.* Baton Rouge: Louisiana State University Press, 1960.

Hudson, Linda S. *Mistress of Manifest Destiny: A Biography of Jane McManus Storm Cazneau, 1807–1878.* Austin: Texas State Historical Association, 2001.

Hyman, Harold M. *A More Perfect Union: The Impact of the Civil War and Reconstruction on the Constitution.* Reprint, Washington, D.C.: The National Archives and Records Administration, 1986.

Johnson, Thomas H. *The Oxford Companion to American History.* New York: Oxford University Press, 1966.

Kelly, Patrick J. *Creating a National Home: Building the Veterans' Welfare State, 1860–1900.* Cambridge, Mass.: Harvard University Press, 1997.

Kirshner, Ralph. *The Class of 1861: Custer, Ames, and Their Classmates after West Point.* Carbondale: Southern Illinois University Press, 1999.

Klein, Maury. *The Flowering of the Third America: The Making of an Organizational Society, 1850–1920.* The American Ways Series. Chicago: Ivan R. Dee, 1993.

Klein, Philip Shriver. *President James Buchanan, a Biography.* State College: Pennsylvania State Press, 1961.

Kruschke, Earl R. *Encyclopedia of Third Parties in the United States.* Santa Barbara, Calif.: ABC Clio, 1991.

Kutler, Stanley I. *Judicial Power and Reconstruction.* Chicago: University of Chicago Press, 1968.

Linton, Calvin D., ed. *A Diary of America: The American Almanac.* Rev. ed. Nashville: Thomas Nelson, 1977.

Litwack, Leon F. *Been in the Storm So Long: The Aftermath of Slavery.* New York: Knopf, 1979.

Magrath, C. Peter. *Morrison R. Waite: The Triumph of Character.* New York: Macmillan, 1963.

Merk, Frederick. *Manifest Destiny and Mission in American History: A Reinterpretation.* Cambridge, Mass.: Harvard University Press, 1995.

Morison, Samuel Eliot, Henry Steele Commager, and William E. Leuchtenburg. *The Growth of the American Republic.* 6th ed. 2 vols. New York: Oxford University Press, 1969.

Morrison, Michael A. *Slavery and the American West: The Eclipse of Manifest Destiny and the Coming of the Civil War.* Chapel Hill: University of North Carolina Press, 1999.

Murrin, John M., et al. *Liberty, Equality, Power: A History of the American People.* Fort Worth, Tex.: Harcourt Brace, 1996.

Nichols, Roy Franklin. *The Disruption of American Democracy.* Reprint, New York: Macmillan, 1996.

———. *Franklin Pierce: The Young Hickory of the Granite Hills.* 2d ed. Philadelphia: University of Pennsylvania Press, 1958.

Oates, Stephen B. *To Purge This Land with Blood.* New York: Harper & Row, 1970.

Parks, Robert, et al. *From Jackson to Lincoln: Democracy and Dissent.* (Exhibit Catalogue). New York: The Pierpont Morgan Library, 1995.

Peterson, Svend. *A Statistical History of the American Presidential Elections.* New York: Frederick Ungar, 1963.

Potter, David M. *The Impending Crisis, 1848–1861.* New York: Harper Collins, 1977.

———. *The South and Sectional Conflict.* Baton Rouge: Louisiana State University Press, 1968.

Scarry, Robert J. *Millard Fillmore.* Jefferson, N.C.: McFarland, 2001.

Skelton, William B. *The American Profession of Arms.* Lawrence: University Press of Kansas, 1992.

Smith, Elbert B. *The Presidencies of Zachary Taylor and Millard Fillmore.* Lawrence: University Press of Kansas, 1988.

———. *The Presidency of James Buchanan.* Lawrence: University Press of Kansas, 1975.

Stampp, Kenneth M. *America in 1857: A Nation on the Brink.* New York: Oxford University Press, 1990.

———. *And the War Came: The North and Secession Crises, 1860–1861.* Reprint, Baton Rouge: Louisiana State University Press, 1985.

Stewart, James Brewer. *Holy Warriors: The Abolitionists and American Slavery.* Reprint, New York: Hill & Wang, 1981.

Swisher, Carl B. *Roger B. Taney.* New York: Macmillan, 1935.

Treaties, Conventions, International Acts, Protocols, and Agreements between the United States of America and Other Powers. . . ., compiled by William M. Malloy under resolution of the U.S. Senate. 4 vols. Washington, D.C.: U.S. Government Printing Office, 1910–38.

Trefousse, Hans L. *Historical Dictionary of Reconstruction.* Westport, Conn.: Greenwood Press, 1991.

———. *The Radical Republicans: Lincoln's Vanguard for Racial Justice.* New York: Twayne, 1969.

Trelease, Allen W. *White Terror: The Ku Klux Klan Conspiracy and Southern Reconstruction.* New York: Harper & Row, 1971.

U.S. Bureau of the Census. *A Century of Population Gowth: From the First Census of the United States to the Twelfth, 1790–1900.* Washington, D.C.: U.S. Government Printing Office, 1909.

———. *Historical Statistics of the United States, Colonial Times to 1970.* 2 parts. Washington, D.C.: U.S. Government Printing Office, 1975.

Van Doren, Charles, and Robert McHenry, eds. *Webster's Guide to American History.* Springfield, Mass.: G. & C. Merriam, 1971.

Wallace, Edward S. *Destiny and Glory.* New York: Coward-McCann, 1957.

Warren, Charles. *Supreme Court in U.S. History.* 2 vols. Littleton, Colo.: Fred B. Rothman, 1987.

Weber, Gustavus A. *The Bureau of Pensions, Its History, Activities and Organization.* Baltimore: The Johns Hopkins Press, 1923.

———. *The Bureau of Standards, Its History, Activities and Organization.* Baltimore: The Johns Hopkins Press, 1925.

———. *The Patent Office, Its History, Activities and Organization.* Baltimore: The Johns Hopkins Press, 1924.

———. *The Weather Bureau, Its History, Activities and Organization.* New York: D. Appleton, 1922.

Williams, Lou Falkner. *The Great South Carolina Ku Klux Klan Trials, 1871–72.* Athens: University of Georgia Press, 1997.

Chapter 10: The Civil War

Adams, Charles. *When in the Course of Human Events: Arguing the Case for Southern Secession.* New York: Rowman & Littlefield, 2000.

The American Almanac and Repository of Useful Knowledge for the Year 1860. Boston: Crosby, Nichols, 1860.

Astor, Gerald. *The Right to Fight.* Novato, Calif.: Presidio Press, 1998.

Berkin, Carol, et al. *Making America: A History of the United States.* Boston: Houghton Mifflin, 1995.

Boatner, Mark M., III. *The Civil War Dictionary.* New York: David McKay, 1959.

Boyer, Paul S., et al. *The Enduring Vision: A History of the American People.* 2d ed. 2 vols. Lexington, Mass.: D. C. Heath, 1993.

Burd, Frank, ed. *Civil War Book of Facts.* Gettysburg, Pa.: Americana Souvenirs & Gifts, n.d.

Burton, William L. *Melting Pot Soldiers: The Union's Ethnic Regiments.* 2d ed. New York: Fordham University Press, 1998.

The Civil War Book of Lists. Conshohocken, Pa.: Combined Books, 1993.

Cochran, Thomas C., ed. *Concise Dictionary of American History.* New York: Charles Scribner's Sons, 1962.

Conlin, Joseph. *The American Past.* Part 1, *A Survey of American History to 1877.* San Diego, Calif.: Harcourt Brace Jovanovich, 1984.

Cook, Chris, and David Waller. *The Longman Handbook of Modern American History, 1763–1996.* New York: Addison Wesley Longman, 1998.

Davis, Burke. *Our Incredible Civil War.* New York: Holt, Rinehart & Winston, 1960.

Davis, Kenneth C. *Don't Know Much about History: Everything You Need to Know about American History but Never Learned.* New York: Crown, 1990.

Denney, Robert E. *Civil War Prisons and Escapes, A Day-by-Day Chronicle.* New York: Sterling, 1993.

Dunnigan, James F., and Albert A. Nofi. *Dirty Little Secrets of the Vietnam War.* New York: St. Martin's Press (Thomas Dunne Books), 1999.

Dupuy, Trevor N. *The Evolution of Weapons and Warfare.* New York: DaCapo Press, 1990.

Faragher, John Mack, et al. *Out of Many: A History of the American People.* 2d ed., combined. Upper Saddle River, N.J.: Prentice Hall, 1997.

Faust, Patricia L., ed. *Historical Times Illustrated Encyclopedia of the Civil War.* New York: Harper & Row, 1986.

Fox, William F. *Regimental Losses in the American Civil War, 1861–1865.* Albany, N.Y.: Albany Publishing Company, 1889.

Garrison, Webb. *Amazing Women of the Civil War.* Nashville: Rutledge Hill Press, 1999.

Goldfield, David, et al. *The American Journey: A History of the United States.* Brief edition, combined volume. Upper Saddle River, N.J.: Prentice Hall, 1998.

Henig, Gerald S., and Eric Niderost. *Civil War Firsts: The Legacies of America's Bloodiest Conflict.* Mechanicsburg, Pa.: Stackpole Books, 2001.

Henretta, James A., David Brody, and Lynn Dumenil. *America: A Concise History.* Vol. 1: *To 1877.* Boston: Bedford/St. Martin's Press, 1999.

Hesseltine, William B., ed. *Civil War Prisons.* Kent, Ohio: Kent State University Press, 1992.

Jones, Howard. *Abraham Lincoln and a New Birth of Freedom: The Union and Slavery in the Diplomacy of the Civil War.* Lincoln: University of Nebraska Press, 1999.

Jones, Wilmer L. *After the Thunder: Fourteen Men Who Shaped Post–Civil War America.* Dallas: Taylor, 2000.

Katcher, Philip. *The American Civil War Source Book.* London: Arms and Armour Press, 1991.

Leonard, Elizabeth D. *All the Daring of the Soldier: Women of the Civil War Armies.* New York: W. W. Norton, 1999.

Livermore, Thomas L. *Numbers and Losses in the Civil War in America, 1861–1865.* Boston: Houghton Mifflin, 1900.

Long, E. B. *The Civil War Day by Day; An Almanac 1861–1865.* Garden City, N.Y.: Doubleday, 1971.

Luraghi, Raimondo. *A History of the Confederate Navy,* trans. Paolo E. Coletta. Annapolis, Md.: Naval Institute Press, 1996.

Massey, Mary Elizabeth. *Ersatz in the Confederacy: Shortages and Substitutions on the Southern Homefront.* 1952. Reprint, Columbia: University of South Carolina Press, 1993.

McPherson, James M. *Battle Cry of Freedom: The Civil War Era.* Vol. 4: *Oxford History of the United States.* New York: Oxford University Press, 1988.

———. *Ordeal by Fire: The Civil War and Reconstruction.* New York: Alfred A. Knopf, 1982.

Morison, Samuel Eliot, Henry Steele Commager, and William E. Leuchtenburg. *The Growth of the American Republic.* 6th ed. 2 vols. New York: Oxford University Press, 1969.

Mulhall, Michael G. *The Dictionary of Statistics.* London: George Routledge and Sons, 1899.

Murrin, John M., et al. *Liberty, Equality, Power: A History of the American People.* Fort Worth, Tex.: Harcourt Brace, 1996.

Neely, Mark E., Jr. *Southern Rights: Political Prisoners and the Myth of Confederate Constitutionalism.* Charlottesville: University Press of Virginia, 2000.

Nofi, Albert A. "Foreigners in the Armies," *North & South Magazine* 2, no. 5 (June 1999): 8.

Paludan, Phillip Shaw. *A People's Contest: The Union and Civil War, 1861–1865.* 2d ed. Lawrence: University Press of Kansas, 1996.

Phisterer, Frederick. *Statistical Record: A Treasury of Information about the U.S. Civil War.* 1883. Reprint, Carlisle, Pa.: John Kallmann, 1996.

Price, William H. *Civil War Handbook.* Civil War Research Associates Series. Fairfax, Va.: Prince Lithograph, 1961.

Reidy, Joseph P. "Black Civil War Sailors Project," *Columbiad: A Quarterly Review of the War between the States* 3, no. 2 (summer 1999): 17–20.

Ringle, Dennis J. *Life in Mr. Lincoln's Navy.* Annapolis, Md.: Naval Institute Press, 1998.

Rosen, Robert N. *The Jewish Confederates.* Columbia: University of South Carolina Press, 2000.

Schrader, Charles R., ed. *Reference Guide to U.S. Military History, 1815–1865.* New York: Facts On File, 1993.
Sifakis, Stewart. *Who Was Who in the Civil War.* New York: Facts On File, 1988.
Silverstone, Paul H. *Warships of the Civil War Navies.* Annapolis, Md.: Naval Institute Press, 1989.
Speer, Lonnie, R. *Portals to Hell: Military Prisons of the Civil War.* Mechanicsburg, Pa.: Stackpole Books, 1997.
Trefousse, Hans L. *Historical Dictionary of Reconstruction.* Westport, Conn.: Greenwood Press, 1991.
U.S. Dept. of Commerce. *Thirteenth Census of the United States, 1860.*
Varhola, Michael J. *Everyday Life during the Civil War: A Guide for Writers, Students and Historians.* Cincinnati: Writer's Digest Books, 1999.
Volo, Dorothy Denneen, and James M. Volo. *Daily Life in Civil War America.* Westport, Conn.: Greenwood Press, 1998.
Weigley, Russell F. *A Great Civil War: A Military and Political History, 1861–1865.* Bloomington: Indiana University Press, 2000.
Wood, Robert C. *Confederate Hand-Book: A Compilation of Important Data and Other Interesting and Valuable Matter Relating to the War between the States.* New Orleans: Graham Press, 1900.

Chapter 11: States and Territories

Austin, Erik W. *Political Facts of the United States since 1789.* New York: Columbia University Press, 1986.
Berkin, Carol, et al. *Making America: A History of the United States.* Boston: Houghton Mifflin, 1995.
De Bow, J. D. B. *Statistical View of the United States: Compendium of the 7th Census.* Washington, D.C.: U.S. Census Office, 1854.
Dodd, Donald B., compiler. *Historical Statistic of the States of the United States: Two Centuries of the Census, 1790–1990.* Westport, Conn.: Greenwood Press, 1993.
Dodd, Donald B, and Wynelle S. Dodd. *Historical Statistics of the South, 1790–1970.* University: University of Alabama Press, 1973.
Horner, Edith R., ed. *Almanac of the 50 States: Basic Data Profiles with Comparative Tables.* Palo Alto, Calif.: Information Publications, 1998.
Kane, Joseph Nathan, Steven Anzorrin, and Janet Podell, eds. *Facts about the States.* New York: H. W. Wilson, 1993.
Kurian, George Thomas, ed. *Datapedia of the United States, 1790–2000: America Year by Year.* Lanham, Md.: Bernan Press, 1994.
Lamar, Howard R., ed. *The Reader's Encyclopedia of the American West.* New York: Thomas Y. Crowell, 1977.
Lands and Peoples: North America. Vol. 5. Danbury, Conn.: Grolier, 1993.
Meltzer, Ellen. *The New Book of American Rankings.* Rev. ed. New York: Facts On File, 1998.
Mitchell, B. R. *International Historical Statistics: The Americas and Australasia.* Detroit: Gale Research, 1983.
Trefousse, Hans L. *Historical Dictionary of Reconstruction.* Westport, Conn.: Greenwood Press, 1991.
The United States Dictionary of Places. New York: Somerset, 1988.
U.S. Bureau of the Census. *Historical Statistics of the United States, Colonial Times to 1970.* 2 parts. Washington, D.C.: U.S. Government Printing Office, 1975.
U.S. Census Office. *A Compendium of the 9th Census, June 1, 1870,* compiled by Francis Amasa Walker. Washington, D.C.: U.S. Government Printing Office. 1872. Reprint, New York: Arno, 1976.
U.S. Department of the Interior. *Statistics of the United States in 1860: Eighth Census.* Washington, D.C.: Government Printing Office, 1866.
Van Doren, Charles, and Robert McHenry. *Webster's Guide to American History: A Chronological, Geographical, and Biographical Survey and Compendium.* Springfield, Mass.: B. & C. Merriam, 1971.
Wilson, Vincent, Jr. *The Book of the States.* 3d ed. Brookeville, Md.: American History Research Associates, 1992.
Worldmark Encyclopedia of the States. 4th ed. Detroit: Gale Research, 1998.
Yanak, Ted, and Pam Cornelison. *The Great American History Fact-Finder.* Boston: Houghton Mifflin, 1993.

Chapter 12: Major Cities

Burrows, Edwin G., and Mike Wallace. *Gotham: A History of New York City to 1898.* New York: Oxford University Press, 1999.
Burton, William L. *Melting Pot Soldiers: The Union's Ethnic Regiments.* 2d ed. New York: Fordham University Press, 1998.
Catchpole, Brian. *A Map History of the United States.* 2d ed. Oxford: Heinemann Educational, 1981.
The Civil War Book of Lists. Conshohocken, Pa.: Combined Books, 1993.
Compendium of 9th U.S. Census. 1870. Reprint, New York: Arno Press, 1976.
Cook, Chris, and David Waller. *The Longman Handbook of Modern American History, 1763–1996.* New York: Addison Wesley Longman, 1998.
Divine, Robert A., et al. *America Past and Present.* Vol. 1: *To 1877.* 5th ed. New York: Addison Wesley Longman, 1999.
Foner, Eric, and John A. Garraty, eds. *The Reader's Companion to American History.* Boston: Houghton Mifflin, 1991.
Foster, George G. *New York by Gas-Light,* ed. Stuart M. Blumin. 1850. Reprint, Berkeley: University of California Press, 1990.
Glaab, Charles N., and A. Theodore Brown. *A History of Urban America.* New York: Macmillan, 1967.
Homberger, Eric. *The Historical Atlas of New York City: A Visual Celebration of Nearly 400 Years of New York City's History.* New York: Henry Holt, 1994.
Jackson, John Brinckerhoff. *American Space, the Centennial Years: 1865–1876.* New York: W. W. Norton, 1972.
Jackson, Kenneth T., and Stanley K. Schultz, eds. *Cities in American History.* New York: Alfred A. Knopf, 1972.
Lynch, Jacqueline T. "Louisa May Alcott and the Transcendence of War." *Civil War Magazine* 71 (December 1998), pp. 35–41.
McKelvey, Blake. *The Urbanization of America, 1860–1915.* New Brunswick, N.J.: Rutgers University Press, 1963.
Mitchell, B. R. *International Historical Statistics: The Americas and Australasia.* Detroit: Gale Research, 1983.
New York Public Library. *The NYPL American History Desk Reference.* New York: Macmillan (Stonesong Press), 1997.
Parker, Sybil P., ed. *World Geographical Encyclopedia.* Vol. 2: *The Americas.* New York: McGraw-Hill, 1995.
Porter, Glenn, ed. *Encyclopedia of American Economic History.* 3 vols. New York: Charles Scribner's Sons, 1980.
Report of the Commissioner of Agriculture for the Year 1863. House Exec. Doc. No. 91, 38th Congress, 1st Session. Washington, D.C.: U.S. Government Printing Office, 1863.
Report of the Secretary of Agriculture, 2nd Session, 54th Congress. Washington, D.C.: U.S. Government Printing Office, 1896.
Roller, David C., and Robert W. Twyman, eds. *The Encyclopedia of Southern History.* Baton Rouge: Louisiana State University Press, 1979.
Rybczynski, Witold. *A Clearing in the Distance: Frederick Law Olmsted and America in the Nineteenth Century.* New York: Simon & Schuster (Touchstone Books), 2000.
Schultz, Stanley K. *Constructing Urban Culture: American Cities and City Planning, 1800–1920.* Philadelphia: Temple University Press, 1989.
United States Almanac, 1873. New York: New York World, 1873.
U.S. Department of Commerce. *Historical Statistics of the United States, Colonial Times to 1970.* Bicentennial edition. 2 parts. Washington, D.C.: Dept. of Commerce, 1975.

Chapter 13: Representative Americans

Appleton's Cyclopaedia of American Biography. ed. James Grant Wilson and John Fiske. New York: Appleton, 1888.

Bailey, Thomas A. *Voices of America: The Nation's Story in Slogans, Sayings, and Songs.* New York: The Free Press, 1976.

Berson, Robin Kadison. *Marching to a Different Drummer: Unrecognized Heroes of American History.* Westport, Conn.: Greenwood Press, 1994.

Dorsey, Florence. *Road to the Sea: The Story of James B. Eads and the Mississippi River.* 1947. Reprint, Gretna, La.: Pelican, 1998.

Dupuy, Trevor, Curt Johnson, and David L. Bongard. *The Harper Encyclopedia of Military Biography.* New York: Harper Collins, 1992.

Gale, Robert L. *A Cultural Encyclopedia of the 1850s in America.* Westport, Conn.: Greenwood Press, 1993.

Gies, Joseph, and Frances Gies. *The Ingenious Yankees.* New York: Thomas Y. Crowell, 1976.

Hine, Darlene Clark, ed. *Black Women in America: An Historical Encyclopedia.* 2 vols. Brooklyn, N.Y.: Carlson, 1993.

Holbrook, Stewart H. *Dreamers of the American Dream.* Mainstream of America Series, edited by Lewis Gannett. Garden City, N.Y.: Doubleday, 1957.

Hudson, Winthrop S. *Religion in America.* New York: Charles Scribner's Sons, 1965.

Jackson, John Brinckerhoff. *American Space: The Centennial Years, 1865–1876.* New York: W. W. Norton, 1972.

Klement, Frank L. *The Limits of Dissent: Clement L. Vallandigham and the Civil War.* Lexington: University of Kentucky Press, 1970.

Klepper, Michael, and Robert Gunther. *The Wealthy 100.* Secaucus, N.J.: Carol Publishing Group (Citadel Press), 1996.

Lamar, Howard R., ed. *The Reader's Encyclopedia of the American West.* New York: Thomas Y. Crowell, 1977.

Logan, Rayford W., and Michael R. Winston, eds. *Dictionary of American Negro Biography.* New York: W. W. Norton, 1982.

Meier, Matt S. *Mexican American Biographies: A Historical Dictionary, 1836–1987.* Westport, Conn. Greenwood Press, 1988.

Read, Phyllis J., and Bernard L. Witlieb. *The Book of Women's Firsts.* New York: Random House, 1992.

Sifakis, Stewart. *Who Was Who in the Civil War.* New York: Facts On File, 1988.

Wilson, Vincent, Jr. *The Book of Distinguished American Women.* 2d ed. Brookeville, Md.: American History Research Associates, 1992.

Chapter 14: Education

Abbott, Martin. *The Freedman's Bureau in South Carolina, 1865–1872.* Chapel Hill: University of North Carolina Press, 1967.

The American Almanac and Repository of Useful Knowledge. 32 vols. Boston: David H. Williams; New York: Collins, Keese, and Co., 1830–61.

Bergman, Peter M. *The Chronological History of the Negro in America.* New York: Harper & Row, 1969.

Bullock, Henry A. *A History of Negro Education in the South.* Cambridge, Mass.: Harvard University Press, 1967.

Carruth, Gorton, *The Encyclopedia of American Facts and Dates.* 8th ed. New York: Harper & Row, 1987.

Conlin, Joseph R. *The American Past.* 2 vols. New York: Harcourt Brace Jovanovich, 1984.

Cremin, Lawrence A. *American Education: The National Experience, 1783–1876.* New York: Harper & Row, 1980.

Cunliffe, Marcus. *Soldiers and Civilians: The Martial Spirit in America, 1775–1865.* Boston: Little, Brown, 1968.

Gale, Robert L. *A Cultural Encyclopedia of the 1850s in America.* Westport, Conn.: Greenwood Press, 1993.

Graff, Harvey J. *The Legacies of Literacy: Continuities and Contradictions in Western Culture and Society.* Bloomington: Indiana University Press, 1987.

Hornsby, Alton, Jr. *Chronology of African American History, from 1492 to the Present.* 2d ed. Detroit: Gale Research, 1997.

Hoxie, Frederick E., ed. *Encyclopedia of North American Indians.* Boston: Houghton Mifflin, 1996.

Kaestle, Carl F. *Pillars of the Republic: Common Schools and American Society, 1780–1860.* New York: Hill & Wang, 1983.

Lamar, Howard R., ed. *The Reader's Encyclopedia of the American West.* New York: Thomas Y. Crowell, 1977.

Leigh, Edwin. "Illiteracy in the United States." In *Report of the Commissioner of Education, 1870,* 467–502. Washington, D.C.: U.S. Government Printing Office, 1875.

Logan, Rayford W., and Michael R. Winston, eds. *Dictionary of American Negro Biography.* New York: W. W. Norton, 1982.

Mark, Michael L., and Charles L. Gary. *A History of American Music Education.* New York: Schirmer Books, 1992.

Mitchell, B. R. *International Historical Statistics: The Americas and Australasia.* Detroit: Gale Research, 1983.

Morison, Samuel Eliot, Henry Steele Commager, and William E. Leuchtenburg. *The Growth of the American Republic.* 6th ed. 2 vols. New York: Oxford University Press, 1969.

Newcomer, Mabel. *A Century of Higher Education for American Women.* New York: Harper & Row, 1959.

Power, Edward J. *A History of Catholic Higher Education in the United States.* Milwaukee: Bruce, 1958.

Report of the United States Commissioner of Education, 1870. Washington, D.C.: Government Printing Office, 1875.

Rudolph, Frederick. *The American College and University: A History.* Athens: University of Georgia Press, 1962.

Salzman, Jack, David L. Smith, and Cornel West, eds. *Encyclopedia of African-American Culture and History.* 5 vols. New York: Simon & Schuster Macmillan, 1996, 2001.

Solomon, Barbara Miller. *In the Company of Educated Women: A History of Women and Higher Education in America.* New Haven, Conn.: Yale University Press, 1985.

Stuart, Paul. *The Indian Office: Growth and Development of an American Institution, 1865–1900.* Ann Arbor, Mich.: UMI Research Press, 1979.

Ticknor, George. *Life, Letters, and Journals of George Ticknor.* 2 vols. 1876. Reprint, Boston: Houghton Mifflin, 1909.

U.S. Bureau of the Census. *Historical Statistics of the United States, Colonial Times to 1970.* 2 vols. Washington, D.C.: U.S. Government Printing Office, 1975.

U.S. Census Office. *A Compendium of the Ninth Census (1870).* 1872. Reprint, New York: Arno Press, 1976.

Wiggin, Gladys A. *Education and Nationalism: An Historical Interpretation of American Education.* New York: McGraw-Hill, 1962.

Williams, George W. *History of the Negro Race in America, 1619–1880.* New York: Arno Press and The New York Times, 1968.

Chapter 15: Arts, Letters, Music, and Theater

Abel, E. Lawrence. "And the Generals Sang!" *Civil War Times Illustrated* (March 2000), pp. 45–50.

———. *Singing the New Nation: How Music Shaped the Confederacy, 1861–1865.* Mechanicsburg, Pa.: Stackpole Books, 2000.

American Life: A Social History. Macmillan Information Now Encyclopedias Series. New York: Charles Scribner's Sons, 1993.

Anderson, Nancy K. *Thomas Moran.* New Haven, Conn.: Yale University Press (in association with the National Gallery of Art), 1997.

Andrews, William L., and Henry Louis Gates, Jr., eds. *Slave Narratives.* New York: Library of America, 2000.

Bassham, Ben L. *Conrad Wise Chapman, Artist and Soldier of the Confederacy.* Kent, Ohio: Kent State University Press, 1998.

Bode, Carl. *The Anatomy of American Popular Culture, 1840–1861.* Berkeley: University of California Press, 1959.

Branch, E. Douglas. *The Sentimental Years, 1836–1860.* New York: D. Appleton-Century, 1934.

Brooks, Van Wyck, and Otto Bettmann. *Our Literary Heritage: A Pictorial History of the Writer in America.* Reprint, New York: Paddington Press, 1977.

Brown, "Colonel" T. Allston. *A History of the New York Stage, from the First Performance in 1732 to 1901.* 3 vols. New York: B. Blom, 1903.

Chadbourne, Janice H., Karl Gabosh, and Charles O. Vogel, eds. *The Boston Art Club: Exhibition Record, 1873–1909.* Boston: Sound View Press, 1991.

Chase, Gilbert. *America's Music, from the Pilgrims to the Present.* 3d rev. ed. Urbana: University of Illinois Press, 1987.

Collison, Gary. *Shadrach Minkins: From Fugitive Slave to Citizen.* Cambridge, Mass.: Harvard University Press, 1997.

Conway, James. *America's Library: The Story of the Library of Congress, 1800–2000.* New Haven, Conn.: Yale University Press, 2000.

Cortissoz, Royal. *American Artists.* 1923. Reprint, Freeport, N.Y.: Books for Libraries Press, 1970.

Culhane, John. *The American Circus, an Illustrated History.* New York: Henry Holt, 1990.

Davis, Charles T., and Henry Louis Gates, Jr., eds. *The Slave's Narrative.* New York: Oxford University Press, 1985.

Davis, Ronald L. *A History of Music in American Life.* Vol. 1: *The Formative Years, 1620–1865.* Malabar, Fla.: Robert Krieger, 1982.

———. *A History of Music in American Life.* Vol. 2: *The Gilded Years, 1865–1920.* Huntington, N.Y.: Robert Krieger, 1980.

Dormon, James H., Jr. *Theater in the Antebellum South, 1815–1861.* Chapel Hill: The University of North Carolina Press, 1967.

Ellinwood, Leonard. *The History of American Church Music.* New York: Morehouse-Gorham, 1953.

Elson, Louis C. *The History of American Music.* The History of American Art, edited by John C. Van Dyke. New York: Macmillan, 1904.

Emerson, Edwin. *A History of the Nineteenth Century, Year by Year.* New York: P.F. Collier and Son, 1901.

Fahs, Alice. *The Imagined Civil War.* Chapel Hill: University of North Carolina Press, 2000.

Foster, Frances Smith. *Witnessing Slavery: The Development of Ante-Bellum Slave Narratives.* Westport, Conn.: Greenwood Press, 1979.

Garrison, Webb. *Brady's Civil War.* New York: Lyons Press, 2000.

Gutjahr, Paul. *An American Bible: A History of the Good Book in the United States, 1777–1880.* Stanford, Calif.: Stanford University Press, 2001.

Halttunen, Karen. *Murder Most Foul: The Killer and the American Gothic Imagination.* Cambridge, Mass.: Harvard University Press, 1998.

Harris, Neil. *The Artist in American Society: The Formative Years, 1790–1860.* Chicago: University of Chicago Press, 1982.

Hart, James D. *The Popular Book: A History of America's Literary Taste.* Berkeley: University of California Press, 1950.

Haywood, C. Robert. *Victorian West: Class and Culture in Kansas Cattle Towns.* Lawrence: University Press of Kansas, 1991.

Heaps, Willard A., and Porter W. Heaps. *The Singing Sixties: The Spirit of Civil War Days Drawn from the Music of the Time.* Norman: University of Oklahoma Press, 1960.

Hitchcock, H. Wiley. *Music in the United States: A Historical Introduction.* Englewood Cliffs, N.J.: Prentice Hall, 1969.

Holzer, Harold. "The Union's Medal of Honor Artist." *MHQ: The Quarterly Journal of Military History* 13, no. 3 (spring 2001): 32–41.

Holzer, Harold, and Gabor Boritt. *The Confederate Image: Prints of the Lost Cause.* Chapel Hill: University of North Carolina Press, 1987.

Holzer, Harold, and Mark E. Neely, Jr. *Mine Eyes Have Seen the Glory: The Civil War in Art.* New York: Orion Books, 1993.

Hornblow, Arthur. *A History of the Theatre in America from Its Beginnings to the Present Time.* Philadelphia: J. B. Lippincott, 1919.

Howard, John Tasker. *Our American Music.* 3d rev. ed. New York: Thomas Y. Crowell, 1948.

Howard, John Tasker, and George Kent Bellows. *A Short History of Music in America.* New York: Thomas Y. Crowell, 1957.

Hughes, Nathaniel Cheairs, Jr., and Thomas Clayton Ware. *Theodore O'Hara: Poet-Soldier of the Old South.* Knoxville: University of Tennessee Press, 1998.

Hughes, Robert. *American Vision: The Epic History of Art in America.* New York: Alfred A. Knopf, 1997.

Jackson, Richard. *Popular Songs of the Nineteenth Century.* New York: Dover, 1976.

Jacobson, Doranne. *The Civil War in Art: A Visual Odyssey.* New York: Smithmark, 1996.

Jefferson, Joseph. *Autobiography of Joseph Jefferson.* New York: Century, 1897.

Johnson, Thomas H. *The Oxford Companion to American History.* New York: Oxford University Press, 1966.

Johnston, Patricia Condon. "Seth Eastman's West." *American History Illustrated* (September/October 1996), pp. 42–51.

Katz, D. Mark. *Witness to an Era: The Life and Photographs of Alexander Gardner: The Civil War, Lincoln and the West.* Nashville, Tenn.: Rutledge Hill, 1999.

Kingman, Daniel. *American Music, a Panorama.* New York: Simon & Schuster Macmillan (Schirmer Books), 1998.

Knight, Denise D., ed. *Nineteenth-Century American Women Writers: A Bio-Bibliographical Critical Sourcebook.* Westport, Conn.: Greenwood Press, 1997.

Krueger, Karl. *The Musical Heritage of the United States: The Unknown Portion.* New York: Society for the Preservation of the American Musical Heritage, 1973.

Lamar, Howard R., ed. *The Reader's Encyclopedia of the American West.* New York: Thomas Y. Crowell, 1977.

Lang, Paul Henry, ed. *One Hundred Years of Music in America.* New York: Grosset & Dunlap, 1961.

Larkin, Oliver. *Art and Life in America.* New York: Rinehart, 1949.

Lloyd, Norman, and Ruth Lloyd. *The American Heritage Songbook.* New York: American Heritage, 1969.

Logan, Olive. *Before the Footlights and behind the Scenes.* Philadelphia: Parmalee & Co., 1870.

Londré, Felicia Hardison, and Daniel J. Watermeier. *The History of North American Theater, from Pre-Columbian Times to the Present.* New York: Continuum, 1998.

Low, W. Augustus, and Virgil A. Clift, eds. *Encyclopedia of Black America.* New York: Da Capo Press, 1981.

Lynch, Jacqueline T. "Louisa May Alcott and the Transcendence of War." *Civil War Magazine* 71 (December 1998): 35–41.

Mayorga, Margaret G. *A Short History of the American Drama: Commentaries on Plays prior to 1920.* New York: Dodd, Mead, 1932.

McCutcheon, Marc. *The Writer's Guide to Everyday Life in the 1800s.* Cincinnati: Writer's Digest Books, 1993.

Merriam-Webster's Encyclopedia of Literature, edited by Kathleen Kuiper et al. Springfield, Mass.: Merriam-Webster, 1995.

Moody, Richard. *America Takes the Stage: Romanticism in American Drama and Theatre, 1750–1900.* Bloomington: Indiana University Press, 1977.

Morrison, Samuel Eliot, ed. *The Development of Harvard University, since the Inauguration of President Eliot, 1869–1929.* Cambridge, Mass.: Harvard University Press, 1930.

Mott, Frank Luther. *Golden Multitudes: The Story of Best-Sellers in the United States.* New York: Bowker, 1947.

Nelson, Randy F. *The Almanac of American Letters.* Los Altos, Calif.: William Kaufmann, 1981.

Panati, Charles. *Panati's Parade of Fads, Follies, and Manias: The Origins of Our Most Cherished Obsessions.* New York: Harper Collins, 1991.

Pattee, Fred Lewis. *The Feminine Fifties.* New York: D. Appleton-Century, 1940.

Payne, Tom. *Encyclopedia of Great Writers.* New York: Barnes & Noble, 1997.

Pearle, R. S. *Library of the World's Best Literature: Synopses of Noted Books.* New York: J. A. Hill, 1896.

Pearson, Edmund. *Dime Novels; or, Following an Old Trail in Popular Literature.* Boston: Little, Brown, 1929.

Quinn, Arthur Hobson. *A History of the American Drama, from the Beginning to the Civil War.* 2d ed. New York: F. S. Crofts, 1943.

———. *A History of the American Drama, from the Civil War to the Present Day.* New York: F. S. Crofts, 1936.

Randel, William Peirce. *The Evolution of American Taste: The History of American Style from 1607 to the Present.* New York: Crown Publishers (Rutledge Books), 1978.

Rawlings, Kevin. "Christmas in the Civil War." *Civil War Times Illustrated* (December 1998), pp. 46–53.

Reps, John W. *Bird's Eye Views: Historic Lithographs of North American Cities.* New York: Princeton Architectural Press, 1998.

Ritter, Frédéric Louis. *Music in America.* 1883. Revised reprint, New York: Johnson Reprint Corporation, 1970.

Rublowsky, John. *Music in America.* New York: Crowell-Collier Press, 1967.

Sablosky, Irving. *American Music.* The Chicago History of American Civilization Series, edited by Daniel J. Boorstin. Chicago: University of Chicago Press, 1969.

———. *What They Heard: Music in America, 1852–1881.* Baton Rouge: Louisiana State University Press, 1986.

Salzman, Jack, David L. Smith, and Cornel West, eds. *Encyclopedia of African-American Culture and History.* 5 vols. New York: Simon & Schuster Macmillan, 1996.

Scharnhorst, Gary. *Bret Harte: Opening the American Literary West.* The Oklahoma Western Biographies Series. Norman: University of Oklahoma Press, 2000.

———. *Horatio Alger, Jr.* New York: Twayne, 1980.

Scherman, David E., and Rosemarie Redlich. *Literary America: A Chronicle of American Writers from 1607–1952.* New York: Dodd, Mead, 1952.

Sears, Stephen W., ed. *The American Heritage Century Collection of Civil War Art.* New York: American Heritage, 1974.

Siegel, Adrienne. *The Image of the American City in Popular Literature, 1820–1870.* Port Washington, N.Y.: Kennikat Press, 1981.

Silverman, Jason H., and Robert M. Gorman. "The Confederacy's Fighting Poet General John Wagener." *North & South Magazine* 2, no. 4 (April 1999): 42–49.

Smith, Bradley. *The USA: A History in Art.* New York: Thomas Y. Crowell, 1975.

Smith, Henry Nash. *Virgin Land: The American West as Symbol and Myth.* 1950. Reprint, New York: Random House, 1970.

Starling, Marion Wilson. *The Slave Narrative: Its Place in American History.* Washington, D.C.: Howard University Press, 1988.

Stevenson, Lauralee Trent. *Confederate Soldier Artists: Painting the South's War.* Shippensburg, Pa.: White Mane, 1998.

Strickland, Carol, and John Boswell. *The Annotated Mona Lisa: A Crash Course in Art History from Prehistoric to Post-Modern.* Kansas City, Mo.: Andrews & McMeel (Universal Press Syndicate), 1992.

Taft, Robert. *Artists and Illustrators of the Old West, 1850–1900.* New York: Charles Scribner's Sons, 1953.

———. *Photography and the American Scene: A Social History, 1839–1889.* 1942. Reprint, New York: Macmillan, 1964.

Taylor, Yuval, ed. *I Was Born a Slave: An Anthology of Classic Slave Narratives.* 2 vols. Vol. 1: *1772–1849*; Vol. 2: *1849–1866.* Chicago: Lawrence Hill Books, 1999.

Tebbel, John. *From Rags to Riches: Horatio Alger, Jr.* New York: Macmillan, 1963.

Ticknor, George. *Life, Letters, and Journals of George Ticknor.* 2 vols. 1876. Reprint, Boston: Houghton Mifflin, 1909.

Toll, Robert C. *Blacking Up: The Minstrel Show in Nineteenth-Century America.* New York: Oxford University Press, 1974.

———. Minstrels/Minstrelsy. In *Encyclopedia of African-American Culture and History,* 5 vols., edited by Jack Salzman, David L. Smith, and Cornel West. Vol. 4: *1810–12.* New York: Simon & Schuster Macmillan, 1996.

Varhola, Michael J. *Everyday Life during the Civil War: A Guide for Writers, Students and Historians.* Cincinnati: Writer's Digest Books, 1999.

Ward, Andrew. *Dark Midnight When I Rise: The Story of the Jubilee Singers Who Introduced the World to the Music of Black America.* New York: Farrar, Straus & Giroux, 2000.

Wharton, H. M. *War Songs and Poems of the Southern Confederacy, 1861–1865.* 1904. Reprint, Edison, N.J.: Castle Books 2000.

Whitcomb, Ian. *After the Ball: Pop Music from Rag to Rock.* New York: Simon & Schuster, 1973.

Wilkins, Thurman. *Thomas Moran, Artist of the Mountains.* 2d ed. Norman: University of Oklahoma Press, 1966.

Wilkins, William. *Charles Dickens in America.* 1911. Reprint, Brooklyn, N.Y.: Haskell House, 1970.

Wilmeth, Don B., and Christopher Bigsby, eds. *The Cambridge History of American Theater.* 2 vols. Vol. 1: *Beginnings to 1870;* Vol. 2: 1870–1945. New York: Cambridge University Press, 1999.

Woloch, Nancy. *Women and the American Experience.* 2d ed. New York: McGraw-Hill, 1994.

Chapter 16: Architecture and Design

Ambrose, Stephen E. *Nothing Like It in the World: The Men Who Built the Transcontinental Railroad, 1863–1869.* New York: Simon & Schuster, 1999.

American National Biography, edited by John A. Garraty et al. 24 vols. New York: Oxford University Press, 1999.

Andrews, Wayne. *American Gothic.* New York: Random House, 1975.

———. *Architecture, Ambition and Americans.* 5th ed. New York: Harper Brothers, 1979.

"Architecture." In *Dictionary of American History,* edited by Louise Bilebofketz et al. 7 vols. New York: Charles Scribner's Sons, 1976.

Burchard, John, and Albert Bush-Brown. *The Architecture of America: A Social and Cultural History.* Abridged ed. Boston: Little, Brown, 1966.

Cochran, Thomas C., et al. *Concise Dictionary of American History.* New York: Charles Scribner's Sons, 1962.

Condit, Carl W. *American Building: Materials and Techniques from the First Colonial Settlements to the Present.* Chicago: University of Chicago Press, 1982.

Conway, James. *America's Library: The Story of the Library of Congress, 1800–2000.* New Haven, Conn.: Yale University Press, 2000.

Doherty, Craig A., and Katherine M. Doherty. *The Washington Monument.* Woodbridge, Conn.: Blackbird Press Books, 1995.

Drury, Ian, and Tony Gibbons. *The Civil War Military Machine.* New York: Smithmark, 1993.

Dupré, Judith. *Bridges.* New York: Black Dog & Leventhal, 1997.

Edwards, Llewellyn Nathaniel. *A Record of the History and Evolution of Early American Bridges.* Orono: University Press of Maine, 1959.

Faude, Wilson H. "Associated Artists and the American Renaissance in the Decorative Arts." *Winterthur Portfolio* 10 (1975): 101–30.

Galloway, John Debo. *The First Transcontinental Railroad.* 1950. Reprint, New York: Dorset Press, 1989.

Gowans, Alan. *Images of American Living.* Philadelphia: Lippincott, 1964.

Green, Constance McLaughlin. *Washington: Village and Capital.* Princeton, N.J.: Princeton University Press, 1962.

Gustaitis, Joseph. "The Lady of the Tower." *American History Magazine* (June 1999), pp. 44–50.

Handlin, David P. *American Architecture.* London: Thames and Hudson, 1985.

Hawke, David Freeman. *Nuts and Bolts of the Past: A History of American Technology, 1776–1860.* New York: Harper & Row, 1988.

Hayden, Dolores. *Seven American Utopias: The Architecture of Communitarian Socialism, 1790–1975.* Cambridge: Massachusetts Institute of Technology Press, 1976.

Hill, Forest G. *Roads, Rails, and Waterways: The Army Engineers and Early Transportation.* Reprint, Westport, Conn.: Greenwood Press, 1977.

Hitchcock, Henry-Russell, and William Seale. *Temples of Democracy.* San Diego, Calif.: Harcourt, 1976.

Humphrey, Effingham P. "The Churches of James Renwick, Jr." M.A. thesis, New York University, 1942.

Katcher, Philip. *The Army of Robert E. Lee.* London: Arms and Armour Press, 1994.

Kirkbride, Thomas Story. *On the Construction, Organization, and General Arrangements of Hospitals for the Insane.* Philadelphia: Lippincott, 1880. Reprint, New York: Arno Press, 1973.

Lewis, Emanuel Raymond. *Seacoast Fortifications of the United States, an Introductory History.* Annapolis, Md.: Leeward, 1979.

Liscombe, R. Windsor. *Altogether American: Robert Mills, Architect and Engineer, 1781–1855.* New York: Oxford University Press, 1994.

McCullough, David. *The Great Bridge: The Epic Story of the Building of the Brooklyn Bridge.* New York: Simon & Schuster, 1972.

Mendelowitz, Daniel M. *A History of American Art.* New York: Holt, Rinehart & Winston, 1960.

Morgan, Mark. "Forts and Fortifications." In *Encyclopedia of the Confederacy.* Vol. 2, edited by Richard N. Current et al. 616–24. New York: Simon & Schuster, 1993.

Morrison Hugh Sinclair. *Louis Sullivan, Prophet of Modern Architecture.* 5th ed. New York: W. W. Norton, 1998.

Oliver, John W. *History of American Technology.* New York: Ronald Press, 1956.

Perkins, J. R. *Trails, Rails and War—The Life of General G. M. Dodge.* Indianapolis, Ind.: Bobbs-Merrill, 1929.

Pierson, William H., Jr. *American Buildings and Their Architects.* Vol. 1: *The Colonial and Neoclassical Styles*; Vol. 2: *Technology and the Picturesque.* Garden City, N.Y.: Doubleday, 1970.

Rybczynski, Witold. *A Clearing in the Distance: Frederick Law Olmsted and America in the Nineteenth Century.* New York: Scribner's, 1999.

Stanton, Phoebe B. *The Gothic Revival and the American Church.* Baltimore, Md.: Johns Hopkins University Press, 1968.

Steinman, D. B. *The Builders of the Bridge: The Story of John Roebling and His Son.* New York: Harcourt Brace, 1945.

Strickland, Carol. *The Annotated Arch: A Crash Course in the History of Architecture.* Kansas City, Mo.: Andrews McMeel, 2001.

Trachtenberg, Alan. *Brooklyn Bridge, Fact and Symbol.* 2d ed. Chicago: University of Chicago Press, 1979.

Trudeau, Noah André. *The Last Citadel: Petersburg, Virginia, June 1864–April 1865.* Boston: Knopf, 1991.

Upjohn, Everard M. *Richard Upjohn, Architect and Churchman.* New York: Columbia University Press, 1939.

Weinberger, Jill Knight. "Time Traveler: The Mark Twain House." *American History Magazine* (April 1999), pp. 60–61.

Zabel, Craig. "Public Architecture." In *Information Now Encyclopedia of American Life: A Social History.* New York: Macmillan Library Reference USA, 1993.

Chapter 17: Science and Technology

Bellesiles, Michael A. *Arming America: The Origins of a National Gun Culture.* New York: Alfred Knopf, 2000.

Boatner, Mark M. *The Civil War Dictionary.* New York: David McKay, 1959.

Bright, Charles. *Submarine Cables: Their History, Construction and Working.* 1898. Reprint, New York: Arno Press, 1974.

Cookson, Gillian. "The Transatlantic Telegraph Cable: Eighth Wonder of the World." *History Today* 50, no. 3 (March 2000): 44–51.

Cravens, Hamilton, Alan I. Marcus, and David M. Katzman, eds. *Technical Knowledge in American Culture: Science, Technology, and Medicine since the Early 1800s.* History of American Science and Technology Series. Tuscaloosa: University of Alabama Press, 1996.

Daniels, George H. *American Science in the Age of Jackson.* Tuscaloosa: University of Alabama Press, 1994.

Davis, Lance E., and J. R. T. Hughes. "A Dollar-Sterling Exchange, 1809–1895." *The Economic History Review* 13, no. 1 (August 1960): 52–78.

Gies, Joseph, and Frances Gies. *The Ingenious Yankees: The Men, Ideas, and Machines That Transformed a Nation, 1776–1876.* New York: Thomas Y. Crowell, 1976.

Haskins, Jim. *Outward Dreams: Black Inventors and Their Inventions.* New York: Walker, 1991.

Havlik, Robert J. "Hellfire from the Heavens." *Civil War Times Illustrated* (October 1999), pp. 34–37.

Hawke, David Freeman. *Nuts and Bolts of the Past: A History of American Technology, 1776–1860.* New York: Harper & Row, 1988.

Headrick, Daniel R. *The Invisible Weapon: Telecommunications and International Politics, 1851–1945.* New York: Oxford University Press, 1991.

Henig, Gerald S., and Eric Niderost. *Civil War Firsts: The Legacies of America's Bloodiest Conflict.* Mechanicsburg, Pa.: Stackpole Books, 2001.

Hindle, Brooke, and Steven Lubar. *Engines of Change: The American Industrial Revolution, 1790–1860.* Baltimore, Md.: Johns Hopkins University Press, 1986.

Hirschfield, Charles. "America on Exhibition: The New York Crystal Palace." *American Quarterly* 9 (1972): 101–16.

Hoehling, Mary. *Thaddeus Lowe: America's One-Man Air Corps.* New York: Messner, 1958.

Hounshell, David A. *From the American System to Mass Production, 1800–1932: The Development of Manufacturing Technology in the United States.* Baltimore, Md.: Johns Hopkins University Press, 1984.

Ives, Patricia Carter. *Creativity and Inventions.* Arlington, Va.: Research Unlimited, 1987.

Kaempffert, Waldemar, ed. *A Popular History of American Invention.* Vol. 2. New York: Charles Scribner's Sons, 1924.

Macdonald, Anne L. *Feminine Ingenuity: How Women Inventors Changed America.* New York: Ballantine Books, 1992.

Marcus, Alan I., and Howard P. Segal. *Technology in America: A Brief History.* San Diego, Calif.: Harcourt Brace Jovanovich, 1989.

Mayr, Otto, and Robert C. Post, eds. *Yankee Enterprise: The Rise of the American System of Manufactures.* Baltimore, Md.: Johns Hopkins University Press, 1982.

Mitchell, B. R. *British Historical Statistics.* Cambridge: Cambridge University Press, 1988.

———. *International Historical Statistics: The Americas and Australasia.* Detroit: Gale Research, 1983.

Mulhall, George G. *The Dictionary of Statistics.* 4th rev. ed. London: George Routledge and Sons, Ltd., 1899.

Oliver, John W. *History of American Technology.* New York: Ronald Press, 1956.

Olsen, Frank H. *Inventors Who Left Their Brands on America.* New York: Bantam Books, 1991.

Patton, Phil. *Made in U.S.A.: The Secret Histories of the Things That Made America.* New York: Grove Weidenfeld, 1992.

Pursell, Carroll W., Jr., ed. *Technology in America: A History of Individuals and Ideas.* Cambridge, Mass.: MIT Press, 1981.

Raab, James W. *America's Daredevil Balloonist—W. H. Donaldson, 1840–1875.* Manhattan, Kans.: Sunflower University Press, 1999.

Reader's Digest. *Stories behind Everyday Things.* Pleasantville, N.Y.: Reader's Digest Association, 1980.

Ross, Charles. *Trial by Fire: Science, Technology and the Civil War.* Shippensburg, Pa.: White Mane, 2000.

Sanders, Stuart W. "Le Mat: Unique Firearms for a New Country." *Civil War Times Illustrated* (December 1998), pp. 66–70.

Taft, Robert. *Photography and the American Scene: A Social History, 1839–1889.* New York: Dover, 1938.

Thompson, Robert L. *Wiring a Continent: The History of the Telegraph Industry in the United States, 1832–1866.* Princeton, N.J.: Prineton University Press, 1947.

Travers, Bridget, and Jeffrey Muhr, eds. *World of Invention: History's Most Significant Inventions and the People behind Them.* Detroit: Gale Research, 1994.

Trudeau, Noah A. "A Record of Wreckage," *MHQ: Quarterly Journal of Military History* 12, no. 3 (spring 2000): 42–49.

U.S. Department of Commerce. *Historical Statistics of the United States, Colonial Times to 1970.* Bicentennial ed. 2 parts. Washington, D.C.: Department of Commerce, 1975.

———. *The Story of the United States Patent and Trademark Office.* Washington, D.C.: U.S. Government Printing Office, 1988.

———. *The Story of the United States Patent Office.* Washington, D.C.: U.S. Government Printing Office, 1972.

Volo, Dorothy Denneen, and James M. Volo. *Daily Life in Civil War America.* Westport, Conn.: Greenwood Press, 1998.

Waldsmith, John S. *Stereo Views: An Illustrated History and Price Guide.* Radnor, Pa.: Wallace-Homestead, 1991.

Zeller, Bob. *The Civil War in Depth: History in 3-D.* New York: Chronicle Books, 1997.

———. "War in 3-D." *Civil War Times* 38, no. 2 (1999): 28–35.

Chapter 18: Medicine and Psychiatry

Adams, George Worthington. *Doctors in Blue: The Medical History of the Union Army in the Civil War.* 1952. Reprint, Dayton, Ohio.: Morningside Press, 1985.

The American Almanac and Repository of Useful Knowledge. 32 vols. Boston: David H. Williams; New York: Collins, Keese, and Co., 1830–1861.

Barun, Dhiman, and William B. Greenough III, eds. *Cholera.* New York: Plenum Books, 1992.

Beller, Susan Provost. *Medical Practices in the Civil War.* Charlotte, Vt.: OurStory, 1992.

Bettmann, Otto L. *The Good Old Days—They Were Terrible!* New York: Random House, 1974.

Billings, John S. "Literature and Institutions." In *A Century of American Medicine, 1776–1876,* edited by Edward H. Clark et al. Philadelphia: Lea, 1876.

Bordley, James, III, and A. McGehee Harvey. *Two Centuries of American Medicine.* Philadelphia: W. B. Saunders, 1976.

Bray, R. S. *Armies of Pestilence: The Impact of Disease on History.* New York: Barnes & Noble Books, 1996.

Brooks, Stewart. *Civil War Medicine.* Springfield, Ill.: Charles C. Thomas, 1966.

Cartwright, Frederick F. *Disease and History.* New York: Dorset Press, 1972.

Cassedy, James H. *Medicine in America: A Short History.* Baltimore, Md.: Johns Hopkins University Press, 1991.

Cunningham, H. H. *Doctors in Gray: The Confederate Medical Service.* 2d ed. Baton Rouge: Louisiana State University, 1960.

Deutsch, Albert. *The Mentally Ill in America: A History of Their Care and Treatment from Colonial Times.* 2d rev. ed. New York: Columbia University Press, 1949.

Dormandy, Thomas. *The White Death: A History of Tuberculosis.* London: The Hambledon Press, 1999.

Duffy, John. *From Humors to Medical Science: A History of American Medicine.* 2d ed. Urbana: University of Illinois Press, 1993.

———. *The Healers: A History of American Medicine.* Reprint, Urbana: University of Illionois Press, 1979. New York: McGraw-Hill, 1976.

———. *The Sanitarians: A History of American Public Health.* Urbana: University of Illinois Press, 1992.

Dunlop, Richard. *Doctors of the American Frontier.* Reprint, New York: Ballantine Books, 1975. New York: Ballantine, 1965.

Earnest, Ernest Penney. *S. Weir Mitchell, Novelist and Physician.* Philadelphia: University of Pennsylvania Press, 1950.

Freemon, Frank R. *Gangrene and Glory: Medical Care during the Civil War.* Madison, N.J.: Fairleigh Dickinson University Press, 1998.

Garrison, Nancy S. "'Every Condition of Horror' [the U.S. Sanitary Commission in the Civil War]." *North & South Magazine* 3, no. 1 (November 1999): 66–78.

Grob, Gerald N. *The Mad among Us: A History of the Care of America's Mentally Ill.* New York: The Free Press, 1994.

———. *Mental Institutions in America: Social Policy to 1875.* New York: The Free Press, 1972.

Halttunen, Karen. *Murder Most Foul: The Killer and the American Gothic Imagination.* Cambridge, Mass.: Harvard University Press, 1998.

Harrington, T. F. *The Harvard Medical School: A History, Narrative and Documentary, 1782–1905.* Chicago: Lewis, 1905.

Hunt, William R. *Body Love: The Amazing Career of Bernard Macfadden.* Bowling Green, Ohio: Bowling Green State University Popular Press, 1989.

Karolevitz, Robert F. *Doctors of the Old West.* Seattle: Superior, 1967.

Kaufman, Martin, Stuart Galishoff, and Todd L. Savitt, eds. *Dictionary of American Medical Biography.* 2 vols. Westport, Conn.: Grenwood Press, 1984.

King, Lester S. *Transformations in American Medicine, from Benjamin Rush to William Osler.* Baltimore: Md.: The Johns Hopkins University Press, 1991.

Kiple, Kenneth F., ed. *Plague, Pox and Pestilence: Disease in History.* New York: Barnes & Noble Books, 1997.

Kohn, George C., ed. *Encyclopedia of Plague and Pestilence.* New York: Facts On File, 1995.

Leland, R. G. *Distribution of Physicians in the United States.* Chicago: American Medical Association, 1935.

Lovering, Joseph P. *S. Weir Mitchell.* New York: Twayne, 1971.

Lowry, Thomas P., and Jack D. Welsh. *Tarnished Scalpels: The Court-Martials of Fifty Union Surgeons.* Mechanicsburg, Pa.: Stackpole Books, 2000.

Lynch, Jacqueline T. "Louisa May Alcott and the Transcendence of War." *Civil War Magazine* 71 (December 1998): 35–41.

Lynch, John S. "Medical Treatment, or the Lack Thereof, . . ." *America's Civil War* September 1991, pp. 10–12.

Medical and Surgical History of the War of the Rebellion (1861–65): Prepared in Accordance with Acts of Congress under the Direction of Surgeon General Joseph K. Barnes, United States Army. 6 vols. Washington, D.C.: U.S. Government Printing Office, 1875–88. (Reprinted as *Medical and Surgical History of the Civil War.* 12 vols. Wilmington, N.C.: Broadfoot, 1990–91.)

Medicine of the Civil War. The National Library of Medicine. Washington, D.C.: U.S. Government Printing Office, n.d.

Merck Research Laboratories. *The Merck Manual of Diagnosis and Therapy.* 1899. Reprint, Rahway, N.J.: Merck, 1999.

Morris, Roy, Jr. "Germs, Not Bullets, Were a Civil War Soldier's Deadliest Foes." *America's Civil War* (September 1999), p. 6

Moulton, Candy. *The Writer's Guide to Everyday Life in the Wild West.* Cincinnati: Writer's Digest Books, 1999.

Mulhall, Michael G. *The Dictionary of Statistics.* 4th ed., rev. 1899. Reprint, Detroit: Gale Research, 1969.

Norris, David A. "Seagoing Surgeons of the Civil War." *America's Civil War* (January 1999), pp. 34–40.

Norwood, William Frederick. *Medical Education in the United States Before the Civil War.* Philadelphia: University of Pennsylvania Press, 1944.

Oates, Stephen B. *A Woman of Valor: Clara Barton and the Civil War.* New York: The Free Press, 1994.

Ott, Katherine. *Fevered Lives: Tuberculosis in American Culture since 1870.* Cambridge, Mass.: Harvard University Press, 1996.

Packard, Francis R. *History of Medicine in the United States.* 2 vols. New York: Hafner, 1963.

Porter, Roy. *The Greatest Benefit to Mankind: A Medical History of Humanity.* New York: W. W. Norton, 1997.

Rauch, John H. "[Report on] Medical Education in the United States and the Regulation of the Practice of Medicine in the United States and Canada, 1763–1891; Medical Education and the Regulation of the Practice of Medicine in Foreign Countries." Chicago: Illinois State Board of Health, 1891.

Rosenberg, Charles E. *The Cholera Years.* Chicago: University of Chicago Press, 1962.

Rothstein, William G. *American Physicians in the Nineteenth Century, from Sects to Science.* Baltimore, Md.: The Johns Hopkins University Press, 1972.

Schultz, Stanley K. *Constructing Urban Culture: American Cities and City Planning, 1800–1920.* Philadelphia: Temple University Press, 1989.

Shafer, Henry Burnell. *The American Medical Profession, 1783–1850.* 1936. Reprint, New York: AMS Press, 1968.

Shorter, Edward. *A History of Psychiatry: From the Era of the Asylum to the Age of Prozac.* New York: John Wiley & Sons, 1997.

Shyrock, Richard H. *Medicine in America.* Baltimore, Md.: Johns Hopkins University Press, 1966.

Stein, Alice P. "The North's Unsung Sisters of Mercy." *America's Civil War* (September 1999), pp. 38–44.

Steiner, Paul. *Disease in the Civil War.* Springfield, Ill.: Charles C. Thomas, 1968.

Stillé, Charles J. *History of the United States Sanitary Commission in the War of the Rebellion.* 1886. Reprint, Gansevoort, N.Y.: Corner House Historical, 1997.

Taylor, Henry L., and James Russell Parsons, Jr. "Professional Education in the United States." Bulletin No. 8. New York: University of the State of New York, 1900.

U.S. Bureau of the Census. *Historical Statistics of the United States.* 2 vols. Washington, D.C.: U.S. Government Printing Office, 1960.

Wilbur, C. Keith. *Civil War Medicine, 1861–1865.* The Illustrated Living History Series. Philadelphia: Chelsea House, 1995.

Woodward, Grace Steele. *The Man Who Conquered Pain: A Biography of William Thomas Green Morton.* Boston: Beacon Press, 1962.

Wormeley, Katherine Prescott. *The Other Side of War: On the Hospital Transport with the Army of the Potomac.* 1889. Reprint, Gansevoort, N.Y.: Corner House Historical, 1998.

Chapter 19: Popular Culture

American Life, a Social History. New York: Charles Scribner's Sons, 1993. New material by Macmillan Publishing, USA, 1998.

Anzovin, Steve, and Janet Podell. *Famous First Facts.* 5th ed. New York: H. W. Wilson, 1997.

Aron, Cindy. *Working at Play: A History of Vacations in the United States.* New York: Oxford University Press, 1999.

Asbury, Herbert. *Sucker's Progress: An Informal History of Gambling in America from the Colonies to Canfield.* New York: Dodd, Mead, 1938.

Bode, Carl. *The American Lyceum: Town Meeting of the Mind.* Carbondale: Southern Illinois University Press, 1956.

———. *The Anatomy of American Popular Culture, 1840–1861.* Berkeley: University of California Press, 1959.

———, ed. *Midcentury America: Life in the 1850s.* Carbondale: Southern Illinois University Press, 1972.

Braden, Donna R. *Leisure and Entertainment in America.* Dearborn, Mich.: Henry Ford Museum & Greenfield Village, 1988.

Branch, E. Douglas. *The Sentimental Years.* New York: D. Appleton-Century, 1934.

Carruth, Gorton, ed. *The Encyclopedia of American Facts and Dates.* 8th ed. New York: Harper & Row, 1987.

Chindahl, George L. *A History of the Circus in America.* Caldwell, Idaho: Caxton Printers, 1959.

Culhane, John. *The American Circus, An Illustrated History.* New York: Henry Holt, 1990.

Cyclopaedia of Temperance and Prohibition. New York: Funk & Wagnalls, 1891.

Donald, Nevius Bigelow. *William Conant Church and the Army and Navy Journal.* New York: Columbia University Press, 1952.

Dulles, Foster Rhea. *A History of Recreation: America Learns to Play.* New York: Appleton-Century-Crofts, 1965.

Eckley, Wilton. *The American Circus.* Boston: Twayne, 1984.

Fahs, Alice. *The Imagined Civil War.* Chapel Hill: University of North Carolina Press, 2000.

Fox, Charles Philip, and Tom Parkinson. *The Circus in America.* Waukesha, Wis.: Country Beautiful, 1969.

Gale, Robert L. *A Cultural Encyclopedia of the 1850s in America.* Westport, Conn.: Greenwood Press, 1993.

Goodrum, Charles, and Helen Dalrymple. *Advertising in America: The First 200 Years.* New York: Harry N. Abrams, 1990.

Graff, Harvey J. *The Legacies of Literacy: Continuities and Contradictions in Western Culture and Society.* Bloomington: Indiana University Press, 1987.

Groner, Alex. *The History of American Business and Industry.* New York: American Heritage, 1972.

Halttunen, Karen. *Confidence Men and Painted Women: A Study of Middle-Class Culture in America, 1830–1870.* New Haven, Conn.: Yale University Press, 1982.

Handlin, Oscar, ed. *Readings in American History.* New York: Alfred A. Knopf, 1957.

Haywood, C. Robert. *The Victorian West: Class and Culture in Kansas Cattle Towns.* Lawrence: University Press of Kansas, 1991.
Hotaling, Edward. *The Great Black Jockeys.* Rocklin, Calif.: Forum/Prima, 1999.
Janello, Amy, and Brennon Jones. *The American Magazine.* New York: Harry N. Abrams, 1991.
Johnson, Lloyd. *Baseball Book of Firsts.* Philadelphia: Courage Books (Running Press), 1999.
Kaplan, Max. *Leisure in America: A Social Inquiry.* New York: John Wiley & Sons, 1960.
Kasson, John F. *Rudeness and Civility: Manners in Nineteenth-Century Urban America.* New York: Hill & Wang 1990.
Kelly, Patrick J. *Creating a National Home: Building the Veterans' Welfare State, 1860–1900.* Cambridge, Mass.: Harvard University Press, 1997.
Kirsch, George B. "Bats, Balls, and Bullets." *Civil War Times Illustrated* (May 1998), pp. 30–37.
———. *The Creation of American Team Sports: Baseball and Cricket, 1838–1872.* Urbana: University of Illinois Press, 1989.
Laird, Pamela Walker. *Advertising Progress: American Business and the Rise of Consumer Marketing.* Baltimore: Md.: Johns Hopkins University Press, 1998.
Lapham, Lewis, and Ellen Rosenbush, eds. *One Hundred and Fifty Years of* HARPER'S *Magazine.* New York: Franklin Square Press, 2000.
Lehuu, Isabelle. *Carnival on the Page: Popular Print Media in Antebellum America.* Chapel Hill: University of North Carolina Press, 2000.
Light, Jonathon Fraser. *Cultural Encyclopedia of Baseball.* Jefferson, N.C.: McFarland, 1997.
Low, W. Augustus, and Virgil A. Clift, eds. *Encyclopedia of Black America.* New York: Da Capo Press, 1981.
Loxton, Howard. *The Golden Age of the Circus.* New York: Smithmark Publishers (U.S. Media Holdings), 1997.
Macdonald, Anne L. *Feminine Ingenuity: Women and Invention in America.* New York: Ballantine Books, 1992.
Matthews, Glenna. *"Just a Housewife": The Rise and Fall of Domesticity in America.* New York: Oxford University Press, 1987.
May, Earl Chapin. *The Circus from Rome to Ringling.* 1932. Revised, New York: Dover, 1963.
McCutcheon, Marc. *The Writer's Guide to Everyday Life in the 1800s.* Cincinnati; Writer's Digest Books, 1993.
Mott, Frank Luther. *American Journalism: A History, 1690–1960.* 3d ed. New York: Macmillan, 1962.
———. *A History of American Magazines.* 4 vols. Cambridge, Mass.: Harvard University Press, 1938–68.
Mulhall, Michael G. *Dictionary of Statistics.* 4th ed., rev. 1899. Reprint, Detroit: Gale Research, 1969.
Murray, Marian. *Circus! From Rome to Ringling.* Westport, Conn.: Greenwood Press, 1956.
Panati, Charles. *Extraordinary Origins of Everyday Things.* New York: Harper & Row, 1987.
Peverelly, Charles. *The Book of American Pastimes, Containing a History of the Principal Baseball, Cricket, Rowing, and Yachting Clubs of the United States.* New York: Author, 1866.
Reader's Digest. *Stories behind Everyday Things.* Pleasantville, N.Y.: The Reader's Digest Association, 1980.
Rorabaugh, W. J. *The Alcoholic Republic: An American Tradition.* New York: Oxford University Press, 1979.
Rousmaniere, John. "The America's Cup." *American Heritage Magazine* (February/March 2000), pp. 68–79.
Rushing, S. Kittrell, David B. Sachsman, and Debra Reddin van Tuyll, eds. *The Civil War and the Press.* New Brunswick, N.J.: Transaction, 2000.
Salzman, Jack, David L. Smith, and Cornel West, eds. *Encyclopedia of African-American Culture and History.* 5 vols. New York: Simon & Schuster Macmillan, 1996.
Shaw, William Harlan. *American Men's Wear, 1861–1982.* Baton Rouge, La.: Oracle Press, 1982.
Slotkin, Richard. *Regeneration through Violence: The Mythology of the American Frontier, 1600–1860.* Norman: University of Oklahoma Press, 2000.
Smithsonian Institution. *The Books of the Fairs: Materials about World's Fairs, 1834–1916.* Chicago: American Library Association, 1992.
Tebbel, John, and Mary Ellen Zuckerman. *The Magazine in America, 1741–1990.* New York: Oxford University Press, 1991.
Toll, Robert C. *Blacking Up: The Minstrel Show in Nineteenth-Century America.* New York: Oxford University Press, 1974.
Volo, Dorothy Denneen, and James M. Volo. *Daily Life in Civil War America.* Westport, Conn.: Greenwood Press, 1998.
Winkler, Allan M. "Drinking on the American Frontier." *Quarterly Journal of Studies on Alcohol* 29 (1968): 413–45.
Wright, Marshall D. *Nineteenth Century Baseball: Year-by-Year Statistics for the Major League Teams, 1871 through 1900.* Jefferson, N.C.: McFarland, 1996.

Chapter 20: Crime, Vice, and Violence

Ackerman, S. J. "A Riot in Washington." *American History Magazine* (June 2001), pp. 56–64.
Axelrod, Alan, Charles Phillips, and Kurt Kemper. *Cops, Crooks, and Criminologists: An International Biographical Dictionary of Law Enforcement.* New York: Facts On File, 1996.
Bellesiles, Michael A. *Arming America: The Origins of a National Gun Culture.* New York: Alfred A. Knopf, 1999.
———, ed. *Lethal Imagination: Violence and Brutality in American History.* New York: New York University Press, 2000.
Brown, Richard M. *Violence in America: An Encyclopedia.* New York: Scribner's Sons, 1999.
Cahalan, Margaret Werner. *Historical Corrections Statistics in the United States, 1850–1984.* Washington, D.C.: United States Department of Justice, 1987.
Carruth, Gorton. *The Encyclopedia of American Facts and Dates.* 8th ed. New York: Harper & Row, 1987.
Duane, Charles P. ("Dutch Charley"). *Against the Vigilantes: The Recollections of Dutch Charley Duane,* edited by John Boessenecker. Norman: University of Oklahoma Press, 1999.
Gilje, Paul A. *Rioting in America.* Bloomington: Indiana University Press, 1996.
Gilmore, Donald L. "When the James Gang Ruled the Rails." *Wild West Magazine* (August 2000), pp. 38–44.
Halttunen, Karen. *Murder Most Foul: The Killer and the American Gothic Imagination.* Cambridge, Mass.: Harvard University Press, 1998.
Hollandsworth, James G. *An Absolute Massacre: The New Orleans Race Riot of July 30, 1866.* Baton Rouge: Louisiana State University Press, 2000.
Hornsby, Alton, Jr. *Chronology of African American History, from 1492 to the Present.* 2d ed. Detroit: Gale Research, 1997.
Kenny, Kevin. *Making Sense of the Molly Maguires.* New York: Oxford University Press, 1998.
Mancini, Matthew J. *One Dies, Get Another: Convict Leasing in the American South, 1866–1928.* Columbia: University of South Carolina Press, 1996.
Moody, Richard. *The Astor Place Riot.* Bloomington: University of Indiana Press, 1958.
O'Neal, Bill. *Encyclopedia of Western Gunfighters.* Norman: University of Oklahoma Press, 1979.
Patterson, Richard. *The Train Robbery Era: An Encyclopedic History.* Boulder, Colo.: Pruett, 1991.

Pritchard, James M. "Missouri Outlaws' Raid in West Virginia." *Wild West Magazine* (December 1998), pp. 48–52.

Rugoff, Milton. *America's Gilded Age: Intimate Portraits from an Era of Extravagance and Change, 1850–1890.* New York: Henry Holt, 1989.

———. *Prudery and Passion.* London: Rupert Hart-Davis, 1972.

Sifakis, Carl. *The Encyclopedia of American Crime.* New York: Facts On File, 1982.

Stampp, Kenneth M. *The Peculiar Institution: Slavery in the Ante-Bellum South.* New York: Alfred A. Knopf, 1956.

U.S. Department of Commerce. *Historical Statistics of the United States, Colonial Times to 1970.* Bicentennial ed. 2 parts. Washington, D.C.: Department of Commerce, 1975.

Vandal, Gilles. *New Orleans Riot of 1866: The Anatomy of a Tragedy.* Lafayette: University of Louisiana at Lafayette Press, 1983.

Walker, Samuel. *Popular Justice: A History of American Criminal Justice.* New York: Oxford University Press, 1980.

White, Walter. *Rope and Faggot: A Biography of Judge Lynch.* New York: Alfred A. Knopf, 1929.

Chapter 21: Selected Documents

Alger, Horatio, Jr. *Ragged Dick and Mark, the Match Boy.* Edited by Richard Fink, 39–44. New York: Collier Books, 1962.

Arthur, Timothy Shay. *Ten Nights in a Bar-Room, and What I Saw There.* Edited by Donald A. Koch, 7–16, 232–34. Cambridge, Mass.: Harvard University Press, the Belknap Press, 1964.

Berlin, Ira, et al., eds. *Freedom: A Documentary History of Emancipation 1861–1867.* Series 1, Vol. 1: *The Destruction of Slavery,* 450–53. New York: Cambridge University Press, 1985.

Chesnut, Mary. *A Diary from Dixie.* Edited by Isabella D. Martin and Myrta Lockett Avary. New York: D. Appleton, 1905.

Custer, George A. *My Life on the Plains,* Edited by Milo Milton Quaife, 80–85. Reprint, Chicago: R. R. Donnelly & Sons, Lakeside Press, 1952.

Eddy, Mary Baker G. *Science and Health, with Key to the Scriptures.* 81st ed., 1–52. Boston: E. J. Foster Eddy, 1894.

Montgomery Ward & Company. Catalogue No. 10 (January 1874). Laramie: University of Wyoming American Heritage Center.

Northrup, Solomon. *Twelve Years a Slave: A Narrative of Solomon Northrup, a Citizen of New York, Kidnaped in Washington City in 1841, and Rescued in 1853 from a Cotton Plantation near the Red River, in Louisiana,* 170–79. Auburn, N.Y.: Derby and Miller, 1853.

United States Congress. *The Statutes at Large of the United States.* Vol. 12, 392–94. Washington, D.C.: U.S. Government Printing Office, 1875–1936.

United States Congress. *The Statutes at Large of the United States.* Vol. 12, 1268–69. Washington, D.C.: U.S. Government Printing Office, 1875–1936.

United States Congress. *The Statutes at Large of the United States,* Vol. 15, xiii (XIV). Washington, D.C.: U.S. Government Printing Office, 1875–1936.

United States Congress. *The Statutes at Large of the United States.* Vol. 44. Part 1, 1860 (XIII). Washington, D. C.: U.S. Government Printing Office, 1875–1936.

United States Congress. *The Statutes at Large of the United States.* Vol. 44. Part 1, 1861 (XV). Washington, D.C.: U.S. Government Printing Office, 1875–1936.

Van Woodward, C., and Elisabeth Muhlenfeld, eds. *The Private Mary Chesnut: The Unpublished Civil War Diaries,* 98–105. New York: Oxford University Press, 1984.

Whitman, Walt. *Leaves of Grass.* Comprehensive reader's ed., Edited by Harold W. Blodgett and Sculley Bradley, 28–29, 282–84, 337–38. New York: New York University Press, 1965.

APPENDIX: List of Tables

Index

This index is arranged alphabetically letter by letter. Page numbers in *italic* indicate illustrations or captions. Page numbers in **boldface** indicate biographical profiles. Page numbers followed by *t* indicate tables, by *g* indicate graphs, by *m* indicate maps, and by *n* indicate notes.

G

M